WL 700 G

80025 7554

D1393606

75.60

Neuropsychological Assessment of
Neuropsychiatric and Neuromedical Disorders

Neuropsychological Assessment of Neuropsychiatric and Neuromedical Disorders

Third Edition

Edited by

Igor Grant, M.D., F.R.C.P.(C)

Distinguished Professor and Executive Vice Chair
Department of Psychiatry
Director, HIV Neurobehavioral Research Center
University of California, San Diego School of Medicine
La Jolla, California

Kenneth M. Adams, Ph.D., A.B.P.P

Professor of Psychology and Psychiatry
The University of Michigan, Ann Arbor
Associate Chief, Mental Health and Chief Psychologist
Veterans Affairs Ann Arbor Healthcare System
Ann Arbor, Michigan

OXFORD
UNIVERSITY PRESS
2009

OXFORD
UNIVERSITY PRESS

Oxford University Press, Inc., publishes works that further
Oxford University's objective of excellence
in research, scholarship, and education.

Oxford New York
Auckland Cape Town Dar es Salaam Hong Kong Karachi
Kuala Lumpur Madrid Melbourne Mexico City Nairobi
New Delhi Shanghai Taipei Toronto

With offices in
Argentina Austria Brazil Chile Czech Republic France Greece
Guatemala Hungary Italy Japan Poland Portugal Singapore
South Korea Switzerland Thailand Turkey Ukraine Vietnam

Published by Oxford University Press, Inc.
198 Madison Avenue, New York, New York 10016
www.oup.com

The first and second editions were entitled
Neuropsychological Assessment of Neuropsychiatric Disorders.

Library of Congress Cataloging-in-Publication Data
Neuropsychological assessment of neuropsychiatric and neuromedical
disorders / edited by Igor Grant, Kenneth M. Adams.—3rd ed.
p. ; cm.
Includes bibliographical references and index.
ISBN 978-0-19-537854-2
1. Mental illness—Diagnosis. 2. Nervous system—Diseases—Diagnosis.
3. Neuropsychological tests. I. Grant, Igor, 1942- II. Adams, Kenneth M., 1948-
[DNLM: 1. Central Nervous System Diseases—diagnosis. 2. Delirium, Dementia,
Amnestic, Cognitive Disorders—diagnosis. 3. Neuropsychological Tests.
WM 141 N494 2009]
RC473.N48N47 2009
616.89'075—dc22
2008034750

3 4 5 6 7 8 9

Printed in the United States of America
on acid-free paper

To JoAnn Nallinger Grant
and
To the memory of Carol Bracher Adams

Contents

III.   Psychosocial Consequences of Neuropsychological Impairment

List of Color Illustrations

8-1 The neuropathology of Alzheimer's disease. Grossly apparent cortical atrophy in Alzheimer's disease (Figure 1A) compared to normal aging (Figure 1B), and neocortical amyloid plaques (Figure 2), neurofibrillary tangles (Figure 3), and cerebrovascular amyloid angiopathy (Figure 4).

8-2 Histopathologic abnormalities in the limbic system and neocortex in Dementia with Lewy Bodies (DLB). The typical appearance of vacuolization in the entorhinal cortex, cortical Lewy bodies in the temporal lobe neocortex, and Lewy neurites (i.e., neurons containing abnormal alpha-synuclein filaments) in the CA3 region of the hippocampus.

12-1 Ictal SPECT scan of a 19-year-old patient with unusual episodes of fidgeting, mumbling, and rubbing her legs. She has bilateral epileptiform activity, but the SPECT scan shows clear right temporal hyperperfusion during a seizure (radiological convention: right is on the left).

13-1 Axial MRI scans of a 42-year-old female with relapsing—remitting MS and an Expanded Disability Status Scale of 3.5. The patient's disease duration is 11 years and she is not being managed with any disease modifying therapy. From left to right: T2-weighted, FLAIR and T1-weighted post-gadolinium contrast images. Periventricular hyperintense lesions and frontoparietal lesions are noted on the T2 and FLAIR images; a gadolinium-enhancing lesion is also apparent.

17-1 Structural morphometry in an individual infected with HIV. These two coronal sections highlight regions of abnormality in the white matter (shown in yellow), which may be related to markers of HIV disease and neurobehavioral performance. Dark blue = cortex, light blue = subcortical gray, purple = sulcal/subarachnoid CSF, red = ventricular fluid, yellow = abnormal white matter, dark gray = normal appearing white matter, light gray = cerebellum, maroon = infratentorial CSF.

17-2 Diffusion tensor images from Gongvatana et al. (2008) showing that individuals with HIV-associated neurocognitive disorders (HAND) have lower fractional anisotropy in the anterior callosal region (shown in blue) relative to HIV-infected comparison participants without HAND. Images are presented in axial sections moving from inferior (upper left) to superior (lower right) slices.

18-2 Brain MRI showing loss of brain volume in alcoholic (A) versus healthy control (B). Note reduced cortical thickness and increased sulcal volume.

18-4 Cartoon showing some typical facial features in child with fetal alcohol syndrome.

18-5 One anomaly seen in FAS is agenesis, or absence, of the corpus callosum. The top left MRI scan (A), is a control brain. The other images are from children with FAS. In the top middle the corpus callosum is present, but it is very thin at the posterior section of the brain (B, arrow). In the upper right the corpus callosum is essentially missing (C, arrow). The bottom two pictures (D, E) are from a 9-year old girl with FAS. She has agenesis of the corpus callosum and the large dark area in the back of her brain (E, arrow) above the cerebellum is a condition known as colpocephaly. It is essentially empty space.

18–6   MRI brain images of two cases. Case 1 was abstinent 1 week (A) and rescanned after 8 months of continued abstinence (B). Note lessening prominence of suci and ventricles in B. Case 2 was abstinent 30 days (C) and rescanned at 10 months after relapsing in the interim. Note tissue loss in D, particularly in periventricular white matter, cerebellar vermis, and surrounding IV ventricle.

18–7   Color coded images representing intensity of uptake of the tracer HMPAO during a cognitive activation task in a nonalcoholic control (A), alcoholic abstinent over 18 months (B), and a recently detoxified alcoholic (C) abstinent 4 weeks. Cooler colors indicate less perfusion, especially in frontal areas in C versus A. Case B has values intermediate between A and C, suggesting recovery.

19–1   Cocaine abusers tend to show decreased glucose metabolism in areas of prefrontal cortex (A) relative to healthy controls.

19–2   Decreased rCBF in putamen (A) and frontal (B) white matter of a methamphetamine user compared to a healthy control. Increased rCBF in a methamphetamine user compared to a healthy control in parietal brain regions (C).

20–1   Activation during a Task of Photic Stimulation. (a) The figure shows activation for the high exposure group during a task of photic stimulation predominantly in the primary occipital cortex bilaterally (Brodmann's area 17). (b) The low exposure group shows bilateral activation primarily in the occipital association cortex (Brodmann's areas 18 and 19). (c) When the two groups are compared there is greater activation in the primary occipital cortex in the high exposure group than the low exposure group, representing recruitment of different neuronal resources in the two groups.

22–1   Frequent Regions of Interest Reported in Structural and Imaging Studies Relevant to Understanding Depression and Related Psychiatric Disorders. Numbers indicate center of foci, although some foci are collapsed across the left-right axis to reduce the number of images necessary to display these foci.

22–2   Activation to emotionally salient stimuli for those with Major Depressive Disorder (MDD, $n = 13$) compared to control (CON, $n = 15$) participants. Mean Hamilton Depression Rating Scale-17 Item score for the MDD group was 19.2 (SD = 7.6). The Emotion Word Stimulus Test is nine blocks each of positive (Pos), Negative (Neg) and Neutral (Neut) words (from the Affective Norms for Emotional Words set; Bradley and Lang, 1999) presented to participants during 3 Tesla functional MRI (GE Scanner). Images were analyzed with Statistical Parametric Mapping 2 (SPM2; Friston, 1996, thresholds $p<.001$, minimum cluster size = 120 mm^3) and Region of Interest (ROI) posthoc analyses were conducted using the MARSBAR tool from SPM2 (Brett et al., 2002). Panels A–F (radiological orientation) represent group differences with red indicating CON>MDD and blue indicating MDD>CON. Panels A–C illustrate group comparisons for Neg-Neut and panels D–F represent contrasts for Pos-Neut. There was an area of increased activation for both contrasts, MDD>CON in right middle frontal gyrus (MFG—Brodmann area 9/46, Panels C, F) that was further explored in posthoc analyses. Panel G illustrates the spherical ROI created in the right MFG (in green). An identical spherical ROI was created in the left MFG to test the laterality theory of MDD. The theory states that there will be increased activation in right MFG for Neg-Neut and decreased activation in left MFG for Pos-Neut in MDD compared to CON (Davidson, 2002). This theory is not supported (Panel H bars) with increased right MFG activation for both emotion contrasts (MDD>CON: left bar set = CON; right bar set = MDD). Left MFG was not different between groups in any contrast. We interpret these findings as increased emotion regulatory demand for emotional words in MDD irrespective of Pos or Neg valence.

Preface

The first edition of this book, published in 1986, attempted to capture in one book the dynamic developments in neuropsychology with a fundamental focus on methodological approaches and clinical applications, particularly to neuropsychiatric conditions. The first edition had two sections, one devoted to methods of comprehensive neuropsychological assessment and the second to neuropsychiatric disorders.

On the basis of the positive responses to this work, the second edition, published in 1996, followed in broad scope the general plan envisioned in the first edition. Two important changes were made, however. The first had to do with adding a third section on functional consequences of neuropsychological impairment. This addition recognized the growing interest in the clinical community of understanding how neuropsychological deficits impacted life quality and everyday functioning. The second edition also added new chapters to reflect areas of significant and increasing interest to neuropsychology such as Huntington's disease, hypoxemia, and HIV infection.

This third edition once again follows the general plan of the 1996 work, organizing our information in terms of methods, disorders, and psychosocial consequences. The book also hopefully reflects the enormous developments in neuropsychology in terms of research, clinical applications, and growth of new talent that has occurred in the past decade. As an example, in the preface to the first edition we noted that societies such as the International

Neuropsychological Society (INS) had jumped to about 2000 members. By 2008, the membership of the INS stood at well over 4000 members. Many other organizations of various disciplinary or scientific focus have grown too. These organizations all share a common interest in neuropsychological research, education, and practice. This expansion of neuropsychological talent has been accompanied by an explosive growth in the neuropsychological literature. Indeed, research in neuropsychology, which was at one time concentrated on mapping the cognitive sequelae of brain injuries and attendant "brain–behavior relationships," has now expanded to much broader considerations of the effects of systemic disease, infection, medications, and inflammatory processes on neurocognition and emotion. The third edition of this work attempts to coalesce these currents while continuing to adhere to the objective of presenting them in a concise manner in a single book.

The third edition is a thoroughly revised and updated work. It contains seven entirely new chapters on new topics that were not in the first two editions, including consideration of common sources of neurocognitive morbidity such as multiple sclerosis, diabetes, and exposure to heavy metals. There are also new chapters in an expanded Part III, which deals with psychosocial consequences of neuropsychological impairment. These include chapters on psychiatric and behavioral disorders associated with traumatic brain injury, neuropsychology in relation to everyday functioning, the effects of cognitive impairment on driving skills, and adherence to medical treatments.

There are also five chapters covering content that was in the second edition, but which represents completely new work by new contributors. Included are new chapters on the neuropsychology of epilepsy, hypoxia including sleep apnea, drug abuse, schizophrenia, and depression. As a consequence, approximately 50% of the third edition represents entirely new work. The remaining 50% consists of chapters by contributors to the second edition who have all updated their work. We are also pleased that the third edition has attracted 34 new authors and co-authors, which underscore our commitment to bringing fresh points of view while maintaining overall thematic continuity.

Finally, readers may note a small change in the title of book where we have added "neuro-medical" to be seen alongside our original "neuropsychiatric" focus of our book. This change is intended to capture the increasing presence and importance of neuropsychological assessment

in medical specialties and problems of a very wide variety.

In bringing forward this third edition we wish to thank all the many contributors and supporters who have taken time out of their busy schedules to provide major updates of their work, or to provide entirely new chapters. We are deeply indebted also to Ms. Felicia Roston, Igor Grant's Executive Assistant, for helping us in the many phases of the development of the third edition, including facilitating author communication, compilation of the works, editorial assistance, and coordination with our publisher, Oxford University Press. On the side of the publisher, we are most grateful to Ms. Shelley Reinhardt for her strong encouragement and support of the development of the third edition. Her enthusiasm for this process was essential in bringing this project to fruition.

Igor Grant, M.D.   La Jolla, CA
Kenneth M. Adams, Ph.D.   Ann Arbor, MI

Contributors

KENNETH M. ADAMS, PH.D., A.B.P.P.
Professor of Psychology and Psychiatry,
The University of Michigan,
Associate Chief, Mental Health and Chief
Psychologist, VA Ann Arbor Healthcare
System, Ann Arbor, Michigan

MARK S. ALOIA, PH.D.
Associate Professor,
Department of Medicine,
Director of Sleep Research,
National Jewish Health;
Denver, Colorado

SONIA ANCOLI-ISRAEL, PH.D.
Professor, Department of Psychiatry,
University of California,
San Diego School of Medicine,
La Jolla

TERRY R. BARCLAY, PH.D.
Clinical Neuropsychologist,
Department of Psychology,
Neurovascular Institute and Health
East Hospitals, St. Paul, Minnesota

LINAS A. BIELIAUSKAS, PH.D.
Associate Professor, Neuropsychology Section,
Department of Psychiatry,
The University of Michigan,
Staff Psychologist, Mental Health,
VA Ann Arbor Healthcare System,
Ann Arbor, Michigan

MARK W. BONDI, PH.D.
Professor, Department of Psychiatry,
University of California, San Diego School of
Medicine, La Jolla

AUGUSTINA M. A. BRANDS, PH.D.
Senior Lecturer, Department of Experimental
Psychology, Utrecht University,
Neuropsychologist, Neuropsychology Regional
Psychiatric Center, Zuwe Hofpoort Hospital,
Woerden, The Netherlands

JASON BRANDT, PH.D.
Professor and Director, Division of Medical
Psychology, Departments of Psychiatry and
Behavioral Sciences and Neurology,
The John Hopkins University School of
Medicine, Affiliate Staff, Psychiatry and
Behavioral Sciences, The John Hopkins
Hospital, Baltimore, Maryland

GREGORY G. BROWN, PH.D.
Professor, Department of Psychiatry,
University of California, San Diego School of
Medicine, La Jolla, Associate Director, VISN 22
MIRECC, Psychology Service, VA San Diego
Healthcare System

AMANDA SCHURLE BRUCE, PH.D.
Postdoctoral Fellow, Hoglund Brain Imaging
Center, University of Kansas School of
Medicine, Kansas City

HENRY A. BUCHTEL, PH.D.
Associate Professor of Psychology,
Departments of Psychiatry and Psychology,
The University of Michigan, Staff Psychologist,
Neuropsychology Section, Mental Health
Service, VA Ann Arbor Healthcare System
Ann Arbor, Michigan

CATHERINE L. CAREY, PH.D.
Postdoctoral Scholar, Department of
Psychiatry, University of California, San Diego
School of Medicine, La Jolla

STEVEN A. CASTELLON, PH.D.
Associate Research Psychologist, Department
of Psychiatry and Biobehavioral Sciences,
David Geffen School of Medicine at the,
University of California, Los Angeles, Director,
Postdoctoral Training in Psychology, Mental
Health, and Psychiatry, VA Greater Los
Angeles Healthcare System

ANDREA E. CAVANNA, M.D.
Honorary Research Fellow
Sobell Department of Motor Neuroscience and
Movement Disorders, Institute of Neurology,
London, Consultant in Behavioral Neurology,
Department of Neuropsychiatry, Birmingham
and Solihull Mental Health NHS Foundation
Trust, Birmingham, United Kingdom

THOMAS H. CROOK, PH.D.
Affiliate Professor, Department of Psychiatry,
and Behavioral Medicine, University of
South Florida College of Medicine, Tampa,
Chief Executive Officer, Cognitive Research,
Corporation, St. Petersburg, Florida

JEFFREY CUMMINGS, M.D.
August Rose Professor and Director,
Mary S. Easton Center for Alzheimer's Disease
Research, Department of Neurology, David
Geffen School of Medicine at the University of
California, Los Angeles

VANESSA G. DeFREITAS, M.A.
Candidate for Doctor of Philosophy degree,
Simon Fraser University, Burnaby, British
Columbia, Canada

LISA DELANO-WOOD, PH.D.
Assistant Professor, Department of Psychiatry,
University of California, San Diego School of
Medicine, La Jolla, Research Psychologist, VA
San Diego Healthcare System

SUREYYA DIKMEN, PH.D.
Professor, Department of Rehabilitation
Medicine, University of Washington School of
Medicine, Seattle

CHRISTINE FENNEMA-NOTESTINE, PH.D.
Assistant Adjunct Professor, Department
of Psychiatry and Radiology, University of
California, San Diego School of Medicine,
La Jolla

RAUL GONZALEZ, PH.D.
Assistant Professor of Psychology in
Psychiatry, Department of Psychiatry,
University of Illinois College of Medicine,
Chicago

IGOR GRANT, M.D., F.R.C.P.(C)
Distinguished Professor and Executive
Vice-Chair, Department of Psychiatry;
Director, HIV Neurobehavioral Research
Center, University of California, San Diego
School of Medicine, La Jolla, California

PHILIP D. HARVEY, PH.D.
Professor, Department of Psychiatry, Emory
University School of Medicine, Atlanta,
Georgia

ROBERT K. HEATON, PH.D., ABPP-CN
Professor, Department of Psychiatry,
University of California, San Diego School of
Medicine, La Jolla

NANCY HEBBEN, PH.D.
Clinical Professor in Psychology, Department
of Psychiatry, Harvard Medical School, Boston,
Clinical Associate, Department of Psychology,
McLean Hospital, Belmont,
Massachusetts

CHARLES H. HINKIN, PH.D., ABPP-CN
Professor In Residence, Department of
Psychiatry and Biobehavioral Sciences,
David Geffen School of Medicine at the
University of California, Los Angeles, Director,
Neuropsychology Assessment Laboratory,
Mental Health and Psychiatry, VA Greater Los
Angeles Healthcare System

JENNIFER E. IUDICELLO, B.A.
Doctoral Candidate, Departments of
Psychology and Psychiatry, San Diego State
University and University California,
San Diego Joint Doctoral Program in Clinical
Psychology

PATRICIA A. JANULEWICZ, M.P.H., D.SC.
Clinical Project Coordinator, Epidemiology
Department, Boston University School of
Public Health, Boston, Massachusetts

EDITH KAPLAN, PH.D.
Associate Professor of Psychiatry and
Neurology, Boston University School of
Medicine, Boston, Massachusetts, Affiliate
Professor, Department of Psychology, Clark
University, Worcester, Massachusetts,
Consulting Neuropsychologist, Department of
Psychology, Baycrest Center for Geriatric Care,
North York, Ontario, Canada

ALFRED W. KASZNIAK, PH.D.
Professor and Head, Department of
Psychology, University of Arizona, Tucson

GARY G. KAY, PH.D.
Associate Professor, Department of Neurology,
Georgetown University School of Medicine,
Washington, DC

RICHARD S. E. KEEFE, PH.D.
Professor of Psychiatry and Behavioral Sciences
and Psychology and Neuroscience, Departments
of Psychiatry and Psychology, Duke University
School of Medicine, Durham, North Carolina

ROY P. C. KESSELS, PH.D.
Professor of Neuropsychology, Donders
Institute for the Brain, Cognition, and
Behavior, Radboud University, Nijmegen, The
Netherlands; Clinical Neuropsychologist,
Departments of Medical Psychology and
Geriatric Medicine, Radboud University
Nijmegen Medical Centre, Nijmegen,
The Netherlands

SCOTT A. LANGENECKER, PH.D.
Assistant Professor, Department of Psychiatry,
The University of Michigan, Ann Arbor

GLENN J. LARRABEE, PH.D., ABPP-CN
Independent practice, Sarasota, Florida

RONALD M. LAZAR, PH.D., PAHA
Professor of Clinical Neuropsychology
in Neurology and Neurological Surgery,
Department of Neurology, Columbia,
University College of Physicians and Surgeons;
Attending Neuropsychologist, Division of
Stroke and Critical Care, Department of
Neurology, New York Presbyterian Hospital at

Columbia University Medical Center,
New York, New York

H. JIN LEE, PH.D.
Adjunct Research Investigator,
Neuropsychology Section, Department of
Psychiatry, The University of Michigan,
Ann Arbor

SCOTT L. LETENDRE, M.D.
Associate Professor in Residence, Department
of Medicine, University of California,
San Diego School of Medicine, La Jolla

JOAN MACHAMER, M.A.
Department of Rehabilitation Medicine,
University of Washington School of Medicine,
Seattle

THOMAS D. MARCOTTE, PH.D.
Associate Professor, Department of Psychiatry,
University of California, San Diego School of
Medicine, La Jolla

FRANZISKA MAIER, M.S.
Department of Neurology, University Hospital
Cologne, Cologne, Germany

PAT MCKENNA, PH.D.
Consultant Clinical Neuropsychologist,
Rookwood Hospital, Cardiff, Wales, United
Kingdom

SUSAN MCPHERSON, PH.D.
Associate Clinical Professor of Neurology,
Department of Neurology, University of
Minnesota School of Medicine, Minneapolis

WILLIAM P. MILBERG, PH.D.
Associate Professor of Psychology, Department
of Psychiatry, Harvard Medical School;
Director, Geriatric Neuropsychology
Laboratory, Geriatric Research, Education,
and Clinical Center, VA Boston Healthcare,
Jamaica Plain, Boston, Massachusetts

MAURA MITRUSHINA, PH.D.
Professor, Department of Psychology,
California State University, Northridge;
Associate Clinical Professor, Psychiatry and
Biobehavioral Sciences, Semel Institute for
Neuroscience and Human Behavior,
University of California, Los Angeles

ERIN E. MORGAN, M.S.
Graduate Student Researcher, Departments of
Psychology and Psychiatry, San Diego

State University and University California, San Diego Joint Doctoral Program in Clinical Psychology

GEORGE P. PRIGATANO, PH.D.
Newsome Chair, Clinical Neuropsychology, Barrow Neurological Institute, Phoenix, Arizona

RALPH M. REITAN, PH.D.
Reitan Neuropsychology Laboratory, South Tucson, Arizona

MARY M. ROBERTSON, M.B.CH.B., M.D., D.SC. (MED), D.P.M., F.R.C.P. (UK), F.R.C.P.C.H., F.R.C.PSYCH.
Emeritus Professor in Neuropsychiatry, University College London; Visiting Professor and Honorary Consultant, St George's Hospital and Medical School, London, United Kingdom

SEAN B. ROURKE, PH.D.
Associate Professor, Department of Psychiatry, University of Toronto; Director of Research, Mental Health Service, and Scientist, St. Michael's Hospital, Toronto, Ontario, Canada

LEE RYAN, PH.D.
Associate Professor, Department of Psychology, University of Arizona, Tucson, Arizona

DAVID P. SALMON, PH.D.
Professor in Residence, Department of Neuroscience, University of California, San Diego School of Medicine, La Jolla

J. COBB SCOTT, M.S.
Graduate Student Researcher, Departments of Psychology and Psychiatry, San Diego State University and University of California, San Diego, Joint Doctoral Program in Clinical Psychology

LINDA M. SELWA, M.D.
Professor, Department of Neurology, The University of Michigan, Ann Arbor

LARRY R. SQUIRE, PH.D.
Professor, Departments of Psychiatry, Neuroscience, and Psychology, University of California, San Diego School of Medicine,

La Jolla; Research Career Scientist, VA San Diego Healthcare System

NANCY TEMKIN, PH.D.
Professor, Department of Neurological Surgery, University of Washington School of Medicine, and Department of Biostatistics, University of Washington School of Public Health and Community Medicine, Seattle

ALLEN E. THORNTON, PH.D.
Associate Professor, Department of Psychology, Simon Fraser University, Burnaby, British Columbia, Canada

DANIEL TRANEL, PH.D.
Professor, Departments of Neurology and Psychology, University of Iowa; Chief, Benton Neuropsychology Laboratory, University of Iowa Hospitals & Clinics, Iowa City

JASMIN VASSILEVA, PH.D.
Research Assistant Professor, Department of Psychiatry, University of Illinois College of Medicine, Chicago

ELIZABETH K. WARRINGTON, B.SC., D.SC.
Professor, Dementia Research Centre, Institute of Neurology, London, United Kingdom

ROBERTA F. WHITE, PH.D.
Professor and Chair, Associate Dean for Research, Department of Environmental Health, Boston University School of Public Health; Attending Neuropsychologist, Department of Neurology, Boston University School of Medicine, Boston, Massachusetts

DEBORAH WOLFSON, PH.D.
Reitan Neuropsychology Laboratory, South Tucson, Arizona

STEVEN PAUL WOODS, PSY.D.
Assistant Professor, Department of Psychiatry, University of California, San Diego School of Medicine, La Jolla

MATTHEW J. WRIGHT, PH.D.
Director of Neuropsychology, Psychology Division, Department of Psychiatry, Harbor/University of California, Los Angeles Medical Center

Part I

Methods of Comprehensive Neuropsychological Assessment

1

The Halstead–Reitan Neuropsychological Test Battery for Adults—Theoretical, Methodological, and Validational Bases

Ralph M. Reitan and Deborah Wolfson

The development of the Halstead–Reitan Neuropsychological Test Battery (HRB) began in 1935 when Ward C. Halstead founded, at the University of Chicago, the first full-time laboratory for studying brain–behavior relationships. Halstead used a model based on inferring behavioral functions from observations and test results representing differences between persons with known brain lesions and non-brain-damaged controls. At this time there were essentially only individual tests designed to detect "brain damage" rather than batteries developed to provide comprehensive assessment of the individual person. Thus, Halstead's first step in evaluating brain-damaged patients was to observe them in their everyday living situations and to attempt to discern which aspects of their behavior were different from the behavior of normal individuals. His observations of persons with cerebral lesions made it apparent at the very beginning that brain-damaged individuals had a wide range of deficits and that a single test would not be able to adequately identify and evaluate the nature and severity of their deficits. Some patients had specific language deficits representing dysphasia. Other individuals were confused in a more general yet pervasive way (even though in casual contact they often appeared to be quite intact).

As Halstead studied brain-damaged persons in their typical everyday living situations, he observed that most of them seemed to have difficulties in understanding the essential nature of complex problem situations, in analyzing

the circumstances that they had observed, and in reaching meaningful conclusions about the situations they faced in everyday life.

The initial orientation and approach to a research program may have long-term implications. For example, Binet and Simon (1916) began developing intelligence tests using academic competence as the criterion. IQ tests, though used to assess cerebral damage, are probably still best known for their relationship to school success. It was important and fortuitous that Halstead decided to observe the adaptive processes and difficulties that brain-damaged persons demonstrated in everyday life. If he had focused only on academic achievement or classroom activities, it is probable that the tests he eventually developed would have been quite different. The tests that were finally included in the HRB emanated from a consideration of neuropsychological impairment and, as a result, have much more general relevance than IQ measures to practical aspects of rehabilitation and adaptive abilities.

On the basis of these observations, Halstead began to devise and experiment with a great number of psychological testing procedures. The design of the resulting procedures placed some of them more in the context of standardized experiments than conventional psychometric tests.

The culmination of Halstead's efforts resulted in 10 tests that ultimately formed the principal basis for his concept of biological intelligence. Only 7 of the original 10 tests have withstood the rigors of both clinical and experimental evaluation.

Halstead (1947) described his 10 tests and presented his studies of persons with and without cerebral lesions in his book, *Brain and Intelligence: A Quantitative Study of the Frontal Lobes*. Following this publication, his research and writing largely turned to other aspects of brain–behavior relationships, with illness, which led to his death in 1969, being the limiting factor of his scientific efforts.

Halstead's initial work constituted the first organized attempt to measure and understand the complexities and diversification of higher-level abilities of the human brain and, in this sense, can be thought of as representing the beginning of the discipline of clinical neuropsychology.

Unique Features of the HRB

The HRB has a number of features that are not shared by any other batteries or approaches to the assessment of brain impairment. These distinctive properties arise from the way the battery was developed, the research studies that over the years provided extensive validity findings, and the widespread testing of clinical applicability in many different geographical areas and through use by thousands of clinicians.

The Process Followed in Developing the HRB

The development of many tests and approaches in neuropsychology, such as those followed by Strauss and Werner (1941) in the early phases of child neuropsychology, focused on the behavioral characteristics of persons presumed to have damaged brains. In contrast, Halstead, working in conjunction with neurosurgeons, began his formal studies by examining persons with known brain lesions. The focus was to develop an understanding of brain–behavior relationships, which was possible only when the condition (pathology) of an individual's brain was well described and the behavior was examined and tested under well-defined and controlled conditions.

When Reitan started his laboratory at the Indiana University Medical Center, it soon became clear that Halstead's 10 tests represented only a beginning toward effective and valid clinical evaluation of the individual person.

The eventual development of the HRB was the product of a long-term experiment conceived by Ralph Reitan and Robert F. Heimburger, MD, a neurological surgeon, and implemented over a course of about 15 years with the support and participation of a number of neuropsychologists, neurologists, neurosurgeons, and neuropathologists. The plan was basically simple: patients with definitively diagnosed brain disease or damage would be referred for neuropsychological testing; the testing would be done without knowledge of the patient's history or diagnosis; a report would be written on the basis of the test results alone; this report would be compared with an independent summary of the medical and neurological findings, up to and including autopsy when available (which served as the criterion); and inaccuracies or limitations of the neuropsychological test results in reflecting the brain disease or damage would thereby become apparent.

The neuropsychological testing began using Halstead's 10 tests. These tests usually permitted a correct conclusion about whether the patient was brain damaged or a control, but inferences about lateralization, chronicity, recovery potential, type of lesion or disease, and so forth could not be done with any degree of accuracy. At this point, it was clear that additional tests were needed, as well as a framework for these additional tests, including the complementary use of various testing approaches (level of performance, specific deficits, right–left comparisons, and patterns of test relationships). Tests were added experimentally and, on a case-by-case basis, evaluated for their contribution to correct insights about the patient's brain condition. Many of the tests included on an experimental basis, when evaluated across many patients, did not contribute significantly to the neuropsychological inferences, and were discontinued (as were 3 of Halstead's 10 tests). Other tests, however, provided verified insights about involvement of one hemisphere or the other as well as about more focal cerebral involvement, chronicity, and type of lesion or disease, and these tests were added as the battery was gradually expanded. This process required testing of many patients as well as controls. The controls were primarily inpatients and were not identified as controls at the time of testing, so in these cases the testing and report writing proceeded in exactly the same manner as with patients who had brain disease or damage.

This process continued for about 15 years and included thousands of cases. Over this period tests were added, evaluated, and discarded or included, and we finally reached a point at which the various neurological (medical) findings were usually correctly inferred from the independently collected neuropsychological test results. Correct inferences covered the entire range of brain damage and disease, including neoplasms, vascular disorders, traumatic injury, infectious diseases, demyelinating diseases, degenerative diseases, and toxic exposure. The fact that the final battery, which was completed in the early 1960s, reflected the neuropsychological effects of this broad range of neurological conditions in such a large number of patients lent confidence to our belief that the test battery (which had become rather extensive) encompassed the broad range of abilities subserved by the brain. Only after the battery was complete were we in a position to review the tests that had emerged as overall brain indicators and, on that basis, propose a neuropsychological model of brain functions (now referred to as the Reitan–Wolfson model).

Meier (1985) described the HRB as having "a long and illustrious history of clinical research and application in American clinical neuropsychology," and noted that it "has had perhaps the most widespread impact of any approach in clinical neuropsychology." If these words are correct, this outcome is due to the rigorous implementation, over the years, of the grand experiment planned by Reitan and Heimburger.

It is interesting to note that the approach that laid the foundation for the development of the HRB is quite different from the current popular tendency in the field to base a neuropsychological evaluation on tests selected to measure presumed dimensions of brain functions and, if they measure enough functions, to merit designation as being comprehensive, or, alternatively, to base an evaluation on the client's own complaints or perceived cognitive deficits. This latter approach is essentially a procedure that accepts the client's self-diagnosis as a basis for composing a test battery.

The Extensive Research Supporting the Validity of the HRB

The HRB has a very long paper trail consisting of hundreds of published studies of its effectiveness. Dean (1985), in his review of the HRB, noted that it is the "most researched" battery in the United States. Reitan and his colleagues alone have published more than 300 books, chapters, and research papers, mainly on the HRB. It is not possible to review all of these studies in the present context, but some studies can be mentioned briefly.

Our initial study (Reitan, 1955b), concerned with the sensitivity of tests included in the HRB, used results obtained on Halstead's 10 tests to compare a group of 50 subjects with documented cerebral damage or disease and a group of 50 controls who showed no past or present symptoms of cerebral disease or dysfunction. A heterogeneous and diverse group of subjects with cerebral damage was deliberately included to ensure that an extensive range of neurological conditions would be represented.

The study also intentionally included a number of controls with medical conditions other than brain damage. Twenty-four percent of the control group was composed of normally functioning individuals. The remaining 76% of the control group was composed of patients hospitalized for a variety of difficulties *not* involving impaired brain functions. A substantial number of paraplegic and neurotic patients were included in this group in an attempt to minimize the probability that any differences between the groups could be attributed to variables such as hospitalization, chronic illness, or affective disturbances.

The two groups were composed by matching pairs of individuals on the basis of race and gender and, as closely as possible, on chronological age and years of formal education. The difference in mean age for the two groups was 0.06 years, and the difference in mean education was 0.02 years. The two groups were therefore closely matched for age and education, and the standard deviations for age and education in the two groups were nearly identical.

Although the two groups should have produced essentially comparable results on the basis of the controlled variables, the presence of brain damage in one group was responsible for a striking difference in the test results. Seven of the measures devised by Halstead showed differences between the mean scores for the two groups, with relation to variability estimates, which achieved striking significance from a statistical point of view. In fact, according to the most detailed tables we have seen, the probability estimates not only exceeded the .01 or .001 level, but also exceeded 10^{-12}. However, even these tables were inadequate to express the appropriate statistical probability level for these seven tests. These seven measures were the Category Test, the Tactual Performance Test (TPT; Total Time, Memory, and Localization components), Finger Tapping–Preferred Hand, Speech-sounds Perception Test (SSPT), and the Rhythm Test.

As noted in the preceding paragraph, statistical comparisons of the two groups reached extreme probability levels on 7 of the 10 measures contributing to the Halstead Impairment Index. The most striking intergroup differences were shown by the Halstead Impairment Index (even though 3 of the 10 measures contributing to it were not particularly sensitive) and the Category Test. Not a single brain-damaged subject performed better than his or her matched control on the Impairment Index (although the Impairment Indices were equal in 6 of the 50 matched pairs). The Category Test was the most sensitive of any single measure to the effects of cerebral damage. In three instances the subjects with brain lesions performed better than their matched control subjects, but in the 47 remaining pairs of subjects the controls performed better on the Category Test.

Many years later, Reitan and Wolfson (1988) did a similar study based on 42 variables that summarized results of the entire HRB. These variables comprised the General Neuropsychological Deficit Scale (GNDS), which was based on a standard score from each of 42 variables. Each standard score reflected the degree of normality or impairment on each test.

Data analyses, based on comparisons of 169 persons with independent evidence of brain damage and 41 controls, identified a GNDS cutoff score of 25/26 that yielded a 90% accuracy rate in identifying brain-damaged persons (sensitivity) and a 90% accuracy rate in identifying non–brain-damaged (control) persons (specificity). These sensitivity and specificity findings clearly indicate the power of brain damage as an independent variable in determining the GNDS scores. In fact, 85% of the 169 brain-damaged persons earned GNDS scores of 35 or more, and every control subject earned a GNDS score of 34 or less. In clinical practice, this finding often represents a relatively absolute cutoff for concluding that brain damage is present in the individual case, although evaluation of the results of the entire HRB is obviously necessary to explicate the nature and pattern of the individual's neuropsychological impairment.

One of the most comprehensive studies of the HRB (Wheeler et al., 1963) used discriminant functions to predict whether subjects, on the basis of their test scores, fell in the category of presence of brain damage or that of absence of brain damage. Test data consisted of results for each subject on 11 Wechsler subtests and 13 scores from the HRB. In some instances, combinations of variables were also evaluated (e.g., the 24-variable discriminant function, the Impairment Index, the sum of Verbal and Performance weighted scores from the Wechsler Scale, and other combinations of possible interest) as well as age and education. Comparisons were made between 61 non–brain-damaged control subjects and 79 persons with unequivocal neurological, neurosurgical, or autopsy evidence of cerebral disease or damage. These 79 persons with brain damage were subdivided according to the location of lesions (left hemisphere, $N = 25$; right hemisphere, $N = 31$; and diffuse or bilateral involvement, $N = 23$). The principal comparisons were between the controls and each brain-damaged group as well as controls and the total group of brain-damaged persons.

The discriminant function in each comparison produced a single weighted score for each subject, an optimum least squares type of separation between pairs of groups. The distributions of summed weighted scores in each comparison of pairs of groups were then inspected to determine the point of least overlap. The weighted score for each person, falling above or below this point of least overlap, determined whether the individual belonged to one group or the other in the pair of groups being compared. These assignments were then compared with the group to which the subjects actually belonged (as based on definitive neurological diagnoses), and expressed as percentages of correct predictions.

The results of this study yielded validity findings that have never been equaled by any other neuropsychological test battery. The Impairment Index, evaluated as a single score, was correct in about 9 of 10 cases. The percentage of correct classifications by the Impairment Index in various pairs of groups was as follows: controls versus the entire group of brain-damaged subjects, 87.2%; controls versus diffuse brain damage, 94.5%; controls versus left cerebral damage, 90.2%; and controls versus right cerebral damage, 87.9%. Even higher accuracy rates were achieved with the 24-variable discriminant function. The percentage of correct classifications was as follows: controls versus all brain-damaged cases, 90.7%; controls versus diffuse brain damage, 98.8%; controls versus left cerebral damage, 93.0%; controls versus right cerebral damage, 92.4%; and right cerebral damage versus left cerebral damage, 92.9%. These results demonstrate the sensitivity of the tests in the HRB as they relate differentially to scores produced by normal controls versus brain-damaged groups.

These publications dated back many years, but neurological diagnostic methods at that time were quite capable of identifying brain disease and damage, and persons included in the brain-damaged group had definitive diagnoses in every case. The controls had also been carefully examined by neurologists and neurosurgeons, and none had a history or examination findings that suggested prior brain disease or damage.

The Value of Using Complementary Approaches to Assessment of the Various Ways that Brain Damage Is Expressed

The HRB was deliberately designed to incorporate various methods or approaches to assessment that can be applied in a complementary manner in evaluation of the individual person. The first of these methods concerned level of performance, or how well the subject performed on each test. This is the method customarily used by neuropsychologists in producing data either for clinical evaluation or for research analyses. This method is based on tests that produce continuous distributions, which, of course, cover a range of variability in normal as well as brain-damaged samples. The distributions for these two groups invariably overlap because level of performance is invariably influenced and determined by many factors. This overlap complicates the use of the method in attempting to differentiate individual members of each group.

Another approach frequently used by neuropsychologists compares the subject's scores on various tests and evaluates these relationships as possible indicators of impairment. Clinical interpretation of the HRB is also facilitated by including tests of intelligence and academic achievement as well as measures of personality traits or disturbances.

The aforementioned methods are routinely used and have a long history. We realized early in our evaluation of persons with brain damage that additional approaches, though not necessarily useful in every case, often provided definitive evidence of brain damage, analogous to evidence obtained from specialized neurological tests such as computed tomography and magnetic resonance imaging of the brain. Not infrequently, neuropsychological tests based on the presence or absence of brain-related deficits produce unequivocal evidence of brain dysfunction that is of great specificity in identifying the examinee as brain damaged. In such cases, persons with brain damage manifest deficits on simple tasks that are performed easily and adequately by persons without brain damage. These tests are represented in the HRB by the Reitan–Indiana Aphasia Test and the Reitan–Kløve Sensory-Perceptual Test.

Investigation of such deficits in various groups of brain-damaged and control subjects has a long history in clinical use of the HRB, having shown that certain specific deficits, while rarely judged to be present among non–brain-damaged controls, were not infrequently found among persons with brain disease or damage and, in addition, were sometimes quite specific in their relationship to one cerebral hemisphere or the other (Wheeler & Reitan, 1962).

It may be noted that these approaches to neuropsychological assessment were derived from the field of neurology rather than psychology, and this may be the basic reason that they have been relatively neglected by neuropsychologists. In fact, many medical procedures produce "presence" or "absence" (binary or dichotomous) conclusions (such as computed tomography and magnetic resonance imaging of the brain) in contrast to the continuous distributions produced by most psychological tests. This difference in the two disciplines may stem, in turn, from the need in medicine to identify categorically and accurately various diseases, whereas in psychology the tradition in measurement has been to rate the comparative level of an individual's performance with relation to normative standards. In the very beginning we recognized the potential for integrating these two approaches in a complementary manner; the HRB therefore included methods derived both from neurology and psychology, integrating them as a single assessment procedure. The HRB is still the only neuropsychological testing method to have been developed in this manner.

Another approach to assessment, derived from neurology but deliberately adapted for inclusion in the HRB, was based on the anatomy of the central nervous system and more specifically on the differential functional relationship of each cerebral hemisphere to the contralateral side of the body. Many, if not most, brain disorders affect one hemisphere to a greater extent than the other hemisphere. In turn, one side of the body is often more impaired than the other side with regard to sensory-perceptual and/or motor functions. In the early stages of development of the HRB, tests were developed and included to assess these lateralized deficits in a formal manner. These

test results were compared for the individual subject, producing intraindividual scores that were then validated through correlation with independent neurological findings. Currently, these intraindividual difference scores can be converted into Neuropsychological Deficit Scale scores that range through four categories from perfectly normal to clinically severe deficits (Reitan & Wolfson, 1993).

The Theoretical Model and Content of the Halstead–Reitan Neuropsychological Test Battery

As noted previously in this chapter, the content of the HRB was not derived from presumptions about what *should* be measured but, instead, from a very practical consideration—what tests were needed to differentiate persons with and without independent neurological evidence of brain disease or damage and to discern, from the test results alone, the many additional aspects of the patient's condition (diffuse versus focal disease; right versus left involvement; anterior versus posterior involvement; acute versus chronic disorders; and finally, the specific disease entity or type of damage). Our purpose was to establish a firm, empirical relationship of neuropsychological test results to the complete diagnosis derived from the history, neurological examination, results of specialized neurological tests, findings at surgery of the brain, and finally, autopsy of the brain.

A basic presumption was that when we had developed a neuropsychological battery that permitted accurate predictions of the many aspects of brain disease and damage we would inevitably have included—measurement of the fundamental cognitive, intellectual, motor, and sensory-perceptual aspects of brain function. Many tests, including the Wechsler Memory Scale (but *not* the Wechsler–Bellevue Intelligence Scale), were found to add little (if any) uniqueness. This led to a conceptualization that memory, in a clinically meaningful sense and distinct from immediate reproduction, was a very complex function that was already represented in tests of registration through the various avenues of sensory input, scanning against the body of knowledge already possessed by the brain, related to the principal specialized functions of the cerebral hemispheres (language and speech in a broad sense and visual–spatial and auditory–temporal abilities ranging from simple registration and reproduction to immensely complex interactions) and, perhaps most important, to basic ability in abstraction, reasoning, establishing relationships, logical analysis, and so forth. All of these abilities, in the aggregate, contribute to and compose memory in its complete dimensions.

The long-term process of developing a set of tests that permitted prediction of the presence, nature, and extent of damage to the brain led to the development of a general theory of brain–behavior relationships, referred to as the Reitan–Wolfson model of neuropsychological functioning (see Figure 1–1).

A neuropsychological response cycle first requires input to the brain from the external environment via one or more of the sensory avenues. Primary sensory areas are located in each cerebral hemisphere, indicating that this level of central processing is widely represented in the cerebral cortex and involves the temporal, parietal, and occipital areas particularly

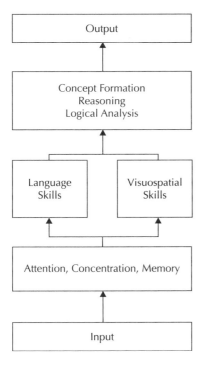

Figure 1–1. A graphic representation of the Reitan–Wolfson model of neuropsychological functioning.

(see Reitan & Wolfson, 1993, for a description of the anatomical structures and systems for each of the elements of the Reitan–Wolfson model).

Once sensory information reaches the brain, the first step in central processing is the "registration phase" and represents alertness, attention, continued concentration, and the ability to screen incoming information in relation to prior experiences (immediate, intermediate, and remote memory). When evaluating this level of functioning, the neuropsychologist is concerned with answering questions such as the following: How well can this individual pay attention to a specified task? Can he or she utilize past experiences (memory) effectively and efficiently to reach a reasonable solution to a problem? Can the person understand and follow simple instructions?

If an individual's brain is not capable of registering incoming information, relating the new information to past experiences (memory), and establishing the relevance of the information, the subject is almost certainly seriously impaired in everyday behavior. A person who is not able to maintain alertness and a degree of concentration is likely to make very little progress as he or she attempts to solve a problem. Persons with such severe impairment have limited opportunity to effectively utilize any of the other higher-level abilities that the brain subserves, and they tend to perform quite poorly on almost any task presented to them.

Because alertness and concentration are necessary for all aspects of problem solving, a comprehensive neuropsychological test battery should include measures that evaluate the subject's attentiveness. Such tests should not be complicated and difficult, but should require the person to pay close attention over time to specific stimulus material. The Halstead-Reitan Battery evaluates this first level of central processing primarily with two measures: the Speech-sounds Perception Test (SSPT) and the Rhythm Test.

The SSPT consists of 60 spoken nonsense words that are variants of the "ee" sound. The stimuli are presented on a tape recording, and the subject responds to each stimulus by underlining one of four alternatives printed on an answer sheet. The SSPT requires the subject to maintain attention through the 60 items, perceive the spoken stimulus through hearing, and relate the perception through vision to the correct configuration of letters on the test form.

The Rhythm Test requires the subject to differentiate between 30 pairs of rhythmic beats. The stimuli are presented by a standardized tape recording. After listening to a pair of stimuli, the subject writes "S" on the answer sheet if he or she thinks the two stimuli sounded the same, and writes "D" if they sounded different. The Rhythm Test requires alertness to nonverbal auditory stimuli, sustained attention to the task, and ability to perceive and compare different rhythmic sequences. Although many psychologists have presumed that the Rhythm Test is dependent on the integrity of the right hemisphere (because the content is nonverbal), the test is actually an indicator of generalized cerebral functions (apparently because of the requirement of attention and concentration) and has no lateralizing significance (Reitan & Wolfson, 1989).

After an initial registration of incoming material, the brain customarily proceeds to process verbal information in the left cerebral hemisphere and visual–spatial information in the right cerebral hemisphere. At this point the specialized functions of the two hemispheres become operational.

The left cerebral hemisphere is particularly involved in speech and language functions or the use of language symbols for communication purposes. It is important to remember that deficits may involve simple kinds of speech and language skills as well as sophisticated higher-level aspects of verbal communication. It must also be recognized that language functions may be impaired in terms of expressive capabilities, receptive functions, or both (Reitan, 1984). Thus, the neuropsychological examination must assess an individual's ability to express language as a response, to understand language through both the auditory and visual avenues, and to complete the entire response cycle, which consists of perception of language information, central processing and understanding of its content, and the development of an effective response.

The HRB measures both simple and complex verbal functions. The Reitan–Indiana Aphasia Screening Test (AST) is used to evaluate language functions such as naming common objects, spelling simple words, reading, writing, enunciating, identifying individual numbers and letters, and performing simple arithmetic computations.

The AST is organized so that performances are evaluated in terms of the particular sensory modalities through which the stimuli are perceived. Additionally, the receptive and expressive components of the test allow the neuropsychologist to judge whether the limiting deficit for a subject is principally receptive or expressive in character. The verbal subtests of the WAIS are also used to obtain information about verbal intelligence.

Right cerebral hemisphere functions are particularly involved with spatial abilities (mediated principally by vision but also by touch and auditory function) and spatial and manipulatory skills (Reitan, 1955a; Wheeler & Reitan, 1962). It is again important to remember that an individual may be impaired in the expressive aspects or the receptive aspects of visual–spatial functioning, or both. It must also be kept in mind that we live in a world of time and space as well as in a world of verbal communication. Persons with impairment of visual–spatial abilities are often severely handicapped in terms of efficiency of functioning in a practical, everyday sense.

The HRB assesses visual–spatial functions with simple as well as complex tasks. Particularly important are the drawings of the square, cross, and triangle of the Aphasia Screening Test (AST), the WAIS Performance subtests, and to an extent, Parts A and B of the Trail Making Test.

In evaluating the drawings on the AST, the criterion of brain damage relates to specific distortions of the spatial configurations rather than to artistic skill. The square and triangle are relatively simple figures, and do not usually challenge an individual's appreciation and production of spatial configurations. The cross involves many turns and a number of directions, and can provide significant information about a subject's understanding of visual–spatial form.

Comparisons of performances on the two sides of the body, using both motor and sensory-perceptual tasks, provide information about the integrity of each cerebral hemisphere, and more specifically, about areas within each hemisphere. Both finger tapping and grip strength yield information about the posterior frontal (motor) areas of each cerebral hemisphere.

The Tactual Performance Test (TPT) requires complex problem-solving skills and can provide information about the adequacy of each cerebral hemisphere. The subject is blindfolded before the test begins and is not permitted to see the formboard or blocks at any time. The first task is to fit the blocks into their proper spaces on the board using only the preferred hand. After completing this task (and without having been given prior warning), the subject is asked to perform the same task using only the nonpreferred hand. Finally, and again without prior warning, the task is repeated a third time using both hands. The amount of time required to perform each of the three trials provides a comparison of the efficiency of performance of the two hands. The Total Time score of the test reflects the amount of time needed to complete all three trials.

After the subject has completed the third trial, the board and blocks are taken out of the testing area and the blindfold is removed. The subject is then asked to draw a diagram of the board with the blocks in their proper spaces. The Memory score is the number of shapes correctly remembered; the Localization score is the number of blocks correctly identified by both shape and position on the board.

An important aspect of the TPT relates to the neurological model. The test's design and procedure allow the functional efficiency of the two cerebral hemispheres to be compared and provide information about the general efficiency of brain functions. During the first trial, data is being transmitted from the preferred hand to the contralateral cerebral hemisphere (usually from the right hand to the left cerebral hemisphere). Under normal circumstances, positive practice effect results in a reduction of time of about one-third from the first trial to the second trial. A similar reduction in time occurs between the second trial and the third trial.

The TPT is undoubtedly a complex task in terms of its motor and sensory requirements, and successful performance appears to be principally dependent on the middle part of the cerebral hemispheres. Ability to correctly place the variously shaped blocks on the board depends on tactile form discrimination, kinesthesis, coordination of movement of the upper extremities, manual dexterity, and an appreciation of the relationship between the spatial configuration of the shapes and their location on the board. Obviously, the TPT is considerably more complex in its problem-solving requirements than either finger tapping or grip strength.

The components of the HRB sensory-perceptual examination include tests for bilateral simultaneous sensory stimulation including tactile, auditory, and visual stimuli presented unilaterally and then, without warning, simultaneously on both sides. Impaired perception of stimulation occurs on the side of the body contralateral to a damaged hemisphere. The Tactile Form Recognition Test requires the subject to identify shapes through the sense of touch and yields information about the integrity of the contralateral parietal area (Reitan & Wolfson, 2002b). Finger localization and finger-tip number writing perception also provide information about the parietal area of the contralateral cerebral hemisphere. Finger-tip number writing requires considerably more alertness and concentration, or perhaps even more general intelligence, than finger localization (Fitzhugh et al., 1962).

In the Reitan–Wolfson theory of neuropsychological functioning, the highest level of central processing is represented by abstraction, reasoning, concept formation, and logical analysis skills. Research evidence indicates that these abilities have a general rather than a specific representation throughout the cerebral cortex (Doehring & Reitan, 1961). The generality and importance of abstraction and reasoning skills may be suggested biologically by the fact that these skills are distributed throughout the cerebral cortex rather than being limited as a specialized function of one cerebral hemisphere or a particular area within a hemisphere. Generalized distribution of abstraction abilities throughout the cerebral cortex may also be significant in the interaction of abstraction with more specific abilities (such as language) that are represented more focally.

Impairment at the highest level of central processing has profound implications for the adequacy of neuropsychological functioning. Persons with deficits in abstraction and reasoning functions have lost a great deal of the ability to profit from their experiences in a meaningful, logical, and organized manner. However, since their deficits are general rather than specific in nature, such persons may appear to be relatively intact in casual contact. Because of the close relationship between organized behavior and memory, these subjects often complain of "memory" problems and are grossly inefficient in practical, everyday tasks. They are not able to organize their activities properly, and frequently direct a considerable amount of time and energy to elements of a situation that are not appropriate to the nature of the problem.

This nonappropriate activity, together with an eventual withdrawal from attempting to deal with problem situations, constitutes a major component of what is frequently (and imprecisely) referred to as "personality" change. On clinical inquiry, such changes are often found to consist of erratic and poorly planned behavior, deterioration of personal hygiene, a lack of concern and understanding for others, and so forth. When examined neuropsychologically, it is often discovered that these behaviors are largely represented by cognitive changes at the highest level of central processing rather than emotional involvement per se.

Finally, in the solution of problems or expression of intelligent behavior, the sequential element from input to output frequently involves an interaction of the various aspects of central processing. Visual–spatial skills, for example, are closely dependent on registration and continued attention to incoming material of a visual–spatial nature, but analysis and understanding of the problem also involves the highest element of central processing, represented by concept formation, reasoning, and logical analysis. Exactly the same kind of arrangement between areas of functioning in the Reitan–Wolfson model would relate to adequacy in using verbal and language skills. In fact, the speed and facility with which an individual carries out such interactions within the content categories of central processing probably in itself represents a significant aspect of efficiency in brain functioning.

The HRB uses several measures to evaluate abstraction skills, including the Category Test, the Trail Making Test, and the overall efficiency of performance demonstrated on the TPT.

The Category Test has several characteristics that make it unique compared to many other tests. The Category Test is a relatively complex test of concept formation that requires ability (1) to note recurring similarities and differences in stimulus material, (2) to postulate reasonable hypotheses about these similarities and differences, (3) to test these hypotheses by receiving positive or negative information (bell or buzzer), and (4) to adapt hypotheses on the basis of the information received after each response.

The Category Test is not particularly difficult for most normal subjects. Since the subject is required to postulate solutions in a structured (rather than permissive) context, the Category Test appears to require particular competence in abstraction ability. The test in effect presents each subject with a learning experiment in concept formation. This is in contrast to the usual situation in psychological testing, which requires solution of an integral problem situation.

The primary purpose of the Category Test is to determine the subject's ability to use both negative and positive experiences as a basis for altering and adapting his or her performance (i.e., developing different hypotheses to determine the theme of each subtest). The precise pattern and sequence of positive and negative information (the bell or buzzer) in the Category Test is probably never exactly the same for any two subjects (or for the same subject on repetition of the test). Since it can be presumed that every item in the test affects the subject's response to ensuing items, the usual approaches toward determination of reliability indices may be confounded. Nevertheless, the essential nature of the Category Test, as an experiment in concept formation, is clear.

The Category Test is probably the best measure in the HRB of abstraction, reasoning, and logical analysis abilities, which in turn are essential for organized planning. As noted earlier, subjects who perform especially poorly on the Category Test often complain of having "memory" problems. In fact, the Category Test requires organized memory (as contrasted with the simple reproduction of stimulus material required of most short-term memory tests), and is probably a more meaningful indication of memory in practical, complex, everyday situations than most so-called memory tests, especially considering that memory, in a purposeful behavioral context, necessarily depends on relating the various aspects of a situation to each other (see Reitan & Wolfson, 1988, 1993, for a discussion of this concept).

The Trail Making Test is composed of two parts, Part A and Part B. Part A consists of 25 circles printed on a sheet of paper. Each circle contains a number from 1 to 25. The subject's task is to connect the circles with a pencil line as quickly as possible, beginning with the number 1 and proceeding in numerical sequence. Part B consists of 25 circles numbered from 1 to 13 and lettered from A to L. The task in Part B is to connect the circles, in sequence, alternating between numbers and letters. The scores represent the number of seconds required to complete each part.

The Trail Making Test requires immediate recognition of the symbolic significance of numbers and letters, ability to scan the page continuously to identify the next number or letter in sequence, flexibility in integrating the numerical and alphabetical series, and completion of these requirements under the pressure of time. It is likely that the ability to deal with the numerical and language symbols (numbers and letters) is sustained by the left cerebral hemisphere, the visual scanning task necessary to perceive the spatial distribution of the stimulus material is represented by the right cerebral hemisphere, and speed and efficiency of performance may reflect the general adequacy of brain functions. It is therefore not surprising that the Trail Making Test, which requires simultaneous integration of these several abilities, is one of the best measures of general brain functions (Reitan, 1955c, 1958).

Clinical Inferences Regarding Individual Persons

Inferences about average performances for groups of subjects are of little relevance when only a single person is involved. The accuracy of conclusions about the individual person is an inescapable consideration whenever the conclusion is actually applied to the individual person. This statement is obviously a truism. Yet, many (if not most) neuropsychological methods of examination have never been submitted to a test of accuracy regarding the identification of brain damage in the individual person. The HRB has always focused on the individual person through research that has rigorously evaluated the accuracy of clinical conclusions.

Realizing that clinical accuracy was a major objective in neuropsychological testing, the HRB long ago was evaluated in this respect (Reitan, 1964). The first step in this validational procedure was to identify subjects with criterion-quality frontal, nonfrontal, or diffuse cerebral lesions based on all available information from the neurologists and neurosurgeons who had treated them, as well as from neuropathological findings. In order to provide a rigorous test of the generality of any conclusion relating to these various groups, we designed the study so that each group had the same number of subjects with different types of lesions. Each regional localization group was therefore composed of equal numbers of subjects with intrinsic tumors, extrinsic tumors, cerebral vascular lesions, and focal traumatic lesions. Classification of these subjects was based solely on medical findings and with no reference to their HRB test results. In total, we identified 64 persons with focal lesions (16 in each quadrant) and 48 persons with diffuse cerebral damage, for a total of 112 persons.

The next step was to refer only to the HRB test results, and rate each of the 112 persons with regard to focal or diffuse involvement, the type of brain disease or lesion, and, if focal, identify the quadrant involved. On the basis of the HRB results alone, 46 of the 48 persons with diffuse involvement and 57 of the 64 persons with focal damage were identified correctly.

The number of correct classifications based on HRB results regarding type of lesion was as follows: intrinsic tumor, 13 of 16; extrinsic tumor, 8 of 16; cerebral vascular disease, 28 of 32; head injury, 30 of 32; and multiple sclerosis, 15 of 16. Thus, 94 of the 112 patients were classified correctly according to type of lesion.

This degree of concurrence between neurological and neuropsychological ratings could scarcely have happened by chance. The results confirmed that HRB test results are differentially influenced by (1) focal and diffuse lesions, (2) the cerebral hemisphere that is damaged, (3) frontal and nonfrontal lesions within the hemisphere involved, (4) intrinsic tumors, extrinsic tumors, cerebral vascular lesions, head injuries, and multiple sclerosis, (5) focal occlusion as compared with generalized insufficiency in cerebral vascular disease, and (6) focal as compared with diffuse damage from head injuries.

Forensic and Clinical Implications of Validity Studies of the HRB

The United States Supreme Court identified four considerations for trial judges to use in evaluating expert testimony, or in some cases, in deciding whether to admit expert testimony. This directive requires that neuropsychologists carefully consider their testing methodology in accordance with whether their procedures meet these four criteria. Briefly, these include the following:

1. Has the method been tested?
2. Has the method been subjected to peer review and publication?
3. What is the error rate in applying the method?
4. To what extent has the method received general acceptance in the relevant scientific community?

In our experience, trial judges and lawyers are giving increased consideration to these guidelines, and give serious consideration to the admissibility of testimony based on whether these guidelines have been met. In the main, concerns have centered around (3) and (4) aforementioned, namely, the error rate and the question of general acceptance.

It would seem perfectly legitimate, and even necessary, to know how accurate a method is in achieving its purpose. Acceptance in the scientific community, however, would carry with it a time factor, inasmuch as newer methods would need time to be incorporated into the knowledge, experience, and practical testing that might be required for acceptance. Neuropsychological tests and procedures, which have been subject to peer review and publication in acceptable outlets, however, might well be viewed as having appropriate acceptance by the scientific community.

Our recent experiences have mainly concerned (3) above—the error rate. The error rate is quite a different matter than the statistical probability of accepting the null hypothesis (or a chance effect), which some neuropsychologists have referred to in responding to this requirement. Even supplying a probability statement for multiple tests is hardly an answer, inasmuch as the independence of the tests is unknown and, in any case, this kind of information says nothing about the rate of errors in conclusions about the individual person. In legal matters concerning personal injury, data relating to the probability that groups of subjects are, or are not, drawn from the same population are essentially irrelevant, because the matter concerns the individual person rather than inferential statistics based on group comparisons.

In fact, the customary models of statistical analyses—the ones we all learned in school and are usually required to meet publication standards—have limited meaning when judgments, diagnoses, and conclusions must be made about the individual person, particularly when based on tests that produce continuous score distributions. We often offer "more probable than not" statements with little or no hard evidence to support these conclusions. If knowledge of the error rate concerning the question of brain damage or impairment was actually required to permit one to testify as an expert, not many neuropsychologists would be allowed to testify. Few studies on individual tests, or even conclusions based on batteries of tests, even report the number of false-positives and false-negatives. Such data are published for other diagnostic methods that require conclusions about the individual person (such as computed tomography and magnetic resonance imaging), and questions of accuracy were among the first issues studied when these procedures were developed and became available.

Why have psychologists failed to produce such data, when it clearly is so necessary as a basis for giving neuropsychological methods a degree of credence? There are a number of possible answers to this question, a principal one being that a specified procedure or set of tests is required, applied to each subject in a precise and standardized manner, in order to evaluate the accuracy of the method, as shown by concurrence with independent criterion information. In cases involving litigation, neuropsychologists appear to be shying away from such specified and standardized procedures in favor of so-called flexible batteries, apparently wanting (or needing) to give whatever tests they wish and to thereby gain the right to draw whatever conclusions they wish (or that may be requisite in terms of the role they have accepted and the conclusions they have committed themselves to support).

In a recent case a federal judge was asked, on the basis of a Daubert challenge, to dismiss the testimony of a prominent neuropsychologist who was testifying on behalf of a plaintiff who had sustained a head injury. In many prior instances, both in his publications and sworn testimony, this neuropsychologist had supported the use of neuropsychological tests in evaluating individual persons. In this case, however, the extensive set of tests that had been administered under his direct supervision fell essentially in the normal range. He admitted that the test findings were essentially normal, and, in fact, this conclusion was readily subject to documentation, inasmuch as they were based on the HRB. However, he insisted that the plaintiff had sustained significant and serious impairment. There was strong evidence against this conclusion, such as the plaintiff having earned a greater income the year after the injury than the year before the injury. However, this prominent neuropsychologist pointed out that he had interviewed the plaintiff, his relatives, and a few friends, all of whom cited a host of complaints and problems that they attributed to the injury.

When asked about the disparity between his conclusions and the normal neuropsychological test results, the neuropsychologist replied that neuropsychological tests contributed no more than 10% to his conclusions and that his clinical impressions were the primary basis for his testimony. The opposing attorney then appealed to the judge to exclude the neuropsychologist's testimony on the grounds that his methodology had not been adequately tested, had not been subjected to peer review, and had an error rate that was unknown. The attorney argued that the neuropsychological community would disagree that neuropsychological tests should count for 10% and clinical impressions for 90%. The defense attorney said that, in his opinion, the judge "came very close to excluding the neuropsychologist's testimony, but in the end felt that he did not have enough information about prevailing practices in neuropsychology to make such a decision." Another consideration may have been that the judge was reluctant to make a ruling that would have devastated the plaintiff's case since, aside from the neuropsychologist's opinion, there was little additional credible evidence of brain impairment.

It seems clear that the time has come for neuropsychologists to support their conclusions with scientific evidence. We can hardly be proud that it is the legal processes that are forcing us in this direction rather than a feeling of clinical responsibility to our clients and patients.

The issue of testing the accuracy of neuropsychological test data must receive much more critical consideration than it has up to this point. One approach might be to make predictive judgments using whatever test data was available for each subject, and checking the accuracy of these predictions against criterion information. The problem with this approach would lie in the fact that there would be no clear definition of the test data used for making the predictions, inasmuch as the tests administered would surely vary from one subject to another.

Neuropsychologists who use so-called flexible batteries would face exactly this problem, because their test batteries, designed according to the supposed complaints or deficits of the client, necessarily vary from one client to another. In fact, a procedure that first discerns the client's area of possible deficit via history information, relatives' observations of the client, or interview information, and then seeks to confirm or refute such hypotheses through selection of a range of tests judged to be appropriate, is clearly circular and can only be considered to be relevant to the complaints initially deemed to be significant.

Under these circumstances, there can be no assurance that the battery of tests selected for each client represents a comprehensive, balanced, and validated set of measures of brain function or dysfunction. Of course, if *each* of these many symptom-oriented batteries had been checked for accuracy in correlating with and identifying brain lesions of a diffuse and/or focal nature, in varying locations of the brain, representing the full range of types of brain disease and injury in identifying both chronic and stabilized brain lesions versus acute and progressive brain conditions and effectively differentiating this entire cadre of people with brain involvement from non–brain-damaged people, there would be no problem. The field of *neuropsychology* (the discipline based on establishing brain–behavior relationships) would be secure. Obviously, though, the diverse collections of tests used by many neuropsychologists have not been tested in this manner.

There is no likely prospect that *multiple* test batteries can be checked out in the detail necessary to establish their relationships to the broad range of conditions that, in total, represent brain damage. Yet, unless there is evidence that all the categories of brain damage are reflected by a particular neuropsychological battery (or that the battery validly differentiates between brain-damaged persons and non-brain-damaged persons regardless of all of the variations that occur under the rubric of brain damage), one cannot presume that the battery validly reflects brain pathology.

In the absence of evidence supporting this presumption, we clearly lose the claim that identifies the essential nature of our field as the area of psychology that relates behavioral measurement to the biological status of the brain. Without a firm anchor to the brain, we become clinical psychologists, school psychologists, consulting psychologists, educational psychologists, or whatever type of psychologist appropriate to our particular interest. Of course, if we have not been intensively trained in these areas, we will also find ourselves failing to compare favorably to the experts who have been so trained and experienced.

It is apparent that we cannot have it both ways. We either have to respect the brain as the basis for behavior, and validate our measures in accordance to the many things that go wrong with the brain, or recognize that the *neuro* part of neuropsychology is added for respectability alone. If we are unable to document valid relationships to brain status, in terms of our scientific methods and procedures, as responsible professionals we should at least admit that the Supreme Court was quite reasonable and correct in requiring that the error rate in *neuro*psychology be specified with respect to individual subjects. Such an admission for many neuropsychologists would also verify their inadequacy to function as expert witnesses.

One way to resolve this dilemma would be competently to use a neuropsychological test battery for which published evidence is available that meets the four criteria identified by the Supreme Court as necessary for admission as an expert witness. The Halstead–Reitan Neuropsychological Test Battery meets these four criteria, but competent interpretation (which can be judged by the many published examples of test interpretation) is required over and beyond training in test administration. Fortunately, detailed information is available for both administration and interpretation of these batteries of neuropsychological tests for adults, older children, and young children (Reitan & Wolfson, 1988, 1990, 1992, 1993), and the interested neuropsychologist can learn much of the basics of HRB test interpretation from the many case examples that have been provided.

Recent Research and Current Issues in Neuropsychology

The development, content, and design of the HRB allow its continual use in pursuing many theoretical, practical, and clinical issues in neuropsychology.

The General Neuropsychological Deficit Scale (GNDS)

The GNDS is a summary score based on 42 variables from the HRB. In addition to tests based on level of performance, the GNDS also includes additional variables that reflect the ways in which the brain expresses its deficits, including the occurrence of specific signs (as opposed to general indicators) of brain damage, relationships among test results that deviate from normal expectation, and intra-individual differences on the two sides of the body.

Since the variables contributing to the GNDS, in themselves, yield significant differences in groups of brain-damaged persons and controls, it is not surprising that the GNDS is highly effective in this regard. Reitan and Wolfson (1988, 1993) found that only about 10% of a group of brain-damaged persons and 10% of a group of controls were misclassified by the GNDS, without any adjustments for age, education, or IQ, demonstrating a very striking degree of sensitivity as well as specificity.

Rojas and Bennett (1995) compared a group with mild head injuries with a group of control subjects and found that the GNDS correctly identified 92% of the subjects, whereas the Stroop Neuropsychological Screening Test did not differentiate the groups. Despite the many studies of the Impairment Index over the years, indicating its sensitivity to brain damage, Rojas and Bennett found in their study that the GNDS was more sensitive than the Impairment Index. Perhaps this is to be expected, considering that the GNDS summarizes results on 42 variables versus the seven variables that contribute to the Impairment Index.

Oestreicher and O'Donnell (1995) compared the GNDS in three groups of young adults: (1) subjects with traumatic brain injuries, (2) subjects with learning disabilities, and (3) volunteer controls. The groups were equivalent in gender and Full Scale IQ. The controls all had GNDS scores of 27 or lower (normal range is 25 or lower); 49% of the learning-disabled persons had GNDS scores of 27 or higher and 97% of the brain-injured subjects had GNDS scores of 27 or higher. This study confirmed earlier findings by O'Donnell and his coworkers and also demonstrated that many young adults with learning disabilities also show evidence of neuropsychological impairment on the GNDS.

Inasmuch as the GNDS is a summary measure, it must be noted that while it provides an overall indication of neuropsychological status, it cannot be substituted for the detailed information provided by the individual tests on which it is based. It serves a valuable purpose

in neuropsychology, however, much as the Full Scale IQ, based on the Wechsler Scales, does for general intelligence. While the IQ has been criticized as lacking specificity because it averages various scores (as does the GNDS), any reasonably intelligent psychologist would review the individual test scores (which are obviously available) if greater specificity of abilities is needed. The same situation applies to the GNDS in neuropsychological evaluation of the individual person. The GNDS stood as the only validated neuropsychological summary score available for a number of years. Recently, however, Heaton et al. (2006) have developed a summary score that is similar to the GNDS, but utilizes demographic adjustments.

Traumatic Brain Injury

The HRB has a long history in the area of traumatic brain injury, with two volumes summarizing published research regarding its sensitivity, specificity, and clinical interpretation (Reitan & Wolfson, 1986, 1988). More recently, a number of studies reported in the literature have found that mild head injury may result in neuropsychological deficits, but that these deficits usually resolve completely in two to three months. These studies have been cited and reviewed in the book *Mild Head Injury: Intellectual, Cognitive, and Emotional Consequences* (Reitan & Wolfson, 2000b). Having examined many hundreds of persons over the years with traumatic head injuries, we were aware that while many persons with mild head injuries recover quite well, many also had persistent and essentially permanent complaints, supported by findings on testing with the HRB.

Our procedure of correlating test results with findings from neurological evaluation indicated that some persons with mild head injuries (including even a few persons who had not lost consciousness) did have definitive evidence of brain damage resulting from intracranial bleeding. There was obviously something wrong with the conclusion of "full recovery" reported in the neuropsychological literature. These observations led to a series of studies reported in the book cited above as well as in other sources (Reitan & Wolfson, 1999b, 2000b). Our main focus was on the method used to compose head-injured groups. In research studies, the procedure had usually been to admit subjects to a study in consecutive order when they met predetermined criteria. No reference was usually made about whether the subjects had continuing or even increasing signs and symptoms following the head injury. Since most persons with a mild head injury recover rather routinely (estimated at 85%–90%), the persons with more serious and persisting deficits would likely "fall between the cracks" when included in the total group.

A study was needed to compare subjects who were accessed into the study according to predetermined criteria with a group of persons with equivalently mild injuries who later sought medical care because of persisting complaints, deficits, and sometimes evidence of brain lesions when finally examined neurologically. Fortunately, we had available both such groups from our large pool of head-injured persons who had been given the HRB. The HRB results showed only mild but statistically significant deficits in the group that had been routinely accessed into the ongoing research study (much in accordance with results reported in the literature), but the group composed of persons who had returned months after their mild head injuries with significant complaints (persisting headaches, loss of efficiency at work, significantly lower school grades, and in some instances, development of posttraumatic epilepsy) performed significantly poorer on the HRB, showing definite neuropsychological impairment. Although these patients represented only a fraction of any total group of persons with head injuries (our estimate was 13%), they were being lost in the routine research practices being reported in the literature, even though they were the persons in need of comprehensive evaluation and treatment. Our studies, while being quite definitive, appear still to be unappreciated by many neuropsychologists, judging from the frequency with which statements are being made regarding full recovery among persons with mild head injuries.

Malingering and Dissimulation

Most published studies of malingering are based on results obtained from participants who were instructed, with varying degrees of thoroughness, to act as if they were brain-injured or otherwise impaired. Malingering in real life undoubtedly is a complex behavior, arising from a host of complex stressors and determinants and expressed in a variety of ways and to different degrees. Thus, to ask normal and often naive participants to simulate the complex behavior represented by malingering, and to expect such playacting to produce valid results, is at least somewhat naive. Brain damage, in its range of pathological characteristics and its varied manifestations, is at least equally complex. The field of clinical neuropsychology is indeed fortunate that its knowledge base was not derived principally by evaluation of persons instructed to pretend that they were brain damaged. Clinical psychology and psychiatry would be similarly skewed in their knowledge base had they been developed from normal persons feigning mental and emotional illnesses.

This approach to the development of knowledge regarding malingerers has undoubtedly arisen from the fact that on one hand, the problem is important and, on the other hand, no one has been able to compose a group of "true" malingerers; generally, they do not confess.

More recently, neuropsychologists have developed what is called a "known-group design," presumably because it is deemed capable of definitively identifying malingerers as well as non-malingerers. This method was recently reviewed by Greve et al. (2006), particularly with respect to documentation of the validity of the Test of Memory Malingering. The method initially requires identification of an external incentive, supplemented by judged disparities between self-report of the history and documented history, information given by other informants, behavioral observations, and judgments regarding exaggeration or fabrication of psychological dysfunction. All of these circumstances depend, of course, on the information (complete or incomplete) that is available and the subjective judgments of the psychologist who happens to be involved in the evaluation. These subjective conclusions are supplemented by psychological testing, requiring "positive findings" on any one of five tests of malingering. These five tests, however, have never been validated on any actually known malingerers. Finally, if a conclusion of malingering is reached using this known-group design, the findings supporting the conclusion must not be *fully* accounted for by psychiatric, neurological, or developmental factors, to the extent that they are known or judged to be applicable.

The essential impossibility of defining criteria for accurate identification of malingerers based on available information (which may be incomplete, biased, or inaccurate) as judged by a psychologist (whose judgments are not subject to any tests of reliability or validity and certainly will differ from other psychologists to at least a degree), supplemented by results from psychological tests using results from "presumed" non-malingerers, with all of the above classifying persons as malingerers without a shred of evidence or data having been gained from actual known malingerers, certainly becomes clear.

The HRB has also been studied regarding the validity of psychological test data, but rather than to try to label people as malingerers in the absence of any data on known malingerers, Reitan and Wolfson (2002a) developed procedures that focused on determining the reliability of the test data. The procedure requires two testings of each individual, and compares the scores and responses on the two testings to see if the individual is responding at the same level and in the same manner on the second testing as on the first. Two scales were developed: one scale to assess the consistency of test scores and another scale to assess the consistency of responses to individual test items. If, for example, a person's test score became worse on the second testing, as if the person had given a correct response initially to a test item followed on the second testing by an incorrect answer or "I don't know" response, the results would contribute to the inconsistency score. These two scales were then combined to form a Dissimulation Index.

The Dissimulation Index was evaluated for two head-injured groups: one group involved in litigation and another group who had never even considered litigation. The mean Dissimulation Indexes for the two groups were decidedly different. The group in litigation had a Dissimulation Index that was almost twice as large as the Index for the group not in litigation.

In fact, there was scarcely any ov score distributions for the two gr results indicate that head-injured persons in litigation, often under the pressure of financial strain with a great deal depending on the outcome of the second testing (and often probably even without a conscious realization that they are not putting forth a maximal effort) do not perform consistently on two examinations (which in this study were separated by about one year). There is a great advantage in using the individual as his or her own control in deriving data about the reliability and validity of test results. The full details, including the tests and test items used, the score-transformation procedures used for the two Indexes, and other data and procedures are presented in several papers (Reitan & Wolfson, 1995b, 1996d, 1997a) and in the book entitled *Detection of Malingering and Invalid Test Scores* (Reitan & Wolfson, 1997b).

Conation: A Neglected Aspect of Neuropsychological Functioning

Conation, also referred to as mental fatigue (Boring, 1942), has a long history in psychology. A more complete definition would describe conation as the ability to apply oneself persistently, diligently, and constructively over a period of time in solution of a problem or completion of a task. This ability, although probably central to performance capabilities in everyday living, has essentially been neglected in neuropsychology and, to a large extent, in the field of psychology as a whole. The HRB, however, was developed with this ability in mind. Halstead, in conversation and in his publications, often referred to the frequent clinical observation of disparities between high general intelligence and limited professional contributions and productive capabilities, citing an apparent lack of intellectual energy or persistence on an observational level and the power factor in his concept of biological intelligence on a scientific level. We felt that it was important, in assessing the effects of brain impairment, to use a broad sampling of functions, ranging from simple tasks to ones that were fairly complex and demanding. In accordance with the concept of composing tests to evaluate the intraindividual aspects of neuropsychological functioning, which also has been a basic aim in using the HRB, we felt that it was important to discern the individual's ability to apply continuing effective energy to the solution of complex tasks. In a sense, the HRB was designed not only to assess possible impairment in various areas of neuropsychological functioning, but also to assess conation.

Our first study of conative ability (Reitan & Wolfson, 2000a) evaluated the differences between a brain-damaged group and a control group on tests that required little conation (Information and Vocabulary from the Wechsler Scale) and tests that required sustained attention, concentration, and effort over time (SSPT and the Henmon–Nelson Test of Intelligence). Although the Henmon–Nelson Test never had been considered a test for brain damage, it did require the subject to work diligently and independently for 30 minutes, thus obviously tapping conation. The results indicated that the largest difference between the two groups occurred on the Henmon–Nelson Test, suggesting that conative ability had a powerful effect in determining the impairment of persons with brain damage.

A second study by Reitan and Wolfson (2004a) compared brain-damaged and control groups regarding IQ differences in tests that required relatively little conation (Wechsler Verbal IQ) with the Henmon–Nelson Test, using a standard score transformation that permitted comparative evaluations based on actual performances. The Henmon–Nelson Test differentiated the groups more effectively than Wechsler Verbal IQ. Conation seemed to be a significant factor in determining IQ values.

Finally, we were interested in the extent to which conation was a general determinant of deficits due to brain damage across a broad range of neuropsychological tests (Reitan & Wolfson, 2005). Nineteen tests from the HRB were rated according to the degree that they appeared to require conation. These 19 tests were then ranked according to their sensitivity (t-ratios) in comparing a group of controls and a group of brain-damaged persons. A rank-difference correlation was completed between the two sets of ratings, yielding a coefficient of 0.86. This result indicated that the extent to which a test required conation was almost perfectly correlated with its sensitivity to brain damage. The tests studied seemed to be increasingly sensitive

to brain damage depending on the degree to which they were dependent on conation.

These results raise a serious question about the current emphasis on "effort" tests as indicators of possible malingering. Is reduced effort an indicator of the invalidity of test results, or is it due to brain damage? Most "effort" tests require the subject to focus attention to paired symbols, establish an association (learning), and then be tested on what has been learned. There seems to be little question that such requirements depend upon conation. However, given the current emphasis and climate in neuropsychology, failure of one effort test is considered to be a sign of invalid results on *all* tests administered, if not actual malingering. Under these circumstances, a person with brain damage could well be penalized for being brain damaged.

Although there have been published claims that mentally retarded, learning-disabled, and other impaired persons can pass "effort" tests that require close attention, concentration, and paired-associate learning, it would appear that this overall situation is quite complex and requires much further evaluation. It may not generally be remembered, but tests of paired-associate learning, using both words and designs pairs, were among the first ever formally proposed for the assessment of brain damage, rather than lack of effort (Hunt, 1943).

Screening Tests to Predict When Comprehensive Testing Is Needed

Our next research effort was motivated by the profession's need for an objective and validated method to identify, on the basis of brief testing, those persons who would show brain-related deficits, and be in obvious need of comprehensive neuropsychological testing. A basic requisite for solving this problem would be the availability of data on a brief set of screening tests for every potential person to be included in the study and the results of comprehensive testing for these same persons. These data would be needed for a non–brain-damaged control group and for a comparable group of persons evaluated neurologically (medically) and found to have unequivocal evidence of mild or more severe brain damage or disease. A criterion value, such as the GNDS score, would be needed as a marker representing the comprehensive testing and a summary value for the many tests administered. Finally, considering the overall age range involved among brain-damaged people, the above requirement would need to be duplicated by a factor of three (young children, older children, and adults).

Fortunately, HRB results were available that met all of these requirements. This study could never have been done without the input of neurologists, neurosurgeons, and neuropathologists, nor would it have been possible were it not for administration of a comprehensive neuropsychological test battery to every potential candidate for inclusion in the research project. (It was necessary to have a much larger pool initially in order to compose age-comparable groups in each of the three age ranges.) While clinical application of the research results would require use of the predictor tests, the comprehensive evaluation could, of course, be done with any tests of the neuropsychologist's choice, even though the outcome of comprehensive testing in the project had been based on the HRB.

Three studies were done based on young children, older children, and adults. The "predictor," or screening tests, was selected from the corresponding HRB for each age range, and in each age range required only 30 to 45 minutes to administer. Thus, the problem became one of predicting the outcome of the comprehensive HRB from a short but diversified group of tests which in each age range included measures of sensory-perceptual abilities, motor functions, and higher-level aspects of brain functioning.

The results for young children (Reitan & Wolfson, 2008a) indicated that the brief screening tests correctly identified as impaired 92% of the brain-damaged children when compared to results obtained on comprehensive testing; 85% of the control children were correctly identified as having scores in the normal range on comprehensive testing. In total, 11.5% of children were misclassified. However, these "misclassified" children had borderline scores, and recommendations were given about the need to consider carefully all additional sources of information, especially when borderline screening scores were obtained.

The study of older children (Reitan & Wolfson, 2008b) correctly identified 92% of the brain-damaged children as needing comprehensive testing and correctly placed 88% of the controls in the normal range. Again, when borderline scores occurred in each group, even though falling just within the appropriate score range, recommendations were given to appraise all additional sources of information.

The study based on adults (Reitan & Wolfson, 2008c) indicated that the screening tests correctly identified 82% of the controls as having normal scores on comprehensive testing. The majority of controls who deviated from expectation based on the screening results were older, and previous studies of the HRB have indicated that some older people, classified as controls on the basis of neurological examination, earn impaired neuropsychological test scores. In the brain-damaged group, however, 96% of the sample were correctly classified by the screening tests as showing impairment on comprehensive testing. In total, 89% were correctly identified by screening tests. Again, in terms of clinical application of the results, recommendations were given to consider all additional information (including age) in evaluating borderline scores on the screening tests. Horton (personal communication) performed a study of adults in which he found an overall correct rate of 92% using the cutoff points presented by Reitan and Wolfson.

It would appear from the above findings that preliminary testing, requiring only a relatively short time, may well provide an objective basis for recommending comprehensive neuropsychological evaluations across a broad age range. The availability of such information may be a factor in gaining approval and payment for comprehensive testing.

It should be clearly recognized that brief screening is in no way a substitute for comprehensive evaluation, since the range of relevant domains, necessary for evaluation of the individual client, have not been examined with the screening tests proposed for use in the aforementioned studies. It is quite likely that many potential candidates for neuropsychological evaluation, as based on available clinical referral information, are not being examined because the complaints are personal, subjective, not subject to independent confirmation, and in many cases, not supported by medical (neurological) findings. Many such persons, especially with prior head injuries or toxic exposure, have deficits which can be described, classified, and documented by neuropsychological examination, with results that provide a basis for treatment and intervention. Perhaps the greatest benefit of validated screening procedures will accrue to this group of people.

There are additional recent studies that have derived from the development and content of the HRB that can be mentioned only briefly because of space limitations. The availability of a strongly sensitive and specific summary measure of the HRB (the GNDS) permitted a number of studies concerned with the possible differential relationship among groups with and without evidence of brain damage of age and education to neuropsychological test results. These studies compared groups of adults (Reitan & Wolfson, 1995d), older children (Reitan & Wolfson, 1995c), children with learning disabilities (Reitan & Wolfson, 1996a, 1996c), and adults with mild head injuries (Reitan & Wolfson, 1996b, 1997c, 1999a). In each of these studies the effects of age and education on neuropsychological test scores were diminished (if not essentially eliminated) by brain trauma or learning disabilities. In computing IQ values, impaired children were affected adversely in using norms developed for normal children because the development of their abilities did not match the rate of normal children. Chronological age advanced at a standard rate for all children, but development of abilities was slower for impaired children, resulting in progressive lowering of their IQ's the older they became (Reitan & Wolfson, 1996a, 1996c). Obviously, the practice of applying normative standards developed for normal persons to impaired persons is fraught with problems.

Additional publications have dealt with the difficulties in producing specific evidence of selective deficits in persons with frontal lobe lesions (Reitan & Wolfson, 1994, 1995a), the validity and clinical usefulness of individual tests (Reitan & Wolfson, 2002b, 2004b, 2004c), the interaction of emotional status and neuropsychological capabilities (Reitan & Wolfson, 2000b), and assessment of specific deficits (Reitan & Wolfson, 2008d), and differences in performances on the two sides of one's

body (Reitan & Wolfson, 2008e) as methods of unequivocal identification of brain damage in a substantial proportion of brain-damaged samples.

Readers wishing more information on these and other topics are referred to complete descriptions of the HRB tests for young children, older children, and adults that have been provided in Reitan and Wolfson (1992, 1993), together with a review of many research studies and many instructional examples of interpretation of results for individual persons.

References

Binet, A., & Simon, T. (1916). *The development of intelligence in children*. Baltimore: Williams & Wilkins.

Boring, E. G. (1942). *Sensation and perception in the history of experimental psychology*. New York: D. Appleton-Century Co.

Dean, R. S. (1985). Review of Halstead–Reitan Neuropsychological Test Battery. In J. V. Mitchell (Ed.), *The ninth mental measurements yearbook* (pp. 642–646). Highland Park, NJ: The Gryphon Press.

Doehring, D. G., & Reitan, R. M. (1961). Certain language and non-language disorders in brain-damaged patients with homonymous visual field defects. *AMA Archives of Neurology and Psychiatry, 5*, 294–299.

Fitzhugh, L. C., Fitzhugh, K. B., & Reitan, R. M. (1962). Sensorimotor deficits of brain-damaged subjects in relation to intellectual level. *Perceptual and Motor Skills, 15*, 603–608.

Greve, K. W., Bianchini, K. J., Black, F. W., Heinly, M. T., Love, J. M., Swift, D. A., et al. (2006). Classification accuracy of the Test of Memory Malingering in persons reporting exposure to environmental and industrial toxins: Results of a known-groups analysis. *Archives of Clinical Neuropsychology, 21*, 439–448.

Halstead, W. C. (1947). *Brain and intelligence: A quantitative study of the frontal lobes*. Chicago: University of Chicago Press.

Heaton, R. K., Miller, S. W., Taylor, M. J., & Grant, I. (2006). *Revised comprehensive norms for an expanded Halstead–Reitan Battery: Demographically adjusted neuropsychological norms for African American and Caucasian adults. Professional Manual.* Lutz, FL: Psychological Assessment Resources, Inc.

Hunt, H. F. (1943). A practical clinical test for organic brain damage. *Journal of Applied Psychology, 27*, 375–381.

Meier, M. J. (1985). Review of Halstead–Reitan Neuropsychological Test Battery. In J. V. Mitchell (Ed.), *The ninth mental measurements yearbook* (pp. 646–649). Highland Park, NJ: The Gryphon Press.

Oestreicher, J. M., & O'Donnell, J. P. (1995). Validation of the General Neuropsychological Deficit Scale with nondisabled, learning-disabled, and head-injured young adults. *Archives of Clinical Neuropsychology, 10*, 185–191.

Reitan, R. M. (1955a). Certain differential effects of left and right cerebral lesions in human adults. *Journal of Comparative and Physiological Psychology, 48*, 474–477.

Reitan, R. M. (1955b). An investigation of the validity of Halstead's measures of biological intelligence. *Archives of Neurology and Psychiatry, 73*, 28–35.

Reitan, R. M. (1955c). The relation of the Trail Making Test to organic brain damage. *Journal of Consulting Psychology, 19*, 393–394.

Reitan, R. M. (1958). The validity of the Trail Making Test as an indicator of organic brain damage. *Perceptual and Motor Skills, 8*, 271–276.

Reitan, R. M. (1964). Psychological deficits resulting from cerebral lesions in man. In J. M. Warren & K. A. Akert (Eds.), *The frontal granular cortex and behavior.* New York: McGraw-Hill.

Reitan, R. M. (1984). *Aphasia and sensory-perceptual deficits in adults.* Tucson, AZ: Neuropsychology Press.

Reitan, R. M., & Wolfson, D. (1986). *Traumatic brain injury. Vol. I. Pathophysiology and neuropsychological evaluation.* Tucson, AZ: Neuropsychology Press.

Reitan, R. M., & Wolfson, D. (1988). *Traumatic brain injury. Vol. II. Recovery and rehabilitation.* Tucson, AZ: Neuropsychology Press.

Reitan, R. M., & Wolfson, D. (1989). The Seashore Rhythm Test and brain functions. *The Clinical Neuropsychologist, 3*, 70–77.

Reitan, R. M., & Wolfson, D. (1990). *Neuropsychological evaluation of young children. Manual.* Tucson, AZ: Neuropsychology Press.

Reitan, R. M., & Wolfson, D. (1992). *Neuropsychological evaluation of older children.* Tucson, AZ: Neuropsychology Press.

Reitan, R. M., & Wolfson, D. (1993). *The Halstead–Reitan Neuropsychological Test Battery: Theory and clinical interpretation* (2nd ed.). Tucson, AZ: Neuropsychology Press.

Reitan, R. M., & Wolfson, D. (1994). A selective and critical review of neuropsychological deficits and the frontal lobes. *Neuropsychology Review, 4*, 161–198.

Reitan, R. M., & Wolfson, D. (1995a). The Category Test and Trail Making Test as measures of frontal lobe functions. *The Clinical Neuropsychologist, 9*, 50–56.

Reitan, R. M., & Wolfson, D. (1995b). Consistency of responses on retesting among head-injured subjects in litigation versus head-injured subjects not in litigation. *Applied Neuropsychology, 2*, 67–71.

Reitan, R. M., & Wolfson, D. (1995c). Influence of age and education on neuropsychological test performances of older children. *Child Neuropsychology, 1*, 165–169.

Reitan, R. M., & Wolfson, D. (1995d). Influence of age and education on neuropsychological test results. *The Clinical Neuropsychologist, 9*, 151–158.

Reitan, R. M., & Wolfson, D. (1996a). Can WISC–R IQ values be computed validly for learning-disabled children? *Applied Neuropsychology, 3*, 15–20.

Reitan, R. M., & Wolfson, D. (1996b). Differential relationships of age and education to WAIS subtest scores among brain-damaged and control groups. *Archives of Clinical Neuropsychology, 11*, 303–311.

Reitan, R. M., & Wolfson, D. (1996c). The diminished effect of age and education on neuropsychological performances of learning-disabled children. *Child Neuropsychology, 2*, 11–16.

Reitan, R. M., & Wolfson, D. (1996d). The question of validity of neuropsychological test scores among head-injured litigants: Development of a Dissimulation Index. *Archives of Clinical Neuropsychology, 11*, 573–580.

Reitan, R. M., & Wolfson, D. (1997a). Consistency of neuropsychological test scores of head-injured subjects involved in litigation compared with head-injured subjects not involved in litigation: Development of the Retest Consistency Index. *The Clinical Neuropsychologist, 11*, 69–76.

Reitan, R. M., & Wolfson, D. (1997b). *Detection of malingering and invalid test scores.* Tucson AZ: Neuropsychology Press.

Reitan, R. M., & Wolfson, D. (1997c). The influence of age and education on neuropsychological performances of persons with mild head injuries. *Applied Neuropsychology, 4*, 16–33.

Reitan, R. M., & Wolfson, D. (1999a). The influence of age and education on neuropsychological performances of persons with mild traumatic brain injuries. In M. J. Raymond, T. L. Bennett, L. C. Hartlage, & C. M. Cullum (Eds.), *Mild traumatic brain injury.* Austin: Pro-ed.

Reitan, R. M., & Wolfson, D. (1999b). The two faces of mild head injury. *Archives of Clinical Neuropsychology, 14*, 191–202.

Reitan, R. M., & Wolfson, D. (2000a). Conation: A neglected aspect of neuropsychological functioning. *Archives of Clinical Neuropsychology, 15*, 443–453.

Reitan, R. M., & Wolfson, D. (2000b). *Mild head injury: Intellectual, cognitive, and emotional consequences.* Tucson, AZ: Neuropsychology Press.

Reitan, R. M., & Wolfson, D. (2002a). Detection of malingering and invalid test results using the Halstead–Reitan Battery. *Journal of Forensic Neuropsychology, 3,* 275–314.

Reitan, R. M., & Wolfson, D. (2002b). Using the Tactile Form Recognition Test to differentiate persons with brain damage from control subjects. *Archives of Clinical Neuropsychology, 17,* 117–121.

Reitan, R. M., & Wolfson, D. (2004a). The differential effect of conation on intelligence test scores among brain-damaged and control subjects. *Archives of Clinical Neuropsychology, 19,* 29–35.

Reitan, R. M., & Wolfson, D. (2004b). The Trail Making Test as an initial screening procedure for neuropsychological impairment in older children. *Archives of Clinical Neuropsychology, 19,* 281–288.

Reitan, R. M., & Wolfson, D. (2004c). Use of the Progressive Figures Test in evaluating brain-damaged children. *Archives of Clinical Neuropsychology, 19,* 305–312.

Reitan, R. M., & Wolfson, D. (2005). The effect of conation in determining the differential variance among brain-damaged and non-brain-damaged persons across a broad range of neuropsychological tests. *Archives of Clinical Neuropsychology, 20,* 957–966.

Reitan, R. M. & Wolfson, D. (2008a). The use of serial testing to identify young children in need of comprehensive neuropsychological evaluation. *Applied Neuropsychology, 15,* 1–10.

Reitan, R. M., & Wolfson, D. (2008b). Serial testing of older children as a basis for recommending comprehensive neuropsychological evaluation. *Applied Neuropsychology, 15,* 11–20.

Reitan, R. M., & Wolfson, D. (2008c). The use of serial testing in evaluating the need for comprehensive neuropsychological testing of adults. *Applied Neuropsychology, 15,* 21–32.

Reitan, R. M., & Wolfson, D. (2008d). Can neuropsychological testing produce unequivocal evidence of brain damage? I. Testing for specific deficits. *Applied Neuropsychology, 15,* 33–38.

Reitan, R. M., & Wolfson, D. (2008e). Can neuropsychological testing produce unequivocal evidence of brain damage? II. Testing for right versus left differences. *Applied Neuropsychology, 15,* 39–43.

Rojas, D. C., & Bennet, T. L. (1995). Single versus composite score discriminative validity with the Halstead–Reitan Battery and the Stroop Test in mild head injury. *Archives of Clinical Neuropsychology, 10,* 101–110.

Strauss, A. A., & Werner, H. (1941). Disorders of conceptual thinking in the brain-injured child. *Journal of Nervous and Mental Diseases, 96,* 153–172.

Wheeler, L., Burke, C. J., & Reitan, R. M. (1963). An application of discriminant functions to the problem of predicting brain damage using behavioral variables. *Perceptual and Motor Skills, [Monograph supplement], 16,* 417–440.

Wheeler, L., & Reitan, R. M. (1962). The presence and laterality of brain damage predicted from responses to a short Aphasia Screening Test. *Perceptual and Motor Skills, 15,* 783–799.

2

The Analytical Approach to Neuropsychological Assessment

Pat McKenna and Elizabeth K. Warrington

Today, it is taken for granted that, of all human biological systems, the brain represents the most complex and highly organized—indeed, the quest to map its organization is a twenty-first-century challenge, resulting in an explosion of fMRI studies mapping brain–behavior correlates. This was not always the case. Until the late 1950s, clinicians felt forced to concede that the brain was characterized by homogeneity of function. Less pervasive equipotentialist thinking can still be found, but this is confined to selective aspects of organization such as proposing that semantic representation is dependent on neural networks spread over a distributed (and large) area of the cerebrum. For the most part, however, clinicians and neuroscientists agree about the broad functional specialization and localization along the dimensions of language, perception, memory, movement, and executive function.

Beyond this point, however, any further investigation encounters diverse schools of thought, a proliferation of documented syndromes of cognitive disorders, and an unwieldy empirical literature without, more often than not, any clear theoretical basis, and certainly not one that is shared throughout the field. This state of the science clearly limits the contribution of clinical neuropsychologists to the diagnosis, assessment, and treatment of patients because the efficiency of clinical tools must ultimately depend on the progress of research. Indeed, Yates (1954) and Piercy (1959) very clearly described the frustration of being a clinician at this stage of development and lamented the lack of an adequate

theory of brain function and the concomitant limitations of clinical tests.

The present academic climate is far more optimistic: developments in neuropsychological research are accelerating, and we are now attempting to incorporate the new levels of understanding into an expanding battery of more efficient and specific tests of brain function. These developments have resulted from a method that combines traditional neurological observation with the modern empiricism of cognitive psychology, which we claim overcomes the very real barrier posed by the notions of equipotentiality. The analytic approach and theoretical orientation outlined in this chapter is one that has arisen from our practice as clinical neuropsychologists and is based on intense and regular clinical work with patients. However, many clinical neuropsychologists practice without a coherent theoretical background and still use a cookbook, test-based approach, acting as test administrators. Often, few tests are used and performance on these tests may rely on the integrity of many different cognitive functions. The method of interpretation relies on normative data and there is little room for qualitative features or improvisation in the use of clinical materials, nor of experience of the examiner. The test is determinative, not the examiner, so the conclusion may just be that "there is a 67% chance of abnormality," rather than a reasoned, clinical opinion such as "assessment reveals clear features of the early stages of a semantic dementia."

Until the 1970s, clinical tests fell into one of two categories. First, experimental psychologists provided formal tests based on global facets of cognitive behavior along gross dimensions such as aptitudes and intelligence. These tests were really measures of complex behavioral skills—the final orchestrated result of many different cognitive functions. They were originally intended for, and far better suited to, group studies within the normal population. Second, a "hunch" led the more innovative clinicians to improvise test stimuli to collect samples of behavior that indicated more skill-specific difficulties in particular patients. This latter approach underlies the anecdotal evidence of neurologists who, though providing new insights, could not progress without formal tests to validate and replicate results. Our method is a synthesis of both the empirical and intuitive styles and is one that started to evolve during the 1960s and still continues to do so. In this chapter, we attempt to describe how this methodology has affected the theoretical orientation, research techniques, and clinical tests resulting from our approach, and finally to explain their application to our assessment of neurological and neuropsychiatric patients. We have not attempted to be comprehensive and have not discussed, for example, action systems nor systems that support propositional speech.

Theoretical Orientation

Evidence is rapidly accumulating to show that the organization of cognitive functions is more complex than has hitherto been supposed. Beyond the first sensory levels of analysis, the cumulative evidence for higher stages of information processing has not revealed any parallel processing between the hemispheres but, instead, increasingly points to their independent organization and specialization. This appears to be particularly applicable to the temporal and parietal lobes, those areas that subserve functions with which we have made the most progress. The focus of this research has been on memory (short-term, semantic, and event), perception and reading and writing, and executive processes, as well as how these systems interrelate. The benefits of a commitment to the theory of cerebral specialization are already evident in the analysis of complex neurological syndromes. For example, constructional apraxia,

most commonly observed in a patient's inability to draw, is often described as arising from either left or right hemisphere damage. It now seems clear that such deficits arising as a result of right hemisphere damage are secondary to impaired space perception, which precludes the ability to draw, whereas left hemisphere lesions give rise to primary praxis deficits, the inability to carry out purposeful voluntary movements or to perform these in the correct sequence (McCarthy & Warrington, 1990; Warrington, 1969).

Some of the most persuasive evidence for hemisphere specialization comes from the relationship between perception and meaning. It has been shown that the post–Rolandic regions of the right hemisphere appear to be critical for visuospatial and perceptual analysis, whereas the post–Rolandic regions of the left hemisphere are implicated in the semantic analysis of perceptual input. Furthermore, if one accepts this differentiation of modalities, certain controversies are resolved. For example, a deficit in word comprehension (e.g., not understanding the word "cat" when one hears it) is generally acknowledged to be a predominantly left hemisphere dysfunction, but the visual equivalent, visual object agnosia (e.g., being able to see a cat perfectly well but no longer recognizing what it is), is often denied (Riddoch et al., 1988), ignored (Caramazza & Hillis, 1990), or implicitly attributed to the right hemisphere (Farah, 1990). This state of affairs provides enormous scope for clinicians and researchers alike to communicate at cross-purposes and, like the constructional apraxia example above, illustrates the conceptual and terminological confusion that often serves to fuel and perpetuate controversies in the literature.

The degree and complexity of specialization of brain functioning are even more striking when one investigates a particular cognitive system. The following sections outline some of the evidence for the delineation of complex behaviors into systems and their subsystems and illustrate that the deficits witnessed in patients with cerebral pathology can be analyzed in terms of a greater degree of functional specialization than has hitherto been supposed.

A major consequence of this theoretical orientation has been a reappraisal of the role of traditional neurological syndromes—which tend to be clusters of commonly occurring symptoms in neurological patients—as the basis for research. This basis of classification may reflect no more than the facts of anatomy, such as the distribution of the arterial system, and may contribute little to the understanding of the cerebral organization of the components of complex skills. The commonly adopted strategy of comparing patients with Broca's and Wernicke's aphasia is a clear example. The traditional syndromes of language breakdown are now seen to fractionate. As an early example, we found conduction aphasia to be a double deficit of at least two partially unrelated functions—articulation and short-term memory (Shallice & Warrington, 1977a). The already quoted example of constructional apraxia is a further illustration of how different sets of components can give rise to the same traditional neurological syndrome, and while it is understandable how neurologists came to give the same label to such fundamentally different deficits there is little justification for neuropsychologists to perpetuate the confusion. A syndrome should now be function based rather than symptom based and should serve to elucidate the nature of a neurobehavioral system or one of its subsystems.

In summary, it is our experience that cognitive functions can best be studied and understood by an information-processing approach to the analysis of a complex skill into its functional components and subcomponents. This approach has resulted in a commitment to a theory of differentiation and localization between and within cognitive functions that overrides notions of equipotentiality.

Research Methods

There are three stages in our approach: first, the use of a single case study to observe and document properties of a neurological syndrome or cognitive deficit; second, the validation of significant findings in appropriate clinical groups to test their pragmatic strength in terms of frequency of occurrence, detectability, and their localization value; and third, the harnessing of results of these validation studies to new tests that have greater specificity and sensitivity

for diagnosis and assessment, the ultimate aim being to provide an exhaustive battery of function- and subfunction-specific tests.

Shallice (1979, 1988) has provided a full discussion of the single case study approach, but for the purpose of this chapter it will suffice to say that given a patient with an observed deficit that appears to be selective (to a system or subsystem) and is consistent and quantifiably significant, then a series of exhaustive experiments can be prepared and repeated to specify the nature and extent of the deficit. One important aspect of single case study methodology is the notion of dissociation. For example, given a patient who has a specific difficulty in reading abstract words as opposed to concrete ones (Shallice & Warrington, 1975), the conclusion that concrete and abstract words are organized separately requires the prediction that it is equally possible to observe the reverse deficit, such that a patient cannot read concrete words but can read abstract words (Warrington, 1981a). Thus, for any particular hypothesis of functional organization, it is possible to draw up a table of predictions of double or even triple dissociations (Warrington, 1979). Without the use of single case studies, it would be impossible, or extremely difficult, to progress in mapping out the organization of cognitive skills.

The second, or intermediate, stage in our research is, when appropriate, to prepare a series of tests based on the results of a single case study for a group study to provide information on lateralization, localization, and frequency of the observation in the clinical population. For example, having described single incidents of material-specific deficits of topographical and face recognition (Whiteley & Warrington, 1977, 1978), a consecutive series of patients with right hemisphere lesions were tested using the same stimulus materials to determine the frequency of these dissociations (Warrington, 1982).

The third stage aims to standardize tests that have been successfully validated in order to provide more appropriate tools for clinical use in the diagnosis and assessment of cognitive deficits. Examples of these standardized tests in the areas of perception, semantics, literacy, memory, and reasoning will be described in the following sections, all of which have evolved from our analytical research investigations.

Clinical Testing of Cognitive Functions

Intelligence and General Factors

Despite our increasing awareness of and sensitivity to individual variation in strengths and weaknesses of different cognitive skills, it is undoubtedly the case that patients can still usefully be screened according to the general level of their intellectual ability. Though age affects many skills to their detriment, an individual's intelligence level remains constant in relation to his age group. Furthermore, in any given individual, levels of performance in different aspects of cognitive behavior will tend to be more similar than not. Many clinical neuropsychologists use the concept of IQ as measured by the various reformulations of the Wechsler Adult Intelligence Scale (WAIS) for a preliminary overview of the patient (Wechsler, 1955, 1981, 1997). Though it is an example of a test and subtests that are sampling patterns of skills rather than specific functions, it is able to give a rough guide to some of the more commonly occurring functional deficits. In our view, the full version of the test has not proved helpful in the neuropsychological setting. For example, Information and Comprehension are considered to be tests of general and social knowledge respectively and thus too culturally determined to be helpful in terms of brain-behavior correlates. Within the shortened version of the WAIS-III that we utilized in prior work, there are patterns of subtest results that can help highlight a lateralized and localized deficit (Warrington et al., 1986). For instance, a much reduced Digit Span backwards, compared to forwards, indicates an executive difficulty and if this is accompanied by a selective difficulty in Similarities and/or Picture Arrangement, the evidence for a dysexecutive syndrome is even greater. A disproportionate difficulty with Picture Completion can indicate a semantic processing deficit implicating the left temporal lobe, even though Picture Completion is a subtest within the Performance Scale. Selective difficulty with Arithmetic and Digit Span may highlight a left parietal dysfunction. Experience based on clinical practice and observation may override the statistically based formulae of cognitive domains contained in the WAIS-III (e.g., Perceptual Organizational Index and Working Memory Index). The subtest Digit Symbol Coding is a Performance subtest but is directly influenced by a left parietal lesion resulting in acquired dyslexia. Thus, blind following of the full WAIS-III formulation could produce a false picture of left versus right hemisphere functioning or even verbal versus nonverbal functioning given the medley of both verbal and nonverbal skills seen in some tests within both the Verbal and Performance Scales. We have traditionally evolved a short form, which minimizes these errors and on which we base correlational data with evolving tests. Whereas before, we would have used the Raven's Matrices for a purer test of nonverbal ability (Raven, 1960), a similar test has been usefully incorporated within the WAIS-III. Kaplan and her colleagues (Kaplan, 1988; Kaplan et al., 1991) also emphasize a qualitative interpretation, which they term a "process approach," to the interpretation of the WAIS-III. Recognizing a need for tests of general intellectual ability within verbal and nonverbal domains that do not rely on rich motor or articulatory response, we standardized and validated a test of inductive reasoning that has parallel verbal and spatial forms (Langdon & Warrington, 1995).

At this general level of clinical assessment, the overriding and growing problem is to detect an incipient decline in intellectual powers over and above the aging process, and often in the presence of depression. Our efforts to provide some indication of a premorbid level of functioning have resulted in a formula based originally on the Schonell Reading Test, which can predict optimal level of functioning up to IQ 115, and in the National Adult Reading Test (NART), which has a higher ceiling of IQ 131 (Nelson, 1992; Nelson & McKenna, 1975). These tests were made viable in the first instance on the finding that reading vocabulary is IQ related (reinforcing the point made above that performances on different tests tend to be correlated) and that reading is one of the most resistant skills in any process of cognitive decline (Paque & Warrington, 1995). The NART resulted from research on dyslexic syndromes that showed word knowledge to be essential for reading irregularly spelled words.

Of note, the revised versions of WAIS (e.g., WAIS-III) has followed this methodology to produce the Wechsler Test of Adult Reading (WTAR).

Visual Perception

We are often so preoccupied with the complexity of meaning that it renders us insensitive to our remarkable (and probably more perfected) skill in organizing our visual world. This is in spite of there being a comparable, if not greater, area of brain serving the visual function. Our evidence indicates that the perceptual systems are capable of equating diverse percepts of a single stimulus object and of categorizing certain visual stimuli *before*, and independently of, any investment of meaning in the percept. Should this appear paradoxical, it is only because semantic identification is the more conscious aspect of the process and the essential criterion of intelligent behavior. Our evidence points to two distinct stages of visual perception prior to semantic analysis, and individual case studies show dissociations between and within all three stages. The more complex processes of the second stage of perceptual analysis appear to be functions lateralized to the right hemisphere. Two major systems have been identified—one subserving space perception and the other subserving form perception. The overriding conclusion from research to date is that these two classes of deficit can dissociate (for review see McCarthy & Warrington, 1990). Furthermore, recent findings suggest that each of these may fractionate into subcomponents.

Early Visual Processing

Before implicating a deficit at the level of categorical perception, it is necessary to establish that visual analysis is intact. It is known that lesions of the primary and secondary visual cortex give rise to, in the first place, impaired brightness and acuity discrimination and, in the second, deficits of color, contour, and location. Visual disorientation, sufficiently marked to be a handicap in everyday life, is invariably associated with bilateral lesions. However, more detailed investigation has revealed unilateral visual disorientation can occur just within the right or left half field of vision in patients with a lesion in the contralateral hemisphere (Cole et al., 1962). This also appears to be the case for color imperception (Albert et al., 1975). The inference from such observations is that the functions of the secondary visual cortex, as is the case for the primary visual cortex, maintain a retinotopic organization. Thus, there appears to be no lateralization at this stage of visual analysis, and the identification of such deficits with "free" vision indicates bilateral dysfunction.

This level of visual analysis is automatic and subconscious, which is why those people who have sudden brain disturbances can be unaware that they cannot see properly. In mild cases, the individual may go to the optician only to be told their acuity is normal and they do not need new glasses. To screen for difficulties at this level of analysis, we produced the Cortical Vision Screening Test (CORVIST, James et al., 2001). This battery consists of 10 screening tests that focus on occipital lobe damage. As this taps the sensory automatic level of processing, no normative data were considered necessary as normal subjects would be expected to score at ceiling. In the more severe cases, which often occur in the context of sudden and severe brain injury, it is as if the higher levels of more conscious analysis interpret the deranged input sensibly but, inevitably, incorrectly. These people think they can see but become distressed when this is put to the test and they become aware that they cannot see an object placed in front of them. This phenomenon of denial of cortical blindness is termed Anton's syndrome and is often, incorrectly in our opinion, thought to represent a psychiatric syndrome.

Space Perception

The concept of space perception implies more than the location of a single point in space; it implies the integration of successive or simultaneous stimuli in a spatial schema. The essential principle guiding our methods of testing for spatial disorders is that the involvement of other cognitive skills be minimized—in particular, praxis skills, including drawing. The test we have evolved, the Visual Object and Space Perception (VOSP) battery (Warrington & James, 1991), has incorporated four such tests ranging in level of difficulty from counting scattered dots to fine position discrimination (the subject is required to make a fine comparison of two locations). The ability to perform such tests has been shown to be selectively impaired in patients with right parietal lesions (Taylor & Warrington, 1973). The more abstract facility of spatial imaging is assessed in the Cube Analysis test. This test, derived from an early version of the Stanford Binet battery, was first applied clinically by O. L. Zangwill at the National Hospital, and later incorporated in a group study of patients with unilateral lesions and of right and left hemisphere lesions. Patients with right parietal lesions got the highest error score (Warrington & Raven, 1970). Thus, this test was incorporated in the VOSP. The degree to which this test also implicates executive functioning is still to be determined.

Form Perception

This stage of visual perceptual analysis—postsensory but presemantic—is difficult to conceptualize and is best introduced by the research findings that led it to being postulated. First, we have shown that although some patients were able to identify and name prototypical views of common objects, they were significantly impaired in identifying the same object from an unfamiliar orientation or less typical view (Warrington & Taylor, 1973). In a further experiment, it was shown that when a prototypical view (equivalent to a flat two-dimensional side view) was paired with a less usual view patients with a right parietal lesion were unable to judge whether the two had the same *physical* identity (Warrington & Taylor, 1978). It was on the basis of these studies that an unusual-view photograph test was devised. Comparing perception of objects, faces, letters, and buildings in 50 patients with right hemisphere lesions, we have observed 9 of the possible 12 single dissociations (Warrington, 1982). Again, these deficits are all held to be at a postsensory but presemantic perceptual processing stage, lateralized to the right hemisphere. Furthermore, it has been shown in both individual cases and group studies that patients with unilateral lesions of the left hemisphere resulting in impaired semantic processing can do these tests in a relatively normal manner (e.g., Warrington, 1975; Warrington &

Taylor, 1978), even though they may not be able to identify the stimulus item. A final set of tests that manipulate the angle of view of silhouettes of objects was derived from these earlier studies and is also incorporated in the VOSP. A further test, based on similar principles of departure from the prototype, using letters as stimuli, is also included in the VOSP. In addition to providing a more comprehensive measure of form perception, discrepancies in the performance of some individuals alerted us to the possibility of further fractionation of this perceptual function, namely, the material selectivity of perceptual categorization.

The Semantic System

Our phylogenetic and ontogenetic development as primates would support the primacy of vision as our dominant sense and the notion that we first master the world in visual terms before the verbal. Language, or linguistics, is a second-order development, which arises from our visual understanding and is intimately connected with it. Visual and verbal semantics, which we believe to be dissociable, are nonetheless closely connected and form the major part of the semantic system. Experimental psychologists have also found it theoretically necessary to differentiate semantics and word retrieval in research on language, and there is much evidence to show that these are dissociable aspects of language in aphasic patients. Finally, we shall complete this section with a discussion on literacy skills, a third-order development.

We take the view that verbal semantics is built on the bedrock of visual semantics and with development and usage achieves a degree of independence. Thus, there will be references to visual semantics in this section where appropriate. The function of the semantic system is to process visual and auditory percepts at the level of meaning. It is not a reasoning system but a store of concepts, perhaps analogous to a thesaurus or encyclopedia. In the domain of nonverbal knowledge systems in humans, the visual modality is by far the most important as opposed to touch, taste, or smell. Extensive knowledge of the visual world is a very early acquisition and, almost certainly, precedes verbal knowledge. However, language, par excellence, illustrates a system that subserves meaning. Our approach to investigating and assessing the verbal semantic system has been to focus on single-word comprehension, thus mirroring an early manifestation of language acquisition.

Our evidence to date suggests that there can be a double dissociation between deficits of visual and verbal knowledge, indicating that the semantic system fractionates into at least two independent modality-specific systems and that they are both associated with damage to the posterior dominant hemisphere (for a review see Gainotti, 2007; McKenna & Warrington, 1993). This conclusion, is based on evidence from (1) patients with intact visual representations of a concept but not its verbal representation; (2) patients with intact verbal representations of a concept but not its visual representation; and (3) studies of patients in whom both verbal and visual representatives of a concept are intact but a disconnection between the two systems (optic aphasia) can be demonstrated (e.g., Lhermitte & Beauvois, 1973; Manning & Campbell, 1992). Furthermore, the emergence of patients with specific-category loss restricted to one modality has further strengthened the argument for multiple representations of concepts in separate modality stores (e.g., Kartsounis & Shallice, 1996; McCarthy & Warrington, 1988).

Within these two domains, the predominant and recurrent findings are a hierarchical organization and category specificity. These findings derive from two lines of investigation. The first draws on evidence of the pattern of loss of conceptual knowledge in patients, where it is shown that superordinate information is often relatively preserved. The order of the loss of conceptual knowledge appears to be constant, going from the particular to the general. Thus, a canary can be identified as living, animal, and a bird but not as yellow, small, and a pet. These effects have been demonstrated for visual as well as verbal knowledge and also for comprehension of the written word (Hodges et al., 1995; Warrington, 1975; Warrington & Shallice, 1979). Second, our investigations suggest that the selective impairment of particular semantic categories in comprehension tasks occurs much more commonly than has hitherto been supposed. It has long been accepted in the neurological literature that selective

anomias for objects, symbols, colors, and body parts can occur, and our own growing evidence from individual case studies would add proper names with further subdivision of people and place names (McKenna & Warrington, 1978, 1980), animate and inanimate, and concrete and abstract dimensions (Warrington, 1981b; Warrington & McCarthy, 1987; Warrington & Shallice, 1984). We would interpret these data in terms of the categorical organization of the semantic knowledge systems.

These categorical effects are also observed at the level of word retrieval as if the organization of the semantic systems provides a blueprint for organization of the lexical output systems. Selective impairments of relatively fine grain categories have been observed in word retrieval tasks in patients in whom comprehension is claimed to be intact (Farah & Wallace, 1992; Hillis & Caramazza, 1991; McKenna & Warrington, 1980).

In summary, it is held that there are modality-specific semantic systems that are hierarchically and categorically organized (Warrington & McCarthy, 1987). This is evidenced in the pattern of difficulties that patients have in visual recognition, verbal comprehension, and word retrieval. Our understanding of these systems is still too incomplete as yet to other than speculate on the range of modality-specific subsystems and categories and on their interaction with episodic memory, reasoning, and linguistics. However, the disproportionate difficulty in later life of learning new "facts" and skills compared with the recall of ongoing "events" would possibly be explained in maturational terms by the capacity of the semantic system to reach its asymptote by the time adulthood is attained.

The clinical relevance of our findings is twofold. First, at a conceptual level, it has enabled us to differentiate and delineate a deficit of semantic processing, as opposed to sensory or perceptual processing, and a deficit of word retrieval in the context of intact semantic processing. Second, new tests have been developed based on our findings. A simple two-choice word comprehension test was included within the embryonic Coughlan and Warrington (1978) language battery that was validated in patients with unilateral cerebral lesions. A new abstract and concrete synonym test was developed to improve and expand on this first attempt (Warrington et al., 1998). Further justification for this dissociation between abstract and concrete concepts is now reported. Crutch and Warrington (2005) describe very different organizational principles for concrete and abstract vocabularies inasmuch as a concrete vocabulary is organized by similarity (categories) and abstract vocabularies are organized by associative links.

The proper names/common nouns dissociation led to the development of our graded-difficulty naming test that has a matched graded-difficulty proper nouns naming test (McKenna & Warrington, 1980). The evidence of category dissociations within the concrete world vocabulary led to the development of four matched category-specific naming tasks incorporating two categories of natural kinds (30 animals and 30 fruits/vegetables) and two categories of man-made objects, one with 30 objects that reflect the use of culturally skilled movements and one with 30 objects that have no particular skilled movements involved in their use. Comprehension of these items is also tested in a word–picture matching paradigm. Group studies on patients with left hemisphere pathology have provided feedback on the incidence in our clinical population of category-specific impairment (McKenna, 1997; McKenna & Parry, 1994a, 1994b). Equally striking category-specific deficits have been reported in a series of patients with schizophrenia (Laws et al., 2006). Most recently, we have standardized two further category-naming and word–picture matching tests. One, an easy test, probes a very basic vocabulary (10 items from 5 categories), and the other probes an intermediate vocabulary with again 10 items from 5 categories (Crutch et al., 2007).

One of the limitations of picture identification tests for comprehension is that they are clearly cross-modality tests and cannot provide an independent assessment of either visual or verbal knowledge. Although a formal clinical battery of visual semantic tests is not available, the Pyramids and Palm Trees Test can be used to compare visual and verbal semantics (Howard & Patterson, 1992). The differentiation of a deficit at the level of perceptual processing and semantic processing entirely within the visual domain can be tested by comparing the patient's ability to match photographs of objects by physical and functional identity (Warrington & Taylor, 1978) and by the Object Decision Test of the VOSP, a test that requires the viewer to recognize which black shape is actually a real object. More recently, we have developed a within-modality test of semantic knowledge. This test probes attribute knowledge (size and weight) of animals and objects, separately, in the visual and verbal domains (Warrington & Crutch, 2007). This combination of standardized clinical tests and research techniques can thus provide an extensive array of methods with which to explore semantic deficits.

Literacy

Neurologists have long since identified two major syndromes of reading disorders: dyslexia with dysgraphia and dyslexia without dysgraphia. The value of this distinction was to acknowledge some independence of the reading and writing skills, but they did not succeed in developing this taxonomy further. Since the 1960s, there has been a consistent and lively academic interest in this area. Patients with unique reading and writing difficulties have been investigated using experimental methods, and a detailed analysis of their deficits is yielding a coherent perspective of the organization of these skills.

With regard to reading, it has been suggested that acquired dyslexia can arise from "peripheral" or "central" deficits. Peripheral dyslexias share the property of failing to achieve a visual word-form (the integrity of the pattern or gestalt provided by the written word, or part thereof) at a purely visual level of analysis. These include (1) neglect dyslexia, characterized by letter substitutions at either end of the word, usually the beginning (Kinsbourne & Warrington, 1962; Warrington, 1991), (2) attentional dyslexia, when a single letter can be read but not if accompanied by other letters in the visual field (Shallice & Warrington, 1977b; Warrington et al., 1993), and (3) the commonly witnessed word-form or spelling dyslexia, characterized by letter-by-letter reading resulting in greater difficulty reading words written in script than in print (Warrington & Langdon, 1994, 2002; Warrington & Shallice, 1980). We consider these difficulties do not reflect general properties of the perceptual system but are specific to the reading system (for review see Behrmann et al., 1998).

Central dyslexias describe an inability to derive meaning from the written word given intact visual analysis of it. There is little disagreement in the present literature that there appear to be two main reading routes—the phonological and the semantic. These are the inevitable inferences from characteristics from two classes of acquired dyslexias. In the first type, there is complete, or near complete, dependence on the use of phonology for reading. Thus, the patient can read regular words (those that use commonly occurring grapheme–phoneme correspondences) but is unable to read irregular words: the greater the deviation from the regular grapheme–phoneme correspondence, the greater the difficulty in reading. In these patients, in whom the direct semantic route is inoperative, the characteristics of the phonological route are open to inspection. Though some patients in this category can apply only the most regular, grapheme–phoneme rules, others show a much more versatile facility, which led us to believe that the properties of phonological processing were more extensive than at first thought, such patients being able to use irregular rules to some extent (Cipolotti & Warrington, 1995; McCarthy & Warrington, 1986; Shallice et al., 1983). Formal tests of nonword reading are now available (e.g., Snowling).

In the second type of central dyslexia, there is an inability to use phonology, and words are recognized as units analogous to pictures. Patients are able to read real words but cannot begin to read nonsense words. In the extreme case, they are unable to sound single letters or pronounce two-letter combinations. This type of dyslexic has a relatively (sometimes completely) intact semantic route, such that the visual word-form has direct access to verbal semantic systems (Beauvois & Derouesne, 1979; Orpwood & Warrington, 1995). The properties and characteristics of the semantic route can be investigated in patients in whom the phonological route is inoperative and there has been partial damage to the semantic route. For example, category specificity has been observed (Warrington, 1981a) or indeed may be commonly the case as found by McKenna and Parry (1994b). For example, a person with such a deficit was unable to understand spoken names but understand written names of fruit and vegetables, while all other categories were normally processed in both spoken and written forms. Another was able to understand spoken names of man-made objects but not their written names, while simultaneously not understanding the spoken names of natural kinds (fruit and vegetables and animals) but understanding their written names (a double dissociation).

Following these advances in research on dyslexia, data have emerged from investigations on dysgraphic patients that show a similar organization for writing (Baxter & Warrington, 1987). A single case study of a patient who could not write irregular words but could write phonologically regular words, whether real or nonsense words, has been reported (Beauvois & Derouesne, 1979). Evidence for a double dissociation between the inferred phonological and direct routes to writing has now been found. Shallice (1981) has reported a patient who could write both real words and letter names but could write neither nonsense syllables nor letter sounds.

Graded-difficulty irregular-word reading tests are already available for clinical purposes, as described earlier, and a comparable graded-difficulty irregular spelling test is also available (Baxter & Warrington, 1994). The assessment of nonsense-word reading (Snowling et al., 1996) and writing together with these two standard tests is sufficient to identify the majority of acquired central dyslexic syndromes in the neurological population.

Event Memory

Psychologists and lay people alike often use the concepts of knowing and remembering interchangeably. Even repeating a heard word, phrase or sentence is also implicated in commonsense ideas of "being able to remember." Among psychologists, both experimental and clinical, short-term memory is now generally acknowledged to be an independent and dissociable system that can be conceptualized as a limited-capacity system that "holds" auditory–verbal information in an acoustic/phonological code for very short time durations. In this case, the term "memory" is a misnomer, and it is better conceptualized as a measure of the present (or at least, "memory for the here and now"). More controversial is the relationship between "knowing" and "remembering." Indeed, many psychologists argue that the difference is one of degree and that the same cognitive systems subserve, for example, "knowing" a word and "remembering" who telephoned yesterday. However, the evidence now supports the view that memory for facts and memory for events are independent processes that can be selectively impaired. The amnesic syndrome is characterized by an almost total inability to recall or recognize autobiographical events either before or since the onset of illness, yet an amnesic's memory for other classes of knowledge can be on a par with normal subjects, and an amnesic can score normally on tests of intelligence. The complementary syndrome, the impairment of semantic systems, or of memory for facts, has been observed in patients in whom memory for past and present events is relatively well preserved. A triple dissociation between these three systems, short-term memory (memory for the immediate present), memory for facts (semantics), and memory for events, has been documented (for review see Warrington, 1979). In this section we discuss only the investigation and assessment of event memory.

Event memory appears to be an independent system with unique properties for mapping ongoing experiences on to an individual's schemas of events. Contrary to the commonly held assumption that memory for remote events is more stable than memory for recent events, Warrington and Sanders (1971) showed that, although memory for events (tested either by recall or recognition) declined with age in normal subjects, vulnerability was the same for both recent and remote events in the older age groups. Similarly, no sparing of remote memories could be demonstrated in amnesic patients (Sanders & Warrington, 1971). Furthermore, after closed head injuries the severity of the anterograde deficit roughly correlates with the severity of the retrograde deficit (Schacter & Crovitz, 1977). We would interpret this evidence as indicating that a unitary memory system subserves both recent and remote events,

and consequently the assessment of new learning and retention over short recall intervals is appropriate and sufficient to document event memory impairment. This strategy has the additional advantage that artifacts such as differences in salience of past experiences, interference during recall intervals, and differences in rehearsal activity can be avoided. The subjective ease with which well-worn memories from the distant past are continually evoked in older individuals may indicate that they have attained the status of semantic concepts.

This fact-like recall was well illustrated in a patient with global amnesia who would repeat a skeletal account of his main life events such as number of children, education, date of marriage, and so on, in almost identical structure whenever asked (Warrington & McCarthy, 1988). The same patient displayed intact semantic knowledge of famous public figures in the sense that he could designate a famous face in an anonymous group and he could complete the name given a prompt but had no idea of the public events that individual was famous for, nor have any subjective recognition of the person. Finally, he had not only retained semantic concepts (e.g., AIDS, Thatcherism) that he had acquired during the long period for which he had lost autobiographical knowledge but had also learned a new vocabulary that had come into the language since his illness (McCarthy et al., 2005). Another amnesic patient who had no ability to retain ongoing events (McKenna & Gerhand, 2002) was able to learn new vocabulary and new objects in the natural world. Thus, on a family holiday in France, he could spontaneously point out a mouflon, which he had newly learned, but needed to be accompanied at all times in novel surroundings beyond home and previously known places. These observations serve to illustrate the dissociation of memory for facts and memory for events.

Numerous investigations have established the occurrence of modality-specific memory deficits. Since the classic studies of Milner (1966, pp. 109–133) it is widely accepted that verbal memory deficits arise from unilateral lesions of the left hemisphere and nonverbal memory deficits with the right hemisphere. Our aim was to develop a test for specific investigation of event memory that would incorporate the verbal/nonverbal dichotomy. A recognition paradigm was chosen in preference to recall because the former task appears to be much less influenced by executive dysfunction, affective disorders, and the normal aging process; in addition, identical procedures can be used for the separate assessment of verbal and nonverbal material. Consequently, a forced two-choice recognition memory test for 50 common words and 50 unknown faces (previously described by Warrington, 1974, in the context of the analysis of the amnesic syndrome) was standardized to produce the Recognition Memory Test (Warrington, 1984). The normalized scores provide a quantitative measure of performance that can be compared directly with other measures of cognitive skills. Validation studies confirmed that a right hemisphere group was shown to be impaired on the face recognition memory test but not on the word recognition test. By contrast, the left hemisphere group, although mildly impaired on the face recognition, had a clear-cut deficit on the word recognition test. Perhaps of greater relevance for the majority of assessment problems was the fact that the test was sufficiently sensitive to detect memory deficits in patients with only a mild degree of atrophy.

Since then, these techniques were extended to produce the Camden Memory Test battery (Warrington, 1996), which incorporates shorter versions of recognition for words and faces and, in addition, tests of recognition memory for pictorial materials of naturalistic scenes and topography as well as a paired associate memory test. Furthermore, these methods have been adopted by other researchers to produce excellent material-specific visual memory tests (e.g., doors in the Doors and People Test, Baddeley et al., 1994). Thus, the findings of a number of investigations have led to the development of a test with the discriminative power to detect minor degrees of modality-specific memory deficits. An easy version of these tests is also available for assessment of older subjects (Clegg & Warrington, 1994). Other batteries, which include recall as well as recognition, were modeled and later developed based on this methodology (AMIPB; Coughlan & Hollows, 1985).

Further characteristics of the event memory system emerged from investigations of the "pure amnesic syndrome"—a very severe yet circumscribed memory impairment. It became increasingly apparent that the amnesic memory deficit was neither as absolute nor as dense as either clinical impressions or conventional memory test results would suggest. For example, strikingly different results are obtained when retention is tested by cueing recall and prompted learning (now termed "implicit memory"); retention scores can be normal or near normal and learning can occur albeit more slowly than for the normal subject (Warrington & Weiskrantz, 1968, 1970). First, retention of words tested by a yes/no recognition procedure is compared with retention tested by cueing recall with the first three letters of the word (now termed stem completion). A discrepancy in the level of performance on these two tasks (cued recall superior to recognition memory) was interpreted to indicate a subcortical amnesia. Second, perceptual learning was tested by giving repeated trials to identify fragmented visual stimuli. These techniques are now featured in the latest version of the Rivermead Behavioural Memory Test as the Implicit Memory Test (Wilson et al., 2007).

This approach to the assessment of memory deficits illustrates the three stages of investigation we initially outlined. Analytic research studies led to group studies, which in turn have led to the development of standardized tests that can be used in a much broader population of neurological and neuropsychiatric patients.

Reasoning and Behavior: The Executive System

The functions underlying our reasoning, judgment, appropriate social behavior, and organizational skills are those that neuropsychologists find the most baffling and elusive phenomena to study. It is not unusual for a patient to recover from frontal lobe treatment to be sent home with no discernable deficit only to be re-referred a few weeks later with a history of job incompetence or other atypical behavior. Again, performance on formal structured tests of cognitive function can be normal. Even more frustrating for the clinician is to assess the patient's behavior subjectively as somewhat "odd" but unable to be more specific. Blanket terms such as "inappropriate," "apathetic," "impulsive," or even "disinhibited" behavior gives no clue as to what neuropsychological process is implicated. Nevertheless, it is clear that the frontal lobe plays a major, if little understood, part in the planning, orchestration, and adaptation of our cognitive systems in our ongoing behavior, and of the systems subserving affect and initiation.

At a theoretical level, neuropsychological research has clarified to some extent which cognitive operations can be eliminated from the reasoning process. For example, our investigation of a patient with acalculia suggests that the core deficit was assessing the "facts" of arithmetic; that is, given that the sum 3 + 2 is comprehended, the solution 5 can normally be accessed directly, computation being unnecessary (though this presumably need not be the case during acquisition). Indeed, the generally accepted finding that patients with frontal lobe lesions can perform relatively well on intelligence tests that follow the format of the WAIS-R may well be due to its loading on stable, well-practiced cognitive skills, which it seems clear are subserved by post–Rolandic regions of the cerebral hemisphere. We concur with the generally held view that impairment of reasoning abilities in such patients may only emerge, but not invariably, with tests that require relatively novel cognitive strategies. The content of tests of frontal lobe functioning can also be a confounding factor if the individual being tested has a primary deficit in processing that material—for example, testing verbal fluency in an aphasic patient, or attempting the Trail-Making Test with someone who has spatial problems. Such considerations have led Stuss et al. (2005) to use very simple displays in reaction time tasks in order to attempt to map the different components of basic self-monitoring and integration of cognitive processing.

So at this stage of our understanding, batteries are composed of pragmatically validated materials for localization purposes and cannot as yet provide a functional breakdown of the processes that make up reasoning. Examples of such tests are the Weigl Sorting Test (Weigl, 1941), the Wisconsin Card Sorting Test (Berg, 1948), the Stroop Test (Stroop, 1935), the Trail-Making Test (Lezak et al., 2004, pp. 371–374), fluency tests (Lezak et al., 2004, pp. 519–521), and the Cognitive Estimates Test (Shallice &

Evans, 1978). More recently, we have added a further test of executive function, which fine-tunes some aspects of verbal fluency (Warrington, 2000).

Further research into different aspects of "novel" manipulation in problem solving using the methodology of group studies has led to the development of the Behavioral Assessment of the Dysexecutive Syndrome battery (Wilson et al., 1996) and the Hayling and Brixton Tests (Burgess & Shallice, 1997). These tests have incorporated a more ecologically valid theoretical basis in that some of the research methods were based on experiments that actually took place in the community (Alderman et al., 2003). However, we are still no further forward in isolating the subsystems of executive functioning distributed within the frontal lobes, nor in a concomitant theoretically grounded taxonomy. Instead, we can only describe the type of cognitive or behavioral difficulties people experience because of pathology in the frontal lobes. Beyond generalities, how a dysexecutive syndrome might reveal itself in particular behaviors or test performance in any individual is not predictable with one exception—that damage to the suborbital inferior parts of the frontal lobes will affect social behavior whereas damage to the superior lateral areas will affect cognitive processes. Traditionally, tests have concentrated on aspects of cognitive function, and only recently are tests of social executive functioning being explored (e.g., TACIT, Theory of Mind). Thus, the search for more fine-tuned dissection of the subcomponents of executive function continues.

Differential Diagnosis

Most, but not all, of our research efforts are concentrated on the neurological patient population, which has provided a most beneficial, if oblique, approach to differential diagnosis in the neuropsychiatric patient group. The fundamental problem posed by this group is to distinguish between impairments of a predominantly organic nature and impairments of a predominantly functional nature. The most obvious indication is a mismatch between subjective complaints and objective performance. A further indication lies in the recurrent theme in all areas of our research—that cognitive systems not only fractionate but they do so along dimensions that do not necessarily follow commonsense ideas of what constitutes a function. Unless the patient is aware of the "rules" of a breakdown, he cannot produce the correct pattern of disability other than on an organic basis. Thus, it becomes more and more possible, with our increasing understanding of cognitive organization, to differentiate between functional and organic components of a symptom.

Most referrals that touch on this problem request a differential diagnosis between depression and dementia, organic or functional memory loss, and investigation of general complaints of intellectual inefficiency. One test of memory described earlier has proved particularly useful and illustrates the mismatch of common sense and the "rules" of cognitive breakdown, namely, an implicit learning task. This task makes small demands on memory resources, for it has been shown that patients with dementia and those with the amnesic syndrome are able to learn and retain such information for a relatively long time. A gross impairment on this learning task can be accepted as a strong indication of nonorganic factors in the context of otherwise normal cognitive skills. Similarly, intact performance on this test effectively eliminates a memory disorder. The Camden Memory Test also includes a deceptively easy test of pictorial recognition of distinctive pictorial scenes at which normal subjects score at ceiling. A mismatch between performance on this and the graded-difficulty memory tests is a pointer to memory deficit of nonorganic origin. A further example from the amnesic syndrome that has very direct application to this differential diagnosis is the generally accepted "rule" that the degree of anterograde amnesia is highly correlated with the degree of retrograde amnesia. Thus, an early finding was that patients who present with severe anterograde amnesia but no retrograde amnesia do not conform to any known organic pattern (Pratt, 1977). However, later case reports suggest that this formula may be too simplistic (e.g., Hodges & McCarthy, 1993).

An occasional observed mismatch is the patient who is alert and able to perform relatively normally in a day-to-day situation but obtains test scores compatible with a gross degree of intellectual failure. More commonly, the mismatch is the reverse; namely, patients and their relatives complain of failing intellectual and memory skills, which even after exhaustive testing cannot be demonstrated objectively. In the area of word retrieval skills, a failure to show the very robust frequency effects of either accuracy or latency would be a very strong indication for nonorganic factors. A skilled clinician is able to detect a mismatch across tasks in the normal course of assessment. For instance, an apparently impaired performance on the Digits Span forwards test can be checked by administering the modified version of the Token Test, ostensibly a task of verbal comprehension, when the latter test is virtually an impossibility for patients with a reduced auditory span of attention.

Many examples of mismatch in abilities are now formalized in stand-alone tests for malingering such as the Test of Memory Malingering (Tombaugh, 1996) and the Word Memory Test (2001). The increasing use of these tests reflects the current trend to automatically screen for effort testing in both clinical and medical legal assessments.

Sometimes the reverse situation occurs, when our knowledge of a cognitive system confirms that an apparently bizarre or non-common-sense symptom could indeed have an organic base. For example, individual case studies may suggest that infrequently there may be a treble dissociation in the deficits associated with the secondary visual cortices, namely, visual analysis of contour, color, and location. Visual disorientation, the inability to locate in space, is a particularly disabling syndrome that together with normal acuity may suggest a mismatch when in fact none exists.

Summary

We have outlined our approach to neuropsychological assessment that has been developing since the 1960s, when an impasse had been reached in the understanding and measurement of cognitive impairment. In 1954, Yates claimed that "a purely empirical approach is unlikely to yield satisfactory results, nor is an approach based on a theory which has not been adequately tested experimentally." Our strategy attempts to use the findings of analytical research either from single cases or group studies in a clinical situation by devising more specific tests of cognitive function. Thus, we are committed in the first instance to research aimed at furthering the understanding of cognitive functions (albeit still at an embryonic stage of development) and, second, to improved clinical tests based on this knowledge. We have cited investigations that, for the most part, have originated at the National Hospital, Queen Square, to illustrate our approach. A full account of the theoretical orientation and the large body of earlier work emanating from this department is now published (McCarthy & Warrington, 1990). However, our theory, methodology, and test paradigms also underlie group-specific batteries such as the MEAMS (Golding, 1989) for older adults and the Rookwood Driving Assessment Battery (McKenna & Bell, 2007) for predicting fitness to drive. However, it is important that our test procedures in no way override our use of other available tools and techniques. Indeed, we are of the opinion that a flexible and eclectic approach is essential for the assessment of neuropsychological and neuropsychiatric patients.

References

Albert, M. L., Reches, A., & Silverberg, R. (1975). Hemianopic colour blindness. *Journal of Neurology, Neurosurgery and Psychiatry, 38*, 546–549.

Alderman N., Burgess, P. W., Knight, C., & Henman, C. (2003). Ecological validity of the multiple errands shopping task. *Journal of the International Neurological Society, 9*, 31–44.

Baddeley, A. D., Emslie, H., & Nimmo-Smith, I. (1994). *Doors and people test: A test of visual and verbal recall and recognition.* England Bury St Edmunds: Thames Valley Test Co.

Baxter, D. M., & Warrington, E. K. (1987). Transcoding sound to spelling: Single or multiple sound unit correspondence? *Cortex, 23*, 11–28.

Baxter, D. M., & Warrington, E. K. (1994). Measuring dysgraphia: A graded-difficulty spelling test (GDST). *Behavioural Neurology, 7*, 107–116.

Beauvois, M. F., & Derouesne, J. (1979). Phonological alexia: Three dissociations. *Journal of Neurology, Neurosurgery and Psychiatry, 42*, 1115–1124.

Behrmann, M., Plaut, D. C., & Nelson, J. (1998). A literature review and new data supporting an interactive account of letter-by-letter reading. *Cognitive Neuropsychology, 15*, 7–51.

Berg, E. A. (1948). A simple objective technique for measuring flexibility in thinking. *Journal of General Psychology, 39*, 15–22.

Burgess, P. W., & Shallice, T. (1997) *The Hayling and Brixton tests.* England, Bury St. Edmunds: Harcourt Assessment/The Psychological Corporation.

Caramazza, A., & Hillis, A. E. (1990). Where do semantic errors come from? *Cortex, 26*, 95–122.

Cipolotti, L., & Warrington, E. K. (1995). Semantic memory and reading abilities: a case report. *Journal of International Neuropsychology Society, 1*, 104–110.

Clegg, F., & Warrington, E. K. (1994). Four easy memory tests for older adults. *Memory, 2*, 167–182.

Cole, M., Schutta, H. S., & Warrington, E. K. (1962). Visual disorientation in homonymous half-fields. *Neurology, 12*, 257–263.

Coughlan, A. K., & Hollows, S. E. (1985). *The adult memory and information processing battery.*, Leeds, UK: Psychology Department, St. James' University Hospital.

Coughlan, A. K., & Warrington, E. K. (1978). Word-comprehension and word retrieval in patients with localized cerebral lesions. *Brain, 101*, 163–185.

Crutch, S. J., Randlesome, K., & Warrington, E. K. (2007). The variability of country map knowledge in normal and aphasic subjects: Evidence from two new category-specific screening tests. *Journal of Neuropsychology. 1*, 171–187.

Crutch, S. J., & Warrington, E. K. (2005). Abstract and concrete concepts have structurally different representational frameworks. *Brain, 128*, 615–627.

Farah, M. J. (1990). *Visual agnosia: Disorders of object recognition and what they tell us about normal vision.* London: MIT Press.

Farah, M. J., & Wallace, M. A. (1992). Semantically bounded anomia: Implications for the neural implementation of naming. *Neuropsychologia, 30*, 609–621.

Gainotti, G. (2007). The anatomical locus of lesion in category-specific disorders and the format of underlying conceptual representations. In J. Hart & M. A. Kraut (Eds.), *The neural basis of semantic memory* (pp. 28–61). England Cambridge: Cambridge University Press.

Green, P. W., Astner, K., & Allen, L. M. (2001). *The word memory test.* Canada: Green's Publishing.

Golding, E. (1989). *The middlesex elderly assessment of mental states.* England: Thames Valley Test Co.

Hillis, A. E., & Caramazza, A. (1991). Category-specific naming and comprehension impairment: A double dissociation. *Brain, 114*, 2081–2094.

Hodges, J. R., Graham, N., & Patterson, K. (1995). Charting the progression in semantic dementia: Implications for the organisation of semantic memory. *Memory, 3*, 463–495.

Hodges, J. R., & McCarthy, R. A. (1993). Autobiographical amnesia resulting from bilateral paramedian thalamic infarction: A case study in cognitive neurobiology. *Brain, 116*, 921–940.

Howard, D., & Patterson, K. E. (1992). *Pyramids and palm trees*. Bury St. Edmunds: Thames Valley Test Company.

James, M., Plant, G. T., & Warrington, E. K. (2001). *CORVIST: Cortical vision screening test*. England, Bury St. Edmunds: Harcourt Assessment/The Psychological Corporation.

Kaplan, E. (1988). A process approach to neuropsychological assessment. In T. Boll & B. K. Bryant (Eds.), *Clinical Neuropsychology and brain function: Research measurement and practice*. Washington DC: APA.

Kaplan, E., Fein, D., Morris, R., & Delis, D. (1991). *WAIS-R as a neuropsychological instrument*. San Antonio, TX: The Psychological Corporation.

Kartsounis, L. D., & Shallice, T. (1996). Modality specific semantic knowledge loss for unique items. *Cortex, 32*, 109–119.

Kinsbourne, M., & Warrington, E. K. (1962). A variety of reading disabilities associated with right hemisphere lesions. *Journal of Neurology, Neurosurgery and Psychiatry, 25*, 339–344.

Langdon, D. W., & Warrington, E. K. (1995). *VESPAR: A verbal and spatial reasoning test*. Hove, Sussex: Lawrence Erlbaum.

Laws, K. R., Leeson, V. C., & McKenna, P. J. (2006) Domain-specific deficits in schizophrenia. *Cognitive Neuropsychiatry, 11*, 537–556.

Lezak, M. D., Howies, D. B., & Loring, D. W. (2004). *Neuropsychological assessment* (4th ed.). New York: Oxford University Press Inc.

Lhermitte, F., & Beauvois, M. F. (1973). A visual–speech disconnection syndrome: Report of a case with optic aphasia, agnosia, alexia and colour agnosia. *Brain, 96*, 695–714.

Manning, L., & Campbell, R. (1992). Optic aphasia with spared action naming: A description and possible loci of impairment. *Neuropsychologia, 30*, 587–592.

McCarthy, R. A., Kopelman, M. D., & Warrington, E. K. (2005). Remembering and forgetting of semantic knowledge in amnesia: A 16 year follow up of RFR. *Neuropsychologia, 43*, 356–372.

McCarthy, R. A., & Warrington, E. K. (1986). Phonological reading: Phenomena and paradoxes. *Cortex, 22*, 359–380.

McCarthy, R. A., & Warrington, E. K. (1988). Evidence from modality-specific meaning systems in the brain. *Nature, 334*, 428–430.

McCarthy, R. A., & Warrington, E. K. (1990). *Cognitive neuropsychology: A clinical introduction*. London: Academic Press.

McKenna, P. (1997). *The Category Specific Names Test*. Cardiff, Wales, UK: Cardiff and Vale NHS Trust, Psychology Department UK.

McKenna, P., & Bell, V. (2007). Fitness to drive following cerebral pathology: The Rookwood Driving Battery as a tool for predicting on-road driving performance. *Journal of Neuropsychology, 1*, 85–100.

McKenna, P., & Gerhand, S. (2002). Preserved semantic learning in an amnesic patient. *Cortex, 38*, 37–58.

McKenna, P., & Parry, R. (1994a). Category specificity in the naming of natural and manmade objects: Normative data from adults and children. *Neuropsychological Rehabilitation, 4*, 283–305.

McKenna, P., & Parry, R. (1994b). Category and modality deficits of semantic memory in patients with left hemisphere pathology. *Neuropsychological Rehabilitation, 4*, 255–281.

McKenna, P., & Warrington, E. K. (1978). Category specific naming preservation: A single case study. *Journal of Neurology, Neurosurgery and Psychiatry, 41*, 571–574.

McKenna, P., & Warrington, E. K. (1980). Testing for nominal aphasia. *Journal of Neurology, Neurosurgery and Psychiatry, 43*, 781–788.

McKenna, P., & Warrington, E. K. (1993). The neuropsychology of semantic memory. In F. Boller & J. Grafsman (Eds.), *Handbook of Neuropsychology/VIII* (pp. 193–213). Amsterdam: Elsevier Science Publishers.

Milner, B. (1966). Amnesia following operation on the temporal lobes. In C. W. M. Whitty & O. L. Zangwell (Eds.), *Amnesia* (pp. 109–133). London: Butterworth.

Nelson, H. E. (1992). *The National Adult Reading Test Manual/II*. Windsor, England: NFER—Nelson Publishing Company Limited.

Nelson, H. E., & McKenna, P. (1975). The use of current reading ability in the assessment of dementia. *British Journal of Social and Clinical Psychology, 14*, 259–267.

Orpwood, L., & Warrington, E. K. (1995). Word specific impairments in naming and spelling but not reading. *Cortex, 31*, 239–265.

Paque, L., & Warrington, E. K. (1995). A longitudinal study of reading ability in patients suffering from dementia. *Journal of the International Neuropsychological Society, 1*, 517–524.

Piercy, M. (1959). Testing for intellectual impairment—some comments on the test and testers. *Journal of Medical Science, 105*, 489–495.

Pratt, R. T. C. (1977). Psychogenic loss of memory. In C. W. M. Whitty & O. L. Zangwill (Eds.), *Amnesia* (pp. 224–232). London: Butterworth.

Raven, J. C. (1960). *Guide to the standard progressive matrices*. London: H. K. Lewis.

Riddoch, M. J., Humphreys, G. W., Coltheart, M., & Funnel, E. (1988). Semantic system or systems? Neuropsychological evidence re-examined. *Cognitive Neuropsychology, 5*, 3–25.

Sanders, H. I., & Warrington, E. K. (1971). Memory for remote events in amnesic patients. *Brain, 94*, 616–668.

Schacter, D. L., & Crovitz, H. F. (1977). Memory function after closed head injury: A review of the quantitative research. *Cortex, 13*, 150–176.

Shallice, T. (1979). Case study approach in neuropsychological research. *Journal of Clinical Neuropsychology, 1*, 183–211.

Shallice, T. (1981). Phonological agraphia and the lexical route in writing. *Brain, 104*, 413–429.

Shallice, T. (1988). *From neuropsychology to mental structure*. Cambridge: Cambridge University Press.

Shallice, T., & Evans, M. E. (1978). The involvement of the frontal lobes in cognitive estimation. *Cortex, 14*, 294–303.

Shallice, T., & Warrington, E. K. (1975). Word recognition in a phonemic dyslexic patient. *Quarterly Journal of Experimental Psychology A, 27*, 187–199.

Shallice, T., & Warrington, E. K. (1977a). Auditory-verbal short-term memory impairment and conduction aphasia. *Brain and Language, 4*, 479–491.

Shallice, T., & Warrington, E. K. (1977b). The possible role of selective attention in acquired dyslexia. *Neuropsychologia, 15*, 31–41.

Shallice, T., Warrington, E. K., & McCarthy, R. A. (1983). Reading without semantics. *Quarterly Journal of Experimental Psychology, 18*, 643–662.

Snowling, M., Stothard, S., & McLean, J. (1996). *Graded Non-word Reading Test*. Bury St. Edmonds: Thames Valley Test Co. U.K.

Stroop, J. R. (1935). Studies of interference in serial verbal reactions. *Journal of Experimental Psychology, 18*, 643–662.

Stuss, D. T., Alexander, M. P., Shallice, T., Picton, T. W., Binns, M. A., Macdonald, R., et al. (2005). Multiple frontal systems controlling response speed. *Neuropsychologia, 43*, 396–417.

Taylor, A. M., & Warrington, E. K. (1973). Visual discrimination in patients with localized cerebral lesions. *Cortex, 9*, 82–93.

Tombaugh, T. N. (1996). *Test of Memory Malingering*. New York: Multi-Health Systems, Inc.

Warrington, E. K. (1969). Constructional Apraxia. In P. J. Vinkin & G. W. Bruyn (Eds.), *Handbook of clinical neurology/IV* (pp. 66–83). Amsterdam: Elsevier Science Publishers.

Warrington, E. K. (1974). Deficient recognition memory in organic amnesia. *Cortex, 10*, 289–291.

Warrington, E. K. (1975). The selective impairment of semantic memory. *Quarterly Journal of Experimental Psychology A, 27*, 635–657.

Warrington, E. K. (1979). Neuropsychological evidence for multiple memory systems. In *Brain and Mind Ciba foundation Series 69* (pp. 153–166). Exerpta Medica, Elsevier North Holland.

Warrington, E. K. (1981a). Concrete word dyslexia. *British Journal of Psychology, 72*, 175–196.

Warrington, E. K. (1981b). Neuropsychological studies of verbal semantic systems. *Philosophical Transactions of the Royal Society of London (B), 295*, 411–423.

Warrington, E. K. (1982). Neuropsychological studies of object recognition. *Philosophical Transactions of the Royal Society of London (B), 298*, 15–33.

Warrington, E. K. (1984). *Manual for Recognition Memory Tests*. Windsor, England: NFER—Nelson Publishing Company Limited.

Warrington, E. K. (1991). Right neglect dyslexia: A single case study. *Cognitive Neuropsychology, 8*, 193–212.

Warrington, E. K. (1996). *The Camden Memory Tests*. UK: Psychology Press.

Warrington, E. K. (2000) Homophone meaning generation. A new test of verbal switching for the detection of frontal lobe dysfunction. *Journal of the International Neuropsychological Society, 6*, 643–648.

Warrington, E. K., Cipolotti, L., & McNeil, J. (1993). Attentional dyslexia: A single case study. *Neuropsychologia, 31*, 871–855.

Warrington, E. K., & Crutch, S. J. (2007). A within-modality test of semantic knowledge: The size/weight attribute test. *Neuropsychology, 21*, 803–811.

Warrington, E. K., & James, M. (1991). *The Visual Object and Space Perception battery*. Bury St. Edmunds: Thames Valley Test Company.

Warrington, E. K., James, M., & Maciejewski, C. (1986). The WAIS as a lateralising and localising diagnostic instrument. A study of 656 patients with unilateral cerebral lesions. *Neuropsychologia, 24*, 223–239.

Warrington, E. K., & Langdon, D. (1994). Spelling dyslexia: A deficit of the visual word-form. *Journal of Neurology, Neurosurgery and Psychiatry, 57*, 211–216.

Warrington, E. K., & Langdon, D. W. (2002). Does the spelling dyslexic read by recognising orally spelled words? An investigation of a letter-by-letter reading. *Neurocase, 8*, 210–218.

Warrington, E. K., & McCarthy, R. A (1987). Categories of Knowledge: Further fractionations and an attempted interpretation. *Brain, 110*, 1273–1296.

Warrington, E. K., & McCarthy, R. A (1988). The fractionation of retrograde amnesia. *Brain and Cognition, 7,* 184–200.

Warrington, E. K., McKenna, P., & Orpwood, L. (1998). Single word comprehension: A concrete and abstract word synonym test. *Neuropsychological Rehabilitation, 8,* 143–154.

Warrington, E. K., & Raven, P. (1970). Perceptual matching in patients with cerebral lesions. *Neuropsychologia, 8,* 475–487.

Warrington, E. K., & Sanders, H. I. (1971). The fate of old memories. *Quarterly Journal of Experimental Psychology, A, 23,* 432–442.

Warrington, E. K., & Shallice, T. (1979). Semantic access dyslexia. *Brain, 102,* 43–63.

Warrington, E. K., & Shallice, T. (1980). Word-form dyslexia. *Brain, 103,* 99–112.

Warrington, E. K., & Shallice, T. (1984). Category specific semantic impairments. *Brain, 107,* 829–853.

Warrington, E. K., & Taylor, A. M. (1973). The contribution of the right parietal lobe to object recognition. *Cortex, 9,* 152–164.

Warrington, E. K., & Taylor, A. M. (1978). To categorical stages of object recognition. *Perception, 7,* 695–705.

Warrington, E. K., & Weiskrantz, L. (1968). New method of testing long-term retention with special reference to amnesic patients. *Nature, 217,* 972–974.

Warrington, E. K., & Weiskrantz, L. (1970). Amnesic syndrome: Consolidation or retrieval? *Nature, 228,* 628–630.

Wechsler, D. (1955). *The Wechsler Adult Intelligence Scale: Manual.* New York: Psychological Corporation.

Wechsler, D. (1981). *WAIS-R Manual: The Wechsler Adult Intelligence Scale-Revised.* New York: Harcourt, Brace, Jovanovich.

Wechsler, D. (1997). *Wechsler Adult Intelligence Scale-III.* New York: The Psychological Corporation.

Weigl, E. (1941). On the psychology of so-called processes of abstraction. *Journal of Abnormal and Social Psychology, 36,* 3–33.

Whiteley, A. M., & Warrington, E. K. (1977). Proposagnosia: A clinical, psychological and anatomical study of three patients. *Journal of Neurology, Neurosurgery and Psychiatry, 40,* 395–403.

Whiteley, A. M., & Warrington, E. K. (1978). Selective impairment of topographical memory, a single case study. *Journal of Neurology, Neurosurgery and Psychiatry, 41,* 575–578.

Wilson, B. A., Alderman, N., Burgess, P. W., Emslie, H., & Evans, J. J. (1996). *Behavioural assessment of the dysexecutive syndrome.* Harcourt Assessment/ The Psychological Corporation.

Wilson, B. A., Greenfield, E., Clare, L., Baddeley, A., Cockburn, J., Watson, P., et al. (2007). *Rivermead Behavioural Memory Test—Third Edition (RBMT – 3).* Harcourt Assessment. U.K.

Yates, A. (1954). The validity of some psychological tests of brain damage. *Psychological Bulletin, 51,* 4.

3

The Boston Process Approach to Neuropsychological Assessment

William P. Milberg, Nancy Hebben, and Edith Kaplan

The Boston Process Approach is based on a desire to understand the qualitative nature of behavior assessed by clinical psychometric instruments, a desire to reconcile descriptive richness with reliability and quantitative evidence of validity, and a desire to relate the behavior assessed to the conceptual framework of experimental neuropsychology and cognitive neuroscience (see Delis et al., 1990). Before its emergence in the late 1970s, clinical neuropsychology as a discipline had developed as a strongly empirical approach to the problem of the assessment of brain damage, which had for the most part been isolated from what can be seen in retrospect as a paradigm shift from behaviorism to cognitivism in academic psychology. The Boston Process Approach was an important bridge between Post-War Clinical Psychology and the increasingly biological and neuroscience based approaches that characterize contemporary clinical research and practice.

In the past 30 years, the practice of clinical neuropsychology has progressed rapidly. Initially, neuropsychological assessment techniques were known only to a few self-trained clinicians or consisted of test batteries designed with the modest goal of determining the presence of the clinical diagnosis of "organicity." These formerly esoteric practices have grown into a widely respected specialty of clinical assessment based on a growing body of research (Lezak et al., 2004). To its credit, the American tradition of clinical neuropsychology is supported by a bulwark of empirical clinical research directly relating test scores to central nervous system (CNS) damage. It is now possible for an experienced clinician to use a series of test scores to reliably determine the presence or absence of brain damage in nonpsychiatric patients and somewhat less reliably to localize and establish the etiology of this pathology.

Unfortunately, most of the assessment techniques used in clinical neuropsychology evolved with little attention to advances in experimental, cognitive, and developmental psychology and the clinical science of behavioral neurology. The historical separateness of clinical and experimental psychological science has been lamented by many (e.g., Cronbach, 1957), but it could be argued that in no discipline is this separateness more obvious than in the practice of clinical neuropsychology. For example, many of the assessment techniques require the clinician to use norms (Heaton et al., 2006; Reitan & Davison, 1974), keys (Russell et al., 1970), and patterns of scores (Golden, 1981), while little emphasis is given to the cognitive functions that underlie these scores, the way the patient attained these scores, the preserved functions the scores reflect, or the way in which these scores relate to the patient's daily life and rehabilitation program.

Development of the Boston Process Approach

The Boston Process Approach had its origins in the efforts of one of the authors (Kaplan, 1983) to apply Heinz Werner's distinction between "process" and "achievement" in development (Werner, 1937) to understanding the dissolution of function in patients with brain damage. The early studies focused on apraxia. It was observed that the loss of voluntary movement to a command was not a unitary phenomenon in that the clinical subtypes of motor, ideomotor, and ideational apraxia were understood best when one actually observed the incorrect attempts of patients to follow simple commands (Goodglass & Kaplan, 1963).

The quality of the patients' responses differed depending on the size and location of their lesion. Some patients would be unresponsive to certain commands; others attempted to follow the command with a primitive, undifferentiated version of the response, such as using a body part as the object; and still others used well-differentiated but irrelevant responses, such as brushing their teeth when they were asked to comb their hair (paramimia). These early observations permitted precise description of the clinical phenomena and provided important data for understanding the development of gestural behavior (Kaplan, 1968) and the disruption of such behavior in relationship to the locus of the lesion (Geschwind, 1975).

A similar strategy was then applied to analyzing the process by which patients pass or fail various Wechsler Adult Intelligence Scale (WAIS) (Wechsler, 1955) and Wechsler Adult Intelligence Scale-Revised (WAIS-R) (Wechsler, 1981) subtests. This led to the development of the WAIS-R as a Neuropsychological Instrument (WAIS-R NI) (Kaplan et al., 1991). The focus on process also led to modifications in administration and scoring of the Wechsler Memory Scale (WMS) (Wechsler, 1945) subtests, as well as a number of other commonly employed clinical measures.

Another test developed with the process approach in mind, the Boston Diagnostic Aphasia Examination (Goodglass & Kaplan, 1972), allows the precise characterization of the breakdown of language function in patients with aphasia using a series of finely grained quantitative scales. As the Boston group and other investigators developed new and better tests to measure brain function, they were adapted and integrated into the collection of core and satellite tests used clinically as part of the Boston Process Approach.

If one were to examine the literature from the 1940s to the 1970s and later in clinical psychology journals, one would find that many of the tests originally intended as tests of personality (e.g., Rorschach Test: Rorschach, 1942), cognitive development (e.g., Bender-Gestalt Test: Bender, 1938), and cognitive function (e.g., Standard Progressive Matrices: Raven, 1960; Seguin-Goddard Formboard or Halstead Tactual Performance Test: Halstead, 1947; WMS: Wechsler, 1945), were also sensitive to brain damage in both adults and children. Research on neuropsychological applications of the Rorschach continued into the 1990s. Perry et al. (1996), for example, found that a neuropsychological process approach to the analysis of Rorschach responses was sensitive to the types of perseverative and linguistic errors characteristic of the deficits seen in patients with dementia of the Alzheimer type.

A number of principles have been formulated to account for tests that appear to differentiate patients with dysfunction from those without brain dysfunction (Russell, 1981). These include the principles of "complexity" and "fluidity." Complex functions are those composed of a number of simpler subelements; fluid functions are those requiring the native intellectual ability of an individual. Fluid intellectual functions are distinguished from crystallized intellectual functions, the latter being well-learned abilities that are dependent on training and cultural experience (Horn & Cattell, 1967). The tests most sensitive to brain damage are those that measure complex and fluid functions. Unfortunately, although tests of complex functions can be used to measure specific cognitive domains (e.g., abstraction), most are not sufficiently differentiated to allow the clinician to specify what component of intellectual competence is impaired or what cognitive strategies the patient used to solve specific problems. A sorting test developed by Delis et al. (1992) was one of the first that permitted a componential analysis of abstract problem-solving ability.

Modern experimental psychology has demonstrated that each general category of human cognitive function is made up of many subcomponents (Neisser, 1967), and that as information is processed it appears to pass through numerous, distinct subroutines. These subroutines are not necessarily used rigidly by every individual in the same way, and there is variation that naturally occurs in the selection and sequencing of these subcomponents. Subjects vary in their use of the underlying cognitive components, and thus they may be said to differ in their cognitive style (Hunt, 1983), skill (Neisser et al., 1963), or general level of intellect (Hunt, 1983; Sternberg, 1980).

Unfortunately, many of the paradigms of experimental psychology have had limited utility in the clinical setting. The major difficulty has been the relative insensitivity of many experimental procedures to the effects of brain lesions. Although some of the experimental techniques might not be useful on their own, the Boston group believed that they held promise in enhancing existing clinical neuropsychological procedures. With this in mind, they gradually combined tests that had been proven valid in the clinical discrimination of patients with and without brain damage with tests that purported to measure narrow specifiable cognitive functions. They also performed careful systematic observations of the problem-solving strategies used by patients (i.e., the way they successfully solved or failed to solve each problem presented to them). The resulting method allowed both a quantitative assessment of a patient's performance and a dynamic serial "picture" of the information-processing style that each patient used (Kaplan, 1988, 1990).

Description of the Process Approach: Early Developments

General Procedures

Although the Boston Process Approach originally employed a core set of tests for most patients, it is probably best characterized as a "flexible battery approach" because the technique can be used to assess the pattern of preserved and impaired functions no matter which particular tests are used. In addition to the core tests, several "satellite tests" are used to clarify particular problem areas and to confirm the clinical hypotheses developed from early observations of the patient. The satellite tests

may consist of standardized tests or a set of tasks specifically designed for each patient. The only limits to the procedures that are employed (beyond the patient's tolerance and limitations) are the examiner's knowledge of available tests of cognitive function and his or her ingenuity in creating new measures for particular-deficit areas (e.g., Delis et al., 1982; Milberg et al., 1979). Of the patients seen clinically during the final 5 years of Dr. Kaplan's tenure at the Veterans Administration Medical Center in Boston (1983–1987), approximately 90% were given a selection from the basic core set of tests shown in Table 3–1.

When first developed, it was necessary to modify many original test measures to facilitate the collection of data about individual cognitive strategies. In most cases, however, an attempt was made to make modifications that did not interfere with the standard administration of the tests. Thus, one could still obtain reliable and generalizable test scores referable to available normative data because most of the modifications involved techniques of data collection and analyses rather than changes in the test procedures themselves. For example, it was considered critical to keep a verbatim account of a patient's answers in verbal tasks and a detailed account of a patient's performance on visuospatial tasks.

Dr. Kaplan also emphasized "testing the limits" whenever possible. Patients with neuropsychological disorders can meet the criterion for discontinuing a subtest and still be able to answer the more difficult items not yet administered. This may occur for a variety of reasons—for example, because of fluctuations in attention, or because brain damage often does not cleanly disrupt a function. Thus, patients may be forced to use new, less efficient strategies that produce an inconsistent performance. Information can be preserved, but not be reliably accessible (Milberg & Blumstein, 1981). This can be tested only by asking patients to respond to questions beyond the established point of failure, and by simplifying response demands.

In addition, certain forms of damage may produce a loss of the ability to initiate a response rather than a loss of the actual function tested. In these instances it would be critical to push beyond consistent "I don't know" responses

Table 3–1. A Representative Sample of the Tests Used in the Boston Process Approach to Neuropsychological Assessment

Name of Test	Reference
Intellectual and Conceptual Functions	
Wechsler Adult Intelligence Scale-Revised	Wechsler, 1981
Wechsler Adult Intelligence Scale-Revised as a Neuropsychological Instrument	Kaplan et al., 1991
Standard Progressive Matrices	Raven, 1960
Shipley Institute of Living Scale	Shipley, 1940
Wisconsin Card Sorting Test	Grant and Berg, 1948
Proverbs Test	Gorham, 1956
Visual Verbal Test	Feldman and Drasgow, 1960
Memory Functions	
Wechsler Memory Scale	Wechsler, 1945
Wechsler Memory Scale-Revised	Wechsler, 1987
California Verbal Learning Test	Delis et al., 1987
Rey-Osterreith Complex Figure	Osterreith and Rey, 1944
Benton Visual Recognition Test (Multiple Choice Form)	Benton, 1950
Consonant Trigrams Test	Butters and Grady, 1977
Cowboy Story Reading Memory Test	Talland, 1965
Spatial Span	Kaplan et al., 1991
Language Functions	
Narrative Writing Sample	Goodglass and Kaplan, 1972
Boston Naming Test	Kaplan et al., 1983
Tests of Verbal Fluency (Word List Generation)	Thurstone, 1938
Visuoperceptual Functions	
Cow and Circle Experimental Puzzles	WAIS-R NI, Kaplan et al., 1991
Automobile Puzzle	WAIS-R NI, Kaplan et al., 1991
Spatial Quantitative Battery	Goodglass and Kaplan, 1972
Hooper Visual Organization Test	Hooper, 1958
Judgment of Line Orientation	Benton et al., 1983
Academic Skills	
Wide Range Achievement Test	Jastak and Jastak, 1984
Executive-Control and Motor Functions	
Porteus Maze Test	Porteus, 1965
Stroop Color-Word Interference Test	Stroop, 1935
Luria Three-Step Motor Program	Christiansen, 1975
Finger Tapping	Halstead, 1947
Grooved Peg Board	Kløve, 1963
The California Proverb Test	Delis et al., 1984
Boston Evaluation of Executive Functions	Levine et al., 1993
Screening Instruments	
Boston/Rochester Neuropsychological Screening Test	Kaplan et al., 1981
Geriatric Evaluation of Mental Status	Milberg et al., 1992
MicroCog	Powell et al., 1993

and minimal responses of one- or two-word elliptical phrases. Test questions may have to be repeated and patients encouraged to try again or try harder. Testing the limits and special encouragement are critical when it appears that a patient's premorbid level of functioning should have produced a better performance. When done after the subtest had been administered in the standard fashion, it was hoped that this encouragement could occur without substantially affecting the reliability of a test score.

Another procedural modification involves time limits. In most cases, when a patient is near a solution as the time limit approaches, he or she is allowed additional time to complete the problem at hand. Response slowing often accompanies brain damage, and its effects on test performance need to be examined separately from the actual loss of information-processing ability. A patient who consistently fails because of inertia in the initiation of a response or because he or she works too slowly must be distinguished from a patient who cannot complete problems no matter how much time is given. Allowing more time may also identify patients who actually perform more poorly if allowed additional time after their initial response. A record of response latencies is critical so that performance on timed tests can be compared to performance on untimed tasks. This comparison allows one to distinguish general slowing from slowness related to the specific demands of a particular test. Modifications of time limits, however, may decrease the reliability and validity of standardized test scores.

Specific Test Modifications: The First Two Decades

Originally, procedural modifications involved the addition of new components to published tests so that the functions of interest were measured more comprehensively. These additions are described with examples of two of the most commonly used tests of that time: the Wechsler Adult Intelligence Scale-Revised (WAIS-R) (Wechsler, 1981) and the Wechsler Memory Scale (WMS) (Wechsler, 1945, 1987). Following a description of our revised test procedures, we will give examples of the variety of data that can be collected with these techniques, and how these data can be used to answer clinical neuropsychological questions. It should be kept in mind that, though its description is limited here to two tests, the method can be used on all neuropsychological tests.

The WAIS-R as a Neuropsychological Instrument (WAIS-R NI)

The WAIS-R NI (Kaplan et al., 1991) was largely based on the Boston modification of the WAIS-R (Kaplan & Morris, 1985) and was available from 1991 to 2004. In general, fewer modifications were made to the administration of the verbal subtests than to the administration of the performance subtests. This is so because it was difficult to engineer modifications that made the covert processes underlying verbal problem solving accessible within the context of standard test administration.

Overall, the verbal subtests represented an opportunity to analyze the form and content of a patient's speech. On any verbal test it is important to look for basic speech and language difficulties such as dysarthria, dysprosody, agrammatism, press of speech, perseveration, and word-finding problems as evidenced in paraphasias, as well as tendencies to be circumlocutory, circumstantial, or tangential. These lessons, derived from the observations of patients with aphasia, were directly applicable to the verbal subtests of the WAIS-R. In addition, the verbal subtests required a patient to comprehend orally presented information and then to produce an oral response.

Both the verbal and performance subtests can be examined for scatter because the items within most of the subtests are ordered in levels of increasing difficulty. Patients from different clinical populations can have the same total subtest score, but differing amounts of scatter within their protocol require different interpretations of performance.

We turn now to the specific Wechsler Intelligence Scale subtests. We should note that the WAIS-R NI is no longer available from its publisher, and the norms upon which it was based are now out of date. Yet, this instrument captured many of the features of the Boston Process Approach as it was originally developed. Many of Dr. Kaplan's methods have been incorporated into the WISC-III PI (Kaplan, 1989).

Information. The information subtest sampled knowledge gained as part of a standard elementary and high school education. It was thought that a pattern of failure on easy items and success on more difficult items on this subtest might suggest retrieval difficulties. Poor performance that is not due to difficulties in language production usually stems from difficulty retrieving information from long-term memory. Retrieval difficulties may arise because the information was never learned, because overlearned information was not available, or because of a deficit recalling information from one of the specific content areas represented (e.g., numerical information, geography, science, literature, and civics). The latter difficulty may be observed in some patients with functional rather than brain-related dysfunction. Some conditions that characteristically manifest fluctuations in attention, such as attention-deficit disorder and temporal lobe epilepsy, may account for the presence of significant scatter and result in a specific impairment of this subtest (Milberg et al., 1980). In contrast, a poor score may be the result of a preponderance of "don't know" responses. Patients who have sustained a severe traumatic brain injury, or who are clinically depressed, show a marked tendency to be "minimal responders." These individuals may perform considerably better when the information items are presented in a multiple-choice format, thus reducing demands for active retrieval processes. Further, the visual presentation may minimize the effects of inattention and auditory acuity or comprehension problems. Reducing the task to one of recognition provides a better assessment of the fund of information an individual still has in remote memory. Joy et al. (1992) demonstrated the efficacy of using the WAIS-R NI Information Multiple-choice subtest in a population of healthy community-dwelling elderly adults (see Table 3–2).

Comprehension. This subtest addressed a patient's ability to interpret orally presented information. A patient's answers can reveal thinking disorders such as concreteness, perseveration, and disturbed associations. This subtest also can show specific deficits in a patient's knowledge of the various areas represented: personal and social behavior, general knowledge, and social obligations. A number of the questions are rather lengthy, so a patient's performance may be compromised by reduced span of apprehension or inattention. To address this issue, all questions may be visually presented; for those patients who were unable to generate interpretations for the proverbs, a multiple-choice version is available. The foils for this task as well as for all the multiple-choice subtests of the WAIS-R NI were carefully selected to provide rich information regarding the underlying cognitive problems a patient may have.

Arithmetic. This subtest measured the patient's ability to perform computations mentally, and thus a variety of factors that may impair performance should be controlled. On completion of the subtest, patients with a short attention span, for example, are given a visual presentation of the auditorily presented verbal problems that they failed. In this way deficits in the ability to organize the problem and solve it can be separated from short-term memory problems. If a patient still cannot adequately execute the problems mentally, paper and pencil are provided to assess his or her ability to transform the verbal problem into a mathematical representation and to evaluate his or her more fundamental computational skills. In addition, by examining the patient's written formulation, errors due to misalignment can be distinguished from those secondary to impairment in arithmetic functions per se and from difficulties in ordering the series of operations.

Incorrect answers in this subtest are analyzed to learn how a specific answer was derived. A typical error includes the use of numbers without consideration of the content of the problem. This error occurs when a patient is impulsive or becomes stimulus bound and attempts to simplify a multistep problem or when he or she is distracted by the numbers themselves at the expense of the computation required. To isolate primary computation problems, the WAIS-R NI

Table 3–2. The WAIS-R NI Information Subtest Among Healthy Older Adults by Age Group

	50–59 yrs. (n = 40)		60–69 yrs. (n = 51)		70–79 yrs. (n = 52)		80–89 yrs. (n = 34)	
	Mean	SD	Mean	SD	Mean	SD	Mean	SD
Information Standard	22.12	4.65	20.24	3.34	19.94	4.96	18.65	5.21
Information Multiple choice	22.20	3.37	21.67	2.85	22.15	3.69	21.06	2.92

computational form of the arithmetic problems is available in a response booklet form.

Similarities. This test requires the patient to form a superordinate category relating pairs of words. The kind of errors a patient makes will vary. His or her answers might be concrete, or he or she might only be able to provide definitions for each word but not be able to integrate the pairs. He or she might provide an answer related to only one word in a pair or describe differences between the words, while ignoring the task of finding similarities. For patients who have difficulty establishing the set to identify similarities, or who have difficulty articulating or elaborating a response, or who tend to say "I don't know," the foils in the multiple-choice format for this subtest help to clarify the nature of the underlying cognitive problems.

Digit Span. In this subtest we considered it especially important to record the patient's response verbatim. Although we discontinue the subtest after failure of both trials of any series, if a patient is able to recall all of the digits, although in the wrong order, we administer the next series. Because the patient's "span of apprehension," or the number of digits recalled, is separate from the process of making errors in the order of recall, two different scores for both forward and backward recall are available for this subtest: the patient's span with correct order of recall and the patient's span regardless of order. We also note if the patient "chunked" digits by repeating them in sets of 2 or 3 digits or multiple unit integers. In addition, the record indicates impulsive performances, such as patients beginning a series before the examiner is finished or repeating the digits at a very rapid rate.

Although the WAIS-R manual gave equal weight to the number of series successfully repeated forward and backward in computing the digit span-scaled score, we have found that there is a dissociation between the capacity to repeat digits forward and backward in patients with brain dysfunction (Lezak, 1995). Repeating digits forward seems to require only the capacity to briefly hold several bits of simple information in short-term memory. The elementary nature of this process is underscored by the fact that patients with severe amnesia can have normal or even above normal digit spans (Butters & Cermak, 1980). Repeating digits backward makes far greater demands on working memory and requires some cognitive processing of the information. This may be achieved by rehearsing the series of digits again and again, or by transforming the auditorily presented information to a "visual" representation and then successively "reading" the digits backwards. The former strategy is heavily reliant on repetition and is susceptible to interference and perseveration within and between series. The latter requires flexible movement between modalities. In either event, digit span backward is more sensitive to brain dysfunction than digit span forward. In general, digit span forward is usually equal to, or better than, digit span backward. With some patients, however, it is not uncommon to find their backward span to be longer than their forward span because they perceive that the former is a more demanding task and thus requires a mobilization of energy and active engagement in the task. This finding is frequently noted in patients with depression and in patients giving inconsistent effort.

An analysis of the nature of errors such as omissions, additions, substitutions of digits and whether they occur at the beginning or end of the series, may suggest problems that relate to vulnerability to interference effects (proactive and retroactive).

Spatial Span. The WAIS-R NI introduced a 10-cube spatial span test that is now part of the Wechsler Memory Scale-Third Edition (WMS-III) to provide a visual analog to Digit Span. It is scored in the same way as Digit Span is scored. In addition to the error types noted above, evidence of errors in the left visual field versus errors in the right visual field provide lateralizing information.

Vocabulary. This subtest, like Information and Comprehension, taps a patient's established fund of knowledge and is highly related to educational, socioeconomic, and occupational experience. It is generally considered the best single measure of "general intelligence" and is least affected by CNS insult except for lesions directly involving the cortical and subcortical language zones. The standard administration of this test calls for the examiner to point to each word listed on a card while saying the word aloud. Because of the many visual and attentional disorders in patients with CNS dysfunction, we also have available a printed version with enlarged words to help focus patients who become distracted when a word is embedded in a list of other words.

Kaplan surmised that numerous types of errors could occur in this subtest. One interesting observation was the tendency to define a word with its polar opposite. Kaplan suggested that this might be seen in adults who had a history of developmental learning disabilities.

Patients may also be distracted by the phonetic or perceptual properties of words and provide associative responses. A tendency to perseverate may be seen in the presence of the same introduction to each response by a patient. In addition, although a patient can be credited with one of the two score points for responses that use examples to define the word, such responses can reveal CNS dysfunction when they reflect an inability to pull away from the stimulus.

The multiple-choice version of this subtest allows us to determine whether a patient still knows the meaning of a word even though he or she is now unable to retrieve the word to adequately express his or her knowledge of the word. Thus, the WAIS-R NI multiple-choice format for the Vocabulary subtest can effectively provide the best estimate of an individual's premorbid level of intelligence.

Digit Symbol. Adequate performance on this multifactorial subtest is dependent on a number of abilities—for example, motor speed, incidental learning of the digit-symbol pairs, and scanning ability (rapidly moving one's gaze to and from the reference key). To understand the nature of the underlying difficulty a patient may have on this task, we introduced the following procedural modifications. To begin with, we administered this subtest in the usual manner, except that as the patient proceeded with the task, the examiner placed marks on the WAIS-R NI record form every 30 seconds to indicate the patient's progress. This allowed an analysis of changes over time in the rate of transcription, changes that could signal fatigue or practice effects. After the 90-second time limit expires, the examiner allowed the patient to continue until he or she completed at least three full lines of the form. This equalized patient experience

with the symbols used in the subtest. If the patient was proficient enough, however, to complete more than three lines of the form within 90 seconds, then he or she was stopped at 90 seconds. At the end of three complete lines, the patient was provided only the last row, and in the absence of the reference key the patient is required to write the symbol for each of the digits. After this, the patient was instructed to write in any order all the symbols he or she could remember. The measurement of paired and free recall of the symbols permitted examination of the amount of incidental learning that had taken place during the subtest. These changes were ultimately incorporated in the WAIS-III as optional procedures.

Dr. Kaplan found it important to examine the actual symbols produced by the patient. Are they rotated, flipped upside down, or transformed into perceptually similar letters? Are the characters produced by the patient micro- or macrographic? Does the patient use the box as part of the symbol, that is, is the patient "pulled" to the stimulus box? Does the patient consistently make incorrect substitutions, or skip spaces or lines of the task? All these attributes help define the patient's cognitive difficulties and may aid in localizing pathology. For example, we have observed that the systematic inversion of symbols to form alphabetic characters (e.g., V for $\wedge$ or T for $\perp$) may be associated with pathology of the dorsolateral surface of the right frontal lobe, whereas a patient is more likely to become "stimulus bound" with bilateral frontal lobe pathology.

One major change in the Digit Symbol subtest was an addition called Symbol Copy, which was administered later in the evaluation. This version is like the original except that there is no key. The patient copied each symbol in the space directly below the symbol, and 30-second intervals are marked for a total of 90 seconds. This version allowed the dissociation of motor speed in the patient's performance from the process of learning the symbols. This is especially important with older patients because motor slowing can confound interpretation of the test score. Joy et al. (1992) found that healthy, community-dwelling elderly between the ages of 50 and 89 showed motor slowing on the symbol copy condition (70% of the variance was attributable to motor slowing), and that there was a dissociation between paired digit/symbol recall and free recall of just symbols. There was a marked reduction in paired incidental learning with increasing age, while the number of symbols freely recalled was not affected by age (see Table 3–3).

Picture Completion. This subtest required visual discrimination and verbal labeling of, or discrete pointing to, the essential missing component in meaningful visual stimuli. It was felt that failures on specific items could be related to different cognitive factors. A patient's perception of the stimulus item may be impaired due to primary visual problems, or visual or secondary visuo-organizational problems. Complete misidentification of the stimulus may occur in patients with visual agnosia. A patient may have difficulty identifying missing embedded features but no difficulty when the important feature belongs to the contour. A patient may have difficulty with items requiring inferences about symmetry, inferences based on the knowledge of the object, or inferences based on knowledge of natural events. Finally, he or she may have difficulty making a hierarchy of the missing details. Errors may also be analyzed with regard to whether the missing part is on the left or right side of the picture.

Block Design. One of Dr. Kaplan's earliest observations regarded performance on this test. She demonstrated that valuable information could be gained by observing the strategy the patient used in his or her constructions on this subtest. To do this, a flowchart was kept of the exact process a patient went through in completing a design. Information such as (1) the quadrant in which the patient began his or her construction, (2) whether the patient worked in the normally favored directions for a right-hander (left to right and top to bottom), (3) whether the patient rotated the blocks in place or in space, (4) whether the patient broke the 2×2 or 3×3 matrix configurations on the way to solution, (5) whether the patient produced a mirror image or an up-down reversal of the actual design as his or her final product, (6) whether the patient perseverated a design across items, and (7) the side of the design the patient made more errors on was noted. Later in this chapter the strategy of "breaking the configuration" (see point 4 above) will be addressed in more detail.

Picture Arrangement. Visual perception, integration, memory of details, and serial ordering were considered important for success in this subtest. As with the Picture Completion subtest, the examiner had to be sensitive to visual field and visuospatial neglect deficits. The cards might have to be placed in a vertical column in front of the patient to minimize such effects.

After the subtest was completed, the patient was asked to tell the story for each sequence as he or she saw it. Several consequences may result: (1) the patient may provide the appropriate story to a correctly sequenced series; (2) he or she may provide the correct story for a disordered arrangement; or (3) he or she may provide neither the correct story nor the correct sequence of cards. The verbal account following each arrangement permits a closer analysis of the underlying problems in all incorrect arrangements. For some patients, giving a verbal account will bring into focus illogical elements in their arrangements and may guide them to a correct rearrangement. The verbal account may also reveal misperceptions of detail, lack of appreciation of spatial relationships, or overattention to details, which results in the inability to perceive similarities across pictures.

Table 3–3. The WAIS-R NI Digit Symbol Subtest Among Healthy Older Adults by Age Group

	50–59 yrs. (n = 40)		60–69 yrs. (n = 51)		70–79 yrs. (n = 52)		80–89 yrs. (n = 34)	
	Mean	SD	Mean	SD	Mean	SD	Mean	SD
Digit Symbol	50.39	8.94	47.84	10.44	37.98	8.73	28.52	9.04
Time to End	123.34	25.81	133.86	31.31	166.86	40.40	235.27	72.23
Copying Time	59.12	15.55	69.10	15.56	75.08	12.09	98.91	26.08
Incidental learning	5.41	2.69	5.20	2.32	4.62	2.33	3.76	2.74
Symbol free recall	7.41	1.41	7.16	1.34	6.96	1.34	6.39	1.52

By allowing a patient to work past the specified time limits on this subtest, his or her capacity to comprehend and complete the task in spite of motor slowing or scanning deficits could be evaluated. Again, the process by which a patient arranged the cards was observed. Some patients were observed to study the cards and preplan their arrangement. Other patients were observed to arrange them impulsively, and still other patients required the visual feedback of their productions as they arrange the cards, study them, and then rearrange them.

Errors were observed to occur for a variety of reasons. A patient may not move cards from their original location because of a poor strategy or because of attentional deficits. The former suggests a strategy characterized by inertia, which is often seen in patients with frontal lobe dysfunction; the latter suggests a strategy more often seen in posterior damage. A patient may fail because of inattention to detail or a focus on irrelevant details. A patient may misunderstand the task and attempt to align the visual elements within the cards, or he may separate the cards into subgroups based on similar features.

Sentence Arrangement. This task was designed to be a verbal analog to Picture Arrangement so that sequencing ability for verbal material could be contrasted with sequencing for pictorial material. Patients with prefrontal damage have difficulty manipulating information in a flexible manner, and have difficulty shifting from one meaning of a word to another. In addition, these patients are "captured" (Shallice, 1982; Stuss & Benson, 1986) by high-probability, familiar word sequences and become stimulus bound.

Object Assembly. Three additional puzzles were added to the four standard puzzles in this subtest in order to elucidate the effect of certain stimulus parameters such as the presence or absence of internal detail on solutions. As in the Block Design subtest, the actual process employed by the patient to solve each puzzle was recorded. The Automobile puzzle from the Wechsler Intelligence Scale for Children (WISC-III) (Wechsler, 1991) was added because it is rich in internal detail and permits a comparison between the puzzles that rely heavily on edge alignment information (i.e., Hand and Elephant) for solution.

Two other experimental puzzles, the Circle and the Cow (Palmer & Kaplan, 1985), were added to demonstrate a patient's reliance on one of these two strategies to the exclusion of the other. The Circle can only be solved by using contour information, whereas the Cow, constructed so that each juncture is an identical arc, cannot be solved by using contour information and demands, instead, a

Table 3–4. A Sampler of WAIS-R Modifications Included in the WAIS-R NI

Subtest	Modification
Information	Discontinue rule not followed; multiple choice version admin-istered later.
Picture Completion	Time limit is not observed; discontinue rule is not followed.
Digit Span	Discontinue rule is not followed.
Picture Arrangement	Time limit is not observed; discontinue rule need not be followed. Examinee is asked to tell a story for each of his or her arrangements.
Vocabulary	Vocabulary multiple choice version; discontinue rule need not be followed.
Block Design	Extra blocks provided; discontinue rule not followed. Examinee asked to judge correctness of his or her constructions.
Arithmetic	Time limit is not observed; discontinue rules need not be followed. Examinee is pre-sented with printed version of failed items; for items then failed, paper and pencil are provided; for items still failed, computational form is presented.
Object Assembly	Examinee is asked to identify the object as soon as he or she srecognizes it; time limit is not observed.
Comprehension	Multiple choice version for proverbs. Examinee is presented printed version.
Digit Symbol	Examinee is asked to complete third row if he or she has not completed it in 90 sees.; paired and unpaired recall of symbols is requested; symbol copy condition presented.
Similarities	Discontinue rule need not be followed; multiple-choice version is administered later.

Source: Based on Kaplan et al. (1991), p. 5.

piece-by-piece analysis. Patients who rely too heavily on contour information will fail to solve the Cow, and patients who are unable to appreciate the relationship between pieces will fail to solve the Circle. Many of the test modifications described above have been incorporated into the WAIS-R NI (Kaplan et al., 1991). Table 3–4 presents a sample of some of the modifications contained within the WAIS-R NI.

Boston Revision of the Wechsler Memory Scale (WMS)

Many of the changes recommended for the WMS have been obviated by the publication of the Wechsler Memory Scale-Revised (WMS-R) (Wechsler, 1987) and then the Wechsler Memory Scale-Third Edition (WMS-III) (Wechsler, 1997). Because not all of the recommended changes for the WMS were incorporated in the WMS-R, we will describe the additional subtests and procedural modifications that had been introduced to make the WMS a more complete assessment of a patient's ability to learn and recall new verbal and visuospatial information.

General Information and Orientation

A number of items based on autobiographical information were added to these two subtests so that recall of personal, current, and old information could be assessed more fully.

Mental Control

Two items that were found to be useful in the characterization and localization of retrieval deficits (Coltheart et al., 1975) were added to this subtest. After reciting the alphabet, patients are asked to name all the letters of the alphabet that rhyme with the word "key" and then to name all the letters of the alphabet that contain a curve when printed as capital letters. These two items provide specific information about a patient's ability to retrieve information from memory based on specific auditory or visual physical characteristics.

Logical Memory

A number of additions were made to this subtest. First, following the standard immediate recall condition, a cued recall condition was administered. Here, specific questions about the details in the passage served as prompts. For example, if, for the first story, the patient had not spontaneously said the woman's name or where she was from, the examiner queries, "What was the woman's name? Where was she from?" These kinds of direct prompts were helpful in identifying whether the information had indeed registered despite the impoverished account the patient had given spontaneously. Then, following the 20-minute delayed recall, a multiple-choice condition is presented. With these modifications it was then possible to determine whether the information had been registered and what the fate of the information was over time. Patients with adequate attentional and rote memory may do well when they initially recall the information but may show severe deficits on delayed recall and may not even benefit from a recognition task (multiple choice). On the other hand, a patient (depressed or hypoactive) may have had a minimal account initially, but given the structure of the prompts, may perform significantly better after a delay. Impairment after a delay may be due to inadequate retrieval strategies or defective storage abilities.

In addition to the two auditorily presented paragraphs, a third paragraph (viz., the Cowboy Story; Talland, 1965), which was read aloud by the patient, thus assuring registration, was then tested for recall immediately and after a 20-minute delay. This additional paragraph allowed an examination of complaints from patients about an inability to retain information that had been read, as well as testing for selective modality of input differences.

Beyond quantifying how much information is learned and recalled, qualitative features of the responses, such as impoverishment, confabulation, disorganization, and confusion of details across stories were also noted.

Associative Learning

Three major modifications were made to this subtest. First, immediately after the third standard trial, "backward retrieval" was measured. The order of each pair of words was reversed, and the patient was presented with the second word of the pair and asked to recall the first. Second, 20 minutes later, free, uncued recall of the pairs was assessed. Third, following this, the first word of each pair was provided as a cue and paired recall was measured once again. Patients who are able to perform better on the third trial than on the reversed trial have been found to perform less well on delayed recall (Guila Glosser, personal communication). Presumably, these patients demonstrated a more shallow level of information processing (phonemic), whereas patients who do not do more poorly on the reversed condition have a higher level of information processing (semantic). As in the Logical Memory subtest, these recall conditions allowed deficits in immediate recall to be examined separately from those in delayed recall. Patient responses on this task might reflect internal and external intrusions, perseveration, or a simple inability to learn new information.

Visual Reproduction

Dr. Kaplan pointed out that it could not be assumed that the difficulty a patient had reproducing a geometric design that was exposed for a brief period was an indication of poor visual memory. It may be that the patient had difficulty perceiving the design, or had difficulty at the visuomotor execution level. The following conditions served to clarify the source of the patient's problem: After the designs had been drawn (immediate reproduction), a multiple-choice task was presented (immediate recognition), followed by a copy condition, a 20-minute delayed recall, and, finally, a matching condition was presented if any question of a visuoperceptual problem remained. The copy condition provided an opportunity to assess a patient's visuoperceptual analysis of the designs. The delayed recall condition assessed changes in recall following an added exposure to the designs. The recognition and matching conditions removed the possible contamination a visuomotor problem might contribute. For all drawings a flow chart was created—that is, a record of the manner in which the patient produced each design. Such analysis can provide information about brain dysfunction, as will be discussed in

greater detail later in this chapter. In addition, the type of errors a patient makes was noted. Recall could be characterized by impoverishment, simplification and distortion of details, disorganization, and confusion between designs.

The revision of the WMS (WMS-R) contained delayed recall conditions for Logical Memory, Verbal Paired Associates, Visual Reproductions, and for a new subtest called the Visual Paired Associates Test.

Screening Instruments

In the 1990s several screening instruments emerged that attempted to capture some of the features of the procedures used in the Boston Process Approach. Examples of these instruments include the Boston/Rochester Neuropsychological Screening Test (Kaplan et al., 1981), the Geriatric Evaluation of Mental Status (the GEMS) (Milberg et al., 1992), and MicroCog, a computerized assessment of cognitive status (Powell et al., 1993).

The Boston/Rochester, which was the first screening battery designed to allow for the analysis of cognitive processes, includes mental status questions and measures of repetition, praxis, reading comprehension, immediate and delayed verbal and design memory, and a number of other tasks that lend themselves to a detailed analysis of patients' cognitive strategies and abilities. The Boston/Rochester takes 1–2 hours to administer.

The GEMS, developed more recently, was designed to be extremely brief (15–20 minutes) and easily administered to elderly patients. It contains a number of tasks to assess visual and verbal memory, language, and executive functions. A number of these tasks were designed specifically for the GEMS, and contain features that allow the examiner to make inferences about the details of a patient's cognitive abilities. The GEMS continues to undergo formal validation (Hamann et al., 1993), but has already been shown to be considerably more sensitive than the Mini-Mental State Examination (Folstein et al., 1975) in detecting general cognitive impairment (Berger, 1993). It has been shown to accurately classify 96% of a sample of 100 inpatient geriatric patients and age-matched controls with extremely low (7%) false-positive rates (Sachs et al., 1995).

MicroCog was a computer-administered battery of cognitive tests inspired by Process Approach ideas (Powell, 1993). It sampled a broad spectrum of cognitive functions and provided indices for attention/mental control, memory, reasoning/calculation, spatial processing, and reaction time. In addition, it allowed the separation of information-processing speed from information-processing accuracy. The Standard Form contains 18 subtests and takes about an hour; the Short Form has 12 subtests and can be completed in half an hour. It has not gained broad popularity as of this writing.

New Developments

Since the second version of this chapter was published more than a decade ago, a number of new tests have appeared that have incorporated a number of procedures and features of the Boston Process Approach into standardized tests. In recognition of the common critique of the use of qualitative observations as a basis for clinical prediction, these new generation of neuropsychological tests have followed the traditional methods of establishing reliability and validity, and the collection of population-based normative data.

The California Verbal Learning Test (CVLT)

One of the earliest tests to be adapted into the Boston Process Approach was the Rey Auditory Verbal Learning Test (RAVLT) (Rey, 1964), which consisted of a 15-item list that was repeated for five trials, with a second interference list and delayed recall. One of the best known and widely used of these tests derived from or influenced by the Boston Process Approach is the CVLT, which adapted many features of the RAVLT.

This test of verbal memory in its current form (CVLT-II) consists of a list of 16 words that are read aloud to the examinee who is asked to recall as many of the items on the list as possible. The items that comprise the list are derived from four semantic categories. This procedure is repeated for five learning trials, after which the examinee is read a second list of words for recall. Following the second list, they are asked to recall the first list again, and this is followed by a categorically cued recall trial. Free and cued recall is repeated again after a long delay, and there is a delayed YES/NO recognition trial. The CVLT. One of the important modifications of the RAVLT contained in the CVLT is a word list that consists of words drawn from several semantic categories. These words are dispersed in pseudorandom order throughout the list, providing the opportunity to use this information to aid recall. The CVLT and CVLT-II have been widely adopted, and used in hundreds of published research papers. The CVLT in many ways is the first Boston Process Approach–inspired psychological test that has become a gold standard measure of a neuropsychological function. Yet it is important to note that while the basic quantitative measures (items recalled, recognized) have been careful norms and have been used in neuropsychological studies of memory disorders, many of the submeasures (primacy/recency, clustering effects, etc.) though not initially supported by empirical investigations have received increasing attention from investigators. For example, Alexander et al. (2003) reported localization-specific patterns of performance on the CVLT in patients with frontal lobe lesions.

Clock Drawing Task

One of the earliest tasks to find its way into the core batteries originally used at the Boston VA by Dr. Kaplan and her associates was the Clock Drawing Test. Clock Drawing to command appears to have been an old bedside mental status examination technique that became well known when examples of the clocks produced by patients with hemispatial neglect were presented in MacDonald Critchley's 1953 monograph entitled "The Parietal Lobes" (e.g., Critchley, 1953). Many of the procedures described by Critchley were ultimately put together by Dr. Kaplan and her colleagues into a test called the Boston Parietal Lobe Battery, which included Critchley's clock copying drawing task, and time setting tasks. The clock copying and drawing task in the Boston Parietal Lobe Battery required the patient to copy/draw a clock set to the time of "three o'clock." Sometime during the late 1970s, Dr. Kaplan modified the clock drawing task with the instructions to set the time to "ten after eleven." As discussed in Freedman et al. (1995),this had the advantage of requiring the patient to place the hands symmetrically around a central up/down axis, and to employ a greater degree of executive functioning. The latter presumably was derived from the fact that the patient must use a relatively abstract rule for time telling and not get "pulled" or distracted by the actual numerals on the clock (i.e., they must interpret the 2 as 10 minutes after the hour, rather than a 2). The revised clock first appears in print in the second edition of the Boston Diagnostic Aphasia Examination manual (Goodglass, 1983), but an examination of the data files at the Harold Goodglass Aphasia Research Center conducted by the first author found that the "10 after 11" clock appeared in research files as early as 1979.

This task provided much fodder for observers of test behavior "process" as it is a deceptively complex task requiring memory, constructional praxis, and the executive functions mentioned above. Clock drawing has generated much interest among clinicians with many variations and scoring systems (Freedman, 1995; Grande, submitted; Libon, 1993; Royall, 1998). Most of these scoring systems try to capture the various striking "qualitative" features that seem to mark pathological performance in a standardized scoring system. Such features as the shape of the clock face, number placement, and hand length, centering, and placement are captured in these systems. Three of these systems Rouleau (1996), Freedman et al. (1995), and Libon et al. (1996) were shown to be comparably reliable (South et al., 2001).

Several systems have tried to make Clock Drawing more sensitive, particularly to the issue of "executive" functions. For example, the CLOX Text (Royall et al., 1998) compared freehand Clock Drawing to copying to obtain a measure that is claimed to be more sensitive to executive dysfunction than the standard clock drawing.

Recently, Grande and colleagues (submitted) developed a test called the Clock-in-a-Box task, which adds the requirement of having patients draw a freehand clock in one of four color coded boxes. The data from this task is quite encouraging, suggesting that the task may be sensitive to a variety of cognitive problems (Munshi et al., 2006).

The Delis–Kaplan Executive Function System (DKEFS)

The DKEFS is a battery of measures designed to assess a broad range of cognitive control abilities known as "executive functions." It consists of nine subtests that for the most part were adaptations of existing measures. These include trail making, verbal fluency, design fluency, color–word interference, sorting, twenty questions, word context, tower, and proverbs. Rather than relying on direct observations of qualitative features of performances, each task contains modifications designed to allow the examiner direct inferences about the "component functions of higher-level cognitive tasks" (p. 3, Delis et al., 2001).

The Quantified Process Approach

Seeing a need to try to capture some of the qualitative process procedures and observations in a standardized format, Poreh (2000, 2006) developed what he calls the "Quantified Process Approach," modeled to some extent on the Boston Process Approach as described in the previous version of this chapter (Milberg et al., 1996) and other sources (e.g., Kaplan). Poreh (2007) has been working on producing computerized automated versions of many of the original tasks used by Kaplan and her colleagues (as well as several completely original tasks) that allow quantitative scoring of a number of "qualitative" features. Poreh's tasks include an updated version of the original Rey Auditory Verbal Learning Test (Rey, 1964), Regard's Five Point Test, Trail-Making Test, and others. This is a promising approach that will allow for a careful empirical examination of many of Dr. Kaplan's original observations.

Using the Process Approach to Localize Lesions and Describe Functions

The modifications of testing and data-recording procedures specific to the Boston Process Approach that allow the clinician to obtain a dynamic record of a patient's problem-solving strategy were described above. In this section, we will show how the specific strategic information that can be collected with the process approach can be useful in the analysis of brain and behavior relationships and in the prediction of behavior outside the clinical laboratory. For purposes of this discussion we will concentrate on several broad categories of cognitive strategies that can be observed across many different measures.

Featural versus Contextual Priority

Most tasks that are useful in assessing brain damage consist of a series of elements or basic stimuli arranged together within a spatial, temporal, or conceptual framework. One important strategic variable, therefore, is the extent to which patients give priority to processing low-level detail or "featural" information versus higher-level configural or contextual information (see Schmeck & Grove, 1979, for related literature from experimental and educational psychology). There is now a considerable body of literature that supports the observation of part/whole processing differences among patients with unilateral cortical lesions (e.g., Delis et al., 1986; Robertson & Delis, 1986; Thomas & Forde, 2006).

This dichotomy of information, featural on one hand and contextual on the other, can be used to characterize both verbal and visuospatial information within each of the sensory modalities. For example, words and their basic phrase structure within a sentence can be thought of as the basic elements or features important in linguistic analysis. Phrases are put together into sentences, and sentences are put together into a conceptually focused paragraph to create a higher-level context or organization. Aside from simple phonemes and acoustic energy transitions, the word or phrase seems to

represent the first major point at which the basic units of language can be isolated from their use in expressing organized thought. Similarly, a photograph of a street scene can be broken down into low-level categorical units of perception, such as cars, people, or litter, and then organized into relational information placing these disparate elements into a larger conceptual or spatial unit.

To successfully interpret most test material requires the use and integration of both featural and contextual information. Brain damage produces a lawful fractionation of a patient's ability to use both types of information simultaneously. Furthermore, the type of information processing given priority is related to the laterality and location of a patient's lesion. Specifically, patients with damage to the left hemisphere are more likely to use a strategy favoring contextual information, whereas patients with damage to the right hemisphere are more likely to give priority to featural information.

We can infer the type of informational strategy favored by a patient from many of the tasks described earlier. For example, a patient may in the course of assembling a block design shaped like a diagonal rectangle within a square (see Figure 3–1) align pairs of solid blocks to form a diagonal rectangle without regard for the 3 × 3 matrix in which it is placed (Figure 3–1a).

This is an example of a patient giving attentional priority to the internal features of the design without regard for the configuration. Another patient may assemble the same design by retaining the 3 3 shape but drastically simplifying the diagonal rectangle into a line of three solid red blocks (Figure 3–1b). In this case the patient is giving attentional priority to the configuration with little regard for the accuracy of the internal features. Similar performance strategies have been found in analyses of block design performance in normal subjects (Haeberle, 1982; Royer, 1967) though not with the rigidity or consistency found in patients with pathology of the CNS. Normal performance is typically characterized by the integration of featural and configural information, whereas pathological performance is characterized by their dissociation. Thus, normal subjects will rarely neglect one source of information completely while using the other.

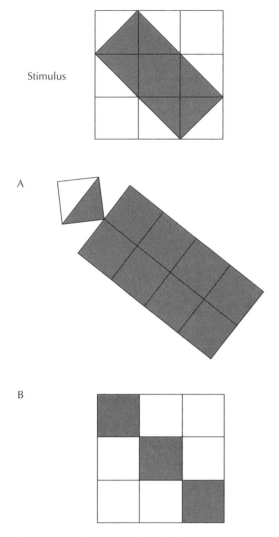

Stimulus

A

B

Figure 3–1. Two examples of informational strategies pursued by patients in solving complex tasks.

Using featural information to the exclusion of contextual information can also be seen on the Rey–Osterreith Complex Figure or Rey Complex Figure (Osterreith & Rey, 1944). By keeping a flowchart of the patient's method of copying or recalling the Rey Figure (Rey, 1964) (see Figure 3–2), evidence about the strategy used by a patient can be obtained. The Rey Complex Figure includes smaller rectangles, squares, and other details placed within and around it.

A normal strategy for copying this complex design makes use of the obvious organizational features, such as the large rectangle and the large diagonals, to organize and guide

performance. Some patients will copy the design as if they were using a random scan path, adding small line segments until their final design resembles the original. Such a painstaking performance can be taken as evidence of a featural priority strategy in the perceptual organization of the design.

Other patients may approach the task of copying the design by producing the entire extreme outline but omitting smaller features. This approach is evidence of a strategy of contextual priority. Additional evidence for the emphasis of one or the other of these strategies can often be seen in the patient's recall of the design after a delay. A patient who is overly dependent on featural information may show a performance like that seen in the left column of Figure 3–3, whereas a patient who directs his attention primarily to configural information may show a production like that seen in the right column of Figure 3–3.

Occasionally, patients will actually retrieve featural information independently of the spatial context in which it originally appeared. For example, a patient may recall one of the designs from the Visual Reproduction subtest of the WMS-III when asked to recall the Rey–Osterreith Complex Figure, or he or she may recombine features from two different designs into one. Stern et al. (1994) have developed a comprehensive qualitative scoring system that provides scoring criteria for configural elements, clusters, details, fragmentation, planning, size (reduction and expansion), rotation, perseveration, confabulation, neatness, and asymmetry. Shorr et al. (1992) have developed a scoring system to analyze perceptual clustering. They found that for a population of neuropsychiatric patients, configural or perceptual clustering on copy was a better predictor of memory performance than was copy accuracy.

Similar deficits in a balance between featural and contextual priorities can be seen in verbal tasks. A patient may show evidence of featural priority when recalling the Logical Memory stories from the WMS. He or she may recall many of the correct items from the original stories but in an incorrect order along with additional irrelevant information based on his or her own associations to the stories or to other stories presented in the course of testing.

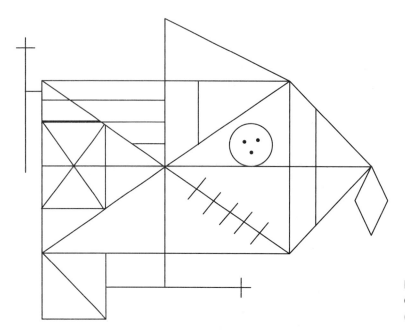

Figure 3–2 The Rey–Osterreith Complex Figure (Osterreith and Rey, 1944).

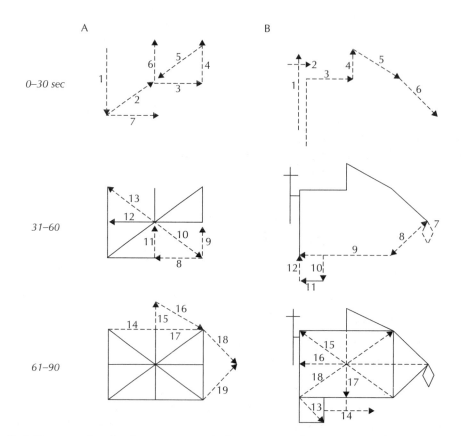

Figure 3–3 Two examples of performance strategies by patients on the Rey–Osterreith Complex Figure.

For example, when recalling the second story from the WMS-III, a patient with a lesion in the right frontal lobe may respond, "Joe Garcia from South Boston did not go out because the temperature was only 56 degrees." In this case, the patient has recombined elements from the two stories into one. Anna Thompson, a character in the first story, was robbed of 56 dollars, and she was from South Boston. This patient has borrowed the elements of 56 and the location from that story and added them to the second story. A patient may also show evidence of configural or contextual priority when recalling the stories. In that case he or she would be able to explain the general theme of the story but would rely too heavily on paraphrases and be unable to recall specific details.

The dimension of featural versus configural priority is useful in predicting behavior outside the clinical laboratory. For example, patients who show an inability to process contextual information despite a preserved ability to process featural information are often found to be handicapped in situations that require an ability to spontaneously organize and direct one's own behavior. This inability to organize personal behavior, along with an impaired ability to detect organization and to interpret complex arrays of information, greatly diminishes large-scale goal-directed behavior. These deficits are subtle, but often manifest in tasks that require responsibility and self-direction.

Thus, the business executive who favors a strategy of "featural" priority after a significant brain injury may begin to experience difficulty in his or her job because he or she is unable to make long-range decisions, give consistent orders, and complete complex assignments. Despite this, the executive may still have an intimate knowledge of the workings of his or her business and be able to function in a minor advisory capacity and perform more circumscribed tasks requiring less long-term planning. It is not unusual for this loss of sensitivity to the overall organization and cohesion of information to have a profound negative effect on social and personal adjustment.

In contrast, patients who have retained their ability to process configural or contextual information but who suffer from a diminished ability to process the "fine details" of their world may

be inefficient and even forgetful, but in many cases they will still be able to make accurate long-range decisions and relate to others in a consistent, appropriate fashion. Patients who have recovered from aphasia often show this latter pattern of deficits.

Professionals who have sustained a head injury that resulted in aphasia may often return to work even though they still have difficulty processing featural information. These patients will be less efficient and need more time to accomplish tasks that they once accomplished easily. Of course, their deficits are likely to be most pronounced in areas requiring verbal competence. Thus, the analysis of strategy can be useful in developing rehabilitation programs. For example, Degutis et al. (2007) successfully used configural processing strategy training to improve face recognition in adults with congenital prosopagnosia.

Hemispatial Priority

Though not strictly a cognitive strategy, the direction in which patients deploy attention in analyzing and solving spatial problems, and the accuracy with which they are able to use information presented visually to the left and right side of space, is an important source of data concerning the integrity of the brain.

It is well known that visual system lesions posterior to the optic chiasm and in the occipital lobe result in visual field losses contralateral to the side of the lesion (Carpenter, 1972). In addition, lesions that occur in the anterior dorsolateral portion of the occipital lobe or in the parietal cortex may result in neglect of, or inattention to, the side of space contralateral to the lesion (Heilman, 1979). Subtle manifestations of "neglect" or "inattention" may be observed in a patient's attempt to solve various spatial problems, even though the full-blown clinical syndrome is not present.

For example, right-handed adults tend to begin scanning spatial problems on the left side of space, although over the course of many problems they may shift from beginning on one side of the stimulus to beginning on the other. In contrast, patients with lesions of the right hemisphere will characteristically scan from right to left on spatial problems, whereas patients with lesions of the left hemisphere will often use a stereotyped left-to-right strategy.

The latter case can be distinguished from a strong normal tendency to scan from left to right because in addition to using an inflexible left-to-right scanning approach to problems a patient with a lesion in the left hemisphere will tend to make more errors and to be slower processing information in the field contralateral to his or her lesion. Hence, patients with lesions in the left hemisphere will often have difficulty completing the right side of a design, or they will omit details from the right side of a design. Adults without brain lesions may show a strong preference for working from left to right on spatial problems but will not tend to make more errors in one particular field.

Other Specific Strategies

The observation of the informational and spatial priorities that a patient uses can be made across materials, modalities, and functions. These are only two of the many possible process variables that have been isolated. They were presented here because of their pervasiveness and ease of observation. Specific cognitive functions, such as memory, praxis, and language, have special sets of process variables related to each of them, and this information has been detailed in Butters and Cermak (1975) and Goodglass and Kaplan (1972).

Strengths of the Process Approach

This method of qualitative analysis affords several advantages over other approaches to the assessment of the neuropsychological sequelae of brain damage. For the purposes of diagnosis, it is as valid for the detection and localization of cortical lesions as other widely used methods (i.e., Halstead–Reitan: Reitan & Davison, 1974; Luria–Nebraska: Golden, 1981). Trained neuropsychologists using the procedures described herein report agreement with radiological evidence in at least 90% of their cases. In some instances, the qualitative data are inconsistent with the quantitative data (i.e., test scores). For example, a patient who works quickly may be able to overcome his use of pathological,

haphazard strategies and achieve a normal test score, so his test score will not reflect impairment. In cases like this, the hit rate using the qualitative analysis method is superior to the hit rate from methods that do not take qualitative information into account. A similar conclusion was reached by Heaton et al. (1981) when they demonstrated that clinicians who rated Halstead–Reitan results had better success in correctly classifying brain-damaged cases than did a psychometric formula approach rooted heavily in level of performance. Heaton et al. (1981) believed that the clinicians' superiority was related to their ability to supplement test scores with consideration of the qualitative and configural features of their data. One of the important limits of the "Process Approach" as originally formulated is the difficulty in subjecting clinical judgments based on "qualitative" observations to quantitative analysis of validity and the ability to correctly classify patients into diagnostic categories. A number of measures that have been inspired by this approach have been found to have excellent psychometric properties (e.g., the CVLT), but the technique of tracking the potentially large base of qualitative observations itself has not been systematically subjected to systematic psychometric analysis.

Clinical Relevance

The greatest strength of this method may be its usefulness in treatment planning and its relevance to patients' daily lives. Qualitative analysis provides the most precise delineation of functions available, and allows the relative strengths and weaknesses of each patient to become obvious in a "face valid" manner.

Resistance to Practice Effect

This method also shares with other methods the advantages of repeatability and comparability across testing intervals (Glosser et al., 1982). Although strategic variables are to some extent more difficult to quantify, they are less susceptible to the practice and repetition effects that can confound interpretation of test scores. This makes qualitative data more useful than test scores alone in the assessment of recovery. Using both qualitative and quantitative data assures the reliable estimate of change that can be evaluated normatively from test scores combined with an estimate of the effects of change independent of the effects of practice.

Effects of Aging

Aging systematically alters neuropsychological test performance. Aging also affects strategic variables, changes that have been discussed in detail by Albert and Kaplan (1980). In brief, it appears that normal aging produces strategic changes akin to those observed among some patients with frontal system disorder, including cognitive slowing and loss of ability to process configural information (Hochanadel, 1991; Hochanadel & Kaplan, 1984).

The methods of the Process Approach have always had the potential for allowing the differentiation of aging from specific asymmetric neuropathologies, such as left frontal or right frontal disease. It is less effective in sorting out aging from mild generalized cerebral disorder, as occurs in very early dementia. In common with other approaches, we based our differentiation partly on estimates of premorbid functioning by considering demographic indices (Karzmark, 1984; Wilson et al., 1979) and performance on tests relatively resistant to the effects of brain damage. We also paid attention to memory impairment that exceeds that to be expected with the benign senescent forgetfulness of normal aging, and to strategic pathologies reflecting frontal lobe dysfunction that are more severe than one ordinarily encounters in the elderly. Regrettably, our normative work is not yet sufficiently advanced to propose specific rules or norms to aid in this important distinction.

Effects of Education

In terms of qualitative information, it was surmised that people who are 50–60 years old and who have completed at least ninth grade show little difference in strategy from individuals who have completed high school and college on most tasks involving visuospatial information. Amount of education does not appear to produce strategic differences in scanning, stimulus selectivity, and contextual or featural sensitivity.

Verbal skills, naturally, are more sensitive to the effects of education.

Sensory Motor Handicaps

Our method emphasizes separating strategic differences from generalized slowing. Being slow must be distinguished from being slowed up by the difficulty of the task (Welford, 1977). Peripheral handicaps often make it difficult to work quickly, but by observing the strategy used by a disabled patient on verbal and visuospatial tasks, one can distinguish the defects caused by peripheral injury from those caused by cognitive dysfunction and inform efforts at rehabilitation.

Psychopathology

Differentiating severe psychopathology from dysfunction related to neurologic processes is one of the most difficult tasks for the neuropsychologist. Patients with severe psychopathology sometimes perform on neuropsychological tests like patients with confirmed lesions of the CNS.

Chronic schizophrenics often have naming problems (Barr et al., 1989), difficulties analyzing details in visuospatial tasks, and difficulty maintaining attention, deficits that we associate with left hemisphere pathology. Patients with severe depression resemble patients with subcortical depression (Massman et al., 1992) and may also be similar to patients with known right hemisphere pathology and, in particular, right frontal lobe dysfunction. These patients can have difficulty analyzing contextual information relative to a preserved ability to use details. In addition, they can have difficulty with visuospatial memory, although their memory for verbal materials is relatively intact in terms of recalling details.

Summary

The Boston Process Approach was a systematic method for assessing qualitative neuropsychological information and was an important step in integrating the "cognitive revolution" occurring in academic experimental psychology with clinical neuropsychological practice. The original method of integrating process-based modifications and observations with traditional test performance data has added sensitivity and meaning to neuropsychological assessment and has evolved into a new generation of tests that incorporate many of the concepts developed by Dr. Kaplan and her colleagues. The original method still has important applications for clinical descriptive uses, but the method itself, by the nature of its complexity, did not result in a significant body of supportive scientific literature. Rather, it served as the groundwork for new approaches, which in fact have become some of the central building blocks of modern cognitive psychology and cognitive neuroscience. We have discussed two strategic elements—featural versus contextual priority and hemispatial priority—to illustrate the possibilities of our approach. As the method we have described is refined both in our laboratory and by other investigators, we foresee that it will help move neuropsychological assessment beyond a reliable cataloging of deficits toward an understanding of the underlying processes. With such an understanding, neuropsychology will be in a better position to assist in the more important task of treatment planning and rehabilitation. As has been emphasized throughout this chapter, the Process Approach as originally formulated, by its nature, has been difficult to be directly used in scientific investigations, though it has had an important impact on the direction of neuropsychological assessment, inspiring a modernization of the practice of the clinical assessment of brain–behavior relationships.

Acknowledgments

The work was supported in part by a VA Merit Review grant to William Milberg at the West Roxbury VA Medical Center and NINDS Program Project Grant NS 26985 to Boston University School of Medicine.

References

Albert, M. S., & Kaplan, E. (1980). Organic implications of neuropsychological deficits in the elderly. In L. W. Poon, J. L. Fozard, L. S. Cermak, D. Arenberg, & L. W. Thompson (Eds.), *New directions in memory and aging* (pp. 403–432). Hillsdale, NJ: Lawrence Erlbaum Associates, Inc.

Alexander, M. P., Stuss, D. T., & Fansabedian, N. (2003). California Verbal Learning Test: Performance by patients with focal frontal and non-frontal lesions. *Brain, 126*(6), 1493–1503.

Barr, W. B., Bilder, R. M., Goldberg, E., & Kaplan, E. (1989). The neuropsychology of schizophrenic speech. *Journal of Communication Disorders, 22*, 327–349.

Bender, L. A. (1938). A visual motor gestalt test and its clinical use. *American Orthopsychiatric Association Research Monographs*, No. 3.

Benton, A. L. (1950). A multiple choice type of visual retention test. *Archives of Neurology and Psychiatry, 64*, 699–707.

Benton, A. L., Hamsher, K. deS., Varney, N. R., & Spreen, O. (1983). *Judgment of line orientation.* New York: Oxford University Press.

Berger, M. (1993). *Sensitivity of neuropsychological instruments.* Unpublished doctoral dissertation. S.U.N.Y., Albany, NY.

Butters, N., & Cermak, L. S. (1975). Some analyses of amnesia syndrome in brain damaged patients. In K. Pribram & R. Isaacson (Eds.), *The hippocampus* (pp. 377–409). New York: Plenum Press.

Butters, N., & Cermak, L. S. (1980). *The Alcoholic Korsakoff's Syndrome. An information processing approach to amnesia.* New York: Academic Press.

Butters, N., & Grady, M. (1977). Effects of predistractor delays on the short-term memory performance of patients with Korsakoff's and Huntington's Disease. *Neuropsychologia, 13*, 701–705.

Carpenter, M. B. (1972). *Core text of neuroanatomy.* Baltimore: Williams and Wilkins.

Christiansen, A. L. (1975). *Luria's neuropsychological investigation: Text, manual, and test cards.* New York: Spectrum.

Coltheart, M., Hull, E., & Slater, D. (1975). Sex differences in imagery and reading. *Nature, 253*, 438–440.

Critchley, M. (1953). *The pareital lobes.* London: Edward Arnold.

Cronbach, L. J. (1957). The two disciplines of scientific psychology. *American Psychologist, 12*, 671–684.

DeGutis, J. M., Bentin, S., Robertson, L. C., & D'Esposito, M. (2007). Functional plasticity in ventral temporal cortex following cognitive rehabilitation of a congenital prosopagnosic. *Journal of Cognitive Neuroscience, 19*(11), 1790–1802.

Delis, D. C., Direnfeld, L., Alexander, M. P., & Kaplan, E. (1982). Cognitive fluctuations associated with the on–off phenomenon in Parkinson's disease. *Neurology, 32*, 1049–1052.

Delis, D. C., Kramer, J. H., Fridland, A. J., & Kaplan, E. (1990). A cognitive science approach to neuropsychological assessment. In P. McReynolds,

J. C. Rosen, & G. Chelune (Eds.), *Advances in psychological assessment* (vol. 7, pp. 101–132). New York: Plenum Press.

Delis, D. C., Kramer, J. H., & Kaplan, E. (1984). *The California proverbs test.* Boston: Boston Neuropsychological Foundation.

Delis, D. C., Kramer, J. H., & Kaplan, E. (2001). *The Delis–Kaplan Executive Function System Test manual.* San Antonio, TX: The Psychological Corporation.

Delis, D. C., Kramer, J. H., Kaplan, E. & Ober, B. A. (1987). *The California Verbal Learning Test. Manual.* San Antonio, TX: The Psychological Corporation.

Delis, D. C., Robertson, L. C., & Efron, R. (1986). Hemisphere specialization of memory for visual hierarchical organization. *Neuropsychologia, 24,* 205–214.

Delis, D. C., Squire, L. R., Bihrle, A., & Massman, P. J. (1992). Componential analysis of problem-solving ability: Performance of patients with frontal lobe damage and amnesic patients on a new sorting test. *Neuropsychologia, 30,* 683–697.

Feldman, M. J., & Drasgow, J. (1960). *The Visual–Verbal Test. Manual.* Beverly Hills, CA: Western Psychological Services.

Folstein, M. F., Folstein, S. E., & McHugh, P. R. (1975). "Mini-mental State." A practical method for grading the cognitive state of patients for the clinician. *Journal of Psychiatric Research, 12,* 189–198.

Freedman, M., Leach, L., Kaplan, E., Winocur, G., Shulman, K., & Delis, D. (1995). *Clock drawing: A neuropsychological analysis.* New York: Oxford University Press.

Geschwind, N. (1975). The apraxias: Neural mechanisms of disorders of learned movement. *American Scientist, 63,* 188–195.

Glosser, G., Kaplan, E., & LoVerme, S. (1982). Longitudinal neuropsychological report of aphasia following left subcortical hemorrhage. *Brain and Language, 15,* 95–116.

Golden, C. J. (1981). A standardized version of Luria's neuropsychological tests. In S. J. Filskov & T. J. Boll (Eds.), *Handbook of clinical neuropsychology* (pp. 608–642). New York: John Wiley and Sons.

Goodglass, H., & Kaplan, E. (1963). Disturbance of gesture and pantomime in aphasia. *Brain, 86,* 708–720.

Goodglass, H., & Kaplan, E. (1972). *The assessment of aphasia and related disorders.* Philadelphia: Lea and Febiger.

Goodglass, H., & Kaplan, E. F. (1983). *Boston diagnostic aphasia examination* (2nd ed.). Media, PA: Williams & Wilkins.

Gorham, D. R. (1956). *Proverbs test.* Missoula: Psychological Test Specialists.

Grande, L., McGlinchey, R., Barber, C., Rudolph, J., & Milberg, W. (Submitted). Detecting cognitive impairment in individuals at risk for cerebrovascular disease: The 90-second "Clock-in-the-Box" Screening Test. *Archives of Clinical Neuropsychology.*

Grant, D. A., & Berg, E. A. (1948). A behavioral analysis of degree of reinforcement and ease of shifting to new responses in a Weigl-type card sorting program. *Journal of Experimental Psychology, 38,* 404–411.

Haeberle, K. C. (1982). Multidimensional scaling of block design patterns. Paper presented at the annual meeting of the Eastern Psychological Association, Baltimore, Maryland.

Halstead, W. C. (1947). *Brain and intelligence: Quantitative study of the frontal lobes.* Chicago: University of Chicago Press.

Hamann, C., McGlinchey-Berroth, R., Minaker, K., & Milberg, W. (1993). *Validation of a neuropsychological screening instrument of older adults.* Geriatric Research Training Center, Project 7 (Core 2), Harvard Division on Aging.

Heaton, R. K., Grant, I., Anthony, W. Z., & Lehman, R. A. W. (1981). A comparison of clinical and automated interpretation of the Halstead–Reitan Battery. *Journal of Clinical Neuropsychology, 3,* 121–141.

Heilman, K. M. (1979). Neglect and related disorders. In K. M. Heilman & C. Valenstein (Eds.), *Clinical neuropsychology* (pp. 268–307). New York: Oxford University Press.

Hochanadel, G. (1991). *Neuropsychological changes in aging: A process oriented error analysis.* Unpublished doctoral dissertation. Clark University, Worcester, MA.

Hochanadel, G., & Kaplan, E. (1984). Neuropsychology of normal aging. In M. L. Albert (Ed.), *Clinical neurology of aging* (pp. 231–244). New York: Oxford University Press.

Hooper, H. E. (1958). *The Hooper Visual Organization Test Manual.* Los Angeles: Western Psychological Services.

Horn, J. L., & Cattell, R. B. (1967). Age differences in fluid and crystallized intelligence. *Acta Psychologica, 26,* 107–129.

Hunt, E. (1983). On the nature of intelligence. *Science, 219,* 141–146.

Jastak, J. F., & Jastak, S. R. (1984). *The Wide Range Achievement Test Manual (Revised).* Los Angeles: Western Psychological Services.

Joy, S., Kaplan, E., & Fein, D. (1992a). The Information Test of the WAIS-R as a Neuropsychological Instrument among healthy older adults. Paper presented at the 14th European Conference of the International Neuropsychological Society, Durham, England.

Joy, S., Kaplan, E., & Fein, D. (1992b). Factors affecting Digit Symbol performance in aging. Paper presented at the 100th Annual Convention, American Psychological Association, Washington, DC.

Kaplan, E. (1968). *Gestural representation of implement usage: An organismic-developmental study.* Unpublished doctoral dissertation. Worcester, MA: Clark University.

Kaplan, E. (1983). Process and achievement revisited. In S. Wapner & B. Kaplan (Eds.), *Toward a holistic developmental psychology* (pp. 143–156). Hillsdale, NJ: Lawrence Erlbaum Associates, Inc..

Kaplan, E. (1988). A process approach to neuropsychological assessment. In T. Boll & B. K. Bryant (Eds.), *Clinical neuropsychology and brain function: Research, measurement, and practice* (pp. 125–167). Washington, DC: American Psychological Association.

Kaplan, E. (1990). The process approach to neuropsychological assessment of psychiatric patients. *Journal of Neuropsychiatry and Clinical Neurosciences, 2,* 72–87.

Kaplan, E., Caine, E., & Morse, P. (1981). *Boston/Rochester Neuropsychological Screening Test.* Unpublished Test.

Kaplan, E., Fein, D., Kramer, J., Delis, D., & Morris, R. (Ed.). (1989). *WISC-111 as a process instrument (WISC-III PI).* San Antonio, TX: The Psychological Corporation.

Kaplan, E., Fein, D., Morris, R., & Delis, D. C. (1991). *WAIS-R as a Neuropsychological Instrument. Manual.* San Antonio, TX: The Psychological Corporation.

Kaplan, E., Goodglass, H., & Weintraub, S. (1983). *The Boston Naming Test* (2nd ed.). Philadelphia: Lea and Febiger.

Kaplan, E., & Morris, R. (1985). *Boston modification of the WAIS-R.* Unpublished Test.

Karzmark, P., Heaton, R. K., Grant, I., & Mathews, C. G. (1984). Use of demographic variables to predict full scale IQ and level of performance on the Halstead–Reitan Battery. *Journal of Consulting and Clinical Psychology, 52,* 663–665.

Kløve, H. (1963). *Grooved pegboard.* Lafayette, IN: Lafayette Instruments.

Levine, B., Milberg, W., & Stuss, D. (1993). *Boston evaluation of executive functions.* Unpublished Test.

Lezak, M. D., Howieson, D. B., & Loring, D. W. (2004). *Neuropsychological assessment* (3rd ed.). New York: Oxford University Press.

Libon, D. J., Swenson, R., Barnoski, E. J., & Sands, L. P. (1993). Clock Drawing as an assessment tool for dementia. *Archives of Clinical Neuropsychology, 8,* 405–415.

Massman, P. J., Delis, D. C., Butters, N., Dupont, R. M., & Gillin, J. C. (1992). The subcortical dysfunction hypothesis of memory deficits in depression: Neuropsychological validation in a subgroup of patients. *Journal of Clinical and Experimental Neuropsychology, 5,* 687–706.

Milberg, W., & Blumstein, S. E. (1981). Lexical decision and aphasia: Evidence for semantic processing. *Brain and Language, 14,* 371–385.

Milberg, W., Cummings, J., Goodglass, H., & Kaplan, E. (1979). Case report: A global sequential processing disorder following head injury: A possible role for the right hemisphere in serial order behavior. *Journal of Clinical Neuropsychology, 1,* 213–225.

Milberg, W., Greiffenstein, M., Lewis, R., & Rourke, D. (1980). Differentiation of temporal lobe and generalized seizure patients with the WAIS. *Journal of Consulting and Clinical Psychology, 48,* 39–42.

Milberg, W., MacDonald, R., Odenheimer, G., McGlinchey-Berroth, R., Hamann, C., Weitzen, S., et al. (1992). *Geriatric evaluation of mental status.* Unpublished Test, Brockton/West Roxbury Geriatric Research, Education, Clinical Center.

Munshi, M., Grande, L., Hayes, M., Ayres, D., Suhl, E., Capelson, N. P., Lin, S., et al. (2006). Cognitive dysfunction is associated with poor diabetes control. *Diabetes Care, 29*(8), 1794–1799.

Neisser, U. (1967). *Cognitive psychology.* New York: Appleton, Century, Crofts.

Neisser, U., Novick, R., & Lager, R. (1963). Searching for ten targets simultaneously. *Perceptual and Motor Skills, 17,* 955–961.

Osterreith, P., & Rey, A. (1944). Le test de copie d'une figure complexe. *Archives de Psychologie, 30,* 206–356.

Palmer, P., & Kaplan, E. (1985). *The cow and circle experimental object assemblies.* New Object Assembly components of the WAIS-R NI. San Antonio, TX: The Psychological Corporation.

Perry, W., Potterat, E., Auslander, L., Kaplan, E., & Jeste, D. (1996). A neuropsychological approach to the Rorschach in patients with dementias of the Alzheimer type. *Assessment, 3,* 351–363.

Poreh, A. M. (2000). The quanitifed process approach: An emerging methodology to neuropsychological assessment. *The Clinical Neuropsychologist, 14*(2), 212–222.

Poreh, A. M. (2006). *The quantified approach to neuropsychological assessment.* New York: Psychology Press.

Porteus, S. D. (1965). *Porteus Maze Test.* Palo Alto: Pacific Books.

Powell, D. H., Kaplan, E., Whitla, D., Weintraub, S., Catlin, R., & Funkenstein, H. H. (1993). *Microcog*

Assessment of Cognitive Functioning Manual. San Antonio, TX: The Psychological Corporation.

Raven, J. C. (1960). *Guide to the standard progressive matrices.* London: H. K. Lewis.

Reitan, R. M., & Davison, L. A. (1974). *Clinical neuropsychology: Current status and applications.* New York: Winston/Wiley.

Rey, A. (1964). *L'Examen Clinique en Psychologie.* Paris Presses Universitaires de France.

Robertson, L. C., & Delis, D. C. (1986). "Part-whole" processing in unilateral brain-damaged patients: Dysfunction of hierarchical organization. *Neuropsychologia, 24,* 363–370.

Rorschach, H. (1942). *Psychodiagnostics: A diagnostic test based on perception* (P. Lemkau and B. Kronenberg, translators). Berne: Huber; U.S. Distributor: Grune and Stratton.

Rouleau, I., Salmon, D. P., & Butters, N. (1996). Longitudinal analysis of clock drawing in Alzheimer's disease patients. *Brain and Cognition, 31,* 17–34.

Royall, D. R., Cordes, J. A., & Polk, M. (1998). CLOX: An executive clock drawing task. *Journal of Neurological Neurosurgery and Psychiatry, 64,* 588–594.

Royer, F. L. (1967). Information processing in the Block Design task. *Intelligence, 1,* 23–50.

Russell, E. W. (1981). Some principles of psychometric neuropsychology and the Halstead–Reitan Battery. *Perspectives in V. A. Neuropsychology Rehabilitation: Proceedings of the Mental Health and Behavioral Sciences Service Conference.* Salt Lake City, Utah.

Russell, E. W., Neuringer, C., & Goldstein, G. (1970). *Assessment of brain damage: A neuropsychological key approach.* New York: John Wiley and Sons.

Sachs, W., Milberg, W., & McGlinchey-Berroth, R. (1995). The detection of cognitive impairment in elderly inpatients using the Geriatric Evaluation of Mental Status. Unpublished Manuscript.

Schmeck, R. R., & Grove, E. (1979). Academic achievement and individual differences in learning processes. *Applied Psychological Measurement, 3,* 43–49.

Shallice, T. (1982). Specific impairment in planning. In D. E. Broadbent & L. Weiskrantz (Eds.), *The neuropsychology of cognitive function* (pp. 199–209). London: The Royal Society.

Shipley, W. C. (1940). A self-administering scale for measuring intellectual impairment and deterioration. *Journal of Psychology, 9,* 371–377.

Shorr, J. S., Delis, D. C., & Massman, P. J. (1992). Memory for the Rey–Osterreith figure: Perceptual clustering, encoding, and storage. *Neuropsychology, 6,* 43–50.

South, M. B., Greve, K. W., Bianchini, K. J., & Adams, D. (2001). Interater reliability of three clock drawing test scoring systems. *Applied Neuropsychology, 8,* 174–179.

Stern, R., Singer, E. A., Duke, L. M., Singer, N. G., Morey, C. E., Daughtrey, E. W., et al. (1994). The Boston Qualitative Scoring System for the Rey–Osterreith Complex Figure: Description and interrater reliability. *The Clinical Neuropsychologist, 8,* 309–322.

Sternberg, R. J. (1980). Sketch of a componential subtheory of human intelligence. *Behavioral Brain Science, 3,* 573–614.

Stroop, J. R. (1935). Studies of interference in serial verbal reactions. *Journal of Experimental Psychology, 18,* 643–662.

Stuss, D. T., & Benson, D. F. (1986). *The frontal lobes.* New York: Raven Press.

Talland, G. A. (1965). *Deranged memory.* New York: Academic Press.

Thomas, R., & Forder, E. (2006). The role of local and global processing in the recognition of living and non-living things. *Neuropsychologia, 44,* 982–986.

Thurstone, L. L. (1938). *Primary mental abilities.* Chicago: University of Chicago Press.

Wechsler, D. A. (1945). A standardized memory scale for clinical use. *Journal of Psychology, 19,* 87–95.

Wechsler, D. A. (1955). *Wechsler Adult Intelligence Scale.* New York: The Psychological Corporation.

Wechsler, D. A. (1981). *Wechsler Adult Intelligence Scale-Revised.* New York: The Psychological Corporation.

Wechsler, D. A. (1987). *Wechsler Memory Scale-Revised.* San Antonio, TX: The Psychological Corporation.

Wechsler, D. A. (1991). *Wechsler Intelligence Scale for Children-III.* San Antonio, TX: The Psychological Corporation.

Wechsler, D. A. (1997). *Wechsler Memory Scale—3rd Edition (WMS-III)* (3rd ed.). San Antonio, TX: The Psychological Corporation.

Welford, A. T. (1977). Causes of slowing of performance with age. *Interdisciplinary Topics in Gerontology, 11,* 43–45.

Werner, H. (1937). Process and achievement: A basic problem of education and developmental psychology. *Harvard Educational Review, 7,* 353–368.

Wilson, R. S., Rosenbaum, G., Brown, G., & Grisell, J. (1979). An index of premorbid intelligence. *Journal of Consulting and Clinical Psychology, 46,* 1554–1555.

4

The Iowa-Benton School
of Neuropsychological Assessment

Daniel Tranel

Historical Introduction

Early Developments

The Iowa-Benton (I-B) school of neuropsychological assessment dates back more than a half century. In 1950, Arthur Benton set up a small neuropsychology unit, at the invitation of Dr. Adolph Sahs, who was the Head of the Department of Neurology at the University of Iowa Hospitals and Clinics. Dr. Benton's service was placed in the Department of Neurology, where it has remained until the current day, and this close affiliation with Neurology has been an important influence in the development of the Iowa approach. In the initial arrangement, Benton agreed to evaluate patients referred by either Dr. Sahs or Dr. Russell Meyers, who was the Chair of the Division of Neurosurgery at UIHC. In return, Benton and his students were permitted to use case material from Neurology and Neurosurgery for research purposes. These strong ties to Neurology and Neurosurgery (the latter now being a department, headed by Dr. Matthew Howard) continue to catalyze both the clinical and research functions of the Benton Laboratory.

In the early days, the Neuropsychology Clinic was a modest operation. Benton was a full-time member of the Department of Psychology and the director of its graduate program in clinical psychology, and these roles occupied most of his time. He typically would spend two afternoons and a Saturday morning each week in the Neuropsychology Clinic. The Neuropsychology operation gradually grew in scope, however, fueled by the labor provided by a succession of graduate students. By 1952, a number of graduate students had begun to receive practicum training in neuropsychological assessment, with their training in neuropsychology supplemented by attendance at the Saturday morning grand rounds of the Neurology and Neurosurgery staffs. In 1953, thesis and dissertation research in neuropsychology was instituted. Benton's first students included Heilbrun, Wahler, Swanson, and Blackburn, all of whom earned their Master's and/or PhD degrees in the mid-1950s. In 1956, Benton initiated a seminar in neuropsychology, aimed at residents in neurology and neurosurgery and also available to graduate students.

During the first several years of the neuropsychology operation, Benton's research focused on development and disturbances of body schema (Benton, 1955a, 1955b; Benton & Abramson, 1952; Benton & Cohen, 1955; Benton & Menefee, 1957; Swanson, 1957; Swanson & Benton, 1955). Another early theme was hemispheric differences in neuropsychological performance patterns (Heilbrun, 1956, 1959). Reaction time was another early research interest (Blackburn, 1958; Blackburn & Benton, 1955), as were qualitative features of performance (Wahler, 1956). In addition, Benton wrote several papers covering historical aspects of the development of neuropsychology (Benton, 1956), including one in which he discussed the Gerstmann syndrome (Benton & Meyers, 1956; for an interesting historical comparison, see Benton, 1992).

Neuropsychology Expands

In 1958, Benton accepted a joint appointment as Professor of Neurology and Psychology, and he moved his main office to the University Hospitals. Thereafter, the Neuropsychology unit expanded considerably, becoming what would be known as the "Neuropsychology Laboratory." A technician and full-time secretary were engaged. In 1961, Otfried Spreen joined the laboratory as a second professional staff member, and the Laboratory became a major center for practicum training and MA and PhD research. Between the years of 1959 and 1978, the Neuropsychology Laboratory sponsored 25 PhD dissertations and 17 MA theses. The research program was highly productive, and the influence of the Laboratory permeated the cognate specialties of behavioral neurology and neuropsychiatry, as well as the field of neuropsychology. During the 1960s and 1970s, the Laboratory produced about 170 scientific and scholarly publications on diverse topics in neuropsychology, many of which are recognized still as standards in the field (cf. Costa & Spreen, 1985; Hamsher, 1985).

Benton achieved emeritus status in 1978, and he remained fully active as a scholar, mentor, and leader in the field of neuropsychology. At that point, the Neuropsychology Laboratory became a core facility in the newly created Division of Behavioral Neurology and Cognitive Neuroscience, established in the late 1970s by Drs. Antonio Damasio and Hanna Damasio. Under the leadership of Paul Eslinger, PhD, the Laboratory played a key role in the development of the ambitious research program in cognitive neuroscience instituted by the Damasios in the early 1980s. In 1986, Daniel Tranel, PhD, assumed direction of the laboratory and, at this point, officially designated the laboratory as the "Benton Neuropsychology Laboratory," a title it keeps to this day. The delivery of clinical services in the Benton Laboratory expanded considerably, to the point where the annual throughput of patients began to number close to 2000. In the late 1990s, the Benton Neuropsychology Laboratory moved to a spacious, newly remodeled area, which included a waiting room, patient check-in, four exam rooms, a rehabilitation laboratory, a driving simulator, and faculty and staff offices.

A Philosophy of Assessment

Virtually all of Benton's professional career had been spent in medical facilities, where he had had the opportunity of watching skilled neurologists and psychiatrists such as Spafford Ackerly, Macdonald Critchley, Raymond Garcin, and Phyllis Greenacre evaluate patients. He noted that, having conducted a brief "mental status" examination, they would probe the diagnostic possibilities by diverse questions and maneuvers (the reasons for which were not always apparent to the auditors at grand rounds!). Benton observed that their evaluations were extremely variable in length. Some were completed in 15 minutes, and others took more than an hour, after which the "chief" would discuss the significance of the findings generated by the questions and procedures in relation to the diagnosis. What forcibly impressed him was the flexibility in choice of procedures and the continuous hypothesis testing that these astute examiners engaged in as they explored the diagnostic possibilities.

Benton was also struck by the essential identity in the approaches of an "organic" neurologist (Critchley) and a psychoanalytically oriented psychiatrist (Greenacre). Both adopted flexible procedures as they pursued one or another lead that might disclose the basic neuropathology or psychopathology underlying a patient's overt disabilities. Benton concluded that neuropsychological assessment should follow the model exemplified by the diagnostic strategy of these eminent physicians. Even though neuropsychological assessment involved the employment of standardized objective tests, it could be flexible. It need not consist of the administration of a standard battery of tests measuring a predetermined set of performances in every patient. In this sense, it was more akin to a clinical examination than to a laboratory procedure. On one occasion, he wrote:

neuropsychological assessment is essentially a refinement of clinical neurological observation and not a 'laboratory procedure' in the same class as serology, radiology, or electroencephalography.... Neuropsychological testing assesses the same behavior that the neurologist observes clinically. It serves the function of enhancing clinical observation.... neuropsychological assessment is very closely allied to clinical neurological evaluation and in fact can be considered to be a special form of it. (Benton, 1975, p. 68)

Subsequently, he restated his position in these words:

The fact is that none of the batteries that are widely used today adequately meet the need for a well focused analysis of the cognitive status of patients with actual or suspected brain disease. Such a battery should provide reliable assessments of a number of learning and memory performances and of at least the semantic aspects of language function as well as of visuoperceptive and visuospatial functions. But even a fairly comprehensive battery of tests cannot be regarded as necessarily being the endpoint of assessment since it cannot possibly answer (or attempt to answer) all the questions that may be raised about different patients. Moreover, the administration of such a battery tends to be wasteful of time and expense.

Instead it may be useful to think in terms of a core battery of modest length, perhaps five or six carefully selected tests that would take not more than 30 minutes to give. Then, depending upon both the specific referral question and the patient's pattern of performance on the core battery, exploration of specific possibilities may be indicated, e.g., an aphasic disorder, a visuoconstructive disability, a visuospatial disorder, or specific impairment in abstract reasoning. For this purpose we should have available a large inventory of well-standardized tests from which a selection can be made in an attempt to answer the diagnostic questions. Administration of the core battery may suffice to answer the referral question in some cases. In other cases, 20 tests may have to be given and even then the answer to the question may not be forthcoming. In short, I think that we should regard neuropsychological assessment in the same way as we view the physical or neurological examination, i.e., as a logical sequential decision-making process rather than as simply the administration of a fixed battery of tests. (Benton, 1985; p. 15)

More recently, he wrote:

Neuropsychological assessment consists essentially of a set of clinical examination procedures and hence does not differ in kind from conventional clinical observation. Both neuropsychological assessment and clinical observation deal with the same basic data, namely, the behavior of the patient. Neuropsychological assessment may be viewed as a refinement and extension of clinical observation—a refinement in that it describes a patient's performances more precisely and reliably, and an extension in that, through instrumentation and special test procedures, it elicits types of performance that are not accessible to the clinical observer. (Benton, 1991; p. 507)

This conception of the nature of neuropsychological assessment was reflected in Benton's Neuropsychology unit at the University of Iowa Hospitals and Clinics. In the 1960s the core battery for a nonaphasic patient would consist typically of three WAIS subtests (Information, Comprehension, Arithmetic) from the Verbal Scale and three (Block Design, Picture Arrangement, Picture Completion) from the Performance Scale. Then, depending upon the referral question and the characteristics of the patient's performance on the core battery, additional tests (which might include some of the remaining WAIS subtests) would be given to explore the diagnostic possibilities. This core battery was gradually modified over the years so that, for example, in the late 1970s, only the Arithmetic and Block Designs subtests of the WAIS were given while other tests such as temporal orientation, the Token Test and the Visual Retention Test found a place in the battery. It was in the context of giving additional tests to answer specific questions that the need for different types of tests emerged. This provided the impetus for the development of the diverse test methods associated with the Iowa laboratory, for example, facial discrimination (Benton & Van Allen, 1968), controlled oral word association (Bechtoldt et al., 1962; Fogel, 1962), three-dimensional constructional praxis (Benton & Fogel, 1962), motor impersistence (Joynt et al., 1962), and judgment of line orientation (Benton et al., 1978).

Current Practice

The I-B School of Neuropsychology

The philosophy of neuropsychological assessment in the current I-B school has evolved over the past several decades from the early tenets established by Benton. In its current practice, the I-B school can be conceptualized as somewhat of a hybrid approach that maintains Benton's emphasis on flexibility, efficiency, and the clinical context, while also incorporating a more formal "laboratory procedure" mentality that emphasizes basic coverage of all higher-order cognitive and behavioral functions by the examination. The principal objective is to obtain quantitative measurements of key domains of cognition and behavior, in a time-efficient manner, in sufficient breadth and depth that the referral question can be answered. The amount of testing required to meet this objective varies considerably across different patients, situations, and referral questions, ranging from a lower figure of 15–30 minutes to a high of 7 hours or even longer. The I-B approach is flexible and hypothesis driven. The selection of tests given to a patient is guided by a number of factors, including the nature of the patient's complaint, the questions raised by the referring entity (physician, family, social agency, etc.), the impressions gained from the initial interview, and, especially, the diagnostic possibilities raised by the patient's performances during the course of the examination. In brief, the procedure involves the administration of relevant tests selected from the rich armamentarium available to neuropsychologists. The results of the tests are interpreted in the context of other contextual and diagnostic information, which typically includes the medical history, neurological findings, and neuroimaging (computed tomography [CT], magnetic resonance imaging [MRI]) data, and may also encompass electroencephalographic (EEG) findings, neurosurgical reports, and functional imaging (e.g., positron emission tomography [PET]) results. The interpretation strategy used in the I-B school is integrative and hypothesis focused, in a manner similar to the neuropsychological testing procedure. Thus, the current practice of the I-B approach is properly considered a laboratory procedure, but one that retains Benton's emphasis on flexibility and efficiency.

The amount of testing used in the I-B approach is not strictly predetermined, although we typically employ a core set of procedures (described below) that usually takes about 3–3½ hours to administer. To some extent, the test protocol is formulated anew for each patient, according to the particular exigencies of the situation, and the examination is pursued to the extent necessary to achieve the main objective of answering the referral question as definitively as possible. And in many cases, our assessments are guided by rehabilitation considerations (cf. Anderson, 1996, 2002). For example, tests are chosen and implemented with an eye toward increasing the type of information that will be especially helpful in the neuropsychological rehabilitation setting, which is in many cases the next stop-off for patients referred for neuropsychological assessment.

Over the years, the segment of the I-B examination that is devoted to providing direct feedback to the patient, family, and other caregivers has increased substantially—in fact, this is probably one of the most notable changes in the I-B examination over the past two decades. In earlier days, the feedback component of the examination was minimal, and the neuropsychologist often left to the referring physician the task of providing feedback on "laboratory tests," including the neuropsychological exam. But this has changed, and it is customary now for the attending neuropsychologist to provide extensive feedback to the patient and relevant persons who accompany the patient to the exam, regarding the nature of the findings from the testing, the meaning of the findings vis-à-vis diagnostic considerations, and the implications of the findings in regard to practical matters such as day-to-day functioning. Recommendations for rehabilitation or related forms of treatment are frequently provided, and an effort is made to identify specific local providers with whom the patient can follow up (e.g., a clinical psychologist). It is common for the neuropsychologist to provide specific recommendations in regard to driving privileges, management of finances, living arrangements, and other important life situations that may be profoundly equivocal in patients with major neurological disease. Oftentimes, this type of feedback is the first time the patient and family will be hearing messages such as this, and a rapport-based, therapeutic context is critical for the feedback to be understood and assimilated. The feedback is often the most challenging aspect of the examination, demanding from the neuropsychologist a full deployment of clinical psychological skills to maximize the chances that the information would yield the largest benefit to the patient and family. Telling a patient that "you should stop driving, and move to a nursing home" is not a trivial matter, and providing feedback of this nature in a tactful, respectful, and effective manner requires a full repertoire of clinical skills. Moreover, we normally provide feedback immediately after the testing, so that patients and families leave our clinic with a full understanding of the outcome of our testing and relevant recommendations. Immediate feedback is widely regarded as very valuable to patients and families, but this service places high demands on the clinical neuropsychologists, who must conceptualize the case on the spot and formulate immediate interpretations and recommendations. Current training in the Benton Laboratory places a high priority on these skills.

A Core Battery. It was noted earlier that Benton developed a core battery of tests, which evolved over the years. This tradition continues in the current I-B school. In fact, Benton has pointed out that one risk of a "flexible" approach is that it can become too flexible, so that no two examinations are the same, and neuropsychologists begin using idiosyncratic sets of tests that have little overlap with those used by other practitioners (not to mention the frequent shortcomings in normative data). To avoid this problem and to provide a structured set of tests that serves as a starting point for neuropsychological assessment, we utilize a Core Battery in the I-B school. The Core Battery is enumerated in Table 4–1 (the tests are listed in order of administration). (As of November 2008, we began using the newly published WAIS-IV (Wechsler, 2008) in our evaluations. Where relevant, the WAIS-III subtests listed in the Core and follow-up procedures below have been replaced by their WAIS-IV counterparts. We have retained the use of Picture Arrangement from the WAIS-III, however, as this subtest was not carried forward in the WAIS-IV battery and we have found Picture Arrangement useful as an index of nonverbal social reasoning.)

All examinations begin with an interview of the patient by the neuropsychologist. Family members are typically present during this phase, and they are called upon to supplement and corroborate the history provided by the patient. The interview is an indispensable and crucial source of information. It provides clues about the nature and cause of the patient's presenting complaints, the patient's capacity and motivation to cooperate with the testing procedures, and the extent to which the patient is aware

Table 4–1. The Iowa-Benton Core Battery[a]

1. Interview
2. Orientation to time, personal information, and place
3. Wide Range Achievement Test-4, Reading Subtest (or Wechsler Test of Adult Reading)
4. Recall of recent presidents
5. Information subtest (WAIS-IV)
6. Complex Figure Test (copy and delayed recall)
7. Auditory Verbal Learning Test (with delayed recall) (or California Verbal Learning Test)
8. Draw a clock
9. Arithmetic subtest (WAIS-IV)
10. Block Design subtest (WAIS-IV)
11. Digit Span subtest (WAIS-IV)
12. Similarities subtest (WAIS-IV)
13. Trail-Making Test
14. Coding subtest (WAIS-IV)
15. Controlled Oral Word Association Test
16. Benton Visual Retention Test
17. Benton Facial Discrimination Test
18. Boston Naming Test
19. Picture Arrangement subtest (WAIS-III)
20. Geschwind-Oldfield Handedness Questionnaire
21. Beck Depression Inventory-II
22. State-Trait Anxiety Inventory

[a] References for tests in the Core Battery are Benton et al. (1983), Lezak et al. (2004), Spreen and Strauss (1998), and Wechsler (2008).

of his or her situation. Typically, the neuropsychologist will formulate a working hypothesis about the case during the initial interview. In keeping with the I-B philosophy, the interview varies considerably in length, depending upon how rapidly and to what degree of certainty the neuropsychologist can formulate a testable hypothesis about the case. During the interview, the neuropsychologist oftentimes administers a few tests to the patient. The examination then proceeds with the collection of formal test data by a technician. Following recommendations and proscriptions of the governing bodies of the field (American Academy of Clinical Neuropsychology; National Academy of Neuropsychology), we use a technician-based method of assessment (DeLuca & Putman, 1993; National Academy of Neuropsychology, 2000a), and the testing is conducted in the absence of third-party observation (American Academy of Clinical Neuropsychology, 2001; National Academy of Neuropsychology, 2000b).

The Core Battery has evolved over the years to satisfy mutual objectives of comprehensiveness and efficiency. The examination is structured to probe all major domains of cognition, including intellectual function, memory, speech and language, visual perception, psychomotor/psychosensory functions, higher-order executive functions (judgment, decision making, planning), and attention and orientation, as well as screening of mood and affect. Strategic sampling of these functions usually suffices to reveal patterns of performance that can be related to particular diagnoses and etiologies, and to provide key information for formulation of a rehabilitation program. Whenever necessary, and depending on a multitude of factors, including the referral question, the patient's stamina, time considerations, and, in particular, the evolving performance profile of the patient, the Core Battery is supplemented with various follow-up procedures. The most frequent procedures utilized for in-depth follow-up are presented in Table 4–2, grouped according to domain of function. The tests are drawn from various sources throughout the field of neuropsychology, and many come from test batteries used in other major neuropsychological assessment approaches.

One area in which the I-B method has traditionally placed less emphasis is the assessment of basic motor and sensory functions. This may be curious, since such testing has received significant emphasis in some neuropsychological assessment philosophies, especially fixed-battery methods. One of the main reasons that the I-B method has de-emphasized this domain is that such testing provides relatively little information for the time investment. This is especially true in the age of modern neuroimaging, which has reduced substantially the extent to which neuropsychology is needed for "lesion localization." For example, there is little point to spending an hour determining that the patient suffers "left hemisphere dysfunction" based on deficient motor and sensory performances with the right hand, when a neuroimaging study (e.g., brain MRI) has revealed clearly that the patient has a left frontal tumor. Of course, neuropsychological testing may reveal signs of hemispheric dysfunction in cases in which neuroimaging is negative, an outcome

not uncommon in the early stages of multiple sclerosis, progressive dementia syndromes (e.g., Alzheimer's disease, Pick's disease (or what is now more commonly called "frontal-temporal dementia")), HIV-related dementia, or mild head injury. However, we have found that most basic motor and sensory tests are less helpful in this regard—and far less economical—than tests aimed at higher-order cognitive capacities. Moreover, the validity of many basic psychomotor and psychosensory tests vis-à-vis brain–behavior relationships has remained elusive.

The Importance of Neuroanatomy. As indicated in the Historical Introduction, the I-B school derives from a strong tradition of neuropsychology practiced in a medical setting. Benton practiced within the medical complex, working closely with Sahs, Van Allen, the Damasios, and other physicians. Tranel has continued that tradition. Influenced by this association and by the long-standing connection to the cognitive neuroscience research program of the Damasios, the Benton Neuropsychology Laboratory has remained decidedly committed to a close connection between neuropsychological assessment and sophisticated neuroanatomical analysis.

In the I-B school, the interpretation of neuropsychological data is informed, to as large an extent as possible, by knowledge of the neuroanatomical findings in a patient. Neuroanatomical information on patients is often available in our facility. Many patients come to the clinic with a neuroimaging study (CT, MR), and we usually have access to both the interpretation of the study (as provided by the radiologist) and the "raw data" (the CT or MR study). Our neuropsychologists frequently can avail themselves of first-hand readings of neuroimaging data, and this information is incorporated directly into the neuropsychological examination, both as a means of guiding test selection and as information to be factored into the impressions, conclusions, and recommendations. In keeping with this tradition, an overarching principle in the I-B method is to generate information that will elucidate and spur hypotheses regarding the status of neural systems in a particular patient's brain. That is, our endeavor is not simply to answer the question, "What is wrong with the patient?" It

Table 4–2. Follow-Up Neuropsychological Tests

1. Intellectual abilities
   Wechsler Adult Intelligence Scale-IV (Wechsler, 2008)
2. Memory
   a. Wechsler Memory Scale-III (Wechsler, 1997)
   b. Recognition Memory Test (Warrington, 1984)
   c. Iowa Autobiographical Memory Questionnaire (Tranel & Jones, 2006)
   d. Iowa Famous Faces Test (Tranel, 2006)
   e. Brief Visuospatial Memory Test—Revised (BVMT-R; Benedict, 1997)
3. Language
   a. Multilingual Aphasia Examination (Benton & Hamsher, 1978)
   b. Boston Diagnostic Aphasia Examination (Goodglass & Kaplan, 1983)
   c. Boston Naming Test (Kaplan et al., 1983)
   d. Benton Laboratory Assessment of Writing (Benton Laboratory)
   e. Iowa-Chapman Reading Test (Manzel & Tranel, 1999)
   f. Category Fluency Test (Benton Laboratory)
4. Academic achievement skills
   Wide Range Achievement Test-4: Reading, Spelling, Arithmetic, and Sentence Comprehension
      subtests (Wilkinson & Robertson, 2006)
5. Perception and attention
   a. Judgment of Line Orientation (Benton et al., 1983)
   b. Hooper Visual Organization Test (Hooper, 1983)
   c. Agnosia Screening Evaluation (Benton Laboratory)
   d. Screening evaluation for visual, auditory, and tactile neglect (Benton Laboratory)
   e. Rosenbaum Visual Acuity Screen
   f. Pelli-Robson Contrast Sensitivity Chart (Pelli et al., 1988)
6. Visuoconstruction
   a. Drawing of a house, bicycle, flower (Lezak et al., 2004, pp. 550-556)
   b. Three-Dimensional Block Construction (Benton et al., 1983)
7. Psychomotor and psychosensory functions
   a. Grooved Pegboard Test (Heaton et al., 1991)
   b. Right–Left Discrimination (Benton et al., 1983)
   c. Finger Localization/Recognition (Benton et al., 1983)
   d. Dichotic Listening (adapted from Kimura, 1967; Damasio & Damasio, 1979)
   e. Line Cancellation Test (Benton et al., 1983)
8. Executive functions
   a. Wisconsin Card Sorting Test (Heaton et al., 1993)
   b. Stroop Color and Word Test (Golden, 1978)
   c. Visual Image (Nonverbal) Fluency (Benton Laboratory)
   d. Category Test (DeFilippis et al., 1979; Halstead, 1947)
   e. Tower of London Test (Shallice, 1982) or Tower of Hanoi Test (Glosser & Goodglass, 1990)
   f. Iowa Gambling Task (Bechara et al., 1994)
   g. Delis–Kaplan Executive Function System (Delis et al., 2001)
9. Personality and affect
   a. Beck Anxiety Inventory (Beck, 1993)
   b. Minnesota Multiphasic Personality Inventory-2 (MMPI-2) (Hathaway & McKinley, 1989)
   c. Iowa Scales of Personality Change (Barrash et al., 2000)
   d. Geriatric Depression Scale (Yesavage et al., 1983)
10. Symptom Validity Testing
    a. Test of Memory Malingering (Tombaugh, 1996)
    b. Forced Choice Memory Assessment (Binder, 1993)
    c. Rey 15-Item Test (Rey, 1964)
    d. Structured Interview of Malingered Symptomatology (Smith & Burger, 1997)
11. Miscellaneous Instruments
    a. Dementia Rating Scale (Mattis, 1988)
    b. Smell Identification Test (Doty et al., 1984)
    c. Useful Field of View Test (Ball & Roenker, 1998)
    d. Repeatable Battery for the Assessment of Neuropsychological Status (RBANS, Randolph, 1998)

goes on to address the more specific question, "What is wrong with the patient's brain?"

Another factor that has been important in influencing the strong anatomical tradition of the I-B school has been the location of the neuropsychological operation in the Department of Neurology, within the University of Iowa Hospitals and Clinics. The Neuropsychology Clinic is situated within the outpatient and inpatient units of Neurology, and the neuropsychologists and technicians have direct access to neurological patients. The neuropsychologists have the opportunity to be involved in the acute management of neurological patients, and are frequently requested to perform examinations at bedside in patients who are only a few hours or days out of a cerebrovascular accident, anoxic/ischemic event, traumatic brain injury, or other brain injury (e.g., Tranel, 1992a).

There are a couple of relatively common scenarios in which neuropsychological data are especially helpful in detecting focal brain dysfunction, and where neuroimaging data may not be immediately contributory. One instance is where neuropsychological findings indicate the presence of focal brain dysfunction, even though early neuroimaging studies have been negative (in a significant number of cases, CT—and even MR—scans conducted within 24 hours of lesion onset are negative). For example, a patient presents with a severe aphasia, with marked defects in both comprehension and speech production; however, the patient has no motor or sensory defect. No lesion is evident on an acute CT conducted the day of onset. Neuropsychological examination the following day indicates that the patient has a severe global aphasia, with marked defects in all aspects of speech and language. The pattern indicates pronounced dysfunction of the perisylvian region, including both Broca's area and Wernicke's area; however, the absence of a right-sided motor defect is unusual and suggests that the lesion is not of the typical middle cerebral artery pattern. The neuropsychologist concludes that the findings suggest the condition of global aphasia without hemiparesis, which typically involves two separate, noncontiguous lesions affecting Broca's and Wernicke's areas, but sparing primary motor cortices. An MR conducted on the sixth day after lesion onset confirms this precise pattern of lesion locus.

Another fairly common scenario is head trauma, or even situations in which brain injury is caused by severe acceleration/deceleration forces in the absence of head trauma per se. Acute structural neuroimaging studies (CT or MR), and even neuroimaging procedures obtained in the chronic epoch, sometimes fail to reveal evidence of structural abnormalities. Detailed neuropsychological examination, however, may furnish clear evidence of significant impairments; for instance, it is not uncommon to see indications of "executive dysfunction," with deficits on tests such as verbal associative fluency, the Wisconsin Card Sorting Test, and the Trail-Making Test. The patient may have a striking postmorbid change in personality. Such data are strongly indicative of dysfunction in the ventromedial prefrontal region, including orbital and lower mesial prefrontal cortices, caused by the shearing and tearing of brain tissues in this region produced by movement of the ventral part of the frontal lobes across bony protrusions from the inferior surface of the cranium (Barrash et al., 2000; Tranel et al., 1994).

Examples such as these indicate that neuropsychological data can furnish important information regarding dysfunction of particular neural systems, even in cases in which neuroimaging studies are negative. However, it should be noted that the use of neuropsychological procedures to localize lesions has declined sharply following the advent of modern neuroimaging techniques, particularly CT in the mid-1970s and MR in the mid-1980s (e.g., Benton, 1989; Boller et al., 1991; Tranel, 1992b). These methods have tremendous power to detect even minimal structural abnormalities, and the "find the lesion" aspect of neuropsychological assessment is no longer much of a mandate.

Empirical tests of the "localizing value" of some of Benton's tests have recently been undertaken, and results from these studies are included in several articles published in a special issue of the *Journal of Clinical and Experimental Neuropsychology* devoted to the legacy of Arthur Benton (Tranel & Levin, in press). In one of the studies, we investigated two of the most successful and widely used Benton tests, the Facial Recognition Test (FRT) and Judgment of Line Orientation (JLO) test, which measure visuoperceptual and visuospatial functions typically associated with right hemisphere structures (Tranel, Vianna, et al., in press). A new lesion-deficit mapping technique was used to investigate the neuroanatomical correlates of FRT and JLO performance. The results showed that failure on the FRT was most strongly associated with lesions in the right posterior-inferior parietal and right ventral occipitotemporal (fusiform gyrus) areas, and failure on the JLO test was most strongly associated with lesions in the right posterior parietal region. These findings extend and sharpen previous work, especially early work by Benton and his students, which had pointed to right posterior structures as being important for FRT and JLO performance (see Benton et al., 1994).

Indications for Neuropsychological Assessment. Some of the common applications of neuropsychological assessment in the Benton Neuropsychology Laboratory are enumerated below.

1. *General appraisal of cognitive and behavioral functioning.* As alluded to earlier, many of our assessments are aimed at characterizing the cognitive capacities of brain-injured patients so as to determine rehabilitation needs, placement, return to work, and recommendations for independent living. For example, in patients who have suffered brain injury due to stroke, head trauma, infection, or anoxia/ischemia, neuropsychological assessment can provide detailed information regarding the cognitive and behavioral strengths and weaknesses of the patients. In most instances, the initial assessment is performed as early in the recovery epoch as possible, provided the patient is awake and alert enough to cooperate with the procedures. This evaluation, termed the "acute epoch" assessment, provides a baseline to which further recovery can be compared, and it initiates contact with the neuropsychologist and related professionals who will figure prominently in the long-term management of the patient. "Chronic epoch" assessments, conducted three or more months following onset of brain injury, assist in monitoring recovery, determining the

effects of therapy, and making long-range decisions regarding educational and vocational rehabilitation.

2. *Monitoring the neuropsychological status of patients who have undergone medical or surgical intervention.* Serial neuropsychological assessments are used to track the course of patients who are undergoing medical or surgical treatment for neurological disease. Typical examples include drug therapy for patients with Parkinson's disease or seizure disorders, and surgical intervention in patients with normal pressure hydrocephalus, brain tumors, or pharmacoresistant seizure disorders (typically temporal lobectomies). Neuropsychological assessment provides a baseline profile of cognitive and behavioral functioning, to which changes can be compared, and it provides a sensitive means of monitoring changes that occur in relation to particular treatment regimens.

3. *Distinguishing organic from psychiatric disease.* Neuropsychological assessment provides crucial evidence to distinguish conditions that are primarily or exclusively "organic" from those that are primarily or exclusively "psychiatric." For example, a common diagnostic dilemma faced by neurologists, psychiatrists, and general practitioners is distinguishing between "true dementia" (e.g., cognitive impairment caused by Alzheimer's disease) and "pseudodementia" (e.g., cognitive impairment associated with depression). Neuropsychological assessment frequently yields definitive evidence to make this distinction. Another common referral is for the assessment of patients with so-called nonepileptic seizure disorders, or what is often referred to as "pseudoseizures," where psychological factors are typically thought to play a role in the patient's condition. Documenting and clarifying the psychological status of such patients can be very helpful to the neurologist, and can factor prominently into treatment decisions.

4. *Medicolegal situations.* Neuropsychological assessment can be very helpful to resolve claims of "brain injury" that are frequent in plaintiffs who sustained head trauma in motor vehicle, slip-and-fall, and other accidents, were exposed to toxic chemicals, suffered carbon monoxide poisoning, or sustained an electrical injury or any other of a variety of "compensable" alleged

insults. In many of these cases, "objective" signs of brain dysfunction (e.g., weakness, sensory loss, impaired balance) are absent, structural neuroimaging and EEG are normal, and the entire case for "brain damage" rests on claims of cognitive deficiencies. Here, neuropsychological data are especially informative to adjudicate the question of whether there is brain dysfunction; moreover, the neuropsychologist is often in the best position to factor the influence of affective variables, the possibility of malingering, and the patient's premorbid status into the diagnostic picture. Teasing out the contributions of physiopathology and psychopathology can be a very challenging endeavor, and neuropsychological data provide one of the best solutions in these situations (Alexander, 1995; Hom, 2003).

5. *Developmental disorders.* Neuropsychological assessment can assist in identifying developmental learning disorders that may influence the cognitive and behavioral presentation of a patient, such as dyslexia, attention-deficit disorder, and nonverbal learning disability.

6. *Conditions in which known or suspected neurological disease is not detected by standard neurodiagnostic procedures.* As noted earlier, there are some situations in which findings from standard neurodiagnostic procedures, including neurological examination, structural neuroimaging, and EEG, are negative, even though the history indicates that brain injury or brain disease is likely. Mild closed head trauma, the early stages of degenerative dementia syndromes (e.g., Alzheimer's disease, frontal-temporal dementia), and early HIV-related dementia are examples. Neuropsychological assessment in such cases frequently provides the most sensitive means of evaluating the patient's brain functioning.

7. *Monitoring changes in cognitive functioning across time.* A situation that warrants special mention is the evolution of cognitive and behavioral changes across time. In the degenerative dementias in particular, it is not uncommon to have equivocal findings in the initial diagnostic workup, or the patient may meet only the criteria for so-called mild cognitive impairment. In such cases, follow-up neuropsychological evaluations can provide important confirming or disconfirming evidence regarding the patient's status. As the disease progresses, the neuropsychological data will be helpful in tracking the trajectory of decline, informing family members about placement and caregiving issues, deciding on the need for supervision, and so on.

8. *Wada testing.* The intracarotid amobarbital procedure (Wada & Rasmussen, 1960) is routinely performed in patients prior to surgery for pharmacoresistant epilepsy to establish hemispheric dominance for language and other verbally mediated functions. Neuropsychological assessment during the Wada procedure is used to measure cognitive functioning in each hemisphere. One hemisphere is anesthetized, and the functions of the other "awake" hemisphere are tested. The procedure allows a determination of whether verbal processing—especially language and to a lesser extent verbal memory—is "localized" to one hemisphere of the brain.

9. *Carbon monoxide poisoning.* We have established a 24-hour, on-call neuropsychology service to respond to emergency situations in which patients have suffered carbon monoxide poisoning and may be in need of treatment in a hyperbaric oxygen chamber. A set of neuropsychological tests is given to the patients to determine whether there is evidence of cognitive dysfunction that might warrant hyperbaric treatment. If the patient is normal on neuropsychological testing, such treatment may be deferred; if the patient is impaired, the treatment may be implemented. Repeated testing is conducted to monitor recovery and determine the need for further hyperbaric treatments.

10. *Driving privileges.* We are called upon frequently to answer the basic question of whether a patient is competent and safe to operate a motor vehicle.

11. *Competence.* The question frequently arises as to whether a patient is mentally competent to execute legal decisions, draw up a will, make decisions about their medical care, and the like. Neuropsychological testing often provides the best means of addressing these issues.

12. *The influence of pain on cognitive functioning.* Many neurological patients suffer debilitating pain syndromes, such as intractable headaches, neck and back pain, or other somatic pain. Neuropsychological testing in such patients can be very helpful in determining the extent to which pain problems are interfering

with cognitive functioning, and in establishing the patient's psychological resources for coping with chronic pain, how the patient will respond to potentially addictive medications, and whether the patient might be capable of developing nonmedical methods of coping with pain.

13. *Obstructive sleep apnea.* Obstructive sleep apnea is a common malady that can have adverse effects on cognition and affective status, and neuropsychological testing in such patients is helpful in sorting out whether there is in fact evidence for genuine cognitive impairment suggestive of brain dysfunction. And of even greater practical importance is the fact that our testing is not uncommonly the juncture at which the basic problem of sleep apnea is identified as a likely etiologic factor in what otherwise appear to be vague, nonspecific complaints of fatigue, poor concentration, lowered energy, and the like.

14. *Information and teaching.* A common and very important function carried out by our neuropsychologists is to provide information to patients and families about neurological, psychological, and neuropsychological conditions. As noted earlier, we spend a significant portion of the overall examination time in feedback, and we arrange the examination schedules so that feedback sessions can run as long as necessary for patients and families to leave with a reasonably complete understanding of the patient's condition—what is wrong, what caused the problem, what can be done about it, what to expect down the road, and so on. Historically, this function too often received short shrift in the context of neuropsychological assessment. And nowadays, when the demands of modern health care have wrung physicians until there is literally not a second to waste on anything that is not directly germane to diagnosis and treatment as dictated by health-care managers whose sole mission seems to be to bolster the profit margin, the role of the neuropsychologist in providing information and in teaching patients and families about neurological diseases has taken on more importance than ever.

Interpretation. The results of the neuropsychological examination are interpreted in the context of other pertinent information. The primary sources of such information are the neurological examination, neuroimaging procedures, EEG studies, and the history. In keeping with the basic philosophy of the I-B school, the interpretation strategy is flexible and hypothesis focused, and varied degrees of efforts are expended to obtain and factor in other information, depending on the particulars of the case. For example, if the premorbid caliber of the patient is equivocal or difficult to estimate, we typically request the patient's academic transcripts from high school and college (if relevant). Other helpful sources of information are patient "collaterals"—that is, spouses, children, and other individuals who know the patient well and who can provide details about the patient's typical behavior in the day-to-day environment (in fact, there are cases in which we devote more time interviewing collateral sources than we do testing the patient). It is also important to mention that interpretation of neuropsychological data takes into account the nature and pattern of the patient's performances, in addition to the actual scores and outcomes.

Training Model

The training required for neuropsychologists who wish to practice according to the I-B school follows, in general, the outline provided by INS/Division 40 task force guidelines, and specifically, the so-called "Houston Model" guidelines (Hannay et al., 1998; see also the American Academy of Clinical Neuropsychology, 2007). We emphasize, in particular, the generic psychology core, the generic clinical core, and training in basic neurosciences (Table 4–3). Our philosophy is that solid graduate student training in these areas is a necessary foundation for postgraduate specialization in neuropsychology. A second important feature is an emphasis on basic research training. The I-B method rests squarely on the scientific principles of hypothesis testing, probabilistic reasoning, and inferential conclusion drawing, and practitioners must be solidly trained in basic research methodology.

All five of the current staff neuropsychologists in the Benton Neuropsychology Laboratory were trained in clinical psychology. For several reasons, this training background is considered in

Table 4–3. Core Graduate Training in Preparation for Clinical Neuropsychology[a]

A. Generic Psychology Core
   1. Statistics and Methodology
   2. Learning, Cognition, and Perception
   3. Social Psychology
   4. Personality Theory
   5. Physiological Psychology
   6. Developmental Psychology
   7. History
B. Generic Clinical Core
   1. Psychopathology
   2. Psychometric Theory
   3. Interview and Assessment Techniques
      i. Interviewing
      ii. Intelligence Assessment
      iii. Personality Assessment
   4. Intervention Techniques
      i. Counseling and Psychotherapy
      ii. Behavior Therapy
   5. Professional Ethics
C. Neurosciences Core
   1. Basic Neurosciences
   2. Advanced Physiological Psychology and Pharmacology
   3. Neuropsychology of Perceptual, Cognitive, and Executive Processes
   4. Neuroanatomy
   5. Neuroimaging Techniques

[a] Reprinted with permission from the Report of the INS-Division 40 Task Force on Education, Accreditation, and Credentialing, *The Clinical Neuropsychologist*, 1987.

our view to be essential for the practice of clinical neuropsychology. First, basic graduate training in psychopathology incorporating issues of theory, assessment, and treatment is of indispensable value. Knowledge about psychopathology becomes essential in neuropsychological practice on several accounts: (1) Many patients bring to the neuropsychological examination some degree of psychopathology, whether that be of an incapacitating degree or simply the distress that often characterizes persons who have sustained cerebral insult. This has an inevitable influence on the manner in which the patient approaches and deals with the neuropsychological assessment situation. Understanding this influence is critical for accurate interpretation of the performances of patients on tests, not to mention the collection of reliable and valid data. (2) The presence of significant psychopathology is often a salient component of the reason for referral. The neuropsychologist is frequently called upon to document such presence, to determine its relationship to other aspects of the patient's cognition and behavior, and finally, to offer impressions about its cause. (3) Typically, referrals to neuropsychologists are from neurologists and psychiatrists. There is considerable overlap in the populations of patients that originate in these two specialty areas, and in the types of signs and symptoms that such patients present. Having the capability of factoring in accurately the contributions of psychopathology to the presentations of such patients is extremely important.

A final rationale for coming to neuropsychology from a clinical psychology background is that such a background furnishes basic training in psychological appraisal, which underlies the standardized nature of clinical neuropsychological assessment. Knowledge about test development and construction, reliability, and validity is crucial when employing standardized psychological tests to measure cognition and behavior.

Other Considerations

Personnel. The Benton Neuropsychology Laboratory is staffed currently by five clinical neuropsychologists and two postdoctoral fellows. There are several neuropsychology technicians and support staff. Practicum training is provided, and at any given time some three to five practicum students (mainly from the clinical psychology or counseling psychology graduate programs) are training in the Benton Laboratory.

Use of Neuropsychology Technicians. The I-B method has utilized neuropsychology technicians since its inception. Technicians are charged with the responsibility for most of the hands-on test administration. They collect pertinent background information, record presenting complaints, and administer the series of tests prescribed by the supervising neuropsychologist. The technicians are specifically trained in the I-B method, and are encouraged to facilitate the flexible, hypothesis-driven approach. This requires that they maintain an awareness of the patient's ongoing performance profile, so that on-line adaptations in the testing procedure can be made. The technicians do not administer a rigid set of tests to a patient if it is obvious that the data being collected are of questionable reliability or validity or, equally important, if the data appear to be uninformative vis-à-vis the referral question. Final decisions regarding changes in testing (e.g., pursuing a particular hypothesis and dropping others) rest with the supervising neuropsychologist; nevertheless, the technicians have the prerogative to raise questions about alternative hypotheses during the course of test administration.

The I-B method places significant demands on the neuropsychology technicians. The method requires a certain degree of decision making, creativity, and vigilance on the part of the technicians; by contrast, administering a prescribed set of tests in adherence to a fixed-battery philosophy is simpler and more straightforward. Accordingly, training technicians in the I-B school probably requires a greater initial investment; however, we have found that once technicians are comfortable with our basic philosophy and the various procedures, they tend to engage the assessment process at a deeper level than might be the case when their charge is simply to collect a specified set of test data.

Technicians are recalibrated annually. Neuropsychologists observe the technicians, with attention to the manner in which the technicians conform to specified instructions for administration of the tests. Departures from standard procedure are discussed and rectified as appropriate. This may involve a reminder to the technician about the standard method of test administration. At times, however, a technician may have developed a procedure that proves to be superior to the standard method, and this may ultimately be incorporated as a revision in the basic method. Making a permanent revision is a sensitive issue, as one must be extremely careful not to create a situation in which the normative information for the test becomes uninformative or misleading because of a different method of administration. We are, however, quite open to the possibility of revising our procedures, and over the years the insightful observations of highly experienced technicians have proven invaluable in making decisions about improving the effectiveness of

a variety of assessment procedures. We also encourage "testing the limits," that is, finding out whether a patient can perform a particular task under conditions that are less demanding than those called for by the formal test protocol. This process often furnishes information about patient capabilities that is not reflected in test scores per se but that has important value for diagnostic purposes and, especially, for designing rehabilitation programs (cf. Kaplan, 1985; Milberg et al., this volume).

The use of technicians offers a distinct advantage in permitting "blind" hypothesis testing in the neuropsychological assessment procedure. The technician has relatively little at stake in the outcome of the procedure; by contrast, the neuropsychologist may have any number of prevailing presuppositions about how the patient might perform, due to forensic issues, research considerations, and so on. Hence, the technician is probably in a better position than the neuropsychologist to collect and record objective findings and to avoid problems related to "experimenter bias."

We find that it is cost and time efficient to utilize technicians. The standard I-B procedure can be performed on two and sometimes even three patients a day by a seasoned technician.

Report Writing. Reports from our Neuropsychology Clinic comprise three main sections: (1) identification and background, (2) data reporting, and (3) impressions and recommendations. The scope of the report varies according to the nature of the situation, but most consultation reports generated for referrals from within the University of Iowa Hospitals and Clinics are relatively brief, on the order of 250–500 words. In more complicated cases, our reports are typically somewhat longer, in the range of 500–750 words. We typically produce longer reports for outside referral agencies, for example, when more detailed questions regarding long-term management of the patient are raised, or in forensic referrals. Such reports may extend up to 1000 or more words.

We have a policy of not including scores and other "raw" data in our reports. The primary reason for this is the potential misuse of such information by persons not trained in neuropsychology or psychological appraisal. Psychological data, particularly IQ scores, memory quotients, and scores reported as "percentiles," are quite vulnerable to misinterpretation, because non-experts frequently fail to appreciate the importance of factors such as the estimated premorbid level of functioning of the patient, the quality of normative information, and the type of population on which the test was standardized. Since reports are usually placed in hospital charts or other sources that can be accessed fairly easily by nonexperts, it seems prudent to omit raw data from such reports. Rather than scores, we emphasize the reporting of interpretations of patient performances—that is, whether the patient performed normally or abnormally, the degree of abnormality, and so forth.

Two additional comments are in order here. First, with regard to IQ scores, the reporting of such scores is not only unwise for the reasons mentioned above, but the use of such scores per se in neuropsychological assessment has been seriously questioned (Lezak, 1988). (We might also note here that the classic "Verbal IQ" and "Performance IQ" indices have been dropped in the most recent version of the WAIS, the WAIS-IV.) Second, the Ethical Principles of the American Psychological Association have outlined a clear position against the release of "raw" data to nonexperts (see Tranel, 1994). Hence, inclusion of data (numbers, scores) in reports that are likely to end up in the hands of nonexperts is hazardous from an ethical point of view as well. There are different views on this issue (e.g., see Freides, 1993), but we have found that refraining from using scores in reports in no way diminishes the quality or usefulness of the reports and, in many cases, actually encourages the authors (neuropsychologists) to provide a higher level of interpretation of the data, which ought to be an objective of a good report. Overall, our approach is generally in line with recent recommendations set forth by the governing bodies of clinical neuropsychology (Attix et al., 2007).

Cognitive Rehabilitation Laboratory

A Cognitive Rehabilitation Laboratory, developed and directed by neuropsychologist Steven Anderson (Anderson, 1996), has been part of the Benton Neuropsychology Laboratory for more than a decade. This service provides on-site rehabilitation programs for brain-injured patients. The approach to cognitive rehabilitation follows the same philosophical approach as the I-B assessment method. Interventions are tailored to individual patients to meet circumscribed goals in a time-efficient manner. Specific interventions are selected from an inventory of empirically supported procedures, with the selection process guided by the findings of the neuropsychological evaluation and by the complaints and goals expressed by the patient and family. Emphasis is placed on education of the patient and family regarding the patient's neuropsychological condition and on compensatory strategies designed to minimize the consequences of the acquired cognitive impairments. Interventions range from a single session or once-a-year consultation (e.g., for the family of a patient with Alzheimer's disease) to daily sessions over several weeks (e.g., for a patient with attention and language impairments from a left hemisphere stroke). Among the services provided are training in the use of compensatory devices (e.g., memory books) and strategies (e.g., use of American Sign Language by severely aphasic patients), computer-assisted attentional training, psychotherapeutic interventions for depression, anxiety, and behavioral control, and awareness training for anosognosia.

Typically, patients are referred to the Cognitive Rehabilitation Laboratory after an initial examination in the Neuropsychology Clinic, when the conclusion has been reached that the patient needs and would probably benefit from cognitive rehabilitation. Thereafter, the Neuropsychology Clinic provides periodic reexaminations, to track the course of the patient's recovery.

Summary

The I-B school of neuropsychological assessment has been developed as a flexible, hypothesis-driven approach to standardized measurement of higher brain functions in patients with known or suspected brain disease. The method is focused on the objective of obtaining quantitative measurements of key domains of cognition and behavior, in a time-efficient manner, in sufficient breadth and depth that the referral question can be answered. Starting from a Core Battery, the selection of tests is guided by a multitude of factors, including the nature of the patient's complaint, the questions raised by the referring agent, the impressions gained from the initial interview, and above all, by the diagnostic possibilities raised by the patient's performances during the course of the examination. A close link to neuroanatomy is maintained, and the neuropsychological data both inform and are informed by neuroanatomical findings. Whenever possible, the neuropsychological findings are used to infer the integrity, or lack of it, of various neural systems in the patient's brain. Interpretation of neuropsychological data is conducted in the context of pertinent historical and diagnostic information regarding the patient. Patients and families are provided immediate feedback about the results of the evaluation, in a detailed feedback session that is incorporated into the end phase of the neuropsychological evaluation. Recommendations for further diagnostic procedures, treatment, and follow-up neuropsychological assessment are provided during feedback.

Acknowledgment

Arthur Benton created the neuropsychological assessment approach that has evolved into the I-B School, and his genius and hard work are why the approach caught on and became a cornerstone in the field of clinical neuropsychology. I had the great good fortune of having Dr. Benton as one of my teachers early in my career. Dr. Benton passed away on December 27, 2006, after living, working, and teaching for the better part of a century. His contributions to our field are prodigious, and his influences live on in the clinic at Iowa that bears his name and in his many students who trained there.

References

Alexander, M. P. (1995). Mild traumatic brain injury: Pathophysiology, natural history, and clinical management. *Neurology, 45,* 1253–1260.

American Academy of Clinical Neuropsychology. (2001). Policy statement on the presence of third party observers in neuropsychological assessments. *Journal of Clinical and Experimental Neuropsychology, 15,* 433–439.

American Academy of Clinical Neuropsychology. (2007). American Academy of Clinical Neuropsychology (AACN) practice guidelines for neuropsychological assessment and consultation. *The Clinical Neuropsychologist, 21,* 209–231.

Anderson, S. W. (1996). Cognitive rehabilitation in closed head injury. In M. Rizzo and D. Tranel (Eds.), *Head injury and postconcussive syndrome* (pp. 457–468). New York: Churchill Livingstone.

Anderson, S. W. (2002). Visuoperceptual impairments. In P. J. Eslinger (Ed.), *Neuropsychological interventions* (pp. 163–181). New York: The Guilford Press.

Attix, D. K., Donders, J., Johnseon-Greene, D., Grote, C. L., Harris, J. G., & Bauer, R. M. (2007). Disclosure of neuropsychological test data: official position of Division 40 (Clinical Neuropsychology) of the American Psychological Association, Association of Postdoctoral Programs in Clinical Neuropsychology, and American Academy of Clinical Neuropsychology. *The Clinical Neuropsychologist, 21,* 232–238.

Ball, K. K., & Roenker, D. L. (1998). *UFOV: Useful Field of View.* San Antonio, TX: Psychological Corporation, Harcourt Brace.

Barrash, J., Damasio, H., Adolphs, R., &Tranel, D. (2000). The neuroanatomical correlates of route learning impairment. *Neuropsychologia, 38,* 820–836.

Barrash, J., Tranel, D., & Anderson, S. W. (2000). Acquired personality disturbances associated with bilateral damage to the ventromedial prefrontal region. *Developmental Neuropsychology, 18,* 355–381.

Bechara, A., Damasio, A. R., Damasio, H., & Anderson, S. W. (1994). Insensitivity to future consequences following damage to human prefrontal cortex. *Cognition, 50,* 7–15.

Bechtoldt, H. P., Benton, A. L., & Fogel, M. L. (1962). An application of factor analysis in neuropsychology. *Psychological Record, 12,* 147–156.

Beck, A. T. (1993). *Beck anxiety inventory.* San Antonio, TX: Psychological Corporation.

Benedict, R. H. B. (1997). *Brief Visuospatial Memory Test—Revised.* Odessa, FL: Professional manual, Psychological Assessment Resources Inc.

Benton, A. L. (1955a). Development of finger localization capacity in school children. *Child Development, 26,* 225–230.

Benton, A. L. (1955b). Right–left discrimination and finger localization in defective children. *Archives of Neurology and Psychiatry, 74,* 383–389.

Benton, A. L. (1956). Jacques Loeb and the method of double stimulation. *Journal of the History of Medicine and Allied Sciences, 11,* 47–53.

Benton, A. L. (1975). Neuropsychological assessment. In D. B. Tower (Ed.), *The nervous system,*

Vol. 2. The clinical neurosciences (pp. 67–74). New York: Raven Press.

Benton, A. L. (1985). Some problems associated with neuropsychological assessment. *Bulletin of Clinical Neurosciences, 50*, 11–15.

Benton, A. L. (1989). Neuropsychology: Past, present and future. In F. Boller & J. Grafman (Eds.), *Handbook of neuropsychology* (vol. 1; pp. 1–27). Amsterdam: Elsevier.

Benton, A. L. (1991). Basic approaches to neuropsychological assessment. In S. R. Steinhauer, J. H. Gruzelier, & J. Zubin (Eds.), *Handbook of schizophrenia* (vol. 5; pp.505–523). Amsterdam: Elsevier.

Benton, A. L. (1992). Gerstmann's syndrome. *Archives of Neurology, 49*, 445–447.

Benton, A. L., & Abramson, L. S. (1952). Gerstmann symptoms following electroshock therapy. *Archives of Neurology and Psychiatry, 68*, 248–257.

Benton, A. L., & Cohen, B. D. (1955). Right–left discrimination and finger localization in normal and brain-injured subjects. *Proceedings of the Iowa Academy of Science, 62*, 447–451.

Benton, A. L., & Fogel, M. L. (1962). Three-dimensional constructional praxis: a clinical test. *Archives of Neurology, 7*, 347–354.

Benton, A. L., & Hamsher, K. (1978). *Multilingual Aphasia Examination.* Iowa City: University of Iowa (Manual, revised).

Benton, A. L., Hamsher, K., Varney, N. R., & Spreen, O. (1983). *Contributions to neuropsychological assessment.* New York: Oxford University Press.

Benton, A. L., & Menefee, F. L. (1957). Handedness and right–left discrimination. *Child Development, 28*, 237–242.

Benton, A. L., & Meyers, R. (1956). An early description of the Gerstmann syndrome. *Neurology, 6*, 838–842.

Benton, A. L., Sivan, A. B., Hamsher, K. deS., Varney, N. R., & Spreen, O. (1994). *Contributions to neuropsychological assessment* (2nd edition). New York: Oxford University Press.

Benton, A. L., & Van Allen, M. W. (1968). Impairment in facial recognition in patients with unilateral cerebral disease. *Cortex, 4*, 344–358.

Benton, A. L., Varney, N. R., & Hamsher, K. (1978). Visuospatial judgment: A clinical test. *Archives of Neurology, 35*, 364–367.

Binder, L. M. (1993). Assessment of malingering after mild head trauma with the Portland Digit Recognition Test. *Journal of Clinical and Experimental Neuropsychology, 15*, 170–182.

Blackburn, H. L. (1958). Effects of motivating instructions on reaction time in cerebral disease. *Journal of Abnormal and Social Psychology, 56*, 359–366.

Blackburn, H. L., & Benton, A. L. (1955). Simple and choice reaction time in cerebral disease. *Confinia Neurologica, 15*, 327–338.

Boller, F., Swihart, A. A., Forbes, M. M., & Denes, G. (1991). Neuropsychology in its daily practice: Past and present. In F. Boller and J. Grafman (Eds.), *Handbook of neuropsychology* (vol. 5; pp. 379–388). Amsterdam: Elsevier.

Costa, L., & Spreen, O. (1985). *Studies in neuropsychology: Selected papers of Arthur Benton.* New York: Oxford University Press.

Damasio, H., & Damasio, A. R. (1979). "Paradoxic" ear extinction in dichotic listening: Possible anatomic significance. *Neurology, 29*, 644–653.

DeFilippis, N. A., McCampbell, E., & Rogers, P. (1979). Development of a booklet form of The Category Test: Normative and validity data. *Journal of Clinical Neuropsychology, 1*, 339–342.

Delis, D. C., Kaplan, E., & Kramer, J. H. (2001). *Delis–Kaplan Executive Function System: Technical manual.* San Antonio, TX: The Psychological Corporation.

DeLuca, J. W., & Putman, S. H. (1993). The professional/technician model in clinical neuropsychology: Deployment characteristics and practice issues. *Professional Psychology: Research and Practice, 24*, 100–106.

Doty, R. L., Shaman, P., Kimmelman, C. P., & Dann, M. S. (1984). University of Pennsylvania Smell Identification Test: A rapid quantitative olfactory function test for the clinic. *Laryngoscope, 94*, 176–178.

Fogel, M. L. (1962). The Gerstmann syndrome and the parietal symptom-complex. *Psychological Record, 12*, 85–90.

Freides, D. (1993). Proposed standard of professional practice: Neuropsychological reports display all quantitative data. *The Clinical Neuropsychologist, 7*, 234–235.

Glosser, G., & Goodglass, H. (1990). Disorders in executive control functions among aphasic and other brain-damaged subjects. *Journal of Clinical and Experimental Neuropsychology, 12*, 485–501.

Golden, C. J. (1978). *Stroop Color and Word Test. A manual for clinical and experimental use.* Chicago, IL: Stoelting Co.

Goodglass, H., & Kaplan, E. (1983). *The assessment of aphasia and related disorders.* 2nd ed. Philadelphia, PA: Lea and Febiger.

Halstead, W. C. (1947). *Brain and intelligence: A quantitative study of the frontal lobes.* Chicago: University of Chicago Press.

Hamsher, K. (1985). The Iowa group. *International Journal of Neuroscience, 25*, 295–305.

Hannay, H. J., Bieliauskas, L. A., Crossen, B. A., Hammeke, T. A., Hamsher, K. deS., & Koffler, S. P.

(1998). Proceedings of the Houston Conference on specialty education and training in clinical neuropsychology. *Archives of Clinical Neuropsychology*, *13*, 157–158.

Hathaway, S. R., & McKinley, J. C. (1989). *The Minnesota Multiphasic Personality Inventory—2*. New York: Psychological Corporation.

Heaton, R., Grant, I., & Matthews, C. (1991). *Comprehensive norms for an expanded Halstead-Reitan neuropsychological battery: Demographic corrections, research findings, and clinical applications*. Odessa, FL: Psychological Assessment Resources.

Heaton, R. K., Chelune, G. J., Talley, J. L., Kay, G. G., & Curtiss, G. (1993). *Wisconsin Card Sorting Test manual: Revised and Expanded*. Odessa, FL: Psychological Assessment Resources, Inc.

Heilbrun, A. B., Jr. (1956). Psychological test performance as a function of lateral localization of cerebral lesion. *Journal of Comparative and Physiological Psychology*, *49*, 10–14.

Heilbrun, A. B., Jr. (1959). Lateralization of cerebral lesion and performance on spatial–temporal tasks. *Archives of Neurology*, *1*, 282–287.

Hom, J. (2003). Forensic neuropsychology: Are we there yet? *Archives of Clinical Neuropsychology*, *18*, 827–845.

Hooper, H. E. (1983). *Hooper Visual Organization Test*. Los Angeles, CA: Western Psychological Services.

Joynt, R. J., Benton, A. L., & Fogel, M. L. (1962). Behavioral and pathological correlates of motor impersistence. *Neurology*, *12*, 876–881.

Kaplan, E. (1985). A process approach to neuropsychological assessment. In T. Boll and B. K. Bryant (Eds.), *Clinical neuropsychology and brain function: Research, measurement, and practice* (pp. 125–167). Washington: American Psychological Association.

Kaplan, E. F., Goodglass, H., & Weintraub, S. (1983). *The Boston naming test*, 2nd edn. Philadelphia: Lea & Febiger.

Kimura, D. (1967). Functional asymmetry of the brain in dichotic listening. *Cortex*, *3*, 163–178.

Lezak, M. D. (1988). IQ: R.I.P. *Journal of Clinical and Experimental Neuropsychology*, *10*, 351–361.

Lezak, M. D., Howieson, D., & Loring, D. W. (2004). *Neuropsychological assessment*, Fourth Edition. New York: Oxford University Press.

Manzel, K., & Tranel, D. (1999). Development and standardization of a reading test for brain-damaged subjects. *Developmental Neuropsychology*, *15*, 407–420.

Mattis, S. (1988). *Dementia Rating Scale: Professional Manual*. Odessa, FL: Psychological Assessment Resources.

National Academy of Neuropsychology. (2000a). The use of neuropsychology test technicians in clinical practice: Official statement of the National Academy of Neuropsychology. *Archives of Clinical Neuropsychology*, *15*, 381–382.

National Academy of Neuropsychology. (2000b). Presence of third party observers during neuropsychological testing: Official statement of the National Academy of Neuropsychology. *Archives of Clinical Neuropsychology*, *15*, 379–380.

Pelli, D. G., Robson, J. G., & Wilkins, A. J. (1988). The design of a new letter chart for measuring contrast sensitivity. *Clinical Vision Sciences*, *2*, 187–199.

Randolph, C. (1998). *Repeatable Battery for the Assessment of Neuropsychological Status Manual*. San Antonio, TX: The Psychological Corporation.

Reports of the INS-Division 40 Task Force on Education, Accreditation, and Credentialing. (1987). *The Clinical Neuropsychologist*, *1*, 29–34.

Rey, A. (1964). *L'examen clinique en psychologie*. Paris: Presses Universitaires de France.

Shallice, T. (1982). Specific impairments of planning. *Philosophical Transactions of the Royal Society of London - Series B: Biological Sciences*, *298*, 199–209.

Smith, G. P., & Burger, G. K. (1997). Detection of malingering: Validation of the structured inventory of malingered symptomatology. *Journal of the American Academy of Psychiatry and the Law*, *25*, 183–189.

Spreen, O., & Strauss, E. (1998). *A compendium of neuropsychological tests: Administration, norms and commentary*. New York: Oxford University Press.

Swanson, R. A. (1957). Perception of simultaneous tactual stimulation in defective and normal children. *American Journal of Mental Deficiency*, *61*, 743–752.

Swanson, R. A., & Benton, A. L. (1955). Some aspects of the genetic development or right–left discrmination. *Child Development*, *26*, 123–133.

Tombaugh, T. (1996). *Test of Memory Malingering (TOMM)*. New York: MultiHealth Systems.

Tranel, D. (1992a). Neuropsychological assessment. In J. Biller and R. Kathol (Eds.), *Psychiatric clinics of North America: The interface of psychiatry and neurology* (pp. 283–299). Philadelphia: W.B. Saunders.

Tranel, D. (1992b). The role of neuropsychology in the diagnosis and management of cerebrovascular disease. In H. P. Adams (Ed.), *Handbook of cerebrovascular diseases* (pp. 613–636). New York: Marcel Dekker.

Tranel, D. (1994). The release of psychological data to non-experts: Ethical and legal considerations. *Professional Psychology: Research and Practice*, *25*, 33–38.

Tranel, D. (2006). Impaired naming of unique landmarks is associated with left temporal polar damage. *Neuropsychology, 20*, 1–10.

Tranel, D., Anderson, S. W., & Benton, A. L. (1994). Development of the concept of "executive function" and its relationship to the frontal lobes. In F. Boller & J. Grafman (Eds.), *Handbook of neuropsychology* (vol. 9; pp. 125–148). Amsterdam: Elsevier.

Tranel, D., & Jones, R. D. (2006). Knowing what and knowing when. *Journal of Clinical and Experimental Neuropsychology, 28*, 43–66.

Tranel, D., & Levin, H. (2009). The legacy of Arthur Benton. *Journal of Clinical and Experimental Neuropsychology, 31*. (in press).

Tranel, D., Vianna, E. P. M., Manzel, K., Damasio, H., & Grabowski, T. (2009). Neuroanatomical correlates of the Benton Facial Recognition Test and Judgment of Line Orientation Test. *Journal of Clinical and Experimental Neuropsychology, 31*. (in press)

Wada, J., & Rasmussen, T. (1960). Intracarotid injection of sodium Amytal for the lateralization of cerebral speech dominance: Experimental and clinical observations. *Journal of Neurosurgery, 17*, 266–282.

Wahler, H. J. (1956). A comparison of reproduction errors made by brain-damaged and control patients on a memory-for-designs test. *Journal of Abnormal Psychology, 52*, 251–255.

Warrington, E. K. (1984). *Recognition memory test*. New Windsor, England: The NFER-Nelson Publishing Co. Ltd.

Wechsler, D. (1997). *Manual for the Wechsler Adult Intelligence Scale-III*. New York: Psychological Corporation.

Wechsler, D. (2008). *Manual for the Wechsler Adult Intelligence Scale-IV*. New York: Psychological Corporation.

Wilkinson, G. S., & Robertson G. J. (2006). *Wide range achievement test—4th Edition*. Odessa FL: Professional Manual, Psychological Assessment Resources Inc.

Yesavage, J. A., Brink, T. L., Rose, T. L., Lum, O., Huang, V., Adey, M. B., et al. (1983). Development and validation of a geriatric depression rating scale: A preliminary report. *Journal of Psychiatric Research, 17*, 37–49.

5

Computer-Based Cognitive Testing

Thomas H. Crook, Gary G. Kay, and Glenn J. Larrabee

More than a decade ago, in the second edition of this book, we described the general merits and limitations of using computers in cognitive testing and went on to describe a number of specific batteries available to clinicians and researchers (Larrabee & Crook, 1996). In looking back, we see that, like old soldiers, several of the test batteries we described have just faded away, while others have been further refined and strengthened, and yet others, many others, have emerged and may provide useful new tools in neuropsychological evaluation. Aside from these new tools, though, the decade has illustrated the limitations of computerized cognitive testing. Principally, that neuropsychological diagnostic testing without a neuropsychologist is probably not a great idea. A number of Web sites and test vendors have purported to do just that and have, thankfully, failed to find acceptance in the marketplace. That is not to say that computerized memory testing via the Internet is not appropriate for preliminary screening, and even repeated testing over time to detect change, but it is not now, and is not likely to become, a substitute for traditional clinical diagnostic evaluation. Moreover, any Internet-based testing should be under the supervision of a qualified psychologist to minimize the chances of misattribution of results and related iatrogenic factors (Mittenberg et al., 1992; Suhr & Gunstad, 2002).

There are so many new computerized cognitive test batteries that a complete review could occupy this entire volume. There is also a great deal of overlap between many batteries. Thus, we have chosen among the available test batteries those with the best psychometric foundations, and those that have taken a novel approach to testing. But, before the review, let us consider the value that computers can bring to clinical neuropsychological evaluation.

Advantages of Computers in Neuropsychology

Even two decades ago, computers were seen as having advantages in testing far beyond data storage. These were said to include data scoring and analysis, analysis of test profiles for diagnostic classification, increased reliability, enhanced capacity to generate complex stimuli, greater accuracy and superior time resolution, standardization of stimulus presentation, and ease of administration, which reduces the need for highly skilled personnel (Adams, 1986; Adams & Brown, 1986). Limitations were also recognized, and these were said to include alterations in the patient's perception of and response to the test when a standardized paper and pencil test is adapted for computerized administration (Adams & Brown, 1986) and differential familiarity of patients with computer manipulanda used in some computerized test batteries (Kapur, 1988). Larrabee and Crook (1991) also emphasized the need to thoroughly validate computerized batteries and not assume that a validated paper and pencil test remains valid when administered via computer, the need for alternate forms and extensive normative data, and the need to develop tests that are "ecologically valid," that is, relevant to the tasks patients perform in everyday life and the symptoms that underlie many neurocognitive disorders.

Although there are advantages to computerized cognitive assessment, there are also limitations. Adapting existing neuropsychological tests to computerized administration changes the nature of the tests. This, in turn, can influence the nature of the patient's perception of the test, which can affect his or her motivation and response style (Adams & Brown, 1986). Kapur (1988) cautions that most computerized measures have significant visuoperceptual demands, which can cause difficulty for patients with reduced visual acuity or neglect. In addition, many computerized test batteries require the patient to utilize manipulanda that may be unfamiliar, such as a mouse or computer keyboard. This may pose particular difficulty for severely impaired patients, especially among the elderly (Larrabee & Crook, 1991).

Finally, it is important that psychologists utilizing computers for evaluation adhere to professional standards regarding such instruments (Division 40 Task Force Report on Computer-Assisted Neuropsychological Evaluation, 1987; Matthews et al., 1991). Computerized neuropsychological evaluation, in general, and memory testing, in particular, should be conducted in line with APA guidelines for test instruments concerning reliability and validity, and user qualifications.

Two basic approaches have been employed in computerized cognitive assessment. The first, exemplified by the MicroCog (Powell et al., 1993), MindStreams (Dwolatzky et al., 2004), CogScreen (Kay, 1995), Cognitive Drug Research (CDR; Wesnes et al., 1987), Cambridge Neuropsychological Tests Automated Battery (CANTAB; Morris et al., 1987), ImPACT (Miller et al., 2007), Automated Neuropsychological Assessment Metrics (ANAM; Reeves et al., 2007), and Cog State (Maruff et al., in press) batteries, adapts standard cognitive tasks for computerized administration and scoring. The second approach, exemplified by the Psychologix Battery developed by Crook, Larrabee, and Youngjohn (e.g., Larrabee & Crook, 1991), makes use of video and computer graphics technologies to simulate memory and other cognitive tasks of everyday life.

Computerized Batteries for Assessing Memory and Related Cognitive Abilities

MicroCog

MicroCog was developed in an effort to identify cognitive status changes in physicians and other professionals that might interfere with occupational performance (Kane, 1995; Powell et al., 1993), but it has subsequently become a general neuropsychological screening instrument. Since 2003, it has been available from Psychological Corporation on a Windows platform. The battery has not been widely accepted by either clinicians or researchers. Nevertheless, in recent years, the program was revised and now operates on a standard PC running the Windows operating system. Responses are entered using a standard keyboard, and this mode, of course, may pose a problem because some testees, particularly older males, may have limited experience with a keyboard.

Five primary neurobehavioral domains are assessed, including Attention/Mental Control, Memory, Reasoning/Calculation, Spatial Processing, and Reaction time. The Attention/Mental Control Domain includes span tasks (numbers forward and reversed), a continuous performance task (Alphabet subtest) requiring identification of letters of the alphabet as they appear in sequence within a series of random letters, and a supraspan word list test (Word Lists subtest) presented in continuous performance format, with subsequent assessment of incidental learning. Memory is assessed for immediate and delayed recognition of the content of two stories read by the examinee and delayed recognition of a street address, assessed in a multiple-choice (i.e., recognition) format. Reaction time assesses visual and auditory simple reaction time. The Spatial Processing domain also includes a visual working memory subtest, in which the subject must reproduce, following a one-second presentation, a grid pattern in a 3 × 3 matrix, in which three, four, or five of the spaces are colored.

MicroCog can be administered in the 18-subtest standard form in one hour or as a 12-subtest short form in 30 minutes. Scores are provided for accuracy, speed, and proficiency (a combination of speed and accuracy). Measures of general cognitive function and proficiency are also computed. There are only two alternate forms, and thus the battery is not appropriate for many research applications or, perhaps, longitudinal clinical follow-up.

A strength of MicroCog is the normative database of 810 adults (45 females and 45 males in each of nine age groups: 18–24, 25–34, 35–44, 45–54, 55–64, 65–69, 70–74, 75–79, 80–89). Test data are also presented for a variety of clinical groups, including dementia, lobectomy, depression, and schizophrenia. Data are provided for percentage correct classification, sensitivity, and specificity for each clinical group. In addition, mean levels of performance for the five neurobehavioral domain index scores, processing speed, processing accuracy, general cognitive function, and proficiency are provided for each clinical group.

Test–retest reliability does not appear to be a great strength of MicroCog, although it is difficult to know from the paper most frequently cited (Elwood, 2001) how it was established. It is not clear whether subjects were tested on different days, with different forms, and so on. In a proper test–retest study in a small sample of 40, normal subjects (Raymond et al., 2006) ranged from .49 to .84 at 2 weeks and from .59 to .83 at 3 months.

Factor analytic data are provided that demonstrate two factors: information-processing accuracy and information-processing speed (Powell et al., 1993). Concurrent validity data are provided that demonstrate the correlation of various MicroCog scales with external test criteria. For example, the MicroCog Attention/Mental Control Index correlates .57 with the Wechsler Memory Scale-Revised (WMS-R; Wechsler, 1987) Attention/Concentration Index and the MicroCog Memory Index correlates .44 with the WMS-R General Memory Index (Powell et al., 1993). These are not impressive correlations. Data relevant to construct validity are provided by Ledbetter and Hurley (1994). In a combined MicroCog WMS-R factor analysis, MicroCog Alphabet, Word List, and Numbers Forward

and Reversed loaded on the same attention factor as WMS-R Digit Span and Visual Memory Span, whereas MicroCog immediate recognition/recall of two stories loaded on a memory factor with WMS-R Logical Memory I. A recent study (Helmes & Miller, 2006) among older subjects in the community found modest correlations between MicroCog and Wechsler Memory Scale-Three (WMS-III; Wechsler, 1997) subtests of the same construct. Correlations between the visual subtests of the two tests were not even statistically significant. So, it seems clear that MicroCog is not a substitute for the WMS-R.

Kane (1995) reviewed MicroCog and noted that its strengths included the computerization of a number of traditional neuropsychological measures, the addition of proficiency scores, the provision of detailed information on standard error of measurement for subtests and general performance indices, and sizable age- and education-based norms. Weaknesses were noted to be the use of a multiple key interface and lack of motor and divided attention tasks. Also, Kane and Kay (1992) noted that much of the psychometric data cited for MicroCog was actually obtained for earlier versions of the test.

MindStreams

MindStreams is an "Advanced Cognitive Health Assessment" battery developed by NeuroTrax, a company founded in Israel in 2000, specifically to develop and commercialize computerized cognitive testing. MindStreams was launched in 2003 and consists of a battery of mostly traditional neuropsychological tests administered and scored by computer. Tests are downloaded over the Internet and scores are transmitted back to a NeuroTrax central computer, where data are processed and scores calculated. Tests can be administered on a standard PC, and a combination mouse/key pad used by the subject in responding during testing is provided by MindStreams.

Individual test scores and index scores for Memory, Executive Function, Visual Spatial and Verbal Function, Attention, Information-Processing Speed, and Motor Skills are calculated and transmitted back to the user within minutes in the form of a detailed report. The report compares an individual's scores with scores in earlier test sessions and with those of subjects matched for age and education within a normative database of 1659 subjects between the ages of 9 and 95. Tests in the Global Assessment Battery include Verbal and Nonverbal Memory, Problem Solving (Nonverbal IQ), Stroop Interference, Finger Tapping, Catch Game, Staged Information-Processing Speed, Verbal Function, and Visual Spatial Processing. Shorter batteries have been developed for research in conditions ranging from attention-deficit hyperactivity disorder (ADHD) to Alzheimer's disease. There are four alternate forms of each test, and they are available in multiple languages. The average time required for completion of the MindStreams Global Assessment Battery is 45–60 minutes.

Test–retest reliability has been demonstrated over hours, weeks, and months, and correlation coefficients cited by NeuroTrax from multiple studies (e.g., Doniger & Simon, 2006; Schweiger et al., 2003) range from .52 for Memory to .83 for Motor Skills. The correlation cited for the Global Cognitive Score is .77. The low reliability on memory performance is a limitation in the battery.

Construct validity has been demonstrated in several studies, including a comparison of MindStreams and standard neuropsychological test performance in a cohort of 54 elderly subjects, some of whom were healthy and others met the criteria for Mild Cognitive Impairment (MCI; Dwolatzky et al., 2003). Correlations between the MindStreams Verbal Memory score and Wechsler Memory Scale-Third Edition (WMS III; Wechsler, 1997) Logical Memory I and II scores as well as Visual Reproduction II were in the range of .70, and the Nonverbal Memory score was correlated at the same level, with eight scores derived from the Rey Auditory Verbal Learning Test (RAVLT; Rey, 1961) and WMS III. Significant correlations were also reported between other MindStreams scores and scores on standard neuropsychological tests designed to measure the same constructs. Construct validity was also demonstrated in children and adolescents (Doniger & Simon, 2006; Schweiger et al., 2007) and in several clinical populations, including patients with movement disorders (Doniger et al., 2006), multiple sclerosis (MS; Simon et al., 2006), schizophrenia

(Ritsner et al., 2006), and Gaucher's disease (Elstein et al., 2005).

There are several versions of the MindStreams battery designed for research in ADHD, MCI and Alzheimer's disease, Parkinson's disease, and schizophrenia. There are also some limited data suggesting that MindStreams tests are sensitive to changes induced by alcohol (Jaffe et al., 2005) and to the effects of stimulant drugs in children with ADHD (Leitner et al., in press) and older patients with Parkinson's disease (Auriel et al., 2006), but these are small sample pilot studies.

In general, MindStreams appears to be a useful battery for the clinician assessing cognitive function and, particularly, attempting to distinguish among the healthy elderly those with MCI and those with mild dementia. In a study of 161 individuals with expert diagnoses (Doniger et al., 2005b), the validity of the battery in making these distinctions was demonstrated convincingly. The value of the battery in some repeated-measures research will be limited by the availability of only four alternate forms. Of interest to clinicians will be the quality of the clinical report generated by MindStreams. In our view, the report is superior in detail and clarity to those produced by the other computerized batteries reviewed.

CogScreen

CogScreen (Kay, 1995) was developed twenty years ago in response to the Federal Aviation Administration's (FAA) need for an instrument that could detect subtle changes in cognitive function relative to poor pilot judgment or slow reaction time in critical flight situations. As such, CogScreen was intended to measure the underlying perceptual, cognitive, and information-processing abilities associated with flying.

In general, CogScreen is focused on measures of attention, concentration, information processing, immediate memory span, and working memory, as would be expected given the origin of the battery. CogScreen includes Backward Digit Span; Mathematical Reasoning; a Visual Sequence Comparison Task, in which the subject must identify two simultaneously presented alphanumeric strings as same or different; a Symbol Digit Coding Task (analogous to WAIS-R Digit Symbol), which also includes immediate and delayed incidental learning trials; a Matching-to-Sample Task involving presentation of a 4 × 4 grid of filled and empty cells, followed by a brief delay and presentation of two new matrices, one of which is identical to the original (requiring visuoperceptual speed, spatial processing, and visual working memory); the Manikin subtest, which presents a male human figure at different orientations holding a flag that the subject must identify as being in the left or right hand; a Divided Attention Task, combining visual monitoring and visual sequencing; an Auditory Sequence Comparison, requiring identification of two tonal sequences as the same or different (analogous to the Seashore Rhythm Test); a Pathfinder Test, similar to the Trail-Making Test; a Shifting Attention Test, requiring subjects to alter their responses dependent on changing rules (involving attribute identification, mental flexibility, sustained attention, deductive reasoning, response interference, and a variety of other cognitive skills); and Dual Task, which presents two tasks (visual-motor tracking and a visual memory span task for numbers) independently, then simultaneously. Most tests are available in 99 alternate forms.

The entire CogScreen battery requires about 45 minutes for administration, and all subject responses are input with a light pen or touch screen except for the tracking component of the Dual Task, which requires the subject to use the keyboard's arrow keys (Kane & Kay, 1992). The test battery runs on PCs with the Windows 98 or 2000 or XP operating system. There are now 10 different versions of CogScreen, which consist of different groupings of CogScreen subtests. These versions of CogScreen were developed for specific research applications. Test instructions are available in English, Spanish, French, and Russian. CogScreen is currently being used in North and South America, Europe, Asia, Africa, and Australia. Scoring is provided for response speed, accuracy, throughput (number of correct responses per minute), and, on certain tasks, process measures (e.g., impulsivity, perseverative errors). CogScreen also provides for entry of important demographic and performance-related

variables (e.g., age, education, flight status, total flight hours logged, and nature of referral, such as alcohol-related or head injury). Norm-based reports are provided. The CogScreen U.S. aviator normative base includes 584 U.S. pilots screened for health status and alcohol and substance abuse. The CogScreen manual includes analysis of age effects, gender, education, and IQ on performance. Gender and education had minimal effects, whereas age and IQ reflected modest degrees of association with CogScreen performance (maximum age effect, 12.3% of the variance with any one measure; maximum IQ effect, 9% of variance).

Validity data are provided in terms of concurrent validity (correlation of CogScreen measures with related WAIS-R tasks, and correlations of CogScreen measures with specialized neuropsychological tasks such as the Wisconsin Card Sorting Test, PASAT, and Trail-Making Test). Several factor analytic studies of CogScreen have explored the factor structure of the battery (Taylor et al., 2000). Additional data are provided contrasting CogScreen performance of pilots selected from the normative base and matched on age and education with nonpilot controls and with patients with mild brain dysfunction. There were no significant differences between pilots and nonpilot controls; however, both groups performed at a superior level compared to the patient group. Additional data are provided on pilot groups with suspicion of alcohol abuse, pilots with questionable proficiency, pilots referred for evaluation of the impact of psychiatric impairment of cognitive function, and pilots with both suspected and confirmed neurologic disorders.

Although developed as a test to be used for the medical certification of pilots with psychiatric or neurological conditions, CogScreen has many other applications. In the aviation world, CogScreen is used for pilot selection by major airlines and by military organizations. The test has been proven to be a good predictor of pilot success. It is also used to periodically monitor the neurocognitive functioning of HIV seropositive pilots. In the area of biomedical research, CogScreen has been used to study the effect of environmental stressors on cognition (e.g., hypoxia and sleep deprivation), the neurocognitive effects of medical treatments (e.g., nasal CPAP treatment for sleep apnea), and for evaluating the adverse or beneficial cognitive effects of medications (e.g., the sedating effect of antihistamines).

The strength of CogScreen is in the area of attention and information-processing speed. The test includes sensitive measures of multitasking, working memory, and executive functions. On the other hand, it provides very limited testing of memory. For this reason, in clinical studies, CogScreen is often administered together with the Psychologix battery, described in later pages (e.g., Kay et al., 2006). CogScreen's use in "high stakes" testing (e.g., job selection, and as primary outcome measure in pharmaceutical and National Institutes of Health studies) is unparalleled. The validity of the test was affirmed by the National Transportation Safety Board (*Hoover v. FAA*). Furthermore, CogScreen results have been used to support drug claims made by pharmaceutical companies (e.g., the "nonsedating" label for Claritin).

Cognitive Drug Research (CDR) Battery

As the name implies, the CDR battery has been used almost exclusively in drug research. The origins of the battery date back to the late 1970s (Wesnes, 1977), and the core tests in the current battery were introduced in the mid-1980s. In the ensuing decades, the CDR was used in hundreds of clinical drug trials aimed at establishing efficacy or assessing unintended cognitive side effects of medication (e.g., Wesnes, 2003). Core tests in the CDR battery and the constructs they are intended to measure are given in Table 5–1.

Each test is brief, usually one to three minutes, and subjects respond in testing by pressing "Yes" or "No" buttons. Fifty alternate forms are available for most tests, and very substantial data are available related to the reliability, validity, and utility of the system (Mohr et al., 1996). The reaction time tasks in the battery require no explanation, but the Articulatory Working Memory Test is based on the Sternberg procedure and involves the subject holding a short series, primarily through self-repetition, and then identifying whether digits presented

Table 5–1. Core Tests in the CDR Battery and the Constructs They Measure

Attention
Simple Reaction Time
Choice Reaction Time

Working Memory
Articulatory Working Memory
Spatial Working Memory

Episodic secondary memory
Word Recall
Word Recognition
Picture Recognition

subsequently are on the list being held. Both speed and accuracy are recorded on this and the other test of working memory. The Spatial Working Memory Test utilizes a three by three array of lights, said to be windows in a house. Four of the nine windows are randomly chosen and lighted, and on subsequent presentations individual windows are lighted and the subject must indicate whether or not that window was among the four initially lighted. The Episodic Secondary Memory tests utilize traditional recall (immediate and delayed) and recognition procedures.

Five factors have been identified among CDR outcome measures using Principal Components Analysis (Wesnes et al., 2000), and these, together with the measures that load on each factor, are shown in Table 5–2.

Although these are very simple and traditional tests, their use for more than two decades in many populations has generated a very significant body of data demonstrating, for example, sensitivity to and the existence of a distinctive test profile for aging, stroke, multiple sclerosis, chronic fatigue syndrome, diabetes, MCI, and many other conditions (Wesnes, 2003). CDR tests have been shown sensitive to the effects of a vast array of drugs and dietary supplements (e.g., Wesnes et al., 2000), but none of these findings has led to drug approval or a change in labeling, and, thus, questions related to specificity may arise.

The CDR battery is provided as a turnkey system consisting of a standard laptop computer with testing software, a proprietary USB key for data storage, and a response pad/box with

Table 5–2. CDR Outcome Measures Using Principal Components Analysis

Speed of Memory Processes
Picture Recognition Speed
Word Recognition Speed
Numeric Working Memory Speed
Spatial Working Memory Speed

Quality of Episodic Secondary Memory
Immediate Word Recall Accuracy
Delayed Word Recall Accuracy
Word Recognition Accuracy
Picture Recognition Accuracy

Power of Attention
Simple Reaction Time
Choice Reaction Time
Digit Vigilance Detection Speed

Continuity of Attention
Digit Vigilance Detection Accuracy
Choice Reaction Time Accuracy
Digit Vigilance False Alarms
Tracking Error

Quality of Working Memory
Numeric Working Memory Accuracy
Spatial Working Memory Accuracy

a separate USB connection. Tests can only be scored at CDR headquarters in England.

Cambridge Neuropsychology Test Automated Battery (CANTAB)

CANTAB, like CDR, comes from a British company that has developed very traditional tests and gathered quite a lot of data with them over the past two decades. Indeed, both companies claim to provide the world's most widely used computerized neuropsychological test battery. In the case of CANTAB, it is reported to be used in 50 countries, at 500 research institutes, with more than 300 publications. Also like CDR, CANTAB tests appear dated, although there is clear value in the databases that have been developed by both companies during the past 20 years. CANTAB, unlike CDR, has not focused primarily on drug development and appears less well suited to that task. CANTAB may be of greater interest to clinicians, however.

A current version of CANTAB, CANTAB eclipse, employs a touch screen as a primary response device, as well as a press pad for measuring reaction time. For many years before this version was introduced, CANTAB was used by researchers in aging, Alzheimer's disease, schizophrenia, depression, and many other conditions and disease states (e.g., Owen et al., 1990; Sahakian, 1990; Sahakian et al., 1988). It has also been shown sensitive to drug effects (e.g., Jones et al., 1992), although far more evidence of drug sensitivity has been shown for the CDR.

The CANTAB battery consists of 19 tests, beginning with two Motor Screening Tests, followed by four Visual Memory Tests. These are a Delayed Matching-to-Sample Test, including perceptual matching, immediate and delayed recall tasks in which the subject is shown a complex visual pattern, followed by four patterns from which he or she must choose the pattern first shown. This is followed by a Paired-Associates Learning Test, in which the subject must remember which patterns are associated with which positions on the touch screen. Still within the Visual Memory construct, a Pattern Recognition Memory Test is given, involving two-choice forced discriminations and a Spatial Recognition Memory Test, also involving two-choice forced discriminations. Moving on to a seemingly heterogeneous "Executive Function, Working Memory, and Planning" domain, the first test is the ID/ED Shift Test, which measures the ability to attend to a specific attribute of a complex visual stimulus and to shift the attribute when required. This is followed by the more colorfully named Stockings of Cambridge Test of spatial planning, based on the Tower of London Test. Next is the Spatial Span test, in which nine white squares appear in random positions on the screen and between two and nine of them are then lighted in different colors in random order. The subject must remember that order. Finally within this domain, the Spatial Working Memory Test involves a series of red boxes on the screen, some of which when touched, reveal a blue box. The object is to remember which red boxes one has touched and find the blue boxes without returning to a red box previously touched.

Performance in the Attention domain is assessed on CANTAB with several simple and complex reaction time tasks, a Matching-to-Sample Visual Search Test, and a Rapid Visual

Information-Processing test, in which the digits 2–9 are presented in a pseudorandom order at the rate of 100 per second. The subject must identify consecutive odd or even digits as quickly as possible.

There are two tests of the Semantic/Verbal Memory construct, the first of which is the Graded Naming Test, in which subjects must identify each of 30 black and white drawings of objects/animals presented in an increasing order of difficulty. The other test of the construct is the Verbal Recognition Memory Test, in which subjects are presented with a list of 12 words, followed by free recall and forced choice recall. A final domain is Emotional Decision Making, and here there are two tests, the Affective Go–No Go Test, in which a subject must recognize the emotional valence of words that are presented on the screen, and the Cambridge Gambling Test, which is intended to assess decision-making and risk-taking behavior outside a learning context. This final test involves betting on the color of the box, among ten, that contains a token and appears appropriately named, but an odd measure of decision making in everyday life.

As noted, more than 300 studies have been reported using the CANTAB tests, and very substantial data on reliability and validity are available. Clinicians comparing MindStreams or CogState test presentation, scoring, and reporting with CANTAB may find the latter dated, particularly because CANTAB test computers must be purchased from the company and the tests cannot be downloaded and scored via the Internet. Also, the cost of the battery and a 10-year license is, as of this writing, US $14,000, and for these reasons the battery is used by few clinicians.

CogState

CogState tests (with one exception) are game-like and entirely lacking in face validity. There has been a serious effort in recent years to establish construct and criterion validity in the absence of face validity. Also, unlike CANTAB, CogState utilizes a technologically sophisticated platform for Internet testing. The company has slightly different batteries for clinical trials, academic studies, use in sports, testing by physicians (and presumably available to neuropsychologists), and use in the workplace. Tests in their Academic Battery, together with the cognitive domain said to be measured and the time required for administration, are listed in Table 5–3.

Table 5–3. Tests in CogState Academic Battery

CogState task	Cognitive domain	Time required (minutes)
Detection*	psychomotor function	2
Identification*	visual attention	2
One Card: learn*	visual learning	5
One Card: delayed recall	visual memory	1.25
One Word: Learn	verbal learning	5
One Word: Recall	verbal memory	1.25
One Back*	working memory	2
Congruent reaction time*	visual attention	2
Monitoring*	Attention	2
Prediction*	executive function	5
Prediction: delayed recall*	visual memory	0.5
Associate learning*	Memory	5
International Shopping List Task (ISLT)	verbal learning	5
ISLT:delayed recall	verbal memory	1
Groton Maze Learning Task (GMLT)	executive function	10
GMLT: delayed recall	spatial memory	2
GMLT: reverse maze	executive function	2

A visual paired-associates learning and recall task, a set-shifting task, and a social–emotional cognition test have recently been added to the battery as well, although data on their reliability and validity have not been published to our knowledge.

CogState measures of test–retest reliabilities ranging from .67 for memory to .89 for psychomotor performance and also for attention have been reported, with playing cards utilized as the stimuli (Collie et al., 2003; Faletti et al., 2003).

Each of the tests above designated with an asterisk uses playing cards as stimuli, and, thus, the measures are remote from both traditional neuropsychological tests and clinical reality. Prior to the addition of the ISLT, the CogState battery was deficient in measures of verbal learning and memory, and this addition clearly strengthens the battery. Many of the tests in the battery also appear far too difficult for many clinical populations. On the other hand, the technology employed in testing and scoring is impressive, and the battery is well suited for use across languages and cultures. It is currently available in 15 languages and is easily translated into others. Also, the CogState battery has been used in a number of creative studies during the past 5 years, and more than 50 peer-reviewed articles have been published or are in press.

Maruff (In Press) has recently attempted to demonstrate construct validity and criterion validity by showing sensitivity to MCI, schizophrenia, and AIDS dementia. This study included only the tests in which playing cards are used as stimuli. One hundred and thirteen healthy young adults participated in the construct validity study, taking both CogState, a battery of standard neuropsychological tests, and a paired-associates memory test from the CANTAB computerized battery. Tests in the standard battery for psychomotor function were Trail Making A and Grooved Pegboard (dominant and nondominant). Attentional function was measured with the Digit Symbol Substitution test, cancellation task, and Trail Making Part B. The standard memory tests were the Paired-Associates Learning Test from the CANTAB, Benton Visual Retention, and delayed recall from the Rey Figure Test. Standard tests of executive function were the Spatial Working Memory Test strategy score,

Spatial Span test, and the Tower of London Test from CANTAB; all tests are described in detail elsewhere (e.g., Lezak, 1995). In the psychomotor domain, correlations between standard and CogState measures ranged from .71 for Trails A to .32 for Grooved Pegboard (dominant). On attentional measures, correlations ranged from .67 on Digit Symbol and .56 on Trails B to .10 on the cancellation task. In the memory domain, all accuracy coefficients were highly significant ($p < .01$), ranging from .86 on the Rey Figure test and .85 on the CANTAB paired-associates test to .73 on Benton Visual Retention. Correlations were also highly significant on measures of executive function. On accuracy scores, the correlations were .86 with strategy on Spatial Working Memory, .69 with Spatial Span, and .67 with Tower of London performance. As to criterion validity, four separate studies reported by Maruff in this same paper demonstrate that CogState performance clearly distinguishes between comparable normals and individuals suffering from mild head injury resulting from auto accidents, MCI, schizophrenia, and AIDS dementia. The pattern of tests distinguishing subjects with each of the disorders from normals was as one would expect. For example, MCI deficits are limited largely to memory, while attentional and executive function deficits are also seen in schizophrenia. Other studies (e.g., Collie et al., 2002; Cysique et al., 2006) have also addressed the validity of Cogstate tests in distinguishing among these and other diagnostic groups. There are also data on the validity of the Groton Maze Learning Test (e.g., Pietrzak et al., 2007), but it is much more limited than that on tests using playing cards as stimuli.

CogState software can be downloaded over the Internet on to most PCs, and the primary response mechanism is the keyboard space bar. Scoring and reporting are done via the Internet.

The Automated Neuropsychological Assessment Metrics (ANAM)

ANAM is described as "a library of computerized tests and test batteries designed for a broad spectrum of clinical and research applications" (Reeves et al., 2007). The current version of ANAM, Version 4, is a Windows-based program that uses a mouse and keyboard as response input devices. There is also a "Web-enabled" and Palm-OS version of the test. The battery is available through C-Shop at the University of Oklahoma. The battery was originally developed by the Department of Defense and is similar to most of the early DOD Performance Assessment Batteries (PABs). There have been numerous iterations of the ANAM battery over the last 20 years. The test is highly configurable with respect to such parameters as inclusion or exclusion of subtests, number of items to include in a subtest, and interstimulus interval. The subtests included in ANAM are shown in Table 5–4.

In addition, there are Tapping, Tower of Hanoi, Stroop, and other standard cognitive tasks. Reeves described a "standard" or "default" version of ANAM that consists of 13 subtests. Although recognized, primarily, as a research tool, the creators of ANAM claim that it is now being developed as a clinical instrument.

A PubMed search of "ANAM" results in 25 citations between 1996 and 2007, with seven of these originating from the recent U.S. Army-sponsored supplement in the Archives of Clinical Neuropsychology. The articles in the supplement document the use of ANAM in "extreme environments," sports medicine, pharmacological studies, and in clinical populations. There are now very extensive norms available for active duty young military individuals ($N = 2371$). Prior publications document the use of ANAM in patients with systemic lupus

Table 5–4. Subtests Included in ANAM

2-Choice Reaction Time
4-Choice Reaction Time
Code Substitution
Grammatical Reasoning
Logical Reasoning
Manikin
Matching Grids
Matching to Sample
Mathematical Processing
Memory Search
Running Memory (CPT)
Simple Reaction Time
Spatial Processing
Continuous Performance Test
Switching
Visual Vigilance

erythematosus, hypothermia and Alzheimer's disease, multiple sclerosis, and traumatic brain injury, as well as individuals exposed to ionizing radiation. ANAM has also been used in evaluating the effects of a nicotine patch for treatment of Age-Associated Memory Impairment. In addition, studies have documented the reliability and validity of ANAM subtests.

In spite of these developments, ANAM remains more of a "performance assessment battery" than a standardized test battery. The test is not widely used by either clinicians or investigators. Until recently, this DOD-funded test was in the "public domain." The test has been acquired by the University of Oklahoma, which now sells and licenses the battery.

ImPACT Test Battery

The ImPACT Test is a computer-administered test battery developed to assess concussion, primarily from sports-related injuries. The ImPACT 2005 is a Windows-based program that claims to measure response times with one-hundredth of a second resolution. The program is capable of creating an unlimited number of alternate forms. The test battery takes approximately 20 minutes and includes 6 "modules," which provide assessment of attention span, working memory, sustained and selective attention, response variability, nonverbal problem solving, and reaction time. There is a 20-minute delayed recall task for the word discrimination and design memory subtests. In addition to these two subtests, there are traditional measures of symbol digit substitution, a choice reaction task, a Sternberg three-letter recall task, and a visual working memory task. Results are immediately available upon completion of the exam in a well-designed report that compares the current scores to the subject's own baseline or to the normative database. The program can be installed on stand-alone PCs and does not require Internet connection for scoring or administration. The test generates a series of scores that are sensitive to head trauma, including five composite scores: Memory Composite (verbal), Memory Composite (visual), Visual Motor Speed, Reaction Time, and Impulse Control. The authors incorporated a Reliable Change Index for identifying meaningful changes in scores across administrations. The test is used by National Football League teams, Major League Baseball teams, and numerous colleges and universities. However, at present, the research base on the ImPACT test is almost entirely limited to sports injury studies (e.g., Miller et al., 2007).

Psychologix Computer-Simulated Everyday Memory Test Battery

The preceding batteries all share the feature of evaluating memory using traditional psychometric stimuli. By contrast, the Psychologix Computer-Simulated Everyday Memory Battery (previously known as the Memory Assessment Clinics Battery) is unique in that stimuli that are immediately relevant to everyday memory tasks are employed. The current battery represents the fifth generation of technology in a test development effort by Crook and colleagues, which began more that 25 years ago (e.g., Crook et al., 1979, 1980). From the outset, the goal was to simulate, in testing, tasks of everyday life that must be performed by virtually everyone, which are frequently affected by trauma, neurological disease, and developmental conditions. Tests were designed, in multiple alternative forms, using computer-imaging technology to simulate demands of everyday life. This heightened everyday realism was combined with traditional memory measurement paradigms such as selective reminding, signal detection, delayed nonmatching to sample, and associate learning.

Procedures include the *Name–Face Association Test* (Crook & West, 1990), in which live video recordings of persons introducing themselves are presented in different paradigms and both immediate and delayed recall are assessed. In the most frequently used paradigm, fourteen individuals appear on the screen, one after another, and each introduces himself/herself by saying, "Hi, I'm (First Name)." Each then reappears in a different order, and the task of the subject is to recall each name. On each recall trial the person to be remembered states the name of the city where he/she lives as a potential recall cue. Depending on the population, there are two or three such acquisition and immediate recall trials, followed by a delayed recall trial 30–40 minutes later. The city "cues" also provide the stimuli for an *Incidental Memory*

Test (Crook et al., 1993), which assesses the subject's recall of the name of the city each person in *Name–Face Association* identifies as his/her home. Associative learning is also evaluated with a primarily nonvisual task, the *First–Last Names Test* (Youngjohn et al., 1991), which measures associate learning and recall of four to six paired first and last names over three to six trials (the subject must recall the first name associated with each last name). *Narrative Recall* measures the subject's ability to answer 25 factual, multiple-choice questions about a 6-minute television news broadcast (Crook et al., 1990a; Hill et al., 1989). *Selective Reminding* uses the paradigm devised by Buschke (1973) to evaluate learning and retention of 15 grocery items over five trials with a 30-minute delayed recall (Youngjohn et al., 1991). *The Misplaced Objects Test* (Crook et al., 1990b) is a visual–verbal associative task in which the subject "places" (by touching the touch-screen) 20 common objects (e.g., shoes, eyeglasses) in a 12-room house; 40 minutes later, the subject is given a first and a second chance at object location recall. Two measures are employed for facial recognition memory assessment (Crook & Larrabee, 1992). The first, *Recognition of Faces—Signal Detection*, employs signal detection procedures for evaluation of recognition memory, employing 156 facial photographs, with scores based on recognition over varying periods of time ranging from no delay to 1 minute, 3 minutes, and 5 minutes to a 40-minute delayed recognition period. The second, *Recognition of Faces—Delayed Nonmatching to Sample*, employs a delayed nonmatching to sample paradigm (Mishkin, 1978), in which the subject must identify, by touching the screen, the new facial photograph added to an array over 25 trials, each successive trial separated by an 8-second delay.

Working memory and attention are evaluated with the *Telephone Dialing Test* and *Reaction Time*. *Telephone Dialing* (West & Crook, 1990) requires the subject to dial 7- or 10-digit numbers on a representation of a telephone dialing pad on the computer screen after seeing them displayed on the screen. The test is also administered with an interference format, in which the subject, after dialing, hears either a ring or a busy signal. If the busy signal is heard, the subject must hang up, and then redial the telephone. *Reaction Time* (Crook et al., 1993) can be administered in one of two formats. First, reaction time can be measured under the single-task condition in which the subject must lift his or her finger off a computer-simulated (on the touchscreen) image of a gas pedal or brake pedal in response to a red or green traffic light. Both lift and travel (from gas to brake pedal or vice versa) reaction times are computed. Second, this task can be administered under the simultaneous processing task (divided attention) condition, where the subject must perform the gas pedal/brake pedal maneuvers while listening to a radio broadcast of road and weather conditions. In this administration, both lift and travel reaction times are computed—as well as the subject's recall of the radio broadcast information.

The Psychologix Battery has undergone extensive standardization and psychometric analysis. Crook and Larrabee (1988) and Tomer and colleagues (1994) factor analyzed a variety of scores from the battery and demonstrated factors of General Memory, Attentional Vigilance, Psychomotor Speed, and Basic Attention. The factor structure did not vary as a function of age, suggesting that although level of performance changed with age, the interrelationships of the tests did not. Hence, one can be assured that the tests are measuring the same constructs, regardless of the adult subject's age. In a second study, Larrabee and Crook (1989a) demonstrated a more varied factor structure, when First–Last Names and Selective Reminding were added to the battery. In this study, both verbal and visual factors emerged, in addition to an attentional factor and psychomotor speed factor. Concurrent validity was established by a combined factor analysis of the Psychologix Battery, WAIS Vocabulary, WMS-R Logical Memory and Paired-Associates Learning, and the Benton Visual Retention Test. Further evidence on validity is provided by many other studies. For example, Larrabee and Crook (1989b) reported cluster analyses that yielded a variety of everyday memory subtypes. Larrabee et al. (1991) demonstrated a significant canonical correlation of 0.528 between memory self-ratings (MAC-S; Crook & Larrabee, 1990) and factor scores from the Psychologix Battery. Youngjohn et al. (1992) reported a discriminant

function analysis that correctly distinguished 88.39% of subjects with Alzheimer's disease from subjects with Age-Associated Memory Impairment. Also, Ivnik and colleagues (1993) demonstrated that the Reaction Time, Name–Face Association, and Incidental Memory procedures were highly sensitive to the cognitive effects of dominant temporal lobectomy. Psychologix tests have been shown highly reliable (Crook et al., 1992) and sensitive to the effects of drugs that both improve (e.g., Crook et al., 1991; Pfizer study) and impair (e.g., Kay et al., 2006; Nickelsen et al., 1999) cognition in many studies. Of greatest significance, because Psychologix tests are used almost exclusively in developing treatments for adult onset cognitive disorders, is the very high sensitivity of all tests to the effects of aging. For example, on the Name–Face Association Test (Crook & West, 1990; Crook et al., 1993), the decline in performance among healthy individuals is approximately 60% between ages 25 and 65. The effects of age on performance of Psychologix tests have been examined in more than 50 peer-reviewed publications, and individual differences that affect test performance have been examined in detail (e.g., West et al., 1992).

Crook et al. (1992) analyzed the equivalency of alternate forms of the various tests. At least six equivalent forms were found for Telephone Dialing, Name–Face Association, First–Last Name Memory, and Selective Reminding. Eight equivalent forms were found for Misplaced Objects and Recognition of Faces—Delayed Nonmatching to Sample.

American normative data for adults ages 18–90 range from 488 (TV News) to 2204 (Name-Face Memory), with sample sizes in the 1300 to 1900 range for most measures (Crook & West, 1990; Larrabee & Crook, 1994; West et al., 1992). Additional data are collected on over 500 persons with Alzheimer's disease and more than 2000 persons with Age-Associated Memory Impairment. The tests are available in several languages including English, a British (Anglicized) version, French, Italian, Swedish, Finnish, Danish, and German, and normative data are available in all these languages. A true random sample of the Italian population, comprising 1800 adults of all ages, is included in the normative database (Crook et al., 1993).

The principal current use of the Psychologix Battery is for evaluation of treatment effects in clinical trials of pharmacologic compounds, with potential benefit for ameliorating age-related memory disorders, and also in trials of drugs for the full range of medical indications where unwanted cognitive impairment may occur (e.g., Ferris et al., 2006; Kay et al., 2006; Seltzer et al., 2004). Although the current version of the Psychologix Battery is run on PCs with the Windows XP operating system and commercially available touchscreens, use of the battery requires specialized support, and, thus, it is not well suited to most clinical applications.

Summary

The test batteries reviewed in this chapter demonstrate the many advantages of computer-assisted cognitive evaluation, but it is important to exercise caution in the application of computers in clinical settings. Despite the technological sophistication of several available computerized memory tests, they do not all meet APA criteria for test instruments concerning reliability, validity, normative data, or with respect to their test manuals.

Nonetheless, significant progress has been made in the application of computers to memory evaluation in recent years. Continued growth can be expected in this area. There is a certain "technological seduction" concerning computerized assessment and remediation, but current as well as future applications of computers with cognitively impaired patients should be carefully considered in relation to the Division 40 guidelines for use of computers in evaluation and rehabilitation (Division 40 Task Force Report on Computer-Assisted Neuropsychological Evaluation, 1987; Matthews et al., 1991).

Future Directions

We believe that the use of computers to administer standard paper and pencil tests is a very early stage in the development of computerized neuropsychological testing. We believe that current technologies can be employed to provide highly realistic simulations of the cognitive tasks that must be performed in everyday life, on which developmental change or the effects of neurological disease or trauma are first noted. For example, we are now using sophisticated multiple-screen, computerized driving simulators that provide quite realistic graphics and representations of driving a car under a wide variety of circumstances. We have validated our driving simulator and shown it sensitive to drug effects (Kay et al., 2004), but beyond this technology lies the entire field of virtual reality. Future testing could allow subjects to enter an interactive world in which they would be called upon to perform a wide variety of cognitive tasks while their performance is precisely measured. Such development efforts are already under way (Rizzo, 2007). At present, we validate computerized tests against standard neuropsychological tests or in their ability to distinguish between groups based on age or disease states. Of course, our ultimate concern is with the individual's ability to function in a cognitively demanding environment, and, in our view, simulating that environment in cognitive testing is an important direction for the future.

References

Adams, K. M. (1986). Concepts and methods in the design of automata for neuropsychological test interpretation. In S. B. Filskov and T. J. Boll (Eds.), *Handbook of clinical neuropsychology* (vol. 2; pp. 561–576). New York: Wiley.

Adams, K. M., & Brown, G. C. (1986). The role of the computer in neuropsychological assessment. In I. Grant and K. M. Adams (Eds.), *Neuropsychological assessment of neuropsychiatric disorders* (pp. 87–89). New York: Oxford.

Auriel, E., Hausdorff, J. M., Herman, T., Simon, E. S., & Giladi, N. (2006). Effects of methylphenidate on cognitive function and gait in patients with Parkinson's disease: A pilot study. *Clinical Neuropharmacology, 29*, 15–17.

Buschke, H. (1973). Selective reminding for analysis of memory and learning. *Journal of Verbal Learning and Verbal Behavior, 12*, 543–549.

Collie, A., Maruff, P., & Currie, J. (2002). Behavioral characterization of mild cognitive impairment. *Journal of Clinical and Experimental Neuropsychology, 24*, 720–733.

Collie, A., Maruff, P., Darby, D. G., & McStephen, M. (2003). The effects of practice on the cognitive test performance of neurologically normal individuals assessed at brief test–retest intervals. *Journal of the International Neuropsychological Society, 9,* 419–428.

Crook, T. H., Ferris, S., & McCarthy, M. (1979). The Misplaced-Objects Task: A brief test for memory dysfunction in the aged. *Journal of the American Geriatrics Society, 27,* 284–287.

Crook, T. H., Ferris, S. H., McCarthy, M., & Rae, D. (1980). Utility of digit recall tasks for assessing memory in the aged. *Journal of Consulting and Clinical Psychology, 48,* 228–233.

Crook, T. H., & Larrabee, G. J. (1988). Interrelationships among everyday memory tests: Stability of factor structure with age. *Neuropsychology, 2,* 1–12.

Crook, T. H., & Larrabee, G. J. (1990). A self-rating scale for evaluating memory in everyday life. *Psychology and Aging, 5,* 48–57.

Crook, T. H., & Larrabee, G. J. (1992). Changes in facial recognition memory across the adult life span. *Journal of Gerontology, 47,* 138–141.

Crook, T. H., Larrabee, G. J., & Youngjohn, J. R. (1993). Age and incidental recall for a simulated everyday memory task. *Journal of Gerontology, 48,* 45–47.

Crook, T. H., Tinklenberg, J., Yesavage, J., Petrie, W., Nunzi, M. G., & Massari, D. C. (1991). Effects of phosphatidylserine in Age Associated Memory Impairment. *Neurology, 41,* 644–649.

Crook, T. H., & West, R. L. (1990). Name recall performance across the adult life span. *British Journal of Psychology, 81,* 335–349.

Crook, T. H., West, R. L., & Larrabee, G. J. (1993). The Driving-Reaction Time Test: Assessing age declines in dual-task performance. *Developmental Neuropsychology, 9,* 31–39.

Crook, T. H., Youngjohn, J. R., & Larrabee, C. J. (1990a). The TV News Test: A new measure of everyday memory for prose. *Neuropsychology, 4,* 135–145.

Crook, T. H., Youngjohn, J. R., & Larrabee, C. J. (1990b). The Misplaced Objects Test: A measure of everyday visual memory. *Journal of Clinical and Experimental Neuropsychology, 12,* 819–833.

Crook, T. H., Youngjohn, J. R., & Larrabee, C. J. (1992). Multiple equivalent test forms in a computerized everyday memory battery. *Archives of Clinical Neuropsychology, 7,* 221–232.

Cysique, L. A., Maruff, P., Darby, D., & Brew, B. J. (2006). The assessment of cognitive function in advanced HIV-1 infection and AIDS dementia complex using a new computerized cognitive test battery. *Archives of Clinical Neuropsychology, 21,* 185–194.

Division 40 Task Force Report on Computer Assisted Neuropsychological Evaluation. (1987). *Clinical Neuropsychologist, 2,* 161–184.

Doniger, G. M., Dwolatzky, T., Zucker, D. M., Chertkow, H., Crystal, H., Schweiger, A., et al. (2005). Computerized cognitive testing battery identifies MCI and mild dementia even in the presence of depressive symptoms. *American Journal of Alzheimer's Disease and Other Dementias, 21,* 28–36.

Doniger, G. M., Okun, M. S., Simon, E. S., Rodriguez, R. L., Jacobson, C. E., Weiss, D., et al. (2006). Validation of a computerized neuropsychological assessment (Mindstreams) in movement disorders: Interim analysis. *20th Annual Symposia on the Etiology, Pathogenesis, and Treatment of Parkinson's Disease and Other Movement Disorders.* Chicago, Illinois, United States, October 8–11, 2006.

Doniger, G. M., & Simon, E. S. (2006). *Construct Validity of Mindstreams: Comparison with Paper-Based Tests.* Internal Document. New York: NeuroTrax Corporation.

Doniger, G. M., Zucker, D. M., Schweiger, A., Dwolatzky, T., & Simon, E. S. (2005). Towards practical cognitive assessment for detection of early dementia: A 30-minute computerized battery discriminates as well as longer testing. *Current Alzheimer Research, 2,* 117–124.

Dwolatzky, T., Whitehead, V., Doniger, G. M., Simon, E. S., Schweiger, A., Jaffe, D, et al. (2003). Validity of a novel computerized cognitive battery for mild cognitive impairment. *BMC Geriatrics, 3,* 4.

Dwolatzky, T., Whitehead, V., Doniger, G. M., Simon, E. S., Schweiger, A., Jaffe, D., et al. (2004). Validity of the Mindstreams computerized cognitive battery. *Journal of Molecular Neuroscience, 24,* 33–44.

Elstein, D., Guedalia, J., Doniger, G. M., Simon, E. S., Antebi, V., Arnon, Y., et al.. (2005). Computerized cognitive testing in patients with type I Gaucher disease: Effects of enzyme replacement and substrate reduction. *Genetics in Medicine, 7,* 124–130.

Elwood, R. W. (2001). MicroCog: Assessment of cognitive functioning. *Neuropsychology Review, 11,* 89–100.

Falleti, M. G., Maruff, P., Collie, A., Darby, D. G., & McStephen, M. (2003). Qualitative similarities in cognitive impairment associated with 24 h of sustained wakefulness and a blood alcohol concentration of 0.05%. *Journal of Sleep Research, 12,* 265–274.

Ferris, S., Schneider, L., Farmer, M., Kay, G., & Crook, T. (2006). A double-blind, placebo-controlled trial of memantine in age-associated memory impairment (memantine in AAMI). *International Journal of Geriatric Psychiatry, 21,* 1–8.

Helmes, E., & Miller, M. (2006). A comparison of MicroCog and the Wechsler Memory Scale (3rd ed.) in older adults. *Applied Neuropsychology, 13,* 28–33.

Hill, R. D., Crook, T. H., Zadeik, A., Sheikh, J., & Yesavage, J. (1989). The effects of age on recall of information from a simulated television news broadcast. *Educational Gerontology, 5,* 607–613.

Ivnik, R. J., Malec, J. F., Sharbrough, F. W., Cascino, G. D., Hirschorn, K. A., Crook, T. H., et al. (1993). Traditional and computerized assessment procedures applied to the evaluation of memory change after temporal lobectomy. *Archives of Clinical Neuropsychology, 8,* 69–81.

Jaffe, D., Doniger, G. M., Simon, E. S., & Neumark, Y. (2005). Computerized cognitive test performance varies with acute alcohol consumption. *158th Annual Meeting of the American Psychiatric Association.* August 18–21, Washington, DC.

Jones, G., Sahakian, B. J., Levy, R., Warburton, D. M., & Gray, J. (1992). Effects of acute subcutaneous nicotine on attention, information processing and short-term memory in Alzheimer's disease. *Psychopharmacology, 108,* 485–494.

Kane, R. L. (1995). MicroCog: A review. *Bulletin of the National Academy of Neuropsychology, 11,* 13–16.

Kane, R. L., & Kay, G. G. (1992). Computerized assessment in neuropsychology: A review of tests and test batteries. *Neuropsychology Review, 3,* 1–117.

Kapur, N. (1988). *Memory disorders in clinical practice.* London: Butterworths.

Kay, G. G. (1995). *CogScreen-Aeromedical Edition. Professional Manual.* Odessa, FL: Psychological Assessment Resources.

Kay, G. G., Crook, T., Rekeda, L., Lima, R., Ebinger, U., Arguinzoniz, M., et al. (2006). Differential effects of the antimuscarinic agents darifenacin and oxybutynin ER on memory in older subjects. *European Association of Urology, 50,* 317–326.

Kay, G. G., Pakull, B., Clark, T. M., Sea, D., Mays, D. A., & Tulloch, S. J. (2004). The effect of Adderall XR® treatment on driving performance in young adults with ADHD. *Paper presented at 17th Annual US Psychiatric and Mental Health Congress,* San Diego, CA, November 2004.

Larrabee, G. J., & Crook, T. H. (1989a). Dimensions of everyday memory in Age Associated Memory Impairment. *Psychological Assessment, 1,* 92–97.

Larrabee, G. J., & Crook, T. H. (1989b). Performance subtypes of everyday memory function. *Developmental Neuropsychology, 5,* 267–283.

Larrabee, G. J., & Crook, T. H. (1991). Computerized memory testing in clinical trials. In E. Mohr and P. Brouwers (Eds.), *Handbook of clinical trials: The neurobehavioral approach* (pp. 293–306). Amsterdam: Swets & Zeitlinger.

Larrabee, G. J., & Crook, T. H. (1994). Estimated prevalence of Age-Associated Memory Impairment derived from standardized tests of memory function. *International Psychogeriatrics, 6,* 95–104.

Larrabee, G. J., & Crook, T. H. (1996). Computers and memory. In I. Grant and K. M. Adams (Eds.). *Neuropsychological assessment of neuropsychiatric disorders (Second Edition)* (pp. 102–117). New York: Oxford University Press.

Larrabee, J. G., West, R. L., & Crook, T. H. (1991). The association of memory complaint with computer-simulated everyday memory performance. *Journal of Clinical and Experimental Neuropsychology, 4,* 466–478.

Ledbetter, M., & Hurley, S. (1994). A construct validation study of the attention and memory domains on the Assessment of Cognitive Functioning Test. *Archives of Clinical Neuropsychology, 9,* 154.

Leitner, Y., Doniger, G. M., Barak, R., Simon, E. S., & Hausdorff, J. M. (In Press). A novel multi-domain computerized cognitive assessment for attention deficit hyperactivity disorder: Evidence for widespread and circumscribed cognitive deficits. *Journal of Child Neurology.*

Lezak, M. D. (1995). *Neuropsychological assessment* (3rd. ed.). New York: Oxford University Press.

Matthews, C. G., Harley, J. P., & Malec, J. F. (1991). Guidelines for computer-assisted neuropsychological rehabilitation and cognitive remediation. *Clinical Neuropsychologist, 5,* 319.

Maruff, P., Thomas, E., Cysique, L., Brew, B., Collie, A., Snyder, P., et al. (In Press). Validity of CogState brief battery: Relationship to standardized tests and sensitivity to cognitive impairment in mild traumatic brain injury and AIDS dementia complex. *Archives of Clinical Neuropsychology.*

Miller, J. R., Adamson, G. J., Pink, M. M., & Sweet, J. C. (2007). Comparison of preseason, midseason, and postseason neurocognitive scores in uninjured collegiate football players. *American Journal of Sports Medicine, 35*(8), 1284–1288.

Mishkin, M. (1978). Memory in monkeys severely impaired by combined but not by separate removal of amygdale and hippocampus. *Nature, 273,* 297–298.

Mittenberg, W., DiGiulio, D. V., Perrin, S., & Bass, A. E. (1992). Symptoms following mild head injury: expectation as etiology. *Journal of Neurology, Neurosurgery, and Psychiatry, 55,* 200–204.

Mohr, E., Walker, D., Randolph, C., Sampson, M., & Mendis, T. (1996). The utility of clinical trial batteries in the measurement of Alzheimer's and Huntington's dementia. *International Psychogeriatrics, 8,* 397–411.

Morris, R. G., Evenden, J. L., Sahakian, B. J., & Robbins, T. W. (1987). Computer-aided assessment of dementia: comparative studies of neuropsychological deficits in Alzheimer-type dementia and Parkinson's disease. In S. M. Stahl, S. D. Iversen, and T. W. Robbins (Eds.). *Cognitive neurochemistry* (pp. 21–36). New York: Oxford University Press.

Nickelsen, T., Lufkin, E. G., Riggs, B. L., Cox, D. A., & Crook, T. H. (1999). Raloxifene hydrochloride, a selective estrogen receptor modulator: Safety assessment of effects on cognitive function and mood in postmenopausal women. *Neuroimmunoendocrinology, 24,* 115–128.

Owen, A. M., Downes, J. J., Sahakian, B. J., Polkey, C. E., & Robbins, T. W. (1990). Planning and spatial working memory following frontal lobe lesions in man. *Neuropsychologia, 28,* 1021–1034.

Pietrzak, R. H., Cohen, H., & Snyder, P. J. (2007). Spatial learning efficiency and error monitoring in normal aging: An investigation using a novel hidden maze learning test. *Archives of Clinical Neuropsychology, 22,* 235–245.

Powell, D. H., Kaplan, E. F., Whitla, D., Weintraub, S., Catlin, R., & Funkenstein, H. H. (1993). *MicroCog. Assessment of Cognitive Functioning. Manual.* Orlando, FL: The Psychological Corporation.

Raymond, P., Hinton-Bayre, A., Radel, M., Ray, M., & Marsh, N. (2006). Test–rest norms and reliable change indices for the MicroCog battery in a healthy community population over 50 years of age. *The Clinical Neuropsychologist, 20,* 261–270.

Reeves, D. L., Winter, K. P., Bleiberg, J., & Kane, R. L. (2007). ANAM® Genogram: Historical perspectives, description, and current endeavors. *Archives of Clinical Neuropsychology, 22S,* S15–S37.

Rey, A. (1961). *L'examen clinique en psychologie.* Paris: Presses Universitaires de France.

Ritsner, M. S., Blumenkrantz, H., Dubinsky, T., & Dwolatzky, T. (2006). The detection of neurocognitive decline in schizophrenia using the Mindstreams Computerized Cognitive Test Battery. *Schizophrenia Research, 82,* 39–49.

Rizzo, A. (2007). T13: Virtual reality in mental health and rehabilitation: An overview. *HCI International 22-27 July 2007, Beijing, China.*

Sahakian B. J. (1990). Computerized assessment of neuropsychological function in Alzheimer's disease and Parkinson's disease. *International Journal of Geriatric Psychiatry, 5,* 211–213.

Sahakian, B. J., Morris, R. G., Evenden, J. L., Heald, A., Levy, R., Philpot, M. P., et al. (1988). A comparative study of visuospatial memory and learning in Alzheimer-type dementia and Parkinson's disease. *Brain, 111,* 695–718.

Schweiger, A., Abramovitch, A., Doniger, G. M., & Simon, E. S. (2007). A clinical construct validity study of a novel computerized battery for the diagnosis of ADHD in young adults. *Journal of Clinical and Experimental Neuropsychology, 29,* 100–111.

Schweiger, A., Doniger, G. M., Dwolatzky, T., Jaffe, D., & Simon, E. S. (2003). Reliability of a novel computerized neuropsychological battery for mild cognitive impairment. *Acta Neuropsychologica, 1,* 407–413

Seltzer, B., Zolnouni, P., Nunez, M., Goldman, R., Kumar, D., Ieni, J., et al. (2004). Efficacy of donepizil in early stage Alzheimer's disease. *Neurology, 61,* 1852–1856.

Simon, E. S., Harel, Y., Appleboim, N., Doniger, G. M., Lavie, M., & Achiron, A. (2006). Validation of the Mindstreams Computerized Cognitive Battery in multiple sclerosis. *Neurology, 66,* A239.

Suhr, J. A., & Gunstad, J. (2002). "Diagnosis threat": The effect of negative expectations on cognitive performance in head injury. *Journal of Clinical and Experimental Neuropsychology, 24,* 448–457.

Taylor, J. L., O'Hara, R., Mumenthaler, M. S., & Yesavage, J. A. (2000). Relationship of CogScreen-AE to Flight Simulator Performance and Pilot Age. *Aviation, Space, and Environmental Medicine, 71,* 373–380.

Tomer, A., Larrabee, G. J., & Crook, T. H. (1994). Structure of everyday memory in adults with Age-Associated Memory Impairment. *Psychology and Aging, 9,* 606–615.

Wechsler, D. A. (1987). *Wechsler Memory Scale Revised: Manual.* San Antonio, TX: The Psychological Corporation.

Wechsler, D. A. (1997). *Wechsler Memory Scale; 3rd Edition (WMS-III).* San Antonio, TX: The Psychological Corporation.

Wesnes, K. A. (1977). The effects of psychotropic drugs on human behaviour. *Modern Problems of Pharmacopsychiatry, 12,* 37–58.

Wesnes, K. A. (2003). The cognitive drug research computerised assessment system: Application to clinical trials. In P. De Deyn, E. Thiery, and R. D'Hooge (Eds.), *Memory: Basic concepts, disorders and treatment* (pp. 453–472).Leuven, Belgium: ACCO.

Wesnes, K. A., Simpson, P. M., & Christmas, L. (1987). The assessment of human information processing abilities in psychopharmacology. In I. Hindmarch and P. D. Stonier (Eds.), *Human psychopharmacology: Measures and Methods, 1,* 79–92.

Wesnes, K. A., Ward, T., McGinty, A., & Petrini, O. (2000). The memory enhancing effects of a Ginko biloba/Panax ginseng combination in healthy middle-aged volunteers. *Psychopharmacology, 152,* 353–361.

West, R. L., & Crook, T. H. (1990). Age differences in everyday memory: Laboratory analogues of telephone number recall. *Psychology and Aging, 5,* 520–529.

West, R. L., Crook, T. H., & Barron, K. L. (1992). Everyday memory performance across the life span: The effects of age and noncognitive individual difference factors. *Psychology and Aging, 7,* 72–82.

Youngjohn, J. R., Larrabee, G. J., & Crook, T. H. (1991). First–last names and the grocery list selective reminding tests: Two computerized measures of everyday verbal learning. *Archives of Clinical Neuropsychology, 6,* 287–300.

Youngjohn, J. R., Larrabee, G. J., & Crook, T. H. (1992). Test–retest reliability of computerized, everyday memory measures and traditional memory tests. *Clinical Neuropsychologist, 6,* 276–286.

6

Cognitive Screening Methods

Maura Mitrushina

Screening for Cognitive Impairment in Medical Settings

Why is Screening Important?

Changes in cognitive status are associated with many medical conditions, including respiratory, cardiovascular, and infectious diseases, as well as autoimmune, renal, liver, kidney, pancreatic, and thyroid dysfunction, diabetes mellitus, other metabolic and systemic diseases, nutritional deficiencies, and toxic exposure (Boswell et al., 2002; Demakis et al., 2000; Elias, 1998; Lal, 2007; Lezak et al., 2004; Murkin, 2005; Ruchinskas et al., 2000; Salik et al., 2007; Sartori et al., 2006; Tarter et al., 2001; Van den Berg et al., 2006). Cognition might also be adversely affected by surgical interventions for cardiovascular diseases, radiation and chemotherapy for cancer, and medications that are given to control physical symptoms. Furthermore, cognitive impairment is a common sequelae of diseases directly affecting the central nervous system. Degenerative diseases of the cerebral cortex, as well as conditions compromising integrity of subcortical structures of the brain, commonly result in notable cognitive deterioration.

Considering the high incidence of cognitive impairment in general medical and neurological conditions, timely detection of cognitive decline may provide a clue to the presence of an underlying physical disorder, as well as to its course and prognosis, and may determine a choice of treatment or medication adjustment.

Timely diagnosis of neuropsychiatric conditions yields the following benefits:

1. Providing indication for treatment of reversible conditions;
2. Preventing a relapse of cognitive impairment through the use of prophylactic measures;
3. Slowing down a progression of cognitive deterioration or achieving improvement through the use of medications that stabilize cognitive functioning;
4. Educating the patient and the family regarding changes in cognition and behavior that lead to reported changes in daily functioning;
5. Allowing the patient and the family to make legal decisions early in the course of the disease and to plan for future care.

Cognitive impairment is commonly viewed in the context of dementia. The definition of dementia captures deterioration of cognitive/intellectual abilities leading to impairment in social and occupational functioning, and in activities of daily life (American Psychiatric Association, 1980; McKhann et al., 1984). Over the years, understanding of clinical profiles associated with dementia has been refined. Whereas in the past the diagnosis of dementia required impairment in memory (as in the case of Alzheimer's disease), it is now believed that memory impairment may not be prominent in several dementing conditions that involve severe deficits in other cognitive domains (e.g., vascular, frontotemporal, and Lewy body dementias). Furthermore, a more recent clinical entity, mild cognitive impairment (MCI), captures less pronounced symptoms of cognitive deterioration that do not interfere considerably with activities of daily life (Gauthier et al., 2006; Petersen & O'Brien, 2006).

As in the case of dementia, MCI can be classified into amnestic and nonamnestic subtypes, depending on the presence of memory impairment.

In geriatric settings, timely detection of insidious dementia is critical for secondary prevention (Ganguli, 1997). Whereas primary prevention of dementia is not currently available, early identification of those individuals who show signs of cognitive impairment allows early diagnosis and treatment, enhancement of functional ability, prevention of complications, community monitoring, and planning of public health services.

Early detection of cognitive impairment, including dementia and MCI, is facilitated by cognitive screening. The goals of cognitive screening can be classified into two categories:

1. To establish the likelihood of global cognitive deterioration in individuals at risk and assess the need for further diagnostic/neuropsychological workup. Screening is typically performed by a primary care physician in response to complaints of cognitive symptoms reported by the patient or other informant. Other risk factors for cognitive deterioration include age, significant medical problems, intake of multiple medications, and family history of dementia. In rehabilitation setting, screening is performed to identify cognitive strengths and weaknesses to aid in rehabilitation efforts, and to monitor the rates of recovery (Ruchinskas & Curyto, 2003).

2. To identify individuals in the community who would benefit from diagnostic evaluation but who have not yet spontaneously sought medical attention for cognitive symptoms. This type of a voluntary screening is typically performed by a trained paraprofessional. Other benefits of voluntary screening programs are freedom from ethical and practical concerns expressed by physicians in respect to routine screening of elderly patients, increasing awareness of the community about issues of aging, providing reassurance to those who are

screening negative, and offering educational opportunities addressing health maintenance issues (Lawrence et al., 2001).

Is There an Ideal Screening Test?

Neuropsychological test batteries are specifically designed to assess cognitive strengths and weaknesses across different functional domains. This information is often used in designing cognitive remediation programs and monitoring effectiveness of treatment. However, use of neuropsychological test batteries for cognitive screening is not feasible due to their high cost, length, need for specially trained examiners, and poor acceptance by the patients. Lengthy test batteries are not well tolerated by medical patients due to their short attention span, fatigability, and, frequently, physical pain and discomfort. Furthermore, it is not practical to use neuropsychological test batteries in assessment of large populations of elderly individuals who are at risk for dementia.

Moreover, a precise measurement of the functional level within different cognitive domains is unnecessary for most medical patients and individuals at risk; the presence versus absence of global cognitive impairment and the domains most severely impaired are of main concern. This task can be accomplished through the use of brief screening measures, which in a limited amount of time allow the examiner to tap important aspects of cognitive abilities.

Many investigators agree that an ideal screening measure should be brief, well tolerated and acceptable to patients, easy to administer and score, free of demographic biases, sensitive to the presence of cognitive dysfunction, and able to assess a wide range of cognitive functions, to identify domains that are in need of further assessment, and to track cognitive changes over time to make them useful in planning for treatment and discharge in rehabilitation setting (Doninger et al., 2006; Ruchinskas & Curyto, 2003; Shulman, 2000; Shulman & Feinstein, 2003).

There is no single screening tool that would meet all of the above criteria. The choice of a screening test depends on the context and the population being screened. Overall, the use of brief screening tests as screening tools for detection of cognitive impairment is well justified in medical settings. The clinical value of screening tests is reflected in their many *strengths*:

1. Such measures are brief and nondemanding for the patient, and can be easily administered at the bedside.

2. They show little practice effect.

3. They can be administered by appropriately trained paraprofessionals and do not require much formal training for their interpretation.

4. They originate from traditional clinical evaluation of mental status, are convenient, and deal with constructs familiar to physicians.

5. They utilize a structured interview format, which provides uniformity in administration and scoring.

6. The test results are quantified, which facilitates decision processes, and allows comparison across time and among different clinicians.

In spite of these assets of cognitive screening tests, a consideration should be given to their *limitations*:

1. They produce high false-negative rates because most of the questions making up screening tests can be answered by a majority of patients, even if they have mild cognitive impairment. Focal brain dysfunctions, especially related to the nondominant cerebral hemisphere, are likely to be missed because cognitive screening measures tend to be constructed mainly of verbal items. In addition, reliance on a global estimate of cognitive functioning makes the detection of isolated deficits less likely. Another source of false-negative identifications is high premorbid intellectual and educational levels of the patient.

2. False-positive errors arise primarily from confounding effects of age and ethnic background, low premorbid intelligence, low education and illiteracy, and poor knowledge of English. Several investigators have attempted to control for these factors by stratifying normative data or using different cutoffs for different demographic groups. Another source of false-positive errors is limited cooperation and motivation, as well as sensory impairment.

3. Estimates of psychometric properties, reported in validation studies as classification rates, are generally evaluated against a "gold standard," such as psychiatric or neurological diagnosis. In spite of the extensive clinical workup that underlies diagnoses made for research purposes, such diagnoses, themselves, have low reliability.

4. Psychometric properties of a test derived on a sample that is representative of a certain population of patients cannot be generalized onto a different population as the test's accuracy in identifying cognitive impairment is affected by the prevalence of the condition and other properties of the population (see below for further discussion).

5. Different studies use different standards for diagnostic determination, which makes comparison of their results misleading. For example, Erkinjuntti et al. (1997) found that the number of subjects classified by a test as having dementia can differ by a factor of 10 across six diagnostic systems used in their study.

6. A comparison of psychometric properties of screening tests across studies is further confounded by the use of different cutoffs for cognitive impairment by different authors. Lorentz et al. (2002) advocate the use of the area under receiver operating characteristic (ROC) curve to overcome this problem.

7. Performance on the cognitive screening instruments is frequently confounded by emotional factors. Cognitive dysfunction may lead to depression and anxiety, whereas affective disturbance is likely to cause or exacerbate cognitive deficits.

8. Cognitive screening instruments do not distinguish between acute and chronic cognitive dysfunction.

9. Cognitive disturbance associated with many neuropsychiatric diseases has a waxing and waning course. Any one evaluation would not provide sufficient information on the course of cognitive changes, and serial evaluations might be warranted.

Performance of screening tests is also affected by the following sources of bias (Gifford & Cummings, 1999):

1. *Spectrum bias* reflects variability in accuracy of detecting cognitive disturbance depending on the severity of the condition.

Consequently, screening tests that have high sensitivity in the populations with more severe disease manifestations do not perform well with less advanced stages of the disease.

2. *Workup (verification) bias* affects accuracy of the results of many validity studies due to preferential referral for the diagnostic workup of those patients who have positive test results. Since patients with negative results do not receive further evaluation, the calculations of sensitivity–specificity of the screening test are not accurate. Failure to include true-negative/false-negative rates into the analysis leads to increased sensitivity and decreased specificity.

3. *Review bias* refers to biased interpretation of the test results, leading to inflated accuracy of the screening test, when both the screening test and diagnostic assessment are performed by the same person.

In addition to these empirically defined test properties, the choice of a screening test should be based on evaluation of its statistically derived psychometric properties in respect to the population being screened.

Review of Psychometric Properties of Screening Tests

Accuracy and utility of cognitive screening examinations with different populations have been reported in numerous validation studies, which differ in design, scoring, and presentation of research findings. In order to facilitate the reader's understanding of the results of different studies described in this chapter, we include a brief review of psychometric properties of tests.

Reliability

When using a screening test, we assume that the test scores would be consistent over repeated administrations, different raters, and different forms of the same test. If an individual sometimes receives high scores and sometimes low scores on the same test, no inferences can be made regarding the level of ability that is measured by this test. In other words, we have to be assured that the test is a reliable measure of a stable construct such as a cognitive ability ("true" variance). However, a certain degree of variability is inherent in test performance due to transient factors associated with the testing situation and the patient's state at the time of testing ("error" variance). Reliability of a test refers to the proportion of "true" variance to "error" variance. In respect to different sources of error, the four most common methods of reliability measurements are described below:

1. *Test–retest reliability* measures the stability of test scores over time. It is presented as a correlation between test scores at different times. The length of time interval between the test probes should be considered in evaluating this statistic.

2. *Alternate form reliability* assesses the correlation between scores obtained by the same subjects on the alternate forms of a test.

3. *Interrater reliability* refers to the rate of agreement (correlation) in test scores, or in ratings on individual items, when obtained by different examiners.

4. *Internal consistency reliability* reflects the extent to which all the test items measure the same underlying construct and is expressed as a degree of relationship between different test items. It is commonly measured with the Cronbach's coefficient alpha, which represents the average of all correlations between each item and all other test items.

Ideally, a highly reliable test would be preferred to a test with low reliability. However, selection of a screening test should weigh heavily on considerations of practicality. Tests with lower reliability might be acceptable since the cost of error in screening situations is lower than in diagnostic decision making. For screening tests, reliability between 0.80 and 0.60 would be acceptable. Reliability estimates below 0.60 are usually judged as unacceptably low as more than 40% of the variability in the test scores is due to measurement error.

Validity

When a test is used to assess cognitive status, it is assumed that the test measures what it is supposed to measure and that the test is useful in making accurate decisions. Different validation strategies are used to understand the meaning and implications of the scores achieved on the test. Content and construct validity indicate whether a test is a valid measure of cognitive status. Criterion-related validity refers to the accuracy of decisions that are based on the test scores.

1. *Content validity* refers to the extent to which the content of the questions adequately taps different aspects of mental status. It is not measured statistically, but is inferred in many studies from clinical relevance of the test and high internal consistency of the test items. Content validity is established if a test *looks* like a valid measure (Murphy & Davidshofer, 1991).

2. *Construct validity* points to agreement between different tests measuring the same construct. The accuracy of the assumption that cognitive screening tests actually measure the underlying hypothetical construct of the cognitive component of mental status is established by documenting high correlations of a particular test with other tests presumably measuring the same construct (*convergent validity*) versus low correlations with tests that are expected to measure different constructs—for example, affective state (*discriminant validity*). Construct validity is established if a test *acts* like a valid measure (Murphy & Davidshofer, 1991).

3. *Criterion-related validity* reflects the relationship between scores on the test and a reference criterion, or "gold standard," that is assumed to represent a "true state" of a patient. Reference criteria vary among different studies and include results of a neuropsychological evaluation, judgment of a clinician, discharge disposition, staff ratings, management problems, self-care capacity, response to treatment, and duration of illness, as well as neuroimaging, EEG, neuropathological, and lab findings. Most studies use clinical diagnosis by a psychiatrist or neurologist as a criterion.

The criterion measures can be obtained *after* decisions are made, based on the test scores in a random sample of the population about which the decisions were made (predictive validity), or *at the same time* when decisions are made in a preselected sample (concurrent validity). Accuracy of decisions in finding individuals to be cognitively impaired or unimpaired as determined by the results of the screening test, judged against the reference criterion in a preselected sample, is addressed by the decision theory approach.

According to the *decision theory*, all patients are classified into cognitively intact (negative) or impaired (positive) groups, based on their test scores. Similar distinction is made according to the criterion (clinical diagnosis). Comparison between these two classifications provides information on the number of correctly identified and misidentified patients on the basis of their test scores. The relative number of cases in each cell representing true (T) or false (F) and negative (N) or positive (P) outcomes (i.e., TP, TN, FP, FN) yields several indices of the test validity.

Sensitivity refers to the ability of a test to correctly identify individuals who have cognitive impairment—the ratio of "true positives" to all impaired patients (true positives/[true positives + false negatives]). *Specificity* indicates the ability of the test to correctly identify absence of cognitive impairment—the ratio of "true negatives" to all intact patients (true negatives/[true negatives + false positives]). These characteristics of the test vary, depending on the "cutoff" points for classification into negative and positive groups, which have been selected by an investigator on the basis of experience.

Manipulation of the cutoffs affects the balance between sensitivity and specificity and, therefore, produces different cost–benefit ratios. For example, if the cutoff is set so that only patients making a very large number of errors are considered impaired, only those patients with pronounced cognitive impairment would be identified. This would result in high specificity and a small number of "false positives." However, many mild cases would be missed, resulting in low sensitivity and a high number of "false negatives." Failure to detect cognitive impairment precludes timely therapeutic intervention that otherwise might allow stabilization or reversal of cognitive symptoms.

Fixing the cutoff at a small number of errors allows the clinician to correctly identify a majority of individuals with even mild signs of cognitive impairment, which ensures high sensitivity of the test and reduces the number of "false negatives." However, this strategy increases the proportion of intact individuals who are identified as "positives," thus lowering the specificity of the test and providing a high number of "false positives." Costs of such an outcome include inappropriate treatment and psychological distress as well as adverse social and economic consequences on the part of intact individuals who are mistakenly identified as cognitively impaired.

Therefore, the cutoff should often be set at values that ensure a reasonable balance between sensitivity and specificity, so that only "borderline" patients will likely be incorrectly classified. Under certain circumstances, however, one would prefer to maximize sensitivity even at the expense of specificity, and vice versa. Setting the optimal cutoff yields the highest *Hit Rate*, that is, ability of the test to correctly identify presence and absence of impairment (expressed as the ratio of [TP + TN] to all individuals in the sample [TP + FP + FN + TN]).

The trade-off between sensitivity and specificity (more precisely, between true-positive and false-positive rates of classification) for all possible cutoff scores is displayed by the ROC curve plot. The area under the ROC curve represents most useful index of diagnostic accuracy (Swets, 1996). The score associated with the largest amount of area under the curve is the most sensitive cutting score. Use of this approach allows one to compute probability of impairment for a certain test score, taking into account different prevalence rates.

Usefulness of screening tests, as reported in different studies, is described by several statistics. Criterion-related validity for most of the screening tests is relatively low, ranging between 0.2 and 0.5, due to the imperfect reliability of the test and the reference criterion. Whereas a criterion is assumed to represent the "true state" of a patient, it is frequently based on subjective clinical judgment, which is inherently unreliable (see discussion of limitations of screening tests in the previous section). To help the reader understand the strength of the relationship expressed by the correlation coefficient, we will use an example. If a correlation coefficient between a test and a criterion is 0.3, the proportion of the variance in the criterion that is accounted for by the test (r^2, coefficient of determination) is 0.09. This means that only 9% of the variability in the criterion can be accounted for by the test scores. Although these numbers

look discouraging, they should be interpreted in the context of other measures that contribute to the accuracy of decisions.

The utility of a test is reflected in its *incremental validity*—the degree of improvement in the accuracy of decisions, that is, frequency of *TP* and *TN* outcomes, beyond the random level, that are made using the test. The contribution of the criterion-related validity of a test to improvement in the accuracy of decisions depends on the base rate and selection ratio.

The *base rate* reflects the proportion of an unselected population who meet the criterion standard. Clinically, this term is used interchangeably with incidence or prevalence of a disorder. In the general population, the base rates for cognitive impairment are usually low and most of the "red flags" represent false alarms. The base rates among elderly, or those individuals who are referred for evaluation due to progressive symptomatology, are higher, and therefore the expected number of false alarms would be lower.

The *selection ratio* is defined as the ratio of *TP + FP* outcomes to the total number of subjects. When the selection ratio is low, a test with even modest validity can make a considerable contribution to the accuracy of decisions.

Thus, incremental validity of a test is highest when the base rate is moderate, selection ratio is low, and the criterion-related validity is high.

In clinical practice, a clinician is concerned with the utility of a test in correctly identifying impairment in an individual patient, that is, in the test's predictive value, rather than in its accuracy in discriminating between groups. *Positive Predictive Value* represents the probability that the patient is indeed impaired, given impaired test score (expressed as the ratio of TP to all individuals identified by the test as impaired [TP + FP]). *Negative Predictive Value* represents the probability that the patient is intact, given nonimpaired test score (expressed as the ratio of TN to all individuals identified by the test as nonimpaired [FN + TN]). Because predictive value is a probabilistic construct relating the number of correctly classified individuals to the total number of individuals falling into a corresponding classification category, it is affected by the prevalence of the disturbance in the population.

Thus, accuracy and usefulness of a cognitive screening test in detecting cognitive impairment depends on the properties of the test and characteristics of a population in which it is being used. The following review provides descriptions and results of validation studies for selected tests.

Description of Selected Screening Tests for Cognitive Impairment

The need for structured measures of mental status was recognized in the beginning of the twentieth century. Adolf Meyer (1918) introduced a uniform method of evaluation of mental status, which required extensive narrative descriptions of the patient's behavior. Toward mid-twentieth century, numeric scales that quantify emotional and cognitive aspects of mental status were developed. Over time, many brief screening measures of cognition were introduced in response to a well-recognized need for early detection of cognitive deterioration. A recent review of the literature by Cullen et al. (2007) identified 39 screening tests for cognitive impairment that met stringent selection criteria, including administration time of less than 20 minutes and availability in English.

Practice guidelines developed by the American Academy of Neurology, following an evidence-based review of the literature, include recommendations for the use of cognitive screening instruments for detection of mild cognitive impairment and dementia in individuals with suspected cognitive impairment (Petersen et al., 2001).

The screening tests summarized in Table 6-1 represent selected measures that are most commonly used with medical and geriatric patients. As statistical properties of tests vary depending on the characteristics of a sample, it is not feasible within the scope of this chapter to provide statistics from different validation studies for all tests reviewed in Table 6-1. A review of selected validation studies is presented for Mini-Mental State Examination and Cognistat.

Mini-Mental State Examination (MMSE) and Related Measures

The MMSE (Folstein et al., 1975) was originally designed for use with psychiatric patients, but was later validated on a broad range of diagnoses. Comprehensive reviews of the history and utility of the MMSE are provided by Anthony et al. (1982), Harvan and Cotter (2006), Mossello and Boncinelli (2006), Tombaugh (2005), and Tombaugh and McIntyre (1992). Findings from selected validation studies for the MMSE are summarized in Table 6-2.

The original version of the MMSE comprises 11 items that have been derived from the mental status examination proposed by Meyer (1918) and yields a total score of 30 (see Table 6-1). Psychometric properties of the test have been extensively investigated with different samples. A review of the literature indicates that performance on the MMSE is influenced by demographic factors, such as age (Almeida, 1998; Crum et al., 1993; Harvan & Cotter, 2006; Magni et al., 1995; Strickland et al., 2005; Tangalos et al., 1996; Tombaugh et al., 1996; Van Gorp et al., 1999), education (Almeida, 1998; Bertolucci et al., 1994; Borson et al., 2005; Crum et al., 1993; Ganguli et al., 1995; Harvan & Cotter, 2006; Lourenco & Veras, 2006; Magni et al., 1995; Mungas et al., 1996; Murden et al., 1991; Ostrosky-Solis et al., 2000; Rosselli et al., 2006; Strickland et al., 2005; Tangalos et al., 1996; Tombaugh et al., 1996; van Gorp et al., 1999), ethnicity and language of test administration (Mungas et al., 1996; Ramirez et al., 2001), intelligence level (MacKenzie et al., 1996), and physical condition (Eslinger et al., 2003; MacKenzie et al., 1996).

Similarly, in a large population-based study sponsored by National Institute of Mental Health (Crum et al., 1993), the MMSE scores for 18,056 adult participants varied as a function of age and education level. The median scores for different age groups ranged from 29 (18–24 years) to 25 (>80 years), and for education groups, from 22 (0–4 years) to 26 (5–8 years) to 29 (>9 years). In a study by Ostrosky-Solis et al. (2000), normal Spanish-speaking illiterate participants obtained scores that correspond to severe cognitive alterations, and those with low education (1–4 years) scored within the range consistent with moderate cognitive alterations. Authors concluded that the MMSE has little diagnostic utility in individuals with low educational level. The effect of demographics on MMSE performance was also documented by

Table 6–1. Descriptions of Cognitive Screening Tests (Presented in the Order of Increasing Administration Time)

Test/Authors, Administration Time	Functions Assessed	Primary Use	Test Properties
General Cognitive Screening Instruments			
Mini-Cog Borson et al. (2000) [3–4 minutes]	Includes Clock Drawing Test and 3-item recall task from CASI	Screening for cognitive impairment in primary care settings	Scores of 0–3 on CDT and on recall task (score of 3—severe impairment); free of education and language bias; used with multiethnic populations; simple administration; sensitive to MCI
Memory Impairment Screen (MIS) Buschke et al. (1999) [4 minutes]	Four-item delayed and cued recall	Screening for dementia	Total score is the sum of items passed on cued recall plus doubled number of items passed on free recall, with range from 0 to 8; test has equivalent forms
General Practitioner Assessment of Cognition (GPCOG) Brodaty et al. (2002) [4–5 minutes]	Two parts: 9 cognitive questions (time orientation, clock drawing, recall of recent event, word recall task); and 6 informant-rated items	Screening for cognitive impairment in primary care settings	Maximum score—9; if the score falls between 5 and 8, informant-rated items should be administered; biased by sociodemographic factors, sensitive to MCI
Abbreviated Mental Test (AMT) Hodkinson (1972) [5 minutes]	Orientation, attention, recent and remote memory, information	Screening for dementia in primary care	10-item test derived from BIMCT; cutoff 7/8; developed in Great Britain; culture-specific; limited validity
Kokmen Short Test of Mental Status (STMS) Kokmen et al. (1987) [5 minutes]	Orientation, attention, learning, calculation, similarities, information, construction, delayed recall	Screening for mild dementia	Score—sum of the subtest scores; maximum score—38
Blessed Orientation-Memory-Concentration Test (OMC) (Short form of BIMC) Katzman et al. (1983) [3–6 minutes] (used as the basis for Halifax Mental Status Scale, HMSS, Fisk et al., 1991)	Orientation, concentration, immediate and delayed memory	Geriatric patients	Score—sum of errors; maximum score—28 on 6 items; cutoff >10 errors
Seven-Minute Screen (7MS) Solomon et al. (1998) [7 minutes]	Benton Temporal Orientation, clock drawing, category fluency, enhanced cued recall	Screening for AD in the primary care setting	Provides indicator of probability of AD: high, low, retest; administration requires considerable training; requires use of a handheld computer to assess likelihood of dementia

(continued)

Table 6–1. Continued

Test/Authors, Administration Time	Functions Assessed	Primary Use	Test Properties
Mini-Mental Status Examination (MMSE) Folstein et al. (1975) [5–10 minutes]	Orientation, concentration, serial 7's, immediate and delayed verbal memory, language, 3-step praxis, copy of geometric design	Broad range of medical and psychiatric diagnoses	Score—sum of the correct responses; maximum score—30 on 11 items
Mental Status Questionnaire (MSQ) Kahn et al. (1960) [5–10 minutes]	Orientation, general and personal information	Institutionalized geriatric patients	Score—sum of errors; 10 items derived from a 31-item version; maximum score—10
Short Portable Mental Status Questionnaire (SPMSQ) Pfeiffer (1975) [5–10 minutes]	Orientation, long-term recall, current event information, serial 3's	Detection of "organic brain syndrome" in geriatric patients	Score—sum of errors with correction for race and education; 10 items
Modified Mini-Mental Status Examination (3MS) Teng and Chui (1987) [10 minutes]	Same as MMSE plus recall of date and place of birth, animal naming, similarities, additional recall task	Broad range of medical and psychiatric diagnoses	Expands range of MMSE scores by allowing for partial credit; maximum score—100 on 15 items
Short and Sweet Screening Instrument (SASSI) Belle et al. (2000) [10 minutes]	Includes MMSE, verbal fluency, and temporal orientation tests	Community screening for dementia	Consists of three cognitive tests statistically derived from a larger battery in MoVIES community study
Cognitive Capacity Screening Exam (CCSE) Jacobs et al. (1977) [5–15 minutes]	Orientation, concentration, serial 7's, immediate and delayed verbal memory, language, verbal concept formation, digit span, arithmetic	Detection of diffuse organic mental syndrome/delirium in medical patients; sensitive to cognitive decline in high-functioning patients	Score—sum of the correct responses; maximum score—30 on 30 items; cutoff <20 correct; as part of CMC is used in combination with MMSE
Blessed Information-Memory-Concentration Test (BIMC) (Fuld's modification) Fuld (1978) [10–20 minutes]	Orientation, concentration, immediate and delayed memory, and unique items	Geriatric patients	Score—sum of errors; maximum score—33 on 28 items; cutoff >7 errors
Addenbrooke's Cognitive Examination-Revised (ACE-R) Mioshi et al. (2006) [12–20 minutes]	Orientation/attention, memory, verbal fluency, language, visuospatial perception/organization	Screening for dementia and mild cognitive impairment, differentiates between AD and FTD profiles	Extension of MMSE; different patterns for types of dementia; Score—sum of subscores on 5 scales; maximum score—100
Cognitive Abilities Screening Instrument (CASI) Teng et al. (1994) [15–20 minutes]	Attention, concentration, orientation, short-term and long-term memory, language, visual construction, verbal fluency, abstraction, judgment	Broad range of medical and psychiatric diagnoses	Based on items from MMSE and 3MS, adapted for cross-cultural use; most individual item scores 0–10; maximum Score—100 on 25 items

(continued)

Table 6–1. Continued

Test/Authors, Administration Time	Functions Assessed	Primary Use	Test Properties
Cognistat, formerly *Neurobehavioral Cognitive Status Examination (NCSE)* Kiernan et al. (1987) [5–30 minutes]	LOC, orientation, attention, comprehension, repetition, naming, construction, memory, calculation, similarities, judgment	Medical, geriatric, and neurological patients	Uses screen and metric approach; allows to plot a profile for 10 domains
Repeatable Battery for the Assessment of Neuropsychological Status (RBANS) Randolph et al. (1998) [20–30 minutes]	Immediate and delayed memory, visuospatial ability, language, attention	Designed as a screening tool to identify and characterize dementia in the elderly; has been used in schizophrenia, TBI, multiple sclerosis, stroke, affective disorders	Provides five indexes, as well as a total cognitive impairment score; sensitive to mild dementia; provides distinct profiles for different types of dementia; has two alternate forms, allowing to track change over time; high test–retest reliability; standardized on U.S. Census-matched population between 20 and 89 years of age; normative data are stratified by demographic groups
High Sensitivity Cognitive Screen (HSCS) Fogel (1991) [20–30 minutes]	Memory, language, attention, concentration, visual and motor skills, spatial perception, self-regulation, planning	Screening for subtle cognitive decline in geriatric and community-dwelling HIV-infected individuals	Scoring is based on interpretive algorithm, classifying each item into normal, borderline, abnormal range (latter is rated as mild, moderate, or severe)
Cambridge CognitiveExamination-Revised (CAMCOG-R) Roth et al. (1999) [25–30 minutes]	Orientation, comprehension, naming, verbal fluency, short-term and long-term memory, attention, calculation, praxis, similarities, visual perception (Original CAMCOG); revised version also includes ideational fluency and visual reasoning	Elderly patients with neurological disorders, for example, Parkinson's disease, post-CVA	105 items; criterion for impairment—score <80; maximum "total executive function score"—28; available for cross-national use
Mattis Dementia Rating Scale (DRS, MDRS) Mattis (1988) [20–45 minutes]	Attention, initiation/perseveration, visuospatial construction, reasoning, memory	Screening for dementia	Score—sum of scores on five subscales; 36 items; maximum score—144; uses screen and metric approach; allows test–retest comparisons; test adaptations used cross-culturally; minimal culture effect

(*continued*)

Table 6–1. Continued

Test/Authors, Administration Time	Functions Assessed	Primary Use	Test Properties
Brief Focused Screening Instruments			
Clock Drawing Test (CDT) Goodglass and Kaplan (1983) [<1–5 minutes]	Visuoperceptual, constructional, conceptual	Screening for dementia	Many administration and scoring systems exist; quantitative scores represent total ratings for clockface, placement of the hands and numbers; qualitative scores are based on the analysis of error types; limited utility as a single screening instrument; used in combination with other tests
Time and Change Test (T&C) Froehlich et al. (1998) [1 minute]	Telling time from a pre-set clock, and making change for a dollar using coins	Screening for dementia	Unaffected by race and education; limited scope of assessed domains
Informant-Based Instruments			
Blessed Dementia Rating Scale (BDRS, BRS, BDS) Blessed et al. (1968)	Caregiver ratings of behavioral, personality, and emotional changes in the preceding six months; frequently used in combination with BIMC or OMC	Screening for dementia	Most items rated present/absent, three items by severity level; 22 items; maximum score—28, highest severity level, cutoff for impairment >4
Informant Questionnaire on Cognitive Decline in the Elderly (IQCODE) Jorm (2004)	Informant ratings of cognitive decline over the previous 10 years	Screening for dementia for individuals who are unable to undergo direct testing, or those with low levels of education and literacy	26 items are rated on a 5-point scale; measures a single factor of cognitive decline; unaffected by education, premorbid ability, language proficiency; affected by informant's depression, anxiety, and quality of relationship; coupled with cognitive tests, improves screening accuracy; several short forms developed; translated into many languages
Deterioration Cognitive Observee (DECO) Ritchie and Fuhrer (1996)	Informant ratings of changes in activity level, long-term and short-term memory, visuospatial processing and new skill learning over the preceding year	Screening for dementia	19 items rated on a 3-point Likert scale ranging from 0 to 2; maximum score 38, indicating no change; cutoff at 30/29

(continued)

111

Table 6–1. Continued

Test/Authors, Administration Time	Functions Assessed	Primary Use	Test Properties
Telephone Screening			
Telephone Interview for Cognitive Status (TICS) Brandt et al. (1988) *(TICS-m)* (modified) Welsh et al. (1993) *Computer-assisted Version of TICS-m* Buckwalter et al. (2002)	Orientation, recall, calculation, information, repetition, verbal reasoning, ability to follow simple commands (TICS-m includes delayed recall item)	Screening for dementia in epidemiological studies; follow-up assessment by telephone after face-to-face assessment with MMSE	11 questions, 17 items; maximum score—41; cutoff score < 27; correlates highly with MMSE in AD

Notes: LOC—level of consciousness; AD—Alzheimer's disease; FTD—frontotemporal dementia; CMC—combined screening test incorporating MMSE and CCSE; MCI—mild cognitive impairment; TBI—traumatic brain injury; CVA—cerebrovascular accident.

Boustani et al. (2003). These findings suggest that demographic factors should be taken into account in interpretation of test scores.

Traditionally, decisions regarding the presence of cognitive impairment or determination of severity ranges are guided by evaluating the patient's total MMSE score in respect to cutoff points for impairment. A score of <23 was originally proposed as the cutoff for cognitive impairment. Kukull et al. (1994) found that the cutoff of <24 has low sensitivity (63%) yet high specificity (96%) relative to a one-year follow-up diagnosis in a sample of outpatients with cognitive complaints. Van Gorp et al. (1999) reported a score of <26 as the optimal cutoff for dementia based on their sample of community-dwelling elders. Tombaugh and McIntyre (1992) expanded the use of cutoff points by dividing the scale into ranges of 18–23 and <17, as indicative of mild and severe impairment, respectively.

However, the uniform criteria for impairment might be misleading when used with different demographic groups. Revised cutoff points for different education levels have been reported in a number of studies. Lourenco and Veras (2006) found the best MMSE performance in detection of dementia at a cutoff of 18/19 for illiterate and 24/25 for literate individuals, based on a sample of elderly Brazilian outpatients. Almeida (1998) proposed a cutoff of 19/20 for individuals with no formal education and 23/24 for those with a history of schooling, based on

a sample of older Brazilian patients. Bertolucci et al. (1994) suggested a cutoff of 13 for illiterate individuals, 18 for those with less than 8 years of education, and 26 for those with 8 or more years, based on a sample of Brazilian adults.

The utility of the MMSE in tracking cognitive changes over time is supported by findings of minimal practice effects. Tombaugh (2005) reported small group changes over 3-month and 5-year test–retest intervals (as measured with a reliable change index) in a large sample of neurologically intact elderly. In raw scores, changes in group means were less than one point over different test–retest intervals, with somewhat greater rate of change in those over the age of 75. In Eslinger et al.'s (2003) large sample of healthy older men, 80% of participants remained within two points of their initial test scores on a 6-year follow-up testing. Tangalos et al. (1996) also emphasized stability of test scores over time and suggested that a decline of at least 4 points in the total MMSE score over a period of 1–4 years represents substantial cognitive deterioration.

The original test underwent a number of modifications in efforts to adapt it to the needs of different populations. Mayeux et al. (1981) developed a modified version of the MMSE that includes Digit Span (forward and backwards), recall of general information, confrontation naming of 10 items from the Boston Naming Test, an additional sentence for repetition, and

Table 6–2. Findings from Selected Validation Studies for the Mini-Mental State Examination and Cognistat

Test /Source	Sample/Setting	Findings
Mini-Mental State Exam (MMSE)		
Strickland et al. (2005)	93 healthy African American older adults	Normative data stratified by age and education are provided
Xu et al. (2002)	351 elderly volunteers with memory complaints	Sensitivity of 61% in identifying MCI, using conversion to dementia at follow-up as a standard
Ostrosky-Solis et al. (2000)	430 intact Spanish-speaking elderly; The sample was stratified into 3 age and 4 education groups	Sensitivity and specificity of the MMSE in both illiterate and 1–4 years of education groups—50% and 72.7%; in >5 years of education group—86.4% and 86.4%
Van Gorp et al. (1999)	22 AD, 19 VaD patients, 12 normal elderly	Discriminatory power was maximized with a cutoff of ≤26, in reference to the NINCDS/ADRDA and DSM-III-R diagnostic criteria for the AD and VaD, respectively
Tombaugh et al. (1996)	Community-dwelling elderly: 406 with no cognitive impairment; 119 with AD	3MS and MMSE scores (derived from the 3MS) were compared as to their accuracy in discriminating between the two groups; The consensus diagnosis by physician and clinical neuropsychologist was used as a reference for AD; psychometric properties of both tests for different age and education groups, as well as normative data stratified by 2 age × 2 education levels are provided
Mungas et al. (1996)	590 elderly participants from a population-based community survey sample; 46.6% Hispanics, 53.4% non-Hispanics	Statistically derived adjusted MMSE score, correcting for age and education is presented; Ethnicity and language of the test administration strongly influenced the raw MMSE score
Tangalos et al. (1996)	3513 elderly patients; Subsample of 185 patients with dementia and 227 age- and sex-matched controls	Cutoff score of 23 yielded 69% sensitivity and 99% specificity; use of age- and education-specific cutoff scores improved sensitivity to 82% with no loss of specificity; With typical base rate for dementia in general medical practice, the PPV < 35%; Determination of substantial cognitive deterioration over a period of 1–4 years requires at least 4-point decline in the total MMSE score
MacKenzie et al. (1996)	150 community-dwelling elderly	Effect of confounding variables (age, social class, hearing acuity, history of stroke, etc.) was assessed; MMSE yielded fewer false positives than other screening tests (sensitivity/specificity of 80%/98%). A cutoff of 20/21 is recommended for routine screening

(continued)

Table 6–2. Continued

Test /Source	Sample/Setting	Findings
Roper et al. (1996)	59 geriatric medical inpatients with diagnosed brain dysfunction, 46 without brain dysfunction	Highest diagnostic accuracy (70%) was achieved at a cutoff score of 26
Cognistat (NCSE)		
Doninger et al. (2006)	120 TBI inpatients 296 community-residing adults with TBI	Rating scale analysis (using Rasch analysis) was used on the original test and modified version by eliminating the easiest items. Three performance strata were identified in both acute and postacute samples
Strickland et al. (2005)	93 healthy African American older adults	Normative data, stratified by age and education, are provided for individual subtests
Schrimsher et al. (2005)	202 African American and 110 Caucasian males admitted to a VA-based residential substance use treatment program	Performance of two ethnic groups on individual subtests and failure rate on screening items are compared
Drane et al. (2003)	108 healthy older adults	Used modified version of the Cognistat; Screen items were not administered; Composite score was introduced; Normative data stratified by age and education are provided; Use of a uniform cutpoint for the classification of impairment is not recommended
Eisenstein et al. (2002)	134 healthy elderly	Normative data for the subtest performance for ages 60–85 are provided
Ruchinskas et al. (2001)	86 urban geriatric rehabilitation patients with medical and neurological conditions	Composite and subtest scores were used; Rate of impaired scores for the composite cutoff of 63 were compared for medical and neurologic groups
Wallace et al. (2000)	48 severe TBI patients >1 year postinjury in postacute rehabilitation	Used impaired score on one scale as a cutoff for impairment; Kappa—0.45, sensitivity—92%, specificity—22% in respect to results of NP evaluation
Van Gorp et al. (1999)	22 AD, 19 VaD patients, 12 normal elderly	Discriminatory power was maximized with a criterion for impairment being a score on at least 1 scale falling in the impaired range, in reference to the NINCDS/ADRDA and DSM-III-R diagnostic criteria for the AD and VaD, respectively
Fladby et al. (1999)	50 psychogeriatric patients with late-onset psychiatric disorder	Sensitivity—81%, specificity—60% in respect to the diagnosis of organic brain disorder made by a physician
Cammermeyer and Prendergast (1997)	804 patients from 20 diagnostic groups	Cognistat profiles for different diagnostic categories are illustarted, based on a multicenter database accumulated from seven medical facilities

(continued)

Table 6–2. Continued

Test /Source	Sample/Setting	Findings
Fals-Stewart (1997)	51 detoxified substance- abusing patients	In reference to the Neuropsychological Screening Battery performance, Cognistat demonstrated low sensitivity (64% false-negative rate), but high specificity (14% false-positive rate); The authors do not recommend use of Cognistat in screening substance-abusing patients
Roper et al. (1996)	59 geriatric medical inpatients with diagnosed brain dysfunction, 46 without brain dysfunction	Highest diagnostic accuracy (69%) was achieved at a cutoff of 2 impaired scales

Notes: AD—Alzheimer's disease; VaD—vascular dementia; NINCDS/ADRDA—National Institute of Neurological and Communicative Disorders and Stroke/Alzheimer's Disease and Related Disorders Association; DSM-III-R—Diagnostic and Statistical Manual of Mental Disorders, Third Edition, Revised; MCI—Mild Cognitive Impairment.

copying of two designs. The maximum score is 57, and the cutoff is <25. Administration of this version requires 30–45 minutes, but the inclusion of additional items improves the validity of the test.

Teng and Chui (1987) introduced the Modified Mini-Mental State Examination (3MS), which includes four added items, utilizes a more graded scoring scale leading to an extended range of scores (0–100), and incorporates other minor changes (see Table 6–1). It retains the brevity but improves the sensitivity of certain items.

Subsequent modification, Cognitive Abilities Screening Instrument (CASI), developed by Teng et al. (1994), incorporates MMSE and 3MS, as an adaptation for cross-cultural use (see Table 6–1). It retains the scale of 0–100, which is based on the scores on 25 items.

A telephone version of the MMSE was developed by Roccaforte et al. (1992) for use with geriatric patients. Another version administered over the telephone, Telephone Interview for Cognitive Status-Modified (TICS-m) (King et al., 2006; Welsh et al., 1993), is based on the MMSE, and is typically used in follow-up assessments to track changes after initial MMSE administration (see Table 6–1).

The standard MMSE, with minor subsequent modifications made by the authors, was recently published by Psychological Assessment Resources. The published materials are available in a variety of languages and include alternative item substitutions for administration in special circumstances. The normative data (in T-scores), stratified by age and education level, are provided in addition to recommended cutoff scores. The printed materials are supplemented with software for scoring, interpretation, and report generation.

The MMSE is frequently used in combination with other screening tests. Belle et al. (2000) introduced Short and Sweet Screening Instrument (SASSI), which combines MMSE with verbal fluency and temporal orientation tests (see Table 6–1). Xu et al. (2002) combined MMSE with Cognitive Capacity Screening Exam (CCSE) (Jacobs et al., 1977; see Table 6–1), which resulted in improved sensitivity of the test to mild cognitive impairment as a prodrome for dementia in nondemented elderly. Improved performance of a combined test was also reported by Ferrucci et al. (1996) and Harvan and Cotter (2006), who used MMSE in combination with the Clock Drawing Test (CDT) (Goodglass & Kaplan, 1983; see Table 6–1).

Based on a review of the literature on the accuracy of screening methods in evaluation of dementia, Harvan and Cotter (2006) concluded that the MMSE has high sensitivity and specificity in outpatients older than 65 years when adjustments for age and education are made. Norms stratified by age and education in samples from different countries have been shown to improve diagnostic accuracy (Grigoletto et al., 1999). Furthermore, sensitivity of the MMSE depends on the degree of impairment, and was found to be satisfactory with moderate to severe levels (Moore et al., 2004; Tombaugh & McIntyre, 1992). Tangalos et al. (1996) and Tombaugh and McIntyre (1992) concluded that the MMSE is not appropriate for routine screening of all elderly, but should be used in populations with high base rates (>10%) of cognitive impairment.

Cognistat (Neurobehavioral Cognitive Status Examination, NCSE)

The Cognistat (Kiernan et al., 1987) provides a profile of cognitive status across 10 domains (see Mueller et al., 1988). Most sections, except for Memory and Orientation, use the screen and metric approach. They begin with a screening item that is rather demanding (producing about 20% failure rate in the normal population). If the examinee passes the screen, the particular skill represented by the item is considered to be intact, and the examiner proceeds to assess another skill. If the screening item is failed, questions of graded difficulty are administered to assess the level of competence in this particular skill. Performance within each domain is scored independently, placing the score into intact versus mildly, moderately, or severely impaired level. The results are presented in the form of a graph. Administration time varies between 5 minutes for cognitively intact individuals and 30 minutes for patients with cognitive impairment. Statistical properties of this test with medical and psychiatric populations and in healthy samples are described in a number of articles. Results of selected validation studies are summarized in Table 6–2.

The Cognistat was found to have adequate psychometric properties in geriatric, psychiatric, medical, and traumatic brain injury/stroke rehabilitation samples, and was more sensitive than MMSE and Cognitive Capacity Screening Examination in various samples (see Doninger et al., 2006; Nabors et al., 1997; Oehlert et al., 1997; Ruchinskas et al, 2001). Poon et al. (2005) reported significant relationship between Cognistat performance at initial inpatient rehabilitation in traumatic brain injury patients and clinical outcome one year postinjury.

In spite of an adequate validity of the overall Cognistat performance, several authors argued against the use of the scale profile comparison as an indication of cognitive strengths and weaknesses, due to significant measurement errors (Doninger et al., 2000, 2006; Karzmark, 1997; Marcotte et al., 1997; Wallace et al., 2000). Furthermore, the scale profile was not useful in distinguishing between Alzheimer's disease and vascular dementia samples (Van Gorp et al., 1999), right- and left-hemisphere stroke, nor cortical versus subcortical stroke (Osmon et al., 1992).

A comparison of psychometric properties of the Cognistat across different validity studies is confounded by a lack of agreement on what constitutes the best criterion for cognitive impairment. According to the test authors, the criterion is met when at least one subtest score falls in the impaired range (Mueller et al., 1988). This criterion is consistent with findings by Van Gorp et al. (1999). However, Osato et al. (1993) reported a cutoff of two subtest scores falling in the impaired range as most sensitive to differences in cognitive profiles between depressed patients and patients with organic mental disorders, which is in agreement with Roper et al.'s (1996) report.

The accuracy of the screen and metric approach was questioned by Drane and Osato (1997), Marcotte et al. (1997), Oehlert et al. (1997), and Schrimsher et al. (2005), as screen results are frequently inconsistent with performance on metric items. Several authors recommended that all metric items be administered regardless of performance on the screening items. Drane et al. (2003) abandoned the screen and metric approach and developed a composite score that represents the sum of scores on all metric items across all scales (out of 82). This approach is consistent with the unitary factor underlying Cognistat scales, derived in factor-analytic studies by Engelhart et al. (1999) and Whiteside et al. (1996), possibly representing attention-based general cognitive function.

There is also little agreement on the effect of demographic variables on Cognistat performance. Whiteside et al. (1996) found that test performance is relatively free of age and education effects in a sample of medical patients. Similarly, Blostein et al. (1997) reported no effect of age on test scores in mild traumatic brain injury patients in acute care setting. On the other hand, effect of age was reported by Drane et al. (2003), Macaulay et al. (2003), and Strickland et al. (2005) in large samples of the healthy elderly. Ruchinskas et al. (2001) found that age correlates with Construction and Memory subtests of the Cognistat. Effect of education on the overall performance and subtest scores was reported by Drane et al. (2003), Ruchinskas et al. (2001), and Strickland et al. (2005). Effect of ethnicity was reported by Schrimsher et al. (2005). According to Lampley-Dallas (2001), further studies investigating the effect of ethnicity on Cognistat performance are needed. Effect of the medical condition on test performance was reported by Ruchinskas et al. (2001).

Other Commonly Used Cognitive Screening Measures

The screening tests, summarized in Table 6–1, are grouped into categories, according to the setting and information sought.

1. *General cognitive screening instruments* are based on a face-to-face structured interview with the individual being assessed. A review of Table 6–1 suggests wide variability in administration time, test structure, domains assessed, and outcome measures in these tests. In choosing a screening test that is most appropriate in a given setting, many factors should be considered. Time required for test administration is frequently an important determinant (General Cognitive Screening Instruments are ordered in Table 6–1 in the order of increasing administration time).

Many screening tests are designed to detect dementia in geriatric populations (or specifically screen for Alzheimer's disease, as in the case of *Seven Minute Screen*). Only a few tests are reported to be sensitive to mild cognitive impairment or mild changes in cognition heralding insidious dementia (Mini-Cog, General Practitioner Assessment of Cognition, Kokmen Short Test of Mental Status, Addenbrook's Cognitive Examination-Revised, Repeatable Battery for the Assessment of Neuropsychological Status). The newest additions to this category are DemTect (Kalbe et al., 2004), Montreal Cognitive Assessment (MoCA) (Nasreddine et al., 2005),

and TE4D-Cog (Mahoney et al., 2005), which are not included in Table 6–1.

Several tests are used with medical and psychiatric patients or in primary care settings (Mini-Cog, General Practitioner Assessment of Cognition, Mini-Mental Status Examination, 3MS, Cognitive Capacity Screening Exam, Cognitive Abilities Screening Instrument, Cognistat, Repeatable Battery for the Assessment of Neuropsychological Status). Several tests assess cognitive decline associated with specific medical conditions, such as HIV infection (High Sensitivity Cognitive Screen, HIV Dementia Scale [van Harten et al., 2004], and CogState [Cysique et al., 2006]; the latter two tests are not included in Table 6–1), diffuse organic brain syndrome/delirium (Short Portable Mental Status Questionnaire, Cognitive Capacity Screening Exam), Parkinson's disease and post-cerebrovascular accident (Cambridge Cognitive Examination-Revised), schizophrenia, traumatic brain injury, multiple sclerosis, stroke, and affective disorders (Repeatable Battery for the Assessment of Neuropsychological Status). Additionally, Immediate Post-Concussion Assessment and Cognitive Testing (ImPACT) (Iverson et al., 2003), a computerized screening test, was developed specifically for detection of cognitive changes in athletes with concussions (not included in Table 6–1).

The majority of screening tests provide a global measure of cognitive functioning, whereas several tests yield performance profile across different domains (Addenbrook's Cognitive Examination-Revised, Cognistat, Repeatable Battery for the Assessment of Neuropsychological Status). As different neuropathological conditions differentially affect cognitive functioning, information about the pattern of impairment helps identify subtypes of dementia. Specifically, Addenbrook's Cognitive Examination-Revised capitalizes on assessment of attention/concentration and executive functioning, which makes it most suitable for distinguishing between Alzheimer's and frontotemporal dementia profiles.

Whereas the effect of demographic variables on test performance commonly confounds screening results, several tests are reported to be useful in assessment of multiethnic populations, as they are free of education and language bias (Mini-Cog) or adapted for cross-cultural use (Cognitive Abilities Screening Instrument, Cambridge Cognitive Examination-Revised, Mattis Dementia Rating Scale). Several tests have normative data stratified by demographic groups or corrected for demographic factors (Short Portable Mental Status Questionnaire, Repeatable Battery for the Assessment of Neuropsychological Status).

Two tests utilize a screen and metric approach that reduces assessment time for intact individuals while allowing thorough assessment of those who demonstrate impairment (Cognistat, Mattis Dementia Rating Scale).

Availability of equivalent forms for use at retest facilitates longitudinal follow-up (Memory Impairment Screen, Repeatable Battery for the Assessment of Neuropsychological Status, Mattis Dementia Rating Scale).

The majority of cognitive screening tests have been intended for use in primary or secondary care settings. In contrast, *Short and Sweet Screening Instrument* is specifically developed for community screening.

2. *Brief focused screening instruments* require little time and assess ability that is thought to be representative of general cognitive status. In addition to *Clock Drawing Test* and *Time and Change Test*, included in Table 6–1, popular neuropsychological tests such as Trail-Making Test, Verbal Fluency, Similarities, and Hopkins Verbal Learning Test (see Lezak et al., 2004) are used to detect global cognitive deterioration. However, considering the limited scope of such assessments, these tests should not be administered in isolation, as this would likely result in false-negative misidentifications.

3. *Informant-based screening instruments* are designed to obtain pertinent information about changes in behavior of an individual being evaluated from a person who knows him/her well. *Blessed Dementia Rating Scale* and *General Practitioner Assessment of Cognition* include informant-rated component. *Informant Questionnaire on Cognitive Decline in the Elderly* and *Deterioration Cognitive Observe* provide informant ratings of cognitive decline and changes in activity level over the previous 10 years and 1 year, respectively. When used in conjunction with cognitive assessment, these

tests improve screening accuracy, as they reflect longitudinal change, and bring into the picture everyday cognitive abilities.

4. *Telephone screening instruments* have been developed for use in the context of large epidemiological studies and for a follow-up after face-to-face screening. *Telephone Interview for Cognitive Status* has been shown to improve screening accuracy when used in conjunction with other tests of cognitive functioning. Other screening interviews administered over the phone have been developed (e.g., *TELE* [Jarvenpaa et al., 2002], and *Minnesota Cognitive Acuity Screen, MCAS* [Knopman et al., 2000], both are not included in Table 6–1).

5. A recently introduced category uses *direct observation* of patient's ability to perform certain task related to activities of daily living, such as ability to learn and use a hypothetical daily medication regimen, as assessed with the Medication Management Test (Gurland et al., 1995; not included in Table 6–1).

The interested reader is referred for further information on the utility of cognitive screening tests to comprehensive reviews by Boustani et al. (2003), Brodaty et al. (1998, 2006), Copersino et al. (2003), Cullen et al. (2007), Demakis et al. (2000), Heun et al. (1998), Lorentz et al. (2002), Malloy et al. (1997), Meng (2004), Petersen et al. (2001), Serper and Allen (2002), and Shulman et al. (2006).

Summary

Timely detection of cognitive impairment and the choice of appropriate treatment are facilitated by cognitive screening of those individuals who suffer from medical and neuropsychiatric conditions that are known to affect cognition or who fall in the "at risk" category for cognitive dysfunction. Screening does not lead to a diagnosis but is useful in assessing the need for further diagnostic/neuropsychological workup. It is performed in two settings: (1) by a primary care physician in response to complaints of cognitive symptoms and (2) by a clinician or trained paraprofessional in order to identify individuals in the community who would benefit from a diagnostic evaluation but who have not yet sought medical attention for cognitive symptoms. Whereas advancing age is a known risk factor for cognitive changes, there is little support in the literature for screening all elderly in a general population. Screening is most useful in the populations with the base rates for cognitive impairment exceeding 10% (e.g., residents of assisted care facilities).

A selection of an assessment instrument should be based on its practicality. The use of cognitive screening tests as tools for the detection of cognitive impairment in medical patients and in large populations of individuals at risk is well justified by their ease in administration, familiarity to the clinician, acceptance by the patient, little practice effect, structured format allowing uniformity in administration and scoring, and quantified presentation of the results.

The chosen screening instrument should also have good psychometric properties in identifying cognitive impairment in a specific population. Typical reliability of a screening test, ranging between .80 and .60, is relatively low. However, it is generally acceptable out of considerations of practicality as the cost of error in screening situations is lower than in diagnostic decision making. Criterion-related validity for most of the screening tests is also relatively low, ranging between .2 and .5, due to the imperfect reliability of the test and the reference criterion. Low validity of the test leads to misclassification of "borderline" patients, whereas intact or moderately/severely impaired individuals are likely to be correctly classified.

False-negative misclassifications are common in assessment of mild cognitive impairment, deficits produced by localized brain dysfunction, and in patients with high educational/intellectual level. This type of errors is of concern to a clinician, as reliance on the screening results might deprive the patient of further diagnostic assessment. False-positive misclassifications are commonly produced by low education/literacy levels, and other demographic and performance factors. Aside from economic and emotional considerations, this type of errors is of a lesser concern to the clinician, because the assumption of cognitive impairment can be ruled out in the course of a subsequent workup.

The best balance of false-positive/false-negative misclassifications and optimal trade-off between sensitivity and specificity can be achieved through adjusting cutoff scores relative to the demographic characteristics of the population being screened, and through the use of the area under the receiver operating characteristic curve in determining the most sensitive cutoff, given the prevalence rate of the condition. Incremental validity of a test is highest when the prevalence (base rate) of the condition in the population is moderate, selection ratio is low, and the criterion-related validity of the test is high.

What are the implications of the above discussion for the individual clinician? Screening for cognitive impairment in primary care setting is indicated in cases of self- or informant-reported complaints of cognitive decline and in those individuals who are "at risk" for cognitive impairment (e.g., secondary to a medical condition). The choice of the instruments would depend on the patient population. As the pattern of cognitive impairment varies depending on the nature of the underlying dysfunction, the selection of a screening instrument should be guided by the usefulness of an individual test in detecting deficits in those cognitive domains that are most vulnerable to decline in those medical conditions that are seen in a given clinic. As follows from the above review, certain screening tests have been identified as most sensitive to cognitive impairments secondary to specific conditions, ranging from different types of dementia (those primarily affecting memory vs. executive abilities) to HIV infection.

Because the predictive value of the instruments depends on the prevalence of the disturbance in a given population, norms should be collected locally (within each clinic using the test), based on the performance of patients who are "typical" for this particular population. The distribution of patients' scores on the screening tests should be validated against the neuropsychological test results for these patients or against other reliable criteria. Separate sets of norms should be developed with respect to different age, education, literacy levels, and race groups. This would allow the clinician to adjust the cutoff scores to achieve a reasonable balance between sensitivity and specificity.

In addition to statistical adjustment of the cutoffs for cognitive impairment, decisions regarding the need for a diagnostic workup, especially for patients falling within the "borderline" category, should take into account the patient's behavior and functional level, history, self-report of cognitive functioning, results of functional disability scales, structured direct observations of the patient's efficiency in performing daily tasks, and informants' perceptions of the patient's cognitive functioning as well as recent changes in functional capacity.

Incremental validity of screening assessments might be further improved by supplementing a standard screening examination with additional measures, particularly with tests tapping nonverbal abilities (e.g., Clock Drawing Test, CDT). Moreover, a combination of cognitive screening with a structured informant report (e.g., Informant Questionnaire on Cognitive Decline in the Elderly, IQCODE) improves screening accuracy as it brings into consideration longitudinal changes and cognitive efficiency in daily functioning.

In many clinical settings, it is important to track progression of cognitive symptoms over time to follow-up on "borderline" changes in cognition, to assess the rate of deterioration in progressive conditions or improvement in treatment, and to plan for treatment and discharge in rehabilitation setting. Furthermore, serial evaluations improve diagnostic accuracy in view of a fluctuating course of cognitive disturbance associated with many medical and neuropsychiatric conditions. Whereas cognitive screening measures generate little practice effect, those tests that have equivalent forms would be preferred in situations in which a retest is intended. Other strategies for follow-up assessments should also be considered. For example, a Telephone Interview for Cognitive Status-Revised (TICS-R) has been shown to improve screening accuracy as a follow-up assessment after a face-to-face administration of the Mini-Mental Status Examination (MMSE).

Acknowledgment

Dr. Mitrushina thanks Dr. Paula Altman Fuld for her coauthorship on the earlier version of this chapter that was published in the second edition of this book.

References

Almeida, O. P. (1998). Mini-Mental State Examination and the diagnosis of dementia in Brazil. *Archives of Neuropsychiatry, 56*(3B), 605–612.

American Psychiatric Association. (1980). *Diagnostic and statistical manual of mental disorders, 3rd edition (DSM-III).* Washington, DC: American Psychiatric Association Press.

Anthony, J. C., LeResche, L., Niaz, U., von Korff, M. R., & Folstein, M. F. (1982). Limits of the "Mini-Mental State" as a screening test for dementia and delirium among hospital patients. *Psychological Medicine, 12*(2), 397–408.

Belle, S. H., Mendelsohn, A. B., Seaberg, E. C., & Ratcliff, G. (2000). A brief cognitive screening battery for dementia in the community. *Neuroepidemiology, 19*(1), 43–50.

Bertolucci, P. H., Brucki, S. M., Campacci, S. R., & Juliano, Y. (1994). The Mini-Mental State Examination in a general population: Impact of educational status. *Archives of Neuropsychiatry, 52*(1), 1–7.

Blessed, G., Tomlinson, B. E., & Roth, M. (1968). The association between quantitative measures of dementia and of senile change in the cerebral grey matter of elderly subjects. *British Journal of Psychiatry, 114*(512), 797–811.

Blostein, P. A., Jones, S. J., Buechler, C. M., & Vandongen, S. (1997). Cognitive screening in mild traumatic brain injuries: Analysis of the neurobehavioral cognitive status examination when utilized during initial trauma hospitalization. *Journal of Neurotrauma, 14*(3), 171–177.

Borson, S., Scanlan, J., Brush, M., Vitaliano, P., & Dokmak, A. (2000). The Mini-Cog: A cognitive "vital signs" measure for dementia screening in multi-lingual elderly. *International Journal of Geriatric Psychiatry, 15*(11), 1021–1027.

Borson, S., Scanlan, J. M., Watanabe, J., Tu, S. P., & Lessig, M. (2005). Simplifying detection of cognitive impairment: Comparison of the Mini-Cog and Mini-Mental State Examination in a multi-ethnic sample. *Journal of the American Geriatrics Society, 53*(5), 871–874.

Boswell, E. B., Anfinson, T. J., & Nemeroff, C. B. (2002). Neuropsychiatric aspects of endocrine disorders. In S. C. Yudofsky and R. E. Hales (Eds.), *Textbook of neuropsychiatry and clinical neurosciences* (4th ed., pp. 851–875). Washington, DC: American Psychiatric Publishing.

Boustani, M., Peterson, B., Hanson, L., Harris, R., & Lohr, K. (2003). Screening for dementia in primary care: A summary of the evidence for the U.S. Preventive Services Task Force. *Annals of Internal Medicine, 138*(11), 927–942.

Brandt, J., Spencer, M., & Folstein, M. (1988). The Telephone Interview for Cognitive Status. *Neuropsychiatry, Neuropsychology, & Behavioral Neurology, 1*(2), 111–117.

Brodaty, H., Clarke, J., Ganguli, M., Grek, A., Jorm, A. F., Khachaturian, Z., et al. (1998). Screening for cognitive impairment in general practice: Toward a consensus. *Alzheimer Disease & Associated Disorders, 12*(1), 1–13.

Brodaty, H., Lee-Fay, L., Gibson, L., & Burns, K. (2006). What is the best dementia screening instrument for general practitioners to use? *American Journal of Geriatric Psychiatry, 14*(5), 391–400.

Brodaty, H., Pond, D., Kemp, N. M., Luscombe, G., Harding, L., Berman, K., et al. (2002). The GPCOG: A new screening test for dementia designed for general practice. *Journal of the American Geriatrics Society, 50*(3), 530–534.

Buckwalter, J. G., Crooks, V. C., & Petitti, D. B. (2002). A preliminary psychometric analysis of a computer-assisted administration of the telephone interview of cognitive status-modified. *Journal of Clinical and Experimental Neuropsychology, 24*(2), 168–175.

Buschke, H., Kuslansky, G., Katz, M., Stewart, W. F., Sliwinski, M. J., Eckholdt, H. M., et al. (1999). Screening for dementia with the Memory Impairment Screen. *Neurology, 52*(2), 231–238.

Cammermeyer, M., & Prendergast, V. (1997). Profiles of cognitive functioning in subjects with neurological disorders. *Journal of Neuroscience Nursing, 29*(3), 163–169.

Copersino, M. L., Serper, M., & Allen, M. H. (2003). Rapid screening for cognitive impairment in the psychiatric emergency service: II. A flexible test strategy. *Psychiatric Services, 54*(3), 314–316.

Crum, R. M., Anthony, J. C., Bassett, S. S., & Folstein, M. F. (1993). Population-based norms for the Mini-Mental State Examination by age and educational level. *Journal of the American Medical Association, 269*(18), 2386–2391.

Cullen, B., O'Neill, B., Evans, J. J., Coen, R. F., & Lawlor, B. A. (2007). A review of screening tests for cognitive impairment. *Journal of Neurology, Neurosurgery, and Psychiatry, 78*(8), 790–799.

Cysique, L. A., Maruff, P., Darby, D., & Brew, B. J. (2006). The assessment of cognitive function in advanced HIV-1 infection and AIDS dementia complex using a new computerised cognitive test battery. *Archives of Clinical Neuropsychology, 21*(2), 185–194.

Demakis, G. J., Mercury, M. G., & Sweet, J. J. (2000). Screening for cognitive impairments in primary care settings. In M.E. Maruish (Ed.). *Handbook of Psychological Assessment in Primary Care Settings* (pp. 555–582). London: Lawrence Erlbaum.

Doninger, N. A., Bode, R. K., Heinemann, A. W., & Ambrose, C. (2000). Rating scale analysis of the neurobehavioral Cognitive Status Examination. *Journal of Head Trauma Rehabilitation, 15*(1), 683–695.

Doninger, N. A., Ehde, D. M., Bode, R. K., Knight, K., Bombardier, C. H., & Heinemann, A. W. (2006). Measurement properties of the neurobehavioral cognitive status examination (cognistat) in traumatic brain injury rehabilitation. *Rehabilitation Psychology, 51*(4), 281–288.

Drane, D. L., & Osato, S. S. (1997). Using the Neurobehavioral Cognitive Status Examination as a screening measure for older adults. *Archives of Clinical Neuropsychology, 12*(2), 139–143.

Drane, D. L., Yuspeh, R. L., Huthwaite, J. S., Klingler, L. K., Foster, L. M., Mrazik, M., et al. (2003). Healthy older adult performance on modified version of the Cognistat (NCSE): Demographic issues and preliminary normative data. *Journal of Clinical and Experimental Neuropsychology, 25*(1), 133–144.

Eisenstein, N., Engelhart, C. I., Johnson, V., Wolf, J., Williamson, J., & Losonczy, M. B. (2002). Normative data for healthy elderly persons with the Neurobehavioral Cognitive Status Exam (Cognistat). *Applied Neuropsychology, 9*(2), 110–113.

Elias, M. (1998). Effects of chronic hypertension on cognitive functioning. *Geriatrics, 53*(Suppl 1), S49–S52.

Engelhart, C. I., Eisenstein, N., Johnson, V., Wolf, J., Williamson, J., Steitz, D., et al. (1999). Factor structure of the Neurobehavioral Cognitive Status Exam (COGNISTAT) in healthy, and psychiatrically and neurologically impaired, elderly adults. *Clinical Neuropsychologist, 13*(1), 109–111.

Erkinjuntti, T., Ostbye, T., Steenhuis, R., & Hachinski, V. (1997). The effect of different diagnostic criteria on the prevalence of dementia. *New England Journal of Medicine, 337*(23), 1667–1674.

Eslinger, P. J., Swan, G. E., & Carmelli, D. (2003). Changes in the Mini-Mental State Exam in community-dwelling older persons over 6 years: Relationships to health and neuropsychological measures. *Neuroepidemiology, 22*(1), 23–30.

Fals-Stewart, W. (1997). Detection of neuropsychological impairment among substance-abusing patients: Accuracy of the Neurobehavioral Cognitive Status Examination. *Experimental and Clinical Psychopharmacology, 5*(3), 269–276.

Ferrucci, L., Cecchi, F., Guralnik, J. M., & Giampaoli, S. (1996). Does the clock drawing test predict cognitive decline in older persons independent of the Mini-Mental State Examination? *Journal of the American Geriatrics Society, 44*(11), 1326–1331.

Fisk, J. D., Braha, R., & Walker, A. (1991). The Halifax Mental Status Scale: Development of a new test of mental status for use with elderly clients. *Psychological Assessment, 3*(2), 162–167.

Fladby, T., Schuster, M., Gronli, O., Sjoholm, H., Loseth, S., & Sexton, H. (1999). Organic brain disease in psychogeriatric patients: Impact of symptoms and screening methods on the diagnostic process. *Journal of Geriatric Psychiatry and Neurology, 12*(1), 16–20.

Fogel, B. S. (1991). The high sensitivity cognitive screen. *International Psychogeriatrics. Special Issue: Delirium Advances in Research and Clinical Practice, 3*(2), 273–288.

Folstein, M. F., Folstein, S. E., & McHugh, P. R. (1975). Mini-mental state: A practical method for grading the cognitive state of patients for the clinician. *Journal of Psychiatric Research, 12*(3), 189–198.

Froehlich, T. E., Robison, J. T., & Inouye, S. K. (1998). Screening for dementia in the outpatient setting: The Time and Change test. *Journal of the American Geriatrics Society, 46*(12), 1506–1511.

Fuld, P. A. (1978). Psychological testing in the differential diagnosis of the dementias. In R. Katzman, R. D. Terry, and K. L. Bock (Eds.). *Alzheimer's Disease: Senile Dementia and Related Disorders* (Vol. 7; pp. 185–193). New York: Raven Press.

Ganguli, M. (1997). The use of screening instruments for the detection of dementia. *Neuroepidemiology, 16*(6), 271–280.

Ganguli, M., Ratcliff, G., Chandra, V., Sharma, S., Gilby, J., Pandav, R., et al. (1995). A Hindi version of the MMSE: The development of a cognitive screening instrument for a largely illiterate rural elderly population in India. *International Journal of Geriatric Psychiatry, 10*(5), 367–377.

Gauthier, S., Reisberg, B., Zaudig, M., Petersen, R. C., Ritchie, K., Broich, K., et al. (2006). Mild Cognitive Impairment. *Lancet, 367*, 1262–1270.

Gifford, D. R., & Cummings, J. L. (1999). Evaluating dementia screening tests: Methodologic standards to rate their performance. *Neurology, 52*(2), 225–227.

Goodglass, H., & Kaplan, E. (1983). *The assessment of aphasia and related disorders* (2nd ed.). Philadelphia: Lea and Febiger.

Grigoletto, F., Zappala, G., Anderson, D. W., & Lebowitz, B. D. (1999). Norms for the Mini-Mental State Examination in a healthy population. *Neurology, 53*(2), 315–320.

Gurland, B. J., Wilder, D. E., Chen, J., Lantigua, R., Mayeux, R., & Van Nostrand, J. (1995). A flexible system of detection for Alzheimer's disease and related dementias. *Aging, 7*, 165–172.

Harvan, J. R., & Cotter, V. (2006). An evaluation of dementia screening in the primary care setting. *Journal of the American Academy of Nurse Practitioners, 18*(8), 351–360.

Heun, R., Papassotiropoulos, A., & Jennssen, F. (1998). The validity of psychometric instruments for detection of dementia in the elderly general population. *International Journal of Geriatric Psychiatry, 13*(6), 368–380.

Hodkinson, H. M. (1972). Evaluation of a mental test score for assessment of mental impairment in the elderly. *Age and Aging, 1*, 233.

Iverson, G. L., Lovell, M. R., & Collins, M. W. (2003). Interpreting change on ImPACT following sport concussion. *Clinical Neuropsychologist, 17*(4), 460–467.

Jacobs, J. W., Bernhard, M. R., Delgado, A., & Strain, J. J. (1977). Screening for organic mental syndromes in the medically ill. *Annals of Internal Medicine, 86*, 40–46.

Jarvenpaa, T., Rinne, J. O., Raiha, I., Koskenvuo, M., Lopponen, M., Hinkka, S., et al. (2002). Characteristics of two telephone screens for cognitive impairment. *Dementia and Geriatric Cognitive Disorders, 13*(3), 149–155.

Jorm, A. F. (2004). The Informant Questionnaire on Cognitive Decline in the Elderly (IQCODE): A review. *International Psychogeriatrics, 16*(3), 275–293.

Kahn, R. L., Goldfarb, A. I., & Pollack, M. (1960). Brief objective measures for the determination of mental status in the aged. *American Journal of Psychiatry, 117*, 326.

Kalbe, E., Kessler, J., Calabrese, P., Smith, R., Passmore, A. P., Brand, M., et al. (2004). DemTect: A new, sensitive cognitive screening test to support the diagnosis of mild cognitive impairment and early dementia. *International Journal of Geriatric Psychiatry, 19*(2), 136–143.

Karzmark, P. (1997). Operating characteristics of the Neurobehavioral Cognitive Status Exam using neuropsychological assessment as the criterion. *Assessment, 4*(1), 1–8.

Katzman, R., Brown, T., Fuld, P., Peck, A., Schlechter, R., & Schimmel, H. (1983). Validation of a short Orientation-Memory-Concentration Test of cognitive impairment. *American Journal of Psychiatry, 140*, 734–739.

Kiernan, R. J., Mueller, J., Langston, J. W., & Van Dyke, C. (1987). The Neurobehavioral Cognitive Status Examination: A brief but differentiated approach to cognitive assessment. *Annals of Internal Medicine, 107*, 481–485.

King, J. T., DiLuna, M. L., Cicchetti, D. V., Tsevat, J., & Roberts, M. S. (2006). Cognitive functioning in patients with cerebral aneurysms measured with the Mini-Mental State Examination and the Telephone Interview for Cognitive Status. *Neurosurgery, 59(4)*, 803–810.

Knopman, D. S., Knudson, D., Yoes, M. E., & Weiss, D. J. (2000). Development and standardization of a new telephonic cognitive screening test: The Minnesota Cognitive Acuity Screen (MCAS). *Neuropsychiatry, Neuropsychology, and Behavioral Neurology, 13*(4), 286–296.

Kokmen, E., Naessens, J. M., & Offord, K. P. (1987). A short test of mental status: description and preliminary results. *Mayo Clinic Proceedings, 62*, 281–288.

Kukull, W. A., Larson, E. B., Teri, L., Bowen, J., McCormick, W., & Pfanschmidt, M. L. (1994). The Mini-Mental State Examination score and the clinical diagnosis of dementia. *Journal of Clinical Epidemiology, 47*, 1061–1067.

Lal, B. K. (2007). Cognitive function after carotid artery revascularization. *Vascular and Endovascular Surgery, 41*(1), 5–13.

Lampley-Dallas, V. T. (2001). Neuropsychological screening tests in African Americans. *Journal of the National Medical Association, 93*(9), 323–328.

Lawrence, J., Davidoff, D., Katt-Lloyd, D., Auerbach, M., & Hennen, J. (2001). A pilot program of improved methods for community-based screening for dementia. *American Journal of Geriatric Psychiatry, 9*(3), 205–211.

Lezak, M. D., Howieson, D. B., & Loring, D. W. (2004). *Neuropsychological Assessment* (4th ed.). New York: Oxford University Press.

Lorentz, W. J., Scanlan, J. M., & Borson, S. (2002). Brief Screening Tests for Dementia. *Canadian Journal of Psychiatry, 47*(8), 723–733.

Lourenco, R. A., & Veras, R. P. (2006). Mini-Mental State Examination: Psychometric characteristics in elderly outpatients. *Revista de Saude Publica, 40*(4), 712–719.

Macaulay, C., Battista, M., Lebby, P. C., & Mueller, J. (2003). Geriatric performance on the Neurobehavioral Cognitive Status Examination (Cognistat) what is normal? *Archives of Clinical Neuropsychology, 18*(5), 463–471.

MacKenzie, D. M., Copp, P., Shaw, R. J., & Goodwin, G. M. (1996). Brief cognitive screening of the elderly: A comparison of the Mini-Mental State Examination (MMSE), Abbreviated Mental Test (AMT) and Mental Status Questionnaire (MSQ). *Psychological Medicine, 26*(2), 427–430.

Magni, E., Binetti, G., Cappa, S., Bianchetti, A., & Trabucchi, M. (1995). Effect of age and education on performance on the Mini-Mental State Examination in a healthy older population and during the course of Alzheimer's disease. *Journal of the American Geriatrics Society, 43*(8), 942–943.

Mahoney, R., Johnston, K., Katona, C., Maxmin, K., & Livingston, G. (2005). The TE4D-Cog: a new test for detecting early dementia in English-speaking populations. *International Journal of Geriatric Psychiatry, 20*(12), 1172–1179.

Malloy, P. F., Cummings, J. L., Coffey, C. E., Duffy, J., Fink, M., Lauterbach, E. C., et al. (1997). Cognitive screening instruments in neuropsychiatry: A report of the committee on research of the American Neuropsychiatric Association. *Journal of Neuropsychiatry & Clinical Neurosciences, 9*(2), 189–197.

Marcotte, T. D., van Gorp, W., Hinkin, C. H., & Osato, S. (1997). Concurrent validity of the Neurobehavioral Cognitive Status Exam subtests. *Journal of Clinical and Experimental Neuropsychology, 19*(3), 386–395.

Mattis, S. (1988). *Dementia Rating Scale: Professional manual*. Odessa, FL: Psychological Assessment Resources.

Mayeux, R., Stern, Y., Rosen, J., & Leventhal, J. (1981). Depression, intellectual impairment, and Parkinson disease. *Neurology, 31*, 645–650.

McKhann, G., Drachman, D., Folstein, M., Katzman, R., Prizce, D., & Stadlan, E. M. (1984). Clinical diagnosis of Alzheimer's disease: Report of the NINCDS-ADRDA Work Group under the auspices of Department of Health and Human Services Task Force on Alzheimer's Disease. *Neurology, 34*, 939–944.

Meng, K. (2004). Dementia screening: New developments and the significance for diagnosis in general practice. *Verhaltenstherapie & Psychosoziale Praxis, 36*(4), 757–765.

Meyer, A. (1918). *Outlines of Examinations*. New York: Bloomingdale Hospital Press.

Mioshi, E., Dawson, K., Mitchell, J., Arnold, R., & Hodges, J. R. (2006). The Addenbrooke's Cognitive Examination Revised (ACE-R): A brief cognitive test battery for dementia screening. *International Journal of Geriatric Psychiatry, 21*(11), 1078–1085.

Moore, D. J., Palmer, B. W., & Jeste, D. V. (2004). Use of the Mini-Mental State Exam in middle-aged and older outpatients with schizophrenia: Cognitive impairment and its associations. *American Journal of Geriatric Psychiatry, 12*(4), 412–419.

Mossello, E., & Boncinelli, M. (2006). Mini-Mental State Examinatation: a 30-year story. *Aging: Clinical and Experimental Research, 18*, 271–273.

Mueller, J., Kiernan, R., & Langston, J. W. (1988). The mental status examination. In H. H. Goldman (Ed.), *Review of General Psychiatry*, (2nd ed.). Los Altos: Lange Medical Publications.

Mungas, D., Marshall, S. C., Weldon, M., Haan, M., & Reed, B. R. (1996). Age and education correction of Mini-Mental State Examination for English-and Spanish-speaking elderly. *Neurology, 46*(3), 700–706.

Murden, R. A., McRae, T. D., Kaner, S., & Bucknam, M. E. (1991). Mini-Mental State Exam scores vary with education in Blacks and Whites. *Journal of the American Geriatrics Society, 39*(2), 149–155.

Murkin, J. M. (2005). Neurocognitive outcomes: The year in review. *Current Opinion in Anesthesiology, 18*(1), 57–62.

Murphy, K. R., & Davidshofer, C. O. (1991). *Psychological testing: Principles and applications* (2nd ed.). Englewood Cliffs, New Jersey: Prentice Hall.

Nabors, N. A., Millis, S. R., & Rosenthal, M. (1997). Use of the Neurobehavioral Cognitive Status Examination (Cognistat) in traumatic brain injury. *Journal of Head Trauma Rehabilitation, 12*(3), 79–84.

Nasreddine, Z. S., Phillips, N. A., Bedirian, V., Charbonneau, S., Whitehead, V., Collin, I., et al. (2005). The Montreal Cognitive Assessment, MoCA: A brief screening tool for mild cognitive impairment. *Journal of the American Geriatrics Society, 53*, 695–699.

Oehlert, M. E., Hass, S. D., Freeman, M. R., Williams, M. D., Ryan, J. J., & Sumerall, S. W. (1997). The Neurobehavioral Cognitive Status Examination: Accuracy of the "screen-metric" approach in a clinical sample. *Journal of Clinical Psychology, 53*, 733–737.

Osato, S. S., Yang, J., & La Rue, A. (1993). The Neurobehavioral Cognitive Status Examination in an older psychiatric population: An exploratory study of validity. *Neuropsychiatry, Neuropsychology, & Behavioral Neurology, 6*(2), 98–102.

Osmon, D. C., Smet, I. C., Winegarden, B., & Gandhavadi, B. (1992). Neurobehavioral Cognitive Status Examination: Its use with unilateral stroke patients in a rehabilitation setting. *Archives of Physical Medicine and Rehabilitation, 73*(5), 414–418.

Ostrosky-Solis, F., Lopez-Arango, G., & Ardila, A. (2000). Sensitivity and specificity of the Mini-Mental State Examination in a Spanish-speaking population. *Applied Neuropsychology. Special Issue: Assessment of Spanish-Speaking Populations, 7*(1), 24–31.

Petersen, R. C., & O'Brien, J. (2006). Mild Cognitive Impairment should be considered for DSM-V. *Journal of Geriatric Psychiatry and Neurology, 19*, 147–154.

Petersen, R. C., Stevens, J. C., Ganguli, M., Tangalos, E. G., Cummings, J. L., & DeKosky, S. T. (2001). Practice parameter: Early detection of dementia:

Mild cognitive impairment (an evidence-based review). *Neurology, 56*(9), 1133–1142.

Pfeiffer, E. (1975). A short portable mental status questionnaire for the assessment of organic brain deficit in elderly patients. *Journal of the American Geriatrics Society, 23*, 433–441.

Poon, W. S., Zhu, X. L., Ng, S. C., & Wong, G. K. (2005). Predicting one year clinical outcome in traumatic brain injury (TBI) at the beginning of rehabilitation. *Acta Neurochirurgica, Supplement, 93*, 207–208.

Ramirez, M., Teresi, J. A., Silver, S., Holmes, D., Gurland, B., & Lantigua, R. (2001). Cognitive assessment among minority elderly: Possible test bias. *Journal of Mental Health and Aging, 7*(1), 91–118.

Randolph, C., Tierney, M. C., Mohr, E., & Chase, T. N. (1998). The Repeatable Battery for the Assessment of Neuropsychological Status (RBANS): Preliminary clinical validity. *Journal of Clinical and Experimental Neuropsychology, 20*(3), 310–319.

Ritchie, K., & Fuhrer, R. (1996). The validation of an informant screening test for irreversible cognitive decline in the elderly: Performance characteristics within a general population sample. *International Journal of Geriatric Psychiatry, 11*(2), 149–156.

Roccaforte, W. H., Burke, W. J., Bayer, B. L., & Wengel, S. P. (1992). Validation of a telephone version of the Mini-Mental State Examination. *Journal of the American Geriatrics Society, 40*(7), 697–702.

Roper, B. L., Bieliauskas, L. A., & Peterson, M. R. (1996). Validity of the Mini-Mental State Examination and the neurobehavioral cognitive status examination in cognitive screening. *Neuropsychiatry, Neuropsychology, & Behavioral Neurology, 9*(1), 54–57.

Rosselli, M., Tappen, R., Williams, C., & Salvatierra, J. (2006). The relation of education and gender on the attention items of the Mini-Mental State Examination in Spanish speaking Hispanic elders. *Archives of Clinical Neuropsychology, 21*(7), 677–686.

Roth, M., Huppert, F., Mountjoy, C., & Tym, E. (1999). *The Cambridge examination for mental disorders of the elderly—revised.* Cambridge: Cambridge University Press.

Ruchinskas, R. A., Broshek, D. K., Crews, W. D., Jr., Barth, J. T., Francis, J. P., & Robbins, M. K. (2000). A neuropsychological normative database for lung transplant candidates. *Journal of Clinical Psychology in Medical Settings, 7*(2), 107–112.

Ruchinskas, R. A., & Curyto, K. J. (2003). Cognitive screening in geriatric rehabilitation. *Rehabilitation Psychology, 48*(1), 14–22.

Ruchinskas, R. A., Repetz, N. K., & Singer, H. K. (2001). The use of the neurobehavioral cognitive status examination with geriatric rehabilitation patients. *Rehabilitation Psychology, 46*(3), 219–228.

Salik, Y., Ozalevli, S., & Cimrin, A. H. (2007). Cognitive function and its effects on the quality of life status in the patients with chronic obstructive pulmonary disease (COPD). *Archives of Gerontology and Geriatrics, 45*(3), 273–280.

Sartori, E., Belliard, S., Chevrier, C., Trebon, P., Chaperon, J., & Edan, G. (2006). From psychometry to neuropsychological disability in multiple sclerosis: A new brief French cognitive screening battery and cognitive risk factors. *Revue Neurologique, 162*(5), 603–615.

Schrimsher, G. W., O'Bryant, S. E., Parker, J. D., & Burke, R. S. (2005). The relation between ethnicity and cognistat performance in males seeking substance use disorder treatment. *Journal of Clinical and Experimental Neuropsychology, 27*(7), 873–885.

Serper, M. R., & Allen, M. H. (2002). Rapid screening for cognitive impairment in the psychiatric emergency service: I. Cognitive screening batteries. *Psychiatric Services, 53*(12), 1527–1529.

Shulman, K. I. (2000). Clock-drawing: Is it the ideal cognitive screening test? *International Journal of Geriatric Psychiatry, 15*(6), 548–561.

Shulman, K. I., & Feinstein, A. (2003). *Quick cognitive screening for clinicians.* London: Taylor and Francis Group.

Shulman, K. I., Herrmann, N., Brodaty, H., Chiu, H., Lawlor, B., Ritchie, K., et al. (2006). IPA survey of brief cognitive screening instruments. *International Psychogeriatrics, 18*(2), 281–294.

Solomon, P. R., Hirschoff, A., Kelly, B., Relin, M., Brush, M., DeVeaux, R. D., et al. (1998). A 7 minute neurocognitive screening battery highly sensitive to Alzheimer's disease. *Archives of Neurology, 55*(3), 349–355.

Strickland, T. L., Longobardi, P. G., Alperson, B. L., & Andre, K. (2005). Mini-Mental State and Cognistat performance in an older African American sample. *Clinical Neuropsychologist, 19*(1), 87–98.

Swets, J. A. (1996). Signal detection theory and ROC analysis in psychology and diagnostics: Collected papers. In *Scientific Psychology Series*: Hilsdale, N.J.: Laurence Erlbaum.

Tangalos, E. G., Smith, G. E., Ivnik, R. J., Petersen, R. C., Kokmen, E., Kurland, L. T., et al. (1996). The Mini-Mental State Examination in general medical practice: Clinical utility and acceptance. *Mayo Clinic Proceedings, 71*, 829–837.

Tarter, R. E., Butters, M., & Beers, S. R. (2001). *Medical neuropsychology* (2nd ed.). New York: Kluwer.

Teng, E. L., & Chui, H. C. (1987). The Modified Mini-Mental State (3MS) examination. *Journal of Clinical Psychiatry, 48*(8), 314–318.

Teng, E. L., Hasegawa, K., Homma, A., Imai, Y., Larson, E., Graves, A., et al. (1994). The Cognitive Abilities Screening Instrument (CASI): A practical test for cross-cultural epidemiological studies of dementia. *International Psychogeriatrics, 6*(1), 45–58.

Tombaugh, T. N. (2005). Test–retest reliable coefficients and 5-year change scores for the MMSE and 3MS. *Archives of Clinical Neuropsychology, 20*(4), 485–503.

Tombaugh, T.N., McDowell, I., Kristjansson, B., & Hubley, A. M. (1996). Mini-Mental State Examination (MMSE) and the Modified MMSE (3MS): A psychometric comparison and normative data. *Psychological Assessment, 8*(1), 48–59.

Tombaugh, T. N., & McIntyre, N. J. (1992). The Mini-Mental State Examination: A comprehensive review. *Journal of the American Geriatrics Society, 40*(9), 922–935.

Van den Berg, E., Kessels, R. P., Kappelle, L. J., de Hann, E. H., Biessels, G. J., Utrecht Diabetic Encephalopathy Study Group. (2006). Type 2 diabetes, cognitive function and dementia: Vascular and metabolic determinants. *Drugs Today, 42*(11), 741–754.

Van Gorp, W. G., Ma rcotte, T. D., Sultzer, D., Hinkin, C., Mahler, M., & Cummings, J. L. (1999). Screening for dementia: Comparison of three commonly used instruments. *Journal of Clinical and Experimental Neuropsychology, 21*(1), 29–38.

Van Harten, B., Courant, M. N. J., Scheltens, P., & Weinstein, H. C. (2004). Validation of the HIV Dementia Scale in an elderly cohort of patients with subcortical cognitive impairment causedby subcortical ischaemic vascular disease or a normal pressure hydrocephalus. *Dementia and Geriatric Cognitive Disorders, 18*(1), 109–114.

Wallace, J. J., Caroselli, J. S., Scheibel, R. S., & High, W. M., Jr. (2000). Predictive validity of the neurobehavioural cognitive status examination (NCSE) in a postacute rehabilitation setting. *Brain Injury, 14*(1), 63–69.

Welsh, K. A., Breitner, J. C., & Magruder-Habib, K. M. (1993). Detection of dementia in the elderly using telephone screening of cognitive status. *Neuropsychiatry, Neuropsychology, & Behavioral Neurology, 6*(2), 103–110.

Whiteside, D. M., Padula, M. A., Jeffrey, L. K., & Zetterman, R. (1996). Cognitive screening with the Neurobehavioral Cognitive Status Examination in a chronic liver disease population. *Clinical Neuropsychologist, 10*(4), 459–463.

Xu, G., Meyer, J. S., Thornby, J., Chowdhury, M., & Quach, M. (2002). Screening for mild cognitive impairment (MCI) utilizing combined mini-mental-cognitive capacity examinations for identifying dementia prodromes. *International Journal of Geriatric Psychiatry, 17*(11), 1027–1033.

7

Demographic Influences and Use of Demographically Corrected Norms in Neuropsychological Assessment

Robert K. Heaton, Lee Ryan, and Igor Grant

A primary goal of clinical neuropsychological assessment is to determine whether a given set of test results suggests brain pathology. This is done by comparing a person's performance to available normative standards, which for most tests are based on the results of a "typical" North American sample of neurologically normal adults. Unfortunately, available norms for most neuropsychological tests do not include adjustment for relevant demographic characteristics of the individual being considered. This state of affairs is, quite clearly, a major impediment to adequate clinical assessment of many patients. Consider, for example, a 60-year-old woman with a grade school education, whose first language was Spanish and who began learning English at age 15. It would be quite inappropriate to compare this patient's performances on most neurobehavioral tests with those of the average adult in North America.

In the first edition of this book, our chapter focused on a study assessing the differences in neuropsychological test performance associated with age, education, and sex (Heaton et al., 1986). The results of the study highlighted the pressing need for more complete normative data that take multiple demographic variables into account. Since the publication of that chapter, a substantial amount of work has been done in this area. For this edition we have expanded and updated the previous presentation by reviewing new studies on the effects of demographic variables and by providing information on several recently available sets of demographically

corrected norms for widely used neuropsychological tests. We have added a discussion of the information available on two groups that are served particularly poorly by most available normative data: the very elderly and ethnic minorities. We begin with a review of general issues related to the use of normative data in neuropsychological assessment.

"Normality" and Adequate

Normative Data

The debate over what constitutes "normal" is clearly a central issue for neuropsychologists. In determining whether an individual's test performance is the result of brain disorder, it is essential to distinguish that performance from normal variations in cognitive ability. Neuropsychological assessment's most straightforward task is to identify a complete *loss of function* secondary to brain damage. The resulting behavior falls well outside the range of ability for the entire normal population and thus is relatively simple to detect. Examples of a loss of function include visual agnosia (the inability to identify common objects visually despite intact visual functioning) and facial apraxia (the loss of motor programs for facial expression). More often, however, neuropsychologists are asked to determine whether an *impairment in function* has occurred; that is, whether test performance constitutes a change in normal functioning *for the individual*. Such a judgment should not be taken lightly as it may have a major impact on an individual's medical evaluation and treatment, self-esteem, family functioning, independence, and access to future opportunities and resources. These judgments are based primarily on tests developed by researchers of a particular cultural, educational, and socioeconomic stratum. An individual's test performance is judged, perforce, in comparison to some standard that the clinician chooses. We espouse a relativistic approach to normality (and hence abnormality), where normal is defined as the range of behaviors and abilities within a group of like individuals who share social, educational, cultural, and generational backgrounds. Western Caucasian middle- to upper-class clinicians cannot assume that their own demographically defined group may be used as a definitive standard.

The purpose of normative data is to provide information on the range of an ability within a specifically defined, neurologically normal population. The clinical utility of norms will depend on several factors, including the representativeness of the normative sample, the goodness of fit between the individual and the normative sample, and the degree to which the norms consider demographic variables that account for normal variations in test performance. Each of these factors will be discussed below.

First, an adequate normative sample must be representative of the general population; that is, the scores included in the data set are assumed to be an unbiased sample of the population of interest. Often, normative standards are derived from small sample sizes that result in poor classification rates when applied to larger samples. For example, the Russell et al. (1970) norms for the Halstead–Reitan Battery (HRB)were originally based on a combination of clinical judgment and the test results of a sample of 26 neurologically normal subjects. Large sample size alone, however, does not ensure representativeness. Methods of recruitment, sampling techniques, inclusion and exclusion criteria, and compliance rates are all critical factors in assessing possible sources of bias in a sample (for discussion, see Anastasi, 1988). Erickson et al. (1992) have pointed out that sampling procedures in normative studies are quite often opportunistic, making use of a population at hand rather than being expressly designed to create an unbiased sample. This practice may result in biases in the sample that are difficult to detect. Publications of standardization samples should thus provide a description of the sampling procedures and subject recruitment procedures employed in the study, as well as rates of subject compliance, so that clinicians may make informed judgments regarding the generalizability of published norms.

Second, assessing whether norms are appropriate for an individual requires sufficient knowledge of the characteristics of the subject sample. The description of the criteria for subject inclusion will define the population from which the sample was drawn, and will essentially constitute the researchers' definition of normality. Important characteristics may include the following: (1) the numbers of subjects in various strata of demographic variables such as age, education, socioeconomic status, and ethnic group; (2) whether the subjects were living independently in the community; (3) current or past histories of factors that might influence cognitive performance, including chronic illness, significant medical history (including head trauma), drug and alcohol use, prescription drug use, and psychiatric diagnoses; and (4) whether there was any independent screening (e.g., mental status exam) to rule out serious cognitive disturbance.

Finally, the utility of norms will depend on whether demographic variables that have a significant impact on test performance have been adequately considered. Performance on most neuropsychological tests are significantly related to the subject's age, education, ethnicity, and, for a few tests, sex (Heaton et al., 1991; Parsons & Prigatano, 1978). The influence of demographic factors is apparent for neurologically normal individuals as well as for those who have cerebral disorders (Finlayson et al., 1977; Reitan, 1955). Unfortunately, as Lezak (1987) notes, despite decades of awareness of the effects of demographic variables, most psychological and neuropsychological tests in common use today do not stratify their samples on or otherwise correct for these variables. Even for test norms that stratify subject groups on age or education, information concerning the effects of such factors in combination often is lacking. Also potentially important is the issue of how recently norms were collected. Demographic and cultural factors cannot be assumed to be comparable for groups of subjects who were tested decades apart. For example, cross-sectional studies may overestimate age effects by confounding these with educational, nutritional, or occupational differences among groups of subjects from different generations (Anastasi, 1988). Successive generations may differ in language patterns and problem-solving styles (Albert, 1981), or perhaps along dimensions that have not yet been identified (Flynn, 1984, 1987). Thus, norms collected 20 years ago, even if they take into account age and education, may contain systematic errors in current use.

While gathering normative data is a time-consuming and labor-intensive enterprise, the importance of such research cannot be overemphasized. Standardization samples that provide adequate descriptions of sampling methods and subject characteristics and that are stratified on or otherwise corrected for important demographic variables are critical to clinical neuropsychology. Expanded and updated norms will continue to be needed as society evolves over time.

Demographic Influences on Test Performance: Age, Education, Sex

Age

Of the instruments considered in this chapter, by far the most well known and widely used are the various versions of the Wechsler Adult Intelligence Scale (Wechsler, 1955, 1981, 1997a) and Wechsler Memory Scale (Wechsler, 1945, 1987, 1997b). Findings with the standardization samples of all of these versions reflect lower average performances for each successive age group tested after their mid-thirties. Age differences are more pronounced for nonverbal than for verbal subtests, reflecting the fact that different abilities change at different rates; in the "classic pattern," verbal skills and well-learned information hold up best over time, while perceptual-integrative and psychomotor skills decline the most with advancing age (Botwinick, 1967; Leckliter & Matarazzo, 1989).

Co-norming of the third editions of the Wechsler Adult Intelligence Scale (WAIS-III)

and Wechsler Memory Scale (WMS-III) has allowed the identification of six cognitive factors that are assessed by the combined Wechsler batteries: Verbal Comprehension, Working Memory, Perceptual Organization, Processing Speed, Auditory Memory, and Visual Memory (Tulsky et al., 2003). Subsequently, Heaton et al. (2003) assessed age effects on education-corrected WAIS-III/WMS-III factor scores of standardization sample subjects over the age of 19 years. Consistent with earlier studies, there was virtually no age effect on the Verbal Comprehension factor (R square < .01), whereas very large age effects were seen on Processing Speed and Visual Memory (R square = .45 in each case). Smaller, but still substantial, age effects occurred on the remaining factors (R squares of .27, .24, and .20 for Perceptual Organization, Working Memory, and Auditory Memory, respectively).

Performances on most of the individual tests in the HRB also show a significant negative relationship with age (Reitan, 1955, 1957; Vega & Parsons, 1967). Reitan warned that after age 45 many normals score in Halstead's brain-damaged range on the Impairment Index. As an illustration, Price et al. (1980) studied a group of 49 retired, healthy schoolteachers (mean age, 72 years) and found that 56% of the subjects scored in the impaired range according to the then-standard norms on the HRB. Considerable variability was seen in the number of subjects misclassified as brain-damaged by the different subtests in the battery (ranging from 18% to 90%). Thus, impaired performance on the HRB appears to occur with most but not all normal elderly subjects, and age-related deficits are more pronounced on some tests than on others. In their review of the literature, Reitan and Wolfson (1986) concluded that age effects on the HRB are found primarily in complex, novel tasks that require reasoning, abstraction, and logical analysis, while tests related to prior learning, past experience, and language ability are generally spared.

Interestingly, Yeudall et al. (1987) did not find a strong association between age and HRB performance with subjects below the age of 40. In a sample of 225 community-recruited males and females between the ages of 15 and 40 years, correlation coefficients ranging from .00 to .27

were reported on various subtests. The evidence suggests that, as with the Wechsler scales, age becomes an increasingly important factor in the fourth decade and beyond. It should be noted, however, that decreased performance in later years may not be solely attributable to age but may also be due to generational differences in education, health services, access to media information, and many other factors. Because the majority of studies in this area are cross-sectional rather than longitudinal, the presence of mediating factors other than age cannot be ruled out.

Education

Performance on the Wechsler Intelligence Scales is strongly correlated with educational achievement, hardly a surprising finding given that the original purpose of intelligence tests was to predict academic success (Anastasi, 1988). Matarazzo (1972) reported a Pearson correlation of .70 between highest grade completed and WAIS IQ; Matarazzo and Herman (1984) reported a correlation of .54 for the WAIS-R standardization sample of 16- to 74-year-olds. The latter correlation appeared to be spuriously lowered because of the inclusion of 16- to 24-year-olds, many of whom had not yet completed their education. When this age group was excluded, the correlation between IQ and years of education increased to .62. Kaufman et al. (1988) also observed that education effects were less prominent in the youngest age group (16–19 years), since education effects are attenuated among individuals who are still actively participating in the educational system. Examining the WAIS-R standardization sample, Reynolds et al. (1987) reported significant differences across education groups for Verbal, Performance, and Full-Scale mean IQs. These IQ scores varied from 26 to 33 points between the lowest education group (less than 8 years) and the highest (16 years or more). In contrast to age effects, Kaufman et al. (1988) found that education had more of an impact on verbal than nonverbal tests.

Heaton et al. (2003) explored education effects on age-adjusted WAIS-III/WMS-III factor scores, again using the joint standardization sample for those batteries. Again, teenagers were excluded because many of them were still in school when they were tested. Significant education effects were seen on all WAIS-III/WMS-III factors. These were largest on Verbal Comprehension (R square = .32), Perceptual Organization (R square = .18), and Processing Speed (R square = .17), but education effects also occurred on Working Memory, Auditory Memory, and Visual Memory (respective R squares = .11, .09, and .08). In general, then, education effects were largest on measures of intellectual abilities, and more modest on measures of episodic memory.

However, how clinically important are these education effects on the WAIS-III/WMS-III factors? To explore this question, Heaton et al. (2003) applied a 1-SD cutoff to define "impairment" on age-corrected factor scores. (The choice of this cutoff is evaluated and discussed in Taylor & Heaton, 2001.) False-positive error rates (normals misclassified as "impaired") were computed for five education subgroups within the national standardization sample: 16+ years (college graduates), 13–15 years (some college), 12 years (high school graduates), 9–11 years (some high school), and ≤9 years (less than high school). The probability of being *misclassified* as impaired in these respective education groups ranged from 2% to 45% for Verbal Comprehension, 4–40% for Perceptual Organization, 3–37% for Processing Speed, 6–31% for Working Memory, 6–28% for Auditory Memory, and 6–27% for Visual Memory. From these results, it is clear that use of the standard, age-corrected factor scores to classify neuropsychological impairment leads to widely different diagnostic accuracy, especially for people with relatively high (16+ years) and low (<9 years) education levels. Although one might be tempted to conclude from these results that classification accuracy is "better" for highly educated persons, it is important to recognize that this is true only for the *specificity* side of the equation. Since specificity and sensitivity of classification cutoffs tend to be inversely related, it can be expected that use of the standard, age-corrected scores will have the "worst" classification accuracy with highly educated persons who have acquired cognitive abnormalities (Taylor & Heaton, 2001).

Historically, the relationship between education and HRB performance has been less well documented. For example, Finlayson et al. (1977) tested normal individuals with grade school (less than 10 years), high school (grade 12, without college experience), and university level (at least 3 years' college experience) education. They found significant differences between the groups on the Category Test, the Seashore Rhythm Test, Speech-Sounds Perception Test, and Trail Making A and B. No effect of education was evident on the Tactual Performance Test or Finger Tapping. With three similar groups of brain-damaged individuals, education effects were less pronounced, and were significant only on the Seashore Rhythm Test and Speech-Sounds Perception Test. Finlayson et al. (1977) suggested that the effects of brain damage may produce sufficient decreases in performance to "wash out" the effects of education.

Vega and Parsons (1967) reported Pearson correlations between years of education and HRB subtest performance as high as .58 for Speech-Sounds Perception Test, .58 for the Seashore Rhythm Test, and .45 for errors on the Category Test. When the effects of education were partialled out, the correlations between the HRB subtests and age weakened, but remained significant, suggesting two independent sources of performance variability. In reviewing the extant literature, Leckliter and Matarazzo (1989) concluded that although correlation coefficients were generally lower between years of education and HRB performance compared to age and HRB performance, highly educated individuals consistently performed better than those individuals with fewer years of education.

The Rate of Age-Related Decline

A question addressed in several previous studies is whether the rate of age-related cognitive decline is linked to subjects' initial level of functioning or socioeconomic status (education, occupation). In reviewing this literature, Botwinick (1967) noted that cross-sectional studies have provided some inconsistent evidence that subjects with lower initial ability and lower occupational status show greater age-related impairment on some tests. The available longitudinal studies do not support this hypothesis. However, these studies are limited by the use of a restricted range of tests over relatively brief age ranges and by the selective attrition of initially less able subjects. Birren and Morrison (1961) found no significant age-by-education interaction effects using data from the WAIS standardization sample. A similar pattern is apparent for the WAIS-R standardization sample (Reynolds et al., 1987), but no statistical analyses were done to assess the interactions between age and education. The possibility of interactions between age and education on the HRB had not been investigated prior to our exploration of the issue for the first edition of this book (see below).

Gender

Research on gender differences in ability has found males and females to be equivalent in general intelligence. Reynolds et al. (1987) did not find that the sexes differed significantly on any of the three summary scores on the WAIS-R. Sex differences on the WAIS and WAIS-R were minimized by design, in that questions that produced clear-cut sex differences were excluded or counterbalanced during the developmental stages of the tests (Matarazzo, 1972, 1986). Nevertheless, on tests of specific ability areas, some sex differences are found. Males tend to do better on tests that involve manipulating spatial relationships, quantitative skills, physical strength, and simple motor speed, whereas females show advantages on tests of certain verbal abilities (for review, see Buffery & Gray, 1972; Maccoby & Jacklin, 1974). For example, on the HRB, Fromm-Auch and Yeudall (1983) found that women were slower on Finger Tapping than men and men had stronger grip strength on the Dynamometer than women for both dominant and nondominant hands.

Heaton et al. (2003) compared males and females within the joint WAIS-III/WMS-III standardization sample on the six-factor scores, which had been corrected for both age and education. Modest mean z-score differences favoring males were seen on Verbal Comprehension ($z = .25$), Perceptual Organization ($z = .17$), and Working Memory ($z = .15$), whereas slightly larger differences favoring women occurred on

Processing Speed ($z = .36$) and the two episodic memory factors (Auditory Memory $z = .25$ and Visual Memory $z = .22$). At most, these gender differences translated into only about a 5% difference in test score specificity for men and women.

Halstead–Reitan Normative Data Pool

In the first edition of this book, we presented a study that highlighted the importance of demographic variables for performance on the WAIS and an extended version of the HRB. The main points of the study will be discussed here; the reader is referred to the original chapter for more details (Heaton et al., 1986). The goal of the study was to address the issue of how performance on the various neuropsychological tests relates to age and education when high and low values of these demographic factors were adequately represented in the subject sample. Which tests are more sensitive to age effects and which appear to be more related to educational attainment? Are there significant age-by-education interaction effects on tests in the battery and, if so, are they consistent with the hypothesis that better-educated groups show less age-related decline in neuropsychological functioning? How well or how poorly does a previously published set of HRB norms work for groups of normal subjects at different age and education levels? Finally, which tests in the battery show significant sex differences, and are these differences large enough to necessitate developing separate norms for males and females?

Subjects and Methods

Subjects consisted of all normal controls (356 males and 197 females) for whom there were complete WAIS and HRB data available at the neuropsychology laboratories of the University of Colorado ($N = 207$), University of California at San Diego ($N = 181$), and the University of Wisconsin ($N = 165$) Medical Schools. None of the subjects had any history of neurological illness, significant head trauma, or substance abuse. Forty subjects (7.2%) were left-handed and

513 were right-handed. Their ages ranged from 15 to 81 years, with a mean of 39.3 (SD = 17.5 years). Years of education ranged from zero (no formal education) to 20 (doctoral degree), with a mean of 13.3 (SD = 3.4) years. For analyses designed to assess age-by-education interaction effects, subjects were divided into three age categories (<40 years, 40–59 years, and ≥60 years) and three education categories (<12 years, 12–15 years, and ≥16 years). Respectively, the total numbers of subjects in the three age categories were 319, 134, and 100, and in the three education categories, 132, 249, and 172. All nine age/education subgroups included over 25 subjects except for the high age/high education category ($n = 17$).

In order to assess sex differences in neuropsychological test performance, males and females were individually matched within 5 years in age and within 2 years in education. This resulted in 177 matched pairs, well matched on mean age (36.6 for males, 36.7 for females) and education (13.2 for males, 13.1 for females).

All subjects were tested by trained technicians, and all were rated as having put forth adequate effort on their evaluations. The 11 subtests of the WAIS and an expanded HRB were administered. The latter battery has been described elsewhere (Reitan & Wolfson, 1986) and included the Category Test, Tactual Performance Test (Time, Memory, and Location components), Seashore Rhythm Test, Speech-Sounds Perception Test, Aphasia Screening Exam, Trail-Making Test, Spatial Relations Assessment, Sensory-Perceptual Exam, Tactile Form Recognition Test, Finger Tapping Test, Hand Dynamometer, and Grooved Pegboard Test.

Scores for the WAIS subtests were regular scaled scores (not age-corrected). The Russell et al. (1970) scoring system was used for the Aphasia Screening Exam, Spatial Relations, Sensory-Perceptual Exam, and Average Impairment Rating. In addition, the cutoff scores provided in the Russell et al. (1970) book were used to determine how many subjects in the different age and education categories were correctly classified as normal by the Average Impairment Rating and each of its component test measures.

Results

Age Effects

Figure 7–1 shows the percentage of variance accounted for by age (R square) on each test measure. All the correlations between test measures and age were significant ($p < .05$), with the exception of Vocabulary and Hand Dynamometer, and consistently indicated poorer performance associated with older age. Among the Wechsler subtests, substantial age effects were apparent on Digit Symbol and Picture Arrangement, whereas age showed minimal relationship with performance on Vocabulary, Information, and Comprehension. Performance on several of the HRB tests was strongly related to age, particularly for measures of psychomotor speed, conceptual ability, flexibility of thought, and incidental memory. In contrast, scores on HRB tests of language skills and simple sensory and motor abilities showed relatively weak associations with age.

Education Effects

Education significantly correlated with all WAIS and HRB measures, indicating better performance with higher education levels. Figure 7–2

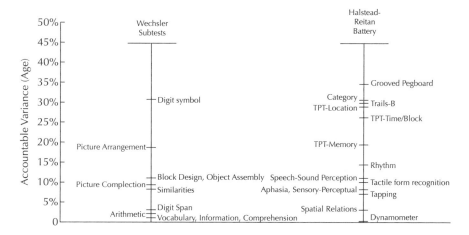

Figure 7–1. Percentage of test variance accounted for by age.

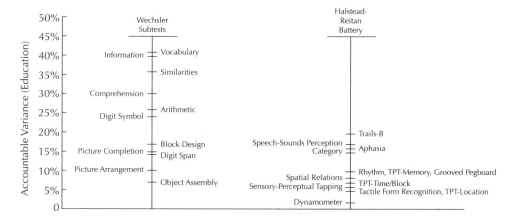

Figure 7–2. Percentage of test variance accounted for by education.

shows the percentage variance in each test accounted for by education (R squared). Even for measures of simple motor and sensory functions, better test performance was associated with higher previous educational attainment. In contrast to the results shown previously for age, education level was most strongly related to scores on the WAIS Verbal subtests, and somewhat less related to scores on the HRB. Consistent with this, within the HRB, correlations were highest with tests of language skills, conceptual ability, and cognitive flexibility.

Tests Showing Relatively Greater Age or Education Sensitivity

Figure 7–3 shows for each test measure the difference between the amount of variance accounted for by age versus education. In general, WAIS subtests tend to be more education related, and the HRB subtests tend to be more age related. Not surprisingly, within both batteries tests of verbal skills and previously accumulated knowledge are more education related, whereas

nonverbal tests of psychomotor speed and/or new problem solving are more age related.

The Interaction Between Age and Education

The 3 × 3 analyses of variance (ANOVAs) performed on all test measures produced age and education main effects that were in agreement with the results of the correlational analysis. That is, tests previously found to be more age related or more education related were similarly classified by these analyses. In addition, significant age-by-education interaction effects were obtained on WAIS Comprehension, Picture Completion, Block Design, Picture Arrangement, as well as on the HRB Impairment Index, Average Impairment Rating, Category Test (errors), Trail Making B, TPT Memory and Location, and Speech-Sounds Perception.

Three possible patterns of age-by-education interaction might be expected: (1) subjects with the most education show less age-related impairment; (2) subjects in the lowest education

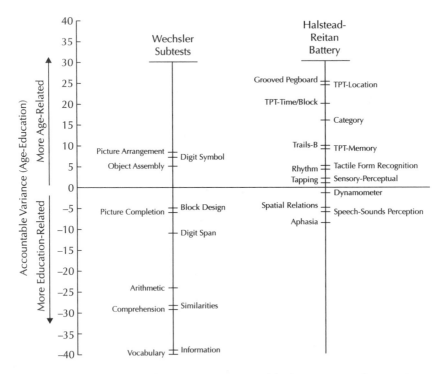

Figure 7–3. Difference in percentage of test variance accounted for by age versus education (i.e., age variance minus education variance).

group show more age-related impairment; and (3) a regression toward the mean occurs, with less effect of education between older groups than between younger groups. These three patterns are not necessarily mutually exclusive. A test may be consistent with pattern (1) or (2) across the first two age levels, but fit pattern (3) between the second and third age levels.

To explore the possible patterns of interaction effects, mean test scores of subgroups at each education level were plotted across the three age levels. While it is tempting to consider this type of graph to be a longitudinal view of how groups at each education level may change with advancing age, it must be recognized that the curves do not reflect *change* in any direct sense, as each point on the graph reflects the performance of a separate subject group that was tested only once.

Several of these graphs are presented here. Figure 7–4 summarizes the data on Vocabulary, a test that is known to show little change in older age groups. The curves for each education level indicated no significant age-related decrease in test performance. Furthermore, the comparability of the three age subgroups within education levels suggests that the subgroups were fairly well matched in terms of previously learned information.

In contrast, consider the graphs for two WAIS subtests that have significant age-by-education interaction effects (see Figures 7–5

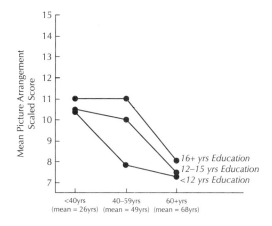

Figure 7–5. Results of groups in nine age/education categories on WAIS Picture Arrangement.

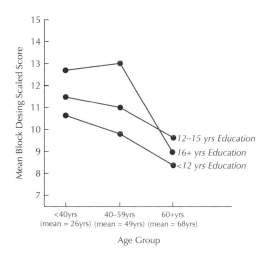

Figure 7–6. Results of groups in nine age/education categories on WAIS Block Design.

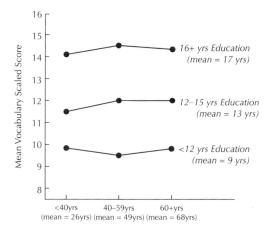

Figure 7–4. Results of groups in nine age/education categories on WAIS Vocabulary test.

and 7–6). On Picture Arrangement, the results across the first two age levels suggested more age-related impairment for the least educated subgroup, consistent with pattern (2) above. On Block Design, the curves across the first two age levels were more consistent with pattern (1), suggesting less age-related impairment for the subgroup with 16+ years of education. On both of these subtests, however, the curves from the second to the third age level fit pattern (3); that is, there was less difference between education subgroups at the older age level. Other tests, including Trail Making B and the Category Test

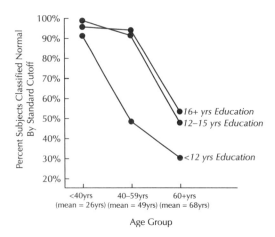

Figure 7–7. Results of groups in age/education categories: percentage classified as normal by Average Impairment Rating.

showed patterns similar to Picture Arrangement; that is, they showed pattern (2) between the first two age levels and pattern (3) between the second and third age levels.

The final graph (Figure 7–7) shows the percentage of subjects classified as normal by the Average Impairment Rating. This pattern was apparent for most standard cutoff scores for the test measures in the HRB. The results indicate that the cutoff scores are adequate for all education subgroups at the first age level. At the second age level the cutoffs misclassify only a few more normal subjects in the two higher education subgroups, but misclassify the majority of the subjects in the lower education subgroup. Finally, although a significant minority of subjects in the oldest subgroup still perform at a level that would be considered normal for a young adult, the vast majority of the subjects in this age group are misclassified as "brain-damaged." It is apparent that the standard cutoffs are not appropriate as norms for most subjects over the age of 60 or, equally important, for most subjects with less than a high school education, regardless of their age.

Sex Effects

T-tests for paired samples were used to compare results of our matched male and female groups on all WAIS and HRB measures. There was virtually no difference between these groups on any WAIS IQ value or HRB summary score. Thus, the males and females were comparable with respect to general intelligence and overall neuropsychological functioning. On individual tests, as expected, males did much better ($p < .001$) with each hand on tests of motor speed (Finger Tapping Test) and grip strength (Hand Dynamometer). Differences were also obtained on the Tactual Performance Test and the Aphasia Screening Exam that were not expected, but are consistent with the general psychological literature on sex differences in normals. Males did significantly better ($p < .05$) on the TPT Total Time score (13.5 minutes versus 15.6 minutes for females). However, the females showed an advantage ($p < .001$) on the Aphasia Screening Exam, obtaining a mean error score of 2.7 versus 4.0 for males. Finally, there was a statistically significant ($p < .05$) but clinically trivial difference on the WAIS Comprehension subtest (mean scores of 12.7 for females and 12.1 for males).

WAIS versus WAIS-R versus WAIS-III Patterns

The WAIS has been replaced in clinical practice by the WAIS-R in 1981 and by the WAIS-III in 1997. Albert and Heaton (1988) reported findings similar to those described above on the WAIS-R subtests. They compared the results of the WAIS-R standardization sample with results of 543 adults who were given the WAIS. Similar relationships were obtained between test performance and both age and education on the two versions of the Wechsler Adult Intelligence Scales. The relationship of scores to education was the inverse of that to age, education correlating more highly with Verbal measures than with Performance measures. Once again, the effect of sex on test performances appeared too small to be of clinical significance. Similar findings have been noted above for the WAIS-III.

Specificity versus Sensitivity

A separate but extremely important issue in developing normative data is to know the usefulness of a test in distinguishing groups with known brain dysfunction from the normative sample group. That is, in addition to knowing the likelihood of correctly classifying normal individuals, the neuropsychologist needs to know the sensitivity of the norms, or the true positive classification rate for people with various cerebral disorders. In the present study, correct classification rates for the normal group (described earlier) were compared with those of the 382 brain-damaged subjects. All subjects in the patient group were clinical referrals for neuropsychological testing, and all had structural brain abnormalities that were verified with appropriate neuroradiological procedures (primarily computerized tomographic scans and magnetic resonance image scans). They had a mean age of 43.7 years (SD = 1.0) and a mean of 12.9 years (SD = 3.1) of formal education; 249 (65.2% of the sample) were males. The most frequent diagnoses were closed head injury ($n = 73$), cerebrovascular accident ($n = 65$), intrinsic tumor ($n = 49$), Alzheimer's disease ($n = 48$), extrinsic tumor ($n = 30$), hydrocephalus ($n = 23$), infectious or toxic encephalopathies ($n = 22$), penetrating head injury ($n = 18$), multiple sclerosis ($n = 9$), and cerebral anoxia ($n = 8$); other etiologies included vascular malformations, epilepsy with structural abnormalities, other dementias, and depressed skull fractures ($n = 37$).

Table 7–1 lists the percentages of the normal and brain-damaged subjects in six age and education subgroups who were correctly classified on the HRB Average Impairment Rating using the Russell et al. (1970) normative criteria. Within the normal group, the percentage of subjects correctly classified as normal decreases with age, but increases with education. In contrast, the *opposite* pattern is evident for the brain-damaged group. Generally, the standard

Average Impairment Rating cutoff is relatively poor at identifying brain-damaged individuals who are young and/or well educated. In the older samples, more brain-damaged subjects are correctly classified (from 55% at <40 years to 94% at 60+ years of age), while as education increases, fewer subjects are correctly classified as brain-damaged (from 87% at <12 years to 60% at 16+ years of education).

This comparison highlights the need for validation of normative data and classification cut points on known brain-damaged groups, as well as on normal controls at different levels of age and education. The Russell et al. (1970) norms obtain fairly good (and balanced) sensitivity and specificity at middle levels of age and education, but at the extremes of these demographic variables, result in unacceptable percentages of false-positive or false-negative errors.

Implications

The results of our study accord well with Cattell's (1963) distinction between "fluid" and "crystallized" intelligence. Crystallized intelligence is measured by tests of knowledge and skills that were acquired in previous learning experiences. Crystallized intelligence develops rapidly during the first 20 years of life and then levels off, remaining relatively stable over the ensuing decades. Thus, performance on tests such as Information or Vocabulary from the various WAIS versions does not decline with age, although it is clearly related to level of education. By contrast, fluid intelligence is considered most dependent upon biological factors such as the normal development and continued integrity of the central nervous system (CNS). This form of intelligence is measured by tasks

Table 7–1. Percentage of Subjects (553 Normal Control Subjects and 382 Brain-damaged Subjects) in Six Age and Education Subgroups who were Correctly Classified as Normal or Brain-Damaged by the Russell et al. (1970) Criteria on the Average Impairment Rating from the Halstead-Reitan Battery

	Age (in years)			Education (in years)		
	<40	40–59	60+	<12	12–15	16+
Normal Controlled Subjects	97% (n = 319)	84% (n = 134)	39% (n = 100)	58% (n = 132)	90% (n = 249)	93% (n = 172)
Brain-Damaged Subjects	55% (n = 167)	83% (n = 138)	94% (n = 77)	87% (n = 99)	71% (n = 191)	60% (n = 92)

requiring learning, conceptual, and problem-solving operations within the context of novel situations. Speed of responding and spatial "visualization" skills may be required in certain tests of fluid intelligence, but are not integral parts of this ability factor. Rather, these might be considered as separate ability factors under the rubric of "information-processing efficiency" (Shallice, 1988). Horn and Cattell (1966) presented data to suggest that fluid intelligence develops as the result of biological maturation and reaches its peak in the late teens or early twenties. This form of intelligence is expected to deteriorate at a rate that is dependent upon various accumulating insults to the CNS that occur during the life span of the individual. Thus, decline in performance on tests such as the Category Test, Block Design, or Picture Arrangement is not attributable to age per se, but to the prevalence of accumulated CNS insults in older groups. Hence, it is possible for healthy older individuals to show very little decline in cognitive functioning.

The results of the study suggest that different patterns of age-related decline in fluid intelligence occur for groups with different educational levels. Groups at the lowest education level showed greatest cognitive decline between the young and middle-age periods. However, the better-educated group tended to "catch up" by the later age period. At older ages, the level of functioning was not much different between the three education levels. Once again, these age-by-education interaction effects occurred only on certain test measures, mostly those of the fluid intelligence variety.

There are several possible explanations why such age-by-education interaction effects might occur. First, subjects with lower education and lower socioeconomic status may tend to have less optimal health care, resulting in a higher prevalence during middle age of health problems that compromise brain function (e.g., high blood pressure). It might also be that people in the higher education groups tend to have better-functioning CNSs to begin with and, as a result, are more resilient to absolute losses in CNS integrity or the presence of pathology associated with disorders of aging, a notion referred to as cognitive reserve (Stern et al., 2003). A third possibility is that subjects in the lower

education subgroups tend to have less intellectually stimulating jobs and general life styles, so that fluid intelligence declines faster due to "disuse" during the middle-age years; better-educated subjects might then catch up due to increasing disuse during their retirement years. The latter hypothesis is attractive because it suggests that intellectually stimulating activities may sustain fluid intelligence in old age. We note once again that these data derive from a cross-sectional design. As such, they demonstrate age-related differences in abilities, but not age-related changes in ability. Longitudinal studies are needed to establish that changes have occurred.

Age- and Education-Corrected Norms

Clearly, demographic variables such as age, education, and sex should be considered together when evaluating neuropsychological test performance. In recent years, norms have been published that present data corrected for both age and education for several widely used tests. The data from the Halstead–Reitan normative data pool described above have been developed into a set of norms for an extended version of the HRB (Heaton et al., 1991). Norms are presented separately for males and females, for 10 age groups (ages 20–34, then in increments of 5 years to age 80), crossed with education level (6–8, 9–11, 12, 13–15, 16–17, and 18+ years).

Heaton (1992) also has developed age, education, and gender corrections for the WAIS-R subtests using the data from the WAIS-R standardization sample (Wechsler, 1981). The norms are presented separately for males and females, with age groups in increments of 3 years, ranging from 18 through 74, crossed with education levels ranging from 0 to 7 years to 16-plus years. In a validation sample of 420 subjects, less than 1% of the variance of the resultant demographically corrected T-scores could be predicted by the demographic variables in question. Thus, the T-scores were found to be essentially free of any linear relationship with age, education, or gender, and did not result in interactions of age-by-education on any WAIS-R variable. A recent study showed that, while raw scores from the WAIS and WAIS-R resulted in appreciable differences between two groups of demographically matched normal subjects, the corrected T-scores showed no differences for the two versions of the test (Thompson et al., 1989). Age, education, gender and ethnicity corrected norms are available for the WAIS-III/WMS-III, and these have been incorporated within The Psychological Corporation's *WAIS-III/ WMS-III/WIAT-II Scoring Assistant* software program.

Age- and education-corrected norms have been published for two summary scores of the Benton Visual Retention Test (BVRT; Youngjohn et al., 1993), namely, number correct and total number of errors. Subjects included 1128 healthy individuals, ranging in age from 17 to 84 years. Unfortunately, subjects with less than a high school education were not included in the study; data are presented for three categories of education, 12–14 years, 15–17 years, and 18-plus years. Sex was not considered in the norms since it did not significantly add to performance prediction in a multiple regression analysis. The BVRT has good discriminant validity for the purposes of differentiating dementia from the effects of normal aging (Youngjohn et al., 1992).

The Mini-Mental State Examination (MMSE; Folstein et al., 1975) is a brief, standardized screening procedure for cognitive impairment that is widely used in both research and clinical settings. A recently published population-based normative study for the MMSE highlights the importance of both age and education in performance on the MMSE (Crum et al., 1993). The study included 18,571 adult participants tested between 1980 and 1984 in five centers across the United States. The age, education, and race distributions of the sample matched those of the 1980 U.S. census. Norms are provided for age groups in increments of 5 years from 18 years to over 85 years, and are stratified by years of education (0–4, 5–8, 9–12, and college experience or higher degree). The total score on the MMSE varied appreciably between educational groups and age groups, ranging from a median score of 19 (out of a possible 30 points) among individuals 85 years and older with 0–4 years of education to a median score of 29 for the youngest group with more than a high school diploma. Scores were also found to be more variable among subjects with fewer years of education.

While the authors suggest several explanations, the larger variance may simply be due to the fact that fewer subjects were included in the 0–4 year education category (with *n* values as small as 17 and 23) than in the high school graduate category (with most cells containing 200 or more subjects). Although the subject sample was selected to reflect the racial distribution of the 1980 census, the study does not present separate data for racial groups, or even describe the percentages of the sample that come from varied ethnic backgrounds. It should be emphasized that these are population-based norms; the survey procedures did not screen out individuals with prior head injury, developmental disorder, or current cognitive dysfunction. Thus, at least some differences in the scores, particularly in the lowest education group and the oldest age group, may be due to the inclusion of these subjects. For example, lower MMSE scores at later ages may partially be attributable to the inclusion of elderly persons who are experiencing dementing diseases. Nevertheless, it is clear that both age and level of education should be considered in interpretation of the MMSE0 score.

Finally, Spreen and Strauss (1998) and Mitrushina et al. (2005) have compiled manuals of norms for many other widely used neuropsychological tests. Their purpose has been to describe each test, present the best normative data available at the time of publication, and comment on issues such as the validity and reliability of the test. In some cases an effort was made to combine normative samples from several sources into one table, thereby increasing the numbers of subjects in each age group. Most welcome is the addition, where available, of norms for children. While these efforts are laudatory, they cannot make up for the basic deficiencies in the field. It remains the case that most tests are sorely lacking in adequate normative data and in information regarding the reliability and discriminant validity of the tests. Nevertheless, the above compendia are useful sources of the most recent references on standardization samples and literature for currently used tests. The clinician employing a particular test is advised to refer to the cited sources if in doubt about the appropriateness of the norms.

Norms for the Very Elderly

Cognitive change is a typical, if not inevitable, consequence of aging. Visual spatial ability, some aspects of memory, speed of processing, and verbal fluency tend to decline with increasing years, particularly over the age of 70 (Labouvie-Vief, 1985; Poon, 1985). Generally, ability on tasks involving basic skills and over-learned information remains stable into very late decades, whereas earlier decline is evident on tasks that involve manipulation of novel situations or materials (Leckliter & Matarazzo, 1989). Generalized slowing of response is the most ubiquitous finding across all cognitive tasks, although the removal of time limits does not improve the performances of older persons to the level of younger adults (Lezak, 1983).

The growing number of the elderly in our society has increased the demand for specialized geriatric medical and psychological services in health-care settings. More and more elderly are being seen in clinics for the assessment of dementing diseases such as Alzheimer's, or for assessment of their ability to continue to function independently in the community. Surprisingly, even for the most thoroughly developed and comprehensively normed neuropsychological instruments, virtually none includes norms for the very elderly. Lezak (1987) notes that "the dearth of... adequate age-graded norms becomes even more astonishing in light of the hundreds of published studies on age-related changes for the full range of discrete to complex cognitive functions, sensory capacities, and motor responses" (p. 2). Normative studies that do exist for a given test often obtain disconcertingly different results. For example, D'Elia et al. (1989) compared studies with normative data for the Wechsler Memory Scale (WMS) that include elderly subjects between the ages of 55 and 89 years (including, among others, Haaland et al., 1983; Hulicka, 1966; Klonoff & Kennedy, 1966). They found wide discrepancies between the obtained means and standard deviations in these studies, most likely due to the influence of other important variables, such as education (Bak & Greene, 1981), that were not considered. The Duke University study (McCarty et al., 1982) has identified sex and race as other important variables on the WMS.

An issue of particular importance to consider when employing norms for the elderly is the health status of the participants in normative studies. Given the frequency of chronic illness in adults over the age of 65, excluding elderly subjects on the basis of current chronic illness such as diabetes or hypertension would likely result in a sample that is not representative of the general elderly population. This poses a dilemma for the researcher gathering normative data. Albert (1981) argues that, on the one hand, the clinician may be concerned with differentiating between the cognitive changes related to chronic illness and those related to aging. Systemic disease such as hypertension or metabolic dysfunction can have an adverse impact on cognitive functions that, in some cases, ameliorates with treatment. Conversely, norms that are based upon data from only healthy older individuals may be setting standards that are unrealistically high for elderly patients. Several projects have dealt with the issue differently. A normative project at the Mayo Clinic (Ivnik et al., 1992b, described below), for example, included in their sample subjects with chronic illness such as hypertension and diabetes, but whose cognitive capacity and daily functioning were not considered to be adversely affected by their illness. Alternatively, Birren et al. (1963) categorized subjects into those who were "optimally healthy" and those "with systemic disease."

The Spreen and Strauss (1998) and Mitrushina et al. (2005) manuals are, once again, worth mentioning as sources of information on normative data for the elderly. In addition, a bibliography of articles containing norms for older persons on a number of neuropsychological instruments is available (Erickson et al., 1992). This bibliography is the result of an extensive search for articles and publications that include norms for persons over 60 years of age. Studies with small sample sizes were not included when comparable larger samples were available. The studies are tabulated under six categories: Mental Status Questionnaires, Intellectual Abilities, Neuropsychological Batteries, Memory Functions, Perceptual Speed and Coordination, and Executive Functions.

As a result of their survey, Erickson et al. (1992) make several observations regarding the state of affairs in the area of norms for the elderly. The authors have come to the sobering conclusion that most of the available norms constituted little more than "rules of thumb," particularly for persons over the age of 75, or for those individuals who do not fit the description of the average North American, namely, White, educated at or beyond the high school level, and middle-class. Too few studies, in their opinion, had been concerned with comparing the ability of various instruments to discriminate between individuals with other demographic characteristics who are normal versus those who have acute neurological conditions or dementing diseases. Even fewer studies provide information on *how* people succeed or fail at a task as well as *what* they achieve and how quickly. Age-related changes in individual cognitive processes may be important diagnostic factors that are not reflected adequately in total scores on complex tests that require the efficient coordination of multiple abilities.

The Mayo Older Americans Normative Studies Project (MOANS)

A major research project that has made a considerable contribution to the area of norms for the elderly has been undertaken at the Mayo Clinic in Rochester, Minnesota. The goal of the project is to provide normative data from a large subject sample that is representative of the elderly in the community. The MOANS project produced excellent age- and education-corrected norms for the WAIS-R, as well as age-corrected norms for the Wechsler Memory Scale–Revised and Rey's Auditory–Verbal Learning Test (Ivnik et al., 1992a, 1992b, 1992c; Malec et al., 1992). The project is worth describing in some detail, not only because of the welcome contribution it makes to the field but because of the excellence of the design and the care the authors have taken in characterizing the normative sample.

The initial MOANS subject sample included 530 subjects between the ages of 54 and 74. The subjects were recruited from the community by random solicitation, with a 34% compliance rate. All the subjects were cognitively capable of independent living, although they had a variety of medical conditions common to the elderly (see Malec et al., 1993). The subjects

considered themselves normal, and were considered normal by their primary care physician. The authors' criteria for normality included the following: no active CNS or psychiatric conditions, no complaint of cognitive difficulty, no findings on physical examination suggesting a disorder with potential to affect cognition, and no psychoactive medication in amounts that would be expected to compromise cognition. Prior history of disorders potentially affecting cognition (e.g., head injury, substance abuse) or current chronic medical illness (e.g., diabetes, hypertension, cardiac problems) did not automatically exclude a subject from the study, as long as the condition was not reported by his or her physician to compromise cognition. A major caveat is that the subject sample was almost exclusively Caucasian with low average to superior intellectual functioning, residing in a predominantly suburban setting with good access to health-care facilities. The use of these norms for an individual with little education, or whose ethnic or socioeconomic background differs markedly from the normative sample, is questionable.

An additional goal of the MOANS project was to provide an extension of the existing normative data for WAIS-R IQ scores (Wechsler, 1981) for subjects beyond age 74. The WAIS-R was administered to 222 subjects over the age of 74 (range 75–97) and to 290 subjects between the ages of 56 and 74. The resultant MOANS norms were derived from age groups defined by overlapping, midpoint age ranges (Pauker, 1988) that maximize the amount of information obtained from the normative sample. Despite relatively small sample sizes for each 5-year interval, the normative data are presented for age ranges with midpoints every 3 years from age 61 to age 88, with a 10-year range in each group. Thus, an individual can be compared to the distribution that most closely fits his or her age, and the subject sample included in each distribution is large enough to provide percentile information for the individual. The MOANS scaled scores and resultant IQs can be further corrected on a set of tables for educational level. Consistent with the research described earlier, the authors show that correction for education level is most necessary at the extremes. In fact, corrections for education for high school graduates or those with up to a few years of college result in little change in scaled scores, and are thus unnecessary.

A second major contribution of the MOANS project has been in the area of memory assessment. Memory decline is typically associated with normal aging (as defined above) but is also an important early manifestation of neurocognitive disorders, such as Alzheimer's disease (Poon, 1985). Difficulty with memory is one of the most common complaints among the elderly on referral for neuropsychological testing, and its evaluation is a critical component of a neuropsychological assessment. The MOANS project has published norms for ages 55–97 on two widely used memory assessment instruments, the Wechsler Memory Scale–Revised (WMS-R; Wechsler, 1987), and the Rey Auditory–Verbal Learning Test (AVLT; Rey, 1964). The instructions give precise information for test administration, scoring, and computation of the subtest scores. Clinicians should familiarize themselves with the instructions in order to use the norms, since several important changes in test administration of the WMS-R were incorporated, so that the delayed recall index of the WMS-R can be computed taking into account the initial level of learning (Cullum et al., 1990). The concordances between the MOANS WMS-R indices and the original WMS-R indices (Wechsler, 1987) were within five points (plus or minus) for 96.4% of the sample on the verbal index, 90.5% on the visual index, 85.8% on the general memory index, and 93.8% on the attention/concentration index. Norms for several summary indices of the AVLT are also published (Ivnik et al., 1992c). These are an expanded version of the norms previously published by this group (Ivnik et al., 1990).

A new, and very significant extension of the Mayo Older American Normative Studies program has been a separate set of norms for elderly African Americans, published in a special issue of *The Clinical Neuropsychologist* (2005, 19, pp. 162–269).

Ethnicity in Neuropsychological Test Performance

Finally, we turn to a discussion of the issue of ethnicity as a variable in neuropsychological test performance. The discussion is by no means exhaustive; our goal is to highlight the pressing need for research in this area and the development of culture-specific normative standards for use in neuropsychological clinical practice. The reader is referred to other sources for a more complete discussion, including Triandis and Berry (1980), Olmedo (1981), Reynolds and Brown (1984), Anastasi (1988), Geisinger (1992), Fletcher-Jansen et al. (2000), Ferraro (2001), Anderson et al. (2004), Manly, Jacobs et al. (2002), and Manly (2005). We should note that our work, and most published observations by others, emanate from experience in the United States. The point of view, and the examples provided, therefore, reflect the North American context. While broader generalizations might not be appropriate from some of the specific data, the general principles should be applicable to other multiethnic and multicultural settings.

At issue, when assessing a patient whose heritage differs from one's own, is whether adequate consideration has been given to the contribution of ethnic and cultural factors to test design and performance. A culturally sensitive assessment has been described as one that balances the application of general population norms with culture-specific norms (Lopez et al., 1989). Unfortunately, not only are normative data nonexistent for most ethnic groups on most tests, but in many cases we do not even know on which tests ethnicity is or is not an important variable to consider. On the other hand, sufficient evidence exists to establish that it is a clinical myth that ethnicity is only an important variable on language- or knowledge-based tests and that the effect of culture can be eliminated if only performance or verbal items were used (for review, see Rosselli & Ardila, 2003). Ethnic background is sometimes, but not always, an important variable even on tests that are supposedly "culture free." Indeed, researchers have sometimes observed even larger group differences across cultural groups in performance and nonverbal tests than in verbal tests (Anastasi, 1988; Irvine & Berry, 1988). For example, Japanese subjects do better than American subjects on the Porteus Mazes and other spatial tests (Lee et al., 1991; Porteus, 1959). In contrast, American and Italian children perform virtually the same on the Judgment of Line Orientation Test (Riva & Benton, 1993).

Whether or not a low test performance is in part due to cultural influences may depend not only on ethnic background but on the individual's level of "acculturation," referring to the degree to which an individual engages in a particular culture's customs, values, beliefs, social practices, and language (Arnold & Orozco, 1989). Integration into the North American cultural setting will depend on numerous factors, some of which include the age at which the person immigrated, the language of origin, the age at which English was learned, and years of education in the American school system. Education and language fluency alone, however, are insufficient to gauge acculturation. Some individuals and some ethnic groups continue to participate fully in the traditions and social milieu of their culture, often continuing to speak their own language at home and in social settings. Collectively, these factors have a significant influence on the degree to which ethnic differences influence cognition (Arnold & Orozco, 1989; Gasquoine, 1999; Harris et al., 2003; Shuttleworth-Edwards et al., 2004; Touradji et al., 2001).

The importance of considering acculturation along with ethnicity or race is highlighted by recent research with Mexican Americans (see also Gonzales & Roll, 1985). For example, in a study by Arnold et al. (1994) three groups of subjects were identified who differed in their level of North American acculturation: Anglo-Americans, Mexican Americans, and Mexicans. Acculturation was assessed using an instrument developed by Cuellar et al. (1980; Acculturation Rating Scale for Mexican Americans, ARSMA) that considers such elements as oral language usage, historical familial identification, contact with Mexico, ease with reading and writing Spanish, and generalized perceptions of identification with the Mexican culture (Orozco et al., 1993). The Mexican group was tested using a Spanish translation of the HRB. The authors found considerable differences among these three groups on the HRB. On the aggregate T-score index, the Anglo-American group scored significantly higher than the Mexican Americans, who in turn scored significantly higher than the Mexican group. However, this was clearly not the case for all tests in the battery. On several tests, including the Trail-Making Test, Location and Memory components of the Tactual Performance Test, and Finger Tapping, similar performances were observed across the groups. In contrast, the Mexican group was significantly slower than either comparison group on Tactual Performance Test, even when age, gender, and SES were controlled for, statistically. On the Category Test, Anglo-Americans scored higher than both Mexican Americans and Mexicans, while on the Seashore Rhythm Test, it was the Mexican American group that scored significantly higher than either Mexicans or Anglo-Americans. The authors suggest this latter finding may be due to an increased sensitivity to auditorily processed materials in bilingual individuals.

More recently, Boone et al. (2007) compared patients referred for neuropsychological evaluation in four racial groups, Caucasian (non-Hispanic), African American, Hispanic, and Asian. Significant group differences were present on some measures of naming, attention and speed, constructional ability, and executive skills. However, these differences depended on several factors, including the number of years in the United States, years of education in the United States, the age at which conversational English was first learned, and whether English was acquired as a second language or learned concurrently with another language.

Clearly, level of acculturation is a significant factor in neuropsychological test performance, and importantly, not always in the direction of "more Anglo-American is better." However, few objective instruments exist for reliably measuring acculturation among members of different ethnic groups. The general paucity of research in this area means that we simply do not know what factors override ethnic differences. Ideally, future normative studies should stratify data according to cultural factors, rather than race alone. In the interim, the best advice remains to use caution when interpreting the test scores of an individual from an ethnic minority. In addition, clinical decisions based on such data should be informed, whenever possible, by the available literature on acculturation so as to avoid mischaracterization of the cognitive abilities of the individual, and should include appropriate caveats regarding sources of measurement error (Pont'on, 2001).

African Americans and Tests of Intelligence

Reynolds et al. (1987) used the WAIS-R standardization sample to investigate the effect of race and its interactions with education on Verbal, Performance, and Full-Scale IQs (VIQ, PIQ, and FSIQ, respectively). The data from 1664 Whites and 192 African Americans were broken into four education categories: 0–8 years, 9–11 years, 12 years, and 13–16 years. Not surprisingly, the FSIQs of individuals with a college education were two standard deviations higher than those with minimal formal schooling. Across all levels of education, a difference of about one standard deviation in favor of Whites over African Americans was found. The pattern of results was similar for VIQ and PIQ measures. The overall difference of one standard deviation in IQ scores is consistent with previous research (for review, see Reynolds & Brown, 1984). The increases in IQ for African Americans across educational levels were substantial but tended to be smaller than corresponding differences for Whites, although this interaction was not statistically significant. African Americans with at least 1 year of college scored 15–16.5 IQ points higher than those with 0–8 years of education; for Whites, the IQ differences were between 18.5 and 24 IQ points; these larger education effects for Whites than African Americans on cognitive tests would be consistent with evidence that many African Americans historically have experienced poorer education *quality* despite similar years of education (Manly et al., 2002). Similar ethnicity effects were reported by Kaufman et al. (1988) on the individual subtests

of the WAIS-R. All subtests produced significant differences in favor of Whites, although the differences were most prominent on Block Design and Vocabulary. One common Wechsler short form that is used for clinical screening is the Vocabulary–Block Design dyad (Sattler, 1982). Examiners should recognize that the use of that dyad as a short form will be particularly penalizing to African Americans.

The differences in IQ scores between African Americans and Whites exist even when scores are corrected for age, years of education, and sex. When Heaton's (1992) T-scores corrected for age, sex, and education are computed for the WAIS-R standardization sample, the differences among ethnic/racial groups are smaller than those described by Kaufman's group but remain appreciable (see Table 7–2).

The significance of these ethnicity differences for diagnostic decision making in neuropsychology is substantial. Heaton et al. (2003) demonstrated this using data from the WAIS-III/WMS-III standardization sample, stratified by ethnicity. By applying a 1-SD cutoff with factor scores corrected for age, education, and sex, these authors observed false-positive error rates for the African American cohort, which were clearly excessive for all six factors: Verbal Comprehension (36% versus 11% for Whites), Perceptual Organization (37% versus 12%), Processing Speed (38% versus 12%), Working Memory (37% versus 11%), Auditory Memory (30% versus 13%), and Visual Memory (25% versus 14%). Similar discrepancies have been seen for the HRB and the California Verbal Learning Test when a single set of norms was applied to test scores of large samples of normal, African American and Caucasian adults (Heaton et al., 2004; Norman et al., 2000). Importantly, in each of these publications it was also demonstrated

Table 7–2. WAIS-R Mean Verbal IQ (VIQ), Performance IQ (PIQ), and Full Scale IQ (FSIQ) Expressed as T scores, for Adult (age 20+) Standardization Sample Subjects in Four Ethnic Groups, Computed Using the Heaton (1992) Age-, Education-, and Sex- Corrected Norms

	Total Sample (n=1680)	White (n=1461)	Black (n=166)	Hispanic (n=34)	Other (n=19)
VIQ	50.0	50.7	44.6	45.9	45.5
PIQ	50.0	50.8	43.8	47.4	46.2
FSIQ	50.1	51.0	43.8	45.8	45.6

that use of ethnicity corrections for the test norms eliminated the previously observed discrepancies in false-positive error rates between Caucasians and African Americans.

The source of these differences has been the subject of intense and often bitter debate. Recent evidence supports the notion that ethnic differences on intellectual testing (and undoubtedly other neuropsychological measures as well) are a barometer of educational, economic, and environmental opportunity. Manly et al. (2002) found that cognitive test score differences between education matched groups of White and African American elders were greatly attenuated when a measure of education *quality* (reading level) was covaried in the analyses. Also, Vincent (1991) has shown that IQ differences between African American and White children in U.S. schools are shrinking. He reviewed pre-1980 and post-1980 studies comparing the performance of African Americans and Whites on various tests of intellectual functioning. Studies with adults included such tests as the WAIS, WAIS-R, and Raven's Progressive Matrices; studies with children employed the WISC-R, Raven's Colored Progressive Matrices, the Kaufman-ABC, and the Stanford-Binet. African American *adults* consistently obtained mean test scores that were approximately one standard deviation below the U.S. general population mean in studies carried out both before and after 1980. In contrast, although African American *children* tested prior to 1980 also scored one standard deviation below the U.S. mean, studies conducted after 1980 obtained group differences that were, on average, less than half as large. In one study (Krohn & Lamp, 1989), no differences were found between African American and White children on the Kaufman-ABC and the Stanford-Binet when socioeconomic factors were controlled. One logical explanation for these findings is that the shrinking ethnicity differences in intellectual test scores of children mirrors improved equity in education *quality* for Whites and African Americans in recent years.

Norms for Spanish-speaking Adults

The United States has the fifth largest Spanish-speaking population in the world, numbering some 29 million, and Hispanic Americans are the fastest-growing minority group in the United States (U.S. Census Bureau, 2004). The population is composed primarily of Latin American immigrant families from Mexico, Puerto Rico, Cuba, and Colombia. For first-generation immigrants, limited English language skills may preclude the use of many tests, regardless of whether or not culture-specific norms exist. In these cases, several Spanish translations of neuropsychological instruments are available that were standardized with Spanish-speaking populations. The most widely used of these tests is the Spanish translation of the WAIS, the Escala de Inteligencia Wechsler para Adultos (EIWA; Wechsler, 1968), standardized on a large sample of Spanish-speaking adults from Puerto Rico. Lopez and Romero (1988) examined the comparability of the EIWA and the WAIS (Wechsler, 1955). They found that in the conversion of raw scores to scaled scores, performance on a given subtest can result in a scaled score difference of up to 5 points, depending on whether one applies the WAIS or EIWA norms. For instance, a raw score of 16 on the Object Assembly, a subtest that is identical on the WAIS and EIWA, translates into a scaled score of 5 for the WAIS and 10 for the EIWA. Lopez and Romero (1988) conclude that for some Spanish-speaking adults, particularly for those with low educational levels, low occupational status, and rural backgrounds, the EIWA may be most appropriate, because this was the combined background of most of the EIWA standardization sample subjects. In interpreting EIWA scores, however, it is important to note that they reflect adequacy of performance with reference to a particular subject sample that differs considerably from the general American population *and* the general Hispanic population within the united States. Thus, if "Spanish speaking" is the only criterion for deciding to use the norms, persons with higher educational and occupational backgrounds than the EIWA standardization sample will produce overestimates of actual versus expected intellectual functioning using this instrument.

Boone et al. (2007) has compiled additional normative data for Hispanic, African American, and Asian individuals who were referred for neuropsychological assessment to a public hospital-affiliated neuropsychology clinic. The test battery included standard neuropsychological tests that were administered in English, such as the WAIS-III, WMS-R, Boston Naming Test, FAS, and Wisconsin Card Sorting Test. Test scores are stratified for individuals with different levels of language acculturation. These authors also provide an extensive list of other recent studies providing normative data for Hispanics, African Americans, and Asians on similar tests.

Rosselli and colleagues (Rosselli et al., 1990, 2000) have made significant contributions to the area of language assessment for Spanish-speaking adults. Rosselli et al. (1990) compiled normative data for the Boston Diagnostic Aphasia Examination (BDAE)—Spanish version (Garcia-Albea et al., 1986). A sample of 180 native Spanish speakers was obtained in Bogota, Colombia, and stratified according to sex, age (16–30, 31–50, and 51–65), and education (0–5, 6–12, and 13 years or more). The results are consistent with the data from U.S. White/Anglophone subject samples (such as Borod et al., 1980) showing that the BDAE is most markedly sensitive to education differences but is affected by age as well. The authors provide means and standard deviations for age and education subgroups, together with cutoff scores for normal performance on each subtest of the BDAE by years of education. The norms may be particularly useful for assessing predominantly Spanish-speaking subjects whose language functioning is in question. While these norms were collected in Colombia, more recently, Rosselli et al. (2000) has obtained normative data for older adults (ages 50–84) who are Spanish bilinguals, Spanish monolinguals, and English speakers on a variety of language tests, including Boston Naming Test, FAS, semantic fluency, and the Boston Diagnostic Aphasia Exam.

As the number of Hispanic individuals within the United States grows, the number of Hispanic elders continues to rise as well. The need for culturally normed screening tools to assess age-related cognitive impairment and early dementia is highlighted by a recent study showing that elderly Hispanics are more likely than Europeans to be identified as demented (Espino et al., 2001) when assessed with the Mini Mental

Status Exam (MMSE; Folstein et al., 1975). Uncorrected, MMSE scores are biased against individuals with lower levels of education, and the use of scoring adjustments for lower educational levels has become standard practice. Rosselli and colleagues (2006) compared MMSE total scores on 102 unimpaired and 58 memory impaired Hispanic individuals (ages 54–98), stratified by education level and gender. They also compared total MMSE scores that were calculated using two approved forms of the tests, one that included the original "serial 7's" item, and one that replaced serial 7's with an apparently less difficult "backwards spelling" task. For all the studied groups, MMSE scores were higher by an average of 1.5 points when using the "backwards spelling" task, and the correlation between serial 7's and backwards spelling was a modest .37. Both education and gender explained significant amount of variance in the MMSE scores. The authors note that the "backwards spelling" and "serial 7's" items do not appear to be equivalent in difficulty when testing Hispanic older adults.

Questions about Use of Demographically Corrected Norms in Neuropsychology

When Should We Use Them and for What Purpose?

Demographically corrected norms are useful for comparing current test performance with what would be expected of the patient if he/she had no brain disorder. Of course, the best way to measure possible changes in neurobehavioral functioning is to have premorbid baseline testing. Unfortunately, this is virtually never available. The next best option is to compare the patient's current test performances with best estimates of normal expectations for people who are as similar as possible to the patient in all characteristics that relate to test performance. This is quite simply, a prediction problem. And it is a fact that demographic characteristics help predict performances on our available neuropsychological tests.

Use of demographic predictions for this purpose may seem objectionable, because we know that demographics, themselves, do not *cause* differences in test performance. Rather, they are surrogates for a complex array of causative factors that are more difficult to reliably measure and use in the norming process. We need to be clear about this: just as correlation coefficients do not tell us anything about cause-effect relationships, demographic adjustments of neuropsychological test norms do not imply anything about the root causes of test performance differences that are associated with demographics. More will be said about this below in relation to individual demographic predictors.

It is generally understood that demographically corrected normative standards are based upon performances of adults who have developed normally, have typical, mainstream educational backgrounds, and have no known history of brain injury or disease. It follows logically from this that such norms should be used with great caution, if at all, to identify acquired brain dysfunctions in patients who have developmental disorders or other-than-mainstream educational backgrounds (e.g., special education). For example, it would be inappropriate to "adjust" a mentally retarded person's IQ upward because of a low education level, thereby potentially depriving him/her of social services or mitigating considerations in criminal prosecution.

As we have noted, demographically corrected norms are used primarily to identify the presence and nature of neurobehavioral *changes* due to known or possible brain insult (injury or disease). Such norms are generally not the best choice for characterizing the individual's *absolute* level of functioning, or functioning in relation to the general population of normal adults (Heaton & Pendleton, 1981). For the latter, we recommend norms that compare the individual's test performance with results of a sample that conforms as closely as possible to census characteristics. For example, with the Heaton et al. (2004) norms for the expanded HRB, uncorrected scaled scores (not demographically corrected T-scores) would be best suited for this purpose.

Normative Adjustments for Age

We have a long history of using age-corrected norms in neuropsychology. Noone would use the same normative standards for a 25-year-old and a 65-year-old. However, it is not age per se

that causes the observed differences. Rather, a variety of complex factors that tend to be associated with age are in various combinations responsible for age-related differences in cognition. These factors obviously are important to study and understand, and perhaps we eventually can measure them in norming to improve predictions of *which* 65-year-olds are likely to show more or less age-related cognitive change. For example, factors like diet and exercise, exposure to adverse environmental influences, frequency with which cognitive abilities are used in everyday functioning, and various age-related health conditions (e.g., hypertension) may all be important. Even genetics, which may help predict successful and unsuccessful cognitive aging, most likely do not *cause* such differences but operate by increasing the likelihood of biological processes, including illnesses, that also correlate with age.

So, when we correct for age, we are using it as a proxy for all these other factors that arguably are more important but that also are much more difficult to evaluate as joint predictors of test performance in individual cases. On the other hand, the proxy of age is readily assessed, it clearly helps in the prediction process, and psychologists have no compunctions about using it.

Normative Adjustments for Education

Education, too, is a useful but very complex predictor of cognitive performance. There is no doubt that it helps predict performance on most of our tests, yet direct causal links are tenuous. To a very limited extent, people with more education do better on our tests because they learned the answers in school. Perhaps more importantly, school experiences (especially early ones) teach basic academic skills and teach how to learn, how to use new facts and skills to solve problems, and how to take tests. Also, school experiences may or may not reinforce these activities as positive features of peoples' lifestyles. Education also is a component of SES, which itself is complex and multifaceted, and years of education completed is a proxy for much of that complexity. There is also a tendency for more cognitively able people to go farther in school: IQ in the second grade is a significant predictor of how many years of school a person ultimately will complete (McCall, 1977). But SES and related experiences certainly affect early IQ measurements, just as they do later in life. In adults, therefore, education is a proxy for all of these factors.

There is no doubt that *quality* of education is important, but this too is complex and may be difficult to assess retrospectively in adult patients (Byrd et al., 2006). Resources devoted to educational systems available to different segments of the U.S. population have varied greatly, especially for African Americans during the era of segregation (Manly et al., 2002). Although this situation has improved somewhat, it would be difficult to argue that the quality of a high school education in poor inner-city or rural areas of the United States is equivalent to that experienced in wealthier suburbs or private schools. Also, because quality of education in the United States has been associated with other complex determinants of cognitive development (i.e., everything that goes with SES), subgroup differences in cognitive outcome might not immediately disappear even if we could achieve complete equality in educational experiences and opportunities.

As was the case with age, years of education completed is an easily obtained proxy for multiple factors that have more direct (causal) effects but also are more difficult to measure and use in prediction models—probably including quality of education. In general, people with better-quality education through high school are more likely to go to college and beyond.

It has been proposed by Manly et al. (2002)—and others as well—that one's current oral reading level may be a good index of the quality of his/her prior education. Although reading level is easily assessed and may in fact have potential value in neuropsychological norms development, this has both conceptual and practical complexities. Conceptually, reading level is multiply- determined and not simply a measure of quality of education. It is probably associated with many other aspects of SES, and obviously relates to years of education completed. From a practical point of view, if the goal of testing is to detect acquired brain impairment, such norms could not be used with patients who may have any disease or injury that could affect oral

reading (e.g., dementing illnesses, or strokes or injuries affecting reading or language functions). Even if reading-corrected norms did exist, considerable clinical judgment may be needed to decide when to use them.

It may not be enough to show that current reading level correlates with performance on other neuropsychological tests in normals, or even that concurrent consideration of reading scores reduces predictive value of demographic variables such as education or ethnicity. Since current reading levels can be affected by some neurologic conditions, and demographic variables are not, we need to know how much reading scores can add to predictions based upon demographic variables alone. Gladsjo et al. (1999) considered this question using data from an ethnically mixed sample of 141 healthy adults, on WAIS-R IQs, the Average Impairment Rating from the HRB, and composite measures of learning and memory. Scores on the American National Adult Reading Test (ANART) did substantially add to the demographic predictions of Verbal IQ, Full-Scale IQ and learning, but provided little help in predicting Performance IQ, the Average Impairment Rating or memory. The major advantage in using reading scores was with people who had at least 13 years of education and relatively poor reading.

Thus, for some patients and for some neuropsychological measures, it may well be helpful to have norms that are adjusted for current reading levels as well as demographics. To do this properly, we need to co-norm all of our neuropsychological tests with a reading test (ideally the same reading test). This has not typically been done and, to our knowledge, no reading-adjusted norms are available at the present time. However, we do recommend that a standard reading test be included in future norming projects.

Normative Adjustments for Gender

At least in the United States and other Western countries, gender does not currently appear to be very confounded with major experiential or biological factors that affect cognition. Since gender is not a proxy for powerful and complex determinants of cognitive performance, it ends up contributing little or nothing to the demographic predictions of performance on most neuropsychological tests. Nevertheless, we see no reason to leave gender out of normative models in which it does add to prediction accuracy (e.g., expectations are slightly lower for males on WAIS-III/WMS-III Processing Speed and measures of episodic memory, but are higher for males on the Finger Tapping Test and Hand Dynamometer test of grip strength).

Normative Adjustments for Ethnicity

Unlike gender, ethnicity in our time, and in Western society, is confounded with many complex and interacting background factors that can affect cognitive test performance. Although the background factors that directly *cause* test performances among different ethnic groups are extremely important, and worthy of careful study, research so far suggests that they are difficult to assess and quantify retrospectively in adults (Byrd et al., 2006). In the absence of currently available methods for quantifying such factors retrospectively and for using them to predict cognitive test performances in individual cases, one can at least avoid excessive false-positive error rates by using norms that are based upon data from normal people who are demographically (including ethnically) similar to the patient. As Manly (2005) has stated, "Increased specificity of cognitive measures is an unmistakable benefit of proper use of normative information..." (p. 271).

It is important to note, however, that culture, values and beliefs can influence neuropsychological testing in subtle but important ways that are difficult to quantify. For clinicians, it is important to keep in mind that cognitive testing represents a social situation that is governed by implicit rules that are not shared by all cultures (Ardila, 2005). To cite several examples, the degree to which the patient is willing to obey instructions may depend on the personal characteristics of the examiner relative to the examinee, such as differences in age, gender, ethnicity, and class or caste. The notion of doing one's best on a test may be important to individuals from a culture that values competition, but not in less competitive societies. Speeded tests may be particularly problematic because of difference in attitudes to timed procedures across

cultures and to the very nature of the concept of time (Munn, 1992). American children are exposed to timed tests from an early age, which reinforces the value that the faster the performance the better the result, while other cultures place more value on accuracy and attention to detail rather than speed (Nell, 2000; Puente & Agranovich, 2003). Neuropsychological testing itself can be construed by some individuals as invasive and inappropriate. For example, Dingfelder (2005) notes that, when dealing with individuals from Latin countries, having the examiner share details of their personal lives would be considered an appropriate way to make the client more comfortable and welcome, but this would likely be an unwelcome level of intimacy for most Americans. But asking the direct question, "Are you feeling depressed?" to the same Latin individual may be regarded an inappropriate invasion of privacy. It is unlikely that these (and other) social variables can ever be captured adequately in normative data, because they depend upon the interaction between the cultural values and individual characteristics and behaviors of both the client and the clinician.

In sum, all of the demographic characteristics that predict neurocognitive test performance are proxies for other more direct, causal influences—influences that are very complex and difficult to objectively assess in individual patients. Nevertheless, use of these readily available proxy corrections does account for substantial amounts of variance in the cognitive test performance of normals. As a result, demographic corrections substantially improve predictions of expected test performance in adults who do not have brain disease. Such norms provide much more *equal* probability of the patient's being correctly classified as normal or abnormal, regardless of whether he/she is young or old, a high school dropout or college graduate, male or female, or White, Black, or Hispanic. For diagnostic questions, this is the major purpose of norms.

How to Assess Validity of Demographically Corrected Norms

We have stated that demographically corrected norms should be most useful in detecting and characterizing acquired brain disorders. Is it therefore reasonable to expect that, compared to uncorrected norms, they will show greater overall specificity (accuracy in classifying the normal population as normal)? *Probably not.* As previously noted, demographic corrections should ensure *equal* probability of being correctly classified as normal, regardless of one's demographic characteristics (age, education, gender, ethnicity). Uncorrected norms are likely to have relatively high specificity with young, well-educated, and mostly Caucasian groups but much lower specificity with people who are older, more poorly educated, and having ethnic minority backgrounds. If the overall population has all of these kinds of people, in relatively balanced proportions, specificity figures for the total groups could be the same for demographically corrected and uncorrected norms (Heaton et al., 1996, 2004).

What about sensitivity to disease? The same concepts apply. Sensitivity is likely to vary according to demographics with uncorrected norms, and much less so with demographically corrected norms (Heaton et al., 1996). The percentages of people in the total population who are classified as "impaired" could be quite similar. Again, the expected benefit of the corrected norms is to have equivalent sensitivity as well as specificity, regardless of the demographics of the people being assessed.

Will corrected and uncorrected norms usually disagree in their classification outcomes? *Not necessarily.* To the extent that patients' demographic characteristics approximate the average member of the adult population (or at least the average member of the normative sample), the classifications are likely to be the same. The largest differences will occur at the extremes of the demographic spectra (e.g., old versus young, very low versus high educational level).

Finally, when comparing diagnostic results with corrected and uncorrected norms, it is most meaningful to use a constant test score cutoff in all cases (e.g., T-score < 40 or standard score < 85). This is similar to the way scores would be interpreted clinically. Use of statistically determined, optimal cutoffs for a particular group or subgroup (e.g., Strong et al., 2005) may obscure differences that would be seen in the clinical situation.

Summary

The adequate assessment of an individual's cognitive functioning entails a knowledge of the demographic variables that relate to neuropsychological test performance. Many of the assumptions that clinicians and researchers sometimes make, such as that Finger Tapping is not associated with education, that "nonverbal" or "performance" tests are culture free, and that matching on age and education level is sufficient to equate performance on tests between people of different ethnic backgrounds, are not warranted. Whenever a subject differs in important characteristics from the "average" person in a set of published norms, caution is the best advice. For a 60-year-old woman with a grade school education, whose first language was Spanish and who began learning English at age 15, the most that neuropsychological tests will tell us for sure is whether and how much she differs from the average American. They will not tell us whether she has experienced a decline in functioning, in what area this decline has occurred, or, if decline has occurred, what impact it will have on her ability to care for herself and her family in the community. In this case, it is particularly important to consider the test results within the context of a detailed and comprehensive history from her family about how she copes with the demands of her daily life and the changes, if any, that have occurred in recent days, weeks, or years. Also, the interpretation of initial neuropsychological results will necessarily rely more on consideration of *pattern* features (e.g., right–left differences on sensory-perceptual, motor, and psychomotor tests) than on *level* of performance, because the expected values for the latter are uncertain. On the other hand, interpreting major changes across successive neuropsychological evaluations is less dependent on baseline norms and can contribute to more secure diagnostic inferences.

Regardless of whether an individual does or does not match the demographic characteristics of the normative samples, the interpretation of neuropsychological test scores will ultimately depend on multiple factors, including one's definition of normal and abnormal, the goal and context of the assessment, the relationship of current test performance and daily functioning to prior levels of functioning, together with a consideration of the likely impact of the results on diagnostic and treatment decisions. As with all clinical information, judgment is required to weigh the importance of a false-positive or false-negative error.

References

Albert, M. S. (1981). Geriatric neuropsychology. *Journal of Consulting and Clinical Psychology, 49,* 835–850.

Albert, M. S., & Heaton, R. K. (1988). Intelligence testing. In M. S. Albert and M. B. Moss (Eds.), *Geriatric neuropsychology* (pp. 13–32). New York: Guilford Press.

Anastasi, A. (1988). *Psychological testing,* 6th ed. New York: Macmillan.

Anderson, N. A., Bulatao, R. A., & Cohen, B. (Eds.). (2004). *Critical perspectives on racial and ethnic differentials in health in late life.* Washington, DC: National Academics Press.

Ardila, A. (2005). Cultural values underlying psychometric cognitive testing. *Neuropsychology Review, 15,* 185–195.

Arnold, B. R., Montgomery, G. T., Castaneda, I., & Longoria, R. (1994). Acculturation and performance of Hispanics on selected Halstead–Reitan neuropsychological tests. *Assessment, 1,* 239–248.

Arnold, B. R., & Orozco, S. (1989). Physical disability, acculturation, and family interaction among Mexican Americans. *Journal of Applied Rehabilitation Counseling, 20,* 28–32.

Bak, J. S., & Greene, R. L. (1981). A review of the performance of aged adults on various Wechsler Memory Scale subtests. *Journal of Clinical Psychology, 37,* 186–188.

Birren, J. E., Butler, R. N., Greenhouse, S. W., Sokoloff, L., & Yarrow, M. R. (1963). *Human aging: A biological and behavioral study.* Washington, DC: U.S. Government Printing Office.

Birren, J. E., & Morrison, D. F. (1961). Analysis of WAIS subtests in relation to age and education. *Journal of Gerontology, 16,* 363–369.

Boone, K. B., Victor, T. L., Wen, J., Razani, J., & Ponton, M. (2007). The association between neuropsychological scores and ethnicity, language, and acculturation variables in a large patient population. *Archives of Clinical Neuropsychology, 22,* 355–365.

Borod, J. C., Goodglass, H., & Kaplan, E. (1980). Normative data on the Boston Diagnostic Aphasia Examination and the Boston Naming Test. *Journal of Clinical Neuropsychology, 2,* 209–215.

Botwinick, J. (1967). *Cognitive processes in maturity and old age.* New York: Springer.

Buffery, A. W., & Gray, J. A. (1972). Sex differences in the development of spatial and linguistic skills. In C. Ounsted and D. C. Taylor (Eds.), *Gender differences: Their ontogeny and significance* (pp. 123–157). Baltimore: Williams and Wilkins.

Byrd, D. A., Miller, S. W., Reilly, J., Weber, S., Wall, T. L., & Heaton, R. K. (2006). Early environmental factors, ethnicity, and adult cognitive test performance. *The Clinical Neuropsychologist, 20,* 243–260.

Cattell, R. B. (1963). Theory of fluid and crystallized intelligence: A critical experiment. *Journal of Educational Psychology, 54,* 1–22.

Crum, R. M., Anthony, J. C., Bassett, S. S., & Folstein, M. F. (1993). Population-based norms for the Mini-Mental State Examination by age and educational level. *Journal of the American Medical Association, 269,* 2386–2391.

Cuellar, I., Harris, L. C., & Jasso, R. (1980). An acculturation scale for Mexican American normal and clinical populations. *Hispanic Journal of Behavioral Sciences, 2,* 199–217.

Cullum, C. M., Butters, N., Troster, A. I., & Salmon, D. P. (1990). Normal aging and forgetting rates on the Wechsler Memory Scale-Revised. *Archives of Clinical Neuropsychology, 5,* 23–30.

D'Elia, L., Satz, P., & Schretlen, D. (1989). Wechsler Memory Scale: A critical appraisal of the normative studies. *Journal of Clinical and Experimental Neuropsychology, 11,* 551–568.

Dingfelder, S. F. (2005). Closing the gap for Latino patients. *Monitor of Psychology, 36,* 58–61.

Erickson, R. C., Eimon, P., & Hebben, N. (1992). A bibliography of normative articles on cognition tests for older adults. *The Clinical Neuropsychologist, 6,* 98–102.

Espino, D. V., Lichtenstein, M. D., Palmer, R. F., & Hazuda, H. P. (2001). Ethnic differences in Mini-Mental State Examination (MMSE) scores: Where you live makes a difference. *Journal of the American Geriatric Society, 49,* 538–548.

Ferraro, F.R. (Ed.). (2001). *Minority and cross-cultural aspects of African Americans.* Lisse, Netherlands: Swets and Zeitlinger.

Finlayson, M. A., Johnson, K. A., & Reitan, R. M. (1977). Relationship of level of education to neuropsychological measures in brain-damaged and non-brain-damaged adults. *Journal of Consulting and Clinical Psychology, 45,* 536–542.

Fletcher-Janzen, E., Strickland, T. L., & Reynolds, C. R. (2000). *Handbook of cross-cultural neuropsychology.* New York: Kluwer Academic/Plenum Publishers.

Flynn, J. R. (1984). The mean IQ of Americans: Massive gains 1932 to 1978. *Psychological Bulletin, 95,* 29–51.

Flynn, J. R. (1987). Massive IQ gains in 14 nations: What IQ tests really measure. *Psychological Bulletin, 101,* 171–191.

Folstein, M. F., Folstein, S. E., & McHugh, P. R. (1975). Mini-Mental State: A practical method for grading the cognitive state of patients for the clinician. *Journal of Psychiatric Research, 12,* 189–198.

Fromm-Auch, D., & Yeudall, L. T. (1983). Normative data for the Halstead–Reitan Neuropsychological Tests. *Journal of Clinical Neuropsychology, 5,* 221–238.

Garcia-Albea, J. E., Sanchez-Bernardos, M. L., & del Viso-Pabon, S. (1986). Test de Boston para el diagnostico de la afasia: Adaptacion Espanola. In H. Goodglass and E. Kaplan (Eds.), *La Evaluacion de la Afasia y de Transtornos Relacionados* (2nd ed., pp. 129–198) (translated by Carlos Wernicke). Madrid: Editorial Medica Panamericana.

Gasquoine, P. (1999). Variables moderating cultural and ethnic differences in neuropsychological assessment: The case of Hispanic Americans. *The Clinical Neuropsychologist, 13,* 376–383.

Geisinger, K. F. (1992). *Psychological testing of hispanics.* Washington, DC: American Psychological Association.

Gladsjo, J. A., Heaton, R. K., Palmer, B. W., Taylor, M. J., & Jeste, D. V. (1999). Use of oral reading to estimate premorbid intellectual and neuropsychological functioning. *Journal of the International Neuropsychological Society, 5*(3), 247–254.

Gonzales, R. R., & Roll, S. (1985). Relationship between acculturation, cognitive style, and intelligence. *Journal of Cross Cultural Psychology, 16,* 190–205.

Haaland, K. Y., Linn, R. T., Hunt, W. C., & Goodwin, J. S. (1983). A normative study of Russell's variant of the Wechsler Memory Scale in a healthy elderly population. *Journal of Consulting and Clinical Psychology, 51,* 878–881.

Harris, J. G., Tulsky, D. S., & Schultheis, M. T. (2003). Assessment of the non-native English speaker: Assimilating history and research findings to guide clinical practice. In S. D. Tulsky, D. H. Saklofske, G. J. Chelune, R. K. Heaton, R. J. Ivnik, R. Bornstein, et al. (Eds.), *Clinical Interpretation of the WAIS-III and WMS-III* (pp. 343–390). San Diego, CA: Academic Press.

Heaton, R. K. (1992). *Comprehensive norms for an expanded Halstead–Reitan Battery: A supplement for the WAIS-R.* Odessa, FL: Psychological Assessment Resources.

Heaton, R. K., Grant, I., & Matthews, C. G. (1986). Differences in neuropsychological test performance associated with age, education, and sex. In I. Grant and K. M. Adams (Eds.), *Neuropsychological assessment of neuropsychiatric disorders* (pp. 100–120). New York: Oxford University Press.

Heaton, R. K., Grant, I., & Matthews, C. G. (1991). *Comprehensive norms for an expanded Halstead–Reitan Battery: Demographic corrections, research findings, and clinical applications.* Odessa, FL: Psychological Assessment Resources.

Heaton, R. K., Matthews, C. G., Grant, I., & Avitable, N. (1996). Demographic corrections with comprehensive norms: An overzealous attempt or a good start? *Journal of Clinical and Experimental Neuropsychology, 18*(3), 449–458.

Heaton, R. K., Miller, W., Taylor, M. J., & Grant, I. (2004). *Revised comprehensive norms for an expanded Halstead–Reitan Battery: Demographically adjusted norms for African American and Caucasian adults.* Lutz, FL: Psychological Assessment Resources, Inc.

Heaton, R. K., & Pendleton, M. G. (1981). Use of neuropsychological tests to predict adult patients' everyday functioning. *Journal of Consulting and Clinical Psychology, 49,* 807–821.

Heaton, R. K., Taylor, M. J., & Manly, J. (2003). Demographic effects and use of demographically corrected norms with the WAIS-III and WMS-III. In D. S. Tulsky, G. C. Chelune, R. J. Irnik, A. Prifitera, D. H. Saklofske, R. K. Heaton, et al. (Eds.), *Clinical interpretation of the WAIS-III and WMS-III* (pp. 181–210). San Diego, CA: Academic Press.

Horn, J. L., & Cattell, R. B. (1966). Age differences in primary mental ability factors. *Journal of Gerontology, 21,* 210–220.

Hulicka, I. M. (1966). Age differences in Wechsler Memory Scale scores. *Journal of Genetic Psychology, 109,* 135–145.

Irvine, S. H., & Berry, J. W. (Eds.). (1988). *Human abilities in cultural context.* New York: Cambridge University Press.

Ivnik, R. J., Malec, J. F., Smith, G. E., Tangalos, E. G., Petersen, R. C., Kokmen, E., et al. (1992a). Mayo's older Americans normative studies: WAIS-R norms for ages 56 to 97. *The Clinical Neuropsychologist, 6*(suppl.), 1–30.

Ivnik, R. J., Malec, J. F., Smith, G. E., Tangalos, E. G., Petersen, R. C., Kokmen, E., et al. (1992b). Mayo's older Americans normative studies: WMS-R norms for ages 56 to 94. *The Clinical Neuropsychologist, 6*(suppl.), 49–82.

Ivnik, R. J., Malec, J. F., Smith, G. E., Tangalos, E. G., Petersen, R. C., Kokmen, E., et al. (1992c). Mayo's older Americans normative studies: Updated AVLT norms for ages 56 to 97. *The Clinical Neuropsychologist, 6*(suppl.), 83–104.

Ivnik, R. J., Malec, J. F., Tangalos, E. G., Petersen, R. C., Kokmen, E., & Kurland, L. T. (1990). The

Auditory–Verbal Learning Test (AVLT): Norms for ages 55 and older. *Psychological Assessment, 2,* 304–312.

Kaufman, A. S., McLean, J. E., & Reynolds, C. R. (1988). Sex, race, residence, region, and education differences on the 11 WAIS-R subtests. *Journal of Clinical Psychology, 44,* 231–248.

Klonoff, H., & Kennedy, M. (1966). A comparative study of cognitive functioning in old age. *Journal of Gerontology, 21,* 239–243.

Krohn, E. J., & Lamp, R. E. (1989). Concurrent validity of the Stanford-Binet Fourth Edition and K-ABC for Head Start children. *Journal of School Psychology, 27,* 59–67.

Labouvie-Vief, G. (1985). Intelligence and cognition. In J. E. Birren and K. W. Schaie (Eds.), *Handbook of the psychology of aging* (2nd ed.; pp. 500–530). New York: Van Nostrand Reinhold Company.

Leckliter, I. N., & Matarazzo, J. D. (1989). The influence of age, education, IQ, gender, and alcohol abuse on Halstead–Reitan Neuropsychological Test Battery performance. *Journal of Clinical Psychology, 45,* 484–512.

Lee, G. P., Sasanuma, S., Hamsher, K. D., & Benton, A. L. (1991). Constructional praxis performance of Japanese and American, normal and brain-damaged patients. *Archives of Clinical Neuropsychology, 6,* 15–25.

Lezak, M. D. (1983). *Neuropsychological assessment* (2nd ed). New York: Oxford University Press.

Lezak, M. D. (1987). Norms for growing older. *Developmental Neuropsychology, 3,* 1–12.

Lopez, S. R., Grover, K. P., Holland, D., Johnson, M. J., Kain, C. D., Kanel, K., et al. (1989). Development of culturally sensitive psychotherapists. *Professional Psychology: Research and Practice, 20,* 369–376.

Lopez, S., & Romero, A. (1988). Assessing the intellectual functioning of Spanish-speaking adults: Comparison of the EIWA and the WAIS. *Professional Psychology: Research and Practice, 19,* 263–270.

Maccoby, E. E., & Jacklin, C. N. (1974). *The psychology of sex differences.* Stanford CA: Stanford University Press.

Malec, J. F., Ivnik, R. J., & Smith, G. E. (1993). Neuropsychology and normal aging: Clinician's perspective. In R. W. Parks, R. F. Zec, & R. S. Wilson (Eds.), *Neuropsychology of Alzheimer's disease and other dementias* (pp. 81–111). New York: Oxford University Press.

Malec, J. F., Ivnik, R. J., Smith, G. E., Tangalos, E. G., Petersen, R. C., Kokmen, E., et al. (1992). Mayo's older Americans normative studies: Utility of corrections for age and education for the WAIS-R. *The Clinical Neuropsychologist, 6*(suppl.), 31–47.

Manly, J. J. (2005). Advantages and disadvantages of separate norms for African Americans. *The Clinical Neuropsychologist, 19*(2), 270–275.

Manly, J.J., Jacobs, D. M., Touradji, P., Small, S. S., & Stern, Y. (2002). Reading level attenuates differences in neuropsychological test performance between African American and White elders. *Journal of the International Neuropsychological Association, 8,* 341–348.

Matarazzo, J. D. (1972). *Wechsler's measurement and appraisal of adult intelligence.* Baltimore: Williams and Wilkins.

Matarazzo, J. D., Bornstein, R. A., McDermott, P. A., & Noonan, J. V. (1986). Verbal IQ vs. performance IQ difference scores in males and females from the WAIS-R standardization sample. *Journal of Clinical Psychology, 42,* 965–974.

Matarazzo, J. D., & Herman, D. O. (1984). Relationship of education and IQ in the WAIS-R standardization sample. *Journal of Consulting and Clinical Psychology, 52,* 631–634.

McCall, R. B. (1977). Childhood IQs as predictors of adult educational and occupational status. *Science, 197,* 482–483.

McCarty, S. M., Siegler, I. C., & Logue, P. E. (1982). Cross-sectional and longitudinal patterns of three Wechsler Memory Scale subtests. *Journal of Gerontology, 37,* 169–175.

Mitrushina, M., Boone, K. B., Razani, J., & D'Elia, L. F. (2005). *Handbook of normative data for neuropsychological assessment* (2nd edition). New York: Oxford University Press.

Munn, N. D. (1992). The cultural anthropology of time: A critical essay. *Annual Review of Anthropology, 21,* 931–923.

Nell, V. (2000). *Cross-cultural neuropsychological assessment: Theory and practice.* Mahwah, NJ: Erlbaum.

Norman, M. A., Evans, J. D., Miller, S. W., & Heaton, R. K. (2000). Demographically corrected norms for the California Verbal Learning Test. *Journal of Clinical and Experimental Neuropsychology, 22,* 80–93.

Olmedo, E. L. (1981). Testing linguistic minorities. *American Psychologist, 36,* 1078–1085.

Orozco, S., Thompson, B., Kapes, J., & Montgomery, G. T. (1993). Measuring the acculturation of Mexican Americans: A covariance structure analysis. *Measurement and Evaluation in Counseling and Development, 25,* 149–155.

Parsons, O. A., & Prigatano, G. P. (1978). Methodological considerations in clinical neuropsychological research. *Journal of Consulting and Clinical Psychology, 46,* 608–619.

Pauker, J. D. (1988). Constructing overlapping cell tables to maximize the clinical usefulness of normative test data: Rationale and an example from neuropsychology. *Journal of Clinical Psychology, 44,* 930–933.

Pont´on, M. O. (2001). Research and assessment issues with Hispanic populations. In M. O. Pont´on and J. Leon-Carrion (Eds.), *Neuropsychology and the hispanic patient: A clinical handbook* (pp. 39–58). Mahwah, NJ: Lawrence Earlbaum.

Poon, L. W. (1985). Difference in human memory with aging: Nature, causes, and clinical implications. In J. E. Birren and K. W. Schaie (Eds.), *Handbook of the psychology of aging* (2nd ed.; pp. 427–462). New York: Van Nostrand Reinhold Company.

Porteus, S. D. (1959). *The maze test and clinical psychology.* Palo Alto: Pacific Books.

Price, L. J., Fein, G., & Feinberg, L. (1980). Neuropsychological assessment of cognitive functioning in the elderly. In L. W. Poon (Ed.), *Aging in the 1980s: Psychological issues* (pp. 78–85). Washington, DC: American Psychological Association.

Puente, A. E., & Agranovich, A. V. (2003). The cultural in crosscultural neuropsychology. In M. Hersen, G. Goldstein, & S. R. Beers (Eds.), *The handbook of psychological assessment* (Vol. 1; pp. 31–332). Wiley, New York.

Reitan, R. M. (1955). The distribution according to age of a psychological measure dependent upon organic brain functions. *Journal of Gerontology, 10,* 338–340.

Reitan, R. M. (1957). Differential reaction of various psychological tests to age. In *Fourth Congress of the International Association of Gerontology* (pp. 158–165). Fidenza: Tito Mattioli.

Reitan, R. M., & Wolfson, D. (1986). The Halstead–Reitan Neuropsychological Test Battery and aging. In T. L. Brink (Ed.), *Clinical gerontology: A guide to assessment and intervention* (pp. 39–61). New York: Haworth Press.

Rey, A. (1964). *L'examen Clinique en Psychologie.* Paris: Presses Universitaires de France.

Reynolds, C. R., & Brown, R. T. (1984). *Perspectives on bias in mental testing.* New York: Plenum Press.

Reynolds, C. R., Chastain, R. L., Kaufman, A. S., & McLean, J. E. (1987). Demographic characteristics and IQ among adults: Analysis of the WAIS-R standardization sample as a function of the stratification variables. *Journal of School Psychology, 25,* 323–342.

Riva, D., & Benton, A. (1993). Visuospatial judgment: A crossnational comparison. *Cortex, 29,* 141–143.

Rosselli, M., & Ardila, A. (2003). The impact of culture and education on non-verbal neuropsychological measurements: A critical review. *Brain & Cognition, 52,* 326–333.

Rosselli, M, Ardila, A., Araugo, K., Weekes, V., Caracciolo, V., Padilla, M., et al. (2000). Verbal Fluency and Repetition Skills in Healthy Older Spanish–English Bilinguals. *Applied Neuropsychology, 7,* 17–24.

Rosselli, M., Ardila, A., Florez, A., & Castro, C. (1990). Normative data on the Boston Diagnostic Aphasia Examination in a Spanish-speaking population. *Journal of Clinical and Experimental Neuropsychology, 12,* 313–322.

Rosselli, M., Tappen, R., Williams, C., & Savatierra, J. (2006). The relation of education and gender on the attention items of the Mini-Mental State Examination in Spanish speaking Hispanic elders. *Archives of Clinical Neuropsychology, 21,* 677–686.

Russell, E. W., Neuringer, C., & Goldstein, G. (1970). *Assessment of brain damage: A neuropsychological key approach.* New York: Wiley-Interscience.

Sattler, J. M. (1982). *Assessment of children's intelligence and special abilities* (2nd ed.). Boston: Allyn and Bacon.

Shallice, T. (1988). *From neuropsychology to mental structure.* Cambridge: Cambridge University Press.

Shuttleworth-Edwards, A., Kemp, R., Rust, A., Muirhead, J., Hartman, N., et al. (2004). Cross-cultural effects on IQ test performance: A review and preliminary normative indications on WAIS-III Test performance. *Journal of Clinical and Experimental Neuropsychology, 26,* 903–920.

Spreen, O., & Strauss, E. (1998). *A compendium of neuropsychological tests: Administration, norms, and commentary* (2nd edition). New York: Oxford University Press.

Stern, Y., Zarahn, E., Hilton, H. J., Flynn, J., DeLa Paz, R., & Rakitin, B. (2003). Exploring the neural basis of cognitive reserve. *Journal of Clinical and Experimental Neuropsychology, 5,* 691–701.

Strong, C. A., Donders, J., & Van Dyke, S. (2005). Validity of demographically corrected norms for the WAIS-III. *Journal of Clinical and Experimental Neuropsychology, 27,* 746–758.

Taylor, M. J., & Heaton, R. K. (2001). Sensitivity and specificity of WAIS-III/WMS-III demographically corrected factor scores in neuropsychological assessment. *Journal of the International Neuropsychological Society, 7*(7), 867–874.

Thompson, L. L., Heaton, R. K., Grant, I., & Matthews, C. G. (1989). A comparison of the WAIS and WAIS-R using T-score conversions that correct for age, education, and sex. *Journal of Clinical and Experimental Neuropsychology, 11,* 478–488.

Touradji, P., Manly, J., Jacobs, D., & Stern, Y. (2001). Neuropsychological test performance: A study of non-Hispanic White elderly. *Journal of*

Clinical and Experimental Neuropsychology, 23, 643–649.

Triandis, H. C., & Berry, J. W. (1980). *Handbook of cross-cultural psychology* (vols. 1 and 2). Boston: Allyn and Bacon.

Tulsky, D. S., Ivnik, R. J., Price, L. R., & Wilkins, C. (2003). Assessment of cognitive functioning with the WAIS-III and WMS-III: Development of a six-factor model. In D. S. Tulsky, G. C. Chelune, R. J. Irnik, A. Prifitera, D. H. Saklofske, R. K. Heaton, et al. (Eds.), *Clinical interpretation of the WAIS-III and WMS-III* (pp. 147–179). San Diego, CA: Academic Press.

U.S. Census Bureau. (2004). Facts for features, hispanic heritage month 2004: September 15–October 15. CB04-FF.14-2.

Vega, A., Jr., & Parsons, O. A. (1967). Cross-validation of the Halstead–Reitan tests for brain damage. *Journal of Consulting Psychology, 31,* 619–625.

Vincent, K. R. (1991). Black/White IQ differences: Does age make the difference? *Journal of Clinical Psychology, 47,* 266–270.

Wechsler, D. (1945). A standardized memory scale for clinical use. *Journal of Psychology, 19,* 87–95.

Wechsler, D. (1955). *Manual for the Wechsler Adult Intelligence Scale.* New York: Psychological Corporation.

Wechsler, D. (1968). *Escala de Inteligencia Wechsler para Adultos.* New York: Psychological Corporation.

Wechsler, D. (1981). *WAIS-R Manual: Wechsler Adult Intelligence Scale-Revised.* New York: Psychological Corporation.

Wechsler, D. (1987). *Wechsler Memory Scale-Revised.* San Antonio, TX: The Psychological Corporation.

Wechsler, D. (1997a). *WAIS-III administration and scoring manual.* San Antonio, TX: The Psychological Corporation.

Wechsler, D. (1997b). *WMS-III administration and scoring manual.* San Antonio, TX: The Psychological Corporation.

Yeudall, L. T., Reddon, J. R., Gill, D. M., & Stefanyk, W. O. (1987). Normative data for the Halstead–Reitan neuropsychological tests stratified by age and sex. *Journal of Clinical Psychology, 43,* 346–367.

Youngjohn, J. R., Larrabee, G. J., & Crook, T. H. (1992). Discriminating age-associated memory impairment from Alzheimer's disease. *Psychological Assessment, 4,* 54–59.

Youngjohn, J. R., Larrabee, G. J., & Crook, T. H. (1993). New adult age- and education-correction norms for the Benton Visual Retention Test. *The Clinical Neuropsychologist, 7,* 155–160.

Part II

Neuropsychiatric Disorders

8

The Neuropsychology of Dementia

Mark W. Bondi, David P. Salmon, and Alfred W. Kaszniak

As an increasing number of people survive into older age, there is growing clinical and research interest in age-associated cognitive decline. This interest has focused to a large extent on the detection and characterization of cognitive deficits associated with age-related neurodegenerative diseases such as Alzheimer's disease (AD), but also includes identification of relatively subtle cognitive changes that take place during the course of normal healthy aging (for reviews, see Hedden & Gabrieli, 2004; Park et al., 2003). Cognitive decline that occurs with healthy aging is particularly evident in information-processing abilities such as effortful encoding of new information, processing speed, inductive reasoning, and working memory. Other cognitive abilities, such as semantic knowledge and vocabulary, autobiographical remote memory, and automatic memory processes (e.g., priming), show little age-related decline. This pattern of decline has led to the development of several psychological and neurological models to account for these changes. One prominent psychological model (Salthouse, 1996) suggests that a general decline in processing speed underlies most of the cognitive decline that occurs with age. According to this model, an age-related decline in information-processing speed reduces the ability to efficiently integrate and organize information, and causes a decline in memory by reducing the efficiency of information encoding, rehearsal, and retrieval. Similar psychological models suggest that cognitive decline in the healthy elderly is caused by

decline in a single factor such as working memory, inhibitory processes, or sensory function (Kramer et al., 2004; Park et al., 2003).

It has also been suggested that specific areas of the brain are particularly vulnerable to aging, and their deterioration leads to a decline in the cognitive abilities they mediate. For example, there is evidence that atrophy of prefrontal cortex and loss of frontal white matter integrity occurs as a normal consequence of aging (Greenwood, 2000; West, 1996). These changes result in age-related declines in so-called frontal functions such as working memory, cognitive flexibility, verbal fluency, directed and divided attention, and self-monitoring performance (Grady & Craik, 2000; Raz, 2005; West, 1996). Aging may also have a particularly adverse effect on white matter tracts that integrate brain regions (Bartzokis, 2004; O'Sullivan et al., 2001; Pfefferbaum et al., 2005; Raz, 2005), which leads to an age-related "disconnection" syndrome that causes cognitive changes beyond those that are usually considered frontal lobe functions (e.g., memory, visuospatial abilities). Other investigators propose that a staggered decline in multiple neurological processes may better explain cognitive changes associated with normal aging than any single neurobiological factor (Band et al., 2002; Buckner, 2004; Kramer et al., 2004).

As our knowledge of the cognitive changes that occur throughout the lifespan has grown, research efforts in the neuropsychology of aging and dementia have focused on differentiating these changes from the cognitive deficits associated with neurodegenerative disorders such as AD. In the remainder of this chapter, we review research that has identified the particular neuropsychological deficits that occur in the earliest stages of AD and show how this knowledge has enhanced the ability to clinically differentiate the early stages of the disease from normal aging. We will also examine the impact of aging on the ability to detect AD, and identify cognitive changes that might foreshadow the development of dementia in those with "prodromal" AD (see Dubois et al., 2007, for discussion). Finally, we will compare and contrast the patterns of cognitive deficits associated with AD and other age-related neurodegenerative disorders, and show how this has improved differential clinical diagnosis and provided important information about the neurological basis of various cognitive abilities. Before embarking on this discussion, it is first important to define the dementia syndrome, identify its prevalence and associated risk factors, and describe the most common age-related neurodegenerative diseases that lead to its manifestation.

The Syndrome of Dementia: Description, Prevalence, and Risk Factors

Definition

Dementia refers to a syndrome of acquired cognitive impairment due to brain dysfunction that is of sufficient severity to interfere with usual social or occupational functioning. According to most definitional schemes (e.g., *Diagnostic and Statistical Manual of Mental Disorders [DSM]— 4th edition*, American Psychiatric Association, 1994; Bayles & Kaszniak, 1987; Cummings & Benson, 1992; NINCDS-ADRDA criteria, McKhann et al., 1984), the syndrome of dementia involves deterioration in memory and one or more of the following domains: language, visuospatial skills, judgment or abstract thinking, or gnosis. These cognitive changes must represent a change from a previously higher level of performance and adversely affect functional abilities. Changes in emotion or personality are also common, but not a necessary component of the dementia syndrome. A Practice Parameter article on the diagnosis of dementia (Knopman

et al., 2001) concludes that these original criteria adopted in the DSM and by McKhann et al. (1984) are sensitive and specific with respect to the diagnosis of the dementia of AD, but may be less than ideal for the detection of dementia associated with other neurodegenerative diseases. Knopman et al. (2001) suggest that consideration of a broader array of cognitive (and behavioral) domains with less emphasis on memory might allow earlier and more accurate detection of vascular dementia (VaD), dementia with Lewy bodies (DLB), and frontotemporal dementia (FTD). As we will describe in subsequent sections, memory impairment is not necessarily a prominent part of the initial presentation of these non-AD dementias and should not be required in the definition of dementia.

Prevalence

Estimates of the prevalence of dementia vary widely due to differences in dementia definitions, sampling techniques, and sensitivity of instruments used to identify cases. In studies of dementia in various countries, prevalence rates have ranged from 2% to 25% for persons over the age of 65 (see Ineichen, 1987; Wancata et al., 2007). Cummings and Benson (1992), calculating the average of prevalence estimates across studies, suggest that approximately 6% of persons over the age of 65 have severe dementia, with an additional 10–15% having mild to moderate dementia. The prevalence of the syndrome of dementia is age-related, doubling approximately every 5 years after age 65 (Jorm et al., 1987). Not surprisingly, the prevalence of dementia is higher among hospital and nursing home residents than among those living within the community (Kramer, 1986; Smyer, 1988).

Risk Factors

Significant advances in our understanding of the epidemiology of dementia have occurred in recent years. Kawas and Katzman (1999) summarize a number of clear-cut findings that have emerged. First, by all accounts, *age* is the single most important risk factor for dementia. Community (population) studies in many different countries have confirmed that the prevalence of the most common causes of dementia, AD and vascular disease, rises in an approximately exponential fashion between the ages of 65 and 85. Importantly, however, data on individuals greater than age 85, who represent the fastest-growing segment of our population, generally show prevalence rates for dementia ranging between 40% and 60%, suggesting that it asymptotes beyond age 85.

Second, *gender* may be a significant risk factor for dementia. A large-scale epidemiological survey in Shanghai identified female gender, along with age and education, as an independent predictor of dementia (Zhang et al., 1990). A number of other studies suggest that women have a slightly greater risk for AD than men (although men may be at somewhat greater risk for vascular dementia). The results of these studies must be considered carefully, however, because the increased prevalence of AD in women may be attributable to differential survival after the onset of dementia due to their longer life expectancy. Although a 2.8:1 (female/male) ratio of AD was observed in the Framingham prevalence study (Bachman et al., 1992), no gender difference in the incidence of either dementia or AD was found in this cohort (Bachman et al., 1993). However, results from the Cache County epidemiological study of dementia demonstrate that incidence rates among women increase after age 80 and exceed the risk among men by more than twofold in late old age (Miech et al., 2002; Zandi et al., 2002).

Third, *low education* and *low occupational attainment* are associated with an increased risk for dementia. An uneducated individual over age 75 has twice the risk for dementia as someone who has completed at least a grade school education (Katzman, 1993; Kawas & Katzman, 1999; Mortimer, 1988; Zhang et al., 1990). Stern and colleagues (1994) demonstrated a similar relationship between risk for dementia and lifetime occupational attainment, and showed that a combination of low education and low lifetime occupational attainment results in a greater relative risk (i.e., close to a threefold increase in risk) than either one alone.

Katzman (1993) and Stern et al. (1992, 1994) were among the first to suggest that the decrease in risk of dementia with increasing levels of educational or lifetime occupational attainment

may occur because these factors are a surrogate for brain or cognitive reserve. Such a reserve would help to delay the onset of the usual clinical manifestations of the disease. Stern et al. (1992) reasoned that if advanced education imparts a reserve, then more severe pathological brain changes would be present in patients with high education than in those with low education at a time when the groups were matched for overall severity of dementia. Consistent with this prediction, they found a significantly greater deficit in parietotemporal blood flow in high-education probable AD patients than in equally demented low-education patients. The relationship between dementia and educational or occupational attainment is now supported by numerous epidemiological and biological studies that show high education, occupational work complexity, and a mentally and socially integrated lifestyle postpones the onset of clinical dementia and AD (for reviews, see Fratiglioni & Wang, 2007; Kawas & Katzman, 1999).

Fourth, a growing literature suggests that environmental influences such as *physical activity* and maintaining involvement in cognitively stimulating *mental activity* buttress cognitive functioning as we age (Hultsch et al., 1999; Kramer et al., 2004; Wilson et al., 2002). Furthermore, there is some evidence that physical and mental activity may result in structural brain changes in animals and humans (Churchill et al., 2002; van Praag et al., 2005), although studies directly investigating the impact of physical and/or mental activity on brain structure in humans have been extremely limited. Long-term benefits of exercise and cardiorespiratory fitness on cognition have been established, and clinical trials have shown that a fitness training intervention has a positive impact on cognitive functioning (particularly executive functions; Barnes et al., 2003). Physical activity has been shown to reduce risk for dementia and improve cognition in both cognitively normal and cognitively impaired older adults (see Fratiglioni et al., 2007; Kramer & Erickson, 2007, for reviews).

Fifth, the risk of developing dementia is increased approximately fourfold by a *family history* of AD in a first-degree relative (i.e., mother, father, brother, or sister; van Duijn et al., 1991). Given the findings of specific point mutations on the amyloid precursor protein gene of chromosome 21 and presenilin gene mutations on chromosomes 1 and 14, there is now little question that this familial association is genetically based and expressed in an autosomal dominant fashion, although a number of newer candidate genes for AD also relate to oxidative stress and inflammatory response (Serretti et al., 2007). Furthermore, the ε4 allele of the *apolipoprotein E (APOE)* gene located on chromosome 19 has been identified as the single most important susceptibility gene for dementia and AD (Corder et al., 1993; Saunders et al., 1993; Strittmatter et al., 1993) because of its overrepresentation in AD relative to healthy elderly.

Finally, *head injury* has been identified as a risk factor for the development of dementia (Jellinger, 2004; Mortimer et al., 1991). Dementia pugilistica may occur in individuals who have suffered repeated blows to the head while boxing (Corsellis et al., 1973), and retired professional football players with histories of recurrent concussions also show increased cognitive impairments in late life compared to retired players without concussive histories (Guskiewicz et al., 2005). The risk of developing AD is doubled for individuals with a history of a single head injury that led to loss of consciousness or hospitalization (Mortimer et al., 1991), and this relationship may be modulated by a gene–environment interaction as Mayeux and colleagues (1995) found a tenfold increase in the risk of AD in people with both the APOE ε4 allele and head injury risk factors. Jordan et al. (1997) also found that possession of an APOE ε4 allele was associated with increased severity of chronic neurologic deficits in high-exposure boxers.

The epidemiological evidence to date suggests that, as the population ages, dementia will increasingly become the dominant disorder in late life. In the short term, advances in identifying risk factors may improve our ability to detect dementia in its earliest stages when palliative treatments may be most effective and, in the long term, may lead to the discovery of specific biological mechanisms that cause the disease. Knowledge of the risk factors for dementia, and particularly AD, is growing rapidly, and now includes not only those imparted in late life but also those that arise across the lifespan. Early-life factors such as perinatal conditions, brain development, body growth, socioeconomic conditions, environmental enrichment, and cognitive reserve can influence the ultimate development of dementia and AD (see Borenstein et al., 2006). Even the major susceptibility gene for AD, the APOE ε4 allele, may have divergent effects on cognition across the lifespan. For example, studies suggest that the presence of the APOE ε4 allele may have a beneficial effect on cognition early in the lifespan (Bloss et al., 2008; Alexander et al., 2007; Han et al., 2007; Hubacek et al., 2001; Keltikangas-Jarvinen et al., 1993; Mondadori et al., 2007; Wright et al., 1993), in contrast to its well-known deleterious effects in late life. These seemingly discrepant effects of the APOE ε4 allele across the lifespan are consistent with the theory of antagonistic pleiotropy (Albin, 1993; Williams, 1957), a concept from evolutionary biology that posits that individual alleles can have different effects on fitness at different ages (see Han & Bondi, 2008; Alexander et al., 2007, for discussion). Regardless, the literature on risk factors for dementia suggests that risk is likely not determined at any single point in time, but results from a complex interplay between genetic and environmental exposures throughout one's life (Bornstein et al., 2006).

Specific Dementing Disorders: Clinical and Neuropathologic Features

Dementia is associated with more than 70 different causes. As mentioned earlier, AD is the most common cause of dementia, accounting for roughly half of all cases (for review, see Cummings & Benson, 1992; Kawas & Katzman, 1999). Vascular dementia (VaD) is usually regarded as the second most common cause, although in some community surveys (particularly, but not exclusively, those in Japan and China), VaD has been found to be as prevalent as AD (Dong et al., 2007). It is not clear whether such differences in relative prevalence estimates reflect actual regional disparities, or rather, methodological variation across studies. Other, less prevalent degenerative neurological diseases (e.g., Huntington's disease [HD], Parkinson's disease [PD], dementia with Lewy bodies [DLB], and frontotemporal dementias [FTD]) may also produce dementia, and they too have been the focus of much neuropsychological research. The neuropathologic and clinical features of some of the more common dementing disorders are briefly presented below (the reader is also referred to other chapters in this volume).

Alzheimer's Disease

AD is a progressive degenerative brain disorder characterized by neuronal atrophy, synapse loss, and the abnormal accumulation of diffuse and neuritic plaques and neurofibrillary tangles (Alzheimer, 1907; See Figure 8–1; see also the color figure in the color insert section). These pathologic changes begin primarily in medial temporal lobe limbic structures (e.g., entorhinal cortex, hippocampus) and then progress to the association cortices of the frontal, temporal, and parietal lobes (Braak & Braak, 1991). Primary motor and sensory cortices and most subcortical structures are relatively spared. Degeneration in the basal forebrain (e.g., the nucleus basalis of Meynert) results in a major decrement in

neocortical and hippocampal levels of the neurotransmitter acetylcholine (Whitehouse et al., 1982). Consistent with these widespread neuropathologic changes, the primary clinical manifestation of AD is a progressive global dementia syndrome that usually begins in later life. The dementia syndrome of AD is usually characterized by prominent amnesia with additional deficits in language and semantic knowledge (i.e., aphasia and agnosia), abstract reasoning, "executive" functions, attention, and constructional (i.e., apraxia) and visuospatial abilities (Salmon & Bondi, 1999). These cognitive deficits and the decline in everyday function they produce are the core features of the AD dementia syndrome.

Vascular Dementia

VaD refers to a cumulative decline in cognitive functioning secondary to multiple or strategically placed infarctions, ischemic injury, or hemorrhagic lesions. The clinical and neuropathologic presentation of VaD is quite heterogeneous, and a variety of conditions fall under the general rubric of VaD (see the chapter by

Pathology of Alzheimer's disease

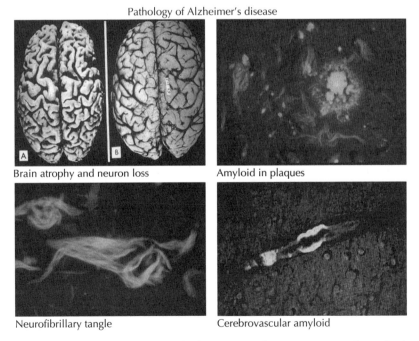

Brain atrophy and neuron loss

Amyloid in plaques

Neurofibrillary tangle

Cerebrovascular amyloid

Figure 8–1. The neuropathology of Alzheimer's disease. Grossly apparent cortical atrophy in Alzheimer's disease (Figure 1A) compared to normal aging (Figure 1B), and neocortical amyloid plaques (Figure 2), neurofibrillary tangles (Figure 3), and cerebrovascular amyloid angiopathy (Figure 4). (Images courtesy of Drs. Eliezer Masliah, Robert Terry, and Larry Hansen).

Brown in this volume). According to Hodges and Graham (2001), these conditions generally fall into three large categories: multi-infarct dementia (MID) associated with multiple large cortical infarctions (usually affecting 10 cc or more of brain tissue), dementia due to strategically placed infarction (e.g., left angular gyrus damage related to infarction of the posterior branch of the medial cerebral artery), and subcortical ischemic vascular dementia due to subcortical small vessel disease that results in multiple lacunar strokes, leukoaraiosis (Binswanger's disease) or diffuse white matter pathology.

Specific research criteria for the diagnosis of VaD have been proposed (e.g., Chui et al., 1992, 2000; Roman et al., 1993). In general, these guidelines require that multiple cognitive deficits (i.e., dementia) occur in the presence of focal neurological signs and symptoms and/ or laboratory (e.g., CT or MRI scan) evidence of cerebrovascular disease that are thought to cause the cognitive impairment (for review, see Chui, 2007). A relationship between dementia and cerebrovascular disease is often indicated if the onset of dementia occurs within several months of a recognized stroke, there is an abrupt deterioration in cognitive functioning, or the course of cognitive deterioration is fluctuating or stepwise. In one set of diagnostic criteria (Roman et al., 1993), VaD can be subcategorized on the basis of the suspected type of vascular pathology (as determined by clinical, radiologic, and neuropathologic features), and possible or probable VaD can be assigned depending on the certainty of the contribution of cerebrovascular disease to the dementia syndrome. Definite VaD is diagnosed only on the basis of histopathologic evidence of cerebrovascular disease that occurs in the absence of neurofibrillary tangles and neuritic plaques exceeding those expected for age and without clinical evidence of any other disorder capable of producing dementia (e.g., Pick's disease, diffuse Lewy body disease).

Huntington's Disease

Huntington's disease (HD) is an inherited autosomal dominant disease that results in the midlife (e.g., ages 30–40) development of movement disorder (e.g., chorea, dysarthria, gait disturbance, oculomotor dysfunction), behavioral changes (e.g., depression, irritability, and anxiety), and dementia. These deficits arise primarily from a progressive deterioration of the neostriatum (caudate nucleus and putamen) (Vonsattel & DiFiglia, 1998) that disrupts "frontostriatal loops" that consist of projections from the frontal neocortex to the striatum, striatum to the globus pallidus, globus pallidus to thalamus, and thalamus back to specific neocortical regions of the frontal lobes (e.g., dorsolateral prefrontal, orbitofrontal, and anterior cingulate cortex) (Alexander et al., 1986). These circuits are believed to have a subcortical influence on both motor control and higher cognitive functions (Alexander et al., 1986). The cognitive and behavioral deficits associated with HD have been described as a "subcortical dementia" syndrome that is broadly characterized by slowness of thought, impaired attention, executive dysfunction, poor learning, visuoperceptual and constructional deficits, and personality changes such as apathy and depression (Albert et al., 1974; McHugh & Folstein, 1975; also see Chapter 10).

Dementia with Lewy Bodies

Dementia with Lewy bodies (DLB) is a clinicopathologic condition characterized by a dementia syndrome that occurs:

• in the presence of cell loss and the deposition of Lewy bodies (abnormal intracytoplasmic eosinophilic neuronal inclusion bodies) in a subcortical pattern similar to that of PD (e.g., in brain stem nuclei including the substantia nigra, locus ceruleus, dorsal motor nucleus of the vagus, and substantia innominata);
• in the presence of Lewy bodies diffusely distributed throughout the limbic system (e.g., cingulate, insula, amygdala, hippocampus, entorhinal cortex, and transentorhinal cortex) and neocortex (e.g., temporal, parietal, and frontal lobes), and in many cases AD pathology (i.e., neuritic plaques, neurofibrillary tangles) that occurs in the same general distribution throughout the brain as in "pure" AD (Gomez-Tortosa et al., 2000; Hansen et al., 1990; Ince et al., 1998; Kosaka et al., 1984; Perry et al., 1990)

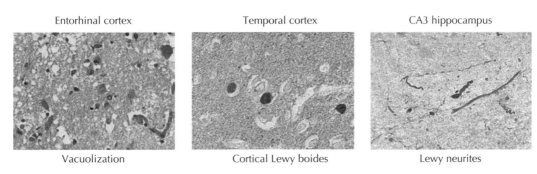

Entorhinal cortex	Temporal cortex	CA3 hippocampus
Vacuolization	Cortical Lewy boides	Lewy neurites

Figure 8–2. Histopathologic abnormalities in the limbic system and neocortex in Dementia with Lewy Bodies (DLB). The typical appearance of vacuolization in the entorhinal cortex, cortical Lewy bodies in the temporal lobe neocortex, and Lewy neurites (i.e., neurons containing abnormal alpha-synuclein filaments) in the CA3 region of the hippocampus. (Images courtesy of Dr. Eliezer Masliah).

(see Figure 8–2; see also color figure in the color insert section).

DLB is associated with widespread depletion of cortical choline acetyltransferase (ChAT) in the neocortex and striatum (e.g., Tiraboschi et al., 2002), and a disruption of dopaminergic input to the striatum due to the loss of pigmented substantia nigra neurons (Ince et al., 1998). Dementia with Lewy bodies is not rare and may occur in approximately 25% of all elderly demented patients.

Frontotemporal Dementia

FTD is a clinicopathologic condition characterized by deterioration of personality and cognition associated with prominent frontal and temporal lobar atrophy (Brun et al., 1994). A number of disorders fall under the rubric of FTD, including Pick's disease (Kertesz et al., 1999; Pick, 1892), familial chromosome 17-linked frontal lobe dementia (Wilhelmsen et al., 1994), dementia lacking distinctive histopathology (DLDH; Knopman et al., 1990), semantic dementia (Snowden et al., 1989), and primary progressive aphasia (Kertesz et al., 1994; Mesulam, 1982). Although each of these disorders has a somewhat unique clinical manifestation, FTD usually begins insidiously with personality and behavioral changes (e.g., inappropriate social conduct, inertia and apathy, disinhibition, perseverative behavior, loss of insight, hyperorality, and decreased speech output). These behavioral changes are accompanied (or soon followed) by cognitive deficits

that include alterations in executive functions and/or aphasia, often with relative sparing of visuospatial abilities and memory (see Weder et al., 2007, for review). Various forms of FTD are thought to account for approximately 3–20% of all cases of dementia (Andreasen et al., 1999; Brun, 1987; Neary, 1999).

Neuropsychological Detection of Alzheimer's Disease

A wealth of neuropsychological research over the past two decades has identified the particular neuropsychological deficits that occur in the earliest stages of AD and enhanced the ability to clinically differentiate the disease from normal aging. Given that the hippocampus and entorhinal cortex are affected in the earliest stages of AD (Braak & Braak, 1991), it is not surprising that measures of the ability to learn and retain new information are among the most effective in differentiating between mildly demented AD patients and normal older adults (e.g., Bayles et al., 1989; Delis et al., 1991; Eslinger et al., 1985; Huff et al., 1987; Kaszniak et al., 1986; Storandt et al., 1984). Patients with early AD are particularly impaired on measures of *delayed recall*, a characteristic that has important clinical utility for the detection and differential diagnosis of the disease (e.g., Butters et al., 1988; Locascio et al., 1995; Welsh et al., 1991). Several studies have shown that *rapid forgetting* expressed as absolute delayed recall scores or "savings" scores (i.e., amount recalled after the delay divided by the amount recalled on the immediate learning trial) can differentiate mildly demented

AD patients from healthy elderly with 85–90% accuracy (Butters et al., 1988; Flicker et al., 1991; Knopman & Ryberg, 1989; Morris et al., 1991; Tröster et al., 1993; Welsh et al., 1991).

The abnormally rapid forgetting shown by patients with AD suggests that their memory disorder may be due to ineffective *consolidation* of information. This possibility is supported by studies that have shown to-be-remembered information is not accessible after a delay even if retrieval demands are reduced by the use of recognition testing (e.g., Delis et al., 1991), and by studies that demonstrate an abnormal *serial position* effect in the episodic memory performance of patients with AD (Bayley et al., 2000; Capitani et al., 1992; Carlesimo et al., 1995; Greene et al., 1996; Massman et al., 1993; Wilson et al., 1983). In these latter studies, patients with early AD consistently show a reduction of the primacy effect (i.e., recall of words from the beginning of a list), suggesting that they cannot effectively transfer information from primary memory (i.e., a passive, time-dependent, limited capacity store that allows the most recent items to be better recalled than other items) to secondary memory (an actively accessed, long-lasting store that allows early list items that received the greatest amount of processing to be better recalled than other items), or that they cannot maintain information in secondary memory after its successful transfer. This deficit has led to the development of several effective clinical tests for early AD that distinguish between primary (or short-term) and secondary (or long-term) memory (e.g., California Verbal Learning Test–2nd edition [CVLT-II]; Delis et al., 2000; Buschke selective reminding procedure; Buschke, 1973).

Impaired *encoding* ability may also adversely affect AD patients' performance on episodic memory tests (Martin et al., 1985). Semantic encoding procedures (Goldblum et al., 1998) or the use of materials that allow the use of semantic encoding strategies (for review, see Backman & Small, 1998) are less effective in improving episodic memory performance in patients with AD than in normal elderly individuals. This semantic encoding deficit is targeted by several clinical memory tests that effectively differentiate between mildly demented AD patients and normal elderly individuals (e.g., Buschke et al., 1997; Knopman & Ryberg, 1989).

A prominent qualitative feature of the memory deficit of patients with AD is an enhanced tendency to produce *intrusion errors* (Butters et al., 1987; Fuld et al., 1982; Jacobs et al., 1990). That is, patients will incorrectly produce old, previously learned information during the attempt to recall new material. The abnormal production of intrusion errors has been interpreted as increased sensitivity to interference or deficient inhibitory processes in patients with AD. Although intrusion errors are not a pathognomonic sign of AD (Jacobs et al., 1990), their occurrence can be a useful adjunct to other memory measures (e.g., total recall, recognition memory, rate of forgetting) in developing clinical algorithms for detecting early AD and differentiating it from other types of dementia (Delis et al., 1991).

Patients with AD often exhibit a severe deficit in the ability to remember past events that were successfully remembered prior to the onset of the disease (i.e., *retrograde amnesia*). The retrograde amnesia of AD is temporally graded with memories from the distant past better retained than memories from the more recent past (Beatty et al., 1988; Hodges et al., 1993; Kopelman, 1989; Sagar et al., 1988; Wilson et al., 1981). This pattern of loss is similar to that of patients with circumscribed amnesia (Albert et al., 1979; Squire et al., 1989) and has been attributed to the interruption of a long-term consolidation process (e.g., shifting memory from an episodic to a semantic form) that is critically dependent upon the hippocampal-diencephalic memory system (Cermak, 1984; Squire, 1987; Zola-Morgan & Squire, 1990; but see Nadel & Moscovitch, 1997). However, AD patients are often impaired even for the most remote time periods, which may result from a combination of the episodic and semantic memory deficits that they suffer (for review, see Salmon, 2000).

Although the episodic memory impairment described above is usually the earliest and most prominent feature of the dementia of AD, a number of higher-order cognitive processes become affected as the neuropathology spreads beyond medial temporal lobe structures to the association cortices of the temporal, frontal, and parietal lobes (Braak & Braak, 1991). For example, *semantic memory* that underlies general knowledge and language is often disturbed relatively early in the course of AD (for reviews, see

Hodges & Patterson, 1995; Nebes, 1989; Salmon et al., 1999). This disturbance is evident in AD patients' reduced ability to recall overlearned facts (e.g., the number of days in a year; Norton et al., 1997), and in their impairment on tests of confrontation naming (Bayles & Tomoeda, 1983; Bowles et al., 1987; Hodges et al., 1991; Huff et al., 1986; Martin & Fedio, 1983), verbal fluency (Butters et al., 1987; Martin & Fedio, 1983; Monsch et al., 1994), and semantic categorization (Aronoff et al., 2006; Chan et al., 1998). In addition, the spontaneous speech of patients with AD is frequently vague, empty of content words, and filled with indefinite phrases and circumlocutions (Nicolas et al., 1985).

The semantic memory deficit exhibited by patients with AD may reflect the loss of semantic knowledge for particular items or concepts during the course of the disease. Studies that have probed for knowledge of particular concepts across different modes of access and output (e.g., fluency, confrontation naming, sorting, word-to-picture matching, definition generation) showed that patients with AD were significantly impaired on all measures of semantic memory, and when a particular stimulus item was missed (or correctly identified) in one task, it was likely to be missed (or correctly identified) in other tasks that accessed the same information in a different way (Chertkow & Bub, 1990; Hodges et al., 1992). A true loss of semantic knowledge (rather than deficient retrieval) in mildly demented patients with AD was also implicated in a longitudinal study by Norton and colleagues (1997) that showed year-to-year consistency in the items missed during progressive decline on a test of general knowledge (i.e., the Number Information Test) that had minimal language demands (also see Salmon et al., 1999).

In addition to memory and language deficits, patients with early AD often exhibit deficits in *"executive" functions* responsible for concurrent mental manipulation of information, concept formation, problem solving, and cue-directed behavior (Perry & Hodges, 1999). A study by Lefleche and Albert (1995) demonstrated that the ability to perform concurrent manipulation of information appears to be particularly vulnerable in early AD. In this study, very mildly demented patients with AD were significantly impaired relative to elderly normal control

subjects on tests that required set-shifting, self-monitoring, or sequencing, but not on tests that required cue-directed attention or verbal problem solving. The executive function deficits associated with AD are also evident on difficult problem-solving tests such as the Tower of London puzzle (Lange et al., 1995) and the modified Wisconsin Card Sorting Task (Bondi et al., 1993), on tests of relational integration (Waltz et al., 2004), and on various other clinical neuropsychological tests such as the Porteus Maze Task, Part B of the Trail-Making Test, and the Raven Progressive Matrices Task (Grady et al., 1988; for review, see Duke & Kasular, 2000).

Some aspects of *attention* are often impaired relatively early in the course of AD. Attention deficits in mildly demented AD patients have been shown by using dual-processing tasks, tasks that require the disengagement and shifting of attention, and working memory tasks that are dependent upon the control of attentional resources (for reviews, see Duke & Kasular, 2000; Parasuraman & Haxby, 1993; Perry & Hodges, 1999). The ability to focus and sustain attention is usually only affected in later stages of the disease, as was shown by the essentially normal performance of mildly demented AD patients on the Attention/Concentration Index of the Wechsler Memory Scale-Revised (WMS-R), a measure derived from performance on tests of digit span (forward and backward), visual memory span (forward and backward), and mental control (Butters et al., 1988).

Patients with AD often exhibit deficits in *visuospatial abilities* that are apparent on visuo-constructional tasks such as the Block Design Test (Mohr et al., 1990; Pandovani et al., 1995; Villardita, 1993), the Clock Drawing Test (for review, see Freedman et al., 1994), or copying a complex figure (Locascio et al., 1995; Mohr et al., 1990; Pandovani et al., 1995; Villardita, 1993). Deficits are also often apparent on tasks that require visuoperception and visual orientation, such as the Judgment of Line Orientation test (Ska et al., 1990), the Money Road Map Test (Locascio et al., 1995), and the Hooper Visual Orientation Test (Paxton et al., 2007). These visuospatial deficits are usually not apparent in the very earliest stages of AD and may have little to contribute to the differentiation of early dementia from normal aging (e.g., Locascio et al.,

1995; Storandt et al., 1984). However, visuospatial abilities decline over time in AD and may be useful for tracking the progression of the disease (see Paxton et al., 2007).

Taken together, the neuropsychological research findings reviewed above suggest that AD usually results in a specific pattern of cognitive deficits that can help differentiate the disease from normal aging. Prominent deficits in episodic memory (e.g., rapid forgetting), certain executive functions (e.g., cognitive set-shifting), and semantic knowledge characterize the disease early on, and are thought to have clinical utility for early detection of AD. This was confirmed in a study that directly compared the ability of a number of sensitive measures of learning and memory, executive abilities, language, and visuospatial abilities to differentiate between 98 patients with mild AD (i.e., scored ≥ 24 on the Mini-Mental State Exam) and 98 gender-, age-, and education-matched normal control subjects (Salmon et al., 2002). The diagnosis of AD was verified in each of the AD patients by subsequent autopsy or longitudinal clinical evaluations that showed a typical course for the disease. Receiver Operating Characteristic (ROC) curve analyses showed excellent sensitivity and specificity for the detection of very mild AD for learning and delayed recall measures from the California Verbal Learning Test (CVLT) (sensitivity: 95–98%, specificity: 88–89%), the category fluency test (sensitivity: 96%, specificity: 88%), and Part B of the Trail-Making Test (sensitivity: 85%, specificity: 83%). A diagnostic model obtained using a nonparametric recursive partitioning procedure (Classification Tree Analysis) showed that a combination of performance on the category fluency test (a measure of semantic memory and executive function) and the delayed recall measure of the Visual Reproduction Test accurately classified 96% of the patients with AD and 93% of the elderly normal control subjects, a level of accuracy higher than achieved with any individual cognitive measure; similar correct classification rates were seen when the Dementia Rating Scale was allowed in the analysis (see Figure 8–3). These findings substantiate the typical pattern of deficits usually observed

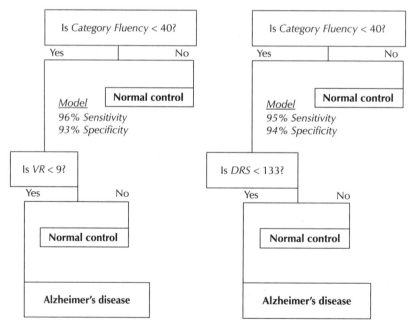

Note: VR = Visual Reproduction Delayed Recall; DRS = Dementia Rating Scale

Figure 8–3. Two classification and regression tree models that were maximally effective in differentiating patients with mild Alzheimer's disease from healthy older adults. The variables retained in the models included a measure of category fluency (i.e., sum of animals, fruits, and vegetables) and either global cognition (i.e., DRS total score) or delayed recall (i.e., Visual Reproduction Test raw score). (Adapted from Salmon et al., 2002).

in AD and attest to the clinical utility of a thorough neuropsychological evaluation for early diagnosis.

There is a growing body of experimental evidence to indicate that the cortical neuropathology of AD results in the loss of effective interaction between distinct and relatively intact cortical information-processing systems (e.g., DeLacoste & White, 1993). Because the neurofibrillary tangle pathology of AD has a strong predilection for cortical layers (e.g., Layer-III and Layer-V) and cell types (e.g., mid-size pyramidal neurons) that support connections between functionally related cortical association areas, it effectively disconnects the hippocampus from neocortex (e.g., Hyman et al., 1984) and disrupts corticocortical pathways that connect cortical association areas (for review, see Hof & Morrison, 1999). This disconnection is evident in marked abnormalities in the interregional pattern of blood-flow activation elicited during the performance of cognitive tasks (e.g., Delbeuck et al., 2003; Grady et al., 2001; Haxby et al., 1985), and reduced coherence (i.e., synchronization) between electroencephalography (EEG) signals measured at different scalp surface electrode sites that correspond to neocortical association areas that must work in concert during integrative cognitive tasks (e.g., crossmodal stimulus processing) (e.g., Dunkin et al., 1995; Hogan et al., 2003; Jelic et al., 1996; Knott et al., 2000; Stevens et al., 2001). Behaviorally, corticocortical disconnectivity in patients with AD is demonstrated by an impaired ability to "bind" distinct visual stimulus features that are effectively processed in different cortical streams (i.e., motion and color; Festa et al., 2005), to identify objects through the integration of perceptual, lexical, and semantic representations mediated by distinct cortical regions (Della Sala et al., 2000; Dobkins & Albright, 1998; Foster et al., 1999; Freedman & Oscar-Berman, 1997; Kurylo et al., 1996; Lakmache et al., 1998; Tales et al., 2002; Tippett et al., 2003), or to perform cross-hemispheric integration of information discretely processed in left- or right-hemisphere cortical regions (Golob et al., 2001). These results suggest that behavioral evidence of cortical disconnectivity may have potential as a cognitive marker for detecting and tracking progression of AD.

Impact of Aging on the Neuropsychological Detection of Alzheimer's Disease

The boundaries between normal age-related cognitive change and early signs of AD are particularly difficult to delineate in very elderly individuals (e.g., over the age of 80). This is because many of the early structural and functional changes of AD overlap with changes that occur in normal aging. Normal aging is associated with mild brain atrophy on structural magnetic resonance imaging (MRI; Jack et al., 1998; Jernigan et al., 2001; Pfefferbaum et al. 1994), decreased hemodynamic response on functional MR imaging (D'Esposito et al., 1999), reduced synaptic density (Masliah et al., 1993), and increased white matter abnormalities (Guttman et al., 1998; Jernigan et al., 2001; Salat et al., 1999). These brain changes are thought to mediate age-related decline in information-processing speed, executive functions, learning efficiency, and effortful retrieval (Corey-Bloom et al., 1996; Desgranges et al., 1998; Grady et al., 1995; Gunning-Dixon & Raz, 2000; Kaszniak & Newman, 2000; Schacter et al., 1996; Ylikoski et al., 1993). Because normal aging detrimentally affects many of the same cognitive abilities affected by AD (see the previous section), the prominence of specific deficits related to AD may be much less evident in the Very-Old than in the Young-Old, especially after performance is standardized to the age-appropriate normal cohort. This may result in a less distinct and somewhat atypical cognitive deficit profile associated with AD in the Very-Old compared to Young-Old.

This possibility was confirmed in a study that directly compared the neuropsychological test performance of AD patients who were over the age of 80 (Very-Old) or below the age of 70 (Young-Old) (Bondi et al., 2003). Despite achieving similar raw scores on all neuropsychological measures, the Young-Old and Very-Old AD patients differed in the severity and pattern of cognitive deficits they exhibited in relation to their age-appropriate control groups (see Figure 8–4). Analysis of composite age-appropriate z-scores in various cognitive domains showed that Young-Old AD patients were generally more impaired than Very-Old patients and

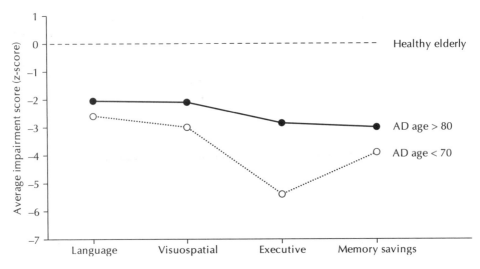

Figure 8–4. The average composite impairment score achieved by Alzheimer's disease (AD) patients older than age 80 or younger than age 70 in the cognitive domains of language, visuospatial abilities, executive functions, and memory (savings scores). The presented scores are z-scores referenced to the patient groups' respective age-appropriate healthy elderly control cohort. (Adapted from Bondi et al., 2003).

had a typical AD profile. That is, they exhibited deficits in executive functions and the retention of episodic memories (i.e., savings scores) that were greater than their deficits in other cognitive domains. By contrast, Very-Old AD patients exhibited a similar level of impairment across all cognitive domains so that their deficit profile lacked the disproportionate saliency of memory and executive function deficits typical of the disease.

It is interesting to note that the distinct cognitive profiles exhibited by Young-Old and Very-Old AD patients actually reflected differences in the respective age-matched normative cohorts. Although the raw scores of the younger and older AD patients were similar, the older control group performed significantly worse than the younger control group on nearly all cognitive tests, with the largest differences apparent on tests of memory, executive functions, and category fluency. Thus, the better z-scores of the Very-Old AD patients compared to the Young-Old AD patients are a function of lower mean performance in the older control group on tests of cognitive abilities that are vulnerable to normal age-related decline. Although increased variability in test performance related to normal aging could also impact the z-scores of the Very-Old AD patients, Bondi and colleagues

(2003) showed that this was not the driving factor in their study because the variance associated with the various cognitive scores did not differ between the older and younger normal control groups.

These and similar results clearly indicate that normal aging can significantly impact the severity and pattern of neuropsychological deficits associated with early AD and reduce the saliency of the deficit profile as a diagnostic marker of the disease. This finding has important clinical implications because it identifies the significant risk of false-negative diagnostic errors in very elderly AD patients if the clinician expects to see the typical deficit pattern characteristic of younger AD patients.

Neuropsychological Detection of "Prodromal" Alzheimer's Disease

It is now commonly accepted that the neurodegenerative changes of AD begin well before the clinical manifestations of the disease become apparent (e.g., Katzman, 1994). As the pathologic changes of AD gradually accumulate, a threshold for the initiation of the clinical symptoms of the disease is eventually reached. Once this threshold is crossed, cognitive deficits associated with AD become evident and

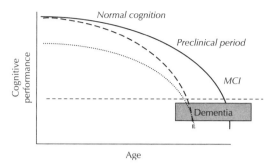

Figure 8–5. Modification of the chronic disease model of Alzheimer's disease first proposed by Katzman (1976). The solid line (—) represents a typical trajectory of cognitive decline for most individuals who do not carry risk factors for the disease. The dotted line (....) represents a trajectory of decline for individuals who have the same degree of neuropathologic changes and contributing causes as those depicted in the solid line but who have less brain reserve capacity perhaps from poorer neural development or interconnectivity. The dashed line (– –) represents individuals with the same relative brain reserve capacity as those depicted in the solid line but who have a genetic or environmental predisposition to AD.

gradually worsen in parallel with continued neurodegeneration. When the cognitive deficits become global and severe enough to interfere with normal social and occupational functioning, established criteria for dementia and a clinical diagnosis of AD are met. It is clear from this sequence of events that subtle cognitive decline is likely to occur in a patient with AD well before the clinical diagnosis can be made with any certainty. Identification of the cognitive changes that occur during this "prodromal" phase of the disease might provide a way to reliably detect AD in its earliest stages, when potential disease-modifying treatments might be most effective (Thal, 1999). Because of the importance of this goal, the attempt to identify prodromal cognitive changes of AD is one of the most active areas of neuropsychological research (see Figure 8–5).

In light of neuropathological evidence that the earliest changes of AD usually occur in the medial temporal lobe structures that are known to be critical for episodic memory (Braak & Braak, 1991), it is not surprising that the search for prodromal cognitive markers of the disease

has focused largely on this aspect of cognition. Indeed, a number of prospective longitudinal studies of cognitive function in nondemented older adults have shown that a subtle decline in episodic memory often occurs prior to the emergence of the obvious cognitive and behavioral changes required for a clinical diagnosis of AD (Bondi et al., 1994; Fuld et al., 1990; Grober & Kawas, 1997; Howieson et al., 1997; Jacobs et al., 1995; Tschanz et al., 2006). In some cases, decline in episodic memory becomes apparent many years prior to the onset of dementia (Backman et al., 2001; Bondi et al., 1999; Kawas et al., 2003; Linn et al., 1995; Schaie et al., 2005; Small et al., 2000). These and similar findings led to the development of formal criteria for *Mild Cognitive Impairment* (MCI; Peterson et al., 1995), a predementia condition in elderly individuals that is characterized by both subjective and objective memory impairment that occurs in the face of relatively preserved general cognition and functional abilities (for reviews, see Albert & Blacker, 2006; Collie & Maruff, 2000; Peterson et al., 2001).

The course of episodic memory change during the prodromal phase of AD has been the focus of a number of studies (Backman et al., 2001; Chen et al., 2001; Rubin et al., 1998; Small et al., 2000; Storandt et al., 2002). These studies suggest that memory performance may be poor but stable a number of years prior to the development of the dementia syndrome in those with AD, and then decline rapidly in the period immediately preceding the dementia diagnosis. Consistent with this plateau model of decline, Small et al. (2000) and Backman et al. (2001) found that episodic memory was mildly impaired 6 years prior to dementia onset, but changed little over the next 3 years. In contrast, Chen et al. (2001) and Lange et al. (2002) showed a significant and steady decline in episodic memory beginning about 3 years prior to the dementia diagnosis in individuals with prodromal AD. These results indicate that an abrupt decline in memory in an elderly individual might better predict the imminent onset of dementia than poor but stable memory ability. Such a plateau model (i.e., mild but stable episodic memory decline followed by more abrupt decline in the years proximal to diagnosis) was validated in a large-scale study by Smith et al.

(2007), who found that the plateau was evident on tests of episodic memory, but not on tests of other cognitive domains.

Although the search for cognitive changes in prodromal AD has largely focused on episodic memory (see also position paper by Dubois et al., 2007), several recent reviews and meta-analyses suggest that there is largely nonspecific cognitive decline in the 2 to 3 years preceding a dementia diagnosis. Although a decline in episodic memory is consistently found in these studies, they also often reveal additional deficits in executive functions, perceptual speed, verbal ability, visuospatial skill, and attention during the prodromal phase of AD (Backman et al., 2004, 2005; Storandt et al., 2006; Twamley et al., 2006). This widespread decline in cognitive abilities mirrors evidence that multiple brain regions (e.g., medial and lateral temporal lobes, frontal lobes, anterior cingulate cortex) are impaired in prodromal AD (Albert et al., 2001; Small et al., 2003) (see Table 8–1).

Several studies suggest that measures of semantic knowledge (i.e., vocabulary, naming, category fluency) decline during the prodromal period of AD, even though they are relatively independent of episodic memory impairment (Koenig et al., 2007) and not particularly susceptible to normal age-related decline (Mickes et al. 2007; see also Cuetos et al., 2007; Powell et al., 2006). Thus, semantic memory impairment may be a promising cognitive marker for prodromal detection of AD in at-risk elderly individuals. This possibility is supported by the results of a recent neuropsychological study that showed that both semantic and episodic memory declined rapidly in a 3 year prodromal period progressing to AD, whereas decline in executive functions was not especially prominent (Mickes et al., 2007; see Figure 8–6). Based upon these findings, Mickes et al. suggested that cognitive functions subserved by the medial and lateral temporal lobes (episodic memory and semantic knowledge, respectively) are substantially more impaired than cognitive functions subserved by the frontal lobes (executive functioning) in early AD. In addition, these results are consistent with a report of decreased semantic access in nondemented older adults at risk for AD owing to the presence of the APOE ε4 allele (Rosen et al., 2005), and with the results of

Table 8–1. Summary of the percentage of studies ($N = 73$) documenting specific cognitive domains affected in the prodromal period of Alzheimer's disease.

Neuropsychological Domain	Percentage of Studies with Affected Domain
Attention	71
Verbal Learning	57
Verbal Memory	50
Executive Functions	44
Processing Speed	43
General Cognition	38
Language	33
Visual Learning	29
Visual Memory	28
Visuospatial Abilities	26
Praxis	17
Motor Speed	17
Working Memory	12

Notes: The cognitive domains most consistently associated with prodromal AD were attention (e.g., 71% of studies in which it was assessed), verbal learning and memory, executive functions, processing speed, and language.

Source: Adapted from Twamley et al. (2006).

a study that demonstrated that language tasks were predictive of AD pathology observed 6 years later (Powell et al., 2006).

A study by Jacobson and colleagues (2002) identified *asymmetric* cognitive profiles as a possible prodromal marker of AD in at-risk older adults. Based upon prior research showing lateralized cognitive deficits (e.g., greater verbal than visuospatial deficits, or vice versa) in subgroups of mildly demented patients with AD, these investigators suggested that inconsistent findings of cognitive markers in at-risk groups occur because subgroups of subjects have asymmetric deficits that cannot be appreciated with the use of a single test. To test this hypothesis, Jacobson and colleagues compared 20 cognitively normal elderly adults who were in a prodromal phase of AD (i.e., they were diagnosed with AD approximately 1 year later) and 20 age- and education-matched normal control subjects on a number of individual cognitive test scores and a derived score that reflected the absolute difference between verbal and visuospatial ability (i.e., a measure of cognitive asymmetry). Although the groups performed similarly on individual cognitive tests of memory, language, and visuospatial ability, the prodromal AD

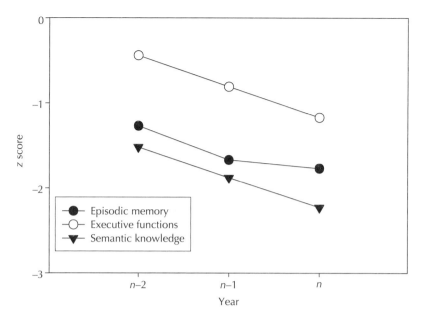

Figure 8–6. Aggregate control-referenced z-scores for prodromal AD patients on tests of episodic memory, semantic memory, and executive functions. Their neuropsychological profiles were examined 1 year ($n–1$) and 2 years ($n–2$) prior to the first year of their non-normal diagnosis (referred to as year n). (Adapted from Mickes et al., 2007).

patients were more likely than normal control subjects to exhibit evidence of cognitive asymmetry in either the verbal or visuospatial direction. These results suggest that a subgroup of prodromal AD patients have asymmetric cognitive changes that are obscured when cognitive scores are averaged over the entire group. Additional evidence of cognitive asymmetry in prodromal AD or in elderly individuals at risk for AD has been shown in subsequent studies that compared auditory versus spatial attention (Jacobson et al., 2005a), verbal versus design fluency (Houston et al., 2005), global versus local item processing (Jacobson et al., 2005b), and response inhibition versus cognitive flexibility (Wetter et al., 2005). Consideration of these nonmemory changes in conjunction with subtle declines in episodic memory may improve the ability to detect AD in its earliest stages.

Differentiating Alzheimer's Disease from Other Dementias

Dementia can arise from a wide variety of etiologically and neuropathologically distinct disorders that give rise to somewhat different patterns of preserved and impaired cognitive abilities. Knowledge of these differences might lead to better understanding of the neurobiological basis of various cognitive disorders, have important implications for the neurobiological basis of normal cognition, and improve differential diagnosis of various neurodegenerative disorders. The remaining sections will review similarities and differences in the cognitive deficits of AD and those of other age-related causes of dementia including HD, DLB, FTD, and VaD.

Alzheimer's Disease vs. Huntington's Disease

Many aspects of cognition are affected in qualitatively distinct ways by AD and HD. One distinction is evident in the nature of the episodic memory deficits associated with the two disorders. As described in the section above, the dementia of AD is usually characterized by a severe deficit in episodic memory that has been attributed to ineffective consolidation (i.e., storage) of new information (Salmon, 2000). In contrast, the dementia of HD is usually characterized by mild to moderate memory impairment that appears to result from a general deficit in the ability to initiate and carry out the systematic retrieval of otherwise successfully stored information (Butters et al., 1985, 1986; Moss et al., 1986). These differences were demonstrated in a study by Delis and colleagues (1991) that directly compared AD and HD patients on a rigorous test of verbal learning and memory (i.e., the CVLT). Despite comparable immediate and delayed recall deficits (based on age-corrected normative data), patients with AD were just as impaired on the recognition trial as they were on the free recall trials, whereas patients with HD were less impaired on the recognition trial than on free recall trials. The benefit of recognition testing for the HD patients suggests that their memory impairment is attenuated when the need for effortful, strategic retrieval is reduced (Butters et al., 1985, 1986), a benefit not shared by patients with AD. In addition, patients with AD exhibited significantly faster forgetting over the 20-minute delay interval than did patients with HD (also see Butters et al., 1988; Troster et al., 1993). Patients with AD retained less than 20% of the initially acquired information, whereas those with HD retained a near-normal 70%. These distinct deficit patterns are consistent with the notion that information is not effectively consolidated by patients with AD because of early damage to medial temporal lobe structures (e.g., hippocampus, entorhinal cortex), whereas information can be successfully stored but not effectively retrieved by patients with HD, presumably owing to disruption of frontostriatal circuits (although some residual memory deficit is apparent even when retrieval demands are reduced; Brandt et al., 1992; for review, see Montoya et al., 2006).

The ineffective retrieval exhibited by patients with HD on tests of episodic memory is also evident in their performance on tests of remote memory. Whereas patients with AD show a severe and temporally graded retrograde amnesia, patients with HD exhibit a relatively mild retrograde amnesia that equally affects all time periods (Albert et al., 1981; Beatty et al., 1988; Sadek et al., 2004). Presumably, episodic memory that was acquired in the past is successfully stored and retained over time by these patients, but retrieval of this information is generally deficient, causing the remote memory deficit to be equally distributed across decades. This interpretation is bolstered by an analysis of cued retrieval in a remote memory task that indicated a preferential cueing benefit for patients with HD compared to patients with AD (Sadek et al., 2004).

A number of qualitative differences exist in the language and semantic knowledge deficits exhibited by patients with AD and HD. For example, patients with AD usually exhibit a significant confrontation naming deficit (e.g., Bayles & Tomoeda, 1983), and the greatest proportion of their naming errors are semantically based (e.g., superordinate errors such as calling a "camel" an "animal"). In contrast, patients with HD usually have little difficulty with confrontation naming (Folstein et al., 1990; Hodges et al., 1991), and the naming errors they make tend to be perceptually based (e.g., calling a "pretzel" a "snake"; Hodges et al., 1991). Differences also exist in the pattern of verbal fluency deficits associated with the two disorders. Patients with HD are severely and equivalently impaired on both letter fluency (i.e., generate words that begin with the letters "F," "A," or "S") and category fluency (i.e., generate exemplars of animals, fruits, or vegetables) tasks, whereas patients with AD are more impaired on category fluency than on letter fluency tasks (Butters et al., 1987; Monsch et al., 1994; for reviews, see Henry et al., 2004, 2005). Studies of the temporal dynamics of retrieval from semantic memory during the letter and category fluency tasks provide some information about the nature of the loss that underlies these distinct deficit patterns (Rohrer et al., 1995, 1999). Patients with AD achieved a lower-than-normal mean latency consistent with the idea that they effectively draw exemplars from a semantic set that is abnormally small due to a loss of semantic knowledge. Patients with HD, in contrast, had a higher-than-normal mean response latency consistent with the notion that they have a normal semantic set size, but draw exemplars abnormally slowly due to ineffective retrieval.

The view that AD and HD differentially impact the integrity of the structure and organization of semantic memory was directly examined by Chan and colleagues using cluster analysis and multidimensional scaling techniques to statistically model a spatial representation of the degree of association between concepts in semantic memory (for review, see Chan et al., 1998). The degree of association between the various exemplars in the category "animals" was estimated from their proximate position when generated in a verbal fluency task, or from the frequency with which they were paired in a triadic comparison task. Modeling showed that the network of semantic associations for patients with HD was virtually identical to that of control subjects, whereas that of patients with AD was characterized by less consistency and weaker and more concrete associations (i.e., size was emphasized rather than domesticity). Thus, AD appears to be characterized by a decline in the structure and organization of semantic knowledge that does not occur in HD. Because the categorization task placed little demand on retrieval processes, the results also support the possibility that HD is characterized by a general retrieval deficit that is not influenced by the demands various tasks place on the structure of semantic memory.

Although memory is usually thought of as a conscious process in which an individual explicitly attempts to remember a specific bit of information, there are some forms of memory that occur without conscious awareness (i.e., implicit memory) and without dependence upon the medial temporal lobe structures important for explicit episodic memory (Schacter, 1987; Squire, 1987). Two forms of implicit memory include priming, a phenomenon in which the ability to identify or to generate a particular stimulus is enhanced simply through prior exposure to an identical or associated stimulus, and motor and cognitive skill learning that occurs with repeated practice. These forms of implicit memory are differentially impaired in AD and HD. Mildly demented patients with AD, but not those with HD, are impaired on various priming tasks including lexical (word stem completion) priming, semantic paired-associate priming, and priming to enhance the identification of fragmented pictures (see Fleischman & Gabrieli, 1998, for review), whereas motor learning is relatively spared (Eslinger & Damasio, 1986). In contrast, mildly demented patients with HD, but not those with AD, are impaired in the ability

to learn and retain certain motor and cognitive skills such as pursuit rotor tracking, adaptation-mediated weight biasing, visual prism adaptation, serial reaction time sequences, reading mirror-reversed text, complex problem solving (e.g., Tower of Hanoi puzzle), and probabilistic classification learning (Gabrieli et al., 1997; Heindel et al., 1989; for review, see Heindel & Salmon, 2001). Taken together, these findings indicate that there is a dissociation in the neural substrates that support various forms of implicit memory. Priming appears to be mediated by the basal forebrain and association cortices damaged in AD, whereas motor and cognitive skill learning is largely mediated by the neostriatal structures (particularly the caudate nucleus) damaged in HD.

Distinct aspects of attention, working memory, and executive functions are differentially affected in AD and HD. In general, a deficit in attention is more salient in HD than in AD (e.g., Butters et al., 1988). The attention deficit in HD is characterized by difficulty in shifting or allocating attention (Hanes et al., 1995; Lange et al., 1995; Lawrence et al., 1996), particularly when attentional shifts must be internally regulated (Sprengelmeyer et al., 1995). Several studies have shown, for example, that the ability to effectively shift attention between stimulus dimensions (e.g., from color to shape) in a visual discrimination task is impaired in moderately to severely demented HD patients, but not in patients with AD or in mildly demented HD patients (Lange et al., 1995; Lawrence et al., 1996).

Alzheimer's disease and HD differentially affect working memory (Baddeley, 1986). Early in the course of HD, working memory deficits are apparent in the ability to maintain information in temporary memory buffers (e.g., as evidenced by poor digit span performance), to inhibit irrelevant information, and to use strategic aspects of memory (e.g., planning, organization) to enhance free recall (Butters et al., 1978; Caine et al., 1977; Lange et al., 1995; Lawrence et al., 1996). Working memory deficits are relatively mild in early AD and are primarily characterized by a disruption of the central executive with sparing of the phonological loop and visuospatial scratchpad (Baddeley et al., 1991; Collette et al., 1999). It is only in the later stages of AD that all aspects of working memory become compromised (Baddeley et al., 1991; Collette et al., 1999).

One of the most salient aspects of the dementia associated with HD is impairment of various "executive" functions involved in planning and problem solving. Patients with HD usually exhibit deficits in goal-directed behavior, the ability to generate multiple response alternatives, the capacity to resist distraction and maintain response set, and the cognitive flexibility needed to evaluate and modify behavior (for review, see Brandt & Bylsma, 1993). These deficits have been documented with a wide variety of tests that assess executive functions, including the Wisconsin Card Sorting Test (Paulsen et al., 1995; Peinemann et al., 2005; Pillon et al., 1991; Ward et al., 2006), the Stroop Test (Peinemann et al., 2005; Ward et al., 2006), the Tower of London Test (Lange et al., 1995), the Gambling Decision Making task (Stout et al., 2001), and tests of verbal concept formation (Hanes et al., 1995). Similar deficits in executive functions occur in AD (for reviews, see Duke & Kaszniak, 2000; Perry & Hodges, 1999), but few studies have directly compared this aspect of cognition in the two disorders. Further research is needed to determine if specific aspects of executive dysfunction are more common in one dementia syndrome than the other, and to establish whether or not this facet of cognitive impairment can differentiate between AD and HD.

Visuospatial processing deficits occur in both AD (for review, see Cronin-Golomb & Amick, 2001) and HD (Brandt & Butters, 1986; Brouwers et al., 1984; Bylsma et al., 1992; Caine et al., 1986; Josiassen et al., 1983; Lawrence et al., 2000; Ward et al., 2006). In one of the few studies to directly compare visuospatial performance in the two disorders, Brouwers and colleagues (1984) showed that AD and HD had differential impacts on personal and extrapersonal orientation abilities. Patients with AD, but not those with HD, were impaired on tests of visuoconstructional ability that required extrapersonal orientation (e.g., copying a complex figure). Patients with HD, but not those with AD, were impaired on visuospatial tasks that required personal orientation (e.g., the Money Road Map Test). This dissociation was supported by the results of a more recent study that examined the ability of AD and HD patients to mentally rotate representations of objects (Lineweaver et al., 2005). Patients with HD were significantly slower than normal control subjects in performing mental rotation, but were as accurate as controls in making the rotation and reporting the correct side of the target. Patients with AD, in contrast, performed the mental rotation as quickly as controls, but were significantly impaired in making an accurate rotation and reporting the correct side of the target. These results were interpreted as showing that HD patients can effectively perform mental rotation of visual representations, but suffer a general bradyphrenia (i.e., slowed thinking) that parallels the bradykinesia that characterizes the disorder. Conversely, patients with AD are impaired in performing mental rotation, perhaps due to extrapersonal visual orientation deficits secondary to neocortical damage in regions involved in processing visual motion (e.g., the middle temporal gyrus).

Another study that directly compared visuospatial abilities in patients with AD or HD examined their ability to draw and copy clocks (Rouleau et al, 1992). The two patient groups were impaired on both conditions of this task, but patients with AD were significantly worse in the draw-to-command condition than in the copy condition, whereas patients with HD were equally impaired in both conditions. A qualitative analysis of the types of errors produced showed that HD patients tended to make graphic, visuospatial, and planning errors in both the command and copy conditions consistent with planning and motor deficits mediated by frontal-subcortical dysfunction. In contrast, AD patients tended to make conceptual or semantically based errors (e.g., drawing a face without numbers, or hands) in the command condition but not the copy condition, consistent with a deficit in accessing knowledge of the attributes and meaning of a clock due to neocortical damage in regions supporting semantic knowledge.

Alzheimer's Disease vs. Dementia with Lewy Bodies (DLB)

The dementia syndromes associated with AD and DLB are quite similar and include insidious onset of cognitive decline with early involvement of memory (Hansen et al., 1990; Hansen & Galasko, 1992; McKeith et al., 1996). Mild parkinsonism (e.g., bradykinesia, rigidity, masked facies), recurrent and well-formed visual hallucinations, and fluctuations in attention or alertness (Cercy & Bylsma, 1997; Galasko et al., 1996; Hansen et al., 1990; McKeith et al., 1996; Merdes et al., 2003) are more prevalent in DLB than in AD, and are the basis for consensus criteria designed to help clinically diagnose DLB and distinguish it from AD (McKeith et al., 1996, 2005). Unfortunately, these clinical features are not ubiquitous in DLB and occur with only about 50% frequency at any time during the course of the disorder (Merdes et al., 2003). Thus, patients found to have DLB at autopsy have often been clinically diagnosed as having probable or possible AD during life (e.g., Hansen et al., 1990; Merdes et al., 2003).

A number of studies have compared the neuropsychological deficits associated with DLB and AD. These studies have consistently shown that the most salient difference between the two disorders is disproportionately severe visuospatial and visuoconstructive deficits in DLB. This distinction has been shown using tests of visual perception (Calderon et al., 2001; Lambon Ralph et al., 2001; Mori et al., 2000), visual search (Cormak et al., 2004), drawing simple and complex two-dimensional figures (Aarsland et al., 2003; Connor et al., 1998; Galasko et al., 1996; Gnanalingham et al., 1996,1997; Hansen et al., 1990; Noe et al., 2003; Salmon et al., 1996), and construction of three-dimensional objects (Hansen et al., 1990; Shimomura et al., 1998). Calderon and colleagues (2001), for example, found that DLB patients performed worse than AD patients on tests of fragmented letter identification, discrimination of "real" objects from nonobjects, and segregation of overlapping figures. These particularly severe deficits in visuospatial and visuoperceptual abilities were apparent even though the DLB patients performed significantly better than the patients with AD on a verbal memory test and at the same level on tests of semantic memory (also see Lambon Ralph et al., 2001). Similar results were obtained by Mori and colleagues (2000), who found that DLB patients performed significantly worse than equally demented AD patients on

tests of visual attention, size and form discrimination, and visual figure-ground segregation. A study of visual search processes (Cormak et al., 2004) showed that DLB patients were more impaired than AD patients in the ability to perform serial search that required feature integration (i.e., detect a single red target circle within arrays of 2, 8, or 16 green circles and red squares distracters) and in "preattentive" parallel search processes that usually elicit the "popout" phenomenon (i.e., detecting a single red target circle within arrays of 2, 8, or 16 green distractor circles). Performance on the parallel search task provided relatively good sensitivity (85%) and specificity (87%) for distinguishing patients with DLB from those with AD.

The disproportionately severe visuospatial deficits exhibited by patients with DLB may be related to occipital cortex dysfunction, which does not usually occur in patients with AD. A number of studies have shown hypometabolism and decreased blood flow in primary visual and visual association cortex in DLB but not in AD (e.g., Minoshima et al., 2001). Neuropathologic studies have identified white matter spongiform change with coexisting gliosis in the occipital cortex of patients with DLB (Higuchi et al., 2000), and in some cases deposition of Lewy bodies is also observed (e.g., Gomez-Tortosa et al., 1999). In contrast, AD pathology in the occipital cortex is rare. The relationship between the structural and metabolic abnormalities in the occipital cortex of patients with DLB and their prominent visuospatial deficits remains unknown.

In addition to disproportionate visuospatial deficits, patients with DLB often have greater deficits in attention and executive functions than patients with AD. Studies have shown that DLB patients perform worse than equally demented AD patients on measures of attention such as the WAIS-R Digit Span subtest (Hansen et al., 1990), the Cancellation Test (Noe et al., 2004), and a computer-based visual search task that assesses the ability to focus attention (Sahgal et al., 1992b). Patients with DLB are also more impaired than AD patients on verbal fluency tests that require initiation and systematic retrieval from semantic memory (Aarsland et al., 2003; Ballard et al., 1996; Connor et al., 1998; Galasko et al., 1998; Hansen et al., 1990), paired-associates learning tests (Galloway et al., 1992), delayed matching-to-sample tests (Sahgal et al., 1992a), and spatial working memory tasks that assess both spatial memory and the ability to use an efficient search strategy (Sahgal et al., 1995). Abstract reasoning abilities assessed by the Raven Colored Progressive Matrices (Shimomura et al., 1998) and the WAIS-R Similarities subtest (Galasko et al., 1998) are more impaired in patients with DLB than in those with AD.

The prominent attention and executive function deficits associated with DLB are similar to those that occur in patients with basal ganglia dysfunction that interrupts frontostriatal circuits (e.g., patients with HD). In DLB, these circuits may be disrupted by substantia nigra pathology that interrupts dopaminergic projections to the striatum, and by direct neocortical Lewy body pathology in the association areas of the frontal lobes. In addition, AD pathology may be superimposed upon the Lewy body pathology in the frontal cortex of patients with DLB. This combination of pathologic processes may induce the disproportionately severe executive function and attention deficits that characterize the disease.

Although deficits in visuospatial abilities, executive functions, and attention are usually greater in patients with DLB than in equally demented patients with AD, memory is often more impaired in patients with AD. Furthermore, qualitative differences in impaired memory processes are evident in the two disorders. These differences were highlighted in a study that directly compared the performances of patients with autopsy-confirmed DLB (all with concomitant AD pathology consistent with Lewy body variant of AD) and patients with autopsy-confirmed AD on the CVLT and the WMS-R Logical Memory Test (Hamilton et al., 2004). Despite equivalent deficits in their ability to learn new verbal information on these tests, the DLB patients exhibited better retention and better recognition memory than patients with AD (also see Ballard et al., 1996; Calderon et al., 2001; Connor et al., 1998; Heyman et al., 1999; Salmon et al., 1996; Shimomura et al., 1998; Walker et al., 1997). These differences are consistent with the particular pathological changes that occur in the two disorders. A number of

studies using neuropathologic (Lippa et al., 1998) or magnetic resonance imaging (Barber et al., 2001; Hashimoto et al., 1998) procedures have shown that the medial temporal lobe structures important for memory (e.g., hippocampus, entorhinal cortex, parahippocampal gyrus) are more severely affected in AD than in DLB. This may account for the poorer retention (i.e., consolidation) exhibited by the AD patients. The greater recognition memory performance of the DLB patients compared to patients with AD suggests that they may have a particular deficit in the ability to initiate and carry out systematic retrieval of successfully stored information. This retrieval deficit may be mediated by the frontostriatal damage that occurs in DLB but not in AD.

The results of the studies reviewed above indicate that visuospatial, attention, and executive function deficits are more prominent in DLB than AD, whereas memory impairment is greater in AD than in DLB. These distinct deficit patterns have been confirmed in a number of recent studies that compared clinically diagnosed or autopsy-confirmed DLB and AD patient groups on relatively extensive batteries of neuropsychological tests (Ferman et al., 2006; Guidi et al., 2006; Johnson et al., 2005; Kraybill et al., 2005; Stavitsky et al., 2006) (see Figure 8–7). The robustness of these deficit patterns (particularly of the disproportionate visuospatial deficits in DLB) may have important clinical utility in distinguishing between AD and DLB in mildly demented patients (Tiraboschi et al., 2006).

Alzheimer's Disease vs. Frontotemporal Dementia

AD and FTD are clinically similar and difficult to distinguish during life (Mendez et al., 1993; Varma et al., 1999). Indeed, Mendez and colleagues (1993) found that 86% of autopsy-confirmed FTD patients had been clinically misdiagnosed with AD during life. Some success has been achieved in differentiating between FTD and AD on the basis of behavioral symptoms (e.g., Barber et al., 1995; Bozeat et al., 2000; Kertesz et al., 2000; Mendez et al., 1998; Miller et al., 1997), but this success has been limited. These findings have led some investigators to

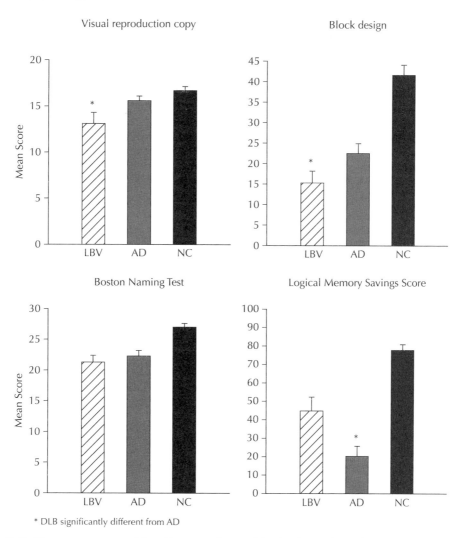

Figure 8–7. The average scores achieved by normal control (NC) subjects (*n* = 24), patients with Alzheimer's disease (AD; *n* = 24), and patients with dementia with Lewy bodies (all with the Lewy body variant (LBV) of AD; *n* = 24) on several neuropsychological tests. The LBV patients were disproportionately impaired compared to the AD patients on tests of visuospatial ability (Visual Reproduction Copy and Block Design), but less impaired on tests of verbal memory (Logical Memory Savings Score). The patient groups did not differ on a test of confrontation naming (Boston Naming Test) (Adapted from Hamilton et al., 2004).

propose that FTD and AD might be differentiated on the basis of the nature and severity of their cognitive deficits. Unfortunately, studies that directly compare neuropsychological deficits in FTD and AD have provided inconsistent results. A number of studies showed a greater verbal fluency deficit in FTD than in AD (Frisoni et al., 1995; Lindau et al., 1998; Mathuranath et al., 2000), but others did not replicate this result (Binetti et al., 2000; Pasquier et al., 1995; Thomas-Anterion et al., 2000). Similarly,

visuospatial and constructional abilities were found to be less impaired in FTD than in AD in some studies (Elfgren et al., 1994; Mendez et al., 1996), but not others (Frisoni et al., 1995; Lindau et al., 1998; Mathuranath et al., 2000; Pachana et al., 1996). Several studies found better visuospatial memory in FTD than in AD (Frisoni et al., 1995; Pachana et al., 1996), but others failed to replicate this finding (Binetti et al., 2000; Lindau et al., 1998; Thomas-Anterion et al., 2000). Reduced verbal output, stereotyped language, and echolalia are observed clinically in FTD (Johanson & Hagberg, 1989; Miller et al., 1997; Neary et al., 1988), but these characteristics have not been formally compared in FTD and AD patients. There appears to be little or no difference between FTD and AD patients on measures of confrontation naming (Binetti et al., 2000; Mendez et al., 1996; Pachana et al., 1996; Thomas-Anterion et al., 2000).

Several studies that examined profiles of cognitive deficits associated with FTD and AD demonstrated a subtle difference in the patterns of deficits engendered by the two disorders (Forstl et al., 1996; Starkstein et al., 1994). In these studies, patients with FTD had a more severe deficit in executive functions than in other cognitive abilities, whereas AD patients had executive dysfunction that was proportional to their deficits in language and visuospatial abilities, and less prominent than their episodic memory deficit. These results were confirmed by a more recent study that directly compared neuropsychological deficit profiles in autopsy-confirmed FTD and AD patients who were matched for level of dementia (i.e., MMSE scores) at the time of testing (Rascovsky et al., 2002). Rascovsky and colleagues (2002) found that FTD patients performed significantly worse than AD patients on word generation tasks sensitive to frontal lobe dysfunction (i.e., letter and category fluency tests), but significantly better on tests of memory (i.e., Mattis DRS Memory subscale) and visuospatial abilities (i.e., Block Design and Clock Drawing tests) sensitive to dysfunction of medial temporal and parietal association cortices, respectively (see Figure 8–8). A logistic regression model using letter fluency, Mattis DRS Memory subscale, and the Block Design test provided good discriminability between the groups, correctly classifying approximately 86% of FTD and AD patients (91% of AD patients and 77% of FTD patients).

In a subsequent study, Rascovsky and colleagues (2007) sought to determine whether or not autopsy-confirmed FTD and AD patients who were matched for level of dementia at the time of testing differed in the pattern of deficits they exhibited on letter and semantic category fluency tasks. Although both verbal fluency tasks engage frontal-lobe-mediated executive processes, distinct patterns were hypothesized

because semantic category fluency requires a search through semantic memory and is critically dependent upon an adequate knowledge of the physical and/or functional attributes that define a particular semantic category. In contrast, letter fluency requires the use of phonemic cues to guide retrieval and may thus require greater effort and more active strategic search than semantic category fluency. Results showed that FTD patients performed worse than AD patients overall, and showed that FTD patients had similar impairment in letter and semantic category fluency, whereas AD patients had greater impairment in semantic fluency than letter fluency. A measure of the disparity between letter and semantic fluency (the Semantic Index) correctly classified 26 of 32 AD patients (82%) and 12 of 16 FTD patients (75%). Interestingly, the misclassified FTD subjects all had clinical presentations of progressive nonfluent aphasia (Mesulam, 1982) or Semantic Dementia (i.e., severe naming and word comprehension impairments in the context of fluent speech; Hodges et al., 1992; Snowden et al., 1989). When these cases were excluded and the analyses repeated, dissociations were apparent in letter worse than semantic fluency for the FTD patients and semantic worse than letter fluency for the AD patients. In addition, the Semantic Index now correctly classified 90% of FTD and AD patients. These unique patterns of fluency deficits may be indicative of differences in the relative contribution of frontal lobe-mediated retrieval deficits and temporal-lobe-mediated semantic deficits in FTD and AD.

Similar levels of discriminability were observed in a number of additional studies that attempted to differentiate between FTD and AD on the basis of tests of executive functions, visuospatial abilities, and memory (Elfgren et al., 1994; Gregory et al., 1997; Libon et al., 2007; Lipton et al., 2005). For example, Grossman et al. (2007) achieved 88% diagnostic accuracy in differentiating between autopsy-confirmed FTD and AD patients on the basis of clinical and neuropsychological features. These results indicate that distinct cognitive profiles are associated with FTD and AD, and suggest that cognitive assessment may provide useful information when making the differential diagnosis of FTD.

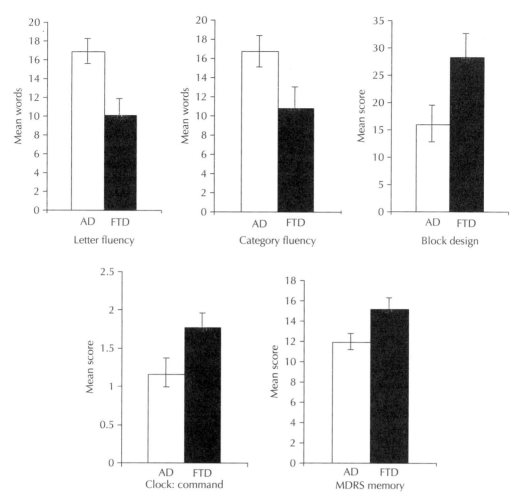

Figure 8–8. Age- and education-adjusted means (and SEM) for the number of words produced in the letter and category fluency tasks and a scores achieved on the WISC-R Block Design test, command condition of the Clock Drawing Test and Mattis Dementia Rating Scale (MDRS) memory subscale by patients with Frontotemporal dementia (FTD) (black bars) or Alzheimer's Disease (AD) (clear bars). Patients with FTD performed significantly worse than those with AD on verbal fluency tasks, but significantly better on tests of memory and visuospatial abilities. All group differences are significant at $p < .05$. (Adapted from Rascovsky et al., 2002).

Alzheimer's Disease vs. Vascular Dementia

Studies of the neuropsychological deficits associated with VaD have primarily focused on differentiating between subcortical VaD and AD (see also chapter by Brown in this volume). For the most part, these studies show that patients with subcortical VaD are more impaired than those with AD on tests of executive functions, whereas patients with AD are more impaired than those with subcortical VaD on tests of

episodic memory (particularly delayed recall) (Desmond, 2004; Graham et al., 2004; Kertesz & Clydesdale, 1994; Lafosse et al., 1997; Lamar et al., 1997). These studies also suggest that executive dysfunction is usually the most prominent deficit in subcortical VaD, presumably because subcortical pathology interrupts frontosubcortical circuits that mediate this aspect of cognition. Consistent with this possibility, Price and colleagues (2005) found that VaD patients with a significant volume of white matter abnormality on imaging exhibited a profile of greater executive and visuoconstructional deficits than impairment of memory and language abilities.

Most of the studies that have shown distinct cognitive profiles in subcortical VaD and AD employed clinically diagnosed patients without autopsy confirmation of diagnosis. The lack of autopsy confirmation may have allowed some degree of diagnostic misclassification since AD and VaD often overlap in their clinical presentations. In a study that avoided this potential confound, Reed and colleagues (2007) found that patients with autopsy-confirmed AD had a deficit in episodic memory (both verbal and nonverbal memory) that was significantly greater than their executive function deficit. In contrast, patients with autopsy-confirmed subcortical VaD had a deficit in executive functions that was greater than their deficit in verbal (but not nonverbal) episodic memory. An analysis of individual patient profiles showed that 71% of AD patients exhibited a profile with memory impairment more prominent than executive dysfunction, whereas only 45% of patients with subcortical VaD exhibited a profile with more prominent executive dysfunction than memory impairment. Interestingly, relatively severe cerebrovascular disease at autopsy was often not associated with clinically significant cognitive decline. When the profile analysis was restricted to those patients who exhibited significant cognitive impairment at their clinical assessment, the distinction between subcortical VaD and AD patients was more pronounced. A low memory profile was exhibited by 79% of AD patients (5% with a low executive profile) and a low executive profile by 67% of subcortical VaD patients (0% with a low memory profile). The results suggest that relatively distinct cognitive deficit profiles might be clinically useful in differentiating between subcortical VaD and AD, but additional research with autopsied patients is needed to further define the deficit profile that will be most useful in this regard.

Chapter Summary

A wealth of neuropsychological research has shown that the cognitive deficits associated with AD are distinct from age-associated cognitive decline. Quantitative and qualitative differences between early AD and normal aging effects are especially apparent in episodic memory (particularly delayed recall), semantic knowledge, and some aspects of executive functions. There is also emerging evidence that the cortical neuropathology of AD causes a loss of functional connectivity that adversely affects interaction between distinct and relatively intact cortical information-processing systems. This loss may cause, for example, an impaired ability to "bind" distinct visual stimulus features that are effectively processed in different cortical streams (i.e., motion and color). The qualitatively distinct pattern of cognitive impairment associated with early AD appears to be less salient in very old patients than in younger patients when they are compared to their age-appropriate cohort. This finding may be driven in large part by the age-associated decline in certain cognitive abilities (e.g., speed of information-processing, retrieval processes) that occurs with normal healthy aging. Progress has been made in identifying cognitive markers of "prodromal" AD that are apparent before the development of the dementia syndrome. Decline in episodic memory is usually the earliest cognitive change that occurs during the prodromal stage of AD, but decline in other cognitive domains, and asymmetry in cognitive abilities (e.g., high verbal vs. low visuospatial performance), may also predict the imminent onset of dementia. Neuropsychological research has also identified patterns of cognitive impairment that might help distinguish AD from other neuropathologically distinct neurodegenerative disorders such as HD, DLB, FTD, and VaD. Knowledge of these differences is clinically important for distinguishing among various causes of dementia, and provides useful information about the brain–behavior relationships that mediate cognitive abilities affected by various neurodegenerative diseases.

Conclusions and Future Directions

Clinical and experimental neuropsychological research has made great strides in differentiating between the cognitive changes that signal the onset of a dementia syndrome and those that occur as a normal consequence of aging. Many of the basic cognitive processes that are adversely affected by AD have been identified, and the prodromal cognitive changes that predict the subsequent development of dementia are being uncovered. Considerable progress has also been made in delineating different patterns of relatively preserved and impaired cognitive abilities that distinguish between AD and other age-associated neurodegenerative disorders. Understanding the cognitive distinctions between these disorders can aid in the development of better differential diagnosis and reveal the nature of brain–behavior relationships underlying memory, language, executive functions, and other cognitive abilities that are affected.

The search for antecedent markers of dementia is predicated on the notion that significant neural dysfunction and cell death occurs well in advance of the clinical diagnosis. It is imperative to reliably identify individuals prior to the development of significant clinical symptoms in order to begin treatments that might halt or slow disease progression. Therefore, the identification and validation of subtle cognitive abnormalities (e.g., poor delayed recall performance, cognitive asymmetry) for prodromal diagnosis of AD remains an extremely important goal. The role of cortical disconnectivity in producing the specific pattern of cognitive deficits that occurs in early AD has only begun to be assessed, but the identification of cognitive processes that are particularly vulnerable to the effects of cortical disconnectivity might provide a useful cognitive marker for the disease and a means by which to assess the effects of interventions that specifically target cortical function (e.g., the NMDA receptor antagonist memantine). Clearly, additional research is needed in this area.

Despite intense research focus, it remains difficult to estimate rate of cognitive decline in AD and other age-related neurodegenerative diseases, although there is promising evidence that certain aspects of current cognitive performance can predict subsequent rate of global cognitive decline in patients with AD (e.g., Chan et al., 1995). Further research is needed to confirm this possibility and to generalize it to other neurodegenerative disorders such as DLB and FTD (e.g., see Wicklund et al., 2007). In addition, there is a continuing need to identify differences in the profiles of cognitive deficits associated with AD and other age-related neurodegenerative diseases

(e.g., DLB, FTD), and to determine how these profiles can be incorporated with other clinical features to improve the accuracy of differential diagnosis in very mildly demented individuals. Accurate early diagnosis is a particularly important goal since the various neurodegenerative disorders are likely to respond differently to potential treatments for dementia that are in development. Finally, the strides made in understanding the neuropsychology of dementia need to be linked to those made in neuroimaging research with consonant goals of early detection and maximization of intervention efforts. This approach will lead to better understanding of the brain–behavior relationships underlying dementia.

Acknowledgments

Preparation of this chapter was supported by funds from NIA grants P50 AG005131 (MWB, DPS), RO1 AG012674 (MWB), K24 AG026431 (MWB), and RO1 AG012963 (DPS) to the University of California San Diego and the Veterans Medical Research Foundation, P30 AG019610 (AWK) to the Arizona Alzheimer's Consortium, and by grant IIRG-07–59343 (MWB) from the Alzheimer's Association. The authors wish to thank their many collaborators at the UCSD Alzheimer's Disease Research Center and the Arizona Alzheimer's Disease Core Center.

References

Aarsland, D., Litvan, I., Salmon, D. P., Galasko, D., Wentzel-Larsen, T., & Larsen, P. (2003). Performance on the dementia rating scale in Parkinson's disease with dementia and dementia with Lewy bodies: Comparison with progressive supranuclear palsy and Alzheimer's disease. *Journal of Neurology, Neurosurgery and Psychiatry, 74*, 1215–1220.

Albert, M. L., Feldman, R. G., & Willis, A. L. (1974). The "subcortical dementia" of progressive supranuclear palsy. *Journal of Neurology, Neurosurgery and Psychiatry, 37*, 121–130.

Albert, M. S., & Blacker, D. (2006). Mild cognitive impairment and dementia. *Annual Review of Clinical Psychology, 2*, 379–388.

Albert, M. S., Butters, N., & Brandt, J. (1981). Development of remote memory loss in patients with Huntington's disease. *Journal of Clinical and Experimental Neuropsychology, 3*, 1–12.

Albert, M. S., Butters, N., & Levin, J. (1979). Temporal gradients in the retrograde amnesia of patients with alcoholic Korsakoff disease. *Archives of Neurology, 36*, 211–216.

Albert, M. S., Moss, M. B., Tanzi, R., & Jones, K. (2001). Preclinical prediction of AD using neuropsychological tests. *Journal of the International Neuropsychological Society, 7*, 631–639.

Albin, R. L. (1993). Antagonistic pleiotropy, mutation accumulation, and human genetic disease. *Genetica, 91*, 279–286.

Alexander, D. M., Williams, L. M., Gatt, J. M., Dobson-Stone, C., Kuan, S. A., Todd, E. G., et al. (2007). The contribution of apolipoprotein E alleles on cognitive performance and dynamic neural activity over six decades. *Biological Psychology, 75*, 229–238.

Alexander, G. E., DeLong, M. R., & Strick, P. L. (1986). Parallel organization of functionally segregated circuits linking basal ganglia and cortex. *Annual Review of Neuroscience, 9*, 357–381.

Alzheimer, A. (1907). Über eine eigenartige Erkrankung der Hirnrinde. *Allg Z Psychiatr Psychol-Gerichtl Med, 64*, 146–148.

American Psychiatric Association. (1994). *Diagnostic and statistical manual of mental sisorders*, 4th ed. Washington DC: American Psychiatric Association.

Andreasen, N., Blennow, K., Sjodin, C., Winblad, B., & Svardsudd, K. (1999). Prevalence and incidence of clinically diagnosed memory impairments in a geographically defined general population in Sweden. The Pitea Dementia Project. *Neuroepidemiology, 18*, 144–155.

Aronoff, J. M., Gonnerman, L. M., Almor, A., Arunachalam, S., Kempler, D., & Andersen, E. S. (2006). Information content versus relational knowledge: Semantic deficits in patients with Alzheimer's disease. *Neuropsychologia, 44*, 21–35.

Backman, L., Jones, S., Berger, A. K., Laukka, E. J., & Small, B. J. (2004). Multiple cognitive deficits during the transition to Alzheimer's disease. *Journal of Internal Medicine, 256*, 195–204.

Backman, L., Jones, S., Berger, A. K., Laukka, E. J., & Small, B. J. (2005). Cognitive impairment in preclinical Alzheimer's disease: A meta-analysis. *Neuropsychology, 19*, 520–531.

Backman, L., & Small, B. J. (1998). Influences of cognitive support on episodic remembering: Tracing the process of loss from normal aging to Alzheimer's disease. *Psychology and Aging, 13*, 267–276.

Backman, L., Small, B. J., & Fratiglioni, L. (2001). Stability of the preclinical episodic memory deficit in Alzheimer's disease. *Brain, 124*, 96–102.

Bachman, D. L., Wolf, P. A., Linn, R., Knoefel, J. E., Cobb, J. L., Belanger, A. J., et al. (1992). Prevalence of dementia and probable senile dementia of the Alzheimer type in the Framingham study. *Neurology, 42*, 115–119.

Bachman, D. L., Wolf, P. A., Linn, R., Knoefel, J. E., Cobb, J. L., Belanger, A. J., et al. (1993). Incidence of dementia and probable Alzheimer's disease in a general population: The Framingham study. *Neurology, 43*, 515–519.

Baddeley, A. D. (1986). *Working memory*. Oxford: Claredon Press.

Baddeley, A. D., Bressi, S., Della Sala, S., Logie, R., & Spinnler, H. (1991). The decline of working memory in Alzheimer's disease: A longitudinal study. *Brain, 114*, 2521–2542.

Ballard, C., Patel, A., Oyebode, F., & Wilcock, G. (1996). Cognitive decline in patients with Alzheimer's disease, vascular dementia and senile dementia of the Lewy body type. *Age and Ageing, 25*, 209–213.

Band, G. P., Ridderinkhof, K. R., & Segalowitz, S. (2002). Explaining neurocognitive aging: Is one factor enough? *Brain and Cognition, 49*, 259–267.

Barber, R., McKeith, I. G., Ballard, C., Gholkar, A., & O'Brien, J. T. (2001). A comparison of medial and lateral temporal lobe atrophy in dementia with Lewy bodies and Alzheimer's disease: Magnetic resonance imaging volumetric study. *Dementia and Geriatric Cognitive Disorders, 12*, 198–205.

Barber, R., Snowden, J. S., & Craufurd, D. (1995). Frontotemporal dementia and Alzheimer's disease: Retrospective differentiation using information from informants. *Journal of Neurology, Neurosurgery and Psychiatry, 59*, 61–70.

Barnes, D. E., Yaffe, K., Satariano, W. A., & Tager, I. B. (2003). A longitudinal study of cardiorespiratory fitness and cognitive function in healthy older adults. *Journal of the American Geriatrics Society, 51*(4), 459–465.

Bartzokis, G. (2004). Age-related myelin breakdown: A developmental model of cognitive decline and Alzheimer's disease. *Neurobiology of Aging, 25*, 5–18.

Bayles, K. A., Boone, D. R., Tomoeda, C. K., Slauson, T. J., & Kaszniak, A. W. (1989). Differentiating Alzheimer's patients from the normal elderly and stroke patients with aphasia. *Journal of Speech and Hearing Disorders, 54*, 74–87.

Bayles, K. A., & Kaszniak, A. W. (1987). *Communication and cognition in normal aging and dementia*. Boston: College Hill/Little-Brown.

Bayles, K. A., & Tomoeda, C. K. (1983). Confrontation naming impairment in dementia. *Brain and Language, 19*, 98–114.

Bayley, P. J., Salmon, D. P., Bondi, M. W., Bui, B. K., Olichney, J., Delis, D. C., et al. (2000). Comparison of the serial position effect in very mild Alzheimer's disease, mild Alzheimer's disease, and amnesia associated with electroconvulsive therapy. *Journal of the International Neuropsychological Society, 6,* 290–298.

Beatty, W. W., Salmon, D. P., Butters, N., Heindel, W. C., & Granholm, E. L. (1988). Retrograde amnesia in patients with Alzheimer's disease or Huntington's disease. *Neurobiology of Aging, 9,* 181–186.

Binetti, G., Locascio, J. J., Corkin, S., Vonsattel, J. P., & Growdon, J. H. (2000). Differences between Pick disease and Alzheimer disease in the clinical appearance and rate of cognitive decline. *Archives of Neurology, 57,* 225–232.

Bloss, C. S., Delis, D. C., Salmon, D. P., & Bondi, M. W. (2008). APOE genotype is associated with left-handedness and visuospatial skills in children. *Neurobiology of Aging* [Epub ahead of print].

Bondi, M. W., Houston, W. S., Salmon, D. P., Corey-Bloom, J., Katzman, R., Thal, L. J., et al. (2003). Neuropsychological deficits associated with Alzheimer's disease in the very old: Discrepencies in raw vs. standardized scores. *Journal of the International Neuropsychological Society, 9,* 783–795.

Bondi, M. W., Monsch, A. U., Butters, N., Salmon, D. P., & Paulsen, J. S. (1993). Utility of a modified version of the Wisconsin Card Sorting Test in the detection of dementia of the Alzheimer type. *Clinical Neuropsychologist, 7,* 161–170.

Bondi, M. W., Monsch, A. U., Galasko, D., Butters, N., Salmon, D. P., & Delis, D. C. (1994). Preclinical cognitive markers of dementia of the Alzheimer type. *Neuropsychology, 8,* 374–384.

Bondi, M. W., Salmon, D. P., Galasko, D., Thomas, R. G., & Thal, L. J. (1999). Neuropsychological function and apolipoprotein E genotype in the preclinical detection of Alzheimer's disease. *Psychology and Aging, 14,* 295–303.

Borenstein, A. R., Copenhaver, C. I., & Mortimer, J. A. (2006). Early-life risk factors for Alzheimer disease. *Alzheimer Disease and Associated Disorders, 20,* 63–72.

Bowles, N. L., Obler, L. K., & Albert, M. L. (1987). Naming errors in healthy aging and dementia of the Alzheimer type. *Cortex, 23,* 519–524.

Bozeat, S., Gregory, C. A., Lambon Ralph, M. A., & Hodges, J. R. (2000). Which neuropsychiatric and behavioral features distinguish frontal and temporal variants of frontotemporal dementia and Alzheimer's disease? *Journal of Neurology, Neurosurgery and Psychiatry, 69,* 178–186.

Braak, H., & Braak, E. (1991). Neuropathological staging of Alzheimer-related changes. *Acta Neuropathologica, 82,* 239–259.

Brandt, J., & Butters, N. (1986). The neuropsychology of Huntington's disease. *Trends in Neuroscience, 9,* 118–120.

Brandt, J., & Bylsma, F. W. (1993). The dementia of Huntington's disease. In R. W. Parks, R. F. Zec, and R. S. Wilson (Eds.), *Neuropsychology of Alzheimer's disease and other dementias* (pp. 265–282). New York: Oxford University Press.

Brandt, J., Corwin, J., & Krafft, L. (1992). Is verbal recognition memory really different in Huntington's and Alzheimer's disease? *Journal of Clinical and Experimental Neuropsychology, 14,* 773–784.

Brouwers, P., Cox, C., Martin, A., Chase, T., & Fedio, P. (1984). Differential perceptual-spatial impairment in Huntington's and Alzheimer's dementias. *Archives of Neurology, 41,* 1073–1076.

Brun, A., Englund, B., Gustafson, L., Passant, U., Mann, D.M.A, Neary, D., & Snowden, J.S. (1994). Clinical and neuropathological criteria for frontotemporal dementia. *Journal of Neurology, Neurosurgery and Psychiatry, 57,* 416–418.

Brun, A. (1987). Frontal lobe degeneration of the non-Alzheimer type I. Neuropathology. *Archives Gerontology and Geriatrics, 6,* 193–208.

Buckner, R. L. (2004). Memory and executive function in aging and AD: Multiple factors that cause decline and reserve factors that compensate. *Neuron, 44,* 195–208.

Buschke, H. (1973). Selective reminding for analysis of memory and learning. *Journal of Verbal Learning and Verbal Behavior, 12,* 543–550.

Buschke, H., Sliwinski, M. J., Kuslansky, G., & Lipton, R. B. (1997). Diagnosis of early dementia by the double memory test. *Neurology, 48,* 989–997.

Butters, N., Granholm, E., Salmon, D. P., Grant, I., & Wolfe, J. (1987). Episodic and semantic memory: A comparison of amnesic and demented patients. *Journal of Clinical and Experimental Neuropsychology, 9,* 479–497.

Butters, N., Salmon, D. P., Cullum, C. M., Cairns, P., Troster, A. I., Jacobs, D., et al. (1988). Differentiation of amnesic and demented patients with the Wechsler Memory Scale—Revised. *Clinical Neuropsychologist, 2,* 133–148.

Butters, N., Sax, D. S., Montgomery, K., & Tarlow, S. (1978). Comparison of the neuropsychological deficits associated with early and advanced Huntington's disease. *Archives of Neurology, 35,* 585–589.

Butters, N., Wolfe, J., Granholm, E., & Martone, M. (1986). An assessment of verbal recall, recognition and fluency abilities in patients with Huntington's disease. *Cortex, 22,* 11–32.

Butters, N., Wolfe, J., Martone, M., Granholm, E., & Cermak, L. S. (1985). Memory disorders associated with Huntington's disease: Verbal recall, verbal recognition and procedural memory. *Neuropsychologia, 23*, 729–743.

Bylsma, F. W., Brandt, J., & Strauss, M. E. (1992). Personal and extrapersonal orientation in Huntington's disease patients and those at risk. *Cortex, 28*, 113–122.

Caine, E. D., Bamford, K. A., Schiffer, R. B., Shoulson, I., & Levy, S. (1986). A controlled neuropsychological comparison of Huntington's disease and multiple sclerosis. *Archives of Neurology, 43*, 249–254.

Caine, E. D., Ebert, M. H., & Weingartner, H. (1977). An outline for the analysis of dementia: The memory disorder of Huntington's disease. *Neurology, 27*, 1087–1092.

Calderon, J., Perry, R. J., Erzinclioglu, S. W., Berrios, G. E., Dening, T. R., & Hodges, J. R. (2001). Perception, attention, and working memory are disproportionately impaired in dementia with Lewy bodies compared with Alzheimer's disease. *Journal of Neurology, Neurosurgery and Psychiatry, 70*, 157–164.

Capitani, E., Della Sala, S., Logie, R., & Spinnler, H. (1992). Recency, primacy, and memory: Reappraising and standardising the serial position curve. *Cortex, 28*, 315–342.

Carlesimo, G. A., Sabbadini, M., Fadda, L., & Caltagirone, C. (1995). Different components in word-list forgetting of pure amnesics, degenerative demented and healthy subjects. *Cortex, 31*, 735–745.

Cercy, S. P., & Bylsma, F. W. (1997). Lewy body and progressive dementia: A critical review and meta-analysis. *Journal of the International Neuropsychological Society, 3*, 179–194.

Cermak, L. S. (1984). The episodic/semantic distinction in amnesia. In L. R. Squire and N. Butters (Eds.), *The neuropsychology of memory* (pp. 52–62). New York: Guilford Press.

Chan, A. S., Salmon, D. P., Butters, N., & Johnson, S. (1995). Semantic network abnormality predicts rate of cognitive decline in patients with Alzheimer's disease. *Journal of the International Neuropsychological Society, 1*, 297–303.

Chan, A. S., Salmon, D. P., & Butters N. (1998). Semantic network abnormalities in patients with Alzheimer's disease. In R. W. Parks, D. S. Levine, and D. L. Long (Eds.), *Fundamentals of neural network modeling* (pp. 381–393). Cambridge, MA: MIT Press.

Chen, P., Ratcliff, G., Belle, S. H., Cauley, J. A., DeKosky, S. T., & Ganguli, M. (2001). Patterns of cognitive decline in presymptomatic Alzheimer disease: A prospective community study. *Archives of General Psychiatry, 58*, 853–858.

Chertkow, H., & Bub, D. (1990). Semantic memory loss in dementia of Alzheimer's type. *Brain, 113*, 397–417.

Chui, H. C. (2007). Subcortical ischemic vascular dementia. *Neurologic Clinics, 25*, 717–740.

Chui, H. C., Mack, W., Jackson, J. E., Mungas, D., Reed, B. R., Tinklenberg, J., et al. (2000). Clinical criteria for the diagnosis of vascular dementia: A multicenter study of comparability and interrater reliability. *Archives of Neurology, 57*, 191–196.

Chui, H. C., Victoroff, J., Margolin, D., Jagust, W., Shankle, R., & Katzman, R. (1992). Criteria for the diagnosis of ischemic vascular dementia proposed by the State of California Alzheimer's Disease Diagnostic Treatment Centers. *Neurology, 42*, 473–480.

Churchill, J. D., Galvez, R., Colcombe, S., Swain, R. A., Kramer, A. F., & Greenought, W. T. (2002). Exercise, experience, and the aging brain. *Neurobiology of Aging, 23*, 941–955.

Collette, F., Van der Linden, M., Bechet, S., & Salmon, E. (1999). Phonological loop and central executive functioning in Alzheimer's disease. *Neuropsychologia, 37*, 905–918.

Collie, A., & Maruff, P. (2000). The neuropsychology of preclinical Alzheimer's disease and mild cognitive impairment. *Neuroscience and Biobehavioral Review, 24*, 365–374.

Connor, D. J., Salmon, D. P., Sandy, T. J., Galasko, D., Hansen, L. A., & Thal, L. (1998). Cognitive profiles of autopsy-confirmed Lewy body variant vs. pure Alzheimer's disease. *Archives of Neurology, 55*, 994–1000.

Corder, E. H., Saunders, A. M., Strittmatter, W. J., Schmechel, D. E., Gaskell, P. C., Small, G. W., et al. (1993). Gene dose of apolipoprotein E type 4 allele and the risk of Alzheimer's disease in late onset families. *Science, 261*, 921–923.

Corey-Bloom, J., Wiederholt, W. C., Edelstein, S., Salmon, D. P., Cahn, D., & Barrett-Connor, E. (1996). Cognitive and functional status of the oldest old. *Journal of the American Geriatrics Society, 44*, 671–674.

Cormak, F., Gray, A., Ballard, C., & Tovee, M. J. (2004). A failure of "pop-out" in visual search tasks in dementia with Lewy bodies as compared to Alzheimer's and Parkinson's disease. *International Journal of Geriatric Psychiatry, 19*, 763–772.

Cronin-Golomb, A., & Amick, M. (2001). Spatial abilities in aging, Alzheimer's disease, and Parkinson's disease. In F. Boller and S. F. Cappa (Eds.), *Handbook of neuropsychology, 2nd edition, (Vol 6): Aging and Dementia* (pp. 119–143). Amsterdam: Elsevier.

Corsellis, J. A. N., Bruton, C. J., & Freeman-Browne, D. (1973). The aftermath of boxing. *Psychological Medicine, 3*, 270–303.

Cuetos, R., Arango-Lasprilla, J. C., Uribe, C., Valencia, C., & Lopera, F. (2007). Linguistic changes in verbal expression: A preclinical marker of Alzheimer's disease. *Journal of the International Neuropsychological Society, 13*, 433–439.

Cummings, J. L., & Benson, D. F. (1992). *Dementia: A clinical approach.* Boston: Butterworth-Heinemann.

De Lacoste, M., & White, C. L. (1993). The role of cortical connectivity in Alzheimer's disease pathogenesis: A review and model system. *Neurobiology of Aging, 14*, 1–16.

Delbeuck, X., Van der Linden, M., & Collette, F. (2003). Alzheimer's disease as a disconnection syndrome? *Neuropsychology Review, 13*, 79–92.

Delis, D. C., Kramer, J. H., Kaplan, E., & Ober, B. A. (2000). *The California Verbal Learning Test-II.* New York: Psychological Corp.

Delis, D. C., Massman, P. J., Butters, N., Salmon, D. P., Cermak, L. S., & Kramer, J. H. (1991). Profiles of demented and amnesic patients on the California verbal learning test: Implications for the assessment of memory disorders. *Psychological Assessment, 3*, 19–26.

Della Sala, S., Kinnear, P., Spinnler, H., & Stangalino, C. (2000). Color-to-figure matching in Alzheimer's disease. *Archives of Clinical Neuropsychology, 15*, 571–585.

Desgranges, B., Baron, J. C., & Eustache, F. (1998). The functional neuroanatomy of episodic memory: The role of the frontal lobes, the hippocampal formation, and other areas. *Neuroimage, 8*, 198–213.

Desmond, D. W. (2004). The neuropsychology of vascular cognitive impairment: Is there a specific cognitive impairment? *Journal of the Neurological Sciences, 226*, 3–7.

D'Esposito, M., Zarahn, E., Aguirre, G. K., & Rypma, B. (1999). The effect of nromal aging on the coupling of neural activity to the BOLD hemodynamic response. *NeuroImage, 10*, 6–14.

Dobkins, K. R., & Albright, T. D. (1998). The influence of chromatic information on visual motion processing in the primate visual system. In T Watanabe (Ed.), *High-level motion processing-computational, neurobiological and psychophysical perspectives* (pp. 53–94). Cambridge: MIT.

Dong, M. J., Peng, B., Lin, X. T., Zhao, J., Zhou, Y. R., & Wang, R. H. (2007). The prevalence of dementia in the People's Republic of China: A systematic analysis of 1980–2004 studies. *Age and Ageing, 36*, 619–624.

Dubois, B., Feldman, H. H., Jacova, C., DeKosky, S. T., Barberger-Gateau, P., Cummings, J., et al. (2007). Research criteria for the diagnosis of Alzheimer's disease: revising the NINCDS-ADRDA criteria. *Lancet Neurology, 6*, 734–746.

Duke, L. M., & Kaszniak, A. W. (2000). Executive control functions in degenerative dementias: A comparative review. *Neuropsychology Review, 10*, 75–99.

Dunkin, J. J., Osato, S., & Leuchter, A. F. (1995). Relationships between EEG coherence and neuropsychological tests in dementia. *Clinical Electroencephalography, 26*, 47–59.

Elfgren, C., Brun, A., Gustafson, L., Johanson, A., Minthon, L., Passant, U., et al. (1994). Neuropsychological tests as discriminators between dementia of Alzheimer's type and Frontotemporal dementia. *International Journal of Geriatric Psychiatry, 9*, 635–642.

Eslinger, P. J., & Damasio, A. R. (1986). Preserved motor learning in Alzheimer's disease: Implications for anatomy and behavior. *Journal of Neuroscience, 6*, 3006–3009.

Eslinger, P. J., Damasio, A. R., Benton, A. L., & Van Allen, M. (1985). Neuropsychologic detection of abnormal mental decline in older persons. *Journal of the American Medical Association, 253*, 670–674.

Ferman, T. J., Smith, G. E., Boeve, B. F., Graff-Radford, N. R., Lucas, J. A., et al. (2006). Neuropsychological differentiation of dementia with Lewy bodies from normal aging and Alzheimer's disease. *Clinical Neuropsychologist, 20*, 623–636.

Festa, E., Insler, R. Z., Salmon, D. P., Paxton, J., Hamilton, J. M., & Heindel, W. C. (2005). Neocortical disconnectivity disrupts sensory integration in Alzheimer's disease. *Neuropsychology, 19*, 728–738.

Fleischman, D. A., & Gabrieli, J. D. E. (1998). Repetition priming in normal aging and Alzheimer's disease: A review of findings and theories. *Psychology and Aging, 13*, 88–119.

Flicker, C., Ferris, S. H., & Reisberg, B. (1991). Mild cognitive impairment in the elderly: Predictors of dementia. *Neurology, 41*, 1006–1009.

Folstein, S. E., Brandt, J., & Folstein, M. F. (1990). Huntington's disease. In J. L. Cummings (Ed.), *Subcortical dementia* (pp. 87–107). New York: Oxford University Press.

Förstl, H., Besthorn, C., Geiger-Kabisch, C., Sattel, H., & Schreitter-Gasser, U. (1996). Frontal lobe degeneration and Alzheimer's disease: A controlled study on clinical findings, volumetric brain changes and quantitative electroencephalography data. *Dementia, 7*, 27–34.

Foster, J. K., Behrmann, M., & Stuss, D. T. (1999). Visual attention deficits in Alzheimer's disease: Simple versus conjoined feature search. *Neuropsychology, 13*, 223–245.

Fratiglioni, L., & Wang, H. X. (2007). Brain reserve hypothesis in dementia. *Journal of Alzheimer's Disease, 12*, 11–22.

Fratiglioni, L., Winblad, B., & von Strauss, E. (2007). Prevention of Alzheimer's disease and dementia. Major finding from the Kungsholmen project. *Physiology and Behavior, 92*, 98–104.

Freedman, M., Leach, L., Kaplan, E., Winocur, G., Shulman, K. I., & Delis, D. C. (1994). *Clock drawing: A neuropsychological analysis.* New York: Oxford University Press.

Freedman, M., & Oscar-Berman, M. (1997). Breakdown of cross-modal function in dementia. *Neuropsychiatry, Neuropsychology, and Behavioral Neurology, 10*, 102–106.

Frisoni, G. B., Pizzolato, G., Geroldi, C., Rossato, A., Bianchetti, A., & Trabucchi, M. (1995). Dementia of the frontal type: Neuropsychological and 99[TC-HMPAO] SPECT features. *Journal of Geriatric Psychiatry and Neurology, 8*, 42–48.

Fuld, P. A., Katzman, R., Davies, P., & Terry, R. D. (1982). Intrusions as a sign of Alzheimer dementia: Chemical and pathological verification. *Annals of Neurology, 11*, 155–159.

Fuld, P. A., Masur, D. M., Blau, A. D., Crystal, H., & Aronson, M. K. (1990). Object-memory evaluation for prospective detection of dementia in normal functioning elderly: Predictive and normative data. *Journal of Clinical and Experimental Neuropsychology, 12*, 520–528.

Gabrieli, J. D. E., Stebbins, G. T., Singh, J., Willingham, D. B., & Goetz, C. G. (1997). Intact mirror-tracing and impaired rotary-pursuit skill learning in patients with Huntington's disease: Evidence for dissociable memory systems in skill learning. *Neuropsychology, 11*, 272–281.

Galasko, D., Katzman, R., Salmon, D. P., Thal, L. J., & Hansen, L. (1996). Clinical and neuropathological findings in Lewy body dementias. *Brain and Cognition, 31*, 166–175.

Galloway, P. H., Sahgal, A., McKeith, I. G., Lloyd, S., Cook, J. H., Ferrier, I. N., et al. (1992). Visual pattern recognition memory and learning deficits in senile dementias of Alzheimer and Lewy body types. *Dementia, 3*, 101–107.

Gnanalingham, K. K., Byrne, E. J., & Thornton, A. (1996). Clock-face drawing to differentiate Lewy body and Alzheimer type dementia syndromes. *Lancet, 347*, 696–697.

Gnanalingham, K. K., Byrne, E. J., Thornton, A., Sambrook, M. A., & Bannister, P. (1997). Motor and cognitive function in Lewy body dementia: Comparison with Alzheimer's and Parkinson's diseases. *Journal of Neurology, Neurosurgery and Psychiatry, 62*, 243–252.

Goldblum, M., Gomez, C., Dalla Barba, G., Boller, F., Deweer, B., Hahn, V., et al. (1998). The influence of semantic and perceptual encoding on recognition memory in Alzheimer's disease. *Neuropsychologia, 36*, 717–729.

Golob, E. J., Miranda, G. G., Johnson, J. K., & Starr, A. (2001). Sensory cortical interactions in aging, mild cognitive impairment, and Alzheimer's disease. *Neurobiology of Aging, 22*, 755–763.

Gomez-Tortosa, E., Newell, K., Irizarry, M. C., Albert, M., Growdon, J. H., & Hyman, B. T. (1999). Clinical and quantitative pathologic correlates of dementia with Lewy bodies. *Neurology, 53*, 1284–1291.

Gómez-Tortosa, E., Irizarry, M. C., Gómez-Isla, T., & Hyman, B. T. (2000). Clinical and neuropathological correlates of dementia with Lewy bodies. *Annals of the New York Academy of Science, 920*, 9–15.

Grady, C. L., & Craik, F. I. (2000). Changes in memory processing with age. *Current Opinion in Neurobiology, 10*, 224–231.

Grady, C. L., Furey, M. L., Pietrini, P., Horwitz, B., & Rapoport, S. I. (2001). Altered brain functional connectivity and impaired short-term memory in Alzheimer's disease. *Brain, 124*, 739–756.

Grady, C. L., Haxby, J. V., Horwitz, B., Sundaram, M., Berg, G., Schapiro, M., et al. (1988). Longitudinal study of the early neuropsychological and cerebral metabolic changes in dementia of the Alzheimer type. *Journal of Clinical and Experimental Neuropsychology, 10*, 576–596.

Grady, C. L., Mcintosh, A. R., Horwitz, B., Maisog, J. M., Ungerleider, L. G., et al. (1995). Age-related reductions in human recognition memory due to impaired encoding. *Science, 269*, 218–221.

Graham, N. L., Emery, T., & Hodges, J. R. (2004). Distinct cognitive profiles in Alzheimer's disease and subcortical vascular dementia. *Journal of Neurology, Neurosurgery and Psychiatry, 75*, 61–71.

Greene, J. D. W., Baddeley, A. D., & Hodges, J. R. (1996). Analysis of the episodic memory deficit in early Alzheimer's disease: Evidence from the doors and people test. *Neuropsychologia, 34*, 537–551.

Greenwood, P. M. (2000). The frontal aging hypothesis evaluated. *Journal of the International Neuropsychological Society, 6*, 705–726.

Gregory, C. A., Orrell, M., Sahkian, B., & Hodges, J. (1997). Can frontotemporal dementia and Alzheimer's disease be differentiated using a brief battery of tests? *International Journal of Geriatric Psychiatry, 12*, 357–383.

Grober, E., & Kawas, C. (1997). Learning and retention in preclinical and early Alzheimer's disease. *Psychology and Aging, 12*, 183–188.

Grossman, M., Libon, D. J., Forman, M. S., Massimo, L., Wood, E., Moore, P., et al. (2007). Distinct antemortem profiles in patients with pathologically defined frontotemporal dementia. *Archives of Neurology, 64(11)*, 1601–1609.

Guidi, M., Paciaroni, L., Paolini, S., DePadova, S., & Scarpino, O. (2006). Differences and similarities in the neuropsychological profile of dementia with Lewy bodies and Alzheimer's disease in the early stage. *Journal of the Neurological Sciences, 248*, 120–123.

Gunning-Dixon, F. M., & Raz, N. (2000). The cognitive correlates of white matter abnormalities in normal aging: A quantitative review. *Neuropsychology, 14*, 224–232.

Guskiewicz, K. M., Marshall, S. W., Bailes, J., McCrea, M., Cantu, R. C., Randolph, C., et al. (2005). Association between recurrent concussion and late-life cognitive impairment in retired professional football players. *Neurosurgery, 57(4)*, 719–726.

Guttman, C. R., Jolesz, F. A., Kikinis, R., Killiany, R. J., Moss, M. B., Sandor, T., et al. (1998). White matter changes with normal aging. *Neurology, 50*, 972–978.

Hamilton, J. M., Salmon, D. P., Galasko, D., Delis, D. C., Hansen, L. A., et al. (2004). A comparison of episodic memory deficits in neuropathologically-confirmed Dementia with Lewy Bodies and Alzheimer's disease. *Journal of the International Neuropsychological Society, 10*, 689–697.

Han, S. D., & Bondi, M. W. (2008). Revision of the apolipoprotein E compensatory mechanism hypothesis. *Alzheimer's & Dementia, 4*, 251–254.

Han, S. D., Drake, A. I., Cessante, L. M., Jak, A. J., Houston, W. S., Delis, D. C., et al. (2007). APOE and Recovery from TBI in a U.S. Military Population: Evidence for a Compensatory Mechanism? *Journal of Neurology, Neurosurgery, and Psychiatry, 78*, 1103–1108.

Hanes, K. R., Andrewes, D. G., & Pantelis, C. (1995). Cognitive flexibility and complex integration in Parkinson's disease, Huntington's disease, and schizophrenia. *Journal of the International Neuropsychological Society, 1*, 545–553.

Hansen, L. A., & Galasko, D. (1992). Lewy body disease. *Current Opinion in Neurology, 5*, 889–894.

Hansen, L., Salmon, D., Galasko, D., Masliah, E., Katzman, R., et al. (1990). The Lewy body variant of Alzheimer's disease: A clinical and pathologic entity. *Neurology, 40*, 1–8.

Hashimoto, M., Kitagaki, H., Imamura, T., Hirono, N., Shimomura, T., et al. (1998). Medial temporal and whole-brain atrophy in dementia with Lewy bodies. *Neurology, 51*, 357–362.

Haxby, J. V., Duara, R., Grady, C. L., Cutler, N. R., & Rapoport, S. I. (1985). Relations between neuropsychological and cerebral metabolic asymmetries in early Alzheimer's disease. *Journal of Cerebral Blood Flow and Metabolism, 5*, 193–200.

Hedden, T., & Gabrieli, J. D. (2004). Insights into the ageing mind: A view from cognitive neuroscience. *Nature Reviews. Neuroscience, 5*, 87–97.

Heindel, W. C., & Salmon, D. P. (2001). Cognitive approaches to the memory disorders of demented patients. In H. E. Adams and P. B. Sutker (Eds.), *Comprehensive handbook of psychopathology, 2nd Edition* (pp. 841–878). New York: Kluwer/Academic-Plenum.

Heindel, W. C., Salmon, D. P., Shults, C. W., Walicke, P. A., & Butters, N. (1989). Neuropsychological evidence for multiple implicit memory systems: A comparison of Alzheimer's, Huntington's, and Parkinson's disease patients. *Journal of Neuroscience, 9*, 582–587.

Henry, J. D., Crawford, J. R., & Phillips, L. H. (2004). Verbal fluency performance in dementia of the Alzheimer's type: A meta-analysis. *Neuropsychologia, 42*, 1212–1222.

Henry, J. D., Crawford, J. R., & Phillips, L. H. (2005). A meta-analytic review of verbal fluency deficits in Huntington's disease. *Neuropsychology, 19*, 243–252.

Heyman, A., Fillenbaum, G. G., Gearing, M., Mirra, S. S., Welsh-Bohmer, K. A., Peterson, B., et al. (1999). Comparison of Lewy body variant of Alzheimer's disease with pure Alzheimer's disease: Consortium to establish a registry for Alzheimer's disease, part XIX. *Neurology, 52*, 1839–1844.

Higuchi, M., Tashiro, M., Arai, H., Okamura, N., Hara, S., et al. (2000). Glucose hypometabolism and neuropathological correlates in brains of dementia with Lewy bodies. *Experimental Neurology, 162*, 247–256.

Hodges, J. R., & Graham, N. L. (2001). Vascular dementias. In J. R. Hodges (Ed.), *Early onset dementia: A multidisciplinary approach* (pp. 319–337). Oxford: Oxford University Press.

Hodges, J. R., & Patterson, K. (1995). Is semantic memory consistently impaired early in the course of Alzheimer's disease? Neuroanatomical and diagnostic implications. *Neuropsychologia, 33*, 441–459.

Hodges, J. R., Salmon, D. P., & Butters, N. (1991). The nature of the naming deficit in Alzheimer's and Huntington's disease. *Brain, 114*, 1547–1558.

Hodges, J. R., Salmon, D. P., & Butters, N. (1992). Semantic memory impairment in Alzheimer's disease: Failure of access or degraded knowledge? *Neuropsychologia, 30*, 301–314.

Hodges, J. R., Salmon, D. P., & Butters, N. (1993). Recognition and naming of famous faces in Alzheimer's disease: A cognitive analysis. *Neuropsychologia, 31*, 775–788.

Hof, P. R., & Morrison, J. H. (1999). The cellular basis of cortical disconnection in Alzheimer's disease and related dementing conditions. In R. D. Terry, R. Katzman, K. L. Bick, & S. S. Sisodia (Eds.), *Alzheimer disease* (pp. 207–232). New York: Raven.

Hogan, M. J., Swanwick, G. R. J., Kaiser, J., Rowan, M., & Lawlor, S. (2003). Memory-related EEG power and coherence reductions in mild Alzheimer's disease. *International Journal of Psychophysiology, 49*, 147–163.

Houston, W. S., Delis, D. C., Lansing, A., Cobell, C., Jacobson, M. W., Salmon, D. P., et al. (2005). Executive function asymmetry in older adults genetically at risk for Alzheimer's disease: Verbal versus design fluency. *Journal of the International Neuropsychological Society, 11*, 863–870.

Howieson, D. B., Dame, A., Camicioli, R., Sexton, G., Payami, H., & Kaye, J. A. (1997). Cognitive markers preceding Alzheimer's dementia in the healthy oldest old. *Journal of the American Geriatric Society, 45*, 84–89.

Hubacek, J. A., Pitha, J., Skodova, Z., Adamkova, V., Lanska, V., & Poledne, R. (2001). A possible role of apolipoprotein E polymorphism in predisposition to higher education. *Neuropsychobiology, 43*, 200–203.

Huff, F. J., Becker, J. T., Belle, S. H., Nebes, R. D., Holland, A. L., & Boller, F. (1987). Cognitive deficits and clinical diagnosis of Alzheimer's disease. *Neurology, 37*, 1119–1124.

Huff, F. J., Corkin, S., & Growdon, J. H. (1986). Semantic impairment and anomia in Alzheimer's disease. *Brain and Language, 28*, 235–249.

Hultsch, D. F., Hertzog, C., Small, B. J., & Dixon, R. A. (1999). Use it or lose it: Engage lifestyle as a buffer of cognitive decline in aging. *Psychology and Aging, 14*(2), 245–263.

Hyman, B. T., Damasio, A. R., Van Hoesen, G. W., & Barnes, C. L. (1984). Alzheimer's disease: Cell specific pathology isolates the hippocampal formation. *Science, 225*, 1168–1170.

Ince, P. G., Perry, E. K., & Morris, C. M. (1998). Dementia with Lewy bodies: A distinct non-Alzheimer dementia syndrome? *Brain Pathology, 8*, 299–324.

Ineichen, B. (1987). Measuring the rising tide. How many dementia cases will there be by 2001? *British Journal of Psychiatry, 150*, 193–200.

Jack, C. R., Petersen, R. C., Xu, Y. C., Waring, S. C., O'Brien, P. C., et al. (1998). Medial temporal atrophy on MRI in normal aging and very mild Alzheimer's disease. *Neurology, 49*, 786–794.

Jacobs, D., Salmon, D. P., Tröster, A. I., & Butters, N. (1990). Intrusion errors in the figural memory of patients with Alzheimer's and Huntington's disease. *Archives of Clinical Neuropsychology, 5*, 49–57.

Jacobs, D. M., Sano, M., Dooneief, G., Marder, K., Bell, K. L., & Stern, Y. (1995). Neuropsychological detection and characterization of preclinical Alzheimer's disease. *Neurology, 45*, 957–962.

Jacobson, M. W., Delis, D. C., Lansing, A., Houston, W. S., Olsen, R., Wetter, S., et al. (2005a). Asymmetries in global and local processing in elderly with the APOE e4 allele. *Neuropsychology, 19*, 822–829.

Jacobson, M. W., Delis, D. C., Bondi, M. W., & Salmon, D. P. (2005b). Asymmetry in auditory and spatial attention span in normal elderly genetically at risk for Alzheimer's disease. *Journal of Clinical and Experimental Neuropsychology, 27*, 240–253.

Jacobson, M. W., Delis, D. C., Bondi, M. W., & Salmon, D. P. (2002). Do neuropsychological tests detect preclinical Alzheimer's disease?: Individual-test versus cognitive discrepancy analyses. *Neuropsychology, 16*, 132–139.

Jelic, V., Shigeta, M., Julin, P., Almkvist, O., Winblad, B., & Wahlund, L. O. (1996). Quantitative electroencephalography power and coherence in Alzheimer's disease and mild cognitive impairment. *Dementia, 7*, 314–323.

Jellinger, K. A. (2004). Head injury and dementia. *Current Opinion in Neurology, 17*, 719–723.

Jernigan, T. J., Archibald, S. L., Fennema-Notestine, C., Gamst, A. C., Stout, J. C., Bonner, J., et al. (2001). Effects of age on tissues and regions of the cerebrum and cerebellum. *Neurobiology of Aging, 22*, 581–594.

Johanson, A., & Hagberg, B. (1989). Psychometric characteristics in patients with frontal lobe degeneration of non-Alzheimer's type. *Archives of Gerontology and Geriatrics, 8*, 129–137.

Johnson, D. K., Morris, J. C., & Galvin, J. E. (2005). Verbal and visuospatial deficits in dementia with Lewy bodies. *Neurology, 65*, 1232–1238.

Jordan, B. D., Relkin, N. R., Ravdin, L. D., Jacobs, A. R., Bennett, A., & Gandy, S. (1997). Apolipoprotein E epsilon4 associated with chronic traumatic brain injury in boxing. *Journal of the American Medical Association, 278*, 136–140.

Jorm, A. F., Korten, A. E., & Henderson, A. S. (1987). The prevalence of dementia: A quantitative integration of the literature. *Acta Psychiatrica Scandinavica, 76*, 465–479.

Josiassen, R. C., Curry, L. M., & Mancall, E. L. (1983). Development of neuropsychological deficits in Huntington's disease. *Archives of Neurology, 40*, 791–796.

Kaszniak, A. W., & Newman, M. C. (2000). Toward a neuropsychology of cognitive aging. In S. H. Qualls and N. Abeles (Eds.), *Psychology and the aging revolution: How we adapt to longer life* (pp. 43–67). Washington, DC: American Psychological Association.

Kaszniak, A. W., Wilson, R. S., Fox, J. H., & Stebbins, G. T. (1986). Cognitive assessment in Alzheimer's disease: Cross-sectional and longitudinal perspectives. *Canadian Journal of Neurological Sciences, 13,* 420–423.

Katzman, R. (1994). Apolipoprotein E and Alzheimer's disease. *Current Opinion in Neurobiology, 4,* 703–707.

Katzman, R. (1993). Education and the prevalence of dementia and Alzheimer's disease. *Neurology, 43,* 13–20.

Kawas, C. H., & Katzman, R. (1999). Epidemiology of dementia and Alzheimer disease. In R. D. Terry, R. Katzman, K. L. Bick, and S. S. Sisodia (Eds.), *Alzheimer disease* (2nd ed., pp. 95–116). New York: Raven Press.

Kawas, C. H., Corrada, M. M., Brookmeyer, R., Morrison, A., Resnick, S. M., Zonderman, A. B., et al. (2003). Visual memory predicts Alzheimer's disease more than a decade before diagnosis. *Neurology, 60,* 1089–1093.

Keltikangas-Jarvinen, L., Raikkonen, K., & Lehtimaki, T. (1993). Dependence between apolipoprotein E phenotypes and temperament in children, adolescents, and young adults. *Psychosomatic Medicine, 55,* 155–163.

Kertesz, A., Davidson, W., & Munoz, D. G. (1999). Clinical and pathological overlap between fronto-temporal dementia, primary progressive aphasia and corticobasal degeneration: The Pick complex. *Dementia and Geriatric Cognitive Disorders, 10*(suppl), 46–49.

Kertesz, A., Hudson, L., Mackenzie, I. R. A., & Munoz, D. G. (1994). The pathology and nosology of primary progressive aphasia. *Neurology, 44,* 2065–2072.

Kertesz, A., Nadkarni, N., Davidson, W., & Thomas, A. W. (2000). The Frontal Behavioral Inventory in the differential diagnosis of frontotemporal dementia. *Journal of the International Neuropsychological Society, 6,* 460–468.

Kertesz, A., & Clydesdale, S. (1994). Neuropsychological deficits in vascular dementia vs. Alzheimer's disease: Frontal lobe deficits prominent in vascular dementia. *Archives of Neurology, 51,* 1226–1231.

Knopman, D. S., DeKosky, S. T., Cummings, J. L., Chui, H., Corey-Bloom, J., Relkin, N., et al. (2001). Practice parameter: Diagnosis of dementia (an evidence-based review). *Neurology, 56,* 1143–1153.

Knopman, D. S., Mastri, A. R., Frey, W., Sung, J. H., & Rustan, T. (1990). Dementia lacking distinctive histologic features: A common non-Alzheimer degenerative dementia. *Neurology, 40,* 251–256.

Knopman, D. S., & Ryberg, S. (1989). A verbal memory test with high predictive accuracy for dementia of the Alzheimer type. *Archives of Neurology, 46,* 141–145.

Knott, V., Mohr, E., Mahoney, C., & Ilivitsky, V. (2000). Electroencephalographic coherence in Alzheimer's disease: Comparisons with a control group and population norms. *Journal of Geriatric Psychiatry and Neurology, 13,* 1–8.

Koenig, P., Smith, E. E., Moore, P., Glosser, G., & Grossman, M. (2007). Categorization of novel animals by patients with Alzheimer's disease and corticobasal degeneration. *Neuropsychology, 21,* 193–206.

Kopelman, M. D. (1989). Remote and autobiographical memory, temporal context memory and frontal atrophy in Korsakoff and Alzheimer patients. *Neuropsychologia, 27,* 437–460.

Kosaka, K., Yoshimura, M., Ikeda, K., & Budka, H. (1984). Diffuse type of Lewy body disease: Progressive dementia with abundant cortical Lewy bodies and senile changes of varying degree: A new disease? *Clinical Neuropathology, 3,* 185–192.

Kramer, M. (1986). Trends of institutionalization and prevalence of mental disorders in nursing homes. In M. S. Harper and B. D. Lebowitz (Eds.), *Mental illness in nursing homes: Agenda for research* (pp. 7–26). Rockville, MD: National Institute of Mental Health (DHHS Publication No. (ADM) 86–1459).

Kramer, A. F., & Erickson, K. I. (2007). Capitalizing on cortical plasticity: Influence of physical activity on cognition and brain function. *Trends in Cognitive Neuroscience, 11*(8), 342–348.

Kramer, A. F., Bherer, L., Colcombe, S. J., Dong, W., & Greenough, W. T. (2004). Environmental influences on cognitive and brain plasticity during aging. *The Journals of Gerontology. Series A, Biological Sciences and Medical Sciences, 59,* 940–957.

Kraybill, M. L., Larson, E. B., Tsuang, D. W., Teri, L., McCormick, W. C., et al. (2005). Cognitive differences in dementia patients with autopsy-verified AD, Lewy body pathology, or both. *Neurology, 64,* 2069–2073.

Kurylo, D. D., Corkin, S., Rizzo, J. F., & Growdon, J. H. (1996). Greater relative impairment of object recognition than of visuospatial abilities in Alzheimer's disease. *Neuropsychology, 10,* 74–81.

Lafosse, J. M., Reed, B. R., Mungas, D., Sterling, S. B., Wahbeh, H., & Jagust, W. J. (1997). Fluency and memory differences between ischemic vascular dementia and Alzheimer's disease. *Neuropsychology, 11,* 514–522.

Lakmache, Y., Lassonde, M., Gauthier, S., Frigon, J-Y., & Lepore, F. (1998). Interhemispheric disconnection syndrome in Alzheimer's disease. *Proceedings of the National Academy of Sciences, 95*, 9042–9046.

Lamar, M., Podell, K., Carew, T. G., Cloud, B. S., Resh, R., et al. (1997). Perseverative behavior in Alzheimer's disease and subcortical ischemic vascular dementia. *Neuropsychology, 11*, 523–534.

Lambon Ralph, M. A., Powell, J., Howard, D., Whitworth, A. B., Garrard, P., & Hodges, J. R. (2001). Semantic memory is impaired in both dementia with Lewy bodies and dementia of Alzheimer's type: A comparative neuropsychological study and literature review. *Journal of Neurology, Neurosurgery and Psychiatry, 70*, 149–156.

Lange, K. L., Bondi, M. W., Salmon, D. P., Galasko, D., Delis, D. C., Thomas, R. G., et al. (2002). Decline in verbal memory during preclinical Alzheimer's disease: Examination of the effect of APOE genotype. *Journal of the International Neuropsychological Society, 8*, 943–955.

Lange, K. W., Sahakian, B. J., Quinn, N. P., Marsden, C. D., & Robbins, T. W. (1995). Comparison of executive and visuospatial memory function in Huntington's disease and dementia of Alzheimer type matched for degree of dementia. *Journal of Neurology, Neurosurgery and Psychiatry, 58*, 598–606.

Lawrence, A. D., Sahakian, B. J., Hodges, J. R., Rosser, A. E., Lange, K. W., & Robbins, T. W. (1996). Executive and mnemonic functions in early Huntington's disease. *Brain, 119*, 1633–1645.

Lawrence, A. D., Watkins, L. H., Sahakian, B. J., Hodges, J. R., & Robbins, T. W. (2000). Visual object and visuospatial cognition in Huntington's disease: Implications for information processing in corticostriatal circuits. *Brain, 123*, 1349–1364.

Lefleche, G., & Albert, M. S. (1995). Executive function deficits in mild Alzheimer's disease. *Neuropsychology, 9*, 313–320.

Libon, D. J., Xie, S. X., Moore, P., Farmer, J., Antani, S., et al. (2007). Patterns of neuropsychological impairment in frontotemporal dementia. *Neurology, 68*, 369–375.

Lindau, M., Almkvist, O., Johansson, S. E., & Wahlund, L. O. (1998). Cognitive and behavioral differentiation of frontal lobe degeneration of the non-Alzheimer's type and Alzheimer's Disease. *Dementia and Geriatric Cognitive Disorders, 9*, 205–213.

Lineweaver, T. T., Salmon, D. P., Bondi, M. W., & Corey-Bloom, J. (2005). Distinct effects of Alzheimer's disease and Huntington's disease on performance of mental rotation. *Journal of the International Neuropsychological Society, 11*, 30–39.

Linn, R. T., Wolf, P. A., Bachman, D. L., Knoefel, J. E., Cobb, J. L., et al. (1995). The "preclinical phase" of probable Alzheimer's disease. *Archives of Neurology, 52*, 485–490.

Lippa, C. F., Johnson, R., & Smith, T. W. (1998). The medial temporal lobe in dementia with Lewy bodies: A comparative study with Alzheimer's disease. *Annals of Neurology, 43*, 102–106.

Lipton, A. M., Ohman, K. A., Womack, K. B., Hynan, L. S., Ninman, E. T., & Lacritz, L. H. (2005). Subscores of the FAB differentiate frontotemporal lobar degeneration from AD. *Neurology, 65*, 726–731.

Locascio, J. J., Growdon, J. H., & Corkin, S. (1995). Cognitive test performance in detecting, staging, and tracking Alzheimer's disease. *Archives of Neurology, 52*, 1087–1099.

Mathuranath, P. S., Nestor, P. J., Berrios, G. E., Rakowicz, W., & Hodges, J. R. (2000). A brief cognitive test battery to differentiate Alzheimer's disease and frontotemporal dementia. *Neurology, 55*, 1613–1620.

Martin, A., Brouwers, P., Cox, C., & Fedio, P. (1985). On the nature of the verbal memory deficit in Alzheimer's disease. *Brain and Language, 25*, 323–341.

Martin, A., & Fedio, P. (1983). Word production and comprehension in Alzheimer's disease: The breakdown of semantic knowledge. *Brain and Language, 19*, 124–141.

Masliah, E., Mallory, M., Hansen, L. A., DeTeresa, R., & Terry, R. D. (1993). Quantitative synaptic alterations in the human neocortex during normal aging. *Neurology, 43*, 192–197.

Massman, P. J., Delis, D. C., & Butters, N. (1993). Does impaired primacy recall equal impaired long-term storage?: Serial position effects in Huntington's disease and Alzheimer's disease. *Developmental Neuropsycholy, 9*, 1–15.

Mayeux, R., Ottman, R., Maestre, G., Ngai, C., Tang, M-X., Ginsberg, H., et al. (1995). Synergistic effects of traumatic head injury and apolipoprotein ε4 in patients with Alzheimer's disease. *Neurology, 45*, 555–557.

McHugh, P. R., & Folstein, M. F. (1975). Psychiatric symptoms of Huntington's chorea: A clinical and phenomenologic study. In D. F. Benson, and D. Blumer (Eds.), *Psychiatric aspects of neurological disease* (pp. 267–285). New York: Raven Press.

McKeith, I. G., Dickson, D. W., Lowe, J., Emre, M., O'Brien, J. T, et al. (2005). Diagnosis and management of dementia with Lewy bodies: Third report of the DLB consortium. *Neurology, 65*, 1863–1872.

McKeith, I. G., Galasko, D., Kosaka, K., Perry, E., Dickson, D., et al. (1996). Clinical and pathological diagnosis of dementia with Lewy bodies (DLB): Report of the Consortium on Dementia with Lewy Bodies (CDLB) International Workgroup. *Neurology, 47,* 1113–1124.

McKhann, G., Drachman, D., Folstein, M., Katzman, R., Price, D., & Stadlan, E.M. (1984). Clinical diagnosis of Alzheimer's disease: Report of the NINCDS-ADRDA Work Group under the auspices of Department of Health and Human Services Task Force on Alzheimer's Disease. *Neurology, 34,* 939–944.

Mendez, M. F., Cherrier, M., Perryman, K., Pachana, N., Miller, B., & Cummings, J. L. (1996). Frontotemporal dementias versus Alzheimer's disease: Differential cognitive features. *Neurology, 47,* 1189–1194.

Mendez, M. F., Perryman, K. M., Miller, B. L., & Cummings, J. L. (1998). Behavioral differences between frontotemporal dementia and Alzheimer's disease: A comparison on the BEHAVE-AD rating scale. *International Psychogeriatrics 10,* 155–162.

Mendez, M. F., Selwood, A., Mastri, A. R., & Frey, W. H. (1993). Pick's disease versus Alzheimer's disease: A comparison of clinical characteristics. *Neurology, 43,* 289–292.

Mesulam, M. M. (1982). Slowly progressive aphasia without generalized dementia. *Annals of Neurology, 30,* 69–72.

Merdes, A. R., Hansen, L. A., Jeste, D. V., Galasko, D., Hofstetter, C. R., et al. (2003). Influence of Alzheimer pathology on clinical diagnostic accuracy in dementia with Lewy bodies. *Neurology, 60,* 1586–1590.

Mickes, L., Wixted, J. T., Fennema-Notestine, C., Galasko, D., Bondi, M. W., Thal, L. J., et al. (2007). Progressive impairment on neuropsychological tasks in a longitudinal study of preclinical Alzheimer's disease. *Neuropsychology, 21(6),* 696–705.

Miech, R. A., Breitner, J. C., Zandi, P. P., Khachaturian, A. S., Anthony, J. C., & Mayer, L. (2002). Incidence of AD may decline in the early 90s for men, later for women: The Cache County study *Neurology, 58,* 209–218.

Miller, B. L., Ikonte, C., Ponton, M., Levy, M., Boone, K., Darby, A., et al. (1997). A study of the Lund-Manchester research criteria for frontotemporal dementia: Clinical and single-photon emission CT correlations. *Neurology, 48,* 937–942.

Minoshima, S., Foster, N. L., Sima, A., Frey, K. A., Albin, R. L., & Kuhl, D. E. (2001). Alzheimer's disease versus dementia with Lewy bodies: Cerebral metabolic distinction with autopsy confirmation. *Annals of Neurology, 50,* 358–365.

Mohr, E., Litvan, I., Williams, J., Fedio, P., & Chase, T. N. (1990). Selective deficits in Alzheimer and Parkinson dementia: Visuospatial function. *Canadian Journal of Neurological Sciences, 17,* 292–297.

Mondadori, C. R. A., de Quervain, D. J-F., Buchmann, A., Mustovic, H., Wollmer, M. A., Schmidt, C. F., et al. (2007). Better memory and neural efficiency in young apolipoprotein E epsilon4 carriers. *Cerebral Cortex, 17,* 1934–1947.

Monsch, A. U., Bondi, M. W., Butters, N. Paulsen, J.S., Salmon, D.P., Brugger, P., et al. (1994). A comparison of category and letter fluency in Alzheimer's disease and Huntington's disease. *Neuropsychology, 8,* 25–30.

Montoya, A., Pelletier, M., Menear, M., Duplessis, E., Richer, F., & Lepage, M. (2006). Episodic memory impairment in Huntington's disease: A meta-analysis. *Neuropsychologia, 44,* 1984–1994.

Mori, E., Shimomura, T., Fujimori, M., Hirono, N., Imamura, T., et al. (2000). Visuoperceptual impairment in dementia with Lewy bodies. *Archives of Neurology, 57,* 489–493.

Morris, J. C., McKeel, D. W., Storandt, M., Rubin, E. H., Price, J. L., et al. (1991). Very mild Alzheimer's disease: Informant-based clinical, psychometric, and pathologic distinction from normal aging. *Neurology, 41,* 469–478.

Mortimer, J. A. (1988). Do psychosocial risk factors contribute to Alzheimer's disease? In A. S. Henderson and J. H. Henderson (Eds.), *Etiology of dementia of the Alzheimer's type* (pp. 39–52). New York: John Wiley and Sons.

Mortimer, J. A., van Duijn, C. M., Chandra, V., Fratglioni, L., Graves, A. B., Heyman, A., et al. (1991). Head trauma as a risk factor for Alzheimer's disease: A collaborative re-analysis of case-control studies. *International Journal of Epidemiology, 20*(suppl.2), S28–S35.

Moss, M. B., Albert, M. S., Butters, N., & Payne, M. (1986). Differential patterns of memory loss among patients with Alzheimer's disease, Huntington's disease and alcoholic Korsakoff's syndrome. *Archives of Neurology, 43,* 239–246.

Nadel, L., & Moscovitch, M. (1997). Memory consolidation, retrograde amnesia and the hippocampal complex. *Current Opinion in Neurobiology, 7,* 217–227.

Neary, D. (1999). Overview of frontotemporal dementias and the consensus applied. *Dementia and Geriatric Cognitive Disorders, 10*(suppl), 6–9.

Neary, D., Snowden, J. S., Gustafson, L. Passant, U., Stuss, D., Black S., et al. (1998). Frontotemporal lobar degeneration: A consensus on clinical diagnostic criteria. *Neurology, 51,* 1546–1554.

Nebes, R. (1989). Semantic memory in Alzheimer's disease. *Psychological Bulletin 106*, 377–394.

Nicholas, M., Obler, L., Albert, M., & Helm-Estabrooks, N. (1985). Empty speech in Alzheimer's disease and fluent aphasia. *Journal of Speech and Hearing Research, 28*, 405–410.

Noe, E., Marder, K., Bell, K. L., Jacobs, D. M., Manly, J. J., & Stern, Y. (2003). Comparison of dementia with Lewy bodies to Alzheimer's disease and Parkinson's disease with dementia. *Movement Disords, 19*, 60–67.

Norton, L. E., Bondi, M. W., Salmon, D. P., & Goodglass, H. (1997). Deterioration of generic knowledge in patients with Alzheimer's disease: Evidence from the Number Information Test. *Journal of Clinical and Experimental Neuropsychology, 19*, 857–866.

O'Sullivan, M., Jones, D. K., Summers, P. E., Morris, R. G., Williams, S. C., & Markus, H. S. (2001). Evidence for cortical "disconnection" as a mechanism of age-related cognitive decline. *Neurology, 57*, 632–638.

Pachana, N. A., Boone, K. B., Miller, B. L., Cummings, J. L., & Berman, N. (1996). Comparison of neuropsychological functioning in Alzheimer's disease and frontotemporal dementia. *Journal of the International Neuropsychological Society, 2*, 505–510.

Pandovani, A., Di Piero, V., Bragoni, M., Iacoboni, M., Gualdi, G. G., & Lenzi, G. L. (1995). Patterns of neuropsychological impairment in mild dementia: A comparison between Alzheimer's disease and multi-infarct dementia. *Acta Neurologica Scandinavica, 92*, 433–442.

Parasuraman, R., & Haxby, J. V. (1993). Attention and brain function in Alzheimer's disease. *Neuropsychology, 7*, 242–772.

Park, H. L., O'Connell, J. E., & Thomson, R. G. (2003). A systematic review of cognitive decline in the general elderly population. *International Journal of Geriatric Psychiatry, 18*, 1121–1134.

Pasquier, F., Lebert, F., Grymonprez, L., & Petit, H. (1995). Verbal fluency in dementia of frontal lobe type and dementia of Alzheimer type. *Journal of Neurology, Neurosurgery and Psychiatry, 58*, 81–84.

Paulsen, J. S., Salmon, D. P., Monsch, A. U., Butters, N., Swenson, M., & Bondi, M. W. (1995). Discrimination of cortical from subcortical dementias on the basis of memory and problem-solving tests. *Journal of Clinical Psychology, 51*, 48–58.

Paxton, J. L., Peavy, G. M., Jenkins, C., Rice, V. A., Heindel, W. C., & Salmon, D. P. (2007). Deterioration of visual–perceptual ability in Alzheimer's disease. *Cortex 43*, 967–975.

Peinemann, A., Schuller, S., Pohl, C., Jahn, T., Weindl, A., & Kassubek, J. (2005). Executive dysfunction in early stages of Huntington's disease is associated with striatal and insular atrophy: A neuropsychological and voxel-based morphometric study. *Journal of the Neurological Sciences, 239*, 11–19.

Perry, R. J., & Hodges, J. R. (1999). Attention and executive deficits in Alzheimer's disease: A critical review. *Brain 122*, 383–404.

Perry, R. H., Irving, D., Blessed, G., Fairbairn, A., & Perry, E. K. (1990). Senile dementia of the Lewy body type: A clinically and neuropathologically distinct form of Lewy body dementia in the elderly. *Journal of the Neurological Sciences, 95*, 119–139.

Petersen, R. C., Doody, R., Kurz, A., Mohs, R. C., Morris, J. C., et al. (2001). Current concepts in mild cognitive impairment. *Archives of Neurology, 58*, 1985–1992.

Petersen, R. C., Smith, G. E., Ivnik, R. J., Tangalos, E. G., Schaid, D. J., et al. (1995). Apolipoprotein E status as a predictor of the development of Alzheimer's disease in memory-impaired individuals. *Journal of the American Medical Association, 273*, 1274–1278.

Pfefferbaum, A., Adalsteinsson, E., & Sullivan, E. (2005). Frontal circuitry degradation marks healthy adult aging: Evidence from diffusion tensor imaging. *Neuroimage, 26*, 891–899.

Pfefferbaum, A., Mathalon, D. H., Sullivan, E. V., Rawles, J. M., Zipursky, R. B., & Lim, K. O. (1994). A quantitative magnetic resonance imaging study of changes in brain morphology from infancy to late adulthood. *Archives of Neurology, 51*, 874–887.

Pick, A. (1892). Uber die Beziehungen der senilen Hirnatrophie zur Aphasie. *Prag. Med. Wschr. 17*, 165–167.

Pillon, B., Dubois, B., Ploska, A., & Agid, Y. (1991). Severity and specificity of cognitive impairment in Alzheimer's, Huntington's, and Parkinson's diseases and progressive supranuclear palsy. *Neurology, 41*, 634–643.

Powell, M. R., Smith, G. E., Knopman, D. S., Parisi, J. E., Boeve, B. F., Petersen, R. C., et al. (2006). Cognitive measures predict pathologic Alzheimer disease. *Archives of Neurology, 63*, 865–868.

Price, C. C., Jefferson, A. L., Merino, J. G., Heilman, K. M., & Libon, D. J. (2005). Subcortical vascular dementia: Integrating neuropsychological and neuroradiologic data. *Neurology, 65*, 376–382.

Rascovsky, K., Salmon, D. P., Ho, G. J., Galasko, D., Peavy, G. M., Hansen, L. A., et al. (2002). Cognitive profiles differ in autopsy-confirmed fronto-temporal dementia and Alzheimer's disease. *Neurology, 58*, 1801–1808.

Rascovsky, K., Salmon, D. P., Hansen, L. A., Thal, L. J., & Galasko, D. (2007). Disparate phonemic and semantic fluency deficits in autopsy-confirmed frontotemporal dementia and Alzheimer's disease. *Neuropsychology, 21,* 20–30.

Raz, N. (2005). The aging brain observed in vivo: Differential changes and their modifiers. In R. Cabeza, L. Nyberg, and D. Park (Eds.), *Cognitive neuroscience of aging: Linking cognitive and cerebral aging* (pp. 19–57). New York: Oxford University Press.

Reed, B. R., Mungas, D. M., Kramer, J. H., Ellis, W., Vinters, H. V., Zarow, C., et al. (2007). Profiles of neuropsychological impairment in autopsy-defined Alzheimer's disease and cerebrovascular disease. *Brain, 130*(Pt3), 731–739.

Rohrer, D., Salmon, D. P., Wixted, J. T., & Paulsen, J. S. (1999). The disparate effects of Alzheimer's disease and Huntington's disease on the recall from semantic memory. *Neuropsychology, 13,* 381–388.

Rohrer, D., Wixted, J. T., Salmon, D. P., & Butters, N. (1995). Retrieval from semantic memory and its implications for Alzheimer's disease. *Journal of Experimental Psychology. Learning, Memory, and Cognition, 21,* 1–13.

Roman, G. C., Tatemichi, T. K., Erkinjuntti, T., Cummings, J.L., Masdeu, J.C., Garcia, J.H., et al. (1993). Vascular dementia: Diagnostic criteria for research studies. Report of the NINDS-AIREN International Workshop. *Neurology, 43,* 250–260.

Rosen, V. M., Sunderland, T., Levy, J., Harwell, A., McGee, L., Hammond, C., et al. (2005). Apolipoprotein E and category fluency: Evidence for reduced semantic access in healthy normal controls at risk for developing Alzheimer's disease. *Neuropsychologia, 43,* 647–658.

Rouleau, I., Salmon, D. P., Butters, N., Kennedy, C., & McGuire, K. (1992). Quantitative and qualitative analyses of clock drawings in Alzheimer's and Huntington's disease. *Brain and Cognition, 18,* 70–87.

Rubin, E. H., Storandt, M., Miller, J. P., Kinscherf, D. A., Grant, E. A., Morris, J. C., et al. (1998). A prospective study of cognitive function and onset of dementia in cognitively healthy elders. *Archives of Neurology, 55,* 395–401.

Sadek, J. R., Johnson, S. A., White, D. A., Salmon, D. P., Taylor, K. I., Delapena, J. H., et al. (2004). Retrograde amnesia in dementia: Comparison of HIV-associated dementia, Alzheimer's disease, and Huntington's disease. *Neuropsychology, 18,* 692–699.

Sagar, H. J., Cohen, N. J., Sullivan, E. V., Corkin, S., & Growdon, J. H. (1988). Remote memory function in Alzheimer's disease and Parkinson's disease. *Brain, 111,* 525–539.

Sahgal, A., Galloway, P. H., McKeith, I. G., Edwardson, J. A., & Lloyd, S. (1992b). A comparative study of attentional deficits in senile dementias of Alzheimer and Lewy body types. *Dementia, 3,* 350–354.

Sahgal, A., Galloway, P. H., McKeith, I. G., Lloyd, S., Cook, J. H., Ferrier, N., et al. (1992a). Matching-to-sample deficits in patients with senile dementias of the Alzheimer and Lewy body types. *Archives of Neurology, 49,* 1043–1046.

Sahgal, A., McKeith, I. G., Galloway, P. H., Tasker, N., & Steckler, T. (1995). Do differences in visuospatial ability between senile dementias of the Alzheimer and Lewy body types reflect differences solely in mnemonic function? *Journal of Clinical and Experimental Neuropsychology, 17,* 35–43.

Salat, D. H., Kaye, J. A., & Janowsky, J. S. (1999). Prefrontal gray and white matter volumes in healthy aging and Alzheimer disease. *Archives of Neurology, 56,* 338–344.

Salmon, D. P. (2000). Disorders of memory in Alzheimer's disease. In L. S. Cermak (Ed.), *Handbook of neuropsychology, 2nd edition (Vol. 2): Memory and its disorders* (pp. 155–195). Amsterdam: Elsevier.

Salmon, D.P., & Bondi, M.W. (1999). Neuropsychology of Alzheimer's disease. In R. D. Terry, R. Katzman, K. L. Bick, and S. S. Sisodia (Eds.), *Alzheimer disease* (pp. 39–56). Philadelphia: Lippincott Williams and Wilkens.

Salmon, D. P., Butters, N., & Chan, A. S. (1999). The deterioration of semantic memory in Alzheimer's disease. *Canadian Journal of Experimental Psychology, 53,* 108–117.

Salmon, D. P., Galasko, D., Hansen, L. A., Masliah, E., Butters, N., Thal, L. J., et al. (1996). Neuropsychological deficits associated with diffuse Lewy body disease. *Brain and Cognition, 31,* 148–165.

Salmon, D. P., Heindel, W. C., & Lange, K. L. (1999). Differential decline in word generation from phonemic and semantic categories during the course of Alzheimer's disease: Implications for the integrity of semantic memory. *Journal of the International Neuropsychological Society, 5,* 692–703.

Salmon, D. P., Thomas, R. G., Pay, M. M., Booth, A., Hofstetter, C. R., Thal, L. J., et al. (2002). Alzheimer's disease can be accurately diagnosed in very mildly impaired individuals. *Neurology, 59,* 1022–1028.

Salthouse, T. A. (1996). The processing-speed theory of adult age differences in cognition. *Psychological Review, 103,* 403–428.

Saunders, A. M., Strittmatter, W. J., Schmechel, D., St. George-Hyslop, P. H., Perick-Vance, M. A., Joo, S. H., et al. (1993). Association of apolipoprotein

E allele e4 with late-onset familial and sporadic Alzheimer's disease. *Neurology, 43*, 1467–1472.

Schacter, D. L. (1987). Implicit memory: History and current status. *Journal of Experimental Psychology. Learning, Memory, and Cognition, 3*, 501–517.

Schacter, D. L., Savage, C. R., Alpert, N. M., Rauch, S. L., & Albert, M. S. (1996). The role of hippocampus and frontal cortex in age-related memory changes: A PET study. *NeuroReport, 7*, 1165–1169.

Schaie, K. W., Caskie, G. I. L., Revell, A. J., Willis, S. L., Kaszniak, A. W., & Teri, L. (2005). Extending neuropsychological assessments into the primary mental ability space. *Aging, Neuropsychology, and Cognition, 12*, 245–277.

Serretti, A., Olgiati, P., & De Ronchi, D. (2007). Genetics of Alzheimer's disease: A rapidly evolving field. *Journal of Alzheimer's Disease, 12*, 73–92.

Shimomura, T., Mori, E., Yamashita, H., Imamura, T., Hirono, N., et al. (1998). Cognitive loss in dementia with Lewy bodies and Alzheimer disease. *Archives of Neurology, 55*, 1547–1552.

Ska, B., Poissant, A., & Joanette, Y. (1990). Line orientation judgement in normal elderly and subjects with dementia of Alzheimer's type. *Journal of Clinical and Experimental Neuropsychology, 12*, 695–702.

Small, B. J., Fratiglioni, L., Viitanen, M., Winblad, B., & Bäckman, L. (2000). The course of cognitive impairment in preclinical Alzheimer disease: Three- and 6-year follow-up of a population-based sample. *Archives of Neurology, 57*, 839–844.

Small, B. J., Mobly, J. L., Laukka, E. J., Jones, S., & Backman, L. (2003). Cognitive deficits in preclinical Alzheimer's disease. *Acta Neurologica Scandinavica Supplementum, 179*, 29–33.

Smith, G. E., Pankratz, V. S., Negash, S., Machulda, M. M., Petersen, R. C., Boeve, B. F., et al. (2007). A plateau in pre-Alzheimer memory decline: Evidence for compensatory mechanisms? *Neurology, 69*, 133–139.

Smyer, M. A. (1988). The nursing home community. In M. A. Smyer, M. D. Cohn, and D. Brannon (Eds.), *Mental health consultation in nursing homes* (pp. 1–23). New York: New York University Press.

Snowden, J. S., Goulding, P. J., & Neary, D. (1989). Semantic dementia: A form of circumscribed cerebral atrophy. *Behavioural Neurology, 2*, 167–182.

Sprengelmeyer, R., Lange, H., & Homberg, V. (1995). The pattern of attentional deficits in Huntington's disease. *Brain, 118*, 145–152.

Squire, L. R. (1987). *Memory and brain.* New York: Oxford University Press.

Squire, L. R., Haist, F., & Shimamura, A. P. (1989). The neurology of memory: Quantitative assessment of retrograde amnesia in two groups of amnesic patients. *Journal of Neuroscience, 9*, 828–839.

Starkstein, S. E., Migliorelli, R., Teson, A., Sabe, L., Vázquez, S., Turjanski, M., et al. (1994). Specificity of changes in cerebral blood in patients with frontal lobe dementia. *Journal of Neurology, Neurosurgery and Psychiatry, 57*, 790–796.

Stavitsky, K., Brickman, A. M., Scarmeas, N., Torgan, R. L., Tang, M-X., et al. (2006). The progression of cognition, psychiatric symptoms, and functional abilities in dementia with Lewy bodies and Alzheimer's disease. *Archives of Neurology, 63*, 1450–1456.

Stern, Y., Alexander, G. E., Prohovnik, I., & Mayeux, R. (1992). Inverse relationship between education and parietotemporal perfusion deficit in Alzheimer's disease. *Neurology, 32*, 371–375.

Stern, Y., Gurland, B., Tatemichi, T. K., Tang, M. X., Wilder, D., & Mayeux, R. (1994). Influence of education and occupation on the incidence of Alzheimer's disease. *Journal of the American Medical Association, 271*, 1004–1010.

Stevens, A., Kircher, T., Nickola, M., Bartels, M., Rosellen, N., & Wormstall, H. (2001). Dynamic regulation of EEG power and coherence is lost early and globally in probable DAT. *European Archives of Psychiatry and Clinical Neuroscience, 251*, 199–204.

Storandt, M., Grant, E.A, Miller, J. P., & Morris, J. C. (2006). Longitudinal course and neuropathologic outcomes in original vs revised MCI and in pre-MCI. *Neurology, 67(3)*, 467–473.

Storandt, M., Botwinick, J., Danziger, W. L., Berg, L., & Hughes, C. P. (1984). Psychometric differentiation of mild senile dementia of the Alzheimer type. *Archives of Neurology, 41*, 497–499.

Storandt, M., Grant, E. A., Miller, J. P., & Morris, J. C. (2002). Rates of progression in mild cognitive impairment and early Alzheimer's disease. *Neurology, 59*, 1034–1041.

Stout, J. C., Rodawalt, W. C., & Siemers, E. R. (2001). Risky decision making in Huntington's disease. *Journal of the International Neuropsychological Society, 7*, 92–101.

Strittmatter, W. J., Saunders, A. M., Schmechel, D., Pericak-Vance, M., Enghild, J., Salvesen, G. S., et al. (1993). Apolipoprotein-E—high-avidity binding to B-amyloid and increased frequency of type 4 allele in late-onset familial Alzheimer disease. *Proceedings of the National Academy of Sciences of the United States of America, 90*, 9649–9653.

Tales, A., Butler, S. R., Fossey, J., Gilchrist, I. D., Jones, R. W., & Troscianko, T. (2002). Visual search in Alzheimer's disease: A deficiency in processing conjunctions of features. *Neuropsychologia, 40*, 1849–1857.

Thal, L. J. (1999). Clinical trials in Alzheimer disease. In R. Terry, R. Katzman, K. L. Bick, and S.

S. Sisodia (Eds.), *Alzheimer disease* (pp. 423–439). Philadelphia: Raven Press.

Thomas-Anterion, C., Jacquin, K., & Laurent, B. (2000). Differential mechanisms of impairment of remote memory in Alzheimer's and frontotemporal dementia. *Dementia and Geriatric Cognitive Disorders, 11*, 100–106.

Tippett, L. J., Blackwood, K., & Farah, M. J. (2003). Visual object and face processing in mild-to-moderate Alzheimer's disease: From segmentation to imagination. *Neuropsychologia, 41*, 453–468.

Tiraboschi, P., Hansen, L. A., Alford, M., Merdes, A., Masliah, E., Thal, L. J., et al. (2002). Early and widespread cholinergic losses differentiate dementia with Lewy bodies from Alzheimer disease. *Archives of General Psychiatry, 59*, 946–951.

Tiraboschi, P., Salmon, D. P., Hansen, L. A., Hofstetter, C. R., Thal, L. J., & Corey-Bloom, J. (2006). What best differentiates Lewy body from Alzheimer's disease in early-stage dementia? *Brain, 129*, 729–735.

Troster, A. I., Butters, N., Salmon, D. P., Cullum, C. M., Jacobs, D., Brandt, J., et al. (1993). The diagnostic utility of savings scores: Differentiating Alzheimer's and Huntington's diseases with the logical memory and visual reproduction tests. *Journal of Clinical and Experimental Neuropsychology, 15*, 773–788.

Tschanz, J. T., Welsh-Bohmer, K. A., Lyketsos, C. G., Corcoran, C., Green, R. C., Hayden, K., et al. (2006). Conversion to dementia from mild cognitive disorder: The Cache county study. *Neurology, 67*, 229–234.

Twamley, E. W., Ropacki, S. A. L., & Bondi, M. W. (2006). Neuropsychological and neuroimaging changes in preclinical Alzheimer's disease. *Journal of the International Neuropsychological Society, 12*, 707–735.

van Duijn, C. M., Stijnen, T., & Hofman, A. (1991). Risk factors for Alzheimer's disease: Overview of the EURODEM collaborative re-analysis of case-control studies. EURODEM Risk Factors Research Group. *International Journal of Epidemiology, 20*(Suppl. 2), S4–S12.

van Praag, H., Shubert, T., Zhao, C., & Gage, F. H. (2005). Exercise enhances learning and hippocampal neurogenesis in aged mice. *Journal of Neuroscience, 25*(38), 8680–8685.

Varma, A. R., Snowden, J. S., Lloyd, J. J., Talbot, P. R., Mann, D. M. A., & Neary, D. (1999). Evaluation of the NINCDS-ADRDA criteria in the differentiation of Alzheimer's disease and frontotemporal dementia. *Journal of Neurology, Neurosurgery and Psychiatry, 66*, 184–188.

Villardita, C. (1993). Alzheimer's disease compared with cerebrovascular dementia. *Acta Neurologica Scandinavica, 87*, 299–308.

Vonsattel, J. P., & Di Figlia, M. (1998). Huntington disease. *Journal of Neuropathology and Experimental Neurology, 57*, 369–384.

Walker, Z., Allen, R., Shergill, S., & Katona, C. (1997). Neuropsychological performance in Lewy body dementia and Alzheimer's disease. *British Journal of Psychiatry, 170*, 156–158.

Waltz, J. A., Knowlton, B. J., Holyoak, K. J., Boone, K. B., Back-Madruga, C., et al. (2004). Relational integration and executive function in Alzheimer's disease. *Neuropsychology, 18*, 296–305.

Wancata, J., Börjesson-Hanson, J., Ostling, S., Sjögren, K., & Skoog, I. (2007). Diagnostic criteria influence dementia prevalence. *American Journal of Geriatrci Psychiatry, 15*, 1034–1045.

Ward, J., Sheppard, J. M., Shpritz, B., Margolis, R. L., Rosenblatt, A., & Brandt, J. (2006). A four-year study of cognitive functioning in Huntington's disease. *Journal of the International Neuropsychological Society, 12*, 445–454.

Weder, N. D., Aziz, R., Wilkins, K., & Tampi, R. R. (2007). Frontotemporal dementias: A review. *Annals of General Psychiatry, 6*, 1–15.

Welsh, K., Butters, N., Hughes, J., Mohs, R., & Heyman, A. (1991). Detection of abnormal memory decline in mild cases of Alzheimer's disease using CERAD neuropsychological measures. *Archives of Neurology, 48*, 278–281.

West, R. L. (1996). An application of prefrontal cortex function theory to cognitive aging. *Psychological Bulletin, 120*, 272–292.

Wetter, S., Delis, D. C., Houston, W. S., Jacobson, M. W., Lansing, A., Cobell, K., et al. (2005). Deficits in inhibition and flexibility are associated with the APOE e4 allele in nondemented older adults. *Journal of Clinical and Experimental Neuropsychology, 27*, 943–952.

Whitehouse, P. J., Price, D. L., Struble, R. G., Clark, A. W., Coyle, J. T., & DeLong, M. R. (1982). Alzheimer's disease and senile dementia: Loss of neurons in the basal forebrain. *Science, 215*, 1237–1239.

Wicklund, A. H., Rademaker, A., Johnson, N., Weitner, B. B., & Weintraub, S. (2007). Rate of cognitive change measured by neuropsychologic test performance in 3 distinct dementia syndromes. *Alzheimer Disease and Associated Disorders, 21*, S70–S78.

Wilhelmsen, K. C., Lynch, T., Pavlou, E., Higgins, M., & Nygaard, T. G. (1994). Localization of disinhibition dementia parkinsonism amyotrophy complex to 17q21–22. *American Journal of Human Genetics, 55*, 1159–1165.

Williams, G. C. (1957). Pleiotropy, natural selection, and the evolution of senescence. *Evolution, 11*(4), 398–411.

Wilson, R. S., Mendes de Leon, C. F., Barnes, L. L., Schneider, J.A., Bienias, J.L., Evans, D.A., et al.

(2002). Participation in cognitively stimulating activities and risk of incident Alzheimer disease. *Journal of the American Medical Association, 287*(6), 742–748.

Wilson, R. S., Bacon, L. D., Fox, J. H., & Kaszniak, A. W. (1983). Primary and secondary memory in dementia of the Alzheimer type. *Journal of Clinical Neuropsychology, 5,* 337–344.

Wilson, R. S., Kaszniak, A. W., & Fox, J. H. (1981). Remote memory in senile dementia. *Cortex, 17,* 41–48.

Wright, R. O., Hu, H., Silverman, E. K., Tsaih, S. W., Schwartz, J., Bellinger, D., et al. (2003). Apolipoprotein E genotype predicts Bayley scales infant development score. *Pediatric Research, 54,* 819–825.

Ylikoski, R., Ylikoski, A., Erkinjuntti, T., Sulkava, R., Raininko, R., & Tilvis, R. (1993). White matter changes in healthy elderly persons correlate with attention and speed of mental processing. *Archives of Neurology, 50,* 818–824.

Zandi, P. P., Carlson, M. C., Plassman, B. L., Welsh-Bohmer, K. A., Mayer, L. S., Steffens, D. C., et al. (2002). Hormone replacement therapy and incidence of Alzheimer disease in older women: The Cache County Study. *Journal of the American Medical Association, 288,* 2123–2129.

Zhang, M., Katzman, R., Salmon, D. P., Jin, H., Cai, G., Wang, Z., et al. (1990). The prevalence of dementia and Alzheimer's disease (AD) in Shanghai, China: Impact on age, gender and education. *Annals of Neurology, 27,* 428–437.

Zola-Morgan, S., & Squire, L. R. (1990). The primate hippocampal formation: Evidence for a time-limited role in memory storage. *Science, 250,* 288–290.

9

Neuropsychological Aspects of Parkinson's Disease and Parkinsonism

Susan McPherson and Jeffrey Cummings

Parkinson's disease (PD) is one of the most common neurological diseases, affecting approximately 350 per 100,000 individuals. Approximately 95% of incident cases of PD occur after the age of 60 making it a common disorder among the elderly (de Lau & Breteler, 2006). At least one study has projected that the number of cases of PD will increase to between 8.7 and 9.2 million patients by 2030 (Dorsey et al., 2007). Behavioral and neuropsychological disorders are common in PD and other parkinsonian syndromes. Patients with PD may have dementia, depression, anxiety, apathy, and a variety of drug-related or surgically induced behavioral alterations.

Significant advances have been made in understanding the pathophysiology of PD. Although depletion of dopamine in the substantia nigra and basal ganglia has been recognized as responsible for the motor disturbances of the disease, evidence suggests that changes in the basal ganglia and frontal–subcortical circuits also play a role in the associated cognitive abnormalities and behavioral changes (Taylor & Saint-Cyr, 1992; Zgaljardic et al., 2006).

The purpose of this chapter is to provide an overview of the neuropsychological and psychiatric features of parkinsonian syndromes, including PD, progressive supranuclear palsy (PSP), and multiple system atrophies (MSA). The clinical characteristics, pathology, treatment and neuropsychological deficits associated with each disorder are described.

Definitions and Classification

Parkinson's disease must be distinguished from the less specific clinical syndrome of parkinsonism. *Parkinsonism* refers to a cluster of motor symptoms consisting of slowness of movement (bradykinesia), difficulty initiating movement (akinesia), hypokinetic speech, masked facies, muscular rigidity, a shuffling or unsteady gait, abnormal posture, and disturbances in equilibrium. Tremor may or may not be present. Parkinson's disease is a neurodegenerative disorder consisting of symptoms of parkinsonism plus a pill-rolling type of resting tremor. PD typically improves with dopaminergic treatment. An absence or paucity of tremor and poor treatment response help differentiate non-PD parkinsonian syndromes from PD (Stacy & Jankovic, 1992).

Classification of Parkinsonism

Parkinsonism can be divided into four subgroups: primary, secondary, multiple system degeneration, and other neurodegenerative conditions (Table 9–1). Primary or idiopathic PD accounts for majority of cases of parkinsonism. Young onset disease (age 21–40) affects 5%–10% of patients and, although onset is rare before the age of 30, there is a juvenile form of the disease with onset before age 21 (Samii et al., 2004). Secondary parkinsonism may occur in a variety of conditions including infections (encephalitis, slow virus), exposure

Table 9–1. Classifications of Parkinsonism

Primary (idiopathic) parkinsonism
    Parkinson's disease
    Juvenile Parkinson's disease
Secondary parkinsonism
    Drug-induced (antipsychotic agents, antiemetics)
    Infections (postencephalitic, slow virus, human
        immunodeficiency virus)
    Vascular (lacunar state)
    Toxins (MPTP[a], manganese, carbon monoxide)
    Metabolic (parathyroid, hypothyroidism)
Trauma (pugilistic encephalopathy)
Tumor, normal pressure hydrocephalus
Multiple System Degeneration (parkinsonian plus
    syndromes)
    Multiple system degeneration-parkinsonism
        (formerly striatonigral degeneration)
    Multiple system degeneration-cerebellar
        (formerly olivopontocerebellar atrophy)
    Multiple system degeneration-autonomic
        (formerly Shy Drager syndrome)
Other neurodegenerative disorders
    Progressive supranuclear palsy
    Lewy body dementia
    Wilson's disease
    Rigid Huntington's disease
    Parkinsonian-ALS dementia complex
    Idiopathic calcification of the basal ganglia
        (Fahr's disease)

---

[a]1-methyl-4-phenyl-1, 2, 3, 6-tetrahydrophyridine (MPTP)

to toxins, drugs (particularly antipsychotic medications), or trauma (pugilistic encephalopathy). There also exists a vascular form of the disease, usually caused by lacunar infarctions of the basal ganglia and characterized by markedly impaired gait with relatively spared upper body motor functioning (Rektor et al., 2006). Multiple system degenerations account for the second largest number of parkinsonian plus disorders and include the parkinsonian (striatonigral degeneration), cerebellar (olivopontocerebellar atrophy) and autonomic (Shy Drager syndrome) forms of the disease. Other degenerative causes of parkinsonism include conditions such as PSP, Lewy body dementia, the rigid form of Huntington's disease, Wilson's disease, and idiopathic basal ganglia calcification.

Parkinson's Disease

Parkinson's disease is ranked among the most common chronic neurological disorders. The prevalence of PD in industrialized countries has been estimated at 0.3% of the population and 1% in persons over age 60 (Nussbaum & Ellis, 2003). The estimated annual incidence rates (number of new cases per year) range from 12 to 15 per 100,000 for all age groups with a significant rise to 160 per 100,000 for persons above age 65 (Hirtz et al., 2007). Recent epidemiological surveys suggest that the disease affects men slightly more than women (Baldereschi et al., 2000; Lai et al., 2003). Community-based studies of PD have varied with some suggesting that the highest rates of the disease are observed in Europe and North America, with markedly lower rates in Japan, China, and Africa (Albin, 2006). Although PD appears to occur at a lower prevalence rate in Blacks and Asians as compared with Whites, differences in these rates may reflect differences in response rates, survival and case-ascertainment rather than real differences across ethnic groups (de Lau & Breteler, 2006).

Clinical Characteristics

Movement disturbance is the hallmark of PD and the primary motor symptoms include akinesia, bradykinesia, rigidity, loss of associated movements, tremor, and neuro-ophthalmic abnormalities. Tremor is probably the best-recognized clinical feature in PD, but other motor disturbances may present as the initial sign. The primary symptom of PD, bradykinesia or hypokinesia, accounts for many of the characteristic features of the disease including difficulty with initiation of movement, expressionless face (masked facies), loss of associated movements, and micrographia. Muscular rigidity involves the upper and lower limbs, producing a lead-pipe rigidity to passive manipulation. The combination of tremor and rigidity bestows a ratchet or cogwheel character to the rigidity. Increase in rigidity also results in the postural changes seen in PD characterized by slight flexion of ankles, knees, hips, elbows, back, and neck and poor balance, leading to an increased risk of falls (Samii et al., 2004). Although hypokinesia is frequently associated with rigidity, the two can be dissociated and the psychomotor retardation of PD is not a result of rigidity. The characteristic tremor of the disease is a pill-rolling alternating contraction of opposing muscles, usually with a frequency of 4–6 cycles per second (cps) and is the first symptom in 70% of patients. The tremor typically develops in one upper extremity and may spread to all four limbs, face, and tongue (Mendez & Cummings, 2003). This tremor is most apparent when the patient is in alert repose, is absent or minimal when the patient is relaxed or asleep, and is exacerbated by stress. In addition to the resting tremor, a minority of PD patients may exhibit an action or postural tremor of 6–12 cps.

Neuro-ophthalmologic changes and autonomic disturbances also occur in PD. Volitional upgaze and convergence are impaired. Rapid volitional eye movements tend to be fragmented into multiple saccades and pursuit movements are broken into a series of small saccadic steps (cogwheel eye movements) (Mendez & Cummings, 2003). Autonomic disturbances often associated with PD include prominent gastrointestinal symptoms, orthostatic hypotension, constipation, impotence, and esophageal spasm (Jost, 2003). Sleep disturbances are also common and arise from a variety of causes including nocturnal stiffness, nocturia, depression, restless leg syndrome, and rapid eye movement (REM) sleep behavior disorder (Stacy, 2002).

Genetics

Studies on the genetics of PD have produced mixed results. While some studies have suggested that only 15% of patients with PD have a first degree relative with the disease (Payami et al., 1994), more recent studies have suggested that individuals with PD are two to three times more likely to have a first degree relative with the disease (Marder et al., 2003). Twin studies have suggested low concordance rates in late-onset PD but increased concordance rates in earlier onset PD (Tanner et al., 1999). Recent genetic investigation has resulted in the discovery of genes and/or genetic loci associated with PD. Nine loci in PD have been identified and five genes for Mendelian PARK loci have been cloned. These include α-synuclein (PARK1); parkin (PARK2), DJ-1 (PARK7), PINK1 (PARK6), and LRRK2 (PARK8) (Hardy et al., 2006). The α-synuclein mutation (PARK1) found on chromosome 4 has been linked to autosomal dominant familial disease (Polymeropoulos et al., 1997). The PARK2 locus which encodes the protein parkin, a key enzyme in the ubiquitin-proteosome system, has been linked to juvenile onset PD (Kitada et al., 1998). An additional loci (PARK5) have been linked to ubiquitin-pathways by encoding ubiquitin terminal hyrolase L1 (UCHl1). Three loci have focused on mitochondrial dysfunction, due to mutations in the proteins PINK1, DJ-1, and LRRK2. Mutations in the *DJ-1* gene (PARK7) have been associated with autosomal recessive early-onset PD and may be linked to oxidative stress (Bonifati et al., 2003). Mutations of the PARK8 (LRRK2) locus produce dominantly inherited PD and may contribute to a small number of cases of typical late-onset disease (Albin, 2006). While the above gene loci have been associated with some forms of the disease, the relationship of these genes to PD is far from conclusive, and they appear to account for only a small number of cases.

Pathology

Characteristic neuropathological changes in PD include neuron loss in the substantia nigra and other brain stem nuclei (locus ceruleus, dorsal vagal nucleus, and sympathetic ganglia) and the presence of Lewy bodies in some of the remaining neurons of the involved nuclei. Lewy bodies are intracellular structures made up of protein and sphingomyelin and consist of loosely packed filaments in an outer zone surrounding a granular core. The principal protein of Lewy bodies is α-synuclein. Although found in highest concentrations in the substantia nigra and locus ceruleus, they also occur in the amygdala, cortex, nucleus basalis, dorsal vagal nucleus, autonomic ganglia, and hypothalamus (Braak et al., 2003).

Parkinson's disease is characterized neurochemically by the loss of dopaminergic projections from the substantia nigra pars compacta to the basal ganglia and associated brain regions. Dopamine content is markedly diminished in the caudal putamen. Dopamine is also depleted in the caudate, frontal lobe cortex, and medial temporal lobes. Other neurotransmitters and modulators are decreased in PD including nor-epinephrine, glutamate decarboxylase, gamma amino butyric acid (GABA), methionine-en-kephalin, cholestokinin, and serotonin and its metabolite 5-hydroxyindoleacetic acid, albeit none to the extent of dopamine (Mendez & Cummings, 2003). Dopamine receptor densi-ties are unaffected. Clinical signs of PD are evi-dent when 80% of striatal dopamine and 50% of nigral neurons are lost (Fearnley & Lees, 1991). Cholinergic deficits are prominent in PD with dementia and are associated with cognitive and neuropsychiatric symptoms (Bohnen et al., 2003; Tiraboschi et al., 2000).

Treatment

Medications

Treatment of PD includes agents used to relieve symptoms and those that may slow progres-sion and preserve neurons. The current main-stay of PD therapy is levodopa, a precursor to dopamine that readily crosses the blood–brain barrier and, once in the substantia nigra, is con-verted into dopamine. Levodopa is typically administered in conjunction with the dopa-decarboxylase inhibitor carbidopa, to mini-mize peripheral side effects. Levodopa has been found to be effective in alleviating the motor symptoms of PD in at least 60% of patients for a period of 1–4 years. Unfortunately, levodopa produces many adverse effects including nau-sea, choreoathetotic dyskinesias, postural hypo-tension, and palpitations. Psychiatric side effects such as sleep disturbances, hallucinations, delu-sions, anxiety, delirium, and hypomania are not uncommon (Mendez & Cummings, 2003). Promipaxole and ropinerole are dopamine receptor agonists that also relieve parkinsonian symptoms and have side effects similar to levo-dopa. It is common to use a receptor agonist in conjunction with levodopa to minimize late-occurring on–off symptoms.

Rasageline (N-propargyl-R-aminoindan) mesylate is a selective, irreversible, second gen-eration monoamine oxidase (MAO-B) inhibitor that has shown effectiveness in early PD when given as an adjunct to levodopa (Parkinson Study Group, 2002). Treatment with rasageline has been shown to reduce "off" time without increasing side effects of confusion, hallucina-tion, and insomnia often observed in patients' taking selegiline. Results of a trial evaluating the efficacy and safety of rasageline as both monotherapy and adjunctive therapy suggested that when compared with patients on placebo, patients treated with rasageline as monotherapy reported only 3% more symtoms of depression as compared with patients on placebo. When used as adjunctive therapy cognitive and behav-ioral adverse events occurred only 1.6% of the time (Elmer et al., 2006) as compared with patients on placebo.

Selegiline and rasageline are MAO-B inhibi-tors that reduce the generation of hydroxyl radicals. Free radicals interfere with the main-tenance of cell membranes and lead to cellular death; reduction of radical presence prevents cell death and may allow partially injured neu-rons to recover. Although consensus is lacking among neuroscientists, administration of sele-giline or rasageline may mitigate cell death and slows disease progression.

One of the newest classes of drugs for the treatment of PD are the peripherally acting catechol-O-methlytransferase (COMT) inhib-itor-entacapone. Administration of a COMT inhibitor such as entacapone concomitantly with levodopa leads to more stable plasma levo-dopa concentrations through out the day and to fewer daily fluctuations (Brooks & Sagar, 2003). Studies with entacapone have shown the drug to be effective in increasing the "on" time in patients with fluctuations and improving activi-ties of daily living in patients without significant "on–off" fluctuations (Brooks & Sagar, 2003).

Studies on rivastigmine, an inhibitor of both acetycholinesterase and butyrylcholin-esterase, have been shown to have meaningful treatment benefits in patients with Lewy body dementia (McKeith et al., 2000) and in patients with dementia associated with PD (Aarsland et al., 2002; Giladi et al., 2003). Rivastigmine produced moderate improvements on global ratings of dementia, attention and executive functions, and behavioral symptoms in patients with dementia associated with PD. Higher rates of nausea, vomiting, and tremor were observed (Emre et al., 2004). Rivastigmine has been approved for use in PD dementia by the U.S. Food and Drug Administration.

Surgical Interventions

Pallidotomy

Surgical treatment for PD began over 60 years ago when thalamotomy was performed to reduce contralateral tremor (Burchiel, 1995) and pallidotomy improved motor symptoms (Guridi & Lozano, 1997). With the introduction of medications in the 1960s, the use of surgical intervention was abandoned until the 1990s when surgical intervention was reintroduced to improve bradykinesia, rigidity, and dyskinesias (Hallett & Litvan, 1999).

The cognitive outcome associated with unilateral pallidotomy has produced mixed results. Some studies have shown no evidence of cognitive impairment (Cahn et al., 1998; Fukuda et al., 2000; Perrine et al., 1998; Soukup et al., 1997) while others have reported improvement in memory (Lacritz et al., 2000). Other studies have reported declines in phonemic and semantic verbal fluency particularly after left-sided pallidotomy in right-handed patients (Alegret et al., 2003; Kubu et al., 2000; Masterman et al., 1998; Obwegeser et al., 2000; Riordan et al., 1997; Trepanier et al., 1998; York et al., 2003). Impairments have been noted in verbal learning and memory, particularly after left-sided pallidotomy (Lombardi et al., 2000; Riordan et al., 1997). Changes in visuospatial functions and visual memory have shown either improvements (Obwegeser et al., 2000; Riordan et al., 1997) or declines (Trepanier et al., 1998) following right-sided surgery. Studies on executive functions have also produced mixed results with some studies reporting no changes in executive functions (Cahn et al., 1998; Demakis et al., 2002; Kubu et al., 2000; Uitti et al., 2000) or slight improvements (Jahanshahi et al., 2002; Rettig et al., 2000) and other studies reporting declines in working memory and/or executive impairments (de Bie et al., 2001; Obwegeser et al., 2000; Stebbins et al., 2000; Trepanier et al., 1998). One recent study showed an isolated deficit on one measure of executive functions only (Wisconsin Card Sorting Test) marked by an increase in the percentage of perseverative errors and a decrease in the conceptual responses percentage (Olzak et al., 2006). Bilateral pallidomy has been associated with cognitive deficits, dysphagia, abulia, and aphonia and is no longer recommended (Ghika et al., 1999).

Deep Brain Stimulation

Deep brain stimulation (DBS) involves high-frequency, bilateral stimulation of deep brain targets including thalamus, globus pallidus, and subthalamic nucleus (STN) and is considered an effective treatment for advanced PD (Limousin et al., 1998) with noted benefits on motor function (Volkmann, 2004) and quality of life (Diamond & Jankovic, 2005). Eligibility for DBS relies on the recommendations of the Core Assessment Program for Surgical Interventional Therapies in Parkinson's disease (CAPSIT-PD; Defer et al., 1999) and requires clinically diagnosed PD, a disease duration of greater than 5 years, age <70, refractory motor complications, Hoehn-Yahr scale ≥3 (bilateral disease with postural impairment) and severe motor disability among other criteria. Exclusion criteria include dementia and poorly controlled psychiatric disorders.

The cognitive effects of STN stimulation have been investigated with majority of studies revealing decline in both semantic and phonemic fluency following STN (Parsons et al., 2006). The effects of STN on other aspects of cognition reveal inconsistent results ranging from no global cognitive deterioration (Funkiewiez et al., 2004), minimal effects on cognition (Ardouin et al., 1999) or mild changes in attention, verbal fluency (Morrison et al., 2004), executive functions, verbal memory, and spatial functions (Alegret et al., 2001; Daniele et al., 2003; Dujardin et al., 2001; Smeding et al., 2006; Trepanier et al., 2000). Studies on STN in older patients have shown decreases in memory, mental speed, and fluency (Saint-Cyr et al., 2000) as well as global cognitive decline or behavior changes (Dujardin et al., 2001).

Neuropsychological Aspects of PD

Patients with PD commonly exhibit deficits in cognitive abilities; in many cases, these deficits are confined to specific functions such as loss of cognitive flexibility, reduced ability for learning and recall of information, and psychomotor slowing. The following section presents the pattern of neuropsychologic deficits exhibited by PD patients without overt dementia.

Attention

Simple attentional skills, as assessed by a patient's ability to repeat a series of digits or register a short list of words, is generally unimpaired in patients with PD, even in patients with severe motor dysfunction. Performance on attentional tasks that demand speeded cognitive processing or require the patient to internally guide their attentional resources are generally impaired (Pahwa et al., 1998; Ridenour & Dean, 1999). Deficits in divided attention have been suggested and are attributed to the inability to filter out interference and ignore distractions (Claus & Mohr, 1996).

Memory

Non-demented patients with PD exhibit deficits in the areas of paired associates, verbal list learning, recall of brief prose passages and recall measures involving reproduction of complex designs. These deficits are independent of anti-parkinsonian medications (Brown & Marsden, 1990; Cooper et al., 1993). Patients are sensitive to the effects of proactive interference (Massman et al., 1990). While free recall of newly learned information is impaired, memory for remote information has been found to be unimpaired. Studies have also suggested that prospective memory, which involves remembering to execute a planned action at some point in the future, is impaired in PD (Katai et al., 2003; Whittington et al., 2006). These results suggest that a specific profile of memory deficit exists in PD patients without overt dementia, as opposed to a more pervasive decline in memory function in patients with overt dementia.

Controversy exists regarding retrieval of information or recognition memory in PD. While some studies suggest that retrieval is intact in PD (Breen, 1993; Emre, 2003; Ivory et al., 1999), other studies have found impaired recognition in non-demented PD patients (Barnes et al., 2003; Stebbins et al., 1999; Woods & Troster, 2003). Some investigators have suggested that the inconsistencies in

literature regarding retrieval deficits may be secondary to task difficulty stating that some recognition tasks may not be sufficiently challenging to reveal deficits in early-stage PD patients (Whittington et al., 2006).

Language

Compared with other areas of cognitive functioning, language skills are relatively spared in PD, particularly vocabulary. There is somewhat greater controversy in the literature concerning confrontation naming with investigations finding mixed results.

Although the literature concerning performance of PD patients on tasks of verbal fluency, as assessed by asking the patient to generate a list of words according to some predetermined criteria (e.g., letters or semantic categories), has produced mixed findings, the preponderance of literature suggests that both semantic and phonemic fluency are impaired in PD patients without dementia (Bayles et al., 1993; Raskin et al., 1992; Troster et al., 1998). It has been suggested that poor performance on tasks of verbal fluency, secondary to deficits in executive function has usually been attributed to frontal/executive deficits (e.g., set shifting or strategy initiation) and not to a breakdown of lexical stores (Zgaljardic et al., 2003).

Deficits have been reported in comprehension of complex commands and grammar and decreased syntactic complexity in spontaneous speech. Difficulties in complex sentence processing have been reported to be present in non-demented PD patients (Grossman, 1999; Skeel et al., 2001) and have been attributed to limitations in working memory and processing speed and the need for greater recruitment of other cortical regions to compensate for depleted working memory resources (Grossman et al., 2003).

Visuospatial Skills

Assessment of visuospatial skills is difficult in patients with profound motor impairment. Even when the effects of motor slowing are taken into account, visuospatial and visuoconstructive skills are among the most frequently reported cognitive disturbances associated with

PD (Brown & Marsden, 1990). Studies of visuospatial functions have found that PD patients exhibit deficits in visual analysis and synthesis (as assessed by performance on embedded figures tasks), visual discrimination and matching, and pattern completion. Patients with PD exhibited impaired performance on tasks of constructional praxis even after the speed component had been eliminated to minimize motor demands. Visuospatial dysfunction may be secondary to demands of visuospatial tasks on executive functions such as planning and shifting of attention (Bondi et al., 1993; Raskin et al., 1992).

Not all aspects of visuospatial functioning are impaired in PD. Studies have suggested that PD patients were as accurate as control subjects in making right/left judgments even on measures requiring mental rotation (Brown & Marsden, 1990). Variable findings have been reported on graphomotor visuoconstructive tasks, such as design copying, with some investigators reporting impairment and others finding no differences between PD patients and controls on either simple or complex design copying.

Executive Functions

The term executive function refers to a group of cognitive skills involved in the initiation, planning, and monitoring of goal-directed behaviors. Executive functions include the ability to establish and maintain set; shift from one set to another; form concepts and reason abstractly; use feedback to monitor behavior; program sequential motor activities; develop strategies to learn and copy complex figures; and exert emotional self-control and maintain socially appropriate behavior.

Impaired performance on tasks of executive functions are among the earliest cognitive deficits observed in patients with PD. Patients without overt dementia have been found to exhibit deficits in areas of planning, set shifting and initiation of responses (Cools et al., 2001a, 2001b; Hozumi et al., 2000). Researchers have found consistently poor performance by PD patients, as compared with matched controls, on the Wisconsin Card Sorting Test (WCST), a task of concept formation and set shifting ability with most studies reporting that PD patients

achieve significantly fewer categories, with disagreement among researchers on the frequency and type of errors. Deficits in abstract reasoning, cognitive flexibility, accuracy of categorization, and problem solving are also prominent (Hodgson et al., 2002; Maddox & Filoteo, 2001; Tomer et al., 2002).

Several authors have suggested that disturbances in frontal systems abilities and set aptitude may be the underlying mechanism accounting for the difficulties manifested by PD patients in the areas of memory, visuospatial skills, language, and perception (Levin et al., 1992) and a recent study has attempted to link the executive dysfunction in PD to frontal subcortical circuit dysfunction (Zgaljardic et al., 2006). Findings suggested that dysfunction of the dorsolateral prefrontal circuit (DLPFC), as defined by neuropsychological measures, influences the overall executive impairment found in non-demented PD patients.

Issues in Neuropsychology of PD

Although it is evident from the studies cited above that patients with PD may exhibit changes in cognitive abilities very early in the course of the disease, additional factors occurring in the course of the illness are likely to further impair the cognitive abilities of the PD patient. The following section will consider several of these factors: disease severity, the effect of "on–off" periods on cognitive functions, and the interaction of depression and anxiety with intellectual function.

Early versus Late PD

Assessment of patients who have not yet begun treatment with anti-parkinsonian medications provides a clearer understanding of the specific impact of the disease on cognitive functioning. Results of studies assessing recently diagnosed PD patients before treatment was begun with anti-parkinsonian medications indicated that deficits in early PD are likely to be confined to the three areas of psychomotor slowing, loss of cognitive flexibility, and mildly reduced learning and recall. Other studies have suggested that deficits in frontally mediated measures including attention and executive functions are among the earliest deficits (Dujardin et al., 1999; Owen et al., 1992). Untreated, newly diagnosed PD patients showed deficits in immediate recall of verbal material, language production and semantic fluency, set-formation, cognitive sequencing and working memory, and visuomotor construction, but they were unimpaired in immediate memory span, long-term forgetting, naming, comprehension, and visual perception (Cooper et al., 1991).

Findings of deficits in memory, attention, and executive functions were reported in newly diagnosed patients who were treated with levodopa as compared with normal controls (Muslimovic et al., 2005). In contrast, patients with moderate to severe PD who have been under treatment for long periods of time often exhibit more marked neuropsychological impairments including deficits in psychomotor speed, visuospatial ability, and both verbal and nonverbal learning and recall.

Cognitive Changes Associated with "On–Off" Periods

The "on–off" phenomenon in PD refers to abrupt fluctuations between relatively mild motor disability or chorea ("on") and relatively severe motor disability ("off") that occur after chronic levodopa therapy and includes end-of-dose deterioration as well as unpredictable shifts between mobile or dyskinetic "on" states and akinetic "off" states unrelated to medication schedules. Prior literature comparing cognition in "on" versus "off" states found no significant differences in the areas of attention, simple reaction time, verbal fluency, visuospatial abilities, executive functions, immediate recall for short stories and paired associates, immediate and delayed recall of nonverbal memory, and delayed recall and recognition on a list learning task. Significant differences were noted between on/off patients on tests of supraspan list learning, delayed recall of short stories and paired associates, and choice reaction time, with optimal results when dopaminergic status was congruent during learning and later retrieval, indicating a state-dependent memory effect (Delis & Massman, 1992). Other studies have reported that dopamine withdrawal in a sample of patients with PD was associated

with impaired performance on frontal/executive neuropsychological tests leading to the suggestion that dopamine might not be directly associated with nonmotor dysfunction but may be operative in an indirect fashion (Zgaljardic et al., 2003).

Neuropsychiatric Features of PD

Depression

Depression ranks as one of most common psychiatric complications of PD and has been estimated to occur in approximately 40% of patients (Aarsland et al., 1999). In a systematic review of the available literature on PD and depression, Cummings (1992) found no consistent relationships between depressive symptoms and patient's current age, age at onset of PD, or duration of PD. Although studies have identified a past history of depression as a risk factor for a major mood disorder after the onset of PD, other investigators have not found a family history of psychiatric illness, or more specifically family history of mood disorder, to be a risk factor (Leentjens et al., 2002; Mayeux et al., 1992). There is no consistently identified relationship between depression and patient gender. Depression is characterized by prominent anxiety and less self-punative ideation, as compared with idiopathic depression and lower suicide rates as seen in the general population (Lauterbach, 2004). Dementia has been found to be more common among those with greater cognitive impairment or dementia (Aarsland et al., 1996).

The pathophysiology of depression in PD has been attributed to a complex combination of abnormalities in the dopaminergic, noradrenergic, and serotonergic transmitters systems (Mayeux, 1990) with an allelic variation in serotonin transporters suggested as a predisposing factor to mood disorders (Mossner et al., 2001).

Anxiety

Anxiety and panic have been noted in up to 40% of PD patients. Anxiety after initiation of levodopa treatment has been reported, with patients experiencing apprehension, nervousness, irritability, feeling of impending disaster, palpitations, hyperventilation, and insomnia (Factor et al., 1995). Several studies have suggested that anxiety symptoms may precede the diagnosis (Lauterbach & Duvoisin, 1991; Shiba et al., 2000) with an exacerbation of symptoms following initiation of treatment with levodopa. Reports have suggested that pergolide and selegiline may be more likely to induce anxiety than other parkinsonian agents (Cummings, 1991). Anxiety has also been linked to "off" periods and was correlated with severity of symptoms and disease duration (Siemers et al., 1993).

In contrast to the above findings, a few studies have reported that anxiety in PD is not related to duration of treatment or levodopa level and may be related to coexistence of depression (Stein et al., 1990). Given the high frequency of depression in PD patients in general, it has been hypothesized that the presence of anxiety in PD patients is a concomitant of depression, and may not be related to pathophysiologic changes associated with PD (Henderson et al., 1992).

Psychosis

Psychotic symptoms have been estimated to occur in up to 50% of PD patients, generally occurring in patients usually those treated with anti-parkinsonian agents. Drug-induced psychosis is more common with dopamine agonists than with L-dopa and is the leading cause of nursing home placement and produces a greater impact on quality of life and caregiver burden than does motor disability (Lauterbach, 2004). Visual hallucinations, misidentifications and paranoid delusions are common and may result from a combination of anti-parkinsonian medications, frontal lobe dysfunction, and REM sleep intrusions during the day (Mendez & Cummings, 2003).

Gambling

Pathological gambling has been reported in PD on dopaminergic treatment (Dodd et al., 2005; Driver-Dunckley et al., 2003; Molina et al., 2000) and is attributed to dopamine dysregulation syndrome that is defined as compulsive use of dopaminergic treatment with secondary cognitive and behavioral disturbances (Giovannoni et al., 2000; Lawrence et al., 2003). At least one

study has suggested that gambling is associated with the use of medications ropinirole, pergolide, and pramipexole (Lu et al., 2006) with one study suggesting that the disorder occurs mainly in patients taking pramipexole (Dodd et al., 2005).

Anatomically, pathological gambling in PD has been hypothesized to be linked to the ventral striatum and ventral prefrontal cortex, both of which have been implicated in reinforcement learning and reward processing (Ardouin et al., 2006; Reuter et al., 2005). Over stimulation of D3 receptors of the limbic areas of the brain have been suggested as another pharmacological substrate of gambling behavior (Dodd et al., 2005) with the development of pathological gambling in PD patients attributed to overstimulation of dopamine receptors receiving projections from relatively spared ventral tegmental area (Cools et al., 2003).

Sleep Disorders

Sleep disorders are common in PD, affecting 60%–98% of patients (Adler & Thorpy, 2005) and occur as a result of a combination of factors including the disease itself, mood disorders and pain (Ferreri et al., 2006). Sleep disorders include insomnia and hypersomnia as well as parasomnias, including vivid dreams, sleep terror disorder, REM sleep disorder including REM behavior disorder (RBD). REM behavior disorder is a syndrome in which patients act out dreams with kicking, grabbing, yelling, shouting, and falling or jumping out of bed (Ferreri et al., 2006). At least one study suggested that RBD may proceed the onset of motor symptoms in PD in up to 33% of patients (Postuma et al., 2006).

Dementia Associated with PD

Dementia affects approximately 40% of patients with PD, and incidence in PD patients is up to six times that in healthy adults (Emre, 2003). The prevalence of dementia in PD ranges from 107 to 187 per 100,000 (Mayeux et al., 1995). Prevalence of dementia among PD patients below age 50 has been noted to be zero while the prevalence in patients above age 80 was 69% (Mayeux et al., 1992). Risk factors for dementia include advanced age at onset of motor symptoms, duration of disease, akinetic-rigid syndrome, early occurrence of levodopa related confusion or psychosis, depression, and poor cognitive test scores, particularly on measures of verbal fluency (Emre, 2003).

Parkinson's disease, the dementia associated with Parkinson's disease (PDD), and dementia with Lewy bodies (DLB) are presently referred to as the "Lewy body diseases" (LBD) (Lippa et al., 2007). The clinical manifestations of PDD and DLB reflect a common pathogenesis, presumably related to misfolding and aggregation of α-synuclein, leading to the conclusion by a recent DLB/PDD workgroup that the two diseases share many features (Lippa et al., 2007). This workgroup accepted the classification of PDD and DLB based on the timing of the onset of dementia in relation to the onset of motor symptoms (Lippa et al., 2007). When the onset of cognitive symptoms precedes motor symptoms, a diagnosis of DLB is appropriate, and when the onset of the cognitive symptoms follows motor symptoms a diagnosis of PDD is appropriate.

Parkinson's Disease Dementia

The clinical features of dementia associated with PDD includes a dysexecutive system in which impairment of executive functions is the primary feature and is more extensive and severe than in patients with PD without dementia. Deficits in attention and concentration are marked by slowed reaction time and vigilance and fluctuations, similar to those found in patients with DLB (Ballard et al., 2002). Studies regarding memory deficits in PDD have suggested that deficits in new learning and memory are present but are less severe than those seen in patients with Alzheimer's disease (Pillon et al., 1991; Stern et al., 1993). Although controversy exists regarding the existence of a retrieval deficit in PDD, early studies suggested that patients with PDD benefited from semantic cuing (Pillon et al., 1991). As discussed above, executive dysfunction deficits are evident in the early stages of PD, with deficits in concept formation, problem solving, set shifting, and the ability to benefit from environmental cuing. Visuospatial dysfunction is also noted in PDD

and is considered more severe than in patients with AD with similar dementia severity (Levin et al., 1991; Stern et al., 1993). Deficits in verbal fluency are more severe than in patients with AD (Stern et al., 1993). Naming difficulties, decreased information content of spontaneous speech, and impaired comprehension of complex sentences have been reported in both demented and non-demented patients with PD although to a lesser extent than in patients with AD (Grossman et al., 1992). One study comparing patients with PDD, DLB, and AD reported the presence of a subcortical-type cognitive impairment profile with marked executive, visuoconstructive, and attentional impairment, but relatively less marked memory impairment in majority of the sample of subjects with PDD and DLB as compared with AD (Janvin et al., 2006). However, 26% of the PDD sample had a pattern of cortical cognitive impairment, similar to most of the AD patients, with relatively more severe memory impairment.

Dementia with Lewy Bodies

Dementia with lewy bodies is considered to be the second most common subgroup of degenerative dementias (McKeith et al., 2005) accounting for 15%–35% of all dementias after AD (Geser et al., 2005). The core features of DLB include fluctuations in cognition with pronounced variation in attention and alertness, recurrent visual hallucinations that are typically well formed and detailed, and the spontaneous features of parkinsonism (McKeith et al., 2005). Other features suggestive of DLB include REM sleep behavior disorder, severe neuroleptic sensitivity, and low dopamine transporter uptake in the basal ganglia as demonstrated by imaging. The cognitive profile of DLB is marked by substantial attentional deficits and executive and visuospatial dysfunction (Calderon et al., 2001; Collerton et al., 2003). In terms of cognitive performance, preservation of confrontation naming, short- and medium-term recall with intact recognition, and greater impairment on verbal fluency, visual perception, and performance tasks helps to differentiate DLB from AD (Connor et al., 1998; Mormont et al., 2003; Walker et al., 1997). The presence of visual hallucinations and visuospatial/constructional dysfunction also helps differentiate DLB from AD in the earliest stages (Tiraboschi et al., 2006). The neuropathological changes associated with the DLB are discussed below.

Neurobiology and Neuropathology of Dementia in Parkinson's Disease

The neurobiological alterations associated with PDD include deficits in dopamine, monoamines, and acetylcholine as well as neuropathological changes including the coexistence of an Alzheimer-type dementia and Lewy body pathology.

Dopaminergic Deficits

Dopaminergic deficit is the main neurochemical impairment in PD and is linked to the motor symptoms of the disease. Marked reductions of dopamine have been noted particularly in the putamen and caudate nuclei. Other areas of dopamine reduction include the substantia nigra, nucleus accumbens, lateral hypothalamus, ventral tegmental area, frontal lobe, cingulate gyrus, entorhinal cortex, and hippocampus.

Evidence suggests that dopaminergic deficit is not alone responsible for the dementia in PD. Although decrease in striatal dopamine concentrations are the same in PD and PDD, decrease in dopamine concentrations is greater in neocortical areas in PDD than PD suggesting a role for degeneration of mesocortical dopaminergic systems in the development of dementia (Emre, 2003). While experimental studies have suggested that treatment with levodopa improves some of the cognitive deficits of PDD, clinical evidence suggests that levodopa treatment does not improve cognition suggesting that the dopaminergic deficit is not the main neurochemical impairment responsible for dementia in PDD (Emre, 2003).

Monoaminergic Deficit

Involvement of ascending noradrenergic and serotoninergic pathways has also been suggested as the cause of cognitive impairment in PD. Research has produced mixed findings with some studies reporting more severe neuronal loss and norepinephrine depletion in the locus coeruleus of patients with PDD and other studies finding no difference in concentrations of norepinephrine in cerebral neocortex and hippocampus between patients with PD and PDD (Emre, 2003). Neuronal loss in raphe nuclei and reduced serotonin concentrations in the striatopallidal complex, hippocampus, and frontal cortex have been described in PD but without differences between demented and non-demented PD patients (Emre, 2003).

Cholinergic Deficit

Substantial evidence exists for a cholinergic deficit due to degeneration of ascending cholinergic pathways contributing to cognitive impairment in patients with PD. Cholinergic deficits associated with degeneration of the basal forebrain is prominent in PDD and more severe than cortical cholinergic losses in other dementias such as AD, vascular or frontotemporal dementia (Lippa et al., 1999; Perry et al., 1994). Level of cognitive impairment and presence of dementia has been described in patients with a decrease in cholinergic innervation of the cerebral cortex and severe cellular loss in the basal nucleus of Meynert (Emre, 2003). Preliminary results from a recent autopsy study of patients with PDD suggested that in patients with onset of dementia more than 10 years after PD, the morphologic changes associated with DLB were less pronounced and the more prominent finding was a marked cholinergic deficit (Aarsland et al., 2005). Cholinergic deficits have been linked to key clinical symptoms such as attentional dysfunction, fluctuation in alertness, and visual hallucinations, and may be an early marker of pathology.

Alzheimer's Disease Pathology

Several investigators have reported that neuropathological changes associated with AD, namely senile plaques and neurofibrillary tangles, are commonly present in the brains of demented PD patients. Concurrent incipient AD with fully developed PD has been suggested as a cause of impaired cognition in some cases of PDD. Presence of moderate to severe dementia in PD patients has been found to correlate highly with AD pathology, including the cortical neuropathological changes of AD (Jellinger et al., 2002). Recent studies suggest that AD type changes are highly specific to PDD, but lack sensitivity. Although Lewy bodies have the greatest correlation with dementia, ß-amyloid load in the brain is thought to be greater in DBL as compared with PDD. Lippa and colleagues (2007) have suggested that the Pittsburgh Compound B (PIB)—PET is potentially valuable for determining ß-amyloid load (Klunk et al., 2004) and may aid in determining ß-amyloid burden associated with PDD and DLB (Lippa et al., 2007).

Studies using glucose PET or single photon emission computed tomography (SPECT) have been used to assess functional changes in PD with dementia and compare PDD to AD. Occipital hypoperfusion was closely correlated with PDD in one study as compared with frontal, parietal and temporal perfusion (Matsui et al., 2005), while measurement of medial occipital regional cerebral blood flow discriminated DLB from AD in another study (Shimizu et al., 2005) suggesting that occipital hypoperfusion may be a useful tool in differentiating PDD and DLB from AD. Other studies have shown globally reduced metabolic activity or a disproportionate involvement of the temporo-parieto-occipital junction regions (Kawabata et al., 1991; Spampinato et al., 1991). Frontal and parietal hypoperfusion have been reported in SPECT studies of demented PDD patients (Bissessur et al., 1997; Sawada et al., 1992).

Lewy Body Pathology

Diffuse cortical Lewy body pathology is commonly found in patients with PDD and correlates with the severity of dementia (Aarsland et al., 2005; Hurtig et al., 2000; Mattila et al., 2000). Lewy body densities in temporal neocortex have been reported to correlate with cognitive impairment in patients with PD pathology and studies using α-synuclein antibodies as a marker of Lewy bodies suggested that frontal cortical Lewy bodies were associated with greater cognitive decline independent of AD pathology (Hurtig et al., 2000; Mattila et al., 2000). Cortical density of Lewy bodies did not distinguish PDD from DLB, although PDD patients had higher densities of Lewy bodies

in the temporal cortex (Harding & Halliday, 2001). Increased distribution of Lewy bodies in the temporal lobe has been associated with well-formed visual hallucinations in all patients (Harding et al., 2002).

Treatment of Parkinson's Disease Dementias

Treatment of PDD includes pharmacological treatments for the motor, neuropsychiatric, and cognitive symptoms. Levodopa has been used for the motor disorder of both DLB and PDD. The use of anticholinergic medications should be avoided. Improvement in visual hallucinations, delusions, anxiety, behavioral disturbance, and cognition can be achieved with the use of cholinesterase inhibitors (CHEIs; McKeith et al., 2005). Although open label studies have generally demonstrated effectiveness of the available CHEIs, donepezil, rivastigmine, and galantamine in PDD and DLB, placebo controlled data from a large trial are available only for rivastigmine (Emre et al., 2004). Rivastigmine produced improvement on measures of cognition, function, and behavior. Apathy is common in PDD and may improve with CHEIs. Atypical antipsychotics may be used but only very cautiously due to severe neuroleptic sensitivity and the use of traditional antipsychotics should be avoided (McKeith et al., 2005). As with PD, depression is common in both PDD and DLB and can be treated with non-anticholinergic antidepressants such as the selective serotonergic reuptake inhibitors (SSRI) or serotonin-norepinephrine reuptake inhibitors (SNRI).

Differential Diagnosis of Parkinsons Disease and Parkinsonian Syndromes

Alzheimer's Disease

The cognitive deficits associated with AD are discussed in the chapter by Bondi et al. As described above, the cognitive changes in PD are distinct from AD with the onset of deficits in attention, executive abilities, and spatial skills as hallmarks (See Table 9–2). Several neuropsychological differences exist between patients with PD and patients with AD. Simple

Table 9–2. Clinical Distinction between Parkinson's Disease with Dementia (PDD), and Alzheimer's Disease (AD)

	PDD	AD
Neuropsychological Features		
Attention		
Mental Speed	Impaired	Intact/slight declines
Simple attention	Fluctuations	Intact
Language skills		
Naming	Intact	Impaired
Phonemic Fluency	Impaired	Intact
Semantic Fluency	Impaired	Impaired
Memory	Retrieval deficit	Storage deficit
Visuospatial	Prominent deficits	Mild to moderate deficits
Executive Functions	Prominent deficits	Mild to moderate deficits
Neuropsychiatric Features		
PD motor features	Present early	Absent early
Neuroleptic sensitivity	Present	Uncommon
Autonomic dysfunction	Common	Uncommon
disorder	Hallucinations/Delusions Uncommon	Common
	REM sleep behavior Common	Absent

attentional skills are intact in AD while patients with PD may show fluctuations in the level of alertness. In AD, certain language skills are initially intact (e.g., phonemic fluency, reading) with more pervasive early deficits in naming, word-finding ability and language comprehension. In PD, language changes include dysarthic speech and difficulty with both semantic and phonemic fluency. Memory is impaired in patients with both PD and AD, although the impairment in AD is more pronounced, with AD patients performing much more poorly on tasks of delayed recall and recognition and PD patients performing better on measures of recognition or retrieval. Visuospatial deficits are exhibited by both PD and AD patients, even when tasks do not involve motor speed or manual dexterity (Levin et al., 1992). In addition, PD patients tend to exhibit visuospatial deficits earlier in the course of the disease as compared to AD. PD and AD patients alike exhibit poor performance on tasks of cognitive flexibility. However, in PD poor performance frontal tests such as those involving planning, sequencing multiple steps, and set shifting is often the sole or most striking deficit, as compared with AD, where memory (learning, accelerated forgetting)

is the most prominent deficit. (See Table 9–2 for neurocognitive and behavioral comparisons).

Parkinsonian Plus Syndromes. There are several hypokinetic neurodegenerative disorders that share clinical similarities with PD. However, patients with these disorders typically exhibit additional neurological abnormalities and thus these syndromes are referred to as multiple system atrophies or *parkinson-plus syndromes.*

Progressive Supranuclear Palsy

Progressive supranuclear palsy is an uncommon disease with a prevalence rate of 5 per 100,000 (Nath et al., 2001). Age at onset is typically in the sixth or seventh decade and progresses to death in 5–10 years. The disease is sporadic and occurs more commonly in males than females. Patients with PSP tend to have an astonished or worried facial expression secondary to rigidity and hypertonicity of the facial muscles.

Postural instability with frequent falls, usually backward, is among the most disabling features. Loss of volitional downward gaze is one of the most important distinguishing features of PSP and is one of the earliest manifestations of the disease. The patient's eyes deviate upward when the head is tilted forward indicating that oculocephalic reflexes remain intact. Upward gaze is progressively impaired and volitional horizontal gaze is also lost as the disease progresses. Clinicopathological studies have reported early postural instability with falls and supranuclear gaze palsy as the most reliable means of differentiating PSP from other parkinsonian disorders (Collins et al., 1995; Litvan et al., 1997). In contrast to the stooped posture, short and shuffling steps, narrow base, and flexed knees seen in patients with PD, patients with PSP assume an erect or hypererect posture and have a stiff and broad-based gait (Mendez & Cummings, 2003). Patients with PSP develop profound bradykinesia during the course of the illness that resembles PD. Rigidity in the PSP patient is more evident in the midline structures such as the neck and trunk, as opposed to the limbs (e.g., axial rigidity). Both resting and action tremor are unusual. Whereas patients with PD often exhibit substantial improvement when treated with levodopa, patients with PSP show little response. Speech in PSP is characterized by a monotonous, hypernasal, low-pitched, spastic dysarthria (Stacy & Jankovic, 1992), and patients may progress to total anarthria or mutism in late stages (Mendez & Cummings, 2003). Changes in personality, including apathy, irritability, and labile mood may be among the first features of PSP.

Neuropathologic changes associated with the disease include brain stem atrophy with neuronal loss, neurofibrillary tangles and glial inclusions in the brain stem, basal ganglia and diencephalon (Litvan et al., 1996). The neurofibrillary tangles of PSP are composed of four repeat tau and have a different distribution from those of AD (Avila et al., 2004). Performance on measures of information processing speed, abstract reasoning, executive functions, retrieval and procedural learning, category fluency and naming have been noted to be worse in PSP than PD (Cordato et al., 2006; Soliveri et al., 2000). Patients are three times more likely to develop dementia than patients with idiopathic PD. Use of cholinesterase inhibitors has not proven efficacious for treatment of cognitive dysfunction (Lauterbach, 2004).

Multiple System Atrophy. Multiple system atrophy refers to a group of sporadic neurodegenerative disorders of adult onset that share the common feature of parkinsonism. The disease is characterized by a combination of parkinsonian, cerebellar, autonomic, and cortical spinal (pyramidal) signs and symptoms with cell loss and gliosis extensively in the basal ganglia, inferior olives, pons, and cerebellum. On neuropathological examination, glial cytoplasmic inclusions consisting primarily of α-synuclein have been described, suggesting that the disease belongs to the group of α-synucleinopathies (Dickson et al., 1999). Estimates of the prevalence of MSA vary from 1.9 to 4.9 per 100,000 (Vanacore, 2005). Approximately 90% of patients with MSA have REM sleep behavior disorder, which has been correlated with nigrostriatal dopaminergic demise (Gilman et al., 2003). Six of the following features have been noted to reliably diagnose MSA: sporadic adult onset, autonomic signs, parkinsonism, cerebellar features, pyramidal signs, lack of response to levodopa treatment, lack of cognitive dysfunction, and lack of downward gaze palsy (Litvan et al., 1998).

Relatively recent consensus criteria (Gilman et al., 1999) have been developed and have proposed new terminology to replace the terms striatonigral degeneration (SND), sporadic olivopontocerebellar atrophy (sOPCA), and Shy Drager syndrome (SDS), previously considered distinct diagnostics subtypes of MSA. The designation MSA-P has been delineated for those patients with the onset of parkinsonism; MSA-C is used when MSA begins with cerebellar ataxia, and MSA-A is used for patients with autonomic disturbances.

Multiple System Atrophy-Parkinsonism. Multiple system atrophy-parkinsonism (MSA-P) is the most common of the MSA subtypes accounting for 40%–66% of cases in various studies (Gilman, 2006). This term has been used to replace the old term striatonigral degeneration. The parkinsonian features of bradykinesia, rigidity, gait unsteadiness, and hypokinetic speech are hallmarks of MSA-P. Improvement in rigidity, bradykinesia, and postural instability with use of levodopa has been noted in only half of the cases with MSA-P (Hughes et al., 1992; Parati et al., 1993), and a lack of reponsiveness to levodopa has been used to differentiate PD from striatonigral degeneration. A significant number of patients show iron deposition appearing as low T2 signal in the putamen (Macia et al., 2001). Diagnosis is confirmed only upon postmortem examination, which is significant for neuronal loss in the putamen and caudate nucleus (O'Brien et al., 1990). Lewy bodies and neurofibrillary tangles are not common.

Neuropsychological studies have suggested mild memory and executive impairments (Pillon et al., 1995) and significant impairments of visuospatial organization in MSA-P (Testa et al., 1993). Patients with MSA-P performed more poorly than PD patients on frontal attention measures (Meco et al., 1996) and on measures of verbal fluency and visual search (Soliveri et al., 2000). Patients with MSA-P exhibited greater difficulties on tasks of learning, recognition, and verbal fluency as compared to controls and patients with both sporadic and autosomal dominant form of OPCA (Berent et al., 2002).

Multiple System Atrophy-Cerebellar.
The cerebellar disorder of MSA-C includes ataxia of gait, limb movements and speech, and ocular motor disorders including gaze-evoked nystagmus, overshoot dysmetria, and cycadic intrusions into smooth pursuit movements. Patients often complain of imbalance, unsteadiness of gait, and deterioration of handwriting and other fine motor skills. Despite recommendations by the consensus conference on MSA, the term olivopontocerebellar atrophy (OPCA) continues to be used in the literature and is applied to disorders characterized clinically by ataxic gait, hypotonia, upper and lower motor neuron signs, limb unsteadiness, and dysarthria. MSA-C accounts for approximately 10%–15% of cases of MSA. The presence of ophthalmoplegia and pyramidal tract signs is used clinically to distinguish OPCA from pure cerebellar atrophy. Onset of OPCA is usually between ages 30 and 50 years and may be sporadic or inherited in an autosomal dominant pattern (dOPCA), with the autosomal dominant form of the disease now

reclassified as a form of spinocerebellar ataxia (SCA) The disease is slowly progressive and may have a 25-year course.

Relatively mild cognitive deficits have been reported in autosomal dominant OPCA (dOPCA), particularly frontal lobe dysfunction (Botez-Marquard & Botez, 1993). Berent and colleagues (2002) have suggested that motor dysfunction appears to account for discrepancies on cognitive tasks between OPCA patients and normal controls. While subjects with OPCA did not differ from normal controls on measures without motor demands such as working mathematical problems without paper and pencil, defining a list or words or identifying the essential missing piece in a picture, subjects did differ from normal controls on three subtests with motor demands such as constructing blocks to match design and quickly copying symbols paired with numbers. At least one recent study (Bürk et al., 2006) suggested that MSA-C subjects performed more poorly on measures of verbal memory (story recall and list learning) and category and letter fluency as compared with normal controls.

Multiple System Atrophy-Autonomic.
The term MSA-A refers to those cases in which the disease presents with parkinsonism and prominent autonomic disturbance. Abnormalities of function of the autonomic nervous system including impotence, orthostatic hypotension, and urinary incontinence appear early in the clinical course. Other symptoms may include anhidrosis, pupillary changes, and decreased tearing. An akinetic, rigid parkinsonian syndrome develops several years after the onset of the autonomic dysfunction. Some patients may present with associated cerebellar, upper motor neuron, and/or lower motor neuron findings. The disease is more common in men and symptoms first begin in the sixth decade of life. Pathological changes include cell loss and gliosis in the pigmented brain stem nuclei, striatum, pontine structures, and the intermediolateral cell column of the spinal cord (Gilman, 2006). Autonomic failure has been correlated with loss of catecholaminergic neurons in the reticular formation of the rostroventrolateral medulla (Benarroch et al., 2000).

Summary

Parkinson's Disease is among the most common neurological illnesses affecting the elderly. It is characterized by motor symptoms including slowness of movement and difficulty initiating movement, masked facies, muscular rigidity, shuffling or unsteady gait, stooped posture, disturbances in equilibrium, and tremor. The use of levodopa continues to be the mainstay of treatment for PD. Other pharmacological therapies include the use of selegiline, rasageline, and entacapone. Stimulation of the STN is considered an effective treatment for advanced PD with noted benefits on motor function and quality of life.

Neuropsychologic deficits in non-demented PD patients include moderate impairment in verbal and nonverbal memory for both immediate and delayed recall, with recent controversy regarding performance on tasks of recognition. Language functions are generally spared. Visuospatial and visuoconstructive skills are among the most frequently cited deficits in PD, even when the effects of motor slowing are taken into account. Executive functions are the earliest and most consistently impaired abilities. Depression is the most common psychiatric syndrome in PD; anxiety and apathy are also frequently observed. The dementia associated with PD is considered to be one of the Lewy body diseases and shares pathological features of misfolding and aggregation of α-synuclein with Lewy body dementia suggesting that the two diseases are similar. Rivastigmine has been approved for treatment of the dementias associated with PD. Neurodegenerative disorders that share clinical similarities with PD include DLB, PSP, and the various subtypes of MSA. Disorders that affect the head of the caudate nucleus or thalamus produce the syndrome of subcortical dementia with executive function abnormalities, memory loss, slowed cognition, and mood and personality changes. The caudate nucleus, globus pallidus, and thalamus are member structures of frontal–subcortical circuits that link these subcortical nuclei with specific regions of the frontal lobe. Disruption of the circuits results in behavioral abnormalities and cognitive deficits similar to those occurring with frontal lobe dysfunction. Many of the intellectual disturbances documented in PD and other basal ganglia syndromes can be ascribed to interruption of frontal–subcortical circuit function. The high frequency of cognitive deficits, mood changes, anxiety, and personality changes among patients with PD and other movement disorders indicate that the basal ganglia play critical roles in human intellectual and emotional function.

Acknowledgment

Supported in part by the Department of Veterans Affairs and National Institute on Aging grants 1P30 AG10123, AG11325–02, P50 AGi6570.

References

Aarsland, D., Laake, K., Larsen, J. P., & Janvin, C. (2002). Donepezil for cognitive impairment in Parkinson's disease: A randomised controlled study. *Journal of Neurology, Neurosurgery and Psychiatry, 72*(6), 708–712.

Aarsland, D., Larsen, J. P., Lim, N. G., Janvin, C., Karlsen, K., Tandberg, E., et al. (1999). Range of neuropsychiatric disturbances in patients with Parkinson's disease. *Journal of Neurology, Neurosurgery and Psychiatry, 67*(4), 492–496.

Aarsland, D., Perry, R., Brown, A., Larsen, J. P., & Ballard, C. (2005). Neuropathology of dementia in Parkinson's disease: A prospective, community-based study. *Annals of Neurology, 58*(5), 773–776.

Aarsland, D., Tandberg, E., Larsen, J. P., & Cummings, J. L. (1996). Frequency of dementia in Parkinson disease. *Archives of Neurology, 53*(6), 538–542.

Adler, C. H., & Thorpy, M. J. (2005). Sleep issues in Parkinson's disease. *Neurology, 64*(12 Suppl 3), S12–S20.

Albin, R. L. (2006). Parkinson's disease: Background, diagnosis, and initial management. *Clinics in Geriatric Medicine, 22*(4), 735–751, v.

Alegret, M., Junque, C., Valldeoriola, F., Vendrell, P., Pilleri, M., Rumia, J., et al. (2001). Effects of bilateral subthalamic stimulation on cognitive function in Parkinson disease. *Archives of Neurology, 58*(8), 1223–1227.

Alegret, M., Valldeoriola, F., Tolosa, E., Vendrell, P., Junque, C., Martinez, J., et al. (2003). Cognitive effects of unilateral posteroventral pallidotomy: A 4-year follow-up study. *Movement Disorders, 18*(3), 323–328.

Ardouin, C., Pillon, B., Peiffer, E., Bejjani, P., Limousin, P., Damier, P., et al. (1999). Bilateral subthalamic or pallidal stimulation for Parkinson's disease affects neither memory nor executive functions: A consecutive series of 62 patients. *Annals of Neurology, 46*(2), 217–223.

Ardouin, C., Voon, V., Worbe, Y., Abouazar, N., Czernecki, V., Hosseini, H., et al. (2006). Pathological gambling in Parkinson's disease improves on chronic subthalamic nucleus stimulation. *Movement Disorders, 21*(11), 1941–1946.

Avila, J., Lucas, J. J., Perez, M., & Hernandez, F. (2004). Role of tau protein in both physiological and pathological conditions. *Physiological Reviews, 84*(2), 361–384.

Baldereschi, M., Di Carlo, A., Rocca, W. A., Vanni, P., Maggi, S., Perissinotto, E., et al. (2000). Parkinson's disease and parkinsonism in a longitudinal study: Two-fold higher incidence in men. ILSA Working Group. Italian Longitudinal Study on Aging. *Neurology, 55*(9), 1358–1363.

Ballard, C. G., Aarsland, D., McKeith, I., O'Brien, J., Gray, A., Cormack, F., et al. (2002). Fluctuations in attention: PD dementia vs DLB with parkinsonism. *Neurology, 59*(11), 1714–1720.

Barnes, J., Boubert, L., Harris, J., Lee, A., & David, A. S. (2003). Reality monitoring and visual hallucinations in Parkinson's disease. *Neuropsychologia, 41*(5), 565–574.

Bayles, K. A., Trosset, M. W., Tomoeda, C. K., Montgomery, E. B., Jr., & Wilson, J. (1993). Generative naming in Parkinson disease patients. *Journal of Clinical and Experimental Neuropsychology, 15*(4), 547–562.

Benarroch, E. E., Schmeichel, A. M., & Parisi, J. E. (2000). Involvement of the ventrolateral medulla in parkinsonism with autonomic failure. *Neurology, 54*(4), 963–968.

Berent, S., Giordani, B., Gilman, S., Trask, C. L., Little, R. J., Johanns, J. R., et al. (2002). Patterns of neuropsychological performance in multiple system atrophy compared to sporadic and hereditary olivopontocerebellar atrophy. *Brain Cognition, 50*(2), 194–206.

Bissessur, S., Tissingh, G., Wolters, E. C., & Scheltens, P. (1997). rCBF SPECT in Parkinson's disease patients with mental dysfunction. *Journal of Neural Transmission Supplement, 50*, 25–30.

Bohnen, N. I., Kaufer, D. I., Ivanco, L. S., Lopresti, B., Koeppe, R. A., Davis, J. G., et al. (2003). Cortical cholinergic function is more severely affected in parkinsonian dementia than in Alzheimer disease: An in vivo positron emission tomographic study. *Archives of Neurology, 60*(12), 1745–1748.

Bondi, M. W., Kaszniak, A. W., Rapcsak, S. Z., & Butters, M. A. (1993). Implicit and explicit memory following anterior communicating artery aneurysm rupture. *Brain Cognition, 22*(2), 213–229.

Bonifati, V., Rizzu, P., Squitieri, F., Krieger, E., Vanacore, N., van Swieten, J. C., et al. (2003). DJ-1 (PARK7), a novel gene for autosomal recessive, early onset parkinsonism. *Journal of the Neurological Sciences, 24*(3), 159–160.

Botez-Marquard, T., & Botez, M. I. (1993). Cognitive behavior in heredodegenerative ataxias. *European Neurology, 33*(5), 351–357.

Braak, H., Del Tredici, K., Rub, U., de Vos, R. A., Jansen Steur, E. N., & Braak, E. (2003). Staging of brain pathology related to sporadic Parkinson's disease. *Neurobiology of Aging, 24*(2), 197–211.

Breen, E. K. (1993). Recall and recognition memory in Parkinson's disease. *Cortex, 29*(1), 91–102.

Brooks, D. J., & Sagar, H. (2003). Entacapone is beneficial in both fluctuating and non-fluctuating patients with Parkinson's disease: A randomised, placebo controlled, double blind, six month study. *Journal of Neurology, Neurosurgery and Psychiatry, 74*(8), 1071–1079.

Brown, R. G., & Marsden, C. D. (1990). Cognitive function in Parkinson's disease: From description to theory. *Trends in Neuroscience, 13*(1), 21–29.

Burchiel, K. J. (1995). Thalamotomy for movement disorders. *Neurosurgery Clinics of North America, 6*(1), 55–71.

Burk, K., Daum, I., & Rub, U. (2006). Cognitive function in multiple system atrophy of the cerebellar type. *Movement Disorders, 21*(6), 772–776.

Cahn, D. A., Sullivan, E. V., Shear, P. K., Heit, G., Lim, K. O., Marsh, L., et al. (1998). Neuropsychological and motor functioning after unilateral anatomically guided posterior ventral pallidotomy. Preoperative performance and three-month follow-up. *Neuropsychiatry, Neuropsychology, and Behavioral Neurology, 11*(3), 136–145.

Calderon, J., Perry, R. J., Erzinclioglu, S. W., Berrios, G. E., Dening, T. R., & Hodges, J. R. (2001). Perception, attention, and working memory are disproportionately impaired in dementia with Lewy bodies compared with Alzheimer's disease. *Journal of Neurology, Neurosurgery and Psychiatry, 70*(2), 157–164.

Claus, J. J., & Mohr, E. (1996). Attentional deficits in Alzheimer's, Parkinson's, and Huntington's diseases. *Acta Neurologica Scandinavica, 93*(5), 346–351.

Collerton, D., Burn, D., McKeith, I., & O'Brien, J. (2003). Systematic review and meta-analysis show that dementia with Lewy bodies is a visual–perceptual and attentional–executive dementia. *Dementia and Geriatric Cognivite Disorders, 16*(4), 229–237.

Collins, S. J., Ahlskog, J. E., Parisi, J. E., & Maraganore, D. M. (1995). Progressive supranuclear palsy: Neuropathologically based diagnostic clinical criteria. *Journal of Neurology, Neurosurgery and Psychiatry, 58*(2), 167–173.

Connor, D. J., Salmon, D. P., Sandy, T. J., Galasko, D., Hansen, L. A., & Thal, L. J. (1998). Cognitive profiles of autopsy-confirmed Lewy body variant vs pure Alzheimer disease. *Archives of Neurology, 55*(7), 994–1000.

Cools, R., Barker, R. A., Sahakian, B. J., & Robbins, T. W. (2001a). Enhanced or impaired cognitive function in Parkinson's disease as a function of dopaminergic medication and task demands. *Cerebral Cortex, 11*(12), 1136–1143.

Cools, R., Barker, R. A., Sahakian, B. J., & Robbins, T. W. (2001b). Mechanisms of cognitive set flexibility in Parkinson's disease. *Brain, 124*(Pt 12), 2503–2512.

Cools, R., Barker, R. A., Sahakian, B. J., & Robbins, T. W. (2003). L-Dopa medication remediates cognitive inflexibility, but increases impulsivity in patients with Parkinson's disease. *Neuropsychologia, 41*(11), 1431–1441.

Cooper, J. A., Sagar, H. J., Jordan, N., Harvey, N. S., & Sullivan, E. V. (1991). Cognitive impairment in early, untreated Parkinson's disease and its relationship to motor disability. *Brain, 114*(Pt 5), 2095–2122.

Cooper, J. A., Sagar, H. J., & Sullivan, E. V. (1993). Short-term memory and temporal ordering in early Parkinson's disease: Effects of disease chronicity and medication. *Neuropsychologia, 31*(9), 933–949.

Cordato, N. J., Halliday, G. M., Caine, D., & Morris, J. G. (2006). Comparison of motor, cognitive, and behavioral features in progressive supranuclear palsy and Parkinson's disease. *Movement Disorders, 21*(5), 632–638.

Cummings, J. L. (1991). Behavioral complications of drug treatment of Parkinson's disease. *Journal of the American Geriatrics Society, 39*(7), 708–716.

Cummings, J. L. (1992). Depression and Parkinson's disease: A review. *American Journal of Psychiatry, 149*(4), 443–454.

Daniele, A., Albanese, A., Contarino, M. F., Zinzi, P., Barbier, A., Gasparini, F., et al. (2003). Cognitive and behavioural effects of chronic stimulation of the subthalamic nucleus in patients with Parkinson's disease. *Journal of Neurology, Neurosurgery and Psychiatry, 74*(2), 175–182.

de Bie, R. M., Schuurman, P. R., Bosch, D. A., de Haan, R. J., Schmand, B., & Speelman, J. D. (2001). Outcome of unilateral pallidotomy in advanced Parkinson's disease: Cohort study of 32 patients. *Journal of Neurology, Neurosurgery and Psychiatry, 71*(3), 375–382.

de Lau, L. M., & Breteler, M. M. (2006). Epidemiology of Parkinson's disease. *The Lancet Neurology, 5*(6), 525–535.

Defer, G. L., Widner, H., Marie, R. M., Remy, P., & Levivier, M. (1999). Core assessment program for surgical interventional therapies in Parkinson's disease (CAPSIT-PD). *Movement Disorders, 14*(4), 572–584.

Delis, D. C., & Massman, P. J. (1992). The effects of dopamine fluctuation on cognition and affect. In S. J. Huber & J. L. Cummings (Eds.), *Parkinson's disease: Neurobehavioral aspects.* New York: Oxford. <AQ: Please provide page range.>

Demakis, G. J., Mercury, M. G., Sweet, J. J., Rezak, M., Eller, T., & Vergenz, S. (2002). Motor and cognitive sequelae of unilateral pallidotomy in intractable Parkinson's Disease: Electronic measurement of motor steadiness is a useful outcome measure. *Journal of Clinical and Experimental Neuropsychology, 24*(5), 655–663.

Diamond, A., & Jankovic, J. (2005). The effect of deep brain stimulation on quality of life in movement disorders. *Journal of Neurology, Neurosurgery and Psychiatry, 76*(9), 1188–1193.

Dickson, D. W., Liu, W., Hardy, J., Farrer, M., Mehta, N., Uitti, R., et al. (1999). Widespread alterations of alpha-synuclein in multiple system atrophy. *American Journal of Pathology, 155*(4), 1241–1251.

Dodd, M. L., Klos, K. J., Bower, J. H., Geda, Y. E., Josephs, K. A., & Ahlskog, J. E. (2005). Pathological gambling caused by drugs used to treat Parkinson disease. *Archives of Neurology, 62*(9), 1377–1381.

Dorsey, E. R., Constantinescu, R., Thompson, J. P., Biglan, K. M., Holloway, R. G., Kieburtz, K., et al. (2007). Projected number of people with Parkinson disease in the most populous nations, 2005 through 2030. *Neurology, 68*(5), 384–386.

Driver-Dunckley, E., Samanta, J., & Stacy, M. (2003). Pathological gambling associated with dopamine agonist therapy in Parkinson's disease. *Neurology, 61*(3), 422–423.

Dujardin, K., Defebvre, L., Krystkowiak, P., Blond, S., & Destee, A. (2001). Influence of chronic bilateral stimulation of the subthalamic nucleus on cognitive function in Parkinson's disease. *Journal of Neurology, 248*(7), 603–611.

Dujardin, K., Degreef, J., Rogelet, P., Defebvre, L., & Destee, A. (1999). Impairment of the supervisory attentional system in early untreated patients with Parkinson's disease. *Journal of Neurology, 246*, 783–788.

Elmer, L., Schwid, S., Eberly, S., Goetz, C., Fahn, S., Kieburtz, K., et al. (2006). Rasagiline-associated motor improvement in PD occurs without worsening of cognitive and behavioral symptoms. *Journal of the Neurological Sciences, 248*(1–2), 78–83.

Emre, M. (2003). Dementia associated with Parkinson's disease. *The Lancet Neurology, 2*(4), 229–237.

Emre, M., Aarsland, D., Albanese, A., Byrne, E. J., Deuschl, G., De Deyn, P. P., et al. (2004). Rivastigmine for dementia associated with Parkinson's disease. *New England Journal of Medicine, 351*(24), 2509–2518.

Factor, S. A., Molho, E. S., Podskalny, G. D., & Brown, D. (1995). Parkinson's disease: Drug-induced psychiatric states. *Advances in Neurology, 65*, 115–138.

Fearnley, J. M., & Lees, A. J. (1991). Ageing and Parkinson's disease: Substantia nigra regional selectivity. *Brain, 114*(Pt 5), 2283–2301.

Ferreri, F., Agbokou, C., & Gauthier, S. (2006). Recognition and management of neuropsychiatric complications in Parkinson's disease. *Canadian Medical Association Journal, 175*(12), 1545–1552.

Fukuda, M., Kameyama, S., Yoshino, M., Tanaka, R., & Narabayashi, H. (2000). Neuropsychological outcome following pallidotomy and thalamotomy for Parkinson's disease. *Stereotactic and Functional Neurosurgery, 74*(1), 11–20.

Funkiewiez, A., Ardouin, C., Caputo, E., Krack, P., Fraix, V., Klinger, H., et al. (2004). Long term effects of bilateral subthalamic nucleus stimulation on cognitive function, mood, and behaviour in Parkinson's disease. *Journal of Neurology, Neurosurgery and Psychiatry, 75*(6), 834–839.

Geser, F., Wenning, G. K., Poewe, W., & McKeith, I. (2005). How to diagnose dementia with Lewy bodies: State of the art. *Movement Disorders, 20*(Suppl 12), S11–S20.

Ghika, J., Ghika-Schmid, F., Fankhauser, H., Assal, G., Vingerhoets, F., Albanese, A., et al. (1999). Bilateral contemporaneous posteroventral pallidotomy for the treatment of Parkinson's disease: Neuropsychological and neurological side effects. Report of four cases and review of the literature. *Journal of Neurosurgery, 91*(2), 313–321.

Giladi, N., Shabtai, H., Gurevich, T., Benbunan, B., Anca, M., & Korczyn, A. D. (2003). Rivastigmine (Exelon) for dementia in patients with Parkinson's disease. *Acta Neurologica Scandinavica, 108*(5), 368–373.

Gilman, S. (2006). Parkinsonian syndromes. *Clinics in Geriatric Medicine, 22*(4), 827–842, vi.

Gilman, S., Koeppe, R. A., Chervin, R. D., Consens, F. B., Little, R., An, H., et al. (2003). REM sleep behavior disorder is related to striatal monoaminergic deficit in MSA. *Neurology, 61*(1), 29–34.

Gilman, S., Low, P. A., Quinn, N., Albanese, A., Ben-Shlomo, Y., Fowler, C. J., et al. (1999). Consensus statement on the diagnosis of multiple system atrophy. *Joural of Neurological Sciences, 163*(1), 94–98.

Giovannoni, G., O'Sullivan, J. D., Turner, K., Manson, A. J., & Lees, A. J. (2000). Hedonistic homeostatic dysregulation in patients with Parkinson's disease on dopamine replacement therapies. *Journal of Neurology, Neurosurgery and Psychiatry, 68*(4), 423–428.

Grossman, M. (1999). Sentence processing in Parkinson's disease. *Brain Cognition, 40*(2), 387–413.

Grossman, M., Carvell, S., Stern, M. B., Gollomp, S., & Hurtig, H. I. (1992). Sentence comprehension in Parkinson's disease: The role of attention and memory. *Brain and Language, 42*(4), 347–384.

Grossman, M., Cooke, A., DeVita, C., Lee, C., Alsop, D., Detre, J., et al. (2003). Grammatical and resource components of sentence processing in Parkinson's disease: An fMRI study. *Neurology, 60*(5), 775–781.

Guridi, J., & Lozano, A. M. (1997). A brief history of pallidotomy. *Neurosurgery, 41*(5), 1169–1180.

Hallett, M., & Litvan, I. (1999). Evaluation of surgery for Parkinson's disease: A report of the Therapeutics and Technology Assessment Subcommittee of the American Academy of Neurology. The Task Force on Surgery for Parkinson's Disease. *Neurology, 53*(9), 1910–1921.

Harding, A. J., Broe, G. A., & Halliday, G. M. (2002). Visual hallucinations in Lewy body disease relate to Lewy bodies in the temporal lobe. *Brain, 125*(Pt 2), 391–403.

Harding, A. J., & Halliday, G. M. (2001). Cortical Lewy body pathology in the diagnosis of dementia. *Acta Neuropathologica (Berlin), 102*(4), 355–363.

Hardy, J., Cai, H., Cookson, M. R., Gwinn-Hardy, K., & Singleton, A. (2006). Genetics of Parkinson's disease and parkinsonism. *Annals of Neurology, 60*(4), 389–398.

Henderson, R., Kurlan, R., Kersun, J. M., & Como, P. (1992). Preliminary examination of the comorbidity of anxiety and depression in Parkinson's disease. *Journal of Neuropsychiatry and Clinical Neurosciences, 4*(3), 257–264.

Hirtz, D., Thurman, D. J., Gwinn-Hardy, K., Mohamed, M., Chaudhuri, A. R., & Zalutsky, R. (2007). How common are the "common" neurologic disorders? *Neurology, 68*(5), 326–337.

Hodgson, T. L., Tiesman, B., Owen, A. M., & Kennard, C. (2002). Abnormal gaze strategies during problem solving in Parkinson's disease. *Neuropsychologia, 40*(4), 411–422.

Hozumi, A., Hirata, K., Tanaka, H., & Yamazaki, K. (2000). Perseveration for novel stimuli in Parkinson's disease: An evaluation based on event-related potentials topography. *Movement Disorders, 15*(5), 835–842.

Hughes, A. J., Colosimo, C., Kleedorfer, B., Daniel, S. E., & Lees, A. J. (1992). The dopaminergic response in multiple system atrophy. *Journal of Neurology, Neurosurgery and Psychiatry, 55*(11), 1009–1013.

Hurtig, H. I., Trojanowski, J. Q., Galvin, J., Ewbank, D., Schmidt, M. L., Lee, V. M., et al. (2000). Alpha-synuclein cortical Lewy bodies correlate with dementia in Parkinson's disease. *Neurology, 54*(10), 1916–1921.

Ivory, S. J., Knight, R. G., Longmore, B. E., & Caradoc-Davies, T. (1999). Verbal memory in non-demented patients with idiopathic Parkinson's disease. *Neuropsychologia, 37*(7), 817–828.

Jahanshahi, M., Rowe, J., Saleem, T., Brown, R. G., Limousin-Dowsey, P., Rothwell, J. C., et al. (2002). Striatal contribution to cognition: Working memory and executive function in Parkinson's disease before and after unilateral posteroventral pallidotomy. *Journal of Cognitive Neurosciences, 14*(2), 298–310.

Janvin, C. C., Larsen, J. P., Salmon, D. P., Galasko, D., Hugdahl, K., & Aarsland, D. (2006). Cognitive profiles of individual patients with Parkinson's disease and dementia: Comparison with dementia with lewy bodies and Alzheimer's disease. *Movement Disorders, 21*(3), 337–342.

Jellinger, K. A., Seppi, K., Wenning, G. K., & Poewe, W. (2002). Impact of coexistent Alzheimer pathology on the natural history of Parkinson's disease. *Journal of Neural Transmission, 109*(3), 329–339.

Jost, W. H. (2003). Autonomic dysfunctions in idiopathic Parkinson's disease. *Journal of Neurology, 250*(Suppl 1), I28–I30.

Katai, S., Maruyama, T., Hashimoto, T., & Ikeda, S. (2003). Event based and time based prospective memory in Parkinson's disease. *Journal of Neurology, Neurosurgery and Psychiatry, 74*(6), 704–709.

Kawabata, K., Tachibana, H., & Sugita, M. (1991). Cerebral blood flow and dementia in Parkinson's disease. *Journal of Geriatric Psychiatry and Neurology, 4*(4), 194–203.

Kitada, T., Asakawa, S., Hattori, N., Matsumine, H., Yamamura, Y., Minoshima, S., et al. (1998). Mutations in the parkin gene cause autosomal recessive juvenile parkinsonism. *Nature, 392*(6676), 605–608.

Klunk, W. E., Engler, H., Nordberg, A., Wang, Y., Blomqvist, G., Holt, D. P., et al. (2004). Imaging brain amyloid in Alzheimer's disease with Pittsburgh Compound-B. *Annals of Neurology, 55*(3), 306–319.

Kubu, C. S., Grace, G. M., & Parrent, A. G. (2000). Cognitive outcome following pallidotomy: The influence of side of surgery and age of patient at disease onset. *Journal of Neurosurgery, 92*(3), 384–389.

Lacritz, L. H., Cullum, C. M., Frol, A. B., Dewey, R. B., Jr., & Giller, C. A. (2000). Neuropsychological outcome following unilateral stereotactic pallidotomy in intractable Parkinson's disease. *Brain Cognition, 42*(3), 364–378.

Lai, B. C., Schulzer, M., Marion, S., Teschke, K., & Tsui, J. K. (2003). The prevalence of Parkinson's disease in British Columbia, Canada, estimated by using drug tracer methodology. *Parkinsonism and Related Disorders, 9*(4), 233–238.

Lauterbach, E. C. (2004). The neuropsychiatry of Parkinson's disease and related disorders. *Psychiatric Clinics of North America, 27*(4), 801–825.

Lauterbach, E. C., & Duvoisin, R. C. (1991). Anxiety disorders in familial parkinsonism. *American Journal of Psychiatry, 148*(2), 274.

Lawrence, A. D., Evans, A. H., & Lees, A. J. (2003). Compulsive use of dopamine replacement therapy in Parkinson's disease: Reward systems gone awry? *The Lancet Neurology, 2*(10), 595–604.

Leentjens, A. F., Lousberg, R., & Verhey, F. R. (2002). Markers for depression in Parkinson's disease. *Acta Psychiatrica Scandinavica, 106*(3), 196–201.

Levin, B. E., Llabre, M. M., Reisman, S., Weiner, W. J., Sanchez-Ramos, J., Singer, C., et al. (1991). Visuospatial impairment in Parkinson's disease. *Neurology, 41*(3), 365–369.

Levin, B. E., Tomer, R., & Rey, G. J. (1992). Cognitive impairments in Parkinson's disease. *Neurologic Clinics, 10*(2), 471–485.

Limousin, P., Krack, P., Pollak, P., Benazzouz, A., Ardouin, C., Hoffmann, D., et al. (1998). Electrical stimulation of the subthalamic nucleus in advanced Parkinson's disease. *New England Journal of Medicine, 339*(16), 1105–1111.

Lippa, C. F., Duda, J. E., Grossman, M., Hurtig, H. I., Aarsland, D., Boeve, B. F., et al. (2007). DLB and PDD boundary issues: Diagnosis, treatment, molecular pathology, and biomarkers. *Neurology, 68*(11), 812–819.

Lippa, C. F., Smith, T. W., & Perry, E. (1999). Dementia with Lewy bodies: Choline acetyltransferase parallels nucleus basalis pathology. *Journal of Neural Transmission, 106*(5–6), 525–535.

Litvan, I., Booth, V., Wenning, G. K., Bartko, J. J., Goetz, C. G., McKee, A., et al. (1998). Retrospective application of a set of clinical diagnostic criteria for the diagnosis of multiple system atrophy. *Journal of Neural Transmission, 105*(2–3), 217–227.

Litvan, I., Campbell, G., Mangone, C. A., Verny, M., McKee, A., Chaudhuri, K. R., et al. (1997). Which clinical features differentiate progressive supranuclear palsy (Steele–Richardson–Olszewski syndrome) from related disorders? A clinicopathological study. *Brain, 120*(Pt 1), 65–74.

Litvan, I., Hauw, J. J., Bartko, J. J., Lantos, P. L., Daniel, S. E., Horoupian, D. S., et al. (1996). Validity and reliability of the preliminary NINDS neuropathologic criteria for progressive supra-nuclear palsy and related disorders. *Journal of Neuropathology and Experimental Neurology, 55*(1), 97–105.

Lombardi, W. J., Gross, R. E., Trepanier, L. L., Lang, A. E., Lozano, A. M., & Saint-Cyr, J. A. (2000). Relationship of lesion location to cognitive outcome following microelectrode-guided pallidotomy for Parkinson's disease: Support for the existence of cognitive circuits in the human pallidum. *Brain, 123*(Pt 4), 746–758.

Lu, C., Bharmal, A., & Suchowersky, O. (2006). Gambling and Parkinson disease. *Archives of Neurology, 63*(2), 298.

Macia, F., Yekhlef, F., Ballan, G., Delmer, O., & Tison, F. (2001). T2-hyperintense lateral rim and hypointense putamen are typical but not exclusive of multiple system atrophy. *Archives of Neurology, 58*(6), 1024–1026.

Maddox, W. T., & Filoteo, J. V. (2001). Striatal contributions to category learning: Quantitative modeling of simple linear and complex nonlinear rule learning in patients with Parkinson's disease. *Journal of the International Neuropsychological Society, 7*(6), 710–727.

Marder, K., Levy, G., Louis, E. D., Mejia-Santana, H., Cote, L., Andrews, H., et al. (2003). Familial aggregation of early- and late-onset Parkinson's disease. *Annals of Neurology, 54*(4), 507–513.

Massman, P. J., Delis, D. C., Butters, N., Levin, B. E., & Salmon, D. P. (1990). Are all subcortical dementias alike? Verbal learning and memory in Parkinson's and Huntington's disease patients. *Journal of Clinical and Experimental Neuropsychology, 12*(5), 729–744.

Masterman, D., DeSalles, A., Baloh, R. W., Frysinger, R., Foti, D., Behnke, E., et al. (1998). Motor, cognitive, and behavioral performance following unilateral ventroposterior pallidotomy for Parkinson disease. *Archives of Neurology, 55*(9), 1201–1208.

Matsui, H., Udaka, F., Miyoshi, T., Hara, N., Tamura, A., Oda, M., et al. (2005). N-isopropyl-p- 123I iodoamphetamine single photon emission computed tomography study of Parkinson's disease with dementia. *Internal Medicine, 44*(10), 1046–1050.

Mattila, P. M., Rinne, J. O., Helenius, H., Dickson, D. W., & Roytta, M. (2000). Alpha-synuclein-immunoreactive cortical Lewy bodies are associated with cognitive impairment in Parkinson's disease. *Acta Neuropathologica (Berlin), 100*(3), 285–290.

Mayeux, R. (1990). Depression in the patient with Parkinson's disease. *Journal of Clinical Psychiatry, 51 Suppl,* 20–23; discussion 24–25.

Mayeux, R., Denaro, J., Hemenegildo, N., Marder, K., Tang, M. X., Cote, L. J., et al. (1992). A population-based investigation of Parkinson's disease with and without dementia. Relationship to age and gender. *Archives of Neurology, 49*(5), 492–497.

Mayeux, R., Marder, K., Cote, L. J., Denaro, J., Hemenegildo, N., Mejia, H., et al. (1995). The frequency of idiopathic Parkinson's disease by age, ethnic group, and sex in northern Manhattan, 1988–1993. *American Journal of Epidemiology, 142*(8), 820–827.

McKeith, I., Del Ser, T., Spano, P., Emre, M., Wesnes, K., Anand, R., et al. (2000). Efficacy of rivastigmine in dementia with Lewy bodies: A randomised, double-blind, placebo-controlled international study. *Lancet, 356*(9247), 2031–2036.

McKeith, I. G., Dickson, D. W., Lowe, J., Emre, M., O'Brien, J. T., Feldman, H., et al. (2005). Diagnosis and management of dementia with Lewy bodies: Third report of the DLB Consortium. *Neurology, 65*(12), 1863–1872.

Meco, G., Gasparini, M., & Doricchi, F. (1996). Attentional functions in multiple system atrophy and Parkinson's disease. *Journal of Neurology, Neurosurgery and Psychiatry, 60*(4), 393–398.

Mendez, M. F., & Cummings, J. L. (2003). *Dementia: A clinical approach, Third Ed.* Boston: Butterworth-Heinemann.

Molina, J. A., Sainz-Artiga, M. J., Fraile, A., Jimenez-Jimenez, F. J., Villanueva, C., Orti-Pareja, M., et al. (2000). Pathologic gambling in Parkinson's disease: A behavioral manifestation of pharmacologic treatment? *Movement Disorders, 15*(5), 869–872.

Mormont, E., Laurier-Grymonprez, L., Baisset-Mouly, C., & Pasquier, F. (2003). The profile of memory disturbance in early Lewy body dementia differs from that in Alzheimer's disease. *Revue Neurologique (Paris), 159*(8–9), 762–766.

Morrison, C. E., Borod, J. C., Perrine, K., Beric, A., Brin, M. F., Rezai, A., et al. (2004). Neuropsychological functioning following bilateral subthalamic nucleus stimulation in Parkinson's disease. *Archives of Clinical Neuropsychology, 19*(2), 165–181.

Mossner, R., Henneberg, A., Schmitt, A., Syagailo, Y. V., Grassle, M., Hennig, T., et al. (2001). Allelic variation of serotonin transporter expression is associated with depression in Parkinson's disease. *Molecular Psychiatry, 6*(3), 350–352.

Muslimovic, D., Post, B., Speelman, J. D., & Schmand, B. (2005). Cognitive profile of patients with newly diagnosed Parkinson disease. *Neurology, 65*(8), 1239–1245.

Nath, U., Ben-Shlomo, Y., Thomson, R. G., Morris, H. R., Wood, N. W., Lees, A. J., et al. (2001). The prevalence of progressive supranuclear palsy (Steele–Richardson–Olszewski syndrome) in the UK. *Brain, 124*(Pt 7), 1438–1449.

Nussbaum, R. L., & Ellis, C. E. (2003). Alzheimer's disease and Parkinson's disease. *New England Journal of Medicine, 348*(14), 1356–1364.

O'Brien, C., Sung, J. H., McGeachie, R. E., & Lee, M. C. (1990). Striatonigral degeneration: Clinical, MRI, and pathologic correlation. *Neurology, 40*(4), 710–711.

Obwegeser, A. A., Uitti, R. J., Lucas, J. A., Witte, R. J., Turk, M. F., & Wharen, R. E., Jr. (2000). Predictors of neuropsychological outcome in patients following microelectrode-guided pallidotomy for Parkinson's disease. *Journal of Neurosurgery, 93*(3), 410–420.

Olzak, M., Laskowska, I., Jelonek, J., Michalak, M., Szolna, A., Gryz, J., et al. (2006). Psychomotor and executive functioning after unilateral posteroventral pallidotomy in patients with Parkinson's disease. *Journal of Neurological Sciences, 248*(1–2), 97–103.

Owen, A. M., James, M., Leigh, P. N., Summers, B. A., Marsden, C. D., Quinn, N. P., et al. (1992). Fronto-striatal cognitive deficits at different stages of Parkinson's disease. *Brain, 115*(Pt 6), 1727–1751.

Pahwa, R., Paolo, A., Troster, A., & Koller, W. (1998). Cognitive impairment in Parkinson's disease. *European Journal of Neurology, 5*(5), 431–441.

Parati, E. A., Fetoni, V., Geminiani, G. C., Soliveri, P., Giovannini, P., Testa, D., et al. (1993). Response to L-DOPA in multiple system atrophy. *Clinical Neuropharmacology, 16*(2), 139–144.

Parkinson Study Group. (2002). A controlled trial of rasagiline in early Parkinson Disease. The TEMPO study. *Archives of Neurology, 59*, 1937–1943.

Parsons, T. D., Rogers, S. A., Braaten, A. J., Woods, S. P., & Troster, A. I. (2006). Cognitive sequelae of subthalamic nucleus deep brain stimulation in Parkinson's disease: A meta-analysis. *Lancet Neurology, 5*(7), 578–588.

Payami, H., Larsen, K., Bernard, S., & Nutt, J. (1994). Increased risk of Parkinson's disease in parents and siblings of patients. *Annals of Neurology, 36*(4), 659–661.

Perrine, K., Dogali, M., Fazzini, E., Sterio, D., Kolodny, E., Eidelberg, D., et al. (1998). Cognitive functioning after pallidotomy for refractory Parkinson's disease. *Journal of Neurology, Neurosurgery and Psychiatry, 65*(2), 150–154.

Perry, E. K., Haroutunian, V., Davis, K. L., Levy, R., Lantos, P., Eagger, S., et al. (1994). Neocortical cholinergic activities differentiate Lewy body dementia from classical Alzheimer's disease. *Neuroreport, 5*(7), 747–749.

Pillon, B., Dubois, B., Ploska, A., & Agid, Y. (1991). Severity and specificity of cognitive impairment in Alzheimer's, Huntington's, and Parkinson's diseases and progressive supranuclear palsy. *Neurology, 41*(5), 634–643.

Pillon, B., Gouider-Khouja, N., Deweer, B., Vidailhet, M., Malapani, C., Dubois, B., et al. (1995). Neuropsychological pattern of striatonigral degeneration: Comparison with Parkinson's disease and progressive supranuclear palsy. *Journal of Neurology, Neurosurgery and Psychiatry, 58*(2), 174–179.

Polymeropoulos, M. H., Lavedan, C., Leroy, E., Ide, S. E., Dehejia, A., Dutra, A., et al. (1997). Mutation in the alpha-synuclein gene identified in families with Parkinson's disease. *Science, 276*(5321), 2045–2047.

Postuma, R. B., Lang, A. E., Massicotte-Marquez, J., & Montplaisir, J. (2006). Potential early markers of Parkinson disease in idiopathic REM sleep behavior disorder. *Neurology, 66*(6), 845–851.

Raskin, S. A., Borod, J. C., & Tweedy, J. R. (1992). Set-shifting and spatial orientation in patients with Parkinson's disease. *Journal of Clinical and Experimental Neuropsychology, 14*(5), 801–821.

Raskin, S. A., Sliwinski, M., & Borod, J. C. (1992). Clustering strategies on tasks of verbal fluency in Parkinson's disease. *Neuropsychologia, 30*(1), 95–99.

Rektor, I., Rektorova, I., & Kubova, D. (2006). Vascular parkinsonism—an update. *Journal of Neurological Sciences, 248*(1–2), 185–191.

Rettig, G. M., York, M. K., Lai, E. C., Jankovic, J., Krauss, J. K., Grossman, R. G., et al. (2000). Neuropsychological outcome after unilateral pallidotomy for the treatment of Parkinson's disease. *Journal of Neurology, Neurosurgery and Psychiatry, 69*(3), 326–336.

Reuter, J., Raedler, T., Rose, M., Hand, I., Glascher, J., & Buchel, C. (2005). Pathological gambling is linked to reduced activation of the mesolimbic reward system. *Nature Neuroscience, 8*(2), 147–148.

Ridenour, T. A., & Dean, R. S. (1999). Parkinson's disease and neuropsychological assessment. *International Journal of Neuroscience, 99*(1–4), 1–18.

Riordan, H. J., Flashman, L. A., & Roberts, D. W. (1997). Neurocognitive and psychosocial correlates of ventroposterolateral pallidotomy surgery in Parkinson's disease. *Neurosurgery Focus, 2*(3), e7.

Saint-Cyr, J. A., Trepanier, L. L., Kumar, R., Lozano, A. M., & Lang, A. E. (2000). Neuropsychological consequences of chronic bilateral stimulation of the subthalamic nucleus in Parkinson's disease. *Brain, 123*(Pt 10), 2091–2108.

Samii, A., Nutt, J. G., & Ransom, B. R. (2004). Parkinson's disease. *Lancet, 363*(9423), 1783–1793.

Sawada, H., Udaka, F., Kameyama, M., Seriu, N., Nishinaka, K., Shindou, K., et al. (1992). SPECT findings in Parkinson's disease associated with dementia. *Journal of Neurology, Neurosurgery and Psychiatry, 55*(10), 960–963.

Shiba, M., Bower, J. H., Maraganore, D. M., McDonnell, S. K., Peterson, B. J., Ahlskog, J. E., et al. (2000). Anxiety disorders and depressive disorders preceding Parkinson's disease: A case-control study. *Movement Disorders, 15*(4), 669–677.

Shimizu, S., Hanyu, H., Kanetaka, H., Iwamoto, T., Koizumi, K., & Abe, K. (2005). Differentiation of dementia with Lewy bodies from Alzheimer's disease using brain SPECT. *Dementia and Geriatric Cognitive Disorders, 20*(1), 25–30.

Siemers, E. R., Shekhar, A., Quaid, K., & Dickson, H. (1993). Anxiety and motor performance in Parkinson's disease. *Movement Disorders, 8*(4), 501–506.

Skeel, R. L., Crosson, B., Nadeau, S. E., Algina, J., Bauer, R. M., & Fennell, E. B. (2001). Basal ganglia dysfunction, working memory, and sentence comprehension in patients with Parkinson's disease. *Neuropsychologia, 39*(9), 962–971.

Smeding, H. M., Speelman, J. D., Koning-Haanstra, M., Schuurman, P. R., Nijssen, P., van Laar, T., et al. (2006). Neuropsychological effects of bilateral STN stimulation in Parkinson disease: A controlled study. *Neurology, 66*(12), 1830–1836.

Soliveri, P., Monza, D., Paridi, D., Carella, F., Genitrini, S., Testa, D., et al. (2000). Neuropsychological follow up in patients with Parkinson's disease, striatonigral degeneration-type multisystem atrophy, and progressive supranuclear palsy. *Journal of Neurology, Neurosurgery and Psychiatry, 69*(3), 313–318.

Soukup, V. M., Ingram, F., Schiess, M. C., Bonnen, J. G., Nauta, H. J., & Calverley, J. R. (1997). Cognitive sequelae of unilateral posteroventral pallidotomy. *Archives of Neurology, 54*(8), 947–950.

Spampinato, U., Habert, M. O., Mas, J. L., Bourdel, M. C., Ziegler, M., de Recondo, J., et al. (1991). (99mTc)-HM-PAO SPECT and cognitive impairment in Parkinson's disease: A comparison with dementia of the Alzheimer type. *Journal of Neurology, Neurosurgery and Psychiatry, 54*(9), 787–792.

Stacy, M. (2002). Sleep disorders in Parkinson's disease: Epidemiology and management. *Drugs and Aging, 19*(10), 733–739.

Stacy, M., & Jankovic, J. (1992). Differential diagnosis of Parkinson's disease and the parkinsonism plus syndromes. *Neurologic Clinics, 10*(2), 341–359.

Stebbins, G. T., Gabrieli, J. D., Masciari, F., Monti, L., & Goetz, C. G. (1999). Delayed recognition memory in Parkinson's disease: A role for working memory? *Neuropsychologia, 37*(4), 503–510.

Stebbins, G. T., Gabrieli, J. D., Shannon, K. M., Penn, R. D., & Goetz, C. G. (2000). Impaired frontostriatal cognitive functioning following posteroventral pallidotomy in advanced Parkinson's disease. *Brain Cognition, 42*(3), 348–363.

Stein, M. B., Heuser, I. J., Juncos, J. L., & Uhde, T. W. (1990). Anxiety disorders in patients with Parkinson's disease. *American Journal of Psychiatry, 147*(2), 217–220.

Stern, Y., Richards, M., Sano, M., & Mayeux, R. (1993). Comparison of cognitive changes in patients with Alzheimer's and Parkinson's disease. *Archives of Neurology, 50*(10), 1040–1045.

Tanner, C. M., Ottman, R., Goldman, S. M., Ellenberg, J., Chan, P., Mayeux, R., et al. (1999). Parkinson disease in twins: An etiologic study. *Journal of the American Medical Association, 281*(4), 341–346.

Taylor, A. E., & Saint-Cyr, J. A. (1992). Executive function. In S. J. Huber & J. L. Cummings (Eds.), *Parkinsons disease: Neurobehavioral aspects* (pp. 74–85). New York: Oxford University Press.

Testa, D., Fetoni, V., Soliveri, P., Musicco, M., Palazzini, E., & Girotti, F. (1993). Cognitive and motor performance in multiple system atrophy and Parkinson's disease compared. *Neuropsychologia, 31*(2), 207–210.

Tiraboschi, P., Hansen, L. A., Alford, M., Sabbagh, M. N., Schoos, B., Masliah, E., et al. (2000). Cholinergic dysfunction in diseases with Lewy bodies. *Neurology, 54*(2), 407–411.

Tiraboschi, P., Salmon, D. P., Hansen, L. A., Hofstetter, R. C., Thal, L. J., & Corey-Bloom, J. (2006). What best differentiates Lewy body from Alzheimer's disease in early-stage dementia? *Brain, 129*(Pt 3), 729–735.

Tomer, R., Fisher, T., Giladi, N., & Aharon-Peretz, J. (2002). Dissociation between spontaneous and reactive flexibility in early Parkinson's disease. *Neuropsychiatry, Neuropsychology, & Behavioral Neurology, 15*(2), 106–112.

Trepanier, L. L., Kumar, R., Lozano, A. M., Lang, A. E., & Saint-Cyr, J. A. (2000). Neuropsychological outcome of GPi pallidotomy and GPi or STN deep brain stimulation in Parkinson's disease. *Brain Cognition, 42*(3), 324–347.

Trepanier, L. L., Saint-Cyr, J. A., Lozano, A. M., & Lang, A. E. (1998). Neuropsychological consequences of posteroventral pallidotomy for the treatment of Parkinson's disease. *Neurology, 51*(1), 207–215.

Troster, A. I., Fields, J. A., Testa, J. A., Paul, R. H., Blanco, C. R., Hames, K. A., et al. (1998). Cortical and subcortical influences on clustering and switching in the performance of verbal fluency tasks. *Neuropsychologia, 36*(4), 295–304.

Uitti, R. J., Wharen, R. E., Duffy, J. R., Lucas, J. A., Schneider, S. L., Rippeth, J. D., et al. (2000). Unilateral pallidotomy for Parkinson's disease: Speech, motor, and neuropsychological outcome measurements. *Parkinsonism & Related Disorders, 6*(3), 133–143.

Vanacore, N. (2005). Epidemiological evidence on multiple system atrophy. *Journal of Neural Transmission, 112*(12), 1605–1612.

Volkmann, J. (2004). Deep brain stimulation for the treatment of Parkinson's disease. *Journal of Clinical Neurophysiology, 21*(1), 6–17.

Walker, Z., Allen, R. L., Shergill, S., & Katona, C. L. (1997). Neuropsychological performance in Lewy body dementia and Alzheimer's disease. *British Journal of Psychiatry, 170*, 156–158.

Whittington, C. J., Podd, J., & Stewart-Williams, S. (2006). Memory deficits in Parkinson's disease. *Journal of Clinical & Experimental Neuropsychology, 28*(5), 738–754.

Woods, S. P., & Troster, A. I. (2003). Prodromal frontal/executive dysfunction predicts incident dementia in Parkinson's disease. *Journal of the International Neuropsychological Society, 9*(1), 17–24.

York, M. K., Levin, H. S., Grossman, R. G., Lai, E. C., & Krauss, J. K. (2003). Clustering and switching in phonemic fluency following pallidotomy for the treatment of Parkinson's disease. *Journal of Clinical & Experimental Neuropsychology, 25*(1), 110–121.

Zgaljardic, D. J., Borod, J. C., Foldi, N. S., & Mattis, P. (2003). A review of the cognitive and behavioral sequelae of Parkinson's disease: Relationship to frontostriatal circuitry. *Cognitive & Behavioral Neurology, 16*(4), 193–210.

Zgaljardic, D. J., Borod, J. C., Foldi, N. S., Mattis, P. J., Gordon, M. F., Feigin, A., et al. (2006). An examination of executive dysfunction associated with frontostriatal circuitry in Parkinson's disease. *Journal of Clinical & Experimental Neuropsychology, 28*(7), 1127–1144.

10

Huntington's Disease

Jason Brandt

For the second edition of *Neuropsychological Assessment in Neuropsychiatric Disorders*, this author co-wrote a chapter on Huntington's disease (HD) with his mentor, colleague, and friend, Nelson Butters. In 1995, shortly before the book's publication, Nelson's illustrious career in neuropsychology was cut short by his premature death from amyotrophic lateral sclerosis. The current chapter, a summary of the neuropsychology of HD and an update on what we have learned in the ensuing years, is dedicated to Nelson's memory.

A Brief Overview of the Syndrome

Among the neuropsychiatric disorders discussed in this volume, HD provides some of the most fertile conditions for neuropsychological investigation. There are several reasons for this. First, the disease is not difficult to diagnose from history (especially family history) and clinical examination. The discovery of the specific genetic mutation responsible for this illness in 1993 allows for diagnostic confirmation. Second, the neuropathology of HD is relatively stereotyped and well understood. HD is a disease primarily of the basal ganglia, with death of particular neuronal populations in the head of the caudate nucleus and the putamen being most prominent. Third, HD causes a dementia syndrome that is more selective than that seen in Alzheimer's disease (AD) or other cortical dementias. Fourth, since the disease typically has onset in mid-

life, the dementia is not confounded by the brain changes associated with normal aging. Finally, HD is inherited as an autosomal dominant trait, and the availability of a definitive genetic test allows for the identification of presymptomatic individuals. This affords us the unique opportunity to study the evolution of a neuropsychiatric syndrome from its latent (presymptomatic) stage, through its 10–20 year course, to the postmortem examination of brain tissue.

HD presents clinically with a triad of symptoms (Folstein, 1989; Harper, 1996; Hayden, 1981). First, and most prominently, there is the movement disorder. HD is characterized by the onset, typically in one's thirties or forties, of involuntary choreiform and athetoid (jerking and writhing) movements, as well as impairments of voluntary action (David et al., 1987; Folstein et al., 1983; Georgiou et al., 1997; Hefter et al., 1987). Second, HD patients develop a dementia syndrome that has served as the prototype for subcortical dementia (Brandt et al., 1988; McHugh & Folstein, 1975; Paulsen et al., 1995). As will be discussed in more detail below, HD patients do not develop frank aphasia, amnesia, agnosia, or apraxia (but cf. Shelton & Knopman, 1991) but rather suffer from marked impairments in aspects of attention and executive control (including retrieval from episodic memory and knowledge stores) and reduced information-processing speed (Brandt, 1991; Brandt & Butters, 1986; Brandt & Bylsma, 1993). Third, patients usually develop emotional disturbances, with depression, irritability, and apathy being most common (Burns et al., 1990; Chatterjee et al., 2005; Folstein et al., 1983; Paulsen et al., 2001a, 2005). Importantly, multiple studies have found that cognitive impairment and emotional/behavioral symptoms are major sources of functional impairment in HD, often more so than the movement disorder (Bamford et al., 1995; Brandt et al., 1984; Hamilton et al., 2003; Mayeux et al., 1986; Nehl et al., 2004; Rothlind et al., 1993).

Although the hereditary nature of HD was recognized by George Huntington in 1872, it was not until Gusella and colleagues discovered a restriction fragment length polymorphism (RFLP) linked to HD in 1983 that its genetic locus was identified (Gusella et al., 1983). This discovery led to the development of a presymptomatic genetic test for persons at risk who had "informative" pedigrees (Brandt et al., 1989; Meissen et al., 1988). Ten years later, the precise mutation was discovered (Huntington's Disease Collaborative Research Group, 1993), allowing for a vastly improved, definitive genetic test. HD was found to be caused by the pathological expansion of a trinucleotide repeat sequence at chromosomal locus 4p16.3. The sequence of DNA bases at this location—cytosine, adenine, and guanine (CAG)—is repeated between 10 and 35 times on healthy chromosomes. On chromosomes from HD patients, this sequence expands to more than 36 CAG repeats. There is now very good evidence that the size of the expansion is negatively correlated with age of clinical onset (Andresen et al., 2006; Andrew et al., 1993; Claes et al., 1995; Duyao et al., 1993; Kieburtz et al., 1994; Stine et al., 1993). Cases of juvenile onset HD, for example, almost always have CAG repeat lengths greater than 60 (Duyao et al. 1993; Nance & Myers, 2001; Ranen et al., 1995). In contrast, people who have expansions in the range of 36–39 typically have such late onset that some live normal lifespans without ever developing signs or symptoms. Furthermore, there is mounting evidence that longer repeat length is correlated with more rapid progression of symptoms (Brandt et al., 1996; Illarioshkin et al., 1994; Mahant et al., 2003; Rosenblatt et al., 1998; but c.f. Kieburtz et al., 1994).

The Dementia of Huntington's Disease

Early studies of the dementia of HD typically compared samples of early- or mid-course HD patients to neurologically normal subjects (either persons unrelated to HD patients or asymptomatic, at-risk offspring of patients) (Bamford et al., 1995; Butters et al., 1978; Fedio et al., 1979; Josiassen et al., 1982; Sax et al., 1983; Strauss & Brandt, 1986). Not surprisingly, these studies typically reported impairments on a wide variety of neuropsychological tests. A meta-analysis by Zakzanis (1998) of 36 published studies found that HD patients performed more poorly than neurologically normal subjects in all seven of the neuropsychological domains examined. Tests of delayed recall (e.g., Visual Reproductions-II and Logical Memory-II from the Wechsler Memory Scale-Revised) and memory acquisition (e.g., learning variables from the California Verbal Learning Test) yielded the largest effect sizes, followed by tests of cognitive flexibility and abstraction (e.g., Wisconsin Card Sorting Test [WCST], Tower of London, Controlled Oral Word Association Test). Tests of "verbal skill" (e.g., Wechsler Adult Intelligence Scale-Revised [WAIS-R] verbal subtests, Boston Naming Test, National Adult Reading Test) yielded the smallest effect sizes. One limitation of this meta-analysis is that several effect size computations were based on data from a single published study.

Other studies examining the neuropsychological profile of HD have taken a comparative approach, juxtaposing the test performances of HD patients to those of patients with other neurological disorders. A major challenge for such studies is the necessity of matching patient groups for stage of disease or dementia severity; none of the methods for doing this is entirely satisfactory. Three studies (Brandt et al., 1988; Paulsen et al., 1995; Salmon et al., 1989) compared groups of HD patients and AD patients, matched on either the Mini-Mental State Exam (Folstein et al., 1975) or the Dementia Rating Scale (Mattis, 1988). The mean profiles of these groups on those same instruments were compared. The results are extremely consistent: across levels of severity, HD patients have greater impairment on tests of attention, mental tracking, and generativity than equivalently demented patients with AD. HD patients are much less impaired than their AD counterparts on items assessing orientation, naming, and new learning/memory.

In one study using the comparative approach (Brandt et al., 2004), 21 patients with HD were compared to 31 patients with primary cerebellar degenerations using neuropsychological tests assessing five domains (motor, verbal, spatial, memory, and executive). HD and cerebellar degeneration are both conditions which produce mid-life onset of a movement disorder, and the groups studied had equivalently severe motor impairment. The HD patients displayed more pervasive and more severe cognitive deficits, with largest effect sizes (compared to normal subjects) in the spatial and the executive domains (see Figure 10–1).

Attention

Although attention is often described as particularly impaired in HD, there have been surprisingly few empirical studies specifically investigating attentional phenomena in this disorder. One reason may be that many aspects of attention can also be conceptualized as aspects of working memory or executive control. For example, the Brief Test of Attention (Schretlen, 1997) requires patients to keep track of the number of spoken letters or spoken numerals in tape-recorded sequences of letters and numerals of increasing length. Schretlen et al. (1996) reported that HD patients of average intellect, all of whom scored 27 or higher on the Mini-Mental State Examination (MMSE), display very severe impairments on this task when compared to normal subjects. This deficit may be due to impairment in auditory working memory (i.e., maintaining information in active storage and operating on it for a single trial only) as much as an impairment in selective attention.

Müller and colleagues (2002) studied HD patients and neurologically normal control subjects on attention tasks chosen to assess three components of a specific attentional model (van Zomeran & Brouwer, 1994): selection, intensity, and supervisory control. Impairments were found in all three domains, with the most severe and pervasive deficits in intensity. Unlike normal subjects, HD patients did not have shorter latencies in a cued than an uncued reaction time task. The authors suggest that this represents a specific deficit in "extrinsic alertness." A somewhat different conclusion was reached by Sprengelmeyer and colleagues (1995). They reported that HD patients were able to maintain attention when provided with external cues, but fail to do so without cues.

Also using a reaction-time paradigm, Stout et al. (2001b) demonstrated that patients with

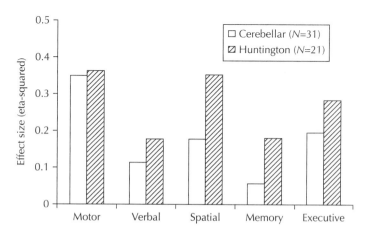

Figure 10–1. Magnitude of cognitive deficits in five domains among patients with Huntington's disease ($N = 21$) and patients with cerebellar degeneration ($N = 31$). Effect sizes (partial eta-squared) for each domain are derived from analyses of variance comparing performance of patient groups to normal control subjects on constituent neuropsychological tests. (From Brandt et al., 2004. Used with permission.)

HD fail to show negative priming. Whereas normal subjects and Parkinson's disease (PD) patients had elevated reaction times when responding to targets that shared features with distractors from previous trials, this was not the case in HD. The authors speculate that the neostriatum, but not the substantia nigra, plays a critical role in selective attention by altering the salience of distractor stimuli.

A specific impairment in shifting attentional set has been described by some investigators as prominent in early HD (Aron et al., 2003; Lawrence et al., 1996). In contrast, no impairment in attentional shifting was observed by Filoteo et al. (1995) using a global–local attention task (e.g., deciding whether a "3" was present when shown a large numeral "1" made up of smaller "3"s). Rather, Filoteo and colleagues found that HD patients, but not PD patients, had abnormally long reaction times on inconsistent trials (a large "1" made up of small "3"s) relative to consistent trials (a large "3" made up of small "3"s) (Roman et al., 1998). Thus, only the HD patients were unusually vulnerable to distraction from the unattended hierarchical level in the global–local paradigm. Maintaining attentional focus was a problem for HD patients, but shifting when appropriate was not.

Language

The most significant obstacle to communication with HD patients is their difficulty with motor control necessary for intelligible speech. Language per se is only mildly affected. Patients make minor syntactic errors (Murray & Lenz, 2001) and have some difficulty comprehending implied meanings (Murray & Stout, 1999). The few errors that HD patients make on tests of visual confrontation naming tend to be due to perceptual misinterpretations rather than impaired access to semantic information (Hodges et al., 1991).

One of the most consistently reported neuropsychological impairments in HD, and one that appears very early in the illness, is in the ability to rapidly generate lists of words conforming to specific rules ("verbal fluency") (Butters et al., 1986; Henry et al., 2005; Ho et al., 2002; Randolph et al., 1993). Whereas the performance failures of AD patients on these tasks

are usually attributed to disorganized semantic networks, HD patients perform poorly due to faulty retrieval mechanisms and strategies (Chan et al., 1993; Randolph et al., 1993; Rohrer et al., 1999).

Two frequently studied characteristics of word list generation performance are clustering (i.e., producing successive words from the same subcategory) and switching among clusters. Clustering on letter-cued word generation tasks is often impaired in temporal lobe disorders, whereas reduced switching has been found in patients with frontal-lobe pathology (Troyer et al., 1998). Rich and colleagues (1999) examined word generation to initial letter cues in 72 patients with HD and 41 healthy participants and found reduced switching but normal clustering in the patients. This was interpreted as reflecting dysfunction in cerebral circuitry linking prefrontal cortex to the striatum. In addition, switching, but not clustering, correlated inversely with disease severity, as measured by both the Quantified Neurological Examination (QNE) (Folstein et al., 1983) and the MMSE. Furthermore, annual follow-ups over 5 years revealed a monotonic decrease in switching over time, whereas clustering performance remained stable. Neurologically normal control participants performed uniformly over time on both measures. These results are consistent with a progressive reduction in cognitive flexibility in HD, attributed to disruption of frontal–subcortical circuits traversing the caudate nucleus.

Spatial Cognition

In addition to their prominent deficits in retrieval from memory and aspects of executive control, HD patients also have very substantial impairments in spatial abilities (Brandt et al., 2004, 2005; Bylsma et al., 1992; Mohr et al., 1991). The severity of these spatial deficits may be overlooked or underappreciated, since patients' difficulties with visuomotor and visuographic tasks are often seen as understandable consequences of their movement disorder. However, HD patients also have difficulty on purely perceptual, entirely nonmotor spatial tasks (Fedio et al., 1979; Gómez-Tortosa et al., 1996; Lawrence et al., 2000) and in situations where the motor impairment has been experimentally or statistically controlled. For example, Brandt et al. (2004) reported that patients with HD had more profound spatial deficits than patients with equivalently severe movement disorders due to cerebellar degeneration.

Mohr and colleagues (1997) addressed the specificity of the spatial deficits in HD. They reported that HD and PD patients share certain visuospatial processing deficits, but only HD patients were impaired on map reading, directional sense, and adjusting their targeted movements to alterations in their body positions. This was interpreted as reflecting a specific impairment in person-centered spatial judgment (see also Bylsma et al., 1992). Davis et al. (2003) reported that the processing and memory of both egocentric and allocentric spatial information is impaired in HD, but only the former (person-centered) is correlated with measures of disease severity.

Lawrence and colleagues (2000) undertook a detailed analysis of visual object and visuospatial cognition in early HD. They administered the Visual Object and Space Perception (VOSP) Battery (Warrington & James, 1991) as well as a number of computerized tasks of visual memory (discussed below) to 19 HD patients and age- and NART-matched normal control subjects. The only VOSP task on which the patient group performed abnormally was the object decision subtest. This task requires subjects to indicate which of four silhouettes is of a real object, but naming or otherwise identifying the object is not necessary. The HD patients were also impaired in both accuracy and reaction time on simultaneous trials (i.e., 0-second delay) of a matching-to-sample task. This suggests that at least some of HD patients' failures on tests of visual pattern and visual spatial memory may be due to perceptual or executive factors.

The neural mechanisms underlying impaired spatial cognition in HD is not fully understood. It has been suggested that one of the functions of the basal ganglia is to update information on spatial relationships from context-relevant sensory input (Lawrence et al., 1998, 2000). In addition, the caudate nucleus receives significant inputs from the inferior parietal sulcus (Yeterian & Pandya, 1993). Thus, the HD striatum may be deprived of critical input from a cortical zone important for spatial localization (Saint-Cyr, 2003).

Memory

Across studies, impaired learning and retrieval of new episodic memories are the most frequently observed cognitive deficits in HD (Zakzanis, 1998). The wordlist and narrative learning impairments of HD patients have been particularly well described (Butters et al., 1986, 1987; Delis et al., 1991; Hodges et al., 1990; Pillon et al., 1993). On list-learning tasks, deficient immediate and delayed free recall with preservation of yes/no or forced-choice recognition is often taken as the *sine qua non* of subcortical dementia (Brandt & Munro, 2001). However, several studies (Brandt et al., 1992; Kramer et al., 1988; Lang et al., 2000), including a recent meta-analysis (Montoya et al., 2006), have questioned whether this pattern really does characterize the memory impairment of HD. In addition, several studies have raised the possibility that the verbal memory difficulties of HD patients are actually secondary to one or more disorders of executive control (Lawrence et al., 1996; Pillon et al., 1993).

Less research has addressed the visuospatial memory impairment of HD patients. Hodges and colleagues (1990) found that HD patients who performed as poorly as AD patients on the immediate recall on the Visual Reproductions subtest of the Wechsler Memory Scale performed significantly better than AD patients on delayed recall. This suggests that rate of forgetting is relatively normal in HD, a conclusion reached earlier by Martone and colleagues (1986) and later by Davis and collaborators (1999).

Lawrence et al. (2000) observed that self-ordered spatial working memory is impaired in early HD while visual object working memory is not. They argued that this difference is primarily due to the greater load the former task places on the development and implementation of search strategies. These same authors also observed that the learning of both visuospatial patterns and spatial positions was impaired in HD but, as in other studies, rate of forgetting was normal. In addition, HD patients were impaired in the simultaneous condition of a match-to-sample task, leading the authors to

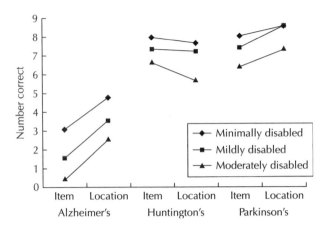

Figure 10–2. Delayed recall of objects (items) and their positions in space (locations) in Alzheimer's disease, Huntington's disease, and Parkinson's disease patients, stratified by level of functional disability. (From Brandt et al., 2005. Used with permission.)

speculate that the primary visuospatial memory deficit in HD was not in memory *per se*, but rather in response selection.

Recently, Brandt et al. (2005) reported that memory for the location of objects in space is more impaired than memory for the objects themselves in HD. Reminiscent of Lawrence et al.'s (2000) finding in working memory, this selective impairment was found across levels of disease severity, and was not seen in AD or PD (see Figure 10–2). It was speculated that this reflects a disruption of parietal lobe's input to the caudate nucleus in HD.

Motor Learning and Other Forms of Nondeclarative Memory

The basal ganglia of primates have extensive reciprocal connections to the motor and premotor areas of the frontal lobe (Alexander et al., 1986), regions that have been implicated in the planning of movements as well as their execution. These corticostriatal connections, as well as the striatum's intrinsic connectivity, have led to the appreciation that the basal ganglia are involved not solely in motor execution, but in motor learning as well (Graybiel et al., 1994).

Patients with HD are, in fact, impaired in acquiring many different motor and sensorimotor skills (Bondi & Kaszniak, 1991; Heindel et al., 1988; Knopman & Nissen, 1991; Martone et al., 1984; Willingham & Koroshetz, 1993).

They are clearly impaired in their ability to learn the pursuit rotor task (Butters, 1984; Heindel et al., 1988) and in learning to adjust their movements to compensate for changes in their body positions (Potegal, 1971) or the displacement of visual stimuli (Paulsen et al., 1993). These deficits are seen very early in the disease, even when baseline motor performance is controlled experimentally or statistically.

Whereas HD patients are impaired in learning the pursuit rotor task, they learn a mirror-reversed tracing task as well as nonpatients (Gabrieli et al., 1997). This has led to the proposal that the neostriatal structures that degenerate in HD are essential for the learning of repetitive motor sequences (as in the pursuit rotor), but not for the learning of new mappings between visual cues and movements (as in the mirror-tracing task) (Willingham et al., 1996). Studies using the serial reaction task to investigate procedural memory have yielded mixed results, with some finding performance deficits in HD (Knopman & Nissen, 1991; Kim et al., 2004; Willingham & Koroshetz, 1993) and others not, at least under some conditions (Brandt, 1994a; Brown et al., 2001). Differences in how task data are analyzed are responsible for some of the differences among studies.

Knowlton and colleagues (1996) extended the nondeclarative learning impairment of HD from the sensorimotor realm to the conceptual realm. They showed that HD patients are poor at learning a probabilistic classification task that, it is argued, requires the type of gradual, trial-by-trial habit acquisition, often outside of awareness, that is the province of the caudate nucleus. In contrast, HD patients were normal in learning an artificial grammar, a task proposed to be more dependent on neocortical mechanisms. Filoteo et al. (2001) also found HD patients to be impaired in learning different types of categorization rules.

Executive Control

The executive functions—those "general purpose control mechanisms that modulate the operation of various cognitive subprocesses and thereby regulate the dynamics of human cognition" (Miyake et al., 2000)—have traditionally been attributed to the prefrontal cortex. However, they are now appreciated as emerging from the integrated activity of cortico-thalamo-striatal circuits, with the caudate nucleus playing a particularly prominent role.

As described earlier, brief selective attention and working memory tasks, often embedded in mental status exams, are sensitive to impairments in executive control in HD (Brandt et al., 1988; Paulson et al., 1995; Rothlind & Brandt, 1993). In addition, well-known clinical tests of executive functioning, including the WCST, Stroop Color-Word Test, and the Tower of London Test, are all impaired in HD patients (Paulsen et al., 1996; Watkins et al., 2000), as are research tasks such as random number generation (Ho et al., 2004) and the CANTAB executive tasks (Lawrence et al., 1996).

There is growing evidence that the executive functions can be behaviorally and neuroanatomically dissociated. For example, lesions of the orbitofrontal and ventromedial prefrontal cortex appear to selectively impair performance on a gambling-type test of decision making, while lesions of the dorsolateral frontal cortex impair a problem-solving task requiring strategy development and working memory (Tower of London; Bechara et al., 1998; Rogers et al., 1998, 1999). Since the caudate nucleus receives its most prominent afferent projections from the dorsolateral prefrontal cortex, it might be expected that HD patients would be impaired earlier, or more severely, on tests of planning and working memory than on tests of risk-taking and decision making. In fact, Watkins and coworkers (2000) found just that. Twenty patients with early HD were impaired on the one-touch version of the Tower of London test of planning, while they performed like neurologically normal subjects on a decision-making task that involved predicting outcomes, and wagering on them, based on their probabilities of occurrence. However, Stout and colleagues (2001a) found HD patients (but not PD patients) to be impaired on the Iowa Gambling Task, the deficit related to difficulties learning the win/lose contingencies. Furthermore, Campbell and colleagues (2004) showed that the autonomic reaction (skin conductance response) displayed by normal subjects upon making a disadvantageous response that costs them money is absent in HD patients. These authors invoke Damasio's somatic marker hypothesis (Damasio, 1996; Tranel et al., 2000) and suggest that the frontostriatal dysfunction of HD renders these patients unable to use physiological cues of success and failure to guide decision making.

Emotional Processing

Even relatively early in the illness, HD patients have difficulty identifying emotions expressed in vocal prosody (Speedie et al., 1990) and in facial expressions (Jacobs et al., 1995; Montagne et al., 2006). One of the most provocative findings in recent years is that these patients may have a selective impairment in the perception of *disgust*. With few exceptions (e.g., Milders et al., 2003), studies have found that patients with HD are more impaired in the recognition of facial expressions of disgust than expressions of fear, anger, and sadness (Hayes et al., 2007; Sprengelmeyer et al., 1996, 1997; Wang et al., 2003). In several studies (Gray et al., 1997; Hennenlotter et al., 2004; Sprengelmeyer et al., 2006), this deficit has been found even in presymptomatic persons carrying the HD mutation. Hayes and colleagues (2007) maintain that this deficit in the perception of facial disgust represents a more general impairment in the *experience* of disgust, as it extends to the labeling of disgusting sounds, the classification of disgust-evoking pictures, the hedonic ratings of disgusting odors, and knowledge of the situational determinants of disgust. These investigators posit that the deficits reflect dysfunction in the insula, a cortical zone with prominent connections to the striatum (Chikama et al., 1997) and which serves as the somatosensory cortex for the olfactory, gustatory, and visceral senses. In support of this supposition, Hennenlotter et al. (2004) reported reduced BOLD responses from the left insula on fMRI among presymptomatic HD mutation carriers during the processing of facial expressions of disgust. This selective deficit in disgust processing in HD stands in contrast to the relatively selective deficit in fear processing among patients with amygdala pathology (Adolphs et al., 1999).

Longitudinal Studies of Huntington's Disease

Although HD is a progressive disorder, there have been relatively few studies of the course of its cognitive impairment. In an early study, Hodges et al. (1990) studied 14 HD patients, 14 AD patients, and 14 normal elderly subjects on two occasions, separated by 1 year. The only neuropsychological task on which HD patients displayed greater decline over time than AD patients was letter-guided wordlist generation (verbal fluency), a finding ascribed to more rapidly progressive retrieval deficits in HD. Snowden and colleagues (2001) reported that relatively automatic tasks with few cognitive demands (e.g., letter fluency, word-reading and color-naming trials of Stroop task) declined more over 1 year than those making greater cognitive demands (e.g., Stroop interference trial, WCST, Road Map Test of Directional Sense). The results were interpreted as reflecting the greater degeneration of striatal nuclei than associative neocortex. However, even for the most sensitive tests, the absolute change in performance over the 1-year study period was extremely modest. Ho and colleagues (2003) reported decline on all the attention and executive function tests administered to HD patients annually for 3–6 years. Timed psychomotor tests (e.g., part A of the Trail-Making Test, and the word-reading and color-naming trials of the Stroop task, but not the SDMT) were particularly sensitive to change. There was no

appreciable change over time on the WCST, probably due to the very strong practice effect on this task (Basso et al., 1999). Similar findings were reported by Bachoud-Lévi and colleagues (2001) using an overlapping test battery.

The role of CAG repeat length in accounting for rate of decline was examined by Brandt and colleagues (1996). At study entry, those HD patients with long mutations were younger and had earlier onsets, but they were no more neurologically or cognitively impaired than those with short mutations. However, the long-mutation group had greater decline over a 2-year period on a cognitive factor reflecting global mental ability. In a much larger sample from 43 sites participating in the Huntington's Study Group, Mahant et al. (2003) examined the correlates of cognitive and functional progression among 1,026 patients followed for an average of 2.7 years. Younger age of onset was associated with more rapid decline on the SDMT, but the effect was not significant for the Controlled Word Association Test or the Stroop Color-Word Test (the only other tests administered). Younger onset was also associated with faster functional decline. It was assumed by the authors that longer CAG repeat lengths underlie this more pernicious disease course in those with earlier onset, but no repeat length data are included in this report.

In one of the more comprehensive recent studies, Ward and colleagues (2006) studied the course of cognitive performance of 70 HD patients over 4 years (i.e., five annual assessments). Using random effects modeling, Ward and collaborators found that, as in many previous studies, the effects of time (visit) on test performance were modest. Statistically significant declines were found on the Trail-Making Test, Brief Test of Attention, Controlled Oral Word Association Test, Hopkins Verbal Learning Test-Revised (HVLT-R), word-reading and color-naming trials of the Stroop task, Developmental Test of Visual-Motor Integration, and WAIS-R Block Design, but there was no significant decline in the WCST, interference trial of the Stroop task or WAIS-R Vocabulary. Neurologic dysfunction (i.e., QNE scores), both at baseline and at each subsequent visit, was the most potent predictor of cognitive performance. In this study, CAG repeat length was not an independent predictor of cognitive decline once the effect of neurologic severity was considered.

Studies of Presymptomatic Huntington's Disease

Since the discovery of the trinucleotide expansion responsible for HD, there have been many attempts to determine whether people who carry the mutation, but are not yet clinically ill, can be distinguished from those without the mutation. Recent brain imaging studies have demonstrated structural and/or metabolic changes in the striatum or cerebral cortex in such individuals (Aylward et al., 2004; Ciarmiello et al., 2006; Feigin et al., 2001; Harris et al., 1999; Paulsen et al., 2004; Reading et al., 2004, 2005; Reynolds et al., 2002; Rosas et al., 2005; van Oostrom et al., 2005). In addition, subtle oculomotor and other movement peculiarities and neuropsychiatric changes have been reported in some mutation-positive individuals prior to the onset of clinical signs and symptoms sufficient for diagnosis (Blekher et al., 2006; Foroud et al., 1995; Golding et al., 2006; Hinton et al., 2007; Kirkwood et al., 1999, 2000; Snowden et al., 2002).

The search for changes in cognition among neurologically normal offsprings of HD patients carrying the gene mutation has met with mixed results. Several investigations have found no differences in neuropsychological test performance between those with and without the CAG expansion (Brandt et al., 2002; Campodonico et al., 1996, 1998; de Boo et al., 1997, 1999). Other investigations have found performance deficits associated with the HD mutation. Impairments have been reported in reaction time, psychomotor and processing speed (Kirkwood et al., 1999; Lemiere et al., 2002; Paulsen et al., 2001b; Snowden et al., 2002; Witjes-Ané et al., 2003), spatial analysis and constructional praxis (Rosenberg et al., 1995), verbal fluency (Lawrence et al., 1998), verbal memory (Hahn-Barma et al., 1998; Solomon et al., 2007), visuospatial memory (Wahlin et al., 2007), mental arithmetic (Kirkwood et al., 1999, 2000), and the perception of disgust (Gray et al., 1997), among others. Much of the discrepancy in findings among studies appears to hinge on the definition of "asymptomatic."

While some studies admitted only persons with no, or only very minimal, nonspecific neurological signs (Hahn-Barma et al., 1998; Paulsen et al., 2001b), others included subjects with "major signs consistent with HD" (Foroud et al., 1995; Kirkwood et al., 2000; Solomon et al., 2007; Witjes-Ané et al., 2003). When the samples in the latter studies are limited to those who are entirely free of even minor motor abnormalities, the cognitive impairments often disappear (Foroud et al., 1995; Solomon et al., 2007). Other factors likely contributing to discrepant research findings include differences in the variety and sensitivity of the specific cognitive tests employed and differences in statistical power to detect group differences (primarily due to sample size).

Brandt et al. (2002) analyzed the results of detailed cognitive testing from 203 neurologically normal offsprings of HD patients who were subsequently tested for the HD mutation. Seventy-five subjects had ≥37 CAG repeats (mutation-positive) and 128 had ≤30 repeats. The mutation-positive cases tended to have one or two very minor neurologic abnormalities, but the QNE scores of the two groups did not differ significantly and both remained well within normal limits. Neuropsychological tests that are very sensitive to early HD failed to detect a significant difference between mutation-positive and mutation-negative groups. Furthermore, among mutation-positive cases, those with shorter mutations (37–43 repeats) and those with longer mutations (≥44 repeats) did not differ on any of the 12 neuropsychological test variables. Proximity to clinical onset of HD was estimated for the mutation-positive cases by computing the difference between chronological age and projected age at onset. Projected age at onset was calculated from CAG repeat length and age at onset of the affected parent, based on a previously derived regression equation (Campodonico et al., 1996). Whereas the close-to-onset subgroup (mean = 4.0 years) and far-from-onset subgroup (mean = 13.1 years) did not differ in QNE score, statistically significant differences were found on 7 of the 12 neuropsychological test variables. The close-to-onset group was most severely impaired on the WAIS-R Block Design subtest ($p = .006$) and the SDMT ($p = .009$), as well as on all three trials of the Stroop Color-Word Test and nondominant hand performance of the Grooved Pegboard Test.

Snowden et al. (2002) also found that performance on psychomotor tasks begins a gradual decline several years prior to clinical onset, while memory performance declines precipitously around symptom onset. A similar conclusion can be drawn from the recent report by Solomon and colleagues (2007). Studying a very large cohort from the Huntington's Study Group, they compared 51 presymptomatic persons with the HD mutation to 423 without the mutation on the HVLT-R (Brandt & Benedict, 2001). Impairments were found on total learning (sum of words correctly recalled on three free-recall trials) and recognition discrimination (hits minus false-positives) only among those mutation-positives with at least minor, nonspecific motor abnormalities. Those who were absolutely symptom-free did not differ from mutation-negatives. Those with the genetic mutation who were judged closer to onset and those who had smaller striatal volumes tended to have poorer HVLT-R scores.

Most studies that have reported cognitive impairment in presymptomatic HD have found it in mutation-positive persons who were *judged* to be close to onset (e.g., Brandt et al., 2002; Paulsen et al., 2004; Wahlin et al., 2007). While informative, studies using estimated years to onset provide less definitive evidence of preclinical cognitive changes than longitudinal investigations of persons who actually develop symptoms of clinical HD (i.e., "convert") during the study period. Paulsen et al. (2001b) analyzed the limited neuropsychological test data available from the 36 centers participating in the Huntington's Study Group. They found that 70 of 260 mutation-positive subjects converted to HD within 2 years of baseline evaluation. These participants performed more poorly on the SDMT and all three trials of the Stroop Color-Word Test (but not a verbal fluency test) than those who did not convert within 2 years.

Brandt et al. (2008) studied longitudinally 237 people at risk who were clinically normal when first examined. Each participant underwent a quantified neurological exam, testing for the *CAG* repeat expansion, and neuropsychological testing. Twenty-one of these individuals tested positive for the mutation, subsequently developed HD symptoms and were diagnosed (i.e., converted) after an average of 7.9 years. These converters did not differ on any neuropsychological variable from the mutation-positive cases who did not convert during the study period ($N = 82$) or those who tested negative for the HD mutation ($N = 134$). However, the converters who developed diagnosable HD soon after genetic testing (between 1.8 and 8.6 years after baseline, with an average of 3.7 years) performed more poorly than those who converted later (between 8.7 and 18.3 years, with an average of 11.8 years) on the WCST. Although the groups have equivalent very low (i.e., normal) scores on the QNE, the "early" converters made more perseverative and nonperseverative errors and were overall less efficient in their problem solving. While the presence of deficits in selective domains of nonverbal cognition may portend earlier emergence of symptoms among those with the *huntingtin* mutation, the data are not yet sufficiently robust for use in counseling individual persons at risk.

Beyond the scope of this chapter, but certainly of great importance to clinicians working with HD patients and their families, is the rich psychological literature on the factors influencing the decision of whether to take the presymptomatic test (Codori et al., 1994; Quaid et al., 1987; Quaid & Morris, 1993), the ethical issues raised by such testing (Bates, 1981; Brandt, 1994b), and the potentially life-altering consequences of presymptomatic diagnosis (Codori & Brandt, 1994; Codori et al., 1997; Wiggins et al., 1992). What we have already learned from the study of this relatively rare neurodegenerative disorder will continue to serves as an important model as the "new genetics" plays an ever-increasing role in the practice of medicine and in neuropsychology.

Acknowledgment

Preparation of this chapter was supported by grant NS 16375 from the National Institute of Neurological Disorders and Stroke.

References

Adolphs, R., Tranel, D., Hamann, S., Young, A. W., Calder, A. J., Phelps, E. A., et al. (1999). Recognition of facial emotion in nine individuals with bilateral amygdala damage. *Neuropsychologia, 37,* 1111–1117.

Alexander, G. E., DeLong, M. R., & Strick, P. L. (1986). Parallel organization of functionally segregated circuits linking basal ganglia and cortex. *Annual Review of Neuroscience, 9,* 357–381.

Andresen, J. M., Gayán, J., Djoussé, L., Roberts, S., Brocklebank, D., Cherny, S. S., et al. (2006). The relationship between CAG repeat length and age of onset differs for Huntington's disease patients with juvenile onset and adult onset. *Annals of Human Genetics, 70,* 1–7.

Andrew, S. E., Goldberg, Y. P., Kremer, B., Telenius, H., Theilmann, J., Adam, S., et al. (1993). The relationship between trinucleotide (CAG) repeat length and clinical features of Huntington's disease. *Nature Genetics, 4,* 398–403.

Aron, A. R., Watkins, L., Sahakian, B. J., Monsell, S., Barker, R. A., & Robbins, T. W. (2003). Task-set switching deficits in early-stage Huntington's disease: Implications for basal ganglia function. *Journal of Cognitive Neuroscience, 15,* 629–642.

Aylward, E. H., Sparks, B. F., Field, K. M., Yallapragada, V., Shpritz, B. D., Rosenblatt, A., et al. (2004). Onset and rate of striatal atrophy in preclinical Huntington disease. *Neurology, 63,* 66–72.

Bachoud-Lévi, A. C., Maison, P., Bartolomeo, P., Boissé, M. F., Dalla Barba, G., Ergis, A. M., et al. (2001). Retest effects and cognitive decline in longitudinal follow-up of patients with early HD. *Neurology, 56,* 1052–1058.

Bamford, K. A., Caine, E. D., Kido, D. K., Cox, C., & Shoulson, I. (1995). A prospective evaluation of cognitive decline in early Huntington's disease: Functional and radiographic correlates. *Neurology, 45,* 1867–1873.

Basso, M. R., Bornstein, R. A., & Lang, J. M. (1999). Practice effects on commonly used measures of executive function across twelve months. *Clinical Neuropsychologist, 13,* 283–292.

Bates, M. (1981). Ethics of provocative test for Huntington's disease. *New England Journal of Medicine, 304,* 175–176.

Bechara, A., Damasio, H., Tranel, D., & Anderson, S. W. (1998). Dissociation of working memory from decision making within the human prefrontal cortex. *Journal of Neuroscience, 18,* 428–437.

Blekher, T., Johnson, S. A., Marshall, J., White, K., Hui, S., Weaver, M., et al. (2006). Saccades in presymptomatic and early stages of Huntington disease. *Neurology, 67,* 394–399.

Bondi, M. W., & Kaszniak, A. W. (1991). Implicit and explicit memory in Alzheimer's disease and Parkinson's disease. *Journal of Clinical and Experimental Neuropsychology, 13,* 339–358.

Brandt, J. (1991). Cognitive impairments in Huntington's disease: Insights into the neuropsychology of the striatum. In F. Boller & J. Grafman (Eds.), *Handbook of neuropsychology* (pp. 241–264). Amsterdam: Elsevier.

Brandt, J. (1994a). Cognitive investigations in Huntington's disease. In L. S. Cermak (Ed.), *Neuropsychological explorations of memory and cognition: Essays in honor of Nelson Butters* (pp. 135–146). New York: Plenum Press.

Brandt, J. (1994b). Ethical considerations in genetic testing: An empirical study of presymptomatic diagnosis of Huntington's disease. In K. W. M. Fulford, J. Soskice, & G. Gillett (Eds.), *Medicine and moral reasoning* (pp. 41–59). Cambridge: Cambridge University Press.

Brandt, J., & Benedict, R. H. B. (2001). *The Hopkins Verbal Learning Test—Revised professional manual.* Odessa, FL: Psychological Assessment Resources, Inc.

Brandt, J., & Butters, N. (1986). The neuropsychology of Huntington's disease. *Trends in Neuroscience, 9,* 118–120.

Brandt, J., & Bylsma, F. W. (1993). The dementia of Huntington's disease. In R. W. Parks, R. F. Zec, & R. W. Wilson (Eds.), *Neuropsychology of Alzheimer's disease and other dementias* (pp. 265–282). New York: Oxford University Press.

Brandt, J., Bylsma, F. W., Gross, R., Stine, O. C., Ranen, N., & Ross, C. A. (1996). Trinucleotide repeat length and clinical progression in Huntington's disease. *Neurology, 46,* 527–531.

Brandt, J., Corwin, J., & Krafft, L. (1992). Is verbal recognition memory really different in Alzheimer's and Huntington's disease? *Journal of Clinical and Experimental Neuropsychology, 14,* 773–784.

Brandt, J., Folstein, S. E., & Folstein, M. F. (1988). Differential cognitive impairment in Alzheimer disease and Huntington's disease. *Annals of Neurology, 23,* 555–561.

Brandt, J., Inscore, A., Ward, J., Shpritz, B., Rosenblatt, A., Margolis, R. L., et al. (2008). Neuropsychological deficits in Huntington's disease gene carriers and predictors of early "conversion." *Journal of Neuropsychiatry and Clinical Neurosciences,* in press.

Brandt, J., Leroi, I., O'Hearn, E., Rosenblatt, A., & Margolis, R. L. (2004). Cognitive impairments in cerebellar degeneration: a comparison with Huntington's disease. *Journal of Neuropsychiatry and Clinical Neurosciences, 16,* 176–184.

Brandt, J., & Munro, C. (2001). Memory in subcortical dementia. In A. Baddeley, B. Wilson, & M. Kopelman (Eds.), *Handbook of memory disorders, 2nd ed.* (pp. 591–614). London: Oxford University Press.

Brandt, J., Quaid, K. A, Folstein, S. E., Garber, P. A., Maestri, N. E., Abbott, M. H., et al. (1989). Presymptomatic diagnosis of delayed-onset disease with linked DNA markers: The experience in Huntington's disease. *Journal of the American Medical Association, 261*, 3108–3114.

Brandt, J., Shpritz, B., Codori, A. M., Margolis, R., & Rosenblatt, A. (2002). Neuropsychological manifestations of the genetic mutation for Huntington's disease in presymptomatic individuals. *Journal of the International Neuropsychological Society, 8*, 918–924.

Brandt, J. Shpritz, B., Munro, C. A., Marsh, L., & Rosenblatt, A. (2005). Differential impairment of spatial location memory in Huntington's disease. *Journal of Neurology, Neurosurgery and Psychiatry, 76*, 1516–1519.

Brandt, J., Strauss, M. E., Larus, J., Jensen, B., & Folstein, S. E. (1984). Clinical correlates of dementia and disability in Huntington's disease. *Journal of Clinical Neuropsychology, 6*, 401–412.

Brown, R. G., Redondo-Verge, L., Chacon, J. R., Lucas, M. L., & Channon, S. (2001). Dissociation between intentional and incidental sequence learning in Huntington's disease. *Brain, 124*, 2188–2202.

Burns, A., Folstein, S., Brandt, J., & Folstein, M. (1990). Clinical assessment of irritability, aggression, and apathy in Huntington's and Alzheimer's disease. *Journal of Nervous and Mental Disease, 178*, 20–26.

Butters, N. (1984). The clinical aspects of memory disorders: Contributions from experimental studies of amnesia and dementia. *Journal of Clinical Neuropsychology, 6*, 17–36.

Butters, N., Granholm, E., Salmon, D. P., Grant, I., & Wolfe, J. (1987). Episodic and semantic memory: A comparison of amnesic and demented patients. *Journal of Clinical and Experimental Neuropsychology, 9*, 479–497.

Butters, N., Sax, D., Montgomery, K., & Tarlow, S. (1978). Comparison of the neuropsychological deficits associated with early and advanced Huntington's disease. *Archives of Neurology, 35*, 585–589.

Butters, N., Wolfe, J., Granholm, E., & Martone, M. (1986). An assessment of verbal recall, recognition and fluency abilities in patients with Huntington's disease. *Cortex, 22*, 11–31.

Bylsma, F. W., Brandt, J., & Strauss, M. E. (1992). Personal and extrapersonal orientation in Huntington's disease and those at risk. *Cortex, 28*, 113–122.

Campbell, M. C., Stout, J. C., & Finn, P. R. (2004). Reduced autonomic responsiveness to gambling task losses in Huntington's disease. *Journal of* the International Neuropsychological Society, 10, 239–245.

Campodonico, J. R., Aylward, E., Codori, A. M., Young, C., Krafft, L., Magdalinski, M., et al. (1998). When does Huntington's disease begin? *Journal of the International Neuropsychological Society, 4*, 467–473.

Campodonico, J. R., Codori, A. M., & Brandt, J. (1996). Neuropsychological stability over two years in asymptomatic carriers of the Huntington's disease mutation. *Journal of Neurology, Neurosurgery, and Psychiatry, 61*, 621–624.

Chan, A. S., Butters, N., Paulsen, J. S., Salmon, D. P., Swenson, M. R., & Maloney, L. T. (1993). An assessment of the semantic network in patients with Alzheimer's disease. *Journal of Cognitive Neuroscience, 5*, 254–261.

Chatterjee, A., Anderson, K. E., Moskowitz, C. B., Hauser, W. A., & Marder, K. S. (2005). A comparison of self-report and caregiver assessment of depression, apathy, and irritability in Huntington's disease. *Journal of Neuropsychiatry and Clinical Neurosciences, 17*, 378–383.

Chikama, M., McFarland, N. R., Amaral, D. G., & Haber, S. N. (1997). Insular cortical projections to functional regions of the striatum correlate with cortical cytoarchitechtonic organization in the primate. *Journal of Neuroscience, 1997, 17*, 9686–9705.

Ciarmiello, A., Cannella, M., Lastoria, S., Simonelli, M., Frati, L., Rubinsztein, D. C., et al. (2006). Brain white-matter volume loss and glucose hypometabolism precede the clinical symptoms of Huntington's disease. *Journal of Nuclear Medicine, 47*, 215–222.

Claes, S., Van Zand, K., Legius, E., Dom, R., Malfroid, M., Baro, F., et al. (1995). Correlations between triplet repeat expansion and clinical features in Huntington's disease. *Archives of Neurology, 113*, 749–753.

Codori, A. M., & Brandt, J. (1994). Psychological costs and benefits of predictive testing for Huntington's disease. *American Journal of Medical Genetics (Neuropsychiatric Genetics), 54*, 174–184.

Codori, A. M., Hanson, R., & Brandt, J. (1994). Self-selection in predictive testing for Huntington's disease. *American Journal of Medical Genetics (Neuropsychiatric Genetics), 54*, 167–173.

Codori, A. M., Slavney, P. R., Young, C., Miglioretti, D. L., & Brandt, J. (1997). Predictors of Psychological adjustment to genetic testing for Huntington's disease. *Health Psychology, 16*, 36–50.

Damasio, A. R. (1996). The somatic marker hypothesis and the possible functions of the prefrontal cortex. *Philosophical Transactions of the Royal Society of London (Biol.)*, 1413–1420.

David, A. S., Jeste, D. V., Folstein, M. F., & Folstein, S. E. (1987). Voluntary movement dysfunction in Huntington's disease and tardive dyskinesia. *Acta Neurologica Scandinavica, 75*, 130–139.

Davis, J. D., Filoteo, J. V., Kesner, R. P., & Roberts, J. W. (2003). Recognition memory for hand positions and spatial locations in patients with Huntington's disease: Differential visuospatial memory impairment? *Cortex, 39*, 239–253.

Davis, J. D., Filoteo, J. V., Rilling, L. M., & Roberts, J. W. (1999). Rate of forgetting for visual spatial information in patients with Huntington's disease. *Archives of Clinical Neuropsychology, 14*, 635–636.

de Boo, G. M., Tibben, A., Hermans, J., Jennekens-Schinkel, A., Maat-Kievit, A., & Roos, R. A. C. (1999). Memory and learning are not impaired in presymptomatic individuals with an increased risk of Huntington's disease. *Journal of Clinical and Experimental Neuropsychology, 21*, 831–836.

de Boo, G. M., Tibben, A., Lanser, J. B., Jennekens-Schinkel, A., Hermans, J., Maat-Kievit, A., et al. (1997). Early cognitive and motor symptoms in identified carriers of the gene for Huntington disease. *Archives of Neurology, 54*, 1353–1357.

Delis, D. C., Massman, P. J., Butters, N., Salmon, D. P., Cermak, L. S., & Kramer, J. H. (1991). Profiles of demented and amnesic patients on the California Verbal Learning Test: Implications for the assessment of memory disorders. *Psychological Assessment, 3*, 19–26.

Duyao, M. P., Ambrose, C. M., & Myers, R. H. (1993). Trinucleotide repeat length: instability and age of onset in Huntington's disease. *Nature Genetics, 4*, 387–392.

Fedio, P., Cox, C. S., Neophytides, A., Canal-Frederick, G., & Chase, T. N. (1979). Neuropsychological profile of Huntington's disease. In T. N. Chase, N. S. Wexler, & A. Barbeau (Eds.), *Advances in neurology, Vol. 23: Huntington's disease* (pp. 239–255). New York: Raven Press.

Feigin, A., Leenders, K. L., Moeller, J. R., Missimer, J., Kuenig, G., Spetsieris, P., et al. (2001). Metabolic network abnormalities in early Huntington's disease: An ¹⁸F fluorodeoxyglucose PET study. *Journal of Nuclear Medicine, 42*, 1591–1595.

Filoteo, J. V., Delis, D. C., Roman, M., Demedura, T., Ford, E., Butters, N., et al. (1995). Visual attention and perception in patients with Huntington's disease: Comparisons with other subcortical and cortical dementias. *Journal of Clinical and Experimental Neuropsychology, 17*, 654–667.

Filoteo, J. V., Maddox, W. T., & Davis, J. D. (2001). A possible role of the striatum in linear and nonlinear category learning: Evidence from patients with Huntington's disease. *Behavioral Neuroscience, 115*, 786–798.

Folstein, M. F., Folstein, S. E., & McHugh, P. R. (1975). "Mini-Mental State": A practical method for grading the cognitive state of patients for the clinician. *Journal of Psychiatric Research, 2*, 189–198.

Folstein, S. E. (1989). *Huntington's disease: A disorder of families.* Baltimore, MD: Johns Hopkins University Press.

Folstein, S. E., Abbott, M. H., Chase, G. A., Jensen, B. A., & Folstein, M. F. (1983). The association of affective disorder with Huntington's Disease in a case series and in families. *Psychological Medicine, 13*, 537–542.

Folstein, S. E., Jensen, B., Leigh, R. J., & Folstein, M. F. (1983). The measurement of abnormal movement: Methods developed for Huntington disease. *Neurobehavioral Toxicology and Teratology, 5*, 605–609.

Foroud, T., Siemers, E., Kleindorfer, B. S., Bill, D. J., Hodes, M. E., Norton, J. A., et al. (1995). Cognitive scores in carriers of Huntington's disease gene compared to noncarriers. *Annals of Neurology, 37*, 657–664.

Gabrieli, J. D., Stebbins, G. T., Singh, J., Willingham, D. B., & Goetz, C. G. (1997). Intact mirror-tracing and impaired rotary-pursuit skill learning in patient's with Huntington's disease: Evidence for dissociable memory systems in skill learning. *Neuropsychology, 11*, 272–281.

Georgiou, N., Phillips, J. G., Bradshaw, J. L., Cunnington, R., & Chiu, E. (1997). Impairments of movement kinematics in patients with Huntington's disease: A comparison with and without a concurrent task. *Movement Disorders, 12*, 386–396.

Golding, C. V., Danchaivijitr, C., Hodgson, T. L., Tabrizi, S. J., & Kennard, C. (2006). Identification of an oculomotor biomarker of preclinical Huntington disease. *Neurology, 67*, 485–487.

Gómez-Tortosa, E., del Barrio, A., Barroso, T., & García Ruiz, P. J. (1996). Visual processing disorders in patients with Huntington's disease and asymptomatic carriers. *Journal of Neurology, 243*, 286–292.

Gray, J. M., Young, A. W., Barker, W. A., Curtis, A., & Gibson, D. (1997). Impaired recognition of disgust in Huntington's disease carriers. *Brain, 120*, 2029–2038.

Graybiel, A. M., Aosaki, T., Flaherty, A. W., & Kimura, M. (1994). The basal ganglia and adaptive motor control. *Science, 265*, 1826–1831.

Gusella, J. F., Wexler, N. S., Conneally, P. M., Naylor, S. L., Anderson, M. A., Tanzi, R. E., et al. (1983). A polymorphic DNA marker genetically linked to Huntington's disease. *Nature, 306*, 234–238.

Hahn-Barma, V., Deweer, B., Durr, A., Dode, C., Feingold, J., Pillon, B., et al. (1998). Are cognitive changes the first symptoms of Huntington's disease? A study of gene carriers. *Journal of Neurology, Neurosurgery and Psychiatry, 64*, 172–177.

Hamilton, J. M., Salmon, D. P. Corey-Bloom, J., Gamst, A., Paulsen, J. S., Jerkins, S., et al. (2003). Behavioral abnormalities contribute to functional decline in Huntington's disease. *Journal of Neurology, Neurosurgery and Psychiatry, 74*, 120–122.

Harper, P. S. (1996). *Huntington disease.* London: W.B. Saunders.

Harris, G. J., Codori, A. M., Lewis, R. F., Schmidt, E., Bedi, A., & Brandt, J. (1999). Reduced basal ganglia blood flow and volume in presymptomatic, gene-tested persons at risk for Huntington's disease. *Brain, 122*, 1667–1678.

Hayden, M. R. (1981). *Huntington's chorea.* New York: Springer-Verlag.

Hayes, C. J., Stevenson, R. J., & Coltheart, M. (2007). Disgust and Huntington's disease. *Neuropsychologia, 45*, 1135–1151.

Hefter, H., Hömberg, V., Lange, H. W., & Freund, H. (1987). Impairment of rapid movement in Huntington's disease. *Brain, 110*, 585–612.

Heindel, W. C., Butters, N., & Salmon, D. P. (1988). Impaired learning of a motor skill in patients with Huntington's disease. *Behavioral Neuroscience, 102*, 141–147.

Hennenlotter, A., Schroeder, U., Erhard, P., Haslinger, B., Stahl, R., Weindl, A., et al. (2004). Neural correlates associated with impaired disgust processing in pre-symptomatic Huntington's disease. *Brain, 127*, 1446–1453.

Henry, J. D., Crawford, J. R., & Phillips, L. H. (2005). A eta-analytic review of verbal fluency deficits in Huntington's disease. *Neuropsychology, 19*, 243–252.

Hinton, S. C., Paulsen, J. S., Hoffman, R. G., Reynolds, N. C., Zimbelman, J. L., & Rao, S. M. (2007). Motor timing variability increases in preclinical Huntington's disease patients as estimated onset of motor symptoms approaches. *Journal of the International Neuropsychological Society, 13*, 539–543.

Ho, A. K., Sahakian, B. J., Brown, R. G., Barker, R. A., Hodges, J. R., Ane, M. N., et al. (2003). Profile of cognitive progression in early Huntington's disease. *Neurology, 61*, 1702–1706.

Ho, A. K., Sahakian, B. J., Robbins, T. W., & Barker, R. A. (2004). Random number generation in patients with symptomatic and presymptomatic Huntington's disease. *Cognitive and Behavioral Neurology, 17*, 208–212.

Ho, A. K., Sahakian, B. J., Robbins, T. W., Barker, R. A., Rosser, A. E., & Hodges, J. R. (2002). Verbal fluency in Huntington's disease: A longitudinal analysis of

phonemic and semantic clustering and switching. *Neuropsychologia, 40*, 1277–1284.

Hodges, J. R., Salmon, D. P., & Butters, N. (1990). Differential impairment of semantic and episodic memory in Alzheimer's and Huntington's diseases: A controlled prospective study. *Journal of Neurology, Neurosurgery and Psychiatry, 53*, 1089–1095.

Hodges, J. R., Salmon, D. P., & Butters, N. (1991). The nature of the naming deficit in Alzheimer's and Huntington's disease. *Brain, 114*, 1547–1558.

Huntington's Disease Collaborative Research Group. (1993). A novel gene containing a trinucleotide repeat that is expanded and unstable on Huntington's disease chromosomes. *Cell, 72*, 971–983.

Illarioshkin, S. N., Igarashi, S., Onodera, O., Markova, E. D., Nikolskaya, N. N., Tanaka, H., et al. (1994). Trinucleotide repeat length and rate of progression of Huntington's disease. *Annals of Neurology, 36*, 630–635.

Jacobs, D. H., Shuren, J., & Heilman, K. M. (1995). Impaired perception of facial identity and facial affect in Huntington's disease. *Neurology, 46*, 1217–1218.

Josiassen, R. C., Curry, L., Roemer, R. A., DeBease, C., & Mancall, E. L. (1982). Patterns of intellectual deficit in Huntington's disease. *Journal of Clinical Neuropsychology, 4*, 173–183.

Kieburtz, K., MacDonald, M., Shih, C., Feigin, A., Steinberg, K., Bordwell, K., et al. (1994). Trinucleotide repeat length and progression of illness in Huntington's disease. *Journal of Medical Genetics, 31*, 872–874.

Kim, J. S., Reading, S. A. J., Brashers-Krug, T., Calhoun, V. D., Ross, C. A., & Pearlson, G. D. (2004). Functional MRI study of a serial reaction time task in Huntington's disease. *Psychiatry Research: Neuroimaging, 131*, 23–30.

Kirkwood, S. C., Siemers, E., Stout, J. C., Hodes, M. E., Conneally, P. M., Christian, J C., et al. (1999). Longitudinal cognitive and motor changes among presymptomatic Huntington disease gene carriers. *Archives of Neurology, 56*, 563–568.

Kirkwood, S. C., Siemers, E., Hodes, M. E., Conneally, P. M., Christian, J. C., & Foroud, T. (2000). Subtle changes among presymptomatic carriers of the Huntington's disease gene. *Journal of Neurology, Neurosurgery and Psychiatry, 69*, 773–779.

Knopman, D., & Nissen, M. J. (1991). Procedural learning is impaired in Huntington's disease: Evidence from the serial reaction time task. *Neuropsychologia, 29*, 245–254.

Knowlton, B. J., Squire, L. R., Paulsen, J. S., Swerdlow, N. R., Swenson, M., & Butters, N. (1996). Dissociations within nondeclarative memory in Huntington's disease. *Neuropsychology, 10,* 538–548.

Kramer, J. H., Delis, D. C., Blusewicz, M. J., Brandt, J., Ober, B. A., & Strauss, M. (1988). Verbal memory errors in Alzheimer's and Huntington's dementias. *Developmental Neuropsychology, 4,* 1–15.

Lang, C. J. G., Majer, M., Balan, P., & Reischies, F. M. (2000). Recall and recognition in Huntington's disease. *Archives of Clinical Neuropsychology, 15,* 361–371.

Lawrence, A. D., Hodges, J. R., Rosser, A. E., Kershaw, A., ffrench-Constant, C., Rubinsztein, D. C., et al. (1998). Evidence for specific cognitive deficits in preclinical Huntington's disease. *Brain, 121,* 1329–1341.

Lawrence, A. D., Sahakian, B. J., Hodges, J. R., Rosser, Lange, K. W., & Robbins, T. W. (1996). Executive and mnemonic functions in early Huntington's disease. *Brain, 119,* 1633–1645.

Lawrence, A. D., Sahakian, B. J., & Robbins, T. W. (1998). Cognitive functions and corticostriatal circuits: insights from Huntington's disease. *Trends in Cognitive Science, 2,* 379–388.

Lawrence, A. D., Watkins, L. H. A., Sahakian, B. J., Hodges, J. R., & Robbins, T. W. (2000). Visual object and visuospatial cognition in Huntington's disease: Implications for information processing in corticostraial circuits. *Brain, 123,* 1349–1369.

Lemiere, J., Decruyenaere, M., Evers-Kiebooms, G., Vandenbussche, E., & Dom, R. (2002). Longitudinal study evaluating neuropsychological changes in so-called asymptomatic carriers of the Huntington's disease mutation after 1 year. *Acta Neurologica Scandinavica, 106,* 131–141.

Mahant, N., McCusker, E. A., Byth, K., Graham, S., & the Huntington Study Group. (2003). Huntington's disease: Clinical correlates of disability and progression. *Neurology, 61,* 1085–1092.

Martone, M., Butters, N., & Trauner, D. (1986). Some analyses of forgetting of pictorial material in amnesic and demented patients. *Journal of Clinical and Experimental Neuropsychology, 8,* 161–178.

Martone, M., Butters, N., Payne, M., Becker, J., & Sax, D. S. (1984). Dissociations between skill learning and verbal recognition in amnesia and dementia. *Archives of Neurology, 41,* 965–970.

Mattis, S. (1988). *Dementia Rating Scale Professional Manual.* Odessa, FL: Psychological Assessment Resources, Inc.

Mayeux, R., Stern, Y., Herman, A., Greenbaum, L., & Fahn, S. (1986). Correlates of early disability in Huntington disease. *Annals of Neurology, 20,* 727–731.

McHugh, P. R., & Folstein, M. F. (1975). Psychiatric syndromes of Huntington's chorea: A clinical

and phenominological study. In D. F. Benson & D. Blumer (Eds.), *Psychiatric aspects of neurologic disease* (pp. 267–286). New York: Grune and Stratton.

Meissen, G., Myers, R., Mastromauro, C., Koroshetz, W., Klinger, K., Farrer, L. et al. (1988). Predictive testing for Huntington's disease with use of a linked DNA marker. *New England Journal of Medicine, 318,* 535–542.

Milders, M., Crawford, J. R., Lamb, A., & Simpson, S. A. (2003). Differential deficits in expression recognition in gene-carriers and patients with Huntington's disease. *Neuropsychologia, 41,* 1484–1492.

Miyake, A., Friedman, N. P., Emerson, M. J., Witzki, A. H., & Howerter, A. (2000). The unity and diversity of executive functions and their contributions to complex "frontal lobe" tasks: A latent variable analysis. *Cognitive Psychology, 41,* 49–100.

Mohr, E., Brouwers, P., Claus, J. J., Mann, U. M., Fedio, P., & Chase, T. N. (1991). Visuospatial cognition in Huntington's disease. *Movement Disorders, 6,* 127–132.

Mohr, E., Claus, J. J., Jules, J., & Brouwers, P. (1997). Basal ganglia disease and visuospatial cognition: Are these disease-specific impairments? *Behavioural Neurology, 10,* 67–75.

Montagne, B., Kessels, R. P. C., Kammers, M. P. M., Kingma, E., de Haan, E. H. F., Roos, R. A. C., et al. (2006). Perception of emotional facial expressions at different intensities in early-symptomatic Huntington's disease. *European Neurology, 55,* 151–154.

Montoya, A., Pelletier, M., Menear, M., Duplessis, E., Richer, F., & Lepage, M. (2006). Episodic memory impairment in Huntington's disease: A meta-analysis. *Neuropsychologia, 44,* 1984–1994.

Müller, S. V., Jung, A., Preinfalk, J., Kolbe, H., Ridao-Alonso, M., Dengler, R., et al. (2002). Disturbance of "extrinsic alertness" in Huntington's disease. *Journal of Clinical and Experimental Neuropsychology, 24,* 517–526.

Murray, L. L., & Lenz, L. P. (2001). Productive syntax abilities in Huntington's and Parkinson's diseases. *Brain and Cognition, 46,* 213–219.

Murray, L. L., & Stout, J. C. (1999). Discourse comprehension in Huntington's and Parkinson's diseases. *American Journal of Speech-Language Pathology, 8,* 137–148.

Nance, M. A., & Myers, R. H. (2001). Juvenile onset Huntington's disease—clinical and research perspectives. *Mental Retardation and Developmental Disabilities Research Reviews, 7,* 153–157.

Nehl, C., Paulsen, J. S., & the Huntington Study Group. (2004). Cognitive and psychiatric aspects of Huntington's disease contribute to functional capacity. *Journal of Nervous and Mental Disease, 192*, 72–74.

Paulsen, J. S., Butters, N., Salmon, D. P., Heindel, W. C., & Swenson, M. R. (1993). Prism adaptation in Alzheimer's and Huntington's disease. *Neuropsychology, 7*, 73–81.

Paulsen, J. S., Como, P., Rey, G., Bylsma, F., Jones, R., Saint-Cyr, J. et al. (1996). The clinical utility of the Stroop test in a multicenter study of Huntington's disease. *Journal of the International Neuropsychological Society, 2*, 35.

Paulsen, J. S., Nehl, C., Hoth, K. F., Kanz, J. E., Benjamin, M., Conybeare, R., et al. (2005). Depression and stages of Huntington's disease. *Journal of Neuropsychiatry and Clinical Neurosciences, 17*, 496–502.

Paulsen, J. S., Ready, R. E., Hamilton, J. M., Mega, M. S., & Cummings, J. L. (2001a). Neuropsychiatric aspects of Huntington's disease. *Journal of Neurology, Neurosurgery and Psychiatry, 71*, 310–314.

Paulsen, J. S., Zhao, H., Stout, J. C., Brinkman, R. R., Guttman, M., Ross, C. A., et al. (2001b). Clinical markers of early disease in persons near onset of Huntington's disease. *Neurology, 57*, 658–662.

Paulsen, J. S., Zimbelman, J. L., Hinton, S. C., Langbehn, D. R., Leveroni, C. L., Benjamin, M. L., et al. (2004). fMRI biomarker of early neuronal dysfunction in presymptomatic Huntington's Disease. *American Journal of Neuroradiology, 25*, 1715–1721.

Paulsen, J. S., Butters, N., Sadek, J. R., Johnson, S. A., Salmon, D. P., Swerdlow, N. R., et al. (1995). Distinct cognitive profiles of cortical and subcortical dementia in advanced illness. *Neurology, 45*, 951–956.

Pillon, B., Deweer, B., Agid, Y., & Dubois, B. (1993). Explicit memory in Alzheimer's, Huntington's, and Parkinson's diseases. *Archives of Neurology, 50*, 374–379.

Potegal, M. (1971). A note on spatial-motor deficits in patients with Huntington's disease: A test of a hypothesis. *Neuropsychologia, 9*, 233–235.

Quaid, K. A., Brandt, J., & Folstein, S. E. (1987). The decision to be tested for Huntington's disease. *Journal of the American Medical Association, 257*, 3362.

Quaid, K. A., & Morris, M. (1993). Reluctance to undergo predictive testing: The case of Huntington's disease. *American Journal of Medical Genetics, 45*, 41–45.

Randolph, C., Braun, A. R., Goldberg, T. E., & Chase, T. (1993). Semantic fluency in Alzheimer's, Parkinson's and Huntington's disease: dissociation of storage and retrieval failures. *Neuropsychology, 7*, 82–88.

Ranen, N. G., Stine, O. C., Abbott, M. H., Sherr, M., Codori, A. M., Franz, M. L., et al. (1995). Anticipation and instability of IT-15 (CAG) repeats in parent–offspring pairs with Huntington disease. *American Journal of Human Genetics, 57*, 593–602.

Reading, S., Dziorny, A. C., Peroutka, L. A., Schrieber, M., Gourley, L. M., Yallapragada, V., et al. (2004). Functional brain changes in presymptomatic Huntington's disease. *Annals of Neurology, 55*, 879–883.

Reading, S. A. J., Yassa, M. A., Bakker, A., Dziorny, A. C., Gourley, L. M., Yallapragada, V., et al. (2005). Regional white matter change in pre-symptomatic Huntington's disease: A diffusion tensor imaging study. *Psychiatric Research: Neuroimaging, 140*, 55–62.

Reynolds, N. C., Jr., Hellman, R. S., Tikofsky, R. S., Prost, R. W., Mark, L. P., Elejalde, B. R., et al. (2002). Single photon emission computerized tomography (SPECT) in detecting neurodegeneration in Huntington's disease. *Nuclear Medicine Commununications, 23*, 13–18.

Rich, J. B., Troyer, A. K., Bylsma, F. W., & Brandt, J. (1999). Longitudinal analysis of phonemic clustering and switching during word list generation in Huntington's disease. *Neuropsychology, 13*, 525–531.

Rogers, R. D., Owen, A. M., Middleton, H. C., Williams, E. J., Pickard, J. D., Sahakian, B. J., et al. (1999). Choosing between small, likely rewards and large, unlikely rewards activates inferior and orbital prefrontal cortex. *Journal of Neuroscience, 20*, 9029–9038.

Rogers, R. D., Sahakian, B. J., Hodges, J. R., Polkey, C. E., Kennard, C., & Robbins, T. W. (1998). Dissociating executive mechanisms of task control following frontal lobe damage and Parkinson's disease. *Brain, 121*, 815–842.

Rohrer, D., Salmon, D. P., Wixted, J. T., & Paulsen, J. S. (1999). The disparate effects of Alzheimer's disease and Huntington's disease on semantic memory. *Neuropsychology, 13*, 381–388.

Roman, M. J., Delis, D. C., Filoteo, J. V., Demedura, T. L., Paulsen, J., Swerdlow, N. R., et al. (1998). Is there a "subcortical" profile of attentional dysfunction? A comparison of patients with Huntington's and Parkinson's diseases on a global–local focused attention task. *Journal of Clinical and Experimental Neuropsychology, 20*, 873–884.

Rosas, H. D., Hevelone, N. D., Zaleta, A. K., Greve, D. N., Salat, D. H., & Fischl, B. (2005). Regional cortical thinning in preclinical Huntington disease and its relationship to cognition. *Neurology, 65*, 745–747.

Rosenberg, N. K., Sorensen, S. A., & Christensen, A. L. (1995). Neuropsychological characteristics of Huntington's disease carriers: a double blind study. *Journal of Medical Genetics, 32,* 600–604.

Rosenblatt, A., Margolis, R. L., Becher, M. W., Aylward, E., Franz, M. L., Sherr, M., et al. (1998). Does CAG repeat number predict rate of pathologic changes in Huntington's disease? *Annals of Neurology, 44,* 708–709.

Rothlind, J. C., & Brandt, J. (1993). A brief assessment of frontal and subcortical functions in dementia. *Journal of Neuropsychiatry and Clinical Neurosciences, 5,* 73–77.

Rothlind, J. C., Bylsma, F. W., Peyser, C., Folstein, S. E., & Brandt, J. (1993). Cognitive and motor correlates of everyday functioning in early Huntington's disease. *Journal of Nervous and Mental Disease, 181,* 194–199.

Saint-Cyr, J. A. (2003). Frontal-striatal circuit functions: Context, sequence, and consequence. *Journal of the International Neuropsychological Society, 9,* 103–128.

Salmon, D. P., Kwo-on-Yuen, P. F., Heindel, W. C., Butters, N., & Thal, L. J. (1989). Differentiation of Alzheimer's disease and Huntington's disease with the Dementia Rating Scale. *Archives of Neurology, 46,* 1204–1208.

Sax, D. S., O'Donnell, B., Butters, N., Menzer, L., Montgomery, K., & Kayne, H. L. (1983). Computed tomographic, neurologic, and neuropsychologic correlates of Huntington's disease. *International Journal of Neuroscience, 18,* 21–36.

Schretlen, D. (1997). *Brief Test of Attention Professional Manual.* Odessa, FL: Psychological Assessment Resources, Inc.

Schretlen, D., Brandt, J., & Bobholz, J. H. (1996). Validation of the Brief Test of Attention in patients with Huntington's disease and amnesia. *The Clinical Neuropsychologist 10,* 90–95.

Shelton, P. A., & Knopman, D. S. (1991). Ideomotor apraxia in Huntington's disease. *Archives of Neurology, 48,* 35–41.

Snowden, J., Craufurd, D., Griffiths, H., Thompson, J., & Neary, D. (2001). Longitudinal evaluation of cognitive disorder in Huntington's disease. *Journal of the International Neuropsychological Society, 7,* 33–44.

Snowden, J. S., Craufurd, D., Thompson, J., & Neary, D. (2002). Psychomotor, executive, and memory function in preclinical Huntington's disease. *Journal of Clinical and Experimental Neuropsychology, 24,* 133–145.

Solomon, A. C., Stout, J. C., Johnson, S. A., Langbehn, D. R., Aylward, E. A., Brandt, J., et al. (2007). Verbal episodic memory declines prior to diagnosis in Huntington's disease. *Neuropsychologia, 45,* 1767–1776.

Speedie, L. J., Brake, N., Folstein, S. E., & Heilman, K. M. (1990). Comprehension of prosody in Huntington's disease. *Journal of neurology, Neurosurgery, and Psychiatry, 53,* 607–610.

Sprengelmeyer, R., Lange, H., & Homberg, V. (1995). The pattern of attentional deficits in Huntington's disease. *Brain, 118,* 145–152.

Sprengelmeyer, R., Schroeder, U., Young, A. W., & Epplen, J. T. (2006). Disgust in pre-clinical Huntington's disease: A longitudinal study. *Neuropsychologia, 44,* 518–533.

Sprengelmeyer, R., Young, A. W., Calder, A. J., Karnat, A., Lange, H., Hömberg, V., et al. (1996). Loss of disgust: Perception of faces and emotions in Huntington's disease. *Brain, 119,* 1647–1665.

Sprengelmeyer, R., Young, A. W., Sprengelmeyer, A., Calder, A. J. Rowland, D., Perrett, D., et al. (1997). Recognition of facial expressions: Selective impairment of specific emotions in Huntington's disease. *Cognitive Neuropsychology, 14,* 839–879.

Stine, O. C., Pleasant, N., Franz, M. L., Abbott, M. H., Folstein, S. E., & Ross, C. A. (1993). Correlation between onset age of Huntington's disease and the length of the trinucleotide repeat in IT-15. *Human Molecular Genetics, 2,* 1547–1549.

Stout, J. C., Rodawalt, W. C., & Siemers, E. R. (2001a). Risky decision making in Huntington's disease. *Journal of the International Neuropsychological Society, 7,* 92–101.

Stout, J. C., Wylie, S. A., Simone, P. M., & Siemers, E. R. (2001b). Influence of competing distractors on response selection in Huntington's disease and Parkinson's disease. *Cognitive Neuropsychology, 18,* 643–653.

Strauss, M. E., & Brandt, J. (1986). Attempt at pre-clinical identification of Huntington's disease using the WAIS. *Journal of Clinical and Experimental Neuropsychology, 8,* 210–218.

Tranel, D., Bechara, A., & Damasio, A. R. (2000). Decision making and the somatic marker hypothesis. In M. S. Gazzaniga (Ed.), *The new cognitive neurosciences, 2nd edition* (pp. 1047–1061). Cambridge, MA: MIT Press.

Troyer, A. K., Moscovitch, M., Winocur, G., Alexander, M. P., & Stuss, D. (1998). Clustering and switching on verbal fluency: The effects of focal frontal and temporal lobe lesions. *Neuropsychologia, 36,* 449–504.

van Oostrom, J. C. H., Maguire, R. P., Verschuuren-Bemelmans, C. C., Veenma-van der Duin, L., Pruim, J., Roos, R. A. C., et al. (2005). Striatal dopamine D2 receptors, metabolism, and volume in preclinical Huntington disease. *Neurology, 65,* 941–943.

van Zomeran, A. H., & Brouwer, W. H. (1994). *Clinical neuropsychology of attention.* New York: Oxford University Press.

Wahlin, T. B. R., Lundin, A., & Dear, K. (2007). Early cognitive deficits in Swedish gene carriers of Huntington's disease. *Neuropsychology, 21,* 31–44.

Wang, K., Hoosain, R., Yang, R. M., Meng, Y., & Wang, C. Q. (2003). Impairment of recognition of disgust in Chinese with Huntington's or Wilson's disease. *Neuropsychologia, 41,* 527–537.

Ward, J., Sheppard, J. M., Shpritz, B., Margolis, R. L., Rosenblatt, A., & Brandt, J. (2006). A four-year prospective study of cognitive functioning in Huntington's disease. *Journal of the International Neuropsychological Society, 12,* 445–454.

Warrington, K. K., & James, M. (1991). *Visual object and space perception battery.* Bury St. Edmunds, U.K.: Thames Valley Test Company.

Watkins, L. H., Rogers, R. D., Lawrence, A. D., Sahakian, B. J., Rosser, A. E., & Robbins, T. W. (2000). Impaired planning but intact decision-making in early Huntington's disease: Implications for specific frontal-striatal pathology. *Neuropsychologia, 38,* 1112–1125.

Wiggins, S., Whyte, P., Huggins, M., Adams, S., Theilmann, J., Bloch, M., et al. (1992). The psychological consequences of predictive testing for Huntington's disease. *New England Journal of Medicine, 327,* 1401–1405.

Willingham, D. B., & Koroshetz, W. J. (1993). Evidence of dissociable motor skills in Huntington's disease patients. *Psychobiology, 21,* 173–182.

Willingham, D. B., Koroshetz, W. J., & Peterson, E. W. (1996). Motor skills have diverse neural bases: Spared and impaired skill acquisition in Huntington's disease. *Neuropsychology, 10,* 315–321.

Witjes-Ané, M. N., Vegter-van der Vlis, M., van Vugt, J. P., Lanser, J. B., Hermans, J., Zwinderman, A. H., et al. (2003). Cognitive and motor functioning in gene carriers for Huntington's disease: A baseline study. *Journal of Neuropsychiatry and Clinical Neurosciences, 15,* 7–16.

Yeterian, E. H., & Pandya, D. N. (1993). Striatal connections of the parietal association cortices in rhesus monkeys. *Journal of Comparative Neurology, 332,* 175–197.

Zakzanis, K. K. (1998). The subcortical dementia of Huntington's disease. *Journal of Clinical and Experimental Neuropsychology, 20,* 565–578.

11

The Neuropsychiatry and Neuropsychology of Gilles de la Tourette Syndrome

Mary M. Robertson and Andrea E. Cavanna

In this chapter, we review the neuropsychiatric and neuropsychological literature on Gilles de la Tourette Syndrome (GTS), which has expanded considerably over the last few years. Comorbid attention-deficit hyperactivity disorder (ADHD), obsessive-compulsive behaviors (OCB) and/or disorder (OCD), and depression, are encountered more frequently, and will be discussed in more detail.

Definition, Epidemiology, Historical Notes

The current internationally recognized diagnostic criteria for GTS include the presence of multiple motor tics and one or more vocal (phonic) tics, both of which must exceed a year's duration (ICD-10, World Health Organization, 1992; *Diagnostic and Statistical Manual of Mental Disorders, 4th edition-Text Revision* [DSM-IV-TR], American Psychiatric Association, 2000). The anatomical location, number, frequency, complexity and severity of the tics characteristically change over time. GTS was once considered to be very uncommon, but to date no less than ten definitive studies have documented remarkably consistent findings and suggested a prevalence of between 0.46% and 1.76% for youngsters between the ages of 5 and 18 years (Comings et al., 1990; Hornsey et al., 2001; Kadesjo & Gillberg, 2000; Khalifa & von Knorring, 2003; Kurlan et al., 2001; Lanzi et al., 2004; Nomoto & Machiyama, 1990; Wang & Kuo, 2003; Wong & Lau, 1992; Zheng et al.,

2004). Of importance is that these studies were worldwide (Sweden [two], United Kingdom, Japan, United States of America [two], Taiwan [two], Italy, mainland China), and they were similar in that they were conducted in mainstream schools, used standard multistaged methods, with both observations and questionnaires about pupils, as well as obtaining information from parents and/or teachers. It is acknowledged that in majority of the "cases" identified, the symptoms are probably mild and undiagnosed, fulfilling current diagnostic criteria but unlikely to cause distress or impairment. The prevalence of GTS in special educational populations, such as those individuals with mental retardation and/or learning difficulties or autistic spectrum disorders, is even higher (e.g., Baron-Cohen et al., 1999; Eapen et al., 1997; Kurlan et al., 2001).

The first clear medical description of GTS was made in 1825, when Itard reported the medical history of a French noblewoman, Marquise de Dampierre (Itard, 1825), whose case was then re-documented by Georges Gilles de la Tourette in 1885 when he described nine cases of GTS, emphasizing the triad of multiple tics, coprolalia (unprovoked, inappropriate swearing), and echolalia (imitating the speech of others) (Gilles de la Tourette, 1885). Of note is that Marquise also manifested symptoms of OCD in addition to a tic disorder. We will return to discuss the association between GTS and OCD later in the chapter.

A convincing case has been made (McHenry, 1967; Murray, 1979) that Dr. Samuel Johnson suffered from GTS with multiple motor tics and a variety of vocal tics including "ejaculations of the Lord's prayer," sounds like the clucking of a hen and a whale exhaling (Boswell, 1867; McHenry, 1967; Murray, 1979). He also exhibited echolalia, mild self-injurious behavior. It has been suggested that Dr. Johnson suffered from severe OCD in addition to his motor and vocal tics. He felt impelled to measure his footsteps, perform complex gestures when he crossed a threshold, and involuntarily touch specific objects (Murray, 1979). The history of GTS has been elegantly reviewed in the scholarly exposition by Kushner (1995).

Neurology

In a large group of patients with GTS examined by Shapiro et al. (1978), subtle neurological deficits were found in 57%, and 20% were left-handed or ambidextrous. Most (78%) had minor motor asymmetry and 20% had chorea or choreoathetoid movements. Other abnormalities included posturing, poor coordination, nystagmus, reflex asymmetry, and unilateral Babinski reflexes. In contrast, Lees et al. (1984), using a standardized handedness questionnaire (Annett, 1970), found 87% of their sample of 53 patients to be right-handed, and other investigators have found minor nonspecific neurological abnormalities only in a few patients (Caine et al., 1988; Erenberg et al., 1986; Lees et al., 1984; Regeur et al., 1986; Robertson et al., 1988). Abnormalities documented have included chorea, dystonia, torticollis, dysphonia, dysdiadochokinesia, postural abnormalities, reflex asymmetry, and motor incoordination.

Assessment

Assessment of patients with GTS requires a thorough personal and family history, as well as mental state and neurological examinations. In terms of clinical diagnosis, special investigations are not useful if the assessor is experienced with the syndrome. Although the exclusion of Wilson's disease with serum assay of copper and caeruloplasmin is considered mandatory, in the authors' experience, no patient presenting with this distinctive picture of GTS has actually had Wilson's disease and certainly more extensive investigation of copper handling is not necessary. Standardized schedules are mandatory for research and are useful for accurately diagnosing GTS and assessing the response to medication. There are many standardized rating scales or schedules that help in the more accurate description of symptoms, including the National Hospital Interview Schedule (Robertson & Eapen, 1996), the Yale Global Tic Severity Scale (Leckman et al., 1989), the MOVES Scale (Gaffney, 1994), the Hopkins Motor and Vocal Tic Severity Scale (Walkup et al., 1992), the Tourette's syndrome videotaped scale (Goetz et al., 1987), and the Diagnostic Confidence Index (Robertson et al., 1999), which specifically highlight the phenomenological characteristics of tics, including suppression, rebound, suggestibility, waxing and waning course, and premonitory urges. For implementing majority of these scales, familiarity with Tourette's syndrome, as well as training by an expert, is important. Many of these scales help not only in accurate diagnosis (e.g., National Hospital Interview Schedule) but also give a likelihood of diagnosis (e.g., Diagnostic Confidence Index), indicate severity (e.g., Yale Global Tic Severity Scale, MOVES Scale), and can be used in research protocols (e.g., Tourette's syndrome videotaped scale).

Etiology

Current etiological theories for GTS include (1) genetic influences, (2) infections, (3) pre- and/or perinatal difficulties, (4) psychosocial stress, and (5) androgen exposure. Originally, however, the etiology of GTS was considered to be psychological and indeed even psychoanalytical (e.g., Ferenczi, 1921; Mahler, 1949), but over the last few years large families were documented (e.g., Kurlan et al., 1986; McMahon et al., 1996; Robertson & Cavanna, 2007; Robertson & Gourdie, 1990; Walkup et al., 1996) with many related people being affected by tic or obsessive-compulsive symptomatology, suggesting a familial nature.

With regard to *genetics*, complex segregation analyses of family history data provided strong evidence that the mode of transmission was compatible with an autosomal dominant model (Curtis et al., 1992; Eapen et al., 1993), but subsequent segregation analyses suggested that the mode of inheritance may be more complex (Pauls, 2006). While the mode of inheritance is not simple, it is clear that GTS has a significant genetic basis and that some individuals with GTS, Chronic Multiple Tics (CMT), and/or OCD manifest variant expressions of the same genetic susceptibility factors (Pauls, 2003). Recently dopamine receptor *D2* gene polymorphisms were shown to be associated with GTS in some individuals (Lee et al., 2005). There have now been five complete genome scans reported in GTS and regions of interest have been shown to be on chromosomes 2, 4, 5, 7, 8, 10, 11, 13, 17, 18, 19, as well as suggestions that the *DRD4* and *MAO-A* genes may also confer an increased risk for developing GTS (Barr et al., 1999; Robertson, 2004 [review]) but no significant linkage results have been obtained and replicated. Most recently, Abelson et al. (2005) reported the association of GTS with the gene *SLITRK1* on chromosome 13q31.1 in a small number of individuals with GTS, which is the first indication of a gene being involved in some cases of GTS. Thus, the genetics of GTS is complex and there is almost certainly genetic as well as clinical heterogeneity.

Deng et al. (2006) and Keen-Kim et al. (2006), on the other hand, have provided evidence that mutations in the *SLITRK1* gene probably are a rare cause of GTS and tests designed to detect variants in the *SLITRK1* gene do not have diagnostic utility in clinical practice.

Neuroimmunological theories operating via the process of molecular mimicry have become of interest in the etiopathogenesis of GTS over the last decade. Swedo et al. (1998) described a group of 50 children with OCD and tic disorders, designated as Pediatric Autoimmune Neuropsychiatric Disorders Associated with Streptococcal (group A beta-hemolytic streptococcal [GABHS] infections), or PANDAS. The best evidence for a relationship between GTS and streptococcal infections comes from the study by Mell et al. (2005). These authors found that patients with GTS, OCD, or tic disorder were more likely than controls to have had prior streptococcal infection in the 3 months before onset date. A few other controlled studies have found laboratory evidence of GABHS infections and/or increased antibasal ganglia antibodies

(ABGAs) in some patients with GTS, supporting a role of GABHS and basal ganglia autoimmunity in GTS (see Leonard & Swedo, 2001; Rizzo et al., 2006), while other groups have failed to confirm these findings (Loiselle et al., 2004; Luo et al., 2004). It seems unlikely that GABHS infections directly cause GTS, but it may well be that individuals inherit a susceptibility to GTS and to the way they react to some infections. Thus, most authors suggest that there is an association between streptococcal infections and GTS in a subgroup of patients.

Leckman (2003 [review]) outlined the potential role of *pre- and perinatal events* in the pathogenesis of GTS, suggesting that the mothers of children with tics were more likely to have experienced a complication during pregnancy than the mothers of children who did not have tics, that the severity of maternal life stress during pregnancy (including severe nausea and/or vomiting during the first trimester) are risk factors for developing tic disorders, and that premature low-birth-weight children as well as those with low Apgar scores and more frequent maternal prenatal visits were associated with having GTS (see also Leckman et al., 1990; Lees et al., 1984; Santangelo et al., 1994). A rigorous controlled study by Burd et al. (1999) involving 92 cases and 460 matched controls identified one categorical variable (trimester prenatal care begun) and three continuous variables (Apgar score at 5 minutes, month prenatal began and number of prenatal visits) as potential risk factors for the development of GTS. However, in a more recent study, when 25 GTS children were compared to 25 healthy controls, there was a nonsignificant increase with regards to the "reduced optimality score" (a measure which takes into account pregnancy, obstetrical, and other relevant medical records) in the pre-, peri- or neonatal periods (Khalifa & von Knorring, 2005).

Finally, clinical experience suggests an association between *stressful life events* and fluctuations in symptom severity of tic disorder patients (see e.g., Hoekstra et al., 2004; Lin et al., 2007), whilst Leckman and his group have raised the hypothesis that androgen exposure ("prenatal masculinization of the brain") may also be important in the etiopathogenesis of GTS and tic-related disorders (Alexander & Peterson, 2004; Peterson et al., 1994, 1998).

Thus, the etiology of GTS is much more complex than previously recognized, with complex genetic mechanisms, some infections possibly having effects, and pre- and perinatal difficulties also affecting the phenotype.

Neuroimaging and Pathophysiology

The previous two decades have seen the birth and maturation of neuroimaging investigations of GTS, aimed at identifying the cerebral bases of the disorder and to define the neural systems that modulate or compensate for the presence of the core symptoms. The results of these investigations, combined with prior clinical and preclinical studies have helped generate specific hypotheses of the neural systems involved in GTS.

Investigations of the structure of the brain using computed tomography (CT) scans (Robertson et al., 1988) and magnetic resonance imaging (MRI) scans (Chase et al., 1986) essentially had not revealed any abnormalities, until 1993, when two independent studies showed reduced basal ganglia volume with MRI (Peterson et al., 1993; Singer et al., 1993). In the largest neuroimaging study in GTS to date, Peterson et al. (2003) demonstrated that the caudate nucleus volumes were significantly smaller in children and adults with GTS, while lenticular nucleus volumes were also smaller in adults with GTS and in children who had comorbid OCD. Bloch et al. (2005) demonstrated that the volumes of caudate nucleus correlated significantly and inversely with severity of tics and OCD in early adulthood and it was suggested that caudate volumes could therefore predict the future severity of GTS. Furthermore, recent MRI studies (Plessen et al., 2004, 2006) showed that the corpus callosum is smaller in children and youngsters with GTS compared with healthy control subjects, resulting in an altered interhemispherical white matter connectivity. On the other hand, an increase in the corpus callosum cross-sectional area has been documented in adult patients with GTS (e.g., Moriarty et al., 1997), thus suggesting plastic changes in response to long-lasting tic symptomatology.

Metabolism and blood flow-related studies using positron emission tomography (PET)

and single-photon emission computed tomography (SPECT) have, with general consistency, reported hypometabolism or low regional cerebral blood flow (rCBF) in basal ganglia regions in subjects with GTS. Likewise, radioligand studies have reported functional abnormalities within the dopaminergic neurotransmitter system in the striatum (Butler et al., 2006; Peterson, 2001). Event-related neuroimaging studies using functional MRI (Bohlhalter et al., 2006) and PET (Lerner et al., 2007; Stern et al., 2000) techniques investigated the neural circuits involved in tic generation in patients with GTS. These studies consistently reported activation in a brain network of paralimbic areas such as anterior cingulate and insular cortex, supplementary motor area, and parietal operculum predominantly before tic onset. In contrast, at the beginning of tic action, significant activities were found in sensorimotor areas including thalamus, putamen, caudate, primary motor cortex, superior parietal lobule bilaterally, and cerebellum.

Mink (2006 [review]) has recently presented a model for the pathophysiology of tics, based on our understanding of basal ganglia function and connectivity, in conjunction with known features of anatomical organization and dopamine neurotransmission. According to this model, clusters of striatal neurons (matrisomes) become abnormally active in inappropriate contexts leading to inhibition of the internal globus pallidus or the substantia nigra (pars reticulata) neurons that would normally be active to suppress unwanted movements. The inhibition of these neurons would then disinhibit thalamocortical circuits, thus leading to the production of tics. Activity-dependent dopamine effects would inappropriately reinforce these activity patterns leading to stereotyped repetition. The overactive striatal neuronal clusters may change under various influences, so that the produced movements change over time. Although directly testable, this model requires confirmation through a valid animal model of tics or higher resolution functional imaging techniques.

In summary, the basal ganglia have consistently been implicated in the pathophysiology of GTS. Nearly all PET and SPECT studies have demonstrated reduced metabolism or blood flow to the basal ganglia in subjects with GTS relative to controls. Reduced flow and metabolism are seen most frequently in the ventral striatum and, within the striatum, most often in the left hemisphere. The radioligand studies have also implicated the basal ganglia in the pathophysiology of GTS, although with less consistency than have the metabolism and blood flow studies. The lack of consistency could be due at least in part to the complexity of the systems regulating dopamine metabolism and dopamine receptor density. Therefore, the blood flow and metabolism studies, along with the radioligand findings, quite strongly implicate pathophysiology of the basal ganglia portions of the CSTC circuits, especially in or around the caudate nucleus portions of the ventral striatum. The basal ganglia are conduits for information-processing streams that serve multiple and diverse functions. The ventral striatum, and particularly the ventral caudate nucleus, tends to subserve temporolimbic and orbitofrontal portions of CSTC circuitry. These regions are thought to subserve, among other things, impulse control, reward contingencies, and executive functions—all of which are behavioral systems that have been hypothesized to be dysfunctional in GTS -related psychopathology. The other CSTC system in which regions differ frequently between GTS and healthy controls is that involving the association cortices, particularly the frontal, parietal, and superior temporal regions, all of which have been consistently implicated in attentional functioning. Clearly more investigations are needed to clarify the relationship between the cortical and basal ganglia findings and GTS symptoms (Frey & Albin, 2006).

Clinical Characteristics

The clinical characteristics of individuals with GTS appear to be independent of culture, as they occur with some degree of uniformity irrespective of the country of origin. The age of onset of GTS symptoms ranges from 2 to 15 years, with a mean of 7 years being commonly reported. The most frequent initial symptoms are tics involving the eyes (such as eye blinking), head nodding, and facial grimacing. GTS is often referred to as a tic disorder, but patients with the syndrome usually exhibit a wide variety of complex movements including touching, hitting, jumping, smelling of the hands or objects, spitting, kicking, stamping, squatting, and a variety of abnormalities of gait (Jankovic, 2001; Leckman, 2002; Robertson, 2000; Singer, 2005).

The onset of vocal tics is usually later than that of the motor tics, with a mean age of 7–11 years. The usual utterances include grunting, coughing, throat-clearing, barking, yelping, snorting, explosive utterances, screaming, humming, hissing, clicking, colloquial emotional exclamations, and inarticulate sounds. Coprolalia (the uttering of obscenities) is reported in approximately one-third of patients and usually has a mean age of onset of 14 years. Copropraxia (the making of obscene gestures) is reported in 3%–21% of GTS patients. Echophenomena (the imitation of sounds, words, or actions of others) occur in 11%–44% of patients (Jankovic, 2001; Leckman, 2002; Robertson, 2000; Singer, 2005).

Premonitory feelings or sensations precede motor and vocal tics in as much as 90% of patients; these may be localized sensations or discomforts (Banaschewski et al., 2003; Kwak et al., 2003; Leckman et al., 1993; Woods et al., 2005). Tics characteristically fluctuate (wax and wane), may be suppressed voluntarily, are suggestible, and persist during sleep (Jankovic, 1997). In addition to changing in severity over weeks and months, both motor and phonic tics arise in bouts (minutes to hours) over the course of a day (Leckman, 2002).

Tics and vocalizations are characteristically aggravated by anxiety, stress, boredom, fatigue, and excitement; while sleep, alcohol, orgasm, fever, relaxation, and concentration lead to temporary disappearance of symptoms (Robertson, 2000). The influence of psychosocial stress on tic expression has been thoroughly investigated in a prospective longitudinal study by Hoekstra et al. (2004). However, the significance of these factors for a causal model of GTS remains unclear.

The long-term outcome of GTS was first suggested to be lifelong, illustrated perhaps best by the marquise de Dampierre, described by both Itard (1825) and Gilles de la Tourette (1885), who was still ticking in her elderly years. More recent follow-up studies of GTS (Bloch et al., 2006; Coffey et al., 2000; Erenger et al., 1987;

Golden, 1984; Leckman et al., 1998) suggest that tics begin around 5–6 years, are worse at 10–12 years and by the age of 18 years many tic symptoms are reduced. In adulthood, a fortunate one-third of children with GTS will be symptom-free; another one-third will have only mild symptom severity that does not require medical attention or pharmacological treatment. Both Coffey et al. (2000) and Bloch et al. (2005) showed that the psychopathology such as OCD increase with increasing age. However, substantial long-term follow-up studies are still needed to document the exact course of GTS.

Majority of studies agree that GTS occurs three to four times more commonly in males than in females and that it is found in all social classes, although Asam (1982) and Robertson et al. (1988) reported respectively that over 60% of their GTS cohorts failed to attain their parental social class. Thus, although GTS is found in all social classes, some studies suggest that GTS patients may well underachieve socially (Robertson et al., 1988; Sandor et al., 1990).

Associated Psychopathology and Comorbidities

In an elegant epidemiological study by Khalifa and von Knorring (2005), the prevalence of GTS was 0.6% of youngsters between 7 and 15 years old. One important finding in this study was that only 8% of the GTS patients had no other diagnosis, while as many as 36% had three or more other diagnoses. In a large clinic-based multicenter study, Freeman et al. (2000) documented that only 12% of GTS patients had no other psychopathology. Thus, both in epidemiological and clinical settings, the finding is remarkably consistent that only 8%–12% of individuals with GTS have no other psychopathology.

Gilles de la Tourette (1899), acknowledging the writings of Guinon (1886), suggested that "tiqueurs" nearly always had associated psychiatric disorders, especially multiple phobias, arithmomania and agoraphobia, habits disorders, hypochondriasis, and enuresis. Grasset (1890) also referred to the obsessions and phobias of patients. To him these were an accompaniment of the tic disorder, representing "psychical" tics. Robertson and Reinstein (1991) translated, for the first time, the writings of

Gilles de la Tourette, Guinon, and Grasset, illustrating early documentation of psychopathology, with special reference to OCD. Subsequent work has confirmed a range of disturbances in patients with GTS (Corbett et al., 1969; Morphew & Sim, 1969). OCD, ADHD, and affective disorders—particularly depression—often represent the problems for which the patient is referred to a physician (Robertson, 2000). In addition, antisocial behavior, inappropriate sexual activity, exhibitionism, aggressive behavior, discipline problems, sleep disturbances, and self-injurious behaviors (SIBs) are found in a substantial percentage of clinic GTS populations (Robertson, 2000; Robertson et al., 1988, 1989). Kurlan et al. (1996) described nonobscene socially inappropriate behaviors in GTS that can be associated in one-third of patients with social difficulties and seem to be related to impulse discontrol.

It has been suggested (Robertson, 2000) that it may be useful to clinically subdivide TS into (1) "pure TS," consisting primarily and almost solely of motor and phonic tics; (2) "full blown TS" that includes coprophenomena (producing swear words and rude gestures), echophenomena (copying other people's actions and words), and paliphenomena (repeating one's own actions and words); (3) "TS-plus" (originally coined by Packer, 1997), in which an individual also has significant obsessive-compulsive symptoms or OCD, ADHD, and SIB (e.g., Cavanna et al., 2006a, 2008). Others with severe psychopathology (e.g., depression, anxiety, personality disorders, and other difficult and antisocial behaviors) may also be included in this group.

ADHD and GTS

Both GTS and ADHD are common neurodevelopmental disorders which tend to occur frequently as comorbid conditions, often accompanied by other psychiatric disorders, such as OCD and mood disorders. In general, it is important that a thorough assessment is conducted to ensure that the youngster has in fact both GTS and ADHD. Some youngsters with GTS are so fidgety with their tics, and are trying to suppress their tics, that they may appear to have poor concentration. ADHD and TS have a close relationship (Robertson, 2006b), as demonstrated by the high rate of comorbidity:

as many as 60%–80% of GTS probands have comorbid ADHD (Freeman et al., 2000; Zhu et al., 2006). These data suggest a shared, but still unknown, neurobiological basis, and the clinical spectrum of the two disorders tends to overlap. Whether tic disorders plus ADHD reflect a separate entity and not merely two-coexisting disorders, as suggested by Gillberg et al. (2004), is still controversial.

There have been both suggestions and refutations that the two disorders are genetically related (e.g., Knell & Comings, 1993; Pauls et al., 1988). Others have shown that there may be two types of GTS with ADHD: those in whom ADHD is independent of GTS and those in whom ADHD is secondary to GTS. Another possibility is that "pure" ADHD and GTS+ADHD are different phenomenologically, but the exact relationship is unclear (for review see Robertson, 2006b). The work of the Rothenberger group has examined the additive effect in detail. Their first study (Yordanova et al., 1996) indicated no additive effect at the psychophysiological level, while the second (Yordanova et al., 1997) only partially supported the additive model. The third (Moll et al., 2001) did provide evidence for additive effects at the level of motor system excitability, while their latest supported the notion that GTS+ADHD was indeed a separate nosological entity (Yordanova et al., 2006). Thus, it would appear that the additive model is becoming more convincing, but these results need to be replicated.

Relatively recently, some research groups have separated individuals with GTS into subgroups, specifically separating those with and without ADHD, demonstrating significant differences. Thus, they have examined cohorts of children including children with GTS-only, and comparing them with other groups such as GTS+ADHD, ADHD only, and unaffected controls (e.g., Carter et al., 2000; Rizzo et al., 2007; Sherman et al., 1998; Spencer et al. 1998; Stephens & Sandor, 1999; Sukhodolsky et al., 2003; Tabori-Kraft, 2007). Overall, these studies generally indicated that youngsters with GTS-only did not differ from unaffected controls on many ratings, including aggression, delinquency and/or conduct difficulties. By contrast, children with GTS+ADHD scored significantly higher than unaffected controls and similar to those with ADHD only, on the indices of disruptive behaviors. Studies further showed that children with GTS+ADHD evidenced more internalizing behavior problems and poorer social adaptation than children with GTS-only or controls. Of importance is that youngsters with GTS-only were not significantly different from unaffected controls on most measures of externalizing behaviors and social adaptation, but did have more internalizing symptoms. Only in one study (Rizzo et al., 2007), the GTS-only group obtained higher scores than controls on "delinquent behavior," which is to some extent in contrast to these previous findings. In summary, individuals with GTS-only appear to be different to those with GTS+ADHD, and this clearly has major management and prognostic implications. In general, the ADHD symptoms encountered in "pure" or "primary" ADHD are similar to the ADHD symptoms encountered in patients with GTS (Robertson, 2006b). The increased prevalence of ADHD among individuals with GTS is not restricted to clinic populations, but has also been identified in epidemiological and community studies (Apter et al., 1993; Hornsey et al., 2001; Khalifa & von Knorring, 2005). Thus, it appears that the ADHD observed in people with GTS is not merely a result of referral or ascertainment bias. In the Apter et al. (1993) epidemiological study, ADHD in the GTS cases identified was significantly elevated above the population point prevalence of ADHD in the Israeli general population at the time of the study.

Robertson (2006b) has recently reviewed the relationships between GTS and ADHD particularly as far as treatment is concerned (see also Robertson & Eapen, 1992) and suggested that when a patient has GTS+ADHD, the clinician should first assess which symptoms are the most problematic, and attempt to treat the target symptoms.

OCD and GTS

Kinnear-Wilson, a neurologist, like Gilles de la Tourette himself, acknowledged a relationship between tics and OCD: "no feature is more prominent in tics than its irresistibility…The element of compulsion links the condition intimately to the vast group of obsessions and fixed ideas" (Kinnear-Wilson, 1927). Modern literature confirmed that OCD and GTS are intimately related, although the percentage of patients with GTS who also show OCD varies from as low as 11% in some reports (Kelman, 1965) to as high as 80% in others (Yaryura-Tobias et al., 1981). Cummings and Frankel (1985) commented on similarities between GTS and OCD, including age of onset; life-long course; waxing and waning of symptoms; involuntary, intrusive, ego-alien behavior and experiences; occurrence in the same families; and worsening with depression and anxiety. Montgomery et al. (1982) further suggested that the obsessive-compulsive symptoms increase in frequency with the duration of GTS.

OCD bears strong similarities to GTS, with the suggestion that certain obsessive-compulsive symptoms (OCS) or behaviors (OCB) form an alternative phenotypic expression of GTS (Eapen et al., 1993; Pauls et al., 1986a, 1986b). A family study by Pauls et al. (1986b) demonstrated that the frequency of OCD in the absence of tics among first-degree relatives was significantly elevated in families of both GTS+OCD and GTS–OCD probands, and that these rates were increased over estimates of the general population and a control sample of adoptive relatives. Studies examining the relationship between age of onset of OCD in probands and their affected relatives have found that childhood onset OCD is a highly familial disorder and that these early onset-cases may represent a valid subgroup, with higher genetic loading and shared vulnerability with chronic tic disorders (Rosario-Campos et al., 2005). Bellodi et al. (1992) suggested that earlier age of onset is associated with greater familiality. Further support for this notion comes from the study of Hemmings et al. (2004), who found a clinical association between early age of onset and an increased frequency of tics and related disorders, and a genetic association between early onset OCD and the dopamine receptor type 4 gene (*DRD4*) suggesting a role for dopaminergic system in the development of early-onset OCD, unlike the serotonergic system that is implicated in adult OCD (see also Robertson, 1995).

Several studies have documented that although the OCB encountered in GTS are integral to GTS (Robertson et al., 1988), they are both clinically and statistically different to those encountered in "pure" or "primary" OCD (e.g., Baer, 1994; Cavanna et al., 2006b; Frankel et al., 1986; George et al., 1993; Leckman et al., 1994, 2003; Miguel et al., 1997, 2000; Mula et al., 2008).

Frankel et al. (1986) reported that the U.S. and U.K. patients with GTS had significantly higher obsessional scores on a specially designed inventory when compared to controls. The obsessional items endorsed by GTS subjects changed with increasing age, in that younger patients endorsed more items to do with impulse control, whereas older subjects endorsed items to do with were more concerned with checking, arranging and fear of contamination. Cluster analysis of the inventory responses comparing OCD and GTS groups revealed a group of seven questions that were preferentially endorsed by GTS patients (blurting obscenities, counting compulsions, impulsions to hurt oneself) and eleven questions elicited high scores from OCD patients (ordering, arranging, routines, rituals, touching one's body, obsessions about people hurting each other). George et al. (1993) demonstrated that patients with GTS+OCD had significantly more violent, sexual and symmetrical obsessions and more touching, blinking, counting, and self-damaging compulsions, compared to patients with OCD-alone who had more obsessions concerning dirt or germs and more compulsions relating to cleaning; the subjects who had both disorders (i.e., GTS+OCD) reported that their compulsions arose spontaneously, whereas the subjects with OCD-alone reported that their compulsions were frequently preceded by cognitions (George et al., 1993). Thus from a clinical point of view, there are differences which in later studies seemed related to family history. Other groups have found similar results in that there were phenomenological differences between the repetitive behaviors encountered in GTS and OCD (e.g., Miguel et al., 1997). Moreover, patients with GTS and OCD reported that their compulsions arose spontaneously or de novo, whereas those with OCD-alone reported that their compulsions were frequently preceded by cognitions. Cavanna et al. (2006b) compared the nature of the OCS in two GTS populations, GTS–OCD and GTS+OCD, and reported that the first group of patients showed a significantly higher prevalence of "impulsive" and harming repetitive behaviors. More recently, Mula et al. (2008) compared the phenomenology of the obsessional thoughts between patients with GTS+OCD and matched patients diagnosed with temporal lobe epilepsy and OCD. The authors found that violent and symmetrical themes were preponderant in the first group, whilst fear of contamination and religious/philosophical ruminations were more frequent in the second group.

Taken together, these data indicate that GTS and OCD are somehow intertwined, and that specific OCS or OCB are likely to be integral to GTS (Hounie et al., 2006 [reviews]; Robertson, 2000).

Depression and GTS

Depression has long been found in association with GTS (e.g., Montgomery et al., 1982). There is now good evidence from controlled and uncontrolled studies recently reviewed by Robertson (2006a) and Robertson and Orth (2006) to support the view that affective disorders are common in patients with GTS, with a lifetime risk of 10%, and prevalence of between 1.8% and 8.9%. In specialist clinics, patients with GTS, depression or depressive symptomatology was found to occur in between 13% and 76% of 5295 individuals. In controlled studies in clinical settings embracing 758 GTS patients, the patients were significantly more depressed than controls in all but one instance. In community and epidemiological studies, depression in GTS individuals was evident in 1/5 investigations. Clinical correlates of the depression in clinical patients with GTS appear to be: tic severity and duration, the presence of echophenomena and coprophenomena, premonitory sensations, sleep disturbances, OCD, SIB, aggression, childhood conduct disorder, and possibly ADHD (Robertson, 2006a; Robertson & Orth, 2006). The depression in people with GTS has been shown to result in a reduced Quality of Life (Elstner et al., 2001), and may lead to hospitalization and even suicide in a few people (Robertson, 2006a). Taken together, the literature indicates that depressive symptoms, and even major depressive disorder, are common in GTS. In contrast, there is no evidence to suggest that the reverse was true, i.e. that GTS is more common in patients with a main diagnosis of major depressive disorder (Eapen et al., 2001).

Depression in GTS is highly likely to be multifactorial in origin, as is the depression in non-GTS populations (e.g., Winokur, 1997). What exactly are the contributory factors of the depression in patients with GTS? GTS can be a distressing condition, particularly if tics are moderate to severe. Thus, depression in GTS patients could be explained, at least in part, by the fact that sufferers have a chronic, socially disabling and stigmatizing disease. Moreover, it has been clearly demonstrated that children who have been bullied at school may also become depressed (Bond et al., 2001; Salmon et al., 1998) and some children with GTS are bullied, teased and given pejorative nicknames, and thus the depression may result from that (Robertson, 2000, 2006a).

Another reason, which might play a part in the etiology of depression in clinic GTS patients, is that in GTS, comorbidity with OCD is high (see this chapter). The most common complication of OCD ranging from 13% to 75% is depression (Perugi et al., 2002), and in a large collaborative study, major depressive disorder was the most common comorbid disorder in OCD patients, occurring in 38% of subjects (Perugi et al., 1999). Next, ADHD is common in GTS (see this chapter) and ADHD has been shown to have a high comorbidity with depression (e.g., Milberger et al., 1995), and thus many GTS patients could be depressed because of the comorbidity with ADHD (Robertson, 2006b).

The depression in clinic GTS patients may also be due to the side effects of both typical and atypical neuroleptic medications. Depression has been reported with, for example, haloperidol, pimozide, fluphenazine, tiapride, sulpiride, and risperidone, as well as tetrabenazine, the calcium antagonist flunarizine, mecamylamine, and clonidine (Robertson, 2000).

Finally, the high levels of depression in some of these studies may reflect the fact that patients that attend specialist clinics (including patients with GTS) often have more than one problem/disorder; this may introduce ascertainment bias. This view would be supported by some of the epidemiological studies, in which individuals with GTS were not rated as having depressed mood when compared to non-GTS subjects or controls. For instance, the study of Sukhodolsky et al. (2003) demonstrated that the "pure" GTS subjects (i.e., those without comorbidity) were not more depressed than the controls.

In summary, the etiology of depression in GTS is highly likely multifactorial, as in primary depressive illness, and less likely to be caused by a single etiological factor. The precise phenomenology and natural history of depression in the context of GTS deserves more research, as well as its contribution to the GTS phenotype(s). Similar to OCD, the phenomenology of depressive symptoms may differ between GTS patients and those with major depressive disorder. In depressed GTS patients, this may help address not only factors of particular relevance to the etiology of their depression and thus improve its recognition but also treatment and outcome.

With regard to psychotic disorders, in particular schizophrenia, it is generally accepted that there is no association between psychosis and GTS apart from a few isolated case reports (Burd & Kerbeshian, 1984; Takeuchi et al., 1986). On the other hand, a recent study by Cavanna et al. (2007) reported a relatively high prevalence of schizotypal personality disorder, especially in association with OCD comorbidity. Finally, there have been suggestions (Berthier et al., 1998; Kerbeshian et al., 1995) that bipolar disorder and GTS could be related; however, numbers are small and it is likely that the relationship is with other comorbid conditions, rather than with GTS per se.

Anxiety Disorders

Anxiety has also been found in substantial proportions of GTS cohorts (e.g., Erenberg et al., 1987; Robertson et al., 1988), and GTS patients have been shown to have increased anxiety when compared to control populations (e.g., Robertson et al., 1993, 1997). In the large multicenter study by Freeman et al. (2000), as high as 18% of the 3500 patients had comorbid anxiety disorders. Thibert et al. (1995) examined responses to a mailed questionnaire and showed that the GTS patients with comorbid OCS/OCB scored higher on social anxiety than did the general population. Carter et al. (1994) found

increased rates of tic disorders, OCS/OCB, and anxiety symptoms in children who had a first-degree relative with GTS.

In summary, it seems that anxiety is common in clinic GTS patients, but its exact relationship to GTS is yet unclear.

Rage and Explosive Outbursts

Explosive outbursts, aggression, "rage attacks" are being more frequently recognized and then documented in people with GTS (Budman et al., 1998, 2000; Stephens & Sander, 1999). It appears that there is a provocation, an extensive reaction to the provocation, and remorse afterwards. These outbursts are related probably to impulsivity and may benefit from SSRI treatment (Bruun & Budman, 1998).

Personality Disorders and Other Neuropsychiatric Disorders

To date, there has been only one investigation of personality disorder in GTS, but it has important clinical implications, and therefore the results will be discussed briefly. Robertson et al. (1997) examined 39 adult GTS patients of moderate severity and 34 age- and sex-matched controls using the Structured Clinical Interview for DSM-III-R Personality Disorders II (SCID-II), plus a self-rated scale for personality disorders. Results showed that 64% of GTS patients had one or more DSM-III-R personality disorders, compared with only 16% of control subjects, which was highly statistically significant. The explanation for this increase in personality disorder may well be the result of the long-term outcome of childhood ADHD, referral bias, or because of other childhood psychopathology.

Other neuropsychiatric disorders associated with GTS include autistic spectrum disorders (Baron-Cohen et al., 1999), people with learning difficulties, disability and "mental retardation" (Eapen et al., 1997; Kurlan et al., 2001), reading disabilities, dyspraxia, dyslexia, and dyscalculia (Comings & Comings, 1987).

Family Psychopathology

Gilles de la Tourette (1899) noted that the family history of patients with GTS was almost invariably "loaded for nervous disorder." Samuel Johnson's father also appeared to suffer from depression, "a general sensation of gloomy wretchedness," and it is thought to be from him that Dr. Johnson "inherited...a vile melancholy" (Boswell, 1867).

Montgomery et al. (1982) found that 70% of 30 first-degree relatives of 15 patients with GTS satisfied Feighner criteria for psychiatric illness, the most common diagnoses being unipolar depression, OC illness, and panic disorder. Subsequently, Green and Pitman (1986), Pauls et al. (1986a, 1986b), and Robertson and Gourdie (1990) found the rate of OCB/OCD significantly higher among relatives of patients with GTS than in control populations. Robertson et al. (1988) reported that 48% of 90 probands had a positive family history of psychiatric illness, of which the most common disorders were depression, schizophrenia, and OCD. More recently Khalifa and von Knorring (2005) described 25/4479 (0.6%) of GTS youngsters in a community sample and compared them to healthy controls. They showed that more parents and siblings of GTS children had an increased prevalence of OCD, ADHD, and depression. Eighty percent had a first-degree relative with a psychiatric disorder. While it is acknowledged that these studies are not controlled, it would appear that there is increased psychiatric morbidity in the relatives of patients with GTS, and that OCD is the most common disorder found in these relatives (see also Robertson & Cavanna, 2007). As suggested earlier, this implicates a common genetic basis to these disorders.

Neuropsychiatry: Preliminary Conclusions

The clinical and epidemiological studies reviewed in this chapter suggest that associated behavioral problems are common in people with GTS, so that it seems reasonable to view this condition as a psychopathological spectrum disorder (e.g., Cavanna et al., 2008).

As mentioned before, the largest investigation to date, embracing 3500 clinic patients with GTS worldwide, demonstrated that at all ages, 88% of individuals had reported comorbidity. The most common was ADHD, followed by OCD. Anger control problems, sleep difficulties, coprolalia, and SIB only reached high levels in individuals with comorbidity; whereas males were more likely than females to have comorbid disorders (Freeman et al., 2000). Moreover, people with GTS have been shown to be more prone to depression, and the severity of this increases with the duration of GTS, possibly as a consequence of having a stigmatizing disorder. OCD, on the other hand, which is also remarkably common in people with GTS, appears to be an integral part of the syndrome. A recent factor analytic study on a large U.K. GTS pedigree supports the view that OCB represent a phenotype of the putative GTS gene(s) (Robertson & Cavanna, 2007). The authors' suggestions as to the relationships between GTS and other various heterogeneous psychopathologies are summarized in Table 11–1.

To date, very few studies have investigated quality of life (QOL) in patients with GTS (Bernard et al. 2006; Elstner et al., 2001; Al Faqih, 2007). According to these preliminary investigations, patients with GTS show significantly worse QOL than the general population. Specifically, correlates of reduced QOL include comorbid OCD and ADHD, rather than tic severity.

Both the DSM and the ICD criteria have dictated that GTS is a unitary condition. However, recent studies using hierarchical cluster analysis (Mathews et al., 2007) and principal component factor analysis (Alsobrook & Pauls, 2002; Robertson & Cavanna, 2007) have demonstrated that there may be more than one GTS phenotype. There are also early suggestions that at least some of the many suggested etiologies may result in different phenotypes. For example, in the Alsobrook and Pauls (2002) study, three out of four factors were heritable. Martino et al. (2007) showed that ABGA positive GTS individuals had significantly less ADHD. Hyde et al. (1992, 1994) showed for monozygotic twins concordant for tics but discordant for severity, the smaller birth weight twin had more severe GTS and more abnormal EEGs. With regard to psychopathology, Eapen et al. (2004) conducted a principal component factor analysis and demonstrated two factors. Thus, both the phenotype of the "tic-part" of GTS and the psychopathology of GTS are not homogeneous unitary entities. There are many causes and many

Table 11–1. Suggested Relationships between Psychopathology and GTS

Neuropsychiatric disorder	Relationship with GTS
OCD	Generally suggested as an integral part of and genetically related to GTS
ADHD	Common in GTS and possibly genetically linked in some cases
Depression	Multifactorial/possibly due to comorbidity with OCD and ADHD, rather than to GTS per se
Dysphoria, anxiety, cognitive impairment, school phobia	Secondary to medication in some cases
Schizophrenia	Uncommon, the association is by chance
Autistic spectrum disorder, rage attacks, learning disability, mental retardation, anorexia nervosa	Relationship is unknown and more research is needed
Huntington's disease, Parkinson's disease, Wilson's disease	No relationship
Bipolar disorder	Few cases described, probably related to comorbidities
Explosive attacks, temper tantrums, "rage" attacks	Related to impulsivity, possibly distinct entity

Note: Only 8%–12% of GTS individuals in epidemiological and clinical settings have "pure" tics and no other diagnosis.
Abbreviations: GTS, Gilles de la Tourette syndrome; OCD, Obsessive-compulsive disorder; ADHD, attention-deficit hyperactivity disorder.
Source: Adapted from Robertson, 2004.

phenotypes. Only time will tell whether or not future studies demonstrate further etiological–phenotypic relationships.

Neuropsychology

We turn now to the neuropsychology of GTS. In our review of this, we restrict our discussion to *cognition* in these patients. This term is both broad enough to include the major psychological processes, and yet focuses enough to exclude such psychological systems as emotion. As will become evident, the neuropsychology of GTS has hardly begun. We suggest that a scientific theory of this disorder must ultimately aim to give a thorough account of how cognition and emotion link with biology and behavior in patients with this condition. The following paragraphs review the studies addressing the main cognitive domains in patients with GTS, namely intelligence, language, attention and executive functions, memory, and visuomotor skills.

Intelligence

More intelligence testing has been carried out in GTS than almost any other kind of cognitive investigation. A range of IQ tests have been used, a key one being the Wechsler Scales (e.g.,

Incagnoli & Kane, 1981; Shapiro et al., 1974). These studies show a relatively consistent set of findings: patients with GTS, as a group, have IQ scores in the normal range (Corbett et al., 1969; Randolph et al., 1993), although GTS and mental handicap can of course coexist (Golden & Greenhill, 1981). In a proportion of the patients with overall IQs in the normal range, statistically significant discrepancies between verbal and performance IQ on the Wechsler Scales have been found (50% in the Shapiro et al. [1974] study). For most patients, performance IQ is significantly worse than verbal IQ, but significant discrepancies in the opposite direction are also sometimes found. Schuerholz et al. (1996), however, did not report any discrepancy between the verbal and performance IQ when comparing patients with GTS-only and patients with GTS and comorbid ADHD. Sherman et al. (1998) compared 21 GTS-only subjects, 14 GTS + ADHD, and 18 controls on the Wechsler Full Scale IQ. The GTS + ADHD group (IQ 99.2) performed significantly worse than the controls (IQ 112.8) and the GTS-only group (106.5). They did not report discrepancies of more than 15 points between the verbal and performance scale.

Within the subtests, Coding, written Arithmetic, and copying tasks (as measured, for example, in the Aphasia Screening Test of the Halstead–Reitan Battery), seem to cluster as a set of severe deficits. Incagnoli and Kane (1981) suggest this may represent dysfunction of "nonconstructional visuopractic abilities" (p. 168), although the relationship between this postulated cognitive deficit in visuographic skills and the symptomatology of the disorder remains to be fully explored. Furthermore, although Incagnoli and Kane stress specifically on *non*constructional visuopractic deficits, deficits have also been found in some constructional abilities, such as those measured by the Block Design or Object Assembly subtests of the Wechsler Scales (Bornstein et al., 1983; Shapiro et al., 1974). These differences may reflect developmental changes, since Shapiro et al. (1974) found deficits on the Block Design subtest in adults with GTS, but not in children.

Overall, GTS patients appear to perform in the normal range on tests of general intelligence (see also Como, 2001 [review]). The authors who reported discrepancies between verbal and performance IQ have noted that they are more common in older GTS subjects (Shapiro et al., 1974; Sutherland et al., 1982). This is in accordance with the findings by Bornstein et al. (1983) and Schuerholz et al. (1996) that neuropsychological abnormalities are more common in older GTS patients and can become more prominent as the disorder progresses.

Language

Vocal tics are, of course, a major diagnostic symptom of GTS. Not all vocal tics are clearly *linguistic*, however. Some vocal tics, for example, are nonverbal (e.g., throat-clearing, barking, or snorting). However, clear verbal tics make up some 35% of vocal tics (Ludlow et al., 1982), and these include coprolalia (unprovoked swearing), palilalia (frequent reiteration of syllables), jargon (production of strings of meaningless syllables), word-tics (interjection of words that are meaningful but are not part of speech), and echolalia (repetition of heard speech). Lees et al. (1984) estimate that coprolalia and echolalia occur in about 40%–50% of patients with GTS. Interestingly, Rickards (2001) reported signing coprolalia and attempts to disguise as a man with prelingual deficits. Most of these language abnormalities have simply been described, but

not systematically studied. Apart from this set of symptoms, some studies also report a history of speech and language problems, even prior to the onset of GTS (O'Quinn & Thompson, 1980), though again, the precise nature of these early language problems remains unspecified.

Given the centrality of language abnormalities in these patients, it is somewhat surprising how few *psycholinguistic* studies of GTS have been carried out. Ludlow et al. (1982) studied 54 patients and 54 normal controls by recording 10 minutes of conversation and picture description from each subject. These authors found that, from the recordings of spontaneous speech, majority of tics were produced at the beginning or end of speech clause production. Tics thus do not seem to interfere *randomly* with speech but are produced in synchrony with overall speech rhythms, mostly at speech boundaries. Motor tics, on the other hand, do not respect word boundaries (Frank, 1978). Second, Ludlow et al. (1982) used a range of language tests on the same patients, all part of the Neurosensory Center Comprehensive Examination of Aphasia (NCCEA), a standardized instrument. These tests included assessments of Visual Naming, Description of Use, Word Fluency, Sentence Construction, Sentence Repetition, Reading, Writing, and Copying. Significant differences between the groups appeared only on language expression, writing (expressive and dictation), and copying. The latter findings are consistent with the visuographic deficits revealed using intelligence tests, reviewed earlier.

In the Ludlow et al. (1982) study, reading was also poorer than normal, but this just failed to reach statistical significance. Although the studies of intelligence reviewed earlier suggested that arithmetic skills are more impaired in GTS than either reading or spelling skills (Bornstein et al., 1983), there are nevertheless a number of other studies reporting high levels of reading problems. Comings and Comings (1987), for example, found severe reading difficulties (dyslexia) in 26.8% of their sample, in contrast to only 4.2% of their control group.

Sutherland et al. (1982) report that performance was low on a Word Fluency Test (naming as many objects, and then animals, as possible in one minute, and then alternating between giving color and bird names as often as possible in 1 minute). This was not explained by any gross anomaly such as abnormal speech lateralization, as a dichotic listening task confirmed a normal left hemisphere dominance for words. It is reasonable to surmise that the difficulties on the Word Fluency Test might be related to impairments in "frontal systems," rather than to purely linguistic factors, given the difficulties that patients with nonfocal frontal lesions have on such tests (Shallice, 1988).

Brookshire et al. (1994) compared GTS patients and controls on the Vocabulary test of the WISC-R and the Oral Fluency Test. Their results showed that the GTS group scored significantly lower on both tests than the control group. Schuerholz et al. (1998) compared a GTS-only, GTS + ADHD, and a control group, showing that the GTS + ADHD group was significantly slower than the GTS-only group on the Rapid Automatized Naming, whereas in the 1996 study the groups did not differ on this measure. On the Letter Word Fluency task, the GTS-only subjects scored significantly lower when compared to the GTS + ADHD. De Nil et al. (2005) analyzed the frequency and type of speech disfluencies in 69 children diagnosed with GTS and compared their results with similar speech data from a control group of 27 individuals. Self-report data on fluency difficulties did not reveal significant group differences; however, detailed analysis of fluency during reading and spontaneous speech revealed an overall higher level of more typical (normal) disfluencies in the GTS group. No overall differences in less typical (stuttering) disfluencies were observed between the two groups of children.

The reviewed studies show that the linguistic skills of GTS patients are relatively intact. The most frequently reported deficit is on the Fluency Tests, which can be accounted for by impairments in executive functions, rather than by linguistic factors entirely.

Attention and Executive Functions

As mentioned earlier, there is now little doubt that GTS is associated strongly with attentional difficulties. Most studies that have looked at the overlap between GTS and ADHD have suggested that the attentional deficits may be a key reason for the ensuing school and learning difficulties that are reported in a proportion of patients, although this explanation is not by itself sufficient to account for the pattern of *specific* deficits (e.g., in visuospatial abilities), unless one posits attentional deficits that are specific to, for example, the visual modality. Some evidence that this may be the case comes from a study by Bornstein et al. (1983), which reported that their patients with GTS scored in the normal range on a test of auditory attention span (from the Wechsler Scales, mean scaled score = 9.6), but in the below average range on a test of visual attention span (using the Knox Cube Test). This pattern once again confirms the dysfunction in the visuospatial and visuomotor systems reviewed earlier.

A further study by Channon et al. (1992) showed that mild deficits were found using "complex" tests of attention, such as serial addition, block sequence span (forwards), the trail-making test, and a letter cancellation vigilance task. Given the very high proportion of GTS patients who show attentional deficits, and given that attention is one of the most well-studied processes in experimental psychology, with a range of paradigms readily available (e.g., Allport, 1987), there is a clear need for more controlled experiments in this area. Important questions that remain to be considered include specifying how attention deficits in patients with GTS differ or compare to those in children without GTS but with ADHD (Taylor, 1985); and whether the behavioral problems that are common in GTS are directly related to attentional deficits, or (as Wilson et al., 1982, found) to other factors such as severity of tics and level of IQ, or to both.

According to Como (2001) executive deficits are also common among GTS patients and can in some cases be more debilitating than the tics characterizing the syndrome. Sutherland et al. (1982) first reported that GTS patients performed significantly worse on the Newcombe Word Fluency Test and on the copy of the Rey Complex Figure compared to controls. Schuerholz et al. (1996) found that GTS-only group performed significantly better on the copy part of the Rey Complex Figure than the control and GTS + ADHD groups. On the other hand, Bornstein (1991) and Bornstein and Yang (1991) found no impairment on the Wisconsin Card Sorting Test (WCST). Bornstein et al.

(1983) revealed an interesting pattern with the GTS patients performing poorly on the Knox Cube Test, a measure of visual attention span. Channon et al. (1992) administered a number of tests measuring attention to GTS subjects and controls. Compared to the control group, GTS patients performed significantly worse on the Corsi Block Test forward, cancellation task, mental arithmetic task, and Trail Making B. Bornstein (1991), however, found no impairment on the Trail Making B among the TS subjects, compared to published norms. Ozonoff et al. (1994) used the Go-NoGo Task and H&S task (in which participants are asked to classify eight different stimulus types, which appear on a computer screen, as either Hs or Ss) to assess the executive functions in GTS-only patients and matched controls. The results revealed no significant differences between the groups on neither the Go-NoGo tasks nor H&S task. The authors presented two explanations for these results. First, it was possible that the Go-NoGo task was too easy for the GTS-only and that a measure with greater cognitive demands might have distinguished between the groups. Alternatively, there are many modalities of inhibition, and GTS may involve a failure of motor inhibition but not deficits in cognitive inhibition. A study by Sherman et al. (1998) compared GTS-only, GTS + ADHD, and a control group on a continuous performance test. Results indicated that the performance of the GTS-only and control group was within the normal limits on measures of attention (number of hits), however the GTS-only performed significantly better than the GTS + ADHD group. Georgiou et al. (1995) tested the ability of GTS patients to respond to relevant (congruent) and irrelevant (incongruent) stimuli. In this study protocol, the subjects had to respond to visuospatial stimuli on a computer screen. Compared to controls, GTS patients were more sensitive to irrelevant stimulus information, and showed difficulty in inhibiting an inappropriate response. The authors concluded that the nature of GTS patients' attentional difficulties might reside in an inability to effectively shift and/or change cognitive sets. This inability to change cognitive sets can be related to basal ganglia-frontal disturbances often seen in GTS, resulting in attentional problems and response inhibition.

Given that the symptoms of GTS seem to involve those systems that are central to the control of action, it is relevant to enquire about the functioning of the so-called frontal systems that are held to control action (and to be impaired in patients with nonfocal frontal lesions). In cognitive psychology the main mechanism that has been described is the Supervisory Attentional System (or the SAS: Shallice, 1988). To understand the SAS, we must first mention what Shallice calls the Contention Scheduling System (CSS), which responds to external stimuli and repeats relevant, routine actions. The SAS oversees the CSS, by activating or inhibiting alternative schemata. The primary function of the SAS is to respond to novelty. Shallice (1988) proposed that the SAS is impaired in patients with frontal lobe syndrome, resulting in disinhibition of actions.

Previous work has shown that children with GTS are impaired in so-called intention editing, a process required whenever two or more intentions are activated simultaneously, only one of which can be executed into action. A study by Baron-Cohen et al. (1994) used two tasks: in the first one they asked the children to simultaneously open one hand while closing the other, and then switch to doing this in the opposite pattern, carrying on this simultaneous alternation for 10 trials (this is Luria's Hand Alternation Task). The second task involved playing the Yes and No Game, in which the children could answer a question in any way they liked, so long as they did not answer with the words "Yes" or "No." On both tasks, children with GTS were severely impaired, relative to normal control groups. These deficits suggest the existence of a mechanism in the normal case (the Intention Editor) that has failed to develop normally in children with GTS (see Baron-Cohen & Moriarty, 1995; Baron-Cohen & Robertson, 1995).

The reviewed studies of executive function ability in GTS patients reveal somewhat inconsistent findings. However, in those studies that have grouped GTS patients according to comorbid conditions such as ADHD or OCD, executive dysfunctions appear to be more common in GTS accompanied by psychiatric disorders (Schuerholz et al., 1996, 1998; Sherman et al., 1998). However, since few studies to date have excluded GTS patients with comorbid conditions, the question arises if the executive dysfunctions are to be considered artefacts of comorbid conditions in GTS rather then specific to GTS itself.

Memory

Only a few studies have focused purely or in depth on memory functions in GTS. Ludlow et al. (1982) report that patients with GTS score in the normal range on tests of auditory memory (Sentence Repetition, Digit Repetition Forwards, and Digit Repetition Backwards). This intact auditory memory system (at least as regards short-term memory) contrasts with Sutherland et al.'s (1982) report that copying and drawing from memory is impaired in GTS, as is delayed recall of visual material (the Wechsler Memory Figures), relative to both mentally handicapped and schizophrenic controls groups. A study by Randolph et al. (1993) using the California Verbal Memory Test and Rey Complex Figure found no difference between performance of severe and less severe GTS patients. Brookshire et al. (1994) used the Verbal and Nonverbal Selective Reminding Test and reported that the GTS group performed in a similar way as the control group on both the verbal and nonverbal part. Likewise, controlled studies by Channon et al. (2003, 2006) and Crawford et al. (2005) found no evidence of impairment in implicit aspects of memory and learning. More recently, Lavoie et al. (2007) demonstrated a specific nonverbal deficit in two cohorts of patients with GTS and chronic tic disorder who completed the Rey–Osterreich Complex Figure and the California Verbal Learning Test.

Whether the memory deficits that have been occasionally identified represent *pure* memory problems, or are secondary to the attentional deficits reviewed above, remains to be established. Since many of the studies that have reported memory impairments in GTS have not divided the patients into groups according to a comorbid condition, it is hard to say whether the impairment is due to GTS solely or to a comorbid condition. For example, Sutherland et al. (1982) speculate that because of the urge many patients report to *repeat* what they hear, which must distract them from the *meaning* of the text being read, poor recall of stories may simply reflect distraction.

Visuomotor Skills

Motor tics are, of course, another pathognomonic symptom of this disorder. The range of motor tics is very wide, from mild blinking to conspicuous flailing of limbs. Perhaps more unusual, though, are motor phenomena that have specific *content*. Echopraxia is a clear example of this, where a patient involuntarily repeats ("echoes") the actions of another person immediately after observing them. Lees et al. (1984) report that echopraxia occurs in 21% of patients with GTS. Here is Gilles de la Tourette's own description of this extraordinary phenomenon:

S. is in the courtyard of the Salpetrière in his usual way. He is moving about, making a few contortions and a few strange sounds, all of which is his ordinary practice. Another patient approaches him and decides to imitate one of his stranger movements, which consists of lifting the right arm and leg and stomping with the left foot, a peculiar position that one can clearly see is apt to cause a loss of balance. At the same time, he mimics one of our patient's more bizarre and characteristic utterances. Soon S., who has been rather calm, starts to imitate the screams and strange mannerisms of his fellow patient, and does it so vigorously that he falls, fortunately not hurting himself. Hospital guards have to stop this game, which could become dangerous. This incident, sadly, has become the source of many cruel episodes where other patients take sadistic advantage of S.'s irresistible imitative compulsion. (Gilles de la Tourette, in Goetz & Klawans [1982], pp. 7–8)

The notion of an "imitative compulsion" dramatically conveys how these movements might be triggered simply by the sight of another person's movements, the resulting imitation being entirely automatic and involuntary. Copropraxia (the gestural equivalent of coprolalia), like echopraxia, is another motor tic with content, and again suggests a single neurological or cognitive deficit may underlie symptoms at both levels, despite earlier arguments against this claim. Copropraxia remains to be studied in more detail.

Bornstein et al. (1983) first reported general motor deficits as measured by the Grooved

Pegboard Test (an index of visuomotor coordination). Golden (1984) reports that half of his patients actually showed superior motor skills, whereas the others showed impaired performance. On the other hand, Bornstein and Yang (1991) did not find a significant difference on the performance of medicated and unmedicated GTS patients on the Grooved Pegboard Test or Trail Making A and B. Randolph et al. (1993) divided twin pairs into twins with less severe and more severe GTS and found that the more severe TS group performed significantly better on the Purdue Pegboard Test, but only with the dominant hand. Brookshire et al. (1994) did not find a significant difference between the GTS group and controls on tests requiring visual-motor skills such as the Block Design and Object Assembly of the WISC. However, the two groups differed significantly on the Coding of WISC, and the GTS group tended to perform worse (nonsignificantly) than the controls on the Grooved Pegboard Test. Finally, in a study by Schultz et al. (1998), GTS patients scored significantly lower than the control group on all three conditions dominant, nondominant, bimanual) of the Purdue Pegboard Test. The question of whether the motor tics in this condition reflect abnormalities in the *planning* of action, or in the control of action, is currently unknown.

Neuropsychology: Preliminary Conclusions

The neuropsychology studies reviewed in this chapter suggested that the level of performance of GTS patients is not indicative of grossly impaired neuropsychological function. GTS individuals score in the average or above average range on intelligence tasks, and on most other measures they are close to normal means. Moreover, where impairments have been reported (especially attentional deficits), they are in most instances linked to a comorbid condition (e.g., ADHD). However, it is important to underscore that the neuropsychology of GTS is still incomplete, in part, because there have been insufficient experimental studies of key psychological systems, and in part because the studies that have been carried out have tended to include a wide mix of subjects, which may mask important neuropsychological differences that may exist between subgroups. For example, some studies have lumped together both old and young patients, or those with tic-related symptoms/comorbid conditions and those without, those with an early and a late onset of GTS, and even those who are receiving medication and those who are not. This variation, in our opinion, prevents a careful comparison of homogenous subgroups within the disorder. It is hoped that future research in this area will adopt a more rigorous experimental approach, drawing on methods available in experimental psychology, and define patient groups more tightly, so that if subgroups do exist, these can be better understood. Such data are needed in order to gain a better insight into the neuropsychological status of GTS.

Summary

In this chapter, we have reviewed some of the neuropsychiatric and neuropsychological studies of GTS. The major finding in the neuropsychiatry field is that there is a high rate of psychiatric comorbidities in GTS, the most commonly encountered being OCD, ADHD, and affective disorders (particularly depression). The exact relationships between psychopathology and GTS are complex, and far from being fully elucidated. However, in recent years a few lines of evidence have started to emerge. For instance, it is now generally accepted that OCB/OCD is unlikely to be a consequence of the disorder and instead appears to be an integral part of it, probably etiologically/genetically related.

With regard to neuropsychology, it appears that the overall level of performance of GTS patients is not indicative of grossly impaired neuropsychological function. They tend to score in the average range on intelligence tasks and most other cognitive measures. However, small sample size, lack of control groups, and ascertainment bias, represent significant limitations of most neuropsychological studies conducted so far. Further studies on specific subgroups of patients are needed in order to answer the question of how cognitive deficits relate to GTS symptoms.

In conclusion, it appears that GTS can no longer be thought of simply as a motor disorder, and, most importantly, that GTS is no longer a unitary condition, as it was previously thought. This change in perspective brings us closer to Georges Gilles de la Tourette's original view of this disorder.

Acknowledgments

The authors wish to thank the Tourettes Action - U.K. and the Tourette Syndrome Association - U.S.A. for their continuing support and encouragement.

References

Abelson, J. F., Kwan, K. Y., O'Roak, B. J., Baek, D. Y., Stillman A. A., Morgan, T. M., et al. (2005). Sequence variants in *SLITRK1* are associated with Tourette's Syndrome. *Science, 310,* 317–320.

Al Faqih, S. S. (2007). Determinants of quality of life in Gilles de la Tourette Syndrome. *Movement Disorders, 22,* S281.

Alexander, G. M., & Peterson, B. S. (2004). Testing the prenatal hormone hypothesis of tic-related disorders: Gender identity and gender role behavior. *Developmental Psychopathology, 16,* 407–420.

Allport, A. (1987). Selection for action: Some behavioral and neurophysiological considerations of attention and action. In H. Heurer & A. Sanders (Eds.), *Perspectives on perception and action* (chap. 15, pp. 395–419). Hillsdale, N.J.: Lawrence Erlbaum.

Alsobrook, J. P. 2nd, & Pauls, D. L. (2002). A factor analysis of tic symptoms in Gilles de la Tourette's syndrome. *American Journal of Psychiatry, 159,* 291–296.

American Psychiatric Association. (2000). *Diagnostic and Statistical Manual of Mental Disorders IV-text revision (DSM-IV-TR).* Washington, DC: American Psychiatric Association.

Annett, M. (1970). A classification of hand preferences by association analysis. *British Journal of Psychology, 61,* 303–321.

Apter, A., Pauls, D. L., Bleich, A., Zohar, A. H., Kron, S., Ratzoni, G., et al. (1993). An epidemiologic study of Gilles de la Tourette's syndrome in Israel. *Archives of General Psychiatry, 50,* 734–738.

Asam, U. (1982). A follow-up study of Tourette syndrome. In A. J. Friedhoff & T. N. Chase (Eds.), *Gilles de la Tourette Syndrome, advances in neurology, vol. 35* (pp. 285–286). New York: Raven Press.

Baer, L. (1994). Factor analysis of symptom subtypes of obsessive compulsive disorder and their relation to personality and tic disorders. *Journal of Clinical Psychiatry, 55,* S18–S23.

Banaschewski, T., Woerner, W., & Rothenberger, A. (2003). Premonitory sensory phenomena and suppressibility of tics in Tourette syndrome: Developmental aspects in children and adolescents. *Developmental Medicine and Child Neurology, 45,* 700–703.

Baron-Cohen, S., Cross, P., Crowson, M., & Robertson, M. (1994). Can children with Gilles de la Tourette syndrome edit their intentions? *Psychological Medicine, 24,* 29–40.

Baron-Cohen, S., & Moriarty, J. (1995). Developmental dysexecutive syndrome: Does it exist? A neuropsychological perspective. In M. Robertson & V. Eapen (Eds.), *Movement and allied disorders in childhood* (pp. 305–316). New York: John Wiley and Sons, Ltd.

Baron-Cohen, S., & Robertson, M. (1995). Children with either autism, Gilles de la Tourette syndrome, or both: Mapping cognition to specific syndromes. *Neurocase, 1,* 101–104.

Baron-Cohen, S., Scahill, V., Izaguirre, J., Hornsey, H., & Robertson, M. M. (1999). The prevalence of Gilles de la Tourette Syndrome in children and adolescents with autism: A large scale study. *Psychological Medicine, 29,* 1151–1159.

Barr, C. L., Wigg, K. G., Pakstis, A. J., Kurlan, R., Pauls, D., Kidd, K. K., et al. (1999). Genome scan for linkage to Gilles de la Tourette Syndrome. *American Journal of Human Genetics, 88,* 437–445.

Bellodi, L., Sciuto, G., Diaferia, G., Ronchi, P., & Smeraldi, E. (1992). Psychiatric disorders in the families of patients with obsessive-compulsive disorder. *Psychiatry Research, 42,* 111–120.

Bernard, B. A., Stebbins, G. T., Siegel, S., Schultz, T. M., Hays, C., Morrissey, M. J., et al. (2006). The impact of co-morbidities on quality of life in Gilles de la Tourette Syndrome. *Neurology, 66*(Suppl 2), A365–A366.

Berthier, M. L., Kulisevsky, J., & Campos, V. M. (1998) Bipolar disorder in adult patients with Tourette's syndrome: A clinical study. *Biological Psychiatry, 43,* 364–370.

Bloch, M. H., Leckman, J. F., Zhu, H., & Peterson, B. S. (2005). Caudate volumes in childhood predict symptom severity in adults with Tourette syndrome. *Neurology, 65,* 1253–1258.

Bloch, M. H., Peterson, B. S., Scahill, L., Otka, J., Katsovich, L., Zhang, H., et al. (2006). Adulthood outcome of tic and obsessive-compulsive symptom severity in children with Tourette syndrome. *Archives of Pediatric and Adolescent Medicine, 160,* 65–69.

Bohlhalter, S., Goldfine, A., Matteson, S., Garraux, G., Hanakawa, T., Kansaku, K., et al. (2006). Neural correlates of tic generation in Tourette syndrome: An event-related functional MRI study. *Brain*, *129*(Pt 8), 2029–2037.

Bond, L., Carlin, J. B., Thomas, L., Rubin, K., & Patton, G. (2001). Does bullying cause emotional problems? A prospective study of young teenagers. *British Medical Journal*, *323*, 480–484.

Bornstein, R. A. (1991). Neuropsychological performance in adults with Tourette Syndrome. *Psychiatry Research*, *37*, 229–236.

Bornstein, R. A., King, G., & Carroll, A. (1983). Neuropsychological abnormalities in Gilles de la Tourette's Syndrome. *Journal of Nervous and Mental Disease*, *171*, 497–502.

Bornstein, R. A., & Yang, V. (1991). Neuropsychological performance in medicated and unmedicated patients with TS. *American Journal of Psychiatry*, *148*, 468–471.

Boswell, J. (1867). *The life of Samuel Johnson*. London: George Routledge and Sons.

Brookshire, B. L., Butler, I. J., Ewing-Cobbs, L., & Fletcher J. M. (1994). Neuropsychological characteristics of children with TS: Evidence for a nonverbal learning disability. *Journal of Clinical and Experimental Neuropsychology*, *16*, 289–302.

Bruun, R., & Budman, C. (1998). Paroxetine as a treatment for anger attacks in patients with Tourette syndrome. *Journal of Clinical Psychiatry*, *59*, 581–588.

Budman, C., Bruun, R., Park, K., Lesser, M., & Olsom, M. (2000). Explosive outbursts in children with Tourette's disorder. *Journal of the American Academy of Child and Adolescent Psychiatry*, *39*, 1270–1276.

Budman, C., Park, K., Olson, M., & Bruun, R. (1998). Rage attacks in children and adolescents with Tourette syndrome: A pilot study. *Journal of Clinical Psychiatry*, *59*, 576–580.

Burd, L., & Kerbeshian, J. (1984). Gilles de la Tourette's syndrome and bipolar disorder. *Archives of Neurology*, *41*, 1236.

Burd, L., Severud, R., Klug, M. G., & Kerbeshian, J. (1999). Prenatal and perinatal risk factors for Tourette disorder. *Journal of Perinatal Medicine*, *27*, 295–302.

Butler, T., Stern, E., & Silbersweig, D. (2006). Functional neuroimaging of Tourette syndrome: Advances and future directions. *Advances in Neurology*, *99*, 115–129.

Caine, E. D., McBride, M. C., Chiverton, P., Bamford, K. A., Rediess, S., & Shiao, J. (1988). Tourette syndrome in Monroe county school children. *Neurology*, *38*, 472–475.

Carter, A. S., O'Donnell, D. A., Schultz, R. T., Scahill, L., Leckman, J. F., & Pauls, D. L. (2000). Social and emotional adjustment in children affected with Gilles de la Tourette's syndrome: Associations with ADHD and family functioning. *Journal of Child Psychology and Psychiatry*, *41*, 215–23.

Carter, A. S., Pauls, D. L., Leckman, J. F., & Cohen, D. J. (1994). A prospective longitudinal study of Gilles de la Tourette syndrome. *Journal of the American Academy of Child and Adolescent Psychiatry*, *33*, 377–385.

Cavanna, A. E., Monaco, F., Mula, M., Robertson, M. M., & Critchley, H. D. (2006a). Uneven focal shoe deterioration in Tourette syndrome. *Neuropsychiatric Disease and Treatment*, *2*, 587–588.

Cavanna, A. E., Robertson, M. M., & Critchley, H. D. (2007). Schizotypal personality traits in Gilles de la Tourette syndrome. *Acta Neurologica Scandinavica*, *116*, 385–391.

Cavanna, A. E., Servo, S., Monaco, F., & Robertson, M. M. (2008). More than tics: The behavioral spectrum of Gilles de la Tourette syndrome. *Journal of Neuropsychiatry and Clinical Neurosciences*, In Press.

Cavanna, A. E., Strigaro, G., Martino D., Robertson, M. M., & Critchley, H. D. (2006b). Compulsive behaviours in Gilles de la Tourette syndrome. *Confinia Neuropsychiatrica*, *1*, 37–40.

Channon, S., Flynn, D., & Robertson, M. (1992). Attentional deficits in Gilles de la Tourette syndrome. *Neuropsychiatry, Neurology, and Behavioral Neurology*, *5*, 170–177.

Channon, S., Gunning, A., Frankl, J., & Robertson, M. M. (2006). Tourette's syndrome (TS): Cognitive performance in adults with uncomplicated TS. *Neuropsychology*, *20*, 58–65.

Channon, S., Pratt, P., & Robertson, M. M. (2003). Executive function, memory, and learning in Tourette's syndrome. *Neuropsychology*, *17*, 247–254.

Chase, T. N., Geoffrey, V., Gillespie, M., & Burrows, G. H. (1986). Structural and functional studies of Gilles de la Tourette syndrome. *Revue Neurologique* (Paris), *142*, 851–855.

Coffey, B. J., Biederman, J., Geller, D. A., Spencer, T., Park, K. S., Shapiro, S. J., et al. (2000). The course of Tourette's disorder: A literature review. *Harvard Review of Psychiatry*. *8*, 192–198.

Comings, D. E., & Comings, B. G. (1987). A controlled study of Tourette's syndrome. 1. Attention-deficit disorder, learning disorders, and school problems. *American Journal of Human Genetics*, *41*, 701–741.

Comings, D. E., Himes, J. A., & Comings, B. G. (1990). An epidemiologic study of Tourette's syndrome in a single school district. *Journal of Clinical Psychiatry*, *51*, 463–469.

Como, P. G. (2001). Neuropsychological function in Tourette syndrome. *Advances in Neurology, 85,* 103–111.

Corbett, J., Mathews, A., Connell, P., & Shapiro, D. (1969). Tics and Gilles de la Tourette's syndrome: A follow-up study and critical review. *British Journal of Psychiatry, 115,* 1229–1241.

Crawford, S., Channon, S., & Robertson M. M. (2005). Tourette's syndrome: performance on tests of behavioural inhibition, working memory and gambling. *Journal of Child Psychology and Psychiatry, 46,* 1327–1336.

Cummings, J. L., & Frankel, M. (1985). Gilles de la Tourette syndrome and the neurological basis of obsessions and compulsions. *Biological Psychiatry, 20,* 1117–1126.

Curtis, D., Robertson, M. M., & Gurling, H. M. (1992). Autosomal dominant gene transmission in a large kindred with Gilles de la Tourette syndrome. *British Journal of Psychiatry, 160,* 845–849.

De Nil, L. F., Sasisekaran, J., Van Lieshout, P. H., & Sandor, P. (2005). Speech disfluencies in individuals with Tourette syndrome. *Journal of Psychosomatic Research, 58,* 97–102.

Deng, H., Le, W. D., Xie, W. J., & Jankovic, J. (2006). Examination of the *SLITRK1* gene in Caucasian patients with Tourette syndrome. *Acta Neurologica Scandinavica, 114,* 400–402.

Eapen, V., Fox-Hiley, P., Banerjee, S., & Robertson, M. (2004). Clinical features and associated psychopathology in a Tourette syndrome cohort. *Acta Neurologica Scandinavica, 109,* 255–260.

Eapen, V., Laker, M., Anfield, A., Dobbs, J., & Robertson, M. M. (2001). Prevalence of tics and Tourette syndrome in an inpatient adult psychiatry setting. *Journal of Psychiatry and Neuroscience, 26,* 417–420.

Eapen, V., Pauls, D., & Robertson, M. (1993). Evidence for autosomal dominant transmission in Tourette's syndrome. *British Journal of Psychiatry, 163,* 593–596.

Eapen, V., Robertson, M. M., Zeitlin, H., & Kurlan, R. (1997). Gilles de la Tourette's Syndrome in special education. *Journal of Neurology, 244,* 378–382.

Elstner, K., Selai, C. E., Trimble, M. R., & Robertson, M. M. (2001). Quality of Life (QOL) of patients with Gilles de la Tourette's syndrome. *Acta Psychiatrica Scandinavica, 103,* 52–59.

Erenberg, G., Cruse, R. P., & Rothner, A. D. (1986). Tourette syndrome: an analysis of 200 pediatric and adolescent cases. *Cleveland Clinic Quarterly, 53,* 127–131.

Erenberg, G., Cruse, R. P., & Rothner, A. D. (1987). The natural history of Tourette syndrome: A follow-up study. *Annals of Neurology, 22,* 383–385.

Ferenczi, S. (1921). Psychoanalytic observations on tic. *International Journal of Psychoanalysis, 2,* 1–30.

Frank, S. (1978). Psycholinguistic findings in Gilles de la Tourette's syndrome. *Journal of Communication Disorders, 11,* 349–363.

Frankel, M., Cummings, J. L., Robertson, M. M., Trimble, M. R., Hill, M. A., & Benson, D. F. (1986). Obsessions and compulsions in Gilles de la Tourette's syndrome. *Neurology, 36,* 378–382.

Freeman, R. D., Fast, D. K., Burd, L., Kerbeshian, J., Robertson, M. M., & Sandor P. (2000). An international perspective on Tourette syndrome: selected findings from 3,500 individuals in 22 countries. *Developmental Medicine and Child Neurology, 42,* 436–447.

Frey, K. A., & Albin, R. L. (2006). Neuroimaging of Tourette syndrome. *Journal of Child Neurology, 21,* 672–677.

Gaffney, G. R. (1994). The MOVES: a self-rating scale for Tourette's syndrome. *Journal of Child Adolescent Psychopharmacology, 4,* 269–280.

George, M. S., Trimble, M. R., Ring, H. A., Sallee, F. R., & Robertson, M. M. (1993). Obsessions in obsessive compulsive disorder with and without Gilles de la Tourette syndrome. *American Journal of Psychiatry, 150,* 93–97.

Georgiou, N., Bradshaw, J. L., Phillips, J. G., Bradshaw, J. A., & Chiu, E. (1995). The Simon effect and attention deficits in Gilles de la Tourette Syndrome and Huntington's disease. *Brain, 118,* 1305–1318.

Gillberg, I. C., Rasmussen, P., Kadesjo, B., Soderstrom, H., Rastam, M., Johnson, M., et al. (2004). Co-existing disorders in ADHD-implications for diagnosis and intervention. *European Child and Adolescent Psychiatry, 13,* 80–89.

Gilles de la Tourette, G. (1885). Etude sur une affection nerveuse caracterisee par de l'incoordination motrice accompagnee d'echolalie et de copralalie. *Archives of Neurology, 9,* 19–42; 158–200.

Gilles de la Tourette, G. (1899). La maladie des tics convulsifs. *La Semaine Medicale, 19,* 153–156.

Goetz, C., & Klawans, H. (1982). Gilles de la Tourette's syndrome. In A. Friedhoff & T. Chase (Eds.), *Gilles de la Tourette's syndrome, advances in neurology,* vol. 35 (pp. 1–16). New York: Raven Press.

Goetz, C. G., Tanner, C. M., Wilson, R. S., & Shannon, K. M. (1987). A rating scale for Gilles de la Tourette's syndrome: Description, reliability, and validity data. *Neurology, 37,* 1542–4.

Golden, G. S. (1984). Psychologic and neuropsychologic aspects of Tourette's syndrome. *Neurologic Clinics, 21,* 91–102.

Golden, G. S., & Greenhill, L. (1981). Tourette syndrome in mentally retarded children. *Mental Retardation, 19,* 17–19.

Grasset, J. (1890). Lecons sur un cas de maladie des tics et un cas de tremblement singulier de la tete et des membres gauches. *Archives of Neurology, 20,* 27–45; 187–211.

Green, R. C., & Pitman, R. K. (1986). Tourette syndrome and obsessive-compulsive disorder. In M. A. Jenike, L. Baer, & W. O. Minichiello (Eds.), *Obsessive-compulsive disorders: Theory and management* (pp. 147–164). Littleton, MA: PSG Publishing Company.

Guinon, G. (1886). Sur la maladie des tics convulsifs. *Revue de Medicine, 6,* 50–80.

Hemmings, S. M., Kinnear, C. J., Lochner, C., Niehaus, D. J., Knowles, J. A., Moolman-Smook, J. C., et al. (2004). Early- versus late-onset obsessive-compulsive disorder: investigating genetic and clinical correlates. *Psychiatry Research, 30,* 175–182.

Hoekstra, P. J., Steenhuis, M. P., Kallenberg, C. G., & Minderaa, R. B. (2004). Association of small life events with self reports of tic severity in pediatric and adult tic disorder patients: A prospective longitudinal study. *Journal of Clinical Psychiatry, 65,* 426–431.

Hornsey, H., Banerjee, S., Zeitlin, H., & Robertson, M. M. (2001). The prevalence of Tourette syndrome in young people in mainstream schools. *Journal of Child Psychology and Psychiatry, 42,* 1035–1039.

Hounie, A. G., do Rosario-Campos, M. C., Diniz, J. B., Shavitt, R. G., Ferrao, Y. A., Lopes, A. C., et al. (2006). Obsessive-compulsive disorder in Tourette syndrome, *Advances in Neurology, 99,* 22–38.

Hyde, T. M., Aaronson, B. A., Randolph, C., Rickler, K. C., & Weinberger, D. R. (1992). Relationship of birth weight to the phenotypic expression of Gilles de la Tourette's syndrome in monozygotic twins. *Neurology, 42*(3 Pt 1), 652–658.

Hyde, T. M., Emsellem, H. A., Randolph, C., Rickler, K. C., & Weinberger, D. R. (1994). Electroencephalographic abnormalities in monozygotic twins with Tourette's syndrome. *British Journal of Psychiatry, 164,* 811–817.

Incagnoli, T., & Kane, R. (1981). Neuropsychological functioning in Gilles de la Tourette's syndrome. *Journal of Clinical Neuropsychology, 3,* 165–169.

Itard, J. M. G. (1825). Memoire sur quelques fonctions involontaires des appareils de la locomotion de la prehension et de la voix. *Archives of General Medicine, 8,* 385–407.

Jankovic, J. (1997). Phenomenology and classification of tics. In J. Jankovic (Ed.), *Neurologic clinics* (pp. 267–275). Philadelphia: WH Saunders Company.

Jankovic, J. (2001). Tourette's syndrome. *New England Journal of Medicine, 345,* 1184–1192.

Kadesjo, B., & Gillberg, C. (2000). Tourette's disorder: epidemiology and comorbidity in primary school children. *Journal of the American Academy of Child and Adolescent Psychiatry, 39,* 548–555.

Keen-Kim, D., Mathews, C. A., Reus, V. I., Lowe, T. L., Herrera, L. D., Budman, C. L., et al. (2006). Overrepresentation of rare variants in a specific ethnic group may confuse interpretation of association analyses. *Human Molecular Genetics, 15,* 3324–3328.

Kelman, D. H. (1965). Gilles de la Tourette's disease in children: A review of the literature. *Journal of Child Psychology and Psychiatry, 6,* 219–226.

Kerbeshian, J., Burd, L., & Klug, M. G. (1995). Comorbid Tourette's disorder and bipolar disorder: an etiologic perspective. *American Journal of Psychiatry, 152,* 1646–1651.

Khalifa, N., & von Knorring, A. L. (2003). Prevalence of tic disorders and Tourette syndrome in a Swedish school population. *Developmental Medicine and Child Neurology, 45,* 315–319.

Khalifa, N., & von Knorring, A. L. (2005). Tourette syndrome and other tic disorders in a total population of children: Clinical assessment and background. *Acta Paediatrica, 94,* 1608–1614.

Kinnear-Wilson, S. A. (1927). Tics and child conditions. *Journal of Neurology and Psychopathology, 8,* 93–109.

Knell, E. R., & Comings, D. E. (1993). Tourette's syndrome and attention-deficit hyperactivity disorder: evidence for a genetic relationship. *The Journal of Clinical Psychiatry, 54,* 331–337.

Kurlan, R., Behr, J., Medved, L., Shoulson, I., Pauls, D., Kidd, J. R., et al. (1986). Familial Tourette's syndrome: Report of a large pedigree and potential for linkage analysis. *Neurology, 36,* 772–776.

Kurlan, R., Daragjati, C., Como, P., McDermott, M. P., Trinidad, K. S., Roddy, S., et al. (1996). Non-obscene complex socially inappropriate behavior in Tourette's syndrome. *Journal of Neuropsychiatry and Clinical Neurosciences, 8,* 311–317.

Kurlan, R., Mc Dermott, M. P., Deeley, C., Como, P. G., Brower, C., Eapen, S., et al. (2001). Prevalence of tics in school children and association with placement in special education. *Neurology, 57,* 1383–1388.

Kushner, H. I. (1995). Medical fictions: the case of the cursing marquise and the (re)construction of Gilles de la Tourette's Syndrome. *Bulletin of the History of Medicine, 69,* 224–254.

Kwak, C., Dat Vuong, K., & Jankovic, J. (2003). Premonitory sensory phenomenon in Tourette's syndrome. *Movement Disorders, 18*(12), 1530–1533.

Lanzi, G., Zambrino, C. A., Termine, C., Palestra, M., Ferrari Ginevra, O., Orcesi, S., et al. (2004). Prevalence of tic disorders among primary school students in the city of Pavia, Italy. *Archives of Disease in Childhood, 89*, 45–47.

Lavoie, M. E., Thibault, G., Stip, E., & O'Connor, K. P. (2007). Memory and executive functions in adults with Gilles de la Tourette syndrome and chronic tic disorder. *Cognitive Neuropsychiatry, 12*, 165–181.

Leckman, J. F. (2002). Tourette's syndrome. *Lancet, 16*, 1577–1586.

Leckman, J. F. (2003). In search of the pathophysiology of Tourette syndrome. In M. A. Bedard, Y. Agid, S. Chouinard, S. Fahn, A. D. Korczyn, & P. Lesperance (Eds.), *Mental and behavioral dysfunction in movement disorders*. (pp. 467–476) Humana Press, Totowa, New Jersey.

Leckman, J. F., Dolnansky, E. S., Hardin, M. T., Clubb, M., Walkup, J. T., Stevenson, J., et al. (1990). Perinatal factors in the expression of Tourette's syndrome: An exploratory study. *Journal of the American Academy of Child and Adolescent Psychiatry, 29*, 220–226.

Leckman, J. F., Grice, D. E., Barr, L. C., de Vries, A. L., Martin, C., Cohen, D. J., et al. (1994–1995). Tic-related vs. non-tic-related obsessive compulsive disorder. *Anxiety, 1*, 208–215.

Leckman, J. F., Pauls, D. L., Zhang, H., Rosario-Campos, M. C., Katsovich, L., Kidd, K. K., et al. (2003). Obsessive-compulsive symptom dimensions in affected sibling pairs diagnosed with Gilles de la Tourette syndrome. *American Journal of Medical Genetics B Neuropsychiatric Genetics, 116*, 60–68.

Leckman, J. F., Riddle, M., & Harden, M. (1989). The Yale global tic severity scale: initial testing of a clinician-rated scale of tic severity. *Journal of the American Academy of Child and Adolescent Psychiatry, 28*, 566–573.

Leckman, J. F., Walker, D. E., & Cohen, D. J. (1993). Premonitory urges in Tourette's syndrome. *American Journal of Psychiatry, 150*, 98–102.

Leckman, J. F., Zhang, H., Vitale, A., Lahnin, F., Lynch, K., Bondi, C., et al. (1998). Course of tic severity in Tourette's syndrome. *Pediatrics, 102*, 14–19.

Lee, C. C., Chou, I. C., Tsai, C. H., Wang, T. R., Li, T. C., & Tsai, F. J. (2005). Dopamine receptor D2 gene polymorphisms are associated in Taiwanese children with Tourette Syndrome. *Pediatric Neurology, 33*, 272–276.

Lees, A., Robertson, M., Trimble, M., & Murray, N. (1984). A clinical study of Gilles de la Tourette's syndrome in the United Kingdom. *Journal of Neurology, Neurosurgery, and Psychiatry, 47*, 1–8.

Leonard, H. L., & Swedo, S. E. (2001). Paediatric autoimmune neuropsychiatric disorders associated with streptococcal infection (PANDAS).

International Journal of Neuropsychopharmacology, 4, 191–198.

Lerner, A., Bagic, A., Boudreau, E. A., Hanakawa, T., Pagan, F., Mari, Z., et al. (2007). Neuroimaging of neuronal circuits involved in tic generation in patients with Tourette syndrome. *Neurology, 68*, 1979–1987.

Lin, H., Katsovich, L., Ghebremichael, M., Findley, D. B., Grantz, H., Lombroso, P. J., et al. (2007). Psychosocial stress predicts future symptom severities in children and adolescents with Tourette syndrome and/or obsessive-compulsive disorder. *Journal of Child Psychology and Psychiatry, 48*, 157–166.

Loiselle, C. R., Lee, O., Moran, T. H., & Singer, H. S. (2004). Striatal microinfusion of Tourette syndrome and PANDAS sera: Failure to induce behavioral changes. *Movement Disorders, 19*, 371–374.

Ludlow, C., Polinsky, R., Caine, E., Bassich, C., & Ebert, M. (1982). Language and speech abnormalities in Tourette's syndrome. In A. Friedhoff and T. Chase (Eds.), *Gilles de la Tourette's Syndrome, Advances in Neurology, vol. 35* (pp. 351–362). New York: Raven Press.

Luo, F., Leckman, J. F., Katsovich, L., Findley, D., Grantz, H., Tucker, D. M., et al. (2004). Prospective longitudinal study of children with tic disorders and/or obsessive-compulsive disorder: Relationship of symptom exacerbations to newly acquired streptococcal infections. *Pediatrics, 113*, e578–e585.

Mahler, M. S. (1949). Psychoanalytic evaluations of tics: A sign and symptom in psychopathology. *Psychoanalytic Study of the Child, 3–4*, 279.

Martino, D., Defazio, G., Church, A. J., Dale, R. C., Giovannoni, G., Robertson, M. M., et al. (2007). Antineuronal antibody status and phenotype analysis in Tourette's syndrome. *Movement Disorders, 22*, 1424–1429.

Mathews, C. A., Jang, K. L., Herrera, L. D., Lowe, T. L., Budman, C. L., Erenberg, G., et al. (2007). Tic symptom profiles in subjects with Tourette Syndrome from two genetically isolated populations. *Biological Psychiatry, 61*, 292–300.

McHenry, L. C., Jr. (1967). Samuel Johnson's tics and gesticulations. *Journal of the History of Medicine, 22*, 152–168.

McMahon, W. M., van de Wetering, B. J., Filloux, F., Betit, K., Coon, H., & Leppert, M. (1996). Bilineal transmission and phenotypic variation of Tourette's disorder in a large pedigree. *Journal of the American Academy of Child and Adolescent Psychiatry, 35*, 672–680.

Mell, L. K., Davis, R. L., & Owens, D. (2005). Association between streptococcal infection and obsessive-compulsive disorder, Tourette's syndrome, and tic disorder. *Pediatrics, 116,* 56–60.

Miguel, E. C., Baer, L., Coffey, B. J., Rauch, S. L., Savage, C. R., O'Sullivan, R. L., et al. (1997). Phenomenological differences appearing with repetitive behaviours in obsessive-compulsive disorder and Gilles de la Tourette's syndrome. *British Journal of Psychiatry, 170,* 140–145.

Miguel, E. C., do Rosario-Campos, M. C., Prado, H. S., do Valle, R., Rauch, S. L., Coffey, B. J., et al. (2000). Sensory phenomena in obsessive-compulsive disorder and Tourette's disorder. *Journal of Clinical Psychiatry, 61,* 150–156.

Milberger, S., Biederman, J., Faraone, S. V., Murphy, J., & Tsuang, M. T. (1995). Attention deficit hyperactivity disorder and comorbid disorders: Issues of overlapping symptoms. *American Journal of Psychiatry, 152,* 1793–1799.

Mink, J. W. (2006). Neurobiology of basal ganglia and Tourette syndrome: Basal ganglia circuits and thalamocortical outputs. *Advances in Neurology, 99,* 89–98.

Moll, G. H., Heinrich, H., Trott, G. E., Wirth, S., Bock, N., & Rothenberger A. (2001). Children with comorbid attention-deficit-hyperactivity disorder and tic disorder: Evidence for additive inhibitory deficits within the motor system. *Annals of Neurology, 49,* 393–396.

Montgomery, M. A., Clayton, P. J., & Friedhoff, A. J. (1982). Psychiatric illness in Tourette syndrome patients and first-degree relatives. In A. J. Friedhoff and T. N. Chase (Eds.), *Gilles de la Tourette Syndrome, Advances in Neurology, vol. 35* (pp. 335–340). New York: Raven Press.

Moriarty, J., Varma, A. R., Stevens, J., Fish, M., Trimble, M. R., & Robertson, M. M. (1997). A volumetric MRI study of Gilles de la Tourette's syndrome. *Neurology, 49,* 410–415.

Morphew, J. A., & Sim, M. (1969). Gilles de la Tourette's syndrome: A clinical and psychopathological study. *British Journal of Medical Psychology, 42,* 293–301.

Mula M., Cavanna, A. E., Critchley, H. D., Robertson, M. M., & Monaco, F. (2008). Phenomenology of obsessive compulsive disorder in patients with temporal lobe epilepsy and Gilles de la Tourette syndrome. *Journal of Neuropsychiatry and Clinical Neurosciences, 20,* 223–226.

Murray, T. J. (1979). Dr. Samuel Johnson's movement disorders. *British Medical Journal, 1,* 1610–1614.

Nomoto, F., & Machiyama, Y. (1990) An epidemiological study of tics. *Journal of Psychiatry and Neurology, 44,* 649–655.

O'Quinn, A., & Thompson, R. (1980). Tourette's syndrome: An expanded review. *Pediatrics, 66,* 420–424.

Ozonoff, S., Strayer, D. L., McMahon, W. M., & Filloux, F. (1994). Executive function abilities in autism and Tourette syndrome: An information processing approach. *Journal of Child Psychology and Psychiatry, 35,* 1015–1032.

Packer, L. E. (1997). Social and educational resources for patients with Tourette syndrome. *Neurologic Clinics, 15,* 457–473.

Pauls, D. L. (2003). An update on the genetics of Gilles de la Tourette Syndrome. *Journal of Psychosomatic Research, 55(1),* 7–12.

Pauls, D. L. (2006). A genome-wide scan and fine mapping in Tourette syndrome families. *Advances in Neurology, 99,* 130–135.

Pauls, D. L., Cohen, D. J., Kidd, K. K., & Leckman, J. F. (1988). Tourette syndrome and neuropsychiatric disorders: Is there a genetic relationship? *American Journal of Human Genetics, 43,* 206–217.

Pauls, D. L., Leckman, J., Towbin, K. E., Zahner, G. E., & Cohen, D. J. (1986a). A possible genetic relationship exists between Tourette's syndrome and obsessive-compulsive disorder. *Psychopharmacology Bulletin, 22,* 730–733.

Pauls, D. L., Towbin, K. E., Leckman, J. F., Zahner, G. E., & Cohen, D. J. (1986b). Gilles de la Tourette's syndrome and obsessive compulsive disorder. *Archives of General Psychiatry, 43,* 1180–1182.

Perugi, G., Akiskal, H. S., Ramacciotti, S., Nassini, S., Toni, C., Milanfranchi, A., et al. (1999). Depressive comorbidity of panic, social phobic, and obsessive-compulsive disorders re-examined: Is there a bipolar II connection? *Journal of Psychiatric Research, 33,* 53–61.

Perugi, G., Toni, C., Frare, F., Traverso, M. C., Hantouche, E., & Akiskal, H. S. (2002). Obsessive-compulsive-bipolar comorbidity: A systematic exploration of clinical features and treatment outcome. *Journal of Clinical Psychiatry, 63,* 1129–1134.

Peterson, B. S. (2001). Neuroimaging studies of Tourette syndrome: a decade of progress. In D. J. Cohen, C. G. Goetz, and J. Jankovic (Eds.), *Tourette Syndrome.* (pp. 179–196) Philadelphia: Lippincott Williams & Wilkins.

Peterson, B. S., Leckman, J. F., Scahill, L., Naftolin, F., Keefe, D., Charest, N. J., et al. (1994). Steroid hormones and Tourette's syndrome: Early experience with antiandrogen therapy. *Journal of Clinical Psychopharmacology, 14,* 131–135.

Peterson, B. S., Riddle, M., & Cohen, D. (1993). Reduced basal ganglia volumes in Tourette's syndrome using 3D reconstruction techniques from MRI. *Neurology, 43,* 941–949.

Peterson, B. S., Thomas, P., Kane, M. J., Scahill, L., Zhang, H., Bronen, R., et al. (2003). Basal ganglia volumes in patients with Gilles de la Tourette syndrome. *Archives of General Psychiatry, 60,* 415–424.

Peterson, B. S., Zhang, H., Anderson, G. M., & Leckman, J. F. (1998). A double-blind, placebo-controlled, crossover trial of an antiandrogen in the treatment of Tourette's syndrome. *Journal of Clinical Psychopharmacology, 18,* 324–331.

Plessen, K. J., Gruner, R., Lundervold, A., Hirsch, J. G., Xu, D., Bansal, R., et al. (2006). Reduced white matter connectivity in the corpus callosum of children with Tourette syndrome. *Journal of Child Psychology and Psychiatry, 47,* 1013–1022.

Plessen, K. J., Wentzel-Larsen, T., Hugdahl, K., Feineigle, P., Klein, J., Staib, L. H., et al. (2004). Altered interhemispheric connectivity in individuals with Tourette's disorder. *American Journal of Psychiatry, 161,* 2028–2037.

Randolph, C., Hyde, T. M., Gold, J. M., Goldberg, T. E., & Weinberger, D. R. (1993). TS in monozygotic twins. Relationship of tic severity to neurospychological functions. *Archives of Neurology, 50,* 725–728.

Regeur, L., Pakkenberg, B., Fog, R., & Pakkenberg, H. (1986). Clinical features and long term treatment with pimozide in 65 patients with Gilles de la Tourette's syndrome. *Journal of Neurology, Neurosurgery and Psychiatry, 49,* 791–795.

Rickards, H. (2001). Signing coprolalia and attempts to disguise in a man with prelingual deafness. *Movement Disorders, 16,* 790–791.

Rizzo, R., Curatolo, P., Gulisano, M., Virzi, M., Arpino, C., & Robertson, M. M. (2007). Disentangling the effects of Tourette syndrome and attention deficit hyperactivity disorder on cognitive and behavioral phenotypes. *Brain and Development, 29,* 413–420.

Rizzo, R., Gulisano, M., Pavone, P., Fogliari, F., & Robertson, M. M. (2006). Increased antistreptoc-cal antibody titres and anti-basal ganglia antibodies in Tourette's syndrome: A controlled study. *Journal of Child Neurology, 21,* 747–753.

Robertson, M. M. (1995). The relationship between Gilles de la Tourette's syndrome and obsessive compulsive disorder. *Journal of Serotonin Research, Suppl. 1,* 49–62.

Robertson, M. M. (2000). Invited Review. Tourette Syndrome, associated conditions and the complexities of treatment. *Brain, 123,* 425–462.

Robertson, M. M. (2004). Tourette Syndrome; an update. Psychiatry 111, The Medicine Publishing Company Group (ed Littlewood RL). *Psychiatry, 3*(8), 3–7.

Robertson, M. M. (2006a). Mood disorders and Gilles de la Tourette's syndrome: An update on prevalence, etiology, comorbidity, clinical associa-tions, and implications. *Journal of Psychosomatic Research, 61,* 349–358.

Robertson, M. M. (2006b). Attention deficit hyperactivity disorder, tics and Tourette's syndrome: The relationship and treatment implications. *European Child and Adolescent Psychiatry, 15,* 1–11.

Robertson, M. M., Banerjee, S., Fox-Hiley, P. J., & Tannock, C. (1997). Personality disorder and psychopathology in Tourette's syndrome: A controlled study. *British Journal of Psychiatry, 171,* 283–286.

Robertson, M. M., Banerjee, S., Kurlan, R., Cohen, D. J., Leckman, J. F., McMahon, W., et al. (1999). The Tourette syndrome diagnostic confidence index: Development and clinical associations. *Neurology, 53,* 2108–2112.

Robertson, M. M., & Cavanna, A. E. (2007). The Gilles de la Tourette syndrome: A principal component factor analytic study of a large pedigree. *Psychiatric Genetics, 17,* 143–152.

Robertson, M. M., Channon, S., Baker, J., & Flynn, D. (1993). The psychopathology of Gilles de la Tourette syndrome: a controlled study. *British Journal of Psychiatry, 162,* 114–117.

Robertson, M. M., & Eapen, V. (1992). Pharmacologic controversy of CNS stimulants in Gilles de la Tourette's syndrome. *Clinical Neuropharmacology, 15,* 408–425.

Robertson, M. M., & Eapen, V. (1996). The National Hospital Interview Schedule for the assessment of Gilles de la Tourette syndrome. *International Journal of Methods in Psychiatric Research, 6,* 203–226.

Robertson, M. M., & Gourdie, A. (1990). Familial Tourette's syndrome in a large British pedigree: Associated psychopathology, severity of Tourette's and potential for linkage analysis. *British Journal of Psychiatry, 156,* 515–521.

Robertson, M. M., & Orth, M. (2006). Behavioral and affective disorders in Tourette syndrome. *Advances in Neurology, 99,* 39–60.

Robertson, M. M., & Reinstein, D. Z. (1991). Convulsive tic disorder. Georges Gilles de la Tourette, Guinon, and Grasset on the phenomenology and psychopathology of Gilles de la Tourette syndrome. *Behavioral Neurology, 4,* 29–56.

Robertson, M. M., Trimble, M. R., & Lees, A. J. (1988). The psychopathology of the Gilles de la Tourette syndrome: A phenomenological analysis. *British Journal of Psychiatry, 152,* 383–390.

Robertson, M. M., Trimble, M. R., & Lees, A. J. (1989). Self-injurious behavior and the Gilles de la Tourette syndrome. A clinical study and review of the literature. *Psychological Medicine, 19,* 611–625.

Rosario-Campos, M. C., Leckman, J. F., Curi, M., Quadrano, S., Katsovich, L., Miguel, E. C., et al. (2005). A family study of early-onset obsessive-compulsive disorder. *American Journal of Medical Genetics. Part B, Neuropsychiatric Genetics, 136,* 92–97.

Salmon, G., James, A., & Smith, D. M. (1998). Bullying in schools: Self reported anxiety, depression, and self esteem in secondary school children. *British Medical Journal, 317,* 924–925.

Sandor, P., Musisi, S., Moldofsky, H., & Lang, A. (1990). Tourette syndrome: A follow-up study. *Journal of Clinical Psychopharmacology, 10,* 197–199.

Santangelo, S. L., Pauls, D. L., Goldstein, J. M., Faraone, S. V., Tsuang, M. T., & Leckman, J. F. (1994). Tourette's syndrome: What are the influences of gender and comorbid obsessive-compulsive disorder? *Journal of the American Academy of Child and Adolescent Psychiatry, 33,* 795–804.

Schuerholz, L. J., Baumgardner T. L., Singer, S. S., Reiss, A. L., & Denckla, M. B. (1996). Neuropsychological Status of Children with Tourette's syndrome with and without attention deficit hyperactivity disorder. *Neurology, 46,* 958–965.

Schuerholz, L. J., Singer, H. S., & Denckla, M. B. (1998). Gender study of neuropsychological and neuromotor function in children with Tourette syndrome with and without attention-deficit hyperactivity disorder. *Journal of Child Neurology, 13,* 277–282.

Shallice, T. (1988). *From neuropsychology to neural structure.* Cambridge: Cambridge University Press.

Shapiro, A., Shapiro, E., & Clarkin, J. (1974). Clinical psychological testing in Tourette's syndrome. *Journal of Personality Assessment, 38,* 464–478.

Shapiro, A. K., Shapiro, E. S., Bruun, R. D., & Sweet, R. D. (1978). *Gilles de la Tourette Syndrome.* New York: Raven Press.

Sherman, E. M., Shepard, L., Joschko, M., & Freeman, R. D. (1998). Sustained attention and impulsivity in children with Tourette syndrome: Comorbidity and confounds. *Journal of Clinical and Experimental Neuropsychology, 20,* 644–657.

Schultz, R. T., Carter, A. S., Gladstone, M., Scahill, L., Leckman, J. F., Peterson, B. S., et al. (1998). Visual-motor functioning in children with Tourette syndrome. *Neuropsychology, 12,* 134–145.

Singer, H. S. (2005). Tourette's syndrome: From behaviour to biology. *Lancet Neurology, 4,* 149–159.

Singer, H. S., Reiss, A., Brown, J., Aylward, E. H., Shih, B., Chee, E., et al. (1993). Volumetric MRI changes in basal ganglia of children with Tourette's syndrome. *Neurology, 43,* 950–956.

Spencer, T., Biederman, J., Harding, M., O'Donnell, D., Wilens, T., Faraone, S., et al. (1998). Disentangling the overlap between Tourette's disorder and ADHD. *Journal of Child Psychology and Psychiatry, 39,* 1037–1044.

Stephens, R. J., & Sandor, P. (1999). Aggressive behaviour in children with Tourette syndrome and comorbid attention-deficit hyperactivity disorder and obsessive-compulsive disorder. *Canadian Journal of Psychiatry, 44,* 1036–1042.

Stern, E., Silbersweig, D. A., Chee, K. Y., Holmes, A., Robertson, M. M., Trimble, M., et al. (2000). A functional neuroanatomy of tics in Tourette syndrome. *Archives of General Psychiatry, 57,* 741–748.

Sukhodolsky, D. G., Scahill, L., Zhang, H., Peterson, B. S., King, R. A., Lombroso, P. J., et al. (2003). Disruptive behavior in children with Tourette's syndrome: Association with ADHD comorbidity, tic severity, and functional impairment. *Journal of the American Academy of Child and Adolescent Psychiatry, 42,* 98–105.

Sutherland, R., Kolb, B., Schoel, W., Whishaw, I., & Davies, D. (1982). Neuropsychological assessment of children and adults with Tourette's syndrome: A comparison with learning difficulties and schizophrenia. In A. Friedhoff and T. Chase (Eds.), *Gilles de la Tourette's Syndrome, Advances in Neurology, vol. 35* (pp. 311–322). New York: Raven Press.

Swedo, S. E., Leonard, H. L., Garvey, M., Mittleman, B., Allen, A. J., Perlmutter, S., et al. (1998). Pediatric autoimmune neuropsychiatric disorders associated with streptococcal infections: Clinical description of the first 50 cases. *American Journal of Psychiatry, 155,* 264–271.

Tabori-Kraft, J. (2007). Clinical features of children with tic disorders: A population based study of children aged 9–11. *International Scientific Symposium on Tourette Syndrome Lillehammer,* Norway, 66.

Takeuchi, K., Yamashita, M., Morikiyo, M., Takeda, N., Morita, K., Tamura, T., et al. (1986). Gilles de la Tourette's syndrome and schizophrenia. *Journal of Nervous and Mental Disease, 174,* 247–248.

Taylor, E. (1985). Syndromes of overactivity and attention deficit. In M. Rutter and L. Hersov (Eds.), *Child and adolescent psychiatry: Modern approaches/II* (pp. 424–443). Oxford/Boston: Blackwells Scientific Publications.

Thibert, A. L., Day, H. I., & Sandor, P. (1995). Self-concept and self-consciousness in adults with Tourette syndrome. *Canadian Journal of Psychiatry, 40,* 35–39.

Walkup, J. T., LaBuda, M. C., Singer, H. S., Brown, J., Riddle, M. A., & Hurko, O. (1996). Family study and segregation analysis of Tourette syndrome: Evidence for a mixed model of inheritance. *American Journal of Human Genetics, 59,* 684–693.

Walkup, J. T., Rosenberg, L. A., Brown, J., & Singer, H. S. (1992). The validity of instruments measuring tic severity in Tourette's syndrome. *Journal of the American Academy of Child and Adolescent Psychiatry, 31,* 472–477.

Wang, H. S., & Kuo, M. F. (2003). Tourette's syndrome in Taiwan: An epidemiological study of tic disorders in an elementary school at Taipei County. *Brain Development, 25*(Suppl 1), 29–31.

Wilson, R. S., Garron, D.C., Tanner, C. M., & Klawans, H. L. (1982). Behavior disturbance in children with Tourette syndrome. In A. J. Friedhoff and T. N. Chase (Eds.), *Gilles de la Tourette's syndrome, advances in neurology, vol. 35* (pp. 329–334). New York: Raven Press.

Winokur, G. (1997). All roads lead to depression: Clinically homogeneous, etiologically heterogeneous. *Journal of Affective Disorders, 45,* 97–108.

Woods, D. W., Piacentini, J., Himle, M. B., & Chang, S. (2005). Premonitory Urge for Tics Scale (PUTS): Initial psychometric results and examination of the premonitory urge phenomenon in youths with tic disorders. *Journal of Developmental Behavioural Pediatrics, 26,* 397–403.

Wong, C. K., & Lau, J. T. (1992). Psychiatric morbidity in a Chinese primary school in Hong Kong. *Australian and New Zealand Journal of Psychiatry, 26,* 459–466.

World Health Organization. (1992). *International classification of diseases and health-related problems/X.* Geneva: World Health Organization.

Yaryura-Tobias, J. A., Neziroglu, F., Howard, S., & Fuller, B. (1981). Clinical aspects of Gilles de la Tourette syndrome. *Journal of Orthomolecular Psychiatry, 10,* 263–268.

Yordanova, J., Dumais-Huber, C., & Rothenberger, A. (1996). Coexistence of tics and hyperactivity in children: No additive at the psychophysiological level. *International Journal of Psychophysiology, 21,* 121–133.

Yordanova, J., Dumais-Huber, C., Rothenberger, A., & Woerner, W. (1997). Frontocortical activity in children with comorbidity of tic disorder and attention-deficit hyperactivity disorder. *Biological Psychiatry, 41,* 585–594.

Yordanova, J., Heinrich, H., Kolev, V., & Rothenberger, A. (2006). Increased event-related theta activity as a psychophysiological marker of comorbidity in children with tics and attention-deficit/hyperactivity disorders. *Neuroimage, 32,* 940–955.

Zheng, R. Y., Jin, R., Xu, H. Q., Huang, W. W., Chen, H., Shao, B., et al. (2004). Study on the prevalence of tic disorders in schoolchildren aged 16 years old in Wenzhou. *Zhongua Liu Xing Bing Za Zhi, 25,* 745–747.

Zhu, Y., Leung, K. M., Liu, P. Z., Zhou, M., & Su, L. Y. (2006). Comorbid behavioral problems in TS are persistently correlated with the severity of tic symptoms. *Australian and New Zealand Journal of Psychiatry, 40,* 67–73.

12

The Neuropsychology of Epilepsy

Henry A. Buchtel and Linda M. Selwa

Seizures, Stigma, Localization, and Treatment

Epilepsy was defined in 2005 by the International League Against Epilepsy as "a disorder of the brain characterized by an enduring predisposition to generate epileptic seizures and by the neurological, cognitive, psychological and social consequences of this condition" (Fisher et al., 2005). This new interpretation of the illness emphasizes the importance of the neuropsychological and behavioral aspects of epilepsy. For many years the behavioral manifestations of acute seizures, which can include fear, inattention, anger, or mood changes, have attracted the attention of behavioral neurologists, psychiatrists, and neuropsychologists. In recent years, the importance of cognitive and psychological assessments has been recognized in the evaluation of epilepsy surgery patients. Social factors have been recognized as significant determinants of the quality of life of epilepsy patients. This chapter will provide a brief description of the brain substrates that predispose to epilepsy and the classification of epilepsy syndromes. Information about cognitive, social, and behavioral issues for patients with epilepsy will be provided, and psychological syndromes that can mimic epilepsy will be described. Finally, the assessment of and treatment options for patients with epilepsy will be reviewed.

A review of the brain abnormalities causing epilepsy and the specific biochemical events that cause the onset of a particular seizure is beyond the scope of this chapter. An excellent review can be found in Dichter (1998). In general, epilepsy results from hyperexcitability in neuronal circuits, resulting from genetic, structural, or biochemical alterations in fundamental neuronal function. Basic molecular mechanisms of this hyperexcitability are still being studied. Likely factors that are critical to epileptogenesis in various types of epilepsy include dysfunction in sodium, calcium, or potassium channels in excitable membranes, abnormalities in neurotransmitter receptors or transport molecules, and changes in trophic substances that determine cellular growth and plasticity. Specific examples of potential cellular influences of epilepsy include enhanced calcium currents and downregulated potassium currents in mesial temporal lobe epilepsy, which is likely to be influenced by the effects of GABA metabotropic receptors in the cortex and glutamate (AMPA and Kainate) receptors in cortical and hippocampal neurons. Neuronal plasticity and interconnection are also critical for initiation and propagation of many types of seizures and these relationships can be altered through any combination of acquired brain abnormalities and genetic predispositions.

The genetics of epilepsy is complex and only a small proportion of epilepsies have been characterized genetically. Most individuals with epilepsy do not have a first-degree relative with epilepsy, and when a family history is present, a simple Mendelian pattern is not present. However, if an individual has epilepsy without any obvious precipitating cause (e.g., head injury), the chance that a sibling (3.6%) or offspring (10.6%) will have epilepsy is higher than in the general population (1.7%). The risk of epilepsy is not greater in more distant relatives (nieces, nephews, and grandchildren). The evidence that the apparent heritability is genetic rather than, for example, environmental, comes from twin studies. If one of a pair of monozygotic twins has epilepsy, there is about a 49% probability that the other one will also have epilepsy. If the twins are dizygotic, the concordance rate is considerably lower, about 16% (Kjeldsen et al., 2003). Same-sex dizygotic twins have a higher concordance rate than different-sex twins (13% versus 5.5%, Kjeldsen et al., 2003). When both twins have epilepsy, it is almost always of the same kind, that is, partial versus generalized (94%, Berkovic et al., 1998).

Prevalence and incidence: Estimates of the *prevalence* of epilepsy in the general population, that is, the ratio of individuals affected to those unaffected, have ranged from 2 per 1000 to 50 per 1000. The variability may reflect the different definitions of what constitutes epilepsy (Is there a minimum seizure frequency?, Are febrile seizures included?, Is the diagnosis accurate?, and so forth). On average, the most accurate estimates suggest that the prevalence is around 5 per 1000, meaning that in a city of 1,000,000 there would be 5000 individuals with seizures. Thus, in the United States, with a population just above 300,000,000, there are approximately 1.5 million individuals with epilepsy. Some studies have estimated the prevalence to be as high as 50 million, with more than 300,000 children under the age of 14 years and more than 500,000 individuals over the age of 65. With 6.6 billion individuals in the world, approximately 33 million will have epilepsy. Some estimates are as high as 50 million. Twenty to thirty percent of these will have intractable seizures (uncontrollable with current medical treatments). Over a lifetime, 3%–5% of all individuals will have at least one seizure; of those who have a seizure, approximately 12% will develop chronic epilepsy. The cost of this common debilitating illness in terms of medical treatment, mental and emotional disability, and social dysfunction is substantial.

The *incidence* of epilepsy (new cases in a particular time period) has been estimated to be around 0.5 to 1.0 per 1000 per year, meaning that in a group of 1,000,000 individuals there would be about 500–1000 new cases each year. Data from studies in Great Britain indicate that most seizure disorders begin in the age range 0–4 years (0.75/1000). The next most common ages of onset are 15–19 years (0.53/1000), 10–14 years (0.44/1000), and 5–9 years (0.33/1000). All other age groups have incidence rates below 0.23/1000. Males and females appear to be equally affected and there are more left-handers with epilepsy than would be expected by chance.

The diagnosis of epilepsy is made by combining a witnessed description of the behavioral manifestations of brain electrical abnormalities and the results of diagnostic tests, including EEG (electroencephalography) and structural imaging with MRI. The differential diagnosis of epilepsy includes syncope, parasomnias, complicated migraines, and metabolic abnormalities including hyper/hypoglycemia. The EEG is abnormal in 60% of patients with epilepsy between seizures. During an epileptic seizure, if consciousness is impaired the EEG will demonstrate clear abnormalities. In those with psychological episodes resembling seizures, there are clear distinguishing clinical features, and the EEG is normal during the episodes despite apparent loss of consciousness. Essentially, epilepsy is an illness characterized by repetitive seizures. Some seizures are symptomatic of brief systemic changes that are not dependent on specific localized neuronal abnormalities in the brain. Seizures can occur due to drug intoxication, alcohol withdrawal, or glucose or electrolyte imbalances, and these episodes are not considered to be epileptic in the same sense that a spontaneous predisposition to recurrent stereotyped episodes are. Patients with epilepsy have a lasting neuronal predisposition to abnormal electrical discharges that remains even when acute episodes are controlled with medications.

In social terms, the stigma and loss of independence that occurs as a result of the disease are often as or more detrimental to overall quality of life than the cerebral dysfunction that has caused the episodes. The involuntary contractions, unusual vocalizations and behavior, incontinence, and tongue biting that occur during many seizures result in fear and disgust in uneducated observers and lead to a substantial social stigma. In many cultures, those with seizures are considered to be deranged or dangerous, and in some it is even felt that their condition may be infectious. In ancient Greece, these patients were felt to be possessed, and epilepsy was called the "sacred disease" (see Tempkin, 1971 for an excellent historical review). While the attitudes of modern society has improved, epilepsy patients are often denied employment in public positions and are not allowed to drive or operate many kinds of machinery. Seizures are hidden as much as possible; the social isolation of individuals with this disorder means that many in the population have never seen a seizure.

Classification: The most recent discussion from the International League Against Epilepsy about the best scheme for classification and terminology of seizures occurred in 2001 (Engel, 2001). We will attempt to provide a concise summary of the most current terminology about the types of seizures and the epileptic syndromes that exist. In general, seizure types refer to the behavioral phenomenology (semiology) and EEG findings in particular events. Epilepsy syndromes refer to a more specific individual diagnosis that takes into account the cause of the seizures, semiology and EEG findings, and likely prognostic outcome. Further information is available in books and helpful Internet sites listed in Appendix 1. In terms of epilepsy types, seizures with known structural abnormalities or clear preceding brain injury are generally referred to as *symptomatic*. Examples are seizures arising from mesial temporal lobe sclerosis, neuronal migrational errors in the cerebral cortex, stroke, head injury, anoxia, tumors, or cerebral palsy. If the cause is not known, the epilepsy is *idiopathic* or *cryptogenic*. The former term is used when no identifiable cause of the seizures can be found. The latter term is used when the clinicians think that there is an abnormality in brain structure but it has not yet been identified.

A second classification dimension is based on the brain regions felt to be responsible for the generation of the epileptogenic zone. If the epilepsy involves seizures that start in one cortical structure and spread to a variable degree to other structures, it is referred to as a *partial* epilepsy (formerly called focal seizures). The individual may experience unusual emotional, cognitive, sensory, motor, or autonomic phenomena that reflect the area of onset of individual seizures. Examples of focal seizures that can occur with this type of epilepsy include those with olfactory auras, prominent emotional changes, visual symptoms, or involuntary motor movements. Reflex epilepsies are generally partial seizure disorders triggered by activation of the irritable epileptogenic zone (e.g., Heschel's gyrus seizures can begin after exposure to specific trigger sounds). Idiopathic partial epilepsies include benign epilepsy with centrotemporal spikes (BECTS) and benign occipital epilepsy. The most common refractory symptomatic partial epilepsy in adults is mesial temporal epilepsy.

If the entire brain is involved at the outset of ictal events or in the generation of the seizures, the condition is classified as *generalized* epilepsy. Some patients with generalized epilepsies can have both partial onset seizures and generalized seizures. Most patients with generalized epilepsy have generalized electrographic discharges, and most lose consciousness with the majority of their seizures, but exceptions exist in cases where the generator of the seizures is felt to represent a global process. Idiopathic generalized epilepsies include absence epilepsy, epilepsy with generalized tonic-clonic seizures (GTCs), and juvenile myoclonic epilepsy. Symptomatic generalized epilepsies include Lennox-Gastaut syndrome and seizures in patients with early onset injuries.

In the case of partial seizures, if the episode progresses to amnesia for the event or impairment or loss of consciousness, it is referred to as a complex partial seizure. If this initial period is followed by a typical GTC, the event is called a "secondarily generalized partial seizure." Generalized seizure types include GTC, tonic seizures, atonic seizures, myoclonic seizures, and absence seizures.

Most of these seizures are brief: GTCs usually last between 60 and 90 seconds. When an individual seizure lasts longer than 30 minutes, or repeated seizures continue for 30 minutes without resumption of normal behavior, the event is termed "status epilepticus." Status epilepticus with generalized convulsive movements has a mortality of over 20% in several U.S. series, with the worst prognosis in older patients without a prior diagnosis of epilepsy. The sequelae of status epilepticus include cognitive, cerebellar, or even motor deficits.

In adults partial epilepsies are most common, with temporal lobe epilepsy accounting for the majority of those with partial onset seizures. In adults over 50, stroke is the most common cause of epilepsy, with hemorrhagic strokes resulting in the highest incidence of seizures. Idiopathic generalized epilepsies account for roughly 30% of seizure disorders, with absence epilepsies more common in children and adolescents. Idiopathic epilepsy is generally more amenable to treatment with antiepileptic drugs (AEDs) than symptomatic generalized epilepsies.

There is a widespread perception that having seizures is bad for the brain. Clinicians frequently see some of their medically refractory patients (patients whose seizures cannot be controlled by medication) deteriorate over the years, and it is natural to assume that the seizures themselves are the cause. Obvious reasons could be prolonged periods of apnea during the seizure and the increased area of the brain with abnormal neuronal discharges caused by kindling. A less obvious cause is falling during seizures, leading to multiple head injuries. An alternative is that the brain disease that causes the seizures is progressive in some cases. It is also possible that the perceived deterioration is rare and that the vast majority of patients remain stable cognitively despite the continuation of their seizures. Data on both sides of this argument have been published. Helmstaedter et al. (2003) followed 249 patients (147 surgically treated and 102 medically treated) and reported that chronic uncontrolled seizures led to memory decline, consistent with progressive medial temporal lobe atrophy. Most recently, a study has been published showing that the expected practice effect of repeat cognitive testing is absent in patients with intractable seizures (Hermann et al., 2006). The lack of improvement was seen as a decline from expectation. However, it is also possible that these patients do not benefit from practice effects and simply perform at the same level over multiple assessments.

Neuropsychometric Testing in Epilepsy

Choosing the Right Interictal Tests for Localization and Evaluation of the Patient

There are at least four primary reasons for assessing cognitive and noncognitive abilities in patients with epilepsy. Given the difficulties with normal education in children with seizures, it is often valuable to carry out baseline intelligence and memory testing early in the child's school career in order to maximize the chance that the child's educational curriculum is tailored to his or her cognitive abilities. A second reason for assessing and monitoring cognitive abilities is to determine whether changes in medication regimen have affected intellectual or attentional abilities. Third, the neuropsychological profile of patients with seizures can provide indications of when to consider seizures of psychogenic origin; see below for further discussion of this distinction. Finally, some patients have medically intractable seizures and may be considered for surgical relief. If so, it is important to carry out a full neuropsychological assessment as a baseline before surgery and to determine whether the pattern of deficits is in correspondence with other sources of evidence for the lateralization and localization of the suspected epileptogenic focus. The tests and procedures for each of these four purposes will vary, but in each case up-to-date intelligence and memory testing is clearly indicated. Objective sensory and motor testing is also clearly needed, and the use of a dynamometer and tapping instrument are used in psychometric evaluations in order to have objective numbers that are reliable. The minimum testing allowable can be inferred from the test battery used in a recently completed study of the benefits from early surgical interventions (ERSET); this had a 90-minute neuropsychological test battery agreed upon by neuropsychologists in 18 different sites around the United States. This abbreviated battery consisted of the following measures: WAIS-III or WISC-III Vocabulary, Block Design, and Digit Span; Rey Auditory Verbal Learning Test (RAVLT); Boston Naming Test (60 item) (BNT); Controlled Oral Word Association Test (COWAT); Brief Visuospatial Memory Test-Revised (BVMT-R); Trail-Making Test (A & B) (TMT); Grooved Pegboard (full board, one trial): and the Multiple Ability Self-Report Questionnaire (MASQ). The last measure is used to assess subjective changes in cognition by asking questions about the existence and frequency of real-life cognitive failures (e.g., "I forget important things I was told just a few days ago.").

At the University of Michigan, as at many other centers evaluating patients for seizure surgery, we add to this list a number of cognitive, sensory, motoric, and mood measures. We include the other WAIS-III subtests for full Verbal and Performance IQ measures, the Wechsler Memory Scale-III, Grip Strength and Finger Oscillation, the expanded Halstead–Reitan Neuropsychological Inventory (Tapping, Tactual Performance Test, Speech Perception, Seashore Rhythm Test, Category Test), Aphasia Screening, and Trail-Making Test (A&B). To assess mood and personality variables, we give the MMPI-2, Miale-Holsopple Sentence Completion, the Washington Psychosocial Seizure Inventory, and a Self-Rating Questionnaire.

Inferences about the location(s) of neurocognitive dysfunction are based on the pattern of strengths and weaknesses in the results of the neuropsychological assessment. The examiner first has to take into account educational and psychosocial influences on this pattern. Once this is done, the presence or absence of language deficits, visual–spatial problems, executive function, and motor deficits can be used to identify regions of abnormal functioning. Naming problems are usually seen when the epileptogenic focus involves the functions of the language-dominant hemisphere (usually left hemisphere in right-handers and most of left-handers); verbal memory problems are usually seen with mesial temporal lobe focus in the language-dominant hemisphere; if naming problems do not accompany these verbal memory deficits, the dysfunction is probably mesial alone, without involvement of the neocortex. Visual–spatial and somatosensory disorders are usually indicative of parietal dysfunction, and abnormal scores on motor and executive function tasks usually indicate a disturbance of functions of anterior brain regions. Many patients have neurocognitive deficits in more than one area, indicating that the process or injury causing their seizures has affected more than one part of the brain. This does not mean that there are multiple epileptogenic foci, but if the individual is being considered for epilepsy surgery, the best candidates for successful control of seizures after surgery are those whose neurocognitive deficits are restricted to the region that has been identified as abnormal by other means (EEG, imaging).

The Wada Test

One of the most fruitful procedures performed during the evaluation for seizure surgery is a test during which a neuroradiologist injects an anesthetic (sodium amobarbital or methohexital) into the internal carotid artery of one hemisphere and then the other. This temporarily inactivates large portions of the hemisphere on the side of the injection, either directly or indirectly (e.g., visual cortex is deafferented by interruption of neuronal activity in the lateral geniculate). This allows the clinicians to determine whether language abilities are on the side being injected and to allow an assessment of the likelihood that surgery on that side would lead to postsurgery amnesia. The test frequently goes by the name intracarotid amobarbital procedure (IAP), but the increasing use of methohexital (Brevital; see Buchtel et al., 2002) has led to the adoption of a more generic term, the Wada test, which honors its inventor and leaves unstated the drug used. The procedure was developed initially at the Montreal Neurological Institute, where the neurologist Juhn Wada was a fellow in the 1950s. In addition to its clinical usefulness, this procedure has allowed testing of various cognitive abilities when only one hemisphere is working. The patient receives a cerebral angiogram in order to know where the drug is going to go. Then a small quantity of sodium amobarbital or methohexital is injected slowly while the clinicians monitor motor and cognitive abilities. Expected neurological changes include contralateral hemiplegia, hemianopsia, and loss of tactile sensation. If the language hemisphere is injected, the patient stops talking and then after some time may speak but with paraphasias and naming difficulties. Understanding what the examiner is saying is usually, but not invariably, absent. Several minutes after injection of the anesthetic, the patient will begin to recover motor and sensory functions, and, if the language hemisphere was injected, language functions will return to baseline. In addition to assessment of language functions during the action of the drug, the clinician will present new information to the patient for later recall in order to determine whether the noninjected hemisphere is capable of forming new memories on its own. When the nonlanguage hemisphere is injected, speech may be slurred because of contralateral facial weakness, but the person can follow commands using the unaffected hand and can understand speech and talk. Patients are typically unaware of the neurological and neuropsychological deficits during the test, although there are occasional exceptions, usually when the language hemisphere is injected. The reason patients are sometimes aware of right-sided hemiplegia and language problems has never been established with certainty, but one theory is that the right hemisphere has more awareness of what is happening on the right side of the body than the left hemisphere has of the left side. It is also possible, though less likely, that the loss of language and the use of the dominant hand is more striking and therefore more likely to be remembered afterwards.

Surgery

Sometimes the seizure is the first manifestation of the presence of a brain tumor. Even when resection of the tumor is the most appropriate option, localization of the ictal onset zone can help to tailor the resection to provide the highest chance of seizure freedom after the lesion is removed. Neuropsychometric testing can be particularly helpful in cases where the lesion affects the mesial temporal structures,

and a Wada test or cortical mapping procedure (either intraoperative or extraoperative) can help to define safe margins of resection that will not impair memory, language, or motor function.

In patients with other types of lesions, including vascular anomalies (arteriovenous malformations [AVMs], venous angiomas, etc.), dysembryoplastic neuroepithelial tumor (DNET), or cortical dysplasia including hamartomas, resections can also be tailored to presurgical tests of ictal onset and functional testing of the most electrically active regions to determine safe margins of resection when these structures are determined to be related to the ictal onset zone.

For those patients with mesial temporal sclerosis, one of the most common indications for epilepsy surgery for those refractory to medications, neuropsychometric testing, and the Wada test can be important in verifying the area of seizure onset. These tests can be strong corroborating features that identify the lateralization of the most epileptogenic area, and can provide information about the likelihood of memory or language deficits after surgery. For instance, if visuospatial memory is significantly more impaired than verbal memory, it is likely that the seizure onset is in the right (or nondominant) hemisphere. If verbal memory is impaired, it may be a bit more likely that seizures begin in the dominant mesial temporal region, but this association is less strong and therefore less specific. The degree of verbal memory difficulty can help predict the amount of initial deficit after resection of the dominant mesial temporal structures—those with better verbal skills tend to lose more functional ability. The Wada test is critical in these patients to the localization of language and memory function, and usually serves as a final check to ensure that the outcome of the proposed surgery is anticipated and any modifications in the surgical plan can be made. Up to 75% of those with mesial temporal sclerosis and concordant neuropsychometric testing, EEG, and clinical findings can go on to have complete control of all seizures that might affect consciousness after appropriate resective procedures.

In patients who are refractory to medical management and who have no clear lesions on imaging (usually epilepsy protocol MRI), surgical treatment may still be possible. In this case, a localizing neuropsychological profile may be even more helpful. Combined with a positron emission tomography (PET) scan to identify possible areas of hypometabolism, a single photon emission computed tomography (SPECT) scan to localize the ictal onset zone as precisely as possible (see Figure 12–1; see also the color version in the color insert section), evidence of focal language, visuospatial, or memory dysfunction can be very valuable. The Wada test is also useful in this context, as in other lesional epilepsies. The likelihood of success in these cases depends on the focality of the onset zone, the clarity of EEG and semiological findings, and the absence of a functionally important cortex in the area of resection. After careful evaluation, the patient is usually quoted a 30%–50% likelihood that consciousness-altering seizures will be controlled, depending on the individual factors identified.

Finally, another type of surgical procedure that can be helpful in the treatment of epilepsy is the insertion of a vagal nerve stimulator (VNS). This is a simple procedure during which a pacemaker-like device in the chest wall is attached to an electrode winding around the vagus nerve. This device helps reduce seizure frequency in up to 30%–40% of those who have it implanted; the rate of complete seizure freedom after implantation is less than 1%, and this procedure is usually performed when other surgical options are limited. An additional benefit of VNS treatment is that the patient and family are provided with a magnetic device that can activate higher stimulation settings and, in some cases, abort a seizure before it spreads, causes falls, and leads to status epilepticus. In patients with prolonged seizures or clusters of seizures, this feature can be very valuable.

Nonepileptic Seizures

Some patients who appear to have refractory epilepsy on initial history and evaluation are actually suffering from a conversion disorder with paroxysmal events of interrupted behavior or motor function that will not respond to treatment of electrical hyperirritability because electrophysiological function in the brain is, in

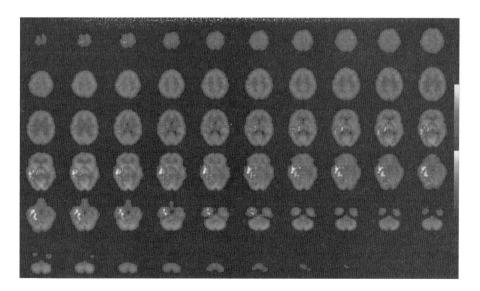

Figure 12–1. Ictal SPECT scan of a 19-year-old patient with unusual episodes of fidgeting, mumbling, and rubbing her legs. She has bilateral epileptiform activity, but the SPECT scan shows clear right temporal hyperperfusion during a seizure (radiological convention: right is on the left). Neuropsychological test results showed that she had a relatively low IQ (full-scale IQ = 68), and had difficulty learning and remembering both verbal and pictorial information. The findings suggested bilateral deficits without clear lateralizing significance.

fact, normal. The vast majority of seizures have an organic basis, and mental health workers should assume that a patient with seizures has no control over their frequency, duration, or form. However, some paroxysmal events that have been presumed to be epileptic are actually psychological and may respond to psychotherapy or psychoactive medications. In the vast majority of cases, patients with events that suddenly appear to impair consciousness without electrographic correlates (nonepileptic seizures, NES) do not have any conscious knowledge of their behavior, and therefore the event should not be considered an example of malingering. These episodes almost always occur in the setting of a substantial childhood trauma, with between 90% and 100% of these patients having a history of physical or sexual abuse in various series. When the seizure is considered to be nonorganic in origin, it has sometimes been called a "pseudoseizure" or "hysterical" seizure, though these terms are generally discouraged because their pejorative connotations may interfere with effective communication with the individual and his/her family.

In some cases, EEGs can remain normal when the patients with epilepsy do not lose consciousness if the focus is too deep in the brain to be discerned using scalp electrodes. In some of those cases, a SPECT scan can be helpful in identifying a focal area of increased metabolism during the ictal event. Nonepileptic psychogenic seizures are only diagnosed when the patient clearly loses consciousness, responsiveness to the environment, and/or is amnestic for information presented during the episode. Although some individuals with nonepileptic seizures also have organically determined epileptic seizures, the use of tight diagnostic criteria has shown that the coexistence of PNES and genuine epilepsy is not very common. Roy Martin and colleagues (Martin et al., 2003; see also Benbadis et al., 2001) studied 1590 patients who received a definitive diagnosis after video monitoring of their spells. Of these, 514 (32.3%) were diagnosed with PNES, and only 29 (5.3%) of them also had epilepsy. The majority of these patients are diagnosed only after video-EEG monitoring allows their physicians to be certain of the nature of each type of episode experienced. The history can provide some helpful clues to prompt early consideration of NES. Table 12–1 shows typical differences between psychogenic and epileptic seizures.

The most reliable historical features for differentiating seizures from NES in several series are descriptions of motionless unresponsiveness that last over 20–30 minutes. In this situation, the likelihood of NES is very high, but monitoring on an inpatient epilepsy unit remains the gold standard of diagnosis. Unfortunately, authors have described an average duration of illness before accurate diagnosis of up to 7 years, and the prognosis for remission of the events is best for those who can be diagnosed in the first year of illness, and for patients with a younger age at onset (Reuber & Elger, 2003).

Other neuropsychological features that distinguish NES patients from those with epilepsy include sometimes a display of less effort on psychometric testing, a high incidence of elevations in scales 1 and 3 of the MMPI (Hs and Hy; Wilkus & Dodrill, 1989), and a variety of different personality patterns. In one study, the personality types included groups of borderline, avoidant, and overly controlled personalities in NES patients (Reuber et al., 2004). Treatments with various types of dialectical and behavioral therapies have been attempted, and group therapy is also gaining popularity.

The diagnosis of nonepileptic seizures is also critical because of significant comorbidities. In one series, 52% met the criteria for depression, 39% had suicidal ideation, and 20% had attempted suicide (Ettinger et al., 1999). These patients have very refractory episodes of loss of consciousness with many series indicating remission rates between 40% and 50%, and treatment remains difficult (LaFrance, Alper, Babcock, Barry, Benbadis, Caplan, Gates, Jacobs, Kanner, Martin, Rundhaugen, Stewart & Vert (for the NES Treatment Workshop participants), 2006). Up to 18% of patients with NES have been treated for status epilepticus (Dworetzky et al., 2006).

Social Issues (Vocational Counseling, Driving, Legal, etc.)

Particularly important for the mental health clinician is the increased risk for serious

Table 12–1. Distinguishing Characteristics of Epileptic and Nonepileptic Seizures[a]

Epileptic seizure	Nonepileptic seizure
Duration of GTC is 90 seconds, partial seizures up to a few minutes	NES can last between seconds and hours. Events that last longer than 10 minutes are suspicious for NES
Nearly always stereotyped description of seizure onset	Some have a more diverse range of ictal phenomena, but may also have stereotyped spells
Almost never includes long periods of motionless unresponsiveness	Up to 30%–40% of events consist of long periods of motionless unresponsiveness
Eyes often open	Eyes often closed
Incontinence and tongue biting in 30% of seizures	Incontinence and tongue biting more rare, but may occur
Ictal cries often occur after seizure is well established	If an ictal cry occurs, it is often the first manifestation of the event
Often rising epigastric sensations in aura	Very rare rising epigastric sensation
Status epilepticus not frequent	Often very long seizures (up to hours)
Bilateral synchronous tonic and clonic jerks, with rare bicycling movements in frontal epilepsy	Asynchronous movements of the extremities more common
Head and body slow version of 90 degrees or more are common	More than 90 degree turning of body is very rare, head shaking ("no") may be seen
Fine amplitude tremor is rare	Tremor is fairly common
Directed violence does not occur except in the postictal state	Bystanders may be hit or kicked
With bilateral tonic-clonic seizure, no speech	Massive jerks together with speech
After tonic-clonic seizures, minutes of coma	Consciousness after massive jerks
Seldom crying afterwards	Often crying afterwards
Usually some benefit from anticonvulsants	No or inconsistent reaction to AEDs
Sometimes occurs during sleep	Rarely occurs during sleep, most often occurs in public places and MD offices
Paucity of other medical problems	History of many other drugs taken, and often many other illnesses

[a] The presence of characteristics in the nonepileptic column cannot be taken as sufficient evidence that the seizures have a psychogenic origin. However, a preponderance of characteristics in this column would certainly raise the question that spells are nonorganic in origin.

depression (around 5% across all kinds of epilepsy; 3–4 times the national average). Among persons with epilepsy, suicide is listed as cause of death in 7%–22% of deaths. Studies since the turn of the century have consistently shown that the life expectancy of persons with epilepsy is shorter than in the rest of the population; the death rate of children with epilepsy 0–5 years of age is 1.3 times greater than that of the general population; from 5 to 24 years of age, the rate is 6.6 times greater; from 25 to 45 years of age, the rate is 3.7 times greater. During the period when persons with epilepsy were typically institutionalized, as many as 50% of them died of causes either directly or indirectly associated with their seizures. Among those whose deaths were directly attributed to seizures, around 12% died of status epilepticus (a continuous and uncontrollable seizure); many others died

of the accumulative effects of multiple injuries sustained during seizures.

Still important but not directly life threatening, childhood epilepsy also negatively affects educational achievement and, regardless of the age of onset, impacts on the person's eventual employment level. About a third of children with epilepsy receive special educational support, and IQ increases linearly as a function of age of onset (from 83 for adults whose seizures began in infancy to 102 for those with adult onset). Equally serious, and probably not unrelated to the person's educational experiences, one's ability to find employment is greatly reduced by epilepsy. In a 1973 survey, almost half of persons with epilepsy reported that they had been turned down for a job because of their epilepsy, and 30% reported that they had lost at least one job because of seizures. Various studies over this century have shown the unemployment rate among working-age persons with epilepsy is between 2 and 7 times the rate of unemployment in the general population. In general, an employer has the right to ask a prospective employee if he/she has any medical condition that will interfere with successful carrying out of the duties, so reduction in employment opportunities may not be entirely the product of a prejudice against epilepsy itself. Loss of the ability to drive a car is mentioned by most persons with epilepsy as a major loss (the seizure-free period before driving again differs from place to place; for example, in Michigan it is 6 months while in Ontario, Canada, it is 1 year).

Pregnancy and genetic aspects: There have been reported cases of birth defects for women who use AEDs. In the overall population, the rate of birth defects is 2%–3%, and the rate is slightly higher (0.5%) for women with epilepsy who are not taking medication. Women taking a single AED have a risk of about 6%–7%, with some medications being more problematic than others. Taking several AEDs increases the risk even more. Unfortunately, seizure frequency may go up during pregnancy, so the need for AEDs may even increase. In some cases, the person's physician may feel that the risks of pregnancy are too great for the mother and child, and recommend that pregnancy be avoided. Finally, some AEDs reduce the effectiveness of oral birth control pills. As mentioned below, the genetics of epilepsy suggest that children may inherit a predisposition to epilepsy, but not epilepsy itself. This means that, for example, a head injury would more likely lead to a seizure disorder if the person has close relatives with epilepsy.

Persons with epilepsy frequently suffer because people do not know what to do when they see a seizure occur. It was once believed that a soft object should be inserted between the teeth to prevent biting the tongue during a seizure. This is now highly discouraged. The proper response, if any, depends on the kind of seizure. In general, only a person having a GTC needs attention, and in this case the greatest help consists of remaining calm, helping the person gently to the floor, and loosening any tight clothing. Hot or sharp objects that could cause harm should be moved away. Placing a cushion or folded piece of clothing beneath the person's head can reduce the chance of a head injury, and turning the head to one side so the saliva can escape is a good idea. It is useless to try to interrupt the seizure; when the seizure is over, the person may need to rest or sleep. Seizures usually stop within several minutes, but if the seizure continues for 10 minutes or more, or if seizures follow in succession without a period of complete recovery, then medical attention should be sought (this could signal the beginning of status epilepticus). Focal (simple partial) seizures do not require any action on the part of observers. A person having a complex partial seizure should not be restrained unless the person is placing himself/herself in danger. As in the case of a generalized seizure, hot or sharp objects should be removed. Partial seizures sometimes progress to a generalized seizure ("secondarily generalized"), so further precautions may be necessary.

Pharmacological Treatment

A wide variety of medications have proven useful in the treatment of epilepsy. The armamentarium of available agents has expanded steadily, and each AED medication has a specific set of indications and possible pitfalls. First, the type of epilepsy must be carefully characterized in order to determine the most effective medication. Primary generalized epilepsies, usually generic syndromes beginning in childhood or adolescence, typically respond much more completely to valproic acid than to other agents. Levetiracetam, topiramate, and zonisamide have also been documented to have some efficacy for these patients. On the other hand, several of the medications designed for partial epilepsies can worsen the frequency and duration of generalized seizures—these include carbamazepine, tiagabine, and oxcarbamazepine.

Carbamazepine is the most widely prescribed medication for partial epilepsies in developed countries, but several other medications have documented substantial efficacy as add-on or adjunctive therapy, including lamotrigine, topiramate, and levetiracetam. Several of the newer agents developed for partial epilepsy have been found to have relatively weak antiepileptic properties and are currently even more widely prescribed for treatment of pain—these include gabapentin and pregabalin (Lyrica).

AEDs are often selected because of their associated side effects and how those relate to the wishes and predispositions of patients. Lamotrigine seems to have very little in the way of cognitive effects—in that sense it is perhaps the best tolerated medication, but it can lead to a life-threatening rash if titrated up too rapidly. Topiramate now has well-documented negative effects on verbal memory in some patients, and most AEDs can cause sedation and attention problems. Levetiracetam and topiramate can

each precipitate psychosis in a small percentage of patients. Topiramate and Zonisamide can cause weight loss, while weight gain is a fairly common side effect of valproic acid, especially at higher doses.

The ability to titrate a medication rapidly can be a significant advantage in certain circumstances—in new frequent or prolonged seizures, phenytoin and levetiracetam can each be rapidly titrated to therapeutic doses, whereas with many of the other newer AEDs, gradual introduction is advisable.

Please see Table 12–2 for usual indications, doses, and side effects.

Table 12–2. Comparison of the Important Characteristics of New Antiepileptic Agents

Medication and usual dose range	Effective in partial epilepsy	Effective in generalized epilepsy	Usual side effects	Special cautions
Phenytoin (Dilantin) 300–500 mg/d	++	++	Sedation, hirsuitism, gingival hyperplasia	Supplement vitamin D to prevent osteoporosis, check LFTs
Carbamazepine (Tegretol) 600–1600 mg/d	++	+ (Avoid in absence)	Blurred vision, imbalance, fatigue	Check CBC and SGOT/PT regularly
Phenobarbital (Luminal) 90–150 mg/d	+	++	Sedation, dizziness	Strong P 450 inducer
Valproic Acid (Depakote) 1500–3000 mg/d	+	+++	Weight gain, tremor, sedation	May cause thrombocytopenia or liver problems, regular blood work needed
Lamotrigine (Lamictal) 300–500 mg/d	++	+?	Headache, fatigue	Stevens Johnson rash if started too rapidly
Levetiracetam (Keppra) 1500–3000 mg/d	++	++	Anxiety, depression, edema, tremor	Occasionally causes psychosis
Topiramate (Topamax) 200–400 mg/d	++	++	Selective verbal memory impairment, renal stones	Occasionally causes psychosis
Gabapentin (Neurontin) 1200–3600 mg/d	+		Edema, tremor, sedation	Used also in pain syndromes, very safe
Zonisamide (Zonegran) 200–400 mg/d	+	++ (Useful in absence)	Kidney stones, weight loss	Rash can be severe
Oxcarbamazepine (Trileptal) 1200–2400 mg/d	+	(May worsen absence)	Sedation, dizziness, diplopia	May cause hyponatremia
Tiagabin (Gabatril) 8–32 mg/d	+	(May worsen absence)	Sedation, dizziness	Spike wave stupor reported in some gen epi pts

Appendix 1

International League against Epilepsy: http://www.ilae-epilepsy.org
Epilepsy Foundation:
    http://www.epilepsyfoundation.org/about/
American Epilepsy Society: http://www.aesnet.org/
Support Groups (one among many): http://www.geocities.com/epilepsy911/

Appendix 2

Seizure types (from http://www.ilae-epilepsy.org)
EPILEPTIC SEIZURE TYPES
Self-limited seizure types
Generalized seizures

- Tonic-clonic seizures (includes variations beginning with a clonic or myoclonic phase)
- Clonic seizures
  - Without tonic features
  - With tonic features
- Typical absence seizures
- Atypical absence seizures
- Myoclonic absence seizures
- Tonic seizures
- Spasms
- Myoclonic seizures
- Massive bilateral myoclonus
- Eyelid myoclonia
- Without absences
- With absences
- Myoclonic atonic seizures
- Negative myoclonus
- Atonic seizures
- Reflex seizures in generalized epilepsy syndromes
- Seizures of the posterior neocortex
- Neocortical temporal lobe seizures
- Focal seizures
- Focal sensory seizures
  - With elementary sensory symptoms (e.g., occipital and parietal lobe seizures)
  - With experiential sensory symptoms (e.g., temporoparieto-occipital junction seizures)
- Focal motor seizures
  - With elementary clonic motor signs
  - With asymmetrical tonic motor seizures (e.g., supplementary motor seizures)
  - With typical (temporal lobe) automatisms (e.g., mesial temporal lobe seizures)
  - With hyperkinetic automatisms
  - With focal negative myoclonus
  - With inhibitory motor seizures
- Gelastic seizures
- Hemiclonic seizures
- Secondarily generalized seizures
- Reflex seizures in focal epilepsy syndromes
Continuous seizure types
Generalized status epilepticus
- Generalized tonic-clonic status epilepticus
- Clonic status epilepticus
- Absence status epilepticus
- Tonic status epilepticus
- Myoclonic status epilepticus
Focal status epilepticus
- Epilepsia partialis continua of Kojevnikov
- Aura continua
- Limbic status epilepticus (psychomotor status)
- Hemiconvulsive status with hemiparesis

References

Benbadis, S.R., Agrawal, V. & Tatum, W.O. (2001). How many patients with psychogenic nonepileptic seizures also have epilepsy? *Neurology, 57*, 915–917.

Berkovic, S. F., Howell, R. A., Hay, D. A., & Hopper, J. L. (1998). Epilepsies in twins: Genetics of the major epilepsy syndromes. *Annals of Neurology, 43*, 435–445.

Buchtel, H. A., Passaro, E., Selwa, L. M., Deveikis, J., & Gomez-Hassan, D. (2002). Sodium methohexital (Brevital) as anesthetic in the Wada Test. *Epilepsia, 43*, 1056–1061.

Dichter, M. A. (1998). In J. Engel and T. A. Pedley (Eds.), *Epilepsy: A comprehensive textbook* (Chapters 21–25). Philadelphia : Lippincott-Raven.

Dworetzky, B. A., Mortati, K. A., Rossetti, A. O., Vaccaro, B., Nelson, A., & Edward B. Bromfield E. B. (2006). Clinical characteristics of psychogenic nonepileptic seizure status in the long-term monitoring unit. *Epilepsy and Behavior, 9*, 335–338.

Engel, J. (2001). A proposed diagnostic scheme for people with epileptic seizures and epilepsy: Report of the ILAE task force on classification and terminology. *Epilepsia, 42*, 796–803.

Ettinger, A., Devinsky, O., Weisbrot, D. M., Ramakrishna, R. K., & Goyal, A. (1999). A comprehensive profile of clinical psychiatric and psychosocial characteristics of patients with psychogenic nonepileptic seizures. *Epilepsia, 40*, 1292–1298.

Fisher, R. S., van Emde Boas, W., Blume, W., Elger, C., Genton, P., Lee, P., et al.. (2005). Epileptic seizures and epilepsy: Definitions proposed by the

International League Against Epilepsy (ILAE) and the International Bureau for Epilepsy (IBE). *Epilepsia, 46*, 470–472.

Helmstaedter, C., Kurthen, M., Lux, S., Reuber, M., & Elger, C. E. (2003). Chronic epilepsy and cognition: A longitudinal study in temporal lobe epilepsy. *Annals of Neurology, 54*, 425–432.

Hermann, B. P., Seidenberg, M., Dow, C., Jones, J., Rutecki, P., Bhattacharya, A., et al. (2006). Cognitive prognosis in chronic temporal lobe epilepsy. *Annals of Neurology, 60*, 80–87.

Kjeldsen, M. J., Corey, L. A., Christensen, K., & Friis, M. L. (2003). Epileptic seizures and syndromes in twins: the importance of genetic factors. *Epilepsy Research, 55*, 137–146.

LaFrance, W.C., Alper, K., Babcock, D., Barry, J.J., Benbadis, S., Caplan, R., Gates, J., Jacobs, M., Kanner, A., Martin, R., Rundhaugen, L., Stewart, R., & Vert, C., (for the NES Treatment Workshop participants) (2006). Nonepileptic seizures treatment workshop summary. *Epilepsy and Behavior, 8*, 451–461.

Martin, R., Burneo, J. G., Prasad, A., Powell, T., Faught, E., Knowlton, R., Mendez, M. & Kuzniecky, R. (2003). Frequency of epilepsy in patients with psychogenic seizures monitored by video-EEG. *Neurology, 61*, 1791–1792.

Reuber, M., Pukrop, R., Bauer, J., Derfuss, R. & Elger, C.E. (2004). Multidimensional analysis of personality in pateints with NES. *Journal of Neurology, Neurosurgery & Psychiatry, 75*, 743–748.

Reuber, M., & Elger, C. E. (2003). Psychogenic nonepileptic seizures: Review and update. *Epilepsy and Behavior, 4*, 205–216.

Temkin, O. (1971). *The falling sickness: A history of epilepsy from the Greeks to the beginnings of modern neurology*, 2nd ed. Baltimore: Johns Hopkins University Press.

Wilkus, R. J., & Dodrill, C. B. (1989). Factors affecting the outcome of MMPI and neuropsychological assessments of psychogenic and epileptic seizure patients. *Epilepsia, 30*, 339–347.

13

The Neuropsychology of Multiple Sclerosis

Allen E. Thornton and Vanessa G. DeFreitas

Multiple sclerosis (MS) is one of the most common neurological disorders of the central nervous system (CNS), affecting approximately 250,000–400,000 individuals in the United States and 2.5 million people worldwide (Anderson et al., 1992; www.nationalmssociety.org). Although its etiology has not been clearly established, evidence indicates that MS involves autoimmune inflammatory processes and results in widespread demyelination of axons and the formation of sclerotic plaques (Keegan & Noseworthy, 2002). Unlike many other degenerative diseases, MS typically begins during early adulthood, with a mean age of onset approximating 30 years (Vukusic & Confavreux, 2001). Given its early onset and accruement of CNS injury throughout a nearly normal life span (Sadovnick et al., 1992), it is not surprising that MS can significantly alter one's quality of life (Murray, 2005).

Neuropathology

While the precise mechanism(s) triggering the autoimmune response in MS remains unclear, T lymphocytes appear to be crucial in the development of MS lesions (Compston & Coles, 2002; Keegan & Noseworthy, 2002; Noseworthy et al., 2000; Rinker II et al., 2006). Specifically, these cells cross the blood–brain barrier from the circulatory system and penetrate the CNS. The T cells encounter the proteins of the myelin and secrete cytokines that in turn recruit macrophages and microglia that attack and damage the myelin covering neuronal axons and the oligodendrocytes that produce myelin. The result is widespread demyelination of axons and the formation of plaques by astrocytes, which slows or blocks the conduction of nerve impulses. Although MS primarily affects the myelin sheath that covers axons, there does appear to be some evidence of axonal loss (Keegan & Noseworthy, 2002). Symptom attenuation appears to result from the clearing of edema, partial remyelination of axons, and a redistribution of sodium channels along demyelinated axon segments (Noseworthy et al., 2000). Following increased illness progression, however, damage to some axons may be irreversible, and the production of myelin by oligodendrocytes may become exhausted (Noseworthy et al., 2000).

Although MS lesions can be found in any myelinated area of the CNS, the distribution of plaques is not altogether random. Regions preferentially damaged in MS include the white matter surrounding the ventricles, corpus callosum, optic nerves, brainstem, cerebellum, and spinal cord (Ge, 2006; Lucchinetti & Parisi, 2006; Noseworthy et al., 2000). MS lesions predominantly affect white matter, but lesions also appear in the gray–white matter junctions and in the gray matter itself (Kidd et al., 1999). Preferential damage includes cortical sulci and the cingulate, temporal, insular, and cerebellar cortices (Lucchinetti & Parisi, 2006). As illustrated in Figure 13-1 (see also the color figure in the color insert section), periventricular and frontoparietal lesions are very common in MS and these lesions

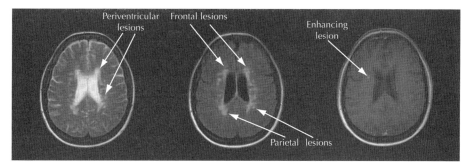

Figure 13–1. Axial MRI scans of a 42-year-old female with relapsing—remitting MS and an Expanded Disability Status Scale of 3.5. The patient's disease duration is 11 years and she is not being managed with any disease modifying therapy. From left to right: T2-weighted, FLAIR and T1-weighted post-gadolinium contrast images. Periventricular hyperintense lesions and frontoparietal lesions are noted on the T2 and FLAIR images; a gadolinium-enhancing lesion is also apparent. (Images are courtesy of Cornelia Laule, PhD, Department of Radiology, University of British Columbia MRI Research Centre).

are associated with neurocognitive impairments (e.g., Sperling et al., 2001). Brain atrophy also occurs in MS and begins early. It occurs at a rate of 0.6%–1.0% annually, and manifests as enlarged ventricles and decreased brain volume (Bermel & Bakshi, 2006; Ge, 2006). Wallerian degeneration, or the degeneration of axons that become detached from their cell bodies, may contribute to tissue loss (Bermel & Bakshi, 2006).

Disease Manifestation, Course, and Diagnosis

Symptoms

MS involves a spectrum of neurological symptoms that reflect the presence and distribution of damage in the CNS and vary considerably across individuals (Compston & Coles, 2002; Feinstein, 1999). Common initial symptoms of MS include vertigo, numbness or tingling in the limbs, gait or balance disturbance, limb weakness, loss of vision in one or both eyes, and diplopia (i.e., double vision) (Beatty, 1996; Joy & Johnston, 2001; Vukusic & Confavreux, 2001). Other symptoms such as spasticity, Lhermitte's sign (i.e., tingling that radiates down the arms, back, or neck evoked by neck flexion), facial numbness, dysarthria, pain, sexual dysfunction, and loss of bowel or bladder control are also commonly observed (Miller, 2006; Mohr et al., 2004). Moreover, both mental and physical fatigue occurs in the majority of persons with MS, and is generally worse in

the afternoon and following exercise (Ford et al., 1998; Noseworthy et al., 2000). Cortical signs such as aphasia, apraxia, and recurrent seizures are only rarely experienced (Noseworthy et al., 2000).

Diagnosis

In general, the diagnosis of MS is based on a detailed clinical history, findings of clinical abnormalities observed on neurological examination (described above), and objective evidence of pathology obtained from magnetic resonance imaging (MRI; see Figure 13–1), cerebrospinal fluid (CSF) analysis, or visual evoked potentials (VEP) (Keegan & Noseworthy, 2002; McDonald et al., 2001; Miller, 2006). The addition of these radiological and laboratory investigations is invaluable in the detection of MS neuropathology. MRI, in particular, is helpful in identifying the presence of CNS lesions (Ge, 2006), and abnormalities in the CSF analysis (e.g., an elevated immunoglobin G [IgG] index, mildly elevated CSF white blood cell count, or the identification of unique oligoclonal IgG bands) support the presence of an inflammatory process (Joy & Johnston, 2001). Furthermore, findings of delayed but well-preserved VEP waveforms are consistent with the slowed nerve impulses seen in demyelinated axons (Joy & Johnston, 2001; McDonald et al., 2001).

Until recently, the diagnosis of MS was based on the Poser classification system (Poser et al.,

1983). Specifically, the Poser criteria divided MS patients into those with *definite MS* and those with *probable MS*, and further subdivided these categories into *clinical* and *laboratory supported*. Criteria for *clinically definite MS* included either (1) two attacks and clinical evidence of two separate lesions, or (2) two attacks, clinical evidence of one lesion, and more objective evidence of a second separate lesion. A diagnosis of *laboratory-supported definite MS* was given in individuals with (1) two attacks, either clinical or objective evidence of one lesion, and CSF IgG or oligoclonal bands, (2) one attack, clinical evidence of two separate lesions, and IgG or oligoclonal bands, or (3) one attack, clinical evidence of one lesion, objective evidence of a second, separate lesion, and CSF IgG or oligoclonal bands. *Clinically probable MS* was defined as having (1) two attacks and clinical evidence of one lesion, (2) one attack and clinical evidence of two separate lesions, or (3) one attack, clinical evidence of one lesion, and objective evidence of a second, separate lesion. Finally, a diagnosis of *laboratory-supported probable MS* was given if the patient had two attacks and evidence of IgG or oligoclonal bands.

In 2001, the International Panel on the Diagnosis of MS further refined the recommended diagnostic criteria for MS (McDonald et al., 2001). According to the McDonald criteria, a diagnosis of MS is typically given if there have been two or more distinct attacks consistent with MS, as well as objective evidence of at least two CNS lesions (i.e., in the cerebral white matter, cerebellum, optic nerves, brain stem, or spinal cord) that are separated in time and space. However, a diagnosis of MS can also be given when there has been only one attack as long as it is accompanied by objective evidence of at least two CNS lesions that are disseminate in time and space. Moreover, the physician must determine that there is "no better explanation" for the observed abnormalities before giving a diagnosis of MS. Failure to meet the diagnosis of MS results in the classification of either *not MS* or *possible MS* (i.e., when a patient clinically presents as having MS but has not yet been diagnostically evaluated, or if the evidence of the diagnostic examination is inconclusive). The Panel also recommends against the use of the terms *clinically definite MS* and *probable MS*. The utility of the McDonald diagnostic criteria has since been established,

demonstrating high sensitivity (83%) and specificity (83%) (Dalton et al., 2002).

Course

A striking feature of MS is that symptom manifestations vary markedly across persons with MS and fluctuate over time within an individual. Accordingly, widely accepted subtypes of MS have been established on the basis of clinical course (Feinstein, 1999; Joy & Johnston, 2001; Lublin & Reingold, 1996; Miller, 2006). More specifically, approximately 80%–85% of persons with MS initially suffer from *relapsing-remitting MS* (RRMS), which is characterized by acute episodes of neurological deterioration interspersed with full or partial recovery between relapses, and a lack of disease progression during periods of recovery. Of these individuals, approximately 10%–20% experience *benign MS*, with only a few relapses and minimal impairment or disability 15 years after onset. However, at least 50% of individuals with an initial relapsing-remitting course will eventually develop *secondary-progressive MS* (SPMS), which is characterized by steady worsening of symptoms over time with or without occasional relapses, minor remissions, or plateaus. In contrast, 10%–15% of individuals suffer from *primary-progressive MS* (PPMS), which is marked by chronic disease progression that begins at onset with only occasional and transient plateaus or minor improvements. Although rare, 5% of individuals with initial PPMS will go on to develop *progressive-relapsing MS*, which is characterized by a progressive disease onset followed by distinct acute exacerbations and continual disease progression between relapses. Also rare is *malignant MS*, whereby the disease progresses rapidly, leading to significant disability and even death in a relatively short period of time. It is important to note that, until recently, PPMS and SPMS were classified under the same category (i.e., *chronic progressive MS*; CPMS) (Montalban & Rio, 2006), and therefore much of the research in this area has employed the CPMS course.

Prognosis

Although the prognosis of MS is quite variable, there is evidence that numerous demographic and clinical factors predict overall outcome (Compston & Coles, 2002; Kantarci & Weinshenker, 2001; Keegan & Noseworthy, 2002; Naismith et al., 2006; Noseworthy et al., 2000; Tremlett & Devonshire, 2006). Indicators of relatively good prognosis include being female, winter birth, younger onset age, primarily sensory and visual disturbances, complete recovery from relapses, few relapses, and longer intervals between relapses. On the other hand, being male or African American, having primarily motor and cerebellar disturbances, incomplete recovery from relapses, frequent relapses during the initial years, a progressive course at onset, and short intervals between relapses predict poorer prognosis. Moreover, relapses have also been associated with increasing number of stressful life events and limited social support (Brown et al., 2006; Mohr et al., 2004). Although life expectancy in MS is only slightly reduced as a result of disease-related factors, there is an increased rate of suicide in afflicted individuals (Sadovnick et al., 1992).

Etiology and Risk Factors

While the precise etiology remains unknown, it is generally accepted that MS results from an interaction between genetic predisposition and environmental factors. Familial studies demonstrate concordance rates for monozygotic twins that approximate 30%–35%, while those for dizygotic twins and non-twin siblings are between 3% and 5% (Hillert & Masterman, 2001; Pryse-Phillips & Sloka, 2006; Sadovnick et al., 1993). Similarly, as genetic relatedness becomes more distant (e.g., parents, second-degree relatives, adopted siblings), the risk of developing MS is further reduced (Compston, 1999; Ebers et al., 1995). Genetic linkage studies have also shown that several genes can predispose one to developing MS (GAMES and Transatlantic Multiple Sclerosis Genetics Cooperative, 2003).

The risk of developing MS is two to three times greater for females than males, and is more prevalent in Caucasians (Joy & Johnston, 2001; Pryse-Phillips & Sloka, 2006). Prevalence rates of MS increase as geographic latitude becomes more extreme at the northern and southern hemispheres, and those who migrate from a high to low risk region maintain the risk of their birthplace only if they relocate when at least 15 years of age (Kurtzke, 2000). Viral exposure may increase susceptibility to MS, as persons who develop MS contract more childhood infections after age 6 than healthy individuals and show increased levels of antibodies of several viruses in the CSF (Marrie, 2004). Although conclusive evidence regarding the association between specific viruses and susceptibility to MS is generally limited, past research has shown that infectious mononucleosis appears to be a risk factor (Thacker et al., 2006), *Chlamydia pneumoniae* is more common in persons who develop MS (Bagos et al., 2006), and there is an increased risk of relapse following infection (Rutschmann et al., 2002).

Influenza immunization does not appear to increase the risk of relapse (Rutschmann et al., 2002). Other potential risk factors include exposure to organic solvents and reduced vitamin D and sun exposure (Kantarci & Wingerchuk, 2006).

Neurocognition in Multiple Sclerosis

Neurocognitive dysfunction in MS is common, with estimates of impairment approximating 40%–50% in community-based samples (Brassington & Marsh, 1998; Rao et al., 1991a). These deficits are meaningful and are one of a few disease manifestations predictive of vocational status (Benedict et al., 2005a, 2006b; Rao et al., 1991b). Furthermore, MS-related deficits have a negative influence on several components of daily functioning, including social and avocational activities (Higginson et al., 2000; Rao et al., 1991b).

The heterogeneous neurocognitive manifestations of MS precludes there being a typical pattern of impairment. Indeed, the variability in deficits expression is striking even in persons with RRMS and minimal disability (Ryan et al., 1996; also see Hannay et al., 2004). For instance, based upon the fifth percentile impairment cutoff, 35% of a sample of 177 persons with RRMS showed no impairments. However, 33% of the sample exhibited impairment on three or more tests, with 5% of individuals appearing relatively globally impaired (Ryan et al., 1996). Often cognitive impairments emerge early in the disease (Schulz et al., 2006; Zivadinov et al., 2001) and longitudinal work suggests that persons with MS may frequently experience both a broadening of their initial impairments and the development of new impairments over longer durations (Amato et al., 2001; Bergendal et al., 2007). Indeed, the prevalence rates of significant neurocognitive impairment show remarkable increases, even early in the disease (Amato et al., 2001; Zivadinov et al., 2001). Recent work suggests that information-processing speed may be particularly vulnerable to this decline over time, especially in persons with SPMS (Bergendal et al., 2007).

Several comprehensive quantitative reviews have elucidated the "average" neurocognitive deficit severities across various domains. Although in both single-sample studies and quantitative reviews it might seem counterintuitive to consider the aggregated neurocognitive impairments in a heterogeneous disorder such as MS, quantitative reviews are valuable in that they yield information regarding the breadth of dysfunction that the disease entails, as well as identifying lesser or less frequent impairments that may go unrecognized in individuals. Relative to single-sample studies, quantitative reviews capture a broader spectrum of the disorder in terms of clinical factors, research settings, and methodologies. Consequently, a more complete picture of the impairment MS entails is elucidated.

The effect size statistic most often used in meta-analyses is essentially an aggregate measure of Cohen's d and represents the magnitude of the differences in neurocognitive performance between two groups of participants. This statistic indexes the strength of impairment in MS relative to a control group, typically composed of healthy individuals. The extent of distributional overlap between persons with MS and controls is also signified by d (Cohen, 1988). For instance, what conventionally is categorized as a large-effect size of $d = 0.80$, corresponds to a 53% overlap (47% nonoverlap) in the distributions of two groups on a given performance measure (Cohen, 1988).

Regardless of variation in methodology, the extant meta-analytic studies (Henry & Beatty, 2006; Prakash et al., 2008; Thornton & Raz, 1997; Wishart & Sharpe, 1997; Zakzanis, 2000) produce fairly consistent neurocognitive results that are selectively summarized in Table 13–1. Note that the effect estimates are presented so that larger values represent greater impairment in persons with MS. The estimates are also complemented with results from relevant single-sample studies. Furthermore, when available (Nocentini et al., 2006; Rao et al., 1991a), observations of the frequency of persons with MS exhibiting impairment below the fifth percentile of healthy individuals are noted for a given neurocognitive domain. As illustrated in Table 13–2, the frequency of these significantly impaired individuals is useful to consider given the heterogeneity of the manifestations of the disorder.

Intelligence

Intelligence as indexed by contemporary IQ measures is composed of a multitude of dissociable abilities. The most frequently employed IQ measures are derived from the Wechsler Adult Intelligence Scales (WAIS; Kaufman & Lichtenberger, 2006). On these scales, persons suffering from MS exhibit greater deficits in Performance Intelligence (PIQ) than Verbal Intelligence (VIQ). As illustrated in Table 13–1, quantitative summaries of the literature reveal that PIQ is robustly impacted ($d = 0.77$), approaching the conventional definition of large (Cohen, 1988). There is perhaps some attenuation of the effect in the Prakash et al. (2008) study ($d = 0.60$), which is comprised of only RRMS samples. VIQ is more moderately affected. Nonetheless, Table 13–2 indicates that 10% of a large sample of persons with RRMS suffering minimal neurological disability (Expanded Disability Status Scale; EDSS) were significantly impaired in fluid intelligence (Raven Progressive Matrices; RPM), whereas, approximately 20% of individuals with a variety of courses and relatively severe disability exhibit fairly broad intellectual impairments.

Verbal Abilities

Modest-to-moderate losses are often observed on select and narrower verbal ability measures, which are consistent with the aforementioned overall VIQ effect. Table 13–1 illustrates that on these select subtests, estimates are always less than 0.50. In relatively severely disabled community participants the frequency of MS-related impairments across WAIS Verbal subscales range from 8% to 19% (see Table 13–2).

In terms of neurocognitive measures of language functioning, moderate effects size estimates are apparent in confrontation naming (Table 13–1). In contrast, marked reductions in verbal fluency are evident with effect magnitudes occasionally approximating 1.00. Table 13–2 illustrates that in these select samples approximately 20% of persons with MS exhibit significant fluency deficits relative to controls. Often these deficits are conceptualized as executive in nature. Meta-analytic findings suggest that fluency deficits may be greater in CPMS and when disability is greater (Henry & Beatty, 2006; Zakzanis, 2000). Although longer duration of illness, increased age, and greater disability level mitigated the association between CPMS and reduced fluency (Henry & Beatty, 2006), these confounded illness features are fundamental to CPMS.

Visuospatial and Constructional Skills

Overall, basic visuoperceptual and constructional abilities are moderately affected by MS despite the fact that these skills, like many measures, are partially reliant on primary sensory and/or motor functions (see Table 13–1). In a community sample of persons with MS, 12%–19% of individuals showed significant impairments on various tasks of visual discrimination, visuospatial integration, and on the more complex task of facial recognition matching (see Table 13–2). In a less disabled sample of RRMS, 14%–16% of persons exhibited significant impairments on visual copying tasks. Importantly, visuoperceptual and constructional tasks often contain multiple operations that may contribute to these deficits, including motor skills, perceptual abilities, and executive processes (Hannay et al., 2004).

Information Processing

Marked impairments are evident in information-processing speed in persons with MS. These losses are most robust on visuomotor scanning tasks, including the Digit Symbol subtest from the WAIS scales and the Symbol-Digits Modalities Test (SDMT). Processing-speed reductions are associated with an effect size of approximately one standard deviation on these tests (only 45% joint MS-control distributional overlap). In a less impaired sample of RRMS, 43% of persons exhibited significant impairments on the oral version of the SDMT (see Table 13–2). Interestingly, impairments on the Trail-Making Tests (TMT) appear relatively attenuated compared with other processing-speed measures (see Table 13–1). The TMT, the Digit Symbol subtest, and the SDMT tax visual search and visuomotor speed significantly; however, the latter two tests place greater demands on memory (Laux & Lane, 1985; Lezak et al., 2004; Strauss et al., 2006), perhaps contributing to the differential impairment.

Effect estimates capturing the loss of processing efficiency with measures of reaction time are moderate to large ($d = 0.65$) even in RRMS samples (see Prakash et al. 2008: Table 13–1). In single-sample studies, deficits in information-processing speed have also been reported on various laboratory tasks, including reaction time, response inhibition, visual search, psychomotor speed and speeded arithmetic (Archibald & Fisk, 2000; Denney et al., 2005; Kail, 1998; Kujala et al., 1994; Rao et al., 1989c). For instance, impairment in divided, focused, and sustained attention has been noted in a hospital catchment sample of persons with MS who experienced fairly severe disability (De Sonneville et al., 2002). Executive aspects of attentional regulation were also impaired in this sample and deficits increased with greater task complexity, suggesting that motor dysfunction itself was not solely responsible for the impairments. Overall, participants in this study exhibited a 40% slowing in processing speed relative to healthy persons.

Tests of attention and psychomotor speed often involve visual and motor components that may contribute to poor task performance in MS (Benedict et al., 2002b; Bruce et al., 2007). The Sternberg Memory Scanning Test (Sternberg, 1969) produces response speed measures that are minimally contaminated by motor and sensory deficits (Gontkovsky & Beatty, 2006). In this paradigm subjects are presented with a set of items to hold in short-term memory (STM). A probe item is then presented, and the subject

Table 13–1. Effect Size Estimates from Meta-analytic Reviews.

Cognitive Domain	Wishart and Sharpe (1997)			Thornton and Raz (1997)			Zakzanis (2000)			Henry and Beatty (2006)			Prakash et al. (2008)		
	d	k	OL	d	k	OL	d	k	OL	d	k	OL	d	k	OL
Intellectual Abilities															
Verbal (VIQ)	0.47	9	69%	-	-	-	0.50	8	67%	0.37	11	74%	0.30	9	79%
Performance (PIQ)	0.77	5	54%	-	-	-	-	-	-	-	-	-	0.60	6	62%
Verbal & Language Abilities															
Information (WAIS)	-	-	-	-	-	-	0.23	5	83%	-	-	-	0.08	13	94%
Comprehension (WAIS)	-	-	-	-	-	-	0.30	5	79%	-	-	-	-	-	-
Similarities (WAIS)	0.32	7	78%	-	-	-	0.43	7	71%	-	-	-	0.28	7	80%
Vocabulary (WAIS)	-	-	-	-	-	-	0.40	7	73%	-	-	-	-	-	-
Semantic Fluency	-	-	-	-	-	-	0.99	7	45%	0.93	16	47%	-	-	-
Phonemic Fluency	0.68	19	58%	-	-	-	0.78	18	54%	0.93	16	47%	-	-	-
Verbal Fluency (omnibus)	-	-	-	-	-	-	-	-	-	-	-	-	0.69	26	57%
Boston Naming Test	0.39	7	73%	-	-	-	0.54	8	65%	0.45	11	70%	0.34	20	76%
Visuospatial & Construction Skills															
Block Design	-	-	-	-	-	-	0.50	6	67%	-	-	-	-	-	-
Visuoperceptual	0.43	11	71%	-	-	-	-	-	-	-	-	-	0.55	11	64%
Visuoconstructional	0.52	19	66%	-	-	-	-	-	-	-	-	-	0.54	22	65%
Attention & Working Memory															
Digit/Spatial Span	-	-	-	0.35	22	76%	-	-	-	-	-	-	0.43	27	71%
Digit Span (total)	0.45	19	70%	-	-	-	-	-	-	-	-	-	-	-	-
Digit Span Forward	0.63	6	60%	-	-	-	0.37	15	74%	-	-	-	-	-	-
Digit Span Backward	-	-	-	-	-	-	0.42	13	72%	-	-	-	-	-	-
Arithmetic (WAIS)	-	-	-	-	-	-	0.33	6	77%	-	-	-	-	-	-
Verbal Working Memory	-	-	-	0.72	11	56%	0.30	5	79%	-	-	-	0.52	85	66%
Trail-Making Test—Form A	-	-	-	-	-	-	-	-	-	-	-	-	-	-	-
Trail-Making Test—Form B	0.65	10	59%	-	-	-	0.41	6	72%	-	-	-	-	-	-
Processing Speed (SDMT and/ or Digit Symbol)	0.93	9	47%	-	-	-	1.03	8	44%	0.90	6	48%	-	-	-

Test	d	k	OL	d	k	OL	d	k	OL	d	k	OL	d	k	OL
Processing Efficiency (Reaction Time)	–	–	–	–	–	–	–	–	–	–	–	–	0.65	13	59%
Verbal LTM															
List/Pairs Learning (multiple trials)	0.82	19	52%	–	–	–	–	–	–	–	–	–	–	–	–
Immediate Recall (single trial)	0.80	12	53%	–	–	–	–	–	–	–	–	–	–	–	–
Delayed Recall	0.68	16	58%	0.81	32	52%	–	–	–	–	–	–	0.78	44	54%
Free Recall	–	–	–	0.69	13	57%	–	–	–	–	–	–	–	–	–
Cued Recall	–	–	–	0.54	13	65%	–	–	–	–	–	–	–	–	–
Recognition	–	–	–	–	–	–	–	–	–	–	–	–	0.49	17	67%
Nonverbal LTM															
List/Pairs Learning (multitrial)	0.93	8	47%	–	–	–	–	–	–	–	–	–	–	–	–
Immediate Recall	0.65	9	59%	–	–	–	–	–	–	–	–	–	0.52	39	66%
Delayed Recall	0.39	10	73%	–	–	–	–	–	–	–	–	–	0.55	14	64%
Free Recall	–	–	–	0.55	12	64%	–	–	–	–	–	–	–	–	–
Cued Recall	–	–	–	0.75	9	55%	–	–	–	–	–	–	–	–	–
Executive/Conceptual Skills															
WCST (pers. errors and/or responses)	0.43	9	71%	–	–	–	0.57	11	63%	0.52	8	66%	–	–	–
WCST (categories)	–	–	–	–	–	–	0.52	10	66%	0.52	9	66%	–	–	–
WCST (sorting and shifting)	–	–	–	–	–	–	–	–	–	–	–	–	0.35	25	76%
Halstead Category Test	0.45	5	70%	–	–	–	–	–	–	–	–	–	–	–	–

Notes: d = Cohen's *d*; *k* = the number of contributing observations; *OL* = approximate percentage of overlap of the distributions; WAIS = Wechsler Adult Intelligence Test; SDMT = Symbol-Digits Modalities Test; LTM = long term memory; WCST = Wisconsin Card Sorting Task. To facilitate comparisons, all effect estimates have been converted to *d* when given in the original article as *r* (see Friedman, 1968). Also for Beatty et al. (2006), with the exception of fluency tasks, the effects reported were not based upon a comprehensive review of the literature. Additionally, the Prakash et al. (2008) meta-analysis was restricted to RRMS samples; the other estimates illustrated were derived from MS samples that were not restricted to a particular course. The WM *d* of Thornton and Raz (1997) is based upon the Constant Trigrams and Paced Auditory Serial Addition Test; the WM *d* of Prakash et al., 2008 is based upon the Digit Span (backward) test, the Sternberg Test, the *n*-Back Test, and the Letter-Number Sequencing Test (WAIS-III).

TABLE 13–2. Frequency Estimates of Cognitive Impairment in MS

Cognitive domain	Nocentini et al. (2006) n = 461 RRMS. EDSS: M= 2.6; SD = 1.3	Rao et al. (1991a) n = 39 RRMS; 19 CPMS; 42 CSMS. EDSS: M = 4.1; SD = 2.2
	% Impaired	% Impaired
Overall Intellectual Abilities		
WAIS-R Verbal Intelligence	-	21
Raven Progressive Matrices	10	19
Verbal and Language Abilities		
Information (WAIS)	-	8
Comprehension (WAIS)	-	18
Similarities (WAIS)	-	19
Vocabulary (WAIS)	-	16
Phonemic Fluency	19	22
Boston Naming Test	-	9
Oral Comprehension	-	9
Visuospatial & Construction Skills		
Hooper Visual Organization Test	-	13
Judgment of Line Orientation Test	-	14
Visual Form Discrimination Test	-	12
Facial Recognition Test	-	19
Visual Design Copy	14–16	-
Attention and Working Memory		
Digit Span Forward (WAIS)	-	8
Digit Span Backward (WAIS)	-	7
Arithmetic (WAIS)	-	15
Sternberg Memory Scanning Task	-	11
Paced Auditory Serial Addition Test	-	22–25
Stroop Interference Test	-	12
Symbol Digit Modalities Test (oral)	43	-
Memory		
Selective Reminding Test	-	-
Long-term storage	-	22
Consistent long-term retrieval	-	31
RAVLT (sum of trials 1–5)	25	-
RAVLT (delayed trial)	23	-
Prose Recall	-	25
7/24 Spatial Recall Test	-	31
Immediate Visual Memory (recog.)	3	-
President's Test	-	10
Executive/Conceptual Skills		
Card Sorting (preservations)	14	8
Card Sorting (categories)	10	13
Halstead Category Test	-	14

Notes: The "percent impaired" is the percentage of persons with MS that fall at or below the fifth percentile of healthy persons. EDSS = Expanded Disability Status Scale; RRMS = relapsing-remitting multiple sclerosis; CPMS = chronic progressive multiple sclerosis; CSMS = chronic-stable multiple sclerosis; WAIS = Wechsler Adult Intelligence Scale; RAVLT = Rey Auditory-Verbal Learning Test.

must judge whether the probe falls within the memory set. Subjects are administered a number of item sets that vary in size (e.g., 1–6 digits). Findings from healthy individuals indicate that as the STM set size is increased, there is a corresponding linear increase in the latency to judge whether an item falls within the memory set (Sternberg, 1969).

A few studies have evaluated the speed of STM search using the Sternberg Paradigm in participants with MS relative to healthy control subjects (Archibald & Fisk, 2000; Rao et al., 1989c, 1991a). In a community sample, 11% of individuals with MS showed significant slowing in memory scanning (see Table 13–2) and this finding was subsequently replicated at a university-associated MS research clinic. In contrast, one study failed to detect any significant MS-control difference in memory search efficiency (Litvan et al., 1988a). However, the sample size of the study was small, which may have contributed to the null finding.

More generally, MS-associated deficits in information-processing speed have often been associated with both clinical and pathological aspects of the disease. Compared to RRMS, information-processing inefficiency appears to be greatest in persons with progressive MS, and in those with greater disability levels and longer illness duration (De Sonneville et al., 2002). Other research has suggested that both higher lesion load, and particularly reduced brain volume, are associated with attention inefficiency and increased response speed variability (Lazeron et al., 2006).

Short-term and Working Memory

Modest-to-moderate deficits are seen in less complex aspects of short-term and working memory (WM) such as memory span and mental arithmetic (see Table 13–1). Table 13–2 indicates that only 7%–8% of community-residing persons with MS experienced significant Digit Span impairments; whereas, 15% of this sample showed impairments in Arithmetic, which is more apt to challenge WM processes. These processes involve manipulating, integrating, and simultaneously holding items in STM while processing information.

There is ample evidence supporting WM impairments in persons with MS that are most apparent when rapid information processing is required. Verbal WM, as operationalized by the Paced Auditory Serial Addition Test (PASAT) and Consonant Word Trigrams tasks (see Ozakbas et al., 2004), is substantially diminished in persons with MS ($d = 0.72$, see Thornton & Raz, 1997; Table 13–1). Table 13–2 indicates that in a community sample, 22%–25% of persons with MS are significantly impaired on the PASAT task, which involves both processing speed and WM (see Demaree et al., 1999). More moderate WM deficits are apparent in samples comprised of only RRMS patients ($d = 0.52$, see Prakash et al., 2008; Table 13–1), when using a compilation of tests that tax WM and processing speed to a lesser degree (e.g., Digit Span (backward), Letter-Number Sequencing). Indeed, the extent to which a task makes demands upon WM appears to be crucial. On the n-back task, an experimental WM procedure that requires identifying whether the current stimulus matches a previous stimulus presented a given number of trials back, persons with RRMS exhibit increasing impairment at higher complexity levels even after accounting for simple motor speed (e.g., Parmenter et al., 2007a).

The impairments discussed above reflect a general characterization of WM; however, WM has been more precisely formulated into a multicomponent theory (Baddeley, 1986, 1992). In Baddeley's model, a set of limited-capacity slave subsystems process different types of information, which are controlled by a central executive supervisor. The subsystems include the visuospatial sketchpad and phonological loop. The latter comprises two components: (1) the phonological store, which holds speech-based information for a very brief duration, and (2) articulatory control, which refreshes the phonological store through subvocal rehearsal. Under dual-task conditions, the limited capacity central executive controller appears degraded in MS relative to healthy controls (D'Esposito et al., 1996). Articulatory control processes within the phonological slave subsystems also appear to be diminished in persons with MS, as suggested by an exaggerated word length effect (Litvan et al., 1988b; Rao et al., 1993; Ruchkin et al., 1994). In contrast, the phonological store itself appears intact (Litvan et al., 1988b).

Disease course and underlying brain pathology clearly influences the expression of neurocognitive deficits, particularly impairments involving processing speed and WM capacities (e.g., Archibald & Fisk, 2000; Sperling et al., 2001). WM deficits are relatively greater in persons with a progressive MS course (Thornton & Raz, 1997). Although patients with either RRMS or SPMS often exhibit impairments in processing speed, progressive MS is associated with increased risk for WM impairments. There is an apparent precipitous increase in STM and WM impairments in samples comprised of CPMS participants relative to samples comprised of RRMS participants (see Thornton & Raz, 1997; Zakzanis, 2000). This latter observation does not appear to be attributable to greater disability levels in the progressive MS participants (Archibald & Fisk, 2000).

DeLuca and colleagues (2004) have made a similar observation regarding the relative prevalence of impairment in WM and information-processing speed in participants seen at a tertiary referral center. Information-processing speed was significantly impaired (fifth percentile cutoff) in 22% of individuals with RRMS and 77% of persons with SPMS. In contrast, only 6% of persons with RRMS were significantly impaired in WM, whereas 32% of the participants with SPMS showed WM deficits. Importantly, these associations might be proxies for the underlying neuropathology. For example, greater total lesion load and the specific loads in the frontal and parietal cortex have been associated with poorer performance on the PASAT and SDMT and lesion load was marginally greater in SPMS compared to RRMS (Sperling et al., 2001).

Indeed, there has been interest in distinguishing WM deficits from those of information processing speed in persons with MS. Interestingly, when PASAT-type tasks, which are noted to involve WM and processing speed, are set at slower presentation speeds, the recall accuracy of most individuals with MS is equal to that of healthy participants (Demaree et al., 1999; Lengenfelder et al., 2006). This finding is argued to be consistent with a fundamental deficit in speed of information processing over WM accuracy (DeLuca et al., 2004). DeLuca

and colleagues (2004) discuss potential explanations for the processing speed observations in MS. From the perspective of the *Relative Consequence Model*, fundamental processing-speed impairment may underlie deficits on other more complex neurocognitive tasks (e.g., WM) when a critical threshold of processing-speed impairment is reached. This is contrasted with the *Independent Consequence Model*, which holds that processing-speed deficits and WM impairments may arise from independent sources (DeLuca et al., 2004). While support has been generated for both of these models (DeLuca et al., 2004; Demaree et al., 1999; Lengenfelder et al., 2006), there is nevertheless substantial evidence suggesting that information-processing speed may be a fundamental deficit in MS (e.g., De Sonneville et al., 2002). Deficits in information-processing speed appear common in MS generally (e.g., ¼ of persons with RRMS experienced such deficits); whereas WM deficits are relatively rare in RRMS but become increasingly common with a progressive MS course.

Processing speed and WM capacity also appear related to performance deficits on other more complex neurocognitive tasks. Whether these abilities are mechanisms for more complex neurocognitive deficits or markers for such deficits remains unclear. Nonetheless, reduced WM capacity and decreased processing speed are frequently associated with impairments in long-term memory (LTM; DeLuca et al., 1994; Gaudino et al., 2001; Litvan et al., 1988b; Thornton et al., 2002). In addition, greater vulnerability to retrograde interference (RI) is apparent in persons with MS, which presumably entails WM processes (Griffiths et al., 2005). Likewise, attenuated processing speed is associated with poor performance on a variety of other cognitive tasks (Denney et al., 2004, 2005).

Long-Term Memory

Over the last several decades, MS-related LTM deficits have been observed in both clinical (Carroll et al., 1984; Grant et al., 1984; Rao et al., 1984) and community-based samples (Rao et al., 1989b, 1991a). While a small subgroup of persons with MS exhibit amnesia and dementia (Beatty et al., 1996; Fischer, 1988; Rao et al., 1984), generally persons with MS have the capacity to learn new information (Beatty et al., 1988; DeLuca et al., 1994; Minden et al., 1990; Rao et al., 1984).

Whether persons with MS exhibit a reduction in their rate of information acquisition is less obvious. On multitrial lists, individuals with MS recall fewer items on each trial; the overall impact on recall corresponds to a large-effect estimate (see Table 13–1, List and Pairs Learning). This observation confounds raw recall with learning rate, as normal recall gains may occur after poor initial trial recall. MS-related deficits in learning have also been reported in paradigms that involve a tally of the number of trials required to meet a criterion performance level (e.g., DeLuca et al., 1994; Grant et al., 1984; Heaton et al., 1985). However, these measures are also sensitive to both raw recall and learning rate. Alternatively, the rate of recall improvement (learning slope) over multiple trials gauges acquisition more directly. Observations suggest that the overall learning slope is relatively intact in group studies of individuals with MS (Beatty et al., 1989b; Jennekens-Schinkel et al., 1990; Rao et al., 1984, but also see Beatty & Gange, 1977).

Typically, persons with MS do not show a pattern of rapid forgetting; rather deficits are apparent at the time of immediate recall (e.g., van den Burg et al., 1987). Indeed, Table 13–1 indicates that effect estimates for immediate and delayed recall are fairly consistent. This lack of differential forgetting suggests that attention, WM, encoding, and/or retrieval processes are candidate operations underlying LTM impairment in MS.

Long-term declarative memory impairment in MS has often been conceptualized as primarily involving attenuated effortful retrieval of information, while encoding and storage appear relatively preserved (Caine et al., 1986; Grafman et al., 1990; Rao et al., 1989b, 1993). For example, the recall pattern generated by persons with MS during verbal fluency and selective reminding tasks (Buschke, 1973; Buschke & Fuld, 1974) implicates retrieval as a viable mechanism in the LTM impairment in MS. Semantic and lexical fluency induce retrieval processes in accessing memory stores (Grafman et al., 1990; Rao et al., 1989b). As noted earlier, verbal fluency is markedly impaired in MS; nevertheless,

this evidence is indirect because it is observed during the rapid access of highly consolidated information, not in retrieving recently encoded long-term declarative memories.

In selective reminding paradigms, an inconsistent recall pattern in persons with MS is observed relative to that of healthy individuals (Rao et al., 1989b, 1991a, 1993). This recall inconsistency occurs after items have presumably been entered into long-term storage, which suggests that retrieval falters. Table 13–2 indicates that 31% of a community-based sample of persons with MS showed significant impairments in their LTM retrieval consistency. A retrieval-focused interpretive framework has also been applied to the pattern of recognition and recall performance in persons with MS. Recognition is thought to minimize demands on retrieval and capture the encoding and storage processes (Grafman et al., 1990). The meta-analytic findings in Table 13–1 indicate that verbal LTM recognition is moderately affected in MS. In the verbal domain, this effect is attenuated relative to the more robust losses in free recall.

Consistent with the retrieval-focused interpretation of MS-related memory, dysfunction is evidence of preserved encoding. For instance, encoding that involves semantic as opposed to perceptual processing enhances LTM performance in MS (Carroll et al., 1984). Like healthy individuals, persons with MS also recall highly imaginable words more readily than difficult to imagine words (Caine et al., 1986). Nevertheless, encoding may also be a source of memory failure. When persons with MS use semantic study strategies, a loss in the distinctiveness of information within the memory trace is observed (Carroll et al., 1984). Individuals with MS also have difficulty utilizing contextual information presented during encoding to retrieve information later (Thornton et al., 2002) and they exhibit reduced semantic clustering, which might reflect poor semantic encoding (Arnett et al., 1997; Diamond et al., 1997).

Interference may also contribute to compromised LTM encoding in MS. Proactive interference (PI) occurs when prior learning impedes retention of subsequent materials (Postman & Underwood, 1973). Versions of the Wicken's paradigm (Wickens, 1970) have been used to study interference in MS. In this paradigm, semantically related items administered across multiple learning trials is associated with a decline in recall as interference increases. Recall recovers ("release" from PI) with the introduction of a new semantic category. Increased PI is associated with poorer WM ability (Blusewicz et al., 1996), while attenuated release from PI has been related to mnemonic and executive deficits (Cermak et al., 1974; Randolph et al., 1992; Squire, 1982).

Individuals with MS generally demonstrate normal accumulation and release from PI on Wicken's-type paradigms (Beatty et al., 1989a; Johnson et al., 1998; Rao et al., 1993), even though they often exhibit WM and executive impairments and lesions to frontoparietal regions (see Figure 13–1; e.g., Foong et al., 1997; Parmenter et al., 2007b; Sperling et al., 2001). But the Wicken's paradigm may be insensitive to interference abnormalities (Dobbs et al., 1989). Recently, our laboratory revisited interference in MS, using the California Verbal Learning Test (CVLT; Delis et al., 1987; Kramer & Delis, 1991), and replicated findings suggesting that individuals with MS are no more susceptible to accumulation of PI than healthy individuals (Griffiths et al., 2005). In contrast, attenuated release from PI was observed, which might reflect a loss in the semantic distinctiveness of LTM (Carroll et al., 1984). This loss may also be manifested in the reduction of semantic categorization during recall (Arnett et al., 1997).

In addition, we evaluated RI, which refers to the decrement in retention of prior learning by subsequent learning (Postman & Underwood, 1973). Findings suggested that persons with MS have increased susceptibility to RI (Griffiths et al., 2005). These results appear to be germane to ultimate LTM, as accumulated RI predicted long-delay free recall in MS, but not in healthy participants. We speculate that increased RI in MS may reflect a reduction in their ability to register distinctiveness in memory. Persons with MS might readily register gist (general) information, rather than contextual and semantic details (Goldstein et al., 1992; Thornton et al., 2002). Consequently, information may be more vulnerable to interference from new entries that activate similar general target attributes.

In summary, it appears that an increased vulnerability to LTM retrieval failure is indicated by aggregated group studies, but this breakdown is not necessarily the only source of LTM impairment. Further, in individuals with MS a variety of recall patterns emerge, with a small minority of persons meeting a strict definition of retrieval deficit (Beatty et al., 1996). Operations that tax either encoding and retrieval processes appear central to the deficits observed. Memory taxing cognitive operations deployed during LTM warrant further research attention as they likely contribute to the impairment patterns observed on traditional clinical memory tests.

Implicit and Procedural Memory

Contrasting the broad impairments noted in declarative LTM, findings have consistently indicated relatively normal abilities in nondeclarative memory. In an earlier study, three tasks of implicit memory were administered to a community-based sample of persons with MS and healthy individuals (Rao et al., 1993). On a degraded word-priming task, individuals with MS identified words in fewer trials than healthy controls, while exhibiting explicit memory impairment for these words. In addition, MS and control participants derived equal RT benefits from the repeated serial presentation of stimuli on a four-choice RT test. Finally, repeated stimulus exposure facilitated performance equally in MS patient and control subjects on an implicit reversed-mirror word-reading task. More severely disabled persons with MS also perform well on nondeclarative memory tasks. For example, regardless of disability level MS participants perform normally on word stem-priming and pursuit motor-learning tasks (Beatty et al., 1990; Scarrabelotti & Carroll, 1999; Seinela et al., 2002). In summary, when memory is based upon presumably nonconscious performance measures, persons with MS benefit from having had previous exposure to the stimulus material to a degree that is similar to that of healthy individuals.

Remote Memory

Persons with MS experience remote memory impairment. For example, the ability to identify famous individuals from various decades is impaired in persons with MS, with deficits that are consistent across the decades (Beatty et al.,

1988, 1989b). Nonetheless, these participants recalled past US presidents in order as readily as healthy individuals, which might arise from a lesser difficulty level for this test relative to identifying famous faces (Beatty et al., 1988, 1989b; Paul et al., 1997). Information on both tests is of an impersonal nature; consequently, it has been noted that conclusions are constrained by the presumption that MS and healthy participants had acquired the relevant information and were equally familiar with it in their past (Paul et al., 1997). This limitation is overcome by autobiographic memory paradigms (Kenealy et al., 2000; Paul et al., 1997).

The Autobiographical Memory Interview (AMI) evaluates semantic and episodic autobiographical memory by verifying memories through the use of collateral interview of significant others. Two past studies using this protocol have produced divergent findings, but the MS participant samples were substantially different. In a sample of relatively mildly disabled persons with MS, findings revealed semantic, not episodic, autobiographic impairments (Paul et al., 1997). Specifically, impairment was limited to generic (semantic) facts such as recalling the name of the high school attended. Participants with MS did not exhibit autobiographic impairments of personal memory episodes. Furthermore, autobiographical knowledge of semantic facts was disrupted equally across all periods. In contrast, 60% of individuals with more severe and long-standing MS exhibited autobiographical memory deficits, with impairment in both episodic and semantic autobiographical knowledge (Kenealy et al., 2000). These impairments were associated with intellectual level and conformed to Ribet's law, with deficits being greater for more recent events.

Executive Functions and Metacognition

Perhaps the most intangible of all neurocognitive abilities are executive functions. Fundamentally, these abilities entail planning, monitoring, and adaptive/flexible responding to novel or emergent circumstances (Lezak et al., 2004; Luria, 1966; Strauss et al., 2006). Metacognitive capacities are closely related to executive functions, as the former involves both knowledge regarding cognition as well as the coordination of cognition itself by means of regulatory processes (see Fernandez-Duque et al., 2000).

Traditional executive functioning tasks have been used in the investigation of neuropsychological deficits in MS. The most commonly employed tests are the Wisconsin Card Sorting Test (WCST) and Halstead Category Test (HCT), both of which require abstract concept formation, mental flexibility, and response to feedback. Quantitative integrations of this literature suggest that the WCST and the HCT are moderately affected by MS, with some suggestion that samples containing only RRMS might be more mildly impacted (i.e., Prakash et al., 2008; see Table 13–1). Estimates of the number of individuals with MS who are significantly impaired on card sorting tasks range from 8% to 14% (see Table 13–2). It has been suggested that these difficulties primarily reflect a fundamental MS-related weakness in identifying sorting concepts (Beatty & Monson, 1996), but this issue has by no means been resolved.

In addition to deficits on tasks of sorting and set shifting, persons with MS generally exhibit impairment on tests that require planning a sequence of moves to reach a goal, while inhibiting prepotent incorrect responses (e.g., tower tasks; Arnett et al., 1997; Foong et al., 1997). Particularly remarkable are MS-related deficits are on the Stroop task, which requires both information-processing speed and prepotent response inhibition (Deloire et al., 2005; Foong et al., 1997; Rao et al., 1991a; also see Vitkovitch et al., 2002). Recently, Prakash et al. (2008) reported meta-analytic observation from RRMS that indicated surprisingly large Stoop-related deficits of $d = 0.79$ in these samples. However, for both the tower task and the Stroop test, processing speed may be fundamental to the underpinnings of these MS-related deficits (Denney et al., 2004, 2005).

Persons with MS exhibit a variety of other deficits presumed to reflect executive dysfunction. For instance, temporal order memory impairment has been reported in MS (Armstrong et al., 1996; Beatty & Monson, 1991a; but also see Arnett et al., 1997). In addition, impairments have been observed in the novel sequencing of pictorial information (Beatty & Monson, 1994). Both temporal memory and cognitive sequencing difficulties are related to poor performance in various other cognitive domains, including traditional executive tasks (Beatty & Monson, 1991a, 1994).

Researchers have also examined the accuracy of feeling-of-knowing (FOK) judgments in MS participants (Beatty & Monson, 1991b). In this case, FOK judgments were predictions made by the subject as to whether an item that was not recalled would be subsequently recognized. In persons with MS, poor FOK accuracy on select measures was associated with impairment on "frontal lobe tasks" and LTM recognition. Relative to healthy individuals, persons with MS also overestimate the occurrence of infrequently presented words and underestimate the occurrence of frequently presented words (Grafman et al., 1991). Additionally, MS participants have difficulty in cognitive estimation. Specifically, they show limitations in their ability to use known information to make accurate abstractions that generate a solution to a novel problem (e.g., "What is the average length of a man's (or women's) spine?"; Foong et al., 1997). Finally, persons with MS benefit from the use of imagery mnemonics, but most notably when the mnemonics are experimenter-generated versus self-generated (Canellopoulou & Richardson, 1998). MS patients apparently abandon the use of self-generated mnemonics (i.e., at follow-up) when explicit directions were absent.

More generally, these findings are related to the concept of insight. Findings are equivocal regarding how insightful persons with MS are regarding their true memory and cognitive abilities. Although individuals with MS may be as accurate as informants in predicting their memory (Randolph et al., 2001), other observations indicate that memory predictions made by persons with MS occasionally appear degraded (Higginson et al., 2000; Taylor, 1990). An earlier report revealed that, relative to controls, persons with MS exhibited reduced correspondence between their subjective memory judgments and their true memory (Beatty & Monson, 1991b); nonetheless, there are positive associations between memory complaints and objective measures of memory and cognition (Randolph et al., 2001, 2004).

Regardless, the above findings clearly imply a deficit in the metacognition of persons with MS (Canellopoulou & Richardson, 1998). Metamemory and metacognition refers to the knowledge an individual has about their cognitive capabilities as well as the control over cognitive processes (Fernandez-Duque et al., 2000). Awareness of one's abilities and their limitations and the implementation/control of relevant cognitive processes may improve performance when cognitive demands are extensive. Importantly, degradation in these oversight and control aspects of cognition in MS likely contributes to the losses observed in other abilities. Depression and depressive attitudes appear to play an important role in the accuracy of metamemory judgments in MS (Randolph et al., 2001, 2004; Taylor, 1990). Increased depression often emerges as a significant associate of perceived compared with objective cognitive dysfunction (Lovera et al., 2006). The relationships between metamemory and executive function, and metamemory and depression, are mediated via depressive attitudes, suggesting that depression and depressive attitudes further intensifies memory complaints (Randolph et al., 2004).

Finally, the ability to remember to complete a task in the future appears compromised in patient with MS. This prospective memory ability requires not only remembering an intention at a future time but retrospectively recalling the required task (Cohen et al., 2001). Although prior findings have suggested deficits in retrospective over prospective memory in MS (Bravin et al., 2000), more recent research that matched persons with MS and controls on the retrospective recall of information (as well as on aspects of STM) indicates that these prospective deficits extend beyond retrospective impairments (Rendell et al., 2007).

Risk Factors Associated with Neurocognitive Dysfunction

Generally, greater disability levels, a progressive course, and the presence of depression and fatigue are all modestly associated with increased MS-related neurocognitive impairments (e.g., Arnett, 2005; Beatty et al., 1988, 1989b; De Sonneville et al., 2002; Gaudino et al., 2001; Grossman et al., 1994; Heaton et al., 1985; Hildebrandt et al., 2006; Huijbregts et al., 2006; Kessler et al., 1992; Lynch et al., 2005; Thornton &

Raz, 1997; Wallin et al., 2006; Zakzanis, 2000). In addition, active disease processes are associated with increased neurocognitive impairment, particularly on attention-demanding tasks (Foong et al., 1998; Grant et al., 1984). Further, it is important to recognize that impaired scores on tasks involving motor and sensory functioning may partially reflect primary deficits in these areas rather than in cognition (Benedict et al., 2002b; Bruce et al., 2007).

Neurocognitive dysfunction in MS is strongly associated with total lesion burden (e.g., Benedict et al., 2006a; Lazeron et al., 2005, 2006; Rao et al., 1989a; Rovaris et al., 2000). The distribution of lesions in MS has also been related to select neurocognitive deficits that are cogent within established neuropsychological frameworks (Arnett et al., 1994; Huber et al., 1992; Lazeron et al., 2005; Sperling et al., 2001). Recently, the role of brain atrophy has been recognized as an important feature associated with the expression of neurocognitive impairments in MS (Benedict et al., 2004, 2006a; Lanz et al., 2007; Lazeron et al., 2006; Parmenter et al., 2007b). Longitudinally, progression of brain atrophy has been identified as a significant predictor in the development of physical disability and neurocognitive dysfunction in early MS, whereas changes in brain lesion volumes were not (Zivadinov et al., 2001).

Regional lobar atrophy has been linked to impairments in a variety of neurocognitive functions (Benedict et al., 2002a; Lazeron et al., 2005, 2006) and temporal lobar atrophy was recently found to be specifically predictive of MS-related declarative LTM impairment (Benedict et al., 2005b; Hildebrandt et al., 2006). However, for both regional atrophy and localized lesion volumes, neurocognitive dysfunction is often also strongly associated with total brain pathology. This raises the possibility that the selective associations are proxies for overall pathology (Foong et al., 1997; Merelli & Casoni, 2000).

Despite the covariation between neurocognition and neuropathology, a significant portion of the pattern and severity of deficits remain unexplained by conventional imaging techniques. One possibility is that these techniques fail to capture pathology in tissue that appears normal (Merelli & Casoni, 2000). Thus, once fully established, some of the newer techniques (e.g., magnetization transfer, magnetic resonance spectroscopy, diffusion tensor imaging) may further explicate variations in neurocognition in MS (Comi et al., 2001; Merelli & Casoni, 2000).

Finally, neurocognitive deficits in MS appear to emerge when physiological compensatory capacity is exceeded, as evaluated by activation patterns during cognitive tasks on functional MRI (fMRI; Cader et al., 2006; Cifelli & Matthews, 2002; Penner et al., 2007; Staffen et al., 2002; Wishart et al., 2004). The ability of individuals with MS to reorganize cortical network activations to compensate for underlying structural brain damage may contribute to the variability in the severity of neurocognitive manifestations in persons with MS (Rocca & Filippi, 2007). Deficits may be most pronounced on tasks that both tax cognitive abilities and exceed the general compensatory capacity of individuals with MS (Penner et al., 2007).

Emotional Functioning in MS

Evidence of emotional disturbances is apparent in a considerable proportion of persons with MS. Major depression, in particular, has a lifetime prevalence of approximately 50% in persons with MS, following diagnosis (Sadovnick et al., 1996), which is notably higher than that seen in the general population (American Psychiatric Association, 1994; Dalton & Heinrichs, 2005; Schubert & Foliart, 1993). A recent quantitative review comparing the depression scores of person with MS to those of healthy persons indicate differences in excess of one standard deviation that favor greater depression in persons with MS (Dalton & Heinrichs, 2005). Interestingly, in RRMS samples the effect estimates observed are somewhat less ($d = 0.70$) and apparently equivalent to that of anxiety ($d = 0.69$; Prakash et al., 2008).

It has been suggested that depression in MS can result from either an emotional reaction to having the disease or as a result of neuropathology (Mohr et al., 2001; Zorzon et al., 2001). In terms of neuropathological underpinnings, extensive lesions in the left medial inferior prefrontal region in conjunction with left anterior temporal lobe atrophy were recently found to be particularly strong predictors of depression, accounting for 42% of the variance in depression scores (Feinstein et al., 2004). Other studies also suggested that pathology within the cortex and white matter tracks are associated with depression and psychiatric disorders in MS (Bakshi et al., 2000; Benedict et al., 2004; Berg et al., 2000; Honer et al., 1987; Pujol et al., 2000; Zorzon et al., 2001). Temporal cortex lesions have been related to poor cognitive-behavioral treatment response in depressed persons with MS (Mohr et al., 2003). Furthermore, attenuated treatment gains at a 6-month follow-up were related to greater total lesion volume, mediated through neuropsychological functioning. These findings indicate the complex relationships between cognition, depression, and emotional recovery.

Depression is associated with greater risk for MS-related cognitive impairment, particularly on tasks involving effort, WM, processing speed, and executive abilities (Arnett, 2005; Arnett et al., 1999a, 1999b, 2001; Demaree et al., 2003; Feinstein, 2006; Gilchrist & Creed, 1994; Landro et al., 2004; Maor et al., 2001; Thornton & Raz, 1997; Wallin et al., 2006). Given the fact that many of the neurological symptoms of MS overlap with vegetative symptoms of depression, the multisymptomatic nature of depression and its association with neurocognition has been scrutinized more closely (Arnett, 2005). In this longitudinal work, negative evaluative symptoms (e.g., inferiority feelings, worthlessness) were strongly and most consistently associated with neurocognitive impairment, relative to mood (e.g., sad, glum) and vegetative (e.g., exhausted, poor appetite) symptoms (Arnett, 2005). Furthermore, poor coping style interacted with depression as their joint occurrence increased the likelihood of cognitive impairment (Arnett et al., 2002).

There is also an increased lifetime prevalence rate of bipolar disorder in MS that is approximately 13 times higher than that of the general population (Feinstein, 1999). The lifetime prevalence rate of any anxiety disorder is elevated and approximates 36%, with panic disorder, obsessive compulsive disorder, and generalized anxiety disorder among the most common (Korostil & Feinstein, 2007). Anxiety appears to be more reactive in nature, and not strongly related to MRI-revealed brain pathology (Zorzon et al., 2001). Approximately 8%–10% of persons with MS experience pathological laughing or crying, which appears to be related to more severe

disability (Feinstein & Feinstein, 2001; Feinstein et al., 1997) and lesions in the cerebro-ponto-cerebellar pathways (Parvizi et al., 2001).

Executive deficits in MS have been specifically associated with neuropsychiatric aspects of the disorder. Persons with MS exhibiting a neurocognitive pattern consistent with frontal lobe pathology (impairments on executive tasks), also tend to exhibit increased euphoria, impaired empathy, and reduced altruism. Relative to the reports of collateral informants, persons with MS overestimate their conscientiousness and empathy toward others and experience increased neuroticism, suggesting that these individuals suffer a loss of insight into their personality alterations (Benedict et al., 2001). Interestingly, euphoria and disinhibition are strongly associated with brain atrophy and lesion burden (Benedict et al., 2004).

Summary

MS is a heterogeneous disease that affects individuals differently over a spectrum of physical, emotional, and neurocognitive domains. The manifestations of the disease vary both within an individual over time and between individuals. This likely reflects the fact that the pathological changes of the central nervous system in persons with MS are dynamic, widespread, and distinctive.

Five prior meta-analytical reviews have provided a wealth of consistent data suggesting that the most pronounced MS-related neuropsychological deficits emerge in the areas of verbal fluency, information processing speed, and in aspects of WM and LTM. Deficits in all of these areas are conventionally characterized as moderate to large. These prominent deficits emerge when cognitive effort and processing speed are critical to effective performance (see D'Esposito et al., 1996; Lengenfelder et al., 2006). Additionally, impairments appear to be amplified by capacity-reducing conditions such as depression (Arnett et al., 1999b, 2001), and when compensatory capacity (as evaluated by activation patterns during cognitive tasks on fMRI) has been exceeded (Cader et al., 2006; Cifelli & Matthews, 2002; Staffen et al., 2002; Wishart et al., 2004). Deficits may be most pronounced on tasks that both tax cognitive abilities and exceed the general compensatory capacity of individuals with MS.

There are several potential areas in which interventions might mitigate the neurocognitive impairments experienced by persons with MS. Specifically, treatments to alleviate depression and improve coping appear to be promising. Techniques to retrain brain function by establishing viable compensatory networks that overcome impairments may also be fruitful (Penner et al., 2006; Penner et al., 2007). Furthermore, curtailing disease progression and enhancing cognition through pharmacological interventions and rehabilitation might reduce the ultimate neurocognitive deficits incurred, but clearly more evidence supporting these treatments is crucial (Pierson & Griffith, 2006).

Acknowledgment

The authors wish to acknowledge Donna Lang for consultation on neuroimaging aspects of this paper and Wendy Loken Thornton for her comments on an earlier version of this manuscript. We also thank the meta-analytic authors who provided additional information to assist in effect size reporting.

References

Amato, M. P., Ponziani, G., Siracusa, G., & Sorbi, S. (2001). Cognitive dysfunction in early-onset multiple sclerosis: A reappraisal after 10 years. *Archives of Neurology, 58*(10), 1602–1606.

American Psychiatric Association. (1994). *Diagnostic and statistical manual of mental disorders* (4th ed.). Washington, DC: Author.

Anderson, D. W., Ellenberg, J. H., Leventhal, C. M., Reingold, S. C., Rodriguez, M., & Silberberg, D. H. (1992). Revised estimate of the prevalence of multiple sclerosis in the United States. *Annals of Neurology, 31*(3), 333–336.

Archibald, C. J., & Fisk, J. D. (2000). Information processing efficiency in patients with multiple sclerosis. *Journal of Clinical and Experimental Neuropsychology, 22*(5), 686–701.

Armstrong, C., Onishi, K., Robinson, K., D'Esposito, M., Thompson, H., Rostami, A., et al. (1996). Serial position and temporal cue effects in multiple sclerosis: Two subtypes of defective memory mechanisms. *Neuropsychologia, 34*(9), 853–862.

Arnett, P. A. (2005). Longitudinal consistency of the relationship between depression symptoms and cognitive functioning in multiple sclerosis. *CNS Spectrums, 10*(5), 372–382.

Arnett, P. A., Higginson, C. I., & Randolph, J. J. (2001). Depression in multiple sclerosis: Relationship to planning ability. *Journal of the International Neuropsychological Society, 7*(6), 665–674.

Arnett, P. A., Higginson, C. I., Voss, W. D., Bender, W. I., Wurst, J. M., & Tippin, J. M. (1999a). Depression in multiple sclerosis: Relationship to working memory capacity. *Neuropsychology, 13*(4), 546–556.

Arnett, P. A., Higginson, C. I., Voss, W. D., Randolph, J. J., & Grandey, A. A. (2002). Relationship between coping, cognitive dysfunction and depression in multiple sclerosis. *Clinical Neuropsychologist, 16*(3), 341–355.

Arnett, P. A., Higginson, C. I., Voss, W. D., Wright, B., Bender, W. I., Wurst, J. M., et al. (1999b). Depressed mood in multiple sclerosis: Relationship to capacity-demanding memory and attentional functioning. *Neuropsychology, 13*(3), 434–446.

Arnett, P. A., Rao, S. M., Bernardin, L., Grafman, J., Yetkin, F. Z., & Lobeck, L. (1994). Relationship between frontal lobe lesions and Wisconsin Card Sorting Test performance in patients with multiple sclerosis. *Neurology, 44*(3), 420–425.

Arnett, P. A., Rao, S. M., Grafman, J., Bernardin, L., Luchetta, T., Binder, J. R., et al. (1997). Executive functions in multiple sclerosis: An analysis of temporal ordering, semantic encoding, and planning abilities. *Neuropsychology, 11*(4), 535–544.

Baddeley, A. (1986). *Working memory*. Oxford: Clarendon Press.

Baddeley, A. (1992). Working memory. *Science, 255*(5044), 556–559.

Bagos, P. G., Nikolopoulos, G., & Ioannidis, A. (2006). Chlamydia pneumoniae infection and the risk of multiple sclerosis: A meta-analysis. *Multiple Sclerosis, 12*(4), 397–411.

Bakshi, R., Czarnecki, D., Shaikh, Z. A., Priore, R. L., Janardhan, V., Kaliszky, Z., et al. (2000). Brain MRI lesions and atrophy are related to depression in multiple sclerosis. *Neuroreport, 11*(6), 1153–1158.

Beatty, P. A., & Gange, J. J. (1977). Neuropsychological aspects of multiple sclerosis. *Journal of Nervous and Mental Disease, 164*(1), 42–50.

Beatty, W. W. (1996). Multiple sclerosis. In R. L. Adams, O. A. Parsons, J. L. Culbertson, & S. J. Nixon (Eds.), *Neuropsychology for clinical practice: Etiology, assessment, and treatment of common neurological disorders* (pp. 225–242). Washington, DC: American Psychological Association.

Beatty, W. W., Goodkin, D. E., Beatty, P. A., & Monson, N. (1989a). Frontal lobe dysfunction and memory impairment in patients with chronic progressive multiple sclerosis. *Brain and Cognition, 11*(1), 73–86.

Beatty, W. W., Goodkin, D. E., Monson, N., & Beatty, P. A. (1989b). Cognitive disturbances in patients with relapsing remitting multiple sclerosis. *Archives of Neurology, 46*(10), 1113–1119.

Beatty, W. W., Goodkin, D. E., Monson, N., & Beatty, P. A. (1990). Implicit learning in patients with chronic progressive multiple sclerosis. *International Journal of Clinical Neuropsychology, 12*(3), 166–172.

Beatty, W. W., Goodkin, D. E., Monson, N., Beatty, P. A., & Hertsgaard, D. (1988). Anterograde and retrograde amnesia in patients with chronic progressive multiple sclerosis. *Archives of Neurology, 45*(6), 611–619.

Beatty, W. W., & Monson, N. (1991a). Memory for temporal order in multiple sclerosis. *Bulletin of the Psychonomic Society, 29*(1), 10–12.

Beatty, W. W., & Monson, N. (1991b). Metamemory in multiple sclerosis. *Journal of Clinical and Experimental Neuropsychology, 13*(2), 309–327.

Beatty, W. W., & Monson, N. (1994). Picture and motor sequencing in multiple sclerosis. *Journal of Clinical and Experimental Neuropsychology, 16*(2), 165–172.

Beatty, W. W., & Monson, N. (1996). Problem solving by patients with multiple sclerosis: Comparison of performance on the Wisconsin and California Card Sorting Tests. *Journal of the International Neuropsychological Society, 2*(2), 134–140.

Beatty, W. W., Wilbanks, S. L., Blanco, C. R., Hames, K. A., Tivis, R., & Paul, R. H. (1996). Memory disturbance in multiple sclerosis: Reconsideration of patterns of performance on the selective reminding test. *Journal of Clinical and Experimental Neuropsychology, 18*(1), 56–62.

Benedict, R. H., Bakshi, R., Simon, J. H., Priore, R., Miller, C., & Munschauer, F. (2002a). Frontal cortex atrophy predicts cognitive impairment in multiple sclerosis. *Journal of Neuropsychiatry and Clinical Neurosciences, 14*(1), 44–51.

Benedict, R. H., Bruce, J. M., Dwyer, M. G., Abdelrahman, N., Hussein, S., Weinstock-Guttman, B., et al. (2006a). Neocortical atrophy, third ventricular width, and cognitive dysfunction in multiple sclerosis. *Archives of Neurology, 63*(9), 1301–1306.

Benedict, R. H. B., Carone, D. A., & Bakshi, R. (2004). Correlating brain atrophy with cognitive dysfunction, mood disturbances, and personality disorder in multiple sclerosis. *Journal of Neuroimaging, 14*(Suppl 3), 36S–45S.

Benedict, R. H., Cookfair, D., Gavett, R., Gunther, M., Munschauer, F., Garg, N., et al. (2006b). Validity of the Minimal Assessment of Cognitive Function in Multiple Sclerosis (MACFIMS). *Journal of the International Neuropsychological Society, 12*(4), 549–558.

Benedict, R. H., Fischer, J. S., Archibald, C. J., Arnett, P. A., Beatty, W. W., Bobholz, J., et al. (2002b). Minimal neuropsychological assessment of MS patients: A consensus approach. *Clinical Neuropsychologist, 16*(3), 381–397.

Benedict, R. H. B., Priore, R. L., Miller, C., Munschauer, F. E., & Jacobs, L. (2001). Personality disorder in multiple sclerosis correlates with cognitive impairment. *Journal of Neuropsychiatry and Clinical Neurosciences, 13*(1), 70–76.

Benedict, R. H., Wahlig, E., Bakshi, R., Fishman, I., Munschauer, F., Zivadinov, R., et al. (2005a). Predicting quality of life in multiple sclerosis: Accounting for physical disability, fatigue, cognition, mood disorder, personality, and behavior change. *Journal of the Neurological Sciences, 231*(1), 29–34.

Benedict, R. H., Weinstock-Guttman, B., Fishman, I., Sharma, J., Tjoa, C. W., & Bakshi, R. (2004). Prediction of neuropsychological impairment in multiple sclerosis: Comparison of conventional magnetic resonance imaging measures of atrophy and lesion burden. *Archives of Neurology, 61*(2), 226–230.

Benedict, R. H., Zivadinov, R., Carone, D. A., Weinstock-Guttman, B., Gaines, J., Maggiore, C., et al. (2005b). Regional lobar atrophy predicts memory impairment in multiple sclerosis. *American Journal of Neuroradiology, 26*(7), 1824–1831.

Berg, D., Supprian, T., Thomae, J., Warmuth-Metz, M., Horowski, A., Zeiler, B., et al. (2000). Lesion pattern in patients with multiple sclerosis and depression. *Multiple Sclerosis, 6*(3), 156–162.

Bergendal, G., Fredrikson, S., & Almkvist, O. (2007). Selective decline in information processing in subgroups of multiple sclerosis: An 8-year longitudinal study. *European Neurology, 57*(4), 193–202.

Bermel, R. A., & Bakshi, R. (2006). The measurement and clinical relevance of brain atrophy in multiple sclerosis. *Lancet Neurology, 5*(2), 158–170.

Blusewicz, M. J., Kramer, J. H., & Delmonico, R. L. (1996). Interference effects in chronic alcoholism. *Journal of the International Neuropsychological Society, 2*(2), 141–145.

Brassington, J. C., & Marsh, N. V. (1998). Neuropsychological aspects of multiple sclerosis. *Neuropsychology Review, 8*(2), 43–77.

Bravin, J. H., Kinsella, G. J., Ong, B., & Vowels, L. (2000). A study of performance of delayed intentions in multiple sclerosis. *Journal of Clinical and Experimental Neuropsychology, 22*(3), 418–429.

Brown, R. F., Tennant, C. C., Sharrock, M., Hodgkinson, S., Dunn, S. M., & Pollard, J. D. (2006). Relationship between stress and relapse in multiple sclerosis: Part II. Direct and indirect relationships. *Multiple Sclerosis, 12*(4), 465–475.

Bruce, J. M., Bruce, A. S., & Arnett, P. A. (2007). Mild visual acuity disturbances are associated with performance on tests of complex visual attention in MS. *Journal of the International Neuropsychological Society, 13*(3), 544–548.

Buschke, H. (1973). Selective reminding for analysis of memory and learning. *Journal of Verbal Learning and Verbal Behavior, 12*(5), 543–550.

Buschke, H., & Fuld, P. A. (1974). Evaluating storage, retention, and retrieval in disordered memory and learning. *Neurology, 24*(11), 1019–1025.

Cader, S., Cifelli, A., Abu-Omar, Y., Palace, J., & Matthews, P. M. (2006). Reduced brain functional reserve and altered functional connectivity in patients with multiple sclerosis. *Brain, 129*, 527–537.

Caine, E. D., Bamford, K. A., Schiffer, R. B., Shoulson, I., & Levy, S. (1986). A controlled neuropsychological comparison of Huntington's disease and multiple sclerosis. *Archives of Neurology, 43*(3), 249–254.

Canellopoulou, M., & Richardson, J. T. (1998). The role of executive function in imagery mnemonics: Evidence from multiple sclerosis. *Neuropsychologia, 36*(11), 1181–1188.

Carroll, M., Gates, R., & Roldan, F. (1984). Memory impairment in multiple sclerosis. *Neuropsychologia, 22*(3), 297–302.

Cermak, L. S., Butters, N., and Moreines, J. (1974). Some analyses of the verbal encoding deficit of alcoholic Korsakoff patients. *Brain and Language, 1*(2), 141–150.

Cifelli, A., & Matthews, P. M. (2002). Cerebral plasticity in multiple sclerosis: Insights from fMRI. *Multiple Sclerosis, 8*(3), 193–199.

Cohen, A. I., West, R., & Craik, F. I. M. (2001). Modulation of the prospective and retrospective components of memory for intentions in younger and older adults. *Aging, Neuropsychology, and Cognition, 8*(1), 1–13.

Cohen, J. (1988). *Statistical power analysis for the behavioral sciences* (2nd ed.). Hillsdale, NJ: Lawrence Erlbaum.

Comi, G., Rovaris, M., Leocani, L., Martinelli, V., & Filippi, M. (2001). Clinical and MRI assessment of brain damage in MS. *Neurological Sciences, 22*(8), S123–S127.

Compston, A. (1999). The genetic epidemiology of multiple sclerosis. *Philosophical Transactions of the Royal Society of London, 354*(1390), 1623–1634.

Compston, A., & Coles, A. (2002). Multiple sclerosis. *Lancet, 359*(9313), 1221–1231.

Dalton, C. M., Brex, P. A., Miszkiel, K. A., Hickman, S. J., MacManus, D. G., Plant, G. T., et al. (2002). Application of the new McDonald criteria to patients with clinically isolated syndromes suggestive of multiple sclerosis. *Annals of Neurology, 52*(1), 47–53.

Dalton, E. J., & Heinrichs, R. W. (2005). Depression in multiple sclerosis: A quantitative review of the evidence. *Neuropsychology, 19*(2), 152–158.

De Sonneville, L. M. J., Boringa, J. B., Reuling, I. E. W., Lazeron, R. H. C., Ader, H. J., & Polman, C. H. (2002). Information processing characteristics in subtypes of multiple sclerosis. *Neuropsychologia, 40*(11), 1751–1765.

Delis, D. C., Kramer, J. H., Kaplan, E., & Ober, B. A. (1987). *The California Verbal Learning Test*. San Antonio, TX: Psychological Corporation.

Deloire, M. S., Salort, E., Bonnet, M., Arimone, Y., Boudineau, M., Amieva, H., et al. (2005). Cognitive impairment as marker of diffuse brain abnormalities in early relapsing remitting multiple sclerosis. *Journal of Neurology, Neurosurgery, and Psychiatry, 76*(4), 519–526.

DeLuca, J., Barbieri-Berger, S., & Johnson, S. K. (1994). The nature of memory impairments in multiple sclerosis: Acquisition versus retrieval. *Journal of Clinical and Experimental Neuropsychology, 16*(2), 183–189.

DeLuca, J., Chelune, G. J., Tulsky, D. S., Lengenfelder, J., & Chiaravalloti, N. D. (2004). Is speed of processing or working memory the primary information processing deficit in multiple sclerosis? *Journal of Clinical and Experimental Neuropsychology, 26*(4), 550–562.

Demaree, H. A., DeLuca, J., Gaudino, E. A., & Diamond, B. J. (1999). Speed of information processing as a key deficit in multiple sclerosis: Implications for rehabilitation. *Journal of Neurology, Neurosurgery, and Psychiatry, 67*(5), 661–663.

Demaree, H. A., Gaudino, E., & DeLuca, J. (2003). The relationship between depressive symptoms and cognitive dysfunction in multiple sclerosis. *Cognitive Neuropsychiatry, 8*(3), 161–171.

Denney, D. R., Lynch, S. G., Parmenter, B. A., & Horne, N. (2004). Cognitive impairment in relapsing and primary progressive multiple sclerosis: Mostly a matter of speed. *Journal of the International Neuropsychological Society, 10*(7), 948–856.

Denney, D. R., Sworowski, L. A., & Lynch, S. G. (2005). Cognitive impairment in three subtypes of multiple sclerosis. *Archives of Clinical Neuropsychology, 20*(8), 967–981.

D'Esposito, M., Onishi, K., Thompson, H., Robinson, K., Armstrong, C., & Grossman, M. (1996). Working memory impairments in multiple sclerosis: Evidence from a dual-task paradigm. *Neuropsychology, 10*(1), 51–56.

Diamond, B. J., DeLuca, J., Kim, H., & Kelley, S. M. (1997). The question of disproportionate impairments in visual and auditory information processing in multiple sclerosis. *Journal of Clinical and Experimental Neuropsychology, 19*(1), 34–42.

Dobbs, A. R., Aubrey, J. B., & Rule, B. G. (1989). Age-associated release from proactive interference: A review. *Canadian Psychology, 30*(3), 588–595.

Ebers, G. C., Sadovnick, A. D., & Risch, N. J. (1995). A genetic basis for familial aggregation in multiple sclerosis. Canadian Collaborative Study Group. *Nature, 377*(6545), 150–151.

Feinstein, A. (1999). *The clinical neuropsychiatry of multiple sclerosis.* New York: Cambridge University Press.

Feinstein, A. (2006). Mood disorders in multiple sclerosis and the effects on cognition. *Journal of the Neurological Sciences, 245*(1), 63–66.

Feinstein, A., & Feinstein, K. (2001). Depression associated with multiple sclerosis. Looking beyond diagnosis to symptom expression. *Journal of Affective Disorders, 66*(2), 193–198.

Feinstein, A., Feinstein, K., Gray, T., & O'Connor, P. (1997). Prevalence and neurobehavioral correlates of pathological laughing and crying in multiple sclerosis. *Archives of Neurology, 54*(9), 1116–1121.

Feinstein, A., Roy, P., Lobaugh, N., Feinstein, K., O'Connor, P., & Black, S. (2004). Structural brain abnormalities in multiple sclerosis patients with major depression. *Neurology, 62*(4), 586–590.

Fernandez-Duque, D., Baird, J. A., & Posner, M. I. (2000). Executive attention and metacognitive regulation. *Consciousness and Cognition, 9,* 288–307.

Fischer, J. S. (1988). Using the Wechsler Memory Scale - Revised to detect and characterize memory deficits in multiple sclerosis. *The Clinical Neuropsychologist, 2*(2), 149–172.

Foong, J., Rozewicz, L., Quaghebeur, G., Davie, C. A., Kartsounis, L. D., Thompson, A. J., et al. (1997). Executive function in multiple sclerosis: The role of frontal lobe pathology. *Brain, 120*(1), 15–26.

Foong, J., Rozewicz, L., Quaghebeur, G., Thompson, A. J., Miller, D. H., & Ron, M. A. (1998). Neuropsychological deficits in multiple sclerosis after acute relapse. *Journal of Neurology, Neurosurgery, and Psychiatry, 64*(4), 529–532.

Ford, H., Trigwell, P., & Johnson, M. (1998). The nature of fatigue in multiple sclerosis. *Journal of Psychosomatic Research, 45*(1), 33–38.

Friedman, H. (1968). Magnitude of experimental effect and a table for its rapid estimation. *Psychological Bulletin, 70*(4), 245–251.

GAMES, & Transatlantic Multiple Sclerosis Genetics Cooperative. (2003). A meta-analysis of whole genome linkage screens in multiple sclerosis. *Journal of Neuroimmunology, 143*(1), 39–46.

Gaudino, E. A., Chiaravalloti, N. D., DeLuca, J., & Diamond, B. J. (2001). A comparison of memory performance in relapsing-remitting, primary progressive and secondary progressive, multiple sclerosis. *Neuropsychiatry, Neuropsychology, and Behavioral Neurology, 14*(1), 32–44.

Ge, Y. (2006). Multiple sclerosis: The role of MR imaging. *American Journal of Neuroradiology, 27*(6), 1165–1176.

Gilchrist, A. C., & Creed, F. H. (1994). Depression, cognitive impairment and social stress in multiple sclerosis. *Journal of Psychosomatic Research, 38*(3), 193–201.

Goldstein, F. C., McKendall, R. R., & Haut, M. W. (1992). Gist recall in multiple sclerosis. *Archives of Neurology, 49*(10), 1060–1064.

Gontkovsky, S. T., & Beatty, W. W. (2006). Practical methods for the clinical assessment of information processing speed. *International Journal of Neuroscience, 116*(11), 1317–1325.

Grafman, J., Rao, S., Bernardin, L., & Leo, G. J. (1991). Automatic memory processes in patients with multiple sclerosis. *Archives of Neurology, 48*(10), 1072–1075.

Grafman, J., Rao, S. M., & Litvan, I. (1990). Disorders of memory. In S. M. Rao (Ed.), *Neurobehavioral aspects of multiple sclerosis* (pp. 102–117). New York: Oxford University Press.

Grant, I., McDonald, W. I., Trimble, M. R., Smith, E., & Reed, R. (1984). Deficient learning and memory in early and middle phases of multiple sclerosis. *Journal of Neurology, Neurosurgery, and Psychiatry, 47*(3), 250–255.

Griffiths, S. Y., Yamamoto, A., Boudreau, V. G., Ross, L. K., Kozora, E., & Thornton, A. E. (2005). Memory interference in multiple sclerosis. *Journal of the International Neuropsychological Society, 11*(6), 737–746.

Grossman, M., Armstrong, C., Onishi, K., Thompson, H., Schaefer, B., Robinson, K., et al. (1994). Patterns of cognitive impairment in relapsing-remitting and chronic progressive multiple sclerosis. *Neuropsychiatry, Neuropsychology, and Behavioral Neurology, 7*(3), 194–210.

Hannay, H. J., Howieson, D. B., Loring, D. W., Fischer, J. S., & Lezak, M. D. (2004). Neuropathology for neuropsychologists. In M. D. Lezak, D. B. Howieson, D. W. Loring, H. J. Hannay, and J. S. Fischer (Eds.), *Neuropsychological Assessment* (4th ed., pp. 157–285). New York: Oxford University Press.

Heaton, R. K., Nelson, L. M., Thompson, D. S., Burks, J. S., & Franklin, G. M. (1985). Neuropsychological findings in relapsing-remitting and chronic-progressive multiple sclerosis. *Journal of Consulting and Clinical Psychology, 53*(1), 103–110.

Henry, J. D., & Beatty, W. W. (2006). Verbal fluency deficits in multiple sclerosis. *Neuropsychologia, 44*(7), 1166–1174.

Higginson, C. I., Arnett, P. A., & Voss, W. D. (2000). The ecological validity of clinical tests of memory and attention in multiple sclerosis. *Archives of Clinical Neuropsychology, 15*(3), 185–204.

Hildebrandt, H., Hahn, H. K., Kraus, J. A., Schulte-Herbrüggen, A., Schwarze, B., & Schwendemann, G. (2006). Memory performance in multiple sclerosis patients correlates with central brain atrophy. *Multiple Sclerosis, 12*(4), 428–436.

Hillert, J., & Masterman, T. (2001). The genetics of multiple sclerosis. In S. D. Cook (Ed.), *Handbook of multiple sclerosis* (3rd ed., pp. 33–66). New York: Marcel Dekker Inc.

Honer, W. G., Hurwitz, T., Li, D. K., Palmer, M., & Paty, D. W. (1987). Temporal lobe involvement in multiple sclerosis patients with psychiatric disorders. *Archives of Neurology, 44*(2), 187–190.

Huber, S. J., Bornstein, R. A., Rammohan, K. W., Christy, J. A., Chakeres, D. W., & McGhee Jr., R. B. (1992). Magnetic resonance imaging correlates of executive function impairments in multiple sclerosis. *Neuropsychiatry, Neuropsychology, and Behavioral Neurology, 5*(1), 33–36.

Huijbregts, S. C., Kalkers, N. F., de Sonneville, L. M., de Groot, V., & Polman, C. H. (2006). Cognitive impairment and decline in different MS subtypes. *Journal of the Neurological Sciences, 245*(1), 187–194.

Jennekens-Schinkel, A., van der Velde, E. A., Sanders, E. A., & Lanser, J. B. (1990). Memory and learning in outpatients with quiescent multiple sclerosis. *Journal of the Neurological Sciences, 95*(3), 311–325.

Johnson, S. K., DeLuca, J., Diamond, B. J., & Natelson, B. H. (1998). Memory dysfunction in fatiguing illness: Examining interference and distraction in short-term memory. *Cognitive Neuropsychiatry, 3*(4), 269–285.

Joy, J. E., & Johnston, R. B. (Eds.). (2001). *Multiple sclerosis: Current status and strategies for the future.* Washington, DC: National Academy Press.

Kail, R. (1998). Speed of information processing in patients with multiple sclerosis. *Journal of Clinical and Experimental Neuropsychology, 20*(1), 98–106.

Kantarci, O., & Wingerchuk, D. (2006). Epidemiology and natural history of multiple sclerosis: New insights. *Current Opinion in Neurology, 19*(3), 248–254.

Kantarci, O. H., & Weinshenker, B. G. (2001). Prognostic factors in multiple sclerosis. In S. D. Cook (Ed.), *Handbook of multiple sclerosis* (3rd ed., pp. 449–463). New York: Marcel Dekker Inc.

Kaufman, A. S., & Lichtenberger, E. O. (2006). *Assessing adolescent and adult intelligence* (3rd ed.). New York: John Wiley and Sons, Inc.

Keegan, B. M., & Noseworthy, J. H. (2002). Multiple sclerosis. *Annual Review of Medicine, 53,* 285–302.

Kenealy, P. M., Beaumont, G. J., Lintern, T., & Murrell, R. (2000). Autobiographical memory, depression and quality of life in multiple sclerosis. *Journal of Clinical and Experimental Neuropsychology, 22*(1), 125–131.

Kessler, H. R., Cohen, R. A., Lauer, K., & Kausch, D. F. (1992). The relationship between disability and memory dysfunction in multiple sclerosis. *The International Journal of Neuroscience, 62*(1), 17–34.

Kidd, D., Barkhof, F., McConnell, R., Algra, P. R., Allen, I. V., & Revesz, T. (1999). Cortical lesions in multiple sclerosis. *Brain, 122,* 17–26.

Korostil, M., & Feinstein, A. (2007). Anxiety disorders and their clinical correlates in multiple sclerosis patients. *Multiple Sclerosis, 13*(1), 67–72.

Kramer, J. H., & Delis, D. C. (1991). Interference effects on the California Verbal Learning Test: A construct validation study. *Psychological Assessment, 3*(2), 299–302.

Kujala, P., Portin, R., Revonsuo, A., & Ruutiainen, J. (1994). Automatic and controlled information processing in multiple sclerosis. *Brain, 117,* 1115–1126.

Kurtzke, J. F. (2000). Multiple sclerosis in time and space--geographic clues to cause. *Journal of Neurovirology, 6*(Suppl 2), S134–S140.

Landro, N. I., Celius, E. G., & Sletvold, H. (2004). Depressive symptoms account for deficient information processing speed but not for impaired working memory in early phase multiple sclerosis (MS). *Journal of the Neurological Sciences, 217*(2), 211–216.

Lanz, M., Hahn, H. K., & Hildebrandt, H. (2007). Brain atrophy and cognitive impairment in multiple sclerosis: A review. *Journal of Neurology, 254*(Suppl 2), II43–II48.

Laux, L. F., & Lane, D. M. (1985). Information processing components of substitution test performance. *Intelligence, 9*(2), 111–136.

Lazeron, R. H. C., Boringa, J. B., Schouten, M., Uitdehaag, B. M. J., Bergers, E., Lindeboom, J., et al. (2005). Brain atrophy and lesion load as explaining parameters for cognitive impairment in multiple sclerosis. *Multiple Sclerosis, 11*(5), 524–531.

Lazeron, R. H. C., de Sonneville, L. M. J., Scheltens, P., Polman, C. H., & Barkhof, F. (2006). Cognitive slowing in multiple sclerosis is strongly associated with brain volume reduction. *Multiple Sclerosis, 12*(6), 760–768.

Lengenfelder, J., Bryant, D., Diamond, B. J., Kalmar, J. H., Moore, N. B., & DeLuca, J. (2006). Processing speed interacts with working memory efficiency in multiple sclerosis. *Archives of Clinical Neuropsychology, 21*(3), 229–238.

Lezak, M. D., Howieson, D. B., Loring, D. W., Hannay, H. J., & Fischer, J. S. (2004). *Neuropsychological Assessment* (4th ed.). New York: Oxford University Press.

Litvan, I., Grafman, J., Vendrell, P., & Martinez, J. M. (1988a). Slowed information processing in multiple sclerosis. *Archives of Neurology, 45*(3), 281–285.

Litvan, I., Grafman, J., Vendrell, P., Martinez, J. M., Junque, C., Vendrell, J. M., et al. (1988b). Multiple memory deficits in patients with multiple sclerosis. Exploring the working memory system. *Archives of Neurology, 45*(6), 607–610.

Lovera, J., Bagert, B., Smoot, K. H., Wild, K., Frank, R., Bogardus, K., et al. (2006). Correlations of Perceived Deficits Questionnaire of Multiple Sclerosis Quality of Life Inventory with Beck Depression Inventory and neuropsychological tests. *Journal of Rehabilitation Research and Development, 43*(1), 73–82.

Lublin, F. D., & Reingold, S. C. (1996). Defining the clinical course of multiple sclerosis: Results of an international survey. National Multiple Sclerosis Society (USA) Advisory Committee on Clinical Trials of New Agents in Multiple Sclerosis. *Neurology, 46*(4), 907–911.

Lucchinetti, C. F., & Parisi, J. E. (2006). Pathology: What may it tell us? In S. D. Cook (Ed.), *Handbook of multiple sclerosis* (4th ed., pp. 113–152). New York: Taylor and Francis.

Luria, A. R. (1966). *Higher cortical functions in man* (2nd ed.). New York: Basic Books, Inc.

Lynch, S. G., Parmenter, B. A., & Denney, D. R. (2005). The association between cognitive impairment and physical disability in multiple sclerosis. *Multiple Sclerosis, 11*(4), 469–476.

Maor, Y., Olmer, L., & Mozes, B. (2001). The relation between objective and subjective impairment in cognitive function among multiple sclerosis patients: The role of depression. *Multiple Sclerosis, 7*(2), 131–135.

Marrie, R. A. (2004). Environmental risk factors in multiple sclerosis aetiology. *Lancet Neurology, 3*(12), 709–718.

McDonald, W. I., Compston, A., Edan, G., Goodkin, D., Hartung, H. P., Lublin, F. D., et al. (2001). Recommended diagnostic criteria for multiple sclerosis: Guidelines from the International Panel on the Diagnosis of Multiple Sclerosis. *Annals of Neurology, 50*(1), 121–127.

Merelli, E., & Casoni, F. (2000). Prognostic factors in multiple sclerosis: Role of intercurrent infections and vaccinations against influenza and hepatitis B. *Neurological Sciences, 21*(4), S853–S856.

Miller, A. E. (2006). Clinical features. In S. D. Cook (Ed.), *Handbook of multiple sclerosis* (4th ed., pp. 153–178). New York: Taylor and Francis.

Minden, S. L., Moes, E. J., Orav, J., Kaplan, E., & Reich, P. (1990). Memory impairment in multiple sclerosis. *Journal of Clinical and Experimental Neuropsychology, 12*(4), 566–586.

Mohr, D., Hart, S., Julian, L., Cox, D., & Pelletier, D. (2004). Association between stressful life events and exacerbation in multiple sclerosis: A meta-analysis. *British Medical Journal, 328*(7442), 731–733.

Mohr, D. C., Boudewyn, A. C., Goodkin, D. E., Bostrom, A., & Epstein, L. (2001). Comparative outcomes for individual cognitive-behavior therapy, supportive-expressive group psychotherapy, and sertraline for the treatment of depression in multiple sclerosis. *Journal of Consulting and Clinical Psychology, 69*(6), 942–949.

Mohr, D. C., Epstein, L., Luks, T. L., Goodkin, D., Cox, D., Goldberg, A., et al. (2003). Brain lesion volume and neuropsychological function predict efficacy of treatment for depression in multiple sclerosis. *Journal of Consulting and Clinical Psychology, 71*(6), 1017–1024.

Montalban, X., & Rio, J. (2006). Interferons and cognition. *Journal of the Neurological Sciences, 245*(1), 137–140.

Murray, T. J. (2005). *Multiple sclerosis: The history of a disease*. New York: Demos Medical Pub.

Naismith, R. T., Trinkaus, K., & Cross, A. H. (2006). Phenotype and prognosis in African-Americans with multiple sclerosis: A retrospective chart review. *Multiple Sclerosis, 12*(6), 775–781.

Nocentini, U., Pasqualetti, P., Bonavita, S., Buccafusca, M., De Caro, M. F., Farina, D., et al. (2006). Cognitive dysfunction in patients with relapsing-remitting multiple sclerosis. *Multiple Sclerosis, 12*(1), 77–87.

Noseworthy, J. H., Lucchinetti, C., Rodriguez, M., & Weinshenker, B. G. (2000). Multiple sclerosis. *The New England Journal of Medicine, 343*(13), 938–952.

Ozakbas, S., Ormeci, B., Akdede, B. B., Alptekin, K., & Idiman, E. (2004). Utilization of the auditory consonant trigram test to screen for cognitive impairment in patients with multiple sclerosis: Comparison with the Paced Auditory Serial Addition Test. *Multiple Sclerosis, 10*(6), 686–689.

Parmenter, B. A., Shucard, J. L., & Shucard, D. W. (2007a). Information processing deficits in multiple sclerosis: A matter of complexity. *Journal of the International Neuropsychological Society, 13*(3), 417–423.

Parmenter, B. A., Zivadinov, R., Kerenyi, L., Gavett, R., Weinstock-Guttman, B., Dwyer, M. G., et al. (2007b). Validity of the Wisconsin Card Sorting and Delis–Kaplan Executive Function System (DKEFS) sorting tests in multiple sclerosis. *Journal of Clinical and Experimental Neuropsychology, 29*(2), 215–223.

Parvizi, J., Anderson, S. W., Martin, C. O., Damasio, H., & Damasio, A. R. (2001). Pathological laughter and crying: A link to the cerebellum. *Brain, 124*(9), 1708–1719.

Paul, R. H., Blanco, C. R., Hames, K. A., & Beatty, W. W. (1997). Autobiographical memory in multiple sclerosis. *Journal of the International Neuropsychological Society, 3*(3), 246–251.

Penner, I. K., Kappos, L., Rausch, M., Opwis, K., & Radu, E. W. (2006). Therapy-induced plasticity of cognitive functions in MS patients: Insights from fMRI. *Journal of Physiology, 99*(4), 455–462.

Penner, I. K., Opwis, K., & Kappos, L. (2007). Relation between functional brain imaging, cognitive impairment and cognitive rehabilitation in patients with multiple sclerosis. *Journal of Neurology, 254*(Suppl 2), II53–II57.

Pierson, S. H., & Griffith, N. (2006). Treatment of cognitive impairment in multiple sclerosis. *Behavioural Neurology, 17,* 53–67.

Poser, C. M., Paty, D. W., Scheinberg, L., McDonald, W. I., Davis, F. A., Ebers, G. C., et al. (1983). New diagnostic criteria for multiple sclerosis: Guidelines for research protocols. *Annals of Neurology, 13,* 227–231.

Postman, L., & Underwood, B. J. (1973). Critical issues in interference theory. *Memory and Cognition, 1*(1), 19–40.

Prakash, R.S., Snook E.M., Lewis, J.M., Motl, R.W., & Kramer, A.F. (2008). Cognitive impairments in relapsing-remitting multiple sclerosis: A meta-analysis. *Multiple Sclerosis, 14*(9), 1250–1261.

Pryse-Phillips, W., & Sloka, S. (2006). Etiopathogenesis and epidemiology: Clues to etiology. In S. D. Cook (Ed.), *Handbook of multiple sclerosis* (4th ed., pp. 1–40). New York: Taylor and Francis.

Pujol, J., Bello, J., Deus, J., Cardoner, N., Martí-Vilalta, J. L., & Capdevila, A. (2000). Beck Depression Inventory factors related to demyelinating lesions of the left arcuate fasciculus region. *Psychiatry Research, 99*(3), 151–159.

Randolph, C., Gold, J. M., Carpenter, C. J., Goldberg, T. E., & Weinberger, D. R. (1992). Release from proactive interference: Determinants of performance and neuropsychological correlates. *Journal of Clinical and Experimental Neuropsychology, 14*(5), 785–800.

Randolph, J. J., Arnett, P. A., & Freske, P. (2004). Metamemory in multiple sclerosis: Exploring affective and executive contributors. *Archives of Clinical Neuropsychology, 19*(2), 259–279.

Randolph, J. J., Arnett, P. A., & Higginson, C. I. (2001). Metamemory and tested cognitive functioning in multiple sclerosis. *The Clinical Neuropsychologist, 15*(3), 357–368.

Rao, S. M., Grafman, J., DiGiulio, D., Mittenberg, W., Bernardin, L., Leo, G. J., et al. (1993). Memory dysfunction in multiple sclerosis: Its relation to working memory, semantic encoding, and implicit learning. *Neuropsychology, 7*(3), 364–374.

Rao, S. M., Hammeke, T. A., McQuillen, M. P., Khatri, B. O., & Lloyd, D. (1984). Memory disturbance in chronic progressive multiple sclerosis. *Archives of Neurology, 41*(6), 625–631.

Rao, S. M., Leo, G. J., Bernardin, L., & Unverzagt, F. (1991a). Cognitive dysfunction in multiple sclerosis. I. Frequency, patterns, and prediction. *Neurology, 41*(5), 685–691.

Rao, S. M., Leo, G. J., Ellington, L., Nauertz, T., Bernardin, L., & Unverzagt, F. (1991b). Cognitive dysfunction in multiple sclerosis. II. Impact on employment and social functioning. *Neurology, 41*(5), 692–696.

Rao, S. M., Leo, G. J., Haughton, V. M., St Aubin-Faubert, P., & Bernardin, L. (1989a). Correlation of magnetic resonance imaging with neuropsychological testing in multiple sclerosis. *Neurology, 39*(2), 161–166.

Rao, S. M., Leo, G. J., & St. Aubin-Faubert, P. (1989b). On the nature of memory disturbance in multiple sclerosis. *Journal of Clinical and Experimental Neuropsychology, 11*(5), 699–712.

Rao, S. M., St. Aubin-Faubert, P., & Leo, G. J. (1989c). Information processing speed in patients with multiple sclerosis. *Journal of Clinical and Experimental Neuropsychology, 11*(4), 471–477.

Rendell, P. G., Jensen, F., & Henry, J. D. (2007). Prospective memory in multiple sclerosis. *Journal of the International Neuropsychological Society, 13*(3), 410–416.

Rinker II, J. R., Naismith, R. T., & Cross, A. H. (2006). Multiple sclerosis: An autoimmune disease of the central nervous system? In S. D. Cook (Ed.), *Handbook of multiple sclerosis* (4th ed., pp. 95–112). New York: Taylor and Francis.

Rocca, M. A., & Filippi, M. (2007). Functional MRI in multiple sclerosis. *Journal of Neuroimaging, 17*(Suppl 1), 36S–41S.

Rovaris, M., Filippi, M., Minicucci, L., Iannucci, G., Santuccio, G., Possa, F., et al. (2000). Cortical/subcortical disease burden and cognitive impairment in patients with multiple sclerosis. *American Journal of Neuroradiology, 21*(2), 402–408.

Ruchkin, D. S., Grafman, J., Krauss, G. L., Johnson Jr., R., Canoune, H., & Ritter, W. (1994). Event-related brain potential evidence for a verbal working memory deficit in multiple sclerosis. *Brain, 117*(2), 289–305.

Rutschmann, O. T., McCrory, D. C., Matchar, D. B., & Immunization Panel of the Multiple Sclerosis Council for Clinical Practice Guidelines (2002). Immunization and MS: A summary of published evidence and recommendations. *Neurology, 59*(12), 1837–1843.

Ryan, L., Clark, C., Klonoff, H., Li, D., & Paty, D. (1996). Patterns of cognitive impairment in relapsing-remitting multiple sclerosis and their relationship to neuropathology on magnetic resonance images. *Neuropsychology, 10*(2), 176–193.

Sadovnick, A. D., Armstrong, H., Rice, G. P., Bulman, D., Hashimoto, L., Paty, D. W., et al. (1993). A population-based study of multiple sclerosis in twins: Update. *Annals of Neurology, 33*(3), 281–285.

Sadovnick, A. D., Ebers, G. C., Wilson, R. W., & Paty, D. W. (1992). Life expectancy in patients attending multiple sclerosis clinics. *Neurology, 42*(5), 991–994.

Sadovnick, A. D., Remick, R. A., Allen, J., Swartz, E., Yee, I. M. K., Eisen, K., et al. (1996). Depression and multiple sclerosis. *Neurology, 46*(3), 628–632.

Scarrabelotti, M., & Carroll, M. (1999). Memory dissociation and metamemory in multiple sclerosis. *Neuropsychologia, 37*(12), 1335–1350.

Schubert, D. S., & Foliart, R. H. (1993). Increased depression in multiple sclerosis patients. A meta-analysis. *Psychosomatics, 34*(2), 124–130.

Schulz, D., Kopp, B., Kunkel, A., & Faiss, J. H. (2006). Cognition in the early stage of multiple sclerosis. *Journal of Neurology, 253*(8), 1002–1010.

Seinela, A., Hamalainen, P., Koivisto, M., & Ruutiainen, J. (2002). Conscious and unconscious uses of memory in multiple sclerosis. *Journal of the Neurological Sciences, 198*(1), 79–85.

Sperling, R. A., Guttmann, C. R. G., Hohol, M. J., Warfield, S. K., Jakab, M., Parente, M., et al. (2001). Regional magnetic resonance imaging lesion burden and cognitive function in multiple sclerosis:

A longitudinal study. *Archives of Neurology, 58*(1), 115–121.

Squire, L. R. (1982). Comparisons between forms of amnesia: Some deficits are unique to Korsakoff's syndrome. *Journal of Experimental Psychology: Learning, Memory, and Cognition, 8*(6), 560–571.

Staffen, W., Mair, A., Zauner, H., Unterrainer, J., Niederhofer, H., Kutzelnigg, A., et al. (2002). Cognitive function and fMRI in patients with multiple sclerosis: Evidence for compensatory cortical activation during an attention task. *Brain, 125*(6), 1275–1282.

Sternberg, S. (1969). Memory-scanning: Mental processes revealed by reaction-time experiments. *American Scientist, 57*(4), 421–457.

Strauss, E., Sherman, E. M. S., & Spreen, O. (2006). *A compendium of neuropsychological tests: Administration, norms, and commentary* (3rd ed.). New York: Oxford University Press.

Taylor, R. (1990). Relationships between cognitive test performance and everyday cognitive difficulties in multiple sclerosis. *The British Journal of Clinical Psychology, 29*, 251–253.

Thacker, E. L., Mirzaei, F., & Ascherio, A. (2006). Infectious mononucleosis and risk for multiple sclerosis: A meta-analysis. *Annals of Neurology, 59*(3), 499–503.

Thornton, A. E., & Raz, N. (1997). Memory impairment in multiple sclerosis: A quantitative review. *Neuropsychology, 11*(3), 357–366.

Thornton, A. E., Raz, N., & Tucker, K. A. (2002). Memory in multiple sclerosis: Contextual encoding deficits. *Journal of the International Neuropsychological Society, 8*(3), 395–409.

Tremlett, H. L., & Devonshire, V. A. (2006). Does the season or month of birth influence disease progression in multiple sclerosis? *Neuroepidemiology, 26*(4), 195–198.

van den Burg, W., van Zomeren, A. H., Minderhoud, J. M., Prange, A. J., & Meijer, N. S. (1987). Cognitive impairment in patients with multiple sclerosis and mild physical disability. *Archives of Neurology, 44*(5), 494–501.

Vitkovitch, M., Bishop, S., Dancey, C., & Richards, A. (2002). Stroop interference and negative priming in patients with multiple sclerosis. *Neuropsychologia, 40*(9), 1570–1576.

Vukusic, S., & Confavreux, C. (2001). The natural history of multiple sclerosis. In S. D. Cook (Ed.), *Handbook of multiple sclerosis* (3rd ed., pp. 433–447). New York: Marcel Dekker Inc.

Wallin, M. T., Wilken, J. A., & Kane, R. (2006). Cognitive dysfunction in multiple sclerosis: Assessment, imaging, and risk factors. *Journal of Rehabilitation Research and Development, 43*(1), 63–72.

Wallin, M. T., Wilken, J. A., Turner, A. P., Williams, R. M., & Kane, R. (2006). Depression and multiple sclerosis: Review of a lethal combination. *Journal of Rehabilitation Research and Development, 43*(1), 45–62.

Wickens, D. D. (1970). Encoding categories of words: An empirical approach to meaning. *Psychological Review, 77*(1), 1–15.

Wishart, H., & Sharpe, D. (1997). Neuropsychological aspects of multiple sclerosis: A quantitative review. *Journal of Clinical and Experimental Neuropsychology, 19*(6), 810–824.

Wishart, H. A., Saykin, A. J., McDonald, B. C., Mamourian, A. C., Flashman, L. A., Schuschu, K. R., et al. (2004). Brain activation patterns associated with working memory in relapsing-remitting MS. *Neurology, 62*(2), 234–238.

Zakzanis, K. K. (2000). Distinct neurocognitive profiles in multiple sclerosis subtypes. *Archives of Clinical Neuropsychology, 15*(2), 115–136.

Zivadinov, R., Sepcic, J., Nasuelli, D., De Masi, R., Bragadin, L. M., Tommasi, M. A., et al. (2001). A longitudinal study of brain atrophy and cognitive disturbances in the early phase of relapsing-remitting multiple sclerosis. *Journal of Neurology, Neurosurgery, and Psychiatry, 70*(6), 773–780.

Zorzon, M., de Masi, R., Nasuelli, D., Ukmar, M., Mucelli, R. P., Cazzato, G., et al. (2001). Depression and anxiety in multiple sclerosis. A clinical and MRI study in 95 subjects. *Journal of Neurology, 248*(5), 416–421.

14

Cerebrovascular Disease

Gregory G. Brown, Ronald M. Lazar, and Lisa Delano-Wood

Cerebrovascular Disease

Although early Greek physicians described stroke, it was not until 1658 that Johanne Jacob Wepfer attributed the symptoms of stroke to disorders of circulation (Benton, 1991; Clarke, 1963). In his *Observationses Anatomicae*, Wepfer was the first author to show that stroke could be caused by occlusion of cerebral vessels or by subdural or intracerebral hemorrhage (Benton, 1991). Wepfer's distinction between cerebrovascular occlusive disease and cerebral hemorrhage remains a central clinical distinction in the differential diagnosis of stroke (Wiebe-Velazquez & Hachinski, 1991). As the pathophysiological basis of stroke has become more refined, the disorders of the content of blood, primary blood diseases, and abnormalities of blood vessels underlying the neuropsychological abnormalities of cerebrovascular disease (CVD) have become increasingly clarified. This chapter is a review of CVD for neuropsychologists who wish to do clinical work or research with patients who have experienced stroke, transient ischemic attack, ischemic white matter disease, or vascular dementia (VaD). We limit our review to studies that highlight neuropsychological aspects of CVD per se, and do not review studies that use stroke patients to draw conclusions about localization of function. Although we do not thoroughly review the effects of stroke on affective brain systems, we comment on the impact of CVD on emotional functioning as part of broader neuropsychological syndromes.

Readers might wish to consult Kales et al. (2005) for a discussion of CVD and depression. Although we do not thoroughly review studies of the neuropsychological effects of treatment, we comment on cerebrovascular treatment in discussions of neuropsychological outcome.

The Distribution of Cerebral Vessels and Their Collaterals

The topography of major brain arteries and their connections determine the location of brain dysfunction caused by a cerebrovascular event. Paired carotid and vertebral arteries bring blood to the brain from the heart (Figure 14–1). Each common carotid artery divides into external and internal segments at about the upper border of the thyroid cartilage (Gilroy & Meyer, 1969, p. 478). At the level of the optic nerve, the internal carotid artery divides into the anterior and middle cerebral arteries. The vertebral arteries ascend through the spinal vertebrae and join in the lower pons to form the basilar artery. At the Circle of Willis at the medial base of the cerebral hemispheres, the basilar artery divides to form the posterior cerebral arteries, which ascend to provide blood to the inferior temporal gyrus, portions of the occipital lobe, and parts of the superior parietal lobule (Sasaki & Kassell, 1990). Whereas the carotid arteries and the anterior and middle cerebral arteries supply blood to the forebrain, the vertebrobasilar circulation and the posterior cerebral arteries supply the brain stem, the cerebellum, much of the thalamus, the occipital lobes, and the posterior medial temporal lobes.

Thomas Willis (1664) was the first author to describe the functional significance of cerebrovasculature connections as collateral paths of blood flow when a single artery is blocked (Meyer & Hierons, 1962). One path, the Circle of Willis, connects the anterior and posterior cerebral arteries at the base of the brain (Figures 14–1 and 14–3). Additional connections result from the joining of small branches of the anterior, middle, and posterior cerebral arteries as they pass through the leptomeninges (Sasaki & Kassell, 1990). Although the external carotid artery generally provides blood to tissue external to the skull and the internal carotid artery provides blood to brain tissue, the external and internal carotid arteries form connections at several points, most prominently through branches of the ophthalmic artery, which arises from the internal carotid artery (Osborn, 1980, pp. 78–85). Examples of these connections included the anastomoses between the anterior branch of the superficial temporal artery, a branch of the external carotid system, and the supraorbital and frontal branches of the ophthalmic artery (Pick & Howden, 1977). Individual variation in collateral supply is an important determinant of the pattern and severity of damage in stroke (Nilsson et al., 1979; Toole, 1990, p. 9).

Ischemic Stroke

Definitions of stroke require the rapid onset of nonconvulsive neurological deficits (Victor & Ropper, 2001). How focal the symptoms must be to be called a stroke varies among experts, with some authorities considering sudden and nonconvulsive loss of consciousness a form of stroke, while other authorities emphasizing the focality of the neurological deficit (Victor & Ropper, 2001; Wiebe-Velazquez & Hachinski, 1991). Ischemic stroke occurs whenever the blood flow through arterial branches is blocked sufficiently to cause cell death (Victor & Ropper, 2001). Common causes of arterial occlusion are embolism—the blockage of a blood vessel by an abnormal particle circulating in the blood—and thrombosis, i.e. blood clots (Victor & Ropper, 2001, p. 870). Although stroke has traditionally been defined by neurological symptoms, modern brain imaging has greatly improved the identification of ischemic infarction (see definition below). Fluid-attenuated inversion recovery (FLAIR) magnetic resonance (MR) images are highly T_2-weighted and have shown greater

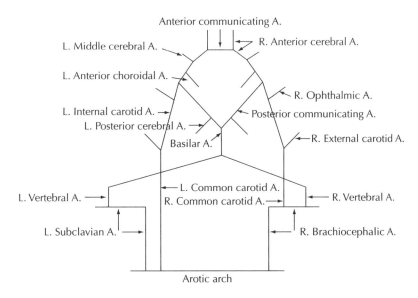

Figure 14–1. A schematic diagram of the major vessels supplying blood to the brain. The polygon shaped like a baseball field at the top of the diagram is the circle of Willis. (Reproduced with permission from Brown et al., 1986.)

sensitivity to the detection of infarction than conventional T_2-weighted magnetic resonance images (Shafer et al., 2006). Diffusion-weighted images along with maps of the apparent diffusion coefficient have especially advanced the detection of tissue abnormality within the first 6 hours of cerebral ischemia (Shafer et al., 2006).

Epidemiology

Studies since 1990, completed primarily in Australia, New Zealand, and Europe, have found a median incidence of ischemic stroke of about 5 cases per 1000 per year for populations 45 years and older (Feigin et al., 2003). The incidence of stroke is greatly influenced by age with median incidence worldwide less than 2 cases per 1000 per year between ages 45 and 54 and increasing 10-fold to 20 cases per 1000 per year for individuals 85 years or older (Feigin et al., 2003). The incidence of stroke in the Ukraine—12 per 1000 per year—is among the highest worldwide (Mihalka et al., 2001). Ischemic stroke accounts for 67%–80% of all new strokes (Feigin et al., 2003).

Comprising about 9.7% of all deaths, stroke is the second most common, single cause of death worldwide behind heart disease (Paul et al., 2007). Stroke mortality rate is higher in developed than underdeveloped countries (Paul et al., 2007). Depending on the location of the study, studies have found that ischemic stroke causes death in 12%–20% of cases within one month of the event (Feigin et al., 2003). Considering the medical treatments and lifestyle interventions available to manage stroke risk factors, stroke and cardiovascular disease are the most common causes of preventable mortality and serious long-term disability among middle-aged and older adults (http://www.ninds.nih.gov/news_and_events/press_releases/pressrelease_may_stroke_050801.htm).

Pathophysiology

The brain is about 2% of total body weight, yet receives 15%–20% of the oxygenated blood pumped from the heart (Sokoloff, 1997). Mean gray matter cerebral blood flow (CBF) is approximately 80 ml/100 gm/min or about three to four times the CBF of white matter (22 ml/100 gm/min) (Fieschi & Rosiers, 1976), yielding a mean CBF of about 60 ml/100 gm/min. Blood brings glucose and oxygen to the brain, while dispersing the heat and metabolic products of cerebral activity (Toole, 1990, pp. 28–29). In natural states, the brain can tolerate only a brief cessation of blood flow before neural functioning is disrupted. Cerebral ischemia occurs when blood flow to a brain region is reduced sufficiently to alter neural metabolism and function (Ginsberg, 1997). When the duration and severity of ischemia produces permanent functional and structural changes, infarction occurs. In some animal stroke models and in human stroke, the ischemic region typically has a gradient of viability that varies with CBF. At the core is a locus where blood flow is not more than 10%–20% of controls, neural tissue becomes isoelectric and destined to progress to infarction (Ginsberg, 1997; Welch & Levine, 1991). Surrounding the ischemic core is a penumbral region where CBF is 20%–40% of control values. Neural tissue in the penumbral region is isoelectric, and conditions fluctuate between those favoring and those opposing tissue viability (Astrup et al., 1981; Meyer et al., 1962). Although residual perfusion in the penumbra is probably sufficient to maintain near-normal concentrations of molecular energy, it is insufficient to maintain normal lactate levels, adequate functioning of ionic pumps, and neurotransmitter synthesis (Welch & Levine, 1991). Surrounding the ischemic zone is a hyperemic region where viable neural tissue retains its normal electrical activity and where CBF is higher than control states (Welch & Barkley, 1986). Protecting viable neurons in penumbral and hyperemic regions from progressing to irreversible injury is one focus of current stroke drug development (Fisher, 2006).

Diminished molecular energy appears to be the stimulus for the cascade of events leading to ischemic infarction; bioenergetic failure, however, is not itself a sufficient cause of tissue death. For example, brain infarction does not develop during hypoglycemic coma despite the occurrence of bioenergetic failure (Siesjo & Smith, 1997). The list of candidate causes of neuronal death following ischemia include acidosis, abnormal calcium influx into nerve cells, free radical production, glutamate-mediated excitotoxicity, dysregulated lipid metabolism, nitric oxide neurotoxicity, and activation of proteolytic enzymes, to name some leading candidates. The primer edited by Welch et al. (1997) can be consulted for reviews of each of these potential causes of ischemic neuronal death. Zemke and colleagues provide a current review of the mechanisms of ischemic cell death from the viewpoint of naturally occurring protective factors (Zemke et al., 2004).

The Behavioral Effects of Ischemic Stroke

Strokes often produce focal or multifocal neurobehavioral deficits and disrupt general adaptive neuropsychological functions (Hom, 1991; Victor & Ropper, 2001). Up to 65% of patients experience the new onset or worsening of cognitive deficits following stroke (Donovan et al., 2008; Jin et al., 2006). The prevalence of poststroke cognitive impairment is especially high among individuals more than 75 years of age (Ballard et al., 2003). A thorough review of the focal neuropsychological syndromes produced by stroke would require a discussion of much of the wide-ranging localization literature. As an alternative to a broad review, we refer readers to the literature on the impact of stroke on the specific neuropsychological domains of memory (Snaphaan & de Leeuw, 2007), language (Salter et al., 2006), and visuoperceptual function (Hildebrandt et al., 1999). We discuss executive functions in the following sections.

In a traditional view, stroke impairs performance on two types of general adaptive functioning measures (Hom & Reitan, 1990). The first type is composed of indices, such as the Halstead Impairment Index and the Average Impairment Index, that sum over scores obtained from separate tests or from individual items. These indices measure the additive as well as synergistic effects of impairment of discrete functions. The second type of index, such as the Halstead Category Test, the Trail-Making Test, especially part B, and the Digit Symbol subtest from the Wechsler intelligence scales, reflect the integrated, interactive behavior of several brain systems (Reitan & Davison, 1974). Perhaps because stroke can have remote as well as focal effects, both additive and integrative indices of general adaptive function are diminished by lateralized stroke (Fujishima et al., 1974; Hom & Reitan, 1990). General measures of adaptive

functioning have been frequently shown to be more sensitive to brain dysfunction than tests of specific neuropsychological domains and might be especially useful in detecting subtle cerebrovascular impairment (Hom, 1991). The extent to which this traditional view can be confirmed in stroke groups with homogenous arteriographic lesions remains to be tested.

Given the large variety of ways that stroke might impair cognitive functioning, how should stroke patients be evaluated? Recently an NINDS (*National Institute of Neurological Disorders and Stroke) and* Canadian Stroke Network consensus panel recommended a battery of brief tests that measure executive function and attention, visuospatial performance, language and lexical retrieval, memory and learning, neuropsychiatric and depressive symptoms, and premorbid status (Hachinski et al., 2006). The consensus group recommended specific tasks within each domain after reviewing candidate tasks for quality of standardization, psychometric properties (e.g., reliability and lack of ceiling and flow effects), brevity and portability, cost and ease of use, domain specificity, cross-cultural generalizability, and previous use among patients with vascular cognitive impairment (VCI; Hachinski et al., 2006). After considering these test selection criteria, the consensus working group recommended test batteries that vary in duration and assessment focus (see Table 14–1). The 5-minute battery was intended for use in epidemiological studies, especially those studies involving assessment over the telephone. The 60-minute battery was developed to provide reliable information about the integrity of functioning in specific neuropsychological domains. The 30-minute battery was designed to clinically screen patients suspected of having vascular cognitive deficit (Hachinski et al., 2006).

Although the tests selected by the consensus group have been individually validated as sensitive measures of vascular cognitive impairment, the usefulness of these tests as components of an integrated test battery remains to be determined.

Transient Ischemia

A sudden focal neurological symptom presumably due to vascular disease, limited to the

Table 14–1. NINDS–Canadian Stroke Network Neuropsychological Test Protocols

Neuropsychological doman & recommended tests	Targeted battery length (minutes)		
	60	30	5
Executive/Activation			
Animal Naming (semantic fluency)	Recommended	Recommended	Supplemental
Controlled Oral Word Association Test	Recommended	Recommended	
WAIS-III Digit Symbol Coding	Recommended	Recommended	
Trail-Making Test: Parts A and B	Recommended	Supplemental	Supplemental
Montreal Cognitive Assessment 1-Letter Verbal Fluency			Recommended
Learning Strategies from Hopkins Verbal Learning Test	Recommended		
Simple and Choice Reaction Time	Future Development		
Self-Regulation and Metacognition	Future Development		
Language/Lexical Retrieval			
Boston Naming Test (2nd ed.)[a]	Recommended		
Visuospatial			
Rey–Osterrieth Complex Figure—Copy Condition	Recommended		
Rey–Osterrieth Complex Figure—Memory Condition	Supplemental		
Memory/Learning			
Hopkins Verbal Learning Test—Revised	Recommended	Recommended	
California Verbal Learning Test—2	Alternative		
Boston Naming Test Recognition	Future Development		
Digit Symbol Coding Incidental Learning	Supplemental		
Montreal Cognitive Assessment 5-Word Test			Recommended
Neuropsychiatric/Depressive Symptoms			
Neuropsychiatric Inventory—Questionnaire Version	Recommended	Recommended	
Center for Epidemiological Studies—Depression Scale	Recommended	Recommended	
Premorbid Status			
Informant Questionnaire for Cognitive Decline in the Elderly[a]	Recommended		
Mental Status			
Mini-Mental State Examination	Supplemental	Supplemental	Supplemental
Orientation			
Cognitive Assessment 6-Item Orientation			Recommended

Notes: See Hachinski, et al., 2006 for test references and suggested standardization sources. Remaining tests from the Montreal Cognitive Assessment could be administered as part of the 5-minute battery. The Mini-Mental State Examination should be administered on a different day, from the 5-minute test, or at least 1-hour later.
[a] Short form.

Source: Adapted from Hachinski et al. (2006).

eye or to a brain region perfused by a specific artery and resolving within 24 hours, has traditionally been diagnosed as a transient ischemic attack (TIA) ("A Classification and Outline of Cerebrovascular Diseases," 1975). The long-standing observation that the majority of neurological symptoms associated with TIAs resolve within 30–60 minutes raised concerns about the legitimacy of the 24-hour criterion among critics of this definition (Albers et al., 2002; Pessin et al., 1977). Modern imaging methods and current drug treatments for acute infarction have rendered the 24-hour duration criterion obsolete (Albers et al., 2002). The current definition of TIA, advanced by the TIA Working Group, defines TIA as a brief episode of neurological dysfunction due to retinal or focal brain ischemia with clinical symptoms usually lasting less than one hour and occurring in the absence of evidence of acute infarction (Albers et al., 2002). If imaging studies show characteristic signs of acute brain infarction, the diagnosis of stroke is made regardless of symptom duration (Albers et al., 2002). This definition focuses clinical attention on the investigation of the causes of ischemia rather than symptom duration. The new definition of TIA is also compatible with neuropsychological evidence of cognitive deficits that persist after their clinical symptoms subside (Brown et al., 1996a). Although the TIA Working Group recommended diffusion-weighted magnetic resonance imaging to investigate structural brain changes, a negative diffusion-weighted image does not necessarily rule out persistent neuronal dysfunction. Lazar and colleagues, for example, have observed the reemergence of resolved hemiparesis and aphasia after administration of a benzodiazepine to TIA patients with negative diffusion-weighted images (Lazar et al., 2003). The extent to which neuropsychological evaluations provide additional information to imaging studies when attempting to rule out subtle but persistent brain dysfunction among TIA patients remains an open research question.

Patients with TIAs are at high risk of stroke in the days and weeks following the episode. A meta-analysis of 11 very well-screened studies of stroke risk following a TIA found that 3.5%, 8.0%, and 9.2% of TIA patients experience stroke, respectively, 3, 30, and 90 days after the episode (Wu et al., 2007). In the three studies where patients had face-to-face evaluations with medical personnel three months following TIA, the risk of early stroke was found to be even higher: 9.9%, 13.4%, and 17.3% at 2, 30, and 90 days, respectively (Wu et al., 2007). Half of patients receiving neuropsychological assessments following TIAs have neuropsychological deficits (e.g., Bakker et al., 2003). These deficits are usually mild and are often not easily recognizable as a specific neuropsychological syndrome (Bakker et al., 2003). Because it is rare for neuropsychological data to

be available prior to a patient's TIA, it is difficult to dissociate the neurobehavioral effects of TIA from the effects of stroke-risk factors or from the impact of previous ischemic events. Nonetheless, TIAs are not benign and require rapid evaluation and management to prevent stroke and subsequent neuropsychological morbidity (Johnston & Hill, 2004).

Outcome of Stroke

House et al. (1990) found in a community-based study that 26% of patients with first-ever stroke displayed impaired mental status on the Mini-Mental State Examination (MMSE) 1 month following stroke. The percentage of patients with impaired mental status dropped to 21 at the 6-month follow-up and remained at this level at the 12-month evaluation as well. Tatemichi and colleagues (1994) investigated memory, orientation, verbal function, visuospatial ability, abstract reasoning, and attention in a sample of 227 patients studied 3 months following stroke. These investigators defined cognitive failure as a score at or less than the fifth percentile of a stroke-free control group after adjusting all test scores for demographic factors. If cognitive impairment was defined as failure on 4 or more of the 17 test items, 35.2% of the stroke patients and 3.8% of controls experienced cognitive impairment. Dependent living status was more than twice as likely if cognitive impairment was present, even after controlling for age and degree of physical impairment (Tatemichi et al., 1994). In a longitudinal study, Ballard and colleagues studied 115 stroke survivors more than 74 years of age who were without dementia 3 months poststroke (Ballard et al., 2003). Patients were evaluated 3 months and again 15 months following stroke with a neuropsychological battery measuring memory, attention, executive performance, and language (Ballard et al., 2003). At the 12-month follow-up, 9% of older stroke patients significantly deteriorated in global cognition, memory, and attention. Level of expressive language performance and vigilance at 3 months predicted general cognitive decline at 12 months. Delayed improvement of cognitive functioning was observed in 50% of poststroke patients with significant gains seen in orientation, language expression, memory, abstract thinking, perception, and executive function (Ballard et al., 2003). The largest improvements were seen on composite measures of mental status, where gains among improvers were equal to two-thirds of the baseline standard deviation. A study of a younger stroke cohort with a mean age of 60 years found that about 30% of patients who had mild cognitive impairment between 0 and 6 months after stroke normalized their cognitive function by 12–18 months (Tham et al., 2002). A third study found delayed improvement in only 10% of stroke patients (mean age, 70 years) between 3 and 15 months after stroke (Desmond et al., 1996). The neurobiological processes underlying delayed cognitive impairment or delayed improvement remain unknown, although correlates of global cognitive impairment following stroke include older age; low education attainment; prestroke cognitive impairment; the severity, location, and recurrence of stroke; neuroradiological features such as extent of white matter lesions (WMLs) and medial temporal lobe atrophy; and medical comorbidities, including diabetes mellitus, myocardial infarction, atrial fibrillation, and pneumonia (Cherubini & Senin, 2003).

Investigators have used measures of general brain function and indices of specific neurobehavioral domains to study the neuropsychological prediction of functional outcome following stroke (Barker-Collo & Feigin, 2006). In samples of patients poststroke, the MMSE total score at admission has been found to predict motor impairment at discharge (Ozdemir et al., 2001) and to correlate highly with anosognosia (Wagner & Cushman, 1994). More specific neuropsychological domains predictive of dependent functional outcome include sustained attention (Robertson et al., 1997), praxis and emotional control (Sundet et al., 1988), and memory (Goldstein et al., 2001; MacNiel & Lichtenberg, 1997). A recent expert panel has made recommendations about which neuropsychological domains should be assessed when assessing functional outcome from stroke (Donovan et al., 2008). Like the NINDS and Canadian Stroke Network consensus panel, the functional outcome panel recommended assessment of the domains of executive, visuospatial, language, memory, and emotional functioning. The functional outcome panel did not separate learning from memory, as did the Stroke panel, nor did the outcome panel specifically list the assessment of premorbid functioning. Instead, the functional outcome panel specifically listed limb parixs and the instrumental language domains, reading, writing, and numeric calculation as neuropsychological domains useful in predicting functional outcome (Donovan et al., 2008).

Vascular Dementia

Despite the considerable degree of accuracy in diagnosing Alzheimer's disease (AD), the clinical differentiation of vascular disease remains one of the most difficult and challenging issues for neuropsychologists and neurologists in clinical settings. In the sections that follow, an overview of the neuroanatomical and neuropsychological aspects of vascular dementia (VaD) will be provided. Additionally, the newer concept of VCI will be presented with an emphasis on vascular risk factors, WML pathology, and the clinical differentiation of vascular-related cognitive syndromes.

Epidemiology

VaD is the second most common form of dementia in the United States, and its prevalence is expected to rise dramatically, especially as the aging population continues to expand at unprecedented rates (*Statistical Abstract of the United States, 2006: The National Data Book*, 2005). VaD is emerging as a major public health concern and increased attention is currently being focused on this particular dementia syndrome for many reasons, including (1) increasing prevalence of VaD, particularly in eastern populations such as Japan, China, and Russia where VaD appears to be more common than AD (Fratiglioni et al., 1999); (2) greater risk for increased short-term morbidity, mortality, and institutionalization associated with VaD versus AD (Bennett, 2001); and (3) indications that VaD might be more amenable than other dementia types to early intervention given that vascular risk factors such as hypertension and diabetes are better established and are more likely to be modifiable (Bowler, 2002; Rockwood et al., 2003).

Clinicopathological Classification

VaD can arise from either ischemic or hemorrhagic damage to the brain and includes several different subtypes (Roman, 2002). Since there are numerous neuropathologic mechanisms that can lead to VaD, clinical and neuropsychological sequelae are known to be heterogeneous in nature. Depending on several factors, including size, location, and type of cerebral damage, common neurologic signs and symptoms include hemiparesis, visual field deficits and visual disturbances, hemisensory loss, brain stem abnormalities, and sensory and/or motor symptoms. Given the different subgroupings of VaD, it has been somewhat challenging to identify homogeneous populations for neuropsychological studies. Most research to date has focused on multi-infarct dementia and, although there is some overlap between the major subgroups, efforts to distinguish them according to dementia onset have clinical merit. For example, early identification of insidious-onset VaD (subcortical VaD) introduces an opportunity for clinical interventions such as control of vascular risk factors that may minimize, arrest, or even reverse cognitive deterioration (Bowler & Hachinski, 2003).

Diagnostic Considerations

In contrast to AD—which is characterized by a slow, degenerative progression of cognitive and functional capacity—VaD has been traditionally thought of as having an abrupt onset of dementia symptoms, followed by stepwise deterioration of cognitive performance reflecting neurological signs and symptoms consistent with focal brain lesions (Roman, 1999). VaD is thought to primarily affect subcortical and frontal-lobe functions (Bowler, 2002; Rockwood et al., 2003), and patients with this dementia type have been described in the literature to exhibit early executive impairment, slowed psychomotor functioning, and frequent depressive features (Libon et al., 2001; Naarding et al., 2003). Frontal-subcortical circuits have been an area of recent research interest (Bigler et al., 2003; Libon et al., 2001) and the specific circuits disrupted in VaD appear to include the dorsolateral prefrontal neuronal circuit mediating executive functioning, the orbitofrontal circuit mediating emotional lability, and the anterior cingulate circuit responsible for motivation and initiation (Cummings, 1994). Moreover, imaging studies lend support to the

conceptualization of VaD as characterized by a greater degree of frontal-subcortical dysfunction than in AD of comparable severity (Lafosse et al., 1997; Libon et al., 1997).

Current DSM-IV criteria indicate that a diagnosis of VaD is warranted in the context of cognitive and functional loss in combination with evidence of stroke. However, studies have shown that, in contrast with AD, VaD appears to be more heterogeneous in origin, pathogenesis, and clinical course (Erkinjuntti, 2000; Rockwood et al., 1999). In addition, approximately 40% of patients with VaD do not evidence stroke, and only 40% of patients with VaD have such focal signs (Bowler, 2002). Meyer et al. (2002) argue that VaD can be separated into two groups: one group characterized predominantly by multi-infarct, strategic-infarct, or intracranial hemorrhage, with abrupt onset (in line with the traditional view of VaD); and the other form of VaD caused by subcortical small-vessel disease, with an insidious onset mirroring the clinical course of AD. Indeed, recent research has demonstrated that subcortical small-vessel disease appears to be an important etiology for VaD (Chui, 2001; Erkinjuntti et al., 2000), with prevalence rates ranging from 36% to 67% (Cummings, 1994; Erkinjuntti, 1987). Slow progression of neuropsychological deficits in subcortical small-vessel disease is thought to be linked to gradually progressive microvascular brain changes. Specifically, it has been posited that hypertensive arteriolar lipohyalinosis (cerebral microangiopathy) involving small penetrating vessels underlies neuropathological changes that promote the clinical syndrome VaD (Chui, 2001). These neuropathological changes are thought to be associated with various vascular risk factors (i.e., hypertension, hyperlipidemia, and diabetes), which are present well before VaD becomes diagnosable and may cause progressive cognitive impairment over time (Bowler & Hachinski, 2003; Meyer et al., 2002).

Problems with the DSM-IV Vascular Dementia Diagnosis

More recently, the traditional DSM-IV diagnosis of VaD has been challenged as problematic, and the foundations for the diagnosis are under scrutiny (Hachinski, 1994; Nolan et al.,

1998; Rockwood et al., 2000). Indeed, it has been noted that the diagnosis of VaD is clouded by many false perceptions; specifically, these assumptions are (1) that the course of VaD is chronic and progressive, (2) that a large stroke or many strokes must precede VaD, and (3) that VaDs are quite rare (Brust, 1988). Contrary to current DSM-IV criteria, focal neurological signs, sudden onset, stepwise progression, and relationship to known stroke(s) are argued to be unnecessary (Bowler & Hachinski, 2003; Erkinjuntti & Rockwood, 2001; Sachdev & Looi, 2003).

Recently, the DSM-IV criteria for VaD have been criticized as "Alzheimerized" (Sachdev & Looi, 2003) and thus inappropriate since the criteria were based primarily on AD (Hachinksi, 1994; McKhann et al., 1984). First, there is a requirement of memory impairment, which is restrictive when applied to VaD, since recent research has shown that memory impairment may not be an early or most salient feature of this dementia type (Bowler & Hachinski, 2003; Cosentino et al., 2004; Garrett et al., 2004). Second, while individuals with AD typically evidence significant deficits on language and semantic knowledge tasks, patients with VaD rarely demonstrate any such deficits (Cosentino et al., 2004; Garrett et al., 2004). Instead, some studies have shown that, in contrast to AD, VaD is often characterized by dramatic impairment on tests of executive functioning, or higher-order thinking, encompassing domains such as cognitive flexibility, planning, and inhibition (Cosentino et al., 2004; Garrett et al., 2004). Unfortunately, the application of the "Alzheimerized" definition to VaD diagnosis may lead to diagnoses of VaD at a relatively advanced state, or its not being diagnosed at all (Bowler & Hachinski, 2003; Rockwood et al., 2000; Erkinjuntti et al., 2000).

The diagnosis of VaD is also problematic because there is currently no agreed-upon set of criteria (Chui et al., 2000; Gold et al., 2002). Several diagnostic criteria are in widespread use, including cutting scores based on the Hachinski Ischemic Score (HIS) and qualitative criteria based on the Diagnostic and Statistical Manual of Mental Disorders (DSM-IIIR, DSM-IV), International Classification of Diseases (ICD-10), State of California Alzheimer's Disease Diagnostic and Treatment Centers (ADDTC), and the National Institute for Neurological Disorders and Stroke–Association Internationale pour la Recherche et l'Enseignement en Neurosciences (NINDS-AIREN). Unfortunately, the criteria are not interchangeable and can lead to a fivefold difference in the frequency of classifying VaD (Chui et al., 2000; Gold et al., 2002; Wetterling et al., 1996). A recent retrospective analysis using four classification systems for the clinical diagnosis of VaD indicated that classification varied widely as a function of the criteria used: patients diagnosed with VaD using one set of criteria were not similarly diagnosed using other criteria (Cosentino et al., 2004). In contrast to the ICD-10, which allows for a differentiation of vascular dementia into subtypes (i.e., VaD of acute onset, multi-infarct dementia, subcortical VaD, and mixed or unspecified types), most commonly employed diagnostic schemes do not allow for subtyping and require evidence of significant ischemic brain injury on structural neuroimaging (i.e., multiple infarcts). It is thus argued that the problems inherent in the diagnosis of VaD may be associated with inadequate detection and diagnosis (Bowler & Hachinski, 2003). Indeed, the current criteria may fail to identify patients with significant cognitive loss caused by CVD, and the emphasis on dementia may underestimate the burden of disease associated with early VaD (Hachinski, 1992, 1994).

Failing to identify early VaD may detract from the focus on prevention, which may have negative consequences with respect to treatment since, in contrast to AD, vascular risk factors are treatable, and strokes can be prevented (Bowler & Hachinski, 2003; Erkinjuntti et al., 2000). Such patients will likely not have the opportunity for secondary preventive measures to delay or stop their progression to dementia (Bowler, 1993; Bowler & Hachinski, 2003; Erkinjuntti & Hachinski, 1993; Hachinski, 1991, 1992, 1994). Calling for an overhaul of current VaD criteria, Bowler (2002) fervently argued that VaD reflects an "outmoded concept" and urged for increased attention to be focused on subtler forms of vascular-related impairment.

Neuropsychological Functioning along the Continuum of Cerebrovascular Disease

Vascular Cognitive Impairment

Although VaD has been the subject of increased clinical research (Rockwood et al., 2003), far less is known about the factors that contribute to the development of dementia among people with chronic CVD compared to AD. Research has shown that the total burden of cognitive impairment of cerebrovascular origin may be very high. Specifically, 78% of elderly patients at autopsy have evidence of CVD as do over 80% of those who are demented (Bowler & Hachinski, 2002) and about 9 in 1000 people aged 85 years or more may develop VaD each year (Bowler & Hachinski, 2003). Just as subtle cognitive impairment may be present several years before the clinical diagnosis of AD (Masur et al., 1994; Meguro et al., 2001), such understated vascular-related cognitive deficits may be evident in early VaD. The crucial question is whether this common and important problem can be detected and halted before significant cognitive loss has occurred.

It has been argued that vascular-related cognitive impairment (VCI) be used to describe the early stage of VaD (Bowler, 2002; Erkinjuntti & Rockwood, 2001; Hachinski, 1994). However, currently, no universally accepted criteria have been formalized (mostly due to a relative lack of data with respect to early cognitive loss), and it has been suggested that, until formal criteria are proposed, the criteria for VCI should be wide ranging and broad (Bowler & Hachinski, 2003). Specifically, Bowler and Hachinski (2002, 2003) indicate that individuals should be considered for VCI when there is any evidence of CVD (with or without known risk factors or neuroimaging findings) in the presence of associated cognitive impairment that does not reach the level of dementia (Bowler & Hachinski, 2003).

Using these broad criteria, preliminary data appear to support the validity of this concept of VCI (Ballard et al., 2003; Meyer et al., 2002; Wentzel et al., 2001). For example, Wentzel et al. (2001) recently reported that 50% of the subjects in their sample who met criteria for VCI

developed dementia over 5 years. Additionally, Meyer et al. (2002) attempted to answer the question of whether a mild cognitive impairment (MCI) stage precedes some cases of VaD by longitudinally following 291 volunteer subjects over one to seven years. Subjects were initially screened with the MMSE and tested annually with neuroimaging (MRI or CT). Follow-up of the 73 subjects who were diagnosed with MCI occurred every 3–6 months, and results indicated that, of the 27 subjects who developed VaD within 7 years, roughly 56% had prodromal MCI. Similarly, Ballard et al. (2003) showed that approximately 9% of their MCI sample developed VaD over 1 year and almost half of the patients developed dementia over 5 years of follow-up. Taken together, these findings suggest that individuals with cognitive difficulties secondary to CVD are at increased risk for further cognitive decline and conversion to dementia. Indeed, it appears that MCI may represent a clinically heterogeneous group of individuals who are at elevated risk for dementia that is not solely restricted to AD. Thus, the concept of VCI appears to be clinically useful and relevant.

Hachinski (1994) and others (Bowler, 2000; Bowler et al., 1999; Devasenapathy & Hachinski, 2000; Garrett, et al., 2004) proposed that VCI exists on a continuum that comprises three primary stages: brain-at-risk (R-CVD); vascular cognitive impairment—no dementia (VaCIND); and VaD. The first stage—R-CVD—consists of individuals with cardiovascular or other system disease processes who are at risk for developing CVD (with no clinically significant cognitive or functional impairments). VaCIND is the first hypothesized *clinical* stage preceding VaD (Hachinski, 1994) and is analogous to MC) (Bowler & Hachinski, 2003). Like MCI, individuals with VaCIND do not have significant impairment in their ability to complete basic activities of daily living.

Chui et al. (2003) have conceptualized VCI with finer gradations within the course of VaD. Their stages include brain at risk (presence of vascular risk factors); early ischemic brain injury, but clinically asymptomatic; early symptomatic, but prior to diagnosis (cognitive decline by neuropsychological testing); clinical diagnosis of

VCI without dementia (VaCIND); clinical diagnosis of VaD; advanced dementia (severe VaD); and death. According to Chui et al. (2003) and others (Bowler & Hachinski, 2003; Inzitari et al., 2003; Rockwood et al., 2003), detection and attempts at intervention do not typically occur until individuals reach stage five or six of Chui et al.'s (2003) VaD continuum, mostly due to the restrictive nature of the current diagnostic criteria for VaD, as discussed above. Unfortunately, adequate intervention at these stages is futile given that excessive cerebrovascular damage has typically occurred at these later stages. While research on vascular-related cognitive impairment (VCI) is in its infancy and only a few studies have been conducted to date, VaCIND is thought to be the best established concept for identifying at-risk patients with CVD (Stephens et al., 2004). Empirical support for the clinical concept has begun to develop—particularly in Asia and Europe—with a strong interest and emphasis on the early phases of the disease process.

Neuropsychological Impairment in Vascular Cognitive Impairment

A greater understanding of neuropsychological impairment during the early stages of VaD might improve the early detection of neuropsychological deficits and justify interventions to prevent or slow progression to dementia (Bowler, 2000; Devasenapathy & Hachinski, 2000; Garret et al., 2004). However, to date, the neuropsychological profile of VaCIND has not received significant study. It has been shown that neurocognitive difficulties associated with cardiac disease and mild CVD include reduced information-processing speed and reduced cognitive flexibility (Kilander et al., 1998; Waldstein et al., 2001). Additionally, recent neuroimaging studies conclude that the magnitude of cognitive impairment among patients with mild cardiovascular disease is significantly associated with neuropathological changes secondary to vascular damage (Raz et al., 2003). As will be discussed in further detail, research has suggested that cardiac risk factors can be associated with cognitive and neuropathological changes in the absence of frank stroke or dementia (DeCarli et al., 2001; Swan et al., 1998).

The finding that cognitive functions mediated by frontostriatal circuits (i.e., executive functioning) are most disturbed during the late phases of VaD raises the possibility that mild changes in these cognitive functions may occur during the early stages of this dementia process. However, it remains unclear whether clinically meaningful changes are evident among patients in early stages of VaD. Furthermore, it is of clinical interest to determine if the difficulties on measures of frontal-lobe functioning exist in the context of preserved function in other cognitive domains such as memory. As noted by Garrett et al. (2004), a pattern of strengths and weaknesses on cognitive measures may prove to be a critical determinant of diagnostic differentiation between the various stages of vascular-related cognitive impairment, as well as distinguishing vascular etiologies from other dementing conditions. Thus, the identification of a pattern of neuropsychological changes associated with the early stage of VaD (i.e., Va CIND) would greatly benefit diagnosis and facilitate intervention (Garrett et al., 2004).

Outcome of Vascular Cognitive Impairment

VCI is associated with an increased risk for adverse outcomes. Rockwood et al. (2000) found that a failure to consider VCI underestimates the prevalence of impairment and the associated risk for adverse outcomes. Specifically, this study compared the rates of adverse outcomes for older patients with (1) no cognitive impairment, (2) VCI, and (3) probable AD. After reassessment 5 years later, VCI was the most prevalent form of cognitive impairment among older adults aged 65–84 years. Most strikingly, rates of institutionalization for those with VCI were similar to that of those with VaD, and the mortality rate for VCI patients was similar to that of patients with AD. Data such as these support the view that increased attention on subtle vascular-related cognitive impairment is important and clinically relevant. Moreover, the criteria that require the diagnosis of dementia likely underestimate the prevalence and burden of vascular cognitive disease (Hachinski, 1994; Rockwood et al., 1994).

White Matter Lesion Pathology

In 1986, Hachinski coined the term "leukoaraiosis" to describe abnormal cerebral white matter changes as seen on CT scans (Hachinski et al., 1986). At about the same time, Awad, Spetzler, Hodak, Awad, and Carey (1986) characterized these white matter changes as seen on MRI as "incidental subcortical lesions." Initially termed "UBOs," or Unidentified Bright Objects, these changes have more recently been termed WMLs or hyperintensities. They are typically found in deep cerebral areas and as cappings on the lateral ventricles (Drayer, 1988) and are identified as signal hyperintensities on T_2- and proton density-weighted magnetic resonance (MR) scans.

The precise etiology of WML is debated since numerous potential causes have been identified (Brown, 2000; Chui, 2001). For example, it is thought that WML can be caused by either arteriosclerosis causing direct occlusion of small arteries or by partial occlusion of small arteries in combination with cardiovascular failure (orthostatic hypotension, carotid sinus sensitivity, and congestive heart failure) (Chui, 2001). In addition, WML appear to be attributed to normal aging processes, including increased fluid in the white matter around the anterior horns of the lateral ventricles and enlarged perivascular spaces (Munoz et al., 1993). Moreover, WML have been posited to be caused by subclinical ischemia secondary to cerebral hypoperfusion (Brun, 2003). Indeed, the cerebral white matter is the least irrigated compartment of the brain, and thus it may be more vulnerable to the effects of ischemia and hypoperfusion (Brown, 2000). Interestingly, the prefrontal brain regions appear to be most vulnerable given lower vasodilatory capacity versus white matter found in other brain regions (Brown, 2000).

WML have been related to physical illnesses such as diabetes mellitus (Longstreth et al., 2000), hypertension (de Leeuw et al., 2002), stroke or myocardial infarction, atrial fibrillation and carotid artery atherosclerosis (de Leeuw et al., 2000). WML reach their highest prevalence in patients who have VaD (Smith et al., 2000) and depression (Kumar et al., 2000). There is little controversy that WML increases with the aging process (Gunning-Dixon & Raz, 2000; Pantoni & Garcia, 1995; Schmidt et al., 1999), and a threshold effect for cognitive decline has been hypothesized to be present (Libon et al., 2008). However, the debate over identified WML centers on their clinical significance, and it is still unclear whether they represent a pathognomonic sign for brain disease (DeCarli & Scheltens, 2002).

Vascular Cognitive Impairment and White Matter Lesions

The contribution of WML to cognitive impairment is receiving increased attention. Recent research has shown that 33%–97% of cases of VaD demonstrate extensive WML (Campbell & Coffey, 2001; Pohjasvaara et al., 2000; Wetterling et al., 1996) and less extensive WMLs are thought to be evident in VCI (Erkinjuntti & Rockwood, 2001; Pohjasvaara et al., 2000). Bowler and Hachinski (2003) have reported that there is a need for research to focus on WML in terms of their association with subtle forms of cognitive impairment, as well as how best to define the borders between normal aging, VCI, and VaD (Bowler & Hachinski, 2003).

The presence of vascular risk factors or cerebrovascular events in general may be sufficient for a diagnosis of VCI (Erkinjuntti & Rockwood, 2001). Although current criteria require evidence of stroke for a diagnosis of VaD, some studies show that silent infarcts and WMLs are relevant and may represent early cases of VaD, or VCI (Erkinjuntti & Rockwood, 2001). Indeed, it has been shown that evidence of ischemic disease on neuroimaging (in the absence of stroke and atrophy) appear to be associated with cognitive impairment (Bowler, 2002). In fact, some researchers (Emery et al., 1994; Phillips & Mate-Kole, 1997) have argued that WML represent the beginning stage of a series of pathological processes that precede tissue infarction and suggest the term "pre-infarct state" to describe cognitive changes in patients who evidence WML, regardless of whether they evidence cerebral infarcts. Current research is beginning to focus on more subtle lesions, and how they may be associated with neuropsychological impairment (Garrett et al., 2004; Raz et al., 2003; Stephens et al., 2004). According to Sachdev and Looi (2003), more clearly defined differentiation of VaD from AD is likely to be greatly influenced by the extent of WML in the two groups.

In a longitudinal study of 27 individuals with MCI by Wolf et al. (2000), it was demonstrated that subjects who developed dementia after 2–3 years had more severe WMLs. In addition, there was an inverse relationship between WML and the degree of temporal lobe atrophy in those who progressed to dementia during the follow-up interval; thus, high WML severity was associated with lesser degree of temporal lobe atrophy and higher global cognitive performance, as measured by SIDAM (Structured Interview for the Diagnosis of Dementia of Alzheimer Type). This illustrates how subcortical vascular impairment and cortical degenerative dementia seem to differ in their course and clinical picture. Specifically, it appears likely that those with greater levels of WMLs and less medial temporal lobe atrophy may progress to VaD, whereas those with little to no WML and evidence of significant medial temporal lobe atrophy may more likely progress to AD. Thus, WML appear to play a role in the dementia process and may accelerate decline in individuals with mild cognitive impairment.

Neuropsychological Deficits Associated with White Matter Lesions

Early neuropathological research involving WMLs was quite mixed. While some studies pointed to a relationship between such lesions and neuropsychological functioning (Almkvist et al., 1992; Breteler et al., 1994a, 1994b), many found no relationship after controlling for age (Hunt et al., 1989; Tupler et al., 1992). It has been suggested that earlier research was hampered by many factors, including small sample sizes (Mirsen et al., 1991), the use of inadequate and insensitive tests that are rarely used with older populations (Mirsen et al., 1991), differences in subject settings (Hershey et al., 1987; Rao et al., 1989), and the use of CT scans, which are not very sensitive to WML (Diaz et al., 1991; Hershey et al., 1987; Miyao et al., 1992). However, not all of the negative studies can be dismissed as resulting from these limitations (See Hunt et al.'s elegant 1989 neuropsychological and magnetic resonance imaging study).

Contrary to previous studies, more recent reports have demonstrated that WMLs appear to disrupt cognitive functioning and thus may have clinical significance (Breteler et al., 1994a, 1994b; Garrett et al., 2004). Indeed, although the effects are often subtle and mild, there has been a link between early VCI and WMLs and

cognitive loss (Garrett et al., 2004). Consistent with deficits often found in VaD, older individuals with numerous WMLs appear to perform worse on tests of speed and visuospatial function, even after controlling for age (Cosentino et al., 2004; Garrett et al., 2004). Additionally, while few studies have examined the distribution of WML and their effect on cognitive function, there is some evidence that the extent and pattern of WML is important in influencing cognitive performance (Raz et al., 2003). Specifically, associated deficits appear to be of a frontal-subcortical nature, affecting neuropsychological functions such as speed of processing and executive functioning; this relationship appears to be stronger with respect to deep white matter lesions (DWML) versus periventricular (PVL) WML (Garrett et al., 2004; Raz et al., 2003), although data are preliminary.

Recent studies have noted that the neuropsychological impairment sometimes seen in association with WML is similar to other types of subcortical dementing illnesses (Giovannetti-Carew et al., 1997; Libon et al., 2001). Libon et al. (1997) found a dissociation between tests of verbal declarative memory and executive systems functioning; patients with VaD obtained lower scores and made more perseverative errors on executive systems tests, but exhibited less forgetting, obtained higher tests scores on delayed free/cued recall and recognition test conditions, and made fewer intrusion errors than AD patients. This study also found that the pattern of neuropsychological impairment seen in dementia associated with subcortical WML was more similar to other subcortical dementing illnesses, such as Parkinson's disease (PD) and Huntington's disease, than cortical dementing illnesses such as AD. Similar findings have been reported by Doody et al. (1998).

In a more recent study by Libon and colleagues (2001), subjects were assessed with regards to WML quantity independent of clinical diagnosis. Individuals with a diagnosis of either vascular or Alzheimer's dementia were placed in groups representing either minimal-mild WML or significant WML. After being compared to patients with PD, it was found that neuropsychological testing failed to distinguish between those with PD and those with significant WML;

additionally, those with significant WML demonstrated disproportionate impairment on tests of visuoconstruction and executive systems functioning, whereas patients with little WML showed greater impairment on tests of declarative memory and semantic knowledge. These findings point to a pattern of cognitive impairment associated with significant WML as distinctly different when compared to AD.

A cautionary observation about these more recent studies is that they typically have been performed by researchers working in stroke clinics or in stroke centers. Consequently, the base rates for CVD in these settings will be greater than in the general population.

Cerebrovascular Anomalies

The neuropsychological literature discussed above primarily involved patients with brain ischemia. This section focuses on the neuropsychological correlates of brain hemorrhage associated with vascular anomalies, especially cerebral aneurysms and brain arteriovenous malformations (AVMs).

Brain Arteriovenous Malformations

AVMs of the brain are lesions composed of coiled batches of blood vessels located in any part of the brain (cortical, subcortical, dural, or brain stem) (see Figure 14–2). They are made up of a complex tangle of abnormal veins and arteries (The Arteriovenous Malformation Study Group, 1999; Stapf et al., 2001) with a missing capillary bed, and instead are connected by fistulas and characterized by shunting of blood from artery to vein (Bambakidis et al., 2001; Klimo et al., 2007; O'Brien et al., 2006). This shunting mechanism causes hypertension within the AVM and in the draining vein (The Arteriovenous Malformation Study Group, 1999; Iwama et al., 2002; Loring, 1999) and hypotension in the surrounding and feeding vessels (The Arteriovenous Malformation Study Group, 1999), with little apparent clinical effect (Diehl et al., 1994; Fogarty-Mack et al., 1996; Mast et al., 1995; Murphy, 1954).

AVMs are often asymptomatic and go undetected unless there is a clinical event (such as hemorrhage or seizure). Unlike other brain lesions, the AVM itself often does not cause cognitive dysfunction. This phenomenon has been explained by Lazar and his colleagues (Lazar et al., 1997, 2000), who proposed that brain reorganization was due to the chronic nature of the AVM. Rather, it is usually a hemorrhage that is responsible for functional/cognitive changes seen in patients with AVM.

Neuropathology and Pathophysiology

The central point of abnormal development in the AVM is the nidus (Loring, 1999), which is the densest region of the arteries and veins. The feeding arteries can include branches off the main cerebral arteries (e.g., MCA, PCA, ACA), carotid or vertebral arteries, or the choroidal arteries

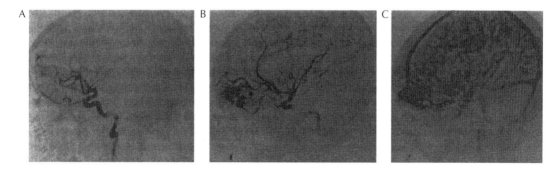

Figure 14–2. Cerebral angiogram of an arteriovenous malformation. (a) Early arterial phase (b) Arterial phase (c) Venous phase (Reprinted with permission from Brown, G. G., Spicer, K. B., and Malik, G., 1991.)

from the subcortical regions (The Arteriovenous Malformation Study Group, 1999). Both parenchymal and dural AVMs have the potential to cause a more focal deficit (similar to that seen in stroke) while dural AVMs have also been shown to cause a more global dementia-like syndrome (Festa et al., 2004; Hurst et al., 1998; Ito et al., 1995; Matsuda et al., 1999; Tanaka et al., 1999). Subcortical (deep) AVMs have been associated with deficits such as neglect and memory disturbance (Buklina, 2001, 2002).

Demographics and Epidemiology

AVMs are an uncommon vascular phenomenon occurring in approximately 4.3% of the population based on 4530 consecutive autopsies (McCormick & Rosenfield, 1973). Pathology data have shown that approximately 12% of AVMs are symptomatic (Hashimoto et al., 2004; McCormick, 1978), and researchers report that approximately 0.1%–1% of the population will have a symptomatic AVM annually (The Arteriovenous Malformation Study Group, 1999; Brown et al., 1996b; Hofmeister et al., 2000; Mohr et al., 2004; Redekop et al., 1998; Singer et al., 2006). Females account for 45%–51% of AVM cases (Hofmeister et al., 2000). The mean age of diagnosis is 31.2 years, with significant variability in reporting across clinical sites. It was reported that 69% to 74% of patients had AVM location in eloquent (functional) brain regions and the majority (52%–59%) showed deep venous drainage (Hofmeister et al., 2000). As for AVM size, 38% were small (<3 cm), 55% were medium (3–6 cm), and 7% were large AVMs (>6 cm) (Hofmeister et al., 2000).

While AVMs are considered to be congenital or developmental, there are currently no in utero reports of AVM, suggesting that it may not be due to embryonic vessel development as once theorized (Stapf et al., 2001). Rather, they are likely formed during the late fetal or immediate postpartum periods (Stapf et al., 2001), although the mechanism is still unknown. Most researchers classify AVM clinical presentation into two major categories, hemorrhagic and nonhemorrhagic, which can present with identical symptoms (e.g., headache, seizure, or neurological deficit) with one significant differentiation: a bleed (Stapf et al., 2006).

Hemorrhage related to AVMs account for approximately 1%–2% of all strokes (Furlan et al., 1979; Gross et al., 1984; Hashimoto et al., 2004; Perret & Nishioka, 1966), and intracranial hemorrhage (ICH) is the most frequent symptom of AVM, (Brown et al., 1990; Graf et al., 1983; Ondra et al., 1990).

Nonhemorrhagic seizures co-occur in 16%–53% of the AVM population (The Arteriovenous Malformation Study Group, 1999; Hofmeister et al., 2000) and are the second most common presentation. The Columbia AVM Database demonstrated 49% of AVM-related seizure activity to be generalized tonic-clonic, 22% are focal, 22% are focal with secondary generalization, 4% are complex partial, and 4% are not classified (Choi & Mohr, 2005; Hofmeister et al., 2000). Most epileptogenic AVMs are superficial and supratentorial, and are fed by the middle cerebral artery (Turjman et al., 1995).

Neurological/Neuropsychological Deficits

Neurological deficit is reported in the AVM population with varying frequencies (1.3%–48%), with reversible deficits significantly more common (8%) than persistent deficits (7%) (Hofmeister et al., 2000; Mast et al., 1995; Wenz et al., 1998). Some researchers have demonstrated significant deficits in neuropsychological functioning of patients, some studies of which unfortunately combine ruptured and unruptured AVMs (Baker et al., 2004; Mahalick et al., 1993; Marshall et al., 2003; Steinvorth et al., 2002; Wenz et al., 1998). Wenz et al. found that AVM patients (both with and without hemorrhage) demonstrated below-normal performance on tests of general IQ (24% of patients), attention (34% of patients), and memory (48% of patients). Mahalick et al. also demonstrated significantly lower performance on tests of neuropsychological functioning for AVM patients as compared to normals, but again did not covary for prior hemorrhage. In another study combining ruptured and unruptured AVM, it was found that AVM patients were again significantly below normal on tests of intelligence, memory, and attention (Steinvorth et al., 2002).

Researchers have demonstrated improvement in neuropsychological functioning postsurgery (Malik et al., 1996; Wenz et al., 1998). Cognitive improvements after AVM treatment have been attributed to improved CBF and reduction of the "steal effect" (Malik et al., 1996; Steinvorth et al., 2002; Wenz et al., 1998). The steal effect refers to the assumption that shunting and hypertension through the AVM decreases cerebral perfusion, thus causing cerebral ischemia and ultimately neurological deficits (Mast et al., 1995). Iwama et al. (2002) demonstrated that intracranial steal and venous hypertension, and not decreased neurological activity or mass effect, are responsible for the hemodynamic changes seen in high-flow AVMs.

Other researchers disagree with the "steal" hypothesis (Mast et al., 1995; Stabell & Nornes, 1994). Stabell and Nornes (1994) reported that AVM patients performed the same as normal controls on cognitive assessment. While some significant improvement was observed, Stabell and Nornes dispute the "steal" hypothesis as an explanation for cognitive improvement after AVM surgery. Mast et al. (1995) were unable to replicate the "steal effect" using their prospective database. They demonstrated, for example, that AVM patients with chronic cerebral hypotension in Wernicke's area did not have any functional cognitive impairment. In addition, they used positron emission tomography (PET) to study 14 AVM patients and demonstrated that while these patients did have hypoperfusion in surrounding tissue, they did not have any parenchymal volume loss and metabolism was normal (Mast et al., 1995). Developmental learning disorders have been found in 66% of adults with AVMs (Lazar et al., 1999). In this study, AVM patients reported four times the rate of learning disability than the normal population (17%). Lazar et al. reported that perhaps these disorders of higher intellectual functioning (e.g., learning) may serve as a marker for subtle developmental cerebral dysfunction in AVM patients.

Related Vascular Anomalies

Dural arteriovenous fistulas consist of shunts that are located within the dural layer, making up approximately 10%–15% of cerebrovascular malformations and account for 1% of all strokes (Festa et al., 2004; Hurst et al., 1998; Kurl et al., 1996; Newton & Cronqvist, 1969). Dural AV fistulas (while located in the dura and not directly associated with eloquent cortex) have been found to cause focal deficits, such as Wernicke's aphasia and transient right hemiparesis, identical to symptoms caused by a focal stroke (Festa et al., 2004). Unlike AVMs located within the parenchyma, which are not likely to cause global neuropsychological dysfunction, dural AV fistulas have also been demonstrated to cause a dementia syndrome, which presents like encephalopathy (Hurst et al., 1998; Matsuda et al., 1999; Tanaka et al., 1999). These authors reported patients with angiographically confirmed dural AV fistulas who presented with global cognitive dysfunction, including progressive memory decline, slowed mentation, low initiation, and almost all patients reported focal headaches. This dementia-like syndrome may be reversible, as indicated by multiple case reports on patients with dural AVM dementia that reversed after treatment of the fistula (Hurst et al., 1998; Tanaka et al., 1999; Zeidman et al., 1995).

Functional Imaging

Functional MRI measures regional CBF and has been used with AVM patients to study brain reorganization and help with presurgical planning (Cannestra et al., 2004). Cannestra et al. found that functional magnetic resonance imaging (fMRI) testing was sensitive when identifying eloquent language regions in patients with left perisylvian AVMs. They were able to categorize the patients into three surgical risk groups from fMRI alone and demonstrated positive surgical outcomes from their classification system. They reported that 75% of patients avoided awake, invasive brain mapping by using fMRI. In 25% of patients, however, they were not able to successfully determine operative risk, and electrocortical stimulation mapping (ESM) was required. In addition, for some patients, ESM confirmed nidus eloquence, which was not initially detected on fMRI.

The utility of fMRI in studying AVM has received mixed reviews. Hemodynamic abnormalities in AVMs make measuring regional CBF on fMRI problematic (Alkadhi et al., 2000;

Cannestra et al., 2004; Lehericy et al., 2002). Therefore, fMRI should be followed up with superselective Wada testing or electrocortical mapping stimulation for AVMs with significant blood flow disruptions or when eloquent cortex is thought to be bordering the AVM (Cannestra et al., 2004; Lehericy et al., 2002).

Treatment and Prognosis

Mahalick et al. (1993) reported that surgical excision of the AVM resulted in significant improvements in tasks involving short- and long-term verbal memory, long-term visual-spatial memory, verbal learning, verbal and nonverbal intelligence. Overall, they found 60% of AVM patients performed in the normal range on neuropsychological examination postsurgery (Mahalick et al., 1993).

Superselective Wada Testing and Electrocortical Stimulation Mapping

Superselective Wada testing and electrocortical stimulation mapping are in vivo procedures used to help interventional neuroradiologists and neurosurgeons to identify eloquent cortex that may be surrounding the AVM, and helps to predict neurological and cognitive changes that would occur as an adverse effect of treatment. Currently, the Spetzler-Martin grading system aids surgeons by establishing a risk model by assessing the size and location of the AVM. The treating physician traditionally assumed eloquence from the location of the AVM (i.e., if the AVM is located in Broca's area, the surgeon will assume this area is crucial for expressive language). However, because brain reorganization has now been associated with AVM (Lazar et al., 1997, 2000), the grading system without empirical data from in vivo testing of eloquence is felt no longer capable of establishing true treatment risk (Lazar, 2001).

Based on techniques used in epilepsy, superselective Wada testing is a clinical procedure that is used to help the interventional neuroradiologist determine prior to embolization whether a feeding artery to an AVM also supplies blood necessary for eloquent function in nearby brain areas. With the microcatheter in place for delivery of embolic material, the neuroradiologist injects a short-acting anesthetic (usually amobarbital or a combination of amobarbital and lidocaine) that lasts for approximately three to four minutes. During the testing period, a neuropsychologist (who has previously collected baseline neurocognitive data for this particular patient) performs tests of cognitive functioning typically associated with the brain region supplied by the feeding vessel. The neuroradiologist will use the results of Wada testing to help determine the course of treatment. If a deficit is apparent during Wada testing, the radiologist may choose to embolize closer to the AVM nidus to diminish neurocognitive damage, or perhaps decide not to embolize at all. A negative Wada test result allows the neuroradiologist to embolize the feeding vessel with diminished risk for significant neurological damage. Evaluation for cognitive function during superselective Wada is typically adapted from well-known neuropsychological tests (i.e., Boston Diagnostic Aphasia Tests, Wechsler Memory Scale) with well-established norms (Fitzsimmons et al., 2003; Goodglass & Kaplan, 1983; Wechsler, 1987).

Another in vivo procedure that can be used to determine eloquence of surrounding cortex is electrocortical stimulation mapping (EMS). Electrocortical stimulation mapping is performed intraoperatively during an awake craniotomy. While the patient performs different tasks, the brain is stimulated and essential versus nonessential cortical sites can be mapped out (Cannestra et al., 2004).

Cannestra et al. (2004) compared fMRI, superselective Wada testing, and EMS for efficacy as presurgical tools to identify eloquent cortex surrounding the AVM. They reported that superselective Wada testing was not sensitive in identifying eloquent cortex and that fMRI in combination with EMS was required to adequately predict surgical risk.

Cerebral Aneurysm

Pathophysiology and Epidemiology

Intracranial aneurysms are bulges in the arterial wall, with most in the brain being thin-walled sacs arising out of the Circle of Willis or its major branches (Vates et al., 2004). Those that arise from defects in the media of the blood vessel wall are divided into those which are saccular (berry shaped and the most common) or fusiform in shape; other classifications include those that come about from any infectious (mycotic), traumatic, or neoplastic etiology (Mohr & Gautier, 1995). Because of their weakened state, the walls of these vascular anomalies are vulnerable to rupture, producing spontaneous subarachnoid hemorrhage (SAH), which is the predominant reason that aneurysms come to clinical attention.

Cerebral aneurysms are the fourth leading cause of a cerebrovascular event, accounting for approximately 5%–10% of all strokes (Adams & Davis, 2004), with most unruptured aneurysms detected incidentally and a small proportion found after seizures or III-nerve palsy. It has been estimated, largely on the basis of autopsy findings, that the prevalence of intracranial aneurysm is about 2% of the general population (Hassler, 1961). In the United States, the most common age period for aneurysmal rupture is between 40 and 60 years old (Kassell & Torner, 1982), with occurrence in children and adolescents considered rare. Although SAH can present with different symptoms, it is the presence of the "worst

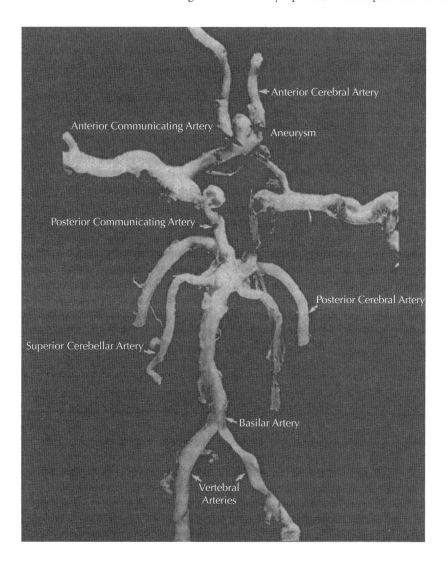

Figure 14–3. Arteries at the base of the brain. The anterior communicating artery and an ACoA aneurysm are indicated by black arrows. The arteries composing the circle of Willis are also seen (see text). (Adapted courtesy of Hirano, 1988, p. 29, Fig. 67.)

headache of my life" that frequently occurs, along with nausea and vomiting. Among the most common clinical tools for rating syndrome severity are the Hunt and Hess Scale (Hunt & Hess, 1968) and Fisher Grade (Fisher et al., 1980). SAH is associated with a significant mortality rate so that 12% have sudden death, 40% die in the first week after hospitalization (Huang & van Gelder, 2002), and 50% in the first 6 months (Schievink, 1997). Risk factors associated with SAH include the size of the aneurysm, female gender and pregnancy, smoking, and excessive alcohol consumption (Weir, 2002). Although the role of sustained hypertension remains a matter of debate as a risk factor, transient increases in blood pressure produced by sudden exertion is considered to be the major immediate cause of rupture (Mohr, 1984). More important, however, is that first-degree relatives are seven times more likely to have a SAH than those in the general population (Raaymakers, 1999). Because the presence of blood in the subarachnoid space is the defining feature of SAH, a lumbar puncture to visualize cerebrospinal was for many years the means for making a diagnosis. With the development of imaging technology, a noncontrast CT is currently the first step for the detection of SAH. The identification of the underlying aneurysm is still most reliability made via cerebral angiography, but now CT angiograms appear capable of high sensitivity in the detection of these lesions (Papke et al., 2007).

The deleterious effects of SAH can be made worse with a number of possible complications. Vasospasm, for example, refers to the narrowing of the intradural subarachnoid arteries that occurs between 4 and 10 days after SAH, and can result in cerebral infarction, with ensuing behavioral and cognitive changes typical of those seen in ischemic stroke. In addition, there can be hydrocephalus, seizures, recurrent hemorrhage, electrolyte imbalance, and cardiopulmonary dysfunction (Stern et al., 2006).

The International Cooperative Study on the Timing of Aneurysm Surgery was instrumental in identifying the predominant sites of intracranial aneurysms (Kassell et al., 1990). Slightly more than one-third of the cases had aneurysms located on the anterior communicating artery, followed by the internal carotid artery (30%) and the middle cerebral artery (19%). Within

the posterior circulation, basilar tip aneurysms are the most common.

Neuropsychological Findings

Improvements in treatment of ruptured aneurysms have improved survival so that quality-of-life concerns have gained increasing relevance in the assessment of patient outcomes. It is now well accepted that despite improvements in physical status, patients who survive SAH can suffer from significant neurobehavioral deficits, even with excellent outcomes as defined by the Glasgow Outcome Scale (Haug et al., 2007). Residual deficits have been reported in patients with "good recovery" even up to 7 years after initial hospitalization (Hellawell & Pentland, 2001). Studies have largely confirmed that aneurysmal clipping of unruptured aneurysm produces few, if any, neuropsychological deficits and that it is the presence of hemorrhage that appears responsible for the neurocognitive sequelae in most patients (Hillis et al., 2000; Tuffiash et al., 2003). What is not yet clear, however, is the nature, extent, and time course of the neuropsychological and emotional changes that arise after hemorrhage and intervention.

There have been a wide range of impairments associated with aneurysmal SAH. The spectrum of disorders measured after hemorrhage has included verbal memory deficits (DeLuca, 1993; Irle et al., 1992), visual disorders (Ogden et al., 1993), and defects in information processing (Bellebaum et al., 2004). Frontal-lobe dysexecutive syndromes are also commonly reported (Bellebaum et al., 2004). But, as has been pointed out by Haug et al. (Haug et al., 2007), follow-up of patients up to 1 year after SAH has demonstrated that various cognitive functions have different courses of recovery. The time point of assessment after SAH therefore appears to be an important factor in the constellation of residual deficits, especially in patients with poor SAH grades (Mocco et al., 2006).

One of the complicating factors in determining the cognitive consequences of SAH is that the majority of patients have also received either surgical or endovascular treatment. Early studies in which patients underwent either intervention and were assessed at one time point showed marginally fewer effects after coiling than postclipping (e.g., Hadjivassiliou et al., 2001). Bellebaum and his colleagues compared two groups of 16 patients, assigned either to clipping or coiling treatment (Bellebaum et al., 2004). Both patient groups showed deficits in verbal and visual memory, with the clipping group demonstrating slightly greater impairment, especially in frontal executive function. But, as pointed out by Haug et al. above, serial measurement of cognitive function can yield other outcomes. Individuals undergoing coiling or clipping were assessed within 2 weeks of treatment and again at 6 months by Frazer et al. (Frazer et al., 2007). They found acute changes in both groups in memory, executive function, and information-processing speed. At follow-up, deficits in both groups were less severe, with residual dysfunction in memory, frontal executive dysfunction, naming skills and information-processing speed. Interestingly, there was no difference in functioning between the treatment groups at both time points. Koivisto et al. found no differences in neuropsychological function across three measurement points, and patients undergoing either coiling or clipping demonstrated improvement over time (Koivisto et al., 2000).

One of the presumed determining factors has been the location of the bleed. As the most common site of SAH, rupture of the anterior communicating artery has been proposed by some investigators to be associated with the triad of an amnestic disorder, confabulation and alteration of personality, collectively labeled the "ACoA syndrome" (Damasio et al., 1985; DeLuca & Diamond, 1995). Comparisons of neurocognitive outcomes of patients with ruptured aneurysms in this and other regions, however, have not yielded consistent behavioral differences. Results of executive function tests, for example, have not uniformly discriminated between patients with anterior and posterior SAH sites (Papagno et al., 2003).

The inconsistency of syndromal findings in patients with similar regions of SAH, similar behavioral manifestations in the context of hemorrhage in different brain areas, and differing long-term outcomes in patients with comparable initial cognitive profiles does suggest the presence of other important factors that affect neurocognition in this setting. It was proposed almost 20 years ago that local bleeding in the subarachnoid causes a more diffuse, global toxic effect on the brain (Laiacona et al., 1989). This notion has received increasing support from clinical outcome studies. Kreiter et al. prospectively evaluated 113 of 248 consecutively admitted nontraumatic SAH patients alive at 3 months (Kreiter et al., 2002). Predictors of cognitive dysfunction in two or more domains in a multivariate model showed that global cerebral edema had the highest predictive value associated with residual cognitive impairment. It is therefore not surprising that the severity of the hemorrhage in other studies as seen on imaging is correlated with more diffuse neuropsychological functions, even when the precise origin of the hemorrhage is unknown (Hutter et al., 1994). Another potential global factor, the presence the apolipoprotein ε4 allele, which has been found important in other neurological conditions, does not appear to be a global risk factor for late cognitive impairment, even 10 years after hemorrhage (Louko et al., 2006).

Final Comments

In an earlier edition of this book, we argued that neuropsychological methods should aim to bridge the anatomical, metabolic, and physiological effects of CVD to the capacity for self-care and independent living (Brown et al., 1996a). How well has recent neuropsychological research done in relating physiology to function? The considerable literature correlating neuropsychological measures to daily functioning has led to standards regarding the neuropsychological prediction of quality of life among patients with CVD (e.g., Donovan et al., 2008). Researchers have done much less work relating neuropsychological measures to physiological functioning. An exception to this negative general trend has been in the presurgical evaluation of patients with cerebrovascular anomalies where fMRI and electrocortical stimulation have been used to map areas of critical neuropsychological function. Hopefully, the increasing availability of fMRI and its success in guiding surgical decisions among patients with vascular anomalies will stimulate other investigators to more closely integrate neuropsychological changes following a cerebrovascular event with measurements of brain metabolism and blood flow. Recent work on the use of fMRI to predict outcome in language rehabilitation following stroke provides further evidence of the utility that accrues from the integration of neuropsychological and functional brain-imaging methods (Crosson et al., 2007).

The past decade has seen remarkable changes in stroke nosology as it relates to neuropsychological function. Advances in cerebrovascular nosology have been stimulated by evidence of subtle neuropsychological deficits that fall short of dementia syndromes, on the one hand, and progressive, usually subcortical VaDs that do not present as multiple strokes, on the other. The current nosology, which often tries to connect subtle forms of vascular change with dementia syndromes, is likely to remain in flux as dimensional models of VCI clash with syndromal models of stroke. Nonetheless, recent changes to nosology have enlarged the field's view about how CVD can affect neuropsychological functioning. One implication of the changing perspective on CVD is that the process of diagnosing degenerative dementias might have to change as well. For example, as more forms of VCI that do not involve stroke symptoms are described, the vascular exclusionary criteria for AD is likely to become more difficult to meet. What is needed is not a definition of dementia for vascular disease that stands parallel to the definition of degenerative dementia, but a rethinking of the concept of dementia from within a broad neuropathological framework.

Given the flux of nosological terms currently found in the literature, how should neuropsychologists assess patients for the cognitive effects of CVD? The literature on CVD over the past several decades indicates that the assessment of these disorders is best performed by combining dimensional and focal-syndrome assessment approaches. Dimensional assessment of CVD should measure general adaptive functions that have an executive component. Neuropsychological measurements that assess these adaptive functions have been described throughout this review. Standards for assessing focal neuropsychological syndromes in CVD have been recently promulgated (Hachinski et al., 2006). A critical question about the relatively brief batteries described in the recent standards is the extent to which their brevity has affected their sensitivity to subtle vascular impairment and their reliability in detecting neuropsychological profiles at the core of focal syndromes. The expert opinions offered by consensus panels need to be validated by classical test selection methods.

The flux of recent ideas about vascular cognitive disorders has highlighted the critical importance of neuropsychological assessment to stroke practice and research. This chapter has aimed to provide neuropsychologists new to the cerebrovascular field the background needed to continue the development of critical neuropsychological methodology.

References

Adams, H. P., & Davis, P. H. (2004). Aneurysmal subarachnoid hemorrhage. In J. P. Mohr, D. W. Choi, J. C. Grotta, B. Weir and P. A. Wolf (Eds.), *Stroke: Pathophysiology, diagnosis, and management* (4th ed., pp. 377–396). New York: Churchill Livingston.

Albers, G. W., Caplan, L. R., Easton, J. D., Fayad, P. B., Mohr, J. P., Saver, J. L., et al. (2002). Transient ischemic attack—proposal for a new definition. *New England Journal of Medicine, 347*, 1713–1716.

Alkadhi, H., Kollias, S. S., Crelier, G. R., Golay, X., Hepp-Reymond, M. C., & Valavanis, A. (2000). Plasticity of the human motor cortex in patients with arteriovenous malformations: A functional MR imaging study. *AJNR American Journal of Neuroradiology, 21*, 1423–1433.

Almkvist, O., Wahlund, L.O., Andersson-Lundman, G., Basun, H., & Backman, L. (1992). White-matter hyperintensity and neuropsychological functions in dementia and healthy aging. *Archives of Neurology, 49*, 626–632.

The Arteriovenous Malformation Study Group. (1999). Arteriovenous malformations of the brain in adults. *The New England Journal of Medicine, 340*, 1812.

Astrup, J., Siejo, B. K., & Symon, L. (1981). Thresholds in cerebral ischema—the ischema penumbra. *Stroke, 12*, 723–725.

Awad, I. A., Spetzler, R. F., Hodak, J. A., Awad, C. A., & Carey, R. (1986). Incidental subcortical lesions identified on magnetic resonance imaging in the elderly: Correlation with age and cerebrovascular risk factors. *Stroke, 17*, 1084–1098.

Ballard, C., Rowan, E., Stephens, S., Kalaria, R., & Kenny, R. A. (2003). Prospective follow-up study between 3 and 15 months after stroke: Improvements and decline in cognitive function among dementia-free stroke survivors > 75 years of age. *Stroke, 34,* 2440–2444.

Baker, R. P., McCarter, R. J., & Porter, D. G. (2004). Improvement in cognitive function after right temporal arteriovenous malformation excision. *British Journal of Neurosurgery, 18,* 541–544.

Bakker, F. C., Klijn, C. J., Jennekens-Schinkel, A., van der Tweel, I., Tulleken, C. A., & Kappelle, L. J. (2003). Cognitive impairment in patients with carotid artery occlusion and ipsilateral transient ischemic attacks. *Journal of Neurology, 250,* 1340–1347.

Bambakidis, N. C., Sunshine, J. L., Faulhaber, P. F., Tarr, R. W., Selman, W. R., & Ratcheson, R. A. (2001). Functional evaluation of arteriovenous malformations. *Neurosurgical Focus, 11*(5), e2.

Barker-Collo, S., & Feigin, V. (2006). The impact of neuropsychological deficits on functional stroke outcomes. *Neuropsychology Review, 16,* 53–64.

Bellebaum, C., Schafers, L., Schoch, B., Wanke, I., Stolke, D., Forsting, M., et al. (2004). Clipping versus coiling: Neuropsychological follow up after aneurysmal subarachnoid haemorrhage (SAH). *Journal of Clinical and Experimental Neuropsychology, 26,* 1081–1092.

Bennett, D. (2001). Public health importance of vascular dementia and Alzheimer's disease with cerebrovascular disease. *International Journal of Clinical Practice, 120,* 41–48.

Benton, A. L. (1991). Cerebral vascular disease in the history of clinical neuropsychology. In R. A. Bornstein and G. G. Brown (Eds.), *Neurobehavioral aspects of cerebrovascular disease* (pp. 3–13). New York: Oxford University Press.

Bigler, E. D., Lowry, C. M., Kerr, B., Tate, D. F., Hessel, C. D., Earl, H. D., et al. (2003). Role of white matter lesions, cerebral atrophy, and APOE on cognition in older persons with and without dementia; the cache county, Utah, Study of Memory and Aging. *Neuropsychology, 17,* 339–352.

Bowler, J. V. (1993). *Cerebral infarction and Tc HMPAO SPECT.* London: University of London.

Bowler, J. V., Steenhuis, R., & Hachinski, V. (1999). Conceptual background to vascular cognitive impairment. *Alzheimer's Disease and Associated Disorders, 13,* S30–S37.

Bowler, J. V. (2000). Criteria for vascular dementia: Replacing dogma with data. *Archives of Neurology, 57,* 170–171.

Bowler, J. V. (2002). The concept of vascular cognitive impairment. *Journal of the Neurological Sciences, 203–204,* 11–15.

Bowler, J. V., & Hachinski, V. (2002). The concept of vascular cognitive impairment. In T. Erkinjuntti and S. Gauthier (Eds.), *Vascular cognitive impairment* (pp. 9–26). London, UK: Informa Healthcare.

Bowler, J. V., & Hachinski, V. C. (2003). Vascular cognitive impairment—a new concept. In J. V. Bowler and V. C. Hachinski (Eds.), *Vascular cognitive impairment: Preventable dementia* (pp. 5–14). New York: Oxford University Press.

Breteler, M. M., van Amerongen, N. M., van Swieten, J. C., Claus, J. J., Grobbee, D. E., van Gijn, J., et al. (1994a). Cognitive correlates of ventricular enlargement and cerebral white matter lesions on magnetic resonance imaging. The Rotterdam Study. *Stroke, 25,* 1109–1115.

Breteler, M. M., van Swieten, J. C., Bots, M. L., Grobbee, D. E., Claus, J. J., van den Hout, J. H., et al. (1994b). Cerebral white matter lesions, vascular risk factors, and cognitive function in a population-based study: The Rotterdam Study. *Neurology, 44,* 1246–1252.

Brown, G., G., Baird, A. D., Shatz, M. W., & Bornstein, R. A. (1996a). The effects of cerebral vascular disease on neuropsychological functioning. In I. Grant and K. M. Adams (Eds.), *Neuropsychological assessment of neuropsychiatric disorders* (2nd ed., pp. 342–378). New York: Oxford University Press.

Brown, M. (2000). White matter changes: Possible cerebral blood flow abnormalities. In L. Pantoni, D. Inzitari, and A. Wallin (Eds.), *The matter of white matter: Clinical and pathological aspects of white matter disease related to cognitive decline and vascular dementia* (pp. 299–312). Utrecht, the Netherlands: Academic Pharmaceutical Publications.

Brown, R. D., Jr., Wiebers, D. O., & Forbes, G. S. (1990). Unruptured intracranial aneurysms and arteriovenous malformations: Frequency of intracranial hemorrhage and relationship of lesions. *Journal of Neurosurgery, 73,* 859–863.

Brown, R. D., Jr., Wiebers, D. O., Torner, J. C., & O'Fallon, W. M. (1996b). Frequency of intracranial hemorrhage as a presenting symptom and subtype analysis: A population-based study of intracranial vascular malformations in Olmsted Country, Minnesota. *Journal of Neurosurgery, 85,* 29–32.

Brun, A. (2003). Vascular burden of the white matter. *International Psychogeriatrics, 15,* 53–58.

Brust, J. C. (1988). Vascular dementia is overdiagnosed. *Archives of Neurology, 45,* 799–801.

Buklina, S. B. (2001). Memory impairment and deep brain structures. *Neuroscience and Behavioral Physiology, 31,* 171–177.

Buklina, S. B. (2002). The unilateral spatial neglect phenomenon in patients with arteriovenous malformations of deep brain structures. *Neuroscience and Behavioral Physiology, 32,* 555–560.

Campbell, J. J., & Coffey, C. E. (2001). Neuropsychiatric significance of subcortical hyperintensity. *Journal of Neuropsychiatry and Clinical Neuroscience, 13,* 261–288.

Cannestra, A. F., Pouratian, N., Forage, J., Bookheimer, S. Y., Martin, N. A., & Toga, A. W. (2004). Functional magnetic resonance imaging and optical imaging for dominant-hemisphere perisylvian arteriovenous malformations. *Neurosurgery, 55*, 804–812; discussion 812–804.

Cherubini, A., & Senin, U. (2003). Elderly stroke patient at risk for dementia: In search of a profile. *Stroke, 34*, 2445.

Choi, J. H., & Mohr, J. P. (2005). Brain arteriovenous malformations in adults. *Lancet Neurology, 4*, 299–308.

Chui, H. C., Mack, W., Jackson, J. E., Mungas, D., Reed, B. R., Tinklenberg, J., et al. (2000). Clinical criteria for the diagnosis of vascular dementia: A multicenter study of comparability and interrater reliability. *Archives of Neurology, 57*, 191–196.

Chui, H. (2001). Vascular dementia: A new beginning. Shifting focus from clinical phenotype to ischemic brain injury. *Clinical Neurology, 18*, 951–977.

Chui, H., Mack, W., Varpetian, A., & Mungas, D. (2003). Evidence-based prognosis of vascular dementia: Survival and rate of cognitive decline. In J. V. Bowler and V. Hachinski (Eds.), *Vascular cognitive impairment; Preventable Dementia* (pp. 33–39). Oxford: Oxford University Press.

Chusid, J. G. (1985). *Correlative neuroanatomy and functional neurology*. Los Altos, CA: Lange Medical Publications.

Clarke, E. (1963). Apoplexy in early Hippocratic writings. *Bulletin of the History of Medicine, 37*, 301–314.

Cosentino, S. A., Jefferson, A. L., Carey, M, Price, C. C., Davis-Garrett, K., Swenson, R., et al. (2004). The clinical diagnosis of vascular dementia: A comparison among four classification systems and a proposal for a new paradigm. *Clinical Neuropsychologist, 18*, 6–21.

Crosson, B., McGregor, K., Gopinath, K. S., Conway, T. W., Benjamin, M., Chang, Y. L., et al. (2007). Functional MRI of language in aphasia: A review of the literature and the methodological challenges. *Neuropsychology Review, 17*, 157–177.

Cummings, J. L. (1994). Vascular subcortical dementias: Clinical aspects. *Dementia, 5*, 177–180.

Damasio, A. R., Graff-Radford, N. R., Eslinger, P. J., Damasio, H., & Kassell, N. (1985). Amnesia following basal forebrain lesions. *Archives of Neurology, 42*, 263–271.

DeCarli, C., Miller, B. L., Swan, G. E., Reed, T., Wolf, P. A., & Carmelli, D. (2001). Cerebrovascular and brain morphologic correlates of mild cognitive impairment in the National Heart, Lung, and Blood Institute Twin Study. *Archives of Neurology, 58*, 643–647.

DeCarli, C., & Scheltens, P. (2002). Structural brain imaging. In T. Erkinjuntti and S. Gauthier (Eds.), *Vascular cognitive impairment* (pp. 433–457). London: Martin Dunitz.

De Leeuw, F. E., de Groot, J. C., Bots, M. L., Witteman, J. C., Oudkerk, M., Hofman, A., et al. (2000). Carotid atherosclerosis and cerebral white matter lesions in a population based magnetic resonance imaging study. *Journal of Neurology, 247*, 291–296.

De Leeuw, F. E., de Groot, J. C., Oudkerk, M., Witteman, J. C., Hofman, A., van Gijn, J., et al. (2002). Hypertension and cerebral white matter lesions in a prospective cohort study. *Brain, 125*, 765–772.

DeLuca, J. (1993). Predicting neurobehavioral patterns following anterior communicating artery aneurysm. *Cortex, 29*, 639–647.

DeLuca, J., & Diamond, B. J. (1995). Aneurysm of the anterior communicating artery: A review of neuroanatomical and neuropsychological sequelae. *Journal of Clinical and Experimental Neuropsychology, 17*, 100–121.

Devasenapathy, A., & Hachinski, V. C. (2000). Vascular cognitive impairment. *Current Treatment Options in Neurology, 2*, 61–72.

Desmond, D. W., Moroney, J. T., Sano, M., & Stern, Y. (1996). Recovery of cognitive function after stroke. *Stroke, 27*, 1798–1803.

Diaz, F., Mersky, H., Hachinski, V. C., Lee, D. H., Boniferro, M., Wong, C. J., et al. (1991). Improved recognition of leukoaraiosis and cognitive impairment in Alzheimer's disease. *Archives of Neurology, 48*, 1022–1025.

Diehl, R. R., Henkes, H., Nahser, H. C., Kuhne, D., & Berlit, P. (1994). Blood flow velocity and vasomotor reactivity in patients with arteriovenous malformations. A transcranial Doppler study. *Stroke, 25*, 1574–1580.

Donovan, N. J. Kendall, D. L., Heaton, S. C., Kwon, S., Velozo, C. A., & Duncan, P. W. (2008). Conceptualize functional cognition in stroke. *Neurorehabilitation and Neural Repair, 22*, 122–135.

Doody, R. S., Massman, P. J., Mawad, N., & Nance, M. (1998). Cognitive consequences of subcortical magnetic resonance imaging changes in Alzheimer's disease: Comparison to small vessel ischemic vascular dementia. *Neuropsychiatry, Neuropsychology, and Behavioral Neurology, 11*, 191–199.

Drayer, B. P. (1988). Imaging of the aging brain. Part I. Normal findings. *Radiology, 166*, 785–796.

Emery, V. B., Gillie, E., & Ramdev, P. T. (1994). Vascular dementia redefined. In T. E. Oxman and V. B. Emery (Eds.), *The Johns Hopkins series in psychiatry and neuroscience. Dementia: Presentations, differential diagnosis, and nosology* (pp. 162–194). Baltimore, MD: Johns Hopkins University Press.

Erkinjuntti, T. (1987). Differential diagnosis between Alzheimer's disease and vascular dementia: Evaluation of some common clinical methods. *Acta Neurologica Scandinavica, 76*, 433–442.

Erkinjuntti, T. (2000). Vascular dementia: An overview. In J. O'Brien and L. Bruns (Eds.), *Dementia* (2nd ed., pp. 623–634). London, UK: Arnold Press.

Erkinjuntti, T., & Hachinski, V. (1993). Rethinking vascular dementia. *Cerebrovascular Disorders, 3*, 3–23.

Erkinjuntti, T., Inzitari, D., Pantoni, L., Wallin, A., Scheltens, P., Rockwood, K., et al. (2000). Research criteria for subcortical vascular dementia in clinical trials. *Journal of Neurological Transmission, 59*, 23–30.

Erkinjuntti, T., & Rockwood, K. (2001). Vascular cognitive impairment. *Psychogeriatrics, 1*, 27–38.

Feigin, V. L. Lawes, C. M., Bennett, D. A., & Anderson, C. S. (2003). Stroke epidemiology: A review of population-based studies of incidence, prevalence, and case-fatality in the late 20th century. *Lancet Neurology, 2*, 43–53.

Festa, J. R., Lazar, R. M., Marshall, R. S., Pile-Spellman, J., Chong, J. Y., & Duong, H. (2004). Dural arteriovenous fistula presents like an ischemic stroke. *Cognitive and Behavioral Neurology, 17*(1), 50–53.

Fieschi, C., & Rosiers, M. D. (1976). Cerebral blood flow measurements in stroke. In: R.W. Ross Russell (Ed.), *Cerebral artery disease* (pp.85–106). New York: Churchill Livingstone.

Fisher, C. M., Kistler, J. P., & Davis, J. M. (1980). Relation of cerebral vasospasm to subarachnoid hemorrhage visualized by computerized tomographic scanning. *Neurosurgery, 6*, 1–9.

Fisher, M. (2006). The ischemic penumbra: A new opportunity for neuroprotection. *Cerebrovascular Diseases, 21*(Suppl 2), 64–70.

Fitzsimmons, B. F., Marshall, R. S., Pile-Spellman, J., & Lazar, R. M. (2003). Neurobehavioral differences in superselective Wada testing with amobarbital versus lidocaine. *American Journal of Neuroradiology, 24*, 1456–1460.

Fogarty-Mack, P., Pile-Spellman, J., Hacein-Bey, L., Osipov, A., DeMeritt, J., Jackson, E. C., et al. (1996). The effect of arteriovenous malformations on the distribution of intracerebral arterial pressures. *American Journal of Neuroradiology, 17*, 1443–1449.

Fratiglioni, L., De Ronchi, D., & Agüero-Torres, H. (1999). Worldwide prevalence and incidence of dementia. *Drugs and Aging, 15*, 365–375.

Frazer, D., Ahuja, A., Watkins, L., & Cipolotti, L. (2007). Coiling versus clipping for the treatment of aneurysmal subarachnoid hemorrhage: A longitudinal investigation into cognitive outcome. *Neurosurgery, 60*, 434–441; discussion 441–432.

Fujishima, M., Tanaka, K., Takeya, Y., & Omae, T. (1974). Bilateral reduction of hemispheric blood flow in patients with unilateral cerebral infarction. *Stroke, 5*, 648–653.

Furlan, A. J., Whisnant, J. P., & Elveback, L. R. (1979). The decreasing incidence of primary intracerebral hemorrhage: A population study. *Annals of Neurology, 5*, 367–373.

Garrett, K. D., Browndyke, J. N., Whelihan, W., Paul, R. H., DiCarlo, M., Moser, D. J., et al. (2004). The neuropsychological profile of vascular cognitive impairment—no dementia: Comparisons to patients at risk for cerebrovascular disease and vascular dementia. *Archives of Clinical Neuropsychology, 19*, 745–757.

Gilroy, J., & Meyers, J. S. (1969). *Medical neurology*. London: The MacMillan Company.

Ginsberg, M. D. (1997). Animal models of global and focal cerebral ischema. In K. M. A. Welch, L. R. Caplan, D. J. Reis, B. K. Siejs, & B. Weir (Eds.), *Premier on cerebrovascular disease* (pp. 165–181). San Diego, CA: Academic Press.

Giovannetti-Carew, T. G., Lamar, M., Cloud, B. S., Grossman, M., & Libon, D. J. (1997). Impairment in category fluency in ischemic vascular dementia. *Neuropsychology, 11*, 400–412.

Gold, G., Bouras, C., Canuto, A., Bergallo, M. F., Herrmann, F. R., Hof, P. R., et al. (2002). Clinicopathological validation study of four sets of clinical criteria for vascular dementia. *American Journal of Psychiatry, 159*, 82–87.

Goldstein, F. C., Levin, H. S., Goldman, W. P., Clark, A. N., & Altonen, T. K. (2001). Cognitive and neurobehavioral functioning after mild versus moderate traumatic brain injury in older adults. *Journal of the International Neuropsychology Society, 7*, 373–383.

Goodglass, H., & Kaplan, E. (1983). *Boston Diagnostic Aphasia Examination (BDAE)*. Philadelphia: Lea and Febiger.

Graf, C. J., Perret, G. E., & Torner, J. C. (1983). Bleeding from cerebral arteriovenous malformations as part of their natural history. *Journal of Neurosurgery, 58*, 331–337.

Gross, C. R., Kase, C. S., Mohr, J. P., Cunningham, S. C., & Baker, W. E. (1984). Stroke in south Alabama: Incidence and diagnostic features—a population based study. *Stroke, 15*, 249–255.

Gunning-Dixon, F. M., & Raz, N. (2000). The cognitive correlates of white matter abnormalities in normal aging: A quantitative review. *Neuropsychology, 14*, 224–232.

Hachinski, V., Potter, P., & Merskey, H. (1986). Leukoaraiosis: An ancient term for a new problem.

Canadian Journal of Neurological Science, 13(4 Suppl), 533–534.

Hachinski, V. C. (1991). Multi-infarct dementia: A reappraisal. *Alzheimer's Disease Associative Disorders, 5*, 64–68.

Hachinski, V. C. (1992). Preventable senility: A call for action against the vascular dementias. *The Lancet, 340*, 645–647.

Hachinski, V. C. (1994). Vascular dementia: A radical redefinition. *Dementia, 5*, 130–132.

Hachinski, V., Iadecola, C., Petersen, R. C., Breteler, M. M., Nyenhuis, D. L., Black, S. E., et al. (2006). National Institute of Neurological Disorders and Stroke-Canadian Stroke Network vascular cognitive impairment harmonization standards. *Stroke, 37*, 2220–2241. Erratum in: (2007). *Stroke, 38*, 1118.

Hadjivassiliou, M., Tooth, C. L., Romanowski, C. A., Byrne, J., Battersby, R. D., Oxbury, S., et al. (2001). Aneurysmal SAH: Cognitive outcome and structural damage after clipping or coiling. *Neurology, 56*, 1672–1677.

Hashimoto, H., Iida, J., Kawaguchi, S., & Sakaki, T. (2004). Clinical features and management of brain arteriovenous malformations in elderly patients. *Acta Neurochirurgica, 146*, 1091–1098; discussion 1098.

Hassler, O. (1961). Morphological studies on the large cerebral arteries, with reference to the aetiology of subarachnoid haemorrhage. *Acta psychiatrica Scandinavica. Supplementum, 154*, 1–145.

Haug, T., Sorteberg, A., Sorteberg, W., Lindegaard, K. F., Lundar, T., & Finset, A. (2007). Cognitive outcome after aneurysmal subarachnoid hemorrhage: Time course of recovery and relationship to clinical, radiological, and management parameters. *Neurosurgery, 60*, 649–656; discussion 656–647.

Hellawell, D. J., & Pentland, B. (2001). Relatives' reports of long term problems following traumatic brain injury or subarachnoid haemorrhage. *Disability and Rehabilitation, 23*, 300–305.

Hildebrandt, H., Giesselmann, H., & Sachsenheimer, W. (1999). Visual search and visual target detection in patients with infarctions of the left or right posterior or the right middle brain artery. *Journal of Clinical and Experimental Neuropsychology, 21*, 94–107.

Hillis, A. E., Anderson, N., Sampath, P., & Rigamonti, D. (2000). Cognitive impairments after surgical repair of ruptured and unruptured aneurysms. *Journal of Neurology, Neurosurgery, and Psychiatry, 69*, 608–615.

Hershey, L. A., Modic, M. T., Greenough, P. G., & Jaffe, D. F. (1987). Magnetic resonance imaging in vascular dementia. *Neurology, 37*, 29–36.

Hofmeister, C., Stapf, C., Hartmann, A., Sciacca, R. R., Mansmann, U., TerBrugge, K., et al. (2000).

Demographic, morphological, and clinical characteristics of 1289 patients with brain arteriovenous malformation. *Stroke, 31*, 1307–1310.

Hom, J. (1991). Contributions of the Halstead-Reitan Battery in the neuropsychological investigation of stroke. In R. A. Bornstein and G. G. Brown (Eds.), *Neurobehavioral aspects of cerebrovascular disease* (pp. 165–181). New York: Oxford University Press.

Hom, J., & Reitan, R. M. (1990). Generalized cognitive function after stroke. *Journal of Clinical and Experimental Neuropsychology, 12*, 644–654.

House, A., Dennis, M., Warlow, C., Hawton, K., & Molyneux, A. (1990). The relationship between intellectual impairment and mood disorder in the first year after stroke. *Psychological Medicine, 20*, 805–814.

Huang, J., & van Gelder, J. M. (2002). The probability of sudden death from rupture of intracranial aneurysms: A meta-analysis. *Neurosurgery, 51*, 1101–1105; discussion 1105–1107.

Hunt, A. L., Orrison, W. W., Yeo, R. A., Haaland, K. Y., Rhyne, R. L., Garry, P. J., et al. (1989). Clinical significance of MRI white matter lesions in the elderly. *Neurology, 39*, 1470–1474.

Hunt, W. E., & Hess, R. M. (1968). Surgical risk as related to time of intervention in the repair of intracranial aneurysms. *Journal of Neurosurgery, 28*, 14–20.

Hurst, R. W., Bagley, L. J., Galetta, S., Glosser, G., Lieberman, A. P., Trojanowski, J., et al. (1998). Dementia resulting from dural arteriovenous fistulas: The pathologic findings of venous hypertensive encephalopathy. *American Journal of Neuroradiology, 19*, 1267–1273.

Hutter, B. O., Gilsbach, J. M., & Kreitschmann, I. (1994). Is there a difference in cognitive deficits after aneurysmal subarachnoid haemorrhage and subarachnoid haemorrhage of unknown origin? *Acta Neurochirurgica, 127*, 129–135.

Inzitari, D., Lamassa, M., & Pantoni, L. (2003). Treatment of vascular dementias. In J. V. Bowler and V. Hachinski (Eds.), *Vascular cognitive impairment: Preventable dementia* (pp. 152–176). New York: Oxford University Press.

Irle, E., Wowra, B., Kunert, H. J., Hampl, J., & Kunze, S. (1992). Memory disturbances following anterior communicating artery rupture. *Annals of Neurology, 31*, 473–480.

Ito, M., Sonokawa, T., Mishina, H., & Sato, K. (1995). Reversible dural arteriovenous malformation-induced venous ischemia as a cause of dementia: Treatment by surgical occlusion of draining dural sinus: case report. *Neurosurgery, 37*, 1187–1191; discussion 1191–1182.

Iwama, T., Hayashida, K., Takahashi, J. C., Nagata, I., & Hashimoto, N. (2002). Cerebral hemodynamics and metabolism in patients with cerebral arterio-venous malformations: An evaluation using positron emission tomography scanning. *Journal of Neurosurgery, 97,* 1314–1321.

Jin, Y. P., Di Legge, S., Ostbye, T., Feightner, J. W., & Hachinski, V. (2006). The reciprocal risks of stroke and cognitive impairment in an elderly population. *Alzheimer's and Dementia, 2,* 171–178.

Johnston, D. C. C., & Hill, M. D. (2004). The patient with transient cerebral ischemia: A golden opportunity for stroke prevention. *Canadian Medical Association Journal, 170,* 1134–1137.

Kales, H. C., Maixner, D. F., & Mellow, A. M. (2005). Cerebrovascular disease and late-life depression. *American Journal of Geriatric Psychiatry, 13,* 88–98.

Kassell, N. F., & Torner, J. C. (1982). Epidemiology of intracranial aneurysms. *International Anesthesiology Clinics, 20,* 13–17.

Kassell, N. F., Torner, J. C., Haley, E. C., Jr., Jane, J. A., Adams, H. P., & Kongable, G. L. (1990). The International Cooperative Study on the Timing of Aneurysm Surgery. Part 1: Overall management results. *Journal of Neurosurgery, 73,* 18–36.

Kilander, L., Andren, B., Nyman, H., Lind, L., Boberg, M., & Lithell, H. (1998). Atrial fibrillation is an independent determinant of low cognitive function: A cross-sectional study in elderly men. *Stroke, 19,* 1816–1820.

Klimo, P., Jr., Rao, G., & Brockmeyer, D. (2007). Pediatric arteriovenous malformations: A 15-year experience with an emphasis on residual and recurrent lesions. *Child's Nervous System, 23,* 31–37.

Koivisto, T., Vanninen, R., Hurskainen, H., Saari, T., Hernesniemi, J., & Vapalahti, M. (2000). Outcomes of early endovascular versus surgical treatment of ruptured cerebral aneurysms. A prospective randomized study. *Stroke, 31,* 2369–2377.

Kreiter, K. T., Copeland, D., Bernardini, G. L., Bates, J. E., Peery, S., Claassen, J., et al. (2002). Predictors of cognitive dysfunction after subarachnoid hemorrhage. *Stroke, 33,* 200–208.

Kumar, A., Bilker, W., Jin, Z., & Udupa, J. (2000). Atrophy and high intensity lesions: Complementary neurobiological mechanisms in late-life major depression. *Neuropsychopharmacology, 22,* 264–274.

Kurl, S., Saari, T., Vanninen, R., & Hernesniemi, J. (1996). Dural arteriovenous fistulas of superior sagittal sinus: Case report and review of literature. *Surgical Neurology, 45,* 250–255.

Lafosse, J. M., Reed, B. R. Mungas, D., Sterling, S. B., Wahbeh, H., & Jagust, W. J. (1997). Fluency and memory differences between ischemic vascular dementia and Alzheimer's disease. *Neuropsychology, 11,* 514–522.

Laiacona, M., De Santis, A., Barbarotto, R., Basso, A., Spagnoli, D., & Capitani, E. (1989). Neuropsychological follow-up of patients operated for aneurysms of anterior communicating artery. *Cortex, 25,* 261–273.

Lazar, R. M. (2001). Neuropsychological function and brain arteriovenous malformations: Redefining eloquence as a risk for treatment. *Neurosurgical Focus, 11,* e4.

Lazar, R. M., Connaire, K., Marshall, R. S., Pile-Spellman, J., Hacein-Bey, L., Solomon, R. A., et al. (1999). Developmental deficits in adult patients with arteriovenous malformations. *Archives of Neurology, 56,* 103–106.

Lazar, R. M., Fitzsimmons, B. F., Marshall, R. S., Mohr, J. P., & Berman, M. F. (2003). Midazolam challenge reinduces neurological deficits after transient ischemic attack. *Stroke, 34,* 794–796.

Lazar, R. M., Marshall, R. S., Pile-Spellman, J., Duong, H. C., Mohr, J. P., Young, W. L., et al. (2000). Interhemispheric transfer of language in patients with left frontal cerebral arteriovenous malformation. *Neuropsychologia, 38,* 1325–1332.

Lazar, R. M., Marshall, R. S., Pile-Spellman, J., Hacein-Bey, L., Young, W. L., Mohr, J. P., et al. (1997). Anterior translocation of language in patients with left cerebral arteriovenous malformation. *Neurology, 49,* 802–808.

Lehericy, S., Biondi, A., Sourour, N., Vlaicu, M., du Montcel, S. T., Cohen, L., et al. (2002). Arteriovenous brain malformations: Is functional MR imaging reliable for studying language reorganization in patients? Initial observations. *Radiology, 223,* 672–682.

Libon, D. J., Bogdanoff, B., Bonavita, J., Skalina, S., Cloud, B. S., Resh, R., et al. (1997). Dementia associated with periventricular deep white matter alterations: A subtype of subcortical dementia. *Archives of Clinical Neuropsychology, 12,* 239–250.

Libon, D. J., Bogdanoff, B., Leopold, N., Hurka, R., Bonavita, J., Skalina, S., et al., (2001). Neuropsychological profiles associated with subcortical white matter alterations and Parkinson's disease: Implications for the diagnosis of dementia. *Archives of Clinical Neuropsychology, 16,* 19–32.

Libon, D. J., Price, C. C., Giovannetti, T., Swenson, R., Magouirk, Bettcher, B., & Heilman, K. M. (2008). Linking MRI hyperintensities with patterns of neuropsychological impairment: Evidence for a threshold effect. *Stroke, 39,* 806–813.

Longstreth, W. T., Arnold, A. M., & Manolio, T. A. (2000). Clinical correlates of ventricular and sulcal size on cranial magnetic resonance imaging of 3301 elderly people. *Neuroepidemiology, 19,* 30–42.

Loring, D. W. (1999). *INS Dictionary of Neuropsychology.* New York: Oxford University Press.

Louko, A. M., Vilkki, J., & Niskakangas, T. (2006). ApoE genotype and cognition after subarachnoid haemorrhage: A longitudinal study. *Acta Neurology Scandavica, 114,* 315–319.

MacNeill, S. E., & Lichtenberg, P. A. (1997). Home alone: The role of cognition in return to independent living. *Archives of Physical Medicine and Rehabilitation, 78,* 755–758.

Mahalick, D. M., Ruff, R. M., Heary, R. F., & U, H. S. (1993). Preoperative versus postoperative neuropsychological sequelae of arteriovenous malformations. *Neurosurgery, 33,* 563–570; discussion 570–561.

Malik, G. M., Seyfried, D. M., & Morgan, J. K. (1996). Temporal lobe arteriovenous malformations: Surgical management and outcome. *Surgical Neurology, 46,* 106–114; discussion 114–105.

Marshall, G. A., Jonker, B. P., Morgan, M. K., & Taylor, A. J. (2003). Prospective study of neuropsychological and psychosocial outcome following surgical excision of intracerebral arteriovenous malformations. *Journal of Clinical Neuroscience, 10,* 42–47.

Mast, H., Mohr, J. P., Osipov, A., Pile-Spellman, J., Marshall, R. S., Lazar, R. M., et al. (1995). "Steal" is an unestablished mechanism for the clinical presentation of cerebral arteriovenous malformations. *Stroke, 26,* 1215–1220.

Masur, D. M., Sliwinski, M., Lipton, R. B., Blau, A. D., & Crystal, H. A. (1994). Neuropsychological prediction of dementia and the absence of dementia in healthy elderly persons. *Neurology, 44,* 1427–1432.

Matsuda, S., Waragai, M., Shinotoh, H., Takahashi, N., Takagi, K., & Hattori, T. (1999). Intracranial dural arteriovenous fistula (DAVF) presenting progressive dementia and parkinsonism. *Journal of the Neurological Sciences, 165,* 43–47.

McCormick, W. (1978). Classification, pathology, and natural history of the central nervous system. *Neurological Neurosurgery, 14,* 2–7.

McCormick, W. F., & Rosenfield, D. B. (1973). Massive brain hemorrhage: A review of 144 cases and an examination of their causes. *Stroke, 4,* 946–954.

McKhann, G., Drachman, D., Folstein, M., Katzman, R., Price, D., & Stadlan, E. M. (1984). Clinical diagnosis of Alzheimer's Disease report of the NINCDS-ADRDA work group under the auspices of Department of Health and Human Services Task Force on Alzheimer's Disease. *Neurology, 34,* 939–944.

Meguro, K., Shimada, M., Yamagushi, S., Ishizaki, J., Ishii, H., Shimada, Y., et al. (2001). Cognitive function and frontal lobe atrophy in normal elderly adults: Implications for dementia not as aging-related disorders and the reserve hypothesis. *Psychiatry and Clinical Neurosciences, 55,* 565–572.

Meyer, J. S., Goto, F., & Tazaki, Y. (1962). Metabolism Following experimental cerebral embolism. *Journal of Neuropathology and Experimental Neurology, 21,* 4–24.

Meyer, A., & Hierons, R. (1962). Observations on the history of the "circle of Willis." *Medical History, 6,* 119–130.

Meyer, J. S., Xu, G., Thornby, J., Chowdhury, M. G., & Quach, M. (2002). Is mild cognitive impairment prodromal for vascular dementia like Alzheimer's Disease? *Stroke, 33,* 1981–1985.

Mihalka, L., Smolanka, V., Bulecza, B., Mulesa, S., & Bereczki, D. (2001). A population study of stroke in West Ukraine: Incidence, stroke services, and 30-day case fatality. *Stroke, 32,* 2227–2231.

Mirsen, T. R., Lee, D. H., Wong, C. J., Diaz, J. F., Fox, A. J., Hachinski, V. C., et al. (1991). Clinical correlates of white-matter changes on magnetic resonance imaging scans of the brain. *Archives of Neurology, 48,* 1015–1021.

Miyao, S., Takano, A., Teramoto, J., & Takahashi, A. (1992). Leukoaraiosis in relation to prognosis for patients with lacunar infarction. *Stroke, 23,* 1434–1438.

Mocco, J., Ransom, E. R., Komotar, R. J., Sergot, P. B., Ostapkovich, N., Schmidt, J. M., et al. (2006). Long-term domain-specific improvement following poor grade aneurysmal subarachnoid hemorrhage. *Journal of Neurology, 253,* 1278–1284.

Mohr, J. H., A., Mast, H., Pile-Spellman, J., Schumacher, H. C., & Stapf, C. (2004). Anteriovenous Malformations and Other Vascular Anomalies. In J. P. Mohr, D. W. Choi, J. C. Grotta, B. Weir, and P. A. Wolf. (Eds.), *Stroke pathophysiology, diagnosis and management* (pp. 397–421). Philadelphia: Churchill Livingstone.

Mohr, J. P. (1984). Intracranial aneuryms. In J. P. Mohr (Ed.), *Manual of clinical problems in neurology* (1st ed., pp. 188–191). Boston: Little, Brown and Company.

Mohr, J. P., & Gautier, J. C. (1995). Subarachnoid hemorrhage: Aneuryms and vascular malformations. In J. P. Mohr and J. C. Gautier (Eds.), *Guide to clinical neurology* (pp. 605–618). New York: Churchill Livingston.

Munoz, D. G., Hastak, S. M., Harper, B., Lee, D., & Hachinski, V. (1993). Pathologic correlates of increased signals of the centrum ovale on magnetic resonance imaging. *Archives of Neurology, 50,* 492–497.

Murphy, J. (1954). Vascular tumors: Arteriovenous malformations of the brain. In J. P. Murphy (Ed.), *Cerebrovascular disease* (pp. 242–262). Chicago: Yearbook Medical Publishers.

Naarding, P., de Koning, I., dan Kooten, F., Dippel, D., Janzing, J., van der Mast, R., et al. (2003). Depression in vascular dementia. *International Journal of Geriatric Psychiatry, 18,* 325–330.

Newton, T. H., & Cronqvist, S. (1969). Involvement of dural arteries in intracranial arteriovenous malformations. *Radiology, 93,* 1071–1078.

Nilsson, B., Cronqvist, S., & Ingvar, D. H. (1979). Regional cerebral blood flow (rCBF) studies in patients to be considered for extracranial-intracranial bypass operations. In J. S. Meyer, H. Lechner, and M. Reivich (Eds.), *Cerebral vascular disease 2* (pp. 295–300). Amsterdam: Excerpta Medica.

Nolan, K. A., Lino, M., Seligmann, A. W., & Blass, J. P. (1998). Absence of vascular dementia in an autopsy series form a dementia clinic. *Journal of the American Geriatrics Society, 46,* 597–604.

O'Brien, P., Neyastani, A., Buckley, A. R., Chang, S. D., & Legiehn, G. M. (2006). Uterine arteriovenous malformations: From diagnosis to treatment. *Journal of Ultrasound in Medicine, 25,* 1387–1392.

Ogden, J. A., Mee, E. W., & Henning, M. (1993). A prospective study of impairment of cognition and memory and recovery after subarachnoid hemorrhage. *Neurosurgery, 33,* 572–586; discussion 586–577.

Ondra, S. L., Troupp, H., George, E. D., & Schwab, K. (1990). The natural history of symptomatic arteriovenous malformations of the brain: A 24-year follow-up assessment. *Journal of Neurosurgery, 73,* 387–391.

Osborn, A. G. (1980). *An introduction to cerebral angiography* (pp. 78–85). New York: Harper and Row.

Ozdemir, F., Birtane, M., Tabatabaei, R., Ekuklu, G., & Kokino, S. (2001). Cognitive evaluation and functional outcome after stroke. *American Journal of Physical Medicine and Rehabilitation, 80,* 410–415.

Pantoni, L., & Garcia, J. H. (1995). The significance of cerebral white matter abnormalities 100 years after Binswanger's report: A review. *Stroke, 26,* 1293–1301.

Papagno, C., Rizzo, S., Ligori, L., Lima, J., & Riggio, A. (2003). Memory and executive functions in aneurysms of the anterior communicating artery. *Journal of Clinical and Experimental Neuropsychology, 25,* 24–35.

Papke, K., Kuhl, C. K., Fruth, M., Haupt, C., Schlunz-Hendann, M., Sauner, D., et al. (2007). Intracranial aneurysms: Role of multidetector CT angiography in diagnosis and endovascular therapy planning. *Radiology, 244,* 532–540.

Paul, S. L., Srikanth, V. K., & Thrift, A. G. (2007). The large and growing burden of stroke. *Current Drug Targets, 8,* 786–793.

Perret, G., & Nishioka, H. (1966). Report on the cooperative study of intracranial aneurysms and subarachnoid hemorrhage. Section VI. Arteriovenous malformations. An analysis of 545 cases of cranio-cerebral arteriovenous malformations and fistulae reported to the cooperative study. *Journal of Neurosurgery, 25,* 467–490.

Pessin, M. S., Duncan, G. W., Mohr, J. P., & Poskanzer, D. C. (1977). Clinical and angiographic features of carotid transient ischemic attacks. *New England Journal of Medicine, 296,* 358–362.

Phillips, N. A., & Mate-Kole, C. C. (1997). Cognitive deficits in peripheral vascular disease: A comparison of mild stroke patients and normal controls. *Stroke, 28,* 777–784.

Pick, T. P., & Howden, R. (Eds.). (1977). *Grey's anatomy* (15th ed.). New York: Bounty Books.

Pohjasvaara, T., Mantyla, R., Ylikoski, R., Kaste, M., & Erkinjuntti, T. (2000). Comparison of different clinical criteria (DSM-III, ADDTC, ICD-10, NINDS-AIREN, DSM-IV) for the diagnosis of vascular dementia. National Institute of Neurological Disorders and Stroke-Association Internationale pour la Recherche et l'Enseignement en Neurosciences. *Stroke, 31,* 2952–2957.

Raaymakers, T. W. (1999). Aneurysms in relatives of patients with subarachnoid hemorrhage: Frequency and risk factors. MARS Study Group. Magnetic Resonance Angiography in Relatives of patients with Subarachnoid hemorrhage. *Neurology, 53,* 982–988.

Rao, S. M., Mittenberg, W., Bernardin, L., Haughton, V., & Leo, G. J. (1989). Neuropsychological test findings in subjects with leukoaraiosis. *Archives of Neurology, 46,* 40–44.

Raz, N., Rodrigue, K. M., & Acker, J. D. (2003). Hypertension and the brain: Vulnerability of the prefrontal regions and executive functions. *Behavioral Neuroscience, 117,* 1169–1180.

Redekop, G., TerBrugge, K., Montanera, W., & Willinsky, R. (1998). Arterial aneurysms associated with cerebral arteriovenous malformations: Classification, incidence, and risk of hemorrhage. *Journal of Neurosurgery, 89,* 539–546.

Reitan, R. M., & Davison, L. A. (1974). *Clinical neuropsychology: Current status and applications.* New York: John Wiley and Sons.

Robertson, I. H., Ridgeway, V., Greenfield, E., & Parr, A. (1997). Motor recovery after stroke depends on intact sustained attention: A 2-year follow-up study. *Neuropsychology, 11,* 290–295.

Rockwood, K., Bowler, J., Erkinjuntti, T., Hachinski, V., & Wallin, A. (1999). Subtypes of vascular dementia. *Alzheimer's Disease and Associated Disorders, 13*(Suppl. 3), S59–S65.

Rockwood, K., Davis, H., MacKnight, C., Vandorpe, R., Gauthier, S., Guzman, A., et al. (2003). The Consortium to Investigate Vascular Impairment of Cognition: Methods and first findings. *Canadian Journal of Neurological Science, 30,* 237–243.

Rockwood, K., Parhad, I., & Hachinski, V. (1994). Diagnosis of vascular dementia: Consortium of Canadian Centres for Clinical Cognitive Research Consensus Statement. *Canadian Journal of Neurological Sciences, 21,* 358–364.

Rockwood, K., Wentzel, C., Hachinski, V., Hogan, D. B., MacKnight, C., & McDowell, I. (2000). Prevalence and outcomes of vascular cognitive impairment. *Neurology, 54,* 447–451.

Roman, G. C. (1999). A historical review of the concept of vascular dementia: Lessons from the past for the future. *Alzheimer Disease and Associated Disorder, 13*(Suppl 3):S4–S8.

Roman, G. C. (2002). Vascular dementia may be the most common form of dementia in the elderly. *Journal of the Neurological Sciences, 203–204,* 7–10.

Sachdev, P. S., & Looi, J. C. L. (2003). Neuropsychological differentiation of Alzheimer's disease and vascular dementia. In J. V. Bowler and V. Hachinski (Eds.), *Vascular cognitive impairment: Preventable dementia* (pp. 152–176). New York: Oxford University Press.

Salter, K., Jutai, J., Foley, N., Hellings, C., & Teasell, R. (2006). Identification of aphasia post stroke: A review of screening assessment tools. *Brain Injury, 20,* 559–568.

Sasaki, T., & Kassell, N. F. (1990). Cerebrovascular system. In G. Paxinos (Ed.), *The human nervous system* (pp. 1135–1149). New York: Academic Press.

Schievink, W. I. (1997). Intracranial aneurysms. *New England Journal of Medicine, 336,* 28–40.

Schmidt, R., Fazekas, F., Kapeller, P., Schmidt, H., & Hartung, H. P. (1999). MRI white matter hyperintensities: Three-year follow-up of the Austrian Stroke Prevention Study. *Neurology, 53,* 132–139.

Shafer, P. W., Roccatagliata, L., & González, R. G. (2006). Stroke and cerebral ischemia. In R. R. Edelman, J. R. Hesselink, M. B. Zlatkin, and J. V. Cures III (Eds.), *Clinical magnetic resonance imaging* (3rd ed., Vol. 2, pp. 1454–1498). Philadelphia: Saunders Elsevier.

Siesjo, B., & Smith, M. L. (1997). Mechanisms of acidosis-related damage. In K. M. A. Welch, L. R. Caplan, D. J. Reis, B. K. Siesjo, and B. Weir (Eds.), *Primer on cerebrovascular diseases* (pp. 223–226). New York: Academic Press.

Singer, R., Ogilvy, C., & Rordorf, G. (2006). Brain Anteriovenous Malformations [Electronic Version]. http://www.uptodate.com/patients/content/topic.do?topicKey=~bxbI9AkWqzJgaDZ

Smith, C. D., Snowdon, D. A., Wang, H., & Markesbery, W. R. (2000). White matter volumes and periventricular white matter hyperintensities in aging and dementia. *Neurology, 54,* 838–842.

Snaphaan, L., & de Leeuw, F. E. (2007). Poststroke memory function in nondemented patients: A systematic review on frequency and neuroimaging correlates. *Stroke, 38,* 198–203.

Sokoloff, L. (1997). Anatomy of cerebral circulation. In K. M. A. Welch, L. R. Caplan, D. J. Reis, B. K. Siesjo, and B. Weir (Eds.), *Primer on cerebrovascular diseases* (pp. 3–5). New York: Academic Press.

Stabell, K. E., & Nornes, H. (1994). Prospective neuropsychological investigation of patients with supratentorial arteriovenous malformations. *Acta Neurochirurgica, 131,* 32–44.

Stapf, C., Mast, H., Sciacca, R. R., Choi, J. H., Khaw, A. V., Connolly, E. S., et al. (2006). Predictors of hemorrhage in patients with untreated brain arteriovenous malformation. *Neurology, 66,* 1350–1355.

Stapf, C., Mohr, J. P., Pile-Spellman, J., Solomon, R. A., Sacco, R. L., & Connolly, E. S., Jr. (2001). Epidemiology and natural history of arteriovenous malformations. *Neurosurgical Focus, 11,* e1.

Steinvorth, S., Wenz, F., Wildermuth, S., Essig, M., Fuss, M., Lohr, F., et al. (2002). Cognitive function in patients with cerebral arteriovenous malformations after radiosurgery: Prospective long-term follow-up. *International Journal of Radiation Oncology, Biology, Physics, 54,* 1430–1437.

Stephens, S., Kenny, R. A., Rowan, E., Allan, L., Kalaria, R. N., Bradbury, M., et al. (2004). Neuropsychological characteristics of mild vascular cognitive impairment and dementia after stroke. *International Journal of Geriatric Psychiatry, 19,* 1053–1057.

Stern, M., Chang, D., Odell, M., & Sperber, K. (2006). Rehabilitation implications of non-traumatic subarachnoid haemorrhage. *Brain Injury, 20,* 679–685.

Sundet, K., Finset, A., & Reinvang, I. (1988). Neuropsychological predictors in stroke rehabilitation. *Journal of Clinical and Experimental Neuropsychology, 10,* 363–379.

Swan, G. E., DeCarli, C., Miller, B. L., Reed, T., Wolf, P. A., & Jack, L. M. (1998). Association of midlife blood pressure to late-life cognitive decline and brain morphology. *Neurology, 51,* 986–993.

Tanaka, K., Morooka, Y., Nakagawa, Y., & Shimizu, S. (1999). Dural arteriovenous malformation manifesting as dementia due to ischemia in bilateral thalami. A case report. *Surgical Neurology, 51,* 489–493; discussion 493–484.

Tatemichi, T. K., Desmond, D. W., Stern, Y., Paik, M., Sano, M., & Bagiella, E. (1994). Cognitive impairment after stroke: Frequency, patterns, and relationship to functional abilities. *Journal of Neurology, Neurosurgery, and Psychiatry, 57,* 202–207.

Tham, W., Auchs, A. P., Thong, M., Goh, M-L., Chang, H-M., Wong, M-C., et al. (2002). Progression of cognitive impairment after stroke: One year results from a longitudinal study of Singaporean stroke patients. *Journal of the Neurological Sciences, 203–204,* 49–52.

Toole, J. F. (1990). *Cerebrovascular disorders* (4th ed.). New York: Raven Press.

Tuffiash, E., Tamargo, R. J., & Hillis, A. E. (2003). Craniotomy for treatment of unruptured aneurysms is not associated with long-term cognitive dysfunction. *Stroke, 34,* 2195–2199.

Tupler, L. A., Coffey, C. E., Logue, P. E., Djang, W. T., & Fagan, S. M. (1992). Neuropsychological importance of subcortical white matter hyperintensity. *Archives of Neurology, 49,* 1248–1252.

Turjman, F., Massoud, T. F., Sayre, J. W., Vinuela, F., Guglielmi, G., & Duckwiler, G. (1995). Epilepsy associated with cerebral arteriovenous malformations: A multivariate analysis of angioarchitectural characteristics. *American Journal of Neuroradiology, 16,* 345–350.

U.S. Census Bureau. (2005). *Statistical Abstract of the United States 2006: The National Data Book.* Washington, DC: United States Government Printing Office.

Vates, G. E., Zabramski, J. M., Spetzler, R. F., & Lawton, M. T. (2004). Intracranial Aneuryms. In J. P. Mohr, D. W. Choi, J. C. Grotta, B. Weir, and P. A. Wolf (Eds.), *Stroke: Pathophysiology, diagnosis, and management* (4th ed., pp. 1279–1335). New York: Churchill Livingston.

Victor, M., & Ropper, A. H. (2001). *Adams and Victor's principles of neurology* (7th ed.). New York: McGraw-Hill.

Wagner, M. T., & Cushman, L. A. (1994). Neuroanatomic and neuropsychological predictors of unawareness of cognitive deficit in the vascular population. *Archives of Clinical Neuropsychology, 9,* 57–69.

Waldstein, S. R., Snow, J., Muldoon, M. F., & Katzel, L. I. (2001). Neuropsychological consequences of cardiovascular disease. In R. E. Tarter, M. Butters, and S. R. Beers (Eds.), *Medical neuropsychology* (2nd ed., pp. 51–84). New York: Kluwer Academic/Plenum Publishers.

Wechsler, D. (1987). *Weschler Memory Scale: Revised manual.* San Antonio: Psychological Corporation/Harcourt Brace Jovanovich.

Weir, B. (2002). Unruptured intracranial aneurysms: A review. *Journal of Neurosurgery, 96,* 3–42.

Welch, K. M. A., & Barkley, G. L. (1986). Biochemistry and pharmacology of cerebral ischemia. In H. J. M. Barnett, J. P. Mohr, B. M., Stein, and F. M. Yatsu (Eds.), *Stroke: Pathophysiology, diagnosis, and management. Vol. 1.* (pp. 75–90). New York: Churchill-Livingstone.

Welch, K. M. A., Caplan, L. R., Reis, D. J., Siesjo, B. K., & B. Weir, B. (Eds.). (1997). *Primer on cerebrovascular diseases.* New York: Academic Press.

Welch, K. M. A., & Levine, S. R. (1991). Focal brain ischemia and stroke: Pathophysiology and acid-base status. In R. A. Bornstein and G. G. Brown (Eds.), *Neurobehavioral aspects of cerebrovascular disease* (pp. 3–13). New York: Oxford University Press.

Wentzel., C., Rockwood, K., MacKnight, C., Hachinski, V. C., Hogan, D. B., & Feldman, H. (2001). Progression of impairment in patients with vascular cognitive impairment without dementia. *Neurology, 57,* 714–716.

Wenz, F., Steinvorth, S., Wildermuth, S., Lohr, F., Fuss, M., Debus, J., et al. (1998). Assessment of neuropsychological changes in patients with arteriovenous malformation (AVM) after radiosurgery. *International Journal of Radiation Oncology, Biology, Physics, 42,* 995–999.

Wetterling, T., Kanitz, R. D., & Borgis, K. J. (1996). Comparison of different diagnostic criteria for vascular dementia (ADDTC, DSM-IV, ICD-10, NINDS-AIREN). *Stroke, 27,* 30–36.

Wolf, H., Ecke, G. M., & Bettin, S., (2000). Do white matter changes contribute to the subsequent development of dementia in patients with mild cognitive impairment? A longitudinal study. *International Journal of Geriatric Psychiatry, 15,* 803–812.

Wiebe-Velazquez, S., & Hachinski, V. (1991). Overview of clinical issues in stroke. In R. A. Bornstein and G. G. Brown (Eds.), *Neurobehavioral aspects of cerebrovascular disease* (pp. 111–130). New York: Oxford University Press.

Willis, T. (1664). *Cerebri Anatome.* London: J. Flesher.

Wu, C. M., McLaughlin, K., Lorenzetti, D. L., Hill, M. D., Manns, B. J., & Ghali, W. A. (2007). Early risk of stroke after transient ischemic attack. *Archives of Internal Medicine, 167,* 2417–2422.

Zeidman, S. M., Monsein, L. H., Arosarena, O., Aletich, V., Biafore, J. A., Dawson, R. C., et al. (1995). Reversibility of white matter changes and dementia after treatment of dural fistulas. *American Journal of Neuroradiology, 16,* 1080–1083.

Zemke, D., Smith, J. L., Reeves, M. J., & Majid, A. (2004). Ischemia and ischemic tolerance in the brain: An overview. *NeuroToxicology, 25,* 895–904.

15

Neuropsychological Effects of Hypoxia in Medical Disorders

Amanda Schurle Bruce, Mark S. Aloia, and Sonia Ancoli-Israel

The human body relies on an adequate supply of oxygen for healthy functioning. The brain is just one organ sensitive to oxygen deprivation, especially when it occurs over extended periods of time. There are several medical conditions commonly associated with limited oxygen supply to the brain, including chronic obstructive pulmonary disease (COPD), obstructive sleep apnea (OSA), and acute respiratory distress syndrome (ARDS). The literature demonstrating the detrimental effects of oxygen deprivation on neuropsychological functioning has developed rapidly over the past few decades. This chapter focuses on the neuropsychological effects of disorders with limited supply of oxygen, addressing questions designed to both summarize the existing literature and theorizing about the potential mechanisms behind the findings and their implications for future research.

Definitions

Hypoxia literally means "deficient in oxygen." It can refer to abnormally low oxygen availability to body as a whole (generalized) or to a specific region of the body (tissue hypoxia). An example of generalized hypoxia is that which is seen at high altitudes, where reduced atmospheric pressure lessens the availability of oxygen in the environment. Generalized hypoxia can occur in otherwise healthy individuals and can result in altitude sickness, high-altitude pulmonary edema or high-altitude cerebral edema. Tissue hypoxia, on the other hand, is described in more local terms. It is generally due to a more specific restriction in blood supply (and therefore oxygen supply) to a specific organ. Hypoxemia, a term commonly confused with hypoxia, refers to deficiency in the concentration of oxygen in *arterial* blood. Anoxia refers to the complete deprivation of oxygen supply. Finally, hypercapnia is an associated state marked by an abnormally high level of carbon dioxide (CO_2) in the blood. Hypercapnia can be the result of a variety of causes such as hypoventilation, lung disease, or diminished consciousness. Hypercapnia is less often the focus of cognitive studies, but it is associated with hypoxia and may be a more sensitive variable in some clinical populations. This chapter focuses on hypoxia and hypoxemia, using the definition that best fits the study in question, but each term is employed to refer to a limitation in oxygen supply to the brain.

Medical Syndromes Associated with Hypoxia

There are many medical conditions that can be associated with limited oxygen supply, but three in particular are associated with hypoxia (or hypoxemia): COPD, OSA, and ARDS.

Chronic Obstructive Pulmonary Disease

COPD primarily encompasses emphysema and chronic bronchitis. The World Health

Organization rated COPD tied with HIV/AIDS as the fourth most common single cause of death. Smoking is estimated to be responsible for 80%–90% of COPD cases in the United States (Rennard, 2004; Strassels, 1999). Nonsmokers, however, can also develop the disorder, even if they are not exposed to second-hand smoke. The National Heart Lung Blood Institute estimates that 12.5 million adults over the age of 25 were diagnosed with COPD in the year 2001. The total estimate cost of COPD in 2002 was $32.1 billion dollars.

Neuropsychological Functioning in COPD. Chronic hypoxemia in COPD has a known and well-studied negative effect on cognition. Systematic investigations of neuropsychological functioning in COPD began in the 1970s, and initially demonstrated deficits on measures of perceptual-motor functioning and simple motor functioning in hypoxic participants with COPD (Krop et al., 1973). These findings were extended by two large multicenter trials conducted in the 1980s, the Nocturnal Oxygen Therapy Trial (NOTT) (Grant et al., 1982) and the Intermittent Positive Pressure Breathing Trial (IPPB) (Prigatano et al., 1983), which demonstrated impairments in perceptual-motor, simple motor, abstracting, executive functioning, and verbal and nonverbal learning and memory abilities in COPD patients. The data from these studies were combined in order to more thoroughly examine the relationship between hypoxemia severity and neuropsychological functioning in a total of 302 COPD patients with varying hypoxemia severity (Grant et al., 1987). Cognitive functioning was impaired in the COPD patients as a whole, with 42% of the combined sample demonstrating neuropsychological impairments. The proportion of cognitively impaired patients increased with worsening hypoxemia, with 27% of the mildly hypoxemic and 61% of the severely hypoxemic patients demonstrating impairments. A factor analysis was performed on the 27 test measures used in these studies, resulting in a four-factor solution. Multivariate analysis of variance on the factors revealed that performance on three of the four factors declined with worsening hypoxemia. The affected factors were perceptual learning and problem solving, alertness and psychomotor speed, and simple motor skills. No group differences emerged on a factor measuring verbal intelligence. Multiple regression analyses demonstrated that hypoxemia had a modest relationship to neuropsychological functioning, and that medical and pulmonary function variables did not significantly contribute to the prediction of neuropsychological impairment. Within the last decade, multiple studies have examined the profile of neuropsychological impairments associated with COPD and potential relationships between cognitive functioning in COPD and other medical or pulmonary variables.

Several studies have sought to characterize the profile of neuropsychological impairments in COPD and compare the pattern to patterns seen in other disorders, Alzheimer's disease (AD) being the most common (Antonelli Incalzi et al., 1993). Antonelli Incalzi and colleagues performed a discriminant function analysis of the cognitive profiles of participants with COPD, AD, multi-infract dementia (MID), and no known cognitive disorders (normal elderly). Of the COPD participants, 48.5% had a specific cognitive profile, with impairments in verbal functions and verbal memory, a diffuse decline in other cognitive functions, and normal visual attention. Relatively equal proportions of the remaining COPD participants were classified as belonging to each of the other groups. Cognitive impairments in the COPD patients were not as severe as documented in previous samples, (e.g., Grant et al., 1982), but all participants with COPD included in this study were on oxygen therapy, which may have ameliorated or slowed the progression of some cognitive deficits. Increasing age and duration of chronic respiratory failure were correlated with cognitive impairment. In a subsequent study, Antonelli Incalzi et al. (1997) again utilized discriminant function analysis to examine memory performance of hypoxic COPD patients, AD patients, older healthy subjects, and controls (Antonelli Incalzi et al., 1997). Only 19% of the participants with COPD were classified as having normal memory, while 38% exhibited a unique memory pattern, 17% were classified as AD, and 26% were classified as older normal controls. The participants with COPD exhibited memory deficits suggesting impairments in both the encoding and retrieval of verbal information.

Findings from studies examining the neuro-psychological profiles of nonhypoxic or mildly hypoxic COPD patients have been less conclusive. Kozora et al. (1999) compared the performance of mildly hypoxemic participants with COPD on oxygen therapy with AD patients normal and elderly (Kozora et al., 1999). The AD group performed significantly more poorly than both the COPD and control groups on most neuropsychological measures, and both the participants with AD and those with COPD performed more poorly than normal controls on verbal fluency to letter cues. However, the performance of the COPD group on this measure was not in the clinically impaired range. Results indicated that mildly hypoxemic participants with COPD who were treated with oxygen therapy and who had no neurologic histories may not exhibit cognitive deficits. This finding contrasted somewhat with findings of neuropsychological impairments documented in samples of untreated mildly hypoxic participants with COPD (e.g., Prigatano et al., 1983) or more severely hypoxic participants with COPD (Antonelli Incalzi et al., 1993). Antonelli Incalzi et al. (2003) examined cerebral perfusion in nonhypoxic participants with COPD, hypoxic participants with COPD, AD participants, and healthy controls. Nonhypoxic COPD participants had normal cerebral perfusion, while hypoxic COPD participants demonstrated an intermediate level of perfusion, between that of the nonhypoxic COPD and AD participants (Antonelli Incalzi et al., 2003). Hypoxic COPD and AD participants had reduced perfusion in anterior areas, while AD participants also had reduced perfusion in association areas. Both the nonhypoxic and hypoxic COPD participants performed better than those with AD on neuropsychological testing, and both groups performed below normative standards on measures of verbal memory, attention, and deductive thinking. The authors hypothesized that differences between the nonhypoxic and hypoxic COPD participants did not emerge because the hypoxic participants did not exhibit severe hypercapnia, which may have a greater link to cognitive dysfunction.

In addition to characterizing the neuropsychological profile associated with COPD, many studies have examined potential relationships between neuropsychological functioning and pulmonary or other medical variables.

In general, findings have been more robust in patients with more advanced disease or greater hypoxemia, and potential associations have been observed between cognitive functioning and measures of blood oxygenation, carbon dioxide, and fitness. An uncontrolled study of 18 COPD participants found that complex attention, information-processing speed, and memory were correlated with measures of carbon dioxide and oxygen partial pressure (Stuss et al., 1997). When participants from this study were divided into mildly hypoxic and severely hypoxic groups, the severely hypoxic group demonstrated poorer memory and attention functioning, and had more evidence of abnormalities on brain CT and EEG. Poorer baseline lung functioning (% predicted forced vital capacity (FVC) and forced expiratory volume in one second (FEV1)) and more depressive symptoms were predictive of decline over a 2-year period on the Mini-Mental Status Exam (MMSE) in a sample of 40 COPD participants, while depressive symptoms and performance of activities of daily living remained stable (Antonelli Incalzi et al., 1998). Findings suggested that more severe lung disease and onset of depression are risk factors for cognitive decline in COPD. Significant relationships between aerobic fitness and pulmonary functioning and measures of fluid intelligence, speed of processing, and working memory were found in a sample of 98 COPD participants, although findings related to pulmonary function were variable (Etnier et al., 1999). Aerobic fitness was felt to be a protective factor, serving to minimize or slow the decline of cognitive functioning. Again, findings from studies investigating the relationship between pulmonary and medical variables and neuropsychological functioning in samples of nonhypoxemic COPD participants have been mixed. Liesker et al. (2004) found poorer performance on measures of information-processing speed and no differences in performance on measures of memory or executive functioning in a group of 30 nonhypoxic COPD participants compared to age- and education-matched normal controls (Liesker et al., 2004).

Posttreatment Neuropsychological Functioning in COPD. Several investigators have examined the association between treatments designed to improve brain oxygenation and changes in neuropsychological functioning in COPD. Studies have focused primarily on three types of intervention: the provision of supplemental oxygen, exercise training and rehabilitation, and lung-volume reduction surgery.

It was initially hypothesized that supplemental oxygen would improve neuropsychological functioning in participants with COPD by alleviating their chronic hypoxia. Early findings suggested improvements following short-term supplemental oxygen therapy (Krop et al., 1973). The NOTT sought to examine the effects of long-term supplemental oxygen therapy on cognition, as a follow-up of these early findings (Heaton et al., 1983). A total of 150 patients were enrolled, 78 of whom received continuous oxygen therapy and 72 of whom received nocturnal oxygen therapy. Following six months of treatment, both groups demonstrated slight improvements compared to normal controls on three individual neuropsychological measures (sequencing ability, simple motor speed, and motor strength). When a subsample of 37 participants was examined following 12 months of treatment, the continuous oxygen therapy group exhibited improved performance relative to the nocturnal therapy group on three of five neuropsychological summary measures (i.e., WAIS Performance IQ, HRB Average Impairment Rating, and Brain Age Quotient). No significant improvement, however, was noted on measures of emotional functioning or quality of life. In a smaller sample of 10 hypoxemic COPD participants followed through three months of treatment, COPD was associated with poorer baseline attention, information-processing speed, and memory relative to age-matched normal controls (Hjalmarsen et al., 1999). Although neuropsychological performance among the COPD participants subjectively improved following treatment, changes were not statistically significant. Findings may have been due to practice effects or insufficient power. There were also no significant changes noted on measures of cerebral blood flow.

With the increasing acceptance of exercise and rehabilitation therapy in the treatment of COPD, investigators began to examine the effect of these treatments on psychological and neuropsychological functioning. Improved cognitive functioning following exercise had been previously observed in older individuals, and potentially related to reduced postexercise sympathetic hyperarousal and improved neurotransmitter regulation associated with greater oxygen carrying capacity of the blood (Dustman et al., 1984). A number of studies have subsequently examined the effects of exercise and rehabilitation on cognitive functioning in COPD patients. Emery et al. (1998) examined psychological and cognitive outcomes in participants with COPD randomized to a 10-week exercise plus education and stress management condition as compared to those randomized to education and stress management only and a wait-list control. While no improvement in pulmonary functioning was observed, the exercise group demonstrated improved physical endurance and reduced symptoms of anxiety and depression. Interestingly, depressive symptoms also declined in the wait-list control group (Emery et al., 1998). Participants in the exercise group demonstrated improved verbal fluency/verbal processing, suggesting some possible improvement in frontal lobe executive functions. No group differences emerged on measures of attention, motor speed, and mental efficiency. The authors hypothesized that changes in the release and re-uptake of neurotransmitters and in sympathetic nervous system activity associated with the exercise intervention may have led to the observed improvements in mood and cognition, but no direct evidence of this was given. Emery et al. (2001) also demonstrated a similar improvement in cognitive functioning in participants with COPD *immediately* following exercise. Both COPD patients and healthy controls completed a brief neuropsychological test battery immediately before and immediately after both an exercise condition (bicycle stress test) and a video-viewing control condition. Neither group improved following the control condition, and the COPD group demonstrated improved verbal fluency/verbal processing postexercise, superior to that seen in the normal controls (Emery et al., 2001). Improved neurotransmitter functioning postexercise was hypothesized to contribute to the changes observed in the COPD participants, but this study remains to be replicated.

Long-term changes in neuropsychological functioning following exercise interventions have also been studied (Emery et al., 2003; Etnier & Berry, 2001). Etnier and Berry (2001) found an apparent association between improved performance on a measure of fluid intelligence and aerobic fitness following a 3-month exercise intervention in participants with COPD. Participants were subsequently randomized into either a 15-month structured exercise program or a control condition in which they were simply encouraged to continue exercising. At follow-up, there were no group differences in cognitive performance, although findings suggested that individual subjects demonstrating the greatest improvement in aerobic fitness also showed the greatest improvement on a measure of fluid intelligence. Their findings suggest that relatively short exercise interventions can lead to improved cognitive functioning. Emery et al. (2003) examined the relationship between adherence and the long-term effects of exercise treatment in a sample of 28 COPD participants who had completed a 10-week exercise intervention. Participants were re-assessed 1 year after treatment and determined to be exercise adherent or nonadherent. While no subsequent improvements were noted, adherent participants maintained gains in physical endurance and cognitive functioning made following the 10-week intervention. In contrast, nonadherent participants exhibited decline at follow-up on measures of physical endurance, cognitive functioning (psychomotor speed and sequencing), and psychological symptoms (increased depression and anxiety). While continued adherence with exercise interventions did not result in continuing improvement in neuropsychological functioning, it may have been a protective factor, maintaining previous gains and preventing further decline.

The National Emphysema Treatment Trial (NETT) demonstrated that non-high-risk COPD patients undergoing lung-volume reduction surgery exhibited significant improvement on measures of both physical functioning and quality of life ("The National Emphysema Treatment Trial [NETT]: How strong is the evidence?," 2003). Kozora et al. (2005) examined neuropsychological functioning in a sample of 39 participants with emphysema and 39 matched controls at baseline, following 6–10 weeks of rehabilitation, and 6 months

post-randomization to either lung-volume reduction surgery ($n = 19$) or continuing medical therapy ($n = 20$). At follow-up, participants undergoing lung-volume reduction surgery improved on measures of delayed verbal recall and sequential psychomotor skills, and had a trend toward improved verbal naming (Kozora et al., 2005). Additionally, lung-volume reduction surgery was associated with reduced depressive symptoms and improved quality of life. Participants in the medical therapy condition improved only on one measure of accuracy of visual attention at follow-up, and also exhibited an increase in depressive symptoms. The potential mechanisms contributing to this change were difficult to identify, as improvements in the surgery group relative to the medical therapy group could not be accounted for by changes in physical endurance, pulmonary function, psychological symptoms, or medication changes, although improved quality of life may have influenced improved neuropsychological functioning.

Obstructive Sleep Apnea

OSA is a sleep disorder that affects at least 4% of middle-aged men and 2% of middle-aged women (Young et al., 1993) and 70% of older men and 56% of older women (Ancoli-Israel et al., 1991). It is a well-recognized clinical disorder characterized by repeated obstructions of the upper airway during sleep. OSA results in sleep fragmentation that disrupts the normal sleep architecture and periodic oxygen desaturations that can drop to dangerously low levels. Sleep fragmentation and hypoxemia are generally inextricably tied in OSA, making it difficult to make explicit statements regarding the independent effects on any single cognitive factor. Primarily correlative techniques have been used to try to tease the effects apart.

Neuropsychological Functioning and OSA. OSA can cause significant daytime behavioral and adaptive deficits. Functional impairments like sleepiness, impaired driving, increased risk of accidents, and decreased quality of life are frequent consequences of sleep apnea (Engleman & Douglas, 2004; George & Smiley, 1999). Behavioral effects of OSA are often referred to as "neurobehavioral" consequences because they are presumed to be directly related to brain function (Beebe, 2005). Neurobehavioral functioning is a broad term that includes several specific cognitive functions. Numerous studies have examined these specific cognitive functions and some have attempted to identify a "pattern" of cognitive dysfunction in OSA. Such patterns, when they exist, will be summarized below. Following that summary, theoretical models describing potential mechanisms involved in this relationship are discussed.

Neurocognitive testing is common in studies involving OSA. The cognitive sequelae of the disorder have been repeatedly discussed, but are not always consistent across studies (e.g., Aloia et al., 2004; Engleman et al., 2000; Sateia, 2003). Some inconsistencies may be associated with the heterogeneity of the samples, while others may be the result of the different tests utilized in the studies. Too few studies utilize the same cognitive tests to draw any definitive conclusions as to the degree or pattern of cognitive deficits in OSA.

Cognition in OSA has been examined as both a unitary function and one divided into several specific domains (e.g., memory, attention, executive functioning, etc.). The utility of each type of examination depends upon the question being asked and the degree to which each approach would adequately address a given hypothesis. Studies of global impairment may be better suited for addressing the overall effects of a particular variable on cognition. Impaired cognition among OSA patients is not, however, global. In fact, apnea patients may exhibit relatively few deficits in the global cognitive domain when compared to normal controls (for review see Aloia et al., 2004). Studies that limit themselves to global functioning may not have a true appreciation for the various components of cognition that contribute to this global score, and specific cognitive deficits can be masked. Domain-specific hypotheses can remedy this problem. Domains can be divided in several ways, but common domain names include executive functioning, memory, attention, vigilance, visuospatial ability, constructional ability, psychomotor functioning, and language. One should remember, however, that each of these domains may also have subdomains that further break apart their complex nature (e.g.,

executive functioning) and that domains are not mutually exclusive in their functions. For OSA patients, the domains of cognitive functioning may be differentially affected. Vigilance, including sustained attention, controlled attention, efficiency of information processing, and response time, is the most commonly assessed cognitive construct in OSA and has been found to be the most consistently affected cognitive domain in apnea patients.

Executive functioning, which includes processes involved in planning, initiation, and the execution of goal-oriented behavior and mental flexibility, is another affected domain. Some argue that it is the most prominent area of cognitive impairment in untreated sleep-disordered breathing and that the dysfunction extends to children with sleep apnea as well as adults (Beebe & Gozal, 2002). The broad construct of executive functioning makes it difficult to accurately describe the deficits and to construct a model explaining causes of the impairment. Examples of executive functioning include working memory, set shifting, perseveration, planning, abstract reasoning, and verbal fluency. Even more, executive functions are in part supported by adequate attention. Therefore, complex attentional problems could represent the root cause of executive dysfunction. Despite its being a broad construct, OSA patients clearly perform consistently more poorly on tests of executive functioning than matched controls (Bedard et al., 1991, 1993; Feuerstein et al., 1997; Naegele et al., 1995; Salorio et al., 2002; Verstraeten et al., 1997). Several investigators have documented executive dysfunction in OSA. Initially, these findings allude to frontal lobe deficits associated with the disorder (Beebe & Gozal, 2002). Such a theory is supported by animal studies and neuroimaging, but foundation functions like attention might also contribute to what is seen to be prominent executive dysfunction. Moreover, the cause of executive dysfunction is often complex.

Learning and memory are also impaired in patients with OSA. Learning and memory constitute a broad, complex domain that includes verbal memory, visual memory, short-term memory, and long-term memory. Memory performance deficits can be attributed to several areas: initial learning, free recall, or forgetfulness, each of which has different implications

(Aloia et al., 2004). OSA patients perform more poorly on tests of memory and learning than matched controls (e.g., Aloia et al., 2004; Feuerstien et al., 1997; Naegele et al., 1995). A recent study, which examined the specific type of memory impairment in OSA by comparing performance on tests of list learning, procedural memory, and working memory (a combination function including executive functions as well as memory), found the most compelling evidence for cognitive dysfunction in OSA exists in working memory. At first glance this finding suggests that executive dysfunction could tip the scales in favor of working memory being the most commonly affected memory impairment in OSA. However, another recent study attempted to parse out the various cognitive functions underlying working memory to determine in fact whether or not working memory deficits were primarily the result of learning impairments, free recall impairments, motor dyscoordination, or executive dysfunction. This study concluded that the impairments were most commonly seen on complete tests of working memory than on any specific cognitive subfunction. This suggests that this construct may be quite sensitive to the consequences of OSA.

Psychomotor performance is a domain that has been assessed less frequently. Most studies, however, show OSA patients to be impaired in psychomotor performance relative to controls (see Aloia et al., 2004 for review). Specifically, OSA patients perform relatively poorer on tests of fine motor coordination (Bédard et al., 1991, 1993; Greenberg et al., 1987; Verstraeten et al., 1997). Not all studies have reported impairment on tests of motor speed (Knight et al., 1987; Verstraeten et al., 1997). Overall, there has been relatively little discussion of this domain as a primary source of impairment. The mechanism for psychomotor dysfunction is not clear. One explanation for psychomotor difficulties is excessive sleepiness, but this does not account for the discrepancy between tests of fine motor skills and motor speed.

Few studies have been conducted examining cognitive dysfunction associated with OSA in older adults. A large-scale study in France reported that participant reports of snoring and/or breathing cessation during sleep were associated with greater impairment on tests of attention and information processing, even after controlling for several extraneous variables (Ohayon & Vecchierini, 2002). These findings were significantly associated with cognition only when daytime sleepiness was also reported. A longitudinal study employed more stringent criteria for diagnosing OSA. Ancoli-Israel and colleagues examined the sleep and global cognitive functioning of 46 community-dwelling older adults over the course of 4 years (Cohen-Zion et al., 2001), finding that increases in apnea severity and daytime sleepiness were associated with respective decreases in global cognitive functioning over time. Moreover, the findings seemed to be driven by daytime sleepiness when regression models were employed. An intriguing study by Antonelli Incalzi and colleagues compared older individuals with sleep apnea to patients with either AD or MID on a battery of neuropsychological tests (Antonelli Incalzi et al., 2004). This study suggested that the cognitive profile of apnea is most like that seen in MID. They relate this finding to the probable involvement of subcortical brain regions in apnea, a relationship that has also been posited by other investigators (Aloia et al., 2003, 2004).

Posttreatment Neuropsychological Functioning in OSA. The most common and effective treatment for OSA is positive airway pressure (PAP). When properly used, PAP has been shown to dramatically reduce morbidity and mortality (Campos-Rodriguez et al., 2005; He et al., 1988; Keenan et al., 1994). Due in part to these encouraging findings, the effect that PAP treatment has on cognition has been an area of interest for many investigators. Long-term adherence to PAP treatment, however, is less than optimal, with approximately 25% of patients discontinuing use within a year (McArdle et al., 1999). Commonly cited reasons for poor adherence include physical discomfort as well as psychosocial factors (Aloia et al., 2001, 2005a; Hoffstein et al., 1992; Kribbs et al., 1993; Waldhorn et al., 1990).

Aloia and colleagues published a critical review of the literature on the neuropsychological sequelae of OSA. They concluded that the majority of studies examining the connection between PAP and OSA have indeed cited a positive relationship between treatment adherence and improved performance on various cognitive tests. Response to treatment, however, may be a factor of the particular test being measured. Just as some tests are more sensitive to dysfunction, some are likely to be more sensitive to the effects of treatment.

Ancoli-Israel and colleagues examined the effect of continuous PAP (CPAP) treatment on cognitive function in patients with mild-to-moderate AD and OSA. Results suggested that 3 weeks of CPAP treatment, with an average of 5 hours of use a night, resulted in improvements in episodic verbal learning and memory and some aspects of executive functioning such as cognitive flexibility, and mental processing speed (Ancoli-Israel et al., 2006).

Two recent studies concluded that the number of hours of CPAP adherence needs to be evaluated when examining other outcome measures. Zimmerman et al. (2006) split a group of memory-impaired OSA patients into three adherence groups based on average PAP use at three months. The reference group for the study comprised poor users—those using 1 or fewer hours per night on average. Moderate users (2–5 hours' use a night) were 3 times as likely to develop normal memory over 3 months with PAP compared to poor users. This was not a significant effect. Optimal users (6 or more hours a night), however, were 8 times as likely to normalize their memory compared to poor users at 3 months. This finding was not due to baseline differences in memory or any other intervening variables, suggesting that it takes as many as 6 hours of use per night to normalize memory in OSA patients who demonstrated memory impairments at baseline.

In a second study of adherence, Weaver et al. (2007) demonstrated that subjective sleepiness can change with as little as 4 hours of CPAP use a night, while objective sleepiness (as measured by the Multiple Sleep Latency Test) might take 6 hours of use, and changes to functional outcomes associated with sleepiness might require over 7 hours of use per night. These two studies demonstrate that adherence as well as test sensitivity and specificity must be incorporated into efficacy trials.

Potential Mechanisms for Neurobehavioral Dysfunction in OSA. The theoretical models discussed below propose certain mechanisms that may be involved in the relationship between OSA and cognition. Beebe and Gozal hypothesized that OSA has a predilection for affecting the frontal lobes of the brain compared to other brain regions. Two primary mechanisms (i.e., sleep fragmentation and hypoxemia) were outlined as the causes of frontal lobe dysfunction (Beebe & Gozal, 2002). The model suggested that OSA has a predilection for affecting the frontal lobes of the brain compared to other brain regions. Hypoxemia is thought to result in cellular changes to the prefrontal cortex that directly affects function, while sleep fragmentation is posited to preferentially affect the frontal lobes of the brain by disrupting the normal restorative process of sleep. Together, hypoxemia and sleep fragmentation adversely affect the executive functioning of the frontal lobes. Sleep deprivation studies provide evidence for this model by showing a strong relationship to executive functions. The executive model has several strengths. First, it was one of the first models to thoughtfully take a neurofunctional approach to explain the cognitive dysfunction seen in OSA. The model also employed both basic and clinical studies as evidence. There were, however, some weaknesses to the model. Data from carbon monoxide poisoning studies and sleep deprivation studies were extrapolated to the conditions of hypoxemia and sleep fragmentation in general. These analogies may or may not be appropriate. In addition, the effects of sleep fragmentation and hypoxemia on brain regions other than frontal lobes were not incorporated into this early model. Finally, as mentioned above, executive dysfunction is complex and multifactorial, something acknowledged by the authors. Regardless of this criticism, the authors undertook a very complex task: to develop a comprehensive, neurofunctional model of OSA.

Another proposed model is the attentional model. Certainly attentional problems have been implicated in OSA. Verstraeten and Cluydts (2004) have recently published two papers making the case that higher-order cognitive dysfunction in OSA can be explained by the impairment of basic attentional processes and slowed mental processing. The first paper proposed a theoretical model of neurocognitive functioning marked by the hierarchical ordering of cognitive processes that can lead to the appearance of higher-order cognitive dysfunction. This theoretical paper is quite interesting as it is the first to recognize that higher-order cognitive processes are complex enough to often rely on more basic attentional and lower-level cognitive processes. The authors made the case that executive dysfunction per se should be interpreted cautiously in the case of sleep apnea, given the potentially profound effects of sleep disruption on arousal, basic processing speed, and attentional ability. The conclusion of this paper is that investigators should consider developing studies that allow them to systematically control for lower-level functions in the assessment of high-order cognitive ability. The second study attempted to demonstrate this theory by fractionating these functions to determine the degree to which the reliance of higher-order functions on attention can lead to the misinterpretation when considering the functional deficits in OSA. Deficits in OSA patients were seen in processing speed, attentional capacity, and short-term memory span, with no differences seen in executive functions per se. The investigators provided these data as evidence for this hierarchical model of dysfunction in OSA, making the case that executive dysfunction may be misinterpreted without knowledge of lower-order skills. This series of studies is quite compelling and encourages investigators to consider cognitive functions in a hierarchical manner (Verstraeten et al., 2004). Indeed, identifying the basic functional deficits that underlie these more complex deficits can lead to a better understanding of the neurofunctional mechanisms impaired in OSA. The one lacking component of this work is the provision of data to support any specific mechanisms related to sleep fragmentation or hypoxemia. Future research will undoubtedly address this gap in the model and may augment the executive model described above.

The microvascular theory as a model for cognitive dysfunction in OSA was first put forth by Aloia and colleagues in 2004, owing in large part to the work of Somers and colleagues (Lanfranchi & Somers, 2001). Aloia and colleagues culled mechanisms of dysfunction from the cardiovascular literature and determined that since cardiovascular dysfunction was a well-supported consequence of OSA it was reasonable that vascular compromise might also exist in the brain. It was determined, on the basis of hypoxia literature (Caine & Watson, 2000), that hypoxemia would preferentially affect regions of the brain that were metabolically active during the event and fed by small vessels. Damage to the small vessels might in fact precede large vessel stroke and may result in a predictable pattern of cognitive dysfunction associated with small vessel brain disease. The pattern would involve deficits in motor speed and coordination, executive dysfunction, memory impairment, and some problems with attention and mental processing speed. After a review of the literature, Aloia and colleagues argued that this pattern of cognitive dysfunction was indeed present in OSA and may represent microvascular disease. Several supporting studies for this model were presented, highlighting the involvement of the white matter in OSA, an area fed primarily by small vessels and susceptible to ischemic disease. Functional and structural studies were presented, though few had been completed at the time of the original publication. In closing the paper, it was demonstrated in a small sample that evidence of microvascular disease could be seen on brain MRI in OSA. Since the publication of this review, several studies have been published to support and refute this model. One supportive study identified a subgroup of OSA patients with cognitive dysfunction that likened a pattern seen in MID. However, other studies have failed to find an association between white matter ischemic disease and OSA severity using large-scale epidemiological data in older adults. One primary limitation of the model was that it did not attend strongly to the differential effects of sleep fragmentation and hypoxemia. The model is promising in that it is parsimonious and incorporates a known mechanism of dysfunction in OSA, vascular compromise, into the cognitive realm. Further research, however, is needed to defend, refute, or expand the model and to relate its effects to complaints of fatigue and sleepiness.

The most recent model, posited by Beebe (Beebe, 2005), is the most comprehensive to date and pulls upon the strengths of previous models to develop a heuristic model of the mechanisms underlying cognitive dysfunction in OSA.

He hypothesized that the effects of sleep fragmentation and hypoxemia are not likely to be effectively isolated from one another. He stated that their interaction may in fact be synergistic. Moreover, he presented the likelihood that these mechanisms interact with certain vulnerable brain regions, highlighting specifically the hippocampus, the prefrontal cortex, subcortical gray matter, and white matter. The inclusion of the subcortical gray and white matter reflects an appreciation for the potential involvement of the small vessels of the brain. Beebe also attended to the possibility that findings in studies of the potential mechanisms of cognitive dysfunction are dependent in part on task demands and the environment under which testing is conducted. This addition shows an appreciation for the complexity of executive dysfunction as multifactorial and broadens the executive and attentional models by including several other cognitive tasks that may be impaired in OSA simply due to the demands that they present for the implicated brain regions. Finally, Beebe went beyond the other models by incorporating two additional areas to consider: (1) risk and resilience factors, and (2) direct effects on cognition outside of those involved in OSA. When discussing risk and resilience, Beebe acknowledged recent work by Alchanatis and colleagues showing that there may be moderators of dysfunction in OSA; for example, intelligence has been proposed as one moderator for vigilance problems in OSA (Alchanatis et al., 2005). This study identified cognitive reserve (high premorbid cognitive ability that results in resistance to cognitive decline with insult) as a resilience factor, but the heuristic model also includes age, sex, sociodemographic factors, and duration of illness. Others have also proposed the inclusion of moderators of dysfunction noting that several patients with severe OSA do not suffer dysfunction at all, while others with mild OSA show significant impairment. Finally, the model incorporates genetic endowment, prior experience with testing, and sociodemographic factors as possible extraneous variables when considering the mechanisms of cognitive dysfunction in OSA. The model needs to be tested, but there are more strengths to this model than there are weaknesses. The model is testable with large datasets and is more inclusive

than previous models. It is not, however, overly inclusive and specifies brain regions likely to be involved without implying that all regions are equally vulnerable. Perhaps most importantly, the model highlights the likely effect of moderating factors for cognitive impairment in OSA, something that has only recently been addressed in the literature.

Acute Respiratory Distress Syndrome

ARDS results from injury to the microvasculature of the lungs, which can lead to leakage of fluid into the alveoli resulting in hypoxemia, dyspnea, and in some cases death. ARDS is generally seen in hospitalized patients with severe illnesses, including sepsis, pneumonia, severe blood loss, chest and head injuries, aspiration of stomach contents, and breathing injurious fumes. The syndrome affects roughly 13–18 people per 100,000, with prevalence rates between 15% and 18% among ventilated patients. ARDS can result in death, with mortality rates between 35% and 70%. Few studies have examined the cognitive effects of ARDS. Hopkins and her colleagues have conducted the majority of these studies in an attempt to provide evidence for cognitive dysfunction, identify the pattern of dysfunction, and address the consequences of such dysfunction in longitudinal designs (Hopkins et al., 2004, 2005, 2006; Hopkins & Herridge, 2006). In general, there are consistent findings of cognitive dysfunction in ARDS. Global cognitive function is impaired in the majority of patients immediately following discharge. There is some recovery of function over the first year after discharge, but Hopkins et al. (2005) have demonstrated that cognitive dysfunction can persist as long as 2 years after discharge. One additional study documented cognitive dysfunction as long as 6 years postdischarge, raising concerns over long-lasting and permanent damage to the brain (Rothenhausler et al., 2001). Indeed, neuroimaging studies have demonstrated early evidence of cortical atrophy (Hopkins et al., 2006). Objective and subjective data suggest that the majority of the cognitive deficits in ARDS fall into the realm of memory, with some impairment occurring in executive functioning, with psychomotor speed and impulsivity contributing to these deficits.

This is surprisingly consistent with the OSA data presented above. Even more compelling is that the ARDS cognitive data do not correlate with illness severity, age, or smoking history. These data mirror much of what has been demonstrated in OSA and call into question the presence of moderators that may make certain individuals more susceptible to the effects of hypoxemia compared to others.

Conclusions and Comments

This chapter covered the effects that hypoxia has on neuropsychological functioning in several different medical conditions. In closing, it appears clear that hypoxemia and hypoxia have unmistakable detrimental effects on cognitive functioning. It is also obvious, however, that these findings are not necessarily pervasive across all patients. The focus of positive studies to date has been on the mediators of cognitive dysfunction in disease states, including hypoxia. Future studies should also attempt to tackle the question of moderators of cognitive dysfunction in persons with hypoxic conditions. For example, studies have demonstrated that high cognitive reserve spares some individuals with OSA from developing cognitive problems (Alchanatis et al., 2005). Investigators have also considered the possibility of substances that are thought to be protective from inflammation (e.g., antioxidants) as potential moderators of dysfunction (Baldwin et al., 2005). Genetic factors are also only now being considered. Probably, our understanding of the role of hypoxia in cognitive dysfunction will only be made clear with these mediator and moderator studies. The future of this line of research is appealing, and the need for additional studies remains strong.

References

Alchanatis, M., Zias, N., Deligiorgis, N., Amfilochiou, A., Dionellis, G., & Orphanidou, D. (2005). Sleep apnea-related cognitive deficits and intelligence: An implication of cognitive reserve theory. *Journal of Sleep Research, 14*, 69–75.

Aloia, M. S., Arnedt, J. T., Davis, J. D., Riggs, R. L., & Byrd, D. (2004). Neuropsychological consequences of sleep apnea: A critical review. *Journal of the International Neuropsychological Society, 10*, 772–785.

Aloia, M. S., Arnedt, J. T., Stepnowsky Jr., C. J., Hecht, J., & Borrelli, B. (2005a). Predicting treatment adherence in obstructive sleep apnea using principles of behavior change. *Journal of Clinical Sleep Medicine, 1*(4), 346–353.

Aloia, M. S., DiDio, P., Ilniczky, N., Perlis, M. L., Greenblatt, D. W., & Giles, D. E. (2001). Improving compliance with nasal CPAP and vigilance in older adults with OSAHS. *Sleep and Breathing, 5*(1), 13–21.

Aloia, M. S., Ilniczky, N., Di Dio, P., Perlis, M. L., Greenblatt, D. W., & Giles, D. E. (2003). Neuropsychological changes and treatment compliance in older adults with sleep apnea. *Journal of Psychosomatic Research, 54*(1), 71–76.

Aloia, M. S., Stanchina, M. L., Arnedt, J. T., Malhotra, A., & Millman, R. P. (2005b). Treatment adherence and outcomes in flexible versus continuous positive airway pressure therapy. *Chest, 127*(6), 2085–2093.

Ancoli-Israel, S., Kripke, D. F., Klauber, M. R., Mason, W. J., Fell, R., & Kaplan, O. (1991). Sleep disordered breathing in community dwelling elderly. *Sleep, 14*(6), 486–495.

Ancoli-Israel, S., Palmer, B. W., Marler, M., Corey-Bloom, J., Loredo, J. S., & Liu, L. (2006). Effect of CPAP on cognition in Alzheimer's patients with apnea. *Sleep, 29*, A106.

Antonelli Incalzi, R., Chiappini, F., Fuso, L., Torrice, M. P., Gemma, A., & Pistilli, R. (1998). Predicting cognitive decline in patients with hypoxaemic COPD. *Respiratory Medicine, 92*, 527–533.

Antonelli Incalzi, R., Gemma, A., Marra, C., Muzzolon, R., Capparella, O., & Carbonin, P. U. (1993). Chronic obstructive pulmonary disease: An original model of cognitive decline. *American Review of Respiratory Diseases, 148*, 418–424.

Antonelli Incalzi, R., Carhonin, P., Gemma, A., Capparella, O., Marra, C., & Fuso, L. (1997). Verbal memory impairment in COPD: Its mechanisms and clinical relevance. *Chest, 112*, 1506–1513.

Antonelli Incalzi, R., Marra, C., Giordano, A., Calcagni, M. L., Cappa, A., Basso, S., et al. (2003). Cognitive impairment in chronic obstructive pulmonary disease: A neuropsychological and SPECT study. *Journal of Neurology, 250*, 325–332.

Antonelli Incalzi, R., Marra, C., Salvigni, B. L., Petrone, A., Gemma, A., Selvaggio, D., et al. (2004). Does cognitive dysfunction conform to a distinctive pattern in obstructive sleep apnea? *Journal of Sleep Research, 13*, 79–86.

Baldwin, C. M., Bootzin, R. R., Schwenke, D. C., & Quan, S. F. (2005). Antioxidant nutrient intake and supplements as potential moderators of cognitive decline and cardiovascular disease in obstructive sleep apnea. *Sleep Medicine Reviews, 9*(6), 459–476.

Bédard, M. A., Montplaisir, J., Malo, J., Richer, F., & Rouleau, I. (1993). Persistent neuropsychological deficits and vigilance impairment in sleep apnea syndrome after treatment with continuous positive airways pressure (CPAP). *Journal of Clinical and Experimental Neuropsychology, 15*(2), 330–341.

Bédard, M. A., Montplaisir, J., Richer, F., Rouleau, I., & Malo, J. (1991). Obstructive sleep apnea syndrome: Pathogenesis of neuropsychological deficits. *Journal of Clinical and Experimental Neuropsychology, 13*(6), 950–964.

Beebe, D. (2005). Neurobehavioral effects of obstructive sleep apnea: An overview and heuristic model. *Current Opinion in Pulmonary Medicine, 11*, 494–500.

Beebe, D., & Gozal, D. (2002). Obstructive sleep apnea and the prefrontal cortex: Towards a comprehensive model linking noctural upper airway obstruction to daytime cognitive and behavioral deficits. *Journal of Sleep Research, 11*, 1–16.

Caine, D., & Watson, J. D. G. (2000). Neuropsychological and neuropathological sequelae of cerebral anoxia: A critical review. *Journal of the International Neuropsychological Society, 6*, 86–99.

Campos-Rodriguez, F., Pena-Grinan, N., Reyes-Nunez, N., De la Cruz-Moron, I., Perez-Ronchel, J., De la Vega-Gallardo, F., et al. (2005). Mortality in obstructive sleep apnea-hypopnea patients treated with positive airway pressure. *Chest, 128*(2), 624–633.

Cohen-Zion, M., Stepnowsky Jr., C. J., Marler, M. R., Shochat, T., Kripke, D., & Ancoli Israel, S. (2001). Changes in cognitive function associated with sleep disordered breathing in older people. *Journal of the American Geriatric Society, 49*(12), 1622–1627.

Dustman, R. E., Rughling, R. O., Russell, E. M., Shearer, D. E., Bonekat, H. W., Shigeoka, J. W., et al. (1984). Aerobic exercise training and improved neuropsychological function of older individuals. *Neurobiology of Aging, 5*(1), 35–42.

Emery, C., Schein, R., Hauck, E., & MacIntyre, N. (1998). Psychological and cognitive outcomes of a randomized trial of exercise among patients with chronic obstructive pulmonary disease. *Health Psychology, 17*, 232–240.

Emery, C., Shermer, R., Hauck, E., Hsiao, E., & MacIntyre, N. (2003). Cognitive and psychological outcomes of exercise in a 1-year follow-up study of patients with chronic obstructive pulmonary disease. *Health Psychology, 22*, 598–604.

Emery, C. F., Honn, V. J., Frid, D. J., Lebowitz, K. R., & Diaz, P. T. (2001). Acute effects of exercise on

cognition in patients with chronic obstructive pulmonary disease. *American Journal of Respiratory and Critical Care Medicine, 164*(9), 1624–1627.

Engleman, H., Kingshott, R. N., Martin, S. E., & Douglas, N. J. (2000). Cognitive function in the sleep apnea/hypopnea syndrome. *Sleep, 23*, S102–S108.

Engleman, H. M., & Douglas, N. J. (2004). Sleepiness, cognitive function, and quality of life in obstructive sleep apnoea/hypopnoea syndrome. *Thorax, 59*, 618–622.

Etnier, J., & Berry, M. (2001). Fluid intelligence in an older COPD sample after short- or long-term exercise. *Medicine and Science in Sports and Exercise, 33*, 1620–1628.

Etnier, J., Johnston, R., Dagenbach, D., Pollard, J., Rejeski, W. J., & Berry, M. (1999). The relationships among pulmonary function, aerobig fitness, and cognitive functioning in older COPD patients. *Chest, 116*, 953–960.

Feuerstein, C., Naegele, B., Pepin, J. L., & Levy, P. (1997). Frontal lobe-related cognitive functions in patients with Sleep Apnea Syndrome before and after treatment. *Acta Neurologica Belgica, 97*, 96–107.

George, C. F., & Smiley, A. (1999). Sleep apnea and automobile crashes. *Sleep, 22*(6), 790–795.

Grant, I., Heaton, R., McSweeney, A., Adams, K., & Timms, R. (1982). Neuropsychologic findings in hypoxemic chronic obstructive pulmonary disease. *Archives of Internal Medicine, 142*, 1470–1476.

Grant, I., Prigatano, G., Heaton, R., McSweeny, A., Wright, E., & Adams, K. (1987). Progressive neuropsychologic impairment and hypoxemia: Relationship in chronic obstructive pulmonary disease. *Archives of General Psychiatry, 44*, 999–1006.

Greenberg, G. D., Watson, R. K., & Deptula, D. (1987). Neuropsychological dysfunction in sleep apnea. *Sleep, 10*(3), 254–262.

He, J., Kryger, M. H., Zorick, F., Conway, W., & Roth, T. (1988). Mortality and apnea index in obstructive sleep apnea: Experience in 385 male patients. *Chest, 94*, 9–14.

Heaton, R., Grant, I., McSweeney, A., Adams, K., Petty, T., & the NOTT Study Group. (1983). Psychologic effects of continuous and nocturnal oxygen therapy in hypoxemic chronic obstructive pulmonary disease. *Archives of Internal Medicine, 143*, 1941–1947.

Hjalmarsen, A., Waterloo, K., Dahl, A., Jorde, R., & Viitanen, M. (1999). Effect of long-term oxygen therapy on cognitive and neurological dysfunction in chronic obstructive pulmonary disease. *European Neurology, 42*, 27–35.

Hoffstein, V., Viner, S., & Mateika, S. (1992). Treatment of obstructive sleep apnea with nasal continuous positive airway pressure. Patient compliance, perception of benefits, and side effects. *American Review of Respiratory Diseases, 145*, 841–845.

Hopkins, R. O., & Herridge, M. S. (2006). Quality of life, emotional abnormalities, and cognitive dysfunction in survivors of acute lung injury/acute respiratory distress syndrome. *Clinical Chest Medicine, 27*(4), 679–689.

Hopkins, R. O., Gale, S. D., & Weaver, L. K. (2006). Brain atrophy and cognitive impairment in survivors of Acute Respiratory Distress Syndrome. *Brain Injury, 20*(3), 263–271.

Hopkins, R. O., Weaver, L. K., Collingridge, D., Parkinson, R. B., Chan, K. J., & Orme, J. F., Jr. (2005). Two-year cognitive, emotional, and quality of life outcomes in acute respiratory distress syndrome. *American Journal of Respiratory and Critical Care Medicine, 171*(4), 340–347.

Hopkins, R. O., Weaver, L. K., Chan, K. J., & Orme, J. F., Jr. (2004). Quality of life, emotional, and cognitive function following acute respiratory distress syndrome. *Journal of the International Neuropsychological Society, 10*(7), 1005–1017.

Keenan, S. P., Burt, H., Ryan, F., & Fleetham, J. A. (1994). Long-term survival of patients with obstructive sleep apnea treated by uvulopalatopharyngoplasty or nasal CPAP. *Chest, 105*, 155–159.

Knight, H., Millman, R. P., Gur, R. C., Saykin, A. J., Doherty, J. U., & Pack, A. I. (1987). Clinical significance of sleep apnea in the elderly. *American Review of Respiratory Disease, 136*(4), 845–850.

Kozora, E., Emery, C., Ellison, M., Wamboldt, F., Diaz, P., & Make, B. (2005). Improved neurobehavioral functioning in emphysema patients following lung volume reduction surgery compared with medical therapy. *Chest, 128*, 2653–2663.

Kozora, E., Filley, C., Julian, L., & Cullum, C. (1999). Cognitive functioning in patients with chronic obstructive pulmonary disease and mild hypoxemia compared with patients with mild Alzheimer disease and normal controls. *Journal of Neuropsychiatry, Neuropsychology, and Behavioral Neurology, 12*, 178–183.

Kribbs, N. B., Pack, A. I., Kline, L. R., Smith, P. L., Schwartz, A. R., Schubert, N. M., et al. (1993). Objective measurement of patterns of nasal CPAP use by patients with obstructive sleep apnea. *American Review of Respiratory Diseases, 147*, 887–895.

Krop, H., Block, A., & Cohen, E. (1973). Neuropsychologic effects of continuous oxygen therapy in chronic obstructive pulmonary disease. *Chest, 64*, 317–322.

Lanfranchi, P., & Somers, V. K. (2001). Obstructive sleep apnea and vascular disease. *Respiratory Research, 2*, 315–319.

Liesker, J., Postma, D., Beukema, R., ten Hacken N., van der Molen, T., Riemersma, R., et al. (2004). Cognitive performance in patients with COPD. *Respiratory Medicine, 98*, 351–356.

McArdle, N., Devereux, G., Heidarnejad, H., Engleman, H. M., Mackay, T. W., & Douglas, N. J. (1999). Long-term Use of CPAP Therapy for Sleep Apnea/Hypopnea Syndrome. *American Journal of Respiratory and Critical Care Medicine, 159*(4), 1108–1114.

Naegele, B., Thouvard, V., Pepin, J. L., Levy, P., Bonnet, C., Perret, J. E., et al. (1995). Deficits of cognitive executive functions in patients with sleep apnea syndrome. *Sleep, 18*(1), 43–52.

The National Emphysema Treatment Trial: How strong is the evidence? (2003). *New England Journal of Medicine, 348*(21), 2059–2073.

Ohayon, M. M., & Vecchierini, M. F. (2002). Daytime sleepiness and cognitive impairment in the elderly population. *Archives of Internal Medicine, 162*, 201–208.

Prigatano, G., Parsons, O., Wright, E., Levin, D. C., & Hawryluk, G. (1983). Neuropsychological test performance in mildly hypoxemic patients with chronic obstructive pulmonary disease. *Journal of Consulting and Clinical Psychology, 51*, 108–116.

Rennard, S. I. (2004). Treatment of stable chronic obstructive pulmonary disease. *Lancet, 364*(9436), 791–802.

Rothenhausler, H. B., Ehrentraut, S., Stoll, C., Schelling, G., & Kapfhammer, H. P. (2001). The relationship between cognitive performance and employment and health status in long-term survivors of the acute respiratory distress syndrome: Results of an exploratory study. *General Hospital Psychiatry, 23*(2), 90–96.

Salorio, C. F., White, D. A., Piccirillo, J., & Uhles, M. L. (2002). Learning, memory, and executive control in individuals with obstructive sleep apnea syndrome. *Journal of Clinical and Experimental Neuropsychology, 24*(1), 93–100.

Sateia, M. J. (2003). Neuropsychological impairment and quality of life in obstructive sleep apnea. *Clinical Chest Medicine, 24*(2), 249–259.

Strassels, S. A. (1999). Economic consequences of chronic obstructive pulmonary disease. *Current Opinion in Pulmonary Medicine, 5*(2), 100–104.

Stuss, D., Peterkin, I., Guzman, D., Guzman, C., & Troyer, A. (1997). Chronic obstructive pulmonary disease: Effects of hypoxia on neurological and neuropsychological measures. *Journal of Clinical and Experimental Neuropsychology, 19*, 515–524.

Verstraeten, E., & Cluydts, R. (2004). Executive control of attention in sleep apnea patients: Theoretical concepts and methodological considerations. *Sleep Medicine Reviews, 8*, 257–267.

Verstraeten, E., Cluydts, R., Pevernagie, D., & Hoffmann, G. (2004). Executive function in sleep apnea: Controlling for attentional capacity in assessing executive attention. *Sleep, 27*(4), 685–693.

Verstraeten, E., Cluydts, R., Verbraecken, J., & De Roeck, J. (1997). Psychomotor and cognitive performance in nonapneic snorers: Preliminary findings. *Perceptual and Motor Skills, 84*, 1211–1222.

Waldhorn, R. E., Herrick, T. W., Nguyen, M. C., O'Donnell, A. E., Sodero, J., & Potolicchio, S. J. (1990). Long-term compliance with nasal continuous positive airway pressure therapy of obstructive sleep apnea. *Chest, 97*, 33–38.

Weaver, T. E., Maislin, G., Dinges, D. F., Bloxham, T., George, C. F., Greenberg, H., et al. (2007). Relationship between hours of CPAP use and achieving normal levels of sleepiness and daily functioning. *Sleep, 30*(6), 711–719.

Young, T., Palta, M., Dempsey, J., Skatrud, J., Weber, S., & Badr, S. (1993). The occurrence of sleep-disordered breathing among middle-aged adults. *New England Journal of Medicine, 328*(17), 1230–1235.

Zimmerman, M. E., Arnedt, J. T., Stanchina, M., Millman, R. P., & Aloia, M. S. (2006). Normalization of memory performance and positive airway pressure adherence in memory-impaired patients with obstructive sleep apnea. *Chest, 130*(6), 1772–1778.

16

Diabetes and the Brain: Cognitive Performance in Type 1 and Type 2 Diabetes

Augustina M. A. Brands and Roy P. C. Kessels

Neuropsychology traditionally examines cognitive impairments due to neurological diseases or psychiatric disorders. However, within the field of internal medicine, neuropsychology has gained attention only recently. The aim of the present chapter is to review the literature on the neuropsychology of diabetes mellitus, one of the most common systemic diseases that is becoming increasingly more prevalent, not only in older people but also in younger adults. First, we briefly introduce the diagnostic criteria for diabetes type 1 and 2, their prevalence and treatment options, and possible complications of this disease. Subsequently, the effects of diabetes on the brain will be discussed, highlighting neuroimaging findings, as well as neuropsychological correlates of diabetes type 1 and 2 and the neuropsychiatric consequences. Furthermore, we discuss possible underlying mechanisms of brain dysfunction and cognitive impairment in diabetes. Finally, we will focus on the clinical implications of these findings and discuss relevant issues that must be addressed in neuropsychological examination of these patients.

Diabetes: Some General Facts

Classification and Prevalence

Diabetes mellitus is a common metabolic disease and is characterized by high blood glucose levels (hyperglycemia). The vast majority of cases of diabetes fall into two broad etiopathogenetic categories. In one category, type 1 diabetes, the cause is an absolute deficiency of insulin secretion. Individuals at increased risk for developing this type of diabetes can often be identified by serological evidence of an autoimmune pathologic process occurring in the pancreatic islets and by genetic markers, and this form of diabetes is often diagnosed during childhood or early adulthood. In the other, much more prevalent category, type 2 diabetes, the cause is a combination of resistance to insulin action and an inadequate compensatory insulin secretory response. In the latter category, a degree of hyperglycemia sufficient to cause pathologic and functional changes in various target tissues, but without clinical symptoms may be present for a long period of time before diabetes is detected. During this asymptomatic period, it is possible to demonstrate an abnormality in carbohydrate metabolism by measurement of plasma glucose in the fasting state or after a challenge with an oral glucose load (American Diabetes Association, 2005). Type 2 diabetes is generally more prevalent in older adults.

Assigning a type of diabetes to an individual often depends on the circumstances present at the time of diagnosis, and many diabetic individuals do not easily fit into a single class. For example, a woman with gestational diabetes mellitus (GDM), which may be present during pregnancy, may continue to be hyperglycemic after delivery and may be determined to have, in fact, type 2 diabetes. Alternatively, a person who acquires diabetes because of large doses of exogenous steroids may become normoglycemic once the glucocorticoids are discontinued, but then may develop diabetes many years later after recurrent episodes of pancreatitis. The global prevalence of diabetes in adults was estimated to be 2.8% in 2000 and is estimated to rise to 4.4% by the year 2030 (Wild et al., 2004). Worldwide, the number of patients is expected to increase from 171 million in 2000 to 366 million in 2030, based solely on demographic changes (Wild et al., 2004). About 90% of these diabetic patients will suffer from type 2 diabetes.

Diagnosis of Diabetes

In diagnosing diabetes, physicians primarily depend upon the results of specific glucose tests (American Diabetes Association, 2005). However, test results are just part of the information that supports the diagnosis of diabetes. Some people who are significantly ill will have transient problems with elevated blood sugars that return to normal after the illness has resolved. In addition, medication may alter blood glucose levels, most commonly steroids and certain diuretics. The two main tests used to measure the presence of blood sugar problems are (1) the direct measurement of fasting plasma glucose (FPG) levels in the blood during an overnight fast, and (2) measurement of the body's ability to appropriately handle the excess sugar presented after consuming a high glucose drink. An oral glucose tolerance test (OGTT) requires that a person being tested performs the test in a fasting state. An initial blood glucose level is drawn and then the person is given a "glucola" bottle containing a high amount of sugar (75 g of glucose). The person then has his or her blood tested again 30 minutes, 1 hour, 2 hours, and 3 hours after drinking the high glucose drink. In a person without diabetes, the glucose levels in the blood rise after intake, but rapidly fall back to normal, because insulin is produced in response to the glucose that lowers the blood glucose. In a diabetic person, glucose levels rise stronger than normal after intake and normalize much slower or not at all. In this case, insulin is either not produced, or is produced but the cells of the body do not respond to it. In an intermediate group of people, glucose levels, although not meeting criteria for diabetes, are nevertheless too high to be considered normal.

This group is defined as having impaired FPG. The categories of FPG values are as follows:

- FPG < 100 mg/dl (5.6 mmol/l) = normal fasting glucose;
- FPG 100–125 mg/dl (5.6–6.9 mmol/l) = IFG (impaired fasting glucose);
- FPG ≥ 126 mg/dl (7.0 mmol/l) = provisional diagnosis of diabetes.

The corresponding categories when the OGTT is used are the following:

- 2-hour postload glucose < 140 mg/dl (7.8 mmol/l) = normal glucose tolerance;
- 2-hour postload glucose 140–199 mg/dl (7.8–11.1 mmol/l) = IGT (impaired glucose tolerance);
- 2-hour postload glucose ≥ 200 mg/dl (11.1 mmol/l) = provisional diagnosis of diabetes.

Patients with IFG or IGT are referred to as having "prediabetes" indicating the relatively high risk for eventual development of diabetes in these patients. In the absence of pregnancy, IFG and IGT are not clinical entities in their own right, but rather risk factors for future diabetes, as well as for cardiovascular disease. IFG and IGT are associated with the so-called metabolic syndrome, which includes obesity (especially abdominal or visceral obesity), dyslipidemia, and hypertension. Medical nutrition therapy aimed at producing 5%–10% loss of body weight, exercise, and certain pharmacological agents prevent or delay the development of diabetes in people with IGT; the potential impact of such interventions to reduce cardiovascular risk, however, has not been examined to date (American Diabetes Association, 2005).

Complications and Treatment Goals

It is well known that both type 1 and type 2 diabetes can result in several complications in the long term. These include retinopathy with potential loss of vision, nephropathy leading to renal failure, peripheral neuropathy with risk of foot ulcers, amputations, and Charcot joints, and autonomic neuropathy causing gastrointestinal, genitourinary, and cardiovascular symptoms, as well as sexual dysfunction. The characteristic clinical signs and symptoms, as well as the techniques to diagnose these complications, are well established (American Diabetes Association, 2002). Patients with diabetes also have an increased incidence of atherosclerotic cardiovascular, peripheral arterial, and cerebrovascular disease. Hypertension and abnormalities of lipoprotein metabolism are often found in people with diabetes. The development of these complications is dependent on the duration of diabetes and the level of metabolic control and are associated with increased mortality. Since both randomized trials and large cohort studies have shown that good control of blood glucose levels is associated with reduced risk of these complications (DCCT Research Group, 1996; Gaede et al., 2003; Reichard & Rosenqvist, 1989), current treatment is aimed at obtaining and maintaining normal glucose levels.

Acute Effects

In contrast to type 1 diabetes, type 2 diabetes is a disease of slow onset. Initially, compensatory increases in insulin secretion (hyperinsulinemia) maintain normal glucose concentrations by counteracting the reduced sensitivity of tissues to insulin. The aim of treatment is to maintain normal glucose levels in order to prevent the occurrence of aforementioned complications. In patients with type 2 diabetes, this treatment initially consists of dietary restrictions and exercise. Oral hypoglycemic drugs or insulin injections are prescribed in later stages.

Patients with type 1 diabetes are treated with exogenous insulin. Unfortunately, even with repeated injections or subcutaneously implanted insulin pumps, these treatments cannot fully compensate for the tightly regulated insulin secretions of a normally functioning pancreas. Therefore, individuals with type 1 diabetes may experience fluctuations in blood glucose levels throughout the day, ranging from low blood glucose levels (hypoglycemia) to high blood glucose levels (hyperglycemia). These fluctuations depend upon the timing, type, dose of insulin administration, the quantity and nutritional content of food ingested, and the amount of physical activity. Since normal cerebral functioning is dependent upon sufficient levels of continuous circulating glucose, these fluctuations can affect functioning of the brain. Symptoms of hypoglycemia include hunger, nervousness and shakiness, perspiration, dizziness or light-headedness, sleepiness, confusion, difficulty speaking, feeling anxious or weak, headache, lack of energy, and an inability to concentrate. Prolonged severe hypoglycemia may result in a hypoglycemic coma.

Symptoms of hyperglycemia are the same as those of untreated diabetes: thirst, frequent urination, vomiting, drowsiness, abdominal pain and pain in the legs, fatigue, impairment of cognitive function, depressive mood, and anxiety. Prolonged severe hyperglycemia may result in ketoacidosis. Acute hypo- and hyperglycemia have disruptive effects on the central nervous system (CNS) and, as a result, on cognitive functioning (for a review see Weinger & Jacobson, 1998).

Relatively less is known about the slowly developing end-organ damage to the CNS that may present itself as electrophysiological and structural changes and impairment of cognitive functioning. These cerebral complications of both type 1 and type 2 diabetes are referred to as "diabetic encephalopathy," a concept introduced several decades ago (Reske-Nielsen et al., 1965). In the next paragraphs, we will highlight some of the recent findings related to diabetic encephalopathy.

Long-Term Effects on the Brain

Cognitive Performance in Adults with Type 1 Diabetes

As early as 1922, it was recognized that patients with diabetes may suffer from cognitive performance deficits (Miles & Root, 1922). Since then, middle-aged individuals with type 1 diabetes have been reported to show deficits on a wide range of neuropsychological tests compared to age-matched controls. Some studies report impairments on tests relying on problem-solving skills (Deary et al., 1993), whereas other studies report deficiencies in psychomotor efficiency (Ryan et al., 1992) or memory and learning (Ryan & Williams, 1993; Sachon et al., 1992) or find no difference at all (Wredling et al., 1990).

Although the results of these studies are relatively heterogeneous with respect to the severity and nature of the affected cognitive domains, a recent meta-analysis clearly shows that cognitive function is mildly impaired in patients with type 1 diabetes relative to controls, mainly reflecting as slowing of mental speed and a diminished mental flexibility (Brands et al., 2005, see Figure 16-1). Meta analyses on case-control studies report findings in terms of effect sizes (Cohen's d) that is, the standardized difference between the experimental and the compared group (Cohen, 1988). This effect size provides information about how large a difference is evident across all studies. Compared to nondiabetic controls, the type 1 diabetic group demonstrated a significant overall lowered performance (Cohen's $d = -0.3$) as well as an impairment on the cognitive domains of overall intelligence ($d = -0.65$), implicit memory ($d = -0.75$), speed of information processing ($d = -0.26$), psychomotor efficiency ($d = -0.56$), motor speed ($d = -0.7$), visual ($d = -0.41$) and sustained attention ($d = -0.31$), cognitive flexibility ($d = -0.54$) and visual perception

($d = -0.4$). No differences in performance could be demonstrated between patients with and without recurrent severe hypoglycemic episodes.

Cognitive Performance in Older People with Type 1 Diabetes

Thus far, all studies addressing cognition in type 1 diabetes examined cognition in children or young adults. However, it could be hypothesized that the effects of type 1 diabetes on cognition might be more pronounced in older individuals. This hypothesis was recently tested in a study in which cognitive performance was assessed in 40 patients with type 1 diabetes with a mean age of 60 years and 40 matched controls. Cognitive performance was related to cerebral magnetic resonance imaging (MRI) findings and measures of psychological well-being (Brands et al., 2006). Cognition was studied by extensive neuropsychological assessment of 11 tests tapping

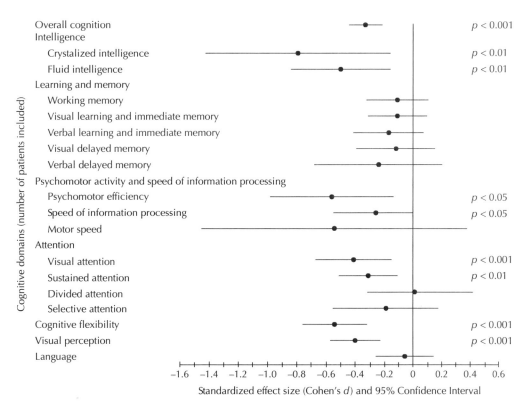

Figure 16–1. Effect sizes (Cohen's d) derived from a meta-analysis on cognitive functioning in type 1 diabetes. Adapted from Brands et al. (2005).

the major cognitive domains in both a verbal and a nonverbal way. Psychological well-being was assessed by two questionnaires. Both cortical and subcortical atrophy and periventricular and deep white matter abnormalities were rated on MRI scans, using standardized rating scales. The diabetic group performed significantly worse than controls only on speed of information processing (Cohen's $d < 0.4$). Neither significant intergroup differences were found on any of the MRI rating scales nor could cognitive performance be related to MRI findings. Type 1 diabetic patients reported significantly more depressive and cognitive complaints, but the depressive symptoms did not correlate with cognitive performance.

The pattern as well as the severity of cognitive dysfunction is comparable with the results of the meta-analysis, which included only studies using adults under the age of 50. These results suggest that there is only limited progression of cognitive deterioration over time in patients with type 1 diabetes. This is in line with the very limited progression of cognitive deterioration reported in very few longitudinal studies on cognitive functioning in type 1 diabetic patients that are available (DCCT Research Group, 1996; Diabetes Control and Complications Trial/Epidemiology of Diabetes Interventions and Complications Study Research Group et al., 2007; Reichard et al., 1996; Ryan, 2003). Future studies should examine the course of cognitive impairment in older people with diabetes type 1 in more detail in order to draw firm conclusions.

MRI Findings in Type I Diabetes

The relation between cognitive impairments and structural changes in the brain has not been investigated systematically. Thus far, only a few MRI studies of the brain in patients with type 1 diabetes have been published (e.g., Dejgaard et al., 1991; Ferguson et al., 2003, 2005; Lobnig et al., 2006; Lunetta et al., 1994; Musen et al., 2006; Perros et al., 1997; Wessels et al., 2006b; Yousem et al., 1991). Radiological abnormalities involving the subcortical white matter and both cortical and subcortical atrophy have been reported, but it has been suggested that the abnormalities based on MRI in diabetes type

1 are within the normal range (Brands et al., 2006) in that similar rates of (silent) infarcts and white matter lesion (WML) severity have been reported in random samples from the general population of the same age group (de Leeuw et al., 2001; Vermeer et al., 2003; Ylikoski et al., 1995). Other studies of brain MRI in type 1 diabetes involved younger patients (average ages 25–40 years) with an earlier disease onset (average ages at onset 10–18 years) (Dejgaard et al., 1991; Ferguson et al., 2003; Lobnig et al., 2006; Lunetta et al., 1994; Musen et al., 2006; Perros et al., 1997; Wessels et al., 2006b; Yousem et al., 1991). Some studies compared measures of cerebral atrophy (Ferguson et al., 2003; Lobnig et al., 2006; Lunetta et al., 1994; Musen et al., 2006; Perros et al., 1997; Wessels et al., 2006b; Yousem et al., 1991) or WML severity (Dejgaard et al., 1991; Lobnig et al., 2006; Yousem et al., 1991) in type 1 diabetic patients with control subjects. One study reported a 3% decrease in total cerebral volume (Lobnig et al., 2006). The most detailed studies on cerebral atrophy so far reported modest regional reductions in cortical gray matter density, using voxel based morphometry (Musen et al., 2006; Wessels et al., 2006b).

A study on WML in type 1 diabetic patients with advanced microvascular complications did not observe WML in any of these patients (Yousem et al., 1991). Others reported WML in a majority of type 1 diabetic patients, but not in controls (Dejgaard et al., 1991). Neither a history of severe hypoglycemia, nor the presence of retinopathy was associated with cerebral atrophy or WML, although retinopathy was associated with an increased occurrence of so-called enlarged perivascular spaces (Ferguson et al., 2003, 2005). Earlier onset of diabetes (<7 years) was associated with a higher ventricular volume, but not with cortical atrophy or WML severity (Ferguson et al., 2005, but see Wessels et al., 2006b). The combined results of these papers indicate that MRI changes in the brain of patients with type 1 diabetes are relatively subtle, and may be more pronounced in patients with an early diabetes onset. Probably, more sensitive neuroimaging paradigms, such as functional magnetic resonance imaging (fMRI) or single photon emission computed tomography (SPECT) could be more informative with respect to more subtle changes in brain functioning. For example, a different pattern of brain activation in a group of patients with type 1 diabetes was found during a cognitively demanding working-memory task (Wessels et al., 2006a); patients with diabetic retinopathy showed significantly less deactivation in the anterior cingulate and the right orbital frontal gyrus than those without retinopathy, which may reflect a compensatory mechanism, although cognitive functioning did not differ between both the groups (Wessels et al., 2006a).

Cognition in Type 2 Diabetes

Numerous studies have been conducted to evaluate the neuropsychological functioning of individuals diagnosed with type 2 diabetes. These studies differ with respect to demographic characteristics of the research participants, such as age or gender distribution, or diabetic characteristics, such as diabetes duration, treatment regime, and comorbidity or complications (Awad et al., 2004; Stewart & Liolitsa, 1999). Studies also varied in neuropsychological domains covered and in methodological designs (cross-sectional or longitudinal, clinic or population based). The most common finding is that type 2 diabetes is associated with mild to moderate impairments of cognitive functioning with lowered performance on speed of information processing, episodic memory and, although less consistently, on mental flexibility (Awad et al., 2004; Stewart & Liolitsa, 1999). Effect sizes are small to moderate (0.4–0.8). Cognitive domains that are less likely to show significant differences between type 2 diabetic patients and controls include visuospatial processing, auditory or visual attention, long-term semantic knowledge and language abilities (Awad et al., 2004).

Apart from differences in design, inconsistencies across studies may also be related to the neuropsychological sensitivity of test measures used. Also, in several studies a selection was made with respect to the cognitive domains that were assessed and a rationale for that selection was not always provided (Awad et al., 2004). The question arises whether inconsistent findings are due to the fact that type 2 diabetes causes a global rather nonspecific decline in all cognitive domains, or that the observed cognitive changes follow a specific pattern in which impairments in one area, such as speed of information processing, explain the performance decline in other cognitive domains. Studies which examined relations between different disease variables and cognitive functioning showed that patients with worse glycemic control were more likely to show cognitive deficits (Strachan et al., 1997). A number of other factors, such as depression, and cardiovascular or cerebrovascular disease, are also thought to increase cognitive deficits (Awad et al., 2004). Moreover, although most studies did not use age as an independent predictor, the largest effect of type 2 diabetes on cognitive function was observed in studies in which patients were older (Ryan & Geckle, 2000). As they age, people with type 2 diabetes develop other related pathologies such as hypertension, atherosclerosis, macro- and microvascular disease that produce further cognitive deficits, which become most apparent in later life.

Two recent studies assessed cognitive performance in elderly patients with type 2 diabetes in relation to MRI findings (Manschot et al., 2006; van Harten et al., 2007). Both studies revealed that type 2 diabetes was associated with both cognitive dysfunction and MRI abnormalities. Patients with type 2 diabetes particularly performed worse on the domains of attention and executive functioning, information processing speed, and memory.

Some data indicate that DM may place elderly at risk for dementia, both Alzheimer's disease and vascular dementia. A report by Biessels et al. (2006) reported that the incidence of dementia was higher in individuals with diabetes than in those without diabetes in seven of ten studies reviewed. This high risk included both Alzheimer's disease and vascular dementia (8 of 13 studies and 6 of 9 studies respectively). Detailed data on modulating and mediating effects of glycemic control, microvascular complications, and comorbidity (e.g., hypertension and stroke) were generally absent.

MRI in Type 2 Diabetes

Only few studies have specifically addressed brain MRI abnormalities in patients with type 2 diabetes. These studies indicate that modest cortical and subcortical atrophy and symptomatic or asymptomatic infarcts are more common in type 2 diabetic patients than in controls (Araki et al., 1994; den Heijer et al., 2003; Longstreth et al., 1998; Schmidt et al., 2004; Vermeer et al., 2003). Generally, cognitive impairments in type 2 diabetes are associated with MRI abnormalities, more specifically with WMLs, infarcts, and atrophy (Garde et al., 2000; Gunning-Dixon & Raz, 2003; Manschot et al., 2006; van Harten et al., 2007). The CT and MRI studies reviewed in a recent review by van Harten and colleagues (2006) show a relation between diabetes and cerebral atrophy and lacunar infarcts but no consistent relation with WMLs.

The relation between cerebral atrophy and hypertension in type 2 diabetic patients is less clear, one study reporting no effects of adjustment for hypertension (den Heijer et al., 2003), whereas other studies indicated that hypertension appeared to be a major determinant of cerebral atrophy in type 2 diabetic patients (Schmidt et al., 2004; van Harten et al., 2007). Results of previous studies on the association between type 2 diabetes and WMLs are inconsistent. The majority of these studies involved selected subgroups of patients with, for example, clinically manifesting cardiovascular disease or stroke (Manolio et al., 1994; Schmidt et al., 1992) and used relatively insensitive measures to rate WMLs. Some of these studies in patients with vascular disease reported relatively more severe WML in patients with type 2 diabetes (Schmidt et al., 1992), whereas others did not find statistically significant relations between type 2 diabetes and WMLs (Manolio et al., 1994). The study on WMLs in older people with diabetes that involved the largest cohort and the most detailed rating method thus far reported no reliable effect of diabetes on periventricular white matter lesion (PWML; Schmidt et al., 2004).

A General Pattern of Cognitive Dysfunction in Diabetes?

Compared to nondiabetic controls, both patients with type 1 and type 2 diabetes exhibit a lowered performance on a range of cognitive tasks, varying from speed of information processing or psychomotor efficiency, aspects of attention and cognitive flexibility to learning and retrieval of recently learned information. In contrast, patients did not show lowered performance on tasks measuring general intelligence or visuoconstructive skills. A recent review of results in type 2 diabetes (Awad et al., 2004) compared to the results of the meta-analyses in type 1 diabetes (Brands et al., 2005) suggests that the profile of cognitive dysfunction in type 1 diabetes is not exactly similar to that seen in type 2 diabetes. Especially learning and memory seem to be relatively spared in type 1 diabetes compared to type 2 diabetes.

These findings suggest that patients with diabetes have difficulty with cognitively demanding, effortful tasks (Kahneman, 1973). Central to the mental-effort hypothesis is a limited attentional capacity. Similar ideas have been formulated to describe the pattern of cognitive deficits seen in normal aging processes (Park et al., 2002; Salthouse, 2004). Germane to this issue is also a large body of literature on cognitive functioning in aging persons, indicating that older persons display deficits in cognitive domains other than memory and processing speed, namely attention and executive function (for overview see Braver & Barch, 2002; Tisserand & Jolles, 2003). That is to say, the cognitive problems we see in diabetes mimic the patterns of cognitive aging and could be viewed as "accelerated aging."

Psychiatric Comorbidity in Diabetes Mellitus

The prevalence of psychiatric disorders, in particular depression and anxiety disorders which are known to have a negative effect on cognition, is increased in type 1 diabetes. In a recent meta-analysis, odds ratios and prevalence of depression were estimated for both type 1 and 2 diabetes, from 42 studies having a combined sample size of 21,351 subjects (Anderson et al., 2001). The main conclusion is that diabetes doubles the odds ratio. A difference in the prevalence of depression in type 1 compared to type 2 diabetes could not be established. This increased prevalence of depression might result from an inability to cope with the stress associated with diabetes and its complicated treatment that requires strict compliance, but neurophysiological alterations in serotonin and dopaminergic activity could also be involved (Broderick & Jacoby, 1988; Lackovic et al., 1990). Disturbances in glucocorticoid metabolism may play an additional role, since several authors have mentioned a relation between type 1 diabetes and a dysregulation of the hypothalamic–pituitary–adrenal axis activity (Prestele et al., 2003; Roy et al., 1991).

In all, the relation between cognition and depression in diabetes is complex. On the one hand the co-occurrence of depression could influence cognitive performance in patients with diabetes negatively, since depressive symptoms have been related to cognitive dysfunction in some studies (Elderkin-Thompson et al., 2003; Lockwood et al., 2002). On the other hand, depression and cognitive dysfunction could each be a different expression of the same underlying encephalopathy. Although it is well known that the burden of a chronic illness in general may result in elevated levels of psychological distress, biomedical factors may also play a role, since it has been reported that depressive symptoms are related to white matter abnormalities (Jorm et al., 2005) and severity of diabetic complications (Leedom et al., 1991). MRI studies of patients with major depression have found a higher prevalence of WMLs, particularly in participants with late-depression onset (Videbech, 1997). It has been suggested that late-onset depression could be regarded as "vascular depression," a late-onset subtype of depression that involves increased cardiovascular risk factors and hyperintensities of deep white matter or subcortical gray matter (Alexopoulos et al., 1997). Others refer to the co-occurrence of cognitive impairments, depressed mood and vascular dysfunction as "vascular dementia" (Baldwin et al., 2006) or "pseudodementia," that is, geriatric depression with reversible cognitive deficits (Alexopoulos et al., 1997). The question of how psychological well-being is related to MRI abnormalities in type 2 diabetes has not been examined yet. Type 2 diabetic patients report more subjective cognitive problems and show higher levels of psychological distress than controls (Anderson et al., 2001), but many somatic complaints reported by these patients appear to be the result of diabetes itself and not from depression (Brands et al., 2007a).

Generally, the percentage of type 2 diabetic patients reporting serious depressive symptoms or high levels of psychological distress is relatively low, compared to what is reported in general in the literature (Anderson et al., 2001). Moreover, levels of psychological distress in type 2 diabetes were not related to levels of cognitive performance or MRI findings (Brands et al., 2007a; Gregg et al., 2000; Lowe et al., 1994). The concept of "vascular depression" is therefore not useful in type 2 diabetic patients.

Risk Factors and Possible Pathophysiological Mechanisms

Taken together, the results of the studies outlined in this chapter indicate that cognitive deficits in diabetic patients are not merely caused by acute metabolic derangements or psychological factors, but point to end-organ damage in the CNS (Gispen & Biessels, 2000). Although some uncertainty remains about the exact pathogenesis, several mechanisms through which diabetic encephalopathy may develop have now been identified more clearly.

No Role for Hypoglycemia in the Pathogenesis

Until recently, most research on the pathophysiological basis of diabetic encephalopathy in type 1 diabetes was aimed at the hypothesis that hypoglycemic events are the primary cause of neurocognitive dysfunction. Several studies reported deleterious effects of repeated episodes of severe hypoglycemia on cognition (Bale, 1973; Sachon et al., 1992; Wredling et al., 1990). One study even reported severe deterioration in cognitive function and personality changes in five patients with diabetes (Gold et al., 1994). However, in a large prospective study a total of 1144 patients with type 1 diabetes enrolled in the Diabetes Control and Complications Trial (DCCT) and its follow-up Epidemiology of Diabetes Interventions and Complications (EDIC) study were examined on entry to the DCCT (at mean age 27 years) and a mean of 18 years later with the same comprehensive battery of cognitive tests. Neither the frequency of severe hypoglycemia nor the previous treatment-group assignment was associated with decline in any cognitive domain (DCCT Research Group, 1996; Diabetes Control and Complications Trial/Epidemiology of Diabetes Interventions and Complications Study Research Group et al., 2007). The combined results of all these studies provide no evidence for a linear relationship between recurrent episodes of hypoglycemia and permanent brain dysfunction. The reason for this may be that, despite the acute energy failure in the brain associated with hypoglycemia, there might be a period in which the CNS is resistant to hypoglycemia-induced damage (Chabriat et al., 1994). This "brain-damage-free-period" contrasts with immediate brain damage caused by other acute effects in the brain, such as hypoxia or ischemia (cf. Chabriat et al., 1994).

This, however, does not imply that low blood glucose levels are always unrelated to neuropsychological function. Apart from the acute risk of a hypoglycemic coma, hypoglycemia contributes to feelings of psychological distress and should therefore be avoided. Furthermore, it could be hypothesized that specific subgroups of diabetic patients (e.g., patients with microvascular complications or young children) are more sensitive to the adverse effects of hypoglycemia on the brain (Frier & Hilsted, 1985; Ryan, 2006b).

The Role of Hyperglycemia in the Pathogenesis of Cognitive Impairments

Evidence for the involvement of microvascular abnormalities in the pathogenesis of diabetic encephalopathy comes from several studies. For example, in a study in which adults with type 1 diabetes were followed up over a 7-year period, it appeared that only patients with significant proliferative retinopathy showed a decline in measures of psychomotor efficiency (Ryan et al., 2003). Also, a higher degree of structural brain damage has been reported in diabetic patients with clinically significant retinopathy (Ferguson et al., 2003; Wessels et al., 2006b). Furthermore, a recent study showed that higher glycated hemoglobin values were associated with moderate declines in motor speed ($P = .001$) and psychomotor efficiency ($P < .001$), but not in any other cognitive domain (Diabetes Control and Complications Trial/Epidemiology of Diabetes

Interventions and Complications Study Research Group et al., 2007). In line with this, a recent study suggested a link between reduced cortical gray matter and increased severity of retinopathy in diabetic patients (Musen et al., 2006). Importantly, microvascular abnormalities (i.e., microaneurysms) are associated with similar patterns of cognitive deficits (namely, psychomotor slowing) in middle-aged adults without diabetes (Wong et al., 2002). In line with this, experimental models of diabetes have demonstrated "neurotoxic" effects due to hyperglycemia (Gispen & Biessels, 2000). These toxic effects directly affect brain tissue and can lead to microvascular changes in the brain (Biessels et al., 2002a, 2002b). Cerebral microvascular pathology in diabetes may result in a decrease of regional cerebral blood flow and an alteration in cerebral metabolism, which could partly explain the occurrence of cognitive impairments (cf. Price et al., 2002).

The Role of Atherosclerotic Risk Factors

Previous studies in type 1 and type 2 diabetes do not invariably find an association between chronic hyperglycemia, as assessed by HbA1c levels, and the severity of cognitive impairments (e.g., see Brands et al., 2004, 2005; Stewart & Liolitsa, 1999; Strachan et al., 1997). Moreover, subtle cognitive dysfunction may already develop in "prediabetic stages," such as impaired glucose tolerance, or in newly diagnosed type 2 diabetic patients who have not yet been exposed to long-term hyperglycemia (Kalmijn et al., 1995; Vanhanen et al., 1998). One important recent finding is that a mean duration of 30 years in type 1 diabetes appears to have a similar effect on the brain as a mean duration of 7 years in type 2 diabetes (Brands et al., 2007b). Thus, hyperglycemia is unlikely to be the only factor in the development of cognitive impairments in diabetes. The results of recent studies (e.g., Brands et al., 2007b; Helkala et al., 1995; Jagusch et al., 1992; Manschot et al., 2006; van den Berg et al., 2006; van Harten et al., 2007) suggest that atherosclerotic risk factors, such as hypercholestrolemia, dyslipidemia, or a history of macrovascular disease, could be also important factors.

Although some studies failed to detect a marked effect of hypertension on cognitive functioning (e.g., Manschot et al., 2006), other studies report otherwise. Blood pressure elevations, particularly elevations in systolic blood pressure, have been associated with cognitive deficits (Ryan et al., 2003; van Harten et al., 2007), cortical atrophy (Schmidt et al., 2004), and WMLs (van Dijk et al., 2004). Hypertension may even have a synergistical effect with diabetes since individuals with diabetes and elevated blood pressure tend to have the worst neurocognitive outcomes (Hassing et al., 2004; Schmidt et al., 2004).

Another Factor to be Considered: Insulin

Insulin receptors are widely distributed in the brain. Classically, the CNS was thought to be an insulin-insensitive tissue, but in the late 1970s, it was demonstrated that insulin receptors were present throughout the CNS (Havrankova et al., 1979) with particular abundance in defined areas, such as the hypothalamus and the hippocampus (Zhao et al., 2004). The cortically distributed insulin receptor has been shown to be involved in cognitive functions. Emerging evidence has suggested that insulin signaling plays a role in synaptic plasticity by modulating activities of excitatory and inhibitory receptors such as glutamate and GABA receptors, and by triggering signal transduction cascades leading to alteration of gene expression that is required for long-term memory consolidation. Furthermore, deterioration of insulin receptor signaling appears to be associated with aging-related brain degeneration such as Alzheimer's disease and cognitive impairment in older persons suffering from type 2 diabetes mellitus (Zhao et al., 2004). Insulin signaling seems to be especially disturbed in type 2 diabetes, as type 1 diabetes is only associated with a fairly limited degree of insulin resistance (DeFronzo et al., 2003). To exert its effects on the brain, insulin has to be transported across the blood–brain barrier, bind to cerebral insulin receptors and convey its signal through an intracellular signaling cascade. Each of these processes may be affected by diabetes. However, variable results in animal studies using models of either type 1 or type 2 diabetes indicate that different degrees of hyperglycemia, hyperinsulinemia, and insulin resistance are associated with clear-cut differential effects on insulin action in the brain (cf. Banks et al., 1997; Baskin et al., 1985; Figlewicz et al., 1985; Marks & Eastman, 1989). Differences in insulin action in the brain between patients with type 1 and type 2 diabetes may therefore explain part of the distinctive cognitive profiles of these two conditions. Acquisition of information over time (i.e., learning) and consolidation of information for long-term storage, for example, seem to be relatively spared in type 1 diabetes compared with type 2 diabetes. These two cognitive domains are critically dependent on the hippocampus (Squire & Alvarez, 1995). This structure has a relatively high density of insulin receptors and may therefore be extra vulnerable for defects in insulin action. The observation that type 2 diabetic patients have more difficulties with learning and retrieval of information than type 1 diabetic patients suggests that these cognitive deficits are not merely another illustration of problems with tasks that require substantial mental effort. It could also be interpreted as the result of an additional specific pathway (e.g., failing insulin signaling in the brain) leading to cognitive impairment, especially in type 2 diabetes.

Interaction of Diabetic Encephalopathy with Aging?

Cerebral hypoperfusion and other vascular changes become more prominent over the course of normal aging. Also, diabetes-related cognitive impairment may be primarily or at least partly vascular in origin. Thus, one might expect to find evidence of clinically significant impairment in patients who have had diabetes for a prolonged period of time, or interaction effects between diabetes and normal aging. Indeed, several processes that have been implicated in brain aging, including oxidative stress, accumulation of so-called advanced glycosilation end-products, microvascular dysfunction, and alterations in cerebral glucose and insulin metabolism that may be accelerated by diabetes (Biessels et al., 2002b). Related to this, studies suggest that cognitive deficits appear to be more pronounced in those individuals with type 2 diabetes who are older than 60–65 years of age (Ryan & Geckle, 2000). In a similar vein, age was found to be related to underperformance in three out of five cognitive domains in patients with type 2 diabetes, and the interaction term of age and group was significant for the domain of memory (Manschot et al., 2006). This points to an interaction between diabetes and aging. It has been hypothesized that cognitive deficits in older patients with type 1 diabetes may also be more pronounced than those in younger type 1 diabetic patients, but empirical findings do not support this hypothesis (Brands et al., 2006; Diabetes Control and Complications Trial/ Epidemiology of Diabetes Interventions and Complications Study Research Group et al., 2007).

The Paradox: Diabetic Encephalopathy versus Evidence of Cognitive Resilience

Although the combined results of all studies provide compelling evidence for the adverse effects of both type 1 and type 2 diabetes on the brain, several observations are incongruent with the concept of slowly progressing end-organ damage. First, the results from the study on older patients with type 1 diabetes (Brands et al., 2006) suggest that although patients suffer from significant peripheral complications, there is only a limited effect on the brain. Second, older patients with type 1 diabetes do not show more pronounced cognitive deficits compared to younger patients (van den Berg et al., 2006). In this context, it is important to note that Ryan (2006a) recently pointed out that the majority of cross-sectional studies on type 1 diabetic patients, including patients with childhood onset, typically have found quite modest cognitive deficits that hardly meet the criteria for "clinical relevance." These observations suggest that diabetic patients have a remarkable level of what might be best conceptualized as neurocognitive resilience (Ryan, 2006a). This line of reasoning counters the concept of "diabetic encephalopathy," which predicts a gradual, but apparently relentless, decline over time as duration of hypoperfusion increases (de Jong, 1950; Reske-Nielsen et al., 1965). If there is no inexorable neurocognitive deterioration in the vast majority of diabetic patients, the question arises as to what protects the brain from further vascular (and nonvascular) damage (Ryan, 2006a). The concept of "cognitive reserve" could be of interest here (Satz, 1993). The notion of reserve against brain damage stems from the repeated observation in clinical research that there is no direct relationship between the degree of brain pathology or brain damage and the clinical manifestation of that damage (Satz, 1993). It could be hypothesized that the brain has specific ways to preserve homeostasis that has been demonstrated in other areas of research (Fehm et al., 2006). It has been argued that the brain actively attempts to cope with or compensate for pathology, which could be based on more efficient utilization of brain networks or on enhanced ability to recruit alternate brain networks as needed (Stern, 2002).

It could also be speculated that diabetes acts as a so-called challenge factor (Satz, 1993) to the amount of brain reserve and, as such, makes an individual more vulnerable to symptom onset or functional impairments if other insults occur. For example, the observation that patients with type 2 diabetes have a twofold increased risk for the development of dementia could be viewed as the aggregate effect of two distinct processes.

Implications for Clinical Practice

The concept of diabetic encephalopathy is probably not a useful one to describe the neurocognitive complications of diabetes, given the relative subtlety of impairments in most cases. Nevertheless, the large variation in cognitive performance indicates that individual patients may present with cognitive impairments that are clinically relevant and hamper everyday functioning. However, reliable and objective criteria to diagnose "diabetic encephalopathy" or diabetes-related cognitive deficits are lacking, making these symptoms difficult to detect in the individual patient. The findings described in this chapter suggest that especially patients with type 2 diabetes are at risk for diabetes-related cognitive decline, but other potentially confounding factors, such as poor glycemic control or illness-related depression, should be always taken into account. However, neuropsychological assessment may help to unravel the underlying deficits that may or may not be related to the diabetic complications or brain alterations. In general, sensitive neuropsychological tests relying on mental effort should be used to detect the subtle cognitive changes that can be expected in diabetes. Although precise diagnostic criteria still need to be developed, we especially recommend the use of sensitive tests focusing on information processing speed, mental flexibility, and learning and retrieval of information.

Summary

Both type 1 and type 2 diabetes mellitus are associated with altered brain function. This chapter focused on the clinical and neuropsychological characteristics of altered CNS functioning in both type 1 and in type 2 diabetes, as well as on the possible underlying mechanisms. Type 1 diabetes is associated with modest cognitive impairments in young to middle-aged adult patients, which is related to long-term glycemic control and its subsequent microvascular complications, but not to the occurrence of severe hypoglycemic episodes. Similar deficits were found in older people with type 1 diabetes, but their magnitude appears to be comparable to the findings in younger adults. Also, in this particular study, these cognitive deficits were not accompanied by brain changes. However, a clear relationship between cognitive deficits and brain abnormalities does exist in older patients with type 2 diabetes. In all, diabetes patients show diabetes-related cognitive decline. Although this is typically subtle in nature and does not match the originally proposed concept of diabetic encephalopathy, these may be clinically relevant in individual patients and can be reliably assessed with sensitive, cognitively demanding neuropsychological tests.

References

Alexopoulos, G. S., Meyers, B. S., Young, R. C., Campbell, S., Silbersweig, D., & Charlson, M. (1997). "Vascular depression" hypothesis. *Archives of General Psychiatry, 54*, 915–922.

American Diabetes Association. (2002). Standards of medical care for patients with diabetes mellitus. *Diabetes Care, 25*, 213–229.

American Diabetes Association. (2005). Diagnosis and classification of diabetes mellitus. *Diabetes Care, 28*, S37–S42.

Anderson, R. J., Freedland, K. E., Clouse, R. E., & Lustman, P. J. (2001). The prevalence of comorbid depression in adults with diabetes: A meta-analysis. *Diabetes Care, 24*, 1069–1078.

Araki, Y., Nomura, M., Tanaka, H., Yamamoto, H., Yamamoto, T., & Tsukaguchi, I. (1994). MRI of the brain in diabetes mellitus. *Neuroradiology, 36*, 101–103.

Awad, N., Gagnon, M., & Messier, C. (2004). The relationship between impaired glucose tolerance, type 2 diabetes, and cognitive function. *Journal of Clinical and Experimental Neuropsychology, 26*, 1044–1080.

Baldwin, R. C., Gallagley, A., Gourlay, M., Jackson, A., & Burns, A. (2006). Prognosis of late life depression: A three-year cohort study of outcome and potential predictors. *International Journal of Geriatric Psychiatry, 21*, 57–63.

Bale, R. N. (1973). Brain damage in diabetes mellitus. *British Journal of Psychiatry, 122*, 337–341.

Banks, W. A., Jaspan, J. B., & Kastin, A. J. (1997). Effect of diabetes mellitus on the permeability of the blood-brain barrier to insulin. *Peptides, 18*, 1577–1584.

Baskin, D. G., Stein, L. J., Ikeda, H., Woods, S. C., Figlewicz, D. P., Porte, D. J., et al. (1985). Genetically obese Zucker rats have abnormally low brain insulin content. *Life Science, 36*, 627–633.

Biessels, G. J., Staekenborg, S., Brunner, E., Brayne, C., & Scheltens, P. (2006). Risk of dementia in diabetes mellitus: A systematic review. *Lancet Neurology, 5*, 64–74.

Biessels, G. J., ter Laak, M. P., Hamers, F. P., & Gispen W. H. (2002a). Neuronal Ca(2+) dysregulation in diabetes mellitus. *European Journal of Pharmacology, 447*, 201–209.

Biessels, G. J., van der Heide, L. P., Kamal, A., Bleys, R. L., & Gispen, W. H. (2002b). Ageing and diabetes: Implications for brain function. *European Journal of Pharmacology, 441*, 1–14.

Brands, A. M. A., Biessels, G. J., de Haan, E. H. F., Kappelle, L. J., & Kessels, R. P. C. (2005). The Effects of Type 1 Diabetes on Cognitive Performance: A meta-analysis. *Diabetes Care, 28*, 726–735.

Brands, A. M. A., Biessels, G. J., Kappelle, L. J., de Haan E. H. F., de Valk, H. W., Algra, A., et al. (2007b). Cognitive functioning and brain MRI in patients with type 1 and type 2 diabetes mellitus: A comparative study. *Dementia and Geriatric Cognitive Disorders, 23*, 343–350.

Brands, A. M. A., Kessels, R. P. C., de Haan, E. H. F., Kappelle L. J., & Biessels, G. J. (2004). Cerebral dysfunction in type 1 diabetes: Effects of insulin, vascular risk factors and blood-glucose levels. *European Journal of Pharmacology, 490*, 159–168.

Brands, A. M. A., Kessels, R. P. C., Hoogma, R. P. L. M., Henselmans, J. M. L., van der Beek Boter, J. W., Kappelle, L. J., et al. (2006). Cognitive performance, psychological well-being and brain MRI in older patients with type 1 diabetes. *Diabetes, 28*, 726–735.

Brands, A. M. A., van den Berg, E., Manschot, S. M., Biessels, G. J., Kappelle, L. J., de Haan, E. H. F., et al. (2007a). A detailed profile of cognitive dysfunction and its relation to psychological distress in patients with type 2 diabetes mellitus. *Journal of the International Neuropsychological Society, 13*, 288–297.

Braver, T. S., & Barch, D. M. (2002). A theory of cognitive control, aging cognition, and neuromodulation. *Neuroscience and Biobehavioral Reviews, 26*, 809–817.

Broderick, P. A., & Jacoby, J. H. (1988). Serotonergic function in diabetic rats: Psychotherapeutic implications. *Biological Psychiatry, 24*, 234–239.

Butters, M., Beers, S. R., Tarter, R. E., Edwards, K. L., & Van Thiel, D. H. (Eds.) (2001). *Medical neuropsychology: The impact of disease on behavior* (2nd ed.). New York: Kluwer Academic.

Chabriat, H., Sachon, C., Levasseur, M., Grimaldi, A., Pappata, S., Rougemont, D., et al. (1994). Brain metabolism after recurrent insulin induced hypoglycemic episodes: A PET study. *Journal of Neurology Neurosurgery and Psychiatry, 57*, 1360–1365.

Cohen, J. (1988). *Statistical power analysis for the behavioral sciences* (2nd ed.).Hillsdale, NJ: Erlbaum.

DCCT Research Group. (1996). Effects of intensive diabetes therapy on neuropsychological function in adults in the Diabetes Control and Complications Trial. *Annals of Internal Medicine, 124*, 379–388.

Diabetes Control and Complications Trial/ Epidemiology of Diabetes Interventions and Complications Study Research Group; Jacobson, A. M., Musen, G., Ryan, C. M., Silvers, N., Cleary, P., et al. (2007). Long-term effect of diabetes and its treatment on cognitive function. *New England Journal of Medicine, 356*, 1842–1852.

Deary, I. J., Crawford, J. R., Hepburn, D. A., Langan, S. J., Blackmore, L. M., & Frier, B. M. (1993). Severe hypoglycemia and intelligence in adult patients with insulin-treated diabetes. *Diabetes, 42*, 341–344.

DeFronzo, R. A., Hendler, R., & Simonson, D. (2003). Insulin resistance is a prominent feature of insulin-dependent diabetes. *Diabetes, 31*, 795–801.

Dejgaard, A., Gade, A., Larsson, H., Balle, V., Parving, A., & Parving H. H. (1991). Evidence for diabetic encephalopathy. *Diabetic Medicine, 8*, 162–167.

de Jong, R. N. (1950). The nervous system complications in diabetes mellitus with special reference to cerebrovascular changes. *Journal of Nervous and Mental Disease, 111*, 181–206.

de Leeuw, F. E., de Groot, J., Achten, E., Oudkerk, M., Ramos, L. M., Heijboer, R., et al. (2001). Prevalence of cerebral white-matter lesions in elderly people: A population based magnetic resonance imaging study. The Rotterdam Scan Study. *Journal of Neurology, Neurosurgery and Psychiatry, 70*, 9–14.

den Heijer, T., Vermeer, S. E., van Dijk, E. J., Prins, N. D., Koudstaal, P. J., Hofman, A., et al. (2003). Type 2 diabetes and atrophy of medial temporal lobe structures on brain MRI. *Diabetologia, 46*, 1604–1610.

Elderkin-Thompson, V., Kumar, A., Bilker, W. B., Dunkin, J. J., Mintz, J., Moberg, P. J., et al. (2003). Neuropsychological deficits among patients with late-onset minor and major depression. *Archives of Clinical Neuropsychology, 18*, 529–549.

Fehm, H. L., Kern, W., & Peters, A. (2006). The selfish brain: competition for energy resources. *Progress in Brain Research, 153*, 129–140.

Ferguson, S. C., Blane, A., Perros, P., McCrimmon, R. J., Best, J. J., Wardlaw, J., et al. (2003). Cognitive ability and brain structure in type 1 diabetes: Relation to microangiopathy and preceding severe hypoglycemia. *Diabetes, 52*, 149–156.

Ferguson, S. C., Blane, A., Wardlaw, J., Frier, B. M., Perros, P., McCrimmon, R. J., et al. (2005). Influence of an early-onset age of type 1 diabetes on cerebral structure and cognitive function. *Diabetes Care, 28*, 1431–1437.

Figlewicz, D. P., Dorsa, D. M., Stein, L. J., Baskin, D. G., Paquette, T., Greenwood, M. R., et al. (1985). Brain and liver insulin binding is decreased in Zucker rats carrying the 'fa' gene. *Endocrinology, 117*, 1537–1543.

Frier, B. M., & Hilsted, J. (1985). Does hypoglycemia aggravate the complications of diabetes? *Lancet, 2*, 1175–1177.

Gaede, P., Vedel, P., Larsen, N., Jensen, G. V., Parving, H. H., & Pedersen, O. (2003). Multifactorial intervention and cardiovascular disease in patients with type 2 diabetes. *New England Journal of Medicine, 348*, 383–393.

Garde, E., Mortensoen, E. L., Krabbe, K., Rostrup, E., & Larsson, H. B. (2000). Relation between age-related decline in intelligence and cerebral white-matter hyperintensities in healthy octogenarians: A longitudinal study. *Lancet, 356*, 628–634.

Gispen, W. H., & Biessels, G. J. (2000). Cognition and synaptic plasticity in diabetes mellitus. *Trends in Neuroscience, 23,* 542–549.

Gregg, E. W., Yaffe, K., Cauley, J. A., Rolka, D. B., Blackwell, T. L., & Narayan, K. M. (2000). Is diabetes associated with cognitive impairment and cognitive decline among older women? Study of Osteoperotic Fractures Research Group. *Archives of Internal Medicine, 160,* 174–180.

Gold, A. E., Deary, I. J., Jones, R. W., O'Hare, J. P., Reckless, J. P., & Frier, B. M. (1994). Severe deterioration in cognitive function and personality in five patients with long-standing diabetes: A complication of diabetes or a consequence of treatment? *Diabetic Medicine, 11,* 499–505.

Gunning-Dixon, F. M., & Raz, N. (2003). Neuroanatomical correlates of selected executive functions in middle-aged and older adults: A prospective MRI study. *Neuropsychologia, 41,* 1929–1941.

Hassing, L. B., Hofer, S. M., Nilsson, L. G., Berg, S., Pedersen, N. L., McClearn, G., et al. (2004). Comorbid type 2 diabetes mellitus and hypertension exacerbates cognitive decline: Evidence from a longitudinal study. *Age and Ageing, 33,* 355–361.

Havrankova, J., Roth, J., & Brownstein, M. J. (1979). Concentrations of insulin and insulin receptors in the brain are independent of peripheral insulin levels. Studies of obese and streptozotocin-treated rodents. *Journal of Clinical Investigations, 64,* 636–642.

Helkala, E. L., Niskanen, L., Viinamaki, H., Partanen, J., & Uusitupa, M. (1995). Short-term and long-term memory in elderly patients with NIDDM. *Diabetes Care, 18,* 681–685.

Jagusch, W., Cramon, D. Y. V., Renner, R., & Hepp, K. D. (1992). Cognitive function and metabolic state in elderly diabetic patients. *Diabetes, Nutrition and Metabolism, 5,* 265–274.

Jorm, A. F., Anstey, K. J., Christensen, H., de Plater, G., Kumar, R., Wen, W., et al. (2005). MRI hyperintensities and depressive symptoms in a community sample of individuals 60–64 years old. *American Journal of Psychiatry, 162,* 699–704.

Kahneman, D. (1973). *Attention and effort.* New Jersey, USA: Prentice-Hall Inc., Englewood Cliffs.

Kalmijn, S., Feskens, E. J., Launer, L. J., Stijnen, T., & Kromhout, D. (1995). Glucose intolerance, hyperinsulinaemia and cognitive function in a general population of elderly men. *Diabetologia, 38,* 1096–1102.

Lackovic, Z., Salkovic, M., Kuci, Z., & Relja, M. (1990). Effect of long-lasting diabetes mellitus on rat and human brain monoamines. *Journal of neurochemistry, 54,* 143–147.

Leedom, L., Meehan, W. P., Procci, W., & Zeidler, A. (1991). Symptoms of depression in patients with type II diabetes mellitus. *Psychosomatics, 32,* 280–286.

Lobnig, B. M., Krömeke, O., Optenhostert-Porst, C., & Wolf, O. T. (2006). Hippocampal volume and cognitive performance in longstanding Type 1 diabetic patients without macrovascular complications. *Diabetic Medicine, 23,* 32–39.

Lockwood, K. A., Alexopoulos, G. S., & van Gorp, W. G. (2002). Executive dysfunction in geriatric depression. *American Journal of Psychiatry, 159,* 1119–1126.

Longstreth, W. T., Jr., Bernick, C., Manolio, T. A., Bryan, N., Jungreis, C. A., & Price, T. R. (1998). Lacunar infarcts defined by magnetic resonance imaging of 3660 elderly people: The Cadiovascular Health Study. *Archives of Neurology, 55,* 1217–1225.

Lowe, L. P., Tranel, D., Wallace, R. B., & Welty, T. K. (1994). Type II diabetes and cognitive function. A population-based study of Native Americans. *Diabetes Care, 17,* 891–896.

Lunetta, M., Damanti, A. R., Fabbri, G., Lombardo, M., Di Mauro, M., & Mughini, L. (1994). Evidence by magnetic resonance imaging of cerebral alterations of atrophy type in young insulin-dependent diabetic patients. *Journal of Endocrinological Investigation, 17,* 241–245.

Manolio, T. A., Kronmal, R. A., Burke, G. L., Poirier, V., O'Leary, D. H., Gardin, J. M., et al. (1994). Magnetic resonance abnormalities and cardiovascular disease in older adults. The Cardiovascular Health Study. *Stroke, 25,* 318–327.

Manschot, S. M., Brands, A. M. A., van der Grond, J., Kessels, R. P. C., Algra, A., Kappelle, L. J., et al. (2006). Brain MRI Correlates of impaired cognition in patients with type 2 diabetes mellitus. *Diabetes, 55,* 1106–1113.

Marks, J. L., & Eastman, C. J. (1989). Effect of starvation on insulin receptors in rat brain. *Neuroscience, 30,* 551–556.

Miles, W. R., & Root, H. F. (1922). Psychologic tests applied in diabetic patients. *Archives of Internal Medicine, 30,* 767–777.

Musen, G., Lyoo, I. K., Sparks, C. R., Weinger, K., Hwang, J., Ryan, C. M., et al. (2006). Effects of type 1 diabetes on gray matter density as measured by voxel-based morphometry. *Diabetes, 55,* 326–323.

Park, D. C., Lautenschlager, G., Hedden, T., Davidson, N. S., Smith, A. D., & Smith, P. K. (2002). Models of visuospatial and verbal memory across the adult life span. *Psychology and Aging, 17,* 299–320.

Perros, P., Best, J. J. K., Deary, I. J., Frier, B. M., & Sellar, R. J. (1997). Brain abnormalities demonstrated by magnetic resonance imaging in adult

IDDM patients with and without a history of recurrent severe hypoglycemia. *Diabetes Care, 20,* 1013–1018.

Prestele, S., Aldenhoff, J., & Reiff, J. (2003). The HPA-axis as a possible link between depression, diabetes mellitus and cognitive dysfunction. *Fortschritte der Neurologie-Psychiatrie, 71,* 24–36.

Price, J. C., Kelley, D. E., Ryan, C. M., Meltzer, C. C., Drevets, W. C., Mathis, C. A., et al. (2002). Evidence of increased serotonin-1A receptor binding in type 2 diabetes: A positron emission tomography study. *Brain Research, 927,* 97–103.

Reichard, P., Pihl, M., Rosenqvist, U., & Sule, J. (1996). Complications in IDDM are caused by elevated blood glucose level: The Stockholm Diabetes Intervention Study (SDIS) at 10-year follow up. *Diabetologia, 39,* 1483–1488.

Reichard P., & Rosenqvist, U. (1989). Nephropathy is delayed by intensified insulin treatment in patients with insulin-dependent diabetes mellitus and retinopathy. *Journal of Internal Medicine, 226,* 81–87.

Reske-Nielsen, E., Lundbaek, K., & Rafaelsen, O. J. (1965). Pathological changes in the central and peripheral nervous system of young long-term diabetics. *Diabetologia, 1,* 233–241.

Roy, M., Collier, B., & Roy, A. (1991). Dysregulation of the hypothalamo-pituitary-adrenal axis and duration of diabetes. *Journal of Diabetic Complications, 5,* 218–220.

Ryan, C. M. (2005). Diabetes, ageing and cognitive decline. *Neurobiology of Aging, 26S,* S21–S25.

Ryan, C. M. (2006a). Diabetes and brain damage: More (or less) than meets the eye? *Diabetologia, 49,* 2229–2233.

Ryan, C. M. (2006b). Why is cognitive dysfunction associated with the development of diabetes early in life? The diathesis hypothesis. *Pediatrics, 7,* 289–297.

Ryan, C. M., & Geckle, M. O. (2000). Why is learning and memory dysfunction in Type 2 diabetes limited to older adults? *Diabetes Metabolism Research and Reviews, 16,* 308–315.

Ryan, C. M., Geckle, M. O., & Orchard, T. J. (2003). Cognitive efficiency declines over time in adults with type 1 diabetes: Effects of micro- and macrovascular complications. *Diabetologia, 46,* 940–948.

Ryan, C. M., & Williams, T. M. (1993). Effects of insulin-dependent diabetes on learning and memory efficiency in adults. *Journal of Clinical and Experimental Neuropsychology, 15,* 685–700.

Ryan, C. M., Williams, T. M., Orchard, T. J., & Finegold, D. N. (1992). Psychomotor slowing is associated with distal symmetrical polyneuropathy in adults with diabetes mellitus. *Diabetes, 41,* 107–113.

Sachon, C., Grimaldi, A., Digy, J. P., Pillon, B., Dubois, B., & Thervet, F. (1992). Cognitive function, insulin-dependent diabetes and hypoglycemia. *Journal of Internal Medicine, 231,* 471–475.

Salthouse, T. A. (2004). What and when of cognitive aging. *Current Directions in Psychological Science, 13,* 140–144.

Satz, P. (1993). Brain reserve capacity on symptom onset after brain injury: A formulation and review of evidence for threshold theory. *Neuropsychology, 7,* 273–295.

Schmidt, R., Fazekas, F., Kleinert, G., Offenbacher, H., Gindl, K., Payer, F., et al. (1992). Magnetic Resonance Imaging signal hyperintensities in the deep and subcortical white-matter. A comparative study between stroke patients and normal volunteers. *Archives of Neurology, 49,* 825–827.

Schmidt, R., Launer, L. J., Nilsson, L. G., Pajak, A., Sans, S., Berger, K., et al. (2004). Magnetic resonance imaging of the brain in diabetes: The Cardiovascular Determinants of Dementia (CASCADE) Study. *Diabetes, 53,* 687–692.

Squire, L. R., & Alvarez, P. (1995). Retrograde amnesia and memory consolidation: A neurobiological perspective. *Current Opinions in Neurobiology, 5,* 169–177.

Stern, Y. (2002). What is cognitive reserve? Theory and research application of the reserve concept. *Journal of the International Neuropsychological Society, 8,* 448–460.

Stewart, R., & Liolitsa, D. (1999). Type 2 diabetes mellitus, cognitive impairment and dementia. *Diabetic Medicine, 16,* 93–112.

Strachan, M. W., Deary, I. J., Ewing, F. M., & Frier, B. M. (1997). Is type II diabetes associated with an increased risk of cognitive dysfunction? A critical review of published studies. *Diabetes Care, 20,* 438–445.

Tisserand, D. J., & Jolles, J. (2003). On the involvement of prefrontal networks in cognitive ageing. *Cortex, 39,* 1107–1128.

van den Berg, E., De Craen, A. J. M., Biessels, G. J., Gusselkloo, J., & Westendorp R. G. J. (2006). The impact of diabetes mellitus on cognitive decline in the oldest of the old: A prospective population-based study. *Diabetologia, 49,* 2015–2023.

van Dijk, E. J., Breteler, M. M., Schmidt, R., Berger, K., Nilsson, L. G., Oudkerk, M., et al. (2004). The association between blood pressure, hypertension, and cerebral white-matter lesions: Cardiovascular determinants of dementia study. *Hypertension, 44,* 625–630.

Vanhanen, M., Koivisto, K., Kuusisto, J., Mykkanen, L., Helkala, E. L., Hanninen, T., et al. (1988). Cognitive function in an elderly population with persistent impaired glucose tolerance. *Diabetes Care, 21*, 398–402.

van Harten, B., de Leeuw, F. E., Weinstein, H. C., Scheltens, P., & Biessels, G. J. (2006). Brain imaging in patients with diabetes: A systematic review. *Diabetes Care, 29*, 2539–2548.

van Harten, B., Oosterman, J., Muslimovic, D., van Loon, B. J., Scheltens, P., & Weinstein, H. C. (2007). Cognitive impairment and MRI correlates in the elderly patients with type 2 diabetes mellitus. *Age and Ageing, 36*, 164–170.

Vermeer, S. E., den Heijer, T., Koudstaal, P. J., Oudkerk, M., Hofman, A., & Breteler, M. M. B. (2003). Incidence and risk factors of silent brain infarcts in the population-based Rotterdam Scan Study. *Stroke, 34*, 392–396.

Videbech, P. (1997). MRI findings in patients with affective disorder: A meta-analysis. *Acta Acta Psychiatrica Scandinavica, 96*, 157–168.

Weinger, K., & Jacobson, A. M. (1998). Cognitive impairment in patients with type 1 (insulin-dependent) Diabetes Mellitus. *CNS Drugs, 9*, 233–252.

Wessels, A. M., Rombouts, S. A., Simsek, S., Kuijer, J. P., Kostense, P. J., Barkhof, F., et al. (2006a). Microvascular disease in type 1 diabetes alters brain activation: a functional magnetic resonance imaging study. *Diabetes, 55*, 334–340.

Wessels, A. M., Simsek, S., Remeijnse, P. L., Veltman, D. J., Biessels, G. J., Barkhof, F., et al. (2006b). Voxel-based morphometry demonstrates reduced grey matter density on brain MRI in patients with diabetic retinopathy 3724. *Diabetologia, 49*, 2474–2480.

Wild, S., Roglic, G., Green, A., Sicree, R., & King, H. (2004). Global prevalence of diabetes: Estimates for the year 2000 and projections for 2030. *Diabetes Care, 27*, 1047–1053.

Wong, T. Y., Klein, R., Sharrett, A. R., Nieto, F. J., Boland, L. L., Couper, D. J., et al. (2002). Retinal microvascular abnormalities and cognitive impairment in middle-aged persons: The Atherosclerosis Risk in Communities Study. *Stroke, 33*, 1487–1492.

Wredling, R., Levander, S., Adamson, U., & Lins, P. E. (1990). Permanent neuropsychological impairment after recurrent episodes of severe hypoglycemia in man. *Diabetologia, 33*, 152–157.

Ylikoski, A., Erkinjuntti, T., Raininko, R., Sarna, S., Sulkava, R., & Tilvis, R. (1995). White-matter hyperintensities on MRI in the neurologically nondiseased elderly. Analysis of cohorts of consecutive subjects aged 55 to 85 years living at home. *Stroke, 26*, 1171–1177.

Yousem, D. M., Tasman, W. S., & Grossman, R. I. (1991). Proliferative retinopathy: Absence of white-matter lesions at MR imaging. *Radiology, 179*, 229–230.

Zhao, W. O., Chen, H., Quon, M. J., & Alkon, D. L. (2004). Insulin and the insulin receptor in experimental models of learning and memory. *European Journal of Pharmacology, 490*, 71–81.

17

Neuropsychological Aspects of HIV Infection

Steven Paul Woods, Catherine L. Carey, Jennifer E. Iudicello, Scott L. Letendre, Christine Fennema-Notestine, and Igor Grant

Neurobiology of HIV: An Overview

The human immunodeficiency virus (HIV) is a lentivirus that can severely compromise immune function by damaging cluster of differentiation 4+ (CD4) lymphocytes (i.e., T-helper cells), thereby increasing the risk of opportunistic infections and cancers. In addition to its striking effects on the immune system, HIV can be highly neurovirulent. That is, the virus is capable of penetrating the blood–brain barrier (BBB) early in the course of infection (Davis et al., 1992), most likely as a consequence of the trafficking of infected circulating white blood cells (e.g., monocytes) across the BBB (Haase, 1986). Once in the brain, HIV does not infect neurons. Instead, HIV primarily replicates in perivascular macrophages and microglia, which can subsequently fuse to form multinucleated giant cells, a hallmark of HIV encephalitis. Moreover, HIV infection indirectly alters neural functioning by triggering a cascade of neurotoxic molecular events, such as the upregulation of chemokines (Gonzalez-Scarano & Martin-Garcia, 2005). The resultant HIV-associated neuronal and glial pathologies are evident in as many as 50% of HIV-infected persons (Budka, 2005), often taking the form of neuronal apoptosis and/or synaptodendritic injury (Ellis et al., 2007).

Early magnetic resonance imaging (MRI) studies of individuals with HIV infection focused on the central nervous system (CNS) opportunistic infections to which such cohorts were highly vulnerable (e.g., Jarvik et al., 1988). However, it became quickly apparent that a subset of HIV-infected individuals with no apparent CNS opportunistic infections exhibited nonspecific evidence of neurodegeneration on MRI, such as white matter hyperintensities and enlarged ventricles and subarachnoid spaces (e.g., Dal Pan et al., 1992). Carefully controlled magnetic resonance (MR) morphometric studies have since helped to define the regional distribution of these HIV-related abnormalities (e.g., Aylward et al., 1993), revealing that the cerebral white matter and fronto-striato-thalamo-cortical circuits are particularly vulnerable (see Figure 17–1; see also the color figure in the color insert section). Indeed, HIV-infected individuals may evidence diffuse white matter abnormalities, including nonspecific hyperintensities, which correspond to the postmortem markers of synaptodendritic injury severity (Archibald et al., 2004). More recent diffusion tensor imaging studies also reveal increased mean diffusivity and reduced fractional anisotropy (e.g., Pomara et al., 2001), with the latter being particularly prominent in individuals with HIV-associated neurocognitive disorders (see Figure 17–2; see also the color figure in the color insert section). Although HIV-associated pathologies are evident throughout the CNS, including the temporolimbic system, a large body of research has focused specifically on the effects of HIV in the frontal cortex and striatum (i.e., caudate

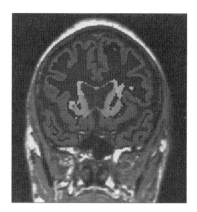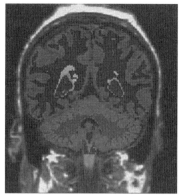

Figure 17–1. Structural morphometry in an individual infected with HIV. These two coronal sections highlight regions of abnormality in the white matter (shown in yellow), which may be related to markers of HIV disease and neurobehavioral performance. Dark blue = cortex, light blue = subcortical gray, purple = sulcal/subarachnoid CSF, red = ventricular fluid, yellow = abnormal white matter, dark gray = normal appearing white matter, light gray = cerebellum, maroon = infratentorial CSF.

nucleus and putamen). For example, Wiley et al. (1998) reported that the HIV RNA viral load in the caudate nucleus was significantly higher as compared to other brain regions in persons with HIV encephalitis. HIV infection is associated with structural abnormalities in the frontal cortices, including lower volumes (e.g., Jernigan et al., 2005) and neocortical thinning (e.g., Thompson et al., 2005). Moreover, MR spectroscopic markers of neuroinflammation (e.g., elevated myoinositol and choline) are evident in the striatum and frontal gray and white matter in the early stages of HIV infection, with more prominent neuronal damage (i.e., decreased N-acetyl asparate) emerging in the same regions as the disease advances (Chang et al., 2005). Longitudinal studies show that declines in CD4 lymphocytes are associated with atrophy in the caudate nucleus (e.g., Stout et al., 1998). Finally, hypoperfusion and increased blood oxygenation level dependent (BOLD) signal are frequently observed bilaterally in the caudate and prefrontal cortex (e.g., Chang et al., 2000). The apparent susceptibility of the frontostriatal circuits to HIV-associated neural injury may be a function of BBB permeability to HIV trafficking in these regions (e.g., Berger & Arendt, 2000) or the relative involvement of specific neuronal populations (e.g., large spiny neurons) or neurotransmitter systems (e.g., glutamate and dopamine) in the

neuropathogenesis of HIV (e.g., see Langford et al., 2005).

Neuropsychological Profile of HIV

Considering its neurovirulence, it is not surprising that cognitive deficits are a common feature of HIV infection (Grant et al., 1987). Although the use of different diagnostic nomenclatures complicates interpretation of the published prevalence data, it is generally held that HIV-associated neurocognitive disorders are evident in 30%–50% of persons living with HIV (see Figure 17–3).

Among these neuropsychologically impaired individuals, approximately one-half to two-thirds are asymptomatic (e.g., Antinori et al., 2007; Grant et al., 2005), meaning that their cognitive deficits do not interfere with the independent performance of instrumental activities of daily living (IADLs). According to the recently revised nomenclature for HIV-associated neurocognitive disorders (HAND) developed by the Frascati Group (Antinori et al., 2007), these individuals would be diagnosed with Asymptomatic Neurocognitive Impairment (ANI), provided they demonstrate impairment (i.e., 1 SD or more below the normative mean) in two or more cognitive domains that is not better explained by developmental and/or comorbid factors. The remaining proportion of

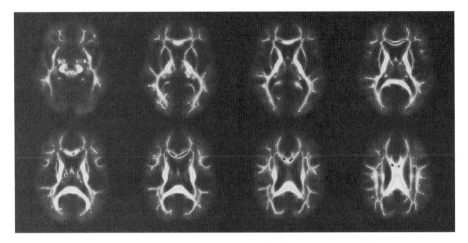

Figure 17–2. Diffusion tensor images from Gongvatana et al. (2008) showing that individuals with HIV-associated neurocognitive disorders (HAND) have lower fractional anisotropy in the anterior callosal region (shown in blue) relative to HIV-infected comparison participants without HAND. Images are presented in axial sections moving from inferior (upper left) to superior (lower right) slices.

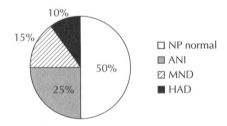

Figure 17–3. Pie chart displaying the estimated prevalence of HIV-associated neurocognitive disorders, including neuropsychologically (NP) normal, asymptomatic (i.e., subsyndromic) neuropsychological impairment (ANI), Mild Neurocognitive Disorder (MND), and HIV-associated Dementia (HAD).

individuals with HIV-associated neurocognitive disorders evidence IADL declines, which may be subclassified as either Mild Neurocognitive Disorder (MND, which was formerly referred to as Minor Cognitive-Motor Disorder [MCMD]) or HIV-Associated Dementia (HAD). Diagnoses of MND and HAD require the presence of HIV-associated impairment in two or more cognitive domains that results in a disruption of IADLs (e.g., financial management); however, MND carries more mild cognitive and functional deficits than HAD, which is typically accompanied by greater cognitive and functional

declines. Table 17–1 displays the revised criteria for HAND.

The epidemiology of MND is not well understood, but the limited data available suggest that the diagnosis is evident in about 5%–20% of HIV-infected persons (Grant et al., 2005). The incidence of HAD has declined as much as 50% in the era of combination antiretroviral therapies (cART), with recent estimates of 10.5/1000 persons per year (e.g., Sacktor et al., 2001). Prevalence rates for HAD fall between 5% and 15% of HIV-infected persons (e.g., Tozzi et al., 2005), with higher estimates among non-immunosuppressed persons in recent years (Grant et al., 2005).

The course of HIV-associated neurocognitive disorders is highly variable across individuals (Antinori et al., 2007), particularly when contrasted against traditional neurodegenerative diseases (e.g., Alzheimer's disease). Many persons with mild impairment do not progress to MCD or HAD; likewise, partial—and even full—remission of HIV-associated neurocognitive disorders in conjunction with effective cART is not uncommon (McArthur, 2004).

Motor and Psychomotor Abilities

Gross motor abnormalities (e.g., parkinsonism, chorea, myoclonus, and dystonia) occur

Table 17–1. Revised Research Criteria for HIV-Associated Neurocognitive Disorders (HAND; Antinori et al., 2007)

HIV-associated Asymptomatic Neurocognitive Impairment (ANI)[a]

1. Acquired impairment in cognitive functioning, involving at least two ability domains, documented by performance of at least 1 SD below the mean for demographically adjusted norms on standardized neuropsychological tests.[b]
2. The cognitive impairment does not interfere with everyday functioning (e.g., work, home life, and social activities).
3. The cognitive impairment does not meet criteria for delirium (e.g., clouding of consciousness is not a prominent feature) or HAD.
4. There is no evidence of another preexisting cause for the ANI.[c]

HIV-associated Mild Neurocognitive Disorder (MND)[a]

1. Acquired impairment in cognitive functioning, involving at least two ability domains, documented by performance of at least 1 SD below the mean for demographically adjusted norms on standardized neuropsychological tests.[b]
2. The cognitive impairment contributes to at least mild interference in everyday functioning as evidenced by at least one of the following:
   a) Self-report of reduced mental acuity, inefficiency in work, homemaking, or social functioning.
   b) Observation by knowledgeable others that the individual has undergone at least mild decline in mental acuity with resultant inefficiency in work, homemaking, or social functioning.
3. The cognitive impairment does not meet criteria for delirium or HAD.
4. There is no evidence of another preexisting cause for the MND.[c]

HIV-associated Dementia (HAD)[a]

1. Marked acquired impairment in cognitive functioning, involving at least two ability domains (typically the impairment is in multiple domains), documented by performance of at least 2 SD below the mean for demographically adjusted norms on standardized neuropsychological tests.[b] (If neuropsychological testing is not available, standard neurological evaluation and simple bedside testing may be used, but this should be done according to the algorithm provided by Antinori, et al., 2007).
2. The cognitive impairment contributes to marked interference with everyday functioning (e.g., work, home life, and social activities).
3. The pattern of cognitive impairment does not meet criteria for delirium; or, if delirium is present, criteria for HAD were met on a prior examination when delirium was not present.
4. There is no evidence of another, preexisting cause for HAD.[c]

---

[a]A diagnosis of HAND "in remission" may be applicable if the individual has a prior diagnosis of HAND, but does not currently meet criteria.
[b]The neuropsychological assessment must survey the ability areas of language, episodic memory, attention/working memory, executive functions, information-processing speed, sensory-perception, and motor skills.
[c]See Table 17–1A.

relatively infrequently, but can manifest in individuals with advanced HIV disease, likely arising from nigrostriatal dopaminergic dysregulation (e.g., Tse et al., 2004). Bradykinesia (i.e., slowed movement) is one of the earliest identified and most striking features of neuroAIDS; for example, tests of gait velocity (e.g., timed gait; Robertson et al., 2006) and fine motor speed and dexterity (e.g., Grooved Pegboard; Carey et al., 2004) are sensitive indicators of HIV-associated neurocognitive disorders. Bradyphrenia, or the slowing of mental faculties, may be observed on tasks with a wide variety of information-processing demands, particularly in more severe stages of illness (Reger et al., 2002) and when controlled attentional processes are required (e.g., choice versus simple reaction time; see Martin et al., 1999). It has been posited that psychomotor slowing may mediate the expression of HIV-associated neuropsychological deficits (Hardy & Hinkin, 2002), even for ability areas that are not expressly speeded (e.g., Becker & Salthouse, 1999). Such data highlight the importance of accounting for motor and psychomotor slowing when interpreting performance on higher-cognitive functions.

Attention, Working Memory, and Executive Functions

Attention. Attentional deficits are well documented in HIV (Hardy & Hinkin, 2002) and generally increase in magnitude with advancing disease severity (Grant et al., 2005). Regarding specific aspects of attention, several studies have demonstrated impairment in selective attention, including deficits on complex visual search and discrimination tasks (Hardy & Hinkin, 2002), covert orienting (Maruff et al., 1995), and global versus local visual processing (Martin et al., 1995) in HIV. Similarly, deficits in divided attention are observed in individuals with HIV infection (e.g., Hinkin et al., 2000; cf. Law et al., 1994), and are robust predictors of motor vehicle accidents (Marcotte et al., 2006). Although several studies have reported sustained attention deficits in HIV (e.g., Fein et al., 1995), it is unclear whether these deficits are mediated by psychomotor slowing.

Working Memory. Given the predominant frontostriatal dysfunction in HIV, there has been considerable interest in working memory, which involves the mental representation and manipulation of information for temporary information processing and storage (e.g., Baddeley & Hitch, 1994). Studies of working memory in HIV reveal impairment across multiple modalities (i.e., auditory, spatial, visual, and verbal), irrespective of the type of information being processed (Bartok et al., 1997; Farinpour et al., 2000; Martin et al., 2001). Converging evidence further suggests that HIV-associated working memory deficits are not limited to any one component process but rather are associated with several aspects of working memory, such as the mental operations involved in short-term memory storage, information maintenance across time delays, and/or immediate "online" memory manipulations (Martin et al., 2001).

Executive Functions. Definitions of executive functioning vary widely in the literature, but generally refer to a group of higher-order cognitive abilities involved in complex goal-directed behavior (e.g., planning and self-monitoring) and are commonly linked to frontal systems. Executive dysfunction is apparent even in the early stages of HIV disease, increasing in prevalence and magnitude in persons with AIDS (e.g., Heaton et al., 1995). Neuropsychological studies of HIV infection have typically revealed these executive deficits using standard clinical measures of abstraction and problem solving (e.g., Category Test errors), cognitive flexibility and set-shifting (e.g., perseverative errors on the Wisconsin Card Sort Test), and response inhibition (e.g., interference effects on the Stroop Color-Word Test). In addition, deficits in both cognitive (e.g., Bartok et al., 1997) and social (e.g., Benedict et al., 2000) planning may be evident in HIV. More recently, research on HIV-associated executive dysfunction has focused on decision-making processes using the Iowa Gambling Task, which was adapted from research on persons with ventromedial prefrontal lesions (e.g., Bechara et al., 1997). These early studies indicate that HIV-infected individuals are prone to selecting larger immediate rewards that are associated with more severe long-term consequences as compared to smaller immediate rewards with lesser negative outcomes (Hardy et al., 2006; Martin et al., 2004b). Martin and colleagues (2004b) suggested that such risky response styles among persons with HIV might reflect increased vulnerability to cognitive impulsivity, which has important implications for the identification and remediation of risky behavioral choices in everyday life (e.g., unprotected sex).

Learning and Memory

Declarative—Episodic Memory. Deficits in both verbal and visual episodic memory are present in approximately 50% of individuals infected with HIV (e.g., Heaton et al., 1995). Driven largely by frontostriatal circuit dysfunction (Wiseman et al., 1999), HIV-associated episodic (i.e., retrospective recall) memory impairment is typically characterized by deficient executive control of encoding and retrieval (e.g., Murji et al., 2003). Specifically, HIV-infected individuals demonstrate diminished free recall, increased repetition errors, and limited use of organizational encoding strategies (e.g., Delis et al., 1995). For example, HIV-associated semantic clustering deficits during list learning and recall are associated with executive dysfunction (e.g., Gongvatana et al., 2007) and are evident in relatively immunocompetent persons (e.g., Woods et al., 2005b), with impairment increasing in a stepwise manner in individuals with asymptomatic neurocognitive impairment, MCMD, and HAD (Gongvatana et al., 2007). Nevertheless, episodic memory deficits generally improve (although not necessarily to the normal range of functioning) when retrieval demands are minimized, particularly on recognition trials (e.g., Delis et al., 1995). Genuine consolidation impairment is rarely observed in HIV, except among persons with HAD who may evidence rapid forgetting, perhaps secondary to shallow encoding as indicated by an elevated recency effect (Scott et al., 2006).

A recent series of studies has begun to elucidate the nature and extent of prospective memory (ProM) impairment in HIV. ProM is a form of episodic memory involving the ability to successfully encode, retrieve, and execute future intentions, or "remember to remember," and as such, has important implications for daily functioning (e.g., medication management). Self-reported ProM complaints are elevated in HIV, particularly on daily tasks that require self-initiated cue detection and retrieval (Woods et al., 2007a). Objective ProM performance is also impaired in HIV infection and is characterized by mild to moderate deficits in both time- (Martin, et al., 2007) and event-based (Carey et al., 2006b) tasks. HIV-associated ProM deficits reflect impaired strategic encoding and retrieval of future intentions, as evidenced by increased rates of task substitution and no response errors in the setting of normal recognition of cue-intention pairings (Carey et al., 2006b). Interestingly, biomarkers of HIV disease severity such as macrophage activation (e.g., monocyte chemoattractant protein-1 [MCP-1]) and neuronal injury (e.g., tau) are associated with ProM, but not retrospective memory, suggesting that the neuropathogenesis of HIV-associated ProM impairment may be dissociable (Woods et al., 2006b). Of greater clinical relevance, HIV-associated ProM impairment demonstrates incremental ecological validity as a predictor of IADL declines (Woods et al., 2008a) and antiretroviral nonadherence (Woods et al., 2008b; in press).

Declarative—Semantic Memory. Few studies to date have specifically examined the effects of HIV on semantic memory, which refers to memory for generalized or factual knowledge that is not linked to a specific learning experience. Sadek et al. (2004) investigated the temporal pattern of HAD-associated retrograde semantic memory, finding that memory for famous faces and public events was mildly impaired in HAD relative to seronegative comparison subjects, with relatively comparable deficits in recall across time periods. This pattern was similar to that of persons with Huntington's disease, but contrasted with that of individuals with Alzheimer's disease, who demonstrated a temporal gradient of memory loss (i.e., poorer memory for recent versus remote events). The mild severity and temporal pattern of semantic memory loss in HAD was interpreted to reflect retrieval deficits arising from frontostriatal dysfunction, rather than a degradation of semantic memory stores, which would be more consistent with posterior cortical involvement.

Nondeclarative Memory. Nondeclarative memory refers to those aspects of memory that are implicit, or not directly altered within consciousness. Consistent with research on procedural memory deficits in populations with frontal systems dysfunction (e.g., Parkinson's disease; Harrington et al., 1990), Martin et al. (1993) reported that persons with MCMD demonstrate impaired motor skills learning. Kalechstein and colleagues (1998) went on to suggest that, in contrast to episodic memory deficits, HIV-associated procedural memory impairment may be associated with increased affective/cognitive symptoms of depression. Priming (i.e., the implicit effect of prior stimulus exposure on subsequent processing) is another important aspect of nondeclarative memory. Individuals with HIV-associated neurocognitive impairment demonstrate deficits on semantic, but not perceptual priming tasks (e.g., Nielsen-Bohlman et al., 1997), which is consistent with conceptual models suggesting that semantic priming is primarily mediated by frontal systems, whereas perceptual priming is more closely linked to the posterior neocortex.

Language Abilities

In the absence of severe HAD or focal CNS opportunistic infections, gross aphasia is rare in HIV. Although no large-scale, comprehensive assessments of basic speech and language functioning have been published on adults with HIV, it is widely held that receptive language abilities are relatively unaffected. In contrast, specific aspects of expressive language may be mildly to moderately impaired. For example, a small case-controlled study (Lopez et al., 1994) suggested that HIV might cause a motor speech disorder characterized by ataxic dysarthria (e.g., irregular articulatory rhythm). General expressive language deficits are mild in asymptomatic HIV infection, but may increase to medium effect sizes in persons with AIDS (Reger et al., 2002).

Verbal fluency is perhaps the most widely studied aspect of expressive language in HIV infection, with a recent meta-analysis revealing comparable, but modest deficits in both letter and category fluency (Iudicello et al., 2007). HIV-associated verbal fluency deficits appear to be characterized by impairment in strategic search and retrieval from lexico-semantic memory stores, perhaps reflecting a frontostriatal circuit neuropathogenesis. In support of this hypothesis, deficiencies in switching (i.e., the number of times an individual disengages from one lexico-semantic cluster and switches to another) but not clustering (i.e., the average number of consecutively generated words within a category) are evident in the verbal fluency protocols of persons with advanced HIV infection (Millikin et al., 2004; Woods et al., 2004). Moreover, HIV-associated category switching deficits are exacerbated in alternating fluency paradigms (Iudicello et al., 2008b).

Recent data suggest that action (verb) fluency (Piatt et al., 1999b) may be singly dissociable from noun fluency (e.g., animal fluency) in HIV (Woods et al., 2005a). Informed by the neural dissociation between noun and verb networks (Damasio & Tranel, 1993), action fluency (i.e., rapid oral generation of "things...that people do") demonstrates construct validity as a measure of frontal systems functions in Parkinson's disease (e.g., Piatt et al., 1999a) and healthy

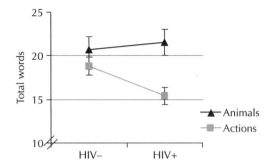

Figure 17–4. Line graph showing the significant interaction between HIV serostatus and verbal fluency cue (adapted from Woods et al., 2005).

adults (e.g., Woods et al., 2005c). In fact, an interaction between HIV serostatus and verbal fluency cue exists (Woods et al., 2005a), whereby HIV-infected individuals generate disproportionately fewer verbs than nouns (i.e., animals) relative to demographically comparable seronegative volunteers (see Figure 17–4), which may be selectively driven by astrocytosis (i.e., elevated S-100β; Iudicello et al., 2008a). Importantly, action fluency is sensitive to HIV-associated neurocognitive disorders (Woods et al., 2005a) and may provide incremental ecological validity in predicting IADL declines as compared to traditional letter- and noun-based fluency tasks (Woods et al., 2006a).

Spatial Cognition

Spatial cognition refers to the diverse set of cognitive abilities required to perceive, process, and mentally manipulate visual stimuli, often in the service of motor functions (e.g., visuoperception). It is widely held that spatial cognition is not affected in HIV disease (e.g., (Cysique et al., 2006). However, the posterior parietal cortex and parieto-striato-frontal circuits play an important role in spatial cognition (e.g., Lawrence et al., 2000), thereby raising questions as to whether prior HIV studies were too cursory in their measurement of this construct. To this end, Martin (1994) reported impairment in egocentric spatial cognition in HIV, which involved the analysis of objects in relation to a frame of reference that is based on an observer's point of view, rather than the participant's (i.e., allocentric). More recently, Olesen and colleagues (2007) observed deficits in mental rotation (i.e., the mental manipulation of visual images in space) in a small sample of HIV-infected men, which were particularly pronounced at greater degrees of rotation. The cognitive (e.g., spatial working memory and/or visuoperceptual impairment) and neurobiological (e.g., frontostriatal and/or posterior parietal dysfunction) underpinnings of HIV-associated impairment in mental rotation await further examination.

General Cognitive Functioning

Mental Status. Delirium (i.e., acute, fluctuating alterations in the sensorium) may be evident in as many as one-half of hospitalized patients with HIV infection (e.g., Breitbart et al., 1996). A variety of factors may cause delirium in HIV, such as opportunistic infections (e.g. meningitis), medication side effects (e.g., benzodiazepines), and metabolic disturbances (e.g., electrolyte imbalance) (Atkinson et al., 2005). Although research is limited, delirium in HIV is generally associated with poorer disease outcomes, including higher mortality rates (e.g., Uldall et al., 2000).

Cognitive Screening. The HIV Dementia Scale (HDS) was designed to screen for global cognitive deficits in HIV, specifically HAD (Power et al., 1995). As compared to other mental status tests (e.g., the Mini-Mental State Examination), the HDS is more sensitive to HAD, perhaps given its relatively stronger demands on information-processing speed (e.g., timed written alphabet and cube copy). Nevertheless, the HDS has been criticized for its poor negative predictive power (Carey et al., 2004). In response, Morgan et al. (2008) developed age- and education-adjusted normative standards for the HDS. When applied to a validation cohort of 135 HIV-infected participants, the normed HDS significantly improved the sensitivity and overall classification of the HDS for identifying HIV-associated neurocognitive disorders. Nevertheless, false negative errors were still problematic for individuals with very mild neurocognitive impairment (positive predictive power = 34%), indicating that other validated screening approaches (e.g., Grooved Pegboard) and/or referral for comprehensive evaluation are needed for such cases (e.g., Carey et al., 2004).

Intellectual Functioning. It is widely known that certain aspects of fluid intelligence (e.g., information-processing speed) are sometimes impaired in adults with HIV infection. In addition, studies have also indicated that crystallized intellectual abilities (e.g., general fund of knowledge) might also be negatively affected (e.g., Egan et al., 1990). Questions have arisen as to whether such differences reflect low premorbid IQ, rather than the consequences of HIV infection itself. Indeed, premorbid IQ estimates are oftentimes lower in HIV-infected adults relative to demographically comparable seronegatives (e.g., Basso & Bornstein, 2000). Lower premorbid IQ, perhaps by way of diminished cognitive reserve, is likely an important source of variability in HIV-associated neuropsychological impairment (e.g., van Gorp et al., 1993). HIV-infected individuals with minimal cognitive reserve show increased prevalence (Stern et al., 1996) and incidence (Basso & Bornstein, 2000) of cognitive deficits. Whether cognitive reserve explains the subset of cases in which neuropsychological functioning is normal, but extensive HIV-associated neuropathologies are present upon postmortem examination, remains to be determined by future research.

Sensory-Perception

Basic sensory-perceptual functions (e.g., tactile sensation) can be compromised by HIV and threaten interpretation of deficits in higher-level cognitive abilities. Approximately 28% of individuals with HIV-associated neuropsychological impairment show sensory-perceptual deficits as measured by the Reitan-Kløve Sensory-Perceptual Exam, specifically in bilateral tactile form recognition (Heaton et al., 1995). Distal sensory polyneuropathy (DSPN), involving the distal degeneration of long axons, affects up to 50% of patients with AIDS (Simpson et al., 2006). Symptoms of DSPN include painful dysesthesias, paresthesias, and numbness (most often in the lower extremities), all of which may compromise IADLs and quality of life. Risk factors for DSPN include older age, lower CD4 counts, neuromedical comorbidity (e.g., hepatitis C infection), and neurotoxic antiretroviral drugs (e.g., d4T; Keswani et al., 2005). With regard to ocular functions, infectious (e.g., cytomegalovirus) and noninfectious (e.g., cotton wool spots [CWS]) retinopathies may manifest in HIV-infected individuals in the advanced stages of the disease. The destruction of retinal ganglion cells by multiple microinfarcts can manifest clinically as CWS, the presence of which is associated with reduced visual acuity, as well as neuropsychological impairment (e.g., Geier et al., 1993; cf. Freeman et al., 2004). Otologic and audiologic abnormalities also frequently occur in HIV. Early studies indicated that up to 33% of HIV-infected patients have ear disease and many present with otitis media (Chandrasekhar et al., 2000). In addition, high-frequency sensorineural hearing loss is commonly observed and tends to be more severe in patients with more advanced HIV disease. Finally, deficits in odor detection (Razani et al., 1996) and identification (Westervelt et al., 1997) have also been reported in HIV infection.

Effort and Symptom Validity

Approximately 20% of persons with HIV infection in the United States receive Social Security disability benefits (Centers for Disease Control and Prevention, 2001), including some specifically for HIV-associated neurocognitive disorders. As such, the possibility that a small subset of HIV-infected claimants might feign or exaggerate cognitive deficits in an effort to secure monetary compensation and/or service benefits must be considered (Sweet et al., 2002). Suboptimal effort, perhaps secondary to constitutional symptoms (e.g., fatigue), might also confound the interpretation of neuropsychological data in HIV. Using an "embedded" effort index from within the Wechsler Memory Scale-Revised (WMS-R; Mittenberg et al., 1993; Psychological Corporation, 1987), Slick and colleagues (2001) observed false positive rates ranging from 7%-18% in a small sample of persons with HIV infection, with the greatest number of false positives among individuals with higher general memory abilities. Woods et al. (2003) reported that as few as 2% of non-

compensation-seeking individuals with HIV-associated neurocognitive disorders fail the Hiscock Digit Memory Test (HDMT; a symptom validity test, test designed to detect suboptimal effort, etc.; Hiscock & Hiscock, 1989). Although these preliminary studies provide important information regarding specificity, prospective data regarding the sensitivity and positive predictive power of various symptom validity tests in well-characterized compensation-seeking HIV samples would also be useful.

Everyday Consequences of Neuropsychological Impairment in HIV

A variety of factors associated with HIV infection can contribute to reduced independence in performing IADLs, including constitutional symptoms, affective distress, and substance-related disorders. For example, HIV-infected individuals with substance dependence are at risk for poor antiretroviral (ARV) medication adherence (e.g., Arnsten et al., 2002), which in turn contributes to poorer health outcomes (e.g., medication resistant viral strains). In this section, we focus on the impact of HIV-associated neurocognitive impairment on health-related quality of life (HRQOL), risk behaviors, and IADLs (i.e., employment, automobile driving, and medication adherence), and mortality rates.

Health-Related Quality of Life

HRQOL is a multifaceted construct delineating an individual's ability to function and successfully perform daily activities (e.g., employment), and their mental, physical and emotional well-being. Research has consistently found poorer physical, emotional, and mental HRQOL in HIV infection, particularly among individuals with AIDS (e.g., Ruiz Perez et al., 2005) and comorbid affective disorders (e.g., Trepanier et al., 2005). The literature also supports a correspondence between reduced HRQOL and several aspects of HIV-associated neuropsychological impairment, including deficits in fine motor coordination, episodic memory, executive functions, and information-processing speed (Tozzi et al., 2003). Cognitive impairment in these ability areas also increases the risk of dependence in IADLs, which ostensibly reduces HRQOL. In addition, it has been suggested that individuals with HIV-associated neurocognitive disorders may utilize ineffective coping strategies (e.g., confrontive coping; Manly et al., 1997), thereby reducing HRQOL by limiting their ability to effectively manage stressful life events (e.g., Pukay-Martin et al., 2003).

Risk Behaviors

HIV infection is associated with a number of risky behaviors (e.g., injection drug use and unprotected sex). As such, understanding the underlying neuropsychological deficits that may predispose individuals to developing and engaging in risky behaviors may have important implications for prevention and treatment of both "at risk" and already HIV-infected individuals. Although HIV-infected individuals evidence risky decision-making styles (Hardy et al., 2006), the limited research to date in HIV-infected substance users has not identified a strong relationship between self-reported risk behavior and measures of executive functions (e.g., Gonzalez et al., 2005) or working memory (Martin et al., 2004b). Nevertheless, Martin et al. (2007) recently reported an association between risky behaviors in HIV-infected substance-dependent individuals and impaired time-based ProM, which may moderate the relationship between one's intention to implement HIV prevention strategies and actual participation in risky HIV transmission behaviors.

Instrumental Activities of Daily Living (IADL)

Employment. Retaining gainful employment is a critical issue for individuals living with HIV infection, especially vis-à-vis the debilitating physical (e.g., fatigue), affective (e.g., depression), and cognitive complications of the disease. HIV-related neuropsychological impairment is associated with poor performance on standardized work samples, higher rates of unemployment, and incident work disability over time, even after controlling for HIV disease severity (e.g., Heaton et al., 2004). Individuals with deficits in learning efficiency and executive functions (i.e.,

set-shifting and response inhibition) are perhaps at greatest risk of reducing or discontinuing work (van Gorp et al., 1999). The advent of cART has extended survival rates and HRQOL, but has also introduced the possible challenges of returning to work, often after significant periods of unemployment and/or disability. van Gorp et al. (2007) reported that verbal learning and memory abilities were the strongest predictors of returning to work, such that individuals with the highest memory scores had greater than a 70% chance of being employed at a 2-year follow-up. These findings may have implications for cognitive and vocational rehabilitation, as a number of cognitive interventions have been designed to improve learning and memory (e.g., spaced retrieval) in various clinical populations (e.g., dementia).

Automobile Driving. Driving an automobile requires a complex combination of multiple cognitive domains including perception, sustained and selective attention, visual and psychomotor processing speed, motor sequencing, judgment, and planning, many of which may be adversely affected in HIV. In fact, individuals with HIV-associated neurocognitive disorders perform significantly worse on computerized driving simulators and are more likely to fail on-road driving evaluations (Marcotte et al., 2004) than their unimpaired HIV counterparts. Deficits in executive functions, complex attention, speed of information processing, fine motor dexterity, and sensory-perceptual functions are most closely associated with poor driving performance (Marcotte et al., 1999, 2004). Although these findings highlight the potential impact of HIV-associated neurocognitive deficits on driving ability, one must also weigh the relative risk of on-road accidents to the potential impact of lost driving privileges on HRQOL. As such, evidence of neuropsychological impairment may warrant referral for an on-road evaluation, but should not be the sole arbiter of a recommendation to suspend driving privileges.

Medication Adherence. Optimal adherence to cART regimens is associated with dramatic reductions in morbidity and mortality, whereas nonadherence has potentially life-threatening consequences (e.g., development of drug-resistance). The literature consistently reveals that HIV-associated cognitive deficits are associated with deficient medication adherence. In fact, cognitive impairment confers a twofold greater risk of cART nonadherence, which is driven primarily by episodic memory deficits and executive dysfunction (e.g., Hinkin et al., 2002). Furthermore, individuals with HIV-associated neurocognitive disorders who are prescribed more complex cART regimens may be at greater risk for nonadherence (Gallant & Block, 1998; Hinkin et al., 2002). A recent study demonstrated the importance of HIV-associated ProM impairment to medication adherence in 79 volunteers who were followed for approximately 1 month using medication event monitoring caps (Woods et al., in press). As shown in Figure 17–5, nonadherent individuals ($n = 31$) demonstrated significantly poorer prospective memory functioning as compared to adherent persons ($n = 48$), particularly on an index of time-based ProM (i.e., elevated loss of time errors). Importantly, time-based ProM impairment remained significant, independent predictor of non-adherence, even after considering demographics, disease severity, affective distress, and general cognitive impairment, suggesting that cART adherence may be particularly dependent on the self-initiated cognitive processes involved in retrieving future intentions (e.g., time monitoring; see also Woods et al., 2008b).

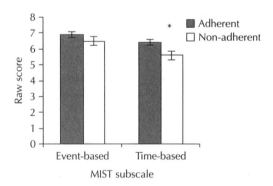

Figure 17–5. Bar chart showing the time- and event-based prospective memory scores from the Memory for Intentions Screening Test (MIST) in antiretroviral adherent ($n = 48$) and nonadherent ($n = 31$) participants (adapted from Woods et al., in press).
* $p < .05$, Cohen's $d = -0.6$.

Mortality

HIV-associated neurocognitive disorders are potentially a harbinger of mortality (Ellis et al., 1997a). Global cognitive impairment is significantly associated with lower survival rates, even prior to progression to AIDS (Ellis et al., 1997a; Mayeux et al., 1993). Studies from both the pre- and post-cART eras show higher rates of mortality among HIV-infected persons with a range of cognitive impairment severity (e.g., Mayeux et al., 1993; Sevigny et al., 2007). There is a particularly strong association between HAD and time to death, independent of disease progression (e.g., CD4 count), treatment effects (e.g., ARV use) and demographic factors (Sevigny et al., 2007). Future research should investigate possible mediators of the relationship between neuropsychological impairment and death (e.g., medication adherence) in an effort to develop effective interventions and further improve survival rates.

Biomarkers of HIV-Associated Neurocognitive Disorders

CDC Staging

The Center for Disease Control and Prevention, (CDC, 1993) defined a set of staging guidelines based on three ranges of CD4 lymphocyte counts (i.e., ≥ 500, 499–200, and < 200 cells/μL) and three severities of symptomatology (i.e., A, B, and C), which comprise nine exclusive categories. The prevalence and severity of neurocognitive impairment generally increases in a stepwise fashion as the disease advances (e.g., Reger et al., 2002). Despite early controversies over whether cognitive impairment existed in the asymptomatic phase (e.g., CDC A; Janssen et al., 1989), subsequent research shows that approximately 30% of persons in this stage evidence overall mild cognitive impairment across numerous domains of functioning (Heaton et al., 1995). An important future direction of this research is examination of the CNS effects of acute (i.e., the period between transmission and seroconversion) and early (i.e., < 1 year posttransmission) HIV infection, a period in which rapid viral replication and neuroinflammatory responses are present in animal and cellular models (e.g., Greco et al., 2004).

CNS Opportunistic Infections

Although less common in the cART era, several of the AIDS-defining opportunistic infections (OIs) have implications for CNS functioning. Typically occurring when an individual is immunosuppressed (i.e., CD4 count < 200 cells/ μL), CNS OIs include Toxoplasma encephalitis, JC virus encephalitis (i.e., progressive multifocal leukoencephalopathy), Cytomegalovirus encephalitis, and primary CNS lymphoma. The most common CNS OI is Cryptococcal meningitis, which has been reported to occur in up to 10% of persons with AIDS, particularly in untreated individuals or in international settings (Chayakulkeeree & Perfect, 2006; Mirza et al., 2003).

CD4 Lymphocyte Count

A primary target of HIV, CD4 lymphocytes are a type of white blood cell (i.e., leukocytes) that are vital to immune function by assisting in the destruction of bacteria, viruses, fungi, and parasites. The normal CD4 count range varies by laboratory, but is generally between 500 to 1,500 cells/μL. The specific neuropathological processes that underlie the relationship between the number of circulating CD4 lymphocytes and the risk for HIV-associated neurological complications are still not well understood. For example, CD4 lymphocyte counts among individuals recently diagnosed with HAD appears to be higher than those reported in the pre-cART era (Brew, 2004), suggesting that current CD4 lymphocyte count may now be less useful as a clinical biomarker of neuroAIDS. In light of this, several research groups have investigated the predictive value of self-reported CD4 nadir (i.e., the lowest ever CD4 count) in neuroAIDS. For example, Valcour et al. (2006) demonstrated that nadir CD4 count significantly predicted HAD and MCMD, even after modeling the effects of demographics, current CD4 count, and HIV disease duration. Specifically, a difference of 100 cells/μL was associated with a 40% increased risk of HAD. These findings replicate others that have identified lower nadir CD4 counts as a risk factor for neurocognitive impairment (Tozzi et al., 2005) and neuropathy

(Watters et al., 2004), thereby supporting the possible utility of this measure as a marker of nervous system disease.

HIV RNA

HIV RNA, an indicator of HIV replication or "viral load" can be quantified in blood plasma or cerebrospinal fluid (CSF). Although plasma viral load is integral to monitoring general immune health and treatment efficacy, it is not reliably predictive of HIV-associated neuropsychological impairment (e.g., Reger et al., 2005). Evidence of viral compartmentalization in the CNS (e.g., Ellis et al., 1997b) inspired the hypothesis that CSF viral load may provide a clearer window onto the CNS burden of HIV infection. In further support of this notion, Ellis et al. (2002) found that detectable CSF viral load was a stronger predictor of incident cognitive impairment than plasma HIV RNA. Despite these encouraging findings from the pre-cART era, more recent findings have identified weakened relationships between CSF viral loads and cognitive outcomes (e.g., Sevigny et al., 2004). CSF viral load may still provide insights into pathologic events in the CNS, but it is not currently considered an optimal surrogate marker (McArthur et al., 2004).

Host Biomarkers

Biomarkers that reflect host processes that may contribute to HIV neuropathogenesis have also been explored (see Gonzalez-Scarano & Martin-Garcia, 2005), including chemokines (e.g., MCP-1), neuroprotective factors (e.g., FGF-1), and markers of monocyte activation (e.g., beta-2 microglobulin), excitotoxicity (e.g., quinolinic acid), astrocytosis (e.g., S-100β), neuroinflammation (e.g., tumor necrosis factor-alpha), oxidative stress (e.g., ceramide), and neuronal damage (e.g., neurofilament-light). One of the most widely studied biomarkers of HIV neuropathogenesis is MCP-1 (i.e., CC chemokine ligand 2), which is produced by astrocytes, is a marker of mononuclear phagocyte (e.g., macrophages) trafficking, and is associated with higher CSF viral loads (e.g., Monteiro de Almeida et al., 2005), HAD (e.g., Kelder et al., 1998), and HIV encephalitis (Cinque et al., 1998). Although concerns regarding the specificity of biomarkers to HIV disease persist, their value in delineating the neuropathogenic mechanisms of HIV-associated neurocognitive disorders is nonetheless compelling.

Genetic Factors

The past 10 years have witnessed an increased effort to understand the viral and host genetic factors involved in HIV-associated neurocognitive disorders. Extending the HIV biomarker research described above, several investigators have begun to examine the role of genetic variants of various chemokines and chemokine receptors in neuroAIDS. For example, Gonzalez et al. (2002) demonstrated that variability in the promoter region of the gene encoding MCP-1 was associated with a 4.5-fold increased risk of HAD. In addition, Singh et al. (2004) reported that variability in the gene encoding CCR2, the receptor for MCP-1, was associated with a twofold increased risk of incident neuropsychological impairment, perhaps reflecting increased susceptibility to neurotoxic inflammatory processes. Several studies have also examined the role of apolipoprotein E ε4 allele (APOE-ε4) in the expression of neuroAIDS. Corder et al. (1998) were the first to describe an association between APOE-ε4 and increased frequency of neurological symptoms in HIV, including HAD. More recently, Valcour et al. (2004b) demonstrated that APOE-ε4 was associated with a threefold increased risk for HAD in older adults with HIV. Postmortem studies suggest that, among persons with HAD, APOE-ε4 is associated with increased susceptibility of neurons to lipid metabolism pathologies (e.g., increased concentrations of sphingolipids in the prefrontal cortex) (Cutler et al., 2004). Considering the neuropathogenesis of HIV-associated neurocognitive disorders and prior research on the genetics of cognition (Goldberg & Weinberger, 2004), numerous other candidate genes might be considered, including brain derived neurotrophic factor (BDNF), catechol-O-methyltransferase (COMT), monoamine oxidase A (MAOA), and serotonin 2A receptor (5-HT2A).

Comorbidities of HIV-Associated Neurocognitive Disorders

Affective Disorders

Depression. Major Depressive Disorder (MDD) is perhaps the most common comorbid psychiatric disorder found in HIV-infected individuals, with estimated prevalence rates as high as 50% (Ciesla & Roberts, 2001). The etiology of depressive symptoms may be either primary (e.g., premorbid) or secondary (e.g., associated with the psychological impact of HIV infection or due to organic causes related to infection of the CNS) to HIV infection (Treisman et al., 1998). Depression in HIV infection is of particular clinical importance as a predictor of poorer treatment outcomes, reduced medication adherence, and everyday functioning (Heaton et al., 2004) as well as increased mortality (Mayeux et al., 1993). In seronegative groups, MDD is associated with neuropsychological impairment, including deficits in attention, learning and memory, psychomotor speed and executive functions. In HIV, MDD and neuropsychological impairment are independently associated with HRQOL (Trepanier et al., 2005), IADLs (Heaton et al., 1996), and mortality (Ellis et al., 1997a). Depressed mood is also often associated with increased cognitive complaints in HIV, even though neuropsychological performance may be within normal limits(Rourke et al., 1999). However, research on the potential additive effects of MDD on HIV-associated neuropsychological impairment has been largely negative. Despite their similar pathological features (e.g., frontostriatal circuits) and neuropsychological profiles, the majority of studies have failed to identify significant additive effects of MDD and HIV on cognition (e.g., Grant et al., 1993), suggesting possibly dissociable neuropathogenic mechanisms (Cysique et al., 2007).

Anxiety Disorders. HIV-infected individuals are also at risk of developing anxiety disorders, with comorbid prevalence estimates as high as 38% (Elliott, 1998). Typically, symptoms of anxiety found in HIV infection result from a premorbid condition, or from a preoccupation with HIV and difficulties in coping with the illness, rather than from an organic basis resulting directly from infection (Grant & Atkinson, 1999). Comorbid anxiety disorders in HIV infection are predictive of medication nonadherence and poorer HRQOL (Tucker et al., 2003). This is a potentially important area of research because neuropsychological impairments are evident in a subset of anxiety disorders, including Obsessive-Compulsive Disorder, Post-traumatic Stress Disorder, and Generalized Anxiety Disorder (e.g., Airaksinen et al., 2005). Mapou et al. (1993) found that higher self-reported anxiety symptoms in HIV were associated with subjective cognitive complaints, but not performance-based neuropsychological impairment. Similarly, diagnoses of Generalized Anxiety Disorder were not associated with neuropsychological impairment in a large HIV sample (Heaton et al., 1995). Considering the prevalence of anxiety disorders in HIV infection and their independent effects on the CNS, HRQOL, and IADLs, research on the neurocognitive consequences of comorbid anxiety disorders and HIV infection is clearly indicated.

Bipolar Disorder. HIV-infected individuals may also display either primary or secondary symptoms of mania. Although Bipolar Disorder and HIV affect similar neural systems (i.e., frontostriatal and limbic networks), little is known about their potential additive effects on the CNS or how frequently these conditions co-occur. Importantly, Bipolar Disorder and HIV and are each associated with increased risk-taking behavior (e.g., unprotected sex), neuropsychological deficits (e.g., executive dysfunction), and medical noncompliance, suggesting that investigation into their combined effects is highly relevant. To this end, Moore and colleagues (2006) recently reported evidence of additive effects of HIV and Bipolar Disorder in a sample of polysubstance users, such that global neuropsychological impairment was more prevalent in individuals with comorbid Bipolar Disorder and HIV infection (70%) as compared to demographically comparable subjects with only one risk factor (i.e., HIV or Bipolar Disorder alone; 61%) or neither condition (24%). Prospective research regarding the prevalence and neurobiological mechanisms of Bipolar Disorder in

HIV, along with the neuropsychiatric, cognitive, and functional (e.g., medication adherence and HIV transmission risk) consequences of comorbidity is needed.

Substance-Related Disorders

Alcohol. Alcohol-related disorders (i.e., abuse and/or dependence) often accompany HIV infection, with the rate of heavy drinking almost twice that of the general population (Galvan et al., 2002). In addition, alcohol abusers have a 5%–10% higher risk of acquiring HIV (Meyerhoff, 2001) as consumption has been linked to risk behaviors (e.g., sexual disinhibition) associated with HIV transmission (Stein et al., 2005) and reduced medication compliance (Braithwaite et al., 2005). Furthermore, alcohol has been shown to influence the progression of HIV infection by altering the immune response (Wang et al., 2002), diminishing the effectiveness of cART (Miguez et al., 2003), and potentiating the neurotoxicity of HIV-specific protein-induced gp120 apoptosis (Chen et al., 2005). Alcohol use can also exacerbate HIV-associated white matter damage (e.g., fractional anisotropy in the corpus callosum; Pfefferbaum et al., 2007) and interacts with disease severity with respect to volume reduction in the corpus callosum and enlargement of the supratentorial ventricles (Pfefferbaum et al., 2006). Metabolic abnormalities (i.e., reduced N-acetyl aspartate and creatine) are also evident in HIV-infected individuals with alcohol dependence (Pfefferbaum et al., 2005).

Previously, neuropsychological studies of alcohol use in the context of HIV infection were confounded by the inclusion of polysubstance dependent individuals or limited cognitive assessments, thereby limiting reliable conclusions about the potential interaction. Three recent studies, however, have addressed this limitation by excluding comorbid substance users in their sample. Each demonstrated evidence for an additive effect of alcohol and HIV, specifically on measures of selective attention (Schulte et al., 2005), verbal reasoning and auditory processing (Green et al., 2004), and psychomotor speed (Durvasula et al., 2006). Whether such elevated rates of impairment in these cohorts are associated with increased risk of IADL dependence, HRQOL, and/or mortality remains to be determined.

Marijuana. Marijuana use is widespread among HIV-infected individuals (Whitfield et al., 1997), both in terms of recreational and medicinal (e.g., analgesia, increasing appetite, and nausea control) consumption. Importantly, marijuana suppresses immune function and may have an additive effect in the context of already immunocompromised systems (e.g., Ongradi et al., 1998). A meta-analysis of the residual effects of long-term cannabis use on neurocognitive functioning found only a small effect in the ability to learn and remember new information (Grant et al., 2003), but to our knowledge, only one study has examined the effects of marijuana use on cognition in HIV-infected individuals. Cristiani et al. (2004) stratified groups according to self-reported marijuana use over the past 12 months with the "no/minimal use" group reporting using less than once per month as compared to the "frequent use" group who reported use at least once a week, as well as HIV disease stage. A significant interaction was observed, suggesting that frequent marijuana use was associated with greater memory impairment among symptomatic participants. Further study is needed regarding the cognitive and neurobiological sequelae of marijuana use in HIV-infected individuals, particularly considering evidence that marijuana may be neuroprotective in HIV (Croxford, 2003), and is a potentially effective treatment for chronic neuropathic pain from HIV-associated sensory neuropathy (Abrams et al., 2007).

Cocaine. Animal model studies suggest that chronic cocaine abuse may hasten the progression of the HIV disease process. For instance, cocaine-injected mice also inoculated with HIV-infected macrophages demonstrated increased astrogliosis and microgliosis, more impaired cognitive performance on a spatial learning task, and recovered more slowly from fatigue in comparison to uninfected mice (Griffin et al., 2007). The possible additive effects of cocaine and HIV may be secondary to their combined neurotoxic effects, particularly with respect to dopaminergic dysfunction (e.g., Wang et al.,

2004). Other proposed mechanisms include increased neuroinvasion and neurovascular complications secondary to cocaine's direct effects on microvascular endothelial cells in the BBB (e.g., Zhang et al., 1998), amplification of HIV replication (e.g., Peterson et al., 1991), and augmented expression of inflammatory cytokines, leukocyte transmigration, and adhesion molecules (e.g., Gan et al., 1998).

Human cognitive studies have been primarily limited to polysubstance abusers who use cocaine, making it difficult to isolate cocaine-specific deficits. In a sample of African American men with comorbid HIV infection and cocaine abuse, Durvasula and colleagues (2000) reported that, with the exception of an association between moderate to heavy recent cocaine use and slower psychomotor speed, cocaine use did not contribute to HIV-associated neuropsychological deficits. Another study found that cocaine-dependent individuals with HIV reported significantly more cognitive impairment than seronegative cocaine users (Avants et al., 1997); however, performance-based cognitive abilities were not investigated. Finally, a study of active stimulant users (cocaine and/or amphetamines) with HIV infection found impairment in sustained attention (Levine et al., 2006). Prospective research, perhaps using a parametric study design is needed to more clearly articulate the possible combined effects of cocaine use in HIV infection.

Methamphetamine. Methamphetamine dependence is frequent among HIV-infected individuals and in persons at high-risk for HIV infection (Woody et al., 1999). Methamphetamine dependence and HIV infection are both independently associated with cognitive dysfunction (e.g., Reger et al., 2002; Scott et al., 2007) and converge in their neuropathophysiological effects on frontostriatal circuits (e.g., Nath et al., 2002). Interestingly, it appears that structural brain alterations associated with methamphetamine dependence and HIV are distinct, yet overlapping with opposing effects on brain volume. Specifically, HIV is associated with volume atrophy (e.g., frontal cortex and caudate nucleus), whereas methamphetamine is associated with cortical (e.g., parietal) and basal ganglia volume increases

(Jernigan et al., 2005). Nevertheless, additive effects are evident using MR spectroscopy, specifically reductions in N-acetyl aspartate (NAA) in the basal ganglia, frontal white matter, and frontal gray matter, diminished creatine in the basal ganglia, and *myo*inositol reductions in the frontal white matter (Chang et al., 2005). Not surprisingly, comorbid HIV and methamphetamine dependence are associated with a compounding of adverse neurocognitive effects (Rippeth et al., 2004), particularly in a subset of immunosuppressed individuals (Carey et al., 2006a). Episodic memory is perhaps most susceptible to the additive effects of HIV and methamphetamine, the cellular basis for which may be a severe loss of calbindin and parvalbumin interneurons in the frontal cortex (Chana et al., 2006).

Opioids. Injection opioid (i.e., heroin) users are at significantly increased risk for acquiring HIV infection. Opioids readily cross the BBB and are associated with feelings of euphoria, but the research on possible neuropsychological deficits in seronegative persons dependent on heroin are generally inconclusive (e.g., Pau et al., 2002). Although some studies show an independent effect of heroin use on cognitive impairment in HIV-infected individuals (e.g., Margolin et al., 2002), there is no clear evidence that heroin necessarily exacerbates HIV-associated neuropsychological impairment (Selnes et al., 1997). However, the neuroAIDS research on heroin users is difficult to interpret given multiple confounding factors, including polysubstance abuse (especially cocaine), psychiatric comorbidity, premorbid CNS vulnerabilities, demographic effects, and various (often unmeasured) health-related factors, such as nutritional deficiencies and co-infection with the hepatitis C virus.

Hepatitis C Co-Infection

Between 15% and 50% of persons living with HIV are co-infected with the Hepatitis C Virus (HCV), with the highest rates of co-infection among HIV-seropositive injection drug users (e.g., Mohsen et al., 2005). HCV is a single-stranded RNA Flavivirus that has infected approximately 3 million adults in the United States and is associated with chronic

liver disease. Research increasingly supports the neurovirulence of chronic HCV infection: HCV RNA is detectable in brain parenchyma (e.g., Radkowski et al., 2002), and elevated metabolic markers of neuronal injury and neuroinflammation are evident in the basal ganglia and frontal cerebral white matter of HCV-infected individuals (e.g., Forton et al., 2005). Cognitive deficits, most notably slowed information-processing speed and complex attentional impairments, have also been associated with HCV (e.g., Forton et al., 2005), even after controlling for potentially confounding comorbidities (e.g., substance abuse; Cherner et al., 2005). HCV-associated deficits in motor coordination and information-processing speed are correlated with declines in the independent performance of basic and instrumental ADLs, respectively (Vigil, et al., 2008).

Since HIV and HCV each adversely affect cognition, several groups have posited that co-infection may confer additive risks of neurocognitive impairment, perhaps by way of inflammatory mechanisms (e.g., Letendre et al., 2005). Individuals with HIV–HCV co-infection may be particularly vulnerable to neuropsychiatric disturbances (e.g., affective distress; von Giesen et al., 2004) and psychomotor slowing (e.g., Clifford et al., 2005). For example, Martin et al. (2004a) reported that HIV and HCV were additively associated with slower reaction times to both congruent and incongruent Stroop trials. Nevertheless, the limited data published to date on the possible additive neuropsychological effects of co-infection are mixed (e.g., Ryan et al., 2004). Multidisciplinary studies designed to clarify the prevalence, mechanisms, and functional impact of co-infection on the CNS are warranted and should give consideration to potential confounds, such as alcohol and drug use, socioeconomic status, developmental disorders (e.g., learning disabilities), liver disease severity, and antiviral medications.

Normal Aging

With the advent of more effective cART, the mortality rates in HIV have decreased dramatically, resulting in an increased prevalence of older adults living with HIV infection (CDC, 2005). Eighteen percent of the incident

AIDS cases and 32% of AIDS-related deaths in the United States are among HIV-infected individuals aged 50 years and older (CDC, 2005). Although controversy exists regarding the impact of normal aging on HIV disease (Casau, 2005), older adults with HIV may be at greater risk for premorbid immune down-regulation (e.g., Fagnoni et al., 2000), more rapid HIV disease progression (e.g., Goetz et al., 2001) and morbidity (Perez & Moore, 2003). Numerous CNS risk factors also accompany normal aging, including cardiovascular disease (e.g., hypertension), cerebrovascular comorbidity, metabolic dysregulation (e.g., insulin resistance), and non-HIV-associated dementias (e.g., Alzheimer's disease) (Valcour et al., 2004a). Indeed, older age may confer an increased risk of HIV-associated neurocognitive disorders. Valcour et al. (2004a) reported that older adults (aged ≥ 50 years) were three times more likely to be diagnosed with HAD than their younger counterparts, even after controlling for demographics, HIV disease severity, psychiatric comorbidities, and cART. Among nondemented older HIV-infected adults, individuals with detectable CSF viral loads evidence a twofold risk of neurocognitive impairment (Cherner et al., 2004). Whether the profile of HIV-associated neuropsychological deficits is different in older adults remains to be determined, but the increased prevalence of argyrophilic amyloid plaques (Esiri et al., 1998) and possible expression of APOE-ε4 genotype (Valcour et al., 2004b) suggest that cognitive sequelae of medial temporal pathology may be more prominent in this cohort (Brew, 2004). Finally, the contribution of neurocognitive deficits to everyday functioning (e.g., automobile driving and HRQOL) in HIV-infected older adults deserves exploration. Although older age is generally associated with better cART compliance (Wutoh et al., 2001), older adults with HIV-associated cognitive impairment (e.g., executive dysfunction) may be at increased risk for nonadherence (Hinkin et al., 2004).

The revised criteria for HAND begin to address the issue of diagnosis of HAND in the context of potential confounds. Table 17–1A provides an approach to classifying such confounds which was developed by the Frascati Group (see also Antinori et al., 2007).

Treatment of HIV-Associated Neurocognitive Disorders

Antiretroviral Therapies

Although cART has reduced the incidence of HAD (Sacktor et al., 2006), HIV-associated neuropsychological impairment is still highly prevalent and continues to adversely affect HRQOL and IADLs (Tozzi et al., 2004). Research generally supports the positive impact of cART initiation on HIV-associated neuropsychological deficits (e.g., psychomotor slowing) (e.g., Ferrando et al., 1998); however, the literature is not entirely consistent in this regard (e.g., Cysique et al., 2004). In fact, a very recent study identified that neuropsychological performance may improve when cART is discontinued, although the mechanisms for this observation are not yet understood (Robertson et al., 2007). One complexity of observational research on the effects of cART is that many patients are not prescribed ARVs until their CD4 counts fall below 200 cells/μL (e.g., Powderly, 2002), possibly increasing the risk of cognitive impairment associated with immunocompromise (Munoz-Moreno et al., 2007).

The discrepant findings regarding the effectiveness of cART in improving HIV-associated cognitive deficits could be due to the differences in the distribution of ARVs into the CNS. The effectiveness of ARVs in the CNS can be estimated by their molecular and chemical properties, their concentrations in CSF, or their effectiveness in reducing viral loads in CSF or treating neurocognitive impairment (see Letendre et al., 2008). Cross-sectional research indicates that ARVs with better penetration characteristics are associated with better episodic memory performance among HIV-infected persons with generalized neuropsychological impairment (Cysique et al., 2004). In a single-group longitudinal study, Letendre et al. (2004) reported that the regimens that included ARVs with better CNS penetration characteristics were associated with greater reductions in CSF viral load, which in turn was related to improvement in global HIV-associated neuropsychological impairment. Randomized clinical trials are needed to more thoroughly investigate the potential relationship between optimized CNS penetration of

Table 17–1A. Published Guidelines for Classifying Confounds to HIV-Associated Neurocognitive Disorders (Antinori et al., 2007)

Comorbid Condition	Recommendation
Depression	
Secondary	Depressed mood and/or major depressive disorder but without psychotic features, and no clinical indication of inadequate effort/motivation on cognitive testing (NP or MSE). Normal performance on ≥1 effort-demanding cognitive test (e.g., PASAT).
Contributing	Major depressive disorder with psychotic features or some clinical evidence of fluctuating or suboptimal effort on cognitive testing. Nevertheless, impairment is present on non-speeded tests or on tests on which patient appeared to put forth good effort. Patient responds well to task demands with some examiner encouragement.
Confounding	Major depressive disorder with psychotic features and/or persisting clinical evidence of suboptimal effort in the cognitive testing process. Patient does not respond well to examiner prompting or encouragement.
Traumatic brain injury (TBI)	
Secondary	Mild TBI with no apparent functional decline (return to independent living; resumed successful employment and/or schoolwork, as appropriate to prior level of functioning). Subsequent cognitive and functional decline within the context of HIV.
Contributing	Mild TBI with some evidence of persisting mild functional decline or Severe TBI with no more than mild functional sequelae. Subsequent additional decline within the context of HIV.
Confounding	Mild or Severe TBI without return to work/school (as appropriate to prior level of functioning), and with increased dependence on others for IADLs. No clear subsequent cognitive or functional decline within the context of HIV.
Developmental disability	
Secondary	Isolated mild academic problem, but with passing performance in regular academic classes (not "special education"), and no repeated grades, followed by vocational and/or IADL independence. Subsequent cognitive and functional decline within the context of HIV.
Contributing	Mild to moderate cognitive/educational disability (lifelong): Some regular academic classes with passing performance, and no more than 1 repeated grade, followed by IADL independence. Subsequent cognitive and functional decline within the context of HIV.
Confounding	Mental Retardation and/or severe educational disability, followed by some dependence in IADLs and no employment with significant cognitive demands. Cognitive or functional decline with HIV is difficult or impossible to establish.
History of alcohol or other substance use disorder	
Secondary	Past history of substance use disorder, but patient does not meet DSM-IV criteria for abuse or dependence during last 6 months. No clinical evidence of intoxication or withdrawal at the time of evaluation. No prior overdoses with significant sequelae. Despite substance use disorder, patient has maintained adequate employment and/or independence of IADLs in the past (during or after the period of abuse or dependence). Evidence of cognitive and functional decline within the context of HIV, which began during or extended into the recent period when the patient did not meet criteria for abuse or dependence.

(continued)

Table 17–1A. Continued

Comorbid Condition	Recommendation
Contributing	Past history of substance use disorder but patient does not meet DSM-IV criteria for abuse or dependence within the last 30 days. Cognitive and functional decline within the context of HIV appears worse than in the past (even with ongoing substance use disorder in the past) and extends to the current time. No clinical evidence of intoxication or withdrawal at the time of the current evaluation. *OR* Ongoing substance use disorder, which would be considered a "confounding condition" in a baseline or cross-sectional assessment (see next row), but there is strong, longitudinal evidence of an additional HIV effect: Without any change in the pattern of substance use, a stable or progressive worsening in both neurocognitive performance and everyday functioning is documented over at least 3 longitudinal assessments (baseline and at least 2 follow-ups). This worsening occurs within the context of HIV infection, and cannot be explained by a drug overdose, by evidence of intoxication or withdrawal at the times of the evaluations, or by any other neuromedical or psychiatric confound.
Confounding	Ongoing substance use disorder with significant impact on everyday functioning. Difficult or impossible to determine whether cognitive or functional decline is due to substance use and/or HIV. *OR* Patient gave clinical evidence of intoxication or withdrawal during the time of the current evaluation.

HIV-related opportunistic CNS disease

Secondary	History of space-occupying brain lesions with contrast enhancement and edema, such as tumor or abscess; space-occupying lesions without enhancement and edema, such as progressive multifocal leukoencephalopathy (PML); symptomatic meningitis, such as due to Cryptococcus and syphilis. Patient returned to normal functioning but then experienced subsequent cognitive and functional decline within the context of HIV.
Contributing	History of space-occupying brain lesions with contrast enhancement and edema, such as tumor or abscess; space-occupying lesions without enhancement and edema, such as PML; symptomatic meningitis, such as due to Cryptococcus and syphilis. Patient did not return to normal cognition but experienced subsequent additional cognitive and functional decline within the context of HIV.
Confounding	Acutely symptomatic space-occupying brain lesions with contrast enhancement and edema, such as tumor or abscess; space-occupying lesions without enhancement and edema, such as PML; symptomatic meningitis, such as due to Cryptococcus and syphilis.

Non-HIV-related Neurologic Condition

Secondary	Prior stroke or cardiac bypass surgery with return to normal cognition after the event, no intervening event (another stroke or bypass surgery) but with subsequent cognitive and functional decline within the context of HIV.
Contributing	Prior stroke or cardiac bypass surgery without return to normal cognition after the event, no intervening event (another stroke or bypass surgery) but subsequent cognitive and functional decline within the context of HIV.

(continued)

Table 17–1A. Continued

Comorbid Condition	Recommendation
Confounding	As in HIV-related opportunistic CNS disease, but not a direct consequence of HIV. Other considerations include acutely symptomatic primary or metastatic brain tumor, brain abscess, symptomatic meningitis, uncontrolled epilepsy, progressive multiple sclerosis, stroke, and dementia due to causes other than HIV (e.g., Alzheimer's disease for older persons).
Systemic disease	
Secondary	Chronic, stable systemic condition such as hypertension or asthma, with no apparent cognitive sequelae or significant loss of function but with subsequent cognitive and functional decline within the context of HIV.
Contributing	Chronic, stable systemic illness (e.g., chronic obstructive pulmonary disease) associated with mild cognitive and/or functional impairment, but with subsequent additional cognitive and functional decline within the context of HIV.
Confounding	Constitutional illness (e.g., persistent unexplained fever, diarrhea, significant weight loss, disabling weakness). These could be due to factors related or unrelated to HIV or to medication side effects. Symptomatic new AIDS-related opportunistic conditions. Newly diagnosed nutritional abnormality including B12 or thiamine deficiency or newly diagnosed malnutrition. In these cases, direct effects of HIV on cognitive or functional decline are difficult or impossible to establish.
Co-infection with Hepatitis-C Virus (HCV)	
Secondary	Evidence of prior HCV infection with successful clearance (i.e., seropositive, but HCV RNA undetectable in plasma), either spontaneously or with treatment, and absence of decompensated liver disease (defined by total serum bilirubin $\geq$ 1.5 mg/dL; INR $\geq$ 1.5; albumin $\leq$ 3.4 g/dL; platelet count < 75,000 K/MM^3; or evidence of hepatic encephalopathy or ascites). Evidence of subsequent cognitive and functional decline within the context of HIV.
Contributing	Evidence of current HCV infection (i.e., HCV RNA present in plasma) but without decompensated liver disease (defined by total serum bilirubin $\geq$ 1.5 mg/dL; INR $\geq$ 1.5; albumin $\leq$ 3.4 g/dL; platelet count < 75,000 K/MM^3; or evidence of hepatic encephalopathy or ascites). In this situation, HIV and HCV may be associated with independent risks for cognitive impairment and functional decline.
Confounding	Evidence of current HCV infection (i.e., HCV RNA present in plasma) with severe or decompensated liver disease (defined by total serum bilirubin $\geq$ 1.5 mg/dL; INR $\geq$ 1.5; albumin $\leq$ 3.4 g/dL; platelet count < 75,000 K/MM^3; or evidence of hepatic encephalopathy or ascites). In this situation, any cognitive impairments and functional decline cannot be confidently attributed to HIV because of higher risk of hepatic encephalopathy.

cART regimens and the amelioration of HIV-associated neurocognitive disorders.

Non-antiretroviral Treatments

A variety of adjunctive, non-antiretroviral drugs have been evaluated as possible treatments for HIV-associated neurocognitive disorders, including psychostimulants, N-methyl-D-aspartic acid (NMDA) antagonists (e.g., memantine), antioxidants (e.g., CPI-1189), anti-inflammatory agents (e.g., lexipafant), mood stabilizers, and antidepressants. Methylphenidate, for example, has demonstrated modest effects in improving psychomotor slowing in HIV (e.g., Hinkin et al., 2001). Extending *in vitro* research on the possible neuroprotective effects of lithium (viz., inhibition of gp120-mediated neurotoxicity; Everall et al., 2002), Letendre et al. (2006) reported that low doses of oral lithium improved neuropsychological functioning in a small, single-arm, open-label study of eight individuals with HIV-associated neurocognitive disorders. Another class of psychotropic agents, serotonin reuptake inhibitors (SRIs; e.g., citalopram), were associated with a reduced HIV replication in the CSF and better neurocognitive performance in a large, observational cohort study (Letendre et al., 2007). Importantly, the cognitive benefits of these psychotropic drugs do not appear to be a function of improvements in depressive symptomatology, which (as noted above) is not reliably related to neuropsychological impairment in HIV (Goggin et al., 1997). Nevertheless, the veracity of these preliminary findings regarding the effectiveness of adjunctive therapies for HIV-associated neurocognitive disorders remains to be systematically evaluated in larger clinical trials. For example, Selegiline (i.e., L-deprenyl) is a monoamine oxidase inhibitor with neuroprotective potential (e.g., Turchan-Cholewo et al., 2006) that ameliorated deficits in delayed list recall and motor speed in a small pilot study (Sacktor et al., 2000), but was generally ineffective in a phase II clinical trial (Schifitto et al., 2006). More recent novel agents of interest for treating HIV-associated cognitive disorders include Substance P, a neuropeptide with an affinity for the neurokinin-1 receptor (Ho & Douglas, 2004), and Minocycline, an antibacterial with potent anti-inflammatory and neuroprotective properties (Zink et al., 2005), which is the focus of a new, randomized, placebo-controlled clinical trial.

Cognitive Rehabilitation

Cognitive remediation is a form of rehabilitation therapy used to treat individuals with neurological deficits, typically those recovering from brain injury. Cognitive rehabilitation techniques have generally emphasized strategies to compensate for residual cognitive deficits ("strategy training"), rather than attempting to directly restore the underlying impaired function ("restitution training"). Although systematic reviews generally support the effectiveness of cognitive remediation in brain injury (Cicerone et al., 2005), there has been virtually no research investigating its effectiveness in persons with HIV-associated neurocognitive disorders. One small pilot study examined an intervention based on Spaced Retrieval (SR), a memory technique that teaches individuals to recall information over progressively longer intervals of time, in combination with external memory aids in ten older adults with HIV. Among those who identified at least one goal (e.g., remembering appointments), 90% initially mastered the correct response and procedure, 60% retained the correct response and procedure over a 2-month interval (demonstrating retention of mastery), and 100% self-reported that the intervention had helped them achieve their goal (Neundorfer et al., 2004). In another recent study, Andrade and colleagues (2005) employed a randomized controlled trial to investigate the effect of an electronic memory prompting device on adherence to cART and found that the device, which provided electronic verbal reminders at dosing times, improved medication adherence in HIV-infected individuals with memory impairment.

HIV-Associated Neurocognitive Disorders in the Developing World

The HIV pandemic is not restricted to the developed world as approximately 40 million people are living with HIV infection worldwide, with the low- and middle-income countries in Africa and Asia being particularly affected (UNAIDS, 2006). Accompanying the much-needed humanitarian efforts to increase access to HIV prevention strategies and antiretroviral therapies in these resource-limited areas, there has been considerable scientific interest in international neuroAIDS. Basic science observations regarding the differential neurovirulence of genetic variations in viral clades have stimulated interest in the prevalence, mechanisms, and functional impact of HIV-associated CNS dysfunction in these settings. Although findings so far are inconsistent, some research suggests that B clade virus (more prevalent in the

United States and Europe) may be more neuro-virulent than non-B clade variants (e.g., C clade virus in Africa, India, and Brazil) perhaps as a function of differing chemotactic properties (Ranga et al., 2004) or glutamate production in infected macrophages (Zheng et al., 2007). Of course, investigation of the cognitive sequelae of HIV infection in resource-limited countries is a complex undertaking for which a sophisticated and collaborative cross-cultural approach is necessary. The HIV Dementia Scale, for example, was recently adapted by Sacktor and colleagues (2005) for international use in persons not fluent in English by replacing its language-based subtests with finger tapping and alternating hand position tests. Preliminary data suggest that the International HDS may be useful for basic screening and monitoring of HAD in resource-limited settings (e.g., Sacktor et al., 2006). However, in addition to the obvious linguistic complexities of test translation and adaptation, the myriad socioeconomic and cultural factors that ostensibly influence the validity of cognitive testing in these settings must also be considered in future international neuroAIDS research efforts (e.g., the relevance of some cognitive constructs, such as speeded motor and information processing, may vary widely across cultures).

References

Abrams, D. I., Jay, C. A., Shade, S. B., Vizoso, H., Reda, H., Press, S., et al. (2007). Cannabis in painful HIV-associated sensory neuropathy: A randomized placebo-controlled trial. *Neurology, 68,* 515–521.

Airaksinen, E., Larsson, M., & Forsell, Y. (2005). Neuropsychological functions in anxiety disorders in population-based samples: Evidence of episodic memory dysfunction. *Journal of Psychiatric Research, 39,* 207–214.

Andrade, A. S., McGruder, H. F., Wu, A. W., Celano, S. A., Skolasky, R. L., Jr., Selnes, O. A., et al. (2005). A programmable prompting device improves adherence to highly active antiretroviral therapy in HIV-infected subjects with memory impairment. *Clinical Infectious Diseases, 41,* 875–882.

Antinori, A., Arendt, G., Becker, J. T., Brew, B. J., Byrd, D. A., Cherner, M., et al. (2007). Updated research nosology for HIV-associated neurocognitive disorders. *Neurology, 69,* 1789–1799.

Archibald, S. L., Masliah, E., Fennema-Notestine, C., Marcotte, T. D., Ellis, R. J., McCutchan, J. A., et al. (2004). Correlation of in vivo neuroimaging abnormalities with postmortem human immunodeficiency virus encephalitis and dendritic loss. *Archives of Neurology, 61,* 369–376.

Arnsten, J. H., Demas, P. A., Grant, R. W., Gourevitch, M. N., Farzadegan, H., Howard, A. A., et al. (2002). Impact of active drug use on antiretroviral therapy adherence and viral suppression in HIV-infected drug users. *Journal of General Internal Medicine, 17,* 377–381.

Atkinson, J. H., Person, C., Young, C., Deitch, D., & Treisman, G. (2005). Psychiatric disorders. In H. E. Gendelman, I. Grant, I. Everall, S. A. Lipton, and S. Swindells (Eds.), *The Neurology of AIDS* (2nd edition, pp. 553–564). New York: Oxford University Press.

Avants, S. K., Margolin, A., McMahon, T. J., & Kosten, T. R. (1997). Association between self-report of cognitive impairment, HIV status, and cocaine use in a sample of cocaine-dependent methadone-maintained patients. *Addictive Behaviors, 22,* 599–611.

Aylward, E.H., Henderer, J.D., McArthur, J.C., Brettschneider, P.D., Harris, G.J., Barta, P.E., et al. (1993). Reduced basal ganglia volume in HIV-1-associated dementia: Results from quantitative neuroimaging. *Neurology, 43*(10), 2099–2104.

Baddeley, A. D., & Hitch, G. J. (1994). Developments in the concept of working memory. *Neuropsychology, 8,* 485–493.

Bartok, J.A., Martin, E. M., Pitrak, D. L., Novak, R. M., Pursell, K. J., Mullane, K. M., et al. (1997). Working memory deficits in HIV-seropositive drug users. *Journal of the International Neuropsychological Society, 3,* 451–456.

Basso, M. R., & Bornstein, R. A. (2000). Estimated premorbid intelligence mediates neurobehavioral change in individuals infected with HIV across 12 months. *Journal of Clinical and Experimental Neuropsychology, 22,* 208–218.

Bechara, A., Damasio, H., Tranel, D., & Damasio, A. R. (1997). Deciding advantageously before knowing the advantageous strategy. *Science, 275,* 1293–1295.

Becker, J. T., & Salthouse, T. A. (1999). Neuropsychological test performance in the acquired immunodeficiency syndrome: Independent effects of diagnostic group on functioning. *Journal of the International Neuropsychological Society, 5,* 41–47.

Benedict, R. H. B., Mezhir, J. J., Walsh, K., & Hewitt, R. G. (2000). Impact of human immunodeficiency virus type-1-associated cognitive dysfunction on activities of daily living and quality of life. *Archives of Clinical Neuropsychology, 15,* 535–544.

Berger, J. R., & Arendt, G. (2000). HIV dementia: The role of the basal ganglia and dopaminergic systems. *Journal of Psychopharmacology, 14*, 214–221.

Braithwaite, R. S., McGinnis, K. A., Conigliaro, J., Maisto, S. A., Crystal, S., Day, N., et al. (2005). A temporal and dose-response association between alcohol consumption and medication adherence among veterans in care. *Alcoholism: Clinical and Experimental Research, 29*, 1190–1197.

Breitbart, W., Marotta, R., Platt, M. M., Weisman, H., Derevenco, M., Grau, C., et al. (1996). A double-blind trial of haloperidol, chlorpromazine, and lorazepam in the treatment of delirium in hospitalized AIDS patients. *American Journal of Psychiatry, 153*, 231–237.

Brew, B. J. (2004). Evidence for a change in AIDS dementia complex in the era of highly active antiretroviral therapy and the possibility of new forms of AIDS dementia complex. *AIDS, 18*(Suppl 1), S75–S78.

Budka, H. (2005). The neuropathology of HIV-associated brain disease. In H. E. Gendelman, I. Grant, I. Everall, S. A. Lipton, and S. Swindells (Eds.), *The neurology of AIDS* (2nd ed., pp. 375–391). New York: Oxford University Press.

Carey, C. L., Woods, S. P., Rippeth, J. D., Gonzalez, R., Heaton, R. K., & Grant, I. (2006a). Additive deleterious effects of methamphetamine dependence and immunosuppression on neuropsychological functioning in HIV infection. *AIDS and Behavior, 10*, 185–190.

Carey, C. L., Woods, S. P., Rippeth, J. D., Gonzalez, R., Moore, D. J., Marcotte, T. D., et al. (2004). Initial validation of a screening battery for the detection of HIV-associated cognitive impairment. *The Clinical Neuropsychologist, 18*, 234–248.

Carey, C. L., Woods, S. P., Rippeth, J. D., Heaton, R. K., & Grant, I. (2006b). Prospective memory in HIV-1 infection. *Journal of Clinical and Experimental Neuropsychology, 28*, 536–548.

Casau, N. C. (2005). Perspective on HIV infection and aging: Emerging research on the horizon. *Clinical Infectious Diseases, 41*, 855–863.

Centers for Disease Control and Prevention. (1993). Classification system for HIV infection and expanded surveillance case definition for AIDS among adolescents and adults. *Journal of the American Medical Association*, 269,729–730.

Centers for Disease Control and Prevention. (2001). *HIV/AIDS surveillance report.* Atlanta, GA: Author.

Centers for Disease Control and Prevention. (2005). *HIV/AIDS surveillance report, 2004.* Atlanta, GA: Author.

Chana, G., Everall, I. P., Crews, L., Langford, D., Adame, A., Grant, I., et al. (2006). Cognitive deficits and degeneration of interneurons in HIV+ methamphetamine users. *Neurology, 67*, 1486–1489.

Chandrasekhar, S. S., Connelly, P. E., Brahmbhatt, S. S., Shah, C. S., Kloser, P. C., & Baredes, S. (2000). Otologic and audiologic evaluation of human immunodeficiency virus-infected patients. *American Journal of Otolaryngology, 21*, 1–9.

Chang, L., Ernst, T., Leonido-Yee, M., & Speck, O. (2000). Perfusion MRI detects rCBF abnormalities in early stages of HIV-cognitive motor complex. *Neurology, 54*, 389–396.

Chang, L., Ernst, T., Speck, O., & Grob, C. S. (2005). Additive effects of HIV and chronic methamphetamine use on brain metabolite abnormalities. *American Journal of Psychiatry, 162*, 361–369.

Chayakulkeeree, M., & Perfect, J. R. (2006). Cryptococcosis. *Infectious Disease Clinics of North America, 20*, 507–544, v–vi.

Chen, W., Tang, Z., Fortina, P., Patel, P., Addya, S., Surrey, S., et al. (2005). Ethanol potentiates HIV-1 gp120-induced apoptosis in human neurons via both the death receptor and NMDA receptor pathways. *Virology, 334*, 59–73.

Cherner, M., Ellis, R. J., Lazzaretto, D., Young, C., Mindt, M. R., Atkinson, J. H., et al. (2004). Effects of HIV-1 infection and aging on neurobehavioral functioning: Preliminary findings. *AIDS, 18*(Suppl 1), S27–S34.

Cherner, M., Letendre, S., Heaton, R. K., Durelle, J., Marquie-Beck, J., Gragg, B., et al. (2005). Hepatitis C augments cognitive deficits associated with HIV infection and methamphetamine. *Neurology, 64*, 1343–1347.

Cicerone, K. D., Dahlberg, C., Malec, J. F., Langenbahn, D. M., Felicetti, T., Kneipp, S., et al. (2005). Evidence-based cognitive rehabilitation: Updated review of the literature from 1998 through 2002. *Archives of Physical Medicine and Rehabilitation, 86*, 1681–1692.

Ciesla, J. A., and Roberts, J. E. (2001). Meta-analysis of the relationship between HIV infection and risk for depressive disorders. *American Journal of Psychiatry, 158*, 725–730.

Cinque, P., Vago, L., Mengozzi, M., Torri, V., Ceresa, D., Vicenzi, E., et al. (1998). Elevated cerebrospinal fluid levels of monocyte chemotactic protein-1 correlate with HIV-1 encephalitis and local viral replication. *AIDS, 12*, 1327–1332.

Clifford, D. B., Evans, S. R., Yang, Y., & Gulick, R. M. (2005). The neuropsychological and neurological impact of hepatitis C virus co-infection in HIV-infected subjects. *AIDS, 19*(Suppl 3), S64–S71.

Corder, E. H., Robertson, K., Lannfelt, L., Bogdanovic, N., Eggertsen, G., Wilkins, J., et al.

(1998). HIV-infected subjects with the E4 allele for APOE have excess dementia and peripheral neuropathy. *Nature Medicine, 4,* 1182–1184.

Cristiani, S. A., Pukay-Martin, N. D., & Bornstein, R. A. (2004). Marijuana use and cognitive function in HIV-infected people. *The Journal of Neuropsychiatry and Clinical Neurosciences, 16,* 330–335.

Croxford, J. L. (2003). Therapeutic potential of cannabinoids in CNS disease. *CNS Drugs, 17,* 179–202.

Cutler, R. G., Haughey, N. J., Tammara, A., McArthur, J. C., Nath, A., Reid, R., et al. (2004). Dysregulation of sphingolipid and sterol metabolism by APOE4 in HIV dementia. *Neurology, 63,* 626–630.

Cysique, L. A., Deutsch, R., Atkinson, J. H., Young, C., Marcotte, T. D., Dawson, L., et al. (2007). Incident major depression does not affect neuropsychological functioning in HIV-infected men. *Journal of the International Neuropsychological Society, 13,* 1–11.

Cysique, L. A., Maruff, P., & Brew, B. J. (2004). Antiretroviral therapy in HIV infection: Are neurologically active drugs important? *Archives of Neurology, 61,* 1699–1704.

Cysique, L. A., Maruff, P., & Brew, B. J. (2006). The neuropsychological profile of symptomatic AIDS and ADC patients in the pre-HAART era: A meta-analysis. *Journal of the International Neuropsychological Society, 12,* 368–382.

Damasio, A. R., & Tranel, D. (1993). Nouns and verbs are retrieved with differently distributed neural systems. *Proceedings of the National Academy of Sciences of the United States of America, 90,* 4957–4960.

Davis, S. J., Schockmel, G. A., Somoza, C., Buck, D. W., Healey, D. G., Rieber, E. P., et al. (1992). Antibody and HIV-1 gp120 recognition of CD4 undermines the concept of mimicry between antibodies and receptors. *Nature, 358,* 76–79.

Delis, D. C., Peavy, G., Heaton, R., Butters, N., Salmon, D. P., Taylor, M., et al. (1995). Do patients with HIV-associated minor cognitive/motor disorder exhibit a "subcortical" memory profile? Evidence using the California Verbal Learning Test. *Assessment, 2,* 151–165.

Durvasula, R. S., Myers, H. F., Mason, K., & Hinkin, C. (2006). Relationship between alcohol use/abuse, HIV infection and neuropsychological performance in African American men. *Journal of Clinical and Experimental Neuropsychology, 28,* 383–404.

Durvasula, R. S., Myers, H. F., Satz, P., Miller, E. N., Morgenstern, H., Richardson, M. A., et al.

(2000). HIV-1, cocaine, and neuropsychological performance in African American men. *Journal of the International Neuropsychological Society, 6,* 322–335.

Egan, V. G., Crawford, J. R., Brettle, R. P., & Goodwin, G. M. (1990). The Edinburgh cohort of HIV-positive drug users: Current intellectual function is impaired, but not due to early AIDS dementia complex. *AIDS, 4,* 651–656.

Elliott, A. (1998). Anxiety and HIV infection. *STEP Perspective, 98,* 11–14.

Ellis, R., Langford, D., & Masliah, E. (2007). HIV and antiretroviral therapy in the brain: Neuronal injury and repair. *Nature Reviews. Neuroscience, 8,* 33–44.

Ellis, R. J., Deutsch, R., Heaton, R. K., Marcotte, T. D., McCutchan, J. A., Nelson, J. A., et al. (1997a). Neurocognitive impairment is an independent risk factor for death in HIV infection. *Archives of Neurology, 54,* 416–424.

Ellis, R. J., Hsia, K., Spector, S. A., Nelson, J. A., Heaton, R. K., Wallace, M. R., et al. (1997b). Cerebrospinal fluid human immunodeficiency virus type 1 RNA levels are elevated in neurocognitively impaired individuals with acquired immunodeficiency syndrome. *Annals of Neurology, 42,* 679–688.

Ellis, R. J., Moore, D. J., Childers, M. E., Letendre, S., McCutchan, J. A., Wolfson, T., et al. (2002). Progression to neuropsychological impairment in human immunodeficiency virus infection predicted by elevated cerebrospinal fluid levels of human immunodeficiency virus RNA. *Archives of Neurology, 59,* 923–928.

Esiri, M. M., Biddolph, S. C., & Morris, C. S. (1998). Prevalence of Alzheimer plaques in AIDS. *Journal of Neurology Neurosurgery and Psychiatry, 65,* 29–33.

Everall, I. P., Bell, C., Mallory, M., Langford, D., Adame, A., Rockestein, E., et al. (2002). Lithium ameliorates HIV-gp120-mediated neurotoxicity. *Molecular and Cellular Neurosciences, 21,* 493–501.

Fagnoni, F. F., Vescovini, R., Passeri, G., Bologna, G., Pedrazzoni, M., Lavagetto, G., et al. (2000). Shortage of circulating naive CD8(+) T cells provides new insights on immunodeficiency in aging. *Blood, 95,* 2860–2868.

Farinpour, R., Martin, E. M., Seidenberg, M., Pitrak, D. L., Pursell, K. J., Mullane, K. M., et al. (2000). Verbal working memory in HIV-seropositive drug users. *Journal of the International Neuropsychological Society, 6,* 548–555.

Fein, G., Biggins, C. A., & MacKay, S. (1995). Delayed latency of the event-related brain potential P3A component in HIV disease. Progressive effects with increasing cognitive impairment. *Archives of Neurology, 52,* 1109–1118.

Ferrando, S., van Gorp, W., McElhiney, M., Goggin, K., Sewell, M., & Rabkin, J. (1998). Highly active antiretroviral treatment in HIV infection: Benefits for neuropsychological function. *AIDS, 12,* F65–F70.

Forton, D. M., Allsop, J. M., Cox, I. J., Hamilton, G., Wesnes, K., Thomas, H. C., et al. (2005). A review of cognitive impairment and cerebral metabolite abnormalities in patients with hepatitis C infection. *AIDS, 19*(Suppl 3), S53–S63.

Freeman, W. R., McCutchan, J. A., Arevalo, J. F., Wolfson, T., Marcotte, T. D., Heaton, R. K., et al. (2004). The relationship between AIDS retinal cotton wool spots and neuropsychological impairment in HIV-positive individuals in the pre-highly active antiretroviral therapy era. *Ocular Immunology and Inflammation, 12,* 25–33.

Gallant, J. E., & Block, D. S. (1998). Adherence to antiretroviral regimens in HIV-infected patients: Results of a survey among physicians and patients. *Journal of International Association of Physicians in AIDS Care, 4,* 32–35.

Dal Pan, G.J., McArthur, J.H., Aylward, E., Selnes, O.A., Nance-Sproson, T.E., Kumar, A.J., Mellits, E.D., & McArthur, J.C. (1992). Patterns of cerebral atrophy in HIV-1-infected individuals: results of a quantitative MRI analysis. *Neurology, 42,* 2125–2130.

Galvan, F. H., Bing, E. G., Fleishman, J. A., London, A. S., Caetano, R., Burnam, M. A., et al. (2002). The prevalence of alcohol consumption and heavy drinking among people with HIV in the United States: Results from the HIV cost and services utilization study. *Journal of Studies on Alcohol, 63,* 179–186.

Gan, X., Zhang, L., Newton, T., Chang, S. L., Ling, W., Kermani, V., et al. (1998). Cocaine infusion increases interferon-gamma and decreases interleukin-10 in cocaine-dependent subjects. *Clinical Immunology and Immunopathology, 89,* 181–190.

Geier, S. A., Perro, C., Klauss, V., Naber, D., Kronawitter, U., Bogner, J. R., et al. (1993). HIV-related ocular microangiopathic syndrome and cognitive functioning. *Journal of Acquired Immune Deficiency Syndromes, 6,* 252–258.

Goetz, M. B., Boscardin, W. J., Wiley, D., & Alkasspooles, S. (2001). Decreased recovery of CD4 lymphocytes in older HIV-infected patients beginning highly active antiretroviral therapy. *AIDS, 15,* 1576–1579.

Goggin, K. J., Zisook, S., Heaton, R. K., Atkinson, J. H., Marshall, S., McCutchan, J. A., et al. (1997). Neuropsychological performance of HIV-1 infected men with major depression. *Journal of the International Neuropsychological Society, 3,* 457–464.

Goldberg, T. E., & Weinberger, D. R. (2004). Genes and the parsing of cognitive processes. *Trends in Cognitive Sciences, 8,* 325–335.

Gongvatana, A., Schweinsburg, B. C., Taylor, M. J., Theilmann, R. J., Letendre, S. L., Alhassoon, O., et al. (2008). HIV-associated white matter tract injury and neurocognitive impairment in the HAART era. [abstract]. *Journal of the International Neuropsychological Society, 14* (Suppl. 1), 145–146.

Gongvatana, A., Woods, S. P., Taylor, M. J., Vigil, O., Grant, I., & The HNRC Group. (2007). Semantic clustering inefficiency in HIV-associated dementia. *Journal of Neuropsychiatry and Clinical Neurosciences, 19,* 36–42.

Gonzalez, E., Rovin, B. H., Sen, L., Cooke, G., Dhanda, R., Mummidi, S., et al. (2002). HIV-1 infection and AIDS dementia are influenced by a mutant MCP-1 allele linked to increased monocyte infiltration of tissues and MCP-1 levels. *Proceedings of the National Academy of Sciences of the United States of America, 99,* 13795–13800.

Gonzalez, R., Vassileva, J., Bechara, A., Grbesic, S., Sworowski, L., Novak, R. M., et al. (2005). The influence of executive functions, sensation seeking, and HIV serostatus on the risky sexual practices of substance-dependent individuals. *Journal of the International Neuropsychological Society, 11,* 121–131.

Gonzalez-Scarano, F., & Martin-Garcia, J. (2005). The neuropathogenesis of AIDS. *Nature Reviews. Immunology, 5,* 69–81.

Grant, I., & Atkinson, J. H. (1999). Neuropsychiatric aspects of HIV infection and AIDS. In B. J. Sadock and V. A. Sadock (Eds.), *Kaplan and Sadock's comprehensive textbook of psychiatry VII* (pp. 308–335). Baltimore: Williams and Wilkins.

Grant, I., Atkinson, J. H., Hesselink, J. R., Kennedy, C. J., Richman, D. D., Spector, S. A., et al. (1987). Evidence for early central nervous system involvement in the acquired immunodeficiency syndrome (AIDS) and other human immunodeficiency virus (HIV) infections. Studies with neuropsychologic testing and magnetic resonance imaging. *Annals of Internal Medicine, 107,* 828–836.

Grant, I., Gonzalez, R., Carey, C. L., Natarajan, L., & Wolfson, T. (2003). Non-acute (residual) neurocognitive effects of cannabis use: A meta-analytic study. *Journal of the International Neuropsychological Society, 9,* 679–689.

Grant, I., Olshen, R. A., Atkinson, J. H., Heaton, R., Nelson, J., McCutchan, J. A. et al. (1993). Depressed mood does not explain neuropsychological deficits in HIV-infected persons. *Neuropsychology, 7,* 53–61.

Grant, I., Sacktor, N., & McArthur, J. C. (2005). HIV neurocognitive disorders. In H. E. Gendelman, I. Grant, I. Everall, S. A. Lipton, and S. Swindells (Eds.), *The neurology of AIDS* (2nd ed. pp. 359–373). New York: Oxford University Press.

Greco, J. B., Westmoreland, S. V., Ratai, E. M., Lentz, M. R., Sakaie, K., He, J., et al. (2004). In vivo 1H MRS of brain injury and repair during acute SIV infection in the macaque model of neuroAIDS. *Magnetic Resonance in Medicine, 51,* 1108–1114.

Green, J. E., Saveanu, R. V., & Bornstein, R. A. (2004). The effect of previous alcohol abuse on cognitive function in HIV infection. *American Journal of Psychiatry, 161,* 249–254.

Griffin, W. C., 3rd, Middaugh, L. D., & Tyor, W. R. (2007). Chronic cocaine exposure in the SCID mouse model of HIV encephalitis. *Brain Research, 1134,* 214–219.

Haase, A. T. (1986). Pathogenesis of lentivirus infections. *Nature, 322,* 130–136.

Hardy, D. J., & Hinkin, C. H. (2002). Reaction time performance in adults with HIV/AIDS. *Journal of Clinical and Experimental Neuropsychology, 24,* 912–929.

Hardy, D. J., Hinkin, C. H., Levine, A. J., Castellon, S. A., & Lam, M. N. (2006). Risky decision making assessed with the gambling task in adults with HIV. *Neuropsychology, 20,* 355–360.

Harrington, D. L., Haaland, K. Y., Yeo, R. A., & Marder, E. (1990). Procedural memory in Parkinson's disease: Impaired motor but not visuoperceptual learning. *Journal of Clinical and Experimental Neuropsychology, 12,* 323–339.

Heaton, R., Marcotte, T. D., White, D. A., Ross, D., Meredith, K., Taylor, M. J., et al. (1996). Nature and vocational significance of neuropsychological impairment associated with HIV infection. *The Clinical Neuropsychologist, 10,* 1–14.

Heaton, R. K., Grant, I., Butters, N., White, D. A., Kirson, D., Atkinson, J. H., et al. (1995). The HNRC 500—Neuropsychology of HIV infection at different disease stages. *Journal of the International Neuropsychological Society, 1,* 231–251.

Heaton, R. K., Marcotte, T. D., Mindt, M. R., Sadek, J., Moore, D. J., Bentley, H., et al. (2004). The impact of HIV-associated neuropsychological impairment on everyday functioning. *Journal of the International Neuropsychological Society, 10,* 317–331.

Hinkin, C. H., Castellon, S. A., Durvasula, R. S., Hardy, D. J., Lam, M. N., Mason, K. I., et al. (2002). Medication adherence among HIV+ adults: Effects of cognitive dysfunction and regimen complexity. *Neurology, 59,* 1944–1950.

Hinkin, C. H., Castellon, S. A., & Hardy, D. J. (2000). Dual task performance in HIV-1 infection. *Journal of Clinical and Experimental Neuropsychology, 22,* 16–24.

Hinkin, C. H., Castellon, S. A., Hardy, D. J., Farinpour, R., Newton, T., & Singer, E. (2001). Methylphenidate improves HIV-1-associated cognitive slowing. *The Journal of Neuropsychiatry and Clinical Neuroscience, 13,* 248–254.

Hinkin, C. H., Hardy, D. J., Mason, K. I., Castellon, S. A., Durvasula, R. S., Lam, M. N., et al. (2004). Medication adherence in HIV-infected adults: Effect of patient age, cognitive status, and substance abuse. *AIDS, 18*(Suppl 1), S19–S25.

Hiscock, M., & Hiscock, C. K. (1989). Refining the forced-choice method for the detection of malingering. *Journal of Clinical and Experimental Neuropsychology, 11,* 967–974.

Ho, W. Z., & Douglas, S. D. (2004). Substance P and neurokinin-1 receptor modulation of HIV. *Journal of Neuroimmunology, 157,* 48–55.

Iudicello, J. E., Letendre, S. L, Carey, C. L., Dawson, M. S., Durelle, J., Grant, I., et al. (2008a). HIV-associated deficits in action (verb) fluency reflect astrocytosis [abstract]. *Journal of the International Neuropsychological Society, 14*(Suppl. 1), 146.

Iudicello, J. E., Woods, S. P., Parsons, T. D., Moran, L. M., Carey, C. L., & Grant, I. (2007). Verbal fluency in HIV infection: A meta-analytic review. *Journal of the International Neuropsychological Society, 13,* 183–189.

Iudicello, J. E., Woods, S. P., Weber, E., Dawson, M. S., Scott, J. C., Carey, C. L., et al. (2008b). Cognitive mechanisms of switching in HIV-associated category fluency deficits. *Journal of Clinical and Experimental Neuropsychology, 30*(7), 797–804.

Janssen, R. S., Saykin, A. J., Cannon, L., Campbell, J., Pinsky, P. F., Hessol, N. A., et al. (1989). Neurological and neuropsychological manifestations of HIV-1 infection: Association with AIDS-related complex but not asymptomatic HIV-1 infection. *Annals of Neurology, 26,* 592–600.

Jarvik, J. G., Hesselink, J. R., Kennedy, C., Teschke, R., Wiley, C., Spector, S.,et al. (1988). Acquired immunodeficiency syndrome. Magnetic resonance patterns of brain involvement with pathologic correlation. *Archives of Neurology, 45,* 731–736.

Jernigan, T. L., Gamst, A. C., Archibald, S. L., Fennema-Notestine, C., Mindt, M. R., Marcotte, T. D., et al. (2005). Effects of methamphetamine dependence and HIV infection on cerebral morphology. *American Journal of Psychiatry, 162,* 1461–1472.

Kalechstein, A. D., Hinkin, C. H., van Gorp, W. G., Castellon, S. A., & Satz, P. (1998). Depression predicts procedural but not episodic memory in HIV-1 infection. *Journal of Clinical and Experimental Neuropsychology, 20,* 529–535.

Kelder, W., McArthur, J. C., Nance-Sproson, T., McClernon, D., & Griffin, D. E. (1998). Beta-chemokines MCP-1 and RANTES are selectively increased in cerebrospinal fluid of patients with human immunodeficiency virus-associated dementia. *Annals of Neurology, 44,* 831–835.

Keswani, S., Luciano, C., Pardo, C., Cherry, K., Hoke, A., & McArthur, J. C. (2005). The spectrum of peripheral neuropathies in AIDS. In H. E. Gendelman, I. Grant, I. Everall, S. A. Lipton, and S. Swindells (Eds.), *The neurology of AIDS* (2nd ed., pp. 423–443). New York: Oxford University Press.

Langford, D., Hurford, R., Hashimoto, M., Digicaylioglu, M., & Masliah, E. (2005). Signalling crosstalk in FGF2-mediated protection of endothelial cells from HIV-gp120. *BMC Neuroscience, 6,* 8.

Law, W. A., Martin, A., Mapou, R. L., Roller, T. L., Salazar, A. M., Temoshok, L. R., et al. (1994). Working memory in individuals with HIV infection. *Journal of Clinical and Experimental Neuropsychology, 16,* 173–182.

Lawrence, A. D., Watkins, L. H., Sahakian, B. J., Hodges, J. R., & Robbins, T. W. (2000). Visual object and visuospatial cognition in Huntington's disease: Implications for information processing in corticostriatal circuits. *Brain, 123,* 1349–1364.

Letendre, S. L., Cherner, M., Ellis, R. J., Marquie-Beck, J., Gragg, B., Marcotte, T., et al. (2005). The effects of hepatitis C, HIV, and methamphetamine dependence on neuropsychological performance: Biological correlates of disease. *AIDS, 19*(Suppl 3), S72–S78.

Letendre, S. L., Marquie-Beck, J., Capparelli, E., Best, B., Clifford, D. B., Collier, A. C., et al. (2008). Validation of the CNS Penetration-Effectiveness rank for quantifying antiretroviral penetration into the central nervous system. *Archives of Neurology, 65,* 65–70..

Letendre, S. L., Marquie-Beck, J., Woods, S. P., Best, B., Clifford, D. B., Collier, A. C., et al. (2007). The role of cohort studies in drug development: Clinical evidence of antiviral activity of serotonin reuptake inhibitors and HMG-CoA reductase inhibitors in the central nervous system. *Journal of Neuroimmune Pharmacology, 2,* 120–127.

Letendre, S. L., McCutchan, J. A., Childers, M. E., Woods, S. P., Lazzaretto, D., Heaton, R. K., et al. (2004). Enhancing antiretroviral therapy for human immunodeficiency virus cognitive disorders. *Annals of Neurology, 56,* 416–423.

Letendre, S. L., Woods, S. P., Ellis, R. J., Atkinson, J. H., Masliah, E., van den Brande, G., et al. (2006). Lithium improves HIV-associated neurocognitive impairment. *AIDS, 20,* 1885–1888.

Levine, A. J., Hardy, D. J., Miller, E., Castellon, S. A., Longshore, D., & Hinkin, C. H. (2006). The effect of recent stimulant use on sustained attention in HIV-infected adults. *Journal of Clinical and Experimental Neuropsychology, 28,* 29–42.

Lopez, O. L., Becker, J. T., Dew, M. A., Banks, G., Dorst, S. K., & McNeil, M. (1994). Speech motor control disorder after HIV infection. *Neurology, 44,* 2187–2189.

Manly, J. J., Patterson, T. L., Heaton, R., Semple, S. J., White, D. A., Velin, R. A., et al. (1997). The relationship between neuropsychological functioning and coping activity among HIV-positive men. *AIDS and Behavior, 1,* 81–91.

Mapou, R. L., Law, W. A., Martin, A., Kampen, D., Salazar, A. M., & Rundell, J. R. (1993). Neuropsychological performance, mood, and complaints of cognitive and motor difficulties in individuals infected with the human immunodeficiency virus. *The Journal of Neuropsychiatry and Clinical Neurosciences, 5,* 86–93.

Marcotte, T. D., Heaton, R. K., Wolfson, T., Taylor, M. J., Alhassoon, O., Arfaa, K., et al. (1999). The impact of HIV-related neuropsychological dysfunction on driving behavior. *Journal of the International Neuropsychological Society, 5,* 579–592.

Marcotte, T. D., Lazzaretto, D., Scott, J. C., Roberts, E., Woods, S. P., & Letendre, S. (2006). Visual attention deficits are associated with driving accidents in cognitively-impaired HIV-infected individuals. *Journal of Clinical and Experimental Neuropsychology, 28,* 13–28.

Marcotte, T. D., Wolfson, T., Rosenthal, T. J., Heaton, R. K., Gonzalez, R., Ellis, R. J., et al. (2004). A multimodal assessment of driving performance in HIV infection. *Neurology, 63,* 1417–1422.

Margolin, A., Avants, S. K., Warburton, L. A., & Hawkins, K. A. (2002). Factors affecting cognitive functioning in a sample of human immunodeficiency virus-positive injection drug users. *AIDS Patient Care and STDs, 16,* 255–267.

Martin, A. (1994). HIV, cognition, and the basal ganglia. In I. Grant and A. Martin (Eds.), *Neuropsychology of HIV infection* (pp. 234–259). New York: Oxford University Press.

Martin, E. M., Nixon, H., Pitrak, D. L., Weddington, W., Rains, N. A., Nunnally, G., et al. (2007). Characteristics of prospective memory deficits in HIV-seropositive substance-dependent individuals: Preliminary observations. *Journal of Clinical and Experimental Neuropsychology, 29,* 496–504.

Martin, E. M., Novak, R. M., Fendrich, M., Vassileva, J., Gonzalez, R., Grbesic, S., et al. (2004a). Stroop performance in drug users classified by HIV and hepatitis C virus serostatus. *Journal of the International Neuropsychological Society, 10,* 298–300.

Martin, E. M., Pitrak, D. L., Novak, R. M., Pursell, K. J., & Mullane, K. M. (1999). Reaction times are faster in HIV-seropositive patients on antiretroviral therapy: A preliminary report. *Journal of Clinical and Experimental Neuropsychology, 21,* 730–735.

Martin, E. M., Pitrak, D. L., Robertson, L. C., Novak, R. M., Mullane, K. M., & Pursell, K. J. (1995). Global-local analysis in HIV-1 infection. *Neuropsychology, 9,* 102–109.

Martin, E. M., Pitrak, D. L., Weddington, W., Rains, N. A., Nunnally, G., Nixon, H., et al. (2004b). Cognitive impulsivity and HIV serostatus in substance dependent males. *Journal of the International Neuropsychological Society, 10,* 931–938.

Martin, E. M., Robertson, L. C., Sorensen, D. J., Jagust, W. J., Mallon, K. F., & Chirurgi, V. A. (1993). Speed of memory scanning is not affected in early HIV-1 infection. *Journal of Clinical and Experimental Neuropsychology, 15,* 311–320.

Martin, E. M., Sullivan, T. S., Reed, R. A., Fletcher, T. A., Pitrak, D. L., Weddington, W., et al. (2001). Auditory working memory in HIV-1 infection. *Journal of the International Neuropsychological Society, 7,* 20–26.

Maruff, P., Malone, V., McArthur-Jackson, C., Mulhall, B., Benson, E., & Currie, J. (1995). Abnormalities of visual spatial attention in HIV infection and the HIV-associated dementia complex. *The Journal of Neuropsychiatry and Clinical Neurosciences, 7,* 325–333.

Mayeux, R., Stern, Y., Tang, M. X., Todak, G., Marder, K., Sano, M., et al. (1993). Mortality risks in gay men with human immunodeficiency virus infection and cognitive impairment. *Neurology, 43,* 176–182.

McArthur, J. C. (2004). HIV dementia: An evolving disease. *Journal of Neuroimmunology, 157,* 3–10.

McArthur, J. C., McDermott, M. P., McClernon, D., St Hillaire, C., Conant, K., Marder, K., et al. (2004). Attenuated central nervous system infection in advanced HIV/AIDS with combination antiretroviral therapy. *Archives of Neurology, 61,* 1687–1696.

Meyerhoff, D. J. (2001). Effects of alcohol and HIV infection on the central nervous system. *Alcohol Research and Health, 25,* 288–298.

Miguez, M. J., Shor-Posner, G., Morales, G., Rodriguez, A., & Burbano, X. (2003). HIV treatment in drug abusers: Impact of alcohol use. *Addiction Biology, 8,* 33–37.

Millikin, C. P., Trepanier, L. L., & Rourke, S. B. (2004). Verbal fluency component analysis in adults with HIV/AIDS. *Journal of Clinical and Experimental Neuropsychology, 26,* 933–942.

Mirza, S. A., Phelan, M., Rimland, D., Graviss, E., Hamill, R., Brandt, M. E., et al. (2003). The changing epidemiology of cryptococcosis: An update from population-based active surveillance in 2 large metropolitan areas, 1992–2000. *Clinical Infectious Diseases, 36,* 789–794.

Mittenberg, W., Azrin, R., Millsaps, C., & Heilbronner, R. (1993). Identification of malingered head injury on the Wechsler Memory Scale—Revised. *Psychological Assessment, 5,* 34–40.

Mohsen, A. H., Murad, S., & Easterbrook, P. J. (2005). Prevalence of hepatitis C in an ethnically diverse HIV-1-infected cohort in south London. *HIV Medicine, 6,* 206–215.

Monteiro de Almeida, S., Letendre, S., Zimmerman, J., Lazzaretto, D., McCutchan, A., & Ellis, R. (2005). Dynamics of monocyte chemoattractant protein type one (MCP-1) and HIV viral load in human cerebrospinal fluid and plasma. *Journal of Neuroimmunology, 169,* 144–152.

Moore DJ, Woods SP, Lazzaretto DL, Depp CA, Atkinson JH, Heaton RK, Grant I, and the HNRC group. (2006). Cognitive impairment among individuals with Bipolar Disorder and HIV infection. *Journal of the International Neuropsychological Society, 12*(Suppl 1), 150..

Morgan, E. E., Woods, S. P., Childers, M., Marquie-Beck, J., Ellis, R. J., Grant, I., et al. (2008). Predictive validity of demographically-adjusted normative standards for the HIV Dementia Scale. *Journal of Clinical and Experimental Neuropsychology, 30,* 83–90.

Munoz-Moreno, J. A., Rodriguez, C., Prats, A., Ferrer, M., Negredo, E., Garolera, M., et al. (2007). *Recommended earlier initiation of ART based on nadir CD4 cell count as a risk factor for HIV-related neurocognitive impairment (abstract 383).* Paper presented at the 14th Conference on Retroviruses and Opportunistic Infections, Los Angeles, CA.

Murji, S., Rourke, S. B., Donders, J., Carter, S. L., Shore, D., & Rourke, B. P. (2003). Theoretically derived CVLT subtypes in HIV-1 infection: Internal and external validation. *Journal of the International Neuropsychological Society, 9,* 1–16.

Nath, A., Hauser, K. F., Wojna, V., Booze, R. M., Maragos, W., Prendergast, M., et al. (2002). Molecular basis for interactions of HIV and drugs of abuse. *Journal of Acquired Immune Deficiency Syndromes, 31*(Suppl 2), S62–S69.

Neundorfer, M. M., Camp, C. J., Lee, M. M., Skrajner, M. J., Malone, M. L., & Carr, J. R. (2004). Compensating for cognitive deficits in persons aged 50 and over with HIV/AIDS: A pilot study of a cognitive intervention. *Journal of HIV/AIDS and Social Services, 3,* 79–97.

Nielsen-Bohlman, L., Boyle, D., Biggins, C., Ezekiel, F., & Fein, G. (1997). Semantic priming impairment in HIV. *Journal of the International Neuropsychological Society, 3,* 348–358.

Olesen, P. J., Schendan, H. E., Amick, M. M., & Cronin-Golomb, A. (2007). HIV infection affects parietal-dependent spatial cognition: Evidence from mental rotation and heirarchical pattern perception. *Behavioral Neuroscience, 121,* 1163–1173.

Ongradi, J., Specter, S., Horvath, A., & Friedman, H. (1998). Combined in vitro effect of marijuana and retrovirus on the activity of mouse natural killer cells. *Pathology Oncology Research, 4,* 191–199.

Pau, C. W., Lee, T. M., & Chan, S. F. (2002). The impact of heroin on frontal executive functions. *Archives of Clinical Neuropsychology, 17,* 663–670.

Perez, J. L., & Moore, R. D. (2003). Greater effect of highly active antiretroviral therapy on survival in people aged > or =50 years compared with younger people in an urban observational cohort. *Clinical Infectious Diseases, 36,* 212–218.

Peterson, P. K., Gekker, G., Chao, C. C., Schut, R., Molitor, T. W., & Balfour, H. H., Jr. (1991). Cocaine potentiates HIV-1 replication in human peripheral blood mononuclear cell cocultures. Involvement of transforming growth factor-beta. *Journal of Immunology, 146,* 81–84.

Pfefferbaum, A., Adalsteinsson, E., & Sullivan, E. V. (2005). Cortical NAA deficits in HIV infection without dementia: Influence of alcoholism comorbidity. *Neuropsychopharmacology, 30,* 1392–1399.

Pfefferbaum, A., Rosenbloom, M. J., Adalsteinsson, E., & Sullivan, E. V. (2007). Diffusion tensor imaging with quantitative fibre tracking in HIV infection and alcoholism comorbidity: Synergistic white matter damage. *Brain, 130*s, 48–64.

Pfefferbaum, A., Rosenbloom, M. J., Rohlfing, T., Adalsteinsson, E., Kemper, C. A., Deresinski, S., et al. (2006). Contribution of alcoholism to brain dysmorphology in HIV infection: Effects on the ventricles and corpus callosum. *Neuroimage, 33,* 239–251.

Piatt, A. L., Fields, J. A., Paolo, A. M., Koller, W. C., & Troster, A. I. (1999a). Lexical, semantic, and action verbal fluency in Parkinson's disease with and without dementia. *Journal of Clinical and Experimental Neuropsychology, 21,* 435–443.

Piatt, A. L., Fields, J. A., Paolo, A. M., & Troster, A. I. (1999b). Action (verb naming) fluency as an executive function measure: Convergent and divergent evidence of validity. *Neuropsychologia, 37,* 1499–1503.

Pomara, N., Crandall, D. T., Choi, S. J., Johnson, G., & Lim, K. O. (2001). White matter abnormalities in HIV-1 infection: A diffusion tensor imaging study. *Psychiatry Research, 106,* 15–24.

Powderly, W. G. (2002). Sorting through confusing messages: The art of HAART. *Journal of Acquired Immune Deficiency Syndromes, 31*(Suppl 1), S3–S9; discussion S24–S25.

Power, C., Selnes, O. A., Grim, J. A., & McArthur, J. C. (1995). HIV dementia scale: A rapid screening test. *Journal of Acquired Immune Deficiency Syndromes and Human Retrovirology, 8,* 273–278.

Psychological Corporation. (1987). *Wechsler Memory Scale—Revised.* San Antonio, TX: Author.

Pukay-Martin, N. D., Cristiani, S. A., Saveanu, R., & Bornstein, R. A. (2003). The relationship between stressful life events and cognitive function in HIV-infected men. *The Journal of Neuropsychiatry and Clinical Neurosciences, 15,* 436–441.

Radkowski, M., Wilkinson, J., Nowicki, M., Adair, D., Vargas, H., Ingui, C., et al. (2002). Search for hepatitis C virus negative-strand RNA sequences and analysis of viral sequences in the central nervous system: Evidence of replication. *Journal of Virology, 76,* 600–608.

Ranga, U., Shankarappa, R., Siddappa, N. B., Ramakrishna, L., Nagendran, R., Mahalingam, M., et al. (2004). Tat protein of human immunodeficiency virus type 1 subtype C strains is a defective chemokine. *Journal of Virology, 78,* 2586–2590.

Razani, J., Murphy, C., Davidson, T. M., Grant, I., & McCutchan, A. (1996). Odor sensitivity is impaired in HIV-positive cognitively impaired patients. *Physiology and Behavior, 59,* 877–881.

Reger, M., Welsh, R., Razani, J., Martin, D. J., & Boone, K. B. (2002). A meta-analysis of the neuropsychological sequelae of HIV infection. *Journal of the International Neuropsychological Society, 8,* 410–424.

Reger, M. A., Martin, D. J., Cole, S. L., & Strauss, G. (2005). The relationship between plasma viral load and neuropsychological functioning in HIV-1 infection. *Archives of Clinical Neuropsychology, 20,* 137–143.

Rippeth, J. D., Heaton, R. K., Carey, C. L., Marcotte, T. D., Moore, D. J., Gonzalez, R., et al. (2004). Methamphetamine dependence increases risk of neuropsychological impairment in HIV infected persons. *Journal of the International Neuropsychological Society, 10,* 1–14.

Robertson, K., Su, Z., Krambrink, A., Evans, S., Havlir, D., Margolis, D., et al. (2007). *This is your brain off drugs: Neurocognitive function before and after ART discontinuation in patients with high CD4 nadir (ACTG A5170) (abstract 113).* Paper presented at the 14th Conference on Retroviruses and Opportunistic Infections, Los Angeles, CA.

Robertson, K. R., Parsons, T. D., Sidtis, J. J., Hanlon Inman, T., Robertson, W. T., Hall, C. D., et al. (2006). Timed gait test: Normative data for the assessment of the AIDS dementia complex. *Journal of Clinical and Experimental Neuropsychology, 28,* 1053–1064.

Rourke, S. B., Halman, M. H., & Bassel, C. (1999). Neurocognitive complaints in HIV-infection and their relationship to depressive symptoms and neuropsychological functioning. *Journal of Clinical and Experimental Neuropsychology, 21,* 737–756.

Ruiz Perez, I., Rodriguez Bano, J., Lopez Ruz, M. A., del Arco Jimenez, A., Causse Prados, M., Pasquau Liano, J., et al. (2005). Health-related quality of life of patients with HIV: Impact of sociodemographic, clinical and psychosocial factors. *Quality of Life Research, 14,* 1301–1310.

Ryan, E. L., Morgello, S., Isaacs, K., Naseer, M., & Gerits, P. (2004). Neuropsychiatric impact of hepatitis C on advanced HIV. *Neurology, 62,* 957–962.

Sacktor, N., Lyles, R. H., Skolasky, R., Kleeberger, C., Selnes, O. A., Miller, E. N., et al. (2001). HIV-associated neurologic disease incidence changes: Multicenter AIDS cohort study, 1990–1998. *Neurology, 56,* 257–260.

Sacktor, N., Nakasujja, N., Skolasky, R., Robertson, K., Wong, M., Musisi, S., et al. (2006). Antiretroviral therapy improves cognitive impairment in HIV+ individuals in sub-Saharan Africa. *Neurology, 67,* 311–314.

Sacktor, N., Schifitto, G., McDermott, M. P., Marder, K., McArthur, J. C., & Kieburtz, K. (2000). Transdermal selegiline in HIV-associated cognitive impairment: Pilot, placebo-controlled study. *Neurology, 54,* 233–235.

Sacktor, N. C., Wong, M., Nakasujja, N., Skolasky, R. L., Selnes, O. A., Musisi, S., et al. (2005). The international HIV dementia scale: A new rapid screening test for HIV dementia. *AIDS, 19,* 1367–1374.

Sadek, J. R., Johnson, S. A., White, D. A., Salmon, D. P., Taylor, K. I., Delapena, J. H., et al. (2004). Retrograde amnesia in dementia: Comparison of HIV-associated dementia, Alzheimer's disease, and Huntington's disease. *Neuropsychology, 18,* 692–699.

Schifitto, G., Sacktor, N., Zhang, J., Evans, S., Simpson, D., Millar, L., et al. (2006). *A phase ii, placebo-controlled, double-blind study of the selegiline transdermal system in the treatment of HIV-associated cognitive impairment (abstract 364).* Paper presented at the 13th Conference on Retroviruses and Opportunistic Infections, Denver, CO.

Schulte, T., Mueller-Oehring, E. M., Rosenbloom, M. J., Pfefferbaum, A., & Sullivan, E. V. (2005). Differential effect of HIV infection and alcoholism on conflict processing, attentional allocation, and perceptual load: Evidence from a Stroop match-to-sample task. *Biological Psychiatry, 57,* 67–75.

Scott, J. C., Woods, S. P., Patterson, K. A., Morgan, E. E., Heaton, R. K., Grant, I., et al. (2006). Recency effects in HIV-associated dementia are characterized by deficient encoding. *Neuropsychologia, 44,* 1336–1343.

Scott, J. C., Woods, S. P., Matt, G. E., Meyer, R. A., Heaton, R. K., Atkinson, J. H., et al. (2007). Neurocognitive effects of methamphetamine: A critical review and meta-analysis. *Neuropsychology Review, 17,* 275–297.

Selnes, O. A., Galai, N., McArthur, J. C., Cohn, S., Royal, W., Esposito, D., & Vlahov, D. (1997). HIV infection and cognition in intravenous drug users: long-term follow-up. *Neurology, 48,* 223–230.

Sevigny, J. J., Albert, S. M., McDermott, M. P., McArthur, J. C., Sacktor, N., Conant, K., et al. (2004). Evaluation of HIV RNA and markers of immune activation as predictors of HIV-associated dementia. *Neurology, 63,* 2084–2090.

Sevigny, J. J., Albert, S. M., McDermott, M. P., Schifitto, G., McArthur, J. C., Sacktor, N., et al. (2007). An evaluation of neurocognitive status and markers of immune activation as predictors of time to death in advanced HIV infection. *Archives of Neurology, 64,* 97–102.

Simpson, D. M., Kitch, D., Evans, S. R., McArthur, J. C., Asmuth, D. M., Cohen, B., et al. (2006). HIV neuropathy natural history cohort study: Assessment measures and risk factors. *Neurology, 66,* 1679–1687.

Singh, K. K., Ellis, R. J., Marquie-Beck, J., Letendre, S., Heaton, R. K., Grant, I., et al. (2004). CCR2 polymorphisms affect neuropsychological impairment in HIV-1-infected adults. *Journal of Neuroimmunology, 157,* 185–192.

Slick, D. J., Hinkin, C. H., van Gorp, W. G., & Satz, P. (2001). Base rate of a WMS-R malingering index in a sample of non-compensation-seeking men infected with HIV-1. *Applied Neuropsychology, 8,* 185–189.

Stein, M., Herman, D. S., Trisvan, E., Pirraglia, P., Engler, P., & Anderson, B. J. (2005). Alcohol use and sexual risk behavior among human immunodeficiency virus-positive persons. *Alcoholism: Clinical and Experimental Research, 29,* 837–843.

Stern, R. A., Silva, S. G., Chaisson, N., & Evans, D. L. (1996). Influence of cognitive reserve on neuropsychological functioning in asymptomatic human immunodeficiency virus-1 infection. *Archives of Neurology, 53,* 148–153.

Stout, J. C., Ellis, R. J., Jernigan, T. L., Archibald, S. L., Abramson, I., Wolfson, T., et al. (1998). Progressive cerebral volume loss in human immunodeficiency virus infection: A longitudinal volumetric magnetic resonance imaging study. *Archives of Neurology, 55,* 161–168.

Sweet, J. J., King, J. H., Malina, A. C., Bergman, M. A., & Simmons, A. (2002). Documenting the prominence of forensic neuropsychology at national meetings and in relevant professional journals from 1990 to 2000. *The Clinical Neuropsychologist, 16*, 481–494.

Thompson, P.M., Dutton, R.A., Hayashi, K.M., Toga, A.W., Lopez, O.L., Aizenstein, H.J., & Becker, J.T. (2005). Thinning of the cerebral cortex visualized in HIV/AIDS reflects CD4+ T lymphocyte decline. *Proceedings of the National Academy of the Sciences USA, 102*, 15647–15652.

Tozzi, V., Balestra, P., Galgani, S., Murri, R., Bellagamba, R., Narciso, P., et al. (2003). Neurocognitive performance and quality of life in patients with HIV infection. *AIDS Research and Human Retroviruses, 19*, 643–652.

Tozzi, V., Balestra, P., Lorenzini, P., Bellagamba, R., Galgani, S., Corpolongo, A., et al. (2005). Prevalence and risk factors for human immunodeficiency virus-associated neurocognitive impairment, 1996 to 2002: Results from an urban observational cohort. *Journal of Neurovirology, 11*, 265–273.

Tozzi, V., Balestra, P., Murri, R., Galgani, S., Bellagamba, R., Narciso, P., et al. (2004). Neurocognitive impairment influences quality of life in HIV-infected patients receiving HAART. *International Journal of STD and AIDS, 15*, 254–259.

Treisman, G., Fishman, M., Schwartz, J., Hutton, H., & Lyketsos, C. (1998). Mood disorders in HIV infection. *Depression and Anxiety, 7*, 178–187.

Trepanier, L. L., Rourke, S. B., Bayoumi, A. M., Halman, M. H., Krzyzanowski, S., & Power, C. (2005). The impact of neuropsychological impairment and depression on health-related quality of life in HIV-infection. *Journal of Clinical and Experimental Neuropsychology, 27*, 1–15.

Tse, W., Cersosimo, M. G., Gracies, J. M., Morgello, S., Olanow, C. W., & Koller, W. (2004). Movement disorders and AIDS: A review. *Parkinsonism and Related Disorders, 10*, 323–334.

Tucker, J. S., Burnam, M. A., Sherbourne, C. D., Kung, F. Y., & Gifford, A. L. (2003). Substance use and mental health correlates of nonadherence to antiretroviral medications in a sample of patients with human immunodeficiency virus infection. *The American Journal of Medicine, 114*, 573–580.

Turchan-Cholewo, J., Liu, Y., Gartner, S., Reid, R., Jie, C., Peng, X., et al. (2006). Increased vulnerability of ApoE4 neurons to HIV proteins and opiates: Protection by diosgenin and L-deprenyl. *Neurobiology of Disease, 23*, 109–119.

Uldall, K. K., Ryan, R., Berghuis, J. P., & Harris, V. L. (2000). Association between delirium and death in AIDS patients. *AIDS Patient Care and STDS, 14*, 95–100.

UNAIDS. (2006). *Report on the global AIDS epidemic 2006*. Geneva: UNAIDS.

Valcour, V., Shikuma, C., Shiramizu, B., Watters, M., Poff, P., Selnes, O., et al. (2004a). Higher frequency of dementia in older HIV-1 individuals: The Hawaii aging with HIV-1 cohort. *Neurology, 63*, 822–827.

Valcour, V., Shikuma, C., Shiramizu, B., Watters, M., Poff, P., Selnes, O. A., et al. (2004b). Age, apolipoprotein E4, and the risk of HIV dementia: The Hawaii aging with HIV cohort. *Journal of Neuroimmunology, 157*, 197–202.

Valcour, V., Yee, P., Williams, A. E., Shiramizu, B., Watters, M., Selnes, O., et al. (2006). Lowest ever CD4 lymphocyte count (CD4 nadir) as a predictor of current cognitive and neurological status in human immunodeficiency virus type 1 infection-the Hawaii aging with HIV cohort. *Journal of Neurovirology, 12*, 387–391.

van Gorp, W. G., Baerwald, J. P., Ferrando, S. J., McElhiney, M. C., & Rabkin, J. G. (1999). The relationship between employment and neuropsychological impairment in HIV infection. *Journal of the International Neuropsychological Society, 5*, 534–539.

van Gorp, W. G., Lamb, D. G., & Schmitt, F. A. (1993). Methodologic issues in neuropsychological research with HIV-spectrum disease. *Archives of Clinical Neuropsychology, 8*, 17–33.

van Gorp, W. G., Rabkin, J. G., Ferrando, S. J., Mintz, J., Ryan, E., Borkowski, T., et al. (2007). Neuropsychiatric predictors of return to work in HIV/AIDS. *Journal of the International Neuropsychological Society, 13*, 80–89.

Vigil, O., Posada, C., Woods, S. P., Atkinson, J. H., Heaton, R. K., Perry, W., et al. (2008). Impairments in fine-motor coordination and speed of information processing predict dependence in everyday functioning in Hepatitis C infection. *Journal of Clinical and Experimental Neuropsychology, 30*, 805–815.

von Giesen, H. J., Heintges, T., Abbasi-Boroudjeni, N., Kucukkoylu, S., Koller, H., Haslinger, B. A., et al. (2004). Psychomotor slowing in hepatitis C and HIV infection. *Journal of Acquired Immune Deficiency Syndromes, 35*, 131–137.

Wang, G. J., Chang, L., Volkow, N. D., Telang, F., Logan, J., Ernst, T., et al. (2004). Decreased brain dopaminergic transporters in HIV-associated dementia patients. *Brain, 127*, 2452–2458.

Wang, X., Douglas, S. D., Metzger, D. S., Guo, C. J., Li, Y., O'Brien, C. P., et al. (2002). Alcohol potentiates HIV-1 infection of human blood mononuclear phagocytes. *Alcoholism: Clinical and Experimental Research, 26*, 1880–1886.

Watters, M. R., Poff, P. W., Shiramizu, B. T., Holck, P. S., Fast, K. M., Shikuma, C. M., et al. (2004).

Symptomatic distal sensory polyneuropathy in HIV after age 50. *Neurology, 62*, 1378–1383.

Westervelt, H. J., McCaffrey, R. J., Cousins, J. P., Wagle, W. A., and Haase, R. F. (1997). Longitudinal analysis of olfactory deficits in HIV infection. *Archives of Clinical Neuropsychology, 12*, 557–565.

Whitfield, R. M., Bechtel, L. M., and Starich, G. H. (1997). The impact of ethanol and marinol/marijuana usage on HIV+/AIDS patients undergoing azidothymidine, azidothymidine/dideoxycytidine, or dideoxyinosine therapy. *Alcoholism: Clinical and Experimental Research, 21*, 122–127.

Wiley, C. A., Soontornniyomkij, V., Radhakrishnan, L., Masliah, E., Mellors, J., Hermann, S. A., et al. (1998). Distribution of brain HIV load in AIDS. *Brain Pathology, 8*, 277–284.

Wiseman, M. B., Sanchez, J. A., Buechel, C., Mintun, M. A., Lopez, O. L., Milko, D., et al. (1999). Patterns of relative cerebral blood flow in minor cognitive motor disorder in human immunodeficiency virus infection. *Journal of Neuropsychiatry and Clinical Neurosciences, 11*, 222–233.

Woods, S. P., Carey, C. L., Moran, L. M., Dawson, M. S., Letendre, S. L., & Grant, I. (2007a). Frequency and predictors of self-reported prospective memory complaints in individuals infected with HIV. *Archives of Clinical Neuropsychology, 22*, 187–195.

Woods, S. P., Carey, C. L., Troster, A. I., & Grant, I. (2005a). Action (verb) generation in HIV-1 infection. *Neuropsychologia, 43*, 1144–1151.

Woods, S. P., Conover, E., Rippeth, J. D., Carey, C. L., Gonzalez, R., Marcotte, T. D., et al. (2004). Qualitative aspects of verbal fluency in HIV-associated dementia: A deficit in rule-guided lexical-semantic search processes? *Neuropsychologia, 42*, 801–809.

Woods, S. P., Conover, E., Weinborn, M., Rippeth, J. D., Brill, R. M., Heaton, R. K., et al. (2003). Base rate of Hiscock Digit Memory Test Failure in HIV-associated neurocognitive disorders. *The Clinical Neuropsychologist, 17*, 383–389.

Woods, S. P., Dawson, M. S., Weber, E., Gibson, S., Grant, I., Atkinson, J. H., and The HNRC Group. (in press). Timing is everything: Antiretroviral non-adherence is associated with impairment in time-based prospective memory. *Journal of the International Neuropsychological Society.*

Woods, S. P., Iudicello, J. E., Moran, L. M., Carey, C. L., Dawson, M. S., Grant, I., et al. (2008a). HIV-associated prospective memory impairment increases risk of dependence in everyday functioning. *Neuropsychology, 22*, 110–117.

Woods, S. P., Moran, L. M., Carey, C. L., Dawson, M. S., Iudicello, J. E., Gibson, S., et al. (2008b).

Prospective memory in HIV infection: Is "remembering to remember" a unique predictor of self-reported medication management? *Archives of Clinical Neuropsychology, 23*, 257–270.

Woods, S. P., Morgan, E. E., Dawson, M., Scott, J. C., & Grant, I. (2006a). Action (verb) fluency predicts dependence in instrumental activities of daily living in persons infected with HIV-1. *Journal of Clinical and Experimental Neuropsychology, 28*, 1030–1042.

Woods, S. P., Morgan, E. E., Marquie-Beck, J., Carey, C. L., Grant, I., & Letendre, S. L. (2006b). Markers of macrophage activation and axonal injury are associated with prospective memory in HIV-1 disease. *Cognitive and Behavioral Neurology, 19*, 217–221.

Woods, S. P., Scott, J. C., Dawson, M. S., Morgan, E. E., Carey, C. L., Heaton, R. K., et al. (2005b). Construct validity of Hopkins Verbal Learning Test-Revised component process measures in an HIV-1 sample. *Archives of Clinical Neuropsychology, 20*, 1061–1071.

Woods, S. P., Scott, J. C., Sires, D. A., Grant, I., Heaton, R. K., & Troster, A. I. (2005c). Action (verb) fluency: Test–retest reliability, normative standards, and construct validity. *Journal of the International Neuropsychological Society, 11*, 408–415.

Woody, G. E., Donnell, D., Seage, G. R., Metzger, D., Marmor, M., Koblin, B. A., et al. (1999). Non-injection substance use correlates with risky sex among men having sex with men: Data from HIVNET. *Drug and Alcohol Dependence, 53*, 197–205.

Wutoh, A. K., Brown, C. M., Kumoji, E. K., Daftary, M. S., Jones, T., Barnes, N. A., et al. (2001). Antiretroviral adherence and use of alternative therapies among older HIV-infected adults. *Journal of the National Medical Association, 93*, 243–250.

Zhang, L., Looney, D., Taub, D., Chang, S. L., Way, D., Witte, M. H., et al. (1998). Cocaine opens the blood-brain barrier to HIV-1 invasion. *Journal of Neurovirology, 4*, 619–626.

Zheng, J., Lopez, A., Huang, Y., Persidsky, A., He, J., Zhang, H., et al. (2007). *Comparison of different viral strains from clade B and C on macrophage-mediated inflammatory factor and glutamate production and neurotoxicity (abstract 354).* Paper presented at the 14th Conference on Retroviruses and Opportunistic Infections, Los Angeles, CA.

Zink, M. C., Uhrlaub, J., DeWitt, J., Voelker, T., Bullock, B., Mankowski, J., et al. (2005). Neuroprotective and anti-human immunodeficiency virus activity of minocycline. *Journal of the American Medical Association, 293*, 2003–2011.

18

The Neurobehavioral Correlates of Alcoholism

Sean B. Rourke and Igor Grant

In the United States about 10% of adults meet the diagnostic criteria for alcohol abuse or dependence. It is estimated that of those who meet the criteria for alcohol dependence approximately 50% (range 31%–85%) manifest neurocognitive impairments on neuropsychological testing when abstinent for 3–4 weeks (Eckardt & Martin, 1986; Grant et al., 1984; Parsons, 1986a; Rourke & Grant, 1995).

The main goal of this chapter is to delineate the neurobehavioral correlates of alcoholism. We have divided the chapter into seven major sections. In the first, we briefly describe the diagnosis of alcoholism and related disorders, and the clinical course associated with the "typical" alcoholic. Next, we summarize the neurobehavioral findings associated with alcoholism, as well as the neuroimaging, electrophysiological, and neuropathological correlates. In this section, we focus primarily on chronic alcoholics who do not meet the criteria for either an amnestic disorder and/or a dementia associated with alcoholism. A brief description of the models that have been proposed to explain the brain dysfunction associated with alcoholism is presented in the third section. A summary of the neurobehavioral and neuroimaging findings associated with the Wernicke–Korsakoff syndrome is presented in the next section. While there is no doubt that alcohol is a neurotoxic agent, we present a conceptual model in the fifth section to illustrate the multifactorial etiology of the neurobehavioral impairments that are detected in alcoholics. Next, we summarize the

evidence for the recovery of brain structure and function, and identify some of the variables that may mediate this recovery. Finally, we focus on clinical implications and the role of neuropsychological performance in the treatment outcome of alcoholics.

Diagnosis of Alcoholism and Clinical Course

Diagnosis of Alcohol Dependence and Alcohol-Related Disorders

Alcohol dependence, or simply alcoholism, refers to a constellation of symptoms that develop in the context of a maladaptive pattern of alcohol consumption and continue despite adverse life consequences. In the most recent update (the fourth edition) of the *Diagnostic and Statistical Manual of Mental Disorders* (DSM-IV) (American Psychiatric Association, 1994), alcohol dependence falls under substance-related disorders, and more specifically, substance dependence. The diagnosis for alcohol dependence is reproduced in Table 18–1.

According to DSM-IV criteria, a person is diagnosed as having alcohol dependence if he or she has three or more of the above symptoms; in addition, the diagnosis specifies the conditions for physiological dependence, the presence of which is indicated by tolerance and/or withdrawal symptoms. Further course specifiers are used to reflect the amount of time that a person has been abstinent (i.e., early versus sustained remission) and whether there have been any symptoms of dependence or abuse during this time (i.e., partial versus full remission) (American Psychiatric Association, 1994). Alcohol abuse is similar to alcohol dependence in some respects (i.e., both refer to a maladaptive use of alcohol that leads to clinically significant impairment or distress), but the former does not involve tolerance, withdrawal, or a pattern of compulsive use, as is the case with the latter diagnosis (American Psychiatric Association, 1994).

Severe cognitive disorders occur in approximately 10% of persons diagnosed with alcohol dependence (Horvath, 1973). The DSM-IV diagnostic criteria for these disorders are listed below in Table 18–2. (See *Wernicke–Korsakoff syndrome,* below, for a summary of the neurobehavioral and neuroimaging correlates of alcohol-

induced persisting amnestic disorder, and refer to Martin et al. [1986, 1989] for more information regarding alcohol-induced persisting dementia.)

Although most alcoholics do not meet the criteria for either of these severe cognitive disorders listed above, many (i.e., approximately 50%) nevertheless demonstrate significant cognitive deficits that can have important effects on their treatment compliance and everyday functioning (see Figure 18–1). Because the DSM system does not yet admit to concepts like mild neurocognitive disorder, alcoholics with milder deficits might be assigned the vague diagnosis of alcohol-related disorder not otherwise specified (American Psychiatric Association, 1994); see the next section for the neurobehavioral and neuroimaging correlates of alcoholics who meet the latter criteria. Refer also to Figure 18–1

Table 18–1. Alcohol Dependence

A maladaptive pattern of alcohol use, leading to clinically significant impairment or distress by *three* (or more) of the following, occurring at any time in the same 12-month period:
1. tolerance, as defined by either of the following:
   (a) a need for markedly increased amounts of alcohol to achieve intoxication or desired effect
   (b) markedly diminished effect with continued use of the same amount of alcohol
2. withdrawal, as manifested by either of the following:
   (a) the characteristic alcohol withdrawal syndrome that occurs after cessation of (or reduction in) alcohol use that has been heavy and prolonged, and which has two (or more) of the following that develop within several hours to a few days: autonomic hyperactivity (e.g., sweating or pulse rate greater than 100), increased hand tremor, insomnia, nausea or vomiting, transient visual, tactile, or auditory hallucinations or illusions, psychomotor agitation, anxiety, or grand mal seizures.
   (b) the same (or a closely related) substance is taken to relieve or avoid withdrawal symptoms
3. alcohol is often taken in larger amounts or over a longer period than was intended
4. there is a persistent desire or unsuccessful efforts to cut down or control alcohol use
5. a great deal of time is spent in activities necessary to obtain alcohol, use alcohol, or recover from its effects
6. important social, occupational, or recreational activities are given up or reduced because of substance use
7. the alcohol use is continued despite knowledge of having a persistent or recurrent physical or psychological problem that is likely to have been caused or exacerbated by alcohol (e.g., continued drinking despite recognition that an ulcer was made worse by alcohol consumption).

(DSM-IV: pp. 181, 198–199)

Table 18–2. Alcohol-Induced Persisting Amnestic Disorder

A. The development of memory impairment as manifested by impairment in the ability to learn new information or the inability to recall previously learned information.
B. The memory disturbance causes a significant impairment in social or occupational functioning and represents a significant decline from a previous level of functioning.
C. The memory disturbance does not occur exclusively during the course of a delirium or a dementia and persists beyond the usual duration of Alcohol Intoxication and Withdrawal.
D. There is evidence from the history, physical examination, or laboratory findings that the memory disturbance is etiologically related to the persisting effects of alcohol use.

(DSM-IV: p. 162)

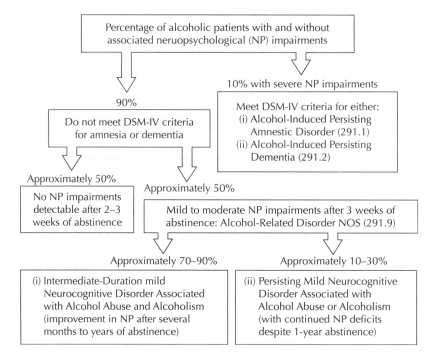

Figure 18–1. Prevalence of neuropsychological deficits associated with alcoholism.

for an additional nosology to better character-ize the neurocognitive status of alcoholics with extended periods of abstinence (Grant et al., 1987b).

Clinical Course Associated with Alcoholism

Understanding the natural history of alcohol-ism has practical usefulness for both clinicians and researchers. For clinicians, it can help iden-tify the time course associated with the emer-gence of various alcohol-related symptoms, and it can dictate when different treatment interven-tions should be implemented depending on the severity of alcohol-related symptoms (Schuckit et al., 1993). For researchers in the field of neu-ropsychology, knowledge of the clinical course of alcoholism is important because of the neu-romedical events and systemic illnesses that can often arise during the course of alcoholism (e.g., head injuries, blackouts, hypertension, diabetes, withdrawal seizures, hepatic dysfunc-tion, chronic obstructive pulmonary disease [COPD]); these can have separate and additive negative effects on the brain, independent of the

neurotoxic effects of alcohol (see *Multifactorial Etiology of Neuropsychological Deficits,* below).

A study by Schuckit and his colleagues (1993) provides useful information about the relative appearance of the various symptoms that occur with alcohol dependence (Schuckit et al., 1993). In their study, 636 male inpatients with primary alcoholism and a mean age and education of 45.0 and 12.8 years, respectively, were admin-istered a structured interview regarding the age at which 21 alcohol-related major life events first occurred; the information from the patients was also further corroborated with at least one resource person. Of the 21 alcohol-related life events, the alcoholics as a group experienced an average of 10.9 events. These alcohol-dependent men experienced several alcohol-related prob-lems by their late twenties (e.g., 96% drank before noon, 74% had binges of drinking lasting for 12 hours straight). By their early thirties, there was evidence that alcohol had begun to interfere with functioning in multiple life areas (e.g., 91% were experiencing a withdrawal syndrome, 82% were having blackouts, 49% were involved in auto accidents, 76% were having morning shakes). By age 34, 86% reported that they had lost control of their drinking. More serious job- and social-related problems occurred in their late thirties (43% had been fired, 61% were divorced or separated). Finally, when alcoholic subjects reached their late thirties and early forties, there was evidence of severe long-term consequences related to alcohol use (i.e., between the ages of 40 and 42, 5% had withdrawal convulsions, 24% had been hospitalized, 37% endorsed that their physician had noted health problems, and 26% had hepatitis/pancreatitis).

Schuckit and his colleagues further explored whether there were any subgroups within this sample that varied in the emergence of alcohol-related symptoms. Interestingly, the order of occurrence of these 21 symptoms of alcohol dependence was consistent across the sample when they were divided according to subjects' age of onset of alcohol dependence (≤30 years, >30 years), or the presence of family history of alcoholism, a secondary diagnosis of drug dependence or depressive disorder, or a primary diagnosis of antisocial personality disorder (ASPD; Schuckit et al., 1993).

Thus, alcohol-related health consequences are extremely common in alcoholic men, especially when they have reached their late thirties and early forties. It is not until this point in time (i.e., after heavy drinking for 10–15 years), that most alcohol-dependent men will seek treatment for their alcohol-related medical problems. If neuropsychological deficits are also present when the alcoholic patient is recently detoxified (i.e., sober for 2–3 weeks), one needs to entertain the possibility that the etiology of these deficits is multifactorial. (See *Multifactorial Etiology of Neuropsychological Deficits,* below, for a review of the medical problems that arise during the course of alcohol abuse, which can contribute in both direct and indirect ways to neurobehavioral dysfunction.)

Neurobehavioral and Neuroimaging Findings Associated with Alcoholism

While damage to or dysfunction of the functional and structural integrity of the human brain is most striking, approximately 10% of alcoholic patients have severe neurocognitive decline (e.g., alcohol-induced amnestic or alcohol-induced dementia disorder). Many of the remaining 90% of alcoholics who do not meet the criteria for either of these disorders nevertheless demonstrate clear evidence of neurocognitive dysfunction after 2–3 weeks of detoxification. Rather consistent findings have emerged regarding the intellectual and neuropsychological ability patterns of such recently detoxified alcoholics.

One of the first systematic neuropsychological studies compared hospitalized alcoholics with nonalcoholic brain-damaged patients and control subjects on the Halstead–Reitan Neuropsychological Test Battery (Fitzhugh et al., 1960). Alcoholics performed at levels similar to those of brain-damaged subjects on the Halstead measures and on the Trail-Making Test, but more like controls on the Wechsler-Bellevue subtests. Furthermore, the alcoholics, when compared with the controls, exhibited worse performance on the Category Test, the Halstead Impairment Index, and the Tactual Performance Test total time. A subsequent study by these investigators, which included a larger number of subjects, revealed similar findings (Fitzhugh et al., 1965). Since these initial studies, other investigators have confirmed that recently detoxified alcoholics can perform at levels similar to those of brain-damaged patients on the Category Test (Jones & Parsons, 1971) and the Halstead–Reitan Battery (HRB; Goldstein & Shelly, 1982; Miller & Orr, 1980). A review of earlier studies by Parsons and Leber (1981) noted that the Halstead Impairment Index (a summary index of impaired performance on the seven measures comprising the Halstead Battery) was either significantly higher (worse) in alcoholics than nonalcoholic controls, or in the impaired range according to normative data, in 18 of 20 studies reviewed.

Intellectual Performance in Recently Detoxified Alcoholics

Despite evidence of neurocognitive dysfunction, recently detoxified alcoholics generally perform at levels comparable to those of nonalcoholic controls on Verbal and Full Scale IQ values, but often show lower Performance IQ values because of inferior performances on Block Design, Object Assembly, and Digit Symbol subtests from the Wechsler-Bellevue or

Wechsler Adult Intelligence Scales (original or revised versions) (Grant, 1987; Kleinknecht & Goldstein, 1972; Miller & Orr, 1980; Parsons & Farr, 1981; Tarter & Van Thiel, 1985). In the review by Parsons and Leber (1981), the mean Verbal and Performance IQ values of alcoholics across 14 studies was 108.7 and 104.7, respectively; in eight of the studies where subtest scores were reported, Block Design, Object Assembly, and Digit Symbol subtest scores from the WAIS were significantly lower than those of controls in 100%, 89%, and 75% of the studies evaluated, respectively (Parsons & Leber, 1981).

Neuropsychological Deficits in Recently Detoxified Alcoholics

Although not all recently detoxified alcoholics show evidence of impairment on formal neuropsychological testing, there is a "typical" neurocognitive profile that is generally observed in chronic detoxified alcoholics who are sober for 2–4 weeks. That is, alcoholics generally display intact verbal skills and have intelligence quotients within the normal range, but often show impairments on tests of novel problem solving and abstract reasoning, learning and memory, visual–spatial analysis, and complex perceptual–motor integration and on tests of simple motor skills.

Much of the research in the field of alcoholism has involved the study of alcoholic men; however, where female comparisons are available both male and female alcoholics generally show similar patterns of neuropsychological deficits (Fabian et al., 1981; Fabian & Parsons, 1983; Silberstein & Parsons, 1981); women, however, often show deficits after shorter drinking histories than men (Acker, 1985; Fabian et al., 1981; Glenn & Parsons, 1990). But in one study of Russian alcoholics, women manifested worse performance than men on tasks of visual working memory, spatial planning, problem solving, and cognitive flexibility (Flannery et al., 2007). Some investigators have reported that alcoholic women may escape deficits on learning and memory tests (Fabian et al., 1984; Sparadeo et al., 1983) even when matched on years of alcoholic drinking (Sparadeo et al., 1983). However, Sullivan et al. (2002) reported both verbal and nonverbal working memory and

visuospatial deficits in their female alcoholics. On balance, both male and female alcoholics, when compared with demographically matched nonalcoholic controls, generally perform less accurately on a broad array of neuropsychological tests and take more time to complete these tests. They also show reduced neurocognitive efficiency on summary measures that consider both accuracy and time together (Glenn & Parsons, 1990, 1991a), as well as on tests that sample verbal skills, learning and memory, problem solving and abstracting, and perceptual–motor skills (Glenn & Parsons, 1992).

Next, we turn to a more detailed description of the neuropsychological ability patterns that have been generally associated with alcoholism. For a more in depth treatment of older literature we refer the reader to a number of excellent reviews (Chelune & Parker, 1981; Eckardt & Martin, 1986; Grant, 1987; Goldman, 1983; Kleinknecht & Goldstein, 1972; Parsons, 1987; Parsons & Farr, 1981; Parsons & Nixon, 1993; Reed & Grant, 1990; Ryan & Butters, 1986; Tarter, 1980; Tarter & Van Thiel, 1985).

Attention and Concentration Skills

Mixed results have been obtained regarding whether alcoholics have deficits in attention and concentration (Miller & Orr, 1980). Tests of attention and concentration from the HRB (Speech Sounds Perception Test and Seashore Rhythm Test) were found to be impaired in 62% and 44% of the alcoholic samples reviewed (Parsons & Leber, 1981). Attentional tasks that place a higher processing demand can reveal deficits (Bartsch et al., 2007; Cairney et al., 2007) and these have been related to imaging indicators of neuronal integrity (Bartsch et al., 2007).

Abstraction, Problem Solving, and Executive Functioning

Alcoholics most frequently perform in the impaired range on neuropsychological tests that place demands on abstraction, reasoning and problem-solving skills, and cognitive flexibility. For example, alcoholics were impaired on the Category Test in 89% of the studies reviewed (i.e., 17 of 19), relative to controls or normative data that indicated impairment (Parsons & Leber,

1981), with degree of impairment related to the length of abstinence (Rourke & Grant, 1999). Alcoholics have the most difficulty on subtest 4 from the Category Test, a subtest requiring spatial discrimination (Jones & Parsons, 1972); in addition, length of drinking history in alcoholics has been shown to be positively associated with the number of errors on the Category Test (Jones & Parsons, 1971). Deficits have also been noted on other nonverbal reasoning and problem-solving tests—for example, the Raven's Progressive Matrices (Jones & Parsons, 1972) and the Levine Hypothesis Testing procedure (Schaeffer et al., 1989; Turner & Parsons, 1988)—as well as on verbal reasoning and problem-solving measures—for example the Conceptual Level Analogy Test (Turner & Parsons, 1988; Yohman & Parsons, 1987), the Word Finding Test (Reitan, 1972; Turner & Parsons, 1988), and the Shipley Institute of Living Scale Abstracting Test (Silberstein & Parsons, 1981; Turner & Parsons, 1988).

Tests of cognitive flexibility (e.g., Part B of the Trail-Making Test) revealed impairments in 80% of the studies reviewed (i.e., 12 of 15) (Parsons & Leber, 1981). Alcoholics have also been shown to be impaired on the Wisconsin Card Sorting Test (WCST). In general, they make more total errors and require more trials to reach the criterion level (Beatty et al., 1993; Joyce & Robbins, 1991; Tarter & Parsons, 1971), and tend to make elevated rates of perseverative responses and errors (Beatty et al., 1993; Joyce & Robbins, 1991; Tarter & Parsons, 1971). It has been suggested that this pattern of performance on the WCST reflects a deficit in the ability to sustain and persist with problem-solving tasks (Tarter & Parsons, 1971). When one examines the effects of age and length of drinking history on WCST performance, younger alcoholics tend to show less deficits (Cynn, 1992), whereas considerably more deficits are evident in older alcoholics and in those with more than 10 years of drinking (Tarter, 1973). Finally, Parsons and colleagues have also demonstrated that alcoholics have problem-solving deficits on ecologically valid measures of abstraction (e.g., on a Piagetian-type task [Nixon & Parsons, 1991]), and on an Adaptive Skills Battery (Patterson et al., 1988). Additional evidence for executive dysfunction is provided by Noël et al. (2007),

who noted reduced response inhibition on the Iowa Gambling Task, and Hildebrand et al. (2004) who noted abnormalities in response to shifting, but not working memory.

Visual–Spatial and Complex Perceptual–Motor Integration

Complex perceptual–motor deficits are common in alcoholics. One of the more common tests that assess this cognitive domain is the Tactual Performance Test from the HRB, which has previously revealed impairments in 84% of the 19 studies reviewed by Parsons and Leber (1981). Deficits in visuoperceptual and visuospatial processing also occur, both on tests with a motor component (e.g., Visual Search [Bertera & Parsons, 1978; Glosser et al., 1977]) and those without (e.g., on the Embedded Figures Test [Brandt et al., 1983; Donovan et al., 1976]). Other tests that have been used in discriminating visuospatial functions of alcoholics include the Gollin Incomplete Pictures Test, Wechsler Memory Scale (WMS) drawings, Rey–Osterrieth Complex Figure, and the Hidden Figures Test (Sullivan et al., 2000). Performance of alcoholics may be impaired on tests of psychomotor speed (Cairney et al., 2007).

Learning and Memory

Initial evaluations of learning and memory performance using the Memory Quotient (MQ) from the WMS revealed that alcoholics generally exhibit intact memory functioning and have comparable MQ relative to their IQ values (Butters et al., 1977; Løberg, 1980a; Parsons & Prigatano, 1977; Ryan & Butters, 1980a). However, although alcoholics without memory complaints were comparable to nonalcoholics on the MQ from the WMS, alcoholics were found to be impaired relative to controls when memory tests were made more difficult (Brandt et al., 1983; Ryan & Butters, 1980a). Later modifications to the original WMS (Russell, 1975), which resulted in separate learning, recall, and retention measures for verbal and visual information, revealed that some alcoholics do have mild deficits in learning and memory for both verbal and figural information (Hightower & Anderson, 1986; Nixon et al.,

1987). In the study by Nixon and colleagues, using Russell's modification to the WMS (Russell, 1975), alcoholics were found to recall less verbal and figural information at immediate and delay conditions, with both verbal and figural learning being affected to the same degree (Nixon et al., 1987). When these investigators calculated savings or retention scores for both groups (i.e., taking into account the amount of information that had been acquired when evaluating recall scores), alcoholics were not found to differ from controls. What this pattern of performance on the revised WMS suggests is that alcoholics have deficits with acquisition and encoding, and possibly with retrieval, but not with retention of information once adjustments are made for the amount of information acquired (Nixon et al., 1987). Deficits in working memory and implicit memory have also been reported (Cairney et al., 2007; Sullivan et al., 2000).

Studies using the WMS-R (Ryan & Lewis, 1988) confirm the WMS results. That is, alcoholics differed from controls in level of performance on all five summary measures from the WMS-R, but not with respect to their pattern of performance. Although the authors of this study did not make a distinction between learning ability and savings or retention of information, the differences between the alcoholics and controls on the memory summary scores (i.e., verbal, visual, and general memory) indicate that alcoholics have a generalized learning impairment, while the difference scores between general memory and delayed memory for each group were virtually identical, thus suggesting similar savings or retention of information across both groups. We would like to stress that it is important to make a distinction between learning and savings or "memory," because if an alcoholic has both a learning *and* a retention problem, a separate neuropathological process may be present (e.g., alcohol-induced persisting dementia or amnestic disorder).

Over the years, there has been controversy in the literature regarding whether alcoholics perform differentially on verbal and visual learning and memory tasks. For example, several studies have indicated that alcoholics are impaired on visual learning (Fabian et al., 1984; Leber et al., 1981), but perform normally on verbal learning tests (Leber et al., 1981; Yohman & Parsons,

1985). More recent studies, however, have shown that alcoholics have deficits also on verbal learning tests. For example, alcoholics were found to have acquisition deficits on the Luria Memory word test, but comparable rates of retention (Sherer et al., 1992). Using the California Verbal Learning Test (CVLT), Kramer and colleagues demonstrated that alcoholics have deficits on immediate and free recall, reduced performance on recognition testing, and produce more intrusions and false-positive errors than expected (Kramer et al., 1989). Consistent with studies using the WMS and WMS-R, alcoholics exhibited comparable retention on the CVLT to that of controls, when adjustments were made for the amount of material acquired. A similar pattern of immediate and free recall and recognition performance has also been obtained using the Rey Auditory Verbal Learning Test (Tuck & Jackson, 1991).

A number of investigators have questioned the external validity of the learning and memory findings obtained in the laboratory with alcoholics, and have subsequently developed more ecologically valid learning and memory tests. For example, Becker and his colleagues compared both young and old alcoholics on an ecologically relevant task (i.e., learning to associate names with faces; Becker et al., 1983). They found that alcoholics made more errors and were not able to achieve the same criterion level as a demographically matched group of controls (Becker et al., 1983). In contrast, their recognition performance for the faces and names, and their retention was similar to controls. Becker and his colleagues attributed the learning problem in alcoholics to a deficit in forming associations during encoding, rather than to a visuoperceptual deficit (Becker et al., 1983). Learning impairments on this face-name test have also been replicated with a VA sample of alcoholics (Schaeffer & Parsons, 1987), as well as with a community sample of male and female alcoholics (Everett et al., 1988).

Simple Motor Skills

Gait and balance disturbances have been reported in recently detoxified alcoholics (Sullivan et al., 2000, 2002). The evidence for simple motor deficits in alcoholics has been inconsistent. While one study showed that alcoholics have deficits on tests of fine-motor coordination, but not necessarily on a test of grip strength (Parsons et al., 1972), another study reported impairments in fine-motor coordination, grip strength, and motor speed (Tarter & Jones, 1971). Impairments in motor speed (finger tapping) have been reported in 29% of studies reviewed (i.e., four of 14 studies) (Parsons & Leber, 1981). Another study showed that alcoholics were 9.3% slower than age-matched controls on motor speed (York & Biederman, 1991). Because polyneuropathy occurs in 20%–74% of alcoholics (Feuerlein, 1977; Franceschi et al., 1984; Neundorfer et al., 1984; Tuck & Jackson, 1991), it is possible that the variability in motor test performance in alcoholics may be the result of a combination of peripheral and/or central nerve dysfunction or deterioration.

Given the robust nature of the neuropsychological deficits observed in alcoholics, we next turn to a summary of the neuroimaging, electrophysiological, and neuropathological correlates associated with alcoholism.

Neuroimaging Findings in Alcoholics

Pneumoencephalographic studies provided the first evidence of ventricular dilatation in alcoholics, reflecting cortical and cerebellar atrophy (Brewer & Perrett, 1971; Haug, 1968). This technique, in which air is exchanged for cerebrospinal fluid (CSF), enabled investigators to examine the contrast between cerebral tissue and CSF-containing spaces. However, because of the associated morbidity and pain to subjects, this technique never achieved widespread use.

The advent of computed tomography (CT) quickly replaced pneumoencephalography. A number of CT reviews have appeared in the 1980s (Bergman, 1987; Carlen & Wilkinson, 1983, 1987; Ron, 1987; Wilkinson, 1982, 1987). These reviews, from groups of investigators in various countries, provide extensive cross-validation of the neuroradiological abnormalities in heterogeneous groups of alcoholics. In general, increases of CSF in subarachnoid spaces and in the ventricular system (i.e., lateral and third ventricles) were interpreted to reflect cortical and subcortical atrophy, respectively. Increases in cortical CSF have generally been observed in

alcoholics of all ages, whereas increased CSF in the ventricular system has predominantly been seen in older and nutritionally compromised alcoholics. Cortical atrophy tends to be more evident bilaterally in frontal and frontal-temporal-parietal areas of the brain, although reduced density only in the left hemisphere of alcoholics has been reported (Golden et al., 1981). In a review of 14 CT studies by Cala and colleagues, the rate of cerebral atrophy ranged from 4% to 100% (Cala & Mastaglia, 1981). The extreme variability in the prevalence rate of atrophy reflects to a large degree the referral source of alcoholics tested; many of the earlier studies either did not screen for adverse neuromedical and neurological abnormalities, or had selected alcoholics patients for clinical suspicion of central nervous system damage (Bergman et al., 1980a; Carlen & Wilkinson, 1980; Ron, 1983).

In one of the largest studies of alcoholics using CT imaging, Bergman and colleagues (1980a) demonstrated that a group of 148 male alcoholic patients had significantly more evidence of cerebral atrophy, relative to a random sample of men ($n = 200$) not diagnosed with alcoholism. Cortical changes were evident across the entire age range in the alcoholics, whereas central changes accelerated with increasing age, particularly in those alcoholics with longer drinking histories (Bergman et al., 1980a).

Using a semiautomated method for estimating CSF volumes obtained from CT imaging (Zatz et al., 1982), Jernigan and her colleagues examined fluid volumes in various intracranial zones in 46 male chronic alcoholics (excluding those with liver disease) and compared them with 31 male normal volunteers (Jernigan et al., 1982). Correcting for cerebral changes that occur with normal aging (i.e., by using z-scores corrected for changes due to aging), these investigators found that alcoholics had significantly more CSF than the control group on all sulcal measures (i.e., sulcal score at low and high convexity sections, and at the level of the ventricles). Group differences, however, on the measure of ventricular CSF volume fell short of significance ($p < 0.06$). No significant correlations were observed between the number of years of alcohol drinking and any CSF measurement. In a subsequent investigation, Pfefferbaum and his colleagues examined the vulnerability of various brain structures to age, level of alcohol consumption, and nutritional status (Pfefferbaum et al., 1988). They utilized a similar semiautomated technique to measure the percentage of fluid at the ventricles and cortical sluci, and found that male alcoholics as a group had more CSF than controls for both ventricular and sulcal CT measures. Interestingly, the ventricular enlargement was evident only in older alcoholics, whereas increases in sulcal CSF were evident across the entire age range. Years of alcoholic drinking were correlated with both cortical and ventricular CT measures. In addition, the central ventricular measure, but not the cortical measure, was significantly associated with measure of body weight, body mass index, hematocrit, and mean corpuscular volume, suggesting that nutritional status may have been compromised in these alcoholics. These results support the theory that cerebral structures (cortical and subcortical) are differentially affected by alcohol. That is, alcohol appears to affect cortical structures, regardless of age, whereas subcortical structures may be more affected by nutritional status (i.e., acute thiamine deficiency) and/or age.

Most of the CT studies have been conducted with alcoholic men, but CT studies carried out in Sweden (Bergman, 1985, 1987), England (Jacobson, 1986a, 1986b), and Germany (Mann et al., 1992) have indicated that women also demonstrate similar abnormal brain morphology, although the abnormalities tend to be evident after a much shorter drinking history and with a lower daily intake of alcohol, than they are with alcoholic men. Given recent reports that drinking patterns of women are changing, and are becoming much more like that of men, this trend could have serious medical and neuropsychological consequences (Mercer & Khavari, 1990).

Increases in CSF in chronic alcoholics have consistently been demonstrated on CT scanning using linear measurements, clinical ratings, and volumetric analyses. While inferences have been made regarding the meaning of these CSF changes, studies using magnetic resonance imaging (MRI) have opened up the possibility of much more detailed in vivo brain structural investigation (See Figure 18–2; see also the color figure in the color insert section).

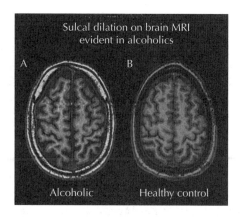

Figure 18–2. Brain MRI showing loss of brain volume in alcoholic (A) versus healthy control (B). Note reduced cortical thickness and increased sulcal volume. (From San Diego VA Alcohol Study, I. Grant, P.I.)

Jernigan and her colleagues examined 28 chronic alcoholics and 36 age- and sex-matched nonalcoholics with MRI and brain morphometric analyses (Jernigan et al., 1991a). The focus of their study was to (1) evaluate the relationship between CSF volume increases and gray matter losses, as well as the signal hyperintensities occurring in the white matter, and (2) correlate the cognitive losses observed in the alcoholics with various MR indices. The results from their study indicated that the increases in CSF (in cortical and ventricular areas) were associated with significant volume reductions in specific cerebral gray matter structures (both cortical and subcortical). Specifically, the chronic alcoholics demonstrated significant volume reductions in subcortical structures (e.g., caudate and diencephalon) as well as in cortical volumes (e.g., mesial temporal cortex, dorsolateral frontal cortex, and parieto-occipital cortex). In addition, the alcoholics had significantly more white matter signal hyperintensities than did the controls. With respect to the relationship between neuropsychological performance and MRI indices, there were substantially more significant correlations between cognitive measures and subcortical fluid volumes (i.e., 6 of 13) than with cortical fluid volumes (i.e., 3 of 13 were significant); gray and white matter volumes did not relate in any significant way to cognitive measures. Jernigan and her colleagues also noted that the reductions in cortical tissue in the superior frontal and parietal areas in alcoholics are consistent with neuropathological reports (see results from Harper's group listed below).

Research at the Palo Alto VA Medical Center and Stanford University (Pfefferbaum et al., 1992) has extended the findings reported by Jernigan and her group in San Diego. A similar semiautomated procedure with MRI was used, which allowed subcortical regions to be segmented into CSF and brain tissue, and cortical regions into CSF, gray matter and white matter. Forty-nine alcoholics were tested 3–4 weeks after their last drink and compared with 43 healthy controls. Adjusting for the effects of aging, the alcoholics had decreased parenchymal volume and increased CSF (alcoholics had 30% more CSF than controls); these included significant reductions in cortical and subcortical gray matter volume, as well as loss of white matter (Pfefferbaum et al., 1992). While some studies report generalized reduction in brain volume, others have noted some regional predilections, including selective frontal and temporal shrinkage (Cardenas et al., 2007; Pfefferbaum et al., 1997) and losses in the insula, thalamus, and cerebellum (Chanraud et al., 2007). The observed losses in white matter volume (Chick et al., 1989; Gallucci et al., 1989) have led to increased interest in exploring the integrity fiber tracts. The emergence of the MRI based technique of diffusion tensor imaging (DTI) has facilitated this line of research. This method quantifies the diffusion properties of white matter, the notion being that within intact white matter tracts, the movement of water in a magnetic field will not be random, but constrained consistent with the orientation of the bundles. Two common indices are computed: fractional anisotropy (FA), which reflects diffusion orientation and coherence, and mean diffusivity (MD) or bulk mean diffusion (Pfefferbaum & Sullivan, 2005). Generally speaking one expects FA to be high, and MD to be low in intact white matter tracts, and this is most readily measured in brain regions where these are regularly oriented, for example, corpus callosum. Studies comparing recently detoxified alcoholics to controls do indeed report lower FA and higher MD in the patient groups, suggesting disruption of white matter

microstructure (Pfefferbaum et al., 2000, 2007; Pfefferbaum & Sullivan, 2005).

Relation of Neuroimaging and Neuropsychological Variables

Attempts to find associations between neuropsychological test performance and CT brain imaging correlates have yielded mixed results (Jernigan et al., 1991a; Pfefferbaum et al., 1988; Rourke, et al., 1993). That is, while Pearson correlations between CT measures and neuropsychological performance with alcoholics were highly significant in most cases (i.e., 33 of 45 were significant), only two of 45 remained significant once age was partialled out (Bergman et al., 1980b). Bergman and colleagues also did not find any significant correlations between alcohol consumption or neuropsychological test performance with CT brain measures in a large random sample of men ($n = 200$) and women ($n = 200$) not diagnosed with alcoholism (Bergman et al., 1983).

Nevertheless, there are reports in the literature of associations between specific neuropsychological tests and CSF volumes, or structures adjacent to these fluid-filled areas. For example, in one study, CT scan measures of the third ventricle, but not the lateral ventricles, were associated with memory performance in male alcoholics (Acker et al., 1987); in another study, mean CT thalamic density was shown to be correlated with verbal and symbol digit paired-associated learning test performance (Gebhardt et al., 1984). Bergman and colleagues reported that learning and memory performance was related to central changes in 106 alcoholics, whereas performance on the Halstead Impairment Index was related to cortical changes (Bergman et al., 1980c).

MRI indices of structural brain changes have yielded more consistent correlates with neuropsychological function. Decline in block design has been related to general brain volume reduction in alcoholics (Schottenbauer et al., 2007), while regional changes in gray and white mater volumes predicted worse performance on tests of executive function (Chanraud et al., 2007). Callosal abnormalities detected with DTI have been linked to measures of working memory and visuospatial ability (Pfefferbaum et al., 2006).

Functional Neuroimaging: Cerebral Blood Flow and Metabolism in Alcoholics

Cerebral blood flow (CBF) is normally proportional to metabolic brain activity (except under severe pathological conditions such as significant cerebrovascular disease), and is therefore a sensitive measure of neuronal function. Blood flow imaging techniques—for example, xenon injection and inhalation, positron emission tomography (PET), and single photon emitted computed tomography (SPECT)—have the advantage over CT and magnetic resonance brain imaging, in that they provide a window through which the brain can be examined in a more functional and dynamic state. Studies of CBF in "normal" healthy volunteers have demonstrated an inverse relationship with age and cerebrovascular status (Gur et al., 1987; Shaw et al., 1984). A gender effect has also been observed, with men showing reduced CBF as compared with women (Mathew et al., 1986), although this effect disappears after the sixth decade of life (Shaw et al., 1984).

Most studies of chronic alcoholics without the Wernicke–Korsakoff syndrome have shown reductions and/or abnormalities, particularly in frontal and parietal areas, using both cerebral blood flow (Berglund et al., 1987; Caspari et al., 1993; Dally et al., 1988; Erbas et al., 1992; Hata et al., 1987; Ishikawa et al., 1986; Mathew & Wilson, 1991; Melgaard et al., 1990; Nicolas et al., 1993; Rogers et al., 1983) and brain metabolism techniques (Adams et al., 1993; Dupont, et al., 1996; Gilman et al., 1990; Sachs et al., 1987; Samson et al., 1986; Volkow et al., 1992, 1994; Wang et al., 1993; Wik et al., 1988), which tend to improve after several weeks of abstinence (Berglund et al., 1987; Caspari et al., 1993; Hata et al., 1987; Ishikawa et al., 1986; Volkow et al., 1994).

Functional Magnetic Resonance (fMRI), with its capacity to detect brief changes in blood flow in circumscribed brain regions in response to cognitive and sensory-motor tasks has opened new avenues in exploring the relationship between specific neural circuitry disturbance and neurocognitive dysfunction. Such studies have revealed, for instance that although alcoholics sometimes perform comparably to controls of some neuropsychological measures, their pattern of brain activation to cognitive tasks differs. For example, Pferrerbaum and Sullivan (summarized in Crews et al., 2005) note that on a visuospatial working memory n-back task controls show activation in the dorsolateral prefrontal cortex; alcoholics activated the ventromedial prefrontal cortex (Pfefferbaum et al., 1998), whereas other research finds that alcoholics activate broader frontal and cerebellar regions to a verbal working memory task (Desmond et al., 2003). Other data indicate that alcoholics recruit more brain regions to accomplish cognitive operations than controls, suggesting the possibility that neural injury from alcohol requires some neural reorganization and recruitment of circuitries that are not typically involved.

Electrophysiological Findings in Alcoholics

Neurophysiological aberrations (EEG and event-related potentials—ERPs) have frequently been observed in alcoholics (Porjesz & Begleiter, 2003). In general, differences on electrophysiological measures in alcoholics seem to depend on the recency and intensity of alcohol use, family history loading for alcoholism, which particular component of the electrophysiological response is examined, and what tasks or stimuli are used to elicit the electrophysiological response.

Data from quantitative EEG analysis (QEEG) have reported alterations in both alpha (Finn & Justus, 1999) and beta (Bauer, 1994; Costa & Bauer, 1997; Rangaswami et al., 2002, 2004; Winterer et al., 1998) frequencies. Increased beta activity has been linked to family history of alcoholism, and has been observed in some first-degree relatives of alcoholics (Ehlers & Schuckit, 1990; Rangaswami et al., 2004). Results concerning slower wave frequencies (theta, delta) have been mixed. For example, Rangaswami et al. (2003) reported increased theta activity, whereas Saletu-Zyhlarz et al. (2004) and Coutin-Churchman et al. (2003, 2006) found reduced power in theta and delta bands. The latter authors also noted that decreased power in the slow bands was correlated with a degree of brain atrophy on MRI.

Alcoholics have been shown to have increased latencies and longer transmission times on auditory brain stem potentials, suggesting possible demyelination (Begleiter et al., 1981; Porjesz & Begleiter, 2003). In one study, 41% of alcoholics had abnormal auditory brain stem responses, which were associated with the age of the subject, CT evidence of cerebral atrophy, and severity of neurological complications (Chu, 1985; Chu et al., 1982). Cadaveira et al. (1994) observed increased latencies for peak V and prolonged III–V and I–V intervals.

Alcoholics have also been shown to have reduced amplitudes of N100, N200, P300, and increased latency of P300 (Emmerson et al., 1987; Kaseda et al., 1994; Miyazato & Ogura, 1993). In a review by Oscar-Berman, reduced P300 amplitude (i.e., a late positive waveform elicited during the discrimination of a stimulus) was found to be the most consistent finding (more reliable than the P300 latency) in abstinent alcoholics (Oscar-Berman, 1987). Reduced P300 has been related to imaging measures of brain shrinkage (Begleiter et al., 1980; Kaseda et al., 1994; Ogura & Miyazato, 1991). There may also be gender effects on ERPs. For example, male alcoholics tend to show reduced N100 and N300 amplitudes whereas females often do not (Parsons et al., 1990b).

There have been several attempts to correlate ERP and neuropsychological test findings. When significant correlations are found, they tend to occur between P300 amplitude and/or P300 latency and tests of perceptual–motor functioning (Parsons et al., 1990b; Patterson et al., 1989), and on tests of delayed figural memory (Patterson et al., 1989). The relationship between ERP and memory may not be as reliable; another group of investigators did not find significant correlations between ERP measures and MQ score from the WMS (Romani & Cosi, 1989).

Abnormal ERP findings, particularly reduced average P300 amplitudes, are more pronounced in alcoholics who are family history positive (FH+)—that is, have alcoholic first-degree relatives—relative to family history negative (FH–) alcoholics (Parsons et al., 1990b; Patterson et al., 1987; Pfefferbaum et al., 1991; Whipple et al., 1988). Because the reduced P300 in the FH+ alcoholics has been shown to be independent of lifetime alcohol consumption, several investigators have suggested that it

may be a biological marker of risk for alcoholism (Begleiter et al., 1984; Pfefferbaum et al., 1991). As such, there is growing evidence that the P300 is genetically determined, and it may also be involved with the dopaminergic system, particularly the D_2 dopamine receptor gene (Noble et al., 1994).

Neuropathology in Alcoholism

A number of autopsy studies have addressed the neuropathological correlates of alcoholism (Courville, 1955; Harper, 1998; Harper et al., 2003; Harper & Kril, 1990; Harper & Matsumoto, 2005; Torvik, 1987; Torvik et al., 1982). These studies indicate that alcoholics have reduced brain weights (Harper & Blumbergs, 1982; Torvik, 1987), as well as increased pericerebral spaces that reflect changes in the proportion of brain volume to intracranial volume (Harper & Kril, 1985; Harper et al., 1990).

Since the mid-1980s, Harper and his colleagues have carried out a number of morphometric and histological examinations of the brains of alcoholics (Harper, 2007). The first study in this series demonstrated that chronic alcoholics have significant reductions in white matter tissue in the cerebral hemispheres, as well as increased ventricular volume, but no significant differences in the mean volume of cortical gray matter, or in the volume of the basal ganglia (Harper et al., 1985). These morphometric differences were also most pronounced in those alcoholics with a history of cirrhosis or Wernicke's encephalopathy (Harper et al., 1988). More specifically, brains of patients with chronic Wernicke–Korsaff syndromes showed substantial neuronal loss in thalamus, mamillary bodies, basal forebrain, dorsal and medial raphe, and cerebellar vermis (Harper, 1998; Harper et al., 2003; Harper & Matsumoto, 2005). Three subsequent studies were carried out and focused on specific white and gray matter volumes. These reported a reduction in the size of the corpus callosum (Harper & Kril, 1988) and a selective loss in the number of neurons in the superior frontal cortex, but not in the motor cortex (Harper et al., 1987; Kril & Harper, 1989), or in the frontal cingulate and temporal cortices (Kril & Harper, 1989); the reductions in the superior frontal cortex occurred mainly in the terminal branches of the arbor (Harper & Corbett, 1990) and in neurons greater than 90 μ² (Harper & Kril, 1989). In addition to the selective loss of superior frontal neurons, a significant reduction in the mean neuronal surface area was also noted in the superior frontal as well as the motor and cingulate cortical areas (Kril & Harper, 1989). The latter data indicate that shrinkage of the neuronal cell body is quite widespread in a number of cortical areas, as compared to actual neuronal loss, and may provide the basis for the clinical improvements on neurobehavioral testing and on neuroimaging in alcoholics, for example, through rearborization once abstinence is achieved (Harper & Kril, 1990). This possibility seems tenable, especially given the results from animal studies showing dendritic alterations with chronic ethanol treatment (Durand et al., 1989; McMullen et al., 1984), as well as recovery in dendritic morphology with abstinence (McMullen et al., 1984) in the hippocampus (King et al., 1988), particularly in the terminal segments of this structure (Pentney, 1991; Pentney et al., 1989).

With respect to changes at the neuroreceptor level, a 40% reduction in the density of cholinergic muscarinic receptors was found in the frontal cortex of alcoholics, following a histological examination that compared the brains of 30 alcoholics to 49 age-matched controls who were nondemented (Freund & Ballinger, 1988). In a follow-up study, these investigators demonstrated similar reductions in the putamen (i.e., 40% of cholinergic muscarinic receptors), but not in receptor densities of benzodiazepine receptors (Freund & Ballinger, 1989). These investigators suggest that neuronal loss and/or the loss of respective receptors in the brains of alcoholics is not random, and that alcohol may affect certain receptors in specific brain areas (Freund & Ballinger, 1989). In another study, muscarinic receptors were found to be reduced by 40% in temporal cortex, as well as in frontal and putamen areas, while benzodiazepine receptors decreased by 30% in the hippocampus, 30% in the frontal cortex, but not in the putamen or the temporal cortex (Freund & Ballinger, 1991).

In addition to cerebral gray matter changes with alcoholism, a number of investigators have

shown that alcohol may also cause a disproportionate atrophy of white matter (de la Monte, 1988; Harper, 1998, 2007; Harper et al., 2003; Jensen & Pakkenberg, 1993). In one study, alcoholics had similar brain weights and subcortical nuclei size, when compared with a demographically matched control group, but had evidence of mild atrophy of the cerebral cortex, enlargement of the ventricular system, and moderate atrophy of white matter that corresponded well to amount of ventricular enlargement (de la Monte, 1988). Support for the differential effects on cerebral white matter with heavy exposure to alcohol is also supported by animal studies (Hansen et al., 1991). The mechanism for white matter vulnerability is not understood, but may involve downregulation of myelin regulating genes (Lewohl et al., 2001).

Efforts to Link Pattern of Neuropsychological Impairment in Alcoholics to Brain Regions

Right Hemisphere Dysfunction Model

In 1972, Jones and Parsons suggested that the right hemisphere might be more vulnerable to long-term alcohol exposure than the left hemisphere (Jones & Parsons, 1972). This led to the right hemisphere dysfunction (RHD) model of alcoholism. In support of the RHD model, prominent difficulties have been observed with visuospatial integration, disproportionately worse Performance IQ than Verbal IQ, and impaired motor regulation of the left hand (Parsons et al., 1972). Subsequent studies by Parsons and colleagues, as well as by other investigators, have provided further support for the RHD model, as indicated by the pattern of performance on the Tactual Performance Test—reduced performance with the left hand by right-handed individuals (Fabian et al., 1981; Jenkins & Parsons, 1981), reduced performance on a visual search test (Chandler & Parsons, 1977), and worse performance on the Rey–Osterrieth Complex Figure Test relative to a verbal learning test performance (Miglioni et al., 1979). Several neuropsychological follow-up studies (Berglund et al., 1987; Page & Schaub, 1977; Schau et al., 1980) also provide support for the RHD model. Using experimental techniques to study brain lateralization, Kostandov et al. (1982) found that using a paradigm to study differences in left and right visual field perception and lateral evoked potentials, both nonalcoholics given alcohol and abstinent alcoholics evidenced a slower processing rate in the right than in the left hemisphere (Kostandov et al., 1982). Consistent with this finding, male alcoholics have also been shown to exhibit a pattern of RHD on a dichotic listening task (Drake et al., 1990).

Despite the research supporting the RHD model, there are, however, a number of problems with this model. For example, tasks generally thought to be "right hemispheric" are not entirely specific to that brain region. Further, many of the "right hemisphere" tasks are inherently harder, or more novel than "left hemisphere" tasks. Thus, what we might be measuring is selective difficulty, which alcoholics experience on more demanding tests. In addition, recovery for such "right hemisphere" functions might also take more time. Sex differences may play a role; in a review of 14 studies in general neuropsychology, men with left and right-sided lesions showed the expected Verbal IQ-Performance IQ differences, whereas women did not show such a pattern (Inglis & Lawson, 1981). Similarly, male alcoholics were found to exhibit the RHD pattern on dichotic listening, but not alcoholic women (Drake et al., 1990). Also, women show less impairment on visuospatial and tactile-spatial tests, which may suggest that less lateralization in brain organization occurs in women; if this were the case, one may also expect less dramatic lateralization differences (Silberstein & Parsons, 1979). Depressive symptomatology, which frequently occurs in alcoholics undergoing detoxification, has been shown to relate significantly to impaired Performance IQ in alcoholics (Løberg, 1980b). Because many "right hemisphere" tests are timed, depression-related lack of motivation and psychomotor retardation might contribute to poor performance, although there is no strong evidence to support this mechanism.

Several additional studies are inconsistent with the RHD model. Prigatano (1980) reported that men tested before disulfiram treatment had higher Performance than Verbal IQ values (Prigatano, 1980). Also, although alcoholics had lower Performance relative to Verbal IQ values, there were no differences in left- or right-hand performance on the Tactual Performance Test, the Finger Tapping Test, or on Finger Agnosia or Finger-Tip Writing tests (Barron & Russell, 1992). Furthermore, in one study, motor speed was found to be slower in the dominant as compared to the nondominant hand, and significantly more static tremor was found in the right than the left hand (Løberg, 1980a). Grant and his colleagues found practically the same level on Performance and Verbal IQ's at initial testing for both recently detoxified and long-term abstinent male alcoholics (Grant et al., 1979a), and a quantitatively higher Performance IQ than Verbal IQ for both groups 1 year later (Adams et al., 1980). The latter, may, of course, be due to the effect of practice on timed performance tests. O'Leary and colleagues found Performance IQ and Verbal IQ to be equal in field-independent alcoholics (O'Leary et al., 1977a). Fitzhugh and colleagues found quantitatively higher Performance than Verbal IQ in both of their studies of alcoholic male subjects (Fitzhugh et al., 1960, 1965). While alcoholics frequently perform poorly on the WAIS Block Design subtest, they do not resemble right hemisphere damaged neurological patients in their pattern of performance (Akshoomoff et al., 1989). Using a dichotic listening paradigm, Ellis (1990) found that both hemispheres were affected by alcoholism and aging. Finally, an extensive review of the RHD model by Ellis and Oscar-Berman (1989) found similar patterns of functional laterality with alcoholism.

Frontal Lobe Dysfunction Model

Another hypothesis that has been proposed to explain the neuropsychological deficits observed in alcoholics is the frontal lobe dysfunction model (Parsons & Leber, 1981) and the frontolimbic-diencephalic dysfunction model (Tarter, 1973, 1975). Tarter suggests that the commonly observed deficits of alcoholics in categorizing or abstraction (in the absence of other severe impairment) is very consistent with selective frontal lobe dysfunction. The finding of Berglund and others that frontal regional blood flow was most clearly related to Block Design performance may also imply that of the different brain systems relevant for such a task, the frontal lobes play a significant part at least in the early abstinence phase in alcoholics. Neuropathological data indicate selective loss of frontal cortical neurons (Harper, 2007; Harper & Matsumoto, 2005), particularly in the superior frontal association cortex (Harper, 1998; Harper et al., 2003), whereas MR spectroscopic studies reveal metabolite changes especially in frontal regions (Bartsch et al., 2007; Schweinsburg et al., 2001). These authors speculated that because frontal structures are particularly heavily innervated by glutamatergic neurons, repeated bouts of withdrawal might induce excitotoxic damage especially in this region. It has also been suggested that due to the relatively late maturation of the frontal lobes, they may be particularly vulnerable to heavy drinking in adolescence and young adulthood. In animal models, adolescent rats fed ethanol showed injury particularly in their frontal association areas, which, according to the authors, correspond to orbital frontal cortex of the human brain (Crews et al., 2000). Some of the neurocognitive deficits noted in alcohol abusing adolescents—for example, difficulties in problem solving and working memory—may reflect frontal lobe involvement (Moss et al., 1994; Tapert & Brown, 1999).

Diffuse or Generalized Dysfunction Model

Two studies carried out by Goldstein and Shelly provide support for the diffuse or generalized dysfunction model associated with alcoholism. Using the neuropsychological key approach, alcoholics have been shown to have a diffuse pattern of deficits (Goldstein & Shelly, 1980). In a subsequent evaluation by Goldstein, right-handed alcoholics were compared with right-handed brain-damaged patients who had well-documented left hemisphere damage, right hemisphere damage, frontal or frontal-temporal lesions, parietal, occipital, or parieto-occipital lesions, and diffuse brain damage not associated with alcoholism (Goldstein & Shelly, 1982). Alcoholics with an average impairment rating greater than 1.55 were included and compared to the brain-damaged patients; all recently detoxified alcoholics performed in the brain-damage

range on the AIR. Two discriminant function analyses were carried out, one including both sensory-motor and cognitive tests, and the other including only the cognitive tests. Alcoholics were often classified as similar to patients with diffuse brain damage of nonalcoholic etiology, when compared with brain-damaged subjects with anterior, posterior, and diffuse pathology. When alcoholics were compared with left, right, and diffuse brain-damaged patients, using both cognitive and sensory-motor measures, alcoholics were more similar to the diffuse brain-damaged group. Eliminating the sensory-motor measures led to a slight indication of right hemisphere dysfunction, but this was not dramatic (Goldstein & Shelly, 1982).

At this point in our understanding, data from NP, imaging, and neuropathological studies converge on the notion that while any area of the brain can be affected by alcoholism, among uncomplicated (non-Wernicke–Korsakoff) alcoholics, gray and white matter injury appears to be more prominent in the frontal lobes, with the possibility that injury to the reciprocal connections between the brain stem and cerebellum might contribute to some of the cognitive motor presentation (Sullivan et al., 2003).

Wernicke–Korsakoff Syndrome/ Alcohol-Induced Persisting Amnestic Disorder

Neurobehavioral Findings

The WKS, also referred to as Alcohol-Induced Persisting Amnestic Disorder in DSM-IV, has been well researched over the past several decades and is described in more detail in several recent reviews (Butters & Granholm, 1987; Butters & Salmon, 1986; Jacobson et al., 1990; Martin et al., 1986, 1989; Salmon & Butters, 1987; Salmon et al., 1993).

The Wernicke part of the syndrome involves the presentation of a clinical triad of symptoms, which include global confusion or delirium, abnormal eye movements (e.g., ophthalmoplegia, nystagmus), and gait ataxia. Confabulation, if present, occurs predominantly in the early stages of the WKS. It is now well established that this clinical triad arises because of a severe thiamine deficiency, and if not properly treated, death may ensue after several weeks. However, with aggressive treatment, involving large doses of thiamine supplementation, the delirium clears, and the ophthalmoplegia and ataxia improve dramatically, although other features such as peripheral neuropathy and amnesia usually persist. These residual symptoms have come to be referred to as the alcoholic Korsakoff syndrome. The residual memory deficits consist of a severe anterograde amnesia (with increased sensitivity to interference) and a temporally graded retrograde amnesia, which are over and above the cognitive deficits (e.g., visuoperceptual, perceptual–motor, abstracting, and problem-solving impairments) that frequently are present secondary to a long history of severe alcohol use (Butters & Salmon, 1986).

It is important to note that while the alcoholic Korsakoff syndrome is the expected sequel to Wernicke's encephalopathy, a recent study indicated that of 44 patients diagnosed with Alcohol Amnestic Disorder (DSM-III-R), 33 of the cases had no obvious neurological symptoms of Wernicke's disease (Blansjaar & van Dijk, 1992). In another study, of 70 cases of Wernicke's encephalopathy that were identified at autopsy (i.e., in 0.8% of all 8735 autopsies and 12.5% of all examined alcoholics), 22 were characterized as active, whereas 48 were inactive (chronic); in addition, one - third of the cases with inactive encephalopathy resembled a pure Korsakoff psychosis, while the remaining cases exhibited a pattern of a global dementia ("alcoholic dementia") (Torvik et al., 1982). These two studies illustrate that WKS may be more heterogeneous than previously thought (see Bowden [1990] for an excellent review of this area of controversy).

One of the hallmark features of WKS is the dramatic difference between the patients' IQ (Wechsler, 1955, 1981), which is often relatively comparable to that of non-WKS alcoholics and controls, and their severely impaired MQ from the WMS (Wechsler & Stone, 1945). It is not uncommon for this difference to be 20–30 points (e.g., IQ = 100, MQ = 70–80) (Butters & Cermak, 1980). In addition, however, because WKS subjects have normal attention and concentration, the revised WMS, which has indices that do not confound attention/concentration with memory, may actually better reflect the severity of their memory performance; this is indicated by

a study by Butters and colleagues that demonstrated that WKS subjects have WMS-R General and Memory indices of 65 and 57, respectively (Butters et al., 1988). Patients with KS also show evidence of frontal lobe dysfunction. That is, patients with frontal lobe lesions, but who are not amnesic, perform similarly to patients with WKS on the WCST, as well as on the initiation and perseveration subtests from the Dementia Rating Scale (Janowsky et al., 1989). This frontal lobe dysfunction may also contribute to impairments in other neuropsychological areas. Finally, the impairments in planning and executive functioning appear to be independent of other impairments in memory and visuoperceptive ability (Joyce & Robbins, 1991).

Neuroimaging and Neuropathology Findings

The neuropathology of WKS is also well established. Specifically, thiamine deficiency is thought to cause hemorrhagic lesions in the brain stem, cell loss in the periaqueductal and periventricular gray matter, and midline diencephalic nuclei, particularly the dorsomedial nucleus of the thalamus and the mammillary bodies (Harper, 2007). In addition, cell loss in the area of the nucleus basalis, which includes the medial septal nucleus, the nucleus of the diagonal band of Broca, and the nucleus basalis Maynert neurons in the substantia inominata, may also occur (Arendt et al., 1983). Recent research has provided data to suggest that there may a genetic predisposition (i.e., an abnormality in the enzyme transketolase) to the development of WKS (Blass & Gibson, 1977), particularly since not all malnourished alcoholics develop WKS.

The majority of WKS cases have occurred in persons with lengthy and heavy alcohol consumption histories, although a number of case studies have emphasized that Korsakoff's syndrome (KS) can develop without any history of alcohol abuse or dependence. For example, Cole and colleagues (1992) presented evidence that KS can develop following a left (dominant) thalamic infarction. Vighetto and colleagues (1991) reported on a 37-year-old man with multiple sclerosis with disseminated white matter lesions especially in both medial temporal lobes, who initially presented with an acute amnestic syndrome consistent with KS. Parkin et al. (1991) reported that the retrograde and anterograde memory deficits of a woman with anorexia nervosa (after intravenous feeding and intestinal surgery) was similar to the memory disorder found in WKS (Parkin et al., 1991, 1993). Other investigators have also found similar findings with other anorexia nervosa patients (Beatty et al., 1989; Becker et al., 1990). The WKS cases that develop secondary to anorexia nervosa (i.e., with severe thiamine deficiency), as well as with thalamic infarcts, and not in the context of serious alcohol consumption, underscore the importance of thalamic structures in the neuropathology of the disorder.

A Comparison of Nonamnesic and Amnesic (Wernicke-Korsakoff) Alcoholics

A few studies have addressed the neuroimaging and neuropathology similarities and differences between nonamnesic (i.e., non-Korsakoff) alcoholics and amnesics (i.e., alcoholics with Korsakoff syndrome). In 1988, Shimamura and colleagues used a quantitative method to compare tissue densities on CT imaging in six areas (thalamus, head of the caudate, putamen, anterior white matter, posterior white matter, and centrum semiovale) and fluid volumes in seven areas (total ventricular space, third ventricle, interventricular region, frontal sulci, peri-sylvian region, medial cerebellum, and vertex) in a small group of patients with Korsakoff syndrome, age-matched alcoholic subjects, and age-matched healthy control subjects (Shimamura et al., 1988). Results from their study revealed that the Korsakoff patients had greater bilateral decreases in the region of the thalamus, as well as increased fluid volumes in the area of the third ventricle, as compared with the non-Korsakoff alcoholics. The lower densities observed in the thalamus of the Korsakoff patients, along with greater fluid volume in the frontal sulci, were correlated with performance on memory tests. Alcoholic and Korsakoff subjects, however, demonstrated similar enlargement of frontal and peri-sylvian sulci (Shimamura et al., 1988). Similar findings have been reported by another group of investigators

who found that many Korsakoff patients show evidence of cerebral damage, particularly frontal shrinkage, in addition to diencephalic lesions; both non-Korsakoff and Korsakoff alcoholics exhibit similar cortical atrophy, as indicated by similar sulcal and sylvian fissure widths (Jacobson & Lishman, 1990).

Jernigan and colleagues have recently replicated their CT findings with Korsakoff and non-Korsakoff alcoholics using MRI (Jernigan et al., 1991b). That is, although both alcoholic groups showed significant increases in CSF in both subarachnoid spaces and the ventricular system as compared to controls, the Korsakoff subjects also showed increased fluid volume in the ventricles relative to the nonamnesic alcoholics. With respect to gray matter volumes, post hoc analyses revealed that both alcoholic groups showed losses of gray matter in diencephalic structures, as well as in the parietal and superior frontal cortices; however, the Korsakoff alcoholics also experienced additional tissue loss in the anterior diencephalon (which included septal nuclei and anterior hypothalamic gray matter) and in the mesial temporal and orbitofrontal cortical areas. These results have been supported by a neuropathological examination of Korsakoff patients; 38 of 43 cases experienced atrophy in the dorsomedial nucleus of the thalamus and all evidenced mamillary body atrophy (Victor et al., 1989).

Although the results from Shimamura et al. (1988) and Jernigan et al. (1991b) provide evidence to support the notion of two distinct and separable neuropathological processes associated with alcoholism, there continues to be a debate whether this distinction can be made clinically (Bowden, 1990). In addition, the neuropathological results presented above, and a recent MRI study showing similar cortical and subcortical lesions in alcoholic Korsakoff patients and chronic alcoholics without cognitive deficits (Blansjaar et al., 1992), further emphasize the heterogeneity of WKS.

The Multifactorial Etiology of Neuropsychological Deficits in Nonamnesic Alcoholics

Several investigators have discussed the possible multifactorial etiology for the neuropsychological deficits observed in alcoholics (Adams & Grant, 1986; Grant, 1987; Tarter & Alterman, 1984; Tarter & Edwards, 1986). Grant (1987) presented a model (Figure 18–3) suggesting a number of variables that could directly or indirectly contribute to the neuropsychological deficits in recently detoxified alcoholics, and we use this model to guide our review of these associated factors.

Drinking Indices and Neuropsychological Performance

There are two main approaches to the issue of predicting neuropsychological performance from drinking history. One approach has been to compare neuropsychological performance of groups with different levels of alcohol consumption (e.g., social drinkers, problem drinkers, and alcoholics). Such studies can be said to be exploring the "continuity" notion: that there is putative progressive neuropsychological decline with amount of drinking, detectable even at the social drinking level. On the other hand, some investigators have utilized the correlational approach of analyzing the relationship between drinking dimensions (e.g., years of excessive drinking, amount consumed at drinking occasion) and neuropsychological measures specifically in abusive drinkers.

In support of the continuity notion of impairment originally proposed by Ryback (1971), Parker and Noble (1977) investigated cognitive functioning in social drinkers. They found that good performance on tests of abstraction and adaptive abilities were negatively associated with the amount of alcohol per drinking occasion in male social drinkers. These results were subsequently confirmed in their laboratory with male college students and social drinkers (Parker et al., 1980, 1983), and replicated by another group of investigators (Mac Vane et al., 1982). Parsons and Fabian (1982), as well as Parker's group (Parker, 1982), have provided valuable comments on the previous studies of social drinkers (Jones & Jones, 1980; Parker et al., 1980; Parker & Noble, 1977, 1980).

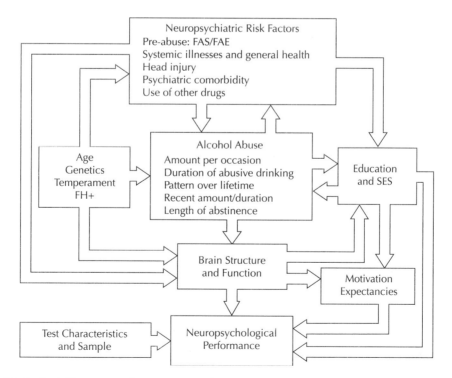

Figure 18–3. Variables to consider in any causal model of alcohol-associated neuropsychological deficit. (Modified from Grant [1987], p. 320).

The findings of Parker and colleagues could be summarized as follows: the abstracting score from the Shipley Institute of Living Scale was found to be negatively associated with the amount of alcohol per drinking occasion in male social drinkers and college students, whereas lifetime consumption and current frequency of drinking was not (Parker et al., 1980, 1983; Parker & Noble, 1977, 1980). A later study by the same group of investigators showed that psychological distress could not account for the differences (Parker et al., 1991). Another group of investigators reported similar findings with social drinking; increased alcohol consumption per occasion and total lifetime consumption was associated with worse neuropsychological performance in college students (Hannon et al., 1983, 1985, 1987), although replication of Parker's studies have not always been consistent (Parsons & Fabian, 1982).

In contrast, a number of reports and reviews have been unable to document social drinking effects on neuropsychological test performance. In a review of the literature on the effects of "social drinking" on neuropsychological test performance, Hill argued that there is no compelling evidence that moderate intake of alcohol results in permanent alteration in the structural integrity of the brain (Hill & Ryan, 1985). In another review by Bowden, he reiterated the same opinion and proposed that previous associations between social drinking and neuropsychological test performance did not properly account for innate ability, demographics, and variations in drinking behavior (Bowden, 1987); similar conclusions have also been reached in Grant's (1987) review. In a prospective study of the development of alcohol and other drug use behaviors in adolescents and young adults (Rutgers Health and Human Development Project), there was little direct relation between cognitive performance and "social" drinking in a young sample (Bates & Tracy, 1990). Although most of the research with social drinking has been carried out with men, there does not appear to any relationship between social drinking and neurocognitive performance in women (Carey & Maisto, 1987), even with mild to moderate social drinking (Waugh et al., 1989). Finally, according to an extensive review of the literature by Parsons

(1986b), there does not appear to be any consistent evidence to suggest that social drinking causes neuropsychological impairment.

Correlational studies relating length of excessive drinking to neuropsychological impairment in alcoholics have also generally been disappointing (i.e., correlations are usually in the 0.20–0.30 range). One possibility for the attenuated correlations may be inaccuracy of self-report of drinking (Fuller et al., 1988). Nevertheless, when relationships are found, they are most often in the expected direction: the greater the intake or length of drinking, the worse the neuropsychological test performance (Parsons, 1989). The maximum quantity frequency (MQF) of alcohol consumption over the past 6 months has often been demonstrated to be the best predictor of neuropsychological impairment (Schaeffer & Parsons, 1986), although some studies have shown that longer alcohol consumption leads to more neuropsychological deficits (Jones & Parsons, 1971; Tarter, 1973). Some investigators (e.g., Eckardt and colleagues, 1978), have argued for the use of nonlinear regression models (i.e., curvilinear) to explain the relationship between cognitive measures in alcoholics and various consumption scores. However, Adams and his colleagues have been unable to replicate Eckardt's results using analogous quadratic equations, and they have suggested that linear models may be more parsimonious (Adams & Grant, 1984).

Finally, Parsons and Stevens (1986) reported that in 57% of the studies they reviewed (i.e., 16 of 28), one or more significant correlations were observed between duration of alcohol abuse and neuropsychological test performance; however, in 12 of the 28 studies (or 43%), there was no relationship. Furthermore, Parsons and Stevens did not find that demographics (i.e., age, education, and sex) or length of abstinence (i.e., difference of less than 10 days or greater than 10 days of abstinence) influenced these results. In contrast to their review of the human studies, their review of animal literature did provide convincing evidence that performance deficits and neuroanatomical changes occur in detoxified animals that are fed alcohol whose nutrition is comparable to control animals. Parsons and Stevens further reported that the animal studies suggest a duration threshold effect for impairment. That is, impairments are not detected until a certain point, but after a consumption threshold has been reached, there is a negative inverse relation between amount of alcohol and performance. They also suggest that impairments may increase with age but reach an asymptote, after which no further increase in consumption is associated with a further decrease in performance (Parsons & Stevens, 1986).

The Influence of Age on Neuropsychological Test Performance

There continues to be controversy about when neuropsychological deficits can first be detected, and which variables seem to mediate this emergence. Some investigators have suggested that neuropsychological impairments are not detectable in alcoholics until they reach their mid- to late forties (Adams et al., 1980; Eckardt et al., 1995; Grant et al., 1979a; Jones & Parsons, 1971; Klisz & Parsons, 1977), whereas other investigators have reported neuropsychological deficits regardless of age (Brandt et al., 1983; Eckardt et al., 1980b; Ryan & Butters, 1980b). Furthermore, age of onset of heavy alcohol use may also influence neuropsychological test performance, with those beginning at an early age showing more deficits (Portnoff, 1982).

There continues to be a debate as to the degree to which age may interact with alcohol abuse to make elders more vulnerable to neurocognitive insult. There are two variants of the premature-aging model: the accelerated aging hypothesis and the increased vulnerability hypothesis. In the accelerated aging version, both young and old alcoholics perform at inferior levels on neuropsychological tests relative to their age-matched controls (Noonberg et al., 1985). With respect to the increased vulnerability hypothesis, alcoholics and controls perform similarly then later diverge, with the alcoholics showing increasing deficits with age relative to the controls. Much of the support for the premature aging hypothesis has come from studies showing similarities between young alcoholics and old nonalcoholic controls. For example, although alcoholics and controls as a group performed similarly on the Shipley Vocabulary, and the Comprehension and Similarities subtests

from the WAIS, the young alcoholics performed significantly worse than both the young and old controls on the Brain Age Quotient (BAQ), with the latter groups performing similarly. When the individual tests from the BAQ were examined (not corrected for age), the overall pattern on the individual subtests from the BAQ was similar across groups, with the young alcoholics performing intermediate to the young and old controls (Hochla & Parsons, 1982); length of alcoholism history or duration of abstinence was not related to performance in the alcoholics on the BAQ. Although there are a number of other studies that have supported the premature aging model (Blusewicz et al., 1977a, 1977b; Hochla & Parsons, 1982; Parsons & Leber, 1981), more recent studies do not (Burger et al., 1987; Kramer et al., 1989; Ryan & Butters, 1984).

Grant and associates (1984) found that whereas both recently abstinent alcoholic status and age were related to a decline in learning and problem solving, aging but not alcoholism was associated with reduction in psychomotor speed and attention. While this study suggested that age and alcohol effects had somewhat different profiles, an actual age by alcohol interaction was not demonstrated. A morphometric MRI study reported that there was increased brain tissue loss with advanced age in alcoholics relative to controls (Pfefferbaum et al., 1992). The same research group provided evidence for age by alcoholism interaction on bulk diffusivity, a measure of microstructural change in the corpus callosum (Pfefferbaum et al., 2006).

In sum, age and drinking patterns may interact, such that older alcoholics who continue to drink at levels comparable to those of their younger years may suffer more brain injury, particularly in those older alcoholics who have already begun to show neuropsychological deficits.

Genetic and Developmental Factors in Alcoholism Associated Brain Dysfunction. It is generally believed that genetic factors are important in the development of alcoholism (Begleiter & Porjesz, 1999; Prescott & Kendler, 1999; Schuckit, 1987, 1994). The search to determine whether neuropsychological deficits exist prior to the beginning of heavy alcohol use has proceeded along two lines. One approach has been to study individuals at high risk for the development of alcoholism (i.e., children of alcoholics [COA])—mostly sons of male alcoholics), and to compare them to demographically matched individuals without a family history of alcoholism on intellectual and neuropsychological tests, as well as on electrophysiological measures of brain functioning. This approach has been driven largely by the fact that alcoholics who also have a positive family history for alcoholism demonstrate more neuropsychological deficits in some studies than those without alcoholic family members (see below). A second approach has been to administer questionnaires that retrospectively assess childhood behavioral disturbances in adult alcoholics, and to determine if these symptoms and disturbances relate to residual neuropsychological test performance as adults. Ultimately, both approaches have tremendous clinical implications in that they may help to identify individuals who are at risk for a more severe course of alcoholism or for more neurobehavioral impairments, as well as target them for primary prevention and/or intervention (Bates & Pandina, 1992).

Regarding the intellectual or academic deficits in COA, some studies have not revealed any deficits (Bates & Pandina, 1992; Johnson & Rolf, 1988; Ozkaragoz & Noble, 1995); other studies have shown that COA, relative to children without alcoholic family members, have lower verbal ability and academic achievement (Drejer et al., 1985; Parsons, 1989; Sher et al., 1991; Tarter et al., 1984), and more psychiatric distress and alcohol/drug problems (Sher et al., 1991).

With regard to the neuropsychological deficits in COA, some studies have found deficits (Ozkaragoz & Noble, 1995; Tarter et al., 1984, 1989a), while others have not (Bates & Pandina, 1992; Schuckit et al., 1987; Workman-Daniels & Hesselbrock, 1987). In those studies that have found deficits, the pattern of results do not suggest generalized effects (Tarter et al., 1989a), but rather specific deficits on tests measuring verbal skills and language processing (Parsons, 1989; Tarter et al., 1984; Tarter et al., 1989b), visual scanning and attention, planning ability (Ozkaragoz & Noble, 1995; Tarter et al., 1984, 1989a, 1989b), perceptual–motor performance, abstraction (Parsons, 1989; Peterson & Pihl, 1990; Tarter et al., 1984), and memory

(Ozkaragoz & Noble, 1995; Parsons, 1989; Tarter et al., 1984). The fact that adult male COA have deficits in visual–spatial learning that resemble the deficits found in children may suggest that certain deficits may be premorbid (Garland et al., 1993).

While there continues to be controversy regarding the neuropsychological deficits in COA, one possible explanation for the mixture of findings is the failure to consider comorbid psychopathology (Gillen & Hesselbrock, 1992). For example, Gillen and Hesselbrock have shown that neuropsychological deficits in the areas of higher level motor control and verbal concept formation occur in alcoholics with ASPD; however, there was no ASPD and family history interaction. In contrast, another group of investigators demonstrated that young adult COA exhibited more childhood attentional and social problems, but not elevated rates of cognitive problems, drug use, or mental health problems (Alterman et al., 1989a). Alterman and colleagues have suggested that it may be important to consider both drinking and familial alcoholism risk status when performing comparisons on neuropsychological tests (Alterman et al., 1986), although they were unable to find a relationship between heavy drinking and familial risk with neuropsychological performance in college men in one of their subsequent studies (Alterman & Hall, 1989).

Hesselbrock and colleagues (1985b) have reported that Attention Deficit Disorder/hyperactivity and conduct disorder prior to age 12 predicted onset of drinking. However, they were unable to detect any neuropsychological performance differences in young adults who were characterized as being at high or low risk, and there was also no difference between these subjects when the data were broken down according to frequency of intoxication, or when a second cohort similar in age was compared on neuropsychological tests, based on whether neither parent, one parent, or both parents were alcoholics (Hesselbrock et al., 1985b). What these results may suggest is that a higher prevalence of childhood problem behaviors may be related to the development of a variety of psychiatric problems, in addition to alcoholism.

Hesselbrock and his colleagues proposed that the evidence in support of neuropsychological differences between low- and high-risk individuals is not strong and that variations in literature are likely the result of differences in study design and methodology, and in how family history of alcoholism is characterized (Hesselbrock et al., 1991). According to Hesselbrock et al., the strongest differences and deficits in COA, as well as in FH+ alcoholics, occur on tests of verbal ability and abstracting/conceptual reasoning skills. Hesselbrock proposed that a number of additional factors may explain the equivocal results that have been obtained (e.g., drinking of mother, parental psychiatric comorbidity, conduct disorder).

A number of years ago, Tarter and his colleagues developed a 50-item questionnaire that assessed childhood "minimal brain dysfunction" (MBD) symptoms (Tarter et al., 1977). This MBD inventory has been shown to capture four factors: hyperactivity–impulsivity, attentional–socialization problems, antisocial behavior, and learning disability (Alterman & Gerstley, 1986; Alterman & McLellan, 1986). In a series of studies using this inventory, Tarter and his colleagues found that primary alcoholics reported more childhood MBD symptoms than less severe drinkers (secondary alcoholics), psychiatric patients, and controls (Tarter et al., 1977); in addition, he found that alcoholics characterized as essential and reactive differed in their retrospective accounts of symptoms of hyperactivity and MBD, with the former having twice as many symptoms as the latter (Tarter, 1982). This finding has also been replicated (i.e., essential alcoholics scored higher on the Beck Depression Inventory, the Neuropsychological Impairment Scale, and had a tendency to report more symptoms on the MBD questionnaire; Braggio et al., 1991). In another study, alcoholics who scored high on the MBD inventory were found to report more psychopathology on the Minnesota Multiphasic Personality Inventory (MMPI), differed in alcoholism use patterns and consequences, had worse emotional and psychosocial functioning, and were more likely to use other drugs (Alterman et al., 1985a). The results obtained using the MBD questionnaire are generally consistent with previous findings that alcoholics with a positive family history for alcoholism begin drinking at an earlier age and have increased prevalence of childhood history of learning problems, hyperactivity,

conduct disorder, and an adult history of antisocial behavior (Goodwin, 1983). In sum, these results suggest that primary or essential alcoholics, and possibly those with a family history for alcoholism, are more at risk for antecedent neuropsychiatric deficits.

Electrophysiological Findings in Children of Alcoholics. In parallel with the neurocognitive studies of COA, investigators have attempted to determine whether there are electrophysiological abnormalities in COA that may predispose one to develop alcoholism.

Comparisons of EEG activity between individuals at low and high risk for alcoholism have produced mixed results. For example, there were no differences on four measures of EEG activity in a study that compared male COA to those without positive family history for alcoholism, suggesting that EEG does not effectively discriminate between individuals at high and low risk for alcoholism prior to alcohol administration (Cohen et al., 1991). However, EEGs of young male COA do show different EEG wave patterns than those without a positive family history risk when given an alcohol challenge (Ehlers & Schuckit, 1990, 1991).

Far more electrophysiological studies have been carried out examining various waveforms from ERPs in individuals at low versus high risk for alcoholism. Many investigators have reported electrophysiological abnormalities, particularly differences in P300, in adolescent males with FH+ (Begleiter et al., 1984; O'Connor & Tasman, 1990; Porjesz & Begleiter, 1990, 1991, 1993; Whipple et al., 1988) as well as in boys whose fathers are characterized as Type 2 alcoholics (Begleiter et al., 1987). There are, however, some investigators who have not been able to find any family history effect of alcoholism in latency or amplitude of P300, although in some of their studies latency increased and amplitude decreased with an increase in the reported amount of alcohol consumption (Polich & Bloom, 1986, 1988; Polich et al., 1988a, 1988b).

Some investigators have suggested that P300 may provide a phenotypic marker for alcoholism (Begleiter & Porjesz, 1990; Porjesz & Begleiter, 1993), which may also predict later substance (including alcohol) abuse in young boys (Berman et al., 1993). However, Polich and colleagues (1994) have argued that the P300 may not be specific to alcoholism, because it is often abnormal in a number of other neuropsychiatric patient groups. In their recent meta-analysis of the P300 findings in COA, they calculated that the most reliable finding with COA is the reduction in P300 amplitude using the most difficult visual tasks, and that the variability obtained in past studies can be explained by a number of moderator variables (e.g., age of the individual, source of recruitment, stimulus material used to elicit the ERP (task difficulty and modality), and the strength of family history for alcoholism) (Polich et al., 1994).

The Influence of Family History of Alcoholism on Neuropsychological Differences in Alcoholics. In trying to explain the neuropsychological deficits in alcoholics, investigators have compared alcoholics with positive and negative family histories for alcoholism (FH+ and FH–, respectively). In one study, male alcoholics with family histories of alcoholism were found to have an earlier onset of alcoholism, report more symptoms of childhood conduct disorder, tended to have higher level of depressive symptoms, and performed worse on the Shipley Abstraction Test, relative to male alcoholics without such histories (Schaeffer et al., 1988). An earlier study also suggested that alcoholics' deficits in abstracting/problem solving, and possibly learning and memory, may antedate alcohol use in FH+ individuals, and that the lack of interaction between family history and alcohol/control status suggested alcoholism and that family history has additive effects on neuropsychological test performance (Schaeffer et al., 1984). In a review of the family history studies carried out in the Oklahoma laboratory, neuropsychological deficits were found to be more prominent in male alcoholics with an alcoholic father and/or in those with a history of childhood behavioral disorders, although Cloninger's Type 1 and Type 2 classification (i.e., consideration of the course of alcoholism, psychiatric comorbidity, and personality traits; Cloninger, 1987) may have contributed to the variability across studies (Parsons, 1989; Parsons & Nixon, 1993). In contrast to studies demonstrating family history effects, a number of investigators have been unable to find differences between FH+ and FH\ alcoholics using various classification schemes that classified alcoholics according to strength of family history (Alterman et al., 1987; Reed et al., 1987).

The Influence of Pre-Abuse Neuropsychiatric Risk Factors

Fetal Alcohol Syndrome and Fetal Alcohol Effects. Alcohol and other drugs consumed during pregnancy can have a variety of neurological effects on the developing fetus (Riley & McGee, 2005) The more severe manifestation of intrauterine ethanol exposure have been termed fetal alcohol syndrome (FAS) and can range from life threatening brain and other organ deformities in exceptional cases, to more commonly recognized stigmata such as characteristic facial features (e.g., short palpebral fissures, flat midface, short nose, indistinct philtrum, thin upper lip, accompanied by mental retardation, and microcephaly, see Figure 18–4; see also the color figure in the color insert section). However, it is generally acknowledged that FAS is but the more severe form of a spectrum of conditions that ranges from very mild effects of intrauterine alcohol exposure to the most profound. Terms describing these less severe forms include fetal alcohol effects (FAE), alcohol-related neurodevelopment disorders (ARND), and alcohol-related birth defects (ARBD). Riley and colleagues have proposed that FAS, FAE, and other manifestations be grouped as fetal alcohol spectrum disorders (Riley & McGee, 2005). Brain effects in the more severe forms (i.e., the dysmorphic, or FAS type) can include marked reduction in brain volume and thinning or agenesis of the corpus callosum (Archibald et al., 2001). FAE cases can also manifest a variety of milder changes of the same types (Archibald, et al., 2001; Ma et al., 2005; Mattson et al., 1994; Mattson & Riley, 1995; Riley, et al., 1995, 2004; Sowell, et al., 2001; see Figure 18–5; see also the color figure in the color insert section).

There is continued controversy regarding the critical threshold of drinking that leads to fetal effects. Recently, it has been suggested that the threshold may be around 30 to 40

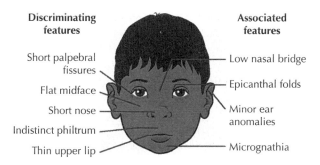

Figure 18–4. Cartoon showing some typical facial features in child with fetal alcohol syndrome. (Modified from Ann Streissguth, PhD, University of Washington and Edward Riley, PhD, San Diego State University. Courtesy of Dr. Riley.)

g/day (above the level generally defined as moderate drinking), though the authors of the study state that current evidence is insufficient (Plant et al., 1993). Several other investigators argue against the use of a cutoff as the critical determinant, and point to the increasing probability of damage with increasing amounts of alcohol. Russell et al. examined growth, dysmorphology, and cognitive development in 6-year-old children exposed to alcohol prenatally (Russell et al., 1991). Even after excluding children born to mothers who drank over seven drinks a day, and children with probable/possible FAE, Russell and colleagues found significant effects of maternal drinking on cognitive functions (and head circumference).

Decrements in intellectual performance, particularly verbal-language skills, have been reported with prenatal alcohol exposure (Caruso & ten Bensel, 1993; Conry, 1990; Mattson et al., 1992, 1998; Nanson & Hiscock, 1990; Smith & Eckardt, 1991; Streissguth et al., 1990) in infants born to mothers with more than one indication of problem drinking (Russell et al., 1991), and in children raised by an alcoholic father (Ervin et al., 1984). Consumption of two or more drinks per day on an average was associated with a 7-point decrement in IQ in 482 7-year-old children (Streissguth et al., 1990). In addition, the effect of prenatal alcohol exposure was exacerbated if parental education was low and with increased number of children in the home; learning problems were associated

with binge drinking (i.e., with more than five drinks per occasion) (Streissguth et al., 1990). A follow-up of these children (*n* = 462) at age 14 revealed that the number of drinks per occasion was the strongest alcohol predictor, and alcohol exposure prenatally was associated with attention and memory deficits in a dose-dependent fashion (Streissguth et al., 1994). Other neuropsychological impairments are also common (Conry, 1990; Mattson et al., 1992; Smith & Eckardt, 1991; Streissguth et al., 1989, 1994), including deficits in executive functioning and working memory (Kodituwakku et al., 2001; Mattson et al., 1999).

The Influence of Concurrent Neuromedical Risk Factors in Alcoholics

The Effects of Hepatic Dysfunction on Neuropsychological Test Performance. It is well established that hepatic dysfunction and disease can result in neuropsychological dysfunction (Tarter et al., 1987). For example, biochemical measures of hepatic dysfunction have been shown to correlate with neuropsychological dysfunction in alcoholics with cirrhosis (Tarter et al., 1986b), particularly on tests of memory performance (Arria et al., 1991a). Psychomotor, visuopractic, and abstracting abilities can recover following liver transplantation; memory deficits, however, may persist (Arria et al., 1991b). The fact that alcoholics and nonalcoholics with cirrhosis display similar

Corpus callosum abnormalities

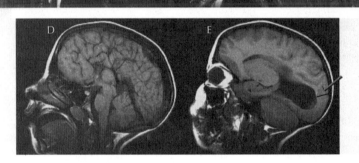

Figure 18–5. One anomaly that has been seen in FAS is agenesis, or absence, of the corpus callosum. While not common, it occurs in FAS cases (~6%) more frequently than in the general population (0.1%) or in the developmentally disabled population (2%–3%). In fact it has been suggested that FAS may be the most common cause of agenesis of the corpus callosum.

The top left MRI scan (A), is a control brain. The other images are from children with FAS. In the top middle the corpus callosum is present, but it is very thin at the posterior section of the brain (B, arrow). In the upper right the corpus callosum is essentially missing (C, arrow). The bottom two pictures (D, E) are from a 9-year old girl with FAS. She has agenesis of the corpus callosum and the large dark area in the back of her brain (E, arrow) above the cerebellum is a condition known as colpocephaly. It is essentially empty space. (Courtesy Edward Riley, PhD, San Diego State University).

neuropsychological deficits (Tarter et al., 1986a, 1988) suggests that alcohol is not the only etiological mechanism for brain dysfunction in alcoholics.

Although less than one-third of alcoholics or heavy drinkers develop serious alcohol-related liver damage (Grant et al., 1988), elevated levels of liver enzymes in noncirrhotic alcoholics have been shown to be significantly related to a number of neuropsychological measures, particularly those that assess visuoperceptual and visuoconceptual abilities.

A study by Irwin and colleagues illustrates the effects of liver enzymes on neuropsychological test performance (Irwin et al., 1989). Blood and serum were collected from 132 primary alcoholic men 24–48 hours after admission, but approximately a mean of 7 days after their last drink. Based on blood and serum values, alcoholics were divided into three groups according to their plasma levels of gamma-glutamyl transferase (GGT, a liver enzyme where plasma level rises during acute heavy drinking) at admission. There were 69 men with normal GGT values (>40 IU/L), 41 men with moderately elevated GGT levels (40 ≤ GGT ≤ 100 IU/L), and 22 with extremely elevated GGT levels (>100 IU/L). There were no differences in age, education, and WAIS-R vocabulary scores, suggesting that the groups were comparable on premorbid neuropsychological functioning. When the three groups were compared on a brief battery of neuropsychological tests, which included the Trail-Making Test (Parts A and B), WAIS-R Digit Symbol, and Visual Search, significant differences emerged as GGT level increased. When multiple regressions were performed to examine the influence of various parameters (i.e., GGT, liver injury tests, demographics, alcohol consumption, and depressive symptoms as measured by the Hamilton Depression Rating Scale) on neuropsychological test performance, it was found that over and above the expected influence of age and education, GGT contributed a significant amount of variance to Trails B and Visual Search. In addition, even when other liver function tests were included in the analyses, GGT continued to explain Visual Search, Digit Symbol, and Trails B performance, suggesting that level of GGT in alcoholics is associated with neuropsychological deficits in the areas of visuoperceptual and visuoconceptual functions (Irwin et al., 1989).

In a later study by Irwin and his colleagues (Schafer et al., 1991), liver function tests and depression at admission were found to be related to neuropsychological dysfunction in alcoholics, but not at discharge several weeks later. In a study by another group of investigators, liver enzyme levels, when collected from alcoholics at hospital admission, were shown to have continued effects on neuropsychological test performance at least 21 days later, particularly on tests of visuoperceptual and conceptual abilities (Richardson et al., 1991).

Persons with alcoholism can also have liver disease by virtue of hepatitis C virus (HCV) infection, which is more common among alcoholics who have concurrend drug abuse, especially injection drug use. There is accumulating evidence that HCV can produce neurocognitive impairment even in the absence of severe liver disease (Forton et al., 2002, 2005, 2006; Hilsabeck et al., 2003). HCV has been identified in astrocytes and macrophages in the brain (Letendre et al., 2007) and neurocognitive disturbance has been linked to systemic inflammatory markers associated with HCV disease (Letendre et al., 2006). Therefore, testing for HCV serostatus may be indicated, especially where apparent alcohol-related neuropsychological deficits persist or worsen despite abstinence.

The Impact of Head Injury on Neuropsychological Test Performance. Head injuries are extremely common in alcoholics and they represent a significant risk factor for neuropsychological impairment independent of the neurotoxic effects of alcohol. Traumatic head injuries appear to be two to four times more prevalent in alcoholics than in the general population (Hillbom & Holm, 1986). Excessive alcohol consumption has been shown to lead to increased susceptibility to head injuries in both alcoholic and control groups (Hillbom & Holm, 1986), as well as worse head injury outcome (Ruff et al., 1990). In fact, heavy alcohol use and head injury severity may lead to independent or interactive effects on neuropsychological performance and outcome (Dikmen et al., 1993; Solomon & Malloy, 1992). For example, one study showed a significant interaction between head injury severity (i.e., length of post-traumatic amnesia) and alcohol use, with increasing memory deficits occurring with increasing alcohol use (Brooks et al., 1989). Several studies have examined whether the degree of intoxication at time of head injury, a history of alcohol abuse, or both contribute to the severity of traumatic brain injury (TBI)-induced brain injury and predicts recovery. Brooks et al. (1989) reported that posttraumatic amnesia was worst among heaviest drinkers at injury, while Wilde et al. (2004) found that both blood alcohol concentration on day of injury and history of chronic use were associated with greater brain atrophy on MRI and worse NP outcome. Other studies report no effect of day of injury drinking on NP outcome (Alexander et al., 2004; Lange et al., 2007). The latter study also considered history of alcohol abuse and noted a significant, but small effect on neurocognitive outcome of head injury. Family history for alcoholism may also be a significant risk factor, because alcoholics with a positive family risk have been shown to have elevated rates of closed head injuries (60% in FH+ versus 35% in FH-) (Alterman & Tarter, 1985).

One group of investigators have found that a history of head injuries independently predicted neuropsychological deficits, particularly on a factor of verbal skills and on a factor that reflected nonverbal learning and problem solving (Grant et al., 1984). In another study, alcoholics with head injuries performed significantly worse than alcoholics without head injuries on the Halstead Impairment Index, the Finger Tapping Test (dominant hand) and on the Location score from the Tactual Performance Test (Hillbom & Holm, 1986). There is no unanimity that mild head injury affects NP in alcoholism, as several studies failed to detect an association (Alterman et al., 1985b; Ryan & Lewis, 1988).

Nutrition. A few studies in the early 1980s examined how nutrition may impact neuropsychological test performance in alcoholics. These studies provided evidence that folic acid level was related to deficits on a number of neuropsychological tests in recently detoxified alcoholics (Albert et al., 1982, 1983). The authors of these studies suggested that nutrition effects may be important only early in the detoxification process, whereas the more long-standing neuropsychological deficits that are detected may be related to the neurotoxic effects of alcohol. In a more recent study, alcoholics who had lower serum levels of thiamine scored lower on intellectual and visual–spatial tasks relative to controls. There were a few significant correlations between thiamine level and neuropsychological test performance; however, regression analyses revealed that duration of alcohol intake and educational level were the major contributors to neuropsychological test performance (Molina et al., 1994).

Possible Effects of Hypoxemia. It is estimated that between 83% and 94% of alcoholics smoke cigarettes (Ayers et al., 1976; DiFranza & Guerrera, 1990). It is well established that COPD can cause significant neuropsychological impairment with increasing severity of hypoxemia (Grant et al., 1987a). Although most neuropsychological studies of alcoholics generally exclude those with obvious lung disease or COPD, it is possible that mild levels of hypoxemia in those who are in the early stages of COPD may contribute to neuropsychological deficits independent of alcohol. In addition, because chronic alcohol consumption can also lead to increasing night time hypoxemia and sleep apnea, particularly in older men. Additional deficits may be observed in alcoholics with such conditions since sleep apnea itself can be associated with NP impairment (Roth et al., 1995; Vitiello et al., 1987).

Sleep Disturbances. Notwithstanding possible nighttime hypoxemia in alcoholics, there are a number of sleep abnormalities

that persist for extended periods of time after detoxification that may also contribute to daytime impairments. For example, young primary alcoholics have been shown to have sleep patterns typical of older controls (Gillin et al., 1990b); in addition, length of abstinence, drinks per drinking day in past 3 months, and maximum number of withdrawal symptoms ever experienced by the patient were related to sleep abnormalities (Gillin et al., 1990b). Furthermore, alcoholics (both primary and those with a secondary depression) have significantly longer sleep latency and less sleep efficiency, less total sleep time, and delta sleep than controls; primary alcoholics with secondary depression have shorter REM latency and less non-REM sleep than alcoholics without secondary depression (Gillin et al., 1990a). Finally, there is also some evidence that decreases in slow wave sleep in alcoholics may be related to increased atrophy of the cerebral cortex (Ishibashi et al., 1987).

Blackouts, Seizures, and Effects of Repeated Withdrawal from Alcohol. There are a number of consequences that result from heavy drinking (e.g., blackouts, seizures, and repeated withdrawals) that could indirectly influence brain functioning. For example, of 135 alcoholics seeking help for an alcohol/drug problem, 86% reported having experienced alcohol-related blackouts (Campbell & Hodgins, 1993); these blackouts were found to be related to the severity of alcohol problems (i.e., those with blackouts started drinking at a younger age, drank larger amounts, had greater dependence, were more likely to have delirium tremens, shakes, and family history of alcoholism). Approximately 14%–21% of hospitalized alcoholics report having had seizures, typically of the grand mal variety (Feuerlein, 1977; Neundorfer et al., 1984; Tuck & Jackson, 1991). Although a small study showed that alcoholics who presented to the hospital experiencing withdrawal seizures (n = 12) were not different from those without (n = 22) intellectual or neuropsychological measures, African American alcoholics were more likely than White alcoholics in this study to experience seizures (Tarter et al., 1983). In another study, African American alcoholics with seizure histories performed worse on intellectual and neuropsychological tests compared to African American alcoholics without such histories; there were no differences among White alcoholics (Goldstein et al., 1983). More recent data indicate lowered N-acetyl aspartate (NAA), a metabolite thought to reflect neuronal integrity, among detoxified alcoholics who reported withdrawal seizures (Schweinsburg, 2002). Regarding repeated alcohol withdrawals uncomplicated by seizures, male and female alcoholics have been shown to perform worse on memory testing when repeated withdrawals occurred in the past year (Glenn et al., 1988).

The Influence of Psychiatric Comorbidity on Neuropsychological Test Performance in Alcoholics. Personality disorders are associated with alcoholism (Løberg & Miller, 1986); one study reported that 78% of alcoholics admitted to an addiction treatment unit ($n = 178$) had at least one personality disorder, with the average being 1.8 per patient (DeJong et al., 1993). Personality disturbances, based on the MMPI, show many significant correlations with drinking variables, but few with neuropsychological test variables; however, alcoholics with severe neuropsychological impairment often show pathological personality profiles (Løberg, 1981; Løberg & Miller, 1986).

ASPD and antisocial traits, for example, as indexed by elevated Pd scale of the MMPI (Løberg, 1981), characterize a subgroup of alcoholics. Although some investigators have shown that alcoholics with ASPD perform worse on neuropsychological testing (Gorenstein, 1982; Hesselbrock et al., 1985a; Malloy et al., 1989, 1990), this has not always been the case (Hoffman et al., 1987; Sutker & Allain, 1987). One possible reason for these discrepant findings may be that some ASPD substance abusers may have histories of "minimal brain dysfunction," Attention Deficit Disorder (ADD), and/or developmental disorders (Tarter & Edwards, 1986) before they begin substance use. Another reason may be that certain deviant behaviors (e.g., drinking-related arrests) may be common to both antisocial personality and alcoholism, and these may carry with them higher neuromedical risks leading to specific neuropsychological deficits (Gorenstein, 1987). That is,

alcoholics with ASPD may have a higher prevalence of neuropsychological deficits because they begin drinking earlier and suffer more alcohol-related problems, including more blackouts, more physical injuries, more frequent sleep disturbances, and engage in more polydrug use than those alcoholics without ASPD (Malloy et al., 1990). Finally, violent, recently detoxified alcoholics have been shown to have more severe neuropsychological impairments (e.g., on abstraction and mental coordination) and more deviant personality profiles on the MMPI, compared with nonviolent alcoholics (Løberg, 1981).

To circumvent the problem of discrete classification associated with the diagnosis of ASPD, Glenn and her colleagues carried out a study to examine how "subclinical" levels of antisocial behaviors influenced neuropsychological impairment in adult alcoholics (i.e., they included subjects who did not meet criteria for ASPD, but nevertheless had a number of symptoms that were characteristic of this disorder); in this study, they also investigated how childhood behavioral disorder symptoms and affective symptomatology affected neuropsychological performance (Glenn et al., 1993). Childhood behavior symptoms proved to be the most consistent predictor of neuropsychological performance for both male and female alcoholics and controls, although childhood affective symptoms were also related.

Goldstein and Shelly used MMPI to classify alcoholics as normal, depressed, or psychotic and then compared them on intellectual and neuropsychological measures (Goldstein et al., 1985). There were no differences in intellectual or neuropsychological performance in alcoholics who were classified as "normal" and "depressed" using the MMPI; however, alcoholics classified as "psychotic" were more impaired with regard to conceptual and visual–spatial skills; 80% of the "psychotic" alcoholics were classified as impaired using an AIR of 1.55, whereas only 50% of the other groups were similarly classified; "psychotic" alcoholics also had lower verbal skills (Goldstein et al., 1985). There are, however, some apparently discrepant findings and infrequent relations between neuropsychological test performances and personality when correlations are performed (Løberg

& Miller, 1986). For example, it may be that certain personality profile types may be associated with elevated levels of neuropsychological impairments, which are not obvious when simple correlations are made between neuropsychological test measures and individual clinical scales from the MMPI (Goldstein et al., 1985; Løberg, 1981).

Psychiatric symptomatology, particularly depressive and anxiety symptoms, is common during heavy drinking and during detoxification in alcoholics. In one study, 82% of alcoholics (350 of 428 patients) presented to treatment with depressive symptomatology (Angelini et al., 1990). Depressive symptomatology may be explained both biochemically, since alcohol is a CNS depressant, and psychologically, due to remorse and guilt over actions not taken, obligations not fulfilled, and actions performed that should not have been undertaken while drinking.

Brown and her colleagues at the San Diego VA Medical Center have documented that significant changes in depressive (Brown & Schuckit, 1988; Brown et al., 1995) and anxiety (Brown et al., 1991) symptoms occur in primary alcoholics during detoxification. For example, whereas 42% of alcoholic men had clinically significant levels of depression within 48 hours of admission into an inpatient unit (i.e., with Hamilton Depression Rating Scores of ≥20), only 6% had elevated levels at discharge 4 weeks later. This level of depressive symptomatology at discharge corresponds well with previous reports that alcohol-dependent men do not have elevated rates for major depressive disorder independent of alcohol-induced mood syndromes (Schuckit et al., 1994). With regard to anxiety, 98% of men (n = 171) reported at least one symptom of anxiety during drinking or withdrawal, but only 4% fulfilled criteria for generalized anxiety disorder with protracted abstinence (i.e., >3 months) (Schuckit et al., 1990). In another report by these investigators, 40% of primary alcoholic men reported significantly elevated levels of anxiety state at admission, which had returned to within the normal range by the second week of treatment, and further reductions were evident with continued abstinence (Brown et al., 1991). For information on how to clinically separate affective and anxiety disorders from the substance-

induced effects of alcohol and drugs, we refer the interested reader to the study of Anthenelli and Schuckit (1993).

A number of investigators have carried out studies to examine how depressive and anxiety symptoms influence neuropsychological test performance. For example, Sinha and colleagues (1992) demonstrated that scores on the Beck Depression Inventory correlated with an overall measure of neuropsychological impairment in both FH+ and FH– alcoholics. Scores on the Hamilton Depression Rating Scale were also shown to be related to Trails B and WAIS Digit Symbol when alcoholics were on average 12 days sober (Schafer et al., 1991). At the 3-month follow-up, estimates of drinking following discharge and severity of depressive symptoms were significantly related to neuropsychological test performance. However, in another study, severity of depressive symptoms (using the Beck Depression Inventory) was not associated with cognitive impairment 7–14 days after admission or at 6 months (Clark et al., 1984).

Alcoholism and alcohol abuse can also be comorbid with other major mental disorders such as schizophrenia, but the combined effects of these disorders on NP are not well understood, since in many NP studies of alcoholics, schizophrenia is an exclusion criterion. Interestingly, Sullivan et al. (2003) reported that there were selective reductions in pontine volumes on MRI in dually affected patients that were not noted in schizophrenics who were not alcoholic. Finally, alcoholics who also use depressants and opiates may have more neuropsychological impairments than those who consume only alcohol (Carlin, 1986; Carlin et al., 1978; Grant et al., 1977, 1978, 1979b).

In sum, though depression and anxiety are frequent correlates of heavy drinking, but these do not consistently relate to NP findings. ASPD has been variably associated with NP deficits, and alcoholics with more severe NP deficits can exhibit substantial personality disturbance that may be secondary to their brain damage.

Education Influences

Certain intellectual and neuropsychological abilities are affected by the level of formal education (Heaton, 1992; Heaton et al., 1991; see also Heaton et al., this volume, Chapter 7). To illustrate this relationship in alcoholics, when 14 samples of alcoholics were ranked according to their level of education and their performance on the Halstead Impairment Index, alcoholics with lower education were more often impaired (Grant et al., 1984). In addition, there may be an interaction between drinking and education, because heavy drinkers with low education generally show more neuropsychological deficits (Williams & Skinner, 1990).

A number of investigators have examined the relationship between premorbid functioning (using in most cases the Vocabulary subtest from the WAIS/WAIS-R) and neuropsychological deficits observed in alcoholics. Some have suggested that neuropsychological deficits in alcoholics may be explained by premorbid differences, because a number of studies have found that the level of neuropsychological deficits parallels Vocabulary level (Cutting, 1988; Draper & Manning, 1982; Emmerson et al., 1988). Lower Vocabulary scores in alcoholics may also be a surrogate indicator of past learning problems in school. Along these lines, 40% of alcohol-dependent male adults were found to have had special education, remedial services, or repeated grade failure (concurrent with a familial history of alcoholism and current indices of learning disability) (Rhodes & Jasinski, 1990). The authors from this study also suggested that having a history of childhood learning disorders may be related to the development of alcoholism (i.e., a compromised central nervous system may make one less resistant to familial or social risk factors for the development of unhealthy drinking practices). Residual learning problems may also explain some of the neuropsychological impairment found among detoxified alcoholics (Løberg, 1989; Rhodes & Jasinski, 1990).

The Influence of Motivation and Expectancies on Neuropsychological Test Performance in Alcoholics

Parsons and his group carried out a number of studies to determine whether motivation or expectancies about one's performance may explain the neuropsychological differences that are often observed between alcoholics and controls. In one of their first studies, his laboratory showed that both alcoholics and controls do show a trend to improve their performance on a face-name learning task when monetary incentives were made contingent on their performance; however, though alcoholics did show deficits on this task, the authors did not find an interaction between group membership and incentive (Schaeffer & Parsons, 1988). A similar paradigm, used to evaluate motivational effects on problem-solving ability in alcoholics, also showed no interaction between incentive and group performance (Schaeffer et al., 1989). In both of the preceding studies, depressive symptoms, as measured by the Beck Depression Inventory, could not account for these differences. Because alcoholics rate themselves as being more impaired cognitively (Errico et al., 1990; Shelton & Parsons, 1987), their reduced expectancies may in some way affect their performance on neuropsychological tests. A study by Sander et al. (1989) addressed this issue and found that alcoholics do have reduced expectancies about their performance, which also correlate with their actual neuropsychological performance; however, neuropsychological differences persist when one statistically removes the variance associated with pretest expectancies (Sander et al., 1989). Finally, both alcoholics and controls respond similarly to experimental manipulations that enhance personal involvement or reduce negative affect, further suggesting that motivation differences do not explain neuropsychological deficits in alcoholics (Nixon et al., 1992).

Sample Selection influences on NP performance

A study by Parsons and his group revealed that community alcoholics performed intermediate to VA alcoholics and controls on a number of neuropsychological measures suggesting that referral source is an important determinant of whether deficits will be present (Tivis et al., 1993). Furthermore, alcoholics who declined participation in a research study on the effects of alcohol on brain functioning performed worse on the Shipley Abstraction Test, suggesting that alcoholics who are enrolled may not be as impaired as those that decline (Nixon et al., 1988).

Neurobehavioral Recovery and Neuroimaging Reversibility in Alcoholics

Neurobehavioral Recovery

The extent to which CNS abnormalities persist in alcoholics, or recover with increasing length of stable abstinence, is an area of continuing debate. Certainly, if one were to focus only on the data from recently detoxified alcoholics tested weeks to several months after their last drink, one might erroneously conclude that alcohol causes chronic and permanent CNS damage in a high percentage of cases. However, studies that have examined alcoholics after longer periods of abstinence have been able to show that neurobehavioral recovery continues for several months, and perhaps years, after a person stops drinking. A nosology that takes into account this time course, as well as the differential rate of neurobehavioral recovery, has been previously described (Grant et al., 1987b) (see Figure 18–1).

Since the first systematic neuropsychological investigation of alcoholics (Fitzhugh et al., 1960), a significant number of studies have focused on the neuropsychological recovery of alcoholics, particularly with respect to the effects that increasing length of abstinence, resumption of drinking, and age at testing may have on the amount of recovery.

Of the studies that have examined alcoholics after short periods of abstinence (i.e., weeks to several months), some have shown improvements in neuropsychological functioning (Ayers et al., 1978; Bean & Karasievich, 1975; Cermak & Ryback, 1976; Ellenberg et al., 1980; Farmer, 1973; Gechter, 1987; Guthrie & Elliott, 1980; Hester et al., 1980; Kish et al., 1980; Leber et al., 1981; McIntyre, 1987; Muuronen et al., 1989; Sharp et al., 1977; Smith & Layden, 1972), particularly with "experience-dependent" stimulation or training (Forsberg & Goldman, 1985, 1987; Goldman & Goldman, 1988; Goldman et al., 1983, 1985; Roehrich & Goldman, 1993; Stringer & Goldman, 1988); others, however, have shown little neuropsychological recovery with short periods of abstinence (Brandt et al., 1983; Claiborn & Greene, 1981; Clarke & Haughton, 1975; de Obaldia et al., 1981; Eckardt

et al., 1979, 1980b; Page & Linden, 1974; Page & Schaub, 1977; Ryan & Butters, 1980b; Unkenstein & Bowden, 1991).

There are also conflicting reports on the extent of neuropsychological recovery in alcoholics who have maintained longer periods of abstinence (i.e., many months to several years). Some investigators have shown that long-term abstinence can be associated with normal or improved neuropsychological functioning (Adams et al., 1980; Berglund et al., 1977; Chaney et al., 1980; Fabian & Parsons, 1983; Fein et al., 2006; Gardner et al., 1989; Grant et al., 1979a, 1984, 1987b; Long & McLachlan, 1974; Marchesi et al., 1992; McLachlan & Levinson, 1974; O'Leary et al., 1977b; Reed et al., 1992; Schau et al., 1980; Templer et al., 1975); others, however, have been unable to demonstrate much change with long-term abstinence (Brandt et al., 1983; Eckardt et al., 1980a; Parsons et al., 1990a; Ryan et al., 1980; Yohman et al., 1985).

With respect to resumption of drinking, a number of longitudinal studies have examined the effects of interim drinking on neuropsychological recovery. Those alcoholics who maintained continuous abstinence, or demonstrated "improved drinking habits" over a follow-up period, showed more neuropsychological recovery and less deficits at follow-up, relative to alcoholics who resumed drinking at moderate or severe levels (Abbott & Gregson, 1981; Adams et al., 1980; Berglund et al., 1977; Eckardt et al., 1980a; Fabian & Parsons, 1983; Grant et al., 1987b; Gregson & Taylor, 1977; Guthrie & Elliott, 1980; McLachlan & Levinson, 1974; Muuronen et al., 1989; Parsons et al., 1990a; Rourke & Grant, 1999; Yohman et al., 1985); however, there are two reports that have not found an effect of level of interim drinking on neuropsychological performance (O'Leary et al., 1977b; Schau et al., 1980).

One of the more comprehensive studies was reported by Rourke and Grant (1999). These authors examined alcoholics at the conclusion of an inpatient treatment program (approximately one month abstinent) and re-evaluated them about 2 years later. Those who relapsed in the interim were compared to those who were constantly sober in the interim (these were termed intermediate duration sobers). In addition, to evaluate possible practice effects, and effects of very long-term abstinence, groups of nonalcoholics and alcoholics who were abstinent for a minimum of 18 months at first assessment were re-examined 2 years later. Change in NP performance was examined with respect to initial group assignment and interim drinking history. The data indicated that all groups registered some NP improvement on 2-year re-evaluation, but that the improvement in the intermediate group (i.e., the alcoholics who maintained abstinence after discharge) was significantly more on measures like the Category Test than for the other groups. This study provided strong evidence in support of the notion that there is continued recovery in brain function after the initial month to 6 weeks of abstinence, indicating that conclusions about persisting alcohol effects ought to be deferred until some months after completion of treatment.

At least four methodological shortcomings likely contribute to the discrepant findings in the literature regarding the rate and amount of neuropsychological recovery in alcoholics. First, many of the longitudinal studies, particularly those in the 1970s and early 1980s, did not include age- and education-matched control groups to correct for demographic differences and the effects of practice (Ayers et al., 1978; Bean & Karasievich, 1975; Berglund et al., 1977; Cermak & Ryback, 1976; Farmer, 1973; Gechter, 1987; Guthrie & Elliott, 1980; Hester et al., 1980; Kish et al., 1980; Long & McLachlan, 1974; McLachlan & Levinson, 1974; Muuronen et al., 1989; Page & Linden, 1974; Page & Schaub, 1977; Smith & Layden, 1972; Unkenstein & Bowden, 1991).

Second, many studies have not screened and/or controlled for adverse neuromedical confounds or risk factors that predate, coexist with, or occur as a consequence of heavy alcohol consumption (Tarter & Edwards, 1986). These risk factors or confounds are likely to contribute or lead to neuropsychological impairments over and above the neurotoxic effects of alcohol. Along these lines, investigators have shown that alcoholics with MBD symptoms (de Obaldia & Parsons, 1984; Tarter, 1982), head injuries (Adams & Grant, 1986; Alterman & Tarter, 1985; Grant et al., 1984; Hillbom & Holm, 1986; Solomon & Malloy, 1992), or liver dysfunction/pathology (Acker et al., 1982; Arria et al., 1991a;

Irwin et al., 1989; Schafer et al., 1991; Tarter et al., 1986b, 1988) perform worse on neuropsychological testing. The extent to which these symptoms, events, and conditions influence the rate and amount of neuropsychological recovery when subjects are followed over time has yet to be addressed.

Third, psychometric evaluations were often conducted during the first 2 weeks of abstinence before acute withdrawal effects and detoxification were complete (Ayers et al., 1978; Bean & Karasievich, 1975; Cermak & Ryback, 1976; Chaney et al., 1980; Claiborn & Greene, 1981; Clarke & Haughton, 1975; Eckardt et al., 1979, 1980b; Ellenberg et al., 1980; Farmer, 1973; Guthrie & Elliott, 1980; Hester et al., 1980; Kish et al., 1980; Long & McLachlan, 1974; McIntyre, 1987; Muuronen et al., 1989; O'Leary et al., 1977b; Page & Linden, 1974; Page & Schaub, 1977; Schau et al., 1980; Sharp et al., 1977; Smith & Layden, 1972).

Fourth, failure to use a number of tests to adequately represent a single neuropsychological ability area, or to sample a wide range of neuropsychological abilities, has most likely led to an inaccurate estimation of neuropsychological deficits. This is particularly salient when performance on one test is used to infer performance on a neuropsychological ability, or when the task difficulty/complexity is manipulated. Relative to all of the studies carried out on the neuropsychological recovery of alcoholics, only a selected number of cross-sectional (Adams & Grant, 1986; de Obaldia et al., 1981; Grant et al., 1984; Reed et al., 1992) and longitudinal studies (Adams et al., 1980; Chaney et al., 1980; Claiborn & Greene, 1981; Eckardt et al., 1979, 1980a, 1980b; Fabian & Parsons, 1983; Grant et al., 1987b; Long & McLachlan, 1974; McIntyre, 1987; Page & Linden, 1974; Page & Schaub, 1977; Parsons et al., 1990a; Rourke & Grant, 1999; Schau, et al., 1980; Yohman et al., 1985) have included a comprehensive sampling of neuropsychological abilities.

Neuroimaging Evidence for Reversibility in Structural Brain Abnormalities

If there is evidence of neurobehavioral recovery in alcoholics, one would also expect to see evidence at the structural and functional level for brain recovery. In fact, several investigators have provided evidence to suggest that brain morphology can improve with stable and increasing length of abstinence.

In 1978, Carlen and his colleagues demonstrated a measurable decrease in the degree of cerebral atrophy using CT, as well as some functional improvement, in four of eight chronic alcoholics who had maintained their abstinence over the interim. These results represented the first report of reversible cerebral "atrophy" in recently abstinent chronic alcoholics using CT scanning. Since this time, there have been a number of CT as well as MRI reports that have documented reductions in cortical and central CSF volumes with extended periods of abstinence or in alcoholics who improve their drinking habits (Artmann et al., 1981; Carlen & Wilkinson, 1983, 1987; Carlen et al., 1984; Drake et al., 1995; Jacobson, 1986a; Mann et al., 1993; Marchesi et al., 1994; Muuronen et al., 1989; Ron, 1983; Ron et al., 1982; Rourke et al., 1993; Shear et al., 1994).

Whereas most of these studies have been with male alcoholics, a cross-sectional comparison of CT parameters in 26 recently detoxified female alcoholics (abstinent for a mean of 33 days) and eight long-term female abstinent alcoholics (abstinent for a mean of 3.3 years) recruited from local AA chapters indicated that female AA members were more comparable to nonalcoholic female controls; in addition, there was some indication that cerebral changes were evident after briefer periods of abstinence than with male AA members (Jacobson, 1986a). Thus, although female alcoholics may experience cerebral structural abnormalities similar to those obtained in male alcoholics that tend to appear after shorter and less intense drinking careers, they may also tend to recover more quickly than their male counterparts.

MRI studies of brain volumes consistently report improvements over time. Mann et al. (1989) reported significant decreases in total CSF, ventricular and subarachnoid volumes in nine chronic alcoholics after 5 weeks of alcohol abstinence. In another study (Zipursky et al., 1989), ventricular volumes from 10 alcoholics were compared to 10 age-matched controls.

Alcoholics had significantly larger ventricles at the time of their first MRI scan (scan within 2 weeks of alcohol withdrawal; mean 7.3 days); however, 19–28 days later (mean 22.6 days), the difference between alcoholics and controls was no longer significant. MRI reports have demonstrated that decreases in CSF were associated with increases in tissue volumes, particularly white matter, in alcoholics who maintained stable abstinence over 3 months (Shear et al., 1994) and 1 year (Drake et al., 1995). Pfefferbaum (1995) and colleagues confirmed that abstaining alcoholics showed reduction in ventricular volume and tended to have increase in gray matter volume after one month of abstinence; in a 2–12 month follow-up, those who remained abstinent had further reduction in third ventricle volume, while those who relapsed had some reduction in gray matter. Other studies have confirmed that white matter recovers with abstinence and that volume gains regress with relapse (Cardenas et al., 2007; O'Neill et al., 2001; Pfefferbaum et al., 1998). Recovery in brain volumes appears to be most rapid in the early part of the abstinence process (e.g., first month), but may continue for a year (Gazdzinski et al., 2005, see Figure 18–6; see also the color figure in the color insert section).

Studies of brain metabolites also note abstinence associated reversal of reduction in NAA and Cho as well as in myoinositol, which may be a marker of inflammation or osmotic stress (Bartsch et al., 2007; Ende et al., 2005; Schweinsburg et al., 2001, 2003). Benzdsus et al. (2001) noted that degree of NAA recovery correlated to NP improvement. Perfusion studies including those using single photon emission computed tomography (SPECT) have noted normalization of tracer uptake in longer term abstainers (Figure 18–7; see also the color figure in the color insert section).

Based on a convergence of evidence from NP, MRI, MRI spectroscopy, and electrophysiological data, it is clear that substantial, and perhaps, among younger alcoholics, complete recovery of structure and function can occur; however the mechanisms of this recovery are unclear. While changes in hydration have been suggested to explain these effects, current insights do not support this notion. In animal models, cessation of heavy ethanol exposure has been

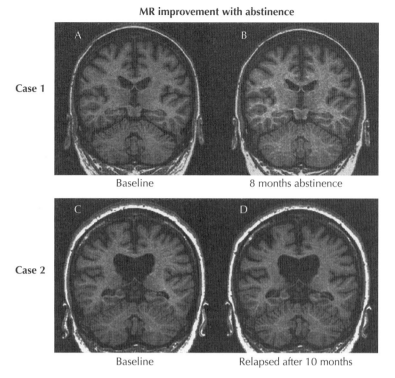

Figure 18–6. MRI brain images of two cases. Case 1 was abstinent 1 week (A) and rescanned after 8 months of continued abstinence (B). Note lessening prominence of suci and ventricles in B. Case 2 was abstinent 30 days (C) and rescanned at 10 months after relapsing in the interim. Note tissue loss in D, particularly in periventricular white matter, cerebellar vermis, and surrounding IV ventricle. (Derived from images shown in Gazdzinski, et al. [2005], *Drug and Alcohol Dependence, 78*, 263–273. Reprinted with permission from Elsevier.)

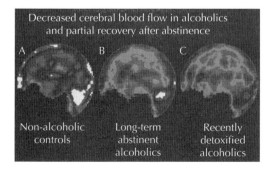

Figure 18–7. Color coded images representing intensity of uptake of the tracer HMPAO during a cognitive activation task in a nonalcoholic control (A), alcoholic abstinent over 18 months (B), and a recently detoxified alcoholic (C) abstinent 4 weeks. Cooler colors indicate less perfusion, especially in frontal areas in C versus A. Case B has values intermediate between A and C, suggesting recovery. (From Grant, Alhassoon, et al., San Diego VA Alcohol Study.)

associated with dendritic regrowth (McMullen et al., 1984). Recovery in NAA, a marker of neuronal integrity, suggests that a comparable mechanism might take place in humans. Animal models also suggest that ethanol can suppress neural progenitor cells, an effect that reversed when ethanol exposure ceased (Nixon & Crews, 2004). Such changes might be linked to reduced availability of trophic factors such as brain derived neurotrophic factor, or their receptors (Climent et al., 2002; Miller et al., 2002). Other brain changes found in animal models include damage to myelin sheaths (Phillips et al., 1991; Vrbaski & Ristic, 1985) and increased lipid peroxidation (Agar et al., 2003) which may provide an insight into the white matter loss observed in humans, and the recovery in choline on MRS with abstinence.

Of interest, studies conducted with human postmortem specimens indicate that expression of genes implicated in control of inflammation, cell survival, and myelin integrity is altered in alcoholism. One of the molecules regulating these genes is Nuclear Factor-kappa B (NF-kB). Among other things, NF-kB mediated gene transcription can alter synaptic signaling and promote cell death. NF-kB is suppressed in acute alcohol exposure, but is elevated in chronic exposure (Ökvist et al., 2007). It seems possible that alcohol-associated modification of glutamate transmission as well as accompanying oxidative stress causes intracytoplasmic release of NF-kB from its binding protein, resulting in its translocation into the cell's nucleus, and activation of genes whose downstream effects are neural dysfunction and injury. If so, abstinence from alcohol may reverse these molecular changes.

Clinical Implications and Treatment Outcome

Even though mild to moderate neuropsychological deficits that are often detected in alcoholics after 2–4 weeks of detoxification are not severe enough to warrant a diagnosis of either an Alcohol-Induced Persisting Dementia or an Alcohol-Induced Amnestic Disorder (American Psychiatric Association, 1994), these deficits can, however, have significant effects on treatment compliance, aftercare success, employment, and everyday functioning of recovering alcoholics (Abbott & Gregson, 1981; Alterman et al., 1989b; Donovan et al., 1984, 1985, 1986; Eckardt et al., 1980a; Glenn & Parsons, 1991b; Goldman, 1990; Gregson & Taylor, 1977; Guthrie & Elliott, 1980; Leber et al., 1985; McCrady & Smith, 1986; O'Leary et al., 1979; Parsons et al., 1990a; Trivedi & Raghavan, 1989).

One limitation in many inpatient alcohol and drug treatment programs is that it is difficult and time consuming to make accommodations for individual patients who might have quite different neuropsychological abilities and deficits. For example, some younger healthy alcoholic patients may be relatively normal from a neurocognitive perspective, and may be more ready to pay attention, assimilate new information (e.g., relapse prevention material), and be able to reason, problem solve, and use their intact abstracting skills to see how a number of factors have contributed to the development of their disease, and how they might make life

changes to help maintain their abstinence and to develop more adaptable behaviors. In contrast, many older alcoholics who have a number of medical complications and neuromedical risk factors may have many neuropsychological deficits that place significant limitations on their ability to utilize the standard treatment modalities for alcoholism. In a recent study, elderly alcoholics were found to experience more severe withdrawal symptoms (i.e., more cognitive impairment, disorientation and confusion, increased daytime sleepiness, weakness, cardiac disease and high blood pressure) than younger alcoholics, despite similar recent drinking history and educational experience (Brower et al., 1994). Overall, these results suggest that treatment for alcoholism may take longer in elderly patients, and interventions should target the medical comorbidity (Brower et al., 1994) as well as develop ways to circumvent the neuropsychological deficits that are often prevalent in elderly alcoholics.

A number of investigators have explored how neuropsychological test performance during inpatient treatment may predict treatment success and compliance, later relapse, and everyday functioning. Some have demonstrated that neuropsychological performance is associated or predictive of time in residence (Fals-Stewart & Schafer, 1992), relapse (Gregson & Taylor, 1977), therapists' ratings of improvement during therapy (Parsons, 1983) as well as prognosis (Leber et al., 1985), length of abstinence, treatment compliance and aftercare success, and later employment (Donovan et al., 1984, 1985, 1986; O'Leary et al., 1979; Walker et al., 1983). In one study, alcoholics who remained sober through 1 year were better educated and had higher memory scores at baseline than those alcoholics who relapsed (George et al., 1992). However, in contrast, there are a number of reports in which neuropsychological test performance is not related to treatment outcome (Alterman et al., 1990; Eckardt et al., 1988; Macciocchi et al., 1989; Prange, 1988).

Glenn and Parsons recently examined how a number of variables collected at baseline (i.e., depressive symptoms, neuropsychological test performance, psychosocial maladjustment, previous treatment, and childhood ADD symptoms) predict resumption of drinking in alcoholics 14

Pathology of Alzheimer's disease

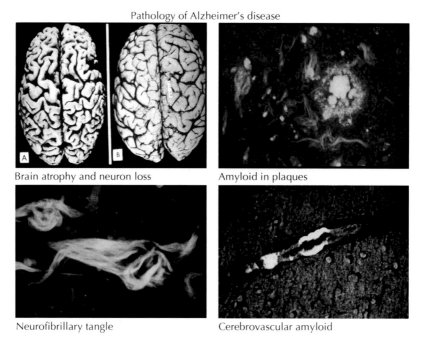

Brain atrophy and neuron loss   Amyloid in plaques

Neurofibrillary tangle   Cerebrovascular amyloid

Figure 8–1. The neuropathology of Alzheimer's disease. Grossly apparent cortical atrophy in Alzheimer's disease (Figure 1A) compared to normal aging (Figure 1B), and neocortical amyloid plaques (Figure 2), neurofibrillary tangles (Figure 3), and cerebrovascular amyloid angiopathy (Figure 4). (Images courtesy of Drs. Eliezer Masliah, Robert Terry, and Larry Hansen).

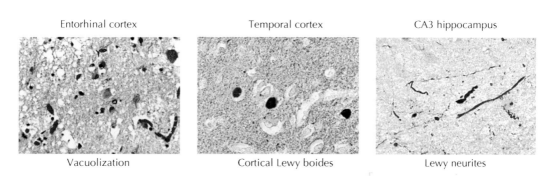

Entorhinal cortex   Temporal cortex   CA3 hippocampus

Vacuolization   Cortical Lewy boides   Lewy neurites

Figure 8–2. Histopathologic abnormalities in the limbic system and neocortex in Dementia with Lewy Bodies (DLB). The typical appearance of vacuolization in the entorhinal cortex, cortical Lewy bodies in the temporal lobe neocortex, and Lewy neurites (i.e., neurons containing abnormal alpha-synuclein filaments) in the CA3 region of the hippocampus. (Images courtesy of Dr. Eliezer Masliah).

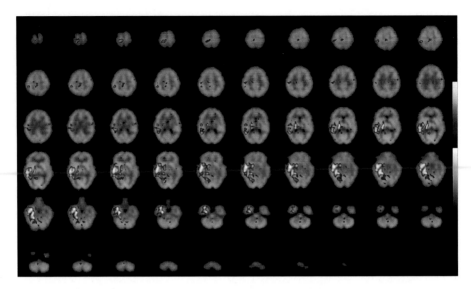

Figure 12–1. Ictal SPECT scan of a 19-year-old patient with unusual episodes of fidgeting, mumbling, and rubbing her legs. She has bilateral epileptiform activity, but the SPECT scan shows clear right temporal hyperperfusion during a seizure (radiological convention: right is on the left). Neuropsychological test results showed that she had a relatively low IQ (full-scale IQ = 68), and had difficulty learning and remembering both verbal and pictorial information. The findings suggested bilateral deficits without clear lateralizing significance.

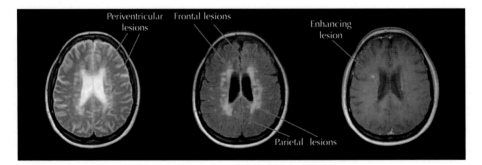

Figure 13–1. Axial MRI scans of a 42-year-old female with relapsing—remitting MS and an Expanded Disability Status Scale of 3.5. The patient's disease duration is 11 years and she is not being managed with any disease modifying therapy. From left to right: T2-weighted, FLAIR and T1-weighted post-gadolinium contrast images. Periventricular hyperintense lesions and frontoparietal lesions are noted on the T2 and FLAIR images; a gadolinium-enhancing lesion is also apparent. (Images are courtesy of Cornelia Laule, PhD, Department of Radiology, University of British Columbia MRI Research Centre).

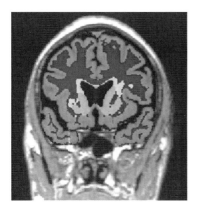 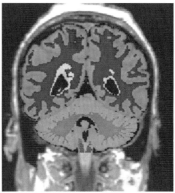

Figure 17–1. Structural morphometry in an individual infected with HIV. These two coronal sections high-light regions of abnormality in the white matter (shown in yellow), which may be related to markers of HIV disease and neurobehavioral performance. Dark blue = cortex, light blue = subcortical gray, purple = sulcal/subarachnoid CSF, red = ventricular fluid, yellow = abnormal white matter, dark gray = normal appearing white matter, light gray = cerebellum, maroon = infratentorial CSF.

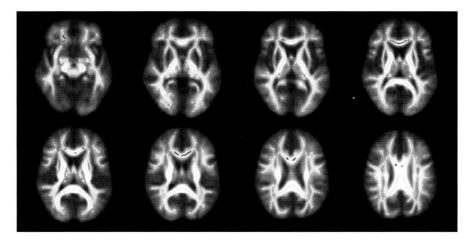

Figure 17–2. Diffusion tensor images from Gongvatana et al. (2008) showing that individuals with HIV-associated neurocognitive disorders (HAND) have lower fractional anisotropy in the anterior callosal region (shown in blue) relative to HIV-infected comparison participants without HAND. Images are presented in axial sections moving from inferior (upper left) to superior (lower right) slices.

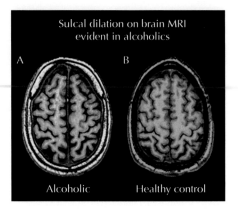

Figure 18–2. Brain MRI showing loss of brain volume in alcoholic (A) versus healthy control (B). Note reduced cortical thickness and increased sulcal volume. (From San Diego VA Alcohol Study, I. Grant, P.I.)

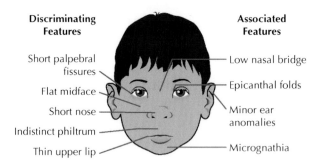

Figure 18–4. Cartoon showing some typical facial features in child with fetal alcohol syndrome. (Modified from Ann Streissguth, PhD, University of Washington and Edward Riley, PhD, San Diego State University. Courtesy of Dr. Riley.)

Corpus Callosum Abnormalities

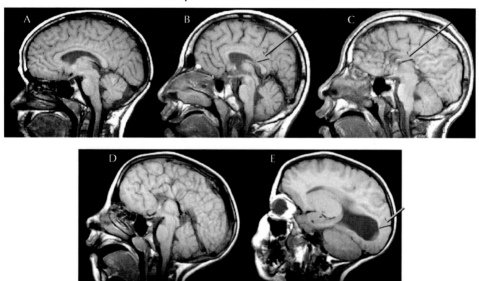

Figure 18–5. One anomaly that has been seen in FAS is agenesis, or absence, of the corpus callosum. While not common, it occurs in FAS cases (~6%) more frequently than in the general population (0.1%) or in the developmentally disabled population (2%–3%). In fact it has been suggested that FAS may be the most common cause of agenesis of the corpus callosum.

The top left MRI scan (A), is a control brain. The other images are from children with FAS. In the top middle the corpus callosum is present, but it is very thin at the posterior section of the brain (B, arrow). In the upper right the corpus callosum is essentially missing (C, arrow). The bottom two pictures (D, E) are from a 9-year old girl with FAS. She has agenesis of the corpus callosum and the large dark area in the back of her brain (E, arrow) above the cerebellum is a condition known as colpocephaly. It is essentially empty space. (Courtesy Edward Riley, PhD, San Diego State University).

MR improvement with abstinence

A B

Case 1

Baseline 8 months abstinence

C D

Case 2

Baseline Relapsed after 10 months

Figure 18–6. MRI brain images of two cases. Case 1 was abstinent 1 week (A) and rescanned after 8 months of continued abstinence (B). Note lessening prominence of suci and ventricles in B. Case 2 was abstinent 30 days (C) and rescanned at 10 months after relapsing in the interim. Note tissue loss in D, particularly in periventricular white matter, cerebellar vermis, and surrounding IV ventricle. (Derived from images shown in Gazdzinski, et al. [2005], *Drug and Alcohol Dependence, 78*, 263–273. Reprinted with permission from Elsevier.)

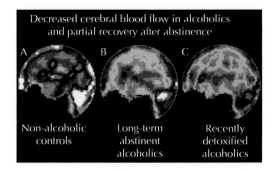

Figure 18–7. Color coded images representing intensity of uptake of the tracer HMPAO during a cognitive activation task in a nonalcoholic control (A), alcoholic abstinent over 18 months (B), and a recently detoxified alcoholic (C) abstinent 4 weeks. Cooler colors indicate less perfusion, especially in frontal areas in C versus A. Case B has values intermediate between A and C, suggesting recovery. (From Grant, Alhassoon, et al., San Diego VA Alcohol Study.)

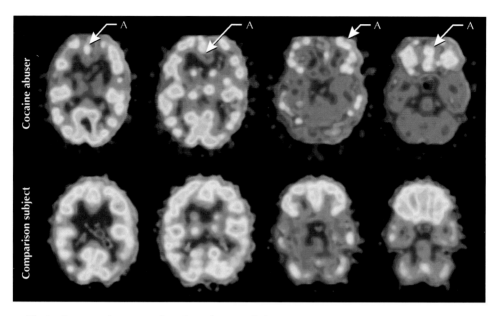

Figure 19–1. Cocaine abusers tend to show decreased glucose metabolism in areas of prefrontal cortex (A) relative to healthy controls. (Image courtesy of Dr. Nora Volkow.)

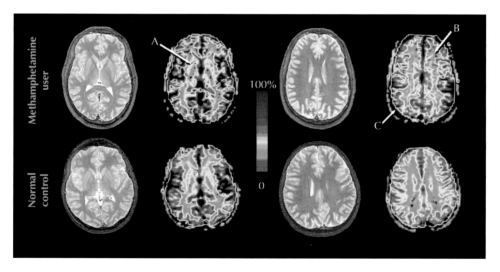

Figure 19–2. Decreased rCBF in putamen (A) and frontal (B) white matter of a methamphetamine user compared to a healthy control. Increased rCBF in a methamphetamine user compared to a healthy control in parietal brain regions (C). (Image courtesy of Dr. Linda Chang.)

a. High MeHg and High PCB exposure

b. Low MeHg and Low PCB exposure

c. Subtraction of Activation of the Low Exposure Group from the High Exposure Group

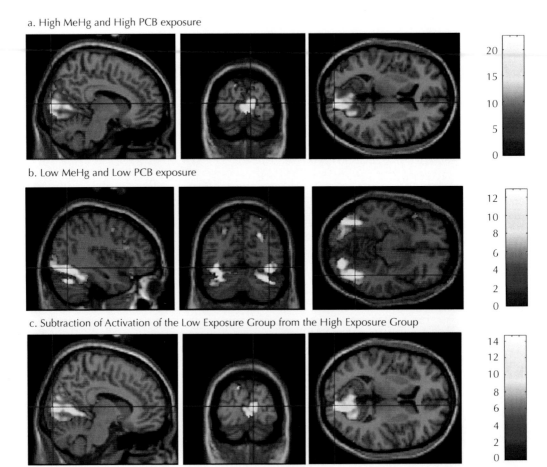

Figure 20–1. Activation during a Task of Photic Stimulation (a) The figure shows activation for the high exposure group during a task of photic stimulation predominantly in the primary occipital cortex bilaterally (Brodmann's area 17). (b) The low exposure group shows bilateral activation primarily in the occipital association cortex (Brodmann's areas 18 and 19). (c) When the two groups are compared there is greater activation in the primary occipital cortex in the high exposure group than the low exposure group, representing recruitment of different neuronal resources in the two groups.

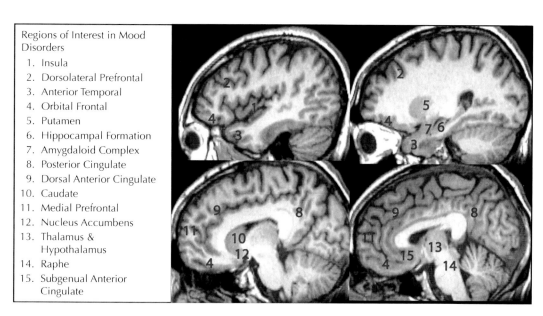

Figure 22–1. Frequent Regions of Interest Reported in Structural and Imaging Studies Relevant to Understanding Depression and Related Psychiatric Disorders. Numbers indicate center of foci, although some foci are collapsed across the left-right axis to reduce the number of images necessary to display these foci.

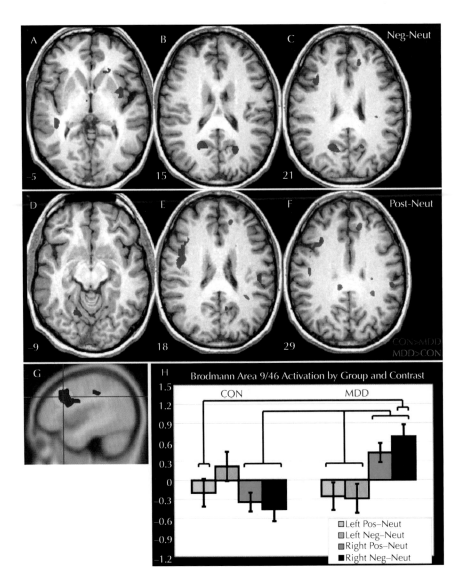

Figure 22–2. Activation to emotionally salient stimuli for those with Major Depressive Disorder (MDD, $n = 13$) compared to control (CON, $n = 15$) participants. Mean Hamilton Depression Rating Scale-17 Item score for the MDD group was 19.2 (SD = 7.6). The Emotion Word Stimulus Test is nine blocks each of positive (Pos), Negative (Neg) and Neutral (Neut) words (from the Affective Norms for Emotional Words set; Bradley and Lang, 1999) presented to participants during 3 Tesla functional MRI (GE Scanner). Images were analyzed with Statistical Parametric Mapping 2 (SPM2; Friston, 1996, thresholds $p<.001$, minimum cluster size = 120 mm³) and Region of Interest (ROI) posthoc analyses were conducted using the MARSBAR tool from SPM2 (Brett et al., 2002). Panels A–F (radiological orientation) represent group differences with red indicating CON>MDD and blue indicating MDD>CON. Panels A–C illustrate group comparisons for Neg-Neut and panels D–F represent contrasts for Pos-Neut. There was an area of increased activation for both contrasts, MDD>CON in right middle frontal gyrus (MFG—Brodmann area 9/46, Panels C, F) that was further explored in posthoc analyses. Panel G illustrates the spherical ROI created in the right MFG (in green). An identical spherical ROI was created in the left MFG to test the laterality theory of MDD. The theory states that there will be increased activation in right MFG for Neg-Neut and decreased activation in left MFG for Pos-Neut in MDD compared to CON (Davidson, 2002). This theory is not supported (Panel H bars) with increased right MFG activation for both emotion contrasts (MDD>CON: left bar set = CON; right bar set = MDD). Left MFG was not different between groups in any contrast. We interpret these findings as increased emotion regulatory demand for emotional words in MDD irrespective of Pos or Neg valence.

months later (Glenn & Parsons, 1991b; Parsons et al., 1990a). They found that alcoholics who later resumed drinking performed significantly worse at baseline on all five factors that explained 27% of the variance. Overall, 75% of the sample was correctly classified, and depressive symptoms at baseline were discovered to be the most predictive of relapse. When they excluded neuropsychological test performance from the model, the classification rate was slightly reduced to 72.5% (Glenn & Parsons, 1991b). These results provide further support that neuropsychological test performance by itself does not significantly predict later relapse or treatment success. We believe that further studies are needed to determine how neuropsychological test performance may be more of a mediator or intervening variable in a model that also incorporates measures of social support, affective symptomatology, and measures of everyday functioning when trying to predict treatment compliance, success, and everyday functioning.

The potential benefits of cognitive stimulation and remediation during treatment, an area that Goldman and his colleagues have advanced (Forsberg & Goldman, 1987; Roehrich & Goldman, 1993), deserves further study. For example, Roehrich and Goldman (1993) reported that alcoholics who received ecologically relevant or neuropsychological remediation during inpatient treatment showed more cognitive improvements over the course of their treatment, decreased affective symptomatology, a decline in their self-reported cognitive complaints, and were able to learn more information on relapse prevention.

Summary

Alcoholism can be associated with brain injury, and this can be reflected in persisting neurocognitive impairment, and associated changes on brain imaging. Disturbances in abstraction-executive abilities are the most consistently reported NP changes, along with reduced verbal and nonverbal learning and perceptual–motor deficits. Language skills tend to be preserved, and accelerated forgetting is uncommon except in cases of Wernicke–Korsakoff syndrome. Other functional changes include reduced regional brain blood flow, especially in

the frontal lobes, and reduced NAA, a metabolite reflecting neuronal integrity on MR spectroscopy. Changes in choline and myoinositol on MRS may reflect white matter injury and inflammatory changes, and these are related to NP performance. Similarly there may be electrophysiological changes, such as reduced P300 evoked potential, perhaps reflecting frontostriatal dysfunction. Structural imaging can reveal reduction in gray and white matter volumes on in vivo MRI, with some studies particularly noting changes in frontal and cerebellar structures. With regard to neuropathology both neuronal injury, and in advanced cases, neuronal loss are evident, with frontal and cerebellar pathology being most prominent. In Wernicke–Korsakoff cases, additional volume loss can be noted in mamillary bodies, hippocampus, and other diencephalic structures. Loss of dendritic arbor may be one of the substrates for the NP impairment. The molecular mechanisms that underlie alcohol's effect are not well understood, but may involve excitotoxic cascades, oxidative stress, and other changes converging to disrupt the balance of neurotrophic and cell injurious pathways. For example, the transcriptional factor NF-kappa B may be released, altering gene expression and initiating apoptotic cascades. Downregulation of genes controlling cytoskeleton and myelin integrity have been suggested as mechanisms. It should be noted that many alcoholics, especially those under 50 without major comorbidities, do not manifest NP deficits at any time. The mechanisms underlying host resistance or vulnerability to effects of alcohol on the brain are largely unstudied. The picture is different for the developing brain, and studies on fetal alcohol exposure document permanent brain injury in cases of prenatal exposure.

Important to recognize is the fact that NP deficits and other brain changes observed in alcoholics who have been recently detoxified are not necessarily permanent. Indeed, neuropsychological recovery occurs throughout the first year of abstinence, and perhaps longer. This brain recovery is observed on NP testing, structural and functional imaging, as well as in electrophysiological indicators. Such recovery may be less complete in older alcoholics, and those with comorbidities such as prior mild head injuries, withdrawal seizures, medical conditions (e.g., HCV infection; liver disease), and other concurrent substance abuse. The mechanisms underlying recovery are not understood; however animal models suggest that dendritic rearborization may be a factor. Thus, we need to view effects of alcoholism on the brain as a dynamic process, whose outcomes vary from no injury in the first place, to reversible injury in the majority of cases of adult alcoholism. Whether the recovery is complete or partial depends on a range of host factors, including developmental stage, conditions of use, and comorbidities.

Acknowledgment

Parts of the work referred to in this chapter were supported by a Department of Veterans Affairs Merit Award, "Alcohol Abuse and Neuropsychological Impairment" (I. Grant, P.I.). The authors wish to acknowledge the contributions of Dr. Tor Løberg to earlier versions of this chapter. The authors thank Ms. Felicia Roston for her editorial assistance in the preparation of this chapter.

References

Abbott, M. W., & Gregson, R. A. M. (1981). Cognitive dysfunction in the prediction of relapse in alcoholics. *Journal of Studies on Alcohol, 42,* 230–243.

Acker, C. (1985). Performance of female alcoholics on neuropsychological testing. *Alcohol and Alcoholism, 20,* 379–386.

Acker, C., Jacobson, R. R., & Lishman, W. A. (1987). Memory and ventricular size in alcoholics. *Psychological Medicine, 17,* 343–348.

Acker, W., Aps, E. J., Majumdar, S. K., Shaw, G. K., & Thomson, A. D. (1982). The relationship between brain and liver damage in chronic alcoholic patients. *Journal of Neurology, Neurosurgery and Psychiatry, 45,* 984–987.

Adams, K. M., Gilman, S., Koeppe, R. A., Kluin, K. J., Brunberg, J. A., Dede, D., et al. (1993). Neuropsychological deficits are correlated with frontal hypometabolism in positron emission tomography studies of older alcoholic patients. *Alcoholism: Clinical and Experimental Research, 17,* 205–210.

Adams, K. M., & Grant, I. (1984). Failure of nonlinear models of drinking history variables to predict neuropsychological performance in alcoholics. *American Journal of Psychiatry, 141,* 663–667.

Adams, K. M., & Grant, I. (1986). Influence of premorbid risk factors on neuropsychological performance in alcoholics. *Journal of Clinical and Experimental Neuropsychology, 8,* 362–370.

Adams, K. M., Grant, I., & Reed, R. (1980). Neuropsychology in alcoholic men in their late thirties: One-year follow-up. *American Journal of Psychiatry, 137,* 928–931.

Agar, E., Demir, S., Amanvermez, R., Bosnak, M., Ayyildiz, M., & Celik, C. (2003). The effects of ethanol consumption on the lipid peroxidation and glutathione levels in the right and left brains of rats. *International Journal of Neuroscience, 13,* 1643–1652.

Akshoomoff, N. A., Delis, D. C., & Kiefner, M. G. (1989). Block constructions of chronic alcoholic and unilateral brain-damaged patients: A test of the right hemisphere vulnerability hypothesis of alcoholism. *Archives of Clinical Neuropsychology, 4,* 275–281.

Albert, M., Butters, N., Rogers, S., Pressman, J., & Geller, A. (1982). A preliminary report: Nutritional levels and cognitive performance in chronic alcohol abusers. *Drug and Alcohol Dependence, 9,* 131–142.

Albert, M., Butters, N., Rogers, S., Pressman, J., & Geller, A. (1983). Nutritional links between cognitive performance and alcohol misuse. *Digest of Alcoholism Theory and Application, 2,* 44–47.

Alexander, S., Kerr, M. E., Yonas, H., & Marion, D. W. (2004). The effects of admission alcohol level on cerebral blood flow and outcomes after severe traumatic brain injury. *Journal of Neurotrauma, 21*(5), 575–583.

Alterman, A. I., Bridges, K. R., & Tarter, R. E. (1986). The influence of both drinking and familial risk statuses on cognitive functioning of social drinkers. *Alcoholism: Clinical and Experimental Research, 10,* 448–451.

Alterman, A. I., & Gerstley, L. J. (1986). Predictive validity of four factors derived from an "Hyperactivity/MBD" questionnaire. *Drug and Alcohol Dependence, 18,* 259–271.

Alterman, A. I., Gerstley, L. J., Goldstein, G., & Tarter, R. E. (1987). Comparisons of the cognitive functioning of familial and nonfamilial alcoholics. *Journal of Studies on Alcohol, 48,* 425–429.

Alterman, A. I., Goldstein, G., Shelly, C., Bober, B., & Tarter, R. E. (1985b). The impact of mild head injury on neuropsychological capacity in chronic alcoholics. *International Journal of Neuroscience, 28,* 155–162.

Alterman, A. I., & Hall, J. G. (1989). Effects of social drinking and familial alcoholism risk on cognitive functioning: Null findings. *Alcoholism: Clinical and Experimental Research, 13,* 799–803.

Alterman, A. I., Holahan, J. M., Baughman, T. G., & Michels, S. (1989b). Predictors of alcoholics' acquisition of treatment-related knowledge. *Journal of Substance Abuse Treatment, 6,* 49–53.

Alterman, A. I., Kushner, H., & Holahan, J. M. (1990). Cognitive functioning and treatment outcome in alcoholics. *Journal of Nervous and Mental Disease, 178,* 494–499.

Alterman, A. I., & McLellan, A. T. (1986). A factor-analytic study of Tarter's "Hyperactivity–MBD" questionnaire. *Addictive Behaviors, 11,* 287–294.

Alterman, A. I., Searles, J. S., & Hall, J. G. (1989a). Failure to find differences in drinking behavior as a function of familial risk for alcoholism: A replication. *Journal of Abnormal Psychology, 98,* 50–53.

Alterman, A. I., & Tarter, R. E. (1985). Relationship between familial alcoholism and head injury. *Journal of Studies on Alcohol, 46,* 256–258.

Alterman, A. I., Tarter, R. E., Baughman, T. G., Bober, B. A., & Fabian, S. A. (1985a). Differentiation of alcoholics high and low in childhood hyperactivity. *Drug and Alcohol Dependence, 15,* 111–121.

American Psychiatric Association. (1994). *Diagnostic and statistical manual of mental disorders* (4th ed.). Washington, DC: American Psychiatric Association.

Angelini, G., Bogetto, F., Borio, R., Meluzzi, A., Mucci, P., Patria, D., et al. (1990). Clinico-nosographic remarks on the relationship between depression and alcoholism in a population of 450 hospitalized alcoholics. *Minerva Psichiatrica, 31,* 41–45.

Anthenelli, R. M., & Schuckit, M. A. (1993). Affective and anxiety disorders and alcohol and drug dependence: Diagnosis and treatment. *Journal of Addictive Diseases, 12,* 73–87.

Archibald, S. L., Fennema-Notestine, C., Gamst, A., Riley, E. P., Mattson, S. N., & Jernigan, T. L. (2001). Brain dysmorphology in individuals with severe prenatal alcohol exposure. *Developmental Medicine & Child Neurology, 43*(3), 148–154.

Arendt, T., Bigl, V., Arendt, A., & Tennstedt, A. (1983). Loss of neurons in the nucleus basilis of Meynert in Alzheimer's disease, paralysis agitans and Korsakoff's disease. *Acta Neuropathologica, 61,* 101–108.

Arria, A. M., Tarter, R. E., Kabene, M. A., Laird, S. B., Moss, H., & Van Thiel, D. H. (1991a). The role of cirrhosis in memory functioning of alcoholics. *Alcoholism: Clinical and Experimental Research, 15,* 932–937.

Arria, A. M., Tarter, R. E., Starzl, T. E., & Van Thiel, D. H. (1991b). Improvement in cognitive functioning of alcoholics following orthotopic liver transplantation. *Alcoholism: Clinical and Experimental Research, 15,* 956–962.

Artmann, H., Gall, M. V., Hacker, H., & Herrlich, J. (1981). Reversible enlargement of cerebral spinal fluid spaces in chronic alcoholics. *American Journal of Neuroradiology, 2,* 23–27.

Ayers, J., Ruff, C. F., & Templer, D. I. (1976). Alcoholism, cigarette smoking, coffee drinking and extraversion. *Journal of Studies on Alcohol, 37,* 983–985.

Ayers, J. L., Templer, D. I., Ruff, C. F., & Barthlow, V. L. (1978). Trail making test improvement in abstinent alcoholics. *Journal of Studies on Alcohol, 39,* 1627–1629.

Barron, J. H., & Russell, E. W. (1992). Fluidity theory and neuropsychological impairment in alcoholism. *Archives of Clinical Neuropsychology, 7,* 175–188.

Bartsch, A. J., Homola, G., Biller, A., Smith, S. M., Weijers, H. G., Wiesbeck, G. A., et al. (2007). Manifestations of early brain recovery associated with abstinence from alcoholism. *Brain, 130* (Pt 1), 36–47.

Bates, M. E., & Pandina, R. J. (1992). Familial alcoholism and premorbid cognitive deficit: A failure to replicate subtype differences. *Journal of Studies on Alcohol, 53,* 320–327.

Bates, M. E., & Tracy, J. I. (1990). Cognitive functioning in young "social drinkers": Is there impairment to detect? *Journal of Abnormal Psychology, 99,* 242–249.

Bauer, L. O. (1994). Electroencephalographic and autonomic predictors of relapse in alcohol-dependent patients. *Alcoholism: Clinical and Experimental Research, 18,* 760–775.

Bean, K. L., & Karasievich, G. O. (1975). Psychological test results at three stages of inpatient alcoholism treatment. *Journal of Studies on Alcohol, 36,* 838–852.

Beatty, W. W., Bailly, R. C., & Fisher, L. (1989). Korsakoff-like amnesic syndrome in a patient with anorexia and vomiting. *International Journal of Clinical Neuropsychology, 11,* 55–65.

Beatty, W. W., Katzung, V. M., Nixon, S. J., & Moreland, V. J. (1993). Problem-solving deficits in alcoholics: Evidence from the California Card Sorting Test. *Journal of Studies on Alcohol, 54,* 687–692.

Becker, J. T., Butters, N., Hermann, A., & D'Angelo, N. (1983). Learning to associate names and faces: Impaired acquisition on an ecologically relevant memory task by male alcoholics. *Journal of Nervous and Mental Disease, 171,* 617–623.

Becker, J. T., Furman, J. M., Panisset, M., & Smith, C. (1990). Characteristics of the memory loss of a patient with Wernicke-Korsakoff's syndrome without alcoholism. *Neuropsychologia, 28,* 171–179.

Begleiter, H., & Porjesz, B. (1990). Neuroelectric processes in individuals at risk for alcoholism. *Alcohol and Alcoholism, 25,* 251–256.

Begleiter, H., & Porjesz, B. (1999). What is inherited in the predisposition toward alcoholism? A proposed model. *Alcoholism: Clinical and Experimental Research*, *23*(7), 1125–1135.

Begleiter, H., Porjesz, B., Bihari, B., & Kissin, B. (1984). Event-related brain potentials in boys at risk for alcoholism. *Science, 225*, 1493–1496.

Begleiter, H., Porjesz, B., & Chou, C. L. (1981). Auditory brainstem potentials in chronic alcoholics. *Science, 211*, 1064–1066.

Begleiter, H., Porjesz, B., Rawlings, R., & Eckardt, M. (1987). Auditory recovery function and P3 in boys at high risk for alcoholism. *Alcohol, 4*, 315–321.

Begleiter, H., Porjesz, B., & Tenner, M. (1980). Neuroradiological and neurophysiological evidence of brain deficits in chronic alcoholics. *Acta Psychiatrica Scandinavica, 62*, 3–13.

Berglund, M., Hagstadius, S., Risberg, J., Johanson, T. M., Bliding, A., & Mubrin, Z. (1987). Normalization of regional cerebral blood flow in alcoholics during the first 7 weeks of abstinence. *Acta Psychiatrica Scandinavica, 75*, 202–208.

Berglund, M., Leijonquist, H., & Horlen, M. (1977). Prognostic significance and reversibility of cerebral dysfunction in alcoholics. *Journal of Studies on Alcohol, 38*, 1761–1770.

Bergman, H. (1985). Cognitive deficits and morphological cerebral changes in a random sample of social drinkers. *Recent Developments in Alcoholism, 3*, 265–276.

Bergman, H. (1987). Brain dysfunction related to alcoholism: Some results from the KARTAD Project. In O. A. Parsons, N. Butters, and P. E. Nathan (Eds.), *Neuropsychology of alcoholism: Implications for diagnosis and treatment* (pp. 21–44). New York: Guilford Press.

Bergman, H., Axelsson, G., Idestrom, C. M., Borg, S., Hindmarsh, T., Makower, J., et al. (1983). Alcohol consumption, neuropsychological status and computer-tomographic findings in a random sample of men and women from the general population. *Pharmacology, Biochemistry, and Behavior, 18*, 501–505.

Bergman, H., Borg, S., Hindmarsh, T., Idestrom, C. M., & Mutzell, S. (1980a). Computed tomography of the brain and neuropsychological assessment of male alcoholic patients and a random sample from the general male population. *Acta Psychiatrica Scandinavica, 286*(Suppl.), 77–88.

Bergman, H., Borg, S., Hindmarsh, T., Idestrom, C. M., & Mutzell, S. (1980b). Computed tomography of the brain, clinical examination and neuropsychological assessment of a random sample of men from the general population. *Acta Psychiatrica Scandinavica, 286*(Suppl.), 47–56.

Bergman, H., Borg, S., Hindmarsh, T., Idestrom, C. M., & Mutzell, S. (1980c). Computed-tomography of the brain and neuropsychological assessment of alcoholic patients. *Advances in Experimental Medicine and Biology, 126*, 771–786.

Berman, S. M., Whipple, S. C., Fitch, R. J., & Noble, E. P. (1993). P3 in young boys as a predictor of adolescent substance use. *Alcohol, 10*, 69–76.

Bertera, J. H., & Parsons, O. A. (1978). Impaired visual search in alcoholics. *Alcoholism: Clinical and Experimental Research, 2*, 9–14.

Blansjaar, B. A., & van Dijk, J. G. (1992). Korsakoff minus Wernicke syndrome. *Alcohol and Alcoholism, 27*, 435–437.

Blansjaar, B. A., Vielvoye, G. J., van Dijk, J. G., & Rijnders, R. J. (1992). Similar brain lesions in alcoholics and Korsakoff patients: MRI, psychometric and clinical findings. *Clinical Neurology and Neurosurgery, 94*, 197–203.

Blass, J. P., & Gibson, G. E. (1977). Abnormality of a thiamine-requiring enzyme in patients with Wernicke–Korsakoff syndrome. *New England Journal of Medicine, 297*, 1367–1370.

Blusewicz, M. J., Dustman, R. E., Schenkenberg, T., & Beck, E. C. (1977a). Neuropsychological correlates of chronic alcoholism and aging. *Journal of Nervous and Mental Disease, 165*, 348–355.

Blusewicz, M. J., Schenkenberg, T., Dustman, R. E., & Beck, E. C. (1977b). WAIS performance in young normal, young alcoholic, and elderly normal groups: An evaluation of organicity and mental aging indices. *Journal of Clinical Psychology, 33*, 1149–1153.

Bowden, S. C. (1987). Brain impairment in social drinkers? No cause for concern. *Alcoholism: Clinical and Experimental Research, 11*, 407–410.

Bowden, S. C. (1990). Separating cognitive impairment in neurologically asymptomatic alcoholism from Wernicke–Korsakoff syndrome: Is the neuropsychological distinction justified? *Psychological Bulletin, 107*, 355–366.

Braggio, J. T., Pishkin, V., Parsons, O. A., Fishkin, S. M., & Tassey, J. R. (1991). Differences between essential and reactive alcoholics on tests of neuropsychological functioning and affect. *Psychological Reports, 69*, 1131–1136.

Brandt, J., Butters, N., Ryan, C., & Bayog, R. (1983). Cognitive loss and recovery in long-term alcohol abusers. *Archives of General Psychiatry, 40*, 435–442.

Brewer, C., & Perrett, L. (1971). Brain damage due to alcohol consumption: An airencephalographic, psychometric and electroencephalographic study. *British Journal of Addiction, 66*, 170–182.

Brooks, N., Symington, C., Beattie, A., Campsie, L., Bryden, J., & McKinlay, W. (1989). Alcohol and other predictors of cognitive recovery after severe head injury. *Brain Injury, 3*, 235–246.

Brower, K. J., Mudd, S., Blow, F. C., Young, J. P., & Hill, E. M. (1994). Severity and treatment of alcohol withdrawal in elderly versus younger patients. *Alcoholism: Clinical and Experimental Research, 18*, 196–201.

Brown, S. A., Inaba, R. K., Gillin, J. C., Schuckit, M. A., Stewart, M. A., & Irwin, M. R. (1995). Alcoholism and affective disorder: Clinical course of depressive symptoms. *American Journal of Psychiatry, 152*, 45–52.

Brown, S. A., Irwin, M., & Schuckit, M. A. (1991). Changes in anxiety among abstinent male alcoholics. *Journal of Studies on Alcohol, 52*, 55–61.

Brown, S. A., & Schuckit, M. A. (1988). Changes in depression among abstinent alcoholics. *Journal of Studies on Alcohol, 49*, 412–417.

Burger, M. C., Botwinick, J., & Storandt, M. (1987). Aging, alcoholism, and performance on the Luria-Nebraska Neuropsychological Battery. *Journal of Gerontology, 42*, 69–72.

Butters, N., & Cermak, L. S. (1980). *Alcoholic Korsakoff's syndrome: An information processing approach to amnesia.* New York: Academic Press.

Butters, N., Cermak, L. S., Montgomery, K., & Adinolfi, A. (1977). Some comparisons of the memory and visuoperceptive deficits of chronic alcoholics and patients with Korsakoff's disease. *Alcoholism: Clinical and Experimental Research, 1*, 73–80.

Butters, N., & Granholm, E. (1987). The continuity hypothesis: Some conclusions and their implications for the etiology and neuropathology of alcoholic Korsakoff's syndrome. In O. A. Parsons, N. Butters, and P. E. Nathan (Eds.), *Neuropsychology of alcoholism: Implications for diagnosis and treatment* (pp. 176–206). New York: Guilford Press.

Butters, N., & Salmon, D. P. (1986). Etiology and neuropathology of alcoholic Korsakoff's syndrome: New findings and speculations. In I. Grant (Ed.), *Neuropsychiatric correlates of alcoholism* (pp. 61–108). Washington, DC: American Psychiatric Press.

Butters, N., Salmon, D. P., Cullum, C. M., Cairns, P., Tröster, A. I., Jacobs, D., et al. (1988). Differentiation of amnesic and demented patients with the Wechsler Memory Scale-Revised. *The Clinical Neuropsychologist, 2*, 133–148.

Cadaveira, F., Corominas, M., Rodríguez Holguín, S., Sánchez-Turet, M., & Grau, C. (1994). Reversibility of brain-stem evoked potential abnormalities in abstinent chronic alcoholics: one year follow-up. *Electroencephalography and Clinical Neurophysiology, 90*(6), 450–455.

Cairney, S., Clough, A., Jaragba, M., & Maruff, P. (2007). Cognitive impairment in Aboriginal people with heavy episodic patterns of alcohol use. *Addiction, 102*(6), 909–915.

Cala, L. A., & Mastaglia, F. L. (1981). Computerized tomography in chronic alcoholics. *Alcoholism: Clinical and Experimental Research, 5*, 283–294.

Campbell, W. G., & Hodgins, D. C. (1993). Alcohol-related blackouts in a medical practice. *American Journal of Drug and Alcohol Abuse, 19*, 369–376.

Cardenas, V. A., Studholme, C., Gazdzinski, S., Durazzo, T. C., & Meyerhoff, D. J. (2007). Deformation-based morphometry of brain changes in alcohol dependence and abstinence. *Neuroimage, 34*(3), 879–887.

Carey, K. B., & Maisto, S. A. (1987). Effect of a change in drinking pattern on the cognitive function of female social drinkers. *Journal of Studies on Alcohol, 48*, 236–242.

Carlen, P. L., & Wilkinson, D. A. (1980). Alcoholic brain damage and reversible deficits. *Acta Psychiatrica Scandinavica, 286*(Suppl.), 103–118.

Carlen, P. L., & Wilkinson, D. A. (1983). Assessment of neurological dysfunction and recovery in alcoholics: CT scanning and other techniques. *Substance and Alcohol Actions/Misuse, 4*, 191–197.

Carlen, P. L., & Wilkinson, D. A. (1987). Reversibility of alcohol-related brain damage: Clinical and experimental observations. *Acta Medica Scandinavica, 717*(Suppl.), 19–26.

Carlen, P. L., Wilkinson, D. A., Wortzman, G., & Holgate, R. (1984). Partially reversible cerebral atrophy and functional improvement in recently abstinent alcoholics. *Le Journal Canadien des Sciences Neurologiques, 11*, 441–446.

Carlin, A. S. (1986). Neuropsychological consequences of drug abuse. In I. Grant and K. M. Adams (Eds.), *Neuropsychological assessment of neuropsychiatric disorders* (pp. 478–497). New York: Oxford University Press.

Carlin, A. S., Stauss, F. F., Adams, K. M., & Grant, I. (1978). The prediction of neuropsychological impairment in polydrug abusers. *Addictive Behaviors, 3*, 5–12.

Caruso, K., & ten Bensel, R. (1993). Fetal alcohol syndrome and fetal alcohol effects: The University of Minnesota experience. *Minnesota Medicine, 76*, 25–29.

Caspari, D., Trabert, W., Heinz, G., Lion, N., Henkes, H., & Huber, G. (1993). The pattern of regional cerebral blood flow during alcohol withdrawal: A single photon emission tomography study with 99mTc-HMPAO. *Acta Psychiatrica Scandinavica, 87*, 414–417.

Cermak, L. S., & Ryback, R. S. (1976). Recovery of verbal short-term memory in alcoholics. *Journal of Studies on Alcohol, 37*, 46–52.

Chandler, B. C., & Parsons, O. A. (1977). Altered hemispheric functioning under alcohol. *Journal of Studies on Alcohol, 38*, 381–391.

Chaney, E. F., O'Leary, M. R., Fehrenbach, P. A., & Donovan, D. (1980). Cognitive deficit in middle-aged alcoholics. *Drug and Alcohol Dependence, 6,* 219–226.

Chanraud, S., Martelli, C., Delain, F., Kostogianni, N., Douaud, G., Aubin, H. J., et al. (2007). Brain morphometry and cognitive performance in detoxified alcohol-dependents with preserved psychosocial functioning. *Neuropsychopharmacology, 32*(2), 429–438.

Chelune, G. J., & Parker, J. B. (1981). Neuropsychological deficits associated with chronic alcohol abuse. *Clinical Psychology Review, 1,* 181–195.

Chick, J. D., Smith, M. A., Engleman, H. M., Kean, D. M., Mander, A. J., Douglas, R. H. B., et al. (1989). Magnetic resonance imaging of the brain in alcoholics: Cerebral atrophy, lifetime alcohol consumption, and cognitive deficits. *Alcoholism: Clinical and Experimental Research, 13,* 512–518.

Chu, N. S. (1985). Computed tomographic correlates of auditory brainstem responses in alcoholics. *Journal of Neurology, Neurosurgery and Psychiatry, 48,* 348–353.

Chu, N. S., Squires, K. C., & Starr, A. (1982). Auditory brain stem responses in chronic alcoholic patients. *Electroencephalography and Clinical Neurophysiology, 54,* 418–425.

Claiborn, J. M., & Greene, R. L. (1981). Neuropsychological changes in recovering men alcoholics. *Journal of Studies on Alcohol, 42,* 757–765.

Clark, D. C., Pisani, V. D., Aagesen, C. A., Sellers, D., & Fawcett, J. (1984). Primary affective disorder, drug abuse, and neuropsychological impairment in sober alcoholics. *Alcoholism: Clinical and Experimental Research, 8,* 399–404.

Clarke, J., & Haughton, H. (1975). A study of intellectual impairment and recovery rates in heavy drinkers in Ireland. *British Journal of Psychiatry, 126,* 178–184.

Climent, E., Pascual, M., Renau-Piqueras, J., & Guerri, C. (2002). Ethanol exposure enhances cell death in the developing cerebral cortex: role of brain-derived neurotrophic factor and its signaling pathways. *Journal of Neuroscience Research, 68*(2), 213–225.

Cloninger, C. R. (1987). Neurogenetic adaptive mechanisms in alcoholism. *Science, 236,* 410–416

Cohen, H. L., Porjesz, B., & Begleiter, H. (1991). EEG characteristics in males at risk for alcoholism. *Alcoholism: Clinical and Experimental Research, 15,* 858–861.

Cole, M., Winkelman, M. D., Morris, J. C., Simon, J. E., & Boyd, T. A. (1992). Thalamic amnesia: Korsakoff syndrome due to left thalamic infarction. *Journal of Neurological Sciences, 110,* 62–67.

Conry, J. (1990). Neuropsychological deficits in fetal alcohol syndrome and fetal alcohol effects. *Alcoholism: Clinical and Experimental Research, 14,* 650–655.

Costa, L., & Bauer, L. (1997). Quantitative electroencephalographic differences associated with alcohol, cocaine, heroin and dual-substance dependence. *Drug Alcohol Dependence, 46*(1–2), 87–93.

Courville, C. B. (1955). *Effects of alcohol on the nervous system of man.* Los Angeles: San Lucas Press.

Coutin-Churchman, P., Añez, Y., Uzcátegui, M., Alvarez, L., Vergara, F., Méndez, L., et al. (2003). Quantitative spectral analysis of EEG in psychiatry revisited: drawing signs out of numbers in a clinical setting. *Clinical Neurophysiology, 114,* 2294–2306.

Coutin-Churchman, P., Moreno, R., Añez, Y., & Vergara, F. (2006). Clinical correlates of quantitative EEG alterations in alcoholic patients. *Clinical Neurophysiology, 117*(4), 740–751.

Crews, F. T., Braun, C. J., Hoplight, B., Switzer, R. C. 3rd, & Knapp, D. J. (2000). Binge ethanol consumption causes differential brain damage in young adolescent rats compared with adult rats. *Alcoholism: Clinical and Experimental Research, 24*(11), 1712–1723.

Crews, F. T., Buckley, T., Dodd, P. R., Ende, G., Foley, N., Harper, C., et al. (2005). Alcoholic neurobiology: changes in dependence and recovery. *Alcoholism: Clinical and Experimental Research, 29*(8), 1504–1513.

Cutting, J. C. (1988). Alcohol cognitive impairment and aging: Still an uncertain relationship. *British Journal of Addiction, 83,* 995–997.

Cynn, V. E. (1992). Persistence and problem-solving skills in young male alcoholics. *Journal of Studies on Alcohol, 53,* 57–62.

Dally, S., Luft, A., Ponsin, J. C., Girre, C., Mamo, H., & Fournier, E. (1988). Abnormal pattern of cerebral blood flow distribution in young alcohol addicts. *British Journal of Addiction, 83,* 105–109.

de la Monte, S. M. (1988). Disproportionate atrophy of cerebral white matter in chronic alcoholics. *Archives of Neurology, 45,* 990–992.

de Obaldia, R., Leber, W. R., & Parsons, O. A. (1981). Assessment of neuropsychological functions in chronic alcoholics using a standardized version of Luria's Neuropsychological Technique. *International Journal of Neuroscience, 14,* 85–93.

de Obaldia, R., & Parsons, O. A. (1984). Relationship of neuropsychological performance to primary alcoholism and self-reported symptoms of childhood minimal brain dysfunction. *Journal of Studies on Alcohol, 45,* 386–392.

DeJong, C. A., van den Brink, W., Harteveld, F. M., & van der Wielen, E. G. (1993). Personality disorders in alcoholics and drug addicts. *Comprehensive Psychiatry, 34,* 87–94.

Desmond, J. E., Chen, S. H., DeRosa, E., Pryor, M. R., Pfefferbaum, A., & Sullivan, E. V. (2003). Increased frontocerebellar activation in alcoholics during verbal working memory: An fMRI study. *Neuroimage, 19*(4), 1510–1520.

DiFranza, J. R., & Guerrera, M. P. (1990). Alcoholism and smoking. *Journal of Studies on Alcohol, 51,* 130–135.

Dikmen, S. S., Donovan, D. M. Løberg T., Machamer, J. E., & Temkin, N. R. (1993). Alcohol use and its effects on neuropsychological outcome in head injury. *Neuropsychology, 7,* 296–305.

Donovan, D. M., Kivlahan, D. R., & Walker, R. D. (1984). Clinical limitations of neuropsychological testing in predicting treatment outcome among alcoholics. *Alcoholism: Clinical and Experimental Research, 8,* 470–475.

Donovan, D. M., Kivlahan, D. R., & Walker, R. D. (1986). Alcoholic subtypes based on multiple assessment domains: Validation against treatment outcome. *Recent Developments in Alcoholism, 4,* 207–222.

Donovan, D. M., Kivlahan, D. R., Walker, R. D., & Umlauf, R. (1985). Derivation and validation of neuropsychological clusters among men alcoholics. *Journal of Studies on Alcohol, 46,* 205–211.

Donovan, D. M., Queisser, H. R., & O'Leary, M. R. (1976). Group embedded figures test performance as a predictor of cognitive impairment among alcoholics. *International Journal of the Addictions, 11,* 725–739.

Drake, A. I., Hannay, H. J., & Gam, J. (1990). Effects of chronic alcoholism on hemispheric functioning: An examination of gender differences for cognitive and dichotic listening tasks. *Journal of Clinical and Experimental Neuropsychology, 12,* 781–797.

Drake, A. I., Jernigan, T. L., Butters, N., Shear, P. K., & Archibald, S. L. (1995). Volumetric changes on magnetic resonance imaging in chronic alcoholics: A one year follow-up. *Journal of the International Neuropsychological Society, 1,* 393–394 (Abst.).

Draper, R. J., & Manning, A. (1982). Vocabulary deficit and abstraction impairment in hospitalized alcoholics. *Psychological Medicine, 12,* 341–347.

Drejer, K., Theilgaard, A., Teasdale, T. W., Schulsinger, F., & Goodwin, D. W. (1985). A prospective study of young men at high risk for alcoholism: Neuropsychological assessment. *Alcoholism: Clinical and Experimental Research, 9,* 498–502.

Dupont, R. M., Rourke, S. B., Grant, I., Lehr, P. P., Reed, R. J., Challakere, K., et al. (1996). Single photon emission computed tomography with iodo-amphetamine-123 and neuropsychological studies in long-term abstinent alcoholics. *Psychiatry Research, 67,* 99–111.

Durand, D., Saint-Cyr, J. A., Gurevich, N., & Carlen, P. L. (1989). Ethanol-induced dendritic alterations in hippocampal granule cells. *Brain Research, 477,* 373–377.

Eckardt, M. J., & Martin, P. R. (1986). Clinical assessment of cognition in alcoholism. *Alcoholism: Clinical and Experimental Research, 10,* 123–127.

Eckardt, M. J., Parker, E. S., Noble, E. P., Feldman, D. J., & Gottschalk, L. A. (1978). Relationship between neuropsychological performance and alcohol consumption in alcoholics. *Biological Psychiatry, 13,* 551–565.

Eckardt, M. J., Parker, E. S., Noble, E. P., Pautler, C. P., & Gottschalk, L. A. (1979). Changes in neuropsychological performance during treatment for alcoholism. *Biological Psychiatry, 14,* 943–954.

Eckardt, M. J., Parker, E. S., Pautler, C. P., Noble, E. P., & Gottschalk, L. A. (1980a). Neuropsychological consequences of posttreatment drinking behavior in male alcoholics. *Psychiatry Research, 2,* 135–147.

Eckardt, M. J., Rawlings, R. R., Graubard, B. I., Faden, V., Martin, P. R., & Gottschalk, L. A. (1988). Neuropsychological performance and treatment outcome in male alcoholics. *Alcoholism: Clinical and Experimental Research, 12,* 88–93.

Eckardt, M. J., Ryback, R. S., & Pautler, C. P. (1980b). Neuropsychological deficits in alcoholic men in their mid thirties. *American Journal of Psychiatry, 137,* 932–936.

Eckardt, M. J., Stapleton, J. M., Rawlings, R. R., Davis, E. Z., & Grodin, D. M. (1995). Neuropsychological functioning in detoxified alcoholics between 18 and 35 years of age. *American Journal of Psychiatry, 152,* 53–59.

Ehlers, C. L., & Schuckit, M. A. (1990). EEG fast frequency activity in the sons of alcoholics. *Biological Psychiatry, 27,* 631–641.

Ehlers, C. L., & Schuckit, M. A. (1991). Evaluation of EEG alpha activity in sons of alcoholics. *Neuropsychopharmacology, 4,* 199–205.

Ellenberg, L., Rosenbaum, G., Goldman, M. S., & Whitman, R. D. (1980). Recoverability of psychological functioning following alcohol abuse: Lateralization effects. *Journal of Consulting and Clinical Psychology, 48,* 503–510.

Ellis, R. J. (1990). Dichotic asymmetries in aging and alcoholic subjects. *Alcoholism: Clinical and Experimental Research, 14,* 863–871.

Ellis, R. J., & Oscar-Berman, M. (1989). Alcoholism, aging, and functional cerebral asymmetries. *Psychological Bulletin, 106,* 128–147.

Emmerson, R. Y., Dustman, R. E., Heil, J., & Shearer, D. E. (1988). Neuropsychological performance of young nondrinkers, social drinkers, and long- and short-term sober alcoholics. *Alcoholism: Clinical and Experimental Research, 12,* 625–629.

Emmerson, R. Y., Dustman, R. E., Shearer, D. E., & Chamberlin, H. M. (1987). EEG, visually evoked and event related potentials in young abstinent alcoholics. *Alcohol, 4,* 241–248.

Ende, G., Welzel, H., Walter, S., Weber-Fahr, W., Diehl, A., Hermann, D., et al. (2005). Monitoring the effects of chronic alcohol consumption and abstinence on brain metabolism: A longitudinal proton magnetic resonance spectroscopy study. *Biological Psychiatry, 58*(12), 974–980.

Erbas, B., Bekdik, C., Erbengi, G., Enunlu, T., Aytac, S., Kumbasar, H., et al. (1992). Regional cerebral blood flow changes in chronic alcoholism using Tc-99m HMPAO SPECT: Comparison with CT parameters. *Clinical Nuclear Medicine, 17,* 123–127.

Errico, A. L., Nixon, S. J., Parsons, O. A., & Tassey, J. (1990). Screening for neuropsychological impairment in alcoholics. *Psychological Assessment, 2,* 45–50.

Ervin, C. S., Little, R. E., Streissguth, A. P., & Beck, D. E. (1984). Alcoholic fathering and its relation to child's intellectual development: A pilot investigation. *Alcoholism: Clinical and Experimental Research, 8,* 362–365.

Everett, M., Schaeffer, K. W., & Parsons, O. A. (1988). Learning impairment in male and female alcoholics. *Archives of Clinical Neuropsychology, 3,* 203–211.

Fabian, M. S., Jenkins, R. L., & Parsons, O. A. (1981). Gender, alcoholism, and neuropsychological functioning. *Journal of Consulting and Clinical Psychology, 49,* 138–140.

Fabian, M. S., & Parsons, O. A. (1983). Differential improvement of cognitive functions in recovering alcoholic women. *Journal of Abnormal Psychology, 92,* 87–95.

Fabian, M. S., Parsons, O. A., & Sheldon, M. D. (1984). Effects of gender and alcoholism on verbal and visual–spatial learning. *Journal of Nervous and Mental Disease, 172,* 16–20.

Fals-Stewart, W., & Schafer, J. (1992). The relationship between length of stay in drug-free therapeutic communities and neurocognitive functioning. *Journal of Clinical Psychology, 48,* 539–543.

Farmer, R. H. (1973). Functional changes during early weeks of abstinence, measured by the Bender-Gestalt. *Quarterly Journal of Studies on Alcohol, 34,* 786–796.

Fein, G., Torres, J., Price, L. J., & Di Sciafani, V. (2006). Cognitive performance in long-term abstinent alcoholic individuals. *Alcoholism, Clinical and Experimental Research, 30*(9), 1538–1544.

Feuerlein, W. (1977). Neuropsychiatric disorders of alcoholism. *Nutrition and Metabolism, 21,* 163–174.

Finn, P. R., & Justus, A. (1999). Reduced EEG alpha power in the male and female offspring of alcoholics. *Alcoholism: Clinical and Experimental Research, 23*(2), 256–262.

Fitzhugh, L. C., Fitzhugh, K. B., & Reitan, R. M. (1960). Adaptive abilities and intellectual functioning in hospitalized alcoholics. *Quarterly Journal of Studies on Alcohol, 21,* 414–423.

Fitzhugh, L. C., Fitzhugh, K. B., & Reitan, R. M. (1965). Adaptive abilities and intellectual functioning of hospitalized alcoholics: Further considerations. *Quarterly Journal of Studies on Alcohol, 26,* 402–411.

Flannery, B., Fishbein, D., Krupitsky, E., Langevin, D., Verbitskaya, E., Bland, C., et al. (2007). Gender differences in neurocognitive functioning among alcohol-dependent Russian patients. *Alcoholism, Clinical and Experimental Research, 31*(5), 745–754.

Forsberg, L. K., & Goldman, M. S. (1985). Experience-dependent recovery of visuospatial functioning in older alcoholic persons. *Journal of Abnormal Psychology, 94,* 519–529.

Forsberg, L. K., & Goldman, M. S. (1987). Experience-dependent recovery of cognitive deficits in alcoholics: Extended transfer of training. *Journal of Abnormal Psychology, 96,* 345–353.

Forton, D. M., Allsop, J. M., Cox, I. J., Hamilton, G., Wesnes, K., Thomas, H. C., et al. (2005). A review of cognitive impairment and cerebral metabolite abnormalities in patients with hepatitis C infection. *AIDS, 19*(Suppl 3), S53–S63.

Forton, D. M., Taylor-Robinson, S. D., & Thomas, H. C. (2006). Central nervous system changes in hepatitis C virus infection. *European Journal of Gastroenterology and Hepatology, 18*(4), 333–338.

Forton, D. M., Thomas, H. C., Murphy, C. A., Allsop, J. M., Foster, G. R., Main, J., et al. (2002). Hepatitis C and cognitive impairment in a cohort of patients with mild liver disease. *Hepatology, 35*(2), 433–439.

Franceschi, M., Truci, G., Comi, G., Lozza, L., Marchettini, P., Galardi, G., et al. (1984). Cognitive deficits and their relationship to other neurological complications in chronic alcoholic patients. *Journal of Neurology, Neurosurgery and Psychiatry, 47,* 1134–1137.

Freund, G., & Ballinger, W. E., Jr. (1988). Loss of cholinergic muscarinic receptors in the frontal cortex of alcohol abusers. *Alcoholism: Clinical and Experimental Research, 12,* 630–638.

Freund, G., & Ballinger, W. E., Jr. (1989). Neuroreceptor changes in the putamen of alcohol abusers. *Alcoholism: Clinical and Experimental Research, 13,* 213–218.

Freund, G., & Ballinger, W. E., Jr. (1991). Loss of synaptic receptors can precede morphologic changes induced by alcoholism. *Alcohol and Alcoholism, 1*(Suppl.), 385–391.

Fuller, R. K., Lee, K. K., & Gordis, E. (1988). Validity of self-report in alcoholism research: Results of a Veterans Administration Cooperative Study. *Alcoholism: Clinical and Experimental Research, 12,* 201–205.

Gazdzinski, S., Durazzo, T. C., & Meyerhoff, D. J. (2005). Temporal dynamics and determinants of whole brain tissue volume changes during recovery from alcohol dependence. *Drug and Alcohol Dependence, 78*(3), 263–273.

Gallucci, M., Amicarelli, I., Rossi, A., Stratta, P., Masciocchi, C., Zobel, B. B., et al. (1989). MR imaging of white matter lesions in uncomplicated chronic alcoholism. *Journal of Computer Assisted Tomography, 13,* 395–398.

Gardner, M. K., Clark, E., Bowman, M. A., & Miller, P. J. (1989). Analogical reasoning abilities of recovering alcoholics. *Alcoholism: Clinical and Experimental Research, 13,* 508–511.

Garland, M. A., Parsons, O. A., & Nixon, S. J. (1993). Visual–spatial learning in nonalcoholic young adults with and those without a family history of alcoholism. *Journal of Studies on Alcohol, 54,* 219–224.

Gebhardt, C. A., Naeser, M. A., & Butters, N. (1984). Computerized measures of CT scans of alcoholics: Thalamic region related to memory. *Alcohol, 1,* 133–140.

Gechter, G. L. (1987). Changes in neuropsychological functions among detoxifying and recovering alcoholics as measured by the Luria Nebraska Neuropsychological Battery. *Dissertation Abstracts International, 48,* 262–B.

George, D. T., Lindquist, T., Rawlings, R. R., Eckardt, M. J., Moss, H., Mathis, C., et al. (1992). Pharmacologic maintenance of abstinence in patients with alcoholism: No efficacy of 5-hydroxytryptophan or levodopa. *Clinical Pharmacology Therapy, 52,* 553–560.

Gillen, R., & Hesselbrock, V. (1992). Cognitive functioning, ASP, and family history of alcoholism in young men at risk for alcoholism. *Alcoholism: Clinical and Experimental Research, 16,* 206–214.

Gillin, J. C., Smith, T. L., Irwin, M., Kripke, D. F., Brown, S., & Schuckit, M. (1990a). Short REM latency in primary alcoholic patients with secondary depression. *American Journal of Psychiatry, 147,* 106–109.

Gillin, J. C., Smith, T. L., Irwin, M., Kripke, D. F., & Schuckit, M. (1990b). EEG sleep studies in "pure" primary alcoholism during subacute withdrawal: Relationships to normal controls, age, and other clinical variables. *Biological Psychiatry, 27,* 477–488.

Gilman, S., Adams, K., Koeppe, R. A., Berent, S., Kluin, K. J., Modell, J. G., et al. (1990). Cerebellar and frontal hypometabolism in alcoholic cerebellar degeneration studied with positron emission tomography. *Annals of Neurology, 28,* 775–785.

Glenn, S. W., Errico, A. L., Parsons, O. A., King, A. C., & Nixon, S. J. (1993). The role of antisocial, affective, and childhood behavioral characteristics in alcoholics' neuropsychological performance. *Alcoholism: Clinical and Experimental Research, 17,* 162–169.

Glenn, S. W., & Parsons, O. A. (1990). The role of time in neuropsychological performance: Investigation and application in an alcoholic population. *The Clinical Neuropsychologist, 4,* 344–354.

Glenn, S. W., & Parsons, O. A. (1991a). Impaired efficiency in female alcoholics' neuropsychological performance. *Journal of Clinical and Experimental Neuropsychology, 13,* 895–908.

Glenn, S. W., & Parsons, O. A. (1991b). Prediction of resumption of drinking in posttreatment alcoholics. *International Journal of the Addictions, 26,* 237–254.

Glenn, S. W., & Parsons, O. A. (1992). Neuropsychological efficiency measures in male and female alcoholics. *Journal of Studies on Alcohol, 53,* 546–552.

Glenn, S. W., Parsons, O. A., Sinha, R., & Stevens, L. (1988). The effects of repeated withdrawals from alcohol on the memory of male and female alcoholics. *Alcohol and Alcoholism, 23,* 337–342.

Glosser, G., Butters, N., & Kaplan, E. (1977). Visuoperceptual processes in brain damaged patients on the digit symbol substitution test. *International Journal of Neuroscience, 7,* 59–66.

Golden, C. J., Graber, B., Blose, I., Berg, R., Coffman, J., & Bloch, S. (1981). Difference in brain densities between chronic alcoholic and normal control patients. *Science, 211,* 508–510.

Goldman, M. S. (1983). Cognitive impairment in chronic alcoholics: Some cause for optimism. *American Psychologist, 38,* 1045–1054.

Goldman, M. S. (1990). Experience-dependent neuropsychological recovery and the treatment of chronic alcoholism. *Neuropsychology Review, 1,* 75–101.

Goldman, M. S., Klisz, D. K., & Williams, D. L. (1985). Experience-dependent recovery of cognitive functioning in young alcoholics. *Addictive Behaviors, 10,* 169–176.

Goldman, M. S., Williams, D. L., & Klisz, D. K. (1983). Recoverability of psychological functioning following alcohol abuse: Prolonged visual–spatial dysfunction in older alcoholics. *Journal of Consulting and Clinical Psychology, 51,* 370–378.

Goldman, R. S., & Goldman, M. S. (1988). Experience-dependent cognitive recovery in alcoholics: A task component strategy. *Journal of Studies on Alcohol, 49,* 142–148.

Goldstein, G., & Shelly, C. (1980). Neuropsychological investigation of brain lesion localization in alcoholism. *Advances in Experimental Medicine and Biology, 126,* 731–743.

Goldstein, G., & Shelly, C. (1982). A multivariate neuropsychological approach to brain lesion localization in alcoholism. *Addictive Behaviors, 7,* 165–175.

Goldstein, G., Shelly, C., Mascia, G. V., & Tarter, R. E. (1985). Relationships between neuropsychological and psychopathological dimensions in male alcoholics. *Addictive Behaviors, 10,* 365–372.

Goldstein, G., Tarter, R. E., Shelly, C., Alterman, A. I., & Petrarulo, E. (1983). Withdrawal seizures in black and white alcoholic patients: Intellectual and neuropsychological sequelae. *Drug and Alcohol Dependence, 12,* 349–354.

Goodwin, D. W. (1983). Familial alcoholism: A separate entity? *Substance and Alcohol Actions/Misuse, 4,* 129–136.

Gorenstein, E. E. (1982). Frontal lobe functions in psychopaths. *Journal of Abnormal Psychology, 91,* 368–379.

Gorenstein, E. E. (1987). Cognitive-perceptual deficit in an alcoholism spectrum disorder. *Journal of Studies on Alcohol, 48,* 310–318.

Grant, B. F., Dufour, M. C., & Harford, T. C. (1988). Epidemiology of alcoholic liver disease. *Seminars in Liver Disease, 8,* 12–25.

Grant, I. (1987). Alcohol and the brain: Neuropsychological correlates. *Journal of Consulting and Clinical Psychology, 55,* 310–324.

Grant, I., Adams, K. M., Carlin, A. S., & Rennick, P. M. (1977). Neuropsychological deficit in polydrug users: A preliminary report of the findings of the collaborative neuropsychological study of polydrug users. *Drug and Alcohol Dependence, 2,* 91–108.

Grant, I., Adams, K. M., Carlin, A. S., Rennick, P. M., Judd, L. L., & Schooff, K. (1978). The collaborative neuropsychological study of polydrug users. *Archives of General Psychiatry, 35,* 1063–1074.

Grant, I., Adams, K., & Reed, R. (1979a). Normal neuropsychological abilities of alcoholic men in their late thirties. *American Journal of Psychiatry, 136,* 1263–1269.

Grant, I., Adams, K. M., & Reed, R. (1984). Aging, abstinence, and medical risk factors in the prediction of neuropsychologic deficit among long-term alcoholics. *Archives of General Psychiatry, 41,* 710–718.

Grant, I., Prigatano, G. P., Heaton, R. K., McSweeny, A. J., Wright, E. C., & Adams, K. M. (1987a). Progressive neuropsychologic impairment and hypoxemia. *Archives of General Psychiatry, 44,* 999–1006.

Grant, I., Reed, R., & Adams, K. M. (1987b). Diagnosis of intermediate-duration and subacute organic mental disorders in abstinent alcoholics. *Journal of Clinical Psychiatry, 48,* 319–323.

Grant, I., Reed, R., Adams, K., & Carlin, A. (1979b). Neuropsychological function in young alcoholics and polydrug abusers. *Journal of Clinical Neuropsychology, 1,* 39–47.

Gregson, R. A., & Taylor, G. M. (1977). Prediction of relapse in men alcoholics. *Journal of Studies on Alcohol, 38,* 1749–1760.

Gur, R. C., Gur, R. E., Obrist, W. D., Skolnick, B. E., & Reivich, M. (1987). Age and regional cerebral blood flow at rest and during cognitive activity. *Archives of General Psychiatry, 44,* 617–621.

Guthrie, A., & Elliott, W. A. (1980). The nature and reversibility of cerebral impairment in alcoholism: Treatment implications. *Journal of Studies on Alcohol, 41,* 147–155.

Hannon, R., Butler, C. P., Day, C. L., Khan, S. A., Quitoriano, L. A., Butler, A. M., et al. (1985). Alcohol use and cognitive functioning in men and women college students. *Recent Developments in Alcoholism, 3,* 241–252.

Hannon, R., Butler, C. P., Day, C. L., Khan, S. A., Quitoriano, L. A., Butler, A. M., et al. (1987). Social drinking and cognitive functioning in college students: A replication and reversibility study. *Journal of Studies on Alcohol, 48,* 502–506.

Hannon, R., Day, C. L., Butler, A. M., Larson, A. J., & Casey, M. (1983). Alcohol consumption and cognitive functioning in college students. *Journal of Studies on Alcohol, 44,* 283–298.

Hansen, L. A., Natelson, B. H., Lemere, C., Niemann, W., De Teresa, R., Regan, T. J., et al. (1991). Alcohol-induced brain changes in dogs. *Archives of Neurology, 48,* 939–942.

Harper, C. (1998). The neuropathology of alcohol-specific brain damage, or does alcohol damage the brain? *Journal of Neuropathology and Experimental Neuroogyl, 57*(2), 101–110.

Harper C. (2007). The neurotoxicity of alcohol. *Human & Experimental Toxicology, 26*(3), 251–257.

Harper, C. , & Blumbergs, P. C. (1982). Brain weights in alcoholics. *Journal of Neurology, Neurosurgery and Psychiatry, 45,* 838–840.

Harper, C., & Corbett, D. (1990). Changes in the basal dendrites of cortical pyramidal cells from alcoholic patients: A quantitative Golgi study. *Journal of Neurology, Neurosurgery and Psychiatry, 53,* 856–861.

Harper, C., Dixon, G., Sheedy, D., & Garrick, T. (2003). Neuropathological alterations in alcoholic brains. Studies arising from the New South Wales Tissue Resource Centre. *Progress in Neuropsychopharmacology and Biological Psychiatry, 27*(6), 951–961.

Harper, C., & Kril, J. (1985). Brain atrophy in chronic alcoholic patients: A quantitative pathological study. *Journal of Neurology, Neurosurgery and Psychiatry, 48,* 211–217.

Harper, C., & Kril, J. J. (1988). Corpus callosal thickness in alcoholics. *British Journal of Addiction, 83,* 577–580.

Harper, C. G., & Kril, J. (1989). Patterns of neuronal loss in the cerebral cortex in chronic alcoholic patients. *Journal of the Neurological Sciences, 92,* 81–89.

Harper, C., & Kril, J. J. (1990). Neuropathology of alcoholism. *Alcohol and Alcoholism, 25,* 207–216.

Harper, C., Kril, J., & Daly, J. (1987). Are we drinking our neurones away? *British Medical Journal (Clinical Research Edition), 294,* 534–536.

Harper, C., Kril, J., & Daly, J. (1988). Does a "moderate" alcohol intake damage the brain? *Journal of Neurology, Neurosurgery and Psychiatry, 51,* 909–913.

Harper, C., Kril, J. J., & Holloway, R. L. (1985). Brain shrinkage in chronic alcoholics: A pathological study. *British Medical Journal, 290,* 501–504.

Harper, C., & Matsumoto, I. (2005). Ethanol and brain damage. *Current Opinion in Pharmacology, 5*(1), 73–78.

Harper, C., Smith, N. A., & Kril, J. J. (1990). The effects of alcohol on the female brain: A neuropathological study. *Alcohol and Alcoholism, 25,* 445–448.

Hata, T., Meyer, J. S., Tanahashi, N., Ishikawa, Y., Imai, A., Shinohara, T., et al. (1987). Three-dimensional mapping of local cerebral perfusion in alcoholic encephalopathy with and without Wernicke–Korsakoff syndrome. *Journal of Cerebral Blood Flow and Metabolism, 7,* 35–44.

Haug, J. O. (1968). Pneumoencephalographic evidence of brain damage in chronic alcoholics: A preliminary report. *Acta Psychiatrica Scandinavica, 203,* 135–143.

Heaton, R. K. (1992). *Comprehensive norms for an expanded Halstead–-Reitan Battery: A supplement for the Wechsler Adult Intelligence Scale-Revised.* Odessa, Florida: Psychological Assessment Resources.

Heaton, R. K., Grant, I., & Matthews, C. G. (1991). *Comprehensive norms for an expanded Halstead–Reitan Battery: Demographic corrections, research findings, and clinical applications.* Odessa, Florida: Psychological Assessment Resources.

Hesselbrock, M. N., Weidenman, M. A., & Reed, H. B. (1985a). Effect of age, sex, drinking history and antisocial personality on neuropsychology of alcoholics. *Journal of Studies on Alcohol, 46,* 313–320.

Hesselbrock, V., Bauer, L. O., Hesselbrock, M. N., & Gillen, R. (1991). Neuropsychological factors in individuals at high risk for alcoholism. *Recent Developments in Alcoholism, 9,* 21–40.

Hesselbrock, V. M., Stabenau, J. R., & Hesselbrock, M. N. (1985b). Minimal brain dysfunction and neuropsychological test performance in offspring of alcoholics. *Recent Developments in Alcoholism, 3,* 65–82.

Hester, R. K., Smith, J. W., & Jackson, T. R. (1980). Recovery of cognitive skills in alcoholics. *Journal of Studies on Alcohol, 41,* 363–367.

Hightower, M. G., & Anderson, R. P. (1986). Memory evaluation of alcoholics with Russell's revised Wechsler Memory Scale. *Journal of Clinical Psychology, 42,* 1000–1005.

Hildebrandt, H., Brokate, B., Eling, P., & Lanz, M. (2004). Response shifting and inhibition, but not working memory, are impaired after long-term heavy alcohol consumption. *Neuropsychology, 18*(2), 203–211.

Hill, S. Y., & Ryan, C. (1985). Brain damage in social drinkers? Reasons for caution. *Recent Developments in Alcoholism, 3,* 277–288.

Hillbom, M., & Holm, L. (1986). Contribution of traumatic head injury to neuropsychological deficits in alcoholics. *Journal of Neurology, Neurosurgery and Psychiatry, 49,* 1348–1353.

Hilsabeck, R. C., Hassanein, T. I., Carlson, M. D., Ziegler, E. A., & Perry, W. (2003). Cognitive functioning and psychiatric symptomatology in patients with chronic hepatitis C. *Journal of the International Neuropsychological Society, 9*(6), 847–854.

Hochla, N. A. N., & Parsons, O. A. (1982). Premature aging in female alcoholics: A neuropsychological study. *Journal of Nervous and Mental Disease, 170,* 241–245.

Hoffman, J. J., Hall, R. W., & Bartsch, T. W. (1987). On the relative importance of "psychopathic" personality and alcoholism on neuropsychological measures of frontal lobe dysfunction. *Journal of Abnormal Psychology, 96*, 158–160.

Horvath, T. B. (1973). Clinical spectrum and epidemiological features of alcoholic dementia. In J. G. Rankin (Ed.), *Alcohol, drugs and brain damage* (pp. 1–16). Toronto, Ontario: Addiction Research Foundation.

Inglis, J., & Lawson, J. S. (1981). Sex differences in the effects of unilateral brain damage on intelligence. *Science, 212*, 693–695.

Irwin, M., Smith, T. L., Butters, N., Brown, S., Baird, S., Grant, I., et al. (1989). Graded neuropsychological impairment and elevated gamma-glutamyl transferase in chronic alcoholic men. *Alcoholism: Clinical and Experimental Research, 13*, 99–103.

Ishibashi, M., Nakazawa, Y., Yokoyama, T., Koga, Y., Miyahara, Y., Hayashida, N., et al. (1987). Cerebral atrophy and slow wave sleep of abstinent chronic alcoholics. *Drug and Alcohol Dependence, 19*, 325–332.

Ishikawa, Y., Meyer, J. S., Tanahashi, N., Hata, T., Velez, M., Fann, W. E., et al. (1986). Abstinence improves cerebral perfusion and brain volume in alcoholic neurotoxicity without Wernicke–Korsakoff syndrome. *Journal of Cerebral Blood Flow and Metabolism, 6*, 86–94.

Jacobson, R. (1986a). The contributions of sex and drinking history to the CT brain scan changes in alcoholics. *Psychological Medicine, 16*, 547–559.

Jacobson, R. (1986b). Female alcoholics: A controlled CT brain scan and clinical study. *British Journal of Addiction, 81*, 661–669.

Jacobson, R. R., Acker, C. F., & Lishman, W. A. (1990). Patterns of neuropsychological deficit in alcoholic Korsakoff's syndrome. *Psychological Medicine, 20*, 321–334.

Jacobson, R. R., & Lishman, W. A. (1990). Cortical and diencephalic lesions in Korsakoff's syndrome: A clinical and CT scan study. *Psychological Medicine, 20*, 63–75.

Janowsky, J. S., Shimamura, A. P., Kritchevsky, M., & Squire, L. R. (1989). Cognitive impairment following frontal lobe damage and its relevance to human amnesia. *Behavioral Neuroscience, 103*, 548–560.

Jenkins, R. L., & Parsons, O. A. (1981). Neuropsychological effect of chronic alcoholism on tactual-spatial performance and memory in males. *Alcoholism: Clinical and Experimental Research, 5*, 26–33.

Jensen, G. B., & Pakkenberg, B. (1993). Do alcoholics drink their neurons away? *Lancet, 342*, 1201–1204.

Jernigan, T. L., Butters, N., DiTraglia, G., Schafer, K., Smith, T., Irwin, M., et al. (1991a). Reduced cerebral grey matter observed in alcoholics using magnetic resonance imaging. *Alcoholism: Clinical and Experimental Research, 15*, 418–427.

Jernigan, T. L., Schafer, K., Butters, N., & Cermak, L. S. (1991b). Magnetic resonance imaging of alcoholic Korsakoff patients. *Neuropsychopharmacology, 4*, 175–186.

Jernigan, T. L., Zatz, L. M., Ahumada, A. J., Jr., Pfefferbaum, A., Tinklenberg, J. R., & Moses, J. A., Jr. (1982). CT measures of cerebrospinal fluid volume in alcoholics and normal volunteers. *Psychiatry Research, 7*, 9–17.

Johnson, J. L., & Rolf, J. E. (1988). Cognitive functioning in children from alcoholic and non-alcoholic families. *British Journal of Addiction, 83*, 849–857.

Jones, B., & Parsons, O. A. (1971). Impaired abstracting ability in chronic alcoholics. *Archives of General Psychiatry, 24*, 71–75.

Jones, B., & Parsons, O. A. (1972). Specific vs generalized deficits of abstracting ability in chronic alcoholics. *Archives of General Psychiatry, 26*, 380–384.

Jones, M. K., & Jones, B. M. (1980). The relationship of age and drinking history to the effects of alcohol on memory in women. *Journal of Studies on Alcohol, 41*, 179–186.

Joyce, E. M., & Robbins, T. W. (1991). Frontal lobe function in Korsakoff and non-Korsakoff alcoholics: Planning and spatial working memory. *Neuropsychologia, 29*, 709–723.

Kaseda, Y., Miyazato, Y., Ogura, C., Nakamoto, H., Uema, T., Yamamoto, K., et al. (1994). Correlation between event-related potentials and MR measurements in chronic alcoholic patients. *The Japanese Journal of Psychiatry and Neurology, 48*, 23–32.

King, M. A., Hunter, B. E., & Walker, D. W. (1988). Alterations and recovery of dendritic spine density in rat hippocampus following long-term ethanol ingestion. *Brain Research, 459*, 381–385.

Kish, G. B., Hagen, J. M., Woody, M. M., & Harvey, H. L. (1980). Alcoholics' recovery from cerebral impairment as a function of duration of abstinence. *Journal of Clinical Psychology, 36*, 584–589.

Kleinknecht, R. A., & Goldstein, S. G. (1972). Neuropsychological deficits associated with alcoholism: A review and discussion. *Quarterly Journal of Studies on Alcohol, 33*, 999–1019.

Klisz, D. K., & Parsons, O. A. (1977). Hypothesis testing in younger and older alcoholics. *Journal of Studies on Alcohol, 38*, 1718–1729.

Kodituwakku, P. W., Kalberg, W., & May, P. A. (2001). The effects of prenatal alcohol exposure on executive functioning. *Alcohol Research & Health, 25*, 192–198.

Kostandov, E. A., Arsumanov, Y. L., Genkina, O. A., Restchikova, T. N., & Shostakovich, G. S. (1982). The effects of alcohol on hemispheric functional asymmetry. *Journal of Studies on Alcohol, 43,* 411–426.

Kramer, J. H., Blusewicz, M. J., & Preston, K. A. (1989). The premature aging hypothesis: Old before its time? *Journal of Consulting and Clinical Psychology, 57,* 257–262.

Kril, J. J., & Harper, C. G. (1989). Neuronal counts from four cortical regions of alcoholic brains. *Acta Neuropathologica, 79,* 200–204.

Lange, R. T., Iverson, G. L., & Franzen, M. D. (2007). Short-term neuropsychological outcome following uncomplicated mild TBI: effects of day-of-injury intoxication and pre-injury alcohol abuse. *Neuropsychology, 21*(5), 590–598.

Leber, W. R., Jenkins, R. L., & Parsons, O. A. (1981). Recovery of visual–spatial learning and memory in chronic alcoholics. *Journal of Clinical Psychology, 37,* 192–197.

Leber, W. R., Parsons, O. A., & Nichols, N. (1985). Neuropsychological test results are related to ratings of men alcoholics' therapeutic progress: A replicated study. *Journal of Studies on Alcohol, 46,* 116–121.

Letendre, S. L., Cherner, M., Ellis, R. J., Marquie-Beck, J., Gragg, B., Marcotte, T., et al. (2006). The effects of hepatitis C, HIV, and methamphetamine dependence on neuropsychological performance: biological correlates of disease. *AIDS, 19*(Suppl 3), S72–S78.

Letendre, S., Paulino, A. D., Rockenstein, E., Adame, A., Crews, L., Cherner, M., et al. (2007). Pathogenesis of hepatitis C virus coinfection in the brains of patients infected with HIV. *Journal of Infectious Diseases, 196*(3), 361–370.

Lewohl, J. M., Dodd, P. R., Mayfield, R. D., & Harris, R. A. (2001). Application of DNA microarrays to study human alcoholism. *Journal of Biomedical Science, 8*(1), 28–36.

Løberg, T. (1980a). Alcohol misuse and neuropsychological deficits in men. *Journal of Studies on Alcohol, 41,* 119–128.

Løberg, T. (1980b). Neuropsychological deficits in alcoholics: Lack of personality (MMPI) correlates. *Advances in Experimental Medicine and Biology, 126,* 797–808.

Løberg, T. (1981). MMPI-based personality subtypes of alcoholics: Relationships to drinking history, psychometrics and neuropsychological deficits. *Journal of Studies on Alcohol, 42,* 766–782.

Løberg, T. (1989). The role of neuropsychology in secondary prevention. In T. Løberg, W. R. Miller,

P. E. Nathan, and G. A. Marlatt (Eds.), *Addictive behaviors: Prevention and early intervention* (pp. 69–86). Amsterdam, The Netherlands: Swets and Zeitlinger.

Løberg, T., & Miller, W. R. (1986). Personality, cognitive, and neuropsychological correlates of harmful alcohol consumption: A cross-national comparison of clinical samples. *Annals of the New York Academy of Sciences, 472,* 75–97.

Long, J. A., & McLachlan, J. F. C. (1974). Abstract reasoning and perceptual–motor efficiency in alcoholics: Impairment and reversibility. *Quarterly Journal of Studies on Alcohol, 35,* 1220–1229.

Ma, X., Coles, C. D., Lynch, M. E., LaConte, S. M., Zurkiya, O., Wang, D., et al. (2005). Evaluation of corpus callosum anisotropy in young adults with fetal alcohol syndrome according to diffusion tensor imaging. *Alcoholism: Clinical & Experimental Research, 29*(7), 1214–1222.

Macciocchi, S. N., Ranseen, J. D., & Schmitt, F. A. (1989). The relationship between neuropsychological impairment in alcoholics and treatment outcome at one year. *Archives of Clinical Neuropsychology, 4,* 365–370.

MacVane, J., Butters, N., Montgomery, K., & Farber, J. (1982). Cognitive functioning in men social drinkers: A replication study. *Journal of Studies on Alcohol, 43,* 81–95.

Malloy, P., Noel, N., Longabaugh, R., & Beattie, M. (1990). Determinants of neuropsychological impairment in antisocial substance abusers. *Addictive Behaviors, 15,* 431–438.

Malloy, P., Noel, N., Rogers, S., Longabaugh, R., & Beattie, M. (1989). Risk factors for neuropsychological impairment in alcoholics: Antisocial personality, age, years of drinking and gender. *Journal of Studies on Alcohol, 50,* 422–426.

Mann, K., Batra, A., Gunthner, A., & Schroth, G. (1992). Do women develop alcoholic brain damage more readily than men? *Alcoholism: Clinical and Experimental Research, 16,* 1052–1056.

Mann, K., Mundle, G., Langle, G., & Petersen, D. (1993). The reversibility of alcoholic brain damage is not due to rehydration: A CT study. *Addiction, 88,* 649–653.

Mann, K., Opitz, H., Petersen, D., Schroth, G., & Heimann, H. (1989). Intracranial CSF volumetry in alcoholics: studies with MRI and CT. *Psychiatry Research, 29,* 277–279.

Marchesi, C., De Risio, C., Campanini, G., Maggini, C., Piazza, P., Grassi, M., et al. (1992). TRH test in alcoholics: Relationship of the endocrine results with neuroradiological and neuropsychological findings. *Alcohol and Alcoholism, 27,* 531–537.

Marchesi, C., De Risio, C., Campanini, G., Piazza, P., Grassi, M., Chiodera, P., et al. (1994). Cerebral atrophy and plasma cortisol levels in alcoholics after short or a long period of abstinence. *Progress in Neuro-Psychopharmacology and Biological Psychiatry, 18,* 519–535.

Martin, P. R., Adinoff, B., Weingartner, H., Mukherjee, A. B., & Eckardt, M. J. (1986). Alcoholic organic brain disease: Nosology and pathophysiologic mechanisms. *Progress in Neuro-Psychopharmacology and Biological Psychiatry, 10,* 147–164.

Martin, P. R., Eckardt, M. J., & Linnoila, M. (1989). Treatment of chronic organic mental disorders associated with alcoholism. *Recent Developments in Alcoholism, 7,* 329–350.

Mathew, R. J., & Wilson, W. H. (1991). Substance abuse and cerebral blood flow. *American Journal of Psychiatry, 148,* 292–305.

Mathew, R. J., Wilson, W. H., & Tant, S. R. (1986). Determinants of resting regional cerebral blood flow in normal subjects. *Biological Psychiatry, 21,* 907–914.

Mattson, S. N., Goodman, A. M., Caine, C., Delis, D. C., & Riley, E. P. (1999). Executive functioning in children with heavy prenatal alcohol exposure. *Alcoholism, Clinical and Experimental Research, 23*(11), 1808–1815.

Mattson, S. N., Riley, E. P., Jernigan, T. L., Ehlers, C. L., Delis, D. C., Jones, K. L., et al. (1992). Fetal alcohol syndrome: A case report of neuropsychological, MRI and EEG assessment of two children. *Alcoholism: Clinical and Experimental Research, 16,* 1001–1003.

Mattson, S. N., Jernigan, T. L., & Riley, E. P. (1994). MRI and prenatal alcohol exposure. *Alcohol Health & Research World, 18*(1), 49–52.

Mattson, S. N., & Riley, E. P. (1995). Prenatal exposure to alcohol: What the images reveal. *Alcohol Health & Research World, 19*(4), 273–277.

Mattson, S. N., Riley, E. P., Gramling, L., Delis, D. C., & Jones, K. L. (1998). Neuropsychological comparison of alcohol-exposed children with or without physical features of fetal alcohol syndrome. *Neuropsychology, 12*(1), 146–153.

McCrady, B. S., & Smith, D. E. (1986). Implications of cognitive impairment for the treatment of alcoholism. *Alcoholism: Clinical and Experimental Research, 10,* 145–149.

McIntyre, B. M. (1987). Functional neuropsychological impairment and recovery in alcoholics. *Dissertation Abstracts International, 47,* 4658–B.

McLachlan, J. F. C., & Levinson, T. (1974). Improvement in WAIS block design performance as a function of recovery from alcoholism. *Journal of Clinical Psychology, 30,* 65–66.

McMullen, P. A., Saint-Cyr, J. A., & Carlen, P. L. (1984). Morphological alterations in rat CA1 hippocampal pyramidal cell dendrites resulting from chronic ethanol consumption and withdrawal. *The Journal of Comparative Neurology, 225,* 111–118.

Melgaard, B., Henriksen, L., Ahlgren, P., Danielsen, U. T., Sørensen, H., & Paulson, O. B. (1990). Regional cerebral blood flow in chronic alcoholics measured by single photon emission computerized tomography. *Acta Neurologica Scandinavica, 82,* 87–93.

Mercer, P. W., & Khavari, K. A. (1990). Are women drinking more like men? An empirical examination of the convergence hypothesis. *Alcoholism: Clinical and Experimental Research, 14,* 461–466.

Miglioni, M., Buchtel, H. A., Campanini, T., & De Risio, C. (1979). Cerebral hemispheric lateralization of cognitive deficits due to alcoholism. *Journal of Nervous and Mental Disease, 167,* 212–217.

Miller, R., King, M. A., Heaton, M. B., & Walker, D. W. (2002). The effects of chronic ethanol consumption on neurotrophins and their receptors in the rat hippocampus and basal forebrain. *Brain Research, 950*(1–2), 137–147.

Miller, W. R., & Orr, J. (1980). Nature and sequence of neuropsychological deficits in alcoholics. *Journal of Studies on Alcohol, 41,* 325–337.

Miyazato, Y., & Ogura, C. (1993). Abnormalities in event-related potentials: N100, N200 and P300 topography in alcoholics. *The Japanese Journal of Psychiatry and Neurology, 47,* 853–862.

Molina, J. A., Bermejo, F., del Ser, T., Jimenez-Jimenez, F. J., Herranz, A., Fernandez-Calle, P., et al. (1994). Alcoholic cognitive deterioration and nutritional deficiencies. *Acta Neurologica Scandinavica, 89,* 384–390.

Moss, H. B., Kirisci, L., Gordon, H. W., & Tarter, R. E. (1994). A neuropsychologic profile of adolescent alcoholics. *Alcoholism: Clinical and Experimental Research, 18*(1), 159–163.

Muuronen, A., Bergman, H., Hindmarsh, T., & Telakivi, T. (1989). Influence of improved drinking habits on brain atrophy and cognitive performance in alcoholic patients: A 5-year follow-up study. *Alcoholism: Clinical and Experimental Research, 13,* 137–141.

Nanson, J. L., & Hiscock, M. (1990). Attention deficits in children exposed to alcohol prenatally. *Alcoholism: Clinical and Experimental Research, 14,* 656–661.

Neundorfer, B., Claus, D., & Burkowski, H. (1984). Neurological complications of chronic alcoholism. *Wiener Klinische Wochenschrift, 96,* 576–580.

Nicolas, J. M., Catafau, A. M., Estruch, R., Lomena, F. J., Salamero, M., Herranz, R., et al. (1993). Regional cerebral blood flow-SPECT in chronic alcoholism:

Relation to neuropsychological testing. *Journal of Nuclear Medicine, 34,* 1452–1459.

Nixon, K., & Crews, F. T. (2004). Temporally specific burst in cell proliferation increases hippocampal neurogenesis in protracted abstinence from alcohol. *Journal of Neuroscience, 24*(43), 9714–9722.

Nixon, S. J., Errico, A. L., Parsons, O. A., Leber, W. R., & Kelley, C. J. (1992). The role of instructional set on alcoholic performance. *Alcoholism: Clinical and Experimental Research, 16,* 949–954.

Nixon, S. J., Kujawski, A., Parsons, O. A., & Yohman, J. R. (1987). Semantic (verbal) and figural memory impairment in alcoholics. *Journal of Clinical and Experimental Neuropsychology, 9,* 311–322.

Nixon, S. J., & Parsons, O. A. (1991). Alcohol-related efficiency deficits using an ecologically valid test. *Alcoholism: Clinical and Experimental Research, 15,* 601–606.

Nixon, S. J., Parsons, O. A., Schaeffer, K. W., & Hale, R. L. (1988). Subject selection biases in alcoholic samples: Effects on cognitive performance. *Journal of Clinical Psychology, 44,* 831–836.

Noble, E. P., Berman, S. M., Ozkaragoz, T. Z., & Ritchie, T. (1994). Prolonged P300 latency in children with the D2 dopamine receptor A1 allele. *American Journal of Human Genetics, 54,* 658–668.

Noël, X., Bechara, A., Dan, B., Hanak, C., & Verbanck, P. (2007). Response inhibition deficit is involved in poor decision making under risk in nonamnesic individuals with alcoholism. *Neuropsychology, 21*(6), 778–786.

Noonberg, A., Goldstein, G., & Page, H. A. (1985). Premature aging in male alcoholics: "Accelerated aging" or "increased vulnerability"? *Alcoholism: Clinical and Experimental Research, 9,* 334–338.

O'Connor, S., & Tasman, A. (1990). The application of electrophysiology to research in alcoholism. *Journal of Neuropsychiatry and Clinical Neuroscience, 2,* 149–158.

Ökvist, A., Johansson, S., Kuzmin, A., Bazov, I., Merino-Martinez, R., Ponomarev, I., et al. (2007). Neuroadaptations in human chronic alcoholics: dysregulation of the NF-kappa B system. *PLoS ONE, 2*(9), e930.

O'Leary, M. R., Donovan, D. M., & Chaney, E. F. (1977a). The relationship of perceptual field orientation to measures of cognitive functioning and current adaptive abilities in alcoholics and nonalcoholics. *Journal of Nervous and Mental Disease, 165,* 275–282.

O'Leary, M. R., Donovan, D. M., Chaney, E. F., & Walker, R. D. (1979). Cognitive impairment and treatment outcome with alcoholics: Preliminary findings. *Journal of Clinical Psychiatry, 40,* 397–398.

O'Leary, M. R., Radford, L. M., Chaney, E. F., & Schau, E. J. (1977b). Assessment of cognitive recovery in alcoholics by use of the Trail-Making Test. *Journal of Clinical Psychology, 33,* 579–582.

O'Neill, J., Cardenas, V. A., & Meyerhoff, D. J. (2001). Effects of abstinence on the brain: quantitative magnetic resonance imaging and magnetic resonance spectroscopic imaging in chronic alcohol abuse. *Alcoholism: Clinical and Experimental Research, 25*(11), 1673–1682.

Ogura, C., & Miyazato, Y. (1991). Cognitive dysfunctions of alcohol dependence using event related potentials. *Japanese Journal of Alcohol and Drug Dependence, 26,* 331–340.

Oscar-Berman, M. (1987). Alcohol-related ERP changes in cognition. *Alcohol, 4,* 289–292.

Ozkaragoz, T. Z., & Noble, E. P. (1995). Neuropsychological differences between sons of active alcoholic and non-alcoholic fathers. *Alcohol and Alcoholism, 30,* 115–123.

Page, R. D., & Linden, J. D. (1974). "Reversible" organic brain syndrome in alcoholics: A psychometric evaluation. *Quarterly Journal of Studies on Alcohol, 35,* 98–107.

Page, R. D., & Schaub, L. H. (1977). Intellectual functioning in alcoholics during six months' abstinence. *Journal of Studies on Alcohol, 38,* 1240–1246.

Parker, D. A., Parker, E. S., Brody, J. A., & Schoenberg, R. (1983). Alcohol use and cognitive loss among employed men and women. *American Journal of Public Health, 73,* 521–526.

Parker, E. S. (1982). Comments on "cognitive functioning in men social drinkers; A replication study." *Journal of Studies on Alcohol, 43,* 170–177.

Parker, E. S., Birnbaum, I. M., Boyd, R. A., & Noble, E. P. (1980). Neuropsychologic decrements as a function of alcohol intake in male students. *Alcoholism: Clinical and Experimental Research, 4,* 330–334.

Parker, E. S., & Noble, E. P. (1977). Alcohol consumption and cognitive functioning in social drinkers. *Journal of Studies on Alcohol, 38,* 1224–1232.

Parker, E. S., & Noble, E. P. (1980). Alcohol and the aging process in social drinkers. *Journal of Studies on Alcohol, 41,* 170–178.

Parker, E. S., Parker, D. A., & Harford T. C. (1991). Specifying the relationship between alcohol use and cognitive loss: The effects of frequency of consumption and psychological distress. *Journal of Studies on Alcohol, 52,* 366–373.

Parkin, A. J., Blunden, J., Rees, J. E., & Hunkin, N. M. (1991). Wernicke–Korsakoff syndrome of nonalcoholic origin. *Brain and Cognition, 15,* 69–82.

Parkin, A. J., Dunn, J. C., Lee, C., O'Hara, P. F., & Nussbaum, L. (1993). Neuropsychological sequelae of Wernicke's encephalopathy in a 20-year-old woman: Selective impairment of a frontal memory system. *Brain and Cognition, 21,* 1–19.

Parsons, O. A. (1983). Cognitive dysfunction and recovery in alcoholics. *Substance and Alcohol Actions/Misuse, 4,* 175–190.

Parsons, O. A. (1986a). Alcoholics' neuropsychological impairment: Current findings and conclusions. *Annals of Behavioral Medicine, 8,* 13–19.

Parsons, O. A. (1986b). Cognitive functioning in sober social drinkers: A review and critique. *Journal of Studies on Alcohol, 47,* 101–114.

Parsons, O. A. (1987). Intellectual impairment in alcoholics: Persistent issues. *Acta Medica Scandinavica, 717*(Suppl.), 33–46.

Parsons, O. A. (1989). Impairment in sober alcoholics' cognitive functioning: The search for determinants. In T. Løberg, W. R. Miller, P. E. Nathan, and G. A. Marlatt (Eds.), *Addictive behaviors: Prevention and early intervention* (pp. 101–116). Amsterdam, The Netherlands: Swets and Zeitlinger.

Parsons, O. A., & Fabian, M. S. (1982). Comments on "Cognitive functioning in men social drinkers: A replication study." *Journal of Studies on Alcohol, 43,* 178–182.

Parsons, O. A., & Farr, S. P. (1981). The neuropsychology of alcohol and drug use. In S. B. Filskov and T. S. Boll (Eds.), *Handbook of clinical neuropsychology* (pp. 320–365). New York: Wiley Press.

Parsons, O. A., & Leber, W. R. (1981). The relationship between cognitive dysfunction and brain damage in alcoholics: Causal, interactive, or epiphenomenal? *Alcoholism: Clinical and Experimental Research, 5,* 326–343.

Parsons, O. A., & Nixon, S. J. (1993). Neurobehavioral sequelae of alcoholism. *Neurologic Clinics, 11,* 205–218.

Parsons, O. A., & Prigatano, G. P. (1977). Memory functioning in alcoholics. In I. M. Birnbaum and E. S. Parker (Eds.), *Alcohol and human memory* (pp. 185–194). Hillsdale, NJ: Lawrence Erlbaum.

Parsons, O. A., Schaeffer, K. W., & Glenn, S. W. (1990a). Does neuropsychological test performance predict resumption of drinking in post-treatment alcoholics? *Addictive Behaviors, 15,* 297–307.

Parsons, O. A., Sinha, R., & Williams, H. L. (1990b). Relationships between neuropsychological test performance and event-related potentials in alcoholic and nonalcoholic samples. *Alcoholism: Clinical and Experimental Research, 14,* 746–755.

Parsons, O. A., & Stevens, L. (1986). Previous alcohol intake and residual cognitive deficits in detoxified alcoholics and animals. *Alcohol and Alcoholism, 21,* 137–157.

Parsons, O. A., Tarter, R. E., & Edelberg, R. (1972). Altered motor control in chronic alcoholics. *Journal of Abnormal Psychology, 80,* 308–314.

Patterson, B. W., Parsons, O. A., Schaeffer, K. W., & Errico, A. L. (1988). Interpersonal problem solving in alcoholics. *Journal of Nervous and Mental Disease, 176,* 707–713.

Patterson, B. W., Sinha, R., Williams, H. L., Parsons, O. A., Smith, L. T., & Schaeffer, K. W. (1989). The relationship between neuropsychological and late component evoked potential measures in chronic alcoholics. *International Journal of Neuroscience, 49,* 319–327.

Patterson, B. W., Williams, H. L., McLean, G. A., Smith, L. T., & Schaeffer, K. W. (1987). Alcoholism and family history of alcoholism: Effects on visual and auditory event-related potentials. *Alcohol, 4,* 265–274.

Pentney, R. J. (1991). Remodeling of neuronal dendritic networks with aging and alcohol. *Alcohol and Alcoholism, 1*(Suppl.), 393–397.

Pentney, R. J., Quackenbush, L. J., & O'Neill, M. (1989). Length changes in dendritic networks of cerebellar purkinje cells of old rats after chronic ethanol treatment. *Alcoholism: Clinical and Experimental Research, 13,* 413–419.

Peterson, J. B., & Pihl, R. O. (1990). Information processing, neuropsychological function, and the inherited predisposition to alcoholism. *Neuropsychology Review, 1,* 343–369.

Pfefferbaum, A., Adalsteinsson, E., & Sullivan, E. V. (2006). Dysmorphology and microstructural degradation of the corpus callosum: Interaction of age and alcoholism. *Neurobiology of Aging, 27*(7), 994–1009.

Pfefferbaum, A., Ford, J. M., White, P. M., & Mathalon, D. (1991). Event-related potentials in alcoholic men: P3 amplitude reflects family history but not alcohol consumption. *Alcoholism: Clinical and Experimental Research, 15,* 839–850.

Pfefferbaum, A., Lim, K. O., Zipursky, R. B., Mathalon, D. H., Rosenbloom, M. J., Lane, B., et al. (1992). Brain gray and white matter volume loss accelerates with aging in chronic alcoholics: A quantitative MRI study. *Alcoholism: Clinical and Experimental Research, 16,* 1078–1089.

Pfefferbaum, A., Rosenbloom, M. J., Adalsteinsson, E., & Sullivan, E. V. (2007). Diffusion tensor imaging with quantitative fibre tracking in HIV infection and alcoholism comorbidity: Synergistic white matter damage. *Brain, 130*(Pt 1), 48–64.

Pfefferbaum, A., Rosenbloom, M., Crusan, K., & Jernigan, T. L. (1988). Brain CT changes in alcoholics: Effects of age and alcohol consumption.

Alcoholism: Clinical and Experimental Research, 12, 81–87.

Pfefferbaum, A., & Sullivan, E. V. (2005). Disruption of brain white matter microstructure by excessive intracellular and extracellular fluid in alcoholism: evidence from diffusion tensor imaging. *Neuropsychopharmacology,* 30(2), 423–432.

Pfefferbaum, A., Sullivan, E. V., Hedehus, M., Adalsteinsson, E., Lim, K. O., & Moseley, M. (2000). In vivo detection and functional correlates of white matter microstructural disruption in chronic alcoholism. *Alcoholism: Clinical and Experimental Research,* 24(8), 1214–1221.

Pfefferbaum, A., Sullivan, E. V., Mathalon, D. H., & Lim, K. O. (1997). Frontal lobe volume loss observed with magnetic resonance imaging in older chronic alcoholics. *Alcoholism: Clinical and Experimental Research,* 21(3), 521–529.

Pfefferbaum, A., Sullivan, E. V., Rosenbloom M. J., Mathalon, D. H., & Lim, K. O. (1998). A controlled study of cortical gray matter and ventricular changes in alcoholic men over a 5-year interval. *Archives of General Psychiatry,* 55(10), 905–912.

Phillips, D. E., Krueger, S. K., & Rydquist, J. E. (1991). Short- and long-term effects of combined pre- and postnatal ethanol exposure (three trimester equivalency) on the development of myelin and axons in rat optic nerve. *International Journal of Developmental Neuroscience,* 9(6), 631–647.

Plant, M., Sullivan, F. M., Guerri, C., & Abel, E. L. (1993). Alcohol and pregnancy. In P. M. Verscuren (Ed.), *Health issues related to alcohol consumption* (pp. 245–262). New York: ILSI Press.

Polich, J., & Bloom, F. E. (1986). P300 and alcohol consumption in normals and individuals at risk for alcoholism: A preliminary report. *Progress in Neuro-Psychopharmacology and Biological Psychiatry,* 10, 201–210.

Polich, J., & Bloom, F. E. (1988). Event-related brain potentials in individuals at high and low risk for developing alcoholism: Failure to replicate. *Alcoholism: Clinical and Experimental Research,* 12, 368–373.

Polich, J., Burns, T., & Bloom, F. E. (1988a). P300 and the risk for alcoholism: Family history, task difficulty, and gender. *Alcoholism: Clinical and Experimental Research,* 12, 248–254.

Polich, J., Haier, R. J., Buchsbaum, M., & Bloom, F. E. (1988b). Assessment of young men at risk for alcoholism with P300 from a visual discrimination task. *Journal of Studies on Alcohol,* 49, 186–190.

Polich, J., Pollock, V. E., & Bloom, F. E. (1994). Meta-analysis of P300 amplitude from males at risk for alcoholism. *Psychological Bulletin,* 115, 55–73.

Porjesz, B., & Begleiter, H. (1990). Event-related potentials in individuals at risk for alcoholism. *Alcohol, 7,* 465–469.

Porjesz, B., & Begleiter, H. (1991). Neurophysiological factors in individuals at risk for alcoholism. *Recent Developments in Alcoholism,* 9, 53–67.

Porjesz, B., & Begleiter, H. (1993). Neurophysiological factors associated with alcoholism. In W. A. Hunt and S. J. Nixon (Eds.), *Alcohol-induced brain damage* (pp. 89–120). Rockville, MD: National Institute on Alcohol Abuse and Alcoholism.

Porjesz, B., & Begleiter, H. (2003). Alcoholism and human electrophysiology. *Alcohol Research and Health,* 27, 153–160.

Portnoff, L. A. (1982). Halstead–Reitan impairment in chronic alcoholics as a function of age of drinking onset. *Clinical Neuropsychology,* 4, 115–119.

Prange, M. E. (1988). Relapsed versus non-relapsed alcohol abusers: Coping skills, stressful life events and neuropsychological functioning. *Dissertation Abstracts International,* 49, 549–B.

Prescott, C. A., & Kendler, K. S. (1999). Age at first drink and risk for alcoholism: A noncausal association. *Alcoholism: Clinical and Experimental Research,* 23(1), 101–107.

Prigatano, G. P. (1980). Neuropsychological functioning of recidivist alcoholics treated with disulfiram: A follow-up report. *International Journal of the Addictions,* 15, 287–294.

Rangaswamy, M., Porjesz, B., Chorlian, D. B., Wang, K., Jones, K., Bauer, L. O., et al. (2002). Beta power in the EEG of alcoholics. *Biological Psychiatry, 52,* 831–842.

Rangaswamy, M., Porjesz, B., Chorlian, D. B., Choi, K., Jones, K. A., Wang, K., et al. (2003). Theta power in the EEG of alcoholics. *Alcoholism: Clinical and Experimental Research,* 27, 607–615.

Rangaswamy, M., Porjesz, B., Chorlian, D. B., Wang, K., Jones, K., Kuperman, S., et al. (2004). Resting EEG in offspring of male alcoholics: Beta frequencies. *International Journal of Psychophysiology,* 51, 239–251.

Reed, R. J., & Grant, I. (1990). The long-term neurobehavioral consequences of substance abuse: Conceptual and methodological challenges for future research. *NIDA Research Monograph, 101,* 10–56.

Reed, R., Grant, I., & Adams, K. M. (1987). Family history of alcoholism does not predict neuropsychological performance in alcoholics. *Alcoholism: Clinical and Experimental Research, 11,* 340–344.

Reed, R. J., Grant, I., & Rourke, S. B. (1992). Long-term abstinent alcoholics have normal memory. *Alcoholism: Clinical and Experimental Research, 16,* 677–683.

Reitan, R. M. (1972). Verbal problem-solving as related to cerebral damage. *Perceptual and Motor Skills, 34,* 515–524.

Rhodes, S. S., & Jasinski, D. R. (1990). Learning disabilities in alcohol-dependent adults: A preliminary study. *Journal of Learning Disabilities, 23,* 551–556.

Richardson, E. D., Malloy, P. F., Longabaugh, R., Williams, J., Noel, N., & Beattie, M. C. (1991). Liver function tests and neuropsychologic impairment in substance abusers. *Addictive Behaviors, 16,* 51–55.

Riley, E. P., & McGee, C. L. (2005). Fetal alcohol spectrum disorders: An overview with emphasis on changes in brain and behavior. *Experimental Biology and Medicine, 230,* 357–365.

Riley, E. P., McGee, C. L., & Sowell, E. R. (2004). Teratogenic effects of alcohol: A decade of brain imaging. *American Journal of Medical Genetics, 127C,* 35–41.

Riley, E. P., Mattson, S. N., Sowell, E. R., Jernigan, T. L., Sobel, D. F., & Jones, K. L. (1995). Abnormalities of the corpus callosum in children prenatally exposed to alcohol. *Alcoholism: Clinical and Experimental Research, 19*(5), 1198–1202.

Roehrich, L., & Goldman, M. S. (1993). Experience-dependent neuropsychological recovery and the treatment of alcoholism. *Journal of Consulting and Clinical Psychology, 61,* 812–821.

Rogers, R. L., Meyer, J. S., Shaw, T. G., & Mortel, K. F. (1983). Reductions in regional cerebral blood flow associated with chronic consumption of alcohol. *Journal of the American Geriatrics Society, 31,* 540–543.

Romani, A., & Cosi, V. (1989). Event-related potentials in chronic alcoholics during withdrawal and abstinence. *Neurophysiology Clinics, 19,* 373–384.

Ron, M. A. (1983). The alcoholic brain: CT scan and psychological findings. *Psychological Medicine Monograph, 3,* 1–33.

Ron, M. A. (1987). The brain of alcoholics: An overview. In O. A. Parsons, N. Butters, and P. E. Nathan (Eds.), *Neuropsychology of alcoholism: Implications for diagnosis and treatment* (pp. 11–20). New York: Guilford Press.

Ron, M. A., Acker, W., Shaw, G. K., & Lishman, W. A. (1982). Computerized tomography of the brain in chronic alcoholism: A survey and follow-up study. *Brain, 105,* 497–514.

Roth, T., Roehrs, T., & Rosenthal, L. (1995). Hypersomnolence and neurocognitive performance in sleep apnea. *Current Opinion in Pulmonary Medicine, 1*(6), 488–490.

Rourke, S. B., Grant, I., Jernigan, T. L., & Reed, R. J. (1993). Negative computed tomography findings in male long-term abstinent alcoholics. *The Clinical Neuropsychologist, 7,* 343.

Rourke, S. B., & Grant, I. (1995). Neuropsychological deficits in male alcoholics: Part II. Using clinical ratings to delineate the effects of interim drinking and length of abstinence on the prevalence of deficits. *Journal of the International Neuropsychological Society, 1,* 327.

Rourke S. B., & Grant, I. (1999). The interactive effects of age and length of abstinence on the recovery of neuropsychological functioning in chronic male alcoholics: A 2-year follow-up study. *Journal of the International Neuropsychological Society, 5*(3), 234–246.

Ruff, R. M., Marshall, L. F., Klauber, M. R., Blunt, B. A., Grant, I., Foulkes, M. A., et al. (1990). Alcohol abuse and neurological outcome of the severely head injured. *Journal of Head Trauma Rehabilitation, 5,* 21–31.

Russell, E. W. (1975). A multiple scoring method for the assessment of complex memory functions. *Journal of Consulting and Clinical Psychology, 43,* 800–809.

Russell, M., Czarnecki, D. M., Cowan, R., McPherson, E., & Mudar, P. J. (1991). Measures of maternal alcohol use as predictors of development in early childhood. *Alcoholism: Clinical and Experimental Research, 15,* 991–1000.

Ryan, C., & Butters, N. (1980a). Further evidence for a continuum-of-impairment encompassing male alcoholic Korsakoff patients and chronic alcoholic men. *Alcoholism: Clinical and Experimental Research, 4,* 190–198.

Ryan, C., & Butters, N. (1980b). Learning and memory impairments in young and old alcoholics: Evidence for the premature-aging hypothesis. *Alcoholism: Clinical and Experimental Research, 4,* 288–293.

Ryan, C., & Butters, N. (1984). Alcohol consumption and premature aging: A critical review. *Recent Developments in Alcoholism, 2,* 223–250.

Ryan, C., & Butters, N. (1986). The neuropsychology of alcoholism. In D. Wedding, A. Horton, and J. Webster (Eds.), *The neuropsychology handbook* (pp. 376–409). New York: Springer-Publishing Co.

Ryan, C., Butters, N., DiDario, B., & Adinolfi, A. (1980). The relationship between abstinence and recovery of function in male alcoholics. *Journal of Clinical Neuropsychology, 2,* 125–134.

Ryan, J. J., & Lewis, C. V. (1988). Comparison of normal controls and recently detoxified alcoholics on the Wechsler Memory Scale-Revised. *The Clinical Neuropsychologist, 2,* 173–180.

Ryback, R. S. (1971). The continuum and specificity of the effects of alcohol on memory: A review.

Quarterly Journal of Studies on Alcohol, 32, 955–1016.

Sachs, H., Russell, J. A. G., Christman, D. R., & Cook, B. (1987). Alteration of regional cerebral glucose metabolic rate in non-Korsakoff chronic alcoholism. *Archives of Neurology, 44,* 1242–1251.

Saletu-Zyhlarz, G. M., Arnold, O., Anderer, P., Oberndorfer, S., Walter, H., Lesch, O. M., et al. (2004). Differences in brain function between relapsing and abstaining alcohol-dependent patients, evaluated by EEG mapping. *Alcohol Alcohol, 39,* 233–240.

Salmon, D. P., & Butters, N. (1987). The etiology and neuropathology of alcoholic Korsakoff's syndrome: Some evidence for the role of the basal forebrain. *Recent Developments in Alcoholism, 5,* 27–58.

Salmon, D. P., Butters, N., & Heindel, W. C. (1993). Alcoholic dementia and related disorders. In R. W. Parks, R. F. Zec, and R. S. Wilson (Eds.), *Neuropsychology of Alzheimer's disease and other dementias* (pp. 186–209). New York: Oxford University Press.

Samson, Y., Baron, J. C., Feline, A., Bories, J., & Crouzel, C. (1986). Local cerebral glucose utilization in chronic alcoholics: A positron tomographic study. *Journal of Neurology, Neurosurgery and Psychiatry, 49,* 1165–1170.

Sander, A. M., Nixon, S. J., & Parsons, O. A. (1989). Pretest expectancies and cognitive impairment in alcoholics. *Journal of Consulting and Clinical Psychology, 57,* 705–709.

Schaeffer, K. W., & Parsons, O. A. (1986). Drinking practices and neuropsychological test performance in sober male alcoholics and social drinkers. *Alcohol, 3,* 175–179.

Schaeffer, K. W., & Parsons, O. A. (1987). Learning impairment in alcoholics using an ecologically relevant test. *Journal of Nervous and Mental Disease, 175,* 213–218.

Schaeffer, K. W., & Parsons, O. A. (1988). Learning and memory test performance in alcoholics as a function of monetary incentive. *International Journal of Neuroscience, 38,* 311–319.

Schaeffer, K. W., Parsons, O. A., & Errico, A. L. (1988). Abstracting deficits and childhood conduct disorder as a function of familial alcoholism. *Alcoholism: Clinical and Experimental Research, 12,* 617–618.

Schaeffer, K. W., Parsons, O. A., & Errico, A. L. (1989). Performance deficits on tests of problem solving in alcoholics: Cognitive or motivational impairment? *Journal of Substance Abuse, 1,* 381–392.

Schaeffer, K. W., Parsons, O. A., & Yohman, J. R. (1984). Neuropsychological differences between male familial and nonfamilial alcoholics and nonalcoholics. *Alcoholism: Clinical and Experimental Research, 8,* 347–351.

Schafer, K., Butters, N., Smith, T., Irwin, M., Brown, S., Hanger, P., et al. (1991). Cognitive performance of alcoholics: A longitudinal evaluation of the role of drinking history, depression, liver function, nutrition, and family history. *Alcoholism: Clinical and Experimental Research, 15,* 653–660.

Schau, E. J., O'Leary, M. R., & Chaney, E. F. (1980). Reversibility of cognitive deficit in alcoholics. *Journal of Studies on Alcohol, 41,* 733–740.

Schottenbauer, M. A., Momenan, R., Kerick, M., & Hommer, D. W. (2007). Relationships among aging, IQ, and intracranial volume in alcoholics and control subjects. *Neuropsychology, 21*(3), 337–345.

Schuckit, M. A. (1987). Biological vulnerability to alcoholism. *Journal of Consulting and Clinical Psychology, 55,* 301–309.

Schuckit, M. A. (1994). A clinical model of genetic influences in alcohol dependence. *Journal of Studies on Alcohol, 55,* 5–17.

Schuckit, M. A., Butters, N., Lyn, L., & Irwin, M. (1987). Neuropsychologic deficits and the risk for alcoholism. *Neuropsychopharmacology, 1,* 45–53.

Schuckit, M. A., Irwin, M., & Brown, S. A. (1990). The history of anxiety symptoms among 171 primary alcoholics. *Journal of Studies on Alcohol, 51,* 34–41.

Schuckit, M. A., Irwin, M., & Smith, T. L. (1994). One-year incidence rate of major depression and other psychiatric disorders in 239 alcoholic men. *Addiction, 89,* 441–445.

Schuckit, M. A., Smith, T. L., Anthenelli, R., & Irwin, M. (1993). Clinical course of alcoholism in 636 male inpatients. *American Journal of Psychiatry, 150,* 786–792.

Schweinsburg, B. C., Alhassoon, O. M., Taylor, M. J., Gonzalez, R., Videen, J. S., Brown, G. G., et al. (2003). Effects of alcoholism and gender on brain metabolism. *The American Journal of Psychiatry, 160,* 1180–1183.

Schweinsburg, B. C., Taylor, M. J., Alhassoon, O. M., Dager, A. D., Tapert, S. F., Patterson, T. L., et al. (2002). Spectroscopy and cognitive functioning in alcoholics with withdrawal seizures (abstract). *Journal of the International Neuropsychological Society, 8* (2), 252.

Schweinsburg, B. C., Taylor, M. J., Alhassoon, O. M., Videen, J. S., Brown, G. G., Patterson, T. L., et al. (2001). Chemical pathology in brain white matter of recently detoxified alcoholics: A 1H magnetic resonance spectroscopy investigation of alcohol-associated frontal lobe injury. *Alcoholism, Clinical and Experimental Research, 25*(6), 924–934.

Sharp, J. R., Rosenbaum, G., Goldman, M. S., & Whitman, R. D. (1977). Recoverability of psychological functioning following alcohol abuse: Acquisition of meaningful synonyms. *Journal of Consulting and Clinical Psychology, 45,* 1023–1028.

Shaw, T. G., Mortel, K. F., Meyer, J. S., Rogers, R. L., Hardenberg, J., & Cutaia, M. M. (1984). Cerebral blood flow changes in benign aging and cerebrovascular disease. *Neurology, 34,* 855–862.

Shear, P. K., Jernigan, T. L., & Butters, N. (1994). Volumetric magnetic resonance imaging quantification of longitudinal brain changes in abstinent alcoholics. *Alcoholism: Clinical and Experimental Research, 18,* 172–176.

Shelton, M. D., & Parsons, O. A. (1987). Alcoholics' self-assessment of their neuropsychological functioning in everyday life. *Journal of Clinical Psychology, 43,* 395–403.

Sher, K. J., Walitzer, K. S., Wood, P. K., & Brent, E. E. (1991). Characteristics of children of alcoholics: Putative risk factors, substance use and abuse, and psychopathology. *Journal of Abnormal Psychology, 100,* 427–448.

Sherer, M., Nixon, S. J., Parsons, O. A., & Adams, R. L. (1992). Performance of alcoholic and brain-damaged subjects on the Luria Memory Word Test. *Archives of Clinical Neuropsychology, 7,* 499–504.

Shimamura, A. P., Jernigan, T. L., & Squire, L. R. (1988). Korsakoff's syndrome: Radiological (CT) findings and neuropsychological correlates. *Journal of Neuroscience, 8,* 4400–4410.

Silberstein, J. A., & Parsons, O. A. (1979). Neuropsychological impairment in female alcoholics. In M. Galanter (Ed.), *Currents in alcoholism* (pp. 481–495). New York: Grune and Stratton.

Silberstein, J. A., & Parsons, O. A. (1981). Neuropsychological impairment in female alcoholics: Replication and extension. *Journal of Abnormal Psychology, 90,* 179–182.

Sinha, R., Bernardy, N., & Parsons, O. A. (1992). Long-term test–retest reliability of event-related potentials in normals and alcoholics. *Biological Psychiatry, 32,* 992–1003.

Smith, J. W., & Layden, T. A. (1972). Changes in psychological performance and blood chemistry in alcoholics during and after hospital treatment. *Quarterly Journal of Studies on Alcohol, 33,* 379–394.

Smith, K. J., & Eckardt, M. J. (1991). The effects of prenatal alcohol on the central nervous system. *Recent Developments in Alcoholism, 9,* 151–164.

Solomon, D. A., & Malloy, P. F. (1992). Alcohol, head injury, and neuropsychological function. *Neuropsychology Review, 3,* 249–280.

Sowell, E. R., Mattson, S. N., Thompson, P. M., Jernigan, T. L., Riley, E. P., & Toga, A. W. (2001). Mapping callosal morphology and cognitive correlates: effects of heavy prenatal alcohol exposure. *Neurology, 57*(2), 235–244.

Sparadeo, F. R., Zwick, W., & Butters, N. (1983). Cognitive functioning of alcoholic females: An exploratory study. *Drug and Alcohol Dependence, 12,* 143–150.

Streissguth, A. P., Barr, H. M., & Sampson, P. D. (1990). Moderate prenatal alcohol exposure: Effects on child IQ and learning problems at age 7 1/2 years. *Alcoholism: Clinical and Experimental Research, 14,* 662–669.

Streissguth, A. P., Bookstein, F. L., Sampson, P. D., & Barr, H. M. (1989). Neurobehavioral effects of prenatal alcohol: Part III. PLS analyses of neuropsychologic tests. *Neurotoxicology and Teratology, 11,* 493–507.

Streissguth, A. P., Sampson, P. D., Olson, H. C., Bookstein, F. L., Barr, H. M., Scott, M., et al. (1994). Maternal drinking during pregnancy: Attention and short-term memory in 14-year-old offspring—A longitudinal prospective study. *Alcoholism: Clinical and Experimental Research, 18,* 202–218.

Stringer, A. Y., & Goldman, M. S. (1988). Experience-dependent recovery of block design performance in male alcoholics: Strategy training versus unstructured practice. *Journal of Studies on Alcohol, 49,* 406–411.

Sullivan, E. V. (2003). Compromised pontocerebellar and cerebellothalamocortical systems: Speculations on their contributions to cognitive and motor impairment in nonamnesic alcoholism. *Alcoholism: Clinical and Experimental Research, 27*(9), 1409–1419.

Sullivan, E. V., Fama, R., Rosenbloom, M. J., & Pfefferbaum, A. (2002). A profile of neuropsychological deficits in alcoholic women. *Neuropsychology, 16*(1), 74–83.

Sullivan, E. V., Rosenbloom, M. J., & Pfefferbaum, A. (2000). Pattern of motor and cognitive deficits in detoxified alcoholic men. *Alcoholism: Clinical and Experimental Research, 24*(5), 611–621.

Sullivan, E. V., Rosenbloom, M. J., Serventi, K. L., Deshmukh, A., & Pfefferbaum, A. (2003). Effects of alcohol dependence comorbidity and antipsychotic medication on volumes of the thalamus and pons in schizophrenia. *American Journal of Psychiatry, 160,* 1110–1116.

Sutker, P. B., & Allain, A. N. (1987). Cognitive abstraction, shifting, and control: Clinical sample comparisons of psychopaths and nonpsychopaths. *Journal of Abnormal Psychology, 96,* 73–75.

Tapert, S. F., & Brown, S. A. (1999). Neuropsychological correlates of adolescent substance abuse: Four-year outcomes. *Journal of the International Neuropsychological Society, 5*(6), 481–493.

Tarter, R. E. (1973). An analysis of cognitive deficits in chronic alcoholics. *Journal of Nervous and Mental Disease, 157,* 138–147.

Tarter, R. E. (1975). Brain damage associated with chronic alcoholism. *Diseases of the Nervous System, 36,* 185–187.

Tarter, R. E. (1980). Brain damage in chronic alcoholics: A review of the psychological evidence. In D. Richter (Ed.), *Addiction and brain damage* (pp. 267–297). Baltimore: University Park Press.

Tarter, R. E. (1982). Psychosocial history, minimal brain dysfunction and differential drinking patterns of male alcoholics. *Journal of Clinical Psychology, 38,* 867–873.

Tarter, R. E. (1988). Are there inherited behavioral traits that predispose to substance abuse? *Journal of Consulting and Clinical Psychology, 56,* 189–196.

Tarter, R. E., & Alterman, A. I. (1984). Neuropsychological deficits in alcoholics: Etiological considerations. *Journal of Studies on Alcohol, 45,* 1–9.

Tarter, R. E., & Edwards, K. L. (1986). Multifactorial etiology of neuropsychological impairment in alcoholics. *Alcoholism: Clinical and Experimental Research, 10,* 128–135.

Tarter, R. E., Goldstein, G., Alterman, A., Petrarulo, E. W., & Elmore, S. (1983). Alcoholic seizures: Intellectual and neuropsychological sequelae. *Journal of Nervous and Mental Disease, 171,* 123–125.

Tarter, R. E., Hays, A. L., Sandford, S. S., & Van Thiel, D. H. (1986a). Cerebral morphological abnormalities associated with non-alcoholic cirrhosis. *Lancet, 2,* 893–895.

Tarter, R. E., Hegedus, A. M., Goldstein, G., Shelly, C., & Alterman, A. I. (1984). Adolescent sons of alcoholics: Neuropsychological and personality characteristics. *Alcoholism: Clinical and Experimental Research, 8,* 216–222.

Tarter, R. E., Hegedus, A. M., Van Thiel, D. H., Edwards, N., & Schade, R. R. (1987). Neurobehavioral correlates of cholestatic and hepatocellular disease: Differentiation according to disease specific characteristics and severity of the identified cerebral dysfunction. *International Journal of Neuroscience, 32,* 901–910.

Tarter, R. E., Hegedus, A. M., Van Thiel, D. H., Gavaler, J. S., & Schade, R. R. (1986b). Hepatic dysfunction and neuropsychological test performance in alcoholics with cirrhosis. *Journal of Studies on Alcohol, 47,* 74–77.

Tarter, R. E., Jacob, T., & Bremer, D. A. (1989a). Cognitive status of sons of alcoholic men. *Alcoholism: Clinical and Experimental Research, 13,* 232–235.

Tarter, R. E., Jacob, T., & Bremer, D. L. (1989b). Specific cognitive impairment in sons of early onset alcoholics. *Alcoholism: Clinical and Experimental Research, 13,* 786–789.

Tarter, R. E., & Jones, B. M. (1971). Motor impairment in chronic alcoholics. *Diseases of the Nervous System, 32,* 632–636.

Tarter, R. E., McBride, H., Buonpane, N., & Schneider, D. U. (1977). Differentiation of alcoholics: Childhood history of minimal brain dysfunction, family history, and drinking pattern. *Archives of General Psychiatry, 34,* 761–768.

Tarter, R. E., & Parsons, O. A. (1971). Conceptual shifting in chronic alcoholics. *Journal of Abnormal Psychology, 77,* 71–75.

Tarter, R. E., & Van Thiel, D. H. (1985). *Alcohol and the brain: Chronic effects.* New York: Plenum Press.

Tarter, R. E., Van Thiel, D. H., Arria, A. M., Carra, J., & Moss, H. (1988). Impact of cirrhosis on the neuropsychological test performance of alcoholics. *Alcoholism: Clinical and Experimental Research, 12,* 619–621.

Templer, D. I., Ruff, C. F., & Simpson, K. (1975). Trail making test performance of alcoholics abstinent at least a year. *International Journal of the Addictions, 10,* 609–612.

Tivis, L. J., Parsons, O. A., Glenn, S. W., & Nixon, S. J. (1993). Differences in cognitive impairment between VA and community treatment center alcoholics. *Psychology of Addictive Behaviors, 7,* 43–51.

Torvik, A. (1987). Brain lesions in alcoholics: Neuropathological observations. *Acta Medica Scandinavica, 717*(Suppl.), 47–54.

Torvik, A., Lindboe, C. F., & Rogde, S. (1982). Brain lesions in alcoholics: A neuropathological study with clinical correlations. *Journal of the Neurological Sciences, 56,* 233–248.

Trivedi, S., & Raghavan, R. (1989). Cognitive functioning of alcoholics and its relationship with prognosis. *Drug and Alcohol Dependence, 23,* 41–44.

Tuck, R. R., & Jackson, M. (1991). Social, neurological and cognitive disorders in alcoholics. *Medical Journal of Australia, 155,* 225–229.

Turner, J., & Parsons, O. A. (1988). Verbal and nonverbal abstracting: Problem-solving abilities and familial alcoholism in female alcoholics. *Journal of Studies on Alcohol, 49,* 281–287.

Unkenstein, A. E., & Bowden, S. C. (1991). Predicting the course of neuropsychological status in recently abstinent alcoholics: A pilot study. *The Clinical Neuropsychologist, 5,* 24–32.

Victor, M., Adams, R. D., & Collins, G. H. (1989). *The Wernicke–Korsakoff Syndrome.* Philadelphia: F. A. Davis Company.

Vighetto, A., Charles, N., Salzmann, M., Confavreux, C., & Aimard, G. (1991). Korsakoff's syndrome as the initial presentation of multiple sclerosis. *Journal of Neurology, 238,* 351–354.

Vitiello, M. V., Prinz, P. N., Personius, J. P., Nuccio, M. A., Ries, R. K., & Koerker, R. M. (1987). History of chronic alcohol abuse is associated with increased nighttime hypoxemia in older men. *Alcoholism: Clinical and Experimental Research, 11,* 368–371.

Volkow, N. D., Hitzemann, R., Wang, G. J., Fowler, J. S., Burr, G., Pascani, K., et al. (1992). Decreased brain metabolism in neurologically intact healthy alcoholics. *American Journal of Psychiatry, 149,* 1016–1022.

Volkow, N. D., Wang, G. J., Hitzemann, R., Fowler, J. S., Overall, J. E., Burr, G., et al. (1994). Recovery of brain glucose metabolism in detoxified alcoholics. *American Journal of Psychiatry, 151,* 178–183.

Vrbaski, S. R., & Ristić, M. (1985). Cerebellum lipids in rats after chronic ethanol treatment. *Journal of Neurochemistry, 44*(6), 1868–1872.

Walker, R. D., Donovan, D. M., Kivlahan, D. R., & O'Leary, M. R. (1983). Length of stay, neuropsychological performance, and aftercare: Influences on alcohol treatment outcome. *Journal of Consulting and Clinical Psychology, 51,* 900–911.

Wang, G. J., Volkow, N. D., Roque, C. T., Cestaro, V. L., Hitzemann, R. J., Cantos, E. L., et al. (1993). Functional importance of ventricular enlargement and cortical atrophy in healthy subjects and alcoholics as assessed with PET, MR imaging, and neuropsychologic testing. *Radiology, 186,* 59–65.

Waugh, M., Jackson, M., Fox, G. A., Hawke, S. H., & Tuck, R. R. (1989). Effect of social drinking on neuropsychological performance. *British Journal of Addiction, 84,* 659–667.

Wechsler, D. (1955). *Manual for the Wechsler Adult Intelligence Scale.* New York: The Psychological Corporation.

Wechsler, D. (1981). *Wechsler Adult Intelligence Scale-Revised Manual.* New York: The Psychological Corporation.

Wechsler, D., & Stone, C. P. (1945). *Wechsler Memory Scale Manual.* New York: The Psychological Corporation.

Whipple, S. C., Parker, E. S., & Noble, E. P. (1988). An atypical neurocognitive profile in alcoholic fathers and their sons. *Journal of Studies on Alcohol, 49,* 240–244.

Wik, G., Borg, S., Sjogren, I., Wiesel, F. A., Blomqvist, G., Borg, J., et al. (1988). PET determination of regional cerebral glucose metabolism in alcohol-dependent men and healthy controls using ^{11}C-glucose. *Acta Psychiatrica Scandinavica, 78,* 234–241.

Wilde, E. A., Bigler, E. D., Gandhi, P. V., Lowry, C. M., Blatter, D. D., Brooks, J., et al. (2004). Alcohol abuse and traumatic brain injury: Quantitative magnetic resonance imaging and neuropsychological outcome. *Journal of Neurotrauma, 21*(2), 137–147.

Wilkinson, D. A. (1982). Examination of alcoholics by computed tomographic (CT) scans: A critical review. *Alcoholism: Clinical and Experimental Research, 6,* 31–45.

Wilkinson, D. A. (1987). Discussion: CT scan and neuropsychological assessments of alcoholism. In O. A. Parsons, N. Butters, and P. E. Nathan (Eds.), *Neuropsychology of alcoholism: Implications for diagnosis and treatment* (pp. 76–102). New York: Guilford Press.

Williams, C. M., & Skinner, A. E. (1990). The cognitive effects of alcohol abuse: A controlled study. *British Journal of Addiction, 85,* 911–917.

Winterer, G. A., Kloppel, B., Heinz, A., Ziller, M., Dufeu, P., Schmidt, L. G., et al. (1998). Quantitative EEG QEEG predicts relapse in patients with chronic alcoholism and points to a frontally pronounced cerebral disturbance. *Psychiatry Research, 78,* 101–113.

Workman-Daniels, K. L., & Hesselbrock, V. M. (1987). Childhood problem behavior and neuropsychological functioning in persons at risk for alcoholism. *Journal of Studies on Alcohol, 48,* 187–193.

Yohman, J. R., & Parsons, O. A. (1985). Intact verbal paired-associate learning in alcoholics. *Journal of Clinical Psychology, 41,* 844–851.

Yohman, J. R., & Parsons, O. A. (1987). Verbal reasoning deficits in alcoholics. *The Journal of Nervous and Mental Disease, 175,* 219–223.

Yohman, J. R., Parsons, O. A., & Leber, W. R. (1985). Lack of recovery in male alcoholics' neuropsychological performance one year after treatment. *Alcoholism: Clinical and Experimental Research, 9,* 114–117.

York, J. L., & Biederman, I. (1991). Hand movement speed and accuracy in detoxified alcoholics. *Alcoholism: Clinical and Experimental Research, 15,* 982–990.

Zatz, L. M., Jernigan, T. L., & Ahumada, A. J., Jr. (1982). Changes on computed cranial tomography with aging: Intracranial fluid volume. *American Journal of Neuroradiology, 3,* 1–11.

Zipursky, R. B., Lim, K. O., & Pfefferbaum, A. (1989). MRI study of brain changes with short-term abstinence from alcohol. *Alcoholism: Clinical and Experimental Research, 13,* 664–666.

19

Neuropsychological Consequences of Drug Abuse

Raul Gonzalez, Jasmin Vassileva, and J. Cobb Scott

Human beings have used psychoactive substances for thousands of years for spiritual, medicinal, and recreational purposes (Merlin, 2003). Such substances affect neurotransmission, may have associated neuropsychological effects, and often have potential for abuse. With advances in agriculture and technology, coupled with boundless human curiosity, new psychoactive substances with potential for abuse emerge frequently. Use and possession of psychoactive drugs are often legislated due to medical, political, and social influences. Many are available legally (e.g., caffeine, alcohol, nicotine), whereas others may only be obtained through medical prescriptions (e.g., opiates), or are banned outright under most circumstances (e.g., cannabis, MDMA, LSD). The number of substances known to affect neurobehavioral functioning are vast, but scientific research has generally focused on those most frequently used. Preclinical studies, as well as human neuropathological and neuroimaging research, have been conducted to understand how specific drugs affect the brain. Although relevant, a thorough discussion of such topics would result in a voluminous work. In this chapter, we focus on investigations of the neuropsychological sequelae associated with use and misuse of popular psychoactive drugs by human subjects. Neither is it possible to cover all relevant investigations for each substance we review; thus, whenever possible we highlight findings from meta-analyses, large-scale investigations, and/or those with particularly illuminating findings.

Neurobehavioral effects of alcohol use are discussed in a separate chapter of this book.

Understanding the neurobehavioral consequences of substance use and substance use disorders is important from both a research neuroscience and clinical perspective. For example, functional and structural brain changes that occur as a result of acute administration and chronic use of specific substances can provide insights on how modulation of particular neurotransmitter systems affects the brain and behavior of human subjects. Insight into the neuroscience of human volition and reward attribution may be explored through examining the neural underpinnings of the "loss of control" that typically occurs with substance addiction. From a clinical standpoint, understanding the neuropsychological effects of substance use can help clinicians discern its impact in the presentation, diagnosis, and treatment planning of patients. Moreover, the sheer prevalence of licit and illicit substance use ensures that medical professionals in many fields are likely to encounter patients with history of substance use or with current substance use, even if they are referred for other neurobehavioral or mental health disorders. Indeed, almost half (46%) of individuals over 12 years of age in the United States reported using illicit drugs in their lifetime, with 2.8% of the U.S. population meeting criteria for a substance use disorder during 2005 (Substance Abuse and Mental Health Services Administration, 2006a). Substance use disorders are a significant public health issue, with economic impact due to disability, accidents, healthcare, and days missed from work. During 1995, the total economic burden of substance use was estimated to be $428.1 billion (Rice, 1999).

In order to better contextualize the research findings we discuss in this chapter, it is prudent to first discuss some important methodological issues that challenge most retrospective studies on neuropsychological effects of substance use. Although this list is not exhaustive, the reader must consider that: (1) patterns of substance use for any given substance often differ substantially across studies; (2) some studies incorporate samples of substance users that do not meet diagnosis for substance use disorders, whereas others examine performance in such subjects exclusively; (3) substance users often misuse multiple substances, which may have common as well as unique neuropsychological effects; (4) substance users often have other comorbid conditions known to affect neuropsychological functioning (e.g., psychiatric disorders); (5) some neurobehavioral problems may predate substance use or be worsened, rather than caused, by substance use.

Substance use characteristics of participants in research studies differ widely, based on parameters such as length of abstinence, amount of polydrug use, and severity of substance use (e.g., amount, frequency, duration, degree of addiction), which may lead to very discrepant findings across studies. For example, results may vary depending on participants' stage of abstinence; that is, whether they are actively using drugs (acute effects), have very recently stopped (withdrawal), are postwithdrawal but without full brain recovery from the effects of the drug or still have traces of the drug in their body (residual effects), or if much time has elapsed since last use (long term or permanent effects). Furthermore, it is important to note that being a substance user does not mean invariably that one has a substance use disorder, as most individuals that try or use a particular drug do not progress to meeting the criteria for a substance use disorder in their lifetime. The DSM-IV recognizes two general types of substance use disorders (abuse or dependence) for each of several drug classes. Some studies only include participants that have substance use

disorders, whereas others may focus on substance users that have consumed a specific substance a certain number of times (sometimes infrequently). These two populations are likely to be very different in terms of substance use severity, comorbid confounds, whether they are seeking treatment, and other factors that may influence neuropsychological functioning.

In this chapter, we will present research findings on the neuropsychological sequelae of substance use grouped by various major drugs and drug classes. This organizational scheme makes intuitive sense based on the unique pharmacological profiles and actions of these substances on neurotransmitters systems and provides a logical framework for discussion. However, this should not be misconstrued to suggest that the neuropsychological deficits described for a particular drug class are solely the cause of using that substance or are specific only to that substance. Use and abuse of multiple illicit drugs over a lifetime is common among individuals with substance dependence. One of the most formidable obstacles in studying the unique effects of drugs of abuse is the extremely high prevalence of polydrug use among addicts (Darke & Hall, 1995; Leri et al., 2003). Therefore, it is difficult to find subject samples that have predominantly used only one drug, and when such samples are successfully recruited, the ability to generalize from their findings to most drug users is questionable.

Furthermore, substance use disorders and/or substance addiction, regardless of the substance, appear to share a common neuropathophysiology, which involves orbitofrontal cortex and anterior cingulate, as well as parts of basal ganglia and limbic structures (Goldstein & Volkow, 2002). It has also been noted (Rogers & Robbins, 2001) that because all drugs of abuse are known to act on the mesocorticolimbic dopaminergic system, one would expect some common neurocognitive deficits to be associated with the abuse of various classes of drugs. Yet, because specific drugs of abuse also differentially affect other monoaminergic and neuropeptide systems in the brain, impairments in brain and cognitive functioning may differ depending on the specific pharmacological properties of the drug.

Finally, in all but a few of the studies we review, it remains unknown whether the observed neuropsychological deficits in substance users predate the onset of substance use and misuse or whether they are the direct result of substance use. There is a large literature showing genetic and neurobehavioral antecedent risk factors for substance dependence, which suggests that some neuropsychological problems are likely to predate drug use (e.g., Vanyukov et al., 2003). Without the use of twin studies or longitudinal research designs that follow participants through various stages of drug use (before use, during use, and during multiple time points after abstinence), these important questions remain difficult to answer. Despite the challenges presented by the aforementioned issues, much progress has been made in the understanding of how substance use and misuse affects neuropsychological functioning. In addition, it is worth noting that even if many neuropsychological abnormalities may predate substance use, it is also likely that they may be exacerbated with initiation and continuation of drug use.

Cannabis

Cannabis is the most commonly used illicit substance in the United States, with 40% of Americans over the age of 12 reporting lifetime use during 2005, and 8% reporting use during the past month (SAMHSA, 2006b). It is estimated that approximately 3.7% of the world's population has used cannabis—compared to 0.3%–0.4% for cocaine and heroin (United Nations Office on Drugs and Crimes, 2004). Given its widespread use, it is no wonder that the effects of cannabis on neuropsychological functioning have been so avidly researched and debated.

Neuropsychological research on cannabis has been partially yoked to developments in understanding the chemical and neuropharmacological properties of its psychoactive ingredients. In 1964, the discovery of delta-9-tetrahydrocannabinol as the primary psychoactive substance in cannabis (Mechoulam & Gaoni, 1967) incited new research on its effects. It was not until 1988 when the first cannabinoid receptor (CB1) was identified in the mammalian brain (Devane et al., 1988) and later cloned (Matsuda et al., 1990). CB1 is widely distributed

in human brain tissue with densest concentration being in basal ganglia, cerebellum, hippocampus, and amygdala (Breivogel & Childers, 1998; Glass et al., 1997). We now understand that cannabis exerts its psychoactive effects by binding to CB1 receptors.

Cannabis produces its psychoactive effects in minutes when smoked, with peak plasma concentrations achieved in 3–10 minutes and psychoactive effects lasting approximately 2–3 hours (Grotenhermen, 2003). Acute intoxication has been shown to affect neuropsychological functioning. The extant literature on acute effects of cannabis provide substantial evidence for dose-dependent impairments in verbal and nonverbal memory characterized by retrieval based deficits and intrusion errors for information presented during intoxication, but no recall or recognition difficulties with information learned prior to intoxication (Ranganathan & D'Souza, 2006). However, conflicting reports exist on the magnitude of impairments on other neuropsychological abilities (i.e., processing speed, reaction time, executive functions).

Understanding the acute effects of cannabis on neuropsychological functioning is an important endeavor; however, it can be argued that understanding the residual, long-term, or permanent changes in neuropsychological functioning that are brought about by cannabis use is of greater public health significance. Numerous studies have been conducted internationally over the last several decades, which have been the subject of several reviews. But, such qualitative reviews have sometimes come to different conclusions despite substantial overlap in the studies surveyed. For example, some conclude "no evidence that marijuana...leads to functional impairment" (Wert & Raulin, 1986), others note "the data support a 'drug residue' effect...but evidence is as yet insufficient to support or refute a...toxic effect on the CNS" (Pope et al., 1995), and others purport that "long-term use of cannabis leads to a more subtle and selective impairment of cognitive function" (Solowij et al., 2002).

Discrepancies in interpretations of study results are in part fueled by substantial heterogeneity in research designs and by methodological limitations in many of the studies that have been reviewed, which have been previously discussed in detail (Gonzalez et al., 2002; Pope, 2002; Pope et al., 1995). In order to overcome the limitations associated with qualitative reviews, Grant et al. (2003) conducted a meta-analysis on studies examining nonacute (i.e., residual, long-term, permanent) effects of cannabis use, including only those studies that met a liberal (but essential) set of inclusion criteria. These criteria were chosen to represent minimal scientific standards needed to infer that differences in neuropsychological performance were associated with cannabis use, rather than other potential confounds (e.g., neurological disorders, psychiatric comorbidity, other drug use). Of the 40 studies that were found to examine the question of residual effects of cannabis on neuropsychological functioning (Gonzalez et al., 2002), only 11 met all criteria (Block & Ghoneim, 1993; Carlin & Trupin, 1977; Croft et al., 2001; Ehrenreich et al., 1999; Gouzoulis-Mayfrank et al., 2000; Hamil, 1996; Pope & Yurgelun-Todd, 1996; Pope et al., 2001; Rodgers, 2000; Solowij, 1995; Solowij et al., 2002) and an additional 4 (Deif et al., 1993; Grant et al., 1973; Rochford et al., 1977; Wig & Varma, 1977) violated only one criterion. When data from all investigations were subjected to meta-analysis, there was evidence for a small overall detrimental effect of cannabis use history on overall neuropsychological functioning ($d = -.16$), with only two of eight neuropsychological domains (Learning and Recall/Retention) showing significant, albeit small, effect sizes ($d = -.21$ and $-.27$, respectively). This is consistent with approximately a quarter-of-a-standard-deviation difference between cannabis users and nonusers. No significant effect sizes were observed for the domains of simple reaction time, attention, verbal/language, abstraction/executive, perceptual motor, and motor. Subjects in the studies included in the meta-analysis varied substantially in length of abstinence from cannabis, and data points were too few to conduct analyses examining how length of abstinence affected the magnitude of observed effects.

It is worth noting that several studies have been published after the meta-analysis which report neuropsychological problems among abstinent heavy cannabis users in various ability areas (Bolla et al., 2002, 2005; Kelleher et al., 2004; Messinis et al., 2006; Verdejo-Garcia et al., 2007a; Whitlow et al., 2004), including on measures of decision making and inhibitory control. However, findings from one investigation suggested that history of cannabis use may have been neuroprotective in the context of methamphetamine use (Gonzalez et al., 2004). However, like results from the meta-analysis, the aforementioned studies cannot establish a causal link between cannabis use and neuropsychological dysfunction, nor can they confidently determine the course of changes in neuropsychological functioning that may occur after abstinence.

A few investigations have employed longitudinal, within-subjects designs with neuropsychological tests administered at different time points after verified abstinence, in order to strengthen causal inferences between cannabis use and neuropsychological functioning. Pope and colleagues (2001) examined groups of former heavy cannabis users, current heavy cannabis users, and nonusing controls that completed thorough neuropsychological assessments on days 0, 1, 7, and 28 of supervised abstinence. Only current heavy users performed more poorly than controls (on measures of verbal memory); however, these differences were observed only on days 0, 1, and 7, with no significant differences detected by day 28.

Two studies by another research group (Fried et al., 2002, 2005) examined the neuropsychological performance of a large cohort of longitudinally followed individuals at ages 9–12 and again at 17–20 years of age, which were divided into four groups based on their cannabis use status at the second assessment (current regular heavy cannabis smokers, current regular light smokers, former regular smokers, and a nonusing control group). Groups were fairly well matched with adequate control of pertinent confounds, and all cannabis users reported abstinence for at least 1 day prior to testing. Relative to their baseline, only current heavy cannabis users demonstrated a statistically significant decrease in IQ scores, immediate and delayed memory, and information processing speed. However, effect sizes were fairly small. Current light users and former heavy users were not found to differ significantly from controls.

A noteworthy study that overcomes the issue of possible premorbid differences between cannabis users and nonusers employed a comprehensive battery of neuropsychological tests to examine 54 monozygotic male twin pairs discordant for history of cannabis use (Lyons et al., 2004). Twin pairs were genetically identical, raised in the same home, and did not differ on history of alcohol, other drug use, or indices of achievement (e.g., employment, educational attainment, school grades, and academic difficulties). None of the participants reported using cannabis at least 1 year prior to testing, with last regular use occurring about 27 years ago on average. Of over 50 different indices of neuropsychological performance examined, statistically significant differences of very small magnitude were observed only on one measure of visuoconstructional abilities.

Overall, there is ample evidence demonstrating acute effects of cannabis use on neuropsychological functioning, particularly in the areas of learning and memory. Similarly, deficits are also often observed among current, heavy cannabis users when not intoxicated, with less frequent users of cannabis often showing minimal or no deficits. Further, most of the current evidence suggests that neuropsychological consequences of cannabis use appear to dissipate over time, indicative of no permanent neuropsychological effects.

Cocaine

The latest United Nations Office on Drugs and Crime world drug report (UNODC, 2006) estimates that in 2005, there were 13.4 million cocaine users worldwide. The United States remains the single largest cocaine market worldwide, accounting for more than 40% of all cocaine users (UNODC, 2006). Within the United States, there were 2.4 million people estimated to have used cocaine within the past month (SAMHSA, 2006b), which represents an increase of 400,000 more users compared to 2004. Similarly, the number of current crack users in the United States increased from 467,000 in 2004 to 682,000 in 2005. Furthermore, in 2005 there were 1.5 million Americans who met criteria for abuse of or dependence on cocaine.

Cocaine is an alkaloid found in the leaves of *Erythroxylon coca,* a tree indigenous to South America. Currently the two most commonly used forms of cocaine are cocaine hydrochloride, the powdered form of cocaine typically taken intranasally, and crack-cocaine, a freebase form of cocaine which is smoked. Cocaine is a vasoconstrictor known to cause cerebrovascular complications of an ischemic nature (Jacobs et al., 1989), resulting in neuronal damage that may further lead to neuropsychological impairments. There has been a dramatic increase in the number of cases of cocaine-related ischemic and hemorrhagic strokes, particularly with the advent of crack-cocaine use in the early 1980s (Levine et al., 1991). Evidence exists showing greater abuse liability, greater propensity for dependence, and more severe consequences when cocaine is smoked (i.e., crack) when compared with intranasal use (i.e., cocaine hydrochloride; Hatsukami & Fischman, 1996).

Structural neuroimaging studies with cocaine users reveal volume loss primarily in the frontal lobe white matter (Bartzokis et al., 2002) and gray matter (Franklin et al., 2002), but also in the temporal and insular cortices (Bartzokis et al., 2002; Franklin et al., 2002). Functional neuroimaging studies with cocaine addicts document widespread perfusion and activation deficits in frontal and limbic areas (Figure 19–1, see also the color version in the color insert section; Goldstein & Volkow, 2002; Volkow et al., 1993) that may persist even after months of abstinence (Strickland et al., 1993; Volkow et al., 1992). Typically, acute administration of cocaine results in higher dopamine (DA) concentrations in limbic but not in frontal regions (Goldstein & Volkow, 2002). However, discontinuation of cocaine use leads to a marked downregulation of dopaminergic activity and decreased DA receptor availability, perhaps related to the reduced glucose metabolism and cerebral blood flow typically observed in frontal and limbic areas of abstinent cocaine users (Goldstein & Volkow, 2002; Volkow et al., 1993). In addition, these marked structural and functional brain abnormalities in chronic cocaine users have been associated with a variety of impairments in neuropsychological function.

Acute administration of cocaine has been associated with improved attentional performance (Johnson et al., 1998), speed of information processing (Higgins et al., 1990), and

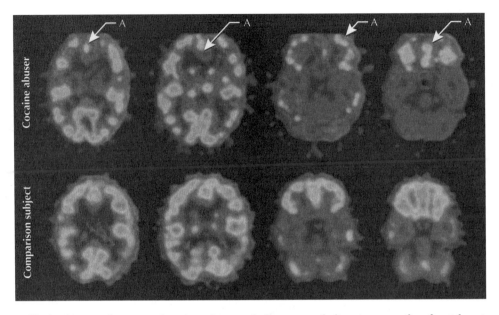

Figure 19–1. Cocaine abusers tend to show decreased glucose metabolism in areas of prefrontal cortex (A) relative to healthy controls. (Image courtesy of Dr. Nora Volkow.)

inhibitory control (Fillmore et al., 2006), consistent with the acute effects of other stimulant drugs on neurocognitive function. A review of the long-term sequelae of chronic cocaine use suggests detrimental effects on cognitive functioning, although the neurocognitive deficits tend to be subtle and specific rather than general. Consistent with the frontal lobe dysfunction seen in neuroimaging studies, the deficits primarily cluster in the domain of executive functioning (Bolla et al., 1998), which are abilities mediated primarily by the prefrontal cortex and its reciprocal cortical and subcortical connections. However, results across studies of chronic cocaine users have often been equivocal. Some studies of abstinent individuals have noted significant deficits in attention (di Schlafani et al., 2002; Roselli & Ardila, 1996), executive functioning (Beatty et al., 1995; di Schlafani et al., 2002; Rosselli et al., 2001), psychomotor speed (Bauer, 1994; O'Malley & Gawin, 1990; Robinson et al., 1999), and visual and verbal memory (Bolla et al., 2000; Roselli & Ardila, 1996; van Gorp et al., 1999), whereas others report negligible effects (Selby & Azrin, 1998; Volkow et al., 1992), and yet others report better performance in chronic cocaine users relative to healthy controls (Bolla et al., 1999). In addition, a number of well-controlled prospective studies indicate

that the neurocognitive deficits associated with cocaine use may persist even after months of abstinence (Ardila et al., 1991; Di et al., 2002; O'Malley & Gawin, 1990).

To our knowledge, there are no meta-analyses on the long-term neurocognitive effects of chronic cocaine use; however, a recent quantitative review (Jovanovski et al., 2005) compared effect sizes across studies and concluded that the most consistent impairments are indeed noted in attention and executive function. The authors analyzed the effect sizes of approximately 140 neuropsychological test indices provided by various clinical neuropsychological measures in 15 studies conducted between 1987 (when cocaine dependence first appeared as a diagnostic category in the DSM-III-R) and 2002. The total combined sample size included 481 cocaine (predominantly crack) users and 586 healthy controls. The median effect size for all tests was 0.35. Across individual studies, the largest effect sizes were observed on measures of attention, followed by measures of working memory, visual memory, and executive function (with the exception of the Wisconsin Card Sorting Test). On the other hand, minimal effect sizes were obtained on tests of language functions including verbal fluency and sensory-perceptual function. However, the results of this quantitative review should nonetheless be interpreted with caution due to the wide variations in length of abstinence (e.g., 0–1075 days) across the studies included in the analysis, which suggests that some studies may have tested individuals during acute intoxication rather than during long-term abstinence from cocaine use. Similarly, several of the studies in the analysis included subjects with other concurrent substance use, most notably alcohol.

It is worth noting that alcohol use is indeed very common among cocaine users, with upto 84% of those with cocaine dependence also being alcohol dependent (Regier et al., 1990). The presence of alcohol and cocaine in the body creates cocaethylene, a psychoactive substance which has a half-life three to five times that of cocaine and carries an 18- to 25-fold increase in the risk of sudden death compared to cocaine alone (Andrews, 1997). However, research to date has been inconclusive regarding the combined effects of alcohol and cocaine on neuropsychological functioning, with some studies suggesting that the vasodilative effects of alcohol may in fact attenuate some of the vasoconstrictive and neuropsychological effects of cocaine (Abi-Saab et al., 2005; Robinson et al., 1999).

It has been suggested that tasks that simulate real-life decision making or inhibitory control would be more sensitive to the neurocognitive impairments associated with drug addiction (Goldstein et al., 2004). Indeed, more recent studies using novel neurocognitive paradigms investigating decision making related to delay and risk (e.g., the Iowa Gambling Task, the Rogers Decision-Making Task, the Delayed Reward Discounting task, the Balloon Analogue Risk Task), as well as tasks assessing the ability to inhibit behavioral responses such as the Stop-Signal and Go/No-Go paradigms, have begun to provide more conclusive evidence of the long-term deficits observed in cocaine users. Recent studies indicate that chronic cocaine use is associated with deficits in response inhibition (Fillmore et al., 2006; Hester et al., 2007), decision making assessed with the Iowa Gambling Task (Bechara et al., 2001; Verdejo-Garcia & Perez-Garcia, 2007), delayed reward discounting (Kirby & Petry, 2004), and risk-taking propensity (using the Balloon Analogue Risk

Task) (Bornovalova et al., 2005). Because most of these tasks measure various dimensions of impulsivity and behavioral inhibition, results indicate that nonacute long-term effects of chronic cocaine use tends to be manifested primarily in impaired impulse control and related functions.

Benzodiazepines

Sedatives and tranquilizers are one of the most common groups of drugs used illicitly in the United States, with 12.4% of individuals reporting lifetime use without a prescription (SAMHSA, 2006b). These figures do not take into account individuals with prescriptions for these drugs, who are also at risk for dependence and possible neuropsychological sequelae. This drug class represents a variety of different chemicals of varying potency, bioavailability, and half-lives, which makes it difficult to generalize results of studies across all substances that can be categorized as sedatives, tranquilizers, and hypnotics. During the twentieth century, barbiturates were some of the most commonly abused sedatives. Although some investigations reported deleterious neurocognitive effects from abuse of these substances (e.g., Grant et al., 1978), results were variable (for review see Grant & Mohns, 1975) and could be attributed in part to the heterogeneity across substances in this drug class. Barbiturates are still used as analgesics and for treatment of some disorders, including epilepsy (for review of neurocognitive side effects in this context see Reynolds & Trimble, 1985); however, prescription and availability of barbiturates has been largely replaced by benzodiazepines. Indeed, the most commonly used drugs in this class currently are the benzodiazepines, which were reported to have been used illicitly by 8.1% of Americans during 2005, with diazepam, alprazolam, and lorazepam most often consumed (SAMHSA, 2006b). The neuropsychological effects of benzodiazepines have also been the most extensively studied. Some authors posit that benzodiazepines have strong potential for abuse, dependence, and addiction based on animal and human studies (Busto & Sellers, 1991); however, others point out that benzodiazepine abuse usually takes place in the context of other substance use and is generally not a drug of choice (O'Brien, 2005). Regardless, during 2005, 0.2% of Americans met a substance use disorder diagnosis for tranquilizers (compare with 0.1% for heroin) (SAMHSA, 2006b). Given their prevalence of use and potential for abuse, combined with the availability of controlled investigations and well-executed quantitative reviews, we focus only on the neuropsychological effects of benzodiazepines in the section below.

Benzodiazepines exert their mind-altering, and therapeutic, effects through their action on GABA receptors (Haefely, 1978). Acute subjective effects of benzodiazepine administration are well known and include sedation, slowing, relaxation, and anterograde amnesia, which clearly have implications for performance on neuropsychological tests (Barker et al., 2003; Buffett-Jerrott & Stewart, 2002). Indeed, benzodiazepines are clinically used to induce anterograde amnesia in patients undergoing surgery. Acutely, benzodiazepines have been associated with neuropsychological deficits in almost every cognitive domain that is typically assessed clinically, including processing speed, explicit and implicit memory, attention, and executive functions (Buffett-Jerrott & Stewart 2002).

Barker, Greenwood, Jackson, and Crowe (2004a, 2004b) conducted two meta-analyses to quantitatively compile results from peer-reviewed studies published between 1980–2000 that examined neuropsychological effects of "long-term" (at least 1 year) benzodiazepine use. In their first meta-analysis (Barker et al., 2004a), they calculated and compiled effect sizes representing differences between groups of "long-term" benzodiazepine users and controls for each of 12 separate neuropsychological domains (sensory processing, nonverbal memory, speed of processing, attention/concentration, general intelligence, working memory, psychomotor speed, visuospatial, problem solving, verbal memory, motor control, and verbal reasoning) across the 15 studies that met their inclusion criteria (Bergman et al., 1980, 1989; Birzele, 1992; Curran, 1992; Gorenstein et al., 1994, 1995; Hendler et al., 1980; Lucki & Rickels, 1986; Petursson et al., 1983; Rickels et al., 1999; Sakol & Power, 1988;

Salzman et al., 1992; Tata et al., 1994; Tonne et al., 1995; Vignola et al., 2000). Among users in the combined data set, benzodiazepines were used for an average of 9.9 years, at an average daily dose of 17.2 mg (diazepam equivalent), with the last daily dose taken ranging from 18 days to 4 hours prior to evaluation. The vast majority of studies included in the meta-analysis excluded individuals with other drug use or heavy alcohol use. Despite using a conservative approach to calculate effect sizes in each study, the authors found statistically significant moderate to large effects, indicating poorer neuropsychological performance by benzodiazepine users across all 12 domains for which data were compiled.

A second meta-analysis was conducted to determine if published studies showed recovery of neuropsychological functioning after abstinence from benzodiazepines. Using similar study inclusion criteria and the same grouping of effect sizes into 12 neuropsychological domains, Barker and colleagues (2004b) examined if neuropsychological functioning improves among "long-term" benzodiazepine users after withdrawal with data from 12 investigations (Bergman et al., 1980, 1989; Birzele, 1992; Curran, 1992; Gorenstein et al., 1994, 1995; Petursson et al., 1983; Rickels et al., 1999; Sakol & Power, 1988; Salzman et al., 1992; Tata et al., 1994; Tonne et al., 1995). Overall, subjects used benzodiazepines for approximately 10 years, with an average daily dose of 15.3 mg (diazepam equivalent). A median of 3 months (range 1–65) elapsed between initial neuropsychological assessment and postwithdrawal assessment. Small to moderate statistically significant effect sizes, indicating improvements in performances, were observed for 5 of the 11 cognitive domains (visuospatial, attention/concentration, general intelligence, psychomotor speed, and nonverbal memory). A second set of analyses with all but one of these studies revealed that even after the postwithdrawal assessment, previous benzodiazepine users still demonstrated significant impairments of small to large effect sizes in 8 ability areas (verbal memory, psychomotor speed, speed of processing, motor control, visuospatial, general intelligence, attention/concentration, and nonverbal memory) compared to controls.

Barker et al. (2003, 2004a, 2004b) have noted that many of the investigations conducted to examine the long-term effects of benzodiazepines (including many of the studies in their meta-analyses) suffer from significant limitations, which include inadequate control for other substance use and lack of a "high anxiety" non-benzodiazepine using control group in addition to a group of healthy controls. They addressed these issues by examining the neuropsychological performance of three groups of carefully recruited (to exclude potential confounds), well-matched subjects: normal healthy controls, individuals with anxiety disorders but no benzodiazepine use (ANX Group), and a group of individuals with anxiety disorders and history of using benzodiazepines for at least 12 months (BZD Group). The group of subjects with history of benzodiazepine use reported on an average approximately 9 years of use with a mean length of abstinence of approximately 42 months, with all reporting more than 6 months of withdrawal from benzodiazepine use. Participants completed several neuropsychological measures assessing five ability areas (verbal memory, motor control, nonverbal memory, visuospatial, and attention/concentration). The BZD group performed significantly worse than the ANX and normal control groups on verbal memory and motor control domains, as well as on one measure of nonverbal memory, despite no significant differences between the BZD and ANX group on self-reported levels of anxiety symptoms (both of these groups reported significantly greater levels of anxiety than controls). No significant differences on neuropsychological measures were observed between the ANX and healthy controls. Thus, differences in neuropsychological performance of benzodiazepine users could not be attributed to anxiety.

Thus, there is compelling evidence to suggest that long-term use of benzodiazepines cause significant and widespread neuropsychological impairments that persist even after many months of abstinence. The majority of participants in the studies reviewed above were long-term users of therapeutic doses of benzodiazepines, not unlike many patients who may present for neuropsychological assessments in clinical settings. In light of the available evidence, it is prudent to expect that long-term use of benzodiazepines alone is likely to impart deficits on neuropsychological assessments conducted in such patients. However, it is difficult to generalize what nonacute effect on neuropsychological functioning would be bestowed by intermittent recreational use of benzodiazepines. Recreational users of benzodiazepines are likely to consume higher doses than those reported in the above studies. One can speculate that chronic, long-term use at doses that are at least in the range of the studies reviewed would yield similar effects.

Methamphetamine (Ice, Crank, Crystal, Meth)

Methamphetamine (MA) is a potent, addictive psychostimulant that has marked effects on the central nervous system (CNS) for up to 12 hours and may be administered in a variety of different ways (e.g., injection, snorting, or smoking). MA use has been increasingly prevalent in recent years, in part due to its easy and cost-efficient synthesis in clandestine laboratories with inexpensive, over-the-counter ingredients. Recent estimates indicate that approximately 10 million people (around 4.5% of the U.S. population) have tried MA at some point in their lives, while 1.3 million persons used MA in the past year (SAMHSA, 2006b). In addition, dramatic increases in both MA-related emergency room visits and MA abusers seeking treatment have occurred from the mid-1990s until the present (SAMHSA, 2006a, 2006c). While some data suggest that MA use in the United States may have, at minimum, plateaued, MA use remains a significant problem in many areas, including the Western region of the United States and Southeast Asia (SAMHSA, 2006b).

The acute effects of MA use can include euphoria, increased respiration, vasoconstriction, tachycardia, appetite suppression, enhanced energy, increased libido, insomnia, irritability, and even paranoid psychosis. Chronic use of MA is associated with a host of adverse psychosocial (e.g., interpersonal, financial), psychiatric (e.g., depression, psychosis), and physical sequelae, including potent effects on CNS functioning due to its rapid transport across the blood–brain barrier (Barr et al.,

2006). Long-term MA use results in significant neurotoxicity, which may occur via a number of processes (e.g., oxidative stress and hyperthermia; Cadet et al., 2005; Davidson et al., 2001). This neurotoxicity is evident in several neurotransmitter systems, but is perhaps most notable on nigrostriatal dopaminergic projections, thus altering the function of the dopamine rich fronto-striato-thalamo-cortical loops (Cass, 1997). To this end, neuroimaging studies have demonstrated various structural (e.g., Thompson et al., 2004), cerebral blood flow (e.g., Chang et al., 2002; Figure 19–2, see also the color version in the color insert section), and metabolic (e.g., Ernst et al., 2000) abnormalities in the prefrontal cortex and striatum of MA dependent persons, and postmortem studies have found reductions in levels of dopamine and its metabolites in the striatum of MA abusers (Moszczynska et al., 2004; Wilson et al., 1996).

Although administration of moderate doses of MA has been shown to enhance certain cognitive abilities, such as attention and speed of information processing (e.g., Johnson et al., 2005; Mohs et al., 1980), chronic MA use is often associated with mild to moderate neuropsychological impairment. Interpretation of the literature remains difficult due to varying methodologies and participant characteristics,

but current estimates suggest that approximately 40% of persons with MA dependence demonstrate global neuropsychological impairment (i.e., deficits in at least two cognitive domains; Rippeth et al., 2004). Commensurate with the hypothesized neurotoxicity to dopaminergic frontostriatal circuits, MA users evidence impairment in cognitive processes highly dependent upon these circuits, including episodic memory, complex information-processing speed, attention/working memory, response inhibition, decision making, and novel problem solving. Comorbid disease conditions such as HIV (Rippeth et al., 2004), Hepatitis C infection (Cherner et al., 2005), or Attention-Deficit/ Hyperactivity Disorder (ADHD; Sim et al., 2002) may further increase the risk of cognitive impairment. Whether the abuse of other substances such as alcohol or cocaine in combination with MA imparts additive risk remains unanswered by the literature; however, comorbid marijuana use may not exacerbate impairment (Gonzalez et al., 2004).

One of the most marked impairments seen with MA abuse is in verbal episodic memory (Hoffman et al., 2006; Rippeth et al., 2004). The severity of this deficit persists into both early (Jaffe et al., 2005; Kalechstein et al., 2003) and sustained (Johanson et al., 2006) MA abstinence. In addition, episodic memory may be

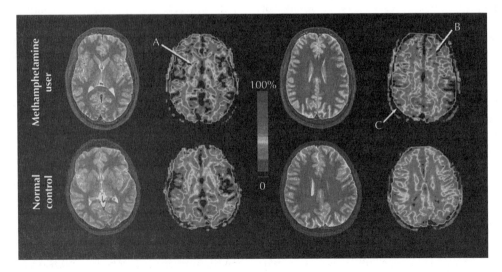

Figure 19–2. Decreased rCBF in putamen (A) and frontal (B) white matter of a methamphetamine user compared to a healthy control. Increased rCBF in a methamphetamine user compared to a healthy control in parietal brain regions (C). (Image courtesy of Dr. Linda Chang.)

particularly susceptible to the effects of MA relapse (Simon et al., 2004). Woods and colleagues (2005) recently investigated the nature of MA-associated verbal learning deficits, finding that inefficiencies in the strategic (i.e., executive) components of encoding and memory likely underlie the impairments observed, supporting a model of MA-associated neurotoxicity in frontostriatal circuits.

Executive dysfunction is also commonly observed in MA-abusing populations, and may contribute to maintenance of drug-seeking behaviors (Bechara & Damasio, 2002). Significant impairments are evident in the ability to switch attentional sets or inhibit responses as assessed by the Stop-Signal Task (Monterosso et al., 2005) and the interference condition of the Stroop task (Salo et al., 2002; Simon et al., 2000, 2002; cf. Hoffman et al., 2006). However, a recent study identified a dissociation between set-shifting and inhibition in an MA dependent population, finding inhibition selectively compromised (Salo et al., 2005), a conclusion bolstered by lack of impairment on another task examining set-shifting abilities, Trail-Making Test, Part B (Chang et al., 2005; Kalechstein et al., 2003; Rippeth et al., 2004; cf. Simon et al., 2000). Interestingly, deficits in selective inhibition in MA abusers may be associated with reduced levels of N-acetyl aspartate (NAA), a brain metabolite commonly regarded as a marker of neuronal integrity, in the anterior cingulate (Salo et al., 2007).

In relation, MA dependent individuals may have marked difficulties with impulsivity, decision making, and conceptualization. While some studies have shown deficits in abstract reasoning and conceptualization (e.g., Simon et al., 2002), others have shown equivocal results (e.g., Rippeth et al., 2004). Similar to other substance dependent individuals (e.g., Coffey et al., 2003), MA dependent individuals evidence elevated rates of "delay discounting," which ostensibly reflects decision-making ability and impulsivity by examining a participant's sensitivity to delayed versus immediate rewards (Hoffman et al., 2006; Monterosso et al., 2006). In addition, MA dependent individuals may evidence fundamental dysfunction during decision-making tasks, including stimulus-driven behavior and elevated rates of disadvantageous and/or impulsive choices (Gonzalez et al., 2007; Paulus et al., 2002). Moreover, hypoactivation in prefrontal, parietal, and insular cortex during a decision-making task, potentially signifying reduced processing resources, has been shown to predict incidence of relapse (Paulus et al., 2005).

MA dependent patients are frequently noted to have variable attention, slowed processing, and increased distractibility. Deficits are most apparent on tests of complex processing, especially when working memory is taxed or some degree of decision making is required, while basic attentional and processing abilities appear unaffected (Chang et al., 2002). For example, deficits in MA abusers are uncommon on tasks such as the Trail-Making Test, Part A or simple digit recognition, but are more pronounced on tests such as the n-back task or Digit Symbol (Johanson et al., 2006; Kalechstein et al., 2003; Simon et al., 2002). Sustained attention may also be particularly susceptible to MA-associated damage (London et al., 2005).

Reduced psychomotor abilities have also been noted in chronic MA abusers, although the incidence has been less than what might be expected given the vulnerability of the striatum to MA-associated neurotoxicity (Moszczynska et al., 2004). Indeed, only a few studies have found impairment in motor functioning, mostly assessed via the Grooved Pegboard test (Chang et al., 2002; Volkow et al., 2001b). Nevertheless, preclinical and case studies suggest the presence of motor abnormalities in MA abusers, and it is possible that the measures employed have not been sensitive enough to detect the subtle nature of impairment (Caligiuri & Buitenhuys, 2005). Alternatively, it is possible that MA-associated damage to dopaminergic systems is more pronounced in cognitive (i.e., caudate) than motor (i.e., putamen) areas of the striatum (Caligiuri & Buitenhuys, 2005; Moszczynska et al., 2004).

It remains unresolved whether the extent of neuropsychological impairment is related to MA use variables and/or extent of dependence. Some studies have reported that rates of cognitive impairment correlate with frequency (Simon et al., 2000) or amount (Monterosso et al., 2005) of MA use, while other studies have found no associations with measures assessing the severity of MA dependence or MA use frequency, amount, or duration (Chang et al., 2002; Hoffman et al., 2006; Johanson et al., 2006; Rippeth et al., 2004). This ambiguity may be due to the unreliability of self-report substance use data, or it may reflect the influence of other, often unmeasured factors (e.g., psychiatric symptomatology).

Although a number of studies have shown at least partial recovery of both dopamine terminal function and brain metabolism with extended abstinence (e.g., Volkow et al., 2001a; Wang et al., 2004), it is still unclear whether this recovery results in any substantive changes in neuropsychological function. In early stages of abstinence, deficits are, at the least, equivalent to those seen in currently abusing individuals, especially in the domains of learning/memory and complex working memory (Hoffman et al., 2006; Kalechstein et al., 2003; Simon et al., 2004; cf. Chang et al., 2005). Volkow and colleagues (2001a) found that deficits in psychomotor and memory performance continued to persist after 9 months of abstinence, albeit in a less severe form, despite a significant degree of recovery in dopamine terminal function. Longer periods of abstinence may lead to further recovery of cognitive function, although some deficits still remain, most notably on episodic memory and cognitive inhibition (Johanson et al., 2006).

MDMA (Ecstasy)

MDMA (3,4-methylenedioxymethamphetamine), or "ecstasy," was first synthesized and patented in the early 1900s, but did not gain popularity until the late 1980s and early 1990s as a recreational drug (Parrott, 2001). The chemical structure of MDMA shares properties of both stimulants and hallucinogens—partly because it does not fit neatly into either of these drug categories and because of its social and emotional effects, it was classified with similar substances (i.e., MBDB, MDA, MDAE) as an "entactogen" (Nichols et al., 1986). During 2005, 4.7% of Americans over 12 years of age reported using "ecstasy" (SAMHSA, 2006b). Tablets of ecstasy are expected to contain MDMA; however, they may contain MDMA combined with other psychoactive substances (e.g., mescaline, heroin, caffeine, dextromethorphan, MA) or may

contain no MDMA at all (Tanner-Smith, 2006), though MDMA is most often present (Parrott, 2004). In the sections below, we will use the terms MDMA and "ecstasy" interchangeably, acknowledging the varying amount of MDMA that may have been consumed by participants in retrospective studies.

MDMA produces its psychoactive effects primarily through its effects on serotonin—but also dopamine and norepinephrine—producing initial effects in humans after oral ingestion in about a half-hour to an hour and lasting about 3 to 4 hours (Green et al., 2003). Preclinical studies suggest that MDMA may produce substantial neurotoxic damage to serotonergic nerve terminals (Green et al., 2003), though its generalizability to recreational MDMA use by humans has been the subject of substantial controversy (Baumann et al., 2007; Gouzoulis-Mayfrank & Daumann, 2006a). Nonetheless, many investigators have sought to document neuropsychological impairments that may arise as a result of MDMA use.

Dumont and Verkes (2006) conducted a systematic semiqualitative review of 29 studies examining acute effects of MDMA using well operationalized criteria for study inclusion, such as: (1) MDMA must be administered to healthy volunteers with known and verified dose; (2) studies must employ a placebo-controlled design; and (3) acute effects must be measured. Many studies examined subjective effects of naïve and experienced users, with the most common effects (reported in more than half of studies) being euphoria, extroversion, improved mood, confusion, liking for the drug, hallucination, and a "drug effect." Studies examining acute effects of MDMA on neuropsychological functions were too few to warrant generalization for most cognitive ability areas. However, a sufficient number of studies were available that examined performance on measures of attention (Cami et al., 2000; Farre et al., 2004; Gamma 2000; Hernandez-Lopez et al., 2002; Lamers et al., 2003; Vollenweider 1998), although none found significant effects of MDMA. Other studies have reported impairments in memory, but these effects appear to be transient (Kuypers & Ramaekers, 2005, 2007).

Substantially more literature is available on residual effects of MDMA use, which have primarily been examined using retrospective designs. Recently, this work has been synthesized in two separate meta-analyses that had substantial overlap in the studies they included. Verbaten (2003) synthesized data from between-group studies examining neuropsychological effects of recreational MDMA use published between 1975 and 2002. The only other criterion for including a study in their analysis was that subjects must be free of MDMA or other illicit drugs for at least 1week prior to their evaluation. The analyses, which were based on a pool of 14 studies (Bhattachary & Powell, 2001; Croft et al., 2001; Fox et al., 2001; Gouzoulis-Mayfrank et al., 2000; McCann et al., 1999; Morgan, 1998, 1999; Morgan et al., 2002; Parrott et al., 1998; Reneman et al., 2001a, 2001b; Rodgers, 2000; Verkes et al., 2001; Wareing et al., 2000), indicated that MDMA users demonstrated significant impairments relative to controls on measures of short-term memory, long-term memory, and attention. More recently, Kalechstein et al. (2007), conducted a meta-analysis of similar scope with studies published until 2004. A liberal criteria that included any study on neuropsychological effects of MDMA with matched controls yielded 23 studies for synthesis, whereas a stricter criteria that required studies to match groups on demographic and premorbid factors and ensured that MDMA users were abstinent at assessment and not treatment seeking winnowed the dataset to 11 investigations (Bhattachary & Powell, 2001; Fox et al., 2001; Gouzoulis-Mayfrank et al., 2000; McCardle et al., 2004; Morgan, 1999; Morgan et al., 2002; Parrott et al., 1998; Reneman et al., 2000; Rodgers, 2000; Verkes et al., 2001; Wareing et al., 2000). Findings indicated significantly poorer performance by MDMA users, with generally moderate effect sizes observed on all domains (i.e., attention/concentration, verbal learning and memory, nonverbal learning and memory, motor/psychomotor speed, and executive functions).

Although most published MDMA investigations make valiant attempts to soundly establish relationships between MDMA use and neuropsychological functions, most are also limited by the many confounds that are inherent in retrospective studies of drug use. Specifically, MDMA users are often frequent users of other

illicit substances with known neuropsychological sequelae, have significant psychiatric comorbidity, and may have neuropsychological deficits that predate drug use, factors that are difficult to address and severely limit inferences (Gouzoulis-Mayfrank & Daumann, 2006b; Gouzoulis-Mayfrank et al., 2006a). Similarly, data provided by meta-analyses are only as good as the studies they examine, and most of the investigations included in the meta-analyses described above employed samples of MDMA users who also used other illicit substances, making it difficult to attribute the deficits observed specifically to MDMA use and not polysubstance use in general.

Stronger causal inferences can be made from longitudinal investigations of changes in neuropsychological functioning among MDMA users after abstinence or continued use, although such studies have reported mixed findings. One study compared subjects after 18 months of abstinence from MDMA and noted no changes in cognitive function (Gouzoulis-Mayfrank et al., 2005). In contrast, other studies have found stable (or improved) memory performances in abstinent users while showing persistent declines in memory performance among continued users at a 1-year (Zakzanis & Young, 2001) and 2-year follow-up (Zakzanis & Campbell, 2006). However, these studies also suffered from samples of MDMA users who also used varied other illicit substances.

In order to avoid issues of polydrug use among MDMA users and to better isolate effects of MDMA on neuropsychological functioning, Halpern et al. (2004) carefully recruited subjects with a very restrictive criteria to obtain two small groups of rave attendees (one group consisting of fairly "pure" users of MDMA) that were very well matched on premorbid and demographic factors. MDMA users were negative on urine toxicology testing for various substances and reported at least 10 days of abstinence from MDMA. Comparisons of both groups showed few significant differences across measures on a very thorough neuropsychological battery, though MDMA users were more likely to perform more poorly. However, stratifying MDMA users into moderate (22–50 lifetime uses) and heavy (60–450 lifetime uses) groups revealed that the heavy group was

significantly worse on some (but not all) measures of processing speed and executive functions. Although this investigation has made
one of the best efforts to date in controlling
for important confounds common in other
MDMA studies, their findings have also been
criticized due to their very small sample size
and likelihood of Type-I errors given the few
statistically significant results found among the
many neuropsychological tests they conducted
to examine between-group differences (Lyvers
& Hasking, 2004).

At this time, preclinical studies appear to
substantiate neurotoxicity from MDMA administration. However, investigations on neuropsychological deficits of recreational MDMA
use have been difficult and inconclusive, partially due to confounds inherent in the manner this drug is often used; that is, usually in
small infrequent quantities and/or in the context of substantial other drug use. Evidence is
persuasive for neuropsychological impairments
among heavy MDMA users; however, whether
the deficits observed can be specifically attributed to MDMA or other confounds remains to
be untangled.

Opiates

Opiates account for the largest proportion of
people in drug treatment services worldwide
(UNODC, 2006). According to the UNODC,
in 2005 almost 16 million people were estimated to abuse opiates worldwide. Within the
United States, an estimated 136,000 Americans
were current heroin users in 2005 (SAMHSA,
2006b). Compared to almost 15 million current marijuana users and 2.4 million current
cocaine users in the United States, the number
of current heroin users does not appear to be
as high, yet opiate addiction is associated with
some of the most devastating health and social
consequences.

In addition to heroin, the past few years
have seen a marked increase in the use of prescription opioid medications such as Vicodin
and OxyContin, with more than 4.7 million
Americans using such medications (SAMHSA,
2006b), more than the number abusing cocaine,
heroin, inhalants, and hallucinogens combined. Alarmingly, 1.5 million Americans meet

criteria for dependence or abuse of prescription
opioid medications, which is about the same as
the number of Americans classified with dependence or abuse of cocaine.

Opiate is an extract derived from the seeds
of the opium poppy plant which has been
cultivated by ancient civilizations in Persia,
Mesopotamia, and Egypt. However, although
opiate drugs have been used for centuries, it was
only in recent decades that their mode of action
began to be elucidated. In 1973, three different
laboratories (Pert & Snyder, 1973; Simon et al.,
1973; Terenius, 1973) almost simultaneously
reported the first evidence of the existence of
stereospecific binding sites or receptors for
opiates in the brain. Currently, three types of
opioid receptors have been identified (μ- [mu],
κ- [kappa], and δ- [delta] opioid receptors).
The presence of such receptors in animal and
human brain further suggested that endogenous opiate-like substances most likely exist in
the body. This led to the discovery of the endogenous opioid neuropeptides (Hughes et al.,
1975), commonly referred to as endorphins (a
contraction of "endogenous" and "morphine").

Neuroimaging findings reveal a plethora of
abnormalities related to chronic opiate use.
Structural neuroimaging studies of opiate
abusers typically show general cortical atrophy
(Pezawas et al., 1998; Strang & Gurling, 1989)
and enlargement of external and internal CSF
spaces (Danos et al., 1998; Kivisaari et al., 2004;
Pezawas et al., 1998). Functional neuroimaging
studies investigating the acute effects of opiates
on brain functioning generally reveal decreases
in blood flow or glucose utilization (Forman
et al., 2004; London et al., 1990; Martin-Soelch
et al., 2001), with some studies (Ersche et al.,
2006; Pezawas et al., 2002) reporting increased
activations in various regions of the prefrontal
cortex. Similarly, most neuroimaging studies
of the withdrawal / abstinence effects of opiates
typically reveal decreased activation in frontal
(Gerra et al., 1998; Krystal et al., 1995; Rose et al.,
1996), parietal (Krystal et al., 1995; Rose et al.,
1996), and temporal cortices (Rose et al., 1996).
There is some indication that the decreased
frontal activations are reversible with increased
length of abstinence (Rose et al., 1996).

Available evidence indicates that chronic
opiate addiction is also associated with

neuropsychological impairments across multiple cognitive domains. Yet, in comparison with cannabis, cocaine, and other stimulants, there has been considerably less research into the neuropsychological impairments related to opiate use. Early investigations examining the effects of narcotics addiction on intelligence testing reported no deficits (Isbell & Fraser, 1950; Pfeffer & Ruble, 1948). However, research into opiate effects did not become more common in the US until the 1970s due to the widespread heroin use by Vietnam veterans. Earlier studies (e.g., Fields & Fullerton, 1975; Hill & Mikhael, 1979; Korin, 1974) typically used traditional neuropsychological batteries consisting of the Bender-Gestalt, Halstead–Reitan, or the Wechsler Adult Intelligence Scale. Results were somewhat inconsistent, with some studies (Hill & Mikhael, 1979; Grant et al., 1978; Korin, 1974) reporting impaired performance of heroin addicts, whereas another (Fields & Fullerton, 1974) found that heroin addicts performed better than a control group.

More recent studies on the acute effects of opiates have typically been conducted with patients on methadone maintenance therapy (MMT) and reveal a wide variety of cognitive deficits including impairments in attention (Darke et al., 2000; Specka et al., 2000), working memory (Mintzer & Stitzer, 2002; Specka et al., 2000), memory (Darke et al., 2000), psychomotor speed (Darke et al., 2000; Mintzer & Spitzer, 2002; Specka et al., 2000), problem solving (Darke et al., 2000), and decision making (Mintzer & Spitzer, 2002; Rotheram-Fuller et al., 2004). Of these, the impairments in psychomotor speed and decision making seem to be the most reliable findings. Other investigators (Guerra et al., 1987; Hill & Mikhael, 1979; Korin, 1974; Rounsaville et al., 1982; Strang & Gurling, 1989) have tested neuropsychological functioning in current heroin users (not on MMT) and have revealed generally mixed results. For example, some studies (e.g., Rounsaville et al., 1982) reported no neuropsychological impairments, whereas others noted impairments in attention (Guerra et al., 1987; Strang & Gurling, 1989), short-term memory (Guerra et al., 1987), verbal fluency (Guerra et al., 1987), and memory (Strang & Gurling, 1989). Studies investigating acute administration effects of prescription opioids such as OxyContin (Zacny & Gutierrez, 2003) and hydrocodone (Zacny, 2003) using a brief cognitive battery have revealed minor impairments in attention and psychomotor functioning, but these effects were much less pronounced and short-lasting than the effects of benzodiazepines.

The long-term residual effects of opiates appear to cluster in the domain of executive functioning (Ersche et al., 2006; Lyvers & Yakimoff, 2003) and most typically include impairments in working memory (Papageoriou et al., 2003) and various dimensions of impulsivity, such as decision making (Fishbein et al., 2007) and delayed reward discounting (Kirby & Petry, 2004; Kirby et al., 1999). With regard to the temporal stability of these impairments, the literature suggests that there tends to be improvement of cognitive functioning over time with abstinence (Guerra et al., 1987). The number of well-designed studies investigating the long-term neurocognitive effects of prescription opioid medication is still limited. A recent review (Chapman et al., 2002) of their effects in patients with chronic pain or cancer concluded that impairments tend to be mild, short-lived and are most often present on simple measures of psychomotor speed but not on more complex cognitive tasks. It should be noted that not all patients in the studies were abstinent at the time of testing and that the participants were typically clinical populations with many confounding variables other than pain.

A number of more recent studies have begun to compare the neuropsychological functioning of current heroin addicts to that of individuals addicted to other substances such as stimulants or cocaine (Bornovalova et al., 2005; Ersche et al., 2006; Kirby & Petry, 2004; Ornstein et al., 2000; Rogers et al., 1999; Verdejo-Garcia & Perez-Garcia, 2007; Verdejo-Garcia et al., 2007b). In general, most studies reveal that the neurocognitive impairments in stimulant users are more severe and extensive than those in heroin users. Studies comparing neuropsychological functioning between users of different drug classes are particularly informative in revealing some of the unique effects of specific drugs on cognition. Overall, the effects of opiates on neurocognitive function are variable and not as consistent as those present in users of other classes of drugs and need to be addressed by meta-analytic studies, which may bring greater clarity of the type of neurocognitive impairments associated with opiate use.

Discussion

Use of illicit substances is a common practice, and abuse of such substances is often associated with neuropsychological deficits that may vary in pattern, severity, and duration. Although many methodological challenges have served to obfuscate our understanding of how specific substances affect neuropsychological functioning, significant improvements in the quality and quantity of such research has occurred in the last decade. In the previous edition of this book, one of the conclusions arrived at by Carlin and O'Malley (1996) was that literature on neuropsychological effects of substance use had many shortcomings at the time. They noted such issues as small sample sizes, lack of well-characterized participant groups, and absence of longitudinal investigations. Further, they identified meta-analysis as a useful technique that deals with the issue of small sample sizes and provides better consensus on available research findings. Since then, the clarity of our knowledge has improved and many of these issues have been addressed, but progress has been somewhat uneven across substances. For example, meta-analyses have furthered our understanding on the nonacute neuropsychological effects of cannabis, benzodiazepines, and MDMA. Unfortunately, to our knowledge, meta-analyses have not been conducted on effects of cocaine or opiates. Typically, meta-analyses have included only studies that meet important methodological criteria to minimize effects of confounds and improve confidence in associations observed between substance use and neuropsychological functioning. Similarly, longitudinal investigations examining long-term effects of substances have emerged for cannabis, benzodiazepines, and MDMA, but remain relatively few. Such studies are critical to our understanding on the persistence of neuropsychological changes due to drug use. Moreover, when participants are tested prior to initiation of substance use and compared to other time points afterwards, the important question of whether some neuropsychological disturbances predated substance use can be examined.

Carlin and O'Malley (1996) also suggested that examining the effects of substance use on neuropsychological functioning was not an actively pursued research topic at the time. Currently, research on effects of substance use and addiction on brain functioning is thriving, and the published manuscripts on the topic have dramatically increased. This is likely in part due to major advances in the understanding of the neuropathophysiology of drug addiction, which have been made in recent years. However, many other factors that differ across substances have also likely served to stimulate research. For example, increase in MA research has been concomitant with increase in use of the drug in the United States. Similarly, MDMA abuse did not receive widespread notoriety until its use became more widespread, and many empirical investigations on its neuropsychological effects have followed thereafter. For cannabis, a significant surge in studies was in part due to characterization of an endogenous cannabinoid signaling system with implications for therapeutic applications. Furthermore, the renewed debate on medicinal use of cannabis and its legal status have strengthened the relevance of understanding its neuropsychological effects. Scientific discoveries and sociopolitical factors will likely continue to steer research priorities on topics of substance use, hopefully resulting in persistent increases in the quality of such studies for decades to come.

References

Abi-Saab, D., Beauvais, J., Mehm, J., Brody, M., Gottschalk, C., & Kosten, T. R. (2005). The effect of alcohol on the neuropsychological functioning of recently abstinent cocaine-dependent subjects. *American Journal on Addictions, 14*, 166–178.

Andrews, P. (1997). Cocaethylene toxicity. *Journal of Addictive Diseases, 16*, 75–84.

Ardila, A., Roselli, M., & Strumwasser, S. (1991). Neuropsychological deficits in chronic cocaine abusers. *International Journal of Neuroscience, 57*, 73–79.

Barker, M. J., Greenwood, K. M., Jackson, M., & Crowe, S. F. (2004a). Cognitive effects of long-term benzodiazepine use: A meta-analysis. *CNS Drugs, 18,* 37–48.

Barker, M. J., Greenwood, K. M., Jackson, M., & Crowe, S. F. (2004b). Persistence of cognitive effects after withdrawal from long-term benzodiazepine use: A meta-analysis. *Archives of Clinical Neuropsychology, 19,* 437–454.

Barker, M. J., Jackson, M., Greenwood, K. M., & Crowe, S. F. (2003). Cognitive effects of benzodiazepine use: A review. *Australian Psychologist, 38,* 202–213.

Barr, A. M., Panenka, W. J., MacEwan, G. W., Thornton, A. E., Lang, D. J., Honer, W. G., et al. (2006). The need for speed: An update on methamphetamine addiction. *Journal of Psychiatry and Neuroscience, 31*(5), 301–313.

Bartzokis, G., Beckson, M., Lu P. H., Edwards, N., Bridge, P., & Mintz, J. (2002). Brain maturation may be arrested in chronic cocaine addicts. *Biological Psychiatry, 51,* 605–611.

Bauer, L. O. (1994). Vigilance in recovering cocaine-dependent and alcohol-dependent patients: A prospective study. *Addictive Behaviors, 19,* 599–607.

Baumann, M. H., Wang, X., & Rothman, R. B. (2007). 3,4-Methylenedioxymethamphetamine (MDMA) neurotoxicity in rats: A reappraisal of past and present findings. *Psychopharmacology, 189,* 407–424.

Beatty, W. W., Katzun, V. M., Moreland, V. J., & Nixon, S. J. (1995). Neuropsychological performance of recently abstinent alcoholics and cocaine abusers. *Drug and Alcohol Dependence, 37,* 247–253.

Bechara, A., & Damasio, H. (2002). Decision-making and addiction (part I): Impaired activation of somatic states in substance dependent individuals when pondering decisions with negative future consequences. *Neuropsychologia, 40,* 1675–1689.

Bechara, A., Dolan, S., Denburg, N., Hindes, A., Anderson, S. W., & Nathan, P. E. (2001). Decision-making deficits, linked to a dysfunctional ventromedial prefrontal cortex, revealed in alcohol and stimulant abusers. *Neuropsychologia, 39,* 376–389.

Bergman, H., Borg, S., Engelbrektson, K., & Vikander, B. (1989). Dependence on sedative-hypnotics: Neuropsychological impairment, field dependence and clinical course in a 5-year follow-up study. *British Journal of Addiction, 84,* 547–553.

Bergman, H., Borg, S., & Holm, L. (1980). Neuropsychological impairment and exclusive abuse of sedatives or hypnotics. *American Journal of Psychiatry, 137,* 215–217.

Bhattachary, S., & Powell, H. (2001). Recreational use of 3, 4-methylenedioxymethamphetamine (MDMA) or "ecstasy": Evidence for cognitive impairment. *Psychological Medicine, 31,* 647–658.

Birzele, H. J. (1992). Benzodiazepine induced amnesia after long-term medication and during withdrawal. *European Review of Applied Psychology, 42,* 277–283.

Block, R. I., & Ghoneim, M. M. (1993). Effects of chronic marijuana use on human cognition. *Psychopharmacology, 110,* 219–228.

Bolla, K. I., Brown, K., Eldreth, D., Tate, K., & Cadet, J. L. (2002). Dose-related neurocognitive effects of marijuana use. *Neurology, 59,* 1337–1343.

Bolla, K. I., Cadet, J., & London, E. D. (1998). The neuropsychiatry of chronic cocaine abuse. *Journal of Neuropsychiatry and Clinical Neurosciences, 10,* 280–289.

Bolla, K. I., Eldreth, D. A., Matochik, J. A., & Cadet, J. L. (2005). Neural substrates of faulty decision-making in abstinent marijuana users. *Neuroimage., 26,* 480–492.

Bolla, K. I., Funderburk, F. R., & Cadet, J. L. (2000). Differential effects of cocaine and cocaine + alcohol on neurocognitive performance. *Neurology, 54,* 2285–2292.

Bolla, K. I., Rothman, R. B., & Cadet, J. L. (1999). Dose-related neurobehavioral effects of chronic cocaine use. *Journal of Neuropsychiatry and Clinical Neurosciences, 11,* 361–369.

Bornovalova, M. A., Daughters, S. B., Hernandez, G. D., Richards, J. B., & Lejuez, C. W. (2005). Differences in impulsivity and risk-taking propensity between primary users of crack cocaine and primary users of heroin in a residential substance-use program. *Experimental and Clinical Psychopharmacology, 13,* 311–318.

Breivogel, C. S., & Childers, S. R. (1998). The functional neuroanatomy of brain cannabinoid receptors. *Neurobiology of Disease, 5,* 417–431.

Buffett-Jerrott, S. E., & Stewart, S. H. (2002). Cognitive and sedative effects of benzodiazepine use. *Current Pharmaceutical Design, 8,* 45–58.

Busto, U. E., & Sellers, E. M. (1991). Anxiolytics and sedative/hypnotics dependence. *British Journal of Addiction, 86,* 1647–1652.

Cadet, J. L., Jayanthi, S., & Deng, X. (2005). Methamphetamine-induced neuronal apoptosis involves the activation of multiple death pathways. Review. *Neurotoxicity Research, 8,* 199–206.

Caligiuri, M. P., & Buitenhuys, C. (2005). Do preclinical findings of methamphetamine-induced motor abnormalities translate to an observable clinical phenotype? *Neuropsychopharmacology, 30,* 2125–2134.

Cami, J., Farre, M., Mas, M., Roset, P. N., Poudevida, S., Mas, A., et al. (2000). Human pharmacology of 3, 4-methylenedioxymethamphetamine ("ecstasy"): Psychomotor performance and subjective effects.

Journal of Clinical Psychopharmacology, 20, 455–466.

Carlin, A. S., & Trupin, E. W. (1977). The effect of long-term chronic marijuana use on neuropsychological functioning. *International Journal of the Addictions, 12,* 617–624.

Carlin, A. S., & O'Malley, S. (1996). Neuropsychological consequences of drug abuse. In I. Grant and K. M. Adams (Eds.), *Neuropsychological assessment of neuropsychiatric disorders* (2nd ed.). New York: Oxford University Press.

Cass, W. A. (1997). Decreases in evoked overflow of dopamine in rat striatum after neurotoxic doses of methamphetamine. *Journal of Pharmacology and Experimental Therapeutics, 280*(1), 105–113.

Chang, L., Cloak, C., Patterson, K., Grob, C., Miller, E. N., & Ernst, T. (2005). Enlarged striatum in abstinent methamphetamine abusers: A possible compensatory response. *Biological Psychiatry, 57*(9), 967–974.

Chang, L., Ernst, T., Speck, O., Patel, H., DeSilva, M., Leonido-Yee, M., et al. (2002). Perfusion MRI and computerized cognitive test abnormalities in abstinent methamphetamine users. *Psychiatry Research, 114*(2), 65–79.

Chapman, S. L., Byas-Smith, M. G., & Reed, B. A. (2002). Effects of intermediate and long-term use of opioids on cognition in patients with chronic pain. *The Clinical Journal of Pain, 18,* S83–S90.

Cherner, M., Letendre, S., Heaton, R. K., Durelle, J., Marquie-Beck, J., Gragg, B., et al. (2005). Hepatitis C augments cognitive deficits associated with HIV infection and methamphetamine. *Neurology, 64*(8), 1343–1347.

Coffey, S. F., Gudleski, G. D., Saladin, M. E., & Brady, K. T. (2003). Impulsivity and rapid discounting of delayed hypothetical rewards in cocaine-dependent individuals. *Experimental and Clinical Psychopharmacology, 11*(1), 18–25.

Croft, R. J., Mackay, A. J., Mills, A. T. D., & Gruzelier, J. G. H. (2001). The relative contributions of ecstasy and cannabis to cognitive impairment. *Psychopharmacology, 153,* 373–379.

Curran, H. V. (1992). Memory functions, alertness and mood of long-term benzodiazepine users: A preliminary investigation of the effects of a normal daily dose. *Journal of Psychopharmacology, 6,* 69.

Danos, P., Van Roos, D., Kasper, S., Bromel, T., Broich, K., Krappel, C., et al. (1998). Enlarged cerebrospinal fluid spaces in opiate-dependent male patients: A stereological CT study. *Neuropsychobiology, 38,* 80–83.

Darke, S., & Hall, W. (1995). Levels and correlates of polydrug use among heroin users and regular amphetamine users. *Drug and Alcohol Dependence, 39,* 231–235.

Darke, S., Sims, J., McDonald, S., & Wickes, W. (2000). Cognitive impairment among methadone maintenance patients. *Addiction, 95,* 687–695.

Davidson, C., Gow, A. J., Lee, T. H., & Ellinwood, E. H. (2001). Methamphetamine neurotoxicity: Necrotic and apoptotic mechanisms and relevance to human abuse and treatment. *Brain Research Reviews, 36*(1), 1–22.

Deif, A., El, S. A., & Fawzy, R. K. (1993). Neurological, psychiatric and C.T. evaluation of chronic cannabis smokers. *Journal of the Medical Research Institute, 14,* 151–160.

Devane, W. A., Dysarz, F. A., Johnson, M. R., Melvin, L. S., & Howlett, A. C. (1988). Determination and characterization of a cannabinoid receptor in rat brain. *Molecular Pharmacology, 34,* 605–613.

Di, S. V., Tolou-Shams, M., Price, L. J., & Fein, G. (2002). Neuropsychological performance of individuals dependent on crack-cocaine, or crack-cocaine and alcohol, at 6 weeks and 6 months of abstinence. *Drug and Alcohol Dependence, 66,* 161–171.

Di Sclafani, V., Tolou-Shams, M., Price, L. J., & Fein, G. (2002). Neuropsychological performance of individuals dependent on crack-cocaine, or crack-cocaine and alcohol, at 6 weeks and 6 months of abstinence. *Drug and Alcohol Dependence, 66,* 161–171.

Dumont, G. J., & Verkes, R. J. (2006). A review of acute effects of 3,4-methylenedioxymethamphetamine in healthy volunteers. *Journal of Psychopharmacology, 20,* 176–187.

Ehrenreich, H., Rinn, T., Kunert, H. J., Moeller, M. R., Poser, W., Schilling, L., et al. (1999). Specific attentional dysfunction in adults following early start of cannabis use. *Psychopharmacology, 142,* 295–301.

Ersche, K. D., Fletcher, P. C., Roiser, J. P., Fryer, T. D., London, M., Robbins, T. W., et al. (2006). Differences in orbitofrontal activation during decision-making between methadone-maintained opiate users, heroin users and healthy volunteers. *Psychopharmacology, 188,* 364–373.

Ernst, T., Chang, L., Leonido-Yee, M., & Speck, O. (2000). Evidence for long-term neurotoxicity associated with methamphetamine abuse: A 1H MRS study. *Neurology, 54*(6), 1344–1349.

Farre, M., de la Torre, R., Mathúna, B. O., Roset, P. N., Peiró, A. M., Torrens, M., et al. (2004). Repeated doses administration of MDMA in humans: Pharmacological effects and pharmacokinetics. *Psychopharmacology, 173,* 364–375.

Fields, S., & Fullerton, J. (1975). Influence of heroin addiction in neuropsychological functioning. *Journal of Clinical and Consulting Psychology, 43,* 114.

Fillmore, M. T., Rush, C. R., & Hays, L. (2006). Acute effects of cocaine in two models of inhibitory control: Implications of non-linear dose effects. *Addiction, 101*, 1323–1332.

Fishbein, D. H., Krupitsky, E., Flannery, B. A., Langevin, D. J., Bobashev, G., Verbitskaya, E., et al. (2007). Neurocognitive characterizations of Russian heroin addicts without a significant history of other drug use. *Drug and Alcohol Dependence, 90*, 25–38.

Forman, S. D., Dougherty, G. G., Casey, B. J., Siegle, G. J., Braver, T. S., Barch, D. M., et al. (2004). Opiate addicts lack error-dependent activation of rostral anterior cingulate. *Biological Psychiatry, 55*, 531–537.

Fox, H. C., Parrott, A. C., & Turner, J. J. (2001). Ecstasy use: Cognitive deficits related to dosage rather than self-reported problematic use of the drug. *Journal of Psychopharmacology, 15*, 273.

Franklin, T. R., Acton, P. D., Maldjian, J. A., Gray, J. D., Croft, J. R., Dackis, C. A., et al. (2002). Decreased gray matter concentration in the insular, orbitofrontal, cingulate, and temporal cortices of cocaine patients. *Biological Psychiatry, 51*, 134–142.

Fried, P., Watkinson, B., James, D., & Gray, F. (2002). Current and former marijuana use: Preliminary findings of a longitudinal study of effects on IQ in Young adults. *Canadian Medical Association Journal, 166*, 887–891.

Fried, P. A., Watkinson, B., & Gray, R. (2005). Neurocognitive consequences of marihuana—a comparison with pre-drug performance. *Neurotoxicology and Teratology, 27*, 231–239.

Gamma, A. (2000). 3,4-Methylenedioxymethamphetamine (MDMA) modulates cortical and limbic brain activity as measured by[H 215 O]-PET in healthy humans. *Neuropsychopharmacology, 23*, 388–395.

Gerra, G., Calbiani, B., Zaimovic, A., Sartori, R., Ugolotti, G., Ippolito, L., et al. (1998). Regional cerebral blood flow and comorbid diagnosis in abstinent opioid addicts. *Psychiatry Research, 83*, 117–126.

Glass, M., Dragunow, M., & Faull, R. L. M. (1997). Cannabinoid receptors in the human brain: A detailed anatomical and quantitative autoradiographic study in the fetal, neonatal and adult human brain. *Neuroscience, 77*, 299–318.

Goldstein, R. Z., Leskovjan, A. C., Hoff, A. L., Hitzemann, R., Bashan, F., Khalsa, S. S., et al. (2004). Severity of neuropsychological impairment in cocaine and alcohol addiction: Association with metabolism in the prefrontal cortex. *Neuropsychologia, 42*, 1447–1458.

Goldstein, R. Z., & Volkow, N. D. (2002). Drug addiction and its underlying neurobiological basis: Neuroimaging evidence for the involvement of the frontal cortex. *American Journal of Psychiatry, 159*, 1642–1652.

Gonzalez, R., Bechara, A., & Martin, E. M. (2007). Executive functions among individuals with methamphetamine or alcohol as drugs of choice: Preliminary observations. *Journal of Clinical and Experimental Neuropsychology, 29(2)*, 155–159.

Gonzalez, R., Carey, C., & Grant, I. (2002). Nonacute (Residual) neuropsychological effects of cannabis use: A qualitative analysis and systematic review. *Journal of Clinical Pharmacology, 42*, 48S–57S.

Gonzalez, R., Rippeth, J. D., Carey, C. L., Heaton, R. K., Moore, D. J., Schweinsburg, B. C., et al. (2004). Neurocognitive performance of methamphetamine users discordant for history of marijuana exposure. *Drug and Alcohol Dependence, 76*, 181–190.

Gorenstein, C., Bernik, M. A., & Pompeia, S. (1994). Differential acute psychomotor and cognitive effects of diazepam on long-term benzodiazepine users. *International Clinical Psychopharmacology, 9*, 145–153.

Gorenstein, C., Bernik, M. A., Pompeia, S., & Marcourakis, T. (1995). Impairment of performance associated with long-term use of benzodiazepines. *Journal of Psychopharmacology, 9*, 313.

Gouzoulis-Mayfrank, E. & Daumann, J. (2006a). Neurotoxicity of methylenedioxyamphetamines (MDMA; ecstasy) in humans: How strong is the evidence for persistent brain damage? *Addiction, 101*, 348–361.

Gouzoulis-Mayfrank, E., & Daumann, J. (2006b). The confounding problem of polydrug use in recreational ecstasy/MDMA users: A brief overview. *Journal of Psychopharmacology, 20*, 188–193.

Gouzoulis-Mayfrank, E., Daumann, J., Tuchtenhagen, F., Pelz, S., Becker, S., Kunert, H. J., et al. (2000). Impaired cognitive performance in drug free users of recreational ecstasy (MDMA). *Journal of Neurology, Neurosurgery and Psychiatry, 68*, 719–725.

Gouzoulis-Mayfrank, E., Fischermann, T., Rezk, M., Thimm, B., Hensen, G., & Daumann, J. (2005). Memory performance in polyvalent MDMA (ecstasy) users who continue or discontinue MDMA use. *Drug and Alcohol Dependence, 78*, 317–323.

Grant, I., Gonzalez, R., Carey, C. L., Natarajan, L., & Wolfson, T. (2003). Non-acute (residual) neurocognitive effects of cannabis use: A meta-analytic study. *Journal of the International Neuropsychological Society, 9*, 679–689.

Grant, I., Adams, K. M., Carlin, A. S., Rennick, P. M., Judd, L. L., & Schooff, K. (1978). The collaborative neuropsychological study of polydrug users. *Archives of General Psychiatry, 35*, 1063–1074.

Grant, I. & Mohns, L. (1975). Chronic Cerebral Effects of Alcohol and Drug Abuse. *Substance Use & Misuse, 10,* 883–920.

Grant, I., Rochford, J., Fleming, T., & Stunkard, A. (1973). A neuropsychological assessment of the effects of moderate marihuana use. *Journal of Nervous and Mental Disease, 156,* 278–280.

Green, A. R., Mechan, A. O., Elliott, J. M., O'Shea, E., & Colado, M. I. (2003). The pharmacology and clinical pharmacology of 3,4-methylenedioxymethamphetamine (MDMA, "ecstasy"). *Pharmacology Review, 55,* 463–508.

Grotenhermen, F. (2003). Pharmacokinetics and pharmacodynamics of cannabinoids. *Clinical Pharmacokinetics, 42,* 327–360.

Guerra, D., Sole, A., Cami, J., & Tobena, A. (1987). Neuropsychological performance in opiate addicts after rapid detoxification. *Drug and Alcohol Dependence, 20,* 261–270.

Haefely, W. E. (1978). Central actions of benzodiazepines: General introduction. *British Journal of Psychiatry, 133,* 231–238.

Halpern, J. H., Pope, H. G., Jr., Sherwood, A. R., Barry, S., Hudson, J. I., & Yurgelun-Todd, D. (2004). Residual neuropsychological effects of illicit 3,4-methylenedioxymethamphetamine (MDMA) in individuals with minimal exposure to other drugs. *Drug and Alcohol Dependence, 75,* 135–147.

Hamil, W. L. (1996). Auditory learning and memory performance among veterans with a history of stimulant abuse. *Dissertation Abstracts International: Section B: The Sciences and Engineering, 56,* 5806.

Hatsukami, D. K., & Fischman, M. W. (1996). Crack cocaine and cocaine hydrochloride. Are the differences a myth or reality? *Journal of the American Medical Association, 276,* 1580–1588.

Hendler, N., Cimini, C., & Ma, T. (1980). A comparison of cognitive impairment due to benzodiazepines and to narcotics. *American Journal of Psychiatry, 137,* 828–830.

Hernandez-Lopez, C., Farre, M., Roset, P. N., Menoyo, E., Pizarro, N., Ortun o, J., et al. (2002). 3,4-Methylenedioxymethamphetamine (Ecstasy) and alcohol interactions in humans: Psychomotor performance, subjective effects, and pharmacokinetics. *Journal of Pharmacology and Experimental Therapeutics, 300,* 236–244.

Hester, R., Simoes-Franklin, C., & Garavan, H. (2007). Post-error behavior in active cocaine users: Poor awareness of errors in the presence of intact performance adjustments. *Neuropsychopharmacology, 32,* 1974–1984.

Higgins, S. T., Bickel, W. K., Hughes, J. R., Lynn, M., Capeless, M. A., & Fenwick, J. W. (1990). Effects of intranasal cocaine on human learning,

performance and physiology. *Psychopharmacology, 102,* 451–458.

Hill, S. Y., & Mikhael, M. A. (1979). Computerized transaxial tomographic and neuropsychological evaluations in chronic alcohol and heroin abusers. *American Journal of Psychiatry, 136,* 598–602.

Hoffman, W. F., Moore, M., Templin, R., McFarland, B., Hitzemann, R. J., & Mitchell, S. H. (2006). Neuropsychological function and delay discounting in methamphetamine-dependent individuals. *Psychopharmacology, 188*(2), 162–170.

Hughes, J., Smith, T. W., Kosterlitz, H. W., Fothergill, L. A., Morgan, B. A., & Morris, H. R. (1975). Identification of two related pentapeptides from the brain with potent opiate agonist activity. *Nature, 258,* 577–580.

Isbell, H., & Fraser, H. F. (1950). Addiction to analgesics and barbiturates. *Pharmacological Reviews, 2,* 355–397.

Jacobs, I. G., Roszler, M. H., Kelly, J. K., Klein, M. A., & Kling, G. A. (1989). Cocaine abuse: Neurovascular complications. *Radiology, 170,* 223–227.

Jaffe, C., Bush, K. R., Straits-Troster, K., Meredith, C., Romwall, L., Rosenbaum, G., et al. (2005). A comparison of methamphetamine-dependent inpatients childhood attention deficit hyperactivity disorder symptomatology. *Journal on Addictive Disorders, 24*(3), 133–152.

Johanson, C. E., Frey, K. A., Lundahl, L. H., Keenan, P., Lockhart, N., Roll, J., et al. (2006). Cognitive function and nigrostriatal markers in abstinent methamphetamine abusers. *Psychopharmacology, 185*(3), 327–338.

Johnson, B. A., Roache, J. D., Ait-Daoud, N., Wallace, C., Wells, L. T., & Wang, Y. (2005). Effects of isradipine on methamphetamine-induced changes in attentional and perceptual-motor skills of cognition. *Psychopharmacology, 178*(2–3), 296–302.

Johnson, B., Overton, D., Wells, L., Kenny, P., Abramson, D., Dhother, S., et al. (1998). Effects of acute intravenous cocaine on cardiovascular function, human learning, and performance in cocaine addicts. *Psychiatry Research, 77,* 35–42.

Jovanovski, D., Erb, S., & Zakzanis K. K. (2005). Neurocognitive deficits in cocaine users: A quantitative review of the evidence. *Journal of Clinical and Experimental Neuropsychology, 27,* 189–204.

Kalechstein, A. D., De La, G. R., Mahoney, J. J., III, Fantegrossi, W. E., & Newton, T. F. (2007). MDMA use and neurocognition: A meta-analytic review. *Psychopharmacology, 189,* 531–537.

Kalechstein, A. D., Newton, T. F., & Green, M. (2003). Methamphetamine dependence is associated with neurocognitive impairment in the initial phases of abstinence. *Journal of Neuropsychiatry and Clinical Neurosciences, 15*(2), 215–220.

Kelleher, L. M., Stough, C., Sergejew, A. A., & Rolfe, T. (2004). The effects of cannabis on information-processing speed. *Addictive Behaviors, 29,* 1213–1219.

Kirby, K. N., & Petry, N. M. (2004). Heroin and cocaine abusers have higher discount rates for delayed rewards than alcoholics or non-drug-using controls. *Addiction, 9,* 461–471.

Kirby, K. N., Petry, N. M., & Bickel, W. K. (1999). Heroin addicts have higher discount rates for delayed rewards than non-drug-using controls. *Journal of Experimental Psychology: General, 128,* 78–87.

Kivisaari, R., Kakhonen, S., Puuskari, V., Jokela, O., Rapeli, P., & Autti, T. (2004). Magnetic resonance imaging of severe, long-term, opiate-abuse patients without neurologic symptoms may show enlarged cerebrospinal spaces but no signs of brain pathology of vascular origin. *Archives of Medical Research, 35,* 395–400.

Korin, H. (1974). Comparison of psychometric measures in psychiatric patients using heroin and other drugs. *Journal of Abnormal Psychology, 83,* 208–212.

Krystal, J. H., Woods, S. W., Kosten, T. R., Rosen, M. I., Seibyl, J. P., van Dyck, C. C., et al. (1995). Opiate dependence and withdrawal: Preliminary assessment using single photon emission computerized tomography (SPECT). *American Journal of Drug and Alcohol Abuse, 21,* 47–63.

Kuypers, K. P., & Ramaekers, J. G. (2005). Transient memory impairment after acute dose of 75mg 3.4-Methylene-dioxymethamphetamine. *Journal of Psychopharmacology, 19,* 633–639.

Kuypers, K. P., & Ramaekers, J. G. (2007). Acute dose of MDMA (75 mg) impairs spatial memory for location but leaves contextual processing of visuospatial information unaffected. *Psychopharmacology (Berl), 189,* 557–563.

Lamers, C. T. J., Ramaekers, J. G., Muntjewerff, N. D., Sikkema, K. L., Riedel, W. J., Samyn, N., et al. (2003). Dissociable effects of a single dose of ecstasy (MDMA) on psychomotor skills and attentional performance. *Journal of Psychopharmacology, 17,* 379.

Leri, F., Bruneau, J., & Stewart, J. (2003). Understanding polydrug use: Review of heroin and cocaine co-use. *Addiction, 98,* 7–22.

Levine, S. R., Brust, J. C., Futrell, N., Brass, L. M., Blake, D., Fayad, P., et al. (1991). A comparative study of the cerebrovascular complications of cocaine: Alkaloidal versus hydrochloride-a review. *Neurology, 41,* 1173–1177.

London, E. D., Berman, S. M., Voytek, B., Simon, S. L., Mandelkern, M. A., Monterosso, J., et al. (2005). Cerebral metabolic dysfunction and impaired vigilance in recently abstinent methamphetamine abusers. *Biological Psychiatry, 58*(10), 770–778.

London, E. D., Broussolle, E. P., Links, J. M., Wong, D. F., Cascella, N. G., Dannals, R. F., et al. (1990). Morphine-induced metabolic changes in human brain. Studies with positron emission tomography and [fluorine 18] fluorodeoxyglucose. *Archives of General Psychiatry, 47,* 73–81.

Lucki, I., & Rickels, K. (1986). The behavioral effects of benzodiazepines following long-term use. *Psychopharmacology Bulletin, 22,* 424–433.

Lyons, M. J., Bar, J. L., Panizzon, M. S., Toomey, R., Eisen, S., Xian, H., et al. (2004). Neuropsychological consequences of regular marijuana use: A twin study. *Psychological Medicine, 34,* 1239–1250.

Lyvers, M., & Hasking, P. (2004). Have Halpern et al. (2004) detected "residual neuropsychological effects" of MDMA? Not likely. *Drug and Alcohol Dependence, 75,* 149–152.

Lyvers, M., & Yakimoff, M. (2003). Neuropsychological correlates of opiate dependence and withdrawal. *Addictive Behaviors, 28,* 605–611.

Martin-Soelch, C., Chevalley, A. F., Kunig, G., Missimer, J., Magyar, S., Mino, A., et al. (2001). Changes in reward-induced brain activation i n opiate addicts. *European Journal of Neuroscience, 14,* 1360–1368.

Matsuda, L. A., Lolait, S. J., Brownstein, M. J., Young, A. C., & Bonner, T. I. (1990). Structure of a cannabinoid receptor and functional expression of the cloned cDNA. *Nature, 346,* 561–564.

McCann, U. D., Mertl, M., Eligulashvili, V., & Ricaurte, G. A. (1999). Cognitive performance in (¦) 3, 4-methylenedioxymethamphetamine (MDMA, "ecstasy") users: A controlled study. *Psychopharmacology, 143,* 417–425.

McCardle, K., Luebbers, S., Carter, J. D., Croft, R. J., & Stough, C. (2004). Chronic MDMA (ecstasy) use, cognition and mood. *Psychopharmacology, 173,* 434–439.

Mechoulam, R., & Gaoni, Y. (1967). The absolute configuration of delta-1-tetrahydrocannabinol, the major active constituent of hashish. *Tetrahedron Letters, 12,* 1109–1111.

Merlin, M. D. (2003). Archaeological evidence for the tradition of psychoactive plant use in the old world. *Economic Botany, 57,* 295–323.

Messinis, L., Kyprianidou, A., Malefaki, S., & Papathanasopoulos, P. (2006). Neuropsychological deficits in long-term frequent cannabis users. *Neurology, 66,* 737–739.

Mintzer, M. Z., & Stitzer, M. L. (2002). Cognitive impairment in methadone maintenance patients. *Drug and Alcohol Dependence, 67,* 41–51.

Mohs, R. C., Tinklenberg, J. R., Roth, W. T., & Kopell, B. S. (1980). Sensitivity of some human cognitive functions to effects of methamphetamine and secobarbital. *Drug and Alcohol Dependence, 5*(2), 145–150.

Monterosso, J. R., Ainslie, G., Xu, J., Cordova, X., Domier, C. P., & London, E. D. (2006). Frontoparietal cortical activity of methamphetamine-dependent and comparison subjects performing a delay discounting task. *Human Brain Mapping, 28,* 383–393.

Monterosso, J. R., Aron, A. R., Cordova, X., Xu, J., & London, E. D. (2005). Deficits in response inhibition associated with chronic methamphetamine abuse. *Drug and Alcohol Dependence, 79*(2), 273–277.

Morgan, M. (1998). Recreational use of Ecstasy (MDMA) is associated with elevated impulsivity. *Neuropsychopharmacology, 19,* 252–264.

Morgan, M., McFie, L., Fleetwood, L., & Robinson, J. (2002). Ecstasy (MDMA): Are the psychological problems associated with its use reversed by prolonged abstinence? *Psychopharmacology, 159,* 294–303.

Morgan, M. J. (1999). Memory deficits associated with recreational use of "ecstasy" (MDMA). *Psychopharmacology, 141,* 30–36.

Moszczynska, A., Fitzmaurice, P., Ang, L., Kalasinsky, K. S., Schmunk, G. A., Peretti, F. J., et al. (2004). Why is parkinsonism not a feature of human methamphetamine users? *Brain, 127*(Pt 2), 363–370.

Nichols, D. E., Hoffman, A. J., Oberlender, R. A., Jacob, P., III, & Shulgin, A. T. (1986). Derivatives of 1-(1,3-benzodioxol-5-yl)-2-butanamine: Representatives of a novel therapeutic class. *Journal of Medicinal Chemistry, 29,* 2009–2015.

O'Brien, C. P. (2005). Benzodiazepine use, abuse, and dependence. *Journal of Clinical Psychiatry, 66*(Suppl 2), 28–33.

O'Malley, S. S., & Gawin, F. H. (1990). Abstinence symptomatology and neuropsychological impairment in chronic cocaine abusers. *NIDA Research Monographs, 101,* 179–190.

Ornstein, T. J., Iddon, J. L., Baldacchino, A. M., Sahakian, B. J., London, M., Everitt, B. J., et al. (2000). Profiles of cognitive dysfunction in chronic amphetamine and heroin abusers. *Neuropsychopharmacology, 23,* 113–126.

Papageorgiou, C., Rabavilas, A., Liappas, I., & Stefanis, C. (2003). Do obsessive-compulsive patients and abstinent heroin addicts share a common psychophysiological mechanism? *Neuropsychobiology, 47,* 1–11.

Parrott, A. C. (2001). Human psychopharmacology of Ecstasy (MDMA): A review of 15 years of empirical research. *Human Psychopharmacology: Clinical and Experimental, 16,* 557–577.

Parrott, A. C. (2004). Is ecstasy MDMA? A review of the proportion of ecstasy tablets containing MDMA, their dosage levels, and the changing perceptions of purity. *Psychopharmacology (Berl), 173,* 234–241.

Parrott, A. C., Lees, A., Garnham, N. J., Jones, M., & Wesnes, K. (1998). Cognitive performance in recreational users of MDMA or "ecstasy": Evidence for memory deficits. *Journal of Psychopharmacology, 12,* 79.

Paulus, M. P., Hozack, N. E., Zauscher, B. E., Frank, L., Brown, G. G., Braff, D. L., et al. (2002). Behavioral and functional neuroimaging evidence for prefrontal dysfunction in methamphetamine-dependent subjects. *Neuropsychopharmacology, 26*(1), 53–63.

Paulus, M. P., Tapert, S. F., & Schuckit, M. A. (2005). Neural activation patterns of methamphetamine-dependent subjects during decision making predict relapse. *Archives of General Psychiatry, 62*(7), 761–768.

Pert, C. B., & Snyder, S. H. (1973). Opiate receptor: Demonstration in nervous tissue. *Science, 179,* 1011.

Petursson, H., Gudjonsson, G. H., & Lader, M. H. (1983). Psychometric performance during withdrawal from long-term benzodiazepine treatment. *Psychopharmacology, 81,* 345–349.

Pezawas, L. M., Fischer, G., Diamant, K., Schneider, C., Schindler, S. D., Thurnher, M., et al. (1998). Cerebral CT findings in male opioid-dependent patients: Stereological, planimetric and linear measurements. *Psychiatry Research: Neuroimaging Section, 83,* 139–147.

Pezawas, L., Fischer, G., Podreka, I., Schindler, S., Brucke, T., Jagsch, R., et al. (2002). Opioid addiction changes cerebral blood flow symmetry. *Neuropsychobiology, 45,* 67–73.

Pfeffer, A. Z., & Ruble, D. C. (1948). Chronic psychosis and addiction to morphine. *Archives of Neurology and Psychiatry, 56,* 665–672.

Pope, H. G., Jr. (2002). Cannabis, cognition, and residual confounding. *Journal of the American Medical Association, 287,* 1172–1174.

Pope, H. G., Gruber, A. J., & Yurgelun-Todd, D. (1995). The residual neuropsychological effects of cannabis—the current status of research. *Drug and Alcohol Dependence, 38,* 25–34.

Pope, H. G., Gruber, A. J., Hudson, J. I., Huestis, M. A., & Yurgelun-Todd, D. (2001). Neuropsychological performance in long-term cannabis users. *Archives of General Psychiatry, 58,* 909–915.

Pope, H. G., Jr., & Yurgelun-Todd, D. (1996). The residual cognitive effects of heavy marijuana use in college students. *Journal of the American Medical Association, 275,* 521–527.

Ranganathan, M., & D'Souza, D. C. (2006). The acute effects of cannabinoids on memory in humans: A review. *Psychopharmacology, 188,* 425–444.

Regier, D. A., Farmer, M. E., Rae, D. S., Locke, B. Z., Keith, S. J., Judd, L. L., et al. (1990). Comorbidity of mental disorders with alcohol and other drug abuse. Results from the Epidemiologic Catchment Area (ECA) Study. *Journal of the American Medical Association, 264,* 2511–2518.

Reneman, L., Booij, J., Schmand, B., van den Brink, W., & Gunning, B. (2000). Memory disturbances in Ecstasy users are correlated with an altered brain serotonin neurotransmission. *Psychopharmacology, 148,* 322–324.

Reneman, L., Lavalaye, J., Schmand, B., de Wolff, F. A., van den Brink, W., den Heeten, G. J., et al. (2001a). Cortical serotonin transporter density and verbal memory in individuals who stopped using 3,4-methylenedioxymethamphetamine (MDMA or "Ecstasy"): Preliminary findings. *Archives of General Psychiatry, 58,* 901–906.

Reneman, L., Majoie, C. B. L. M., Schmand, B., van den Brink, W., & den Heeten, G. J. (2001b). Prefrontal N-acetylaspartate is strongly associated with memory performance in (abstinent) ecstasy users: Preliminary report. *Biological Psychiatry, 50,* 550–554.

Reynolds, E. H., & Trimble, M. R. (1985). Adverse neuropsychiatric effects of anticonvulsant drugs. *Drugs, 29,* 570–581.

Rice, D. P. (1999). Economic costs of substance abuse, 1995. *Proceedings of the Association of American Physicians, 111,* 119–125.

Rickels, K., Lucki, I., Schweizer, E., Garcia-Espana, F., & Case, W. G. (1999). Psychomotor performance of long-term benzodiazepine users before, during, and after benzodiazepine discontinuation. *Journal of Clinical Psychopharmacology, 19,* 107–113.

Rippeth, J. D., Heaton, R. K., Carey, C. L., Marcotte, T. D., Moore, D. J., Gonzalez, R., et al. (2004). Methamphetamine dependence increases risk of neuropsychological impairment in HIV infected persons. *Journal of the International Neuropsychological Society, 10*(1), 1–14.

Rochford, J., Grant, I., & LaVigne, G. (1977). Medical students and drugs: Further neuropsychological and use pattern considerations. *International Journal of the Addictions, 12,* 1057–1065.

Robinson, J. E., Heaton, R. K., & O'Malley, S. S. (1999). Neuropsychological functioning in cocaine abusers with and without alcohol dependence. *Journal of the International Neuropsychological Society, 5,* 10–19.

Rodgers, J. (2000). Cognitive performance amongst recreational users of "ecstasy". *Psychopharmacology, 151,* 19–24.

Rogers, R. D., Everitt, B. J., Baldacchino, A., Blackshaw, A. J., Swainson, R., Wynne, K., et al. (1999). Dissociable deficits in the decision-making cognition of chronic amphetamine abusers, opiate abusers, patients with focal damage to prefrontal cortex, and tryptophan-depleted normal volunteers: Evidence for monoaminergic mechanisms. *Neuropsychopharmacology, 20,* 322–339.

Rogers, R. D., & Robbins, T. W. (2001). Investigating the neurocognitive deficits associated with chronic drug misuse. *Current Opinions in Neurobiology, 11,* 250–257.

Rose, J. S., Branchey, M., Buydens-Branchey, L., Stapleton, J. M., Chasten, K., Werrell, A., et al. (1996). Cerebral perfusion in early and late opiate withdrawal: A technetium-99m-HMPAO SPECT study. *Psychiatry Research, 31,* 39–47.

Roselli, M., & Ardila, A. (1996). Cognitive effects of cocaine and polydrug abuse. *Journal of Clinical and Experimental Neuropsychology, 18,* 122–135.

Rosselli, M., Ardila, A., Lubomski, M., Murray, S., & King, K. (2001). Personality profile and neuropsychological test performance in chronic cocaine-abusers. *International Journal of Neuroscience, 110,* 55–72.

Rotheram-Fuller, E., Shoptaw, S., Berman, S. M., & London, E. D. (2004). Impaired performance in a test of decision-making by opiate-dependent tobacco smokers. *Drug and Alcohol Dependence, 73,* 79–86.

Rounsaville, B. J., Jones, C., Novelly, R. A., & Kleber, H. (1982). Neuropsychological functioning in opiate addicts. *Journal of Nervous and Mental Disorders, 170,* 209–216.

Sakol, M. S. & Power, K. G. (1988). The effects of long-term benzodiazepine treatment and graded withdrawal on psychometric performance. *Psychopharmacology, 95,* 135–138.

Salo, R., Nordahl, T. E., Moore, C., Waters, C., Natsuaki, Y., Galloway, G. P., et al. (2005). A dissociation in attentional control: Evidence from methamphetamine dependence. *Biological Psychiatry, 57*(3), 310–313.

Salo, R., Nordahl, T. E., Natsuaki, Y., Leamon, M. H., Galloway, G. P., Waters, C., et al. (2007). Attentional control and brain metabolite levels in methamphetamine abusers. *Biological Psychiatry, 61,* 1272–1280.

Salo, R., Nordahl, T. E., Possin, K., Leamon, M., Gibson, D. R., Galloway, G. P., et al. (2002). Preliminary evidence of reduced cognitive inhibition in methamphetamine-dependent individuals. *Psychiatry Research, 111*(1), 65–74.

Salzman, C., Fisher, J., Nobel, K., Glassman, R., Wolfson, A., & Kelley, M. (1992). Cognitive improvement following discontinuation in elderly nursing home residents. *International Journal of Geriatric Psychiatry, 7*, 89–93.

Selby, M. J., & Azrin, R. L. (1998). Neuropsychological functioning in drug abusers. *Drug and Alcohol Dependence, 50*, 39–45.

Sim, T., Simon, S. L., Domier, C. P., Richardson, K., Rawson, R. A., & Ling, W. (2002). Cognitive deficits among methamphetamine users with attention deficit hyperactivity disorder symptomatology. *Journal of Addictive Diseases, 21*(1), 75–89.

Simon, S. L., Dacey, J., Glynn, S., Rawson, R., & Ling, W. (2004). The effect of relapse on cognition in abstinent methamphetamine abusers. *Journal of Substance Abuse Treatment, 27*(1), 59–66.

Simon, S. L., Domier, C., Carnell, J., Brethen, P., Rawson, R., & Ling, W. (2000). Cognitive impairment in individuals currently using methamphetamine. *American Journal on Addictions, 9*(3), 222–231.

Simon, S. L., Domier, C. P., Sim, T., Richardson, K., Rawson, R. A., & Ling, W. (2002). Cognitive performance of current methamphetamine and cocaine abusers. *Journal of Addictive Diseases, 21*(1), 61–74.

Simon, E. J., Hiller, J. M., & Edelman, I. (1973). Stereospecific binding of the potent narcotic analgesic [^{3}H]etorphine to rat brain homogenate. *Proceedings of the National Academy of Sciences, 70*, 1947.

Specka, M., Finkbeiner, T., Lodemann, E., Leifert, K., Kluwig, J., & Gastpar, M. (2000). Cognitive-motor performance of methadone-maintained patients. *European Addiction Research, 6*, 8–19.

Solowij, N. (1995). Do cognitive impairments recover following cessation of cannabis use? *Life Sciences, 56*, 2119–2126.

Solowij, N., Stephens, R. S., Roffman, R. A., Babor, T., Kadden, R., Miller, M., et al. (2002). Cognitive functioning of long-term heavy cannabis users seeking treatment. *Journal of the American Medical Association, 287*, 1123–1131.

Strang, J., & Gurling, H. (1989). Computerized tomography and neuropsychological associations in long term heroin addicts. *Addiction, 85*, 1011–1019.

Strickland, T. L., Mena, I., Villanueva-Meyer, J., Miller, B. L., Cummings, J., Mehringer, C. M., et al. (1993). Cerebral perfusion and neuropsychological consequences of chronic cocaine use. *Journal of Neuropsychiatry and Clinical Neuroscience, 5*, 419–427.

Substance Abuse and Mental Health Services Administration. (2006a). *Drug Abuse Warning Network, 2004: National Estimates of Drug-Related Emergency Department Visits* (DAWN Series D-28, DHHS Publication No. SMA 06–4143). Rockville, MD: Office of Applied Studies.

Substance Abuse and Mental Health Services Administration. (2006b). *Results from the 2005 National Survey on Drug Use and Health: National Findings* (Office of Applied Studies, NSDUH Series H-30, DHHS Publication No. SMA 06–4194). Rockville, MD: Office of Applied studies.

Substance Abuse and Mental Health Services Administration. (2006c). *Treatment Episode Data Set (TEDS): 1994–2004* (DASIS Series: S-33, DHHS Publication No. SMA 064180). Rockville, MD: Office of Applied Studies.

Tanner-Smith, E. E. (2006). Pharmacological content of tablets sold as "ecstasy": Results from an online testing service. *Drug and Alcohol Dependence, 83*, 247–254.

Tata, P. R., Rollings, J., Collins, M., Pickering, A., & Jacobson, R. R. (1994). Lack of cognitive recovery following withdrawal from long-term benzodiazepine use. *Psychological Medicine, 24*, 203–213.

Terenius, L., (1973). Stereospecific interaction between narcotic analgesics and a synaptic plasma membrane fraction of rat brain cortex. *Acta Pharmacologica et Toxicologica, 32*, 317.

United Nations Office on Drugs and Crimes. (2004). *World Drug Report.* United Nations Publications.

Thompson, P. M., Hayashi, K. M., Simon, S. L., Geaga, J. A., Hong, M. S., Sui, Y., et al. (2004). Structural abnormalities in the brains of human subjects who use methamphetamine. *Journal of Neuroscience, 24*(26), 6028–6036.

Tonne, U., Hiltunen, A. J., Vikander, B., Engelbrektsson, K., Bergman, H., Bergman, I., et al. (1995). Neuropsychological changes during steady-state drug use, withdrawal and abstinence in primary benzodiazepine-dependent patients. *Acta Psychiatrica Scandanivica, 91*, 299–304.

Van Gorp, W. G., Wilkins, J. N., Hinkin, C. G., Moore, L. H., Hull, J., Horner, M. D., et al. (1999). Declarative and procedural memory functioning in abstinent cocaine abusers. *Archives of General Psychiatry, 56*, 85–89.

Vanyukov, M. M., Tarter, R. E., Kirisci, L., Kirillova, G. P., Maher, B. S., & Clark, D. B. (2003). Liability to substance use disorders: 1. Common mechanisms and manifestations. *Neurosciences and Biobehavioral Reviews, 27*, 507–515.

Verbaten, M. N. (2003). Specific memory deficits in ecstasy users? The results of a meta-analysis. *Human Psychopharmacology, 18*, 281–290.

Verdejo-Garcia, A., Benbrook, A., Funderburk, F., David, P., Cadet, J. L., & Bolla, K. I. (2007a). The differential relationship between cocaine use and marijuana use on decision-making performance over repeat testing with the Iowa Gambling Task. *Drug and Alcohol Dependence, 90*, 2–11.

Verdejo-Garcia, A., & Perez-Garcia, M. (2007). Profile of executive deficits in cocaine and heroin polysubstance users: Common and differential effects on separate executive components. *Psychopharmacology, 190*, 517–530.

Verdejo-Garcia, A. J., Perales, J. C., & Perez-Garcia, M. (2007b). Cognitive impulsivity in cocaine and heroin polysubstance abusers. *Addictive Behaviors, 32*, 950–966.

Verkes, R. J., Gijsman, H. J., Pieters, M. S. M., Schoemaker, R. C., de Visser, S., Kuijpers, M., et al. (2001). Cognitive performance and serotonergic function in users of ecstasy. *Psychopharmacology, 153*, 196–202.

Vignola, A., Lamoureux, C., Bastien, C. H., & Morin, C. M. (2000). Effects of chronic insomnia and use of benzodiazepines on daytime performance in older adults. *Journals of Gerontology Series B: Psychological Sciences and Social Sciences, 55*, 54–62.

Volkow, N. D., Chang, L., Wang, G. J., Fowler, J. S., Franceschi, D., Sedler, M., et al. (2001a). Loss of dopamine transporters in methamphetamine abusers recovers with protracted abstinence. *Journal of Neuroscience, 21*(23), 9414–9418.

Volkow, N. D., Chang, L., Wang, G. J., Fowler, J. S., Leonido-Yee, M., Franceschi, D., et al. (2001b). Association of dopamine transporter reduction with psychomotor impairment in methamphetamine abusers. *American Journal of Psychiatry, 158*(3), 377–382.

Volkow, N. D., Fowler, J. S., Wang, G. J., Hitzemann, R., Logan, J., Schlyer, D. J., et al. (1993). Decreased dopamine D_2 receptor availability is associated with reduced frontal metabolism in cocaine abusers. *Synapse, 14*, 169–177.

Volkow, N. D., Hitzemann, R., Wang, G. J., Fowler, J. S., Wolf, A. P., Dewey, S. L., et al. (1992). Long-term frontal brain metabolic changes in cocaine abusers. *Synapse, 11*, 184–190.

Vollenweider, F. (1998). Psychological and cardiovascular effects and short-term sequelae of MDMA (Ecstasy) in MDMA-naive healthy volunteers. *Neuropsychopharmacology, 19*, 241–251.

Wang, G. J., Volkow, N. D., Chang, L., Miller, E., Sedler, M., Hitzemann, R., et al. (2004). Partial recovery of brain metabolism in methamphetamine abusers after protracted abstinence. *American Journal of Psychiatry, 161*(2), 242–248.

Wareing, M., Fisk, J. E., & Murphy, P. N. (2000). Working memory deficits in current and previous users of MDMA (ecstasy). *British Journal of Psychology, 91*, 181–188.

Wert, R. C., & Raulin, M. L. (1986). The chronic cerebral effects of cannabis use. II. Psychological findings and conclusions. *International Journal of Addictions, 21*, 629–642.

Whitlow, C. T., Liguori, A., Livengood, L. B., Hart, S. L., Mussat-Whitlow, B. J., Lamborn, C. M., et al. (2004). Long-term heavy marijuana users make costly decisions on a gambling task. *Drug and Alcohol Dependence, 76*, 107–111.

Wig, N. N., & Varma, V. K. (1977). Patterns of long-term heavy cannabis use in North India and its effects on cognitive functions: A preliminary report. *Drug and Alcohol Dependence, 2*, 211–219.

Wilson, J. M., Kalasinsky, K. S., Levey, A. I., Bergeron, C., Reiber, G., Anthony, R. M., et al. (1996). Striatal dopamine nerve terminal markers in human, chronic methamphetamine users. *Nature Medicine, 2*(6), 699–703.

Woods, S. P., Rippeth, J. D., Conover, E., Gongvatana, A., Gonzalez, R., Carey, C. L., et al. (2005). Deficient strategic control of verbal encoding and retrieval in individuals with methamphetamine dependence. *Neuropsychology, 19*(1), 35–43.

Zacny, J. P. (2003). Characterizing the subjective, psychomotor, and physiological effects of a hydrocodone combination product (Hycodan) in non-drug-abusing volunteers. *Psychopharmacology, 165*, 146–156.

Zacny, J. P., & Gutierrez, S. (2003). Characterizing the subjective, psychomotor, and physiological effects of oral oxycodone in non-drug-abusing volunteers. *Psychopharmacology, 170*, 242–254.

Zakzanis, K. K., & Campbell, Z. (2006). Memory impairment in now abstinent MDMA users and continued users: A longitudinal follow-up. *Neurology, 66*, 740–741.

Zakzanis, K. K., & Young, D. A. (2001). Memory impairment in abstinent MDMA ("Ecstasy") users: A longitudinal investigation. *Neurology, 56*, 966–969.

20

Neuropsychological, Neurological, and Neuropsychiatric Correlates of Exposure to Metals

Roberta F. White and Patricia A. Janulewicz

The neurotoxic properties of metals have been known for centuries. For example, hatters' use of mercury, with associated behavioral anomalies was known in the 1800s, and the behavioral changes and confusional states associated with occupational and environmental lead exposure were described even earlier. In the first half of the twentieth century, the syndrome of lead poisoning among children with environmental exposures to paint was well described and treated, and dementia and death associated with lead exposure resulting from drinking bootleg liquor produced in lead-bearing equipments were well documented. In the 1960s and 1970s, methylmercury poisoning was identified in Minamata (Japan) and Iraq following environmental exposures of contaminated food, resulting in clinical descriptions of the associated neurological symptoms and in well-defined descriptions of the neuropathological manifestations of methylmercury in the brains of children and adults (Choi, 1989). These instances of metal toxicity were identified from obvious symptoms and sequelae of very large exposures (both acute and chronic), with intoxication/poisoning and clear-cut clinical encephalopathy.

In the latter half of the twentieth century, the application of neuropsychological test methodology to the study of metal neurotoxicity created an explosion of new knowledge regarding effects of metals on brain function in patients with clinical manifestations of encephalopathy, in persons who had histories of environmental or occupational exposures to metals and had symptoms of central nervous system (CNS) dysfunction but did not reach criteria for a clinical diagnosis of intoxication, and in persons who appeared to be asymptomatic with such exposures (Baker, Jr. et al., 1983; Haenninen et al., 1978; Valciukas & Lilis, 1980). For the purposes of epidemiological research on individuals with occupational and environmental exposures to toxicants such as heavy metals, neuropsychological test methods offered sensitive indicators of brain function with outcomes that were based on standardized test administration and scoring rules, validated with regard to the underlying brain–behavior relationships revealed by the tests, and associated with normative data that allowed estimate of effect magnitude and clinical relevance of exposure-associated decrements in test scores. This quantification of subtle brain function was key to uncovering the neurotoxic properties of many toxicants, including metals, whose neurotoxicity was previously unknown.

In addition to their research applications, neuropsychological test methods slowly became accepted as valid clinical indicators of brain dysfunction allowing the diagnosis of encephalopathy among individuals with well-defined exposures to neurotoxic metals.

Research since the early 1900s, particularly using animal models (Feldman, 1999), has led to increased knowledge about the neuropathological, biochemical, and cellular effects of metal exposures. However, a great deal remains unknown concerning the focal and diffuse effects of such exposures on the human brain, especially at low levels of exposure. Newly available magnetic resonance imaging (MRI) methods such as automated quantification of specific brain areas in structural MRI, MR spectroscopy (MRS), diffusion weighted tensor imaging and functional MRI (fMRI) (Janulewicz et al., 2006), positron emission tomography (PET) (Janulewicz et al., 2006), and near infra-red imaging scans (NIRS), may shed more light on these issues in the next decades. While expensive and difficult to apply in epidemiologic settings, effective application of these methods in targeted situations and with well-defined populations may shed important light on the neuropathological underpinnings of the CNS effects of such exposures in humans.

Metals with Known Neurotoxicity

Exposure to several metals (and their associated compounds) has been linked to encephalopathy. It is important to note that most of these substances are found naturally on earth, leading to potential exposure through soil, water, and air. Exposure to them has occurred across centuries of human evolution, and metals have been found in archeological sites and remains of humans buried centuries ago. This section briefly lists some of the most common neurotoxic metals and their sources of exposures. Clinical features of exposure to them are described later in this introduction.

Lead and mercury (and their organic forms) have been investigated most extensively with regard to their clinical, neurological, neurobehavioral, neuropathological, and cellular effects across the lifespan. Industrial and domestic applications of lead that can result in exposure include solders, lead shot/bullets, insecticides, batteries, smelting, paints, leaded glass, pipes and other lead-containing metal structures, and a number of manufacturing processes (some of which use lead in its organic forms-see below). Elemental mercury exposure can result from dental amalgams (in dentists and technicians as well as patients), scientific and other instruments that use mercury indicators, fluorescent lights, electroplating, gold mining, felt making, electrical power production from coal, and other manufacturing processes. A common form of organic mercury exposure (methylmercury) is related to consumption of seafood containing mercury that has been biotransformed into an organic (methylated) form. Seafood consumption is probably the most common source of environmental mercury exposure (see below).

Arsenic is also a well-established neurotoxicant, though studies of exposure effects on human development are just beginning to emerge. Well-water exposures to arsenic are common in the United States and other parts of the world, and exposure can also result from pesticides, pigments, some paints, smelter processes, and manufacturing processes such as electroplating and semi-conductor production. Manganese is similarly emerging as a neurotoxicant of primary research interest. Exposures may be related to iron and steel industry processes, welding, manufacture of fireworks and matches, dry-cell battery production, fertilizers, and welding operations.

Thallium, which is used in rodenticides, fungicides and photoelectric cells, is also found naturally in rock formations and mica. Tin compounds, particularly organotins, are also neurotoxic. Chemists and chemical laboratory workers are especially likely to be exposed to these compounds. Nickel and aluminum are also known to have neurotoxic properties.

Issues in Behavioral Toxicology

How are metals defined as neurotoxic versus non-neurotoxic? Such determinations vary by the individual and/or agency posing the question. For some agencies, the essential criteria include animal and/or tissue models demonstrating neurotoxic effects of experimental exposures and evidence of effects in humans from epidemiologic or experimental research. In many cases, the initial evidence suggesting neurotoxicity has emanated from clinical case reports on individuals or groups of patients with substantial exposure and clinical evidence of CNS disease. These reports may then lead to the development of animal and tissue models of exposure and to epidemiologic investigations of individuals with acute and chronic exposures to the metal in question.

An important concept in understanding the effects of metals and other neurotoxicants is that of *clinical versus subclinical or preclinical* manifestations of toxicant effects. Clinical manifestations of exposure result in obvious disease, with signs, symptoms and/or abnormal laboratory results evident in the context of a well- demonstrated exposure. At the other end of the scale is preclinical or subclinical evidence of neurotoxicity, in which evidence of subtle CNS dysfunction can be discerned in population studies linking an outcome to a range of exposures. An example of the latter is the evidence for decline in Wechsler Intelligence Quotient (IQ) among children with lead exposure: a statistically significant mean 3-point decline in IQ related to low-level exposure might not appear to be "clinically significant" because it is not large enough to diagnose a clinical decline in an individual patient. However, such a finding has great public health importance. First, it demonstrates that lead affects CNS function. Furthermore, it has tremendous implications for populations of individuals: a 3-point shift downward in IQ within a population increases the number of individuals with borderline IQ and decreases the number in the very superior range (Bellinger, 2007; Bellinger & Bellinger, 2006). Such findings also have implications for regulatory agencies in setting standards for acceptable exposures based on lowest level exposure effects. Finally, evidence of sub-clinical effects gives greater credence to patients' symptom complaints in the absence of clinically obvious disease: they may be experiencing subtle exposure effects that cannot be confirmed diagnostically with currently available technology.

Clinical Manifestations of Metal Intoxication

Clinical evidence of neurotoxicity often rests on evidence of encephalopathy within exposed individuals. Encephalopathies resulting from lead and mercury exposures are described in the sections on these metals that follow. These kinds of disorders are usually described in relation to the causative agent (e.g., lead encephalopathy). Often, abnormal neuropsychological test results are used to support these diagnoses. In such cases, it is essential that the supporting neuropsychological data reflect abnormalities within domains that are known to be related to the exposure of interest and that the results cannot be explained by some other factor such as a neurological, psychiatric or developmental disorder, motivational factors, or premorbid cognitive status. When evaluating the effects of neurotoxic insult, it is easy to overestimate exposure effects in persons with borderline premorbid intellectual skills and to underestimate such effects in very bright patients. A nomenclature has been developed for diagnosing toxicant-induced encephalopathies that considers effects of acute versus chronic exposure separately and evaluates the severity of the encephalopathy (from mild, reversible to severe, irreversible brain damage) (White, 1992). In addition to the diagnosis of encephalopathy, some metals exposures result in clinical syndromes. For example, manganese exposure is associated with a parkinsonian syndrome (Feldman, 1999) and neurological disorders such as amyotropic lateral sclerosis and multiple sclerosis have been linked in epidemiologic research to exposure to lead, zinc and other metals (Beal, 1992; Garruto et al., 1985).

Identifying and Quantifying Subclinical Effects of Metal Exposures

Epidemiologic methods have been critical to public health research on metal neurotoxicity. Epidemiologic approaches include cross-sectional, longitudinal, retrospective, and prospective study designs. Population and case-control methodology are both employed in these approaches. Generally, greater credibility is given to prospective data that clearly link exposure (ideally presented as a continuous variable and measured objectively in body tissue such as blood or urine or in environmental samples of air, water or soil) to CNS outcomes. The demonstration *of dose–effect relationships* between exposure and outcome is considered to be the gold standard in such research. Comparisons between exposed and unexposed populations (with no clear quantification of exposure intensity) may produce suggestive or preliminary evidence of effects of a neurotoxicant but are rarely considered to be conclusive. This is partially due to the likelihood of confounding in such studies: membership in the exposed or control group may be systematically linked to another variable that better explains the outcomes than exposure itself. Of course, confounding can also be seen in research that examines dose–effect relationships if intensity of exposure is systematically related to a confounding variable. When neuropsychological test outcomes are used, critical potential confounders or effect modifying variables that must be considered when analyzing outcome data include age, education, history of developmental disorder of learning and/or attention, gender, ethnicity, socioeconomic class, history of neurological disorder or insult, and medications. In the case of exposures occurring in adulthood, an estimate of premorbid intellectual level is essential, and estimates for both the verbal and spatial domains are preferable (personal communications). These are generally based on "hold test" scores on academic skills tests or Wechsler subtests. Other variables that sometimes impact test performance that should be considered include rural versus urban upbringing, familiarity with computers, parental education and/or vocation, and stimulation in the home. Although affective measures such as "depression" are often used as potential confounders in research in behavioral toxicology, it is important to consider such variables quite carefully and critically, since affective changes occur frequently following exposures to neurotoxicants in a dose-dependent manner (Baker, Jr. et al., 1983; White, 1992). Although the use of data transformed through normative values to standard scores might appear to be an attractive means of controlling for some potential confounders, we have consistently found that use of raw score outcomes in data analysis, with statistical control of confounding variables is the most accurate and sensitive approach. Study populations are often unique to themselves, U.S. normative values can introduce unnecessary noise into the data even for Americans, and appropriate norms are not available for many study populations.

Gene–Environment Interactions

Although large population studies can identify dose–effect relationships that confirm the neurotoxic character of metals and neurotoxicity can also be apparent clinically in individuals, these sources of evidence exist despite the fact that there is great interindividual susceptibility to exposure to specific neurotoxicants. The same dosage exposure can produce clinical disease in one person while it has no apparent effects in someone else, individuals seem to vary in the sites of brain lesions following exposure, and exposures to some toxicants seem to be *protective* against development of neurological disease or degeneration. For example, if two siblings carry the same genetic risk for Parkinson's disease (PD) and eventually develop PD, the sibling who smokes is likely to have later onset of the disease (Myers, 2006). This illustration of gene–environment interactions in protection likely applies to the issue of sites of action of toxicants and susceptibility to them. Furthermore, gene–environment–gene interactions and other more complex relationships between exposures and CNS outcomes are almost certainly very important, at least for some diseases and some individuals. The exploration of these relationships is in its earliest, most exploratory stages. But, studies of this kind will likely advance the field of behavioral toxicology dramatically in the future and may shed light on the genetic and environmental risk factors at play in the development of some neurodegenerative disorders such as Alzheimer's disease, cerebrovascular disease, Amyotropic Lateral Sclerosis (ALS), and Parkinson's disease.

Lead and Mercury

This chapter focuses on the two neurotoxic metals that have been studied the most intensively—lead and mercury. We will begin with a review of the neurotoxicity of these metals in their various forms and the neuropathological effects of exposure in adults and children. We will emphasize neuropsychological findings associated with exposures to these metals, though other evidence of neurotoxicity will be mentioned briefly.

Lead

Lead is an ubiquitous metal found naturally (and abundantly) in the earth. It is used extensively in manufacturing and as an additive to various industrial chemicals and compounds, including gasoline, paints, and solders. Both inorganic and organic forms of lead have neurotoxic properties. Forms of inorganic lead include metallic lead as well as compounds such as lead acetate, azide, chloride, chlorate, chromate, fluoride, iodate, nitrate, oxide, sulfate, and sulfide. These lead compounds occur in crystal, powder, and solid forms. Organic lead compounds include tetraethyllead and tetramethyllead, both of which are liquids. Occupational exposure to inorganic lead compounds may occur during smelting, welding, Lead paint manufacture, mining, jewelry and leaded glass production, automobile manufacture, lead foundry work, de-leading operations, and discharge of firearms using lead bullets. Environmental exposures to inorganic lead can occur through occupational sources (e.g., industrial output contaminating soil, water or air; exposure of family members from contaminated clothing of lead-exposed workers). It can also result from lead paint exposure in older homes, lead pipes carrying water, and contamination of soil and water from natural sources of lead. The latter can result in dietary exposure when food is grown in contaminated soil or drinks are made from contaminated water. Occupational and environmental exposure to organic lead compounds was more common in the United States when they were used as additives in gasoline and continue to occur in countries that permit use of leaded gasoline products. Occupational exposures to organic lead continue to occur in some manufacturing operations and during cleaning of storage tanks that have held leaded gasoline. Pollution from industrial organic Lead processes can contaminate seafood and organic lead compounds sometimes enter the food chain by contaminating plant life, resulting in organic lead exposure. Ingestion of alcohol appears to *enhance* the effects of lead exposure. For a detailed description of inorganic and organic lead compounds, exposure sources, and bioavailability, see Feldman (Feldman, 1999).

Lead exposure can be assessed through laboratory measurements of lead in several body media (urine, blood, hair, dentin in teeth, bone). Urine and blood measures most clearly assess recent exposures, while chronic or remote exposures can be detected in hair and tooth dentin.

Bone is the long-term storage compartment in the body for lead. A technique called x-ray fluoroscopy (XRF) applied to the patella or tibia can be used to assess lifetime Lead exposure (Hu et al., 1990, 1995). Bone storage of lead is an important feature of assessing effects of the metal, since lead acquired early in life can be mobilized from bone storage later on, resulting in acute symptoms. This can occur during pregnancy, with development of osteoporosis, or in other unusual circumstances. For example, a patient who developed thyroid disease in adulthood showed symptoms of lead intoxication, high levels of lead on XRF, and abnormal neuropsychological test findings that appeared to reflect childhood lead exposure (Weisskopf et al., 2004a).

Blood lead levels are generally expressed in micrograms per deciliter (ug/dl). The background U.S. lead level is less than 5 ug/dl. Childhood blood lead level recommendations have steadily dropped as research evidence has accumulated. Currently, it appears that a no-effect level (NOEL) does not exist for childhood lead exposure: dose–effect relationships between exposure and cognitive outcomes are significant and, in fact the most steep, at <10 ug/dl (Canfield et al., 2003). Occupational exposures in the United States are now considered to be acceptable at <40 ug/dl, also representing a steady decline from 60 ug/dl in 1965.

Developmental stage at the time of exposure is a key factor influencing the pervasiveness and severity of exposure effects. While acute and chronic exposures to lead in adults affect specific domains of cognitive function, generally sparing language (White, 1992), prenatal and childhood exposures result in a much more diffuse presentation of deficits. Because childhood lead exposures generally occur at the highest dosages at ages 1–2, when mouthing and crawling are dominant behaviors, lead effects have been most extensively documented at these ages. Given the same dosage exposure, earlier exposure is associated with more profound deficits in a wider range of behavioral domains. It has been shown that early childhood exposures affect general intelligence, acquisition of academic knowledge and school completion, personality development, social competency, and occupational success (Bellinger & Dietrich,

1994; Needleman, 2004; Needleman & Bellinger, 1981; Needleman et al., 1982; White et al., 1993a). Furthermore, children who are genetically inclined to develop cognitive deficits in specific domains such as attention, language or visuospatial skills, appear to develop especially prominent deficits in the vulnerable domain(s) following exposure. It should be noted that, in this context, the developing brain is especially susceptible to lead effects through adolescence and into early adulthood during brain myelination and development of prefrontal brain areas. Therefore, exposure effects in adolescence resemble those in early childhood more than they do in those experienced by adults (i.e., they tend to be more diffuse and expressed in vulnerable cognitive domains). While it has been hypothesized that aging may represent another vulnerable period for lead effects on cognition and that lead exposure early in life may be a risk factor for the development of neurodegenerative disorders such as Alzheimer's disease, data on these issues remain sparse at present.

Inorganic lead poisoning from acute and chronic exposures is characterized by gastrointestinal (constipation, vomiting, anorexia), CNS (headache, light-headedness, irritability, fatigue, mood changes), autonomic nervous system (ANS) (sweating) and musculoskeletal (myalgia, arthralgia) symptoms. As encephalopathy develops, seizures, coma, increased intracranial pressure with edema, and death may occur (Feldman, 1999). Peripheral neuropathy is also seen following chronic exposure. Organic lead poisoning was common in the United States before the removal of lead from gasoline, when intoxication was seen in petroleum workers and among individuals who sniffed gasoline as a means of becoming high. Symptoms of organic lead poisoning following acute exposures include prominent behavioral manifestations (hallucinations, irritability, agitation, sleep disturbances, nightmares), gastrointestinal signs (nausea or vomiting, anorexia), and motor disturbances (tremulousness, ataxia). If untreated or severe enough, the patient may develop seizures and die. Chronic exposure to organic lead results in similar symptoms but may include cognitive complaints, abdominal pain, nystagmus, chorea, seizures and hyperactive reflexes (see Feldman, 1999) for detailed descriptions of clinical intoxications with case examples).

Overview of the Neuropsychological Literature on Inorganic Lead Neurotoxicity. As mentioned earlier, lead has received intense examination as a neurotoxicant. This scrutiny has included extensive application of neuropsychological and psychometric test techniques. More than any other neurotoxicant, there is abundant literature concerning effects of lead on both adults and children, which we will consider separately.

Adult Lead Exposures. Table 20–1 summarizes methods and findings from 18 investigations on adult lead exposure effects, divided into occupational and environmental studies.

In the 1970s, Helena Haenninen, a Finish clinician and psychologist, was one of the first investigators to apply clinical psychometric tests to investigate the effects of occupational exposures to lead and other toxicants on brain function and behavior. Her 1978 paper is important for a number of reasons. First, it identifies dose–effect relationships between quantified biomarkers of lead exposure and degree of cognitive change on objective, domain-specific neuropsychological measures, demonstrating lawful decrements in performance related to increased lead level (in this case seen in the absence of statistically significant differences between exposed subjects and the control group). Second, her findings are seen among lead-exposed workers who did not appear to be clinically sick—that is, she demonstrated sub- or preclinical effects of lead exposure. Finally, Hanninen paid attention to the behavioral and affective consequences of exposure to neurotoxicants such as lead, including the fact that there are dose–effect relationships between exposure and affective/behavioral change that cannot be explained as mere indicators of "functional" disorders or psychiatric disease. These principles have been replicated repeatedly in occupational studies of lead neurotoxicity over the decades since this seminal paper.

The table demonstrates that many neuropsychological measures have been employed in epidemiologic research addressing lead toxicity. Domain-specific tests have been used in

Table 20–1. Neuropsychological Research: Occupational and Environmental Lead Exposure in Adults

Authors	Study site	Study type	Sample characteristics	Study assessment battery	Data analytic approach	Positive findings
Occupational Studies						
Haenninen et al., 1978	Finland	Cross-sectional	49 Pb-exposed workers (mean BLL = 11–32 ug/dL); 24 controls	WAIS: Sim, PC, BD, DSp; Benton VOT; Santa Ana pegboard; reaction time; WMS	Exposed versus controls; dose–effect w/in exposed grp	No significant differences exposed versus unexposed; in exposed grp, higher Pb assoc w/lower WAIS BD, DSp; WMS Vis Rep; Santa Ana
Valciukas & Lilis, 1980	New York City, Michigan	Cross-sectional	4 groups w/occupational Pb exposure (N = 141) (mean Pb = 27.5–50.1ug/dL); 265 controls	WAIS BD, DSy; Embedded figures	Dose–effect	Higher BLL associated with worse scores on all 3 tests
Hogstedt et al., 1983	Swedish Lead registry	Cross-sectional	40 Lead exposed; 27 controls	Synonyms, logical functions, perceptual speed, psychomotor function, memory, learning, reaction time	Exposed versus unexposed	Exposed < controls, 11/14 tests; no dose–effect relationship seen
Baker et al., 1984, 1985	U.S. foundry, factory	Longitudinal cohort study	Year 1: N = 106 experience workers, 65 controls; Year 2: N = 43 experience, 34 controls; Year 3: N = 39 experience, 19 controls	WAIS-Voc, Sim, DSp, BD, DSy; WMS; Benton VOT; CPT; Santa Ana; POMS	Dose–effect; score change over time	Year 1: Higher BLL associated with worse WAIS Voc, Sim, DSp; WMS PAL, Vis Rep; POMS; Year 3: Decline in BLL associated with improved POMS
Jeyaratnam et al., 1986	Singapore	Cross-sectional	49 Pb-exposed workers (polyvinyl chloride manufacture), 36 matched controls	WAIS DSy, DSp; Santa Ana; reaction time; TMT; mood	Exposed versus controls	Exposed worse on WAIS DSy; TMT-A; Santa Ana; mood
Parkinson, 1986	Pennsylvania	Cross-sectional	288 Pb-exposed workers, 181 controls	WAIS-Inf, PC, Sim, BD, DSy, DSp; Benton VOT; Embedded Figures; Grooved Pegboard	Exposed versus nonexposed; dose–effect	None

Study	Location	Design	Sample	Tests	Comparison	Findings
Yokoyama et al., 1988	Japan	Prospective longitudinal	17 gun metal factory workers tested 2x; BLL = 30–64 ug/dL year 1, 24–39 year 3; 12 controls (BLL = 20 year 1, 14 year 3)	WAIS- DSy, PC, BD, PA, OA	Dose–effect; change over 2 years (w/exposure decrement)	Year 1: higher BLL associated with lower WAIS-PC; year 3: PC score improved in high BLL group
Schwartz et al., 2002; Schwartz et al., 1999	E. Penn.	Longitudinal cohort study	535–543 former chemical workers exposed to organic Lead; XRF used to measure bone Lead; 118 controls	WAIS-Inf, BD; ROCF; RAVLT; serial digit learning; WAIS-R DSy; TMT; Purdue pegboard; Stroop; FTT; CES-D; SCL-90	Tibial Lead-test performance outcomes; peak tibial Lead-score changes	Higher peak tibial Lead associated with worse serial digit learning, RAVLT, TMT-B, FTT, Purdue pegboard, Stroop; peak tibial Lead predicted decline in performance over time
Osterberg et al., 1997	Swedish secondary smelter	Cross-sectional	38 male Pb-exposed workers, N = 19 high bone Lead (median 32 ug/g); N = 19 low bone Lead (median 16 ug/g); N = 19 controls (median bone Lead 4 ug/g)	Cognitive Scanner Battery (face recognition test, number learning, figure drawing, pen to point, parallelogram, continuous graphics, cancellation, CPT, mood assessment)	High exposure versus low, low exposure versus controls	Negative study
Lucchini et al., 2000	N. Italy	Cross-sectional	71 Pb-exposed workers (mean BLL = 28 ug/dL); 86 controls (mean BLL = 8)	Swedish Performance Evaluation System (SPES); 5 Luria-Nebraska motor subtests	Exposed versus controls	None in SPES or Luria
Kumar et al., 2002	India	Cross-sectional	60 Pb-exposed battery workers (mean BLL = 55.6 ug/dL), 30 controls (mean BLL = 6)	WAIS DSy, DSp; Cancellation; RPM	Exposed versus controls	Exposed had worse scores than controls on virtually all measures; NB: exposure was above U.S. occupational standards

continued

Table 20–1. continued

Authors	Study site	Study type	Sample characteristics	Study assessment battery	Data analytic approach	Positive findings
Schwartz et al., 2005	South Korea	Longitudinal cohort study	576 Lead workers tested 3x/2.2 years; mean BLL = 31 ug/dL	Reaction time; TMT; DSp; DSy; Purdue pegboard; Benton VOT; RCPM; CES-D	Dose–effect, cross-sectional and longitudinal	Cross-sectional: higher BLL associated with lower scores on executive and motor tasks; longitudinal: few + findings
Chen, Dietrich, Ware, Radcliffe, and Rogan, 2005	Taiwan	Cross-sectional	33 highly exposed workers (BLL = 40–80 ug/dL), 28 workers w/"low" exposure (<40), 62 controls	NES2 computerized test battery	Exposed versus controls	Higher exposure associated with worse scores on NES2 FTT, symbol digit, pattern comparison, reaction time, visual digit spans, associate learning, mood scales
Chuang et al., 2005a	Taiwan	Longitudinal cohort study	27 Lead glaze workers followed for 4 years; mean Pb declined from 26.3 ug/dL to 8.3	Chinese NES2	Change in BLL—effect on test score	Decreased Pb associated with improved FTT, Pattern comparison reaction time, memory
Bleecker et al., 2005b	Canada	Occupational cohort study	254 workers median current BLL = 27.7 ug/dL; time weighted average (TWA) BLL (30 ug/dL); integrated BLL index (IBL)	RAVLT	Dose response	TWA, IBL contributed to variance in encoding and retrieval
Environmental Studies						
Muldoon et al., 1996	Baltimore, Monogahela Valley	Cross-sectional	530 women enrolled in Study of Osteoporotic Fractures (SOF), mean age 70.5 years, geometric mean BLL = 4.8 ug/dL	MMSE, TMT-B, WAIS-R DSy; grooved pegboard, reaction time	Dose–effect	In one sample, higher BLL associated with worse TMT-B, WAIS-R DSy

Study	Location	Study type	Subjects	Test	Effect	Result
Nordberg et al., 2000	Kungsholmen district, Stockholm	Longitudinal cohort study	762 subjects (583 women, 179 men); average age 88.4 years; mean BLL = 3.7 ug/dL	MMSE	Dose–effect	No association between BLL and MMSE
Weisskopf et al., 2004b	Boston, MA	Closed cohort study	446 veterans in Normative Aging Study; mean age 67.4; patella median Lead = 27 ug/g, tibia median Lead = 21 ug/g	MMSE	Dose–effect	A one-interquartile range (20 ug/g of bone mineral) associated with −0.24 MMSE score
Krieg et al., 2005	National Health and Nutrition Evaluation Survey (NHANES III) United States	Cross-sectional	Adults aged 20–59; BLLs 0.7–41.8 ug/dL; geometric mean = 2.51 ug/dL; arithmetic mean = 3.3 ug/dL	Simple reaction time, symbol-digit substitution, serial digit learning	Dose–effect	None

BLL = blood Lead level; Pb = Lead; exp. = exposed; ug/dL = micrograms per deciliter; ug/g = micrograms per gram

Benton VOT = Benton Visual Organization Test; CPT = continuous performance test; CES-D = Centers for Disease Control Epidemiology Scale of Depression; FTT = finger tapping test; NES, NES2 = Neurobehavioral Evaluations System; MMSE = Mini-Mental Status Examination; POMS = Profile of Mood States; RAVLT = Rey Auditory Verbal Learning Test; RPM = Raven Progressive Matrices; RCPM = Raven Colored Progressive Matrices; SCL-90 = Symptom Checklist-90 TMT = Trail-making Test (TMT-A = Part A, TMT-B, Part B); WAIS, (WAIS-R) = Wechsler Adult Intelligence Scale (Revised) (subtests: Inf = Information; RCOF = Rey-Osterrieth Complex Figure; Voc = Vocabulary; Sim = Similarities; Com = Comprehension; DSp = Digit Span; BD = Block Design; DSy = Digit Symbol; PC = Picture Completion; PA = Picture Arrangement; OA = Object Assembly); WMS = Wechsler Memory Scale (PAL = Paired Associate Learning, Vis Rep = Visual Reproduction); Santa Ana = Santa Ana Form Board Test order to gain clues about the likely brain sites of the neurotoxic actions of lead. It has been demonstrated repeatedly that lead exposure in adulthood affects executive skills, visuospatial abilities, manual motor speed, short-term memory (both learning and retention), and mood state. Linguistic abilities appear to be spared. These consistent findings suggest that lead preferentially affects the functioning of sub-cortical and limbic areas, with primary or secondary frontal lobe dysfunction (White, 1992). These possible localizations of action receive some support from recent imaging research. One study documented hippocampal effects of lead exposure in elderly men on proton MRS noting higher myoinositol-to-creatine ratios in hippocampus (Weisskopf et al., 2007). A case report described white matter lesions in the structural brain MRIs of lead-exposed 71-year-old monozygotic twins, one of whom had more severe exposure than the other. Neuropsychological findings included executive/working memory deficits in both twins, while the twin with higher exposure demonstrated much worse performance on short-term memory tasks than the sibling. The MRS and neuropsychological findings were interpreted as suggesting hippocampal and frontal lobe dysfunction. In addition, the structural MRIs on the twins identified possible micro-infarcts, suggesting cerebrovascular consequences of lead exposure that would be consistent with the known effects of lead on cardiovascular function (e.g., increased blood pressure) (Weisskopf et al., 2004b).

When the epidemiologic research summarized in this table began in the 1970s–1980s, a blood lead level (BLL) < 60 ug/dL was considered to be acceptable for workers with occupational exposure. By 1985, it was clear that chronic occupational lead exposure is associated with neurocognitive changes in the 40–60 ug/dL BLL range (Baker et al., 1984, 1985). The standard for exposure was lowered to 40 ug/dL. It has since become apparent that effects are seen as low as 20–30 ug/dL in occupational settings (Bleecker et al., 2005a; Chuang et al., 2005b). However, the threshold BLL for chronic occupational lead exposure effects on CNS function has yet to be clearly delineated.

Although BLL is most accurate as a measure of recent and acute exposure, it is often used as an exposure metric in occupational settings where workers have experienced chronic exposures. Since the 1990s, some studies have used XRF methodology to estimate long-term chronic dose effects based on lead uptake in the patella or tibia (Schwartz et al., 1999, 2002). These studies have been better able to define chronic effects of lead exposure than have investigations relying on multiple BLLs collected over a period of time.

In recent years, attention has also been focused on the effects of organic lead exposures, though disentangling the effects of inorganic and organic forms of the metal has been challenging (Schwartz et al., 2002).

Attention has also recently been focused on effects of low-level lead exposure in the elderly, who may be especially vulnerable to lead neurotoxicity. Studies of this issue are sparse, Contradictory results have been observed with regard to effects on the Mini-Mental Status Examination (MMSE) (Nordberg et al., 2000; Weisskopf et al., 2004a). One study reported relationships between poorer performance on Trail-making Test-Part B (TMT-B) and Wechsler Adult Intelligence Scale-Revised (WAIS-R) Digit Symbol (DSy) scores in women whose average BLL was very low (4.8 ug/dL) (Muldoon et al., 1996). Participants in these studies were members of medical cohort studies, not occupationally exposed workers. It is difficult to determine when the critical lead exposures may have occurred developmentally. It remains possible that lead levels late in life are markers for exposure that occurred earlier in adulthood or even in childhood, resulting in cognitive changes that are maintained through a lifetime.

Childhood Exposures. Table 20–2 summarizes data from an extensive epidemiologic literature on lead neurotoxicity in children. Though this body of work has employed domain-specific neuropsychological tests, it has relied more heavily on the use of omnibus tests of intelligence and academic skills to systemically investigate the threshold values of lead exposure required to produce observable exposure-outcome relationships. These tests have included the Wechsler Intelligence Scales for Children (WISC, WISC-R, WISC-III), the McCarthy scale, the Bayley Scales of Infant Development

Table 20–2. Neuropsychological Research: Childhood Lead Exposure

Authors	Study site	Study type	Sample characteristics	Study assessment battery	Data analytic approach	Positive findings
Needleman, 1979	Boston area	Cross-sectional	58 high (>24 ppm) and 100 low (<6 ppm) dentine Pb levels groups; mean age = 7.3 years	WISC-R, Piagetian conversation, Peabody, Sentence repetition, Token, Seashore Rhythm, VMI, Frostig, reaction time, H-R motor tasks. Teacher behavior rating scale	High versus low exposure group comparison	High exposure children worse than low exposure group ($p < .1$) on: WISC-R FSIQ, PIQ, VIQ; WISC subtests (I, Voc, DSp, Com, PC), Seashore Rhythm test, Sentence Repetition and reaction time. Rated more distractible and more behavioral symptoms by teachers
Needleman & Bellinger, 1981	Re-analysis of Needleman et al., 1979	Re-categorized exposure groups into 0–9.9 ppm, 10.0–19.9 ppm, 20.0–29.9 ppm, and 30.0–39.9 ppm	158 working class children	WISC-R	Dose–response	Dentine Pb > 20 ppb associated with decreased IQ
Bellinger et al., 1984	Boston area child cohort f/u	Cross-sectional	141 children. 22 elevated (>20 ppm), 71 midrange (10.0–19.9 ppm), 48 low (<10 ppm) dentine levels	Teacher ratings. Pupil rating scale. Classroom behavior questionnaire	Dose–response	Higher dentine associated with poorer school performance, grade retention most strongly associated with Lead levels. Teacher ratings lower with high exposure
Needleman et al., 1990	Boston area child cohort f/u	Longitudinal follow-up	132 young adults, mean age 18.4 years.	NES subtests; CVLT; BNT; ROCF; word identification test	High (>24ppm) versus low (<6 ppm) exposure; elevated (>20), medium (10–19.9) and low (<10)	Higher dentine Lead levels associated with worse vocabulary and high grammatical reasoning, finger tapping, hand-eye coordination, reaction time, reading scores
Needleman et al., 1982	U.S. children	Cross-sectional	2335 children, grades 1 & 2, median dentine Pb level = 12 ppm	Same as above, Needleman et al., 1979	Dose–response	Controlling for 5/39 possible confounders related to exposure level, Pb related to lower WISC-R FS, P and VIQs; Seashore, sentence repetition, Token, reaction time

continued

Table 20–2. Continued

Authors	Study site	Study type	Sample characteristics	Study assessment battery	Data analytic approach	Positive findings
Bellinger et al., 1986, 1991	Boston	Prospective cohort	Infants; 76 high umbilical BLL (mean = 14.6 ug/dL), 88 medium (mean = 6.5), 85 low (mean = 1.8)	BSID, MDI	Dose–response	High cord BLL associated with lower MDI at 6 and 12 months
Stiles & Bellinger, 1993	Boston neonate	Prospective cohort	148 children recruited at birth, tested at 10 years. Exposure defined as BLL at 24 months: low (<5 ug/dL), medium (5–9.9), high (>10)	WISC-R, K-TEA, CVLT, WCST, ROCF, Story recall, FTT, pegboard	Dose–response	Highest BLL(>10 ug/dL) at 24 months associated with significantly lower FSIQ, VIQ
Hansen et al., 1989	Denmark	Cross-sectional	162 children; average dentin Pb level = 10.7 ug/g. High exposed (dentine Pb >18.7 ug/dL) matched by sex and SES to control children (<5 ug/dL)	WISC, Bender Gestalt Test, Seashore, TMT, sentence repetition test, CPT	High versus controls	High Lead exposure related to lower WISC VIQ + FSIQ, and Bender
Wigg et al., 1988	Port Pirie Cohort Study, Southern Australia	Prospective cohort	723 children BLL at 6, 15, and 24 months (geometric means 14.3, 20.8 and 21.2 ug/dL respectively)	BSID	Dose–response	BLL level at all ages negatively correlated with mental development at 24 months
McMichael et al., 1992	Port Pirie birth cohort, follow-up	Prospective cohort	548 4-year old children	McCarthy GCI	Dose–response	Increases in BLL from 10 ug/dL to 30 associated with 8.3 point decrement in GCI in girls, 0.8 in boys
Baghurst et al., 1992	Port Pirie cohort, follow-up	Prospective cohort	494 seven year old children	McCarthy GCI	Dose–response	Inverse relations btw IQ at 7 and both antenatal and postnatal BLL; increase from 10 ug/dL to 30 = 5.3 IQ point decrease

Author, year	Location	Study design	Sample/BLL	Test	Analysis	Results
Tong et al., 2000	Port Pirie, follow-up children	Prospective cohort	Mean BLL = 21.2 ug/dL at age 2, 7.9 ug/dL at age 11–13 years	BSID, MDI, GCI	Dose–response	Changes in IQ + decline in BLL from age 7 to age13 years suggest slightly better cognition in children whose BLL declined the most
Ernhart & Greene, 1990	U.S. inner city	Cross-sectional	359 infants recruited at birth, tested at 2 years; mean cord blood 6.56 ug/dL; mean 6 month = 10.1; 2 year = 16.7; 3 year =16.7 ug/dL	Receptive and expressive language, taped speech sample at 2 years	Dose–response	No statistically significant results
Dietrich et al., 1991	Cincinnati Lead Study cohort	Prospective cohort	258 urban, inner-city children tested at age 4 years. Mean lifetime Pb levels by quartiles 7.9, 11.4, 15.2, and 23.7 ug/dL	K-ABC	Dose–response	Weak inverse association between postnatal BLL and performance on K-ABC visual-spatial and visual-motor tasks
Dietrich et al., 1992	Lead Study cohort—follow up	Prospective cohort	259 urban, inner-city children tested at age 5 years; mean BLL a 5 years = 11.9 ug/dL	K-ABC	Dose–response	Higher postnatal BLL associated with poorer K-ABC, all subtests; adjustment for home environment + maternal IQ left few statistically significant results
Dietrich et al., 1993	Cincinnati Lead Study cohort	Prospective cohort	253 children tested at age 6.5 years; 3 exp. groups by mean lifetime BLL 0–10, >10–15, >15–20, >20 ug/dL	WISC-R	Dose–response	Higher postnatal BLL associated with lower FSIQ and PIQ, average lifetime BLL >20 ug/dL associated with 7-point decrease in IQ, compared to average lifetime BLL = 10 ug/dL
Coscia et al., 2003	Cincinnati Cohort Study	Longitudinal cohort	196 children, mean prenatal BLL = 8.53 ug/dL, mean BLL age 1–6, 13.46 ug/dL	WISC-R, WISC-3 (BD, Voc)	Dose–response	15 year olds with higher BLL had lower verbal comprehension scores and greater decline in vocabulary
Fergusson et al., 1993	New Zealand	Longitudinal cohort	Children 8–12 years; mean dentine Pb levels at 6–8 years = 6.2 ppm	New Zealand Revision of the Burt Wood Reading Test	Categorical groups (dentine Pb levels 0–3, 4–7, 8+ ppm)	Children with elevated BLL (8+, 4–7 ppm) 4–6 months behind children with 0–3 ppm on word recognition

continued

Table 20–2. Continued

Authors	Study site	Study type	Sample characteristics	Study assessment battery	Data analytic approach	Positive findings
White et al., 1993a	Boston	Cross-sectional	33 middle-aged individuals diagnosed with Lead poisoning before age of 4; 20 controls with no Lead poisoning diagnosis	WAIS, WMS, TMT, COWAT, RPM, FTT, POMS	Lead poisoned versus controls	Exposed worse than controls on all except 3 tests (WMS, Inf, Orien, WAIS DSp); 3 subtests significantly lower in exposed: WAIS PC, WMS LM, RPM
Wasserman et al., 1994	Yugoslavia	Prospective cohort	332 children tested at age 4 years. BLL = 39.9 ug/dL (exposed smelter), and 9.6 ug/dL (controls)	McCarthy GCI	Dose–response	Increase in BLL from 10 to 25 ug/dL associated with 3.8 decrease in GCI
Shen et al., 1998	Yangpu District, China	Prospective Cohort	Newborn children followed 0–12 months, mean cord BLL high group = 13.4 ug/dL, low = 5.3	BSID—MDI, PDI	High versus low comparison groups	High exposure group lower MDI scores at 3, 6, and 12 months
Stokes et al., 1998	Silver Valley, WA	Cohort	Young adults with Pb exposure (n = 281), without Pb exposure (n = 289)	Grooved pegboard, dynamometer, Santa Ana, FTT, simple reaction time, TMT, NES, RPM	Exposed versus unexposed	Exposed group worse hand-eye coordination, simple reaction time, TMT-B, symbol digit latency, serial digit
Mendelsohn et al., 1998	New York,	Cross-sectional	68 children age 6–36 mos; BLL <25 ug/dL	BSID, 2nd ed.	Group 1 (BLL 0–9.9 ug/dL) compared, to group 2 (10–24.9)	BLL 10–24.9 ug/dL associated with mean MDI score 6.2 points lower than BLL 0–9.9
Chiodo et al., 2004	Detroit, Michigan	Longitudinal cohort	246 African American, inner-city children. BLL at 7.5 years	WISC-III, CPT, Talland digit cancellation, WCST, Tower of London, Seashore, WRAML, grooved pegboard, Cosi, VMI	Dose–response	Higher BLL associated with worse FSIQ, VIQ + PIQ, CPT, Seashore, WCST, VMI, pegboard, WRAML
Hu et al., 2006	Mexico City, Mexico	Longitudinal cohort	146 mother–infant pairs recruited at prenatal clinic	BSID	Dose–response	BLL in the first trimester (7.1–>10 ug/dL predicts lower MDI scores

Study	Location	Study design	Sample/BLL	Tests	Dose–response	Findings
Tellez-Rojo et al., 2006	Mexico City, Mexico	Prospective cohort	294 children, BLL at 12 and 24 months <10 ug/dL	BSID	Dose–response	Higher BLL 24 months associated with lower MDI and PDI; BLL 12 months associated with 24-months PDI only
Gomaa et al., 2002	Mexico City, Mexico	Prospective cohort	197 mother– infant pairs. Maternal patella and tibial Pb post delivery (mean patella Pb = 17.9 ug/dL; mean tibia Pb = 11.5 ug/dL). Umbilical cord levels (mean = 6.7 ug/dL)	BSID	Dose–response	Higher maternal tibia + umbilical cord BLL associated with lower MDI scores; 2-fold increase in umbilical BLL associated with 3.1 point MDI decrease
Kordas et al., 2006	Torreon, Mexico	Cross-sectional	602 children mean BLL = 10.2 ug/dL	Math Achievement Test, PPVT, WISC-RM, TMT, Sternberg, Figure matching, Figure design, Visual Search, CAT, stimulus discrimination, visual memory span	Dose–response	For every 1 ug/dL increase in BLL, decreases were seen: 0.17 on Math achievement; −0.36 PPVT; −0.05 Sternberg; −0.05 figure matching
Lanphear et al., 2000	United States	Cross-sectional Meta-analysis	4853 children aged 6–16; geometric mean BLL = 1.9 ug/dL. 172 (2.1%) BLL >10 ug/dL	WRAT; WISC-R (BD, DSp)	Dose–response Four groups <10 ug/dL, <7.5 ug/dL, <5 ug/ dL, <2.5 ug/dL	Lower cognitive and academic skills associated with BLL <5 ug/dL

BLL = blood Lead level; Pb = Lead; exp.=exposed; ug/dL = micrograms per deciliter; ug/g = micrograms per gram

BNT = Boston Naming Test; BSID = Bayley Scales lof Infant Development (MDI = Mental Development Index; PDI = Psychomotor Development Index); CAT = Child Assessment Test; COWAT = Controlled Word Association Test; CPT = continuous performance test; CVLT = California Verbal Learning Test; FTT = finger tapping test; H-R = Halstead Reitan; K-ABC = Kaufman Assessment Battery for Children; K-TEA = Kaufman Test of Educational Achievement; McCarthy GCI = McCarthy Scales Global Cognitive Index; NES, NES2 = Neurobehavioral Evaluation System; POMS = Profile of Mood States; PPVT = Peabody Picture Vocabulary Test; ROCF = Rey–Osterreith Complex Figure; RPM = Raven Progressive Matrices; RCPM = Raven Colored Progressive Matrices; TMT = Trail-making Test (TMT-A = Part A, TMT-B, part B); VMI = Beery Visual Motor Integration test; WCST = Wisconsin Card Sorting Test; WAIS = Wechsler Adult Intelligence Scale (DSp = Digit Span); WISC, WISC-R, WISC-III = Wechsler Scales of Intelligence for Children (Revised, III) (subtests: BD = Block Design; DSp = Digit Span; Voc = Vocabulary); WMS = Wechsler Memory Scale (LM = Logical Memory); WRAML = Wide Range Assessment of Learning and Memory; WRAT = Wide Range Achievement Test; Santa Ana = Santa Ana Form Board Test

(BSID, BSID-2), the Kaufman Assessment Battery for Children (K-ABC), and a myriad of tests of academic achievement and knowledge. In addition, the consequences of lead exposure effects on behavior have been investigated with regard to promotion through grades in school, completing high school, or serving jail time (Bellinger et al., 1984; Needleman, 1979). Several important cohorts have been followed longitudinally for many years as a part of this research, including a group of Boston first and second graders (Needleman, 1979), Boston newborns (Bellinger et al., 1984, 1986), a birth cohort from Port Pirie, Australia (Baghurst et al., 1992; McMichael et al., 1988; Tong et al., 2000; Wigg et al., 1988), and the Cincinnati lead Study cohort (Dietrich et al., 1991, 1992, 1993).

Paralleling the progression of adult lead research, childhood studies began demonstrating dose-related neurotoxicity at levels that would be considered to be unsafe by today's standards, confirming effects at lower and lower dosages and providing detailed data on the shape of the effect curve of lead exposure on intelligence. This line of research culminated in the meta-analysis of data from several studies involving almost 5000 children that demonstrated IQ effects well below BLLs of 10 ug/dL (<5 ug/dL) (Lanphear et al., 2000). In fact, it appears that the *steepest* slope of the lead effect curve on IQ occurs at <10 ug/dL, with continuing dose–effect relationships above that level (Canfield et al., 2003). In these studies, each increase of 10 µg/dL in the lifetime average BL concentration was associated with a 4.6 decrease in IQ. As the blood lead concentration increased from 1 to 10 µg/dL the IQ declined by 7.4 points.

Demonstration of lead effects through IQ measures, which have face validity as measures of cognition among lay people and clinicians and has resulted in the elegant demonstration of lead-associated effects on outcomes, is considered by many to be a major public health achievement of the latter half of the twentieth century.

Mercury

As in the case of lead, the degree of neurotoxicity and specific CNS effects of exposure to mercury depend upon its chemical form. In this section, we will provide a brief background on elemental, inorganic and organic mercury, followed by a detailed discussion on the effects of a form of organic mercury (methylmercury) that has received considerable scientific attention due to its public health importance as a seafood contaminant.

Elemental mercury can be found in thermometers and other scientific and medical instruments; it is utilized in the manufacture of fluorescent light bulbs and in gold mining operations. It is highly lipophilic, easily crosses the blood brain barrier, and appears to remain in the brain for very long periods of time once it accumulates there. Mild effects of acute elemental mercury exposure can include tremor, irritability, emotional lability, depression, and confusion. In cases of serious intoxication, acute exposure to elemental mercury vapor can result in metal fever syndrome. The initial phase of this syndrome is marked by respiratory symptoms, including pneumonitis, bronchiolitis and bronchitis, accompanied by nausea and vomiting, malaise, chills and fever. Onset of neurological symptoms can occur within 24 hours (tremor, delirium, coma). If the initial phase of the syndrome is not fatal, it is followed by an intermediate phase, which includes renal symptoms. In patients who survive this phase, a late phase may occur that is remarkable for persistence of neurological symptoms after the other systemic manifestations have resolved. Chronic exposure to elemental mercury can result in micromercurialism, which is notable for tremor, dysphoria, and diarrhea, which may progress to gingivitis, cognitive complaints, psychotic symptoms, and worsened tremor. Exposure to ethanol appears to *decrease* the effects of elemental mercury exposure by inhibiting its uptake in the red blood cells.

Inorganic mercury compounds are used in plating processes, photography, cosmetics, and embalming. Systemic health effects of acute and chronic exposure to inorganic mercury are similar to those seen in elemental mercury exposure and most likely represent effects of breakdown of the compounds into the elemental form (Feldman, 1999). A case study of elemental mercury poisoning effects in a thermometer worker showed cognitive deficits in several domains (executive, visuospatial, motor, and mood/

behavior, sparing language), accompanied by cortical atrophy and white matter lesions on MRI (White et al., 1993b).

Organic mercurial compounds can be found in several forms that vary widely in neurotoxicity, perhaps related to the ease with which the compound is metabolized into its inorganic form (Feldman, 1999). Some forms of organic mercury are so neurotoxic that even minute quantities of exposure can result in progressive neurologic and systemic decline and death. An interesting characteristic of organic mercury is the occurrence of delayed effects of exposure, with symptoms occurring some time after cessation of exposure that can progress to severe illness and even death. Ethylmercury is a form of organic mercury that is found in thimerosol, a preservative that was used widely in the past in childhood vaccines and is still present in some types of medications and inoculations. This form of mercury has received recent attention as a possible explanation of the increase in diagnosed autism in the United States (Clifton, 2007; "Thimerosal: Updated statement. An advisory committee statement (acs)," 2007) and has been removed from many vaccines.

Methylmercury is an organic mercury compound that is of substantial public health importance. This compound can be manufactured and exposure has occurred through accidental contamination of food or grains. However, exposure most often results from a process in which inorganic mercury contamination of the environment (air, soil, water) leads to methylation by microorganisms in sediment and water. These microorganisms, now contaminated by methylmercury enter the food chain through plants and fish. Organisms higher on the food chain which are large and long-lived carry the greatest risk of methylmercury contamination. Worldwide, the greatest problem resulted from contamination of tuna, swordfish, shellfish, other seafood and land animals that ingest contaminated plants or fish. The environmental pollution leading to this process can occur secondary to manufacturing processes that use mercury, gold mining operations, and electrical power production. Sometimes the pollution is localized and affects a particular area (e.g., gold mining on portions of the Amazon River), but mercury residue can also be carried by winds

and deposited in sites remote from initial release. Degree of methylmercury contamination of seafood varies widely by geographic area and sometimes within different bodies of water in the same geographic region. Persons who consume a great deal of fish are at increased risk to experience symptoms of methylmercury poisoning, and cases of methylmercury intoxication have been reported in California related to consuming large amounts of sushi (Hightower & Moore, 2003).

The clinical syndrome of methylmercury intoxication has been well described due to contamination of Minamata Bay in Japan from a chloralkali plant that used mercury in manufacture, dumping the metal in Minama Bay, where it was transformed through the methylation process described above into methylmercury and contaminated the local food supply of fish. Called Minamata disease, this form of metal poisoning is remarkable for several features. It has a clear-cut developmental trajectory: prenatal exposure to the compound can result in cerebral palsy, blindness, and death; early childhood exposure can produce severe neurological and sensory deficits; exposure in adulthood may result in no obvious symptoms (even in mothers carrying children born with severe deficits) or may be limited to mild sensory disturbances, cognitive change or peripheral neuropathy. These effects of methylmercury were confirmed in a second epidemic of methylmercury poisoning caused by contaminated grain in Iraq in the 1970s (Myers et al., 2000) and in the case history of a farming family who consumed pork from pigs to which they had fed grain accidentally contaminated by the compound. In all of these instances, brain autopsy data and MRI studies revealed severe brain damage in children with prenatal exposure (including small brain size, incomplete development and failure of neurons to migrate properly during development), widely diffuse multifocal lesions in children with postnatal exposure, and a relatively focal picture of posterior brain damage (especially visual cortex) in adults (Choi, 1989).

Methylmercury is known to affect the ANS and is related to increased heart rate variability and to increased blood pressure in a dose–effect manner. Thus, it is likely related to stroke and has been linked to increased risk of heart disease and myocardial infarction (Jain et al., 2007).

Subtle effects of methylmercury , especially preclinical effects of exposure in the absence of obvious clinical disease, have been the topic of intense research in the past 15 years. These studies have sought to determine No Observable Effect Level (NOEL) of methylmercury effect, especially for prenatal and early childhood exposures.

Overview of the Neuropsychological Literature on Methylmercury Neurotoxicity Table 20-3 summarizes the epidemiologic evidence concerning methylmercury (MeHg) neurotoxicity in children using neurocognitive outcomes. Systematic epidemiologic behavioral toxicology research on this compound to date has largely focused on prenatal exposures, due to the remarkable vulnerability of the developing CNS to this toxicant, which was so clearly identified in the poisoning epidemics in Japan and Iraq.

Beginning in the 1980s, investigators became concerned with question of subtle, low-dose effects of MeHg on the developing nervous system. Birth cohorts of children with documented prenatal exposure were developed in New Zealand, the Faroe Islands and the Seychelles Islands, where seafood and fish are an important part of the local diet. Although the New Zealand and Seychelles studies have relied heavily on omnibus tests of intelligence and achievement, other studies of MeHg, including the Faroese investigations, have relied on domain-specific neuropsychological tests. The greater reliance on more focused cognitive outcomes in the MeHg literature compared to Lead research likely reflects greater knowledge about the structural neuropathological effects of MeHg on the brain, at least at higher dose exposures.

The literature on developmental MeHg neurotoxicity in individuals without evidence of clinical poisoning contains some fascinating contradictions. The New Zealand and Faroese studies clearly demonstrate dose–effect relationships between measures of prenatal MeHg exposure and poorer performance on neurocognitive tests during development. Kjellstrom and colleagues measured prenatal exposure using maternal hair collected when their cohort children were born; they found that higher maternal hair MeHg was associated with poorer performance on the Denver Developmental Screening Test (DDST) at age 4 (Kjellstrom et al., 1986) and on WISC-R PIQ and FSIQ, McCarthy perceptual and motor outcomes, and the Test of Language Development (TOLD) at age 6 (Kjellstrom et al., 1989). A team of investigators from the Faroe Islands, Denmark, Japan and the United States examined a large birth cohort of Faroese children ($n = 1022$) at ages 6.5–7.5 and at 14; they reported that higher levels of prenatal MeHg exposure (especially cord blood measures) were associated with poorer performance on tests of attention, memory and naming at age 6.5–7.5 (Grandjean et al., 1997) and on attention, motor, visuospatial and naming tests at age 14 (Debes et al., 2006b). However, very different results have been reported for the Seychelles cohort. This study linked prenatal MeHg exposure, as measured by maternal hair levels at parturition, to performance on a variety of omnibus and domain-specific cognitive tests administered at several points in development (6.5, 19, 29, 66, and 109 mos.). Essentially, no positive findings were reported (Davidson et al., 2000). A study in Great Britain also found no relationship between DDST performance at age 18 mos. and cord tissue Hg (Daniels et al., 2004), though exposure in this cohort was extremely low.

A number of explanations have been offered for these contradictory findings, especially between the two large on-going cohort studies (Faroes and Seychelles). These have included possible confounding from exposure to polychlorinated biphenyls (PCBs) in the Faroes, though these were well documented and ruled out as explaining the findings (Daniels et al., 2004; Grandjean et al., 1997). Other differences between the studies include source of dietary exposure (ocean fish in Seychelles versus whale, ocean fish and shellfish in the Faroes), test administrators (testing was done by clinical specialists in the Faroes, nurses and students in the Seychelles), and exposure assessment differences (the Faroese study used cord blood and maternal hair, finding better associations with cord blood; the Seychelles investigators used only maternal hair). Interestingly, a recent meta-analysis of the New Zealand, Seychelles

Table 20–3. Neuropsychological Research: Childhood Methylmercury Exposure

Authors	Study site	Study type	Sample characteristics	Study assessment battery	Data analytic approach	Positive findings
Kjellstrom et al., 1986	New Zealand	Longitudinal birth cohort	31 high prenatal exposure children (maternal Hg in hair at birth > 6 ug/g); 31 low prenatal exposure (maternal hair 0–5); tested at age 4	DDST	High versus low	Lower DDST scores in high exp. grp.
Kjellstrom et al., 1989	New Zealand cohort f/u		61 high exp., 3 low exp. control grps	WISC-R, TOLD, McCarthy	Dose–effect	Maternal hair Hg associated with WISC-R PIQ, FSIQ; McCarthy percepual, motoric; TOLD
Myers et al., 1995a, 1995b	Seychelle Islands	Longitudinal birth cohort	740 children a. tested at 6.5 months, prenatal exp. measured by maternal hair levels (0.5–26.7 ppm, median = 5.9) b. tested again at 19 months 29 months	a. DDST-R, Fagan test of visual memory b. DDST-R	a. Dose–effect b. Dose–effect	a. None b. None
Davidson et al., 1998; Myers & Davidson, 2000	Seychelles cohort f/u		711 children tested at 66 months	McCarthy, Bender, W-J Letter & Word Rec.; Preschool Language Test; CBC	Dose–effect (using prenatal + postnatal measures)	None
Davidson et al., 2000	Seychelles cohort f/u		87 children tested at 109 months	WISC-III (Inf, Voc, BD, DSp, Coding), CVLT, BNT, VMI, WRAML design memory, Grooved pegboard, TMT, FTT	Dose–effect	None

continued

Table 20–3. continued

Authors	Study site	Study type	Sample characteristics	Study assessment battery	Data analytic approach	Positive findings
Grandjean et al., 1997	Faroe Islands	Longitudinal birth cohort	917 children tested at 7 years; prenatal exp. assessed in cord blood, maternal hair	NES (FTT, Hand-eye coor, Animal CPT), TPT, Bender, CVLT, BNT, WISC-R (DSp,Sim, BD), NAPOMS	Dose–effect	Higher prenatal cord Hg associated with worse CPT, DSp, Bender recall, CVLT, BNT
Debes et al., 2006a	Faroe Islands cohort f/u		878 children tested at age 14 years	NES (FTT, CPT), BNT, S-B Copying Test, CVLT, WISC-R (Sim, DSp), WISC-R + WAIS BD, WMS-III Spatial Span	Dose–effect	Higher cord blood Hg associated with worse FTT, CPT, Spatial span, S-B Copying, BNT
Grandjean et al., 1999	Brazil, Tapajos River Basin	Cross-sectional	351 children from 4 villages, tested age 7–12 years., maternal and child's Hg assessed in hair (mean = 3.8 ug/g–25.4 in 4 villages)	FTT, Santa Ana pegbrd., WISC-III DSp forward; S-B (Copying, Bead Memory)	Dose–effect	Higher hair Hg associated with worse scores on S-B Copying, Santa Ana
Cordier et al., 2002	French Guiana	Cross-sectional	206 children tested age 5–12 years, maternal hair Hg measured; (3 exp. grps: ≤=5, 5–10, >10 ug/g)	FTT, S-B (Copying, Bead memory), McCarthy DSp	Dose–effect	Higher maternal hair Hg associated with lower S-B Copying scores
Daniels et al., 2004	Great Britain	Birth cohort	1054 children tested 15 and 18 months; cord tissue Hg (0–76.5; median = 0.01 ug/g)	MacArthur Communication Development Inventory (15 months); DDST (18 months)	Dose–effect	None

BNT = Boston Naming Test; CBC = Child Behavior Checklist; CPT = continuous performance test; CVLT = California Verbal Learning Test; DDST = Denver Developmental Screening Test; FTT = finger tapping test; H-R = Halstead Reitan; NAPOMS = Nonverbal Analogue Profile of Mood States; NES, NES2 = Neurobehavioral Evaluation System; S–B = Stanford Binet Scale of Intelligence-4; TMT = Trail-making Test; TOLD = Test of Language Development; TMT; VMI = Beery Visual Motor Integration; WAIS = Wechsler Adult Intelligence Scale; WISC-R, WISC-III = Wechsler Scales of Intelligence for Children (Revised, III) (subtests: Inf = Information, BD = Block Design; DSp = Digit Span; Voc = Vocabulary, Sim–Similarities); W-J = Woodcock Johnson; WMS-III = Wechsler Memory Scale-III; WRAML = Wide Range Assessment of Learning and Memory; WRAT = Wide Range Achievement Test; Santa Ana = Santa Ana Form Board Test and Faroese data used WISC subtest scores to generate IQ measures, finding an overall effect of about −0.18 IQ points per 1ppm increase in maternal hair mercury. The authors suggested that a neurotoxic MeHg effect is, in fact, apparent in the data from the Seychelles as well as the other two studies (Axelrad et al., 2007).

Despite the contradictory results, some have called for a reduction in recommended degree of maternal exposure to methylmercury during pregnancy (Gilbert & Grant-Webster, 1995). There has also been considerable controversy in the general press and public health circles about the benefits of fish consumption versus potential risks due to MeHg exposure.

Although the reversibility of effects of prenatal exposure is unknown, some investigators believe that CNS effects are permanent (Debes et al., 2006b; Murata et al., 2004). A functional imaging pilot study of 16-year-old Faroese cohort members indicated significant fMRI differences between boys with high and low prenatal exposures, with highly exposed children having increased activation in more brain areas than children with low exposure (Janulewicz et al., 2006). Figure 20–1 illustrates one example of the findings from this research (see also the color version in the color insert section).

Another debate involves effects of postnatal versus prenatal MeHg exposure on CNS

a. High MeHg and high PCB exposure

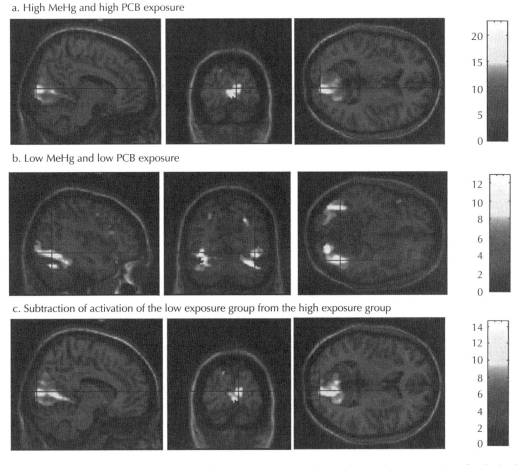

b. Low MeHg and low PCB exposure

c. Subtraction of activation of the low exposure group from the high exposure group

Figure 20–1. Activation during a Task of Photic Stimulation (a) The figure shows activation for the high exposure group during a task of photic stimulation predominantly in the primary occipital cortex bilaterally (Brodmann's area 17). (b) The low exposure group shows bilateral activation primarily in the occipital association cortex (Brodmann's areas 18 and 19). (c) When the two groups are compared there is greater activation in the primary occipital cortex in the high exposure group than the low exposure group, representing recruitment of different neuronal resources in the two groups.

function. In the Faroese cohort, postnatal measures of exposure at the time of testing were largely unrelated to cognitive outcomes. Studies of children living along the Amazon have suggested relationships between current hair mercury level and cognitive performance in children for whom prenatal exposure estimates were unavailable (Cordier et al., 2002; Grandjean et al., 1999). However, these investigators speculate that mercury levels in hair taken at the time of testing in these populations is a marker for prenatal as well as postnatal exposure. Obviously, it is difficult to disentangle pre- versus postnatal effects when data are not available on mercury exposure levels at birth.

Discussion

Epidemiologic research linking neuropsychological outcomes to exposures to metals has been remarkable for positive findings of subtle effects of low-level exposures on brain function. Such findings provide an obvious call to action for preventive measures that will reduce exposure and ultimately result in healthier CNS function in adults and children. In this setting, neuropsychological outcomes have had a powerful public health impact. As imaging techniques improve in resolution and sophistication, it is likely that they will be applied to many of the same issues described in this chapter with, perhaps, new insights into structural and metabolic mechanisms underlying the neurocognitive changes that have already been defined.

Fascinating questions remain. What gene–environment or gene–environment–gene interactions underlie metal effects on cognition? Does early metal exposure lead to later development of neurodegenerative disorders? If so, which metals and which disorders? Are metal effects on the developing of adult brain truly reversible? Are there possible treatments for them? How can subtle changes in cognition and CNS function associated with low-level exposures be more accurately diagnosed and defined clinically in individuals? Which of the metals besides lead and mercury will show similar effects and at what developmental stages? Is aging as vulnerable a developmental stage for low-level metal effects as childhood, or at least more vulnerable than young adulthood and middle age?

Behavioral neurotoxicologists have a great deal of work to do—and neuropsychological assessment methods will certainly play a role in these efforts going forward.

References

Axelrad, D. A., Bellinger, D. C., Ryan, L. M., & Woodruff, T. J. (2007). Dose–response relationship of prenatal mercury exposure and IQ: An integrative analysis of epidemiologic data. *Environmental Health Perspectives, 115*(4), 609–615.

Baghurst, P. A., McMichael, A. J., Wigg, N. R., Vimpani, G. V., Robertson, E. F., Roberts, R. J., et al. (1992). Environmental exposure to lead and children's intelligence at the age of seven years. The Port Pirie cohort study. *New England Journal of Medicine, 327*(18), 1279–1284.

Baker, E. L., Feldman, R. G., White, R. A., Harley, J. P., Niles, C. A., Dinse, G. E., et al. (1984). Occupational lead neurotoxicity: A behavioural and electrophysiological evaluation. Study design and year one results. *British Journal of Industrial Medicine, 41*(3), 352–361.

Baker, E. L., Jr., Feldman, R. G., White, R. F., Harley, J. P., Dinse, G. E., & Berkey, C. S. (1983). Monitoring neurotoxins in industry: Development of a neurobehavioral test battery. *Journal of Occupational Medicine, 25*(2), 125–130.

Baker, E. L., White, R. F., Pothier, L. J., Berkey, C. S., Dinse, G. E., Travers, P. H., et al. (1985). Occupational lead neurotoxicity: Improvement in behavioural effects after reduction of exposure. *British Journal of Industrial Medicine, 42*(8), 507–516.

Beal, M. F. (1992). Does impairment of energy metabolism result in excitotoxic neuronal death in neurodegenerative illnesses? *Annals of Neurology, 31*(2), 119–130.

Bellinger, D., & Dietrich, K. N. (1994). Low-level lead exposure and cognitive function in children. *Pediatric Annals, 23*(11), 600–605.

Bellinger, D., Leviton, A., Rabinowitz, M., Needleman, H., & Waternaux, C. (1986). Correlates of low-level lead exposure in urban children at 2 years of age. *Pediatrics, 77*(6), 826–833.

Bellinger, D., Sloman, J., Leviton, A., Rabinowitz, M., Needleman, H. L., & Waternaux, C. (1991). Low-level lead exposure and children's cognitive function in the preschool years. *Pediatrics, 87*(2), 219–227.

Bellinger, D. C. (2007). Lead neurotoxicity in children: Decomposing the variability in dose–effect relationships. *American Journal of Industrial Medicine, 50*, 720–728.

Bellinger, D. C., & Bellinger, A. M. (2006). Childhood Lead poisoning: The torturous path from science to policy. *Journal of Clinical Investigation, 116*(4), 853–857.

Bellinger, D. C., Needleman, H. L., Leviton, A., Waternaux, C., Rabinowitz, M. B., & Nichols, M. L. (1984). Early sensory-motor development and prenatal exposure to Lead. *Neurobehavioral Toxicology and Teratology, 6*(5), 387–402.

Bleecker, M. L., Ford, D. P., Lindgren, K. N., Hoese, V. M., Walsh, K. S., & Vaughan, C. G. (2005a). Differential effects of lead exposure on components of verbal memory. *Occupational and Environmental Medicine, 62*(3), 181–187.

Bleecker, M. L., Ford, D. P., Vaughan, C. G., Lindgren, K. N., Tiburzi, M. J., & Walsh, K. S. (2005b). Effect of lead exposure and ergonomic stressors on peripheral nerve function. *Environmental Health Perspectives, 113*(12), 1730–1734.

Canfield, R. L., Henderson, C. R., Jr., Cory-Slechta, D. A., Cox, C., Jusko, T. A., & Lanphear, B. P. (2003). Intellectual impairment in children with blood lead concentrations below 10 microg per deciliter. *New England Journal of Medicine, 348*(16), 1517–1526.

Chen, A., Dietrich, K. N., Ware, J. H., Radcliffe, J., & Rogan, W. J. (2005). IQ and blood lead from 2 to 7 years of age: Are the effects in older children the residual of high blood lead concentrations in 2-year-olds? *Environmental Health Perspectives, 113*(5), 597–601.

Chiodo, L. M., Jacobson, S. W., & Jacobson, J. L. (2004). Neurodevelopmental effects of postnatal lead exposure at very low levels. *Neurotoxicology and Teratology, 26*(3), 359–371.

Choi, B. H. (1989). The effects of methylmercury on the developing brain. *Progress in Neurobiology, 32*(6), 447–470.

Chuang, H. Y., Chao, K. Y., & Tsai, S. Y. (2005a). Reversible neurobehavioral performance with reductions in blood lead levels—a prospective study on lead workers. *Neurotoxicology and Teratology, 27*(3), 497–504.

Chuang, H. Y., Chao, K. Y., & Wang, J. D. (2005b). Estimation of burden of lead for offspring of female lead workers: A quality-adjusted life year (qaly) assessment. *Journal of Toxicology and Environmental Health. Part A, 68*(17–18), 1485–1496.

Clifton, J. C., 2nd. (2007). Mercury exposure and public health. *Pediatric Clinics of North America, 54*(2), 237–269, viii.

Cordier, S., Garel, M., Mandereau, L., Morcel, H., Doineau, P., Gosme-Seguret, S., et al. (2002). Neurodevelopmental investigations among meth-ylmercury exposed children in French Guiana. *Environmental Research, 89*(1), 1–11.

Coscia, J. M., Ris, M. D., Succop, P. A., & Dietrich, K. N. (2003). Cognitive development of lead exposed children from ages 6 to 15 years: An application of growth curve analysis. *Child Neuropsychology, 9*(1), 10–21.

Daniels, J. L., Longnecker, M. P., Rowland, A. S., & Golding, J. (2004). Fish intake during pregnancy and early cognitive development of offspring. *Epidemiology, 15*(4), 394–402.

Davidson, P. W., Myers, G. J., Cox, C., Axtell, C., Shamlaye, C., Sloane-Reeves, J., et al. (1998). Effects of prenatal and postnatal methylmercury exposure from fish consumption on neurodevelopment: Outcomes at 66 months of age in the seychelles child development study. *Journal of the American Medical Association, 280*(8), 701–707.

Davidson, P. W., Palumbo, D., Myers, G. J., Cox, C., Shamlaye, C. F., Sloane-Reeves, J., et al. (2000). Neurodevelopmental outcomes of seychellois children from the pilot cohort at 108 months following prenatal exposure to methylmercury from a maternal fish diet. *Environmental Research, 84*(1), 1–11.

Debes, F., Budtz-Jorgensen, E., Weihe, P., White, R. F., & Grandjean, P. (2006a). Impact of prenatal methylmercury exposure on neurobehavioral function at age 14 years. *Neurotoxicology and Teratology, 28*(3), 363–375.

Debes, F., Budtz-Jorgensen, E., Weihe, P., White, R. F., & Grandjean, P. (2006b). Impact of prenatal methylmercury exposure on neurobehavioral function at age 14 years. *Neurotoxicology and Teratology, 28*(5), 536–547.

Dietrich, K. N., Berger, O. G., & Succop, P. A. (1993). Lead exposure and the motor developmental status of urban six-year-old children in the cincinnati prospective study. *Pediatrics, 91*(2), 301–307.

Dietrich, K. N., Succop, P. A., Berger, O. G., Hammond, P. B., & Bornschein, R. L. (1991). Lead exposure and the cognitive development of urban preschool children: The cincinnati lead study cohort at age 4 years. *Neurotoxicology and Teratology, 13*(2), 203–211.

Dietrich, K. N., Succop, P. A., Berger, O. G., & Keith, R. W. (1992). Lead exposure and the central auditory processing abilities and cognitive development of urban children: The Cincinnati lead study cohort at age 5 years. *Neurotoxicology and Teratology, 14*(1), 51–56.

Ernhart, C. B., & Greene, T. (1990). Low-level lead exposure in the prenatal and early preschool periods: Language development. *Archives of Environmental Health, 45*(6), 342–354.

Feldman, R. G. (1999). *Occupational and environmental neurotoxicology*. Philidelphia, PA: Lippincott-Raven Publishers.

Fergusson, D. M., Horwood, L. J., & Lynskey, M. T. (1993). Early dentine lead levels and subsequent cognitive and behavioural development. *Journal of Child Psychology and Psychiatry, and Allied Disciplines, 34*(2), 215–227.

Garruto, R. M., Swyt, C., Fiori, C. E., Yanagihara, R., & Gajdusek, D. C. (1985). Intraneuronal deposition of calcium and aluminium in amyotropic lateral sclerosis of guam. *Lancet, 2*(8468), 1353.

Gilbert, S. G., & Grant-Webster, K. S. (1995). Neurobehavioral effects of developmental methylmercury exposure. *Environmental Health Perspectives, 103*(Suppl 6), 135–142.

Gomaa, A., Hu, H., Bellinger, D., Schwartz, J., Tsaih, S. W., Gonzalez-Cossio, T., et al. (2002). Maternal bone lead as an independent risk factor for fetal neurotoxicity: A prospective study. *Pediatrics, 110*(1 Pt 1), 110–118.

Grandjean, P., Weihe, P., White, R. F., Debes, F., Araki, S., Yokoyama, K., et al. (1997). Cognitive deficit in 7-year-old children with prenatal exposure to methylmercury. *Neurotoxicology and Teratology, 19*(6), 417–428.

Grandjean, P., White, R. F., Nielsen, A., Cleary, D., & de Oliveira Santos, E. C. (1999). Methylmercury neurotoxicity in amazonian children downstream from gold mining. *Environmental Health Perspectives, 107*(7), 587–591.

Haenninen, H., Hernberg, S., Mantere, P., Vesanto, R., & Jalkanen, M. (1978). Psychological performance of subjects with low exposure to lead. *Journal of Occupational Medicine, 20*(10), 683–689.

Hansen, O. N., Trillingsgaard, A., Beese, I., Lyngbye, T., & Grandjean, P. (1989). A neuropsychological study of children with elevated dentine lead level: Assessment of the effect of lead in different socioeconomic groups. *Neurotoxicology and Teratology, 11*(3), 205–213.

Hightower, J. M., & Moore, D. (2003). Mercury levels in high-end consumers of fish. *Environmental Health Perspectives, 111*(4), 604–608.

Hogstedt, C., Hane, M., Agrell, A., & Bodin, L. (1983). Neuropsychological test results and symptoms among workers with well-defined long-term exposure to lead. *British Journal of Industrial Medicine, 40*(1), 99–105.

Hu, H., Aro, A., & Rotnitzky, A. (1995). Bone lead measured by x-ray fluorescence: Epidemiologic methods. *Environmental Health Perspectives, 103*(Suppl 1), 105–110.

Hu, H., Milder, F. L., & Burger, D. E. (1990). X-ray fluorescence measurements of lead burden in subjects with low-level community lead exposure. *Archives of Environmental Health, 45*(6), 335–341.

Hu, H., Tellez-Rojo, M. M., Bellinger, D., Smith, D., Ettinger, A. S., Lamadrid-Figueroa, H., et al. (2006). Fetal lead exposure at each stage of pregnancy as a predictor of infant mental development. *Environmental Health Perspectives, 114*(11), 1730–1735.

Jain, N. B., Potula, V., Schwartz, J., Vokonas, P. S., Sparrow, D., Wright, R. O., et al. (2007). Lead levels and ischemic heart disease in a prospective study of middle-aged and elderly men: The va normative aging study. *Environmental Health Perspectives, 115*(6), 871–875.

Janulewicz, P. A., White, R. F., & Palumbo, C. (2006). *Role of neuroimaging*. New York: Taylor and Francis.

Jeyaratnam, J., Boey, K. W., Ong, C. N., Chia, C. B., & Phoon, W. O. (1986). Neuropsychological studies on lead workers in Singapore. *British Journal of Industrial Medicine, 43*(9), 626–629.

Kjellstrom, T., Kennedy, P., Wallis, S., & Mantel, C. (1986). *Physical and mental development of children with prenatal exposure to mercury from fish. Stage 1: Preliminary tests at age 4. (report 3080)*. Stockholm: National Swedish Environmental Protection Board.

Kjellstrom, T., Kennedy, P., Wallis, S., & Mantel, C. (1989). *Physical and mental development of children with prenatal exposure to mercury from fish. Stage 2: Interviews and psychological tests at age 6. (report 3642)*. Stockholm: National Swedish Environmental Protection Board.

Kordas, K., Canfield, R. L., Lopez, P., Rosado, J. L., Vargas, G. G., Cebrian, M. E., et al. (2006). Deficits in cognitive function and achievement in Mexican first-graders with low blood lead concentrations. *Environmental Research, 100*(3), 371–386.

Krieg, E. F., Jr., Chrislip, D. W., Crespo, C. J., Brightwell, W. S., Ehrenberg, R. L., & Otto, D. A. (2005). The relationship between blood lead levels and neurobehavioral test performance in NHANES III and related occupational studies. *Public Health Reports, 120*(3), 240–251.

Kumar, P., Husain, S. G., Murthy, R. C., Srivastava, S. P., Anand, M., Ali, M. M., et al. (2002). Neuropsychological studies on lead battery workers. *Veterinary and Human Toxicology, 44*(2), 76–78.

Lanphear, B. P., Dietrich, K., Auinger, P., & Cox, C. (2000). Cognitive deficits associated with blood lead concentrations <10 microg/dl in us children and adolescents. *Public Health Reports, 115*(6), 521–529.

Lucchini, R., Albini, E., Cortesi, I., Placidi, D., Bergamaschi, E., Traversa, F., et al. (2000).

Assessment of neurobehavioral performance as a function of current and cumulative occupational lead exposure. *Neurotoxicology, 21*(5), 805–811.

McMichael, A. J., Baghurst, P. A., Vimpani, G. V., Robertson, E. F., Wigg, N. R., & Tong, S. L. (1992). Sociodemographic factors modifying the effect of environmental lead on neuropsychological development in early childhood. *Neurotoxicology and Teratology, 14*(5), 321–327.

McMichael, A. J., Baghurst, P. A., Wigg, N. R., Vimpani, G. V., Robertson, E. F., & Roberts, R. J. (1988). Port Pirie cohort study: Environmental exposure to lead and children's abilities at the age of four years. *New England Journal of Medicine, 319*(8), 468–475.

Mendelsohn, A. L., Dreyer, B. P., Fierman, A. H., Rosen, C. M., Legano, L. A., Kruger, H. A., et al. (1998). Low-level lead exposure and behavior in early childhood. *Pediatrics, 101*(3), E10.

Muldoon, S. B., Cauley, J. A., Kuller, L. H., Morrow, L., Needleman, H. L., Scott, J., et al. (1996). Effects of blood lead levels on cognitive function of older women. *Neuroepidemiology, 15*(2), 62–72.

Murata, K., Weihe, P., Budtz-Jorgensen, E., Jorgensen, P. J., & Grandjean, P. (2004). Delayed brainstem auditory evoked potential latencies in 14-year-old children exposed to methylmercury. *The Journal of Pediatrics, 144*(2), 177–183.

Myers, G. J., & Davidson, P. W. (2000). Does methylmercury have a role in causing developmental disabilities in children? *Environmental Health Perspectives, 108*(Suppl 3), 413–420.

Myers, G. J., Davidson, P. W., Cox, C., Shamlaye, C., Cernichiari, E., & Clarkson, T. W. (2000). Twenty-seven years studying the human neurotoxicity of methylmercury exposure. *Environmental Research, 83*(3), 275–285.

Myers, G. J., Davidson, P. W., Cox, C., Shamlaye, C. F., Tanner, M. A., Marsh, D. O., et al. (1995a). Summary of the seychelles child development study on the relationship of fetal methylmercury exposure to neurodevelopment. *Neurotoxicology, 16*(4), 711–716.

Myers, G. J., Marsh, D. O., Davidson, P. W., Cox, C., Shamlaye, C. F., Tanner, M., et al. (1995b). Main neurodevelopmental study of seychellois children following in utero exposure to methylmercury from a maternal fish diet: Outcome at six months. *Neurotoxicology, 16*(4), 653–664.

Myers, R. H. (2006). Considerations for genomewide association studies in Parkinson disease. *American Journal of Human Genetics, 78*(6), 1081–1082.

Needleman, H. L. (1979). Lead levels and children's psychologic performance. *New England Journal of Medicine, 301*(3), 163.

Needleman, H. L. (2004). Low level lead exposure and the development of children. *The Southeast Asian Journal of Tropical Medicine and Public Health, 35*(2), 252–254.

Needleman, H. L., & Bellinger, D. C. (1981). The epidemiology of low-level lead exposure in childhood. *Journal of the American Academy of Child Psychiatry, 20*(3), 496–512.

Needleman, H. L., Leviton, A., & Bellinger, D. (1982). Lead-associated intellectual deficit. *New England Journal of Medicine, 306*(6), 367.

Needleman, H. L., Schell, A., Bellinger, D., Leviton, A., & Allred, E. N. (1990). The long-term effects of exposure to low doses of Lead in childhood. An 11-year follow-up report. *New England Journal of Medicine, 322*(2), 83–88.

Nordberg, M., Winblad, B., Fratiglioni, L., & Basun, H. (2000). Lead concentrations in elderly urban people related to blood pressure and mental performance: Results from a population-based study. *American Journal of Industrial Medicine, 38*(3), 290–294.

Osterberg, K., Borjesson, J., Gerhardsson, L., Schutz, A., & Skerfving, S. (1997). A neurobehavioural study of long-term occupational inorganic lead exposure. *The Science of the Total Environment, 201*(1), 39–51.

Parkinson, A. (1986). A picture of psychiatric/mental health nursing. *Pro Re Nata PRN, 8*(6), 11.

Schwartz, B. S., Lee, B. K., Bandeen-Roche, K., Stewart, W., Bolla, K., Links, J., et al. (2005). Occupational lead exposure and longitudinal decline in neurobehavioral test scores. *Epidemiology, 16*(1), 106–113.

Schwartz, B. S., Stewart, W., & Hu, H. (2002). Neurobehavioural testing in workers occupationally exposed to lead. *Occupational and Environmental Medicine, 59*(9), 648–649.

Schwartz, B. S., Stewart, W. F., Todd, A. C., & Links, J. M. (1999). Predictors of dimercaptosuccinic acid chelatable lead and tibial lead in former organolead manufacturing workers. *Occupational and Environmental Medicine, 56*(1), 22–29.

Shen, X. M., Yan, C. H., Guo, D., Wu, S. M., Li, R. Q., Huang, H., et al. (1998). Low-level prenatal lead exposure and neurobehavioral development of children in the first year of life: A prospective study in Shanghai. *Environmental Research, 79*(1), 1–8.

Stiles, K. M., & Bellinger, D. C. (1993). Neuropsychological correlates of low-level lead exposure in school-age children: A prospective study. *Neurotoxicology and Teratology, 15*(1), 27–35.

Stokes, L., Letz, R., Gerr, F., Kolczak, M., McNeill, F. E., Chettle, D. R., et al. (1998). Neurotoxicity in young adults 20 years after childhood exposure to lead: The bunker hill experience. *Occupational and Environmental Medicine, 55*(8), 507–516.

Tellez-Rojo, M. M., Bellinger, D. C., Arroyo-Quiroz, C., Lamadrid-Figueroa, H., Mercado-Garcia, A., Schnaas-Arrieta, L., et al. (2006). Longitudinal associations between blood lead concentrations lower than 10 microg/dl and neurobehavioral development in environmentally exposed children in Mexico city. *Pediatrics, 118*(2), e323–330.

Thimerosal: Updated statement. An advisory committee statement (acs). (2007). *Canada Communicable Disease Report, 33*(ACS-6), 1–13.

Tong, S., McMichael, A. J., & Baghurst, P. A. (2000). Interactions between environmental lead exposure and sociodemographic factors on cognitive development. *Archives of Environmental Health, 55*(5), 330–335.

Valciukas, J. A., & Lilis, R. (1980). Psychometric techniques in environmental research. *Environmental Research, 21*(2), 275–297.

Wasserman, G. A., Graziano, J. H., Factor-Litvak, P., Popovac, D., Morina, N., Musabegovic, A., et al. (1994). Consequences of lead exposure and iron supplementation on childhood development at age 4 years. *Neurotoxicology and Teratology, 16*(3), 233–240.

Weisskopf, M. G., Hu, H., Mulkern, R. V., White, R., Aro, A., Oliveira, S., et al. (2004a). Cognitive deficits and magnetic resonance spectroscopy in adult monozygotic twins with lead poisoning. *Environmental Health Perspectives, 112*(5), 620–625.

Weisskopf, M. G., Hu, H., Sparrow, D., Lenkinski, R. E., & Wright, R. O. (2007). Proton magnetic resonance spectroscopic evidence of glial effects of cumulative lead exposure in the adult human hippocampus. *Environmental Health Perspectives, 115*(4), 519–523.

Weisskopf, M. G., Wright, R. O., Schwartz, J., Spiro, A., 3rd, Sparrow, D., Aro, A., et al. (2004b). Cumulative lead exposure and prospective change in cognition among elderly men: The va normative aging study. *American Journal of Epidemiology, 160*(12), 1184–1193.

White, R. F. (1992). *Clinical syndromes in adult neuropsychology: The practitioner's handbook. Neurobehavioral effects of toxic exposures* (Chapter 1). Amsterdam: Elsevier.

White, R. F., Diamond, R., Proctor, S., Morey, C., & Hu, H. (1993a). Residual cognitive deficits 50 years after lead poisoning during childhood. *British Journal of Industrial Medicine, 50*(7), 613–622.

White, R. F., Feldman, R. G., Moss, M. B., & Proctor, S. P. (1993b). Magnetic resonance imaging (MRI), neurobehavioral testing, and toxic encephalopathy: Two cases. *Environmental Research, 61*(1), 117–123.

Wigg, N. R., Vimpani, G. V., McMichael, A. J., Baghurst, P. A., Robertson, E. F., & Roberts, R. J. (1988). Port Pirie cohort study: Childhood blood lead and neuropsychological development at age two years. *Journal of Epidemiology and Community Health, 42*(3), 213–219.

Yokoyama, K., Araki, S., & Aono, H. (1988). Reversibility of psychological performance in subclinical lead absorption. *Neurotoxicology, 9*(3), 405–410.

21

Clinical Neuropsychology of Schizophrenia

Philip D. Harvey and Richard S. E. Keefe

People with schizophrenia have been known since the initial definitions of the condition to manifest an array of cognitive impairments. These impairments appear to be generally moderate to severe in nature and to be accompanied by somewhat smaller changes in global intellectual functioning. It appears as if the majority, if not all, people with schizophrenia show evidence of impairments in performance on neuropsychological (NP) tests and that these impairments are present over the entire course of the illness. These impairments are not caused by medications or psychotic symptoms. NP impairments in schizophrenia are functionally relevant, in that, consistent with other conditions, the severity of cognitive deficits is also associated with impairments in a variety of everyday living skills, including vocational, social, role, and independent living skills.

In trying to understand NP impairments and their importance in schizophrenia, there are several important issues. These include the course of impairment in NP functioning, including when the impairments can be detected and changes over the lifespan, the profile of impairment and whether these impairments are similar to other conditions where brain dysfunction is present, the severity of impairment, the prevalence of impairments and whether any individuals with the illness are spared, and whether these impairments are related in general vs. specific ways to functional deficits. Each of these issues is important for the assessment of functional potential and development of treatment

interventions for people with schizophrenia. Of further relevance is the level of detail and length of assessment required to gain suitable information from an assessment of NP performance.

Course of Cognitive Impairments

Cognitive impairments in schizophrenia are clearly detectable at the time of the first psychotic episode (Bilder et al., 2000; Mohamed et al., 1999). These impairments are similar in severity to those seen in patients with an established course of illness and a history of antipsychotic treatments (Saykin et al., 1994). These data suggest, consistent with several different follow-up studies of first episode patients (e.g., Hoff et al., 1999), that cognitive impairments do not show progressive change in the period immediately after the onset of the illness.

Research on individuals prior to the development of schizophrenia has also suggested that NP impairments are already present at this time. Impairments in a wide array of cognitive functions are also present in individuals who are identified as meeting clinical criteria for being in a prodromal period prior to the onset of schizophrenia (Lencz et al., 2006). While most of the NP ability areas that are impaired in people who meet diagnostic criteria for schizophrenia are also impaired in prodromal cases, it has been argued that there is some variation in the severity impairments prior to the onset of psychosis. Verbal memory and olfactory function may be particularly impaired in those individuals who will later develop a psychotic illness (Brewer et al., 2003). Of further interest is the finding that NP impairments and functional deficits are correlated in cases who do not yet meet diagnostic criteria for schizophrenia. As shown by Cornblatt et al. (2007), social abnormalities and impairments in NP performance are intercorrelated, while neither of these domains of functioning are correlated with the level of severity of "subpsychotic" symptoms shown by these putatively prodromal cases.

Studies that have followed cases who were selected for increased risk for the development of schizophrenia, such as having an affected parent, have also reported NP impairment detectable years before the onset symptoms (Seidman et al., 2006). In specific, impairments in attentional and working memory functions are detectable in children whose parents have schizophrenia as early as the pre-teen years (Cornblatt & Erlenmeyer-Kinling, 1985) and some evidence has suggested that the prevalence of wide-ranging attentional deficits identifies those vulnerable children who are most likely to develop schizophrenia later in life (Cornblatt et al., 1999).

Population-based studies that have related the development of schizophrenia later in life to late-adolescent NP performance have also suggested that a significant number of individuals who are examined at age 16 and are apparently healthy at that time have cognitive changes that predict later schizophrenia. In a series of studies based on the Israeli draft board assessments, Davidson and colleagues have reported on a number of NP impairments that predict the later development of schizophrenia (Davidson et al., 1999). These include intellectual decline across assessments (Reichenberg et al., 2005), excessive variation across different cognitive ability areas (Reichenberg et al., 2006), and generalized cognitive impairments (Weiser et al., 2004). While these impairments do not have high levels of sensitivity to the eventual development of schizophrenia, they do suggest that, for a substantial number of people who eventually develop schizophrenia, NP impairments are detectable when no other signs of illness are immediately apparent.

Turning to the course of cognitive impairments after the development of the illness, the bulk of the evidence suggests that performance on NP tests does not decline, on either a group-mean or case-by-case basis between the period of the first episode until quite later in life. As reviewed by Rund (1998), studies with a variety of NP assessments, younger patient populations, and follow-up periods have not revealed substantial evidence of change in NP performance between the first episode and late life. These data have led some to the conclusion that cognitive impairments in schizophrenia resemble the consequences of a static encephalopathy, at least during the early to middle years of adult life (Goldberg et al., 1993).

In contrast to these findings of stability of performance in early to middle adulthood, there is evidence from a variety of sources indicating that at least a subset of patients with schizophrenia show evidence of decline exceeding normal aging influences later in their life (Arnold et al., 1995; Davidson et al., 1995; Harvey et al., 1999). The majority of the replicated evidence regarding cognitive decline beyond normal aging standards has come from patients with a chronic course of illness, extreme functional disability, and extended stays in chronic psychiatric hospitals, nursing homes, or other full-care facilities. These patients also appear to be affected by treatment-resistant psychotic symptoms, and there is some tentative evidence that the ongoing severity of psychosis is related to risk for decline in NP performance over follow-up periods ranging from 18 to 72 months (Harvey et al., 2003). Even these patients appear to manifest NP decline only after age 65 or so (Friedman et al., 2001), suggesting that with standard NP assessment methods, cognitive decline appears to be detectable only in later life. An exception to these findings are those of Granholm et al. (2000), who noted that patients in the forties and fifties showed evidence of requiring considerably more processing resources than healthy controls (HC) of the same age to perform information processing tasks; in people with schizophrenia, these declines were age related.

In summary of evidence regarding the course of cognitive impairments in schizophrenia, the majority of the evidence suggests that impairments are detectable prior to the onset of the illness, that these impairments at the time of the first episode appear similar in severity and profile to those seen in more chronic patients, and that change over the course of the lifespan is modest until later life. Later life patients appear to be more vulnerable to cognitive decline if they have persistent psychosis and lifelong functional disability.

While these findings have been interpreted as reflecting a static encephalopathy, there is considerable neuroimaging evidence (starting with DeLisi et al., 1997) to suggest that there are active cortical changes occurring over the lifespan in patients with schizophrenia, beginning with the first episode. These declines are detected in cross-sectional studies of patients across the lifespan, particularly during periods of time when NP performance fails to decline, such as immediately after the first episode (DeLisi et al., 2004). Treatment with atypical antipsychotic medications has been reported to be associated with less cortical change (Lieberman et al., 2005), as has good treatment response with conventional medications, resulting in minimal residual negative symptoms (Lieberman et al., 2001). For most patients, however, these data suggest that the encephalopathy in schizophrenia is not static and raise questions about the reasons for the failure to detect changes on NP tests in these same patients. It is possible that either the NP tests are not sensitive to these changes or that these changes do not induce any meaningful cognitive burden in the short term. The patients who show the greatest cortical changes in short-term studies earlier in life (Davis et al., 1998) are the same treatment refractory, consistently disabled patients who show the greatest cognitive declines later. Possibly, some elements of cognitive reserve are protecting patients from showing NP functional declines in the presence of cortical compromise. Later research using a mix of NP and experimental neuroscience tests will be required in order to discriminate between these possibilities.

Profile of Cognitive Impairment

Since NP tests were designed to detect brain dysfunction and there is some evidence of specific relations between NP performance deficits and regional brain dysfunction, there has been considerable interest in the use of profiles of impaired performance to detect possible CNS substrates of impairment. Neuroimaging techniques provide a more direct examination of structural and functional regional brain dysfunction, particularly when paired with evocative cognitive procedures, but interest in the profiles of cognitive impairments has persisted. This interest is focused on several different dimensions: the notion of general versus specific performance deficits, the ability to identify differential performance on potentially separable cognitive ability domains, and the question of whether performance deficits in schizophrenia resemble those seen in disorders with known brain dysfunction (e.g., frontal–striatal abnormalities, cortical dementia, and amnestic syndromes).

The idea of identification of differential performance deficits is an old one in both clinical neuropsychology and schizophrenia research. Often referred to as a "double-dissociation,", the identification of differential patterns of spared and impaired performance across different ability areas as a clue to information about origins of neuropathology has long been an assessment goal. Similarly, cognitively oriented schizophrenia research has focused on the identification of "differential deficits" for at least the last 30 years (Chapman & Chapman, 1978). This goal has been based on the notion that people with schizophrenia often have deficits in performance on multiple cognitive ability domains, so that assessment of a limited number of ability domains may lead to spurious conclusions. For instance, if global intellectual performance, episodic memory, and attentional performance are all impaired compared to healthy people, then assessment of episodic memory alone could lead to the erroneous conclusion of a specific ability deficit when episodic memory is no more impaired than any other ability that would have been assessed.

This problem is also potentially compounded by the fact that intellectual performance is compromised in schizophrenia (David et al., 1997). Since most other cognitive abilities are correlated with scores on intelligence tests, general declines in intellectual functioning could produce poor scores on a whole array of different cognitive abilities. Patients with schizophrenia are also apparently heterogenous in the extent of their intellectual decline, with some patients showing psychometric evidence of decline while others appear to have generally preserved functioning (Weickert et al., 2000). Thus, the challenge in assessment of people with schizophrenia is not in the area of detection of impairment, but rather identification of ability areas that are relatively spared and hence serve as a reference point for differential deficit inferences (Harvey et al., 2000).

Many studies have used factor analysis to identify dimensions of NP performance that could then be evaluated for their differential levels of impairment compared to HC. Recent studies have yielded inconsistent and provocative results. Factor analyses of NP performance on the part of people with schizophrenia have yielded factor solutions ranging from 1 (Keefe et al., 2006) to 6 (Gladsjo et al., 2004) factors. These studies cannot be faulted for small sample sizes (the study with the single-factor solution had over 1331 participants), narrow selection of test batteries, or other major confounds.

Sophisticated studies using confirmatory modeling procedures have been applied to the issue of the dimensional structure of NP deficits in schizophrenia. Perhaps the most sophisticated of those studies (Dickinson et al., 2004), using a broad assessment including complete WAIS and WMS batteries in addition to other tests, demonstrated that the differences in NP performance between HC and schizophrenia patients are best explained by a single "severity" dimension. This dimension did not reflect simple intellectual impairment, but rather tapped a number of apparently independent ability domains. The fit of the unifactorial impairment dimension was considerably better than a multifactorial approach to the differences in performance between schizophrenic and healthy samples.

A question that arises, when the overall profile of performance in schizophrenia and the dimensions of relative impairment compared to HC are found to be unidimensional, is whether there is a single aspect of impairment that accounts for all other measured deficits. Several such impairments have been proposed previously, including working memory impairments (Goldman-Rakic, 1994), overall information processing resource availability (Harvey et al., 2006b), and processing (i.e., psychomotor) speed (Dickinson et al., 2007). Even these ability areas may be interrelated, however, and these domains may not be as separable as they would seem from a superficial examination. Multiple studies have

reported that the single largest correlate of overall cognitive performance in schizophrenia is a measure of the speed of cognitive processing (see Dickinson et al., 2007). For instance, in the baseline results (Keefe et al., 2006) of the large (n = 1035 with full assessments) CATIE study, processing speed as measured by WAIS-III digit symbol accounted for 61% of the variance in the total NP composite score, with an additional measure of psychomotor speed (grooved pegboard) accounting for an additional 7%. In contrast, measures of executive functioning (Wisconsin Card Sorting Test—WCST), attention (Continuous Performance Test—CPT), and spatial working memory accounted for 2% each of the variance in total score.

These data suggest more careful evaluation of the long-held assumption that schizophrenia is marked by a profile of discriminable performance deficits across several critical ability areas (executive functioning, episodic memory, working memory, attention, and processing speed). The possibility has been raised that the profile of impairments seen is actually due to a global performance deficits, combined with the differential ability of different cognitive measures to detect impairment in general. Differential sensitivity to performance deficits, due to reliability, administration issues, and other factors, combined with a generalized performance deficit, might lead to the detection of apparent profiles of impairment.

Related to the emerging questions about whether cognition in schizophrenia truly reflects a profile of variably impaired abilities as compared to a single global deficit are the questions as to whether performance deficits on the part of people with schizophrenia resemble the profile of impairments seen in people with identifiable CNS lesions and resulting cognitive changes. Among the three possibilities proposed to describe the impairments seen in people with schizophrenia are frontostriatal (i.e., subcortical) conditions, cortical dementias, and focal amnestic syndromes. Each will be considered briefly below.

Frontostriatal Conditions

These conditions, with the prototype being Huntington's disease, involve a profile of impairment with reductions in executive functioning, attention, processing speed, and specific changes in episodic memory (Paulsen et al., 1995b). Given the prominence of executive, attention, and processing speed abnormalities, the often-reported sparing of recognition memory in people with schizophrenia has led to the suggestion of resemblance to frontostriatal conditions, in that studies of people with schizophrenia (e.g., Paulsen et al., 1995a; Turetsky et al., 2002) have suggested that a frontostriatal memory profile is more common than a cortical profile (marked by no sparing of recognition memory) or unimpaired profile in patients with schizophrenia. However, it also seems likely that in schizophrenia this profile may also be affected by global severity; when geriatric schizophrenia patients are followed up, a large proportion of patients with frontostriatal profile develop a cortical profile over time (Bowie et al., 2004). Thus, as suggested in the dementia literature, frontostriatal profiles may simply be produced by the presence of less severe global impairments. Further, there was markedly little internal consistency between putative markers of the frontostriatal impairment in patients with schizophrenia in the one study that examined this issue. In patients with frontostriatal conditions, recall memory and verbal fluency are typically impaired while recognition memory and confrontation memory are often spared. Spared recognition memory did not predict spared confrontation naming in a study with 239 schizophrenia patients, leading to only 19% overlap between memory-derived and language-derived frontostriatal profiles (Harvey et al., 2002).

Cortical Dementia

Patients with schizophrenia show pervasive cognitive deficits and most meet the behavioral criteria for dementia. In addition, some proportion of patients with schizophrenia, both younger and older, show evidence of a cortical profile of impairment, with no evidence of recognition memory being spared compared to delayed recall (see above). Yet, when people with schizophrenia are compared to patients with Alzheimer's disease (AD), whether they are younger or older, matched on Mini-Mental State Examination (MMSE) scores or not, they routinely outperform AD patients on delayed recall memory. Interestingly, in two separate studies (Davidson et al., 1996; Heaton et al., 1994) with very different populations of patients with schizophrenia, the global level of impairment across ability areas was greater in people with schizophrenia than those with AD, other than for delayed recall memory, suggesting that the cortical dementia descriptor does not capture the signature of impairment in people with schizophrenia.

Amnesia

People with schizophrenia have grossly impaired episodic memory and may perform in the same range on some tests as people with amnestic conditions. Some studies have suggested that impairments in episodic memory are particularly extreme compared to other ability areas (e.g., Saykin et al., 1991). These results need to be considered in the context of the Dickinson et al. results, which were based on a much broader meta-analysis. Similar to amnesia, patients with schizophrenia show procedural memory deficits that are modest compared to their other impairments (Heinrichs & Zakzanis, 1998). At the same time, it is rare to see a patient with schizophrenia with an isolated impairment in episodic memory. It is our conclusion that schizophrenia is more similar to conditions with wide-ranging cognitive deficits and not to patients with isolated impairments in episodic memory.

Another important issue is whether the profile of NP deficits in schizophrenia reflects specific impairments in regional brain functions. For instance, it has been argued that the cognitive impairments seen in schizophrenia are comparable to those seen in cases with specific frontal lobe lesions. This argument is based both on NP test performance and on evidence from neuroimaging studies suggesting reduced frontal lobe activity (i.e., hypofrontality) during cognitive challenge procedures (e.g., Callicott et al., 1999). While many aspects of NP impairment in schizophrenia are apparently similar to frontal lobe dysfunction, including deficits in abstraction and problem solving (Palmer & Heaton, 2000), working memory (Kim et al., 2004), and attention (Bryson & Bell, 2003), some evidence from clinical NP studies of patients with schizophrenia fail to show evidence of consistent patterns of frontal lobe-like dysfunctions. For instance, Gambini et al. (2003) reported that there were four different clusters of patients that were detected when performance was measured on a battery of frontal-type tests, suggesting a more global profile of performance. Further, questions have been raised about the specificity of classical NP tests to frontal lobe dysfunctions, with considerable data suggesting that deficits may be produced by lesions in a variety of cortical and subcortical areas (Anderson et al., 1991).

Recent intriguing findings from the clinical neuroscience literature show how complex the relationships between schizophrenia, brain activity, and NP test performance are. Research by Callicott and colleagues (Callicott et al., 1999, 2000) has employed a parametric examination of cognitive processing demands, the "n-back" working memory test. In this assessment, subjects are required to maintain information in working memory and respond to information that was presented in the immediately prior stimulus, or separated from the current stimulus by 1, 2, 3, or more items. People with schizophrenia find this test particularly challenging, and, at 2-back conditions, show evidence of grossly diminished activation of the anterior frontal cortex compared to HC performing the same test, much like their performance on other frontal-dependent tests such as WCST. Interestingly, when HC are asked to perform a 3-back version of the test, their cortical activation looks like the performance of people with schizophrenia at the 2-back condition, with reduced anterior activation and excessive activation of posterior regions. When people with schizophrenia perform the 1-back test, their brain activation looks like healthy individuals performing at 2-back.

These findings indicate that altered cortical activation under increased processing demands is not specific to schizophrenia, but rather an apparently normative response. "Hypofrontality" appears not to be a diagnostically sensitive indicator, but rather a behavioral index of processing demands and capacity (Cannon et al., 2005). The origin of the reduced processing capacity seen in schizophrenia is not clear from these results, but it appears that the brain response to processing load is an indicator, not a cause, of alterations in performance.

Summary

The true nature of the profile of cognitive impairments in schizophrenia is still essentially unresolved. It could be concluded that people with schizophrenia do not show marked similarities to people with known neurological disorders or with specific regional brain lesions in the profile of their cognitive impairments and that to compare schizophrenia to identified conditions is unproductive. The dimensional structure of symptoms is an open question, and it is not clear if statistical approaches will provide the answer. As far as global impairment is considered, it seems quite important to determine why processing speed accounts for such a substantial amount of the overall impairment seen in schizophrenia, and why this area accounts for impairments in other areas. Study of processing speed abnormalities seems clearly important and will need to be pursued in order to determine if this should be a primary treatment goal.

Severity of Impairments

Despite our concerns about the statistical and neurobiological validity of different elements of cognitive impairments in schizophrenia, we present our discussion of the severity of impairments using standard ability area definitions. We do this because ability areas are defined by tests and tests are the metric with which cognitive performance data are collected. That said, we note that the severity of impairments detected by different tests may be as much a function of the performance of the tests as that of the patient. These issues are addressed elsewhere in this volume.

In this section we consider performance deficits relative to healthy individuals who are reasonably similar in demographic characteristics that affect cognitive functioning. As has been noted for decades, the changes in educational attainment associated with schizophrenia are substantial, although considerable evidence

Table 21–1. Level of Impairment in Cognitive Abilities in Schizophrenia

	Mild	Moderate	Severe
Long-Term Factual Memory	X		
Perceptual Skills	X		
Manual Dexterity		X	
Attention			
Sustained Attention			X
Selective Attention		X	
Working Memory			
Spatial Working Memory			X
Verbal Working Memory			X
Episodic Memory			
Verbal Learning			X
Nonverbal memory (Spatial Memory)		X	
Delayed Recall		X	
Delayed Recognition	X		
Procedural Memory		X	
Executive Functions		X	
Processing Speed			X
Verbal Skills			
Naming	X		
Verbal Fluency		X	

from large-scale studies shows that the correlation between educational attainment and NP performance is quite similar in HC and schizophrenia samples (e.g., Davidson et al., 1995). Thus, "matching" on education between HC and schizophrenia samples is a mistake; the natural history of schizophrenia leads to reduced educational attainment. Several alternative strategies have been proposed. They include "relative matching," which would select HC and schizophrenia patients as yoked comparisons based on their position in the respective education distribution (Davidson et al., 1996), matching on parental education (Keefe et al., 2005), and using education as a covariate rather than a rigid matching variable.

An additional question in the domain of defining levels of impairment (this is an issue that will return full-force in the next section on normal performance) is how is impairment defined? Clearly a population of people with mental retardation would perform poorly on the tests of classical cognitive abilities in schizophrenia, such as episodic memory and executive functioning. Yet, would they be performing worse than their IQ would predict? Even if they performed more poorly than HC samples, this would not reflect a decline in their performance in these abilities, but a decline in their

performance with consistency across ability areas.

As we mentioned above, there is cognitive decline at the time of the first diagnosis of schizophrenia. Thus, the concept of "premorbid" intellectual functioning refers to the idea that functioning before the onset of the illness is less impaired than after. Thus, comparison of HC and schizophrenia patients needs to consider both the current level of performance of the schizophrenia patients (likely reduced from premorbid functioning) and their impairment compared to their performance prior to the development of the illness (i.e., their premorbid functioning). Thus, the important aspects of cognitive impairment in schizophrenia are those that are impaired compared to premorbid functioning and reflect deterioration in performance subsequent to the development of the illness. For instance, it is possible to identify patients with schizophrenia who appear to vary in their level of intellectual decline (Weickert et al., 2000).

When people with schizophrenia are compared to HC subjects, their performance is consistently impaired, regardless of the standards used. Table 21–1 shows the relative level of impairment across these samples based on several different sources of data (as previously summarized by Gold and Harvey [1993] and Bowie and Harvey [2005]). In this table, data regarding conceptual ability areas are provided. For a detailed assessment looking at individual tests (which is a more desirable strategy) please see Heinrichs and Zakzanis (1998). We define mild impairments as those that are about 0.5 SD compared to expected, moderate impairment as 0.5–1.5 SD compared to expected scores, and severe are more than 1.5 SD compared to standards. These impairments are, whenever possible, indexed relative to premorbid standards, but this is not possible in all cases.

Premorbid intellectual functioning is often estimated by performance on various tests of old learning such as word recognition reading (Gladsjo et al., 1999), as considerable evidence suggests that performance on these tests is least vulnerable to decline, prior to or during the illness (Harvey et al., 2000). While a discussion of the validity of this process could fill this entire chapter, there are several studies providing evidence regarding the congruence of performance on these measures both with data collected prior to illness (Tracy et al., 1996) and evidence regarding resistance to decline (Harvey et al., 2006a). These studies have shown that regardless of whether the follow-up assessments are performed immediately after the development of the illness (Reichenberg et al., 2005) and compared to recent test scores or are compared to relative declines in older patients in the process of deterioration (Harvey et al., 2006a), these scores have the same characteristics.

As can be seen in the table, the general level of impairment is moderate to severe and there are very few mildly impaired areas. Interestingly, the same areas that are moderately to severely impaired are those that are most consistently related to impairments in everyday functional skills (Green, 1996). Most abilities are performed at levels consistent with those seen in cases with traumatic brain injury or dementia, which suggests substantial and functionally relevant levels of impairment. While there is some variability across cases, most people with schizophrenia have impairments in several different ability areas.

Prevalence of Impairment and NP Normality

There has been an ongoing discussion of the prevalence of NP impairments and, conversely, NP normality in people with schizophrenia. For example, estimates of the proportion of neuropsychologically impaired patients have varied from 11% (Torrey et al., 1994) to approximately 73% (Palmer et al., 1997), and up to 98% (Keefe et al., 2005) or 100% (Wilk et al., 2005). These inconsistencies are due, in part, to the different criteria used to classify normality. There have been at least three previously published classification methods. Using the Individual Profile Rating (IPR) procedure presented by Kremen et al. (2000), performance on each ability area is computed as the mean of the z-scores of the individual measures comprising the ability area. Individual NP profiles were then rated for severity of impairment using the classification criteria of Kremen et al. (2000). A profile is generally considered abnormal when at least two functions were more than 2 SDs below the normative mean. However, a profile with only a single impaired function could be rated as abnormal if that function was extremely impaired (i.e., >3 SDs below the normative mean). Sizable discrepancies between domains of function were also considered indicating compromised NP function, even if neither function was more than 2 SDs below the normative mean. Patients are classified into four groups: "neuropsychologically normal," "borderline neuropsychologically normal," "neuropsychologically abnormal," or "neuropsychologically severely impaired." The IPR procedure allows assessment of both the absolute level of performance in each ability area, and the extent of within-subject variability across domains, analogous to the way in which one would clinically evaluate individual NP profiles.

Palmer et al. (1997) suggested that in keeping with accepted definitions of general or clinically significant cognitive impairment (CSCI), impairment had to be observed in at least two specific ability areas in order for patients to be classified as "neuropsychologically impaired." These authors classified impairment as performance of 1 SD or more below the general population mean based on corrected scores.

Another perspective is the Global Deficit Score (GDS) approach for classifying NP impairment (Heaton et al., 1994). The GDS approach begins by converting T-scores to deficit scores that reflect presence and severity of impairment. T-scores greater than 40 represent no impairment (deficit score = 0); whereas a deficit score of 1 reflects mild impairment (T-score = 39 – 35); deficit score of 2 reflects mild to moderate impairment (T-score = 34 to 30); 3 reflects moderate impairment (T-score = 29 to 25); 4 reflects moderate to severe impairment (T-score = 24 to 20), and 5 reflects severe impairment (T-score < 20). Deficit scores on all tests are then averaged to create the GDS. A GDS greater than or equal to 0.5 indicates that, on average, an individual was mildly impaired on half of the NP test measures in the battery.

A final approach was recently suggested to consider the possibility that using global population means may result in biased estimates of individual patient's profiles of impairment. In this alternate approach, performance on current ability areas is compared to the performance of HC matched to the schizophrenia patients on the basis of the same level of intellectual performance (Wilk et al., 2005). Thus, current performance is compared on an individual basis to expected performance based on intellectual intactness and the extent of impaired performance is inferred from discrepancies between expected and achieved levels of performance. In this study, matched pairs of patients and controls, including patients whose current IQ scores were greater than 110, were then compared on other aspects of cognitive functioning. Even patients whose current IQs were 110 and above manifested impaired performance in several ability domains, compared to their matched controls. Thus, these data suggested that even in cases with evidence of intellectual intactness, NP abnormalities could still be detected. Further, this procedure might still underestimate cognitive impairments, as those schizophrenia patients with IQs more than 100 might have still deteriorated from higher, better level of performance.

It is not surprising that these different standards for judging impairment in performance have led to variable estimates of the prevalence of cognitive abnormalities in schizophrenia. What is clear, however, is that the stringency of the definitions of impairment is directly related to the prevalence of impairments detected. In the Wilk et al. definition, where deterioration from current functioning is directly indexed

and impairments compared to HC with similar intellectual performance using a criteria of statistical significance, essentially all patients meet the criteria. When more substantial relative impairments are required, particularly when indexed against general population standards and not controlled for individual intellectual performance, the prevalence of impairment is considerably reduced.

In summary, cognitive impairments are generally moderate to severe across ability areas; with a comprehensive cognitive assessment, few patients are spared from having cognitive impairments. Level of stringency of the definition of NP abnormality and reliance on population norms, instead of directly indexing performance against premorbid functions, leads to reduced estimates of impairment.

Functional Relevance of NP Impairment in Schizophrenia

One likely reason for the increased interest in cognition in schizophrenia in the past 15 years has been the increased appreciation of the functional relevance of NP impairments. Poor performance on NP in tests is associated with greater disability in everyday outcomes, including social functioning, independent living and self-maintenance skills, and a variety of role functioning including work, school, and parenting. While the issues involved in the relationships between functional disability and NP performance across a variety of conditions are considered elsewhere in the volume, there are at least issues that are somewhat specific to schizophrenia: whether there are specific relationships between components of NP impairments and different domains of everyday living skills and whether the treatment of NP deficits would lead to reduction in functional disability.

In terms of the specificity of the relationships between domains of NP and functional dysfunctions, initial suggestions (Green, 1996) that there may be some specificity of relationships have not been consistently replicated. Most studies find a relatively general relationship between measures of everyday living outcomes and most NP ability areas (Evans et al., 2003; Harvey et al., 1997; Twamley et al., 2002). Further, the most substantial correlations in most studies have been between global cognitive ability scores and everyday living domains (Harvey et al., 1998). When functional disability is measured in terms of functional potential, such as with performance-based measures of social and functional skills, there is modest evidence for somewhat greater specificity (McClure et al., 2007), but no clear-cut correlations between deficits in cognitive and functional performance measures.

When treatment of cognitive impairments is considered as a strategy to reduce functional disability, the level of relationship between NP performance and functional disability must be considered. The correlation between everyday outcomes and global scores on NP assessment batteries has been shown to share about 25% variance, while individual ability areas share between 4% and 16%. Changes in single ability areas might not be expected to exert substantial effects on everyday outcomes, although changes in variables that are related this strongly to each other might lead to changes with clinical significance if certain critical threshold levels of performance were crossed during successful treatment. Correlations between performance-based measures and NP performance measures are greater than those with everyday outcomes (Bowie et al., 2006), and as a result, successful cognitive enhancement might lead to greater correlated changes in these types of measures. Other influences on everyday outcomes, such as motivation, opportunities, and various incentives and disincentives toward performance need to be considered as well (Rosenheck et al., 2006).

Cognitive remediation interventions have demonstrated detectable and potentially clinically meaningful changes in everyday outcomes. In two separate studies using randomized clinical trials methods, the addition of cognitive remediation therapy to the ongoing provision of supported employment led to gains in the actively treated group compared to the comparison sample (McGurk et al., 2005; Wexler & Bell, 2005). These improvements had long-term persistence, with differences still evident after 3 years (McGurk et al., 2007). These results make two important points. The first is that NP performance can be altered and these alterations can have direct functional benefits. Second, however, is the point that all

participants in both the studies were receiving specialty employment intervention services. Receipt of these services not only delivers a level of support and encouragement absent from the case management of many people with schizophrenia, but also presupposes a motivation to seek and maintain employment. It is not at all clear that similar cognitive remediation interventions, even with cognitive efficacy, would lead to changes in employment outcomes without the ongoing support provided by additional specialty interventions.

Cognitive impairments are functionally relevant and their treatment, when the cognitive intervention has efficacy and when supports are in place, can lead to functional gains. It is likely an error to assume that cognitive enhancement in isolation would lead to substantial functional gains. It is also unclear what level of improvement is required to be functionally relevant and what the details are of the interaction between support and enhancement. Would greater levels of cognitive change (e.g., complete normalization of functioning) require less concurrent support? Conversely, would a modest enhancement signal be facilitated by consistent and appropriate concurrent supportive interventions? These are empirical questions that will be addressed for years to come.

Assessment Strategies in Schizophrenia

The history of clinical neuropsychology has been marked by controversies over the best approaches to assessment. Differential merits of targeted versus battery-based assessments are discussed elsewhere in this volume. In schizophrenia, like in other neuropsychiatric conditions where motivation and cooperation are affected in some cases, understanding the optimum level of detail required to perform an adequate NP assessment is important. This concern is sharpened by the findings, presented above, that cognitive impairments in schizophrenia may reflect a single, unifactorial severity dimension that can be captured with considerable accuracy using a relatively simple assessment. Given the lack of evidence supporting the idea of (1) potential differential brain dysfunctions or subtypes of the illness defined by different profiles of cognitive deficits or (2) differential functional importance across most NP ability areas, extensive NP assessments may not be needed to characterize the majority of patients with schizophrenia.

The issue of the level of detail required in assessment may be particularly relevant for certain types of NP research, such as cognitive enhancement. In the large schizophrenia trial for the Clinical Antipsychotic Trials of Intervention Effectiveness (CATIE) project, an extensive NP assessment was performed at up to three assessment points. Not only was the majority of the variance in composite scores accounted for by a few measures, all of them paper and pencil, but several of the computerized tests had close to 20% missing data per assessment (Keefe et al., 2006). While this may not be an issue for completion of assessments by experienced sites and testers, clearly clinical trials require assessments that are easily completed. Another interesting issue in the CATIE trial was that some of the briefer tests accounted for substantial variance in the composite NP score, and a set of five tests accounted for almost 90% of the variance. The briefer tests were also more likely to be completed by more subjects. Direct comparisons of abbreviated and extensive assessments in schizophrenia have suggested that longer NP assessments add as little as 1% sensitivity to the detection of cognitive impairments in schizophrenia (Keefe et al., 2004) and that composite scores on brief batteries are just as strongly related to functional disability as those derived from longer assessment procedures (Keefe et al., 2006). Several different batteries with suitable psychometric characteristics are available (e.g., Velligan et al., 2004; Wilk et al., 2004). Given our understanding of the NP characteristics of schizophrenia, we find it difficult to recommend extensive assessments unless an evaluation for additional comorbidities is being performed. Even then, the signal arising from cognitive impairments in schizophrenia is so extensive that it is possible that many concurrent comorbidities might not even be detectable against the background of schizophrenia.

Treatments for Cognitive Impairments

It is well understood that successful treatment of psychotic symptoms in patients with schizophrenia is not reliably associated with improvements in cognitive functioning. It had been proposed that newer antipsychotic medications, referred to as atypical antipsychotics, were superior to conventional medications for cognitive enhancement in schizophrenia (Woodward et al., 2006). Many of these studies have methodological limitations, including small sample sizes, nonrandomized methods, and high doses of the conventional comparator medications (Harvey & Keefe, 2001). Further, the effect sizes of changes in cognitive performance with atypical medications, averaged across several meta-analytic studies, was about 0.25 SD, which is a relatively small effect size compared to the level of deficit described earlier in this chapter. Finally, the results of the large-scale ($N > 1000$ patients) CATIE trial (Keefe et al., 2007) indicated that the effects of atypical medications was consistent with the levels detected in previous meta-analyses, about 0.25 SD, but was also not reliably different from the cognitive benefits of low doses of the conventional antipsychotic medication (perphenazine) employed in the study. The general impression is that atypical antipsychotic medications do not provide substantial added benefits for most patients from a cognitive standpoint.

In contrast, studies of the effects of cognitive remediation interventions have suggested not only that these interventions are quite effective in the short term (e.g., McGurk et al., 2005; Wexler & Bell, 2005), but also that these interventions have long-term functional benefits that are substantial. For instance, in the McGurk et al. sample, a three-year follow-up indicated that the patients randomized to cognitive remediation earned 1100% more money over the follow-up period than similarly employment seeking patients who were randomized to treatment as usual (McGurk et al., 2007). These results, while few in number, do suggest that there is a substantial benefit for cognitive remediation treatment, one that extends even to chronic patients (Lindenmeyer et al., 2008) and is statistically significant in meta-analyses.

Pharmacological cognitive enhancement has been less successful. Treatment failures have been reported for cholinesterase inhibitors (Keefe et al., 2008), atomoxetine (Friedman et al., 2008), selective serotonin reuptake inhibitor (SSRI) antidepressants (Friedman et al., 2005), and glutamatergic agents (Buchanan et al., 2007). While this may appear disappointing, there are multiple additional large-scale trials in process and, unless there are factors associated with other treatments for schizophrenia that interfere with the effectiveness of pharmacological agents, this is an area where new positive developments may be expected in the future.

Conclusions

Schizophrenia is marked by an extensive and functionally relevant set of NP abnormalities that persist over the lifespan. In some patients there is evidence of worsening in functioning with aging, most likely in patients with a lifelong history of poor response to treatment and chronic institutional stay. These impairments are present on many of the tests used to examine other neuropsychiatric conditions, but the impairment profile in schizophrenia does not confirm clearly to a pattern consistent with either focal deficits or profiles of impairment seen in other conditions such as cortical dementias. A current controversy exists as to whether NP impairment in schizophrenia is generalized or specific and as to whether extensive cognitive assessments provide more information than abbreviated evaluations. What is clearly agreed upon is that cognitive impairment in schizophrenia is present in most to all cases and that these impairments are factors that interfere greatly with the life functioning of people with schizophrenia.

References

Anderson, S. W., Damasio, H., Jones, R. D., & Tranel, D. (1991). Wisconsin Card Sorting Test performance as a measure of frontal lobe damage. *Journal of Clinical and Experimental Neuropsychology, 13,* 909–922.

Arnold, S. E., Gur, R. E., Shapiro, R. M., Fisher, K. R., Moberg, P. J., Gibney, M. R., et al. (1995). Prospective clinicopathologic studies of schizophrenia: Accrual and assessment of patients. *American Journal of Psychiatry, 152,* 731–737.

Bilder, R. M., Goldman, R. S., Robinson, D., Reiter, G., Bell, L., Bates, J. A., et al. (2000). Neuropsychology of first-episode schizophrenia:

Initial characterization and clinical correlates. *American Journal of Psychiatry, 157,* 549–559.

Bowie, C. R., & Harvey P. D. (2005). Cognition in schizophrenia: impairments, determinants, and functional importance. *Psychiatric Clinics of North America, 28,* 613–633.

Bowie, C. R., Reichenberg, A., Patterson, T. L., Heaton, R. K., & Harvey, P. D. (2006). Determinants of real world functional performance in schizophrenia: Correlations with cognition, functional capacity, and symptoms. *American Journal of Psychiatry, 163,* 418–425.

Bowie, C. R., Reichenberg, A., Reichmann, N., Parrella, M., White, L., & Harvey, P. D. (2004). Stability and functional correlates of memory-based classification in older schizophrenia patients. *American Journal of Geriatric Psychiatry, 12,* 376–386.

Brewer, W. J., Wood, S. J., McGorry P. D., Francey, S. M., Phillips, L. J., Yung, A. R., et al. (2003). Impairment of olfactory identification ability in individuals at ultra-high risk for psychosis who later develop schizophrenia. *American Journal of Psychiatry, 160,* 1790–1794.

Bryson, G., & Bell, M. D. (2003). Initial and final work performance in schizophrenia: Cognitive and symptom predictors. *Journal of Nervous and Mental Disease, 19,* 87–92.

Buchanan, R. W., Javitt, D. C., Marder, S. R., Schooler, N. R., Gold, J. M., McMahon, R. P., et al. (2007). The Cognitive and Negative Symptoms in Schizophrenia Trial (CONSIST): The efficacy of glutamatergic agents for negative symptoms and cognitive impairments. *American Journal of Psychiatry, 164,* 1593–1602.

Callicott, J. H., Mattay, V. S., Bertolino, A., Finn, K., Coppola, R., Frank, J. A., et al. (1999). Physiological characteristics of capacity constraints in working memory as revealed by functional MRI. *Cerebral Cortex, 9,* 20–26.

Callicott. J. H., Bertolino, A., Mattay, V. S, Langheim, F. J., Duyn, J., Coppola, R., et al. (2000). Physiological dysfunction of the dorsolateral prefrontal cortex in schizophrenia revisited. *Cerebral Cortex, 10,* 1078–1092.

Cannon, T. D., Glahn D. C., Kim, J., Van Erp, T. G., Karlsgodt, K., Cohen, M. S., et al. (2005). Dorsolateral prefrontal cortex activity during maintenance and manipulation of information in working memory in patients with schizophrenia. *Archives of General Psychiatry, 62,* 1071–1080.

Chapman, L. J., & Chapman, J. P. (1978). The measurement of differential deficit. *Journal of Psychiatric Research, 14,* 303–311.

Cornblatt B. A., Auther, A. M., Niendam, T., Smith, C. W., Zinberg, J., Bearden, C. E., et al. (2007).

Preliminary findings for two new measures of social and role functioning in the prodromal phase of schizophrenia. *Schizophrenia Bulletin, 33*, 688–702.

Cornblatt B. A., & Erlenmeyer-Kimling, L. (1985). Global attentional deviance as a marker of risk for schizophrenia: Specificity and predictive validity. *Journal of Abnormal Psychology, 94*, 470–486.

Cornblatt, B., Obuchowski, M., Roberts, S., Pollack S., & Erlenmeyer-Kimling, L. (1999). Cognitive and behavioral precursors of schizophrenia. *Developmental Psychopathology, 11*, 487–508.

David, A. S., Malmberg, A., Brandt, L., Albeck, P., & Lewis G. (1997). IQ and risk for schizophrenia: A population-based cohort study. *Psychological Medicine, 27*, 1311–1323.

Davidson M., Harvey P. D., Powchick P., Parrella, M., White, L., Knobler, H. Y., et al. (1995). Severity of symptoms in chronically institutionalized geriatric schizophrenic patients. *American Journal of Psychiatry, 152*, 197–205.

Davidson, M., Harvey, P. D., Welsh, K., Powchik, P., Putnam, K. M., & Mohs, R. C. (1996). Cognitive impairment in old-age schizophrenia: A comparative study of schizophrenia and Alzheimer's disease. *American Journal of Psychiatry, 153*, 1274–1279.

Davidson, M., Reichenberg, A., Rabinowitz, J., Weizer, M., Kaplan, Z., & Mark M. (1999). Behavioral and intellectual markers for schizophrenia in apparently healthy male adolescents. *American Journal of Psychiatry, 156*, 1328–1335.

Davis, K. L., Buchsbaum, M. S., Shihabuddin, L., Spiegel-Cohen, J., Metzger, M., Frecska, E., et al. (1998). Ventricular enlargement in poor outcome schizophrenia. *Biological Psychiatry, 43*, 783–793.

Delisi, L., Sakuma, M., Mauricio, A. M., Relja, M., & Hoff, A. L. (2004). Cerebral ventricular change over the first 10 years after the onset of schizophrenia. *Psychiatry Research, 130*, 57–70.

Delisi, L., Sakuma, M., Tew, W., Kushrer, M., Hoff, A., & Grimson, R. (1997). Schizophrenia as a chronic active brain process: A study of progressive brain structural change subsequent to the onset of psychosis. *Psychiatry Research Brain Imaging, 74*, 129–140.

Dickinson, D., Iannone, V. N., Wilk, C. M., & Gold, J. M. (2004). General and specific cognitive deficits in schizophrenia. *Biological Psychiatry, 55*, 826–833.

Dickinson, D., Ramsey, M. E., & Gold, J. M. (2007). Overlooking the obvious: A meta-analytic comparison of digit symbol coding tasks and other cognitive measures in schizophrenia. *Archives of General Psychiatry, 64*, 532–542.

Evans, J. D., Heaton, R. K., Paulsen, J. S., Palmer, B. W., Patterson, T., & Jeste, D. V. (2003). The relationship of neuropsychological abilities to specific domains of functional capacity in older schizophrenia patients. *Biological Psychiatry, 53*, 422–430.

Friedman, J. I., Carpenter, D., Lu, J., Fan, J., Tang, C. Y., White, L., et al. (2008). A pilot study of adjunctive atomoxetine treatment to second-generation antipsychotics for cognitive impairment in schizophrenia. *Journal of Clinical Psychopharmacology, 28*, 59–63.

Friedman J. I., Harvey P. D., Coleman T., Moriarty, P. J., Bowie, C., Parrella, M., et al. (2001). A six-year follow-up study of cognitive and functional status across the life-span in schizophrenia: A comparison with Alzheimer's disease and normal aging. *American Journal of Psychiatry, 158*, 1441–1448.

Friedman, J. I., Ocampo, R., Elbaz, Z., Parrella, M., White, L., Bowler, S., et al. (2005). The effect of citalopram adjunctive treatment added to atypical antipsychotic medications for cognitive performance in patients with schizophrenia. *Journal of Clinical Psychopharmacology, 25*, 237–242.

Gambini, O., Campana, A., Garghentini, G., & Scarone, A. (2003). No evidence of a homogenous frontal neuropsychological profile in a sample of schizophrenic subjects. *Journal of Neuropsychiatry and Clinical Neurosciences, 15*, 53–57.

Gladsjo, J. A., Heaton, R. K., Palmer, B. W., Taylor, M. J., & Jeste, D. V. (1999). Use of oral reading to estimate premorbid intellectual and neuropsychological functioning. *Journal of the International Neuropsychological Society, 5*, 247–254.

Gladsjo, J. A, McAdams, L. A., Palmer, B. A., Moore, D. J., Jeste, D. V., & Heaton R. K. (2004). A six-factor model of cognition in schizophrenia and related psychotic disorders: Relationships with clinical symptoms and functional capacity. *Schizophrenia Bulletin, 30*, 739–754.

Gold, J., & Harvey, P. D. (1993). Cognitive deficits in schizophrenia. In: Peter Powchik and S. C. Schultz (Eds.), *Psychiatric clinics of North America* (pp. 295–312). Philadelphia: William B. Saunders.

Goldberg, T. E., Hyde, T. M., Kleinman, J. E., & Weinberger, D. R. (1993). Course of schizophrenia: Neuropsychological evidence for a static encephalopathy. *Schizophrenia Bulletin, 19*, 797–804.

Goldman-Rakic, P. S. (1994). Working memory dysfunction in schizophrenia. *Journal of Neuropsychiatry and Clinical Neurosciences, 6*, 348–357.

Granholm, E., Morris, S., Asarnow, R. F., Chock, D., & Jeste, D. V. (2000). Accelerated age-related decline in processing resources in schizophrenia: Evidence from pupillary responses recorded during the span of apprehension task. *Journal of the International Neuropsychological Society, 6*, 30–43.

Green, M. F. (1996). What are the functional consequences of neurocognitive deficits in schizophrenia? *American Journal of Psychiatry*, *153*, 321–330.

Harvey, P. D., Bertisch, H., Friedman, J. I., Marcus, S., Parrella, M., White, L., et al. (2003). The course of functional decline in geriatric patients with schizophrenia: Cognitive-functional and clinical symptoms as determinants of change. *American Journal of Geriatric Psychiatry*, *11*, 610–619.

Harvey, P. D., Friedman, J. I., Bowie, C., Reichenberg, A., McGurk, S. R., Parrella, M., et al. (2006a). Validity and stability of performance-based estimates of premorbid educational functioning in older patients with schizophrenia. *Journal of Clinical and Experimental Neuropsychology*, *28*, 178–192.

Harvey, P. D., Howanitz, E., Parrella, M., White, L., Davidson, M., Mohs, R. C., et al. (1998). Symptoms, cognitive functioning, and adaptive skills in geriatric patients with lifelong schizophrenia: A comparison across treatment sites. *American Journal of Psychiatry*, *155*, 1080–1086.

Harvey, P. D., & Keefe, R. S. (2001). Studies of cognitive change in patients with schizophrenia following novel antipsychotic treatment. *American Journal of Psychiatry*, *158*, 176–184.

Harvey P. D., Silverman J. M., Mohs R. C., Parrella, M., White, L., Powchik, P., et al. (1999). Cognitive decline in late-life schizophrenia: A longitudinal study of geriatric chronically hospitalized patients. *Biological Psychiatry*, *45*, 32–40.

Harvey, P. D., Sukhodolsky, D., Parrella, M., White, L., & Davidson, M. (1997). The association between adaptive and cognitive deficits in geriatric chronic schizophrenic patients. *Schizophrenia Research*, *27*, 211–218.

Harvey, P. D., Moriarty, P. J., Bowie, C., Friedman, J. I., Parrella, M., White, L., et al. (2002). Cortical and subcortical cognitive deficits in schizophrenia: Convergence of classifications based on language and memory skill areas. *Journal of Clinical and Experimental Neuropsychology*, *24*, 55–66.

Harvey, P. D., Moriarty, P. J., Friedman, J. I., White, L., Parrella, M., Mohs, R. C., et al. (2000). Differential preservation of cognitive functions in geriatric patients with lifelong chronic schizophrenia: Less impairment in reading compared with other skill areas. *Biological Psychiatry*, *47*, 962–968.

Harvey, P. D., Reichenberg, A., Romero, M., Granholm, E., & Siever, L. J. (2006b). Dual-task information processing in schizotypal personality disorder: Evidence of impaired processing capacity. *Neuropsychology*, *20*, 453–460.

Heaton, R. K., Paulsen, J. S., McAdams, L. A., Kuck, J., Zisook, S., Braff, D., et al. (1994). Neuropsychological deficits in schizophrenics: Relationship to age, chronicity, and dementia. *Archives of General Psychiatry*, *51*, 469–476.

Heinrichs, R. W., & Zakzanis, K. K. (1998). Neurocognitive deficit in schizophrenia: A quantitative review of the evidence. *Neuropsychology*, *12*, 426–444.

Hoff, A. L., Sakuma, M., Wieneke, M., Horon, R., Kushner, M., & DeLisi, L. E. (1999). Longitudinal neuropsychological follow-up study of patients with first-episode schizophrenia. *American Journal of Psychiatry*, *156*, 1336–1341.

Keefe, R. S. E., Bilder, R. M., Harvey, P. D., Davis, S. M., Palmer, B. W., Gold, J. M., et al. (2006). Baseline neurocognitive deficits in the CATIE schizophrenia trial. *Neuropsychopharmacology*, *31*, 2033–2046.

Keefe, R. S. E., Bilder, R. M., Davis, S. M., Harvey, P. D., Palmer, B. W., Gold, J. M., et al. (2007). Neurocognitive effects of antipsychotic medications in patients with chronic schizophrenia. *Archives of General Psychiatry*, *64*, 633–647.

Keefe, R. S. E., Eesley, C. E., & Poe, M. P. (2005). Defining a cognitive function decrement in schizophrenia. *Biological Psychiatry*, *57*, 688–691.

Keefe, R. S., Goldberg, T. E., Harvey, P. D., Gold, J. M., Poe, M. P., & Coughenour, L. (2004). The brief assessment of cognition in schizophrenia: Reliability, sensitivity, and comparison with a standard neurocognitive battery. *Schizophrenia Research*, *68*, 283–297.

Keefe, R. S. E., Malhotra, A. K., Meltzer, H. Y., Kane, J. M., Buchanan, R. W., Murthy, A., et al. (2008). Efficacy and safety of donepezil in patients with schizophrenia or schizoaffective disorder: Significant placebo/practice effects in a 12-week, randomized, double-blind, placebo-controlled trial. *Neuropsychopharmacology*, *33*(6), 1217–1228.

Keefe, R. S. E., Poe, M., Walker, T. M., & Harvey, P. D. (2006). The Schizophrenia Cognition Rating Scale SCoRS: Interview based assessment and its relationship to cognition, real world functioning and Functional Capacity. *American Journal of Psychiatry*, *163*, 426–432.

Kim, J., Glahn, D. C., Nuechterlein, K. H., & Cannon, T. D. (2004). Maintenance and manipulation of information in schizophrenia: Further evidence for impairment in the central executive component of working memory. *Schizophrenia Research*, *68*, 173–187.

Kremen, W. S., Seidman, L. J., Faraone, S. V., Toomey, R., & Tsuang, M. T. (2000). The paradox

of normal neuropsychological function in schizophrenia. *Journal of Abnormal Psychology, 109,*
743–752.

Lencz, T., Smith, C. W., McLaughlin, D., Auther, A.,
Nakayama, E., Hovey, L., et al. (2006). Generalized
and specific neurocognitive deficits in prodromal
schizophrenia. *Biological Psychiatry, 59,* 863–871.

Lieberman, J., Chakos, M., Wu, H., Alvir, J., Hoffman,
E., Robinson, D., et al. (2001). Longitudinal study
of brain morphology in first episode schizophrenia. *Biological Psychiatry, 49,* 487–499.

Lieberman, J. A., Tollefson, G. D., Charles, C.,
Zipursky, R., Sharma, T., Kahn, R. S., et al. (2005).
Antipsychotic drug effects on brain morphology
in first-episode psychosis. *Archives of General
Psychiatry, 62,* 361–370.

Lindenmayer, J. P., McGurk, S. R., Mueser, K. T.,
Khan, A., Wance, D., Hoffman, L., et al. (2008). A
randomized controlled trial of cognitive remediation among inpatients with persistent mental illness. *Psychiatric Services, 59,* 241–247.

McClure, M. M., Bowie, C. R., Patterson, T. L.,
Heaton, R. K., Weaver, C., Anderson, H., et
al. (2007). Correlations of functional capacity
and neuropsychological performance in older
patients with schizophrenia: Evidence for specificity of relationships? *Schizophrenia Research, 89,*
330–338.

McGurk, S. R., Mueser, K. T., Feldman, K., Wolfe,
R., & Pascaris, A. (2007). Cognitive training for
supported employment: 2–3 year outcomes of a
randomized controlled trial. *American Journal of
Psychiatry, 164,* 437–441.

McGurk, S. R., Mueser, K. T., & Pascaris, A. (2005).
Cognitive training and supported employment
for persons with severe mental illness: One-
year results from a randomized controlled trial.
Schizophrenia Bulletin, 31, 898–909.

Mohamed, S., Paulsen, J. S., O'Leary, D. Arndt, S.,
& Andreasen N. (1999). Generalized cognitive
deficits in schizophrenia: a study of first-episode patients. *Archives of General Psychiatry, 56,*
749–754.

Palmer, B. W., & Heaton, R. K. (2000). Executive
dysfunction in schizophrenia. In: T. Sharma and
P. D. Harvey (Eds.), *Cognition in schizophrenia:
Impairments, importance and treatment strategies*
(pp. 51–72). New York: Oxford University Press.

Palmer, B. W., Heaton, R. K., Paulsen, J. S., Kuck, J.,
Braff, D., Harris, M. J., et al. (1997). Is it possible
to be schizophrenic yet neuropsychologically normal? *Neuropsychology, 11,* 437–446.

Paulsen, J. S., Heaton, R. K., Sadek, J. R., Perry, W.,
& Jeste, D. V. (1995). The nature of learning and
memory impairments in schizophrenia. *Journal*

of the International Neuropsychological Society, 1,
88–99.

Paulsen, J. S., Salmon, D. P., Monsch, A., Butters,
N., Swenson, M. R., & Bondi, M. W. (1995).
Discrimination of cortical from subcortical dementias on the basis of memory and problem-solving
tests. *Journal of Clinical Psychology, 51,* 48–58.

Reichenberg A., Weiser, M., Rapp, Rabinowitz, J.,
Caspi, A., Schmeidler, J., et al. (2005). Elaboration
on premorbid intellectual performance in schizophrenia: Premorbid intellectual decline and risk
for schizophrenia. *Archives of General Psychiatry,
62,* 1297–1304.

Reichenberg A., Weiser, M., Rapp, M. A., Rabinowitz,
J., Caspi, A., Schmeidler, J., et al. (2006). Premorbid
intra-individual variability in intellectual performance and risk for schizophrenia: A population-
based study. *Schizophrenia Research, 85,* 49–57.

Rosenheck, R., Leslie, D., Keefe, R. S., McEvoy, J.,
Swartz, M., Perkins, D., et al. (2006). Barriers
to employment in people with schizophrenia.
American Journal of Psychiatry, 163, 411–417.

Rund, B. R. (1998). A review of longitudinal studies
of cognitive functions in schizophrenia patients.
Schizophrenia Bulletin, 24, 425–435.

Saykin, A. J., Gur, R. C., Gur, R. E., Mozeley,
D., Mozeley, L. H., & Resnick, S. M. (1991).
Neuropsychological function in schizophrenia:
Selective impairment in memory and learning.
Archives of General Psychiatry, 48, 618–623.

Saykin, A. J., Shtasel, D. L., Gur, R. E., Kester,
D. B., Mozley, L. H., Stafiniak, P., et al. (1994).
Neuropsychological deficits in neuroleptic naive
patients with first-episode schizophrenia. *Archives
of General Psychiatry, 51,* 124–131.

Seidman, L. J., Guiliano, A. J., Smith, C. W.,
Stone, W. S., Glatt, S. J., Meyer, E., et al. (2006).
Neuropsychological functioning in adolescents
and young adults at genetic risk for schizophrenia
and affective psychoses: Results from the Harvard
and Hillside Adolescent High Risk Studies.
Schizophrenia Bulletin, 32, 507–524.

Torrey, E. F., Bowler, A. E., Taylor, E. H., & Gottesman,
I. I. (1994). *Schizophrenia and manic-depressive
disorder: The biological roots of mental illness as
revealed by the landmark study of identical twins.*
New York: Basic Books.

Tracy, J. I., McCrory, A. C., Josiassen, R. C., &
Monaco, C. A. (1996). A comparison of reading
and demographic based estimates of premorbid intelligence in schizophrenia. *Schizophrenia
Research, 22,* 103–109.

Turetsky, B. I., Moberg, P. J., Mozley, L. H., Moelter,
S. T., Agrin, R. N., Gur, R. C., et al. (2002).
Memory-delineated subtypes of schizophrenia:

Relationship to clinical, neuroanatomical, and neurophysiological measures. *Neuropsychology*, *16*, 481–490.

Twamley, E. W., Doshi, R. R., Nayak, G. V., Palmer, B. W., Golshan, S., Heaton, R. K., et al. (2002). Generalized cognitive impairments, ability to perform everyday tasks, and level of independence in community living situations of older patients with psychosis. *American Journal of Psychiatry, 159*, 2013–2020.

Velligan, D. I., DiCocco, M., Bow-Thomas, C. C., Cadle, C., Glahn, D. C., Miller, A. L., et al. (2004). A brief cognitive assessment for use with schizophrenia patients in community clinics. *Schizophrenia Research, 71*, 273–283.

Weickert, T. W., Goldberg, T. E., Gold, J. M., Bigelow, L. B., Egan, M. F., & Weinberger D. R. (2000). Cognitive impairments in patients with schizophrenia displaying preserved and compromised intellect. *Archives of General Psychiatry, 57*, 907–913.

Weiser, M., Reichenberg A., Rabinowitz, J., Knobler, H. Y., Lubin, G., Yazvitzky, R., et al. (2004). Cognitive performance of male adolescents is lower than controls across psychiatric disorders: A population-based study. *Acta Psychatrica Scandinavica, 110*, 471–475.

Wexler, B. E., & Bell, M. D. (2005). Cognitive remediation and vocational rehabilitation for schizophrenia. *Schizophrenia Bulletin, 31*, 931–941.

Wilk, C. M., Gold, J. M., Humber, K., Dickerson, F., Fenton, W. S., & Buchanan, R. W. (2004). Brief cognitive assessment in schizophrenia: Normative data for the Repeatable Battery for the Assessment of Neuropsychological Status. *Schizophrenia Research, 70*, 175–186.

Wilk, C. M., Gold, J. M., McMahon, R. P., Humber, K., Iannone, V. N., & Buchanan, R. W. (2005). No, it is not possible to be schizophrenic yet neuropsychologically normal. *Neuropsychology, 19*, 778–786.

Woodward, N. D., Purdon, S. E., Meltzer, H. Y., & Zald, D. H. (2005). A meta-analysis of neuropsychological change to clozapine, olanzapine, quetiapine, and risperidone in schizophrenia. *International Journal of Neuropsychopharmacology, 8*, 457–472.

22

Neuropsychology of Depression and Related Mood Disorders

Scott A. Langenecker, H. Jin Lee, and Linas A. Bieliauskas

Tremendous strides have been made toward understanding the neuropsychological, neuro-anatomical, and neuroimaging findings associated with depression. Whereas understanding of the neuroanatomical networks involved in depression and related mood disorders remains in an adolescent phase, neuropsychological findings in depression and related mood disorders are fairly well codified at this point. To be sure, there are a number of clinical and demographic features that substantially impact cognitive performance in the context of a mood disorder, including later age of onset, polypharmacy/substance abuse, medical complications, greater severity, and resistance to traditional treatments. Whereas the "causes" for depression-associated cognitive difficulties are heterogeneous, the co-occurrence of features of depression and cognitive difficulties of specific types suggests a common set of neural networks that may be adversely affected, including medial and ventral frontal, limbic, and basal ganglia structures. The present chapter is intended to provide the reader with a blend of traditional neuropsychological investigations of depression and related mood disorders, hereafter referred to generally as mood disorders, in addition to integrating the latest cognitive and affective neuroscience research. We will review the moderating impact of age of onset, effort, subtypes of depression, and medications on cognitive functioning in mood disorders, as well as research using cognitive measures as predictors of treatment response.

The present chapter follows several previous chapters on depression and depression-related cognitive difficulties by King and Caine (1996) and Caine (1986) in earlier editions of this book. As King and Caine note in the previous edition of this book, study of cognition in mood disorders has moved from being a nuisance when studying late-life dementias, also known as pseudo-dementia, to a full fledged area of inquiry. The underlying assumptions about mood disorders as being functional and not organic disorders have now been assailed on a number of different fronts (Tucker et al., 1990). In fact, it is now best to consider mood disorders under a category of "potentially reversible cognitive decrements" (Sobow et al., 2006), although the careful reader of this chapter will come to appreciate that for some individuals, the cognitive difficulties that co-occur with depression are in no way reversible. This characterization may sit poorly with many in a field christened in the tradition of degenerative dementias, wherein dysfunction is the inevitable, and currently irreversible, sequelae of neurological disease. However, as studies of disorders such as multiple sclerosis and Huntington's disease have aptly informed the field, assumptions about "functional" disorders can be largely misplaced (Ghaffar & Feinstein, 2007). This is by no means to associate the frequently present, moderate cognitive inefficiencies observed in depression to those more severe, highly prevalent, and persistent difficulties observed in degenerative conditions. Rather, the purpose is to place the field

523

and the reader in the proper pose of humility when making inferences about the current state of knowledge in brain–behavior relationships in mood disorders. Mood disorders, like any other psychological phenomena, have the central nervous system (CNS) as the wellspring for their existence, and many of the same tracts and systems implicated in neurological disorders are similarly implicated in mood and other psychiatric disorders (Cummings, 1993).

The burgeoning fields of affective and cognitive neuroscience, as well as the expanding body of knowledge on mood disorders from traditional neuropsychological investigations, together make a chapter on the neuropsychology of mood disorders no small endeavor. There are many allied areas of inquiry that are not seamlessly integrated into one theory, model, or basis for understanding of the brain–behavior relationships most typically observed in mood disorders. Given this challenge, we have attempted to balance specific and important areas of inquiry within mood disorders with the more general purview that one might typically expect from a book chapter. We make no pretense of being exhaustive in breadth or depth, but do hope that the present chapter provides an ample overview of general areas along with very specific subtopics that we feel the reader might most benefit from. We begin with an overview of what might be considered a typical cognitive profile of a depressed patient, based largely on the traditional neuropsychological studies of depression. We move from these to discuss neuroanatomical and neuroimaging evidence currently available in mood disorders research. The neuroimaging data largely rely upon cognitive and affective neuroscience research. We then delve into critical mediating factors in understanding brain–behavior relationships in mood disorders. This is a necessary and, we believe, very valuable overview of factors that directly relate to what extent cognitive difficulties might be expected to occur in mood disorders. We will also highlight some specific subtypes of mood disorders that illustrate potential brain–behavior relationships, or where greater prevalence or severity of cognitive difficulties might be expected. We review potential medication effects in depression, as this is likely a frequent question that arises in the neuropsychological

assessment of mood disorders. The chapter closes with several compelling studies that have used neuropsychological and cognitive/affective neuroscience measures to predict treatment response, a summary, and some recommendations for what a "core" battery might be comprised of when assessing a patient with a mood disorder.

Traditional Studies and Cognitive Profile

Major depressive disorder (MDD) is associated with inefficiencies in various cognitive domains (Austin et al., 2001, p. 57; Miller, 1975; for reviews see Elliott, 1998; Rogers et al., 2004) including attention (Cornblatt et al., 1989; Porter et al., 2003; Weiland-Fiedler et al., 2004), psychomotor speed (Sobin & Sackeim, 1997), executive function (Grant et al., 2001; Paelecke-Habermann et al., 2005), and memory (Austin et al., 1992; Brown et al., 1994; Burt et al., 1995; Elliott et al., 1996). It is well known that intragroup heterogeneity of cognitive decrements exist, though the reasons are still not completely clear. Possible mediating factors, some of which are addressed later in this chapter, include the age of onset, age of participants, premorbid level of cognitive function, symptom severity, number of previous depressive episodes, effort and motivation, medication status, patient status (inpatient or outpatient), state of the individual (i.e., remitted or depressed), and history of hospitalization (Elliott, 1998; Fossati et al., 2002; Gualtieri et al., 2006). As such, drawing conclusions regarding cognitive decrements in MDD is challenging because studies often utilize a depressed group of heterogeneous individuals varying in aforementioned characteristics. Furthermore, many such studies are powered only to detect large and very large effect sizes and also typically use tasks designed to assess for obvious brain injury or neurodegenerative conditions.

In this section, we review cognitive decrements in adults who are under the age of 65 as other neurological factors often contribute in the disease process in geriatric or late-onset depression. The specific topic of late-onset depression is discussed in the Age of Onset section in this chapter. Readers can also find several excellent articles on neuropsychological dysfunction in geriatric depression (Bieliauskas, 1993; Elderkin-Thompson et al., 2007; Marcos et al., 2005; Sheline et al., 2006; Wright & Persad, 2007). We focus on domains of attention, psychomotor speed, executive function, and memory, which are the areas that have been most researched and found to be pertinent to MDD (Bulmash et al., 2006; Gualtieri et al., 2006; Landro et al., 2001; Porter et al., 2003). We also understand that sorting neuropsychological measures into different constructs may be arbitrary as one measure usually taps more than one cognitive domain. Furthermore, attention, working memory, processing speed, and executive function mainly involve the common structures in the frontal–subcortical neural networks (Cummings, 1995; Mega & Cummings, 1994).

Attention

Research on attention in MDD suggests that although simpler attentional processes may not be affected in adult depressed patients (Harvey et al., 2004; Ravnkilde et al., 2003), more complex attentional processes such as working memory or sustained attention are often compromised in patients with MDD (Porter et al., 2003; Rose & Ebmeier, 2006) and even in remitted individuals in some cases (Weiland-Fiedler et al., 2004). Hartlage et al. (1993) noted that depressed individuals have more difficulty on tasks that require effortful processing compared to tasks that are simpler or require automatic processing. Indeed, some studies of attentional processing in MDD have shown that short-term attention such as the forward digit span is generally unaffected compared to more difficult working memory tasks (Harvey et al., 2004; Ravnkilde et al., 2003). For example, Harvey et al. (2004) found that short-term attention on forward and backward digit span and forward spatial span did not differ between 22 young inpatients with MDD and 22 normal controls, while poorer performance was found in the patient group on a backward spatial span task and a verbal n-back task. However, their results did not fully support an automatic versus effortful processing hypothesis as they failed to find a group and complexity interaction (i.e., the patient group did not do disproportionately worse as the task became more

difficult). By way of background, the automatic effortful hypothesis states that depressed individuals should incrementally show poorer performance as the degree of effort required on any given task increases (Hasher & Zacks, 1979). Similarly, Rose and Ebmeier (2006) examined working memory in 20 patients with MDD (in or outpatients, most of who were on antidepressant medications) and 20 healthy controls by using a different version of n-back task. The researchers found slower reaction times and reduced accuracy in the MDD group compared to the control group in a linear fashion, again, with no disproportionately slower reaction time and decreased accuracy with increasing cognitive load, suggesting a more uniform pattern of weakness rather than an automatic/effortful continuum.

In tasks of sustained attention, individuals with MDD were shown to make more omission errors (Langenecker et al., 2007a, 2007b; Porter et al., 2003; Sevigny et al., 2003) and commission errors (Farrin et al., 2003; Porter et al., 2003) on continuous performance tests (CPTs). In addition, individuals who were in euthymic or remitted states were also shown to demonstrate persistent difficulty with sustained attention. Recently, Weiland-Fiedler et al. (2004) found decrements in 28 fully remitted, unmedicated individuals with a history of MDD compared to 23 healthy controls on the Rapid Visual Information Processing Task of the Cambridge Neuropsychological Test Automated Battery (CANTAB). Paelecke-Habermann et al. (2005) also found continued attention difficulty in remitted individuals with MDD. Although the aforementioned studies demonstrated attentional inefficiencies in euthymic and depressed states, Grant et al. (2001) did not find differences on the digit span task and a CPT in 123 nonchronic, MDD outpatients and 36 healthy controls. The dependent measures reported by Grant and colleagues were different from the measures reported by other researchers (Harvey et al., 2004; Porter et al., 2003; Sevigny et al., 2003).

Psychomotor Speed

Research on psychomotor speed in mood disorders have shown inconsistent findings. Some studies have shown slowed psychomotor speed in individuals with mood disorders (Bulmash et al., 2006; Sobin & Sackeim, 1997) while other studies have not found any difference between depressed individuals and healthy controls (Grant et al. 2001; Porter et al., 2003). In general, psychomotor slowing has been more commonly associated with melancholic depression (Austin et al., 1999) and/or in older individuals with depression (Beats et al., 1996; Nebes et al., 2000). In medication-free younger individuals, normal performance was found on the Digit Symbol Substitution Test on the *Wechsler Adult Intelligence Scale-Revised* (WAIS-R) and on a CPT in terms of respond latency (Porter et al., 2003). In addition, Harvey et al. (2004) also found no difference between 22 inpatients with MDD and 22 healthy controls on the Trail-Making Test Part A. Perhaps, the level of difficulty or required effort has an effect on psychomotor slowing. Hammar et al. (2003) examined automatic and effortful processing by using a visual search paradigm in 21 individuals with MDD on antidepressant medications and healthy controls. The results indicated no difference in reaction time between the two groups on the task that was thought to only require automatic processing (one distractor task). Nevertheless, reaction time was slower in the MDD group when the task required effortful processing (two distractor task). Another study of 26 patients with MDD reported positive relationships between choice reaction time on the California Computerized Assessment Package clinical depression rating scales (Egeland et al., 2005). Bulmash et al. (2006) examined 18 unmedicated individuals with MDD and 29 controls on a driving simulator for four 30-minute trials throughout the day. The MDD group demonstrated overall slowed steering reaction time and increased number of crashes compared to the control group even after age and sleepiness were controlled.

Executive Functioning

Research has shown that individuals with MDD demonstrate decrements on tasks that are presumed to measure executive function (Grant et al. 2001; Langenecker et al., 2005; Paelecke-Habermann et al., 2005; Porter et al. 2003). Executive function tasks in neuropsychological

assessments involve various functions including concept formation, set-shifting, planning, inhibition, working memory, and fluency (Brown et al., 1994; Miyake et al., 2000). Some of the commonly used tests to assess executive dysfunction both in research and clinical settings include the Wisconsin Card Sorting Test (WCST; Channon, 1996; Grant et al., 2001), tests of verbal fluency (for a review see Henry & Crawford, 2005), the Stroop interference test (Harvey et al., 2004; Markela-Lerenc et al., 2006), Trail-Making Test Part B (Grant et al., 2001; Harvey et al., 2004), the Tower of London test (Naismith et al., 2006; Porter et al., 2003), and the Halstead–Reitan Category test (Grant et al., 2001).

Individuals with depressive symptoms have been shown to complete fewer categories and make more perseverate responses on the WCST (Channon, 1996; Grant et al., 2001), although inconsistently (Fossati et al., 2001; Ravnkilde et al., 2003). Grant et al. (2001) compared 123 outpatients with MDD to 36 healthy controls on the WCST and found that the MDD group completed a fewer number of categories, made more perseverative responses and errors, and more often failed to maintain set and learn. No difference was found, however, on the other measures of executive functioning including the Halstead–Reitan Categories Test, letter fluency, and Trail-Making Test Part B. Ravnkilde et al. (2003) found no difference on the WCST between 40 inpatients with MDD and a group of 49 controls. The researchers did find that Stroop word reading, color naming, and interference were all poorer in the MDD group compared to the healthy control group. Harvey et al. (2004) reported that the depressed group did not differ from the control group on the word reading condition of the Stroop test while they performed worse on the color naming and interference conditions. The researchers also found slower completion times on the Trail-Making Test Part B. Fossati et al. (2001) did not find a significant difference between 22 depressed inpatients and 22 healthy controls on the modified WCST but found a difference on the spontaneous condition of the California Card Sorting Test (Delis et al., 1992). Individuals with MDD were found to generate fewer words on verbal fluency tasks (i.e., a lexical fluency test and on the 'exclude letter' fluency test) in some studies (Porter et al.,

2003) but not in others (Harvey et al., 2004; Naismith et al., 2006). No difference was found between the MDD and normal controls on the Tower of London test (Naismith et al., 2006; Porter et al., 2003).

Memory

Although many studies have shown decreased memory function in patients with MDD (Austin et al., 1992; Bornstein et al., 1991; Brown et al., 1994; Burt et al., 1995; Elliott et al., 1996), the findings again do not show consistent patterns or severity of memory impairment (Basso & Bornstein, 1999; Brand et al., 1992; Fossati et al., 2002). In addition, the initial acquisition process seems to be more affected than retrieval in depressed individuals, as evidenced by decreased initial recall as well as decreased delayed recall and recognition (Austin et al., 1992; Basso & Bornstein, 1999; Ravnkilde et al., 2003). This is likely associated with the affected attentional processes that are interfering with the encoding process. Austin et al. (1992) indicated poorer performance on initial acquisition and delayed recall and recognition portions of the Rey Auditory Verbal Learning Test (RAVLT) in two depressed patient groups ("endogenous" and "neurotic") compared to controls. In contrast, Grant et al. (2001) failed to find differences in memory function in 123 MDD outpatients compared to controls on the Hopkins Verbal Learning Test (HVLT) and on the Visual Reproduction subtest of the WAIS-R. Hasher and Zacks (1979) proposed that memory dysfunction in depression is likely demonstrated with more complex tasks that require effortful encoding rather than less effortful or automatic encoding processes. Rohling and Scogin (1993) examined 30 depressed patients (21 outpatients and 9 inpatients), 20 psychiatric controls, and 30 normal controls on measures that appeared to be more challenging such as paired-associate learning or free recall tasks versus measures that were presumed to be easier such as memory for frequency of occurrence or spatial locations. The researchers noted that as there were no significant correlations between the measures of depression severity and the measures of effortful memory, their results failed to support Hasher and Zacks' hypothesis. Porter et al. (2003)

utilized recall versus recognition memory tasks (presuming that the recall tasks are more difficult than recognition tasks) to examine Hasher and Zacks' hypothesis. The researchers found that the only difference between the medication-free MDD group and the normal group on the RAVLT was the distractor list recall without any evidence of proactive interference. In contrast, the researchers found that the MDD group performed poorer on measures of recognition memory (memory for visual information such as patterns and spatial locations on the CANTAB compared to the control group).

As mentioned, the number of recurrent depressive episodes and inpatient status may be associated with poorer memory function. Basso and Bornstein (1999) studied 20 single-episode depressed inpatients and 46 recurrent depressed inpatients and found a greater memory dysfunction in the recurrent group compared to single-episode patients on the California Verbal Learning Test-Second Edition (CVLT-II) measures including total initial recall, learning curve, short-delay cued recall, long-delay free and cued recall, and recognition discrimination. Ravnkilde et al. (2003) did not find a difference in learning and memory on the Luria Verbal Learning Test but found a difference on the immediate recall of the Logical Memory Test of the WAIS and immediate and delayed recall on the Visual Reproduction Test of the WMR-R between 40 medicated depressive inpatients and 49 normal controls. More positively, memory decrements appear to subside in remitted individuals. Weiland-Fiedler et al. (2004) did not find any difference in memory acquisition on the CVLT-II between a group that consisted of 28 fully remitted, unmediated individuals with a history of MDD and a group of 23 healthy participants.

Neuroanatomy of Mood Disorders

Limbic, frontal, and subcortical areas have been strongly implicated in depression and related mood disorders (Alexopoulos, 2002; Carroll et al., 1976; Drevets & Raichle, 1992; Goldapple et al., 2004; Mayberg et al., 1994; Videbech, 2000), although it should be noted that these areas are implicated in a number of disorders for which dysfunctions in mood and affect are not always present (Nilsson et al., 2002; Owen, 2004;

Van Praag et al., 1975). The relationship of mood and cognitive disturbance to neuroanatomical abnormalities remains somewhat tenuous, as few studies have examined these relationships with sufficient sample size and measurement specificity. This section will review several structures shown to be affected in mood disorders but will not exhaustively review the many studies that have been completed of morphometry in mood disorders. There is specific focus on studies with larger samples, better clinical characterization, and attempts to look at the relationship between cognitive or affective variables and brain morphometry when possible. Functional imaging studies are reviewed in a subsequent section below. Figure 22.1 illustrates brain regions referenced throughout this section, whereas Brodmann areas can be found elsewhere (Kolb & Whishaw, 1996). (See also the color version in the color insert section.) By and large, these areas are all part of a ventral cingulate–medial prefrontal circuit, as described by Cummings (1993) and further subdivided by Rolls (Rolls, 1999) in lateral and medial orbital-frontal circuits. There is also a dorso-lateral prefrontal circuit that is implicated in some of the research described below. We further note that subcortical structures are incorporated within these circuits and are consistent with what was previously described in this book by King and Caine (1996).

Structural Imaging

Structural imaging studies of MDD and related mood disorders, like most morphologic studies, are limited primarily by region of interest (ROI) approaches. For example, many studies only examine one ROI within total brain volume, or a subsection of total brain volume. This approach can provide for a single disassociation, but does not address the possibility of entire systems being disrupted in mood disorders. It does not enable one to understand other parts of the limbic and frontal networks that may be implicated in depression, nor does it address whether there is a global problem or if other systems are unaffected. More recently, voxel-based approaches have been used to do full brain comparisons, but these are limited by heterogeneity in anatomy across subjects and limitations in strategies for anatomical warping to address the heterogeneity. There are a number of brain regions implicated in the neuroanatomy of mood disorders, illustrated in Figure 22.1.

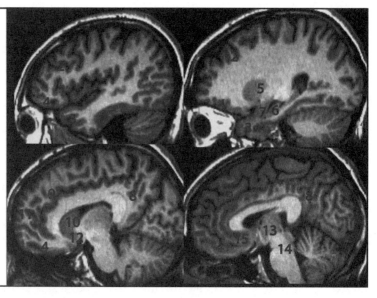

Regions of Interest in Mood Disorders
 1. Insula
 2. Dorsolateral Prefrontal
 3. Anterior Temporal
 4. Orbital Frontal
 5. Putamen
 6. Hippocampal Formation
 7. Amygdaloid Complex
 8. Posterior Cingulate
 9. Dorsal Anterior Cingulate
10. Caudate
11. Medial Prefrontal
12. Nucleus Accumbens
13. Thalamus & Hypothalamus
14. Raphe
15. Subgenual Anterior Cingulate

Figure 22–1. Frequent Regions of Interest Reported in Structural and Imaging Studies Relevant to Understanding Depression and Related Psychiatric Disorders. Numbers indicate center of foci, although some foci are collapsed across the left-right axis to reduce the number of images necessary to display these foci.

The importance of the hippocampus in mood disorders is now accepted, though the specificity and reliability of this relationship has yet to be fully explicated (Caetano et al., 2004; Campbell & MacQueen, 2004; Lee et al., 2002; Lopez et al., 1998; Mervaala et al., 2000; Sapolsky, 2001; Stockmeier et al., 2004). There are several reviews of studies of hippocampal (and amygdalar—see below) volume and depression available and we refer the reader to these (Sheline, 2003; Videbech & Ravnkilde, 2004). A voxel-based morphometry study of 20 patients with treatment resistant depression (TRD), compared to 20 remitted and 20 control subjects revealed atrophy in bilateral hippocampal structures, as well as other areas described in subsequent sections (Shah et al., 2002). Their TRD group had a significantly greater number of hospitalizations compared to the remitted depressives and all had received at least six sessions of electroconvulsive therapy (ECT). An earlier study by this group demonstrated reduced Auditory Verbal Learning performance in treatment resistant depression patients compared to remitted patients (Shah et al., 1998) and a positive correlation between left hippocampal volume and AVLT performance. A study by Vythlingham and colleagues failed to demonstrate differences in hippocampal volume between 38 depressed and 33 control subjects, but the study did show trend level correlations between hippocampal volume and visual immediate and visual delayed recall on the Selective Reminding Test (Vythilingam et al., 2004). In 37 moderate to severe traumatic brain injury (TBI) patients with co-occurring depression, smaller hippocampal volume was associated both with development of mood disorders and poorer vocational outcome at 1 year, suggesting a strong link between hippocampal integrity and affective and cognitive functioning (Pournajafi-Nazarloo et al., 2007). A study of 34 inpatients with depression and 34 control subjects reported reduced hippocampal volume in MDD and a relationship between lower hippocampal volume and poorer performance on the WCST, but not the AVLT (Frodl et al., 2006). Furthermore, there was no association of cognitive measures with frontal volumes. A longitudinal study of 61 depressed patients over the age of 60, compared with 40 age and education matched controls indicated a relationship between right hippocampal volume and persisting memory difficulty 6 months after the initial assessment (O'Brien et al., 2004). Of course, it is unknown if smaller hippocampi placed one at greater risk for mood disorders and reduced cognition due to increased vulnerability, or if these are the result of length and severity of illness.

There is continued debate about whether the amygdala is involved in mood disorders, whereas it is well-established that the amygdala is critical in anxiety disorders. There is a mixture of studies reporting increased as compared to decreased amygdala volume (Sheline, 2003). A study of 30 first-episode patients with MDD demonstrated increased bilateral hippocampal volume compared to the match control group of 30 patients and 27 recurrent depressed patients and was stable over 1 year (Frodl et al., 2003). A larger study of 47 female twins pairs exploring amygdala volumes suggested that there were no differences between those with MDD, those at high risk for MDD, and the control subjects, although there was a significant relationship between twin amygdala volumes suggesting a genetic influence (Munn et al., 2007). Reductions in amygdala volumes have been associated with the short form of the 5-HTTLPR polymorphism in one large study of 114 subjects using voxel-based morphometry (Pezawas et al., 2005), but with the long form in another study of 247 young adult female twins (Chorbov et al., 2007). The data available on relationships between amygdala volume, cognition, and affect measures is limited in morphometry data and may be further complicated by comorbidity between depressed and anxiety subjects in some studies. Whereas there are animal and theoretical models of mood disorders that would suggest an important role for the amygdala in the etiology and maintenance of the mood disorders, the present state of knowledge using morphological techniques is equivocal in this regard. Importantly, there is now some suggestion that amygdala volumes may be enlarged in first onset of mood disorder, yet smaller or not different in size with recurrence of depression and/or treatment with medication.

The frontal lobes have long been implicated in mood disorders (Harlow, 1868; Moniz, 1954).

However, notes of caution for the reader include the following: first, the frontal lobes encompass 33% of the cortical surface, second, there are five, possibly six, frontosubcortical circuits regulating everything from eye movements to emotional functioning, and third, the zeitgeist remains focused on frontal pathology as a cause, or result, of mood disorders. As such, one cannot conclude that the frontal lobes are uniquely involved in mood disorders. Methodological challenges in measuring specific frontal regions are formidable, whether by Brodmann area or by specific landmarks. The subgenual anterior cingulate has been demonstrated to be smaller in several studies (Botteron et al., 2002; Drevets et al., 1997; Ongur et al., 1998, also Coryell et al., 2005) with one of the negative studies showing a functional abnormality in the same region (Pizzagalli et al., 2004). One other group studied both anterior and posterior cingulate volume in 21 unremitted and 10 remitted patients with unipolar depression compared to 31 control subjects, showing reduced volumes in all four (right, left by anterior, posterior) ROIs in those with unremitted depression, but only in the left anterior cingulate in the subset with remitted depression, both compared to the control group (Caetano et al., 2006). The remitted and unremitted groups did not differ in ROI volumes, suggesting that reduced power in the subset analysis may have masked differences between the patient groups, as well as between the remitted patient and control groups. A study of 44 elderly patients with depression showed larger lateral ventricles in those depressed patients with prior ECT compared to those without ECT (Simpson et al., 2001). Furthermore, there were multiple correlations of neuropsychological measures with frontal (reverse digit span), temporal (Trial 1 of the RAVLT, perseverative errors on the WCST, copy of the Rey–Osterrieth Complex Figure Test, and memory for the Rey–Osterrieth Complex Figure Test), and parietal (Digit Symbol Substitution Test, Trial 1 of the RAVLT, and reverse digit span) lobe volumes but not volume of the lateral ventricle. Another study compared 30 elderly depressives and 40 controls, demonstrating a negative relationship between perseverative errors and a positive relationship with total correct on the Benton Visual Memory Test with left orbital frontal cortical

volume (Steffens et al., 2003). These studies suggest that the frontal lobes are indeed relevant when understanding the pathophysiology of depression and the potential for concurrent neuropsychological decrements.

Other brain regions, and related affect and cognitive measures, have received very little research focus thus far in mood disorders. Studies of the basal ganglia are mixed, and there appears to be a distinction in volume between simply depressed (reduced) and bipolar (increased) patients with mood disorders (Anand & Shekhar, 2003; Krishnan et al., 1992). One study of the thalamus with 25 bipolar and 17 unipolar patients showed no differences in thalamic volume from 39 control subjects (Caetano et al., 2001). The insula has also been implicated in mood disorders, although variability in measurement boundaries likely have precluded obtaining strong reliability in morphologic measurements, thus reducing reports in the literature about this region (Nagai et al., 2007). Voxel-based morphometry studies, which are limited in structural specificity, have shown more structural abnormalities in the insula in schizophrenia, and not in mood disorders (Nagai et al., 2007).

Of course, the relevance of subcortical and periventricular hyperintensities in mood disorders are of increasing interest, particularly in elderly or middle-age onset mood disorders, and these patients are more likely to exhibit cognitive difficulties (Bhalla et al., 2006; King et al., 1998; O'Brien et al., 2004; Sobow et al., 2006). One large study of 48 depressed patients and 73 depressed inpatients demonstrated an increasing odds ratio of 5.32 for subcortical hyperintensities in those with depression (Coffey et al., 1993). Another of 37 patients found that white matter hyperintensities were predictors of conversion to dementia syndromes and/or persisting cognitive difficulties (Hickie et al., 1997). A more recent study of 41 MDD patients and 41 control subjects reported inverse relationships between bilateral orbital frontal volumes and subcortical gray matter lesions severity, but not deep white matter lesion severity (Lee et al., 2003). One very large study of 2546 subjects between age 60 and 64 did not find an association between cognitive measures and hippocampal or amygdalar volume, APOE4, or white matter hyperintensities, but rather found these decrements to be associated with psychiatric symptoms, poor physical health, and personality factors (Jorm et al., 2004). A subset analysis of this sample suggested that degree of white matter hyperintensities in 475 elders was related to depressive symptoms, potentially mediated by smoking and physical disability (Jorm et al., 2005). The disruption of networks important for cognitive and affective processing is the likely consequence of white matter hyperintensities, even if the underlying pathology behind white matter hyperintensities remains under debate (Cummings & Benson, 1984; Lamberty & Bieliauskas, 1993).

Functional Neuroimaging and Cognitive and Affective Neuroscience Research

Tremendous progress has been achieved in functional imaging studies of mood disorders in the last decade. Indeed, the field has progressed to the point of trials for deep brain stimulation with subgenual cingulate, ventral striatal and left inferior frontal targets for treatment resistant depression (Mayberg et al., 2005; Schlaepfer et al., 2007), as well as in use of repetitive transcranial magnetic stimulation (rTMS) (McLoughlin et al., 2007). In addition, imaging data are being used to prospectively predict treatment response, highlighting both the heterogeneity in mood disorders and the specificity of actual brain function to illness and treatment parameters (Brody et al., 1999; Langenecker et al., 2007b; Mayberg et al., 1997; Pizzigalli et al., 2001). Herein, we will review very briefly *functional magnetic resonance imaging* (fMRI), positron emission tomography (PET), and single photon emission computed tomography (SPECT) studies of mood disorders, again with specific focus on those studies using larger sample sizes and directly assessing relationships of activation with clinical and cognitive variables. We note that the time and spatial sensitivity for PET/SPECT and fMRI differ, as well as the cognitive/affective/rest paradigms used, which might easily explain the apparent discrepancy between PET/SPECT and fMRI results. In addition, artifact and signal voids in orbital and medial temporal regions in fMRI make imaging these areas more challenging. Finally, due to current funding structures, recruitment difficulties given restrictive exclusion criteria for imaging protocols, and the expense of imaging technology, most, if not all, imaging studies are underpowered, limiting convergence across functional imaging studies, particularly in a biologically heterogeneous set of mood disorders. This section is subdivided into a brief review of neurotransmitter studies, resting glucose/blood flow studies, affective challenges, and cognitive challenges.

Before beginning to review functional imaging studies in mood disorders, it is valuable to review the affective neuroscience literature, as much of this data was the genesis for imaging paradigms described below. In fact, in future chapters on mood disorders, emotion processing may more appropriately be placed under the "traditional" neuropsychological profile of mood disorders. Herein, we differentiate between emotion perception and processing as they might differ from emotional experience. The former denotes a cognitive process in the same vein as visual perception and processing, whereby, the latter refers more broadly to a gestalt of experience. Behavioral studies of emotion processing abnormalities in mood disorders have often focused on aspects of behavior such as mood-congruent memory biases (Gotlib et al., 2004, 2005; Rude et al., 2002), negative processing biases (Danion et al., 1991, 1995; Watkins et al., 1992, 1996; White et al., 1992), memory priming (Bradley et al., 1995; Mogg et al., 1993), and interference effects. These studies indicate a proclivity for processing and remembering negative stimuli, and better delayed memory for such stimuli, in those with mood disorders. Facial emotion stimuli have also been used to determine whether depressed individuals experience difficulty with processing and classifying the emotion expressed in these faces. A majority of these studies indicates that depressed individuals have difficulty in correctly classifying emotions in facial stimuli (Bouhuys et al., 1996, 1999; Gur et al., 1992; Langenecker et al., 2005; Mikhailova et al., 1996; Nandi et al., 1982, Persad & Polivy, 1993). These data have formed a basis for exploring the functional underpinnings of affective irregularities in mood disorders, primarily in fMRI (below), but also in PET and SPECT studies.

Imaging with transmitter-specific ligands using SPECT and PET suggests decreased 5HT1-A and 2-A binding in medial temporal structures in mood disorders, although the data are not consistent, with affects of gender, age of onset, current age, and illness severity all playing a potential role in these discrepancies (Kennedy & Zubieta, 2004). Studies with dopamine ligands, such as DR_{D2} and endogenous opiods, have received relatively less research focus in mood disorders (Kennedy et al., 2006; Larisch et al., 1997), but these studies also suggest relatively decreased binding in mood disorders. There is some suggestion that dopamine binding may differ by mood disorder subtype. In one small study, those with psychomotor retardation and anhedonia associated with decreased DR_{D2} binding, whereas those with impulsivity showed normal binding in left caudate (Martinot et al., 2001). A more recent study of a mixed group of 12 suicide attempters, most with mood disorders, suggested higher impulsivity was related to lower serotonin (5HTT) and dopamine (DAT) binding potential, with relationships most strongly located in the basal ganglia, and extending into insula for serotonin. Unfortunately, there is mixed evidence related to whether treatment of depression results in a significant change in dopamine and serotonin concentrations (Argyelan et al., 2005; Moses-Kolko et al., 2007). Important for the purposes of this chapter, these neurotransmitters are represented quite densely in the same anatomical areas discussed up to this point: frontal, anterior and medial temporal, insular, and subcortical areas.

Fluorodeoxyglucose (FDG), H2(15)O, and resting cerebral blood flow (rCBF) PET studies in depression implicate a network of frontal and limbic areas involved, much like that reported in the section on 'Neuroanatomy of Mood Disorders'. Subgenual anterior cingulate abnormalities in rest and affective paradigms have been reported, with hypometabolism in MDD and in the depressed phase of bipolar disorder (Drevets et al., 1997; Kennedy et al., 1997; Kegeles et al., 2003; Mayberg et al., 1994). The abnormalities in subgenual anterior cingulate resolve with effective treatment (Brody et al., 2001; Kennedy et al., 2007). The same brain regions implicated in anatomical studies

of MDD, prefrontal cortex, basal ganglia, and medial temporal areas are perhaps more consistently shown to deviate from controls using blood flow and glucose studies with PET (Liotti et al., 2000; Milak et al., 2005; Videbech, 2000). One PET study of 40 patients with depression showed diminished rCBF-to-cognitive measures relationships when compared to similar relationships in 49 healthy controls (Ravnkilde et al., 2003). One unique study used acute tryptophan (precursor to serotonin) depletion in eight remitted men, showing diminished ventral anterior cingulate and orbital frontal cortex H2(15)O PET after depletion associated with increased depression symptoms (Smith et al., 1999). Those who exhibited related slowing in verbal fluency had diminished anterior cingulate activity.

Functional imaging studies with cognitive and affective challenges in mood disorders have exploded, particularly within the last 5 years. In addition, increasing sophistication in measure design, combined with tighter recruitment protocols and relatively larger sample sizes, has resulted in exciting new findings within the field. As before, we will highlight studies, with larger sample sizes and attempts to relate functional abnormalities in mood disorders with clinical and cognitive variables, with the goal of increasing confidence about brain regions and systems that are affected in mood disorders.

Affective neuroscience studies in mood disorders using fMRI focused heavily on experiential aspects of emotion processing, for example, passive viewing and resting activation studies (Bench et al., 1993; Dolan et al., 1994; Kalin et al., 1997; Sheline et al., 2001; Whalen, 1998; Wright et al., 2001). Stimuli have included faces, complex visual scenes, and more recently semantic stimuli, some of which are rated as to personal relevance (Canli et al., 2004; Fossati et al., 2003; George et al., 1993, 1994, 1996; Gilboa-Schechtman et al., 2002; Gorno-Tempini et al., 2001; Iidaka et al., 2001; Kensinger & Corkin, 2004; Maddock et al., 2003; Ochsner et al., 2004; Phan et al., 2003; Siegle et al., 2002, see Figure 22.2 for an example from our own work, see also the color version in the color insert section). Physiological reactivity to emotional stimuli and emotion induction is distinctly different in depressed compared to control groups

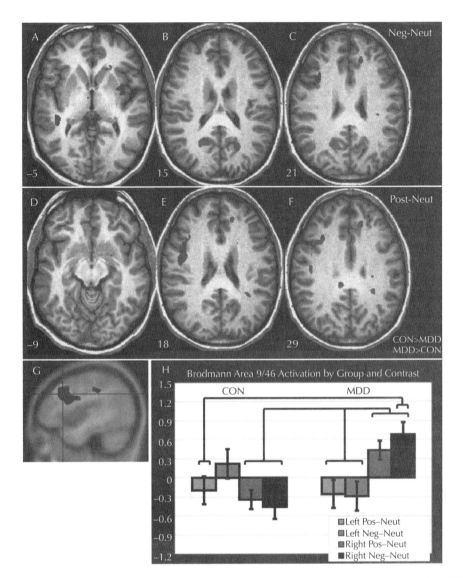

Figure 22–2. Activation to emotionally salient stimuli for those with Major Depressive Disorder (MDD, $n = 13$) compared to control (CON, $n = 15$) participants. Mean Hamilton Depression Rating Scale-17 Item score for the MDD group was 19.2 (SD = 7.6). The Emotion Word Stimulus Test is nine blocks each of positive (Pos), Negative (Neg) and Neutral (Neut) words (from the Affective Norms for Emotional Words set; Bradley and Lang, 1999) presented to participants during 3 Tesla functional MRI (GE Scanner). Images were analyzed with Statistical Parametric Mapping 2 (SPM2; Friston, 1996, thresholds $p<.001$, minimum cluster size = 120 mm³) and Region of Interest (ROI) posthoc analyses were conducted using the MARSBAR tool from SPM2 (Brett et al., 2002). Panels A–F (radiological orientation) represent group differences with red indicating CON>MDD and blue indicating MDD>CON. Panels A–C illustrate group comparisons for Neg-Neut and panels D–F represent contrasts for Pos-Neut. There was an area of increased activation for both contrasts, MDD>CON in right middle frontal gyrus (MFG—Brodmann area 9/46, Panels C, F) that was further explored in posthoc analyses. Panel G illustrates the spherical ROI created in the right MFG (in green). An identical spherical ROI was created in the left MFG to test the laterality theory of MDD. The theory states that there will be increased activation in right MFG for Neg-Neut and decreased activation in left MFG for Pos-Neut in MDD compared to CON (Davidson, 2002). This theory is not supported (Panel H bars) with increased right MFG activation for both emotion contrasts (MDD>CON: left bar set = CON; right bar set = MDD). Left MFG was not different between groups in any contrast. We interpret these findings as increased emotion regulatory demand for emotional words in MDD irrespective of Pos or Neg valence.

(Kalin et al., 1997; Ketter et al., 1996; Kumari et al., 2003; Paradiso et al., 1999; Phillips et al., 2001; Thomas et al., 2001). This disruption in neurophysiological reactions to emotion stimuli is reversible with successful treatment (Brody et al., 2001; Davidson et al., 1999; Davidson et al., 2003; Fu et al., 2004; Kalin et al., 1997; Sheline et al., 2001; see example of our own work in Figure 22.2 below). Although compelling, these studies have just begun to explore the nature of emotion processing difficulties in depression.

Cognitive neuroscience studies of mood disorders in fMRI are perhaps the most intriguing in recent years, with several recent studies indicating increased frontal activation in mood disorders relative to comparison groups. One study of interference resolution reported increased activation for MDD patients (e.g., left DLPFC, AC) compared to the control group (Wagner et al., 2006). Studies utilizing working memory and verbal fluency tasks have generally reported more prominent activation in the control groups in frontal, basal ganglia, and parietal areas compared to MDD patients (Audenaert et al., 2002; Barch et al., 2003; Elliott et al., 1997; Holmes et al., 2005; Hugdahl et al., 2003, 2004; Matsuo et al., 2002; Okada et al., 2003), while three other studies (examining working memory, attention, and interference control, respectively) have noted greater activation in frontal areas for the MDD groups compared to the control groups in the context of preserved behavioral performance (Harvey et al., 2005; Holmes et al., 2005; Wagner et al., 2006). In this same vein, our group has used a parametric Go/No-Go test in 20 patients with MDD compared to 22 control subjects (Langenecker et al., 2007b). The MDD patients exhibited decreased attention and increased inhibitory control accuracy performance in a significant interaction, relative to the control group. The MDD group also exhibited greater subgenual cingulate and bilateral ventral frontal activation compared to the control group during correct rejections of No-Go stimuli (inhibition).

More recently, resting functional connectivity and ROI-linked functional connectivity studies are now on the forefront of studies of mood disorders. There appears to be a disruption in the core, low-frequency "cross-talk" between what

has been termed the default network (including medial, rostral, and posterior cingulate) and more task-oriented structures in depression (lateral prefrontal and parietal, Anand et al., 2005; Greicius et al., 2007), although the specificity and clinical meaning of these findings remain to be seen.

In summary, morphological and functional imaging are strongly suggesting that limbic, frontal, and subcortical regions are involved in mood disorders (see Figure 22.1), converging nicely with the traditional neuropsychological profile described earlier in the chapter. At present, the nature of the relationship is largely correlational—it is unclear if these abnormalities precede onset of the mood disorder and may place individuals at higher risk for development of a mood disorder, or if they are the result of neurobiological changes concurrent with, or resulting from, experience of the mood disorder. Nonetheless, imaging studies of frontal, medial temporal, and subcortical regions will likely continue in mood disorders. There is currently debate about relative increases and decreases in lateral activation bias (right over left), or cortical/subcortical (under activation of cortical, overactivation of subcortical/limbic), but the body of research has not yet converged on a consistently replicable pattern of findings (Davidson et al., 2002; Northoff et al., 2000; Phillips et al., 2003). We strongly urge researchers to more routinely include analysis of structure/function to affective/cognitive relationships, particularly with neuropsychological variables. These can provide better grounding of the significance of any differences between those with mood disorders and control groups.

Critical Mediating Factors in Cognitive Dysfunction related to Depression

Age of Onset

There does not appear to be a gold standard for determining age of onset for depression due to difficulties with individual patient memories, inconsistency of report from one query to the next, and variability in depressive symptoms (Knauper et al., 1999). Authors have reported that early-onset major depression has a mean age of 13.7 (SD = 5.0) and late-onset depression has a mean age of 33.5 (SD = 9.5) (Klein et al., 1999). Early-onset depression is considered more malignant, persistent, and resistant to treatment.

The cognitive changes associated with this adult onset depression are felt to include decreased attention on tasks that require increased effort, decreased initial acquisition of stimuli, and decreased retrieval of information that is encoded (Caine, 1986). Caine (1981) describes these changes as being similar to a subcortical dementia. Interestingly, in their description of the syndrome of subcortical dementia, Cummings and Benson (1984) note depression to be a prominent feature. The cognitive changes, however, are coincident with the severity of the depression and many are lessened if the severity of depressive symptoms is therapeutically ameliorated (Bieliauskas, 1993).

When symptoms of depression occur for the first time in older adults, they are more likely to indicate underlying neurological change than to be manifestations of primary depression (Bieliauskas, 1993). In their review of the literature, Lamberty and Bieliauskas (1993) report that most late-onset depressive symptoms are accompanied by abnormal findings when neuroimaging is employed. In 1992, the NIH Consensus Conference on Diagnosis and Treatment of Depression in Late Life stated:

There is some evidence to suggest that late-onset depression is associated with a lower frequency of family history of depression but a higher frequency of cognitive impairment, cerebral atrophy, deep white matter changes, recurrences, medical comorbidity, and mortality. (NIH Consensus Development Panel on Depression in Late Life, 1992, p. 1019)

Multiple later studies have confirmed the same. Kumar et al. (2000) report that atrophy and high-intensity lesions represent independent pathways to late-life depression, with patients with major depression having larger whole brain lesion volumes than controls and smaller frontal lobe volumes.

As a corollary, depression in the elderly also appears to be predictive of subsequent cognitive decline. Nussbaum et al. (1995) report that 23% of a sample of depressed patients showed cognitive decline over a 25-month period, along with increased white matter MRI, CAT, and EEG abnormalities. This finding was subsequently confirmed in a large longitudinal (Paterniti et al., 2002) and neuropathologic study (Sweet et al., 2004). Similarly, depression in old age is associated with generalized atherosclerosis (Vinkerset al., 2005) and with increased cardiovascular and noncardiovascular mortality (Vinkers et al., 2004).

In sum, while primary depression, generally first occurring in young adulthood, is associated with cognitive dysfunction related to attention, learning, and recall, the initial occurrence of depressive symptoms in the elderly is very likely an indicator of an underlying degenerative or cerebrovascular neurological process. For each depressive symptom observed in the elderly, the rate of cognitive decline has been observed to increase by about 5% predicting cognitive decline in old age (Wilson et al., 2004), though depressive symptoms are not necessarily increased during the prodromal phase of Alzheimer's disease itself (Wilson et al., 2008). From a quality-of-life perspective, late-life depression is treatable by conventional pharmacotherapies, though careful dosing must be observed (Sadavoy, 2004). The positive change in cognitive efficiency that is observed when primary depression is treated, however, is not likely to be seen in the treatment of late-life-onset depressive symptoms (Bieliauskas, 1993).

Severity

It is currently unclear whether severity, as defined by clinician rating or self-report obtained, has any relation to the extent of neuropsychological decrements. There is a suggestion that being seen on an inpatient psychiatry ward is an index of disease severity that would portend greater cognitive difficulties (Burt et al., 1995), as would recurrence of depressive episodes. This section will review studies prototypic of those examining severity according to objective psychometric measures and/or location of treatment service/recruitment. We acknowledge that depression severity gradations assume a dimensional distribution of cognitive decrements, related in a linear fashion. A categorical perspective, such as that used between treatment responders and treatment nonresponders, also provides an index of severity and is reviewed below in a later section. Further, there are some mood disorders (e.g., bipolar disorder) that are often viewed as greater in severity relative to others (MDD). These sorts of subtype gradations, such as comparing MDD to Bipolar disorder or comparing melancholic and nonmelancholic depression, are also conducted in a separate section below.

One large study of elderly patients with minor ($N = 32$) and major depression ($N = 63$) indicated poorer performance compared to a matched control group of 71 participants in initial learning on trial 1 of the CVLT and on List B, as well as in number of correct categories for WCST (minor depression only), and Letter–Number Sequencing (major only (Elderkin-Thompson et al., 2007)). There were no significant effects of severity using this classification. A very large study of 385 elderly patients showed an increase in disruption on the Stroop test between mild and moderate depression, but not with severe depression (Baune et al., 2006). A smaller study of 26 severely depressed patients demonstrated a significant positive relationship between severity of depression and measures of simple and complex reaction time, or processing speed (Egeland et al., 2005) and one measure of memory, with a surprising number of significant negative correlations between 8 a.m. cortisol levels and memory and executive functioning measures.

As is probably well known, those with severe depression have poorer long-term treatment prognosis (Elkin et al., 1995; Saghafi et al., 2007), which may in fact be mediated by extent of neuropsychological decrements in performance. There have been attempts to use chronicity as a measure of severity, including structured interviews to code number of days ill. However, it should be noted that recall bias may significantly affect patient reports of length of illness and number of episodes (Riso et al., 2002). One interesting study used retrospective recall of days of untreated depression to predict hippocampal volume loss in women with recurrent depression (Sheline et al., 2003). It is important to conduct longitudinal studies to determine whether severity of symptoms is related to cognitive performance in a meaningful way (e.g., reflective of permanent underlying disruption of neural networks as an etiological risk factor), or whether depression itself results in significant cognitive decrements and underlying neurological dysfunction (as a chronological sequelae of depression).

A history of inpatient hospitalization and/ or the number of previous depressive episodes appear to be associated with the executive and memory decrements in some studies, both different indices of clinical severity. Purcell et al. (1997) examined 20 depressed patients (19 outpatients and 1 inpatient; 12 medicated) and 20 age and education matched normal controls on the CANTAB and found attentional set-shifting decrements in the depressed group. On closer examination, the researchers found that a history of inpatient hospitalization was associated with poorer performance on the set-shifting task. Paelecke-Habermann et al. (2005) studied 40 euthymic patients with a history of MDD diagnosis (20 individuals with one to two episodes and 20 individuals with three or more episodes) and 20 healthy controls on tasks of executive function (Behavioral Assessment of the Dysexecutive Syndrome, word fluency, and backward visuospatial span) and found worse performance in the MDD group. Furthermore, the severe MDD group performed worse than the mild group, suggesting that individuals with recurrent episodes demonstrate greater decrements than those with one or two episodes.

Studies of the impact of severity of illness as they relate to significance of cognitive decrements are limited in many respects due to nonuniformity in neuropsychological measures employed, clinical measures of severity utilized, and the broader issue of heterogeneity in mood disorders by subtype. Future studies will likely have to further subdivide into different cognitive domains, different depression subtypes, with unique mediating factors.

Effort

Effort, motivation, and abulia continue to be key concepts in understanding mood disorders and related cognitive decrements (King & Caine, 1996). Indeed, the effort-automatic hypothesis of depression had direct roots in beliefs about how depression might affect motivation and effort. For example, early studies indicated that memory tasks that were more automatic (recognition) tended to be performed just fine by depressed patients, whereas more effortful, difficult tasks (recall) tended to be tasks that were more difficult for those with mood disorders (Cohen et al., 1982; Roy-Byrne et al., 1986; Weingartner et al., 1981). As noted in chapter 9 by King and Caine (1996) in the previous edition of this book, there are other theories accounting for cognitive decrements in mood disorders, including decreased resource availability, increased distraction through inefficient inhibitory process, and mood congruent memory biases, though we will not go into these in detail herein.

More recently, there has been a strong and healthy debate about the genesis of cognitive decrements in patients with depression, largely revolving around the old concepts of "functional" and "organic" brain-based cognitive difficulties, particularly within legal contexts (Rohling et al., 2002). In a recent study of primarily legal cases, over 40% of subjects recruited were excluded because of documented poor effort using standardized measures (Rohling et al., 2002). Interestingly, the excluded group had significantly higher depression scores on the Hamilton Depression Rating Scale (HDRS) compared to the group that was not excluded, and performed significantly worse on multiple cognitive measures including learning and memory. A smaller percentage (15%, 8%) of patients filing for workers compensation with depressive symptoms failed formal effort measures in a study of 233 patients (Sumanti et al., 2006). Because anergia and amotivation are key symptoms of depression and these symptoms can adversely affect effort, it is reasonable to assume that for a minority of depressed patients, "amotivation" may result in a failed effort test. One possible interpretation of this finding is that significant primary depression may not result in permanent brain dysfunction, but rather that insufficient engagement of motivational drive (evident in depression) can mimic cognitive decrements on challenging tasks. However, two recent studies have not shown any difficulty in depressed patients or those with anxiety, in passing formal effort measures, suggesting that depression symptoms may have very different etiologies and purposes in legal as opposed to clinical settings (Ashendorf

et al., 2004; Egeland et al., 2005). We have also recently found that depression, as measured by DSM-IV criteria and Geriatric Depression Scale (GDS; Yesavage), was not related to very basic measures of effort such as the Rey 15-Item Test (Lee et al., 1992; Rey, 1964) or the Kaufman Hand Movements Test (Bowen & Littell, 1997; Kaufman & Kaufman, 1983) in a population of elderly medical inpatients (Vadnal, 2005).

These differences in failed versus passed effort tests in "depressed" samples highlight the importance of using formal or informal, but validated, effort measures when assessing those with mood disorders, especially when the possibility of primary and secondary gain becomes crucially important in interpreting the relevance of poor test performance. When no primary or secondary gain can be found, the clinician can correlate self-reported energy levels, depression severity, psychomotor retardation, and so on with observed inefficiencies in performance (everyday functioning), but estimates of optimal functioning levels or inference of underlying neuronal dysfunction in these contexts need to be carefully interpreted.

Subtypes of Mood Disorders

There are a number of different subtypes of depression, wherein cognitive function may be greater (e.g., cerebrovascular, bipolar disorder). Furthermore, there are certain subtype-by-cognitive function distinctions, most notably the prevalence of psychomotor retardation in melancholic but not in atypical depression. A rapidly emerging set of data is in cognitive decrements with co-occurring depression and medical conditions. Cushing's disease is a rare disease with high prevalence of depression, thought to be mediated by hypercortisolism and epitomizing the glucocorticoid cascade hypothesis of depression. Review of these select subtypes exemplifies the variability of cognitive dysfunction in mood disorders.

Cerebrovascular

The increased prevalence of depression among patients with cerebrovascular accidents (CVAs) has long been established, with between 50% and 68% manifesting symptoms of depression

(Eastwood et al., 1989). These estimates rendered the occurrence of "melancholia in up to 25% of patients," with minor or masked depression in 75%–95% of cases (Wiart, 1997). A more recent study has demonstrated that patients with ischemic stroke have double the risk of depression compared with those without stroke (11.2% versus 5.2%) with a greater incidence of depression corresponding to more severe CVAs, particularly in vascular territories supplying limbic structures (Desmond et al., 2003). Though there has been speculation that the distribution of CVAs, especially as related to syndromes of aphasia, may specifically relate to depressive symptoms, more recent evidence suggests that screening for aphasia across studies is highly inconsistent and that conclusions as to relationships between aphasia subtypes and depression are not justified (Townend et al., 2007). Laska et al. (2007) alternatively suggest that depression diagnosis and severity can be reliably made during the acute phases of aphasia and suggest that depression can be identified in at least 24% of such patients.

Nevertheless, there remains little doubt that depression is common following CVA. There has been the suggestion of a vascular depression hypothesis, that is, that cerebrovascular disease may predispose, precipitate, or perpetuate some geriatric depressive syndromes, It is hypothesized that prefrontal systems are disrupted with associated executive dysfunction (Alexopoulos et al., 1997), mechanisms discussed in the section on 'Neuroanatomy of Mood Disorders'.

Secondary to Medical Condition

Depression is a common comorbid condition in medical illnesses including cancer (Chochinov, 2001; McDaniel et al., 1995; Spiegel, 2001), diabetes (Anderson et al., 2001; Ciechanowski et al., 2003), heart disease (Ruo et al., 2003), asthma (Eisner et al., 2005), chronic obstructive pulmonary disease (Yohannes et al., 2000), obesity (Thomsen et al., 2006), migraine headaches (Molgat & Patten, 2005), chronic fatigue syndrome (Patten et al., 2005), fibromyalgia (Ahles et al., 1991; Patten et al., 2005), and chronic pain (McWilliams et al., 2003). A bidirectional relation between depression and medical illnesses appears to exist, with each possibly altering the normal course of illness of the other. In the past, depression associated with a medical illness was considered to be a psychological reaction to having a medical illness and thought to have a less severe course (Boland et al., 2006). However, it is now clear that depression in the medically ill may be more difficult to treat compared to depression in individuals without a comorbid medical condition (Boland et al., 2006). These individuals generally report more medical symptoms even when the severity of the medical disorder is taken into account (for a review, see Katon et al., 2007). Depression can be detrimental in the medically ill in that these individuals are three times less likely to adhere to medical treatment recommendations compared to nondepressed medically ill individuals (Dimatteo et al., 2000). In addition, when the depression is not properly treated, it could negatively impact the morbidity and mortality of the medical illness, especially in older adults (Boland, 2006; Covinsky et al., 1999; Frasure-Smith et al., 1993; Ganzini et al., 1997; Katon, 2003; Lesperance & Frasure-Smith, 1996). For example, Frasure-Smith et al. followed 222 patients who were hospitalized for myocardial infarction for 6 months and found that MDD was an independent risk factor for mortality. Overall, MDD can be identified in 7–17% of patients with chronic medical conditions (Egede, 2007). In contrast, when depression is treated, medical symptoms decrease regardless of the improvement in the medical disease status (Borson et al., 1992).

The cognitive profile of the medically ill individuals with depression should not differ from the traditional profile described above. However, additional physical symptoms including pain and increased fatigue, which are more common in certain medical populations including cancer, chronic pain, and fibromyalgia need to be taken into consideration when interpreting test results. Neuropsychological investigations in the non-neurological, medically ill individuals with depression are scarce with only a few that have focused on fibromyalgia and chronic fatigue syndrome (Johnson et al., 1997; Landro et al., 1997; Suhr, 2003). Nonetheless, it appears that cognitive inefficiencies are generally associated with the individual's presenting symptoms such as fatigue or depression. For example, Suhr investigated 28 individuals with fibromyalgia, 27 individuals with chronic pain, and 21 healthy controls on measures of intellect, memory, executive functioning, attention, and psychomotor speed, as well as on self-reported measures of depression, pain, fatigue, and cognitive complaints. The fibromyalgia group reported more memory complaints, fatigue, pain, and depression than the other groups. Although no difference in performance was found on cognitive measures when fatigue, pain, and depression were taken into account, the severity of depression was associated with memory performance and fatigue was associated with psychomotor speed.

Cushing's Disease and Hypercortisolemic Mood Disorders

One very well-understood model for describing the neurobiological sequelae of mood disorders is the glucocorticoid cascade hypothesis (Sapolsky, 2000). In this model, the increased stress often observed in mood disorders results in excessive release of CRF, signaling release of ACTH, resulting in subsequent release of cortisol. In 33% of individuals with MDD, an abnormal ACTH response to the steroid dexamethasone is indicative of failed feedback mechanism, putatively a result of chronic excessive glucocorticoids (Sonino & Fava, 1996; Young et al., 1991). Cushing's disease is a rare disorder often thought to typify the glucocorticoid model, as there is sustained, elevated cortisol levels for as long as several years before the condition is diagnosed and treated (1961). The excess cortisol levels have been associated with a 60% prevalence of mood irregularities, typically depression. Further, treatment of Cushing's disease typically results in alleviation of depressive symptoms (Sonino et al., 1993; Starkman et al., 1981, 1986). The remission of cognitive difficulties thought to be secondary to Cushing's disease is more equivocal in nature, with some studies showing no improvement, and others showing improvement in memory and executive functioning (Dorn & Cerrone, 2000; Dorn et al., 1997; Forget et al., 2002; Heald et al., 2004; Hook et al., 2007; Mauri et al., 1993; Starkman et al., 2001). One study reported that improvements in memory are positively associated with posttreatment volume increases in the hippocampus, whereas improvements in mood are associated with increases in the caudate (Starkman et al., 1999, 2003, 2007). Cushing's disease provides a model for how excessive stress hormones can have potentially reversible cognitive and affective sequelae, highlighting the deleterious affects of stress hormones, the link between brain morphometry and cognitive and affective symptoms, and the potential for plasticity in brain and neuropsychological functioning in mood disorders (McEwen, 2002). Although focus has been primarily on amygdala, hippocampus, and caudate thus far, future studies by our group are targeted toward effects of hypercortisolism on the entire medial frontal–subcortical circuit.

Studies of hypercortisolemia in other mood disorders have also helped build the connection between cortisol/ACTH levels and cognitive dysfunction. This may be in part due to the heterogeneity in depressive samples and relative variability of neuroendocrine measurements across subjects. Hypercortisolemia occurs in approximately 50% of individuals with depression, and treatment with agents to reduce cortisol levels can result in improved cognitive performance (Golomb et al., 1993; Young et al., 1994, 2001, 2004). One study of 23 severely depressed patients found significant negative correlations between executive and memory functions and 8 a.m. cortisol levels (Egeland et al., 2005). In a study of 102 female outpatients with remitted MDD, those with recurrent depression had higher cortisol levels than the nonrecurrent women (Bos et al., 2005). Elevated cortisol but not ACTH levels have also been reported in a study of 29 participants with psychotic major depression compared to 26 healthy controls and to 24 participants with nonpsychotic major depression (Gomez et al., 2006). Some modest correlations were reported between measures of executive functioning, processing speed, and memory with cortisol levels. Furthermore, in a study of 17 patients with bipolar disorder, euthymic phase, and 16 matched control subjects, post-dexamethasone cortisol was positively correlated with number of errors on a working memory task (Watson et al., 2006). It is unclear whether hypercortisolemia mediates cognitive decrements in mood disorders, and the relationships between HPA axis measures and cognition are not always evident (Caine et al., 1984). As noted before, underlying neural networks that control stress responses and assist in certain aspects of cognition are negatively affected in mood disorders, but variability in presence and degree of disruption, when combined with small sample sizes and variability in clinical characterization and classification, might explain inconsistencies within the literature.

Melancholic Depression

Apart from the studies of psychotic major depression in the context of hypercortisolemia, there are also a subset of studies comparing melancholic and nonmelancholic depression (Cornell et al., 1984). One study demonstrated difficulty in digit symbol and perseverative errors on the WCST on a group of specifically defined patients with melancholic depression, and not on the nonmelancholic group (Austin et al., 1999). A more recent study comparing 11 melancholic with 11 nonmelancholic depressed patients matched on HDRS symptoms, age, age of onset, and education reported poorer performance in intra/extradimensional set-shifting from the CANTAB battery, but not in paired associates learning or stockings of Cambridge (Michopoulos et al., 2006). A smaller study of seven melancholic, eight nonmelancholic, and nine control participants demonstrated slowing on several attention, executive functioning, and processing speed tasks in the patients with melancholic depression but not in the nonmelancholic group (Rogers et al., 2004). It has been hypothesized that frontal dysfunction is greater in melancholic depression (Austin et al., 1999), but no imaging studies to date have tested this hypothesis. Recent neuroimaging studies focusing on anhedonia more specifically have reported decreased ventral striatal/nucleus accumbens response to positive stimuli in depression (Epstein et al., 2006; Keedwell et al., 2005; Knutson et al., 2008).

Bipolar

Individuals with bipolar disorder (BD) often demonstrate worse performance than healthy individuals on measures of learning and memory, executive function, and psychomotor speed (Ferrier et al., 1999; Martinez-Aran et al., 2004; Rubinsztein et al., 2000; Zubieta et al., 2001). Research on individuals with BD often indicates a similar pattern of cognitive inefficiencies that is found in individuals with MDD, with more decrements in general (Borkowska & Rybakowski, 2001; for reviews see Olley et al., 2005; Quraishi & Frangou, 2002). For example, a study examining unmedicated individuals with MDD or BD during acute depressive episodes indicated worse performance in the BD group on the Performance IQ portion of the WAIS-R and on tests of executive function (Borkowska & Rybakowski, 2001). Specifically, the BD group performed worse on the Stroop test (word reading and color–word interference parts), the letter fluency test, and the WCST (more perseverative errors and fewer completed categories). However, contradicting evidence also exists, indicating no difference between MDD and BD patients, at least in depressed states. Fossati et al. (2004) investigated memory performance on a verbal learning task in patients with a first depressive episode, MDD, and BD in depressed states. The researchers found poorer first trial free recall in both MDD and BD groups but not in the first-episode group and concluded that the repetition of depressive episodes affect verbal memory performance in acute depressive phases regardless of the subtype of depression. Similarly, Bearden et al. (2006) did not find any difference in verbal memory performance between the MDD and BD groups although both groups performed worse than the normal control group. The pattern of cognitive decrements in BD patients has also been compared to that of patients with schizophrenia and found to have similarities, although in less severity (Schretlen et al., 2007).

The clinical state or phase of illness in BD appears to affect the neuropsychological function with mixed/manic states showing the greatest decrements and euthymic states displaying the least. Sweeney et al. (2000) examined 35 BD patients (14 in mixed or manic state and 21 in depressed state), 59 MDD patients, and 51 healthy controls on the CANTAB. Decrements in executive function, episodic memory, and spatial span were demonstrated in BD patients in mixed/manic states but only episodic memory decrement was shown in BD patients in depressed states and patients with MDD. A recent meta-analysis of BD individuals in euthymic states (Robinson et al., 2006) revealed greater decrements on measures of executive function and memory compared to measures of attention and processing speed. Specifically, large effect sizes were found for category fluency, backward digit span, and total learning score on the RAVLT and the CVLT; medium effect sizes were found for Stroop Color–Word Inference Test, Trail-Making Test B, WCST (perseverative errors and categories), and short- and long-delay free recall of the memory tests; and a small effect size was found for letter fluency and forward digit span. In a recent review, Robinson and Ferrier (2006) indicated that factors influencing the severity of neuropsychological inefficiencies in euthymic bipolar patients include the number of previous manic episodes, hospitalizations, and length of illness. A consistent finding was the negative relation between the number of manic episodes and performance on tasks of verbal memory and executive function. Specifically, regarding memory function, although encoding is more commonly impaired than retention in euthymic BD individuals, the increasing number of manic episodes was associated with poorer retention. A recent study by Malhi et al. (2007) followed 25 patients with BD over 30 months and assessed them in hypomanic, depressed, and euthymic phases of illness. Decrements in executive functioning, memory, and attention were seen in both hypomanic and depressed states with additional fine motor deficit in the depressed state. In the euthymic phase, mild attention and memory decrements were found. Taken together, although euthymic BD patients show relatively less cognitive inefficiency, persisting decrements, albeit mild, appear to be in components of executive function and memory.

It is worth mentioning that the type of BD also has an effect on cognitive function with BD type I being associated with worse cognitive outcome than compared to BD type II. Relatively few studies have specified the type of BD and a fewer studies have examined the differences between the two types (Malhi et al., 2007;

Zubieta et al., 2001). However, recently Torrent et al. (2006) examined 38 individuals with BD I in euthymic states, 33 individuals with bipolar II in euthymic states, and 35 healthy controls. The two BD groups showed worse performance on tasks of attention and working memory, executive function, and verbal memory compared to the control group, but the type II group was less impaired on tasks of verbal memory and executive function. Future studies need to carefully consider subtype of bipolar disorder, as well as a consideration of mediating factors such as phase of illness and history of substance abuse and suicide attempts.

Medication Effects

The understanding of medication effects in mood disorders poses several challenges in the assessment and interpretation of cognitive and affective data above and beyond the effects of the mood disorder itself. As there is considerable variability on cognitive functioning in mood disorders, and considerable severity of illness in these disorders, understanding any affects of medication becomes quite complex. For example, those with more severe illness may be more likely to receive medications that will affect cognitive functioning, and perhaps even higher doses of these medications than those with less severe illness. As medications are not randomly assigned to patients, there is a potential for medication by severity interactions that may confound interpretation of either one of these alone. As such, the clinician should balance knowledge of the potential cognitive side effects of medication with those that could be a result of the disorder itself. In some cases, it may be advisable to use medication washouts to better determine medication as opposed to illness effects on cognition, while also being aware of greater potential for relapse and/or complications in such instances.

Anticholinergics

Medications with anticholinergic effects are frequently prescribed for depression, particularly tricyclic antidepressants, though this class also includes *selective serotonin reuptake inhibitors* (SSRIs) such as Paroxetine and atypical antidepressants such as Venlafaxine. Caution is urged about use of drugs with anticholinergic properties, especially in the elderly, due to potentially exaggerated side effects such as confusion, and memory and concentration decrements (Sadavoy, 2004). Use of SSRIs may result in subjective memory difficulties, at least in those with significant psychopathology (Wadsworth et al., 2005). Particular attention to dosing in older patients is recommended, with some ranges based on ¼–½ of the general adult dose. We recently found that when careful dosing with drugs with anticholinergic properties in elderly inpatients is followed, significant cognitive side effects do not appear to be of major concern (Harik et al., 2008). Indeed, by and large successful treatment may in fact increase memory, psychomotor, and attentional functioning (Brooks & Hoblyn, 2007).

Benzodiazepines

Patients with mood disorders, perhaps more often those with significant anxiety or insomnia, are frequently prescribed a benzodiazepine in addition to a primary mood medication. The impact of benzodiazepines on cognitive functioning is fairly well understood and is one of the reasons why they are typically used at night or as needed. For example, on-drug driving performance on a simulator in a double-blind, crossover study of 18 healthy volunteers was significantly poorer than nondrug performance with both extended and immediate release alprazolam (Leufkens et al., 2007). There were also effects of immediate release alprazolam on divided attention reaction time at 1-, 2.5-, and 5-hours postadministration, for Stop RT on a stop signal task at the same intervals, and for delayed recall on a word-learning test at 1 hour. Effects for extended release were present on cognitive tests at 1- and 2.5-hour intervals compared to placebo. Lorazepam, and not chlorpromazine, administration to 72 healthy adults resulted in impaired free recall and word-completion in an earlier study (Danion et al., 1992). Furthermore, in a comparison of 328, 65–80 year olds, 57 of whom were chronic benzodiazepine users, chronic benzodiazepine use resulted in higher rates of postoperative confusion (26% compared to 13%), even though measures of anxiety and depression did not differ between the two groups (Kudoh et al., 2004). A comprehensive review of benzodiazepine effects is available, with expected effects of sedation and cognitive decrements in attention, executive functioning, and memory to be expected (Buffett-Jerrott & Stewart, 2002). The effects of benzodiazepines, by way of increasing sleepiness, have been linked to thalamic glucose metabolism in nine healthy control subjects (Volkow et al., 1995). Further, tolerance to detrimental memory effects of benzodiazepines does not appear to occur with long-term use whereas some tolerance to psychomotor effects of diazepam was present (Gorenstein et al., 1994). This was demonstrated using 10-mg diazepam administration on memory in 28 long-term diazepam users with anxiety. Thus, benzodiazepines can affect attention, executive functioning, and memory, while increasing sedation, perhaps further effecting cognitive functioning in those with mood disorders.

Opiates

Given the high rate of mood disorders in individuals with chronic pain or cancer, the evaluation of opioid medications, which are commonly used in these medical populations, on cognitive functioning is necessary (Haythornthwaite et al., 1998; Turk & Brody, 1992). The concern for possible adverse effects of opioid use has been associated with the presence of opiate receptors in the neural structures that are involved in attention, learning, and memory (Payne, 1990). The complexities of research in medical populations using opioids including varying types of opioid medication and doses, interactions with other medications, and participant variables make drawing any firm conclusions regarding the effects of opioids on cognition difficult. However, there is evidence that short-term use of opioid medication in healthy individuals can affect psychomotor performance on tasks such as Digit Symbol Substitution Test, reaction time, and finger tapping (Kerr et al., 1991; Zacny et al., 1994). Some studies suggest that when individuals with chronic pain and healthy individuals are compared on cognitive tasks after taking opioids, the drug has a less deleterious effect on cognition in individuals with chronic pain, likely due to pain relief and/or the pain possibly counteracting the possible effects of opioids in the CNS (Haythornthwaite et al., 1998; Lorenz et al., 1997; Sjogren et al., 2000; Twycross, 1994; Vainio et al., 1995). In patients who take opioid medications on a long-term basis, cognitive inefficiencies are suggested to occur during the first few hours after a dose is given and during the first few days of use (for reviews, see Chapman et al., 2002; Zacny, 1995). A recent study (Byas-Smith et al., 2005) evaluated driving ability in a predetermined route in a community; performance on the Test of Variables of Attention and on the Digit Symbol Substitution Test in 21 patients with chronic pain with stable regimens of opioid analgesics, 11 patients with chronic pain without opioid use, and 50 healthy controls were evaluated. No significant difference in driving ability, sustained attention, or psychomotor speed were found, suggesting that at least some individuals with chronic pain who regularly use opioids do not display significantly diminished cognitive abilities.

Predicting Treatment Response in Mood Disorders

There is an emerging corpus of data suggesting that neuropsychological and cognitive/affective neuroscience techniques may be valuable in prospectively predicting treatment response in mood disorders. There is, however, an uneasy and nonproductive tension between insurance companies mindful of increasing health-care costs, a relative paucity of treatment studies examining alternative treatment predictive models in mood disorders, and a general unwillingness to integrate neuropsychological techniques into psychiatric clinics. This is perhaps a left-over of the remaining stigma toward mental illnesses, as opposed to the "hard" neurological syndromes where permanent, irreversible, and far more severe cognitive sequelae are more frequently observed. It should not be lost on the reader that perhaps one of the greatest areas for impact and improvement in health care could be the timely and judicious application of neuropsychological evaluations in psychiatry clinics. The current trial and error, "cheapest or newest drug first" treatment model for mood disorders can likely be

improved with large clinical trials using demographic, clinical, and neuropsychological measures to predict treatment response, followed up by studies to initiate alternative treatment strategies for those with poor prognosis for positive response to traditional treatments. Screening instruments for use in psychiatry and family medicine clinics are available and can be readily integrated into clinical care settings (Gualtieri et al., 2006; Gur et al., 2001a, 2001b; Langenecker et al., 2007a).

A significant limitation of this section is that most studies of treatment response predictors are much too small in sample size to rule out predictors as being irrelevant in estimating potential for treatment response. This would suggest, however, that any convergence across these small studies is worthy of further and more detailed consideration and study. A study of 53 inpatients with depression who were treated with combined pharmacological and psychotherapeutic treatments used cognitive styles (e.g., dysfunctional attitude and extreme thinking) to predict treatment response at 6 months, noting that less changes in both measures predicted a more rapid return of depressive symptoms (Beevers et al., 2007). In a relatively larger study of 55 depressed patients, better verbal fluency, and poorer Rey–Osterrieth Complex Figure Test, Benton Visual Retention Test, WAIS-R arithmetic, Block Design, and Similarities, as well as poorer Hooper Visual Organization Test performance, were significant predictors of depression remission in HDRS symptoms to SSRIs at 6 weeks of treatment (Kampf-Sherf et al., 2004). Another study of open label SSRI treatment in 35 patients with MDD demonstrated that better verbal fluency performance was a significant, positive prognostic indicator of eventual treatment response (Taylor et al., 2006); this study was supported by a smaller study of 14 middle-aged patients with depression (Dunkin et al., 2000). In the study by Dunkin et al., an omnibus measure of executive functioning including verbal fluency was poorer in the nonresponders ($n = 6$) compared to the responders ($n = 8$). Another study of 45 depressed elderly patients failed to show any differences between responders and nonresponders on the Mattis Dementia Rating Scale (Butters et al., 2000), although this instrument may not be sensitive enough to difficulties observed in mood disorders. A larger study of 112 elderly patients with depression showed poorer Stroop interference and Initiation/Perseveration scores from the Dementia Rating Scale in the nonresponder group ($n = 44$) compared to the responders (Alexopoulos et al., 2005).

Brain imaging studies, including morphologic, EEG, PET, and fMRI have also demonstrated promise in predicting treatment response in mood disorders, most commonly depression. For example, a study comparing 20 subjects with a lengthy depressive episode (greater than 2 years) demonstrated reduced verbal memory performance and decreased left temporal and hippocampal volume when compared to 20 remitted and 20 control subjects (Shah et al., 1998). In a larger PET study of 39 outpatients with MDD, decreasing ventral anterior cingulate and anterior insula activity was associated with improvement in anxiety and tension symptoms, increasing dorsal anterior cingulate activity was associated with improvement in psychomotor retardation, and increasing dorsolateral prefrontal activation was associated with improvement in cognitive symptoms, all from the HDRS and Profile of Mood States (Brody et al., 2001). In our own study of 20 patients with MDD using parametric Go/No-Go task during fMRI, activation during correct rejections of No-Go stimuli at pretreatment in bilateral inferior frontal, right middle frontal, left amygdala and nucleus accumbens, and subgenual anterior cingulate was highly predictive of eventual response to s-citalopram in 15 completers (Langenecker et al., 2007b). An fMRI study using an emotion processing probe also demonstrated that amygdala activation was predictive of treatment response to cognitive behavioral therapy (Siegle et al., 2006). One other PET and an EEG study demonstrated that subgenual and rostral anterior cingulate activity, respectively, were positive predictors of treatment response to SSRIs (Mayberg et al., 1997; Pizzagalli et al., 2004).

The neuropsychological and brain imaging studies predicting treatment response strongly confirm several recurrent themes within this chapter. Disruptions in frontal and limbic activation and in tasks thought to be dependent on these brain circuits are *prospectively*, as well as retrospectively, valuable in predicting and understanding treatment response in mood disorders. Herein, the correlation between structural, functional, and behavioral abnormalities in mood disorders is extended to some extent to include real outcome variables. Future studies can look at correlation of these different dependent variables as they relate to changes with treatment, in order to assess static (trait) versus phasic (state) abnormalities and decrements in function. There is great hope that these measures can be used within clinical settings to inform clinicians about prognosis for treatment response to standard pharmacotherapies, hastening alternative treatments, and aiding in the development of novel treatments.

Conclusions

Neuropsychology, along with cognitive and affective neuroscience research, has taken part in a dramatic transformation in the appreciation for, and understanding of, the neurobiological systems affected in mood disorders. It is increasingly accepted that mood disorders frequently co-occur with cognitive difficulties and further that such difficulties may be reversible in some individuals, but not in others, based on certain characteristics outlined herein (e.g., age of onset, co-occurring medical conditions). Further, genetic and biological risks for developing mood disorders may co-occur with cognitive weaknesses that are evident long before evidence of an affective disorder emerges and are even present to some extent in relatives of those affected with mood disorders.

In the present chapter, we have demonstrated a neuroanatomical network that is affected in a majority of individuals with mood disorders, including amygdala, hippocampus, basal ganglia, thalamus, anterior temporal, insular, ventral, medial, and dorsal prefrontal areas. It should not be lost on the reader that most of these areas are all part of a ventral cingulate–medial prefrontal circuit, as described by Cummings (1993) and further subdivided by Rolls (Rolls, 1999) in lateral and medial orbital–frontal circuits. The exception is dorsolateral prefrontal cortex, which is a distinct dorsal anterior cingulate–dorsal prefrontal circuit that does interact with the corticolimbic circuit. The cognitive and affective findings in mood disorders overlay nicely onto the idea of disruption of these three frontosubcortical circuits, including disruptions in emotion processing, attention, executive functioning, memory, and psychomotor speed. It is also not surprising that measures from these five cognitive/affective domains are implicated in understanding mechanistic issues in mood disorders, such as severity and prognosis for successful treatment response. Medication effects and comorbid medical conditions also play a critical role in understanding the impact of mood disorders on neuropsychological functioning and there are certainly subtypes of mood disorders with greater disease burden and chronicity. In essence, neuropsychological probes can be used to understand disease burden and potential for response to traditional treatments. More importantly, these indexes of disease burden can be ascertained at first episode, thus shifting the treatment plan dependent on risk of recurrence of mood disorders or prognosis of poor response to "front line" treatments.

Neuropsychologists should appreciate that the distinction between "organic" and "functional" disorders is increasingly becoming minimized as our understanding of neurobiological mechanisms of brain function improve. A challenge remains in distinguishing poor effort, decreased goal-directed behavior, decreased efficiency in planning, as secondary to mood disorders, from the same observed phenomena in legal or compensation contexts where primary and secondary gain are highly significant factors. There will be greater expectation that neuropsychologists appreciate the impact of psychiatric and mood symptoms in cognitive functioning. Neuropsychologists can function effectively as consultants in psychiatry and even in primary care clinics, wherein the goal is to understand illness burden and prognosis for treatment success, such that alternative and more effective treatments can be more efficiently and rapidly applied. Finally, neuropsychologists should continue to be mindful of the relevance of, and need for, applied knowledge in clinical, legal, and research settings wherein mood disorders will continue to be prevalent.

Recommendations

We also wish to share with the reader the types of assessment strategies and instruments that will be most beneficial in different settings. Given the traditional and more recent findings in mood disorders, at a minimum we recommend that an assessment of depression-related cognitive functioning include the following:

1. Estimate of baseline functioning less dependent on effort and memory retrieval.
2. Direct or validated indirect measures of effort, regardless of the possibility of primary or secondary gain.
3. Memory measures that rely on repeated exposure to the same stimuli such that a learning curve can be established.
4. Measures of executive functioning that tap into processing speed, short-term memory, sustained attention, and problem-solving areas.
5. Fine motor dexterity and speed.
6. Emotion perception and processing.
7. Objective measures of mood and psychopathology.

Assessments with younger adults should also be attentive to the higher incidence of mood disorders in those with learning and attention deficit disorders, and will likely benefit from judicious use of achievement tests. Evaluations with older adults may benefit from using remote memory measures and cued recall techniques that can help distinguish between mood and amnestic disorders (Dierckx et al., 2007). Finally, the neuropsychologist should be leery of profiles associated with any given psychiatric condition, as at best there is overlap between many different psychiatric conditions, with no validated stable and unique elements for any given mood disorder.

Acknowledgments

We acknowledge the National Alliance for Research on Schizophrenia and Depression (SAL) and NIH K-12 Clinical Research Career Development Award (SAL). We thank Jon-Kar Zubieta, MD, PhD and Sara L. Wright, PhD for their review of this chapter and helpful comments.

References

Depression in Late Life; *NIH Consensus Development Conference on the Diagnosis and Treatment of Depression in Late Life*. (1992). National Institutes of Mental Health.

Ahles, T. A., Khan, S. A., Yunus, M. B., & Spiegel, D. A. (1991). Psychiatric status of patients with primary fibromyalgia, patients with rheumatoid arthritis, and subjects without pain: A blind comparison of DSM-III diagnoses. *American Journal of Psychiatry, 148*(12), 1721–1726.

Alexopoulos, G. S. (2002). Frontostriatal and limbic dysfunction in late-life depression. *American Journal of Geriatric Psychiatry, 10*, 687–695.

Alexopoulos, G. S., Kiosses, D. N., Heo, M., Murphy, C. F., Shanmugham, B., & Gunning-Dixon, F. (2005). Executive dysfunction and the course of geriatric depression. *Biological Psychiatry, 58*, 204–210.

Alexopoulos, G. S., Meyers, B. S., Young, R. C., Campbell, S., Silbersweig, D., & Charlson, M. (1997). "Vascular depression" hypothesis. *Archives of General Psychiatry, 54*, 915–922.

Anand, A., Li, Y., Wang, Y., Wu, J. W., Gao, S. J., Bukhari, L., et al. (2005). Activity and connectivity of brain mood regulating circuit in depression: A functional magnetic resonance study. *Biological Psychiatry, 57*, 1079–1088.

Anand, A., & Shekhar, A. (2003). Brain imaging studies in mood and anxiety disorders—Special emphasis on the amygdala. *Amygdala in Brain Function: Bacic and Clinical Approaches, 985*, 370–388.

Anderson, R. J., Freedland, K. E., Clouse, R. E., & Lustman, P. J. (2001). The prevalence of comorbid depression in adults with diabetes: A meta-analysis. *Diabetes Care, 24*(6), 1069–1078.

Argyelan, M., Szabo, Z., Kanyo, B., Tanacs, A., Kovacs, Z., Janka, Z., et al. (2005). Dopamine transporter availability in medication free and in bupropion treated depression: A 99mTc-TRODAT-1 SPECT study. *Journal of Affective Disorders, 89*, 115–123.

Ashendorf, L., Constantinou, M., & McCaffrey, R. J. (2004). The effect of depression and anxiety on the TOMM in community-dwelling older adults. *Archives of Clinical Neuropsychology, 19*, 125–130.

Audenaert, K., Goethals, I., Van, L. K., Lahorte, P., Brans, B., Versijpt, J., et al. (2002). SPECT neuropsychological activation procedure with the Verbal Fluency Test in attempted suicide patients. *Nuclear Medicine Communications, 23*, 907–916.

Austin, M.-P., Mitchell, P., & Goodwin, G. M. (2001). Cognitive deficits in depression: Possible implications for functional neuropathology. *British Journal of Psychiatry, 178*, 200–206.

Austin, M. P., Ross., M., Murray, C., O'Carroll, R.E., Ebmeier, K.P., Goodwin, G.M. (1992). Cognitive dysfunction in major depression. *Journal of Affective Disorders, 25*, 21–29.

Austin, M.-P., Wilhelm, K., Parker, G., Hickie, I., Brodaty, H., Chan, J. et al. (1999). Cognitive function in depression: A distinct pattern of frontal impairment in melancholia? *Psychological Medicine, 29*, 73–85.

Barch, D. M., Sheline, Y. I., Csernansky, J. G., & Snyder, A. Z. (2003). Working memory and prefrontal cortex dysfunction: Specificity to schizophrenia compared with major depression. *Biological Psychiatry, 53*, 376–384.

Basso, M. R., & Bornstein, R. A. (1999). Relative memory deficits in recurrent versus first-episode major depression on a word-list learning task. *Neuropsychology, 13*(4), 557–563.

Baune, B. T., Suslow, T., Engelien, A., Arolt, V., & Berger, K. (2006). The association between depressive mood and cognitive performance in an elderly general population—the MEMO Study. *Dementia Geriatrics and Cognitive Disorders, 22*, 142–149.

Bearden, C. E., Glahn, D. C., Monkul, E. S., Barrett, J., Najt, P., Villarreal, V., et al. (2006). Patterns of memory impairment in bipolar disorder and unipolar major depression. *Psychiatry Research, 142*, 139–150.

Beats, B. C., Sahakian, B. J., & Levy, R. (1996). Cognitive performance in tests sensitive to frontal lobe dysfunction in the elderly depressed. *Psychological Medicine, 26*(3), 591–603.

Beevers, C. G., Wells, T. T., & Miller, I. W. (2007). Predicting response to depression treatment: The role of negative cognition. *Journal of Consulting and Clinical Psychology, 75*, 422–431.

Bench, C. J., Friston, K. J., Brown, R. G., Frackowiak, R. S., & Dolan, R. J. (1993). Regional cerebral blood flow in depression measured by positron emission tomography: The relationship with clinical dimensions. *Psychological Medicine, 23*, 579–590.

Bhalla, R. K., Butters, M. A., Mulsant, B. H., Begley, A. E., Zmuda, M. D., Schoderbek, B., et al. (2006). Persistence of neuropsychologic deficits in the remitted state of late-life depression. *American Journal of Geriatric Psychiatry, 14*, 419–427.

Bieliauskas, L. A. (1993). Depressed or not depressed? That is the question. *Journal of Clinical and Experimental Neuropsychology, 15*(1), 119–134.

Boland, R., Stein, D. J., Kupfer, D. J., & Schatzberg, A. F. (2006). Depression in Medical Illness (Secondary Depression). In D.J. Stein, D>J. Kupfer, & A.F. Schatzberg (Eds.) *The American Psychiatric*

Publishing Textbook of Mood Disorders. (pp. 639–652). Washington DC: US: American Psychiatric Publishing, Inc.

Borkowska, A., & Rybakowski, J. K. (2001). Neuropsychological frontal lobe tests indicate that bipolar depressed patients are more impaired than unipolar. *Bipolar Disorders, 3,* 88–94.

Bornstein, R. A., Baker, G. B., & Douglass, A. B. (1991). Depression and memory in major depressive disorder. *Journal of Neuropsychiatry & Clinical Neurosciences, 3,* 78–80.

Borson, S., McDonald, G. J., Gayle, T., Deffebach, M., Lakshminarayan, S., & VanTuinen, C. (1992). Improvement in mood, physical symptoms, and function with nortriptyline for depression in patients with chronic obstructive pulmonary disease. *Psychosomatics, 33*(2), 190–201.

Bos, E. H., Bouhuys, A. L., Geerts, E., Van Os, T. W., Van, d. S. I., Brouwer, W. H., et al. (2005). Cognitive, physiological, and personality correlates of recurrence of depression. *Journal of Affective Disorders, 87,* 221–229.

Botteron, K., Raichle, M., Drevets, W., Heath, A., & Todd, R. (2002). Volumetric reduction in the left subgenual prefrontal cortex in early onset depression. *Biological Psychiatry, 51,* 342–344.

Bouhuys, A. L., Geerts, E., Mersch, P. P. A., & Jenner, J. A. (1996). Nonverbal interpersonal sensitivity and persistence of depression: Perception of emotions in schematic faces. *Psychiatry Research, 64,* 193–203.

Bouhuys, A. L., Geerts, E., & Gordijn, M. C. M. (1999). Depressed patients' perceptions of facial emotions in depressed and remitted states are associated with relapse: A longitudinal study. *Journal of Nervous & Mental Disease, 187,* 595–602.

Bowen, M., & Littell, C. (1997). Discriminating adult normals, patients, and claimants with a pediatric test: A brief report. *Clinical Neuropsychologist, 11,* 433–435.

Bradley, B. P., Mogg, K., Millar, N., & White, J. (1995). Selective processing of negative information: Effects of clinical anxiety, concurrent depression, and awareness. *Journal of Abnormal Psychology, 104,* 532–536.

Brand, A. N., Jolles, J., & Gispen-de Wied, C. (1992). Recall and recognition memory deficits in depression. *Journal of Affective Disorders, 25,* 77–86.

Brody, A., Saxena, S., Silverman, D., Alborzian, S., Fairbanks, L., Phelps, M., et al.. (1999). Brain metabolic changes in major depressive disorder from pre- to post-treatment with paroxetine. *Psychiatric Research, 91,* 127–139.

Brody, A. L., Saxena, S., Stoessel, P., Gillies, L. A., Fairbanks, L. A., Alborzian, S., et al. (2001). Regional brain metabolic changes in patients with major depression treated with either paroxetine or interpersonal therapy: Preliminary findings. *Archives of General Psychiatry: Special Issue, 58,* 631–640.

Brooks, J. O., & Hoblyn, J. C. (2007). Neurocognitive costs and benefits of psychotropic medications in older adults. *Journal of Geriatric Psychiatry and Neurology, 20,* 199–214.

Brown, R. G., Scott, L., Bench, C. & Dolan, R.J. (1994). Cognitive function in depression: Its relationship to the presence and severity of intellectual decline. *Psychological Medicine, 24,* 829–847.

Buffett-Jerrott, S. E., & Stewart, S. H. (2002). Cognitive and sedative effects of benzodiazepine use. *Current Pharmaceutical Design, 8,* 45–58.

Bulmash, E. L., Moller, H. J., Kayumov, L., Shen, J., Wang, X., & Shapiro, C. M. (2006). Psychomotor disturbance in depression: Assessment using a driving simulator paradigm. *Journal of Affective Disorders, 93,* 213–218.

Burt, D. B., Zembar, M. J., & Niederehe, G. (1995). Depression and memory impairment: A meta-analysis of the association, its pattern, and specificity. *Psychological Bulletin, 117,* 285–305.

Butters, M. A., Becker, J. T., Nebes, R. D., Zmuda, M. D., Mulsant, B. H., Pollock, B. G., et al. (2000). Changes in cognitive functioning following treatment of late-life depression. *American Journal of Psychiatry, 157,* 1949–1954.

Byas-Smith, M. G., Chapman, S.L., Reed, B., & Cotsonis, G. (2005). The effect of opioids on driving and psychomotor performance in patients with chronic pain. *Clinical Journal of Pain, 21*(4), 345–352.

Caetano, S. C., Hatch, J. P., Brambilla, P., Sassi, R. B., Nicoletti, M., Mallinger, A. G., et al. (2004). Anatomical MRI study of hippocampus and amygdala in patients with current and remitted major depression. *Psychiatry Research-Neuroimaging, 132,* 141–147.

Caetano, S. C., Kaur, S., Brambilla, P., Nicoletti, M., Hatch, J. P., Sassi, R. B., et al. (2006). Smaller cingulate volumes in unipolar depressed patients. *Biological Psychiatry, 59,* 702–706.

Caetano, S. C., Sassi, R., Brambilla, P., Harenski, K., Nicoletti, M., Mallinger, A. G., et al. (2001). MRI study of thalamic volumes in bipolar and unipolar patients and healthy individuals. *Psychiatry Research, 108,* 161–168.

Caine, E.D., (1981). Pseudodementia. Current concepts and future directions. *Archives of General Psychiatry, 38,* 1359–1364.

Caine, E. D., Yerevanian, B. I., & Bamford, K. A. (1984). Cognitive function and the dexamethasone suppression test in depression. *American Journal of Psychiatry, 141,* 116–118.

Caine, E.D., (1986). The Neuropsychology depression The pseudodementia syndrome In I. Grant and K. M. Adams (Eds.), *Neuropsychological assessment of neuropsychiatric disorders* (1st ed., pp. 221–243). New York: Oxford.

Campbell, S., & MacQueen, G. (2004). The role of the hippocampus in the pathophysiology of major depression. *Journal of Psychiatry & Neuroscience, 29*, 417–426.

Canli, T., Sivers, H., Thomason, M. E., Whitfield-Gabrieli, S., Gabrieli, J. D. E., & Gotlib, I. H. (2004). Brain activation to emotional words in depressed vs healthy subjects. *Neuroreport, 15*, 2585–2588.

Carroll, B. J., Curtis, G. C., & Mendels, J. (1976). Neuroendocrine regulation in depression I. Limbic system-adrenocortical dysfunction. *Archives of General Psychiatry, 33*, 1039–1044.

Channon, S. (1996). Executive dysfunction in depression: The Wisconsin card Sorting Test. *Journal of Affective Disorders, 39*, 107–114.

Chapman, S. L., Byas-Smith, M. G., & Reed, B. A. (2002). Effects of intermediate- and long-term use of opioids on cognition in patients with chronic pain. *Clinical Journal of Pain, 18*(4), S83–S90.

Chochinov, H. H. M. (2001). Depression in cancer patients. *The Lancet Oncology, 2*(8), 499–505.

Chorbov, V. M., Lobos, E. A., Todorov, A. A., Heath, A. C., Botteron, K. N., & Todd, R. D. (2007). Relationship of 5-HTTLPR genotypes and depression risk in the presence of trauma in a female twin sample. *American Journal of Medical Genetics-B Neuropsychiatric Genetics, 144B*, 830–833.

Ciechanowski, P. S., Katon, W. J., Russo, J. E., & Hirsch, I. B. (2003). The relationship of depressive symptoms to symptom reporting, self-care and glucose control in diabetes. *General Hospital Psychiatry, 25*(4), 246–252.

Coffey, C., Wilkinson, W., Weiner, R., Parashos, I., & Djang, W. (1993). Quantitative cerebral anatomy in depression. A controlled magnetic resonance study. *Archives of General Psychiatry, 50*, 7–16.

Cohen, R. M., Weingartner, H., Smallberg, S. A., Pickar, D., & Murphy, D. L. (1982). Effort and cognition in depression. *Archives of General Psychiatry, 39*, 593–597.

Cornblatt, B. A., Lenzenweger, M. F., & Erlenmeyer-Kimling, L. (1989). The continuous performance test, identical pairs version: II. Contrasting attentional profiles in schizophrenic and depressed patients. *Psychiatric Research, 29*, 65–85.

Cornell, D. G., Saurex, R., & Berent, S. (1984). Psychomotor retardation in melancholic and non-melancholic depression: Cognitive and motor components. *Journal of Abnormal Psychology, 932*, 150–157.

Coryell, W., Nopoulos, P., Drevets, W., Wilson, T., & Andreasen, N. C. (2005). Subgenual prefrontal cortex volumes in major depressive disorder and schizophrenia: Diagnostic specificity and prognostic implications. *American Journal of Psychiatry, 162*, 1706–1712.

Covinsky, K. E., Kahana, E., Chin, M. H., Palmer, R. M., Fortinsky, R. H., & Landefeld, C. S. (1999). Depressive symptoms and 3-year mortality in older hospitalized medical patients. *Annals of Internal Medicine, 130*(7), 563–569.

Cummings, J. L. (1993). The neuroanatomy of depression. *Journal of Clinical Psychiatry, 54*, 14–20.

Cummings, J. L. (1995). Anatomic and behavioral aspects of fronto-subcortical circuits. *Annals of the New York Academy Sciences, 769*, 1–13.

Cummings, J.L., & Benson, D.F. (1984). Subcortical dementia. Review of an emerging concept. *Archives fof Neurology, 41*, 874–879.

Danion, J. M., Kauffmann-Muller, F., & Grange, D. (1995). Affective valence of words, explicit and implicit memory in clinical depression. *Journal of Affective Disorders, 34*, 227–234.

Danion, J. M., Kauffmann-Muller, F., & Grange, D. (1995). Affective valence of words, explicit and implicit memory in clinical depression. *Journal of Affective Disorders, 34*, 227–234.

Danion, J. M., Peretti, S., Grange, D., Bilik, M., Imbs, J. L., & Singer, L. (1992). Effects of chlorpromazine and lorazepam on explicit memory, repetition priming and cognitive skill learning in healthy volunteers. *Psychopharmacology (Berlin), 108*, 345–351.

Danion, J. M., Willard-Schroeder, D., Zimmermann, M. A., Grange, D., Schlienger, J. L., & Singer, L. (1991). Explicit memory and repetition priming in depression, preliminary findings. *Archives of General Psychiatry, 48*, 707–711.

Davidson, R., Abercrombie, H., Nitschke, J., & Putnam, K. (1999). Regional brain function, emotion and disorders of emotion. *Current Opinion in Neurobiology, 9*, 228–234.

Davidson, R., Pizzigalli, D., Nitschke, J., & Putnam, F. (2002). Depression: Perspectives from affective neuroscience. *Annual Review of Psychology, 53*, 545–574.

Davidson, R. J., Irwin, W., Anderle, M. J., & Kalin, N. H. (2003). The neural substrates of affective processing in depressed patients treated with venlafaxine. *American Journal of Psychiatry, 160*, 64–75.

Delis, D. C., Squire, L.R., Bihrley, A., & Massman, P. (1992). Componential analysis of problem-solving ability: Performance of patients with frontal lobe damage and amnesic patients on a new sorting test. *Neuropsychologia, 30*, 683–697.

Desmond, D. W., Remien, R. H., Moroney, J. T., Stern, Y., Sano, M., & Williams, J. B. W. (2003). Ischemic stroke and depression. *Journal of the International Neuropsychological Society, 9,* 429–439.

Dierckx, E., Engelborghs, S., De, R. R., De Deyn, P. P., & Ponjaert-Kristoffersen, I. (2007). Differentiation between mild cognitive impairment, Alzheimer's disease and depression by means of cued recall. *Psychological Medicine, 37,* 747–755.

Dimatteo, M. R., Lepper, H. S., & Croghan, T. W. (2000). Depression is a risk factor for noncompliance with medical treatment: Meta-analysis of the effects of anxiety and depression on patient adherence. *Archives of Internal Medicine, 160,* 2101–2107.

Dolan, R. J., Bench, C. J., Brown, R. G., Scott, L. C., & Frackowiak, R. S. (1994). Neuropsychological dysfunction in depression: The relationship to regional cerebral blood flow. *Psychological Medicine, 24,* 849–857.

Dorn, L. D., Burgess, E. S., Friedman, T. C., Dubbert, B., Gold, P. W., & Chrousos, G. P. (1997). The longitudinal course of psychopathology in Cushing's syndrome after correction of hypercortisolism. *Journal of Clinical Endocrinology and Metabolism, 82,* 912–919.

Dorn, L. D. & Cerrone, P. (2000). Cognitive function in patients with Cushing's syndrome: A longitudinal perspective. *Clinical Nursing Research, 9,* 420–440.

Drevets, W. C., Price, J., & Simpson, J. (1997). Subgenual prefrontal cortex abnormalities in mood disorders. *Nature, 386,* 824–827.

Drevets, W. C., & Raichle, M. E. (1992). Neuroanatomical circuits in depression: Implications for treatment mechanisms. *Psychopharmacology Bulletin, 28,* 261–274.

Dunkin, J. J., Leuchter, A. F., Cook, I. A., Kasl-Godley, J. E., Abrams, M., & Rosenberg-Thompson, S. (2000). Executive dysfunction predicts nonresponse to fluoxetine in major depression. *Journal of Affective Disorders, 60,* 16–23.

Eastwood, M. R., Rifat, S. L., Nobbs, H., & Ruderman, J. (1989). Mood disorder following cerebrovascular accident. *British Journal of Psychiatry, 154,* 195–200.

Egede, L. E. (2007). Major depression in individuals with chronic medical disorders: Prevalence, correlates, and association with health resource utilization, lost productivity, and functional disability. *General Hospital Psychiatry, 29,* 409–416.

Egeland, J., Lund, A., Landro, N. I., Rund, B. R., Sundet, K., Asbjornsen, A., et al.. (2005). Cortisol level predicts executive and memory function in depression, symptom level predicts psychomotor speed. *Acta Psychiatria Scandinavia, 112,* 434–441.

Eisner, M. D., Katz, P. P., Lactao, G., & Iribarren, C. (2005). Impact of depressive symptoms on adult asthma outcomes. *Annals of Allergy, Asthma and Immunology, 94,* 566–574.

Elderkin-Thompson, V., Mintz, J., Haroon, E., Lavretsky, H., & Kumar, A. (2007). Executive dysfunction and memory in older patients with major and minor depression. *Archives of Clinical Neuropsychology, 22,* 261–270.

Elkin, I., Gibbons, R. D., Shea, M. T., Sotsky, S. M., Watkins, J. T., Pilkonis, P. A., et al. (1995). Initial severity and differential treatment outcome in the National Institute of Mental Health Treatment of Depression Collaborative Research Program. *Journal of Consulting & Clinical Psychology, 63,* 841–847.

Elliott, R. (1998). The neuropsychological profile in unipolar depression. *Trends in Cognitive Sciences, 2*(11), 447–454.

Elliott, R., Baker, S. C., Rogers, R. D., O'Leary, D. A., Paykel, E. S., Frith, C. D., et al. (1997). Prefrontal dysfunction in depressed patients performing a complex planning task: A study using positron emission tomography. *Psychological Medicine, 27,* 931–942.

Elliott, R., Sahakian, B. J., McKay, A. P., Herrod, J. J., Robbins, T. W., & Paykel, E. S. (1996). Neuropsychological impairments in unipolar depression: The influence of perceived failure on subsequent performance. *Psychological Medicine 26,* 975–989.

Epstein, J., Pan, H., Kocsis, J. H., Yang, Y., Butler, T., Chusid, J., et al. (2006). Lack of ventral striatal response to positive stimuli in depressed versus normal subjects. *American Journal of Psychiatry, 163,* 1784–1790.

Farrin, L., Hull, L., Unwin, C., Wykes, T., & David, A. (2003). Effects of depressed mood on objective and subjective measures of attention. *The Journal of Neuropsychiatry and Clinical Neurosciences, 15*(1), 98–104.

Ferrier, I. N., Stanton, B. R., Kelly, T. P., & Scott, J. (1999). Neuropsychological function in euthymic patients with bipolar disorder. *British Journal of Psychiatry, 175,* 246–251.

Forget, H., Lacroix, A., & Cohen, H. (2002). Persistent cognitive impairment following surgical treatment of Cushing's syndrome. *Psychoneuroendocrinology, 27,* 367–383.

Fossati, P., Coyette, F., Ergis, A. M., & Allilaire, J. F. (2002). Influence of age and executive functioning on verbal memory of inpatients with depression. *Journal of Affective Disorders, 68,* 261–271.

Fossati, P., Ergis, A., & Allilaire, J. (2001). Problem-solving abilities in unipolar depressed patients: Comparison of performance on the modified version of the Wisconsin and the California sorting tests. *Psychiatry Research, 104,* 145–156.

Fossati, P., Harvey, P. -O., Bastard, G. L., Ergis, A. -M., Jouvent, R., & Allilaire, J. -F. O. (2004). Verbal memory performance of patients with a first depressive episode and patients with unipolar and bipolar recurrent depression. *Journal of Psychiatric Research, 38*(2), 137–144.

Fossati, P., Hevenor, S., Graham, S. J., Grady, C., Keightley, M. L., Craik, F., et al. (2003). In search of the emotional self: An fMRI study using positive and negative emotional words. *American Journal of Psychiatry, 160,* 1938–1945.

Frasure-Smith, N., Lesperance, F., & Talajic, M. (1993). Depression following myocardial infarction. Impact on 6-month survival. *JAMA, 270*(15), 1819–1825.

Frodl, T., Meisenzahl, E. M., Zetzsche, T., Born, C., Jager, M., Groll, C., et al. (2003). Larger amygdala volumes in first depressive episode as compared to recurrent major depression and healthy control subjects. *Biological Psychiatry, 53,* 338–344.

Frodl, T., Schaub, A., Banac, S., Charypar, M., Jager, M., Kummler, P., et al. (2006). Reduced hippocampal volume correlates with executive dysfunctioning in major depression. *Journal of Psychiatry & Neuroscience, 31,* 316–323.

Fu, C. H. Y., Williams, S. C. R., Cleare, A. J., Brammer, M. J., Walsh, N. D., Kim, J., et al. (2004). Attenuation of the neural response to sad faces in major depression by antidepressant treatment—A prospective, event-related functional magnetic resonance imaging study. *Archives of General Psychiatry, 61,* 877–889.

Ganzini, L., Smith, D. M., Fenn, D. S., & Lee, M. A. (1997). Depression and mortality in medically ill older adults. *Journal of the American Geriatrics Society, 45*(3), 307–312.

George, M. S., Ketter, T., Gill, D., Haxby, J., Ungerleider, L., Herscovitch, P., et al. (1993). Brain regions involved in recognizing facial emotion or identity: An oxygen-15 PET study. *Journal of Neuropsychiatry and Clinical Neuroscience, 5,* 384–394.

George, M. S., Ketter, T. A., Parekh, P. I., Herscovitch, P., & Post, R. M. (1996). Gender differences in regional cerebral blood flow during transient self-induced sadness or happiness. *Biological Psychiatry, 40,* 859–871.

George, M. S., Ketter, T. A., Parekh, P. I., Rosinsky, N., Ring, H., Casey, B. J., et al. (1994). Regional brain activity when selecting a response despite interference: An $H_2^{15}O$ PET study of the Stroop and an emotional Stroop. *Human Brain Mapping, 1,* 194–209.

Ghaffar, O., & Feinstein, A. (2007). The neuropsychiatry of multiple sclerosis: A review of recent developments. *Current Opinion in Psychiatry, 20,* 278–285.

Gilboa-Schechtman, E., Erhard-Weiss, D., & Jeczemien, P. (2002). Interpersonal deficits meet cognitive biases: Memory for facial expressions in depressed and anxious men and women. *Psychiatric Research, 113,* 279–293.

Goldapple, K., Segal, Z., Garson, C., Lau, M., Bieling, P., Kennedy, S., et al. (2004). Modulation of cortical–limbic pathways in major depression—treatment-specific effects of cognitive behavior therapy. *Archives of General Psychiatry, 61,* 34–41.

Golomb, J., deLeon, M. J., Kluger, A., George, A. E., Tarshish, C., & Ferris, S. H. (1993). Hippocampal atrophy in normal aging an association with recent memory impairment. *Archives of Neurology, 50,* 967–973.

Gomez, R. G., Fleming, S. H., Keller, J., Flores, B., Kenna, H., DeBattista, C., et al.. (2006). The neuropsychological profile of psychotic major depression and its relation to cortisol. *Biological Psychiatry, 60,* 472–478.

Gorenstein, C., Bernik, M. A., & Pompeia, S. (1994). Differential acute psychomotor and cognitive effects of diazepam on long-term benzodiazepine users. *International Clinical Psychopharmacology, 9,* 145–153.

Gorno-Tempini, M., Pradelli, S., Serafini, M., Pagnoni, G., Baraldi, P., Porro, C., et al. (2001). Explicit and incidental facial expression processing: An fMRI study. *NeuroImage, 14,* 465–473.

Gotlib, I. H., Krasnoperova, E., Yue, D. N., & Joormann, J. (2004). Attentional biases for negative interpersonal stimuli in clinical depression. *Journal of Abnormal Psychology, 113,* 127–135.

Gotlib, I. H., Traill, S. K., Montoya, R. L., Joormann, J., & Chang, K. (2005). Attention and memory biases in the offspring of parents with bipolar disorder: indications from a pilot study. *Journal of Child Psychology and Psychiatry, 46,* 84–93.

Grant, M. M., Thase, M. E., & Sweeney, J. A. (2001). Cognitive disturbance in outpatient depressed younger adults: Evidence of modest impairment. *Biological Psychiatry, 50,* 35–43.

Greicius, M. D., Flores, B. H., Menon, V., Glover, G. H., Solvason, H. B., Kenna, H., et al. (2007). Resting-state functional connectivity in major depression: Abnormally increased contributions from subgenual cingulate cortex and thalamus. *Biological Psychiatry, 62,* 429–437.

Gualtieri, C. T., Johnson, L. G., & Benedict, K. B. (2006). Neurocognition in depression: Patients on and off medication versus healthy comparison subjects 501. *Journal of Neuropsychiatry and Clinical Neurosciences, 18,* 217–225.

Gur, R. C., Edwin, R., Gur, R., Zwil, A., Heimberg, C., & Kraemer, H. (1992). Facial emotion discrimination: II Behavioral findings in depression. *Psychiatry Research, 42,* 241–251.

Gur, R. C., Ragland, D., Moberg, P., Bilker, W., Kohler, C., Siegel, S., et al. (2001a). Computerized neurocognitive scanning: II The profile of schizophrenia. *Neuropsychopharmacology, 25,* 777–788.

Gur, R. C., Ragland, D., Moberg, P., Turner, T., Bilker, W., Kohler, C., et al. (2001b). Computerized neurocognitive scanning: I Methodology and validation in healthy people. *Neuropsychopharmacology, 25,* 766–776.

Hammar, A., Lund, A., & Hugdahl, K. (2003). Selective impairment in effortful information processing in major depression. *Journal of the International Neuropsychological Society, 9,* 954–959.

Harik, L., Pica, A., Wright, S., Lee, J., & Bieliauskas, L. (2008). Cognitive deficits associated with anticholinergic therapy and drugs with anticholinergic properties in community dwelling veterans. *Journal of the International Neuropsychological Society, 14*(Suppl S1), 106.

Harlow, J. (1868). Recovery from the passage of an iron bar through the head. *Publications of the Massachussetts Medical Society, 2,* 327–347.

Hartlage, S., Alloy, L. B., Vazquez, C., & Dykman, B. (1993). Automatic and effortful processing in depression. *Psychological Bulletin, 113*(2), 247–278.

Harvey, P. O., Le Bastard, G., Poshon, J. B., Levy, R., Allilaire, J. F., Dubois, B., et al. (2004). Executive functions and updating of the contents of working memory in unipolar depression. *Journal of Psychiatric Research, 38,* 567–576.

Harvey, P. O., Fossati, P., Pochon, J-B., Levy, R., Le Bastard, G., et al., (2005). Cognitive control and brain resources in major depression: An fMRI study using the n-back task. *Neuroimage, 26,* 860–869.

Hasher, L., & Zacks, R. T. (1979). Automatic and effortful processes in memory. *Journal of Experimental Psychology: General, 108*(3), 356–388.

Hatfield, R., Langenecker, S. A., Smet, I., Maixner, D., & Giordani, B. (2005). Memory functioning and white matter disease in Treatment Resistant Depression. Presented at the International Neuropsychological Society meeting in St. Louis, MO.

Haythornthwaite, J. A., Menefee, L. A., Quatrano-Piacentini, A. L., & Pappagallo, M. (1998). Outcome of chronic opioid therapy for non-cancer pain. *Journal of Pain and Symptom Management, 15,* 185–194.

Heald, A. H., Ghosh, S., Bray, S., Gibson, C., Anderson, S. G., Buckler, H., et al. (2004). Long-term negative impact on quality of life in patients with successfully treated Cushing's disease. *Clinical Endocrinology, 61,* 458–465.

Henry, J. D., & Crawford, J. R. (2005). A meta-analytic review of verbal fluency deficits in depression. *Journal of Clinical and Experimental Neuropsychology, 27,* 78–101.

Hickie, I., Scott, E., & Wilhelm, K. (1997). Subcortical hyperintensities on magnetic resonance imaging in patients with severe depression-longitudinal evaluation. *Biological Psychiatry, 42,* 367–374.

Holmes, A. J., Macdonald, A., Carter, C. S., Barch, D. M., Stenger, V. A., & Cohen, J. D. (2005). Prefrontal functioning during context processing in schizophrenia and major depression: An event-related fMRI study. *Schizophrenia Research, 76,* 199–206.

Hook, J. N., Giordani, B., Schteingart, D. E., Guire, K., Giles, J., Ryan, K., et al. (2007). Patterns of cognitive change over time and relationship to age following successful treatment of Cushing's disease. *Journal of the International Neuropsychological Society, 3,* 21–29.

Hugdahl, K., Rund, B. R., Lund, A., Asbjornsen, A., Egeland, J., Ersland, L., et al. (2004). Brain activation measured with fMRI during a mental arithmetic task in schizophrenia and major depression. *American Journal of Psychiatry, 161,* 286–293.

Hugdahl, K., Rund, B. R., Lund, A., Asbjornsen, A., Egeland, J., Landro, N. I., et al. (2003). Attentional and executive dysfunctions in schizophrenia and depression: Evidence from dichotic listening performance. *Biological Psychiatry, 53,* 609–616.

Iidaka, T., Omori, M., Murata, T., Kosaka, H., Yonekura, Y., Okada, T., et al. (2001). Neural interactions of the amygdala with the prefrontal and temporal cortices in the processing of facial expressions as revealed by fMRI. *Journal of Cognitive Neuroscience, 13,* 1035–1047.

Johnson, S. K., Lange, G., DeLuca, J., Korn, L. R., & Natelson, B. (1997). The effects of fatigue on neuropsychological performance in patients with chronic fatigue syndrome, multiple sclerosis, and depression. *Applied Neuropsychology, 4*(3), 145–153.

Jorm, A. F., Anstey, K. J., Christensen, H., de Plater, G., Kumar, R., Wen, W., et al. (2005). MRI hyperintensities and depressive symptoms in a community sample of individuals 60–64 years old. *American Journal of Psychiatry, 162,* 699–704.

Jorm, A. F., Butterworth, P., Anstey, K. J., Christensen, H., Easteal, S., Maller, J., et al. (2004). Memory complaints in a community sample aged 60–64 years: Associations with cognitive functioning, psychiatric symptoms, medical conditions, APOE genotype, hippocampus and amygdala volumes, and white-matter hyperintensities. *Psychological Medicine, 34,* 1495–1506.

Kalin, N., Davidson, R., Irwin, W., Warner, G., Orendi, J., Sutton, S., et al. (1997). Functional magnetic resonance imaging studies of emotional processing in normal and depressed patients: Effects of venlafaxine. *Journal of Clinical Psychiatry, 58*, 32–39.

Kampf-Sherf, O., Zlotogorski, Z., Gilboa, A., Speedie, L., Lereya, J., Rosca, P., et al. (2004). Neuropsychological functioning in major depression and responsiveness to selective seretonin reuptake inhibitors antidepressants. *Journal of Affective Disorders 82*, 453–459.

Katon, W., Lin, E. H. B., & Kroenke, K. (2007). The association of depression and anxiety with medical symptom burden in patients with chronic medical illness. *General Hospital Psychiatry, 29*(2), 147–155.

Katon, W. J. (2003). Clinical and health services relationships between major depression, depressive symptoms, and general medical illness. *Society of Biological Psychiatry, 54*, 216–226.

Kaufman, A., & Kaufman, N. (1983). *Kaufman assessment battery for children; administration and scoring manual*. Circle Pines, MA: American Guidance Service.

Keedwell, P., Andrew C., Williams, S. C. R., Bramner, M. J., & Phillips, M. L. (2005). A double dissociation of ventromedial prefrontal cortical responses to sad and happy stimuli in depressed and healthy individuals. *Biological Psychiatry, 58*, 495–503.

Kegeles, L. S., Malone, K. M., Slifstein, M., Ellis, S. P., Xanthopoulos, E., Keilp, J. G., et al. (2003). Response of cortical metabolic deficits to serotonergic challenge in familial mood disorders. *American Journal of Psychiatry, 160*, 76–82.

Kennedy, S. E., Koeppe, R. A., Young, E. A., & Zubieta, J. K. (2006). Dysregulation of endogenous opioid emotion regulation circuitry in major depression in women. *Archives of General Psychiatry, 63*, 1199–1208.

Kennedy, S. E., & Zubieta, J. K. (2004). Neuroreceptor imaging of stress and mood disorders. *CNS Spectrums, 9*, 292–301.

Kennedy, S. H., Javanmard, M., & Vaccarino, F. J. (1997). A review of functional neuroimaging in mood disorders: Positron emission tomography and depression. *Canadian Journal of Psychiatry, 42*, 467–475.

Kennedy, S. H., Konarski, J. Z., Segal, Z. V., Lau, M. A., Bieling, P. J., McIntyre, R. S., et al. (2007). Differences in brain glucose metabolism between responders to CBT and venlafaxine in a 16-week randomized controlled trial 6. *American Journal of Psychiatry, 164*, 778–788.

Kensinger, E. A., & Corkin S. (2004). Two routes to emotional memory: Distinct neural processes for valence and arousal. *Proceedings of the National Academy of Sciences of the United States of America, 101*, 3310–3315.

Kerr, B. B., Hill, H. H., Coda, B. B., Calogero, M. M., Chapman, C. C. R., Hunt, E. E., et al. (1991). Concentration-related effects of morphine on cognition and motor control in human subjects. *Neuropsychopharmacology, 5*(3), 157–166.

Ketter, T. A., Andreason, P. J., George, M. S., Lee, C., & Gill, D. S. (1996). Anterior paralimbic mediation of procaine-induced emotional and psychosensory experiences. *Archives of General Psychiatry, 53*, 59–69.

King, D. A., & Caine, E. D. (1996). Cognitive impairment and major depression. In I. Grant and K. M. Adams (Eds.), *Neuropsychological assessment of neuropsychiatric disorders* (2nd ed., pp. 200–217). New York: Oxford.

King, D. A., Cox, C., Lyness, J. M., Conwell, Y., & Caine, E. D. (1998). Quantitative and qualitative differences in the verbal learning performance of elderly depressives and healthy controls. *Journal of the International Neuropsychological Society, 4*, 115–126.

Klein, D., Schatzberg, A.F., McCullough, J.P., Dowling, F., Goodman, D. et al., (1999). Age of onset in chronic major depression: relation to demographic and clinical variables, family history, and treatment response . *Journal of Affective Disorders , 55* , 149 - 157

Knauper, B. Cannell, CF. Schwarz, N, Bruce, M.L., Kessler, R. (1999). Improving the accuracy of major depression age of onset reports in the US National Comorbidity Survey. *International Journal of Methods in Psychiatric Research,8*:39–48.

Knutson, B., Bhanji, J. P., Cooney, R. E., Atlas, L. Y., & Gotlib, I. H. (2008). Neural responses to monetary incentives in major depression. *Biological Psychiatry, 63*, 686–692.

Kolb, B., & Whishaw, I. (1996). *Human neuropsychology*. New York: W. H. Freeman and Company.

Krishnan, K. R., McDonald, W. M., Escalona, P. R., Doraiswamy, P. M., Na, C., Husain, M. M., et al. (1992). Magnetic resonance imaging of the caudate nuclei in depression. *Archives of General Psychiatry, 49*, 553–557.

Kudoh, A., Takase, H., Takahira, Y., & Takazawa, T. (2004). Postoperative confusion increases in elderly long-term benzodiazepine users. *Anesthesia and Analgesia, 99*, 1674–1678.

Kumar, A., Bilker, W., Jin, Z., Udupa, J. (2000). Atrophy and high intensity lesions: complementary neurobiological mechanisms in late-life major depression. *Neuropsychopharmacology, 22*, 264–274.

Kumari, V., Mittersciffthaler, M., Teasdale, J., Malhi, G., Brown, R., Giampietro, V., et al. (2003). Neural abnormalities during cognitive generation of affect in treatment-resistant depression. *Biological Psychiatry, 54,* 777–791.

Lamberty, G. J., & Bieliauskas, L. A. (1993). Distinguishing between depression and dementia in the elderly: A review of neuropsychological findings. *Archives of Clinical Neuropsychology, 8,* 149–170.

Landro, N. I., Stiles, T. C., & Sletvold, H. (1997). Memory functioning in patients with primary fibromyalgia and major depression and healthy controls. *Journal of Psychosomatic Research, 42*(3), 297–306.

Landro, N. I., Stiles, T. C., & Sletvold, H. (2001). Neurological function in nonpsychotic unipolar major depression. *Neuropsychiatry, Neuropsychology, & Behavioral Neurology, 14*(4), 233–240

Langenecker, S. A., Bieliauskas, L. A., Rapport, L. J., Zubieta, J. K., Wilde, E. A., & Berent, S. (2005). Face emotion perception and executive functioning deficits in depression. *Journal of Clinical and Experimental Neuropsychology, 27,* 320–333.

Langenecker, S. A., Caveney, A. F., Young, E. A., Giordani, B., Nielson, K. A., Rapport, L. J., et al. (2007a). The psychometric properties and sensitivity of a brief computer-based cognitive screening battery in a depression clinic. *Psychiatric Research, 152,* 143–154.

Langenecker, S. A., Kennedy, S. E., Guidotti, L., Briceno, E., Own, L., Hooven, T., et al. (2007b). Frontal and limbic activation during inhibitory control predicts treatment response in Major Depressive Disorder. *Biological Psychiatry, 53,* 46–53.

Larisch, R., Klimke, A., Vosberg, H., Loffler, S., Gaebel, W., & Muller-Gartner, H. W. (1997). In vivo evidence for the involvement of dopamine-D2 receptors in striatum and anterior cingulate gyrus in major depression. *NeuroImage, 5,* 251–260.

Laska, A. C., Martensson, B., Kahan, T., von Arbin, M., & Murray, V. (2007). Recognition of depression in aphasic stroke patients. *Cerebrovascular Diseases, 24,* 74–79.

Lee, A., Ogle, W., & Sapolsky, R. M. (2002). Stress and depression: Possible links to neuron death in the hippocampus. *Bipolar Disorders, 4,* 117–128.

Lee, G. P., Loring, D. W., & Martin, R. C. (1992). Rey's 15-Item Visual Memory Test for the detection of malingering: Normative observations on patients with neurological disorders. *Psychological Assessment, 4,* 43–46.

Lee, S. -H., Payne, M. E., Steffens, D. C., McQuoid, D. R., Lai, T. -J., Provenzale, J. M., et al. (2003). Subcortical lesion severity and orbitofrontal cortex volume in geriatric depression. *Biological Psychiatry, 54,* 529–533.

Lesperance, F., & Frasure-Smith, N. (1996). Negative emotions and coronary heart disease: Getting to the heart of the matter. *Lancet, 347,* 414–415.

Leufkens, T. R., Vermeeren, A., Smink, B. E., van, R. P., & Ramaekers, J. G. (2007). Cognitive, psychomotor and actual driving performance in healthy volunteers after immediate and extended release formulations of alprazolam 1 mg. *Psychopharmacology (Berl), 191,* 951–959.

Liotti, M., Mayberg, H. S., Brannan, S. K., McGinnis, S., Jerabek, P., & Fox, P. T. (2000). Differential limbic–cortical correlates of sadness and anxiety in healthy subjects: Implications for affective disorders. *Biological Psychiatry, 48,* 30–42.

Lopez, J. F., Chalmers, D. T., Little, K. Y., & Watson, S. J. (1998). Regulation of serotonin 1A, glucocorticoid, and mineralocorticoid receptor in rat and human hippocampus: Implications for the neurobiology of depression. *Biological Psychiatry, 43,* 547–573.

Lorenz, J., Beck, H., & Bromm, B. (1997). Cognitive performance, mood and experimental pain before and during morphine-induced analgesia in patients with chronic nonmalignant pain. *Pain, 73,* 369–375.

Maddock, R. J., Garrett, A. S., & Buonocore, M. H. (2003). Posterior cingulate cortex activation by emotional words: fMRI evidence from a valence decision task. *Human Brain Mapping, 18,* 30–41.

Malhi, G. S., Ivanovski, B., Hadzi-Pavlovic, D., Mitchell, P. B., Vieta, E., & Sachdev, P. (2007). Neuropsychological deficits and functional impairment in bipolar depression, hypomania and euthymia. *Bipolar Disorders, 9,* 114–125.

Marcos, T., Portella, M. J., Navarro, V., Gasto, C., Rami, L., Lazaro, L., et al. (2005). Neuropsychological prediction of recovery in late-onset major depression. *International Journal of Geriatric Psychiatry, 20,* 790–795.

Markela-Lerenc, J., Kaiser, S., Fiedler, P., Weisbrod, M., & Mundt, C. (2006). Stroop performance in depressive patients: A preliminary report. *Journal of Affective Disorders, 94,* 261–267.

Martinez-Aran, A., Vieta, E., Colom, F., Torrent, C., Sanchez-Moreno, J., Reinares, M., et al. (2004). Cognitive impairment in euthymic bipolar patients: Implications for clinical and functional outcome. *Bipolar Disorders, 6*(3), 224–232.

Martinot, M. L. P., Bragulat, V., Artiges, E., Dolle, F., Hinnen, F., Jouvent, R., et al. (2001). Decreased presynaptic dopamine function in the left caudate of depressed patients with affective flattening and psychomotor retardation. *American Journal of Psychiatry, 158,* 314–316.

Matsuo, K., Kato, N., & Kato, T. (2002). Decreased cerebral haemodynamic response to cognitive and physiological tasks in mood disorders as shown by near-infrared spectroscopy. *Psychological Medicine, 32*, 1029–1037.

Mauri, M., Sinforiani, E., G., B., Vignati, F., Berselli, M. E., Attanasio, R., et al. (1993). Memory impairment in Cushing's disease. *Acta Neurologica Scandinavia, 87*, 52–55.

Mayberg, H. S., Brannan, S., Mahurin, R., Jerabek, P., Brickman, J., Tekell, J., et al. (1997). Cingulate function in depression: A potential predictor of treatment response. *Neuroreport, 8*, 1057–1061.

Mayberg, H. S., Lewis, P., Regenold, W., & Wagner, H. (1994). Paralimbic hypoperfusion in unipolar depression. *Journal of Nuclear Medicine, 35*, 929–934.

Mayberg, H. S., Lozano, A. M., Voon, V., McNeely, H. E., Seminowicz, D., Hamani, C., et al. (2005). Deep brain stimulation for treatment-resistant depression. *Neuron, 45*, 651–660.

McDaniel, J. S., Musselman, D. L., Porter, M. R., & Reed, D. A. (1995). Depression in patients with cancer: Diagnosis, biology, and treatment. *Archives of General Psychiatry, 52*(2), 89–99.

McEwen, B. S. (2002). Editorial: Cortisol, Cushing's syndrome, and a shrinking brain-new evidence for reversibility. *Journal of Clinical Endocrinology and Metabolism, 87*, 1947–1948.

McLoughlin, D. M., Mogg, A., Eranti, S., Pluck, G., Purvis, R., Edwards, D., et al. (2007). The clinical effectiveness and cost of repetitive transcranial magnetic stimulation versus electroconvulsive therapy in severe depression: A multicentre pragmatic randomised controlled trial and economic analysis. *Health Technology Assessment, 11*, 1–54.

McWilliams, L. A., Cox, B. J., & Enns, M. W. (2003). Mood and anxiety disorders associated with chronic pain: An examination in a nationally representative sample. *Pain, 106*(1), 127–133.

Mega, M. S., & Cummings, J. L. (1994). Fronto-subcortical circuits and neuropsychiatric disorders. *The Journal of Neuropsychiatry and Clinical Neurosciences, 6*, 358–370.

Mervaala, E., Fohr, J., Kononen, M., Valknen-Korhonen, M., & NVainio, P. (2000). Quantitative MRI of the hippocampus and amygdala in severe depression. *Psychological Medicine, 30*, 117–25.

Michopoulos, I., Zervas, I. M., Papakosta, V. M., Tsaltas, E., Papageorgiou, C., Manessi, T., et al. (2006). Set shifting deficits in melancholic vs. non-melancholic depression: Preliminary findings. *European Psychiatry, 21*, 361–363.

Mikhailova, E., Vladimirova, T., Iznak, A., Tsusulkovskaya, E., & Sushko, N. (1996). Abnormal recognition of facial expression of emotions in depressed patients with Major Depression

Disorder and Schizotypal Personality Disorder. *Biological Psychiatry, 40*, 697–705.

Milak, M. S., Parsey, R. V., Keilp, J., Oquendo, M. A., Malone, K. M., & Mann, J. J. (2005). Neuroanatomic correlates of psychopathologic components of major depressive disorder. *Archives of General Psychiatry, 62*, 397–408.

Miller, W. R. (1975). Psychological deficit in depression. *Psychological Bulletin, 82*(2), 238–260.

Miyake, A., Friedman, N. P., Emerson, M. J., Witzki, A. H., & Howerter, A. (2000). The unity and diversity of executive functions and their contributions to complex "frontal lobe" tasks: A latent variable analysis. *Cognitive Psychology, 41*(1), 49–100.

Mogg, K., Bradley, B. P., Williams, R., & Mathews, A. (1993). Subliminal processing of emotional information in anxiety and depression. *Journal of Abnormal Psychology, 102*, 304–311.

Molgat, C. V., & Patten, S. B. (2005). Comorbidity of major depression and migraine—a Canadian Population-Based Study. *The Canadian Journal of Psychiatry/La Revue canadienne de psychiatrie, 50*(13), 832–837.

Moniz, E. (1954). I succeeded in performing the prefrontal leukotomy. *Journal of Clinical and Experimental Psychopathology, 15*, 373–379.

Moses-Kolko, E. L., Price, J. C., Thase, M. E., Meltzer, C. C., Kupfer, D. J., Mathis, C. A., et al. (2007). Measurement of 5-HT1A receptor binding in depressed adults before and after antidepressant drug treatment using positron emission tomography and [11C]WAY-100635. *Synapse, 61*, 523–530.

Munn, M. A., Alexopoulos, J., Nishino, T., Babb, C. M., Flake, L. A., Singer, T., et al. (2007). Amygdala volume analysis in female twins with major depression. *Biological Psychiatry, 62*(5), 415–422.

Nagai, M., Kishi, K., & Kato, S. (2007). Insular cortex and neuropsychiatric disorders: A review of recent literature. *European Psychiatry, 22*(6), 387–394.

Naismith, S. L., Hickie, I. B., Ward, P. B., Scott, E., & Little, C. (2006). Impaired implicit sequence learning in depression: A probe for frontostriatal dysfunction? *Psychological Medicine, 36*, 313–323.

Nandi, D., Saha, G., Bhattacharya, B., & Mandal, M. (1982). A study on perception of facial expression of emotions in depression. *Indian Journal of Psychiatry, 24*, 284–290.

Nebes, R. D., Butters, M. A., Mulsant, B. H., Pollock, B. G., Zmuda, M. D., Houck, P. R., et al. (2000). Decreased working memory and processing speed mediate cognitive impairment in geriatric depression. *Psychological Medicine, 30*, 679–691.

Nilsson, F. M., Kessing, L. V., Sorenson, T. M., Anderson, P. K., & Bolwig, T. G. (2002). Major depressive disorder in Parkinson's disease: A register-based study. *Acta Psychiatrica Scandinavica, 106,* 202–211.

Northoff, G., Richter, A., Gessner, M., Schlagenhauf, F., Fell, J., Baumgart, F., et al. (2000). Functional dissociation between medial and lateral prefrontal cortical spatiotemporal activation in negative and positive emotions: A combined fMRI/MEG study. *Cerebral Cortex, 10,* 93–107.

Nussbaum, P. D., Kaszniak, A. W., Allender, J. A., & Rapcsak, S. Z. (1995). Depression and cognitive deterioration in the elderly: A follow-up study. *The Clinical Neuropsychologist, 9,* 101–111.

O'Brien, J. T., Lloyd, A., McKeith, I., Gholkar, A., & Ferrier, N. (2004). A longitudinal study of hippocampal volume, cortisol levels, and cognition in older depressed subjects. *American Journal of Psychiatry, 161,* 2081–2090.

Ochsner, K., Ray, R. D., Cooper, J. C., Robertson, E. R., Chopra, S., Gabrielli, J. D. E., et al. (2004). For better or worse: Neural systems supporting the cognitive down- and up-regulation of negative emotion. *NeuroImage, 23,* 483–499.

Okada, G., Okamoto, Y., Morinobu, S., Yamawaki, S., & Yokota, N. (2003). Attenuated left prefrontal activation during a verbal fluency task in patients with depression. *Neuropsychobiology, 47,* 21–26.

Olley, A., Malhi, G. S., Mitchell, P. B., Batchelor, J., Lagopoulos, J., & Austin, M. V. (2005). When euthymia is just not good enough. *Nervous and Mental Disease, 193*(5), 323–330.

Ongur, D., Drevets, W. C., & Price, J. L. (1998). Glial reduction in the subgenual prefrontal cortex in mood disorders. *Proceedings of the National Academy of Sciences of the United States of America, 95,* 13290–13295.

Owen, A. M. (2004). Cognitive dysfunction in Parkinson disease: The role of frontostriatal circuitry. *Neuroscientist, 10,* 525–537.

Paelecke-Habermann, Y., Pohl, J., & Leplow, B. (2005). Attention and executive functions in remitted major depression patients. *Journal of Affective Disorders, 89,* 125–135.

Paradiso, S., Johnson, D., Andreasan, N., O'Leary, D., Watkins, G., Ponto, L., et al. (1999). Cerebral blood flow changes associated with attribution of emotional valence to pleasant, unpleasant, and neutral visual stimuli in a PET study of normal subjects. *American Journal of Psychiatry, 156,* 1618–1629.

Paterniti S, Verdier-Taillefer MH, Dufouil C, Alpérovitch A. (2002). Depressive symptoms and cognitive decline in elderly people. Longitudinal study. *British Journal of Psychiatry, 181,* 406–410.

Patten, S. B., Beck, C. A., Kassam, A., Williams, J. V. A., Barbui, C., & Metz, L. M. (2005). Long-term medical conditions and major depression: Strength of association for specific conditions in the general population. *The Canadian Journal of Psychiatry/La Revue canadienne de psychiatrie, 50*(4), 195–202.

Payne, R. (1990). Medication-induced performance deficits: Analgesics and narcotics. *Journal of Occupational Medicine, 32,* 362–369.

Persad, S., & Polivy, J. (1993). Differences between depressed and nondepressed individuals in the recognition of and response to facial emotional cues. *Journal of Abnormal Psychology, 102,* 358–368.

Pezawas, L., Meyer-Lindenberg, A., Drabant, E. M., Verchinski, B. A., Munoz, K. E., Kolachana, B. S., et al. (2005). 5-HTTLPR polymorphism impacts human cingulate-amygdala interactions: A genetic susceptibility mechanism for depression. *Nature Neuroscience, 8,* 828–834.

Phan, K. L., Taylor, S. F., Welsh, R. C., Decker, L. R., Noll, D., Nichols, T. E., et al. (2003). Activation of the medial prefrontal cortex and extended amygdala by individual ratings of emotional arousal: A fMRI study. *Biological Psychiatry, 53,* 211–215.

Phillips, M., Drevets, W., Rauch, S., & Lane, R. (2003). Neurobiology of emotion perception II: Implications for major psychiatric disorders. *Biological Psychiatry, 54,* 515–528.

Phillips, M. L., Medford, N., Young, A. W., Williams, L., Williams, S. C. R., Bullmore, E. T., et al. (2001). Time courses of left and right amygdalar responses to fearful facial expressions. *Human Brain Mapping: Special Issue, 12,* 193–202.

Pizzagalli, D. A., Oakes, T. R., Fox, A. S., Chung, M. K., Larson, C. L., Abercrombie, H. C., et al. (2004). Functional but not structural subgenual prefrontal cortex abnormalities in melancholia. *Molecular Psychiatry, 9,* 393–405.

Pizzigalli, D., Pascual-Marqui, R. D., Nitschke, J., Oakes, T. R., Larson, C. L., Abercrombie, H., et al. (2001). Anterior cingulate activity as a predictor of degree of treatment response in major depression: Evidence from brain Electrical Tomography Analysis. *American Journal of Psychiatry, 158,* 405–415.

Porter, R. J., Gallagher, P., Thompson, J. M., & Young, A. H. (2003). Neurocognitive impairment in drug-free patients with major depressive disorder. *British Journal of Psychiatry, 182,* 214–220.

Pournajafi-Nazarloo, H., Carr, M. S., Papademeteriou, E., Schmidt, J. V., & Cushing, B. S. (2007). Oxytocin selectively increases ERalpha mRNA in the neonatal hypothalamus and hippocampus of female prairie voles. *Neuropeptides, 41,* 39–44.

Purcell, R., Maruff, P., Kyrios, M., & Pantelis, C. (1997). Neuropsychological function in young patients with unipolar major depression. *Psychological Medicine, 27*, 1277–1285.

Quraishi, S., & Frangou, S. (2002). Neuropsychology of bipolar disorder: A review. *Journal of Affective Disorders, 72*, 209–226.

Ravnkilde, B., Videbech, P., Clemmensen, K., Egander, A., Rasmussen, N. A., Gjedde, A., et al. (2003). The Danish PET/depression project: Cognitive function and regional cerebral blood flow. *Acta Psychiatrica Scandinavica, 108*, 32–40.

Rey, A. (1964). *L'examen Clinicque en Psychologie* [The Clinical Examination in Psychology]. Paris: Presses Universitaires de France.

Riso, L. P., Miyatake, R. K., & Thase, M. E. (2002). The search for determinants of chronic depression: A review of six factors. *Journal of Affective Disorders, 70*, 103–115.

Robinson, L. J., & Ferrier, I. N. (2006). Evolution of cognitive impairment in bipolar disorder: A systematic review of cross-sectional evidence. *Bipolar Disorders, 8*, 103–116.

Robinson, L. J., Thompson, J. M., Gallagher, P., Goswami, U., Young, A. H., Ferrier, I. N., et al. (2006). A meta-analysis of cognitive deficits in euthymic patients with bipolar disorder. *Journal of Affective Disorders, 93*, 105–115.

Rogers, M. A., Bellgrove, M. A., Chiu, E., Mileshkin, C., & Bradshaw, J. L. (2004). Response selection deficits in melancholic but not nonmelancholic unipolar major depression. *Journal of Clinical and Experimental Neuropsychology, 26*, 169–179.

Rohling, M. L., Green, P., Allen, L., & Iverson, G. L. (2002). Depressive symptoms and neurocognitive test scores in patients passing symptom validity tests. *Archives of Clinical Neuropsychology, 17*, 205–222.

Rohling, M. L., Scogin, F. (1993). Automatic and effortful memory processes in depressed persons. *The Journals of Gerontology, 48*, 87–95.

Rolls, E. (1999). *The brain and emotion*. Oxford, UK: Oxford University Press.

Rose, E. J., & Ebmeier, K. P. (2006). Pattern of impaired working memory during major depression. *Journal of Affective Disorders, 90*, 149–161.

Roy-Byrne, P. P., Weingartner, H., Bierer, L. M., Thompson, K., & Post, R. M. (1986). Effortful and automatic cognitive processes in depression. *Archives of General Psychiatry, 43*, 265–267.

Rubinsztein, J. S., Michael, A., Paykel, E. S., & Sahakian, B. J. (2000). Cognitive impairment in remission in bipolar affective disorder. *Psychological Medicine, 30*(5), 1025–1036.

Rude, S. S., Wentzlaff, R. M., Gibbs, B., Vane, J., & Whitney, T. (2002). Negative processing biases predict subsequent depressive symptoms. *Cognition & Emotion, 16*, 423–440.

Ruo, B., Rumsfeld, J. S., Hlatky, M. K., Liu, H., Browner, W. S., & Whooley, M. A. (2003). Depressive symptoms and health-related quality of life: The heart and soul study. *JAMA: Journal of the American Medical Association, 290*(2), 215–221.

Sadavoy, J. (2004). *Psychotropic drugs and the elderly*. New York: Norton, & Company.

Saghafi, R., Brown, C., Butters, M. A., Cyranowski, J., Dew, M. A., Frank, E., et al. (2007). Predicting 6-week treatment response to escitalopram pharmacotherapy in late-life major depressive disorder. *International Journal of Geriatric Psychiatry, 11*, 1141–1146.

Sapolsky, R. (2000). Glucocorticoids and hippocampal atrophy in neuropsychiatric disorders. *Archives of General Psychiatry, 57*, 925–935.

Sapolsky, R. M. (2001). Depression, antidepressants, and the shrinking hippocampus. *Proceedings of National Academy of the Sciences of the United States of America, 98*, 12320–12322.

Schlaepfer, T. E., Cohen, M. X., Frick, C., Kosel, M., Brodesser, D., Axmacher, N., et al. (2007). Deep brain stimulation to reward circuitry alleviates anhedonia in refractory major depression. *Neuropsychopharmacology, 33*, 368–377.

Schretlen, D. J., Cascella, N.G., Meyer, S. M., Kingery, L. R., Testa, S. M., Munro, C. A., et al. (2007). Neuropsychological functioning in bipolar disorder and schizophrenia. *Biological Psychiatry, 62*, 179–186.

Sevigny, M., Everett, J., & Grondin, S. (2003). Depression, attention, and time estimation. *Brain and Cognition, 53*, 351–353.

Shah, P., Ebmeier, K., Glabus, M., & Goodwin, G. (1998). Cortical grey matter reductions associated with treatment-resistant chronic unipolar depression: Controlled magnetic resonance imaging study. *British Journal of Psychiatry, 172*, 527–532.

Shah, P. J., Glabus, M. F., Goodwin, G. M., & Ebmeier, K. P. (2002). Chronic, treatment-resistant depression and right fronto-striatal atrophy. *British Journal of Psychiatry, 180*, 434–440.

Sheline, Y. (2003). Neuroimaging studies of mood disorder effects on the brain. *Biological Psychiatry, 54*, 338–352.

Sheline, Y., Barch, D., Donnelly, J., Ollinger, J., Snyder, A., & Mintun, M. A. (2001). Increased amygdala response to masked emotional faces in depressed subjects resolves with antidepressant treatment: An fMRI study. *Biological Psychiatry, 50*, 651–658.

Sheline, Y. I., Barch, D. M., Garcia, K., Gersing, K., Pieper, C., Welsh-Bohmer, K., et al. (2006). Cognitive function in late life depression: Relationships to depression severity, cerebrovascular risk factors, and processing speed. *Biological Psychiatry, 60*, 58–65.

Sheline, Y. I., Gado, M. H., & Kraemer, H. C. (2003). Untreated depression and hippocampal volume loss. *American Journal of Psychiatry, 160*, 1516–1518.

Siegle, G. J., Carter, C. S., & Thase, M. E. (2006). Use of fMRI to predict recovery from unipolar depression with cognitive behavior therapy 145. *American Journal of Psychiatry, 163*, 735–738.

Siegle, G. J., Steinhauer, S. R., Thase, M. E., Stenger, A., & Carter, C. S. (2002). Can't shake that feeling: Event-related fMRI assessment of sustained amygdala activity in response to emotional information in depressed individuals. *Biological Psychiatry, 51*, 693–707.

Simpson, S. W., Baldwin, R. C., Burns, A., & Jackson, A. (2001). Regional cerebral volume measurements in late-life depression: Relationship to clinical correlates, neuropsychological impairment and response to treatment. *International Journal of Geriatric Psychiatry, 16*, 469–476.

Sjogren, P., Olsen, A. K., Thomsen, A. B., & Dalberg, J. (2000). Neuropsychological performance in cancer patients: The role of oral opioids, pain and performance status. *Pain, 86*, 237–245.

Smith, K. A., Morris, J. S., Friston, K. J., Cowen, P. J., & Dolan, R. J. (1999). Brain mechanisms associated with depressive relapse and associated cognitive impairment following acute tryptophan depletion. *British Journal of Psychiatry, 174*, 525–529.

Sobin, C., & Sackeim, H. A. (1997). Psychomotor symptoms of depression. *American Journal of Psychiatry, 154*, 4–17.

Sobow, T., Wojtera, M., & Kloszewska, I. (2006). Prevalence of potentially reversible cognitive function disorders in patients of a memory dysfunction clinic. *Psychiatria Polska, 40*, 845–854.

Sonino, N., & Fava, G. A. (1996). Serotonin, Cushing's disease, and depression. *Psychotherapy and Psychosomatics, 65*, 63–65.

Sonino, N., Fava, G. A., Belluardo, P., Girelli, M. E., & Boscaro, M. (1993). Course of depression in Cushings-Syndrome—response to treatment and comparison with Graves-Disease. *Hormone Research, 39*, 202–206.

Spiegel, D. (2001). Mind matters: Coping and cancer progression. *Journal of Psychosomatic Research, 50*(5), 287–290.

Starkman, M. N., Giordani, B., Berent, S., Schork, M. A., & Schteingart, D. E. (2001). Elevated cortisol levels in Cushing's disease are associated with cognitive decrements. *Psychosomatic Medicine, 63*, 985–993.

Starkman, M. N., Giordani, B., Gebarski, S. S., Berent, S., Schork, M. A., & Schteingart, D. E. (1999).

Decrease in cortisol reverses human hippocampal atrophy following treatment of Cushing's disease. *Biological Psychiatry, 46*, 1595–1602.

Starkman, M. N., Giordani, B., Gebarski, S. S., & Schteingart, D. E. (2003). Improvement in learning associated with increase in hippocampal formation volume. *Biological Psychiatry, 53*, 233–238.

Starkman, M. N., Giordani, B., Gebarski, S. S., & Schteingart, D. E. (2007). Improvement in mood and ideation associated with increase in right caudate volume. *Journal of Affective Disorders, 101*, 139–147.

Starkman, M. N., Schteingart, D. E., & Schork, M. A. (1981). Depressed mood and other psychiatric manifestations of Cushing's syndrome: Relationship to hormone levels. *Psychosomatic Medicine, 43*, 3–18.

Starkman, M. N., Schteingart, D. E., & Schork, M. A. (1986). Cushing's syndrome after treatment: Changes in cortisol and ACTH levels, and amelioration of the depressive syndrome. *Psychiatry Research, 19*, 177–188.

Steffens, D. C., McQuoid, D. R., Welsh-Bohmer, K. A., & Krishnan, K. R. (2003). Left orbital frontal cortex volume and performance on the benton visual retention test in older depressives and controls. *Neuropsychopharmacology, 28*, 2179–2183.

Stockmeier, C. A., Mahajan, G. J., Konick, L. C., Overholser, J. C., Jurjus, G. J., Meltzer, H. Y., et al. (2004). Cellular changes in the postmortem hippocampus in major depression. *Biological Psychiatry, 56*, 640–650.

Suhr, J. A. (2003). Neuropsychological impairment in fibromyalgia: Relation to depression, fatigue, and pain. *Journal of Psychosomatic Research, 55*(4), 321–329.

Sumanti, M., Boone, K. B., Savodnik, I., & Gorsuch, R. (2006). Noncredible psychiatric and cognitive symptoms in a workers' compensation "stress" claim sample. *Clinical Neuropsychologist, 20*, 754–765.

Sweeney, J. A., Kmiec, J. A., & Kupfer, D. J. (2000). Neuropsychologic impairments in bipolar and unipolar mood disorders on the CANTAB neurocognitive battery. *Biological Psychiatry, 48*, 674–685.

Sweet, R.A., Hamilton, R.L., Butters, M.A., Mulsant, B.H., Pollock, B.G. et al. (2004) Neuropathologic correlates of late-onset major depression. *Neuropschopharmacology, 29*, 2242–2250.

Taylor, B. P., Bruder, G. E., Stewart, J. W., McGrath, P. J., Halperin, J., Ehrlichman, H., et al. (2006). Psychomotor slowing as a predictor of fluoxetine nonresponse in depressed outpatients. *American Journal of Psychiatry, 163*, 73–78.

Thomas, K., Drevets, W., Dahl, R. E., Ryan, N., Birmaher, B., Eccard, C., et al. (2001). Amygdala response to fearful faces in anxious and depressed children. *Archives of General Psychiatry, 58,* 1057–1063.

Thomsen, A. F., Kvist, T. K., Andersen, P. K., & Kessing, L. V. (2006). Increased relative risk of subsequent affective disorders in patients with a hospital diagnosis of obesity. *International Journal of Obesity, 30*(9), 1415–1421.

Torrent, C., Martinez-Aran, A., Daban, C., Sanchez-Moreno, J., Comes, M., Goikolea, J. M., et al. (2006). Cognitive impairment in bipolar II disorder. *British Journal of Psychiatry, 189,* 254–259.

Townend, E., Brady, M., & McLaughlan, K. (2007). Exclusion and inclusion criteria for people with aphasia in studies of depression after stroke: A systematic review and future recommendations. *Neuroepidemiology, 29,* 1–17.

Tucker, G., Popkin, M., Caine, E., Folstein, M., & Grant, I. (1990). Reorganizing the "organic" disorders. *Hospital & Community Psychiatry, 41,* 722–724.

Turk, D. C., & Brody, M. C. (1992). What position do APS's physician members take on chronic pain opioid therapy? *APS Bulletin, 2,* 1–5.

Twycross, R. G. (1994). Opioids. In P. D. Wall and R. Melzack (Eds.), *Textbook of pain* (3rd ed., pp. 943–962). Edinburgh, Scotland: Churchill Livingsone.

Vadnal, V. L. (2005). Depression and effort in the elderly. Unpublished senior honor's thesis, University of Michigan.

Vainio, A., Ollila, J., Matikainen, E., Rosenberg, P., & Kalso, E. (1995). Driving ability in cancer patients receiving long-term morphine analgesia. *Lancet, 346,* 667–670.

Van Praag, H. M., Korf, J., Lakke, J., & Schut, T. (1975). Dopamine metabolism in depression, psychoses, and Parkinson's disease: The problem of specificity of biological variables in behavior disorders. *Psychological Medicine, 5,* 138–146.

Videbech, P. (2000). PET measurements of brain glucose metabolism and blood flow in major depressive disorder: A critical review. *Acta Psychiatrica Scandinavica, 101,* 11–20.

Videbech, P., & Ravnkilde, B. (2004). Hippocampal volume and depression: A meta-analysis of MRI studies. *American Journal of Psychiatry, 161,* 1957–1966.

Vinkers, D.J., Stek, M.L., Gussekloo, J., Van Der Mast, R.C., Westendorp, R.G. (2004). Does depression in old age increase only cardiovascular mortality? The Leiden 85-plus Study. *International Journal of Geriatric Psychiatry, 19,* 852–857.

Vinkers, D.J., Stek, M.L., van der Mast, R.C., de Craen, A.J., Le Cessie, S. (2005). Generalized atherosclerosis, cognitive decline, and depressive symptoms in old age. *Neurology, 65,* 107–112.

Volkow, N. D., Wang, G. J., Hitzemann, R., Fowler, J. S., Pappas, N., Lowrimore, P., et al. (1995). Depression of thalamic metabolism by lorazepam is associated with sleepiness. *Neuropsychopharmacology, 12,* 123–132.

Vythilingam, M., Vermetten, E., Anderson, G. M., Luckenbaugh, D., Anderson, E. R., Snow, J., et al. (2004). Hippocampal volume, memory, and cortisol status in major depressive disorder: Effects of treatment. *Biological Psychiatry, 56,* 101–112.

Wadsworth, E. J., Moss, S. C., Simpson, S. A., & Smith, A. P. (2005). SSRIs and cognitive performance in a working sample. *Human Psychopharmacology, 20,* 561–572.

Wagner, G., Sinsel, E., Sobanski, T., Kohler, S., Marinou, V., Mentzel, H. J., et al. (2006). Cortical inefficiency in patients with unipolar depression: An event-related MRI study with the Stroop task. *Biological Psychiatry, 59,* 958–965.

Watkins, P. C., Mathews, A., Williamson, D. A., & Fuller, R. D. (1992). Mood-congruent memory in depression—emotional priming or elaboration. *Journal of Abnormal Psychology, 101,* 581–586.

Watkins, P. C., Vache, K., Verney, S. P., Muller, S., & Mathews, A. (1996). Unconscious mood-congruent memory bias in depression. *Journal of Abnormal Psychology, 105,* 34–41.

Watson, S., Thompson, J. M., Ritchie, J. C., Ferrier, I. N., & Young, A. H. (2006). Neuropsychological impairment in bipolar disorder: The relationship with glucocorticoid receptor function. *Bipolar Disorders, 8,* 85–90.

Weiland-Fiedler, P., Erickson, K., Waldeck, T., Luckenbaugh, D. A., Pike, D., Bonne, O., et al. (2004). Evidence for continuing neuropsychological impairments in depression. *Journal of Affective Disorders, 82,* 253–258.

Weingartner, H., Cohen, R. M., Murphy, D. L., Martello, J., & Gerdt, C. (1981). Cognitive processes in depression. *Archives of General Psychiatry, 38,* 42–47.

Whalen, J. (1998). Masked presentation of emotional facial expressions modulate amygdala activity without explicit knowledge. *Journal of Neuroscience, 18,* 411–419.

White, J., Davison, G. C., Haaga, D. A., & White, K. (1992). Cognitive bias in the articulated thoughts of depressed and nondepressed psychiatric patients. *Journal of Nervous & Mental Disease, 180,* 77–81.

Wiart, L. (1997). Post-cerebrovascular stroke depression. *Encephale, 23,* 51–54.

Wilson, R.S., Mendes De Leon, C.F., Bennett, D.A., Bienias, J.L., Evans, D.A. (2004). Depressive symptoms and cognitive decline in a community population of older persons. *Journal of Neurology, Neurosurgery, and Psychiatry, 75,* 126–129.

Wilson, R.S., Arnold, S.E., Beck, T.L., Bienias, J.L., Bennett, D.A. (2008). Change in depressive symptoms during the prodromal phase of Alzheimer disease. *Archives of General Psychiatry, 65,* 439–445.

Wright, C. I., Fischer, H., Whalen, P. J., McInerney, S. C., Shin, L. M., & Rauch, S. L. (2001). Differential prefrontal cortex and amygdala habituation to repeatedly presented emotional stimuli. *Neuroreport: For Rapid Communication of Neuroscience Research, 12,* 379–383.

Wright, S. L., & Persad, C. (2007). Distinguishing between depression and dementia in older persons: Neuropsychological and neuropathological correlates. *Journal of Geriatric Psychiatry and Neurology, 20*(4), 189–198.

Yohannes, A. M., Baldwin, R. C., & Connolly, M. J. (2000). Mood disorders in elderly patients with chronic obstructive pulmonary disease. *Reviews in Clinical Gerontology, 10*(2), 193–202.

Young, A. H., Gallagher, P., Watson, S., Del-Estal, D., Owen, B. M., & Ferrier, I. N. (2004). Improvements in neurocognitive function and mood following adjunctive treatment with mifepristone (RU-486) in bipolar disorder. *Neuropsychopharmacology, 29,* 1538–1545.

Young, E. A., Carlson, N., & Brown, M. B. (2001). Twenty-four hour ACTH and cortisol pulsatility in depressed women. *Neuropsychopharmacology, 25,* 267–276.

Young, E. A., Haskett, R. F., Grunhaus, L., Pande, A., Weinberg, V. M., Watson, S. J., et al. (1994). Increased circadian activation of the hypothalamic pituitary adrenal axis in depressed patients in the evening. *Archives of General Psychiatry, 51,* 701–707.

Young, E. A., Haskett, R. F., Murphy-Weinberg, V., Watson, S. J., & Akil, H. (1991). Loss of glucocorticoid fast feedback in depression. *Archives of General Psychiatry, 48,* 693–699.

Zacny, J. P. (1995). A review of the effects of opioids on psychomotor and cognitive functioning in humans. *Experimental and Clinical Psychopharmacology, 3*(4), 432–466.

Zacny, J. P., Lichtor, J. L., & Thapar, P. (1994). Comparing the subjective, psychomotor and physiological effects of intravenous butorphanol and morphine in healthy volunteers. *Journal of Pharmacology and Experimental Therapeutics, 270,* 579–588.

Zubieta, J., Huguelet, P., O'Neil, R. L., & Giordani, B. J. (2001). Cognitive function in euthymic bipolar I disorder. *Psychiatry Research, 102,* 9–20.

23

The Neuropsychology of Memory Dysfunction and Its Assessment

David P. Salmon and Larry R. Squire

Introduction

Memory impairment is a common consequence of neurological injury or disease (Strub & Black, 1977) and is often reported in association with affective (Sternberg & Jarvik, 1976; Stromgren, 1977) and other psychiatric (Aleman et al., 1999; Chapman, 1966) disorders. It may also occur as a side effect of treatments such as psychotropic drugs and electroconvulsive therapy (ECT) (Sackeim, 2000; Squire, 1986). Given the pervasive and pernicious nature of memory dysfunction in neuropsychiatric disorders, it is not surprising that memory impairment has been the subject of extensive clinical research. This research has shown that, when memory disorders are evaluated with quantitative methods, it becomes possible to identify the various disorders that can occur, to understand the similarities and differences between them, and to follow their course reliably in individual patients (for reviews, see Butters et al., 1995; Mayes, 1988; Squire & Schacter, 2002; Verfaellie & O'Connor, 2000). These possibilities have been realized largely through the application of principles developed in the field of cognitive neuroscience. Thus, the purpose of this chapter is twofold. First, to elucidate a rationale for the neuropsychological evaluation of memory dysfunction that is grounded in basic cognitive neuroscience research. Second, to identify and describe neuropsychological tools of memory testing that are widely used in clinical settings. Before discussing these issues, we describe the phenomenology of memory dysfunction and its underlying causes.

The Amnesic Syndrome

Although memory dysfunction most often occurs as one of a constellation of disorders of intellectual function, as in depression or dementia, it can sometimes occur as a relatively pure entity. When this occurs, patients with memory dysfunction due to neurological injury or disease can have severe deficits in the ability to learn and retain new information (i.e., anterograde amnesia) but can appear cognitively normal to casual observation. In conversation, they can exhibit appropriate social skills and exhibit normal language ability. They can also have normal intelligence as measured by conventional IQ tests and, importantly, a normal ability to hold information in immediate memory (Butters & Cermak, 1980; Shrager et al., 2008). These characteristics of the amnesic syndrome are illustrated in one of the best known cases of circumscribed amnesia, patient H.M., a man who developed severe anterograde amnesia after neurosurgery carried out to relieve severe epilepsy (Scoville & Milner, 1957). Following bilateral medial temporal lobe resection, H.M. was unable to retain memory for events and information encountered after his surgery. Despite this profound anterograde amnesia, H.M. retained an above-average IQ, intact immediate memory, and normal problem-solving and language functions, including the ability to detect various kinds of linguistic ambiguity (e.g., "Racing cars can be dangerous" or "Charging tigers should be avoided" [Lackner, 1974; also see Schmolck et al., 2000]). H.M. also had acute awareness of his memory deficit and insight into its nature. In an often-quoted passage, he expressed his own experience of his memory disorder:

Right now, I'm wondering. Have I done or said anything amiss? You see, at this moment everything looks clear to me, but what happened just before? That's what worries me. It's like waking from a dream; I just don't remember. (Milner, 1970, p. 37)

Another important feature of the amnesic syndrome exhibited by H.M. was an inability to remember events that occurred prior to the onset of his amnesia (Corkin, 1984). This retrograde amnesia extended back several years prior to his surgery at age 27 but was time-limited, as he was capable of recalling well-formed autobiographical episodes from his adolescence. Subsequent research has shown that retrograde amnesia can be relatively circumscribed and limited to just a few months or years, or it can be extensive and affect many decades prior to the onset of amnesia (Bayley et al., 2006; Squire & Bayley, 2007). In addition, retrograde amnesia is typically temporally graded with older memories less affected than more recent memories. It should be noted, however, that the temporal characteristics of retrograde amnesia are difficult to determine in memory disorders that have a gradual onset (e.g., dementia of Alzheimer's disease) because the distinction between anterograde and retrograde amnesia is always blurred. In these cases, it becomes difficult to determine if information is unavailable because it was not acquired in the first place (anterograde amnesia) or because it was acquired initially and then later lost as the result of the onset of amnesia (retrograde amnesia).

Because many patients with memory dysfunction have insight into their condition, a useful way to obtain information about the scope of their memory loss and the relationship between anterograde and retrograde amnesia is to construct a time line of the deficit with the patient's assistance. This technique was used to good advantage by Barbizet (1970) as a way of identifying what past time periods were affected in an amnesic patient who had suffered a severe closed head injury. The method revealed the approximate duration of both anterograde and retrograde amnesia, and showed how the deficit changed with the passage of time. In this particular case, anterograde amnesia affected about 2 ½ months postinjury and remained fixed for this period of time, even after memory capacities had largely recovered. Presumably, this reflected the time when memories for events could not be formed in the normal way due to the neurologic injury. Retrograde amnesia was initially severe and extensive but gradually shrank to 2 weeks with oldest memories recovering first.

Patient interviews revealed a similar relationship between anterograde and retrograde amnesia in severely depressed patients undergoing a prescribed course of bilateral ECT. Thirty-one patients were interviewed about their memory before ECT, and again 7 months and 3 years after treatment. Before treatment, patients on average reported having difficulty remembering the 5 months prior to ECT, presumably because of their depressive illness. Seven months after ECT, patients reported difficulty remembering events that occurred during the 3 months after treatment and during the 2 years preceding. Three years later, retrograde amnesia had shrunk to about pre-ECT level and anterograde amnesia remained fixed at 2 months (Squire & Slater, 1983).

Although these examples show that there can be recovery of memory function over time following certain amnesia-precipitating events (e.g., ECT, traumatic brain injury), in many cases extensive anterograde and retrograde amnesia are permanent. The profound anterograde amnesia and time-limited retrograde amnesia exhibited by patient H.M., for example, has not abated after more than 50 years (Corkin, 2002). Indeed, it appears that if specific brain structures thought to underlie memory processes are destroyed, the amnesic syndrome will be a permanent condition. If these structures are made temporarily dysfunctional by ECT or vascular deficiencies or only partially or reversibly damaged by a closed head injury, some recovery of memory function can occur. The characteristics of different causes of amnesia are described further in the following section.

Causes of Amnesia

Amnesia can occur for a variety of reasons that include temporal lobe surgery, chronic alcohol abuse, head injury, anoxia or ischemia, encephalitis, epilepsy, tumor, or vascular accident (for review, see Kopelman, 2002). In addition, amnesia is typically a prominent and early sign of dementia associated with Alzheimer's disease and other neurodegenerative disorders (for review, see Salmon, 2000). Although the list of various etiologies for memory dysfunction is long, they have in common their adverse effect on a core set of neurological structures that are critical for memory, as described below.

Medial Temporal Lobe Amnesia

The profound amnesia experienced by patient H.M. following bilateral medial temporal lobe resection to treat severe epilepsy provided the first evidence that structures within this brain region are critical for human memory. Bilateral hippocampal damage was often identified as the critical factor leading to his amnesia, but the medial temporal lobe resection was extensive and damaged not only the hippocampus but also the amygdala and adjacent medial temporal cortex (Scoville & Milner, 1957). The relative importance of these structures for his memory impairment could not be determined.

Subsequent studies of patients with more restricted medial temporal lobe damage have provided additional information about the role of the hippocampus itself in memory (e.g., Zola-Morgan et al., 1986). Patient R.B. became amnesic in 1978 at the age of 52 after an episode of global ischemia that occurred as a complication of open-heart surgery. Extensive neuropsychological assessment during the next 5 years revealed significant memory impairment in the absence of other cognitive dysfunction (see Figure 23–1). Upon his death in 1983, histological examination of R.B.'s brain revealed a discrete bilateral lesion that involved the full rostrocaudal extent of the CA1 field of the hippocampus. Other medial temporal lobe structures and other brain regions were unaffected. This was the first reported case of human amnesia documented by extensive neuropsychological testing that occurred as a consequence of neuropathologically verified damage restricted to the hippocampus. Subsequent neurohistological studies have confirmed the link between memory dysfunction and bilateral hippocampal damage (Gold & Squire, 2006; Rempel-Clower et al., 1996; Victor & Agamanolis, 1990).

The results of these studies indicate that the hippocampus is a critical structure for memory and that damage limited to the hippocampus is sufficient to produce easily detectable and

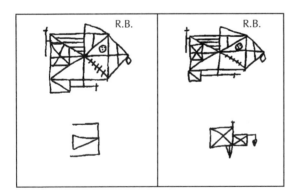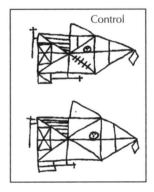

Figure 23–1. Performance of patient R.B. on two separate administrations of the Rey–Osterreith Complex Figure Test. R.B. was first asked to copy the figure (top portions of the left and center panels) and then to reproduce the figure from memory 10–20 minutes later (bottom portion of left and center panels). The two administrations of the test were 6 months (left panel) and 23 months (center panel) after the onset of his amnesia. In both instances, R.B.'s delayed recall of the figure was severely impaired relative to the performance of an age-matched normal control subject (right panel). (Adapted from Zola-Morgan et al., 1986).

clinically significant memory impairment. It is important to note, however, that none of the patients with damage restricted to the hippocampus was as severely amnesic as patient H.M. This suggests that medial temporal lobe structures outside of the hippocampus itself must be important for memory function. This notion was confirmed in studies of an animal model of human amnesia in the monkey (Squire & Zola-Morgan, 1991). This work identified important structures in addition to the hippocampal region itself. (The hippocampal region includes the hippocampus proper, the dentate gyrus, and the subiculum). The additional important structures are the adjacent entorhinal, parahippocampal, and perirhinal cortices. The amygdala is not a component of this memory system.

Diencephalic Amnesia

Damage to the midline of the diencephalon can produce severe amnesia. The most widely studied example of diencephalic amnesia is Korsakoff's syndrome, which can develop after many years of chronic alcohol abuse and nutritional deficiency (Victor et al., 1989). Korsakoff's syndrome is characterized by profound anterograde amnesia and extensive, temporally graded retrograde amnesia (with relative preservation of older remote memories). Neuropathological studies have shown that the syndrome is associated with bilateral damage along the diencephalic midline, especially hemorrhagic lesions in the dorsomedial thalamic and mammillary nuclei (Mair et al., 1979; Mayes, 1988). Additional studies with humans and experimental animals confirm the importance of medial thalamic structures, such as the mediodorsal nucleus, the anterior nucleus, and the connections and structures within the internal medullary lamina (Gold & Squire, 2006; Markowitsch, 1988; Zola-Morgan & Squire, 1993).

The amnesic syndrome associated with Korsakoff's syndrome is similar to that of medial temporal lobe amnesia in many respects (Butters & Cermak, 1980). Although early studies raised the possibility that differences might exist in the rate of forgetting within long-term memory, more recent studies of patients with radiologically confirmed lesions indicated that forgetting from long-term memory occurs at an equivalent rate for patients with diencephalic and medial temporal lobe amnesia (Kopelman & Stanhope, 1997; McKee & Squire, 1992) (see Figure 23–2). This finding is entirely compatible with the well-known observation that in amnesia information is rapidly lost as it moves from short-term to long-term memory (e.g., Isaac & Mayes, 1999).

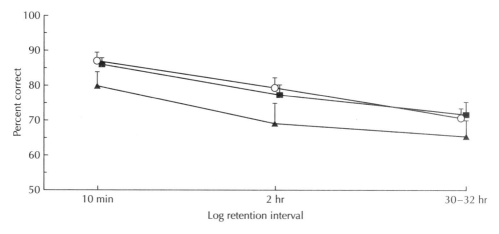

Figure 23–2. The performance of patients with medial temporal lobe amnesia (solid triangles; n = 5), patients with diencephalic amnesia (solid squares; n = 6), and normal control subjects (open circles; n = 10) at three retention delays averaged across four different visual recognition memory tests. The two amnesic patient groups exhibited equivalent rates of forgetting within long-term memory after performance was equated at the shortest delay. (Adapted from McKee & Squire, 1992).

In this sense, all the "organic" amnesias are syndromes of rapid forgetting. At present, there is no compelling basis for separating medial temporal lobe and diencephalic amnesia according to behavioral findings. Certainly, it is reasonable to suppose that the medial temporal lobe and the diencephalic midline should make different contributions to normal memory. However, each region may also be an essential component in a larger functional system such that similar amnesia results from damage to any component.

Although diencephalic and medial temporal lobe damage appear to produce similar memory deficits, there are ways in which Korsakoff's syndrome differs from other forms of amnesia. As one of the first serious students of Korsakoff's syndrome, Talland (1965) wrote that memory dysfunction in these patients "does not present simply a derangement in memory" (p. 108). Similarly, Zangwill (1977) suggested that "other and more extensive psychological dysfunction must coexist with amnesia for the classic picture of Korsakoff's syndrome to emerge" (p. 113). These observations were confirmed in subsequent neuropsychological studies that showed signs of frontal lobe impairment in these patients that influenced memory test performance (Moscovitch, 1982; Oscar-Berman et al., 2004; Schacter, 1987; Shimamura et al., 1991; Squire, 1982). These findings suggest that neuropsychological examination of patients with memory impairment must take into account the idea that etiologically distinct forms of amnesia can present with nonmemory deficits that are superimposed on primary memory dysfunction.

Transient Global Amnesia

Amnesia is not always permanent. Transient global amnesia (TGA) is a disorder quite similar to the neurological amnesia just discussed that usually begins suddenly and lasts for only several hours (Hodges & Ward, 1989; Kritchevsky, 1989; for review, see Jager et al., 2008). The memory impairment is characterized by severe anterograde amnesia and a temporally graded retrograde amnesia that extends over as much as 20 years prior to the onset episode. After the episode, there is full recovery of memory

functions. However, patients are left with a gap in their memory for events that occurred during the period of anterograde amnesia, presumably because usable long-term memory was not being formed. They may also have a permanent retrograde amnesia for events that occurred from a few hours to a day or two just prior to the episode (Kritchevsky, 1989). Although the precise cause of TGA is not known, it generally occurs in persons over age 50 (the annual incidence is 23.5 per 100,000 for persons older than 50) and is thought to be related to vascular factors that affect the medial temporal lobe or diencephalic memory system (Bettermann, 2006; Hodges & Warlow, 1990). However, patients who have had an episode of TGA do not have an increased risk of developing permanent memory dysfunction or of having a subsequent stroke.

Electroconvulsive Therapy

Transient amnesia also occurs after ECT, which is sometimes prescribed for severe depressive illness (for reviews, see Fraser et al., 2008; Sackeim, 2000; Squire, 1986). Anterograde amnesia associated with ECT can be quite severe, particularly in patients who receive bilateral treatments. Retrograde amnesia can also be quite severe and temporally graded with more recent memories most affected (Fraser et al., 2008). New learning capacity recovers within the months following ECT, and persisting impairment in new learning is not detected after this time. Retrograde amnesia also resolves by 6 to 9 months after ECT, although memory for events that occurred during the weeks just preceding ECT can be permanently affected and there may be some spotty memory loss for even earlier time periods. Although the biological basis of ECT-associated memory impairment is not known with certainty, it is likely to be due to transient electrophysiological abnormalities in the medial temporal lobe structures important for memory function (Abrams & Essman, 1982; Lerer et al., 1984; Malitz & Sackeim, 1986).

Alzheimer's Disease

Alzheimer's disease (AD) is an age-related degenerative brain disorder that is characterized by neocortical atrophy, neuron and synapse loss, and abnormal deposition of senile plaques and neurofibrillary tangles (Terry & Katzman, 1983; Terry et al., 1991). These neuropathological changes are thought to usually begin in the hippocampus and entorhinal cortex, and gradually spread to association cortices of the frontal, temporal, and parietal lobes (Braak & Braak, 1991; Hyman et al., 1984). Consistent with this neuropathology, the primary clinical manifestation of AD is a profound global dementia characterized by severe amnesia and additional deficits in language, "executive" functions, attention, and visuospatial and constructional abilities (see Bondi et al., this volume). Because AD is estimated to affect approximately 10% of the population over the age of 65 (Evans et al., 1989), it is the most common cause of severe memory dysfunction.

Despite the global nature of the cognitive dysfunction evident in AD, a disorder of memory is clearly the most prevalent and prominent feature of the early stages of the disease. The memory deficit is similar in many respects to that associated with circumscribed amnesia due to medial temporal lobe damage. For example, neuropsychological testing of AD patients reveals significant declines in their ability to learn and retain new verbal or nonverbal information (i.e., anterograde amnesia), as well as deficits in the ability to recollect information from their recent past (i.e., retrograde amnesia) (Salmon, 2000). Unlike patients with medial temporal lobe amnesia, however, memory for concepts, meaning of words, and remotely acquired factual information may also be impaired in patients with AD, even in the relatively early stages of the disease. In addition, patients with AD have early deficits in certain aspects of implicit memory (see following section on memory systems) that are intact in patients with circumscribed amnesia (Salmon et al., 1988; Shimamura et al., 1987).

A number of prospective longitudinal studies of cognitive function in nondemented older adults have shown that a decline in memory often occurs prior to the emergence of the obvious cognitive and behavioral changes required for a clinical diagnosis of AD (for review, see Twamley et al., 2006). In some cases, memory impairment becomes apparent many years prior to the onset of dementia (e.g., Bäckman et al., 2001). These and similar findings led to the development of formal criteria for amnestic Mild Cognitive Impairment (MCI; Peterson et al., 1995), a predementia condition in elderly individuals that is characterized by both subjective and objective memory impairment, which occurs in the face of relatively preserved general cognition and functional abilities (for reviews, see Albert & Blacker, 2006; Peterson et al., 2001). Presumably, the onset of this circumscribed amnesia corresponds to the development of AD pathology in medial temporal lobe structures (Devanand et al., 2007).

Frontal Lobe Memory Dysfunction

Damage to the prefrontal association cortex can result in memory dysfunction (for review, see Baldo & Shimamura, 2002). The memory deficit usually reflects poor planning and organization that leads to inefficient learning and retrieval strategies, increased susceptibility to interference, and poor retrieval of context (e.g., temporal order) or "source" of to-be-remembered information (Janowsky et al., 1989b). There are also deficits in attention and working memory (i.e., a limited-capacity memory system in which information that is the immediate focus of attention can be temporarily held and manipulated; Baddeley, 1986). The severe deficit in retention that characterizes medial temporal lobe and diencephalic amnesia is not present in frontal lobe memory dysfunction (Kopelman & Stanhope, 1997). Furthermore, patients with frontal lobe damage often show disproportionate deficits in free recall compared to recognition (Janowsky et al., 1989a; Shimamura et al., 1990; Wheeler et al., 1995). For example, Janowsky and colleagues (1989a) found that patients with frontal lobe lesions performed normally on the recognition version of a word list-learning task despite impaired performance on the free-recall version of the same task (see Figure 23–3). Patients with diencephalic or medial temporal lobe damage, in contrast, were impaired at both recall and recognition. These and similar results suggest that the memory impairment associated with frontal lobe damage does not represent a fundamental amnesic syndrome (Kopelman, 2002).

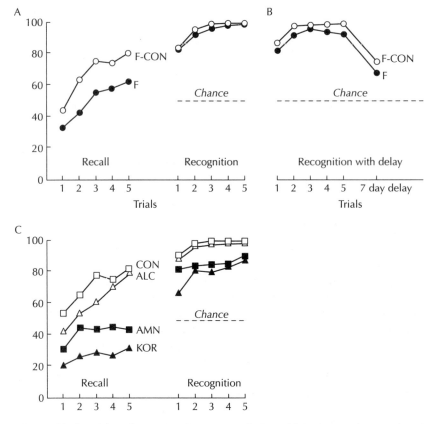

Figure 23–3. The performance of patients with frontal lobe lesions (F; n = 7) and their controls (F-CON; n = 11) on the recall and recognition components of the Rey Auditory Verbal Learning Test (AVLT) (Panel A: recall and recognition; Panel B: a second recognition test that includes a 7-day delay). Although free recall was impaired, recognition memory was not impaired. For comparison, the performance of patients with Korsakoff's syndrome (KOR; n = 7) or other amnesia (AMN; n = 5) and their controls (alcoholic controls, ALC; n = 8, and healthy controls, CON; n = 8, respectively) are also shown (Panel C). The amnesic Korsakoff patients and the other amnesic patients were impaired on both the recall and recognition components of the test. (Adapted from Janowsky et al., 1989a).

Traumatic Brain Injury

Memory dysfunction is common following traumatic brain injury (TBI), but usually occurs in conjunction with other cognitive deficits that may include a reduction in general intellectual capacity, disorders of language and visual perception, apraxia, impairment of attention, and personality change (for reviews, see Levin et al., 1982; Newcombe, 1983; Vakil, 2005). The presence of multiple disorders is consistent with the variable and widespread pattern of cerebral damage that can result from severe head injury.

The immediate aftermath of TBI is usually characterized by a period of posttraumatic amnesia (PTA) that includes confusion, disorientation, impaired attention, and an inability to learn new information or remember day-to-day events (Brooks, 1984). PTA can last from a few hours to several weeks but gradually clears. In some cases, however, residual memory impairment may persist for a number of years. According to Newcombe (1983), approximately 1% of TBI patients have persisting signs of impairment. The duration of PTA is the best available index of severity of injury and is a good predictor of eventual recovery (Jennett, 1976; Russell & Smith, 1961).

A number of studies have examined the long-term effect (beyond the episode of PTA) of moderate-to-severe TBI on learning and memory (for review, see Schacter & Crovitz, 1977; Vakil, 2005). In general, these studies have shown that, relative to healthy control subjects or control subjects with nonbrain traumatic injury (e.g., spinal cord injury), patients with TBI have deficits in both verbal and visual immediate memory, a decreased rate of learning across trials, and a faster rate of forgetting over a delay interval. These findings are illustrated in a study by Zec and colleagues (2001), which compared the performances of patients with TBI (an average of 10 years post-TBI), healthy control subjects and control subjects with spinal cord injury on a battery of memory tests that included the Wechsler Memory Scale-Revised (WMS-R) and the Rey Auditory Verbal Learning Test (AVLT). The TBI patients were impaired relative to the control groups on the Verbal Memory, Visual Memory, General Memory, and Delayed Memory indices of the WMS-R, and on learning rate and delayed recall measures from the Rey AVLT. Other studies have shown that rate of learning is impaired in patients with TBI when measured by free recall, but normal when assessed using cued recall procedures (Vakil & Oded, 2003). Studies using the Buschke-Fuld Selective Reminding Test indicate that the learning deficit may be due to inconsistent recall (Levin et al., 1979). Thus, inefficient organization and learning strategies may be the primary reason for the learning impairment exhibited by patients with TBI (Vakil, 2005). Although faster forgetting in patients with TBI compared to controls has been reported in numerous studies (e.g., Carlesimo et al., 1997; Crosson et al., 1988; Vakil et al., 1992; Vanderploeg et al., 2001), it may not be apparent if groups are equated for initial level of performance in the immediate memory condition (DeLuca et al., 2000). These latter findings have led some investigators to suggest that at least a subset of patients with TBI have memory deficits similar to those associated with prefrontal association cortex damage rather than fundamental anterograde amnesia (Vakil, 2005).

Retrograde amnesia associated with TBI is thought to be quite prevalent (Carlesimo et al., 1998) but has not been widely studied. In one of the few group studies reported, Carlesimo and colleagues (1998) found that 20 patients with TBI were impaired relative to 20 healthy control subjects in recalling remote autobiographical information and well-known public events and people. This retrograde amnesia was extensive but did not follow a temporal gradient typical of medial temporal lobe or diencephalic amnesia. Russell and Nathan (1946) in their classic study of memory impairment associated with head injury make several points about the relationship between anterograde and retrograde amnesia. First, on the basis of 972 of cases of head injury, where information was available about memory loss, it was found that retrograde amnesia was typically brief, covering a period of less than 30 minutes in 90% of the cases. Second, the longer the anterograde amnesia, the longer the retrograde amnesia. Third, retrograde amnesia was more severe in closed (concussive) head injury than in gunshot wounds or other cases of penetrating brain injury. Fourth, during the period of amnesia, neither the anterograde nor retrograde component of memory loss could be influenced significantly by hypnosis or barbiturate drugs. This latter finding suggests that the memory impairment has a neurological rather than functional basis (e.g., compensation neurosis).

Functional Amnesia

Functional amnesia, also known as dissociative amnesia, is a dissociative psychiatric disorder that involves alterations in consciousness and identity (for review, see Brandt & van Gorp, 2006). Although no particular brain structure or brain system is implicated in functional amnesia, the cause of the disorder must be due to abnormal brain function of some kind. Its presentation varies considerably from individual to individual, but in most cases functional amnesia is preceded by physical or emotional trauma and occurs in association with some prior psychiatric history (Kritchevsky et al., 2004; Schacter et al., 1982). In many cases, the patient is in a confused or frightened state at the time of hospitalization. Functional amnesia is usually characterized by severe retrograde amnesia, especially for autobiographical information and personal identity. Semantic or factual knowledge about the world is often preserved, even though factual information about the patient's daily life is unavailable. Despite profound impairment in the ability to recall information about the past, the ability to learn new information is usually intact. The disorder sometimes clears and the lost memories return, but it can be long lasting with sizeable pieces of the past remaining unavailable.

Distinguishing between the "organic" (i.e., those based in physical brain damage) and the functional amnesias is rather straightforward because in the "organic" amnesias anterograde amnesia is severe, but loss of personal identity does not occur. The opposite is true in functional amnesia (Kopelman, 1995; Nemiah, 1980) (see Figure 23–4). Moreover, in "organic" amnesia retrograde amnesia is usually temporally graded, and public event memory and autobiographical memory are similarly affected. In functional amnesia, retrograde memory function is determined more by memory content than by when the information was acquired.

A Cognitive Neuroscience Framework for the Assessment of Memory Disorders

Memory is among the most studied and the best understood of the higher cortical functions (e.g., perception, attention, language, memory, and action). Although still very incomplete, our understanding of memory has grown significantly over the past several decades at both the cellular level in terms of cellular events and synaptic change and the systems (or neuropsychological) level in terms of brain systems and organization (for review, see Squire & Kandel, 2009). Accordingly, a good deal of relevant information about normal memory, and how it is organized in the brain, can be brought to bear when addressing memory disorders from the perspective of clinical neuropsychology. Two important concepts from cognitive neuroscience and cognitive psychology that have had a large impact on the assessment of memory disorders are the identification of neurologically distinct memory systems and the idea that there are psychologically distinct component processes involved in remembering information.

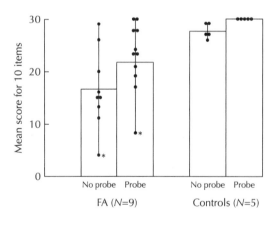
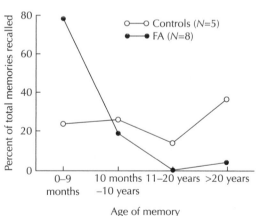

Figure 23–4. Patients with functional amnesia (FA) were impaired relative to healthy controls in their ability to recollect 10 autobiographical episodes (left panel). The quality of the recollections were scored (0 to 3 points) before (No Probe) and after (Probe) encouragement to produce as specific a recollection as possible (left panels; black circles indicate performance of individual subjects). In addition, patients with FA recalled most of their memories (i.e., those scored 3) from recent time periods (0–9 months after the onset of amnesia) and very few from the more distant past (right panel). This pattern is opposite to the temporal gradient often observed in patients with "organic" amnesia. (Adapted from Kritchevsky et al., 2004).

Memory Systems

One of the major contributions of cognitive neuroscience to the study of memory dysfunction and its assessment is the recognition that memory is not a unitary process mediated by a single neuroanatomical system, but rather a compilation of various subsystems that differ from one another in their rules of operation, in the types of information they process, and in their neuroanatomical substrates (for review, see Squire, 2004). These memory subsystems interact but are thought to be relatively independent and can be differentially impaired by disease or injury. Investigations of memory in impaired patient populations have served not only to validate this viewpoint but also to identify the neuroanatomical structures associated with different memory systems. Based on these studies, neuropsychological models of memory have been developed that provided a powerful conceptual framework for the clinical assessment and classification of the distinctive patterns of memory impairment observed in different neuropsychiatric disorders.

One organizational scheme for memory that has generated considerable theoretical and empirical interest is the distinction between declarative (or explicit) and nondeclarative (or implicit or procedural) forms of memory (Cohen & Squire, 1980; Squire & Zola, 1996; see Figure 23–5). Declarative memory refers to knowledge of episodes and facts that can be consciously recalled and related (i.e., declared) by the rememberer. It has been characterized as "knowing that" and includes such things as memory for the words on a recently presented list and knowledge that a dog is an animal. Nondeclarative memory, in contrast, is described as "knowing how" and pertains to an unconscious form of remembering that is expressed only through the performance of the specific operations comprising a particular task. The use of nondeclarative memory is indicated by the performance of a newly acquired motor, perceptual, or cognitive skill, for example, and by the unconscious facilitation in processing a stimulus that occurs following its previous presentation (i.e., priming).

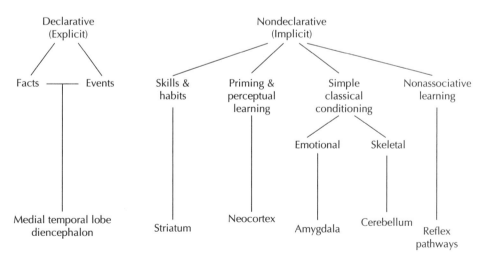

Figure 23–5. Classification of memory. Declarative (explicit) memory refers to conscious recollection of facts and events. Nondeclarative (implicit) memory refers to a heterogeneous collection of abilities that are expressed through performance rather than recollection. Experience alters behavior nonconsciously without providing access to memory content. (Adapted from Squire & Zola, 1996).

The distinction that has been drawn between declarative and nondeclarative memory is based not only on conceptual grounds but also on the dissociation of these two forms of memory in patients with circumscribed amnesia. Despite severe deficits in declarative memory, amnesic patients demonstrate relatively normal lexical and semantic priming (Graf et al., 1984; Levy et al., 2004; Shimamura, 1986; Tulving & Schacter, 1990) and a preserved ability to learn and retain a variety of motor, perceptual, and cognitive skills (e.g., Brooks & Baddeley, 1976; Cohen & Squire, 1980; Corkin, 1968; for review, see Squire, 2004). The preservation of nondeclarative memory in patients with circumscribed amnesia indicates that this form of memory does not rely on the same medial temporal and diencephalic brain structures that are thought to mediate declarative memory. Various forms of nondeclarative memory may be mediated by diverse brain structures, such as the neostriatum, the amygdala, the cerebellum, and the neocortex, structures that are directly involved in the initial processing and performance of particular tasks (Squire, 2004).

Declarative memory has been further dichotomized into episodic and semantic forms (Tulving, 1983). Episodic memory refers to the storage and recollection of temporally dated autobiographical events that depend upon temporal and/or spatial contextual cues for their retrieval. Examples of episodic memory include the ability to recall activities from the previous day and the ability to remember learning a list of words presented 10 minutes earlier. Semantic memory, in contrast, refers to our general fund of knowledge, which consists of overlearned facts and concepts that are not dependent upon contextual cues for retrieval. Knowledge of the meanings of words, the ability to name common objects, or to recollect well-known geographical, historical, and arithmetical facts are all examples of semantic memory.

Memory Processes

Another major contribution from cognitive psychology and neuroscience to the neuropsychological assessment of memory disorders is the notion that "memory" consists of a number of component processes that can be differentially affected by disease or injury in specific brain regions. Research in this area involves the examination of the component processes used in performing episodic memory tasks (e.g., encoding, storage, retrieval) and the relationship between episodic memory and other cognitive functions (e.g., "executive" functions or semantic memory). Two patients who superficially appear to display equivalent memory impairments according to a standardized test can have strikingly different processing deficits underlying their impairments. For example, Butters and colleagues (1985) showed that impairment in different processes may underlie the memory deficits associated with circumscribed amnesia and Huntington's disease (HD), a genetic neurodegenerative disorder producing basal ganglia atrophy that results in a movement disorder (i.e., chorea) and dementia.

Compared to normal control subjects, patients with HD and patients with amnesia were equally impaired on a word list-learning task when free recall was required, but patients with HD were significantly less impaired than the amnesic patients when memory was tested in a recognition format (see Figure 23–6). These results suggest that the memory deficit in HD patients may strongly involve an inability to initiate appropriate and systematic retrieval strategies (the need for which is reduced by recognition testing procedures), whereas the deficit in the amnesic patients, which is not ameliorated by recognition procedures, may involve problems with encoding and consolidation. Indeed, a number of studies have shown that patients with medial temporal lobe amnesia have similar degrees of impairment (relative to healthy controls) on both recall and recognition tasks consistent with an encoding/consolidation deficit (Kopelman et al., 2007; Manns et al., 2003; Wixted & Squire, 2004). As these examples show, experimental neuropsychological studies designed within the theoretical paradigms of cognitive psychology have yielded substantial insights into the processes involved in memory deficits. With these successes in mind, the construction of a number of standardized memory tests such as the California Verbal Learning Test (Delis et al., 1987), the Selective Reminding Tests (Buschke & Fuld, 1974), and the Wechsler Memory Scale-Revised and Wechsler Memory

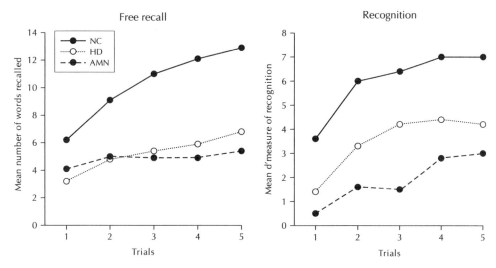

Figure 23–6. The performance of patients with circumscribed amnesia (AMN), patients with Huntington's disease (HD), and normal control (NC) subjects on the free-recall (left panel) and recognition (right panel) components of the Rey Auditory Verbal Learning Test. The HD and AMN patients were similarly impaired in the recall condition, but the HD patients were less impaired than the AMN patients in the recognition condition. This finding suggests that ineffective retrieval (as opposed to encoding or storage deficits) plays a greater role in the memory impairment of the HD patients than in the patients with amnesia. (Adapted from Butters et al., 1985).

Scale-III (Wechsler, 1987, 1997) have been influenced by current cognitive models of memory. In the next section, we illustrate how currently available standardized memory tests can be used to identify distinct processing deficits.

Neuropsychological Assessment of Memory Dysfunction: General Considerations

Formal neuropsychological testing of memory permits one to compare objectively the scores of a given patient to a known group average so that the scope and severity of memory dysfunction can be ascertained. Objective testing with standardized procedures also protects against the natural tendency to rationalize, minimize, or forget clinical observations that do not conform to expectation, or to be influenced by a patient's ability to remember information that might be particularly salient to them. People with memory dysfunction exercise the same denial, suppression, and selection that we all are subject to while learning and remembering, and

they have the same tendencies that we all have (but against the backdrop of reduced retentive capacity) to remember more reliably things that seem important compared to things that seem trivial.

When objectively assessing a memory disorder, two general considerations apply: (1) the need to exceed immediate memory capacity that remains normal in patients with circumscribed amnesia, and (2) the possibility of a material-specific deficit in memory that could arise from lateralized brain damage. These considerations are discussed below.

Exceeding Immediate Memory Capacity

The critical feature of memory tasks that accounts for their sensitivity to amnesia is that information presented to the patient exceeds immediate memory capacity. Even severely amnesic patients can have a normal digit span and a normal ability to report back the relatively small amount of information that can be maintained in "conscious awareness." William James (1890) termed this capacity "primary memory":

An object in primary memory...was never lost; its date was never cut off in consciousness from that of the immediately present moment. In fact it comes to us as belonging to the rearward portion of the present space of time, and not to the genuine past...Secondary memory, as it might be styled, is the knowledge of a former state of mind after it had already once dropped from consciousness...It is brought back, recalled, fished up, so to speak, from a reservoir in which, with countless other objects, it lay buried and lost from view. (pp. 646–648)

This concept of primary memory remains quite useful in understanding the nature of the memory impairment in amnesia. An interesting study of five amnesic patients, including H.M. (Drachman & Arbit, 1966), illustrates this point in a formal way. Patients and control subjects were asked to repeat back digit strings of increasing length until an error occurred. A string of digits of the same length was then given repeatedly until it was reproduced correctly or until 25 repetitions of the same digit string had been given. Each time a correct response was given, a new string of digits was presented that was one digit longer than the preceding string. With this procedure, normal subjects were able to increase their digit span to at least 20 digits. Amnesic patients, however, had great difficulty once their digit span capacity (i.e., the digit string length when their first error occurred) had been reached. Even after 25 repetitions of the same digit string, H.M. was unable to increase his digit span by one digit beyond his primary memory capacity of six digits.

As this example shows, the performance of amnesic patients on tests involving immediate recall depends on whether the amount of information to be remembered exceeds "primary memory" or "immediate memory capacity." It should also be noted that even when the amount of information to be remembered is within immediate memory capacity, memory performance will be poor if active rehearsal is prevented by interposing a delay filled with distraction between learning and retention testing (Cowan et al., 2004). If the delay is very long (e.g., an hour or more), the natural distraction of ongoing activity is sufficient to prevent

rehearsal and to reveal a deficit if one is present. If the delay is short (e.g., seconds or minutes), a formal distraction procedure is needed to prevent rehearsal and expose a deficit. The following observation of patient H.M. makes this point:

Forgetting occurred the instant his focus of attention shifted, but in the absence of distraction his capacity for sustained attention was remarkable. Thus he was able to retain the number 584 for at least 15 minutes, by continuously working out mnemonic schemes. When asked how he had been able to retain the number for so long, he replied: "It's easy. You just remember 8. You see, 5, 8, and 4, add to 17. You remember 8, subtract it from 17 and it leaves 9. Divide 9 in half and you get 5 and 4, and there you are: 584. Easy." (Milner, 1970, p. 37)

Given that "primary memory" is preserved in patients with circumscribed amnesia, it is easy to understand that the hallmark of the disorder is considered to be impaired performance on tests of delayed recall (with interpolated distraction). These tests form the cornerstone of any thorough neuropsychological assessment of memory functions.

Material-Specific Memory Dysfunction and Its Assessment

In addition to addressing the issue of severity, objective neuropsychological testing of memory must also address the fact that memory dysfunction can differ depending on whether the underlying neurological injury or disease is bilateral or left or right unilateral. The effect on memory follows from the asymmetry of hemispheric function with respect to language: verbal impairment from left-sided damage, nonverbal impairment from right-sided damage, "global" impairment from bilateral damage. This point has been best demonstrated in the thorough work of Brenda Milner on temporal lobe function (Milner, 1958, 1971). She observed that patients with left medial temporal lobe resections (which were carried out to relieve epilepsy) complain that they cannot remember what they have read, and they do poorly on verbal memory tests such as delayed recall of short prose passages. Patients who have sustained right medial temporal lobe resections, in contrast, complain that they do not remember where they have put things, and do poorly on tests of memory for faces, spatial relationships, and other stimuli that are not readily encoded in words. Milner termed these conditions material-specific disorders (Milner, 1968) to signify that the side of the brain that is affected determines the kind of material that is difficult to learn and remember. Interestingly, material-specific memory disorders are ordinarily not dependent on the sensory modality through which material is learned (e.g., auditory, visual, or tactile). For example, in the case of left medial temporal lobe injury, a short prose passage will be difficult to remember regardless of whether the patient reads the story or hears it read.

These material-specific effects have been demonstrated for left or right temporal lobe surgical lesions (Milner, 1971); epileptic foci of the left or right temporal lobe (Delaney et al., 1980); left or right unilateral ECT (in which the two electrodes are applied to the same side of the head, in contrast to bilateral ECT, in which one electrode is applied to each temple) (Cohen et al., 1968); unilateral diencephalic lesions (Michel et al., 1982; Speedie & Heilman, 1982; Squire et al., 1989); and unilateral diencephalic brain stimulation (Ojemann, 1971). The existence of material specific memory deficits indicates the need for careful assessment of both verbal and nonverbal memory functions in patients with memory disorders.

Neuropsychological Assessment of Anterograde Amnesia: Verbal Memory Tests

A number of techniques have been developed to assess verbal memory dysfunction. These techniques include tasks that require the recall of meaningful prose passages, word list-learning tasks, and verbal paired-associates learning tasks. Many of these tasks were developed with an eye toward the cognitive neuroscience principles of memory function discussed above. Thus, they often include both immediate and delayed recall components so that consolidation and forgetting can be assessed. They may include both free-recall and recognition components so that retrieval and encoding/consolidation deficits can be distinguished, and they may be structured to encourage semantic encoding and

clustering strategies so that these abilities can be assessed. Several of the more common verbal memory tests that employ these techniques are described below.

Delayed Recall of Prose Materials

There are several formal neuropsychological tests of delayed recall that require memory of prose passages. In general, patients are asked in these tasks to repeat back a short story immediately after hearing it and then again after some delay (Milner, 1958). One of the most widely used of these tasks is the Logical Memory Test from the Wechsler Memory Scales (WMS; WMS-Revised; WMS-III). The Logical Memory Test (as used in the WMS-R; Wechsler, 1987) is a standardized test that assesses free recall of two short stories, which are read aloud to the patient. Each story contains 25 bits of information. In the immediate recall condition, the two stories are presented sequentially with free recall elicited after each presentation. Free recall of the two stories is elicited again after a 30-minute period filled with unrelated testing. The total numbers of bits of information recalled immediately and after the delay interval are recorded. A "savings" score that reflects consolidation (or conversely, forgetting) is computed by dividing the total score achieved during delayed recall by the total score achieved during immediate recall (Troster et al., 1989).

Tests of delayed recall of prose passages are quite sensitive to verbal memory deficits. This principle is illustrated in a study that assessed the performance of 15 patients prescribed a series of bilateral ECT using a test of this type (not the Wechsler Memory Scale) with immediate and 24-hour delayed recall (reported in Weiner et al., 1984) (see Figure 23–7). Memory was assessed before ECT and then again, with an alternate form, 6–10 hours after the fifth treatment of the series. Results showed that ECT had no effect on immediate recall of the prose passage, and by this measure one might have supposed memory functions to be normal. However, delayed recall tests showed that memory functions were markedly impaired. Whereas patients tested before their prescribed series of ECT showed considerable retention 24 hours after hearing the prose passage, only 2 of

15 patients could recall any part of the prose passage after a delay following ECT. The ability to learn and retain prose material recovered 6–9 months after the completion of ECT treatment, as shown in a separate group of patients (see Figure 23–7).

The pattern of deficits exhibited by patients on the prose recall test immediately after ECT (i.e., impaired delayed recall with unimpaired immediate recall) helps to distinguish the "organic" memory disorders from memory disorders caused by depression. Rapid (i.e., greater than normal) forgetting revealed by contrasting immediate and delayed recall is a sensitive marker of neurological dysfunction, whereas depression affects immediate memory (presumably because patients are preoccupied or inattentive) but does not affect delayed recall beyond what would be expected from the level of immediate recall. That is, depression is not associated with rapid forgetting (Cronholm & Ottosson, 1961; Sternberg & Jarvik, 1976).

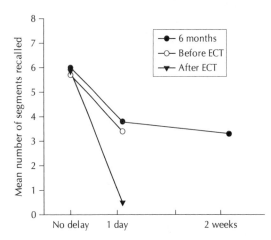

Figure 23–7. Delayed recall of a short prose passage by psychiatric patients administered bilateral electroconvulsive therapy (ECT) for depressive illness. Testing occurred before any treatment (n = 12), 6–10 hours after the fifth treatment (n = 15), and, for a different group of 16 patients, 6–9 months after treatment. Patients were severely impaired at retaining information over a delay when they were tested during the course of treatment, but this ability had recovered by 6 months after treatment. (Adapted from Squire & Chace, 1975).

Word List-Learning Tasks

One of the most powerful techniques for detecting verbal memory dysfunction is the word list-learning task. These tasks are particularly effective when they are designed to assess component processes involved in remembering. Thus, many of the most effective word list-learning tasks incorporate stimulus lists or procedures that encourage deep semantic encoding, allow examination of semantic or serial clustering during recall, assess learning over trials as well as short-delay and long-delay recall, and contrast free recall with cued recall or recognition in order to separate encoding/storage and retrieval deficits. There are a large number of standardized word list-learning tests that are used in the neuropsychological assessment of memory, including the Rey Auditory Verbal Learning Test (AVLT; Rey, 1964), the California Verbal Learning Test (CVLT; Delis et al., 1987), the Hopkins Verbal Learning Test (HVLT; Brandt, 1991), the CERAD Word-List-Learning Test (Welsh et al., 1991), the Selective Reminding Test (Buschke & Fuld, 1974), the Free and Cued Selective Reminding Test (Grober et al., 1997), and the Double Memory Test (Buschke et al., 1997), among others. Several of the most widely used of these tests are described below.

Rey Auditory Verbal Learning Test (Rey, 1964). The AVLT is a list-learning task that assesses multiple cognitive parameters associated with learning and memory. On each of 5 learning trials, 15 unrelated words (all nouns) are presented orally at the rate of one word per second and immediate free recall of the words is elicited after each list presentation. The number of correctly recalled words on each trial is recorded. Following a 20-minute delay filled with unrelated testing, free recall of the original 15-word list is elicited. Finally, a yes/no recognition test is administered using a new word list. After each of 5 list presentations, the original 15 words and 15 interspersed distracter words are presented. The number of target "hits" and false positive responses are recorded. The Rey AVLT has been used in a number of studies that demonstrate the severity of memory impairment in patients with amnesia (e.g., Janowsky et al., 1989a; Squire & Shimamura, 1986; see Figure 23–3).

The California Verbal Learning Test (Delis et al., 1987). The California Verbal Learning Test (CVLT) is a standardized verbal memory test that was explicitly developed to assess a variety of memory processes identified in cognitive psychological studies of normal memory. In the test, subjects are given five presentations/free-recall trials for a list (List A) of 16 words (4 words in each of 4 semantic categories) and are then given a single interference trial for a second, different list (List B) of 16 items. Immediately after the List B trial, subjects are given a free-recall test and then a cued-recall test (utilizing the names of the four categories) for the items on the initial list (List A). Twenty minutes later, the free-

recall and cued-recall tests are repeated for List A, followed by a yes/no recognition test consisting of the 16 List A items and 28 randomly interspersed distractor items. Using this procedure, the CVLT assesses and provides multiple indices for rate of learning, retention after short- and long-delay intervals, semantic encoding ability, recognition (i.e., discriminability), intrusion and perseverative errors (i.e., susceptibility to proactive interference), and response biases. Performance profiles for amnesic patients with Korsakoff's syndrome, patients with Alzheimer's disease, and patients with Huntington's disease have been identified (Delis et al., 1991) (see Figure 23–8). The CVLT was recently updated (as the CVLT-II; Delis

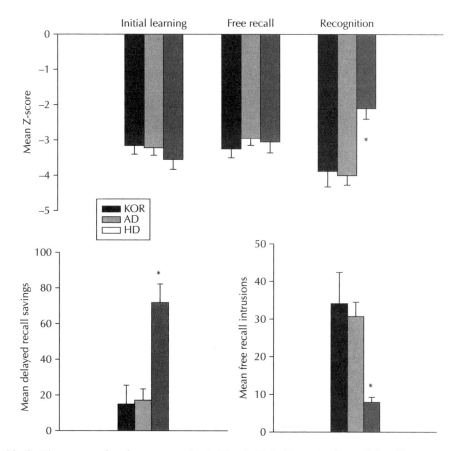

Figure 23–8. The pattern of performance on the California Verbal Learning Test exhibited by amnesic patients with Korsakoff's syndrome (KOR; n = 8), patients with Alzheimer's disease (AD; n = 20), and patients with Huntington's disease (HD; n = 20). The three groups performed similarly on the initial learning and free-recall measures, but HD patients exhibited significantly (*) less impaired recognition (i.e., discriminability), higher savings, and fewer free-recall intrusions than the other two groups. The AD and KOR patients performed similarly on all of the measures. (Adapted from Delis et al., 1991).

et al., 2000) with new word categories, more accurate indices of recognition memory, and expanded normative data.

Selective Reminding Test (Buschke & Fuld, 1974). The selective reminding test is a verbal list-learning task that provides information on storage, retention, and retrieval. It was one of the first standardized verbal memory tests to be designed on the basis of memory processes identified in experimental cognitive psychological studies of normal memory. On the initial trial of a widely used version of the task, patients are read 10 unrelated words and then asked for immediate recall of the entire list. On the second trial, patients are read only those words they failed to recall on the first trial (i.e., selectively reminded) and again are asked for recall of the entire list. This same procedure, presenting only those words not recalled on the preceding trial, is followed for a total of six trials. With this procedure and the scoring methods described by the test authors, it is possible to derive measures of the number of items in short-term storage (i.e., items recalled in the trial immediately after reminding), the number of items in long-term storage (i.e., items recalled even without reminding in the immediately preceding trial), random retrieval (i.e., items recalled inconsistently), and the total number of items recalled during testing. In addition, the patient's performance may be analyzed for intrusion errors (i.e., the production of words that were not on the list) that might be indicative of susceptibility to proactive interference. Several additional tests using selective reminding procedures have been developed, including the Free and Cued Selective Reminding Test (Grober et al., 1997), which uses a semantic encoding procedure that has patients identify the semantic category of each to-be-remembered item during list presentation, and then uses the category name as a cue at the time of recall (in addition to uncued free recall).

Verbal Paired-Associates Learning

Among tests specialized for the detection and quantification of memory dysfunction,

perhaps the most sensitive is paired-associates learning. Paired-associates learning tests have been used experimentally for many years and standardized versions have been incorporated into clinical memory test batteries (e.g., all versions of the Wechsler Memory Scale). In general, these tests involve the initial presentation of pairs of semantically related or unrelated words with the instructions to remember which words go together. Immediately following presentation of the list of word pairs, or after a delay filled with unrelated testing, the first word of each pair is presented and the patient must generate the word with which it was paired. The sensitivity of verbal paired-associates learning tests to memory impairment is illustrated in a study (Janowsky et al., 1989a) that had three kinds of patients with memory problems attempt to learn 10 noun-noun word pairs (e.g., army-table, door-sky). In this case, three consecutive presentations of the word pairs were given, and after each presentation subjects were asked to try to produce the second word of the pair upon hearing the first. As Figure 23–9 shows, patients with alcoholic Korsakoff's syndrome and other amnesic patients all performed poorly on this test, obtaining an average score of less than four correct responses across all 30 learning trials. Patients with frontal lobe lesions and control subjects performed much better. In this same test, patient H.M. was unable to produce any correct responses after three trials, even when he was instructed in the use of imagery techniques for associating the words in each pair (Jones, 1974). The sensitivity of this test derives from the fact that the material to be remembered is too extensive to be retained within immediate memory, the correct associations between the various words must be retained, and the test requires recall rather than recognition of the paired item. A drawback to using paired-associates learning, however, is that poor performance could result from factors other than circumscribed memory loss (e.g., depression, inattention, or dementia). Accordingly, the greatest value of the test may be to rule out memory impairment in persons who perform well. If performance is poor, then further tests are needed to interpret the poor performance.

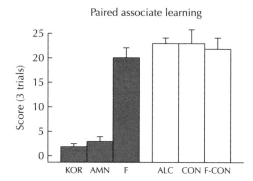

Paired associate learning

Figure 23–9. The performance of patients with Korsakoff's syndrome (KOR; n = 7), other patients with amnesia (AMN; n = 5), patients with frontal lobe lesions (F; n = 7), and their controls (alcoholic controls, ALC; n = 8, healthy controls, CON; n = 8, and frontal controls, F-CON; n = 11, respectively) on a test of paired-associates learning that required learning 10 noun-noun word pairs across three trials. The amnesic patients were severely impaired. (Adapted from Janowsky et al., 1989a).

Neuropsychological Assessment of Anterograde Amnesia: Nonverbal Memory Tests

Two classes of nonverbal memory tests can be used in clinical assessment: those that require retention and free recall of geometric designs that are drawn or reconstructed by the patient and those that require recognition of previously presented visual stimuli such as nonsense figures or unfamiliar faces or objects.

Delayed Recall of Nonverbal Material

There are a number of tests of nonverbal memory that require the patient to draw or reconstruct relatively complex geometric designs that had been studied earlier. The integrity of the reproduced design is usually scored in terms of correctly completed components. Three of the most widely used tests of free recall of nonverbal material are the Rey–Osterrieth Complex Figure Test, the Visual Reproduction Test from the Wechsler Memory Scales (WMS, WMS-Revised, WMS-III), and the Benton Visual Retention Test.

The Rey–Osterrieth Complex Figure (Osterrieth, 1944; Rey, 1941). In this task the subject is asked to copy the Rey–Osterrieth Complex Figure and then to reconstruct it from memory without forewarning. The reconstruction can be requested immediately or after a delay filled with unrelated (preferably verbal) testing. Alternate forms of the figure and various standardized scoring systems have been developed (Lezak et al., 2004; Milner & Teuber, 1968). The sensitivity of the Rey–Osterrieth Complex Figure test to amnesia is shown in the poor performance of patient R.B. discussed earlier (see Figure 23–1).

Visual Reproduction Test (Wechsler, 1945, 1987, 1997). A version of the Visual Reproduction Test is included in all editions of the Wechsler Memory Scales. On each of the three trials of the original version of this test (i.e., in the WMS), the subject must reproduce a complex geometric figure from memory immediately following a 10-second study period. Three increasingly complex stimuli containing from 4 to 10 components are presented on successive trials. The subject's reproductions are scored according to how many components are produced from the original stimulus drawings. To increase the sensitivity of the test to memory dysfunction, two modifications of the original version of the test are often incorporated. First, as a measure of long-term retention, subjects are asked after 30 minutes of unrelated testing to again reproduce the figures from memory. Second, the subject is asked to simply copy the stimulus figures in order to assess any visuoperceptual dysfunction or apraxia that may be contaminating the ability to reproduce the figures from memory. The delayed recall measure from the Visual Reproduction Test has been shown to be quite sensitive to memory impairment in cases of circumscribed amnesia (Troster et al., 1989) and dementia (Salmon et al., 2002), and this measure was incorporated into the newer versions of the test that are included in the WMS-Revised and the WMS-III. These latter versions also modified the number and design of the to-be-remembered geometric figures.

Benton Visual Retention Test. This test consists of a series of 10 stimulus cards that contain geometric figures that must be remembered and drawn by the patient. The first two stimulus cards contain a single figure, and the remaining eight cards contain three figures (generally two large and one small) arranged in a row. In the initial administration format (Form A) each stimulus card is presented for 10 seconds, and drawing begins immediately after its removal. The second administration format (Form B) is identical to the first (with a different set of figures), but each stimulus card is presented for only 5 seconds. The third administration format (Form C) requires the patient to simply copy the figures on each stimulus card (again with a different set of figures). In the final administration format (Form D), each stimulus card is presented for 10 seconds, and drawing begins 15 seconds after its removal. The score for each condition is the number of correctly reproduced three-figure displays (for a maximum of 10 points). An error score can also be computed on the basis of the presence of six error types: omissions, distortions, perseverations, rotations, misplacements, and incorrect size. Extensive normative data for the Benton Visual Retention Test are available (Mitrushina et al., 2005).

Delayed Recognition of Nonverbal Material

Nonverbal memory tests that require patients to draw or reconstruct geometric designs can be adversely influenced by visuoconstructive deficits (i.e., apraxia) or other nonmemory problems that preclude drawing. To avoid this potential problem, some tests require delayed recognition of nonverbal stimuli. These recognition tests have been independently developed as new instruments or have evolved from the free-recall tests described above with the addition of a delayed recognition component in which each target stimulus must be chosen from among an array of similar foils. Examples of the latter include recognition versions of the Visual Reproduction Test and the Benton Visual Retention Test (Amieva et al., 2006). Other nonverbal recognition memory tests require identification of faces (Warrington, 1984) or unfamiliar objects (e.g., front doors of houses; Baddeley et al., 1994). One of the most widely used freestanding nonverbal recognition

memory tests is the memory for faces component of the Recognition Memory Test.

Recognition Memory Test (RMT; Warrington, 1984). This test consists of two forced-choice recognition tests—one for words and one for faces. Memory for words and faces are tested separately. For each test, 50 stimuli are presented sequentially, at the rate of 3 seconds each, and the patient must make a judgment of "pleasant" or "unpleasant" to assure attention and encoding. Immediately following the study phase, each stimulus is paired with a new one, and subjects are asked to indicate which of the two was presented earlier. The score is the number correct out of 50 for both words and faces. The RMT is useful for assessing different levels of severity among memory-impaired patients, and an even more sensitive assessment can be obtained by administering the memory test one day after the study phase (Reed & Squire, 1997; Squire & Shimamura, 1986; see Figure 23–10). Comparison of the faces and words conditions allows evaluation of potential material-specific memory deficits (Warrington, 1984). A modified version of the faces component of the RMT is included in the WMS-III. In this version, there are 24 target faces and both immediate and 30-minute delayed recognition is assessed using a yes/no format rather than the two-alternative forced choice format of the RMT.

Neuropsychological Assessment of Anterograde Amnesia: Memory Test Batteries

A number of comprehensive memory test batteries have been developed and standardized for clinical assessment of memory dysfunction (for review, see Lezak et al., 2004). These batteries usually include an array of tests that evaluate various memory functions such as orientation, learning, and retention, while taking into account the possibility of modality-specific deficits. A benefit of standardized test batteries for clinical use is that they are often grounded in extensive normative data that allow the presence and severity of memory impairment to be reliably identified across the age span, and they may provide index scores that allow straightforward comparisons among various aspects of

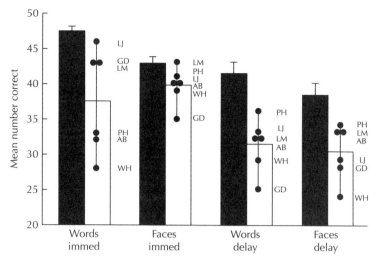

Figure 23–10. The performance of amnesic patients (open bars) and healthy control subjects (dark bars) on the Words and Faces components of the Warrington Recognition Memory Test. Recognition memory was tested immediately (Immed) and in separate tests after a 24-hour delay (Delay). The means (+SEM) are indicated by the bars (maximum possible score = 50), and individual scores of the amnesic patients are indicated by dots and their initials. (Adapted from Reed & Squire 1997).

memory performance and general intellectual abilities. Two of the most widely used memory test batteries are the Wechsler Memory Scale and its various updates (Wechsler, 1945, 1987, 1997) and the Rivermeade Behavioral Memory Test Battery (deWall et al., 1994; Wilson et al., 1989).

The Wechsler Memory Scale

The original Wechsler Memory Scale (WMS; Wechsler, 1945) was among the first standardized memory batteries used to clinically assess memory function. The WMS included seven distinct subtests that measured general orientation, immediate memory, and verbal and nonverbal long-term memory. A memory quotient (MQ) could be calculated on the basis of performance scores for the various subtests. The MQ was designed to parallel the IQ from the Wechsler Adult Intelligence Scale (WAIS) and, therefore, was standardized in the normal population to a mean of 100 with a standard deviation of 15. With the development of the MQ

it became possible and popular to evaluate the severity of memory dysfunction in a patient by comparing their MQ and IQ scores. In both clinical and experimental analyses of memory dysfunction, a large IQ-MQ difference (usually a difference greater than 15 or 20 points) was taken as evidence of a significant and selective amnesic disorder.

As knowledge of the nature of amnesia grew from experimental studies (e.g., Butters & Cermak, 1980; Squire & Shimamura, 1986), it became apparent that the WMS was inadequate for characterizing memory disorders. The scale was limited because (1) scores were combined into one general MQ score that masked dissociations in various memory functions, (2) there was a preponderance of verbal memory tests, (3) there were no measures of delayed memory retention, and (4) some subtests measured functions not typically affected in amnesia (e.g., digit span memory and general orientation). The Wechsler Memory Scale-Revised (WMS-R) was introduced in 1987 with the intention of overcoming some of the limitations of the original test battery (Wechsler, 1987). The WMS-R consists of 13 subtests, which are combined in various ways to produce five indices: Attention/Concentration, General Memory, Verbal Memory, Visual Memory, and Delayed Recall. Each index is normalized to yield a mean score of 100 for normal subjects and a standard deviation of 15. Moreover, for each verbal subtest (e.g., digit span, prose recall, verbal paired-associates learning), there is a corresponding nonverbal subtest (e.g., visual memory span, visual reproduction, visual paired-associates learning). Several verbal and nonverbal tests are administered after a delay of about 30 minutes.

The WMS-R has significant advantages over its predecessor and it provides perhaps the best general assessment of memory dysfunction among readily available test instruments. Among its advantages are distinct indices for verbal and nonverbal memory performance that can elucidate material-specific deficits in patients with unilateral brain damage (Chelune & Bornstein, 1988), a delayed memory index that is particularly sensitive to the rapid forgetting that characterizes many amnesic disorders (Butters et al., 1988), and the development of a separate Attention/Concentration index that incorporates performance scores for subtests that do not depend on the kind of memory that is impaired in amnesia (digit span, visuospatial span, and mental control). Indeed, Janowsky and colleagues (1989a) found that amnesic patients exhibited normal scores on the Attention/Concentration index of the WMS-R, despite severe impairment on the scale's memory indices. Patients with frontal lobe lesions, in contrast, exhibited low scores on the Attention/Concentration index but normal scores on memory indices (Janowsky et al., 1989a). The WMS-R has also been useful in characterizing dementia. Patients with Alzheimer's disease or Huntington's disease exhibited significant impairment on the Attention/Concentration index as well as on the memory indices, whereas patients with amnesic disorders (e.g., patients with Korsakoff's syndrome, hypoxia, or herpes encephalitis) exhibited significant impairment only on the memory indices (Butters et al., 1988).

Although the WMS-R represented a significant advance over the original WMS,

several shortcomings remained. For example, the WMS-R does not provide index scores that fall below 50, and many amnesic patients would obtain scores below this level, particularly on the Delayed Recall Index. Thus, the WMS-R is not suited for discriminating among patients with severe memory impairment. In addition, the WMS-R does not test memory in a recognition format, and that prevents a comparison of retrieval versus encoding/storage processes by measuring the difference between free-recall and recognition test performance.

The newest version of the WMS, the WMS-III (Wechsler, 1997), was developed to address these shortcomings and to provide a balanced approach to memory assessment. While adding measures of recognition memory, the WMS-III reduced the number of core subtests to six (Logical Memory, Verbal Paired-Associates, Spatial Span, Letter-Number Sequencing, Face Recognition Memory, and Family Pictures) and made other subtests optional (Information and Orientation, Mental Control, Digit Span, Visual Reproduction, Word List Learning patterned after the Rey AVLT). Eight primary memory indices that have an expanded lower range can now be generated: Auditory Immediate Memory, Visual Immediate Memory, Immediate Memory, Auditory Delayed Memory, Visual Delayed Memory, Auditory Recognition Memory, General Memory, and Working Memory (formerly Attention/Concentration). It should be noted that the change from verbal memory indices in the WMS-R to auditory memory indices in the WMS-III shifts the focus of these measures from ones that purportedly measure material-specific memory (with a corresponding implication for clinical/anatomical correlations) to ones that measure modality-specific memory (based on the sensory modality of the stimulus presentation) (Lezak et al., 2004). As mentioned previously, material-specific memory disorders are ordinarily not dependent on the sensory modality through which material is learned (e.g., auditory, visual, or tactile) (Milner, 1968). Because of this change, and because several sensitive measures have been given optional status (e.g., Visual Reproductions) and several new, untried subtests have been included (e.g., Family Pictures Recall and Recognition), it is not clear that the WMS-III represents a significant advance beyond the WMS-R for the assessment of memory deficits in patients with amnesia (Lezak et al., 2004).

Rivermead Behavioral Memory Test

The Rivermead Behavioral Memory Test (RBMT) is a test battery that assesses a variety of everyday tasks of memory (deWall et al., 1994; Wilson et al., 1989). Subjects are asked to perform tasks that include associating a name to a face, remembering the location of a hidden object, recalling a spatial route, and distinguishing previously presented faces from new ones. In addition, tasks involving "remembering to remember" (i.e., prospective memory) are given, such as remembering to ask a certain question when an alarm sounds. The test battery is unique among other clinical memory tests in its emphasis on memory demands that are associated with everyday functioning. Accordingly, it has the advantage that it is strongly correlated with the clinical prognosis for rehabilitation (Wilson, 1987). Three forms of the test battery have been constructed so that an individual patient can be assessed at different times after brain injury or disease. The RBMT is particularly well suited to assess progress during rehabilitation of memory impairment (Wilson, 2008). It may be less well suited for neuropsychological studies of memory function, however, because task performance appears to be quite sensitive to the level of attention and the ability to apply mnemonic strategies. Thus, poor performance on the RMBT may be indicative of deficits in attention or general intellectual abilities rather than being indicative specifically of memory impairment.

Neuropsychological Assessment of Retrograde Amnesia

The severity and extent of retrograde amnesia is difficult to assess in a quantitative, standardized fashion because individuals who develop memory disorders differ in their life experiences and in their past exposure to memorable people, events, and information. There have been two approaches to the development of neuropsychological tests for retrograde amnesia: (1) tests based on information about public events

or famous people from specified times in the past to ensure that the information is verifiable and potentially accessible to all subjects; and (2) tests based on an individual patient's autobiographical information from various episodes (e.g., a wedding) and periods of life.

Both types of tests of have provided important information about the nature of remote memory loss in amnesic patients. For example, tests of remote memory for past public events in patients who became amnesic on a known calendar day showed that (1) extensive, temporally graded retrograde amnesia covering more than a decade occurs in patients with medial temporal lobe amnesia, just as it does in patients with diencephalic amnesia (e.g., Korsakoff's syndrome); (2) the impairment reflects a loss of usable knowledge, not a simple difficulty in retrieving an intact memory store that can be overcome given sufficient opportunities for retrieval; and (3) very remote memory for factual information can be intact in amnesia, even when the tests are made so difficult that normal subjects can answer only 20% of the questions (Squire et al., 1989). Similar patterns of retrograde amnesia have been shown for autobiographical information (Kopelman et al., 1989).

Despite their ability to provide significant information about the nature of retrograde amnesia, both types of remote memory tests have limitations in their usefulness as clinical tests for individual patients. Tests based on public events and famous people presume that the individual patient was exposed to the information in question—more specifically, exposed to it only at the time that it occurred. This may not be the case for specific types of information that some people ignore (e.g., sporting events) or for certain events or famous people that are reexposed repeatedly over time (e.g., the attacks of September 11, 2001). Tests of autobiographical knowledge have a different limitation. They rely on information that is often not easily corroborated, although a spouse or relative can sometimes verify reported events and dates. Asking the patient to redate the memories they had recalled and dated in an earlier test session can also provide a check against outright fabrication (Schacter et al., 1982). In addition, both types of retrograde amnesia tests may be susceptible to the contaminating effects of anterograde amnesia, particularly in patients with an insidious onset of memory dysfunction (e.g., patients with Alzheimer's disease). Only when amnesia has a very recent or precise time of onset can one know which test questions assess retrograde amnesia and which assess anterograde amnesia.

Because of these limitations, prospective studies with experimental animals have been needed to reveal the precise shape of the temporal gradient of retrograde amnesia. Such studies have shown that information acquired remote from surgery (e.g., hippocampal ablation) is remembered significantly better than information acquired closer to surgery (Cho et al., 1993; Kim & Fanselow, 1992; Winocur, 1990; Zola-Morgan & Squire, 1990). These results indicate that information that initially depends on the integrity of medial temporal lobe/diencephalic brain structures for its storage and retrieval can eventually become independent of these structures through some process of consolidation or reorganization that results in a more permanent memory (Squire & Alvarez, 1995). These findings with experimental animals provide strong confirmation for the reality of temporal gradients of retrograde amnesia, an idea proposed more than 100 years ago (Ribot, 1881).

Tests of Public Knowledge

The first remote memory tests to explore objectively the nature of memory disorders in amnesic patients consisted of questions about persons or events that had been in the news in Great Britain or involved photographs of famous people who had been prominent in Great Britain at different times in the past (Sanders & Warrington, 1971). By asking questions or presenting faces that covered the past several decades, it was possible to obtain a sampling of an individual's knowledge of past events. Subsequently, similar tests based on public events or famous faces were developed for use in the United States (Albert et al., 1979; Seltzer & Benson, 1974; Squire, 1974). Examples of public event and famous face identification tests are described below.

Public Events Test. Squire and colleagues (Squire et al., 1989) developed a 92-item public events questionnaire that covered events

that had been reported in the news from 1950 to 1985. Testing was first conducted in a free-recall format (e.g., "what was the name of the first satellite to be launched?") and later in a four-alternative forced-choice format (e.g., "Was it Discover, Explorer, Sputnik, or Telstar?"). The test was administered to amnesic patients with Korsakoff's syndrome and their alcoholic controls, and to non-Korsakoff amnesic patients (i.e., patients with medial temporal lobe damage) and their healthy normal controls. The results showed that both patient groups had temporally graded retrograde amnesia with greater impairment for more recent past memories (Squire et al., 1989). This pattern of remote memory loss was observed with both free-recall and recognition test formats (see Figure 23–11). Similar results have been obtained with a variety of other tests of memory for past public events that employed free-recall or recognition formats (Albert et al., 1979; Hodges & Ward, 1989; Kopelman, 1989; McCarthy & Warrington, 1990).

Famous Faces Test (Albert et al., 1979). Albert and colleagues (1979) developed a test of the ability to name or otherwise identify pictured people who were famous at different time periods in the past. In its original form, the test asked for the identification of 8–10 people who were famous in each decade from the 1920s to the 1970s. The test was subsequently updated to extend into the early 1990s (Hodges et al., 1993; Sadek et al., 2004). On each trial, free recall of the name of the pictured person is attempted. Semantic and phonemic cues are provided if free recall is unsuccessful. Faces are presented in a specified order with items from the various decades rotating from earliest to latest. In an attempt to provide some degree of equivalency of difficulty across the items from the various decades, the test items were chosen so that healthy normal control subjects would correctly recall the name of about 75% of the faces in each decade. Using this test, Albert and colleagues (1979) showed the patients with Korsakoff's syndrome have an extensive, temporally graded retrograde amnesia with information from the distant past better retained than information from the more recent past.

Using an updated version of this task, Squire and colleagues (1989) asked amnesic Korsakoff's

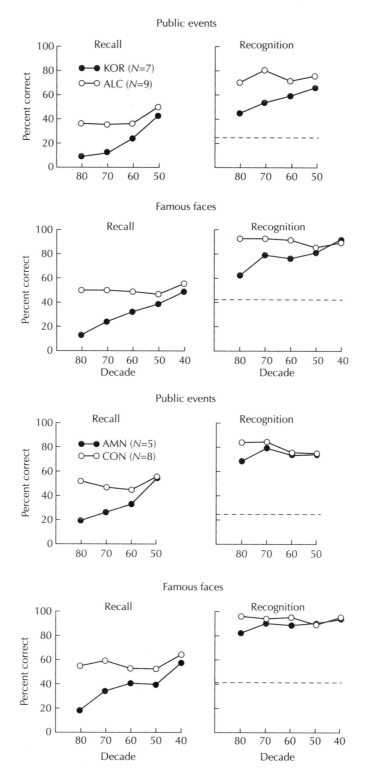

Figure 23–11. Performance of patients with Korsakoff's syndrome and alcoholic control subjects (upper panels), and non-Korsakoff amnesic patients and their control subjects (lower panels), on the recall and recognition versions of the public events test and the famous faces test. (dashed lines indicate chance performance). (Adapted from Squire et al., 1989).

patients and their alcoholic controls, and non-Korsakoff amnesic patients and their controls, to identify 117 photographs of famous people who came into the news between 1950 and 1985. Both free-recall and recognition versions of the task were administered. The results were consistent with those of Albert and colleagues (1979) in showing temporally graded retrograde amnesia in patients with Korsakoff's syndrome, and extended these results to patients with non-Korsakoff's amnesia (i.e., patients with medial temporal lobe damage). In addition, the results paralleled those obtained with the public events questionnaire (Squire et al., 1989) (see Figure 23–11).

It should be noted that remote memory tests cannot be assumed to satisfy the criterion for equivalence just because normal subjects obtain the same score (e.g., 75% correct) across all time periods sampled by the test. As discussed in detail elsewhere (Squire & Cohen, 1982), the events or faces selected from more remote time periods may initially have been more salient and more widely known than those selected from more recent time periods. In addition, the events and faces from more remote periods could have been forgotten more slowly. Thus, such tests may not be particularly well suited to compare performance across time periods.

Television Test (Squire & Slater, 1975). Another remote memory test that has found useful application in the study of memory disorders is a test of former one-season television programs (Squire, 1989; Squire & Slater, 1975). It was designed to overcome an important limitation of other available remote memory tests—the difficulty of comparing scores across different past time periods. To make valid comparisons across time periods, the items selected must satisfy the criterion of equivalence; that is they must sample past time periods in an equivalent way so that the events from different time periods are likely to have been learned to about the same extent, and then forgotten at similar rates. The television test appears to satisfy this criterion (Squire, 1989). However, the television test is limited by the relatively short time span that it can reliably cover (about 20 years), and by the fact that it yields variable results when used clinically to explore the retrograde memory

capacity of a single patient. Despite these limitations, the television test successfully identified temporally graded retrograde amnesia in patients receiving ECT (Squire et al., 1975).

Tests of Autobiographical Knowledge

Although autobiographical memory tests do not have the advantage of being based on verifiable and publicly accessible information, they can be of considerable value in the neuropsychological assessment of memory disorders. Two of the most widely used tests of remote autobiographical knowledge are the Crovitz procedure (sometimes referred to as the Crovitz Test) and the Autobiographical Memory Interview (AMI) (Kopelman et al., 1989).

The Crovitz Test (Crovitz & Schiffman, 1974). Inspired by the early quantitative studies of Galton (1879), the Crovitz Test is designed to obtain autobiographical remote memories about specific past episodes of a patient's life. Patients are given standard cue words (e.g., window, tree, ticket, bird) and are asked in each case to recall a specific memory from the past that involves the word. After recalling a memory for a given cue word, subjects are asked to date the memory as best they can. The responses can be scored on the basis of the quality and quantity of recalled information, and they can provide useful information about the time periods from which recall is possible.

Even amnesic patients who obtain normal scores for recall may draw their memories from different time periods than normal subjects. This was true in the case of patients with alcoholic Korsakoff syndrome who obtained normal or near-normal scores on the recall test but drew their memories from 10 years earlier than their alcoholic control subjects (Zola-Morgan et al., 1983). Similarly, patients who became amnesic as the result of anoxia or ischemia, and had presumed or confirmed bilateral damage to the hippocampal formation, drew fewer memories from the more recent time period than control subjects (MacKinnon & Squire, 1989). Under some conditions, the amnesic patients were able to recollect fully formed autobiographical episodes from their earlier life, which could not be distinguished qualitatively or quantitatively from the recollections of normal subjects. This finding was recently replicated with the Crovitz procedure (Bayley et al., 2005).

Autobiographical Memory Interview (Kopelman et al., 1989). The AMI is a semistructured interview that assesses a patient's ability to recall facts (personal semantic memory) and specific events (autobiographical incidents) from past life. Recall of both types of information is assessed with three questions for each of three time periods: childhood (e.g., "what was the name of your elementary school?"), early adulthood (e.g., "what was your first job?"), and the recent past (e.g., "who was a recent visitor to your home?"). Prompts are provided when the patient cannot give a response. Responses are scored for clarity and specificity on a 0–3 scale. The AMI is sensitive to remote memory loss in patients with circumscribed amnesia. Kopelman and colleagues (Kopelman, 1989; Kopelman et al., 1989), for example, found that patients with amnesia of various etiologies scored significantly below normal control subjects on all components of the AMI, with particularly great impairment for the recent past items in both the autobiographical and personal semantic memory categories. This temporally graded retrograde amnesia revealed by the AMI was observed in several additional studies (with some using a variant of the AMI) that assessed patients with Korsakoff's syndrome (Kopelman et al., 1999) or amnesia related to temporal lobe damage (Bayley et al., 2006; Bright et al., 2006; Kirwan et al., 2008; Reed & Squire, 1998).

Neuropsychological Tests of Nondeclarative Memory

Although tests of nondeclarative memory are not usually used in clinical settings, they can sometimes provide useful information that is not obtained with conventional memory tests. As mentioned previously, patients with circumscribed amnesia arising from diencephalic or medial temporal lobe damage perform normally on these tests, so impairment would suggest the involvement of brain systems beyond the declarative memory system. Indeed, patients with more global cortical involvement, such as those with early stage Alzheimer's disease, are impaired on certain nondeclarative memory tasks (Shimamura et al., 1987; for review, see, Salmon, 2000). In addition, these tests may be particularly useful with patient groups that have a primary memory deficit that involves nondeclarative forms of memory, such as patients with Huntington's disease (Butters et al., 1990; Heindel et al., 1989; Saint-Cyr & Taylor, 1992).

The nondeclarative memory tests of most interest for assessment are those that have been used to demonstrate intact or near-intact performance in amnesic patients. These include tasks involving learning simple conditioned responses, perceptuomotor skills such as mirror drawing and motor pursuit, perceptual skills like reading mirror-reversed words, cognitive skills, adaptation-level effects, probabilistic classification learning, artificial grammar learning, speeded reading of repeated prose passages, and several kinds of priming (for review, see Squire, 2004). Despite normal performance on these nondeclarative memory tasks, memory-impaired patients often show profound amnesia for the declarative memory aspects of the learning situation. For example, patients with circumscribed amnesia exhibit progressive learning and 24-hour retention of a conditioned eye blink response, but they cannot describe the apparatus used in their learning sessions or how it had been used (Daum et al., 1989; Weiskrantz & Warrington, 1979).

Although a description of the various experimental tasks that have been used to assess nondeclarative memory in patients with amnesia is beyond the scope of the present discussion, two types of priming tests, word-stem completion and associative priming, will be briefly described because these are the tests most often used in a quasi-clinical fashion.

Word-Stem Completion Priming

One of the most widely used methods to elicit priming is the word-stem completion task (Graf et al., 1984). In this task, words are presented to the subject (e.g., MOTEL) in the guise of a "likeability" rating task (not as a memory task), and later three-letter word stems (e.g., MOT) are presented. Half of the stems can be completed with one of the previously rated words, and half are novel (to assess baseline guessing rates). Subjects are asked to say the first word that comes to mind that completes each word stem. In a study by Graf and colleagues (1984), the probability of producing previously presented words was increased from about 10% (baseline word-stem completion) to about 50% for both amnesic patients and control subjects. The priming effect indicates that words appear to "pop" into mind, and amnesic patients exhibit this effect as strongly as control

subjects. In contrast, when subjects were asked to use the word stems as cues to recollect words from the study session, the control subjects performed better than amnesic patients. The ability of the word-stem completion priming test to differentiate between patients with circumscribed amnesia or Alzheimer's disease was first shown in a study by Shimamura and colleagues (1987; see Figure 23–12). Although both patient groups had significant and equal deficits

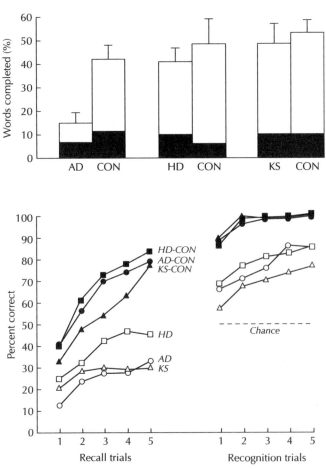

Figure 23–12. The performance of patients with Alzheimer's disease (AD), Huntington's disease (HD), or Korsakoff's syndrome (KS), and their respective controls (CON), on the word-stem completion task (top panel). All groups exhibited priming, as evidenced by the fact that they completed word stems to form previously presented words at above baseline guessing rates (the darkened portion of the bars), but priming was impaired in patients with AD. In contrast, all three patient groups exhibited significant impairment relative to controls on the explicit recall and recognition components of the Rey Auditory Verbal Learning Test (bottom panel). (Adapted from Shimamura et al., 1987).

in explicit memory measured on the Rey AVLT, the patients with amnesia exhibited normal levels of priming above baseline completion rates. Patients with Alzheimer's disease, in contrast, showed less priming than their controls or the amnesic patients.

Associative Priming (Levy et al., 2004; Shimamura & Squire, 1984)

One version of the associative priming task employs a paired-associates procedure in which subjects are first asked to judge the degree of relatedness of categorically or functionally related word pairs (e.g., BIRD-ROBIN, NEEDLE-THREAD) and later to "free-associate" to the first words of the previously presented pairs and to words that were not presented as part of the paired-associates. Shimamura and Squire (1984) showed that amnesic patients and control subjects exhibit a similar bias for using recently presented words (i.e., the second word of the presented word pair) when performing the free association task. In contrast, Salmon and colleagues (1988) found that patients with Alzheimer's disease were significantly less likely to produce the second word of the semantically related pair than were control subjects or patients with Huntington's disease. Similar associative priming deficits in patients with Alzheimer's disease were found by using a variant of the free-association procedure (Brandt et al., 1988). Thus, tests of associative priming may be particularly useful in differentiating memory impairment due to Alzheimer's disease from other causes.

Summary and Recommendations

The preceding sections considered the issues involved in undertaking a clinical neuropsychological evaluation of memory functions. Specialized tests are available for assessing memory dysfunction, including tests of new learning capacity, remote memory, and nondeclarative memory. Of the readily available tests to assess anterograde amnesia, the WMS-R and WMS-III provide a useful general-purpose assessment of new learning ability, the RMT allows effective assessment of the severity of memory impairment, and the CVLT (or CVLT-II) is useful for

obtaining a profile of performance from single patients. Retrograde amnesia can be objectively assessed with tests of remote memory for public events, but more subjective methods based on questions about autobiographical knowledge or a time line of memory loss are also useful. When assessing the patient with memory dysfunction, more than one test of each type can be used if the findings in any one area are ambiguous; additional tests can be used as needed once the clinician becomes familiar with the status of the patient's memory functions.

Neuropsychological testing of memory is most informative when memory tests are supplemented with tests of other cognitive functions. Additional tests establish valuable reference points that help in interpreting memory test scores, and can identify or rule out other kinds of cognitive impairment that could influence memory test performance. For example, the WAIS-R or WAIS-III IQ test can be very helpful because it can identify the general cognitive status and test-taking ability of the patient. Tests that assess language comprehension, confrontational naming, verbal fluency, constructional ability, and executive functions (i.e., frontal lobe functions) can also be valuable in this regard, because deficits in any of these abilities can influence performance on many memory tests (Moscovitch, 1982; Shimamura et al., 1990; for review, see Lezak et al., 2004). The Mattis Dementia Rating Scale (Mattis, 1988) is particularly useful in assessing the basic cognitive status of patients with suspected dementia because it evaluates a wide range of abilities with measures that avoid floor effects in performance.

Having considered the available methods for testing memory, it is worth noting that improvement in neuropsychological testing methods has depended importantly on basic research in cognitive psychology and neuroscience. An enormous amount has been learned over the past two decades about how the brain accomplishes memory storage. An inventory of memory tests has been one of the fruits of this enterprise. The neuropsychological, brain-systems study of memory is part of a broader program of research aimed at understanding the biology of memory at all levels of analysis—from cellular and synaptic events to the complex behavior of animals and humans. A broad, basic research approach to the study of memory and the brain should continue to inform us about mechanisms and organization, and at the same time yield improved methods for the assessment of patients with memory dysfunction. These same research efforts can be expected to suggest strategies for developing treatments for memory dysfunction and methods for evaluating those treatments.

References

Abrams, R., & Essman, W. B. (1982). *Electroconvulsive therapy: Biological foundations and clinical applications*. New York: Spectrum Publications Inc.

Albert, M. S., & Blacker, D. (2006). Mild cognitive impairment and dementia. *Annual Review of Clinical Psychology, 2*, 379–388.

Albert, M.S., Butters, N., & Levin, J. (1979). Temporal gradients in the retrograde amnesia of patients with alcoholic Korsakoff's disease. *Archives of Neurology, 36*, 211–216.

Aleman, A., Hijman, R., de Haan, E. H. F., & Kahn, R. S. (1999). Memory impairment in schizophrenia: A meta-analysis. *American Journal of Psychiatry, 156*, 1358–1366.

Amieva, H., Gaestel, Y., & Dartigues, J. (2006). The multiple-choice formats (form F and G) of the Benton Visual Retention Test as a tool to detect age-related memory changes in population-based studies and clinical settings. *Nature Protocols, 1*, 1936–1938.

Backman, L., Small, B. J., & Fratiglioni, L. (2001). Stability of the preclinical episodic memory deficit in Alzheimer's disease. *Brain, 124*, 96–102.

Baddeley, A. D. (1986). *Working memory*. Oxford: Claredon Press.

Baddeley, A. D., Emslie, H., & Nimmo-Smith, I. (1994). *Doors and People: a test of visual and verbal recall and recognition*. Bury St. Edmunds, England: Thames Valley Test Company.

Baldo, J. V., Shimamura, A. P. (2002). Frontal lobes and memory. In A. D. Baddeley, M. D. Kopelman, and B. A. Wilson (Eds.), *Handbook of memory disorders* (2nd ed., pp. 363–380). Chichester UK: John Wiley.

Barbizet, J. (1970). *Human memory and its pathology*. San Francisco: WH Freeman and Company.

Bayley, P. J., Gold, J. J., Hopkins, R. O., & Squire, L. R. (2005). The neuroanatomy of remote memory. *Neuron, 46*, 799–810.

Bayley, P. J., Hopkins, R. O., & Squire, L. R. (2006). The fate of old memories after medial temporal lobe damage. *Journal of Neuroscience, 26*, 13311–13317.

Bettermann, K. (2006). Transient global amnesia: The continuing quest for a source. *Archives of Neurology, 63*, 1336–1337.

Braak, H., & Braak, E. (1991). Neuropathological staging of Alzheimer-related changes. *Acta Neuropathologica, 82*, 239–259.

Brandt, J. (1991). The Hopkins Verbal Learning Test: development of a new memory test with six equivalent forms. *Clinical Neuropsychologist, 5*, 125–142.

Brandt, J., Spencer, M., McSorley, P., & Folstein, M. F. (1988). Semantic activation and implicit memory in Alzheimer disease. *Alzheimer Disease and Associated Disorders, 2*, 112–119.

Brandt, J., & van Gorp, W. G. (2006). Functional ("psychogenic") amnesia. *Seminars in Neurology, 26*, 331–340.

Bright, P., Buckman, J., Fradera, A., Yoshimasu, H., Colchester, A. C., & Kopelman, M. D. (2006). Retrograde amnesia in patients with hippocampal, medial temporal, temporal lobe, or frontal pathology. *Learning & Memory, 13*, 545–557.

Brooks, D. N. (1984). Cognitive deficits after head injury. In D. N. Brooks (Ed.), *Closed head injury: Psychological, social, and family consequences*. Oxford: Oxford University Press.

Brooks, D. N., & Baddeley, A. D. (1976). What can amnesic patients learn? *Neuropsychologia, 14*, 111–122.

Buschke, H., & Fuld, P. A. (1974). Evaluating storage, retention, and retrieval in disordered memory and learning. *Neurology, 24*, 1019–1025.

Buschke, H., Sliwinski, M. J., Kuslansky, G., & Lipton, R. B. (1997). Diagnosis of early dementia by the double memory test. *Neurology, 48*, 989–997.

Butters, N., & Cermak, L. S. (1980). *Alcoholic Korsakoff's syndrome: An information processing approach*. New York: Academic Press.

Butters, N., Delis, D. C., & Lucas, J. A. (1995). Clinical assessment of memory disorders in amnesia. *Annual Review of Psychology, 46*, 493–523.

Butters, N., Heindel, W. C., & Salmon, D. P. (1990). Dissociation of implicit memory in dementia: Neurological implications. *Bulletin of the Psychonomic Society, 28*, 359–366.

Butters, N., Salmon, D. P., Cullum, C. M., Cairns, P., Troster, A. I., Jacobs, D., et al. (1988). Differentiation of amnesic and demented patients with the Wechsler Memory Scale-Revised. *The Clinical Neuropsychologist, 2*, 133–148.

Butters, N., Wolfe, J., Martone, M., Granholm, E., & Cermak, L. S. (1985). Memory disorders associated with Huntington's disease: Verbal recall, verbal recognition and procedural memory. *Neuropsychologia, 6*, 729–744.

Carlesimo, G. A., Sabbadini, M., Bombardi, P., Di Porto, E., Loasses, A., & Caltagirone, C. (1998).

Retrograde memory deficits in severe closed head injury patients. *Cortex, 34*, 1–23.

Carlesimo, G. A., Sabbadini, M., Loasses, A., & Caltagirone, C. (1997). Forgetting from long-term memory in severe closed head injury patients: Effect of retrieval conditions and semantic organization. *Cortex, 33*, 131–142.

Chapman, J. (1966). The early symptoms of schizophrenia. *The British Journal of Psychiatry, 112*, 225–251.

Chelune, G. J., & Bornstein, R. A. (1988). WMS-R patterns among patients with unilateral brain lesions. *The Clinical Neuropsychologist, 2*, 121–132.

Cho, Y. H., Beracochea, D., & Jaffard, R. (1993). Extended temporal gradient for the retrograde and anterograde amnesia produced by ibotenate entorhinal cortex lesions in mice. *Journal of Neuroscience, 13*, 1759–1766.

Cohen, B. D., Noblin, C. D., Silverman, A. J., & Penick, S. B. (1968). Functional asymmetry of the human brain. *Science, 162*, 475–477.

Cohen, N., & Squire, L. R. (1980). Preserved learning and retention of pattern analyzing skills in amnesia: Dissociation of knowing how and knowing that. *Science, 210*, 207–210.

Corkin, S. (1968). Acquisition of motor skill after bilateral medial temporal lobe excision. *Neuropsychologia, 6*, 255–265.

Corkin, S. (1984). Lasting consequences of bilateral medial temporal lobectomy: Clinical course and experimental findings in H.M. *Seminars in Neurology, 4*, 249–259.

Corkin, S. (2002). What's new with the amnesic patient H.M.? *Nature Reviews: Neuroscience, 3*, 153–160.

Cowan, N., Beschin, N., & Della Sala, S. (2004). Verbal recall in amnesics under conditions of diminished retroactive interference. *Brain, 127*, 825–834.

Cronholm, B., & Ottosson, J. O. (1961). Memory functions in endogenous depression. *Archives of General Psychiatry, 5*, 101–107.

Crosson, B., Novack, T. A., Trenerry, M. R., & Craig, P. L. (1988). California Verbal Learning Test (CVLT) performance in severely head-injured and neurologically normal adult males. *Journal of Clinical and Experimental Neuropsychology, 10*, 754–768.

Crovitz, H. F., & Schiffman, H. (1974). Frequency of episodic memories as a function of their age. *Bulletin of the Psychonomic Society, 4*, 517–518.

Daum, I., Channon, S., & Canavan, A. (1989). Classical conditioning in patients with severe memory problems. *Journal of Neurology, Neurosurgery, and Psychiatry, 52*, 47–51.

Delaney, R. C., Rosen, A. J., Mattson, R. H., & Novelly, R. A. (1980). Memory function in focal epilepsy: A comparison of non-surgical, unilateral temporal lobe and frontal lobe samples. *Cortex, 16*, 103–117.

Delis, D. C., Kramer, J. H., Kaplan, E., & Ober, B. A. (1987). *The California verbal learning test.* New York: Psychological Corporation.

Delis, D. C., Kramer, J. H., Kaplan, E., & Ober, B. A. (2000). *The California verbal learning test, 2nd edition (CVLT-II).* San Antonio: Psychological Corporation.

Delis, D. C., Massman, P. J., Butters, N., Salmon, D. P., Cermak, L. S., & Kramer, J. H. (1991). Profiles of demented and amnesic patients on the California Verbal Learning Test: Implications for the assessment of memory disorders. *Psychological Assessment, 3*, 19–26.

DeLuca, J., Schultheis, M. T., Madigan, N. K, Christodoulou, C., & Averill, A. (2000). Acquisition versus retrieval deficits in traumatic brain injury: Implications for memory rehabilitation. *Archives of Physical Medicine and Rehabilitation, 81*, 1327–1333.

Devanand, D. P., Pradhaban, G., Liu, X., Khandji, A., De Santi, S., Seagal, S., et al. (2007). Hippocampal and entorhinal atrophy in mild cognitive impairment: prediction of Alzheimer disease. *Neurology, 68*, 828–836.

deWall, C., Wilson, B. A., & Baddeley, A. D. (1994). The extended Rivermead Behavioral Memory Test: A measure of everyday memory performance in adults. *Memory, 2*, 149–166.

Drachman, D. A., & Arbit, J. (1966). Memory and the hippocampal complex. II. Is memory a multiple process? *Archives of Neurology, 15*, 52–61.

Evans, D. A., Funkenstein, H. H., Albert, M. S., Scherr, P. A., Cook, N. R., Chown, M. J., et al. (1989). Prevalence of Alzheimer's disease in a community population of older persons. Higher than previously reported. *JAMA, 262*, 2551–2556.

Fraser, L. M., O'Carroll, R. E., & Ebmeier, K. P. (2008). The effect of electroconvulsive therapy on autobiographical memory: a systematic review. *The Journal of ECT, 24*, 10–17.

Galton, F. (1879). Psychometric experiments. *Brain, 2*, 149–162.

Gold, J. J., & Squire, L. R. (2006). The anatomy of amnesia: Neurohistological analysis of three new cases. *Learning & Memory, 13*, 699–710.

Graf, P., Squire, L. R., & Mandler, G. (1984). The information that amnesic patients do not forget. *Journal of Experimental Psychology: Learning, Memory, and Cognition, 10*, 164–178.

Grober, E., Merling, A., Heimlich, T., & Lipton, R. B. (1997). Free and cued selective reminding and selective reminding in the elderly. *Journal of Clinical and Experimental Neuropsychology, 19*, 643–654.

Heindel, W. C., Salmon, D. P., Shults, C. W., Walicke, P. A., & Butters, N. (1989). Neuropsychological evidence for multiple implicit memory systems: A comparison of Alzheimer's, Huntington's, and Parkinson's disease patients. *Journal of Neuroscience, 9*, 582–587.

Hodges, J. R., Salmon, D. P., & Butters, N. (1993). Recognition and naming of famous faces in Alzheimer's disease: A cognitive analysis. *Neuropsychologia, 31*, 775–788.

Hodges, J. R., & Ward, C. D. (1989). Observations during transient global amnesia: A behavioral and neuropsychological study of five cases. *Brain, 112*, 595–620.

Hodges, J. R., & Warlow, C. P. (1990). The etiology of transient global amnesia: A case-control study of 114 cases with prospective follow-up. *Brain, 113*, 639–657.

Hyman, B. T., Van Hoesen, G. W., Damasio, A. R., & Barnes, C. L. (1984). Alzheimer's disease: Cell specific pathology isolates the hippocampal formation. *Science, 225*, 1168–1170.

Isaac, C. L., & Mayes, A. R. (1999). Rate of forgetting in amnesia: Recall and recognition of prose. *Journal of Experimental Psychology: Learning, Memory, and Cognition, 25*, 942–962.

Jager, T., Bazner, H., Kliegel, M., Szabo, K., & Hennerici, M. G. (2008). The transience and nature of cognitive impairments in transient global amnesia: A meta-analysis. *Journal of Clinical and Experimental Neuropsychology, 3*, 1–12.

James, W. (1890). *Principles of psychology*. New York: Holt.

Janowsky, J. S., Shimamura, A. P., Kritchevsky, M., & Squire, L. R. (1989a). Cognitive impairment following frontal lobe damage and its relevance to human amnesia. *Behavioral Neuroscience, 103*, 548–560.

Janowsky, J. S., Shimamura, A. P., & Squire, L. R. (1989b). Source memory impairment in patients with frontal lobe lesions. *Neuropsychologia, 27*, 1043–1056.

Jennett, B. (1976). Assessment of the severity of head injury. *Journal of Neurology, Neurosurgery, and Psychiatry, 39*, 647–655.

Jones, M. K. (1974). Imagery as a mnemonic aid after left temporal lobectomy: Contrasts between material-specific and generalized memory disorders. *Neuropsychologia, 12*, 21–30.

Kim, J. J., & Fanselow, M. S. (1992). Modality-specific retrograde amnesia of fear. *Science, 256*, 675–677.

Kirwan, C. B., Bayley, P. J., Galvan, V. V., & Squire, L. R. (2008). Detailed recollection of remote autobiographical memory after damage to the medial temporal lobe. *Proceedings of the National Academy of Sciences of the United States of America, 105*, 2676–2680.

Kopelman, M. D. (1989). Remote and autobiographical memory, temporal context memory, and frontal atrophy in Korsakoff and Alzheimer patients. *Neuropsychologia, 27*, 437–460.

Kopelman, M. D. (1995). The assessment of psychogenic amnesia. In A. D. Baddeley, B. A. Wilson, and F.N. Watts (Eds.), *Handbook of memory disorders* (pp. 427–448). Chichester UK: John Wiley.

Kopelman, M. D. (2002). Disorders of memory. *Brain, 125*, 2152–2190.

Kopelman, M. D., Bright, P., Buckman, J., Fradera, A., Yoshimasu H., Jacobson C., & Colchester C. F. (2007). Recall and recognition memory in amnesia: Patients with hippocampal, medial temporal, temporal lobe, or frontal pathology. *Neuropsychologia, 45*, 1232–1246.

Kopelman, M. D., & Stanhope, N. (1997). Rates of forgetting in organic amnesia following temporal lobe, diencephalic, and frontal lobe lesions. *Neuropsychology, 11*, 343–356.

Kopelman, M. D., Stanhope, N., & Kingsley, D. (1999). Retrograde amnesia in patients with diencephalic, temporal lobe or frontal lesions. *Neuropsychologia, 37*, 939–958.

Kopelman, M. D., Wilson, B. A., & Baddeley, A. D. (1989). The Autobiographical Memory Interview: A new assessment of autobiographical and personal semantic memory in amnesic patients. *Journal of Clinical and Experimental Neuropsychology, 11*, 724–744.

Kritchevsky, M. (1989). Transient global amnesia. In F. Boller and J. Grafman (Eds.), *Handbook of neuropsychology* (3rd ed., pp. 167–182). New York: Elsevier.

Kritchevsky, M., Chang, J., & Squire, L. R. (2004). Functional amnesia: Clinical description and neuropsychological profile of 10 cases. *Learning & Memory, 11*, 213–226.

Lackner, J. R. (1974). Observations on the speech processing capabilities of an amnesic patient: Several aspects of H.M.'s language function. *Neuropsychologia, 12*, 199–207.

Lerer, B., Weiner, R. D., & Belmaker, R. H. (1984). *ECT: Basic mechanisms*. London: John Libbey.

Levin, H. S., Benton, A. L., & Grossman, R. G. (1982). *Neurobehavioral consequences of closed head injury*. New York: Oxford University Press.

Levin, H. S., Grossman, R. G., Rose, J. E., & Teasdale, G. (1979). Long-term neuropsychological outcome of closed head injury. *Journal of Neurosurgery, 50*, 412–422.

Levy, D. A., Stark, C. E. L., & Squire, L. R. (2004). Intact conceptual priming in the absence of declarative memory. *Psychological Science, 15*, 680–685.

Lezak, M., Howieson, D. B., & Loring, D. W. (2004). *Neuropsychological assessment*. New York: Oxford University Press

MacKinnon, D., & Squire, L. R. (1989). Autobiographical memory in amnesia. *Psychobiology, 17*, 247–256.

Mair, W. G. P., Warrington, E. K., & Weiskrantz, L. (1979). Memory disorder in Korsakoff's psychosis: A neuropathological and neuropsychological investigation of two cases. *Brain, 102*, 749–783.

Malitz, S., & Sackeim, H. A. (1986). *Electroconvulsive therapy: Clinical and basic research issues.* New York: The New York Academy of Sciences.

Manns, J. R., Hopkins, R. O., Reed, J. M., Kitchener, E. G., & Squire, L. R. (2003). Recognition memory and the human hippocampus. *Neuron, 37*, 171–180.

Markowitsch, H. (1988). Diencephalic amnesia: A reorientation towards tracts? *Brain Research Reviews, 13*, 351–370.

Mattis, S. (1988). *Dementia Rating Scale.* Odessa, FL: Psychological Assessment Resources.

Mayes, A. (1988). *Human organic memory disorders.* New York: Oxford University Press.

McCarthy, R. A., & Warrington, E. K. (1990). Actors but not scripts: The dissociation of people and events in retrograde amnesia. *Neuropsychologia, 30*, 633–644.

McKee, R. D., & Squire, L. R. (1992). Equivalent forgetting rates in long-term memory for diencephalic and medial temporal lobe amnesia. *Journal of Neuroscience, 12*, 3765–3772.

Michel, D., Laurent, B., Foyatier, N., Blanc, A., & Portafaix, M. (1982). Infarctus thalamique paramedian gauche. *Revue Neurologique, 138*, 533–550.

Milner, B. (1958). Psychological deficits produced by temporal lobe excision. *Research Publications – Association for Research in Nervous and Mental Disease, 36*, 244–257.

Milner, B. (1968). Disorders of memory after brain lesions in man. Preface: Material-specific and generalized memory loss. *Neuropsychologia, 6*, 175–179.

Milner, B. (1970). Memory and the medial temporal regions of the brain. In K. H. Pribram and D. E. Broadbent (Eds.), *Biology and memory* (pp. 29–50). New York: Academic Press.

Milner, B. (1971). Interhemispheric differences in the localization of psychological processes in man. *British Medical Bulletin*, 27:272–277.

Milner B., & Teuber H. L. (1968). Alteration of perception and memory in man: Reflection on methods. In L. Weiskrantz (Ed.), *Analysis of behavioral change* (pp. 268–375). New York: Harper and Row.

Mitrushina, M., Boone, K. B., Razani, J., & D'Elia, L. F. (2005). *Handbook of normative data for neuropsychological assessment,* 2nd edition. New York: Oxford University Press.

Moscovitch, M. (1982). Multiple dissociations of function in amnesia. In L. Cermak (Ed.), *Human memory and amnesia* (pp. 337–370). Hillsdale NJ: Lawrence Erlbaum.

Nemiah, J. C. (1980). Dissociative disorders. In H. Kaplan, A. Freedman, and B. Sadock (Eds.), *Comprehensive textbook of psychiatry* (3rd ed., pp. 1544–1561). Baltimore: Williams and Wilkens.

Newcombe, F. (1983). The psychological consequences of closed head injury: Assessment and rehabilitation. *Injury, 14*, 111–136.

Ojemann, G. A. (1971). Alteration in nonverbal short term memory with stimulation in the region of the mammillothalamic tract in man. *Neuropsychologia, 9*, 195–201.

Oscar-Berman, M., Kirkley, S. M., Gansler, D. A., & Couture, A. (2004). Comparisons of Korsakoff and non-Korsakoff alcoholics on neuropsychological tests of prefrontal brain functioning. *Alcoholism, Clinical and Experimental Research, 28*, 667–675.

Osterrieth, P. A. (1944). Le test de copie d'une figure complexe. *Archiv für Psychologie, 30*, 206–256.

Petersen, R. C., Doody, R., Kurz, A., Mohs, R. C., Morris, J. C., et al. (2001). Current concepts in mild cognitive impairment. *Archives of Neurology, 58*, 1985–1992.

Petersen, R. C., Smith, G. E., Ivnik, R. J., Tangalos, E. G., Schaid, D. J., et al. (1995). Apolipoprotein E status as a predictor of the development of Alzheimer's disease in memory-impaired individuals. *JAMA, 273*, 1274–1278.

Ribot, T. (1881). *Les Maladies de la Mémoire* [English translation: Diseases of Memory]. New York: Appleton-Century-Croft.

Reed, L. J., & Squire, L. R. (1997). Impaired recognition memory in patients with lesions limited to the hippocampal formation. *Behavioral Neuroscience, 111*, 667–675.

Reed, L. J., & Squire, L. R. (1998). Retrograde amnesia for facts and events: Findings from four new cases. *Journal of Neuroscience, 18*, 3943–3954.

Rempel-Clower, N., Zola, S. M., Squire, L. R., & Amaral, D. G. (1996). Three cases of enduring memory impairment following bilateral damage limited to the hippocampal formation. *Journal of Neuroscience, 16*, 5233–5255.

Rey, A. (1941). L'examen psychologique dans les d'encephalopathie traumatique. *Archiv für Psychologie, 28*, 286–340.

Rey, A. (1964). *L'examen Clinique Psychologie.* Paris: Presses Universitaires de France.

Russell, W. R., & Nathan, P. W. (1946). Traumatic amnesia. *Brain, 69*, 280–300.

Russell, R., & Smith, N. (1961). Post-traumatic amnesia in closed head injury. *Archives of Neurology, 5*, 16–29.

Sackeim, H. (2000). Memory and ECT: From polarization to reconciliation. *Journal of ECT, 16,* 87–96.

Sadek, J. R., Johnson, S. A., White, D. A., Salmon, D. P., Taylor, K. I., Delapena, J. H., et al. (2004). Retrograde amnesia in dementia: Comparison of HIV-associated dementia, Alzheimer's disease, and Huntington's disease. *Neuropsychology, 18,* 692–699.

Saint-Cyr, J. A., & Taylor, A. E. (1992). The mobilization of procedural learning: The "key signature" of the basal ganglia. In L. R. Squire and N. Butters (Eds.), *Neuropsychology of memory* (2nd ed., pp. 188–202). New York: Guilford Press.

Salmon, D. P. (2000). Disorders of memory in Alzheimer's disease. In L. S. Cermak (Ed.), *Handbook of neuropsychology, 2nd edition (Vol. 2): Memory and its disorders* (pp. 155–195). Amsterdam: Elsevier.

Salmon, D. P., Shimamura, A. P., Butters, N., & Smith, S. (1988). Lexical and semantic priming deficits in patients with Alzheimer's disease. *Journal of Clinical and Experimental Neuropsychology, 10,* 477–494.

Salmon, D. P., Thomas, R. G., Pay, M. M., Booth, A., Hofstetter, C. R., Thal, L. J., et al. (2002). Alzheimer's disease can be accurately diagnosed in very mildly impaired individuals. *Neurology, 59,* 1022–1028.

Sanders, H. I., & Warrington, E. K. (1971). Memory for remote events in amnesic patients. *Brain, 94,* 661–668.

Schacter, D. L. (1987). Implicit memory: History and current status. *Journal of Experimental Psychology: Learning, Memory, and Cognition, 13,* 501–518.

Schacter, D., & Crovitz, H. F. (1977). Memory function after closed head injury: A review of the quantitative research. *Cortex, 13,* 150–176.

Schacter, D., Wang, P. L., Tulving, E., & Freedman, P. C. (1982). Functional retrograde amnesia: A quantitative case study. *Neuropsychologia, 20,* 523–532.

Scoville, W. B., & Milner, B. (1957). Loss of recent memory after bilateral hippocampal lesions. *Journal of Neurology, Neurosurgery, and Psychiatry, 20,* 11–21.

Seltzer, B., & Benson, D. F. (1974). The temporal pattern of retrograde amnesia in Korsakoff's disease. *Neurology, 24,* 527–530.

Shimamura, A. P. (1986). Priming effects in amnesia: Evidence for a dissociable memory function. *The Quarterly Journal of Experimental Psychology: Human Experimental Psychology, 38,* 619–644.

Shimamura, A. P., Janowsky, J. S., & Squire, L. R. (1990). Memory for the temporal order of events in patients with frontal lobe lesions and amnesic patients. *Neuropsychologia, 28,* 803–814.

Shimamura, A. P., Janowsky, J. S., & Squire, L. R. (1991). What is the role of frontal lobe damage in memory disorders? In H. D. Levin, H. M. Eisenberg, and A. L. Benton (Eds.), *Frontal lobe function and dysfunction* (pp. 173–195). New York: Oxford University Press.

Shimamura, A. P., Salmon, D. P., Squire, L. R., & Butters, N. (1987). Memory dysfunction and word priming in dementia and amnesia. *Behavioral Neuroscience, 101,* 347–351.

Shimamura, A .P. & Squire, L. R. (1984). Paired-associate learning and priming effects in amnesia: a neuropsychological study. *Journal of Experimental Psychology: General, 113,* 556–570.

Schmolck, H., Stefanacci, L., & Squire, L. R. (2000). Detection and explanation of ambiguity are unaffected by hippocampal lesions but are impaired by larger temporal lobe lesions. *Hippocampus, 10,* 759–770.

Shrager, Y., Levy, D. A., Hopkins, R. O., & Squire, L. R. (2008). Working memory and the organization of brain systems. *Journal of Neuroscience, 28,* 4818–4822.

Speedie, L. J., & Heilman, K. M. (1982). Amnestic disturbance following infarction of the left dorsomedial nucleus of the thalamus. *Neuropsychologia, 20,* 597–604.

Squire, L. R. (1974). Remote memory as affected by aging. *Neuropsychologia, 12,* 429–435.

Squire, L. R. (1982). Comparisons between forms of amnesia: Some deficits are unique to Korsakoff's syndrome. *Journal of Experimental Psychology: Learning, Memory, and Cognition, 8,* 560–571.

Squire, L. R. (1986). Memory functions as affected by ECT. In S. Malitz and H. Sackeim (Eds.), *Electroconvulsive therapy: Clinical and basic issues* (pp. 307–314). New York: New York Academy of Sciences.

Squire, L. R. (1989). On the course of forgetting in very long-term memory. *Journal of Experimental Psychology: Learning, Memory, and Cognition, 15,* 241–245.

Squire, L. R. (2004). Memory systems of the brain: A brief history and current perspective. *Neurobiology of Learning and Memory, 82,* 171–177.

Squire, L. R., & Alvarez, P. (1995). Retrograde amnesia and memory consolidation: A neurobiological perspective. *Current Opinion in Neurobiology, 5,* 169–177.

Squire, L. R., Amaral, D. G., Zola-Morgan, S. M., Kritchevsky, M., & Press, G. (1989). Description of brain injury in the amnesic patient N.A. based on magnetic resonance imaging. *Experimental Neurology, 105,* 23–35.

Squire, L. R., & Bayley, P. J. (2007). The neuroscience of remote memory. *Current Opinion in Neurobiology, 17,* 185–196.

Squire, L. R., & Chace, P. M. (1975). Memory functions six to nine months after electroconvulsive therapy. *Archives of General Psychiatry, 32,* 1557–1564.

Squire, L. R., & Cohen, N. J. (1982). Remote memory, retrograde amnesia, and the neuropsychology of memory. In L. Cermak (Ed.), *Human memory and amnesia* (pp. 275–303). Hillsdale, NJ: Lawrence Erlbaum.

Squire, L. R., Haist, F., & Shimamura, A. P. (1989). The neurology of memory: Quantitative assessment of retrograde amnesia in two groups of amnesic patients. *Journal of Neuroscience, 9,* 828–839.

Squire, L. R., & Kandel, E. R. (2009). *Memory: From mind to molecules.* 2nd edition. Greenwood Village CO: Roberts & Company.

Squire, L. R., & Schacter, D. L. (2002). *The neuropsychology of memory*, 3rd ed. New York: Guilford Press.

Squire, L. R., & Shimamura, A. P. (1986). Characterizing amnesic patients for neurobehavioral study. *Behavioral Neuroscience, 100,* 866–877.

Squire, L. R., & Slater, P. C. (1975). Forgetting in very long-term memory as assessed by an improved questionnaire technique. *Journal of Experimental Psychology: Human Learning and Memory, 104,* 50–54.

Squire, L. R., & Slater, P. C. (1983). Electroconvulsive therapy and complaints of memory dysfunction: A prospective three-year follow-up study. *The British Journal of Psychiatry, 142,* 1–8.

Squire, L. R., Slater, P. C., & Chace, P. M. (1975). Retrograde amnesia: temporal gradient in very long term memory following electroconvulsive therapy. *Science, 187,* 77–79.

Squire, L. R., & Zola-Morgan, S. (1991). The medial temporal lobe memory system. *Science, 253,* 1380–1386.

Squire, L. R., & Zola, S. M. (1996). Structure and function of declarative and nondeclarative memory systems. *Proceedings of the National Academy of Sciences of the United States of America, 93,* 13515–13522.

Sternberg, D. E., & Jarvik, M. E. (1976). Memory functions in depression. *Archives of General Psychiatry, 33,* 219–224.

Stromgren, L. S. (1977). The influence of depression on memory. *Acta Psychiatrica Scandinavica, 56,* 109–128.

Strub, R. L., & Black, F. W. (1977). *The mental status examination in neurology.* Philadelphia: FA Davis.

Talland, G. A. (1965). *Deranged memory.* New York: Academic Press.

Terry, R. D., & Katzman, R. (1983). Senile dementia of the Alzheimer type. *Annals of Neurology, 14,* 497–506.

Terry, R. D., Masliah, E., Salmon, D. P., Butters, N., DeTeresa, R., Hill, R., et al. (1991). Physical basis of cognitive alterations in Alzheimer's disease: Synapse loss is the major correlate of cognitive impairment. *Annals of Neurology, 30,* 572–580.

Troster, A. I., Jacobs, D., Butters, N., Cullum, M., & Salmon, D. P. (1989). Differentiating Alzheimer's disease from Huntington's disease with the Wechsler Memory Scale-Revised. *Clinics in Geriatric Medicine, 5,* 611–632.

Tulving, E. (1983). *Elements of episodic memory.* New York: Oxford University Press.

Tulving, E., & Schacter, D. L. (1990). Priming and human memory systems. *Science, 247,* 301–306.

Twamley, E. W., Ropacki, S. A., & Bondi, M. W. (2006). Neuropsychological and neuroimaging changes in preclinical Alzheimer's disease. *Journal of the International Neuropsychological Society, 12,* 707–735.

Vakil, E. (2005). The effect of moderate to severe traumatic brain injury (TBI) on different aspects of memory: A selective review. *Journal of Clinical and Experimental Neuropsychology, 27,* 977–1021.

Vakil, E., Arbell, N., Gozlan, M., Hoofien, D., & Blachstein, H. (1992). Relative importance of informational units and their role in long-term recall by closed-head-injured patients and control groups. *Journal of Consulting and Clinical Psychology, 60,* 802–803.

Vakil, E., & Oded, Y. (2003). Comparison between three memory tests: Cued recall, priming and savings in closed-head injured patients and controls. *Journal of Clinical and Experimental Neuropsychology, 25,* 274–282.

Vanderploeg, R. D., Crowell, T. A., & Curtiss, G. (2001). Verbal learning and memory deficits in traumatic brain injury: Encoding, consolidation, and retrieval. *Journal of Clinical and Experimental Neuropsychology, 23,* 185–195.

Verfaellie, M., & O'Connor, M. (2000). A neuropsychological analysis of memory and amnesia. *Seminars in Neurology, 20,* 455–462.

Victor, M., Adams, R. D., & Collins, C. (1989). *The Wernicke-Korsakoff syndrome and related neurologic disorders due to alcoholism and malnutrition.* Philadelphia: FA Davis.

Victor, M., & Agamanolis, J. (1990). Amensia due to lesions confined to the hippocampus: A clinical-pathological study. *Journal of Cognitive Neuroscience, 2,* 246–257.

Warrington, E. K. (1984). *Recognition memory test.* Windsor England: NFER-Nelson Publishing Company LTD.

Wechsler, D. (1945). A standardized memory scale for clinical use. *Journal of Psychology, 19,* 87–95.

Wechsler, D. (1987). *The Wechsler memory scale-revised*. New York: Psychological Corporation.

Wechsler, D. (1997). *The Wechsler Memory Scale, Third Edition (WMS-III) Administration and Scoring Manual*. San Antonio, TX: The Psychological Corporation.

Weiner, R. D., Rogers, H. J., Welch, C. A., Davidson, J. R. T., Miller, R. D., Weir, D., et al. (1984). ECT stimulus parameters and electrode placement: Relevance to therapeutic and adverse effects. In B. Lerer, R. D. Weiner, and R. H. Bellmaker (Eds.), *ECT: Basic Mechanisms* (pp. 139–147). London: John Libbey and Company.

Weiskrantz, L., & Warrington, E. K. (1979). Conditioning in amnesic patients. *Neuropsychologia, 17*, 187–194.

Welsh, K., Butters, N., Hughes, J., Mohs, R., & Heyman, A. (1991). Detection of abnormal memory decline in mild cases of Alzheimer's disease using CERAD neuropsychological measures. *Archives of Neurology, 48*, 278–281.

Wheeler, M. A., Stuss, D. T., & Tulving, E. (1995). Frontal lobe damage produces episodic memory impairment. *Journal of the International Neuropsychological Society, 1*, 525–536.

Wilson, B. A. (1987). *Rehabilitation of memory*. New York: Guilford Press.

Wilson, B. A. (2008). Neuropsychological rehabilitation. *Annual Review of Clinical Psychology, 4*, 141–162.

Wilson, B. A., Cockburn, J., Baddeley, A. D., & Hiorns, R. (1989). The development and validation of a test battery for detecting and monitoring everyday memory problems. *Journal of Clinical and Experimental Neuropsychology, 11*, 855–870.

Winocur, G. (1990). Anterograde and retrograde amnesia in rats with dorsal hippocampal or dorsomedial thalamic lesions. *Behavioral Brain Research, 38*, 145–154.

Wixted, J. T., & Squire, L. R. (2004). Recall and recognition are equally impaired in patients with selective hippocampal damage. *Cognitive, Affective & Behavioral Neuroscience, 4*, 58–66.

Zangwill, O. L. (1977). The amnesic syndrome. In C. W. M. Whitty and O. L. Zangwill (Eds.), *Amnesia: clinical, psychological, and medicolegal aspects* (pp. 104–117). London: Butterworths.

Zec, R. F., Zellers, D., Belman, J., Miller, J., Matthews, J., Ferneau-Belman, D., et al. (2001). Long-term consequences of severe closed head injury on episodic memory. *Journal of Clinical and Experimental Neuropsychology, 23*, 671–691.

Zola-Morgan, S., Cohen, N. J., & Squire, L. R. (1983). Recall of remote episodic memory in amnesia. *Neuropsychologia, 21*, 487–500.

Zola-Morgan, S., & Squire, L. R. (1990). The primate hippocampal formation: Evidence for a time-limited role in memory storage. *Science, 250*, 288–290.

Zola-Morgan, S., & Squire, L. R. (1993). Neuroanatomy of memory. *Annual Review of Neuroscience, 16*, 547–563.

Zola-Morgan, S., Squire, L. R., & Amaral, D. G. (1986). Human amnesia and the medial temporal region: Enduring memory impairment following a bilateral lesion limited to field CA1 of the hippocampus. *Journal of Neuroscience, 6*, 2950–2967.

Part III

Psychosocial Consequences of Neuropsychological Impairment

24

Neurobehavioral Consequences of Traumatic Brain Injury

Sureyya Dikmen, Joan Machamer, and Nancy Temkin

Traumatic brain injury (TBI) is of major public health significance, affecting approximately 1.4 million people in the United States each year (Langlois et al., 2004; Thurman et al., 1999). Of these about 50,000 die and 230,000 are admitted to an acute care hospital and survive until discharge (Thurman et al., 1999). About 1.1 million are seen in emergency rooms and discharged, and countless others are either not reported or are seen in private doctor's offices. An estimated 80,000–90,000 persons are left with long-term disability (Sosin et al., 1995) (See Figure 24–1).

Hospitalization rates for TBI have decreased steadily since 1980s as seen in Figure 24–2. It is noteworthy that the most dramatic decline has been for those with mild TBI. Although various factors may be responsible for the decline seen for those with mild TBI, such as lower incidence rates due to prevention efforts, it appears that this decline might be primarily due to changes in hospital admission policies (Thurman et al., 1999).

Of all TBIs, approximately 75%–80% are considered mild (Centers for Disease Control and Prevention, 2004—www.cdc.gov/injury) While the majority of individuals with a mild brain injury recover within days to months after injury, others, including a fraction of the milds and those with more severe TBIs, experience long-term impairments that affect their ability to resume their prior social roles and responsibilities.

Figure 24–3 shows rates of TBI per 100,000 by age and gender. Males outnumber females in all age groups except perhaps after age 75.

Figure 24–4 shows the rates by age, gender, and external cause. Falls are most frequent in children and in those older than 75. Moving vehicle accidents and assaults are relatively even across age groups with perhaps higher rates for ages 10–35. While head injuries can affect anyone, the rates are higher in those with less education, minority status, and lower socioeconomic status. Alcohol intoxication is involved in 1/3–1/2 of the hospitalized cases of TBI. History of substance abuse predating the injury is also high (Bombardier et al., 2003; Corrigan, 1995; Dikmen et al., 1995a).

Perhaps the definition of consequences of TBI as formulated by the Consensus Conference in 1998 captures best the enormity and variety of consequences:

Regardless of severity, consequences rarely are limited to one set of symptoms, clearly delineated impairments or a disability that affects only part of a person's life. Rather, consequences of TBI often affect human functions along a continuum: from altered physiological functions of cells; through neurological, neuropsychological and psychological impairments; to medical problems and disabilities that affect the individual with TBI, family, friends, community as well as society in general. (Consensus conference. Rehabilitation of persons with traumatic brain injury. NIH Consensus Development Panel on Rehabilitation of Persons with Traumatic Brain Injury, 1999)

Given the rate of mortality and disabilities, TBI costs are very high both economically and in terms of the suffering engendered. Max et al.

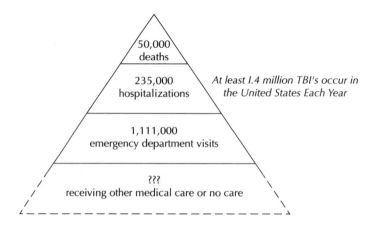

Figure 24–1. Average annual number of traumatic brain injury-related emergency department visits, hospitalizations, and deaths, United States, 1995–2001. (From: Centers for Disease Control and Prevention, 2004 [http://www.cdc.gov/ncipc/pub-res/TBI_in_US_04/TBI in the US_Jan_2006.pdf]).

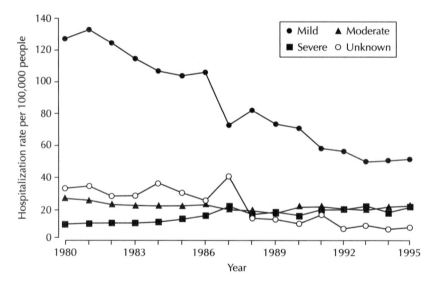

Figure 24–2. Incidence rates of TBI-related hospitalizations in the United States by category of severity, 1980–1995. (From: National Hospital Discharge Survey, National Center for Health Statistics, Centers for Disease Control and Prevention from: Thurman D, Guerrero J. [1999]. Trends in hospitalization associated with traumatic brain injury. *JAMA*, 282, 954–957. Copyright © 1999, American Medical Association. All rights reserved.)

(1991) estimated the lifetime costs of head injuries sustained in 1985 to be $44 billion in 1988 dollars. The majority of the cost (54%) was not for direct health care but was rather incurred by lost productivity and dependency of survivors. More recent estimates put the cost at $60 billion in 2000 (Finkelstein et al., 2006).

Over the last 20–25 years considerable information has accumulated regarding the nature

of impairments, disabilities, and participation problems that occur in the survivors of such injuries. This chapter is a selective review of neuropsychological and psychosocial outcome following TBI and some of the factors that contribute to these outcomes with emphasis on the results of our studies. We will also briefly review selected topics of recent interest: genetic factors in relation to outcome, whether TBI presents a

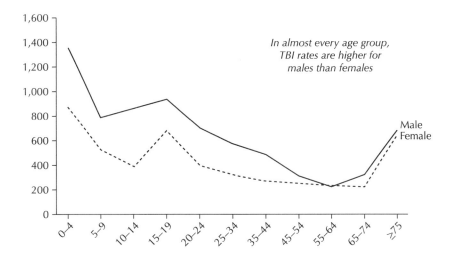

Figure 24–3. Average annual traumatic brain injury-related rates for emergency department visits, hospitalizations, and deaths, by age group and sex, United States, 1995–2001. (From: Centers for Disease Control and Prevention, 2004 [http://www.cdc.gov/ncipc/pub-res/TBI_in_US_04/TBI in the US_Jan_2006.pdf]).

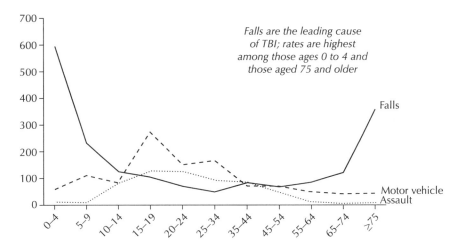

Figure 24–4. Average annual traumatic brain injury-related rates for emergency department visits, hospitalizations, and deaths, by age group and external cause, United States, 1995–2001. (From: Centers for Disease Control and Prevention, 2004 [http://www.cdc.gov/ncipc/pub-res/TBI_in_US_04/TBI in the US_Jan_2006.pdf]).

risk factor for later neurodegenerative diseases, and aging with TBI.

Outcome and Determinants of Outcome

Outcome following TBI ranges from death to full recovery. Time to maximal recovery may range from days or weeks to years, depending on the severity of injury, the age at the time of injury, and the type of function in question, among other factors. The outcome is determined by a host of factors including severity of the brain injury, characteristics of the person injured, time since injury, and a number of factors after the injury that may facilitate or hinder recovery.

A brief review of indices used to assess severity of injury is in order. Severity of closed/blunt injuries most often sustained in civilian TBIs is typically measured by various indices of degree of altered state of consciousness, reflecting the degree of diffuse brain injury. Glasgow Coma

Table 24–1. Glasgow Coma Scale

Best Eye Opening		Best Motor	
Code		Code	
4	Spontaneous	6	Obeys commands
3	To verbal stimulation	5	Localizes to pain
2	To pain	4	Abnormal withdrawal to pain
1	None	3	Flexion to pain
		2	Extension to pain
		1	No response to pain
Best Verbal		TBI Classification by Total GCS	
Code			
5	Oriented	Mild	13–15
4	Confused	Moderate	9–12
3	Inappropriate words	Severe	3–8
2	Unintelligible sounds	Complicated	
1	No verbalization	Mild	13–15 with CT abnormalities

Scale (GCS; Teasdale & Jennett, 1974), the most commonly used measure, is an index of depth of coma at a specified time after injury (see Table 24-1). This scale assesses eye opening, verbal responses, and motor responses to stimulation, with scores ranging from 3 to 15. Severe injuries are considered to be those with GCS of 8 or less. Moderate TBI is considered when the GCS is between 9 and 12, and mild TBI when the GCS is 13 or greater. Generally, the lowest score obtained in the first 24 hours after resuscitation is used for classification purposes. Patients with GCS of 13–15 with CT abnormalities are considered as complicated mild and thought to have outcomes similar to those with moderate injuries (Williams et al., 1990), although more research is needed in this area.

Measures of duration of impaired consciousness typically are better predictors of outcome than measures of depth of coma such as the GCS. These measures include posttraumatic amnesia (PTA) and time from injury to consistently follow commands. PTA is the period of time from injury to the time when regular memory for day-to-day events return. PTA can be determined retrospectively (Levin, 1995) or prospectively (Russell & Smith, 1961). Prospectively assessed PTA may be a better predictor but much more difficult to assess, or less likely to be available to the clinician as it requires daily monitoring of the return of

memory to more normal levels. Time to follow commands is the time from injury to the point when the individual is able to follow simple commands consistently as defined by the motor component of the GCS (Teasdale & Jennett, 1974). This index can be often obtained from careful review of nursing notes during acute hospitalization.

Other indices of severity of brain injury that have been examined include CT abnormalities and pupilary size and reactivity. Secondary insults such as hypoxia, hypotension, and increased intracranial pressure also relate to outcome. TBIs manifest themselves in various combinations of these severity indicators. Unfortunately, there is no higher-order classifications system developed to date that takes into account some combination of these severity indices and relates them to outcome, in a clinician user friendly manner. An exception is the work of the International Mission on Prognosis and Analysis of Clinical Trials in Traumatic Brain Injury (IMPACT), which uses multiple factors including demographics and severity indicators to provide predictions of outcomes for individual cases through a Web site. However, the outcome predicted is a very global index of overall functioning at 6 months postinjury (e.g., dead versus alive; unfavorable (dead, vegetative, and severe disability) versus favorable outcome (moderate disability and good recovery).

Challenges to the Determination of TBI-Related Losses in Civilian Injuries

Unavailability of Baseline Information

One of the biggest challenges to studying neurobehavioral outcomes of civilian TBI is the absence of adequate information (i.e., baseline) about the condition in which the individual started prior to the injury. Important questions regarding outcomes of TBI include the determination of the nature and severity of the losses sustained, the recovery trajectory, and, ultimately, the nature and degree of residual deficits if any and how to predict them. These questions can be more accurately and efficiently answered if one has good information about where the individual started from. Unfortunately, for the majority of the civilian injuries such information is unavailable.

Two injury circumstances where baseline information has been available and have shown the value of such information are those of war and sports injuries. In the case of war injuries, the Army General Classification Test (AGCT) scores used in World War II and the later developed Armed Forces Qualification Test (AFQT), which are correlated with indices of general intelligence and were administered at induction into the army, were used as baseline information (Grafman et al., 1986; Schwab et al., 1993). The results of these studies have elucidated important information about the role of preinjury intelligence on outcome from head injury. To give a couple of examples, Grafman et al. (1986) studied Vietnam veterans with penetrating head injuries of either right or left hemisphere lesions and compared structural lesion location, total brain tissue volume loss, and preinjury AFQT scores with postinjury intellectual functioning. Their results showed that preinjury intelligence was a more significant predictor of tests requiring a number of complementary cognitive processes than either the volume of brain tissue loss or lesion location, highlighting the importance of baseline cognitive functioning in explaining postinjury cognitive outcome. Weinstein and Teuber (1957) provided information about a different question. They examined whether there was a differential decline in intellectual functioning postinjury based on the preinjury intellectual or educational level of the person with TBI. They compared the change in intellectual function on the AGCT from pre- to postinjury to see if those who had low educational levels or performed poorly on the AGCT before the injury showed a greater decline than those who did better initially. They found no evidence to support a relationship between higher level of functioning preinjury and less decline after the injury.

In the case of civilian TBIs, obtaining baseline information has been possible in sports injuries. In these studies players are examined preseason. This design has allowed researchers to examine those injured versus those who have not been injured, consider change in performance from pre- to postinjury in the two groups, and, by monitoring performance over days, ascertain when the results of those injured normalize. A fair amount of literature has accumulated regarding neuropsychological recovery from sports injuries. Please see Belanger and Vanderploeg (2005) and Cernich et al., (2007) for reviews. These studies suggest that recovery of neuropsychological deficits from mild sports injuries seem to occur over about 7–14 days. The most significant finding is that those sustaining TBI seem to fail to benefit from practice effects expected from repeated exposure to the tests.

While the war injuries or sports injuries benefit from the availability of baseline information, they represent very specialized subgroups of TBI. Those studied with injuries from previous conflicts have had penetrating injuries with major and distinct localized brain damage. Sports injuries tend to be very mild, and in both cases the population tends to be principally healthy young adults.

Choice of Control Groups

In the absence of baseline information, performance of a comparison group allows determination of deficits in a group with TBI. The choice of comparison group to be used is important. One needs to consider comparability on a number of dimensions not only on age, education, and gender but also on sometimes difficult-to-define temperamental and sociodemographic factors that may predispose or characterize those injured. Such groups may include friends or family members of the injured based on the assumption that "birds of a feather flock together" (Dikmen et al., 1986; Dikmen & Temkin, 1987; McLean et al., 1993). Another type of comparison group is a general trauma group, which includes persons who sustained injury to other body parts but not to the brain. This kind of a group, although not as good as a baseline in some respects, may take into account lifestyle similarities as well as injuries to other body parts which could impact neurobehavioral functioning. Because of differences in the populations, use of normative samples to judge patient results in clinical work can be also misleading, particularly when the patient has sustained a mild TBI and the consequences are mild and subtle. Normal variation in performance can mimic or mask TBI effects (Dikmen et al., 2001).

Representativeness of the Cases with TBI Studied

If we are interested in the nature and magnitude of limitations due to TBI, the samples studied need to be representative of persons with TBI. Enrollment in the study needs to be based on the characteristics of the injury, rather than on outcome. For instance, a clinic population seen for impairments and disabilities associated with TBI is inappropriate. The latter type of a sample may provide very useful information about the type of problems that may happen after injury but will inflate the magnitude of the problems as was seen in earlier mild TBI studies (e.g., Rimel et al., 1981).

Loss to Follow-up

Finally, another big challenge is performing longitudinal studies with minimal loss to follow-up. This is a big problem in TBI studies as the population injured tend to be young and mobile. Enrolling and maintaining subjects in the studies is a difficult, labor-intensive, and expensive yet critical endeavor because loss to follow-up is not random (Barber, 2003; Corrigan et al., 2003), and thus, if the loss to follow-up rate is high, the results could over- or underestimate head injury

effects. Those more likely to be lost to follow-up, not unexpectedly, tend to be those with lower education and problematic psychosocial histories such as drug and alcohol abuse. Results based on those that can be followed may not provide an accurate picture of head injury effects.

Although these challenges are formidable, they are not insurmountable, and considerable effort has been put into obtaining useful outcome information for the broad class of civilian injuries. Choice of control group and adequate sample size are critical. The 1800 TBI cases and 230 controls in our data repository is the largest series of cases enrolled at injury and followed longitudinally with neuropsychological and functional status measures of outcome and will provide the basis for much of what follows.

Neuropsychological Outcomes

Neuropsychological impairments refer to cognitive difficulties such as problems with attention, working memory, episodic memory, information-processing speed, executive functions, language, and visual-spatial skills. Neuropsychological difficulties are sensitive to the effects of TBI and have received considerable research attention because of their importance in compromising the functioning of individuals in everyday life and their quality of life. Various factors influence the nature and severity of cognitive impairment, such as the characteristics of the person injured, severity of the brain injury, and time from injury to the time of testing, which reflects recovery.

The severity of the brain injury clearly has a decisive effect on neuropsychological outcome. Severity indices such as coma length (Dikmen et al., 1995b), coma depth (Teasdale & Jennet, 1974), one or both nonreactive pupils, and presence and severity of mass lesions have significant impact on outcome.

In one of our studies (Dikmen et al., 1995b) we examined the neuropsychological functioning of a group of 436 persons with TBI on a comprehensive battery of neuropsychological measures 1 year after injury. These patients were nonselect, representative cases enrolled in the study at the time of injury and followed to 1 year with a high follow-up rate of 85%. Functions assessed ranged from motor to higher-level executive functions and included finger tapping speed, sustained and divided attention, memory and learning, verbal and performance intelligence, processing speed, reasoning, and overall neuropsychological competency index. The performances of these subjects, as a group, and also subdivided by various severity indices, were compared with a group of general trauma subjects who had sustained injury but not to the head.

Table 24–2 shows the performances of the TBI cases divided by time from injury to follow simple commands (TFC), an index of length of impaired consciousness. Overall, the TBI subjects as a group performed significantly more poorly than the general trauma group. The impairments were not restricted to attention, memory, or speed of information processing, abilities thought to be sensitive to TBI. Rather, the impairments were diffuse, and also involved motor skills, general intellectual functions, new problem solving, and overall impairments. The magnitude and the pervasiveness of impairments, however, depended on severity of the brain injury. There was clearly a relationship between TFC and level of cognitive impairments 1 year after injury. As a group, the performances of the subgroup with TFC less than 1 hour were comparable to those of the general trauma group. Selective impairments on measures of attention and memory start to emerge with longer TFC of 1–24 hours. With longer TFC lengths such as 1–2 weeks or more, nearly all measures are impaired, with pronounced and consistent impairments observed in the groups with 2–4 weeks or more. It is interesting to note that more consistent differences between the TBI subgroups and the control group are on measures of speed (simple and psychomotor) and composite measures (Performance Intelligence Quotient—PIQ, Halstead Impairment Index) rather than more specific measures of attention and memory. While the constructs of attention and memory are clearly impacted by TBI, measures of these constructs are not very reliable (Dikmen et al., 1999). Composite measures may derive their significance because of increased measurement reliability due to the multiplicity of the observations they are based on. The construct of speed (or processing speed) holds promise as an important area of investigation from both theoretical and clinical perspectives

in explaining the difficulties in everyday life of persons with TBI. In the employment literature, simple and complex motor speed measures have been shown as being important in the employability of both head-injured persons and those with epilepsy (Dikmen & Morgan, 1980; Fraser et al., 1988).

Dose–response relationships can be observed on other measures of brain injury severity. Figure 24–5 shows the relationship between overall neuropsychological impairment (Halstead Impairment Index) and several brain injury severity indices including GCS (an index of depth of coma), neurosurgical intervention for evacuation of space-occupying lesions, and number of nonreactive pupils. Halstead Impairment index, which is based on performance on seven measures, ranges from 0 to 1, with 0 indicating that none of the measures was in the impaired range and 1 that all were. Dose–response relationship between this index and the various severity indicators are obvious. What is noteworthy is the range of variability in performance within each of the severity steps across the different severity indicators. Those with the least or less severity are quite homogenous in their performances, similar to the trauma controls. The performances of those with greater severities are quite heterogeneous, with the exception of the very severe group as represented with TFC of 1 month or more. These results indicate that although there is a dose–response relationship between severity and neuropsychological performance, there is great variability within each of the severity levels indicating that other factors are at play to either exacerbate or mitigate the impact of severity on performance or the recovery potential.

The degree of neuropsychological impairments is greater soon after injury with recovery occurring over days, weeks, months, and maybe years. Degree of improvement and degree of residuals relate to degree of original loss. Figure 24–6 shows recovery of WAIS-PIQ (Wechsler Adult Intelligence Scale-Performance Intelligence Quotient) from 1 to 12 months in subgroups of patients divided on the basis of time to follow commands. Those with more severe brain injury show greater loss at 1 month compared to trauma controls. Those with greater loss have more room to improve with the

Table 24–2. Median Scores for Trauma Controls and Subjects with TBI Divided by Time to Follow Commands.[a]

Measure	Trauma controls[b]	<1 hour[c]	1–24 hours[d]	25 hours–6 days[e]	7–13 days[f]	14–28 days[g]	≥29 days[h]	r[i]
Motor Functions								
Finger Tapping, dominant hand	53	51	52	47***	49**	42***	11***	−.51
Finger Tapping, nondominant hand	50	48	48	44***	45**	38***	16***	−.47
Namewriting, dominant hand	0.50	0.50	0.53	0.60	0.60*	0.69***	3.15***	.49
Namewriting, nondominant hand	1.30	1.41	1.44	1.87*	1.64***	1.82***	3.60***	.43
Attention and flexibility								
Seashore Rhythm Test	27	27	26	27	26	24***	16***	−.42
Trail Making Test, Part A	23	22	25	27**	26*	40***	101***	.57
Trail Making Test, Part B	56	57	72*	63	71	132***	301***	.50
Stroop Color and Word Test, Part 1	42	42	46	44	48***	70***	151***	.51
Stroop Color and Word Test, Part 2	96	98	108	107	122***	162***	300***	.49
Memory								
WMS-LM	11	10.5	10	10	9	8**	0.50***	−.39
WMS-VR	11	12	10	11	11	9*	4***	−.38
SR-RCL	89	89	84*	86*	75***	69***	24***	−.53
WMS-LM, delayed	9	9	8	7*	7*	6***	0***	−.46
WMS-VR, delayed	10	11	10	9	10	6***	0***	−.45
SR-RCL 30-minute delay	9	8	8*	8	7***	5***	0***	−.45
SR-RCL, 4-hour delay	8	8	7	8	5***	4***	0***	−.46
Verbal								
WAIS-VIQ	106	106	101	101	98	92***	57***	−.45
Performance Skills								
WAIS-PIQ	112	110	106	102***	102**	90***	56***	−.55
TPT-T	0.36	0.35	0.40	0.61***	0.51***	1.10***	5.75***	.61
Reasoning								
Category Test	24	22	28	41	32	72***	112***	.54
Overall								
Halstead Impairment Index	0.1	0.1	0.3	0.4***	0.4**	0.7***	1.0***	.59

Notes: WMS-LM = Wechsler Memory Scale Logical Memory. WMS-VR = Wechsler Memory Scale Visual Reproduction. SR-RCL = Selective Reminding Test Total Recall. TPT-T = Tactual Performance Test time per block. WAIS-VIQ = Wechsler Adult Intelligence Scale Verbal Intelligence Quotient. WAIS-PIQ = Wechsler Adult Intelligence Scale- Performance Intelligence Quotient.

[a]For example, the median WAIS-PIQ for subjects with TBI who took less than 1 hour to follow commands is 110. The median decreases systematically as time to follow commands increases and subjects with TBI -injured who took 29 days or more to follow commands have a median WAIS-PIQ of 56.

[b]$n = 121$. [c]$n = 161$. [d]$n = 100$. [e]$n = 52$. [f]$n = 37$. [g]$n = 32$. [h]$n = 53$; median is untestable, lowest observed score recorded.

[i]All significant at $p < .001$.

*$p < .05$. **$p < .01$ ***$p < .001$.

Source: Dikmen et al. (1995b). Published by APA, reprinted with permission.

slopes of improvement appearing to be proportional to the degree of initial loss. An exception is the most severe group (i.e., TFC greater than 29 days). This group also showed improvement, but the improvement is difficult to observe due to floor effects of the measure. Those with milder injuries have lost less and, thus, have less room to improve. In spite of greater improvement, those with greater initial loss end up with greater impairments 1 year after injury. These

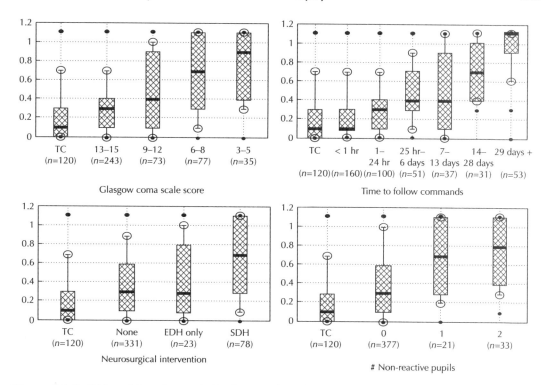

Figure 24–5. Halstead Impairment Index by neurological severity indices. (From: Dikmen et al. [1995]. Neuropsychological outcome at 1-year post head injury. *Neuropsychology,* 9(1), 80–90. Published by APA, reprinted with permission.)

Note: TC = Trauma Control, EDH = Epidural Hematoma, SDH = Subdural Hematoma. Halstead Impairment Index = 1.1 is the value assigned to untestable subjects.

results suggest that the degree of initial deficit is a significant determinant of the subsequent amount of recovery and the residual deficits (Dikmen et al., 1983).

Of the demographic factors, age has a major impact on outcome. The clearest evidence for age effects comes from studies based on severe TBI and using global outcomes, as will be reviewed later under psychosocial outcomes. Neuropsychological studies showing differential neuropsychological impairments as a function of age have been fewer perhaps due to small sample sizes in any given study because of higher mortality among older individuals and difficulties in obtaining appropriate controls. We have examined the impact of age on an extensive battery of neuropsychological measures in a group of 219 subjects with TBI (Ross et al., 1994). There is clear evidence for differential head injury effect as a function of age after

adjusting for normal aging. There was evidence of a greater negative effect of age in more severe injuries. This was seen in two ways. The difference in performance between young and older individuals was greater in more severe injuries, and the youngest age at which one could begin to see worse performance was lower with increased severity. The age effect on neuropsychological functioning may be the result of the fact that head injury effects on an older brain are comparatively worse than on a younger one, or because of greater plasticity of the younger brain to recover compared with an older brain (Dikmen & Machamer, 1995).

While no one would doubt the negative neuropsychological consequences of moderate or more severe TBIs, the neuropsychological sequelae of mild traumatic brain have been much more controversial. Interest and controversy regarding mild TBI derives from the fact

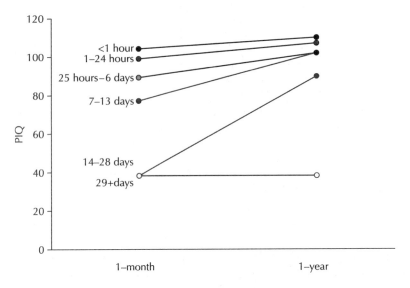

Figure 24–6. Median PIQ score by time to follow command groups. (From: Dikmen et al. [1995]. Neuropsychological outcome at 1-year post head injury. *Neuropsychology,* 9(1), 80–90. Published by APA, reprinted with permission.)

Note: Time to follow commands is the time from injury to when the individual is able to follow simple commands consistently as defined by the motor component of the Glasgow Coma Scale. Time to follow commands group < 1 hour n = 161, 1–24 hours n = 100, 25 hours to 6 days n = 52, 7–13 days n = 37, 14–28 days n = 32, ≥ 29 days n = 53.

that they constitute the majority of the injured, and determination of whether or not a mild TBI has occurred is often based on subtle findings and self-reports. Also, oftentimes the disability is not easily explained on the basis of objective findings. Based on information available in the literature, most would agree that mild head injuries are indeed associated with early neuropsychological difficulties that resolve by 1–3 months postinjury in the majority of the cases (Binder et al., 1997; Dikmen et al., 1986; Gronwall & Wrightson, 1974; Levin et al., 1987; Macciocchi et al., 1996; Ponsford et al., 2000). After conducting meta-analysis of published data Binder et al. (1997) concluded that the effect size of mild head injury on neuropsychological measures is small. This is the case in single uncomplicated head injury in previously healthy young people. Less agreement exists, however, regarding the persistence of neuropsychological impairments, their cause if they persist, and whether or not they are able to explain long-term disabilities.

The topic of mild TBI is too rich and broad to be adequately covered in this chapter.

Interested readers are referred to other publications (Belanger et al., 2005; Carroll et al., 2004; Cassidy et al., 2004).

Psychosocial/Functional Status Outcomes

TBIs can leave those who survive them with various limitations or disabilities in everyday life. These limitations may involve basic areas of functioning such as personal care and ambulation to higher-level functions such as social relationships, work, and leisure. While the nature of the disabilities is multifarious, some important questions are how often do these problems occur and what are the predictors of those who are likely to have them?

The most commonly used index to describe overall outcome in TBI is the Glasgow Outcome Scale (GOS; Jennett & Bond, 1975) and, more recently, its revised version, the GOSE (Wilson et al., 1998). The GOS has five categories: death, persistent vegetative state, severe disability, moderate disability, and good recovery. The differentiation between the last two categories is based on the patient's dependence on others for self-care activities and the patient's ability to participate in normal social life. The GOSE subdivides the *three better* GOS categories into upper and lower good recovery, moderate disability, and severe disability categories. The best data on overall outcome and its predictors in patients with severe head injury based on the GOS are those contributed by three large multicenter studies: the International Coma Data Bank, the Pilot Phase of the National Coma Data Bank, and the Full-Phase Coma Data Bank (Chesnut et al., 2000; Foulkes et al., 1991; Marshall et al., 1991). Severe head injury was defined as a GCS of 8 or less at 6 hours of injury. On the basis of large series of cases with severe TBI, approximately 45% of patients die early and half of those surviving sustain sufficiently severe impairments to make them totally or significantly dependent on others. Even the good recovery category of the GOS, which includes approximately 50% of the surviving patients, does not assure close to preinjury level of functioning (Tate et al., 1989). It is important to point out that persons with severe head injuries who survive long enough to be hospitalized constitute approximately 20% of all hospitalized cases for TBI. The rest have a spectrum of less severe injuries.

Factors that predict outcome on the GOS have recently been examined in the IMPACT study, which combined data collected over the past 20 years on TBI into one large database of over 9000 patients (Marmarou et al., 2007a). These data came from eight clinical trials and three epidemiological studies, and consist of information collected from time of injury to postresuscitation with outcome on the GOS evaluated at 6 months postinjury. The results of a series of univariate and multivariate analyses revealed that poorer outcome on the GOS is related to age at the time of injury (as age increases, outcome gets worse), low GCS scores, especially the motor score, one or more nonreactive pupils, and CT findings including traumatic subarachnoid hemorrhage, swelling, midline shift, and presence of mass lesions (Marmarou et al., 2007b; Maas et al., 2007; Murray et al., 2007; Mushkudiani et al., 2007). Other variables related to poor outcome on the GOS were hypotension, hypoxia, and laboratory values at hospital admission such as glucose, platelets, and hemoglobin levels (McHugh et al., 2007; Murray et al., 2007; Van Beek et al., 2007). The IMPACT study Web site (http://mgzlx4.erasmusmc.nl/impact/index.php?id=1,0,0,1,0,0) allows one to calculate global outcome for individual cases based on demographic and severity variables.

More detailed information on outcome for survivors of TBI, and with a broader spectrum of TBI severity, is shown in Figure 24–7 as assessed by the Sickness Impact Profile (Dikmen et al., 1995c). The subjects were 410 hospitalized adults with a brain injury severity ranging from mild to severe and prospectively followed to 1 year .The SIP results of this group were compared with a group of friends and a group of trauma controls (i.e., a group who had sustained an injury that spared the head). The results on this measure represent percent dysfunction in various areas of everyday life the subject endorses as a result of health or injury. Thus, higher scores mean worse performance. As can be seen, friend controls in this age group do not endorse much health-related dysfunction. In contrast, TBI cases do endorse problems in almost all areas, especially in the areas of employment, recreation, and cognitive functioning. Note, however, that trauma controls also endorse problems but not to the same extent, which suggests that some of the disabilities seen in TBI cases might be related to other injuries sustained in the same accident.

The effects of these injuries can be long lasting and permanent in the more severely injured persons. Long-term outcome at 3–5 years after injury was examined in a group of adults with moderate to severe TBI using the Functional Status Examination (Dikmen et al., 2003). The Functional Status Examination, through a structured interview, assigns a rating ranging from no difference as compared to preinjury to difficulty performing the activity but independent, and needing partial or total help. Figure 24–8 shows the limitations reported by the subjects. Significant limitations were reported by subjects in nearly all areas of daily living assessed. Recovery to preinjury levels ranged from 65% in personal care to about 40% in cognitive competency, major activity, and leisure and recreation. The degree of limitations,

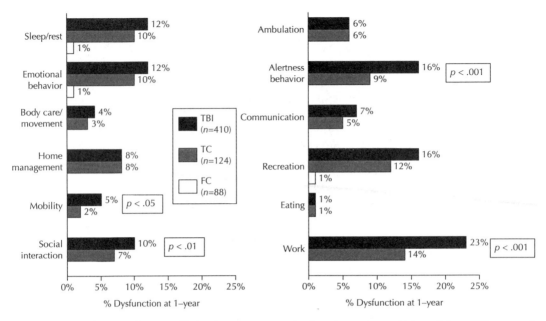

Figure 24–7. Sickness impact profile (SIP): Mean percent dysfunction at 1-year. (Adapted from: Dikmen et al. [1995]. One year psychosocial outcome in head injury. *Journal of the International Neuropsychological Society, 1,* 67–77. Reprinted with permission.)

Note: TBI = Traumatic Brain Injury, TC = Trauma Control, FC = Friend Control. Significance levels refer to the results of the comparisons between TBI and TC on individual Scales.

however, was related to the severity of injury (Dikmen et al., 2003).

A functional area that has received considerable attention is employment. Return to work is clearly compromised after the injury due to the various impairments and disabilities resulting from the injury to the brain as well as injuries sustained to other parts of the body in the same accident.

Doctor et al. (2005) examined, among those working preinjury, the risk of unemployment 1 year after TBI relative to expected risk of unemployment for the sample under a validated risk-adjusted econometric model of employment in the US population. The sample included 418 preinjury workers hospitalized for a head injury, with the severity ranging from mild to severe. The results indicated that for the overall group 42% of TBI cases were unemployed versus 9% expected. After accounting for underlying risk of unemployment in the general population, the relative risk of unemployment varied as a function of demographics. For example, it was higher for males. It also varied as a function of severity of the brain injury as determined by

GCS, global functional status on the GOS, and performance on neuropsychological measures at one month after injury as seen in Table 24–3. For example, the relative risk of unemployment was about 6 times as high as expected for those with GCSs of 3–8, and about 3.5 for those with GCSs of 13–15. With respect to functional status at 1 month, those with good recovery were 1.83 more likely while those with severe disability were 6.79 times more likely to be unemployed at 1 year. Table 24–3 also shows different levels of performance on WAIS-PIQ at 1 month in relation to employment status at 1 year. Note the increasing levels of risk of unemployment at 1 year as compared to expected with increasing levels of difficulties on PIQ at 1 month.

The importance of the same factors was demonstrated, not only in the rates of unemployment at 1 year but also in the timing of return to work in another study (Dikmen et al., 1994), using some of the same subjects and analyzed with survival methodology. Figure 24–9 shows rates of return to work over time as a function of severity of injury as evaluated by the GCS, pre-injury job stability, peripheral extremity injury

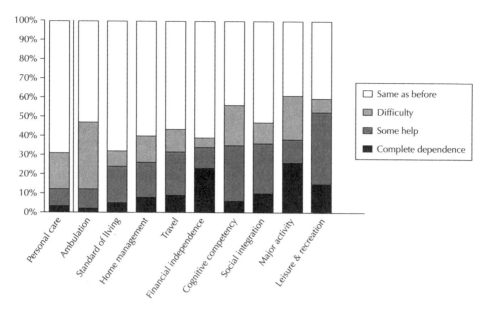

Figure 24–8. Functional Status Examination endorsements at 3–5 years after TBI. (Reprinted from *Archives of Physical Medicine and Rehabilitation, 84*(10), Dikmen et al., Outcome 3 to 5 years after moderate to severe traumatic brain injury, 1449–1457, Copyright © 2003, with permission from Elsevier.)

Note: The percentage of cases at different levels of functioning within each area of everyday life is shown.

Table 24–3. Relative and Excess Risk Values as a Function of Glasgow Coma Scale, GOS, and PIQ

	Actual Unemployed (%)	Expected Unemployed (%)	Risk Difference (%) (95% CI)	Relative Risk (95% CI)
Glasgow Coma Score				
13–15	31.1	8.8	22.3 (16.3, 28.7)	3.46 (2.87, 4.28)
9–12	46.4	9.6	36.8 (25.8, 48.0)	4.85 (3.71, 6.02)
3–8	62.1	10.4	51.7 (40.6, 61.8)	5.98 (4.92, 6.96)
GOS at 1 month				
Good	15.6	8.5	7.1 (0.8, 15.2)	1.83 (1.10, 2.79)
Moderate	39.8	8.3	31.5 (21.4, 42.1)	4.81 (3.60, 6.10)
Severe	66.7	9.8	56.8 (48.0, 64.9)	6.79 (5.89, 7.61)
PIQ at 1 month				
110 and over	18.7	6.8	11.9 (4.0, 22.2)	2.76 (1.60, 4.28)
100–109	18.1	8.7	9.4 (1.2, 20.1)	2.08 (1.15, 3.33)
90–99	41.2	9.9	31.2 (20.7, 42.4)	4.14 (3.08, 5.27)
80–89	38.6	8.7	29.9 (15.6, 45.8)	4.44 (2.80, 6.26)
Below 80	61.4	11.0	50.3 (34.4, 64.6)	5.57 (4.13, 6.86)

Source: Adapted from Doctor et al. (2005). Reprinted with the permission of Cambridge University Press.

and neuropsychological status at 1 month after injury assessed by the Halstead Impairment Index, a composite measure of performance on Halstead's Neuropsychological Test Battery. As shown in Figure 24–9, the rate of return to work varies systematically by severity of injury. About 80% of TBI with GCS of 13–15 have returned to work at least for a short time by 1-year postinjury, compared to 25% of TBI with severe injuries represented by GCS of 3–8. Note also that the rate of return to work is faster for the mild as compared to the severe TBIs. The rate of return to work is slightly better for trauma comparison subjects than for the mild TBI subjects. Preinjury stability of employment, severity of extremity injury, and neuropsychological competency at 1 month after injury—all these impact the rate of return to work, as well as the fraction who have returned at least briefly by 1 or 2 years postinjury. Many additional factors influence the rate and timing of return to work, such as age, education, and gender (Dikmen et al., 1994). These results are consistent with findings by others regarding the importance of injury severity, preinjury productivity, educational levels, and early cognitive status on postinjury employment (Boake et al., 2001; Nakase-Richardson et al., 2007; Sherer et al., 2002).

Although substantial information exists about factors related to who returns, and time taken to return to work after TBI, less is known about the stability of the work experience after the injury. Machamer et al. (2005) studied 165 preinjury workers with TBI, who were followed for 3–5 years postinjury. Injury severity ranged

from complicated mild (GCS 13–15 with CT abnormalities) to severe, with the majority of the cases having complicated mild injuries. Work stability definitions included amount of time worked (amount of time worked divided by time observed postinjury) and maintenance of uninterrupted employment once a person returned to work. Amount of time worked was significantly and systematically related to brain injury severity, neuropsychological functioning at 1-month postinjury, and preinjury characteristics such as prior work stability and earnings. For example, all of the neuropsychological measures examined showed highly significant differences with amount of time worked postinjury. On the other hand, once persons returned to work, the ability to maintain uninterrupted employment was largely related to premorbid characteristics such as older age, higher income before the injury, or a preinjury job with benefits. It was also related to higher neuropsychological

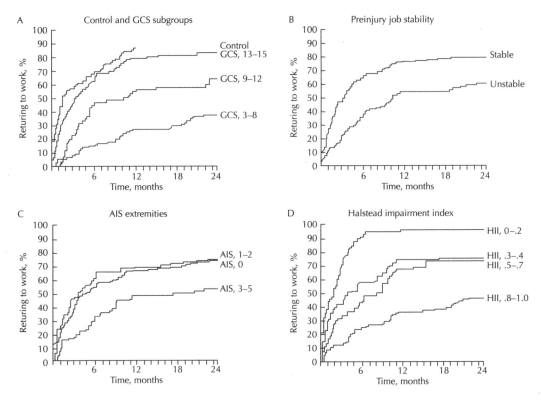

Figure 24–9. Time to return-to-work by various severity and demographic measures. (From: Dikmen et al. [1994]. Employment following traumatic head injuries. *Archives of Neurology, 51,* 177–186. Copyright © 1994, American Medical Association. All rights reserved.)

Note: GCS = Glasgow Coma Scale, AIS = Abbreviated Injury Scale, HII = Halstead Impairment Index.

functioning 1-month postinjury (reflecting the combined effects of premorbid functioning and TBI severity), but not related to neurologic indices of severity (Machamer et al., 2005). Another study examined job stability post-TBI by defining stability as employment at each of three evaluation points 1, 2, and 3 or 4 years postinjury. They also reported that job stability was related to multiple factors, including TBI severity, age, and functional outcome ratings (Kreutzer et al., 2003).

Areas of Research of Current Interest

Genetic Factors (APOE4) and Outcome

Recent evidence has indicated that genetic factors may play a role in outcome following TBI. One of the most studied is the apolipoprotein E gene that is involved with transporting lipids within the central nervous system. There are three allelic variants in humans, apoE2, apoE3, and apoE4. The apoE4 variant has been associated with poor outcome following TBI (Teasdale et al., 1997). The reason why apoE4 should be associated with worse outcome is not known, but is hypothesized to have something to do with the neural response to injury that in some way results in increased neurodegeneration (Diaz-Arrastia & Baxter, 2006). Teasdale and colleagues studied 89 prospectively recruited traumatic brain-injured subjects admitted to a neurosurgery unit and representing a range of brain injury severity. They compared the presence or absence of apoE4 with outcome on the GOS at 6 months postinjury. The findings showed a significant difference in outcome ($p < .01$) with 57% of the participants with apoE4 having poor outcome defined as death, vegetative state, or severe disability versus only 27% with poor outcome in the group without apoE4. This finding remained significant after controlling for age, GCS, and CT scan findings. Other studies, conducted later have also found poor outcome with apoE4 although they have all had small sample sizes (Ariza et al., 2006; Chiang et al., 2003; Crawford et al., 2002; Friedman et al., 1999; Lichtman et al., 2000; Sundstrom et al., 2004). However, the results have not been uniformly positive in finding this association at 6 months postinjury on the GOS/GOSE (Diaz-Arrastia et al., 2003; Nathoo et al., 2003). Teasdale et al., (2005) in a follow-up study involving 984 consecutive head injury admissions failed to find their earlier reported association between apoE4 and poor outcome on the GOS at 6 months. They did report an interaction between age and apoE4 on outcome such that children and young adults with apoE4 had worse outcome. Lack of an association has also been reported for long-term outcomes, on average, 18 years postinjury (Millar et al., 2003) and for other 6-month outcomes following mild to moderate TBI, including neuropsychological functioning, emotional distress, depression, global functioning, and psychosocial outcome and symptoms (Chamelian et al., 2004).

Undoubtedly, this is an area of great interest to many. However, more research is needed to unravel the role of apoE4 and other genetic factors on outcome following TBI.

Aging with Traumatic Brain Injury

This is a topic of current interest although only a few studies have addressed it. The issue here is whether or not the effect of aging is accelerated or abnormal in a previously injured brain. This kind of study is extremely difficult and costly to do since it requires a lengthy longitudinal investigation and has been most typically carried out in military populations (Corkin et al., 1989; Walker & Blumer, 1989). Corkin et al. (1989) presented some of the first evidence of exacerbation of cognitive decline in World War II veterans with penetrating head injuries. They compared 57 head-injured and 27 veterans with peripheral nerve injuries on measures of cognitive functioning first assessed in the 1950s (approximately 10 years after injury) and again 30 years later. The veterans with head injuries showed significantly greater decline in cognitive functioning between testing at time 1 and 2 compared to those with peripheral nerve injuries. However, subsequent studies in military (Newcombe, 1996) and civilian (Wood & Rutterford, 2006) populations have not found evidence for late accelerated cognitive decline after TBI. Conflicting results across studies may in part be due to the sample of cases available for long-term follow-up. Assessments that occur decades after the injury will likely have sample attrition due to death and may also suffer from other biases such as loss of subjects with better or worse late outcome potentially influencing the findings. For example, Wood and Rutterford (2006) were only able to perform late evaluations on 21% of their original sample. Another possible reason for discrepant findings is whether the follow-up period is long enough to capture differential age-related changes in functioning. Potentially, even a lengthy follow-up period of 20–25 years may not be long enough if subjects are injured in their teens or young adult years.

A separate but related area of research is the possible association between TBI and later development of Alzheimer's disease. Whether or not TBI is a risk factor for Alzheimer's disease is not clear although there have been numerous studies to investigate this association. One of the common ways this association has been explored is with prospective cohort studies. These studies follow a group of healthy older people longitudinally and compare risk factors between those who develop dementia and those who do not. The advantage of this type of study is that it is less likely to suffer from recall bias since history of TBI is evaluated before dementia occurs. The results of these studies have generally shown that TBI is a significant risk factor for Alzheimer's disease (Luukinen et al., 2005; Plassman et al., 2000; Schofield et al., 1997). For example, Schofield et al. (1997) followed 271 people for 5 years, and 39 cases developed probable or possible Alzheimer's disease. Alzheimer's disease was significantly associated with a history of TBI, and those reporting loss of consciousness of more than 5 minutes were at significantly increased risk. Plassman et al. (2000) studied 1776 World War II veterans who had sustained either a nonpenetrating head injury or an unrelated condition resulting in hospitalization during their military service. These veterans were contacted approximately 50 years later and evaluated for dementia. The results found that both moderate and severe head injury was associated with significantly increased risk of dementia. On the other hand, Nemetz et al. (1999), using the resources of the Rochester Epidemiology Project to examine all documented cases of TBI that occurred from 1935 to 1984 in Olmsted County, Minnesota, found no association between TBI and Alzheimer's disease. However, time to onset of Alzheimer's was less than expected, which suggested that TBI may reduce the time to develop dementia. Other prospective cohort studies found no significantly increased risk of dementia for those with a history of TBI (Katzman et al., 1989; Mehta et al., 1999; Williams et al., 1991). Follow-up periods that were too short and/or an average age of sample that was lower than the expected age of dementia onset, in some of the studies, may help account for discrepant findings (Starkstein & Jorge, 2005).

The association between TBI and Alzheimer's disease has also been examined using case-control studies, which have generally supported this association. In this design, subjects with Alzheimer's disease are identified, a matched control group without dementia is recruited, risk factors are examined retrospectively, and odds ratios are calculated to determine relative risk. Many of these studies have found a significant association between TBI and Alzheimer's disease (French et al., 1985; Graves et al., 1990; Heyman et al., 1984; Kondo et al., 1994; Mayeuz et al., 1993; Rasmusson et al., 1995; Sullivan et al., 1987) with the odds of prior head injury ranging from 2 (Sullivan et al., 1987) to 13.75 (Rasmusson et al., 1995). The Canadian Study of Health and Aging (1994) examined a large population-based sample of Alzheimer's disease and controls aged 65 years and older in ten Canadian provinces. Their results indicate that head injury was a borderline significant risk factor for Alzheimer's disease. Other case-control studies have failed to find a significant association (Amaducci et al., 1986; Broe et al., 1990; Chandra et al., 1989; Chandra et al., 1987; Mayeux et al., 1995). Possible reasons for the discrepant findings may be the result of methodological problems including varied definitions of head injury across studies, the likelihood of misdiagnosed Alzheimer's disease since this condition can only be verified at autopsy, and recall bias. The history of TBI is determined in these studies by recall, with limited or no means of verification. It is possible that relatives of dementia patients may have overreported a history of TBI. Finally, another problem of some of the case-control studies may have involved inadequate statistical power to detect a significant association between TBI and Alzheimer's disease (Lye & Shores, 2000; Starkstein & Jorge, 2005). Meta-analyses of case-control studies (Fleminger et al., 2003; Mortimer et al., 1991) had a high level of statistical power, and the results showed a significant association between TBI and Alzheimer's disease in men (but not women). However, the problem of possible recall bias remains.

It may also be possible that some of the inconsistencies between studies are the results of factors that are poorly understood and thus uncontrolled. For example, the role of the apoE4 allele and the association of TBI and Alzheimer's disease are not clear. Mayeux et al. (1995) reported that a history of head injury and the apoE4 allele increased the risk of Alzheimer's tenfold, while head injury without the apoE4 allele did not significantly increase the risk of Alzheimer's. Plassman et al. (2000), on the other hand, found only a nonsignificant trend for the apoE4 allele. This is another area of research that is going to continue and, hopefully, produce more definitive results.

Conclusions

Traumatic brain injury represents a significant public health problem. The importance of this problem derives from the high incidence rates, young previously healthy people compromising a large proportion of those injured, survivors having normal life spans, and, depending on the severity of injury, the possibility of a variety of persistent impairments and disabilities that compromise the quality of life of those who survive. Over the last 25 years considerable information has accumulated regarding the nature of impairments, disabilities, and participation problems that occur in the survivors of such injuries. Much has also been learned about factors that relate to outcome, such as severity of the brain injury, the characteristics of the person injured (in particular, age), time since injury (reflecting recovery), and the type of function in question. Although various factors that are important with respect to outcome have been identified, prediction on an individual level is limited due to much unexplained variability.

Prediction of global outcome and employment are two areas that have received more attention and where more gains have been made.

While no one would doubt the negative neuropsychological and psychosocial consequences of moderate or more severe TBIs, the sequelae of mild traumatic brain have been much more controversial. Less agreement exists regarding the persistence of neuropsychological impairments, their cause if they persist, and whether or not they are able to explain long-term disabilities in those with mild injuries.

Areas of more recent research interest in TBI include the effects of genetic factors on outcome (*apolipoprotein E* gene, which is the most studied), and whether TBI accelerates normal aging or may be a harbinger for Alzheimer's disease. These areas of research are in their infancy, and their full value for understanding outcome of TBI is not yet clear.

References

Amaducci, L. A., Fratiglioni, L., Rocca, W. A., Fieschi, C., Livrea, P., Pedone, D., et al. (1986). Risk factors for clinically diagnosed Alzheimer's disease: A case-control study of an Italian population. *Neurology, 36*(7), 922–931.

Ariza, M., Pueyo, R., Matarin, M. d. M., Junque, C., Mataro, M., Clemente, I., et al. (2006). Influence of APOE polymorphism on cognitive and behavioural outcome in moderate and severe traumatic brain injury. *Journal of Neurology, Neurosurgery, and Psychiatry, 77*, 1191–1193.

Barber, J. (2003). *Adjusting for bias caused by missing outcomes in studies of traumatic brain injury: An application and evaluation of three methods.* Unpublished Master, University of Washington.

Belanger, H. G., Curtiss, G., Demery, J. A., Lebowitz, B. K., & Vanderploeg, R. D. (2005). Factors moderating neuropsychological outcomes following mild traumatic brain injury: A meta-analysis. *Journal of the International Neuropsychological Society, 11*(3), 215–227.

Belanger, H. G., & Vanderploeg, R. D. (2005). The neuropsychological impact of sports-related concussion: A meta-analysis. *Journal of the International Neuropsychological Society, 11*(4), 345–357.

Binder, L. M., Rohling, M. L., & Larrabee, G. J. (1997). A review of mild head trauma. Part I: Meta-analytic review of neuropsychological studies. *Journal of Clinical and Experimental Neuropsychology, 19*, 421–431.

Boake, C., Millis, S. R., High, W. M., Jr., Delmonico, R. L., Kreutzer, J. S., Rosenthal, M., et al. (2001). Using early neuropsychologic testing to predict long-term productivity outcome from traumatic brain injury. *Archives of Physical Medicine and Rehabilitation, 82*(6), 761–768.

Bombardier, C. H., Temkin, N. R., Machamer, J., & Dikmen, S. S. (2003). The natural history of drinking and alcohol-related problems after traumatic brain injury. *Archives of Physical Medicine and Rehabilitation, 84*(2), 185–191.

Broe, G. A., Henderson, A. S., Creasey, H., McCusker, E., Korten, A. E., Jorm, A. F., et al. (1990). A case-control study of Alzheimer's disease in Australia. *Neurology, 40*(11), 1698–1707.

Carroll, L. J., Cassidy, J. D., Peloso, P. M., Borg, J., von Holst, H., Holm, L., et al. (2004). Prognosis for mild traumatic brain injury: Results of the WHO Collaborating Centre Task Force on Mild Traumatic Brain Injury. *Journal of Rehabilitation Medicine,* February (43 Suppl), 84–105.

Cassidy, J. D., Carroll, L. J., Peloso, P. M., Borg, J., von Holst, H., Holm, L., et al. (2004). Incidence, risk factors and prevention of mild traumatic brain injury: Results of the WHO Collaborating Centre Task Force on Mild Traumatic Brain Injury. *Journal of Rehabilitation Medicine,* February (43 Suppl), 28–60.

Cernich, A., Reeves, D., Sun, W., & Bleiberg, J. (2007). Automated Neuropsychological Assessment Metrics sports medicine battery. *Archives of Clinical Neuropsychology, 22*(Suppl 1), S101–S114.

Chamelian, L., Reis, M., & Feinstein, A. (2004). Six-month recovery from mild to moderate Traumatic Brain Injury: The role of APOE-epsilon4 allele. *Brain, 127*(Pt 12), 2621–2628.

Chandra, V., Philipose, V., Bell, P. A., Lazaroff, A., & Schoenberg, B. S. (1987). Case-control study of late onset "probable Alzheimer's disease". *Neurology, 37*(8), 1295–1300.

Chandra, V., Kokmen, E., Schoenberg, B. S., & Beard, C. M. (1989). Head trauma with loss of consciousness as a risk factor for Alzheimer's disease. *Neurology, 39*(12), 1576–1578.

Chesnut, R. M. (2000). Evolving models of neurotrauma critical care: An analysis and call to action. *Clinical Neurosurgery, 46,* 185–195.

Chiang, M. F., Chang, J. G., & Hu, C. J. (2003). Association between apolipoprotein E genotype and outcome of traumatic brain injury. *Acta Neurochir (Wien), 145*(8), 649–653; discussion 653–644.

Consensus conference. Rehabilitation of persons with traumatic brain injury. NIH Consensus Development Panel on Rehabilitation of Persons with Traumatic Brain Injury. (1999). *Journal of the American Medical Association, 282*(10), 974–983.

Corkin, S., Rosen, T. J., Sullivan, E. V., & Clegg, R. A. (1989). Penetrating head injury in young adulthood exacerbates cognitive decline in later years. *The Journal of Neuroscience, 9*(11), 3876–3883.

Corrigan, J. D. (1995). Substance abuse as a mediating factor in outcome from traumatic brain injury. *Archives of Physical Medicine and Rehabilitation, 76*(4), 302–309.

Corrigan, J. D., Harrison-Felix, C., Bogner, J., Dijkers, M., Terrill, M. S., & Whiteneck, G. (2003). Systematic bias in traumatic brain injury outcome studies because of loss to follow-up. *Archives of Physical Medicine and Rehabilitation, 84*(2), 153–160.

Crawford, F. C., Vanderploeg, R. D., Freeman, M. J., Singh, S., Waisman, M., Michaels, L., et al. (2002). APOE genotype influences acquisition and recall following traumatic brain injury. *Neurology, 58*(7), 1115–1118.

Diaz-Arrastia, R., & Baxter, V. K. (2006). Genetic factors in outcome after traumatic brain injury: What the human genome project can teach us about brain trauma. *Journal of Head Trauma Rehabilitation, 21*(4), 361–374.

Diaz-Arrastia, R., Gong, Y., Fair, S., Scott, K. D., Garcia, M. C., Carlile, M. C., et al. (2003). Increased risk of late posttraumatic seizures associated with inheritance of APOE epsilon4 allele. *Archives of Neurology, 60*(6), 818–822.

Dikmen, S., & Machamer, J. E. (1995). Neurobehavioral outcomes and their determinants. *Journal of Head Trauma Rehabilitation, 10*(1), 74–86.

Dikmen, S., Machamer, J., & Temkin, N. (2001). Mild head injury: Facts and artifacts. *Journal of Clinical and Experimental Neuropsychology, 23*(6), 729–738.

Dikmen, S., Machamer, J. E., Winn, H. R., & Temkin, N. R. (1995b). Neuropsychological outcome at 1-year post head injury. *Neuropsychology, 9*(1), 80–90.

Dikmen, S., McLean, A., & Temkin, N. (1986). Neuropsychological and psychosocial consequences of minor head injury. *Journal of Neurology, Neurosurgery, and Psychiatry, 49*(11), 1227–1232.

Dikmen, S., & Morgan, S. (1980). Neuropsychological factors related to employability and occupational status in persons with epilepsy. *Journal of Nervous and Mental Disease, 168*(4), 236–240.

Dikmen, S., Reitan, R. M., & Temkin, N. R. (1983). Neuropsychological recovery in head injury. *Archives of Neurology, 40*(6), 333–338.

Dikmen, S., & Temkin, N. (1987). Determination of the effects of head injury and recovery in behavioral research. In H. S. Levin, J. Grafman, and H. M. Eisenberg (Eds.), *Neurobehavioral recovery from head injury* (pp. 73–88). New York: Oxford University Press.

Dikmen, S. S., Heaton, R. K., Grant, I., & Temkin, N. R. (1999). Test-retest reliability and practice effects of expanded Halstead- Reitan Neuropsychological Test Battery. *Journal of the International Neuropsychological Society, 5*(4), 346–356.

Dikmen, S. S., Machamer, J. E., Donovan, D. M., Winn, H. R., & Temkin, N. R. (1995a). Alcohol use before and after traumatic head injury. *Annals of Emergency Medicine, 26*(2), 167–176.

Dikmen, S. S., Machamer, J. E., Powell, J. M., & Temkin, N. R. (2003). Outcome 3 to 5 years after moderate to severe traumatic brain injury. *Archives of Physical Medicine and Rehabilitation, 84*(10), 1449–1457.

Dikmen, S. S., Ross, B. L., Machamer, J. E., & Temkin, N. R. (1995c). One year psychosocial outcome in head injury. *Journal of the International Neuropsychological Society, 1*(1), 67–77.

Dikmen, S. S., Temkin, N. R., Machamer, J. E., Holubkov, A. L., Fraser, R. T., & Winn, H. R. (1994). Employment following traumatic head injuries. *Archives of Neurology, 51*(2), 177–186.

Doctor, J. N., Castro, J., Temkin, N. R., Fraser, R. T., Machamer, J. E., & Dikmen, S. S. (2005). Workers' risk of unemployment after traumatic brain injury: A normed comparison. *Journal of the International Neuropsychological Society, 11*(6), 747–752.

Finkelstein, E., Corso, P., Miller, T., & associates. (2006). *The incidence and economic burden of injuries in the United States.* New York: Oxford University Press.

Fleminger, S., Oliver, D. L., Lovestone, S., Rabe-Hesketh, S., & Giora, A. (2003). Head injury as a risk factor for Alzheimer's disease: The evidence 10 years on; a partial replication. *Journal of Neurology, Neurosurgery, and Psychiatry, 74*(7), 857–862.

Foulkes, M. A., Eisenberg, H. M., Jane, J. A., Marmarou, A., Marshall, L. F., & Traumatic Coma Data Bank Research Group. (1991). The Traumatic Coma Data Bank: Design, methods, and baseline characteristics. *Journal of Neurosurgery, 75,* S8–S13.

Fraser, R., Dikmen, S., McLean, A., Jr., Miller, B., & Temkin, N. (1988). Employability of head injury survivors: First year post-injury. *Rehabilitation Counseling Bulletin, 31,* 276–288.

French, L. R., Schuman, L. M., Mortimer, J. A., Hutton, J. T., Boatman, R. A., & Christians, B. (1985). A case-control study of dementia of the Alzheimer type. *American Journal of Epidemiology, 121*(3), 414–421.

Friedman, G., Froom, P., Sazbon, L., Grinblatt, I., Shochina, M., Tsenter, J., et al. (1999). Apolipoprotein E-epsilon4 genotype predicts a poor outcome in survivors of traumatic brain injury. *Neurology, 52*(2), 244–248.

Grafman, J., Salazar, A., Weingartner, H., Vance, S., & Amin, D. (1986). The relationship of brain-tissue loss volume and lesion location to cognitive deficit. *The Journal of Neuroscience, 6*(2), 301–307.

Graves, A. B., White, E., Koepsell, T. D., Reifler, B. V., van Belle, G., Larson, E. B., et al. (1990). The association between head trauma and Alzheimer's disease. *American Journal of Epidemiology, 131*(3), 491–501.

Gronwall, D., & Wrightson, P. (1974). Delayed recovery of intellectual function after minor head injury. *Lancet, 2*(7881), 605–609.

Heyman, A., Wilkinson, W. E., Stafford, J. A., Helms, M. J., Sigmon, A. H., & Weinberg, T. (1984). Alzheimer's disease: A study of epidemiological aspects. *Annals of Neurology, 15*(4), 335–341.

Jennett, B., & Bond, M. (1975). Assessment of outcome after severe brain damage. *Lancet, i,* 480–484.

Katzman, R., Aronson, M., Fuld, P., Kawas, C., Brown, T., Morgenstern, H., et al. (1989). Development of dementing illnesses in an 80-year-old volunteer cohort. *Annals of Neurology, 25*(4), 317–324.

Kondo, K., Niino, M., & Shido, K. (1994). A case-control study of Alzheimer's disease in Japan—significance of life-styles. *Dementia, 5*(6), 314–326.

Kreutzer, J. S., Marwitz, J. H., Walker, W., Sander, A., Sherer, M., Bogner, J., et al. (2003). Moderating factors in return to work and job stability after traumatic brain injury. *The Journal of Head Trauma Rehabilitation, 18*(2), 128–138.

Langlois, J. A., Rutland-Brown, W., & Thomas, K. E. (2004). *Traumatic brain injury in the United States: Emergency department visits, hospitalizations, and deaths.* Atlanta (GA): Centers for Disease Control and Prevention, National Center for Injury Prevention and Control.

Levin, H. S., Mattis, S., Ruff, R. M., Eisenberg, H. M., Marshall, L. F., Tabaddor, K., et al. (1987). Neurobehavioral outcome following minor head injury: A three-center study. *Journal of Neurosurgery, 66,* 234–243.

Levin, H. S. (1995). Neurobehavioral outcome of closed head injury: Implications for clinical trials. *Journal of Neurotrauma, 12*(4), 601–610.

Lichtman, S. W., Seliger, G., Tycko, B., & Marder, K. (2000). Apolipoprotein E and functional recovery from brain injury following postacute rehabilitation. *Neurology, 55*(10), 1536–1539.

Luukinen, H., Viramo, P., Herala, M., Kervinen, K., Kesaniemi, Y. A., Savola, O., et al. (2005). Fall-related brain injuries and the risk of dementia in elderly people: A population-based study. *European Journal of Neurology, 12*(2), 86–92.

Lye, T. C., & Shores, E. A. (2000). Traumatic brain injury as a risk factor for Alzheimer's disease: A review. *Neuropsychology Review, 10*(2), 115–129.

Maas, A. I., Steyerberg, E. W., Butcher, I., Dammers, R., Lu, J., Marmarou, A., et al. (2007). Prognostic value of computerized tomography scan characteristics in traumatic brain injury: Results from the IMPACT study. *Journal of Neurotrauma, 24*(2), 303–314.

Macciocchi, S. N., Barth, J. T., Alves, W., Rimel, R. W., & Jane, J. A. (1996). Neuropsychological functioning and recovery after mild head injury in collegiate athletes. *Neurosurgery, 39*(3), 510–514.

Machamer, J., Temkin, N., Fraser, R., Doctor, J., & Dikmen, S. (2005). Stabililty of employment after traumatic brain injury. *Journal of the International Neuropsychological Society, 11*(7), 807–816.

Marmarou, A., Lu, J., Butcher, I., McHugh, G. S., Mushkudiani, N. A., Murray, G. D., et al. (2007a). IMPACT database of traumatic brain injury: Design and description. *Journal of Neurotrauma, 24*(2), 239–250.

Marmarou, A., Lu, J., Butcher, I., McHugh, G. S., Murray, G. D., Steyerberg, E. W., et al. (2007b). Prognostic value of the Glasgow Coma Scale and pupil reactivity in traumatic brain injury assessed pre-hospital and on enrollment: An IMPACT analysis. *Journal of Neurotrauma, 24*(2), 270–280.

Marshall, L. F., Gautille, T., Klauber, M. R., Eisenberg, H. M., Jane, J. A., Luerssen, T. G., et al. (1991). The outcome of severe closed head injury. *Journal of Neurosurgery, 75*, S28–S36.

Max, W., MacKenzie, E. J., & Rice, D. P. (1991). Head injuries: Costs and consequences. *Journal of Head Trauma Rehabilitation, 6*(2), 76–91.

Mayeux, R., Ottman, R., Tang, M. X., Noboa-Bauza, L., Marder, K., Gurland, B., et al. (1993). Genetic susceptibility and head injury as risk factors for Alzheimer's disease among community-dwelling elderly persons and their first-degree relatives. *Annals of Neurology, 33*(5), 494–501.

Mayeux, R., Ottman, R., Maestre, G., Ngai, C., Tang, M. X., Ginsberg, H., et al. (1995). Synergistic effects of traumatic head injury and apolipoprotein-epsilon 4 in patients with Alzheimer's disease. *Neurology, 45*(3 Pt 1), 555–557.

McHugh, G. S., Engel, D. C., Butcher, I., Steyerberg, E. W., Lu, J., Mushkudiani, N., et al. (2007). Prognostic value of secondary insults in traumatic brain injury: Results from the IMPACT study. *Journal of Neurotrauma, 24*(2), 287–293.

McLean, A., Jr., Dikmen, S., & Temkin, (1993). Psychosocial recovery after head injury. *Archives of Physical Medicine and Rehabilitation, 74*, 1041–1046.

Mehta, K. M., Ott, A., Kalmijn, S., Slooter, A. J., van Duijn, C. M., Hofman, A., et al. (1999). Head trauma and risk of dementia and Alzheimer's disease: The Rotterdam Study. *Neurology, 53*(9), 1959–1962.

Millar, K., Nicoll, J. A., Thornhill, S., Murray, G. D., & Teasdale, G. M. (2003). Long term neuropsychological outcome after head injury: Relation to APOE genotype. *Journal of Neurology, Neurosurgery, and Psychiatry, 74*(8), 1047–1052.

Mortimer, J. A., van Duijn, C. M., Chandra, V., Fratiglioni, L., Graves, A. B., Heyman, A., et al. (1991). Head trauma as a risk factor for Alzheimer's disease: A collaborative re-analysis of case-control studies. EURODEM Risk Factors Research Group. *International Journal of Epidemiology, 20*(Suppl 2), S28–S35.

Murray, G. D., Butcher, I., McHugh, G. S., Lu, J., Mushkudiani, N. A., Maas, A. I., et al. (2007). Multivariable prognostic analysis in traumatic brain injury: Results from the IMPACT study. *Journal of Neurotrauma, 24*(2), 329–337.

Mushkudiani, N. A., Engel, D. C., Steyerberg, E. W., Butcher, I., Lu, J., Marmarou, A., et al. (2007). Prognostic value of demographic characteristics in traumatic brain injury: Results from the IMPACT study. *Journal of Neurotrauma, 24*(2), 259–269.

Nakase-Richardson, R., Yablon, S. A., & Sherer, M. (2007). Prospective comparison of acute confusion severity with duration of post-traumatic amnesia in predicting employment outcome after traumatic brain injury. *Journal of Neurology, Neurosurgery, and Psychiatry, 78*(8), 872–876.

Nathoo, N., Chetry, R., van Dellen, J. R., Connolly, C., & Naidoo, R. (2003). Apolipoprotein E polymorphism and outcome after closed traumatic brain injury: Influence of ethnic and regional differences. *Journal of Neurosurgery, 98*(2), 302–306.

Nemetz, P. N., Leibson, C., Naessens, J. M., Beard, M., Kokmen, E., Annegers, J. F., et al. (1999). Traumatic brain injury and time to onset of Alzheimer's disease: A population-based study. *American Journal of Epidemiology, 149*(1), 32–40.

Newcombe, F. (1996). Very late outcome after focal wartime brain wounds. *Journal of Clinical and Experimental Neuropsychology, 18*(1), 1–23.

Plassman, B. L., Havlik, R. J., Steffens, D. C., Helms, M. J., Newman, T. N., Drosdick, D., et al. (2000). Documented head injury in early adulthood and risk of Alzheimer's disease and other dementias. *Neurology, 55*(8), 1158–1166.

Ponsford, J., Willmott, C., Rothwell, A., Cameron, P., Kelly, A.M., Nelms, R., et al. (2000). Factors influencing outcome following mild traumatic brain injury in adults. *Journal of the International Neuropsychological Society, 6*(5), 568–579.

Rasmusson, D. X., Brandt, J., Martin, D. B., & Folstein, M. F. (1995). Head injury as a risk factor in Alzheimer's disease. *Brain Injury, 9*(3), 213–219.

Rimel, R. W., Giordani, B., Barth, J. T., Boll, T. J., & Jane, J. A. (1981). Disability caused by minor head injury. *Neurosurgery, 9*(3), 221–228.

Ross, B., Temkin, N., & Dikmen, S. (1994). *The effects of aging on neuropsychological outcome following traumatic head injury.* Paper presented at the International Neuropsychological Society, Cincinnati, Ohio.

Russell, W. R., & Smith, A. (1961). Post-traumatic amnesia in closed head injury. *Archives of Neurology, 5*, 4–17.

Schofield, P. W., Tang, M., Marder, K., Bell, K., Dooneief, G., Chun, M., et al. (1997). Alzheimer's disease after remote head injury: An incidence study. *Journal of Neurology, Neurosurgery, and Psychiatry, 62*(2), 119–124.

Schwab, K., Grafman, J., Salazar, A. M., & Kraft, J. (1993). Residual impairments and work status 15 years after penetrating head injury: Report from the Vietnam Head Injury Study. *Neurology, 43*(1), 95–103.

Sherer, M., Sander, A. M., Nick, T. G., High, W. M., Jr., Malec, J. F., & Rosenthal, M. (2002). Early cognitive status and productivity outcome after traumatic brain injury: Findings from the TBI model systems. *Archives of Physical and Medical Rehabilitation, 83*(2), 183–192.

Sosin, D. M., Sniezek, J. E., & Waxweiler, R. J. (1995). Trends in death associated with traumatic brain injury, 1979 through 1992. Success and failure. *Journal of the American Medical Association, 273*(22), 1778–1780.

Starkstein, S. E., & Jorge, R. (2005). Dementia after traumatic brain injury. *International Psychogeriatrics, 17*(Suppl 1), S93–S107.

Sullivan, P., Petitti, D., & Barbaccia, J. (1987). Head trauma and age of onset of dementia of the Alzheimer type. *Journal of the American Medical Association, 257*(17), 2289–2290.

Sundstrom, A., Marklund, P., Nilsson, L. G., Cruts, M., Adolfsson, R., Van Broeckhoven, C., et al. (2004). APOE influences on neuropsychological function after mild head injury: Within-person comparisons. *Neurology, 62*(11), 1963–1966.

Tate, R. L., Lulham, J. M., Broe, G. A., Strettles, B., & Pfaff, A. (1989). Psychosocial outcome for survivors of severe blunt head injury: The results from a consecutive series of 100 patients. *Journal*

of Neurology, Neurosurgery, and Psychiatry, 52, 1128–1134.

Teasdale, G., & Jennett, B. (1974). Assessment of coma and impaired consciousness: A practical scale. *Lancet, ii*, 81–84.

Teasdale, G. M., Murray, G. D., & Nicoll, J. A. (2005). The association between APOE epsilon4, age and outcome after head injury: A prospective cohort study. *Brain, 128*(Pt 11), 2556–2561.

Teasdale, G. M., Nicoll, J. A., Murray, G., & Fiddes, M. (1997). Association of apolipoprotein E polymorphism with outcome after head injury. *Lancet, 350*(9084), 1069–1071.

The Canadian Study of Health and Aging: Risk factors for Alzheimer's disease in Canada. (1994). *Neurology, 44*(11), 2073–2080.

Thurman, D. J., Alverson, C., Dunn, K. A., Guerrero, J., & Sniezek, J. E. (1999). Traumatic brain injury in the United States: A public health perspective. *Journal of Head Trauma Rehabilitation, 14*(6), 602–615.

Van Beek, J. G., Mushkudiani, N. A., Steyerberg, E. W., Butcher, I., McHugh, G. S., Lu, J., et al. (2007). Prognostic value of admission laboratory parameters in traumatic brain injury: Results from the IMPACT study. *Journal of Neurotrauma, 24*(2), 315–328.

Walker, A. E., & Blumer, D. (1989). The fate of World War II veterans with posttraumatic seizures. *Archives of Neurology, 46*(1), 23–26.

Weinstein, S., & Teuber, H. L. (1957). The role of preinjury education and intelligence level in intellectual loss after brain injury. *Journal of Comparative and Physiological Psychology, 50*, 535–539.

Williams, D. B., Annegers, J. F., Kokmen, E., O'Brien, P. C., & Kurland, L. T. (1991). Brain injury and neurologic sequelae: A cohort study of dementia, Parkinsonism, and amyotrophic lateral sclerosis. *Neurology, 41*(10), 1554–1557.

Williams, D. H., Levin, H. S., & Eisenberg, H. M. (1990). Mild head injury classification. *Journal of Neurosurgery, 27*(3), 422–428.

Wilson, J. T., Pettigrew, L. E., & Teasdale, G. M. (1998). Structured interviews for the Glasgow Outcome Scale and the extended Glasgow Outcome Scale: Guidelines for their use. *Journal of Neurotrauma, 15*(8), 573–585.

Wood, R. L., & Rutterford, N. A. (2006). Long-term effect of head trauma on intellectual abilities: A 16-year outcome study. *Journal of Neurology, Neurosurgery, and Psychiatry, 77*(10), 1180–1184.

25

Neuropsychiatric, Psychiatric, and Behavioral Disorders Associated with Traumatic Brain Injury

George P. Prigatano and Franziska Maier

Introduction and Historical Background

Numerous clinical and research reports have emphasized that changes in patients' emotional and motivational characteristics, as well as their behavioral reactions after traumatic brain injury (TBI) are especially distressful to family members (Hawley et al., 2003; Winstanley et al., 2006) and pose the most serious barriers to successful (neuropsychological) rehabilitation (Prigatano, 1999). These disturbances are often associated with changes in cognitive functioning (Goldstein, 1952; Max et al., 2000), but often cannot be purely explained on the basis of such impairments. Understanding the mechanisms responsible for these disturbances following TBI has attracted much attention over the years. Yet our knowledge remains incomplete.

At the turn of the last century, Adolf Meyer (1904), the "father of American psychiatry," described the "anatomical facts" underlying the "traumatic insanities." Paul Schilder (1934), the psychoanalyst, described the "deep disturbances in the emotional attitude" observed in TBI patients "which we cannot measure" (p. 159). Kurt Goldstein (1952), a neurologist and psychiatrist who was actively involved in the rehabilitation of soldiers who had suffered war-induced brain injuries, emphasized the important distinction between a direct versus indirect symptom. Influenced by the work of John Hughlings Jackson, Goldstein (1952) noted that "the symptomatology which these patients

present is very complex" (p. 245). He suggested that "the personality structure is disturbed, particularly by lesions of the frontal lobes, the parietal lobes, and the insula Reili, but it is also disturbed by diffuse damage to the cortex..." (pp. 246–247). However, he noted that a basic cognitive disturbance—"impairment of the abstract attitude"—was responsible for some of the psychiatric and behavioral disturbances seen in these patients. Impulsive responding, emotional lability, and the lack of "joy" were all related to the inability of the patient to grasp the complexity of the situation and to tolerate normal tensions associated with problem solving. His eloquent description of the "catastrophic reaction" has been especially helpful to rehabilitationists when teaching patients how to understand and manage their emotional reactions (Klonoff & Lage, 1991; Prigatano et al., 1986).

Later assessment of World War II soldiers who had suffered TBIs also emphasized the complex relationship between lesion location, lesion size, changes in cognition, and the emergence of various neuropsychiatric disorders (Lishman, 1968). This later led Lishman (1978) to identify eleven factors (i.e., mental constitution, premorbid personality, emotional impact of the injury, circumstances, setting and repercussions of injury, iatrogenic factors, environmental factors, compensation and litigation, response to intellectual impairments, development of epilepsy, amount of brain damage incurred, and location of brain damage incurred) that potentially could contribute to the psychiatric and

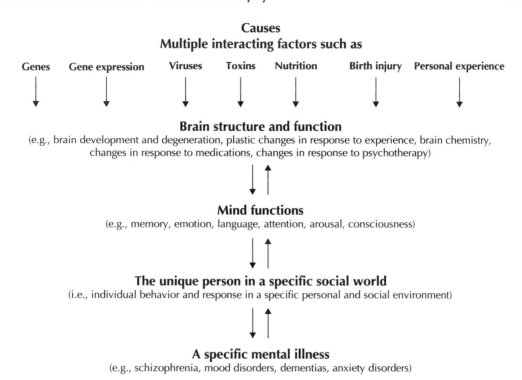

Figure 25–1. A synthetic model of the development of mental illness (reprinted with permission from Andreasen, 2001).

behavioral disturbances observed following head (brain) trauma.

Since that time, several reviews have appeared on the neuropsychiatric aspects of traumatic brain injury (e.g., Jorge, 2005; Silver et al., 2005). These papers emphasized the complexity of the problem (something Goldstein noted over 65 years ago) and have suggested that we apply the technology of the time to help unravel it. In her insightful book, Andreasen (2001) reminds us that specific psychiatric disorders or mental illness reflect a complex, multifactorial outcome. Brain injury (type, size, distribution, location, etc.) potentially interacts with multiple variables to produce the symptom picture (see Figure 25–1).

Our present technological advances include static and dynamic neuroimaging of the brain and our capacity to apply molecular biology to map the genome. Thus, the analysis of emotional, motivational, and behavioral disturbances after TBI has become progressively more "biological" and "neurological" in nature. Careful clinical description of individual patients has given way to the use of standardized questionnaires and structured interviews to understand the psychiatric and behavioral problems of children (Max et al., 2001) and adults (Dikmen et al., 2004) after TBI. In this chapter, we will review findings from this approach.

Due to the extensive literature that has appeared over the last 10–15 years, selected papers will be reviewed for the following disturbances: depression, anxiety, paranoid ideation, a lack of empathy, irritability, impulsiveness, and socially inappropriate comments. Due to space limitations, we will not address other important topics such as posttraumatic stress disorders or pathological laughter and crying after TBI (Tateno et al., 2004). While the focus will be on the TBI literature, studies with other patient groups that have specific bearing on topics to be discussed will be briefly considered. Before reviewing these papers, a few methodological problems facing this research will be considered.

Methodological Problems

Recent studies have used neuroimaging to relate changes of brain structure (as recorded by computed tomography [CT] or magnetic resonance imaging [MRI]) to psychiatric disturbances after TBI. To date they repeatedly have failed to show a strong relationship between brain neuroimaging findings and DSM-IV diagnoses that are applied to TBI patients. Even when neuroimaging techniques try to relate dynamic brain activity, as reflected by functional MRI (fMRI), positron emission tomography (PET), or single photon emission computed tomography (SPECT) studies to psychiatric disturbances, the findings are often difficult to interpret. It is seldom that a specific brain lesion and/or a specific metabolic finding correlates with specific neuropsychiatric disorders.

We believe this is due to several fundamental problems underlying research in this area. First, researchers seldom, if ever, explicitly discuss the important distinction of a direct versus indirect effect of brain dysfunction on the psychiatric disorders seen in TBI patients. Second, the American Psychiatric Association Diagnostic and Statistical Manual of Mental Disorders (DSM-IV; American Psychiatric Association, 1994) may be helpful when classifying traditional psychiatric disturbances, but is limited when describing the varied emotional and motivational disturbances that can be witnessed after TBI. Thus, studies that classify TBI patients using DSM-IV terminology may not capture the most relevant psychiatric features that have the potential to be related to specific neuropsychologic, neuroanatomical, neurophysiologic, or neurotransmitter disturbances observed in TBI patients. A third major difficulty that faces researchers in this field was recently emphasized by Jorge (2005). He notes: "The neuropsychiatry of TBI encompasses a broad spectrum of cognitive, emotional, and behavioral disturbances occurring during the acute, post-acute, and chronic phases of the illness" (p. 291). "TBI is characterized by widespread neuropathological changes in diverse cortical areas, subcortical nuclei, and white matter tracts …" (p. 293). Fourth, although the classification of TBI severity by the Glasgow Coma Scale (GCS) (Teasdale & Jennett, 1974) is an objective, easily applied method of recording unresponsiveness to the environment following brain trauma, this system might be oversimplified at times. It has progressively become clear that GCS scores need to be supplemented with neuroimaging findings to obtain a clearer picture of the severity of TBI (Prigatano et al., 2008).

A true neuropsychiatry of TBI must wrestle with these realities and conduct studies that allow one to specifically relate neuropathological changes with neuropsychological changes that can change with time and occur with varying degrees of severity of injury. Premorbid characteristics of the patients, as well as their psychosocial and cultural backgrounds, need to be considered (Yeates et al., 1997).

Finally, clinicians and researchers should share a common terminology when at all possible. We would suggest the following definitions be utilized. The term *neuropsychiatric* refers to changes in the patient's psychiatric status that is a direct effect (i.e., caused) of brain dysfunction. The term *psychiatric* refers to disturbances in the mental or emotional (and motivational) features of the person that either preexisted the brain disorder (i.e., are characterological) or are in reaction to the limitations a person experiences in their functional capacities following brain injury. The term *behavioral* is used to identify changes in responding that are not a part of a constellation of symptoms that would warrant a specific psychiatric diagnosis.

Depression

Depressive mood is common among patients with a history of moderate-to-severe TBI, but estimates of the percentage of TBI patients who present with acute versus chronic major depressive disorder (MDD) as defined by the DSM-IV vary. Jorge and Starkstein (2005) suggested, however, that "major depression is present in about 40% of patients hospitalized for a TBI" (p. 482). Fedoroff et al. (1992) demonstrated a significant relationship between location of brain lesions and the development of major depression in acute TBI patients using CT scans of the brain within the first 24 hours, and again 1–2 weeks postinjury. "The presence of left dorsolateral frontal lesions and/or left basal ganglia lesions and, to a lesser extent, parietal, occipital, and right hemisphere lesions was associated with an increased probability of developing major depression" (p. 918).

The same sample of patients was then followed at 3, 6, and 12 months postinjury (Jorge et al., 1993). Using the previous CT scan findings, these researchers failed to reveal a significant relationship between lesion location and the presence of major depression during these time frames. The strength of the relationship between depression and regional brain lesions seemed to alter with time.

In a further comparison, Jorge et al. (1993) specifically compared a TBI patient group that was depressed in the hospital, but whose symptoms improved to a nondepressive state by the 3-month follow-up ($N = 7$), with TBI patients who remained depressed. The acute-onset transient depressed patients demonstrated not only significantly higher injury severity but also significantly higher rates of left anterior lesion locations than the other patient group.

In perhaps the first comprehensive prospective study on major depression following TBI, Jorge et al. (2004) reports several interesting findings. Major depression was observed in approximately 33% of 91 patients during the first year following brain trauma. A history of premorbid mood disturbance and anxiety disorders was common in these patients. Depressed TBI patients tended to perform worse on neuropsychological tests, especially measures sampling "executive functions." Their volumetric MRI findings were perhaps the most interesting of all findings reported. TBI patients with major depression "showed significant decreased left lateral frontal cortex volumes" (p. 47). "This difference was owing to significantly smaller left inferior frontal gyrus volumes…as well as small left superior frontal gyrus volumes…and left middle frontal gyrus volumes" (p. 47). They later cautioned, however, that "it is unclear if the reduced prefrontal volumes observed in patients with major depressive disorder are the result of the pathophysiological mechanisms initiated by TBI or they constitute a preexistent trait associated with an increased risk to develop mood disorders. Brain atrophic changes can be observed among patients with chronic mood disorders …" (p. 48). These studies clearly document the interaction effects of preinjury personality disturbances and neuropathological/neuropsychological disturbances observed in TBI patients.

Dikmen et al. (2004) using a behavioral approach documented that "the rates of moderate to severe depression ranged from 31% at 1 month to 17% at 3 to 5 years" (p. 1457) posttrauma. Their study also noted that premorbid factors such as a history of mood disorders and unstable work history was related to postinjury depression. They note, as others have (see Silver et al., 2005), that "these data do not support a simple dose-response relation between TBI severity and severity of depressive symptoms" (p. 1461). They go on to remark "that educational, vocational, and psychologic factors do predict depressive symptom severity, especially at 1 year after injury" (p. 1461). This conclusion is in keeping with the clinical observations that psychotherapy and medications are both helpful in treating depression in postacute TBI patients (Prigatano, 2005; Prigatano & Summers, 1997).

Levin et al. (2005) conducted the first prospective study on the development of a major depressive episode (MDE) following mild TBI in adults (i.e., admitting GCS score 13–15 on arrival to the hospital with no later deterioration below a GCS score of 13). They report that the presence of an abnormal brain CT finding coupled with these GCS scores increased the odds of an MDE by over 7 to 1. They demonstrate that a combination of GCS scores and neuroimaging findings may be helpful in predicting later MDE, even following mild TBI.

Not all neuroimaging studies, however, have been able to relate abnormal findings to depression after TBI. The positive findings observed often relate to the acute period following trauma. Studies that examined patients several years post-TBI often do not report these correlations. Koponen et al. (2006) attempted to relate MRI findings to Axis I and Axis II psychiatric disorders following TBI 30 years posttrauma. Major depression was surprisingly related to an absence of cerebral contusions. Citing Fann et al. (2004) epidemiological study, these authors suggest that the risk of depression several years posttrauma may be associated with milder TBIs.

As interesting as these (generally) well-designed studies are, they have not substantially brought us any closer to understanding MDD in postacute TBI patients. A history of mood or psychiatric disorders plus an unstable work history may be as predictive of post-TBI depression as any neuroimaging correlate found to date. The patients' perception of how the injury affected them and their assessment of the extent and nature of their neuropsychological impairment are seldom, if ever, described in these technically well-designed studies. The patients' experiences are often excluded from the data analysis, leaving the clinician unclear as to what role the premorbid factors and the patients' present existential situation contribute to their major depression.

Before leaving the topic of neuroimaging correlates of mood disorders after TBI, a recent study by Jorge et al. (2007) examined the association between mood disorders following TBI and lesions of the hippocampus. Hippocampal atrophy is common after severe TBI (Bigler, 2005). In a sample of 37 TBI patients, 19 were diagnosed with major depression or mixed features during the first 3 months after injury. MRI scans at the 3-month follow-up showed that TBI patients who had developed a mood disorder had significantly lower right and left hippocampal volumes than TBI patients without mood disorders. They also note that reduced hippocampal volume was related to poor vocational outcome, after controlling for severity of TBI and the presence of mood disorders. It does not appear, however, that the authors specifically assessed the impact of vocational outcome on depression. If major depression after TBI is a direct outcome of hippocampal volume, and not an indirect result of poor vocational outcome, the severity of depressive symptoms should correlate with hippocampal volume when vocational outcome is held constant in statistical analyses. One could also ask the question, Are the patients with low hippocampal volume depressed even if they are able to return to a productive lifestyle? Research on the effects of TBI on depression has still not adequately separated the potential direct versus indirect effects of the TBI on this psychiatric disturbance. We would predict that those patients who are able to maintain a productive lifestyle several months after TBI will have lower rates of depression despite their neuroimaging findings (Prigatano et al., 1986). A key moderating variable will be, however, whether depression was a major problem prior to the TBI.

Anxiety after Traumatic Brain Injury

The prevalence of a generalized anxiety disorder (GAD) in the population has been estimated to be approximately 5.1% (see Hiott & Labbate, 2002). The prevalence of GAD after TBI is unknown. Some studies report a low prevalence (2.5%; Deb et al., 1999) while others report a higher prevalence (10.2%; see Hiott & Labbate, 2002).

Like depression, anxiety disorders encompass a wide range of behavioral difficulties. There is often a sense of "panic" and excessive worrying associated with restlessness, difficulties concentrating, easy fatigability, and irritability. The later problems are especially common after mild TBI and often compose part of a post-concussion syndrome (Ruff & Richards, 2003). Efforts to relate neuropathological changes in the brain to anxiety disorders have repeatedly run into difficulties (Hiott & Labbate, 2002), with a lack of consensus regarding how different lesions of the brain may affect this complicated psychiatric problem.

Clinically, anxiety often seems to be associated with the patients' awareness that there has been some disturbance in their functioning and their inability to return to preinjury role activities. Concerns about the future and inability to support oneself and one's family after TBI may result in increased self-reports of anxiety.

A pathological absence of anxiety, however, may reflect a disturbance of frontal lobe function in which individuals do not experience tension over a given situation when they should (see Luria, 1948/1963, for a discussion of this important problem). For example, Vasa et al. (2004) noted that in children with TBI "greater volume and number of OFC (or orbitofrontal cortex) lesions correlated with decreased risk for anxiety" (p. 208). This is in keeping with Luria's (1948/1963) earlier observations. To date, no specific brain lesion has been shown to substantially increase anxiety after varying levels of severity of TBI. Following Goldstein's (1952) observation, anxiety often appears to be a part of the catastrophic reaction. It may reflect a patient's inability to cope with the environmental demands secondary to reduced cognitive capacity.

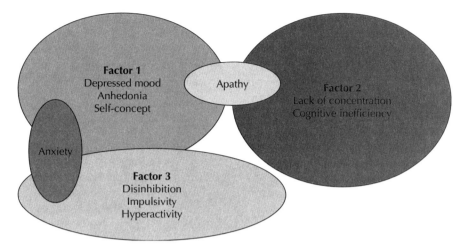

Figure 25–2. Factor structure of psychiatric symptoms elicited by the Present State Examination for persons with traumatic brain injury (reprinted with permission from Jorge & Starkstein, 2005).

Jorge and Starkstein (2005) recently reported data and a theoretical model that links anxiety after TBI with depression, as well as other commonly observed cognitive and behavioral difficulties. Using patients' subjective reports of their present status, they note that reports of anxiety and depression coexist in approximately 60% of the TBI subjects that they studied. They analyzed the factor structure of the psychiatric symptoms reported by persons with TBI (see Figure 25–2 taken from their work). The first factor accounted for 27% of the variance and comprised mainly symptoms associated with depression. The second factor accounted for 12% of the variance. It reflected primarily subjective complaints of cognitive difficulty. The third factor accounted for 11% of the variability and appeared to reflect the problem of psychomotor agitation and disinhibition. The figure highlights the important clinical observation that many of these symptoms overlap in a given patient, as observed in group data as well.

Psychosis and Paranoid Ideation after TBI

While uncommon, psychotic thought processes and behavior have been observed by a number of investigators several months and years post-severe TBI (Fujii et al., 2004; Hillbom, 1960; Lishman, 1968; Thomsen, 1984; Zhang &

Sachdev, 2003). Epidemiological studies suggest schizophrenic-like disorders are 2–3 times more common when the patient has had a history of TBI (Arciniegas et al., 2003; Silver et al., 2001). A consistent and as yet unanswered question is, Does TBI put a person at risk for psychosis or can it cause psychosis several years posttrauma?

At the heart of this problem has been the failure to find a direct neuropathological link between a person's TBI and his or her psychosis. McAllister and Ferrell (2002) shed light, however, on the key observation relative to this controversy:

Although no single brain region has been identified as the site or cause of schizophrenia, several brain regions appear to play important roles in the genesis and phenomenology of this disorder, and these regions overlap with those vulnerable to injury in the typical TBI. (p. 361)

A number of clinical reports have implicated damage to the left hemisphere of the brain, particularly involving the temporal lobes, with psychotic-like behavior, including paranoid ideation (see McAllister & Ferrell, 2002). Acute frontal lobe damage, however, has been consistently linked to confusional disorders (DeLuca & Cicerone, 1991), and may play a role in late onset of delusions.

Prigatano (1988) suggested that unresolved anosognosia or impaired self-awareness (ISA) may contribute to paranoid ideation several years post-TBI. The senior author has followed TBI patients who have developed frank paranoid ideation several years posttrauma. One patient was a 26-year-old male who suffered a severe TBI with an admitting GCS score of 6. He was first examined at age 31, approximately 5 years posttrauma. He demonstrated during the clinical interview, as well as on neuropsychological tests, significant neurocognitive impairment. He insisted, however, that he was perfectly normal in all areas except for motor difficulties. He insisted he was able to work. He reported no major difficulties in his cognitive functioning or changes in his personality. Using the Patient Competency Rating Scale (PCRS) (Prigatano et al., 1986), the patient reported performing almost all tasks with little or no difficulty. His total score on the PCRS was 143 out of 150 possible points. (A score of 150 points means the patient is stating that of 30 items he can do each activity with absolutely no difficulty.) In contrast, his mother rated him on the PCRS-Relative's form with a score of 85 out of 150 points, reflecting significant restrictions in his day-to-day life.

The patient was then seen 13 years later because of the onset of paranoid ideation. He continued to insist that he was perfectly normal in his ability to remember and to think logically. He viewed himself as having no major limitations that would preclude him from returning to work. He explained his failure to return to work on the basis that others did not give him appropriate opportunities. He explained his social isolation and lack of friends on the basis that he lived with his mother in a rural town outside of the Greater Phoenix area. He did not present with any delusions of grandeur or believe that he had any special role to play in life. He was not plagued by hearing voices that urged him to carry out certain actions. He did not have an elaborate set of beliefs that underlined his paranoid ideation as is sometimes seen in true schizophrenia.

On the PCRS-Patient's form, his total score was 138 out of 150 points. The only change in his ratings was that he now felt he could not drive a car because of his motor difficulties and associated visual problems. His mother's ratings on the PCRS-Relative's form produced a

raw score of 84 out of 150 points. These scores are highly reliable from both the patient's and mother's perspective. Despite the patient's insistence that he could do everything well 13 years postinjury, his Wechsler Verbal IQ score was 84 with a Performance IQ of 64. He was clearly cognitively impaired but could not explain his difficulties in everyday life. His conclusion was that others were mistreating him and this was the basis of his personal failures and misery.

Koponen et al. (2002) noted that, in the 30-year follow-up study, paranoid ideation was observed in 8.3% of their study sample. These authors report that delusions are often associated with bilateral brain lesions frequently involving the thalamus. Mizrahi et al. (2006) also have reported a relationship between anosognosia and delusions in Alzheimer patients.

Loss of Empathy After Traumatic Brain Injury

The DSM-IV (1994) does not classify loss of empathy, commonly observed in clinical practice, as a specific neuropsychiatric disorder. A recent study by Woods and Williams (2008) found that individuals with TBI reported a significantly higher proportion of low emotional empathy (60.7%; 54 of 89 participants) than normal controls (31%; 26 of 84 participants). This problem can be especially devastating because it substantially interferes with one's ability to sustain interpersonal relationships. Early severe TBI may have especially negative consequences for the individual (Prigatano, 1999). Eslinger, Parkinson and Shamay (2002) note that empathy "... has been described as a 'binding force' that permits individuals to share experiences and exchange understanding, a fundamental building block for most interpersonal relationships and social groups" (p. 95). When there is a loss of empathy, the individual is often described as "self-centered" and insensitive to the needs of others. As reviewed by Eslinger et al. (2002), a series of studies suggest that damage to the prefrontal cortex and the right posterior cortical regions may significantly alter the person's capacity for empathy. Moreover, "deep white matter lesions of the frontal lobe, disconnecting frontal limbic pathways, have been associated with impaired empathetic capabilities and negative social adaptation …" (p. 95). This may help explain why this problem is common in TBI patients since the pathological changes associated with a loss of empathy are common after severe TBI (Silver et al., 2005).

Lawrence et al. (2006) studied patterns of brain activation, using fMRI, in twelve healthy volunteers who described their and others' feelings during a social perception task. Several areas of the brain were activated during these times. The authors, however, suggest that activation of the anterior cingulate was especially pronounced during those episodes in which the individuals seemed to appear to have an empathetic response. Whether this activation is secondary to the attentional demands of an empathetic response or is associated with empathy per se is unclear. However, broad neurocircuits involving frontal, temporal, parietal, and cingulate gyrus become activated in these tasks. Damage to any of these areas may result in a lack of empathy or a reduction of empathy for TBI patients.

Irritability and Disinhibited Behavior After TBI

It has long been recognized that irritability is a common sequelae of TBI (van Zomeren, 1981). A recent study by Deb and Burns (2007) reported that 37% of TBI participants ages 18–65 (*n* = 120) endorsed problems with irritability. This is consistent with the existing literature, which suggests that about one-third of patients with mild to moderate injuries experience increased irritability (Alderman, 2003).

Early efforts to relate irritability to measures of severity of TBI or location of TBI have repeatedly been unsuccessful (van Zomeren & van den Burg, 1985). Ratings of irritability, ratings of forgetfulness, and ratings of tiring easily around people, however, load on a single factor (Hinkley & Corrigan, 1990). The failure to find a relationship between severity and location of brain injury and yet observations that irritability correlates essentially with failures in coping in everyday life suggest that irritability may be a reactionary problem. This obviously requires further research before firm conclusions can be made.

In their factor analytic studies, Jorge and Starkstein (2005) identified a third factor that

accounted for approximately 11% of the variance as noted above. This factor loaded highly on irritability, as well as other problems associated with disinhibition, agitation, etc. In clinical practice, many patients with TBI describe themselves as being easily irritable. This irritability, at times, is associated with disinhibited behavior.

Have there been any new insights in understanding these behaviors? Koponen et al. (2006) note in their 30-year follow-up study that 17 out of 58 patients (29.3%) studied had definite personality disorders or an organic personality syndrome (using DSM-IV classification system). Many of these patients were described as demonstrating disinhibited behavior. These patients were more likely to have contusions in the frontal regions of the brain. This observation is compatible with earlier reports (Prigatano, 1992). Frontal lobe dysfunction often produces a disinhibited state in some patients. This disinhibited state seems to involve an inability to control one's emotional reactions, particularly angry feelings, and therefore the individual may be described as "more irritable."

Research on children and adults with hypothalamic hamartomas may provide, however, new insights into the etiology of irritability in TBI patients (Prigatano, 2007). Patients with this rare congenital anomaly often have refractory epilepsy. A recent report suggests that when epilepsy is stopped via surgical intervention, these patients may be less irritable. They are likely to be described by their family members as showing a reduction in their rage reactions. The mechanism underlying this change, however, remains unclear. Irritability after TBI may be related to damage to deep brain structures that influence behavior in complicated ways.

Davidson et al. (2003) summarized several findings that are relevant to the topic of irritability and disinhibition after TBI. The orbital frontal cortex plays an important role in inhibitory control. Ventral medial lesions may negatively affect the ability of the person to use feelings to guide decision making. This can lead to a variety of behavioral abnormalities, from excessive gambling to failure to be sensitive to others' feelings (i.e., empathy). Damage to the dorsolateral prefrontal cortex, particularly on the left side of the brain, may predispose a person to depression because of a fundamental disturbance in approach behavior. Lesions to the anterior cingulate may disturb the basic connection between attention and feelings, which again can provide a wide variety of cognitive and behavioral disorders.

Psychiatric and Behavioral Problems in Children with TBI

Rutter and colleagues (Rutter et al., 1983) have demonstrated that TBI in children can result in considerable psychiatric and behavioral difficulties. Brown et al. (1981) demonstrated that "new psychiatric disorders" may dramatically appear during the first year following TBI. Shaffer et al. (1975) recognized that an adverse family environment may greatly contribute to these disorders.

Over the last 20 years, a number of important and well-designed studies have documented and supported these earlier observations. Some of the more seminal findings from these studies include the following observations. Children who present with behavioral problems (perhaps not surprisingly) have much more difficulty succeeding in school (Hawley, 2004). TBI children with behavioral problems typically perform at lower levels on measures of intelligence (Hawley, 2004; Max et al., 1997, 2000). Children described as showing personality change after TBI have consistently been shown to have severe injuries, as judged by a combination of GCS scores and neuroimaging findings (Max et al., 2001). Interestingly, however, the number of contusions versus diffuse injuries to the brain have not specifically identified those children who were described as having personality changes.

The psychiatric disorders frequently reported in children include attentional deficit disorder, obsessive-compulsive disorder, oppositional-defiant disorder, anxiety, and depression. Bloom et al. (2001) suggested that attentional deficit disorders and depressive disorders were, in fact, most common. Max (2004) has emphasized, however, that oppositional-defiant disorders are frequently observed in these children, particularly after mild injury. Prevalence rates are not reported. Max and colleagues (1998) report that oppositional-defiant disorder symptoms are frequently related to preinjury family function, social class, and the presence of preinjury oppositional-defiant disorder symptoms.

There is a high incidence of premorbid psychiatric disorders in children that may not be reported by their parents but become obvious when structured psychiatric interviews are conducted (see Bloom et al., 2001; Max et al., 2001). The family environment appears to substantially contribute to the behavioral problems of these children (Shaffer et al., 1975; Taylor et al., 2001), but the role of brain damage is clearly present. How these two interact becomes a challenging clinical question in individual cases.

Socially Inappropriate Comments after TBI

The final behavioral disorder to be discussed is that of socially inappropriate comments or behavior following TBI. Such behavioral difficulties are seen in both children (Rutter et al., 1983) and adults (Prigatano, 1999). The problem is not just one of disinhibition. The TBI child or adult may make comments that reflect a lack of appreciation of what are the "do's" and the "don'ts" of different social situations. A child may comment on how fat a fellow child is without realizing that the comment would offend that child. A young adult male may comment in public how beautiful a young woman's legs are without knowing her or recognizing that the comments would embarrass or offend her. Middle-aged men or women with severe TBI may tell a spouse that they want a divorce followed by the comment, "have a nice day." The last comment is not said sarcastically. It is simply disjointed and reveals that the patient fails to cognitively understand and affectively experience what the words mean. Not uncommonly, the problem of socially inappropriate comments is associated with significant bilateral frontal lobe dysfunction with associated impairment of self-awareness, particularly awareness of one's problems with planning and social interaction (Prigatano, 1999).

Molecular Biology, Genes, and Psychiatric Disorders After TBI

Since the genetic underpinnings of various diseases are starting to be unraveled (e.g., Corder et al., 1993; Fazekas et al., 2001), it is natural that the methodologies of molecular biology be applied to the study of psychiatric disorders after TBI (McAllister & Summerall, 2003). Several studies have examined how a person's genetic makeup could be related to various markers of recovery after TBI (e.g., Chiang et al., 2003; Diaz-Arrastia et al., 2003; Sorbi et al., 1995; Teasdale et al., 1997). Most of these studies have analyzed the relationship between the Apolipoprotein E4 allele (*APOE ε4*) and outcome after brain trauma (Diaz-Arrastia & Baxter, 2006). Poorer neuropsychological outcome after TBI has also been associated with presence of *APOE ε4* (Liberman et al., 2002; Teasdale et al., 2000), positive findings being reported for attention and facial recognition (Sundstrom et al., 2004), memory (Crawford et al., 2002), and executive functioning (Ariza et al., 2006). Also, the development of posttraumatic dementia has been related to *APOE ε4* (Koponen et al., 2004).

Other authors, however, were not able to find an influence of *APOE ε4* on cognitive outcome after TBI (Chamelian et al., 2004; Millar et al., 2003). For example, Nathoo et al. (2003) studied 110 African patients and could not find an association between *APOE ε4* presence and TBI outcome.

Phenomenological Experiences of Persons with Traumatic Brain Injury

Due to the wide variety of disturbances in brain function that can be induced by TBI, it is not possible to classify the varied phenomenological experiences of patients who suffer such injuries. Yet there are common descriptions that have been repeated by many patients. Following a mild TBI, patients often sense that their brain function has been altered. They may experience headache and nausea. They are easily fatigued. They note that any kind of physical activity may exacerbate a somatic complaint (such as a headache). These individuals are frightened, and anxiety is often a part of their symptom picture. As they progressively improve, their anxiety diminishes, but many do not forget the horrifying experience of not having one's brain function normally.

With severe TBI, in which frontal temporal contusions are common as well as diffuse

axonal injury, the symptoms may appear polar opposite. These individuals may not experience any anxiety. In fact, they may appear to be unaware of their actual limitations. However, they can become easily angry and frequently show memory and processing-speed difficulties. Compatible with Goldstein's (1952) observations, they have a loss of the "abstract attitude." When they fail in day-to-day life activities, they may become overwhelmed by intense anxiety and depression (i.e., show the catastrophic reaction). These individuals, however, often do not ruminate over how bad they are or how unimportant or meaningless their life is. Rather, they have repeated experiences of failure and do not know why they fail. Unlike patients with major depressive disorder they are likely to minimize their description of cognitive limitations. Their depressive affect, therefore, appears quite different from what is seen in major depressive disorder. After TBI, the individual may simply not be able to cope with their environment, and anxiety and depression reflect their failure in coping.

Patients with moderate TBI, particularly those with focal brain damage, provide the most varied subjective reports of what they experience. When lesions involve the mesial left temporal lobe, language and memory functions are often affected, and patients may report worrying that they are "going crazy" (Prigatano & Smith, 2000). Their ability to communicate with others and remember what has been said has been altered, and they may not have an easy explanation for this change in functional capacity that they perceive.

Patients with focal lesions to the right hemisphere, particularly the parietal lobes, however, may have a curious lack of awareness of their difficulties with a euphoric quality to their affect. This is not true happiness, but rather a childlike giddiness over life's events. Few clinicians or theorists, however, have been able to capture exactly what these phenomenological experiences are, but Goldstein's work comes the closest (Goldstein, 1952). While it is important to apply the methods of science to understand the emotional, motivational, and behavioral problems associated with TBI, it is equally important to understand their phenomenological experience in order to engage them in the rehabilitation process (Prigatano, 1999).

Summary, Conclusions, and Reflections

The study of the neuropsychiatric, psychiatric, and behavioral problems of children and adults after TBI has produced a complicated literature. The growing use of neuroimaging studies often report a relationship between neuroimaging findings and depression during the acute-phase posttrauma, but not during the postacute phase. Premorbid factors seem to play a predominant role in postacute depression. The absence of anxiety, especially in children, appears to relate to the severity of frontal lobe damage. There may be a link between the development of paranoid ideation and residual signs of anosognosia. Irritability, once thought to be primarily an indirect effect of brain trauma, may ultimately be found to be related to disturbances in deep brain structures. Socially inappropriate comments are common after frontal lobe lesions.

The potential contribution of genetic factors to the recovery process after TBI and specifically the neuropsychological sequelae is beginning to be appreciated. The data presently available, however, are sparse and do not specifically address neuropsychiatric problems after TBI.

The more biological approach to studying the emotional and motivational disturbances after TBI has produced many interesting findings. However, the translation of these findings into more effective rehabilitation strategies has yet to occur. Failure to separate a direct (i.e., neuropsychiatric, behavioral) disturbance from an indirect one (e.g., reactionary anxiety) has continued to hamper progress in the field. Such a description may help clinicians focus on different strategies for treating these disturbances (Prigatano, 1999). Direct neuropsychiatric disturbances may be especially responsive to pharmacological therapies, while the indirect psychiatric and behavioral problems may well benefit from a combination of psychotherapy and pharmacological interventions.

References

Alderman, N. (2003). Contemporary approaches to the management of irritability and aggression following TBI. *Neuropsychological Rehabilitation, 13*, 211–240.

American Psychiatric Association. (1994). *Diagnostic and statistical manual of mental disorders* (4th ed.). Washington, DC: Author.

Andreasen, N. C. (2001). *Brave new brain: Conquering mental illness in the era of the genome.* New York: Oxford University Press.

Arciniegas, D. B., Harris, S. N., & Brousseau, K. M. (2003). Psychosis following traumatic brain injury. *International Review of Psychiatry, 15*(4), 328–340.

Ariza, M., Pueyo, R., Matarín, Mdel M., Junqué, C., Mataró, M., Clemente, I., et al. (2006). Influence of APOE polymorphism on cognitive and behavioural outcome in moderate and severe traumatic brain injury. *Journal of Neurology, Neurosurgery, and Psychiatry, 77*(10), 1191–1193.

Bigler, E. D. (2005). Structural Imaging. In J. M. Silver, T. W. McAllister, and S. C. Yudofsky (Eds.), *Textbook of traumatic brain injury* (pp. 79–105). Washington, DC: American Psychiatric Publishing, Inc.

Bloom, D. R., Levin, H. S., Ewing-Cobbs, L., Saunders, A. E., Song, J., Fletcher, J. M., et al. (2001). Lifetime and novel psychiatric disorders after pediatric traumatic brain injury. *Journal of the American Academy of Child and Adolescent Psychiatry, 40*(5), 572–579.

Brown, G., Chadwick, O., Shaffer, D., Rutter, M., & Traub, M. (1981). A prospective study of children with head injuries: III. Psychiatric sequelae. *Psychological Medicine, 11*(1), 63–78.

Chamelian, L., Reis, M., & Feinstein, A. (2004). Six-month recovery from mild to moderate traumatic brain injury: The role of APOE-epsilon4 allele. *Brain: A Journal of Neurology, 127*(Pt 12), 2621–2628.

Chiang, M. F., Chang, J. G., & Hu, C. J. (2003). Association between apolipoprotein E genotype and outcome of traumatic brain injury. *Acta Neurochirurgica, 145*(8), 649–654.

Corder, E. H., Saunders, A. M., Strittmatter, W. J., Schmechel, D. E., Gaskell, P. C., Small, G. W., et al. (1993). Gene dose of apolipoprotein E type 4 allele and the risk of Alzheimer's disease in late onset families. *Science, 261*(5123), 921–923.

Crawford, F. C., Vanderploeg, R. D., Freeman, M. J., Singh, S., Waisman, M., Michaels, L., et al. (2002). APOE genotype influences acquisition and recall following traumatic brain injury. *Neurology, 58*(7), 1115–1118.

Davidson, R. J., Pizzagalli, D., Nitschke, J. B., & Kalin, N. H. (2003). Parsing the subcomponents of emotion and disorders of emotion: Perspectives from affective neurosciences. In R. J. Davidson, K. R. Scherer, and H. H. Goldsmith (Eds.), *Handbook of Affective Sciences* (pp. 8–24). New York: Oxford University Press.

Deb, S., & Burns, J. (2007). Neuropsychiatric consequences of traumatic brain injury: A comparison between two age groups. *Brain Injury, 21*, 301–307.

Deb, S., Lyons, I., Koutzoukis, C., Ali, I., & McCarthy, G. (1999). Rate of psychiatric illness 1 year after traumatic brain injury. *The American Journal of Psychiatry, 156*(3), 374–378.

DeLuca, J., & Cicerone, K. D. (1991). Confabulation following aneurism of the anterior communicating artery. *Cortex, 27*, 417–423.

Diaz-Arrastia, R., & Baxter, V. K. (2006). Genetic factors in outcome after traumatic brain injury: What the human genome project can teach us about brain trauma. *The Journal of Head Trauma Rehabilitation, 21*(4), 361–374.

Diaz-Arrastia, R., Gong, Y., Fair, S., Scott, K. D., Garcia, M. C., Carlile, M. C., et al. (2003). Increased risk of late posttraumatic seizures associated with inheritance of APOE epsilon4 allele. *Archives of Neurology, 60*(6), 818–822.

Dikmen, S. S., Bombardier, C. H., Machamer, J. E., Fann, J. R., & Temkin, N. R. (2004). Natural history of depression in traumatic brain injury. *Archives of Physical Medicine and Rehabilitation, 85*(9), 1457–1464.

Eslinger, P. J., Parkinson, K., & Shamay, S. G. (2002). Empathy and social-emotional factors in recovery from stroke. *Current Opinion in Neurology, 15*(1), 91–97.

Fann, J. R., Burington, B., Leonetti, A., Jaffe, K., Katon, W. J., & Thompson, R. S. (2004). Psychiatric illness following traumatic brain injury in an adult health maintenance organization population. *Archives of General Psychiatry, 61*(1), 53–61.

Fazekas, F., Strasser-Fuchs, S., Kollegger, H., Berger, T., Kristoferitsch, W., Schmidt, H., et al. (2001). Apolipoprotein E epsilon 4 is associated with rapid progression of multiple sclerosis. *Neurology, 57*(5), 853–857.

Fedoroff, J. P., Starkstein, S. E., Forrester, A. W., Geisler, F. H., Jorge, R. E., Arndt, S. V., et al. (1992). Depression in patients with acute traumatic brain injury. *The American Journal of Psychiatry, 149*(7), 918–923.

Fujii, D., Ahmed, I., & Hishinuma, E. (2004). A neuropsychological comparison of psychotic disorder following traumatic brain injury, traumatic brain injury without psychotic disorder, and schizophrenia. *The Journal of Neuropsychiatry and Clinical Neurosciences, 16*(3), 306–314.

Goldstein, K. (1952). The effect of brain damage on the personality. *Psychiatry, 15*(3), 245–260.

Hawley, C. A. (2004). Behaviour and school performance after brain injury. *Brain Injury, 18*(7), 645–659.

Hawley, C. A., Ward, A. B., Magnay, A. R., & Long, J. (2003). Parental stress and burden following traumatic brain injury amongst children and adolescents. *Brain Injury, 17*(1), 1–23.

Hillbom, E. (1960). After-effects of brain-injuries. *Acta Psychiatrica et Neurologica Scandinavica, S142*, 1–195.

Hinkeldey, N. S., & Corrigan, J. D. (1990). The structure of head-injured patients' neurobehavioural complaints: A preliminary study. *Brain Injury, 4*(2), 115–133.

Hiott, D. W., & Labbate, L. (2002). Anxiety disorders associated with traumatic brain injuries. *NeuroRehabilitation, 17*(4), 345–355.

Jorge, R. E. (2005). Neuropsychiatric consequences of traumatic brain injury: A review of recent findings. *Current Opinion in Psychiatry, 18*(3), 289–299.

Jorge, R. E., Acion, L., Starkstein, S. E., & Magnotta, V. (2007). Hippocampal volume and mood disorders after traumatic brain injury. *Biological Psychiatry, 62*(4), 332–338.

Jorge, R. E., Robinson, R. G., Arndt, S. V., Starkstein, S. E., Forrester, A. W., & Geisler, F. (1993). Depression following traumatic brain injury: A 1 year longitudinal study. *Journal of Affective Disorders, 27*(4), 233–243.

Jorge, R. E., Robinson, R. G., Moser, D., Tateno, A., Crespo-Facorro, B., & Arndt, S. (2004). Major depression following traumatic brain injury. *Archives of General Psychiatry, 61*(1), 42–50.

Jorge, R. E., & Starkstein, S. E. (2005). Pathophysiologic aspects of major depression following traumatic brain injury. *The Journal of Head Trauma Rehabilitation, 20*(6), 475–487.

Klonoff, P. S., & Lage, G. A. (1991). Narcissistic injury after traumatic brain injury. *Journal of Head Trauma Rehabilitation, 6*, 11–21.

Koponen, S., Taiminen, T., Kairisto, V., Portin, R., Isoniemi, H., Hinkka, S., et al. (2004). APOE-epsilon4 predicts dementia but not other psychiatric disorders after traumatic brain injury. *Neurology, 63*(4), 749–750.

Koponen, S., Taiminen, T., Kurki, T., Portin, R., Isoniemi, H., Himanen, L., et al. (2006). MRI findings and Axis I and II psychiatric disorders after traumatic brain injury: A 30-year retrospective follow-up study. *Psychiatry Research, 146*(3), 263–270.

Koponen, S., Taiminen, T., Portin, R., Himanen, L., Isoniemi, H., Heinonen, H., et al. (2002). Axis I and II psychiatric disorders after traumatic brain injury: A 30-year follow-up study. *The American Journal of Psychiatry, 159*(8), 1315–1321.

Lawrence, E. J., Shaw, P., Giampietro, V. P., Surguladze, S., Brammer, M. J., & David, A. S. (2006). The role of 'shared representations' in social perception and empathy: An fMRI study. *NeuroImage, 29*(4), 1173–1184.

Levin, H. S., McCauley, S. R., Josic, C. P., Boake, C., Brown, S. A., Goodman, H. S., et al. (2005). Predicting depression following mild traumatic brain injury. *Archives of General Psychiatry, 62*(5), 523–528.

Liberman, J. N., Stewart, W. F., Wesnes, K., & Troncoso, J. (2002). Apolipoprotein E epsilon 4 and short-term recovery from predominantly mild brain injury. *Neurology, 58*(7), 1038–1044.

Lishman, W. A. (1968). Brain damage in relation to psychiatric disability after head injury. *The British Journal of Psychiatry: The Journal of Mental Science, 114*(509), 373–410.

Lishman, W. A. (1978). *Organic psychiatry: The psychological consequences of cerebral disorder.* Boston: Blackwell Scientific Publications.

Luria, A. R. (1948/1963). *Restoration of function after brain trauma* (in Russian). Moscow: Academy of Medical Science; London: Pergamon.

Max, J. E. (2004). Psychiatric sequelae of traumatic brain injury in children and adolescents. American Academy of Physical Medicine and Rehabilitation, Course Handouts, www.aapmr.org.

Max, J. E., Castillo, C. S., Bokura, H., Robin, D. A., Lindgren, S. D., Smith, W. L., et al. (1998). Oppositional defiant disorder symptomatology after traumatic brain injury: A prospective study. *The Journal of Nervous and Mental Disorders, 186,* 325–332.

Max, J. E., Koele, S. L., Castillo, C. C., Lindgren, S. D., Arndt, S., Bokura, H., et al. (2000). Personality change disorder in children and adolescents following traumatic brain injury. *Journal of the International Neuropsychological Society, 6*(3), 279–289.

Max, J. E., Robertson, B. A., & Lansing, A. E. (2001). The phenomenology of personality change due to traumatic brain injury in children and adolescents. *The Journal of Neuropsychiatry and Clinical Neurosciences, 13*(2), 161–170.

Max, J. E., Robin, D. A., Lindgren, S. D., Smith, W. L., Sato, Y., Mattheis, P. J., et al. (1997). Traumatic brain injury in children and adolescents: Psychiatric disorders at two years. *Journal of the American Academy of Child and Adolescent Psychiatry, 36*(9), 1278–1285.

McAllister, T. W., & Ferrell, R. B. (2002). Evaluation and treatment of psychosis after traumatic brain injury. *NeuroRehabilitation, 17*(4), 357–368.

McAllister, T. W., & Summerall, L. (2003). Genetic polymorphisms in the expression and treatment of neuropsychiatric disorders. *Current Psychiatric Reports, 5*(5), 400–409.

Meyer, A. (1904). The anatomical facts and clinical varieties of traumatic insanity. *American Journal of Insanity, 60,* 373–441.

Millar, K., Nicoll, J. A., Thornhill, S., Murray, G. D., & Teasdale, G. M. (2003). Long term neuropsychological outcome after head injury: Relation to APOE genotype. *Journal of Neurology, Neurosurgery, and Psychiatry, 74*(8), 1047–1052.

Mizrahi, R., Starkstein, S. E., Jorge, R., & Robinson, R. G. (2006). Phenomenology and clinical correlates of delusions in Alzheimer disease. *The American Journal of Geriatric Psychiatry, 14*(7), 573–581.

Nathoo, N., Chetry, R., van Dellen, J. R., Connolly, C., & Naidoo, R. (2003). Apolipoprotein E polymorphism and outcome after closed traumatic brain injury: Influence of ethnic and regional differences. *Journal of Neurosurgery, 98*(2), 302–306.

Prigatano, G. P. (1988). Anosognosia, delusions, and altered self-awareness after brain injury. *BNI Quarterly, 4*(3), 40–48.

Prigatano, G. P. (1992). Personality disturbances associated with traumatic brain injury. *Journal of Consulting and Clinical Psychology, 60*(3), 360–368.

Prigatano, G. P. (1999). *Principles of neuropsychological rehabilitation.* New York: Oxford University Press.

Prigatano, G. P. (2005). Therapy for emotional and motivational disorders. In W. M. High, A. M. Sander, M. A. Struchen, and K. A. Hart (Eds.), *Rehabilitation for traumatic brain injury* (pp. 118–130). New York: Oxford University Press.

Prigatano, G. P. (2007). Cognitive and behavioral dysfunction in children with a hypothalamic hamartoma syndrome. *Seminars in Pediatric Neurology, 14*(2), 65–72.

Prigatano, G. P., Fordyce, D. J., Zeiner, H. K., Roueche, J. R., Pepping, M., & Wood, B. C. (1986). *Neuropsychological rehabilitation after brain injury.* Baltimore: Johns Hopkins University Press.

Prigatano, G. P., Gray, J. A., & Gale, S. D. (2007). Individual case analysis of processing speed difficulties in children with and without traumatic brain injury. *The Clinical Neuropsychologist, 22,* 603–619.

Prigatano, G. P., & Smith, K. (2000). The role of psychotherapy in a neurological institute. *BNI Quarterly, 16*(3), 7–11.

Prigatano, G. P., & Summers, J. (1997). Depression in patients with brain dysfunction. In M. Robertson and C. Katona (Eds.), *Depression and physical illness* (pp. 341–357). Sussex, England: John Wiley and Sons, Ltd.

Ruff, R. M., & Richards, P. M. (2003). Neuropsychological assessment and management of patients with persistent postconcussional disorders. In G. P. Prigatano and N. H. Pliskin (Eds.), *Clinical neuropsychology and cost outcome research: A beginning* (pp. 61–81). New York: Psychology Press.

Rutter, M., Chadwick, O., & Shaffer, D. (1983). Head injury. In M. Rutter (Ed.), *Developmental neuropsychiatry* (pp. 83–111). New York: The Guilford Press.

Schilder, P. (1934). Psychic disturbances after head injuries. *American Journal of Psychiatry, 91,* 155–188.

Shaffer, D., Chadwick, O., & Rutter, M. (1975). Psychiatric outcome of localized head injury in children. *Ciba Foundation Symposium, 34,* 191–213.

Silver, J. M., Kramer, R., Greenwald, S., & Weissman, M. (2001). The association between head injuries and psychiatric disorders: Findings from the New Haven NIMH Epidemiologic Catchment Area Study. *Brain Injury, 15*(11), 935–945.

Silver, J. M., McAllister, T. W., & Yudofsky, S. C. (Eds.). (2005). *Textbook of traumatic brain injury.* Washington, DC: American Psychiatric Publishing, Inc.

Sorbi, S., Nacmias, B., Piacentini, S., Repice, A., Latorraca, S., Forleo, P., et al. (1995). ApoE as a prognostic factor for post-traumatic coma. *Nature Medicine, 1*(9), 852.

Sundstrom, A., Marklund, P., Nilsson, L. G., Cruts, M., Adolfsson, R., Van Broeckhoven, C., et al. (2004). APOE influences on neuropsychological function after mild head injury: Within-person comparisons. *Neurology, 62*(11), 1963–1966.

Tateno, A., Jorge, R. E., & Robinson, R. G. (2004). Pathological laughing and crying following traumatic brain injury. *The Journal of Neuropsychiatry and Clinical Neurosciences, 16*(4), 426–434.

Taylor, H. G., Yeates, K. O., Wade, S. L., Drotar, D., Stancin, T., & Burant, C. (2001). Bidirectional child-family influences on outcomes of traumatic brain injury in children. *Journal of the International Neuropsychological Society, 7*(6), 755–767.

Teasdale, G., & Jennett, B. (1974). Assessment of coma and impaired consciousness. A practical scale. *Lancet, 2*(7872), 81–84.

Teasdale, G. M., Nicoll, J. A., Murray, G., & Fiddes, M. (1997). Association of apolipoprotein E polymorphism with outcome after head injury. *Lancet, 350*(9084), 1069–1071.

Teasdale, T. W., Jorgensen, O. S., Ripa, C., Nielsen, A. S., & Christensen, A.-L. (2000). Apolipoprotein E and subjective symptomatology following brain injury rehabilitation. *Neuropsychological Rehabilitation, 10,* 151–166.

Thomsen, I. V. (1984). Late outcome of very severe blunt head trauma: A 10–15 year second follow-up. *Journal of Neurology, Neurosurgery, and Psychiatry, 47*(3), 260–268.

van Zomeren, A. H. (1981). *Reaction time and attention after closed head injury.* Lisse: Swets and Zeitlinger.

van Zomeren, A. H., & van den Burg, W. (1985). Residual complaints of patients two years after severe head injury. *Journal of Neurology, Neurosurgery, and Psychiatry, 48*(1), 21–28.

Vasa, R. A., Grados, M., Slomine, B., Herskovits, E. H., Thompson, R. E., Salorio, C., et al. (2004). Neuroimaging correlates of anxiety after pediatric traumatic brain injury. *Biological Psychiatry, 55*(3), 208–216.

Winstanley, J., Simpson, G., Tate, R., & Myles, B. (2006). Early indicators and contributors to psychological distress in relatives during rehabilitation following severe traumatic brain injury: Findings from the Brain Injury Outcomes Study. *The Journal of Head Trauma Rehabilitation, 21*(6), 453–466.

Wood, R. L. L., & Williams, C. (2008). Inability to empathize following traumatic brain injury. *Journal of the International Neuropsychological Society, 14,* 289–296.

Yeates, K. O, Taylor, H. G., Drotar, D., Wade, S. L., Klein, S., Stancin, T., et al. (1997). Preinjury family environment as a determinant of recovery from traumatic brain injuries in school-age children. *Journal of the International Neuropsychological Society, 3,* 617–630.

Zhang, Q., & Sachdev, P. S. (2003). Psychotic disorder and traumatic brain injury. *Current Psychiatry Reports, 5*(3), 197–201.

26

Neuropsychology in Relation to Everyday Functioning

Erin E. Morgan and Robert K. Heaton

Overview: The Neuropsychological Approach to Predicting Everyday Functioning

The field of clinical neuropsychology has historically been concerned with detecting and characterizing the nature of cerebral disorders, which has resulted in a well-established role for neuropsychologists in the diagnosis of brain pathology. Although increasing use of advanced neuroimaging techniques has somewhat reduced the need for neuropsychological test data as an ancillary diagnostic tool, the diagnostic role of the neuropsychologist remains valuable in cases where neuroimaging is inconclusive (e.g., after brain trauma or in suspected cases of early dementia). Furthermore, the field has evolved from its early diagnostic focus, and, arguably, today the most important contribution of neuropsychology is the identification and delineation of cognitive and behavioral consequences of cerebral pathology. An accurate understanding of such consequences often is as important as an accurate diagnosis (Chelune & Moehle, 1986; Heaton & Pendleton, 1981). As focus has shifted from organic brain integrity to brain–behavior relationships, standardized assessments have been developed to successfully measure relationships between brain dysfunction and its cognitive and behavioral outcomes in everyday life (Chaytor & Schmitter-Edgecomb, 2003; Chelune & Moehle, 1986). The defining feature of this shift was the focus on assessment of ability as a primary goal, rather than lesion

identification, and another important shift that is still under way is the need to provide an understanding of the relationship of basic abilities to adequacy of everyday functioning (Chelune & Moehle, 1986). Whereas "basic ability" refers to an individual's skill or talent, "functioning" refers to enacting the ability in the environment (Goldstein, 1996). Evaluation of ability lends itself to assessment in the laboratory with standardized tests, but referral questions have changed to require "prescriptive statements" in which inferences are made from an individual's pattern of strengths and deficits to predict his/her ability to carry out everyday activities in the real world (Chelune & Moehle, 1986). For example, the major clinical questions often concern the impact of the brain insult or disorder on the patient's ability to live independently, his/her prospects for employment and rehabilitation, and identification of a need for environmental support (Heaton & Pendleton, 1981).

Initially, questions about the functional impact of cerebral disorders were addressed by considering performance on neuropsychological tests that were developed for primarily diagnostic purposes (Chelune & Moehle, 1986). An important question that arises from this practice is whether the same test procedures that were used for lesion identification and localization can also be used for making predictions of patient's capabilities and limitations in carrying out everyday tasks and activities (Heaton & Pendleton, 1981). Accordingly, concerns about the ecological validity of neuropsychological tests have been raised—namely, the degree to which basic abilities assessed in controlled laboratory settings relate to real-world performance (Franzen & Wilhelm, 1996; Tupper & Cicerone, 1990). Many methods of defining such real-world functional outcomes have been utilized, including self-report, proxy/caregiver reports, and clinician ratings. However, these subjective, report-based measures have limitations that may obscure relationships between basic abilities and adequacy of functioning in everyday life. In order to address these limitations, recent work has focused on development of objective tests of *functional capacity*, or a person's level of competence with specific everyday activities. These tests, which are performance-based instruments that simulate real-world activities, are intended to bridge the gap between the laboratory and the environment. Performance-based tests of functional capacity have more face validity compared to traditional neuropsychological tests with regard to real-world relevance, and therefore address some concerns regarding ecological validity. A review of the types of everyday functioning measures that are available, as well as their strengths, limitations, and indications, appears later in this chapter.

Despite the limited face validity of traditional neuropsychological tests for this purpose, ongoing research has provided considerable evidence regarding the predictive validity of the neuropsychological approach for estimating success in important aspects of everyday functioning. This research has major clinical applications for predicting whether an individual's brain disorder will affect his/her functional abilities, such as returning to work or driving a car. This is especially true in the context of forensic neuropsychology, in which a neuropsychologist's predictions can directly influence the legal outcomes in a patient's case, such as disability claims or compensation awarded (Long & Collins, 1997). Accurate prediction of the impact of ability deficits on functioning is also necessary to inform rehabilitation professionals and family members regarding likely areas of impaired everyday functioning and potential for developing compensatory strategies. Although not reviewed within this chapter, neuropsychological rehabilitation is an important clinical application that is based upon an accurate understanding of the cognitive factors that influence everyday functioning.

Methodological Considerations for Predicting Everyday Functioning

Defining Predictors

On the basis of a neuropsychological approach to prediction of everyday functioning, if a patient demonstrates impairment of a test involving a particular ability, he/she is assumed to be at risk of experiencing difficulty in everyday tasks and activities in which the same ability is required (Heaton & Pendleton, 1981). Although seemingly straightforward, linking cognition to everyday functioning is complicated by the need to understand which abilities are essential for successful performance of which everyday tasks, and under what circumstances. In fact, although the process of "functional analysis" of complex everyday activities has been previously described (Goldstein, 1996), to date there is no well-established account of the specific abilities that are required for various everyday tasks, such as managing money and keeping appointments. Also, specific demands for these classes of activities vary considerably from person to person; for example, complexity of "financial management" can vary considerably with the number, types, and predictability of income sources and expenses, and the associated budgeting and accounting that is required. In the absence of a firmly established understanding of specific abilities required by specific daily functions, and how they relate to our standard neuropsychological tests, considerable clinical judgment is still required.

Many early studies focused solely on the relationship between general intelligence (IQ) and various aspects of functioning. This work clearly demonstrated that IQ as a sole predictor does have some validity with respect to many aspects of functioning. However, consideration of more specific cognitive abilities assessed within a comprehensive battery not only provides more information regarding the nature of a patient's deficits but also allows for the potential to utilize the patient's strengths to compensate for impairments. One widely used "fixed battery" (a standard, comprehensive set of tests administered to all patients regardless of suspected diagnosis or impairment) is an expanded Halstead–Reitan Battery (HRB), such as that described by Heaton and Taylor (2004). Another approach is to focus on the six ability domains that have been identified through confirmatory factor analysis of the Wechsler Adult Intelligence Scale-III (WAIS-III; Psychological Corporation, 1997) and Wechsler Memory Scale-III (WMS-III; Psychological Corporation, 1997) test batteries, including verbal comprehension, perceptual organization, working memory, auditory learning/memory, visual learning/memory, and speed of information processing (Tulsky & Price, 2003).

Despite a persisting lack of evidence linking specific abilities with specific everyday tasks, findings in the literature generally reveal that neuropsychological tests do measure abilities that are relevant for everyday functioning. For example, performances on various sets of neuropsychological tests have been shown to be predictive of academic success, current and future employment status, requirements of jobs at which patients can succeed, successful performance of activities necessary for independent living, medication management, driving ability, and social and community adjustment. Given the complexity of these everyday activities and the likelihood that different patterns of ability deficits could similarly interfere with their successful performance, it may be that multifactorial summary measures will always provide the best predictions. However, more information is still needed regarding the basic abilities that should be represented in these summary measures, as well as the most efficient ways to assess them, and the severity of impairment that is needed to interfere with the outcome of interest. In addition, a consideration of the motivational abilities that may not be well represented in such summary ability (or deficit) scores will be needed to plan rehabilitation and/or compensation strategies.

Defining Outcomes

Everyday functioning is a broad concept encompassing numerous activities and behaviors. Also, in studies examining everyday functioning outcomes, the criterion must be operationally defined in such a way that allows for measurement and empirical study. In examining everyday functioning, behavior in the natural environment is the criterion, and this introduces numerous challenges to finding outcome measures that are reliable, comparable, and meaningful across different patients (Heaton & Pendleton, 1981). The most obvious challenge is the fact that the "environment" is quite variable across patients, and the factors that determine functional success are complex and vary with the demands of an individual's environment. Numerous ability deficits, alone or in various combinations, can result in failure in performing a previously successful activity. Similar deficits, alone or in combination, could have a very different impact on different people, making it difficult to make global predictions about functional status (Farias et al., 2003; Heaton & Pendleton, 1981).

Data collected through *direct observation* of individuals in their natural environments arguably would be the most accurate measure of everyday functioning, because there would be no need for inferences from basic abilities to functional performance. However, this requires considerable time, effort, and cost, and is therefore not feasible in most cases. Also, direct observation of everyday functioning can be intrusive and can actually change the phenomena being observed; for example, the presence of a clinician observing a patient's vocational behavior in a job setting can influence what the patient does, what his/her coworkers and supervisors do, or both.

After direct observation, another straightforward method of gathering information about an individual's level of functioning in activities of daily living (ADL) is to ask for his/her own assessment, or *self-report*. In addition to its convenience, most would agree that the individual's own perception of functioning is central to quality of life and is therefore quite important (Awad et al., 1997). Numerous self-report measures have been developed and used with a wide variety of patient populations. However, many factors that can reduce the accuracy of self-report have been well documented, including level of insight, psychopathology, and situational factors (Williams, 1994). With regard to a patient's level of insight, the cognitive impairment that the person is experiencing may lead the individual to underreport deficits and functional problems (e.g., Cahn-Weiner et al., 2003). The validity of self-report measures is especially questionable in demented and severely mentally ill populations, in which a patient's level of insight is likely to be most compromised (Farias et al., 2003; Patterson et al., 2001). Psychopathology, especially depression, very often distorts the cognitive and emotional experiences upon which judgments about everyday functioning are based. Even individuals who do not meet criteria for Major Depressive Disorder are greatly influenced by their depressive mood symptoms when completing self-report measures. This effect has been demonstrated in various populations, including individuals with HIV infection (Cysique et al., 2007; Heaton et al., 2004; Rourke et al., 1999) and normal aging (Kliegel & Zimprich, 2005).

Another illustration of the effect of psychopathology on self-report is a finding from a diverse group of individuals referred for clinical evaluation, in which complaints of cognitive difficulties were more related to their emotional status than to objective measures of their cognitive abilities (Heaton et al., 1978). Patient self-report was measured with the Patient's Assessment of Own Functioning (PAOFI; Chelune et al., 1986), a questionnaire containing 32 items on which patients rate their difficulties with everyday functioning in four domains: general cognitive abilities, memory, language and communication, and sensorimotor skills. Multiple regression analyses revealed that patient self-report was more related to results from the Minnesota Multiphasic Personality Inventory (MMPI; Hathaway & McKinley, 1951) than to those from an extended HRB. In fact, the MMPI results accounted for 42.8% of the variance in cognitive complaints, as compared to only 6.6% for neuropsychological test scores. Additionally, situational factors such as secondary gain could influence the accuracy of a patient's reported problems.

Collateral/proxy reports from caregivers, spouses, or family members are often assumed to be more accurate than patient self-report. However, not all patients will have someone to provide the report, and for those patients who do have someone available, that person may not be entirely appropriate to report on the patient's

level of functioning (e.g., Patterson et al., 2001). Individuals with a close relationship to the patient may be biased by their feelings for the patient or may only observe the patient in settings in which the problems with functioning are less likely to occur, such as the home (Heaton & Pendleton, 1981). Loewenstein et al. (2001) found that caregivers of Alzheimer's disease (AD) patients frequently failed to predict their relatives' difficulties on fairly simple ADLs (e.g., telling time, letter preparation, identifying and counting currency, making change, and using eating utensils). Other studies have similarly reported that caregivers tend to overestimate the functional abilities of the patients in their care (e.g., Doble et al., 1999). On the other hand, recent contrary evidence has been reported by Davis et al. (2006), who found that caregivers in their study were generally accurate in reporting the functional abilities of the AD patients in their care and were not heavily influenced by their own characteristics (e.g., level of depressive symptoms) or the quality of their relationship with the patients. However, the authors also noted that most of the caregivers in their study were spouses with high levels of education, and minorities were underrepresented in their sample. Additionally, caregivers and family members may be disproportionately affected by particular patient deficits. For example, one study reported that caregiver ratings of memory were more influenced by language problems such as word finding deficits than by actual memory impairment (Cahn-Weiner et al., 2003). A more recent informant-based questionnaire, the Dementia Severity Scale (DSS; Harvey et al., 2005), has been developed as a brief, simple tool for gathering meaningful clinical information from caregivers. The sound psychometric properties of the questionnaire suggest that this instrument may be useful in research as well as clinical settings (Harvey et al., 2005). Collateral reports are frequently used in conjunction with self-report in an effort to assess reliability of patient reports, but in many cases there may be little agreement between the two sets of judgments of the patient's functioning. In such cases it can be difficult to determine the causes of the disagreements and the relative accuracy of the two reports.

Functional ratings by clinicians based on observation of a patient during an interview in a hospital, clinician's office, or research setting have also been used to measure everyday functioning. However, these ratings may not directly relate to the individual's functioning in his/her everyday environment. Clinicians' interaction with patients is often brief and limited in scope, and clinicians typically do not have the opportunity to observe the everyday behaviors of interest. In fact, their ratings are most often based on or greatly influenced by the reports of the patient and/or family, and as a result clinician ratings often are not independent or necessarily more objective.

Molar outcomes, such as employed versus unemployed, are commonly utilized functional outcome measures that generally show a robust association with neuropsychological indices (e.g., Heaton et al., 2004). Results from a battery of tests, often calculated as a summary score such as an average impairment rating or global deficit score (GDS; e.g., Heaton et al., 2004), appear to be the best at predicting such molar outcomes (employed versus unemployed; independent versus dependent living status) because a combination of abilities is responsible for both the predictor measure and outcome classification (Franzen & Wilhelm, 1996). As such, discrete categories of functional outcome often reflect a wide range of actual functioning. Even the seemingly straightforward categorical variable of employment status (employed vs. unemployed) can vary greatly, depending on the nature of the job requirements and whether employment is defined full-time, part-time, or intermittent (Guilmette & Kastner, 1996; Heaton et al., 1978).

Neuropsychological Predictors of Everyday Functioning

Neuropsychological test results have typically been examined as predictors of everyday functioning in three major classes of functional outcomes: academic achievement, independent living, and vocational functioning. Overall, studies have demonstrated that neuropsychological test results are significantly related to success in all of these areas.

Academic Achievement

The relationship between cognitive test performance and the ability to succeed academically

has been studied extensively. Much of the work that has been done in this area has focused on the relationship between results of intelligence tests and academic performance indices such as years of education completed and grades. Several reviews of the relevant literature are available, such as those by Fishman and Pasanella (1960), Lavin (1965), Matarazzo (1972), and Heaton and Pendleton (1981).

Generally, the literature indicates that the relationship between IQ and academic success is robust (e.g., Heaton & Pendleton, 1981). Matarazzo's review (1972) demonstrated that the approximate correlation between intelligence and academic success (i.e., grades) was $r = 0.50$ when averaged across various studies and populations. Despite the consistent relationship between IQ and academic success, IQ alone is not sufficient for explaining academic outcomes, especially in clinical populations. Heaton and Pendleton (1981) advocated the use of a comprehensive neuropsychological battery with adult neurological patient populations, noting that deficits associated with brain disorders may impact academic performance regardless of pre- and postmorbid IQ. Matarazzo also noted that, with only 25% of the variance in academic success explained for neuropsychologically normal individuals, other cognitive and noncognitive factors must play important roles. On the basis of the findings of his review, Matarazzo suggested that a minimum IQ threshold for completion of successive educational degrees (i.e., high school diploma, Bachelor's degree, graduate school) might exist, and that once that threshold has been met, nonintellective factors (e.g., motivation) may be more influential in determining academic success in neuropsychologically normal persons. However, other reports have indicated that accounting for nonintellective variables in addition to intellective factors only modestly improved predictive accuracy (for reviews see Fishman & Pasanella, 1960; Lavin, 1965).

Independent Living

The functions that have been conceptualized as ADLs vary in the literature, depending on the nature and purpose of the study. Some commonalities in the context of brain injury include self-care skills, ambulation, mobility, vision, health and safety, and communication. In general, ratings (such as those assigned in rehabilitation settings) and structured instruments used to assess basic ADLs have been shown to be moderately related to neuropsychological test results. For example, WAIS subtest scores have been related to both current self-care skills as well as future self-care performance in patients who suffered cerebrovascular accidents (Lehmann et al., 1975). Neuropsychological test results also have been related to prognosis for independent living in both psychiatric and neurological patients (Lehmann et al., 1975; Rioch & Lubin, 1959). More recent evidence has linked memory dysfunction to declines in ADLs in patients with AD (e.g., Drachman et al., 1990) and vascular dementia (e.g., Jefferson et al., 2006).

Given that basic ADLs are relatively simple, overlearned skills that tend to have a significant motor component (such as grooming and mobility), they may be more associated with physical illness than cognitive dysfunction. Accordingly, there is evidence to suggest that neuropsychological test results may be most useful for estimating patients' ability to carry out complex tasks that draw more heavily upon cognitive abilities (e.g., money management) than other, more routine and motor-based daily activities, such as bathing (McCue et al., 1990; Richardson et al., 1995). Thus, researchers have also focused on instrumental activities of daily living (IADLs), which are more complex everyday tasks that have been surveyed with a modified version of the Lawton and Brody (1969) scale. A modified version of this scale consists of 13 items, which require the individual to separately rate his/her current level of independence and highest previous level of independence in the following functional categories: financial management, home repair, medication management, laundry, transportation, grocery shopping, comprehension of reading/TV materials, shopping, housekeeping (cleaning), cooking, bathing, dressing, and telephone use. The total score indicates the number of activities for which the individual currently requires increased assistance. Increased dependence in two or more areas, determined from the distribution found in a normal sample, has been proposed as a cut score in defining clinically

significant IADL dependence (e.g., Heaton et al., 2004).

Several recent studies have linked more specific neuropsychological abilities to IADL performance. For example, IADLs have been shown to be strongly related to executive functioning in normal aging (Bell-McGinty et al., 2002; Cahn-Weiner et al., 2000), AD (e.g., Boyle et al., 2003; Cahn-Weiner et al., 2003), vascular dementia (e.g., Boyle et al., 2004; Jefferson et al., 2006), and schizophrenia (e.g., Green, 1996). A study of HIV-infected individuals demonstrated that deficits in learning, abstraction/executive function, and attention/working memory domains accounted for a considerable proportion of the variance in predicting IADL failures and functional dependence, overall (as indicated by failure on a performance-based functional battery; Heaton et al., 2004). Also, a more recent study of HIV-infected individuals revealed that a new verbal fluency measure (action fluency) by itself was significantly predictive of IADL dependence (Woods et al., 2006).

Vocational Functioning

One of the most common and important neuropsychological referral questions involving prediction of functioning concerns the patient's ability to maintain employment and perform work functions. Much research has been conducted to investigate the relationship between neuropsychological data and vocational functioning, and generally the literature reveals that neuropsychological predictions of employment status and job performance are quite good.

Early studies in this area revealed that in the healthy adults IQ was related to type of job obtained, mean income level, ratings of occupational prestige, and job performance (reviews by Heaton & Pendleton, 1981; Matarazzo, 1972). Research conducted with more comprehensive neuropsychological test batteries has revealed that these tests can discriminate between employed and unemployed individuals having either neurologic and psychiatric disorders, strongly suggesting that current employment status is dependent upon the level of neuropsychological functioning. In the first prospective study of the relationship between neuropsychological functioning and employment status,

Newnan et al. (1978) examined the ability of an expanded HRB and MMPI to predict future employment in patients with stable neurologic conditions who were followed for six months. The results of that study revealed that the Average Impairment Rating from the HRB was the best single predictor of employment status, and that the MMPI showed less predictive ability with regard to future employment than it had to current employment status in a previous study (Heaton et al., 1978). Similarly, employed HIV-infected individuals who eventually experienced work disability demonstrated significantly poorer performance at baseline on a variety of neuropsychological tests (Albert et al., 1999). More recently, a study of HIV-infected individuals examined numerous predictors of return to work and revealed that the California Verbal Learning Test (CVLT; Delis et al., 1987), a measure of learning and memory, was a significant and robust predictor of becoming employed, even when effects of IQ and medical measures of disease severity were controlled (van Gorp et al., 2007). Other studies demonstrating the significant associations between neuropsychological test data and employment status and job performance have been conducted in various populations, such as traumatic brain injury (Rao & Kilgore, 1992), multiple sclerosis (Pierson & Griffith, 2006; Rao et al., 1991), and schizophrenia (Heaton et al., 1994).

It is important to note that neuropsychologists are often asked to judge not only whether a person can work in general, but specifically what kind of work that individual is capable of doing. Although findings in the literature generally support a relationship between neuropsychological test results and global vocational potential, the differing cognitive demands of specific occupations should be considered when basing predictions of vocational functioning on an individual's pattern of neuropsychological strengths and deficits (Chelune & Moehle, 1986). The high level of cognitive demands of certain vocations, such as those experienced by corporate executives, attorneys, scientists, and physicians, are more likely to result in significant changes in job performance in response to cognitive decline than in vocations with fewer cognitive demands. There are challenges to conducting research that would guide decisions regarding specific requirements

of specific occupations. Many types of abilities are required for most jobs, and variable patterns of deficits may significantly interfere. Also, patterns of deficits seen with brain disorders are extremely variable, if not unique, even within groups of patients with a common etiology (e.g., traumatic brain injury, multiple sclerosis, HIV disease). It is not possible to research the effects of a single deficit in isolation (which is rarely seen) or every possible pattern of deficits. Therefore, it is likely that there will always be a substantial role for "clinical judgment" in these decisions. Still, research can be directed at determining the accuracy of such decisions and the patient, job, and environmental factors that contribute to success or failure.

In general, the research so far suggests that, as the number and severity of deficits increase, the likelihood of obtaining and holding competitive employment decreases. For example, the Average Impairment Rating from the HRB appears to serve as a good single predictor of employment status (Newnan et al., 1978), but may be improved upon by adding measures of episodic memory and other abilities underrepresented by the core HRB (Heaton et al., 1978). Further, evidence in the literature suggests that although neuropsychological variables do have predictive power in discriminating employed and unemployed individuals, these data in isolation are often not adequate predictors and may be improved upon by also considering personality variables (reviewed in Guilmette & Kastner, 1996; Heaton & Pendleton, 1981).

General Conclusions and Limitations of the Neuropsychological Approach

Taken together, studies of academic achievement, independent living (ADLs and IADLs), and vocational functioning demonstrate that neuropsychological test results generally relate to adequacy of everyday functioning and can be useful in the prediction of success or failure in these important everyday activities. However, use of neuropsychological data to predict functional outcomes is an iterative process resting on the assumption that demonstration of an impaired ability in the laboratory indicates difficulty or failure with functions that rely upon that ability in the natural environment (Heaton &

Pendleton, 1981). Furthermore, research has still not fully delineated the cognitive abilities that are necessary for success in specific everyday tasks (Farias et al., 2003), and the reported correlations between test scores and functional outcomes generally do not exceed 40% of explained variance (see Goldstein, 1996). The relatively modest amount of variance accounted for by neuropsychological tests alone indicates that other variables, such as demographics, health status, level of experience with the activities in question, and psychiatric and environmental factors, may be highly important when predicting everyday functioning.

Several trends have been revealed in the literature. Generally, the neuropsychological indices that are best for making global predictions, such as employment status, are those that are the most sensitive to brain dysfunction. These are typically summary scores such as the Average Impairment Rating from the HRB or the GDS from the expanded HRB and other test batteries (e.g., Carey et al., 2004; Heaton et al., 2004). Another trend that has previously been noted is that complex cognitive tests can better predict functioning in complex everyday lives than can simpler tests of specific abilities (Goldstein, 1996; McCue et al., 1990; Richardson et al., 1995). One multifactorial ability domain that likely relates to functioning across patient groups is executive functioning. The relationship between executive functioning and everyday functioning has been reported frequently in both patient and healthy populations, leading some authors to suggest that this is an especially important area to focus future research on the predictors of functioning (Cahn-Weiner et al., 2003; Guilmette & Kastner, 1996). Recent research has also indicated that learning and memory also have particularly important roles in daily functioning (Heaton et al., 2004; van Gorp et al., 2007). In a review of studies investigating the neurocognitive deficits associated with functional disability in patients with schizophrenia, verbal episodic memory was revealed to be associated with all types of functional outcome studied (Green, 1996). Whether this relates specifically to the verbal nature of the tests in these studies is unclear, because visual episodic memory typically has not been assessed in the relevant studies. Interestingly, the review also indicated

that negative symptoms were related only to social problem solving and positive psychotic symptoms were not related to any functional outcome measure, providing additional support for the important independent role of cognitive abilities in functional outcomes (Green, 1996).

The use of neuropsychological test results to predict everyday functioning has several limitations. Importantly, as stated above, the demands of home and work environments vary widely, and therefore the types and degrees of impairment that will significantly impact performance of daily activities will also vary with the situation. This is true of more general aspects of functioning, such as ability to work or live independently, as well as functioning in specific activities, since there is also variation in the demands of the same class of activities (e.g., driving, financial management, or writing tasks) for different people. Additionally, an individual who shows no impairment in routine aspects of everyday functioning may nevertheless be unable to adequately respond to less common, high-demand, or emergency-type situations (e.g., for airline pilots or physicians), which could put the individual or others at significant risk. Such situations in the home or on the job, though infrequent, may be critical for the safety of the patient or others. It is also important to consider that an individual's previous experience with a particular task or activity may influence the degree to which an acquired cognitive deficit affects success in future task performance. Compensation for impaired abilities or functioning may also be possible, but this will vary depending on an individual's strengths and environmental demands. In light of these limitations, the relationship between performance on specific laboratory measures of cognitive abilities and functioning in the natural environment still needs to be clarified with further research, but neuropsychological predictors may always rely heavily on clinical judgment.

Direct Assessment of Everyday Functioning: Performance-Based Measures

As noted above, individual differences in cognitive deficits, preserved strengths, past experiences, and specific environmental demands present significant challenges for the measurement and prediction of ability to perform everyday tasks. Rather than abandoning standardized assessment, however, a potential solution to this problem is to develop new assessment instruments that provide better insight into an individual's functioning (Franzen & Wilhelm, 1996). Another impetus in the development of new assessment tools is the above-mentioned question of the ecological validity of neuropsychological tests. In the context of neuropsychological assessment, ecological validity generally refers to the degree to which controlled laboratory assessments mirror requirements of everyday life. With regard to the neuropsychological approach to the prediction of everyday functioning, ecological validity is particularly important because the purpose of the evaluation is to predict behaviors that occur in the natural environment (i.e., "extra-test behavior;" Franzen & Wilhelm, 1996). As neuropsychologists are increasingly presented with referral questions that require predictions of everyday task performance, an understanding of the empirical relationship between existing neuropsychological tests and measures of everyday functioning is important. This approach to ecological validity, known as veridicality, involves statistically relating neuropsychological test findings to various functional outcome measures, and is the method utilized in the research that has been summarized in this chapter thus far. In this approach, a deficit in a particular cognitive ability or a summary score is first identified with neuropsychological testing, and then is related to a selected functional outcome measure. Although this process has demonstrated that existing tests do have some utility in the prediction of real-world functioning, the limited variance accounted for by the neuropsychological test data in functional outcomes and the limited face validity of neuropsychological tests for the measurement of everyday functioning have been addressed by a newer line of research that takes a different approach to ecological validity, known as verisimilitude. With this approach, functional capacity (i.e., ability to perform an everyday task) is directly and objectively assessed. This improves the degree to which the demands of the test are

similar to the demands of the skills required to perform that activity in the natural environment (Chaytor & Schmitter-Edgecombe, 2003; Franzen & Wilhelm, 1996) and avoids or minimizes possible effects of factors other than patient ability (e.g., intereference or assistance by other people in the natural environment). Performance-based tests have been developed to measure what a person is capable of doing in a way that resembles the tasks that the person is required to complete in everyday life.

In comparison with standard neuropsychological tests, performance-based tests of everyday activities provide a more direct assessment of an individual's functional capacity. Rather than measuring cognitive abilities in the abstract and generalizing from deficits in those cognitive abilities to an estimation of how an individual would be able to perform on a given everyday task, the individual demonstrates what he or she is capable of doing by engaging in an actual everyday task in the laboratory. Performance-based everyday functioning tests attempt to objectively measure skills that are required to function independently in the natural environment, such as performing household chores, cooking, and management of finances and medications (Heaton et al., 2004; Patterson et al., 2001). The greater face validity of these performance-based everyday functioning measures makes the results of the tests more readily interpretable as predictors of functional outcomes. Furthermore, the direct and objective assessment of functional abilities and the lack of reliance on the individual's or caregiver's insight into the patient's functioning are compelling advantages to the use of performance-based tests results as functional outcome measures. Scores on standardized versions of everyday tasks may also tend to have good psychometric properties, which would enhance their ability to detect changes in functional abilities related to disease progression or treatment (Heaton et al., 2004).

As is the case with neuropsychological predictors, there are potential limitations for drawing conclusions from performance-based measures. An important limitation is based on the distinction between what a person is capable of doing and what the person actually does in the real world. What an individual is capable of doing is only one piece of the puzzle, because numerous other factors influence what the individual will actually do in everyday life, including motivation and environment-specific factors such as opportunity to carry out certain activities, finances, social support, secondary gain, and the like. Additionally, the fact that functional capacity is being measured in a contrived environment may raise questions about the validity of conclusions drawn from these assessments (Patterson et al., 2001). The fact that performance-based tests are conducted in a controlled setting may result in an overestimation of a individual's real-world functioning because of the lack of distractions in the laboratory that are typically found in the real world. Also, in his/her natural environment, an individual may be forced to manage several activities simultaneously or for extended periods of time, whereas the testing situation usually requires that the individual focus only on a single task and does not last long enough to demonstrate the effects of fatigue. On the other hand, an individual's ability to perform in everyday life could be underestimated at times because in the laboratory he/she is not able to use compensatory strategies that may aid functional performance in the real world (Franzen & Wilhelm, 1996). The verisimiltude approach is not considered to be as rigorous as the veridicality approach because the similarity of a testing situation is not empirically compared to the real-life situation it is intended to represent (Chaytor & Schmitter-Edgecombe, 2003). Despite these limitations, performance-based measures have demonstrated promise in the prediction of everyday functioning.

Earlier work examined the relationships between neuropsychological test results and performance-based measures that had previously been developed for specific populations or in other disciplines. For example, Searight and colleagues (1989) investigated the relationship between performance on the WAIS-R and results from a modified version of the Community Competence Scale (CCS; Loeb, 1984) in older adults with suspected dementia. The CCS combines structured interview with performance-based measures, and was originally designed to determine competence in elderly individuals. Their study revealed that the CCS subscales were significantly correlated with Full-Scale IQ ($r = .72$, $p < .01$), Verbal IQ ($r = .77$, $p < .01$), and Performance IQ ($r = .55$, $p < .01$). The pattern of correlations with WAIS-R subtests was not interpreted, but stronger correlations (moderately to highly correlated) were shown between the CSS subscales and WAIS-R verbal subtests (Searight et al., 1989). The CCS has also been shown to be moderately associated with neuropsychological functioning as measured by the HRB (Dunn et al., 1990). Also the Occupational Therapy Evaluation of Performance and Support (OTEPS) is a standardized performance-based measure containing several functional domains (i.e., hygiene/self-care, safety, medication administration, cooking/nutrition, money management, and community access/utilization). In samples of older adults referred for neurological testing, OTEPS scores have been significantly related to performance on the Dementia Rating Scale (DRS; Mattis, 1988) (Nadler et al., 1993), and to visuospatial functioning (Richardson et al., 1995).

Loewenstein and colleagues (1989) developed a performance-based measure, the Direct Assessment of Functional Status (DAFS), for the purpose of assessing functional abilities in older adults with suspected functional impairments (e.g., due to various dementing conditions). As functional impairment is an essential criterion for the diagnosis of dementia according to the Diagnostic and Statistical Manual-IV (DSM-IV; American Psychiatric Association, 1994), a clear picture of functional deficits is particularly important in this population. High interrater and test–retest reliability have been reported for the DAFS, as well as convergent and discriminant validity (reviewed in Loewenstein et al., 2001). The DAFS consists of several tasks that simulate higher- and lower-order functional activities, including reading a clock, preparing a letter for mailing, identifying currency, counting currency, writing a check, balancing a checkbook, making change for a purchase, and eating skills. The time orientation task involves reading a series of clock settings, and for the communication task the patient prepares a letter for mailing. Loewenstein and colleagues (2001) compared caregiver reports of AD patients' functional abilities with the patients' performance on the DAFS, demonstrating that caregivers overestimated the abilities of those who were functionally impaired on the DAFS. The results of another study of AD patients indicated that performance-based tests, including the DAFS, were more valid and reliable than caregiver reports (Farias et al., 2003).

The DAFS has also been validated for demonstrating functional consequences of cognitive impairment in schizophrenic populations. Findings have generally indicated that global indices of cognitive functioning were the best predictors of functional capacity (e.g., Green, 1996; Harvey, et al., 1997; Klapow et al., 1997). For example, in one study the global DRS score was the best predictor of performance on the DAFS, even after controlling for potentially confounding demographic and illness variables (Patterson et al., 1998). Also, in a study of older patients with schizophrenia, general cognitive functioning (based on a battery of tests) was the strongest predictor of DAFS performance, and specific cognitive domains were inconsistent in predicting DAFS subscales (Evans et al., 2003). Although these studies support the importance of considering cognitive impairment in predicting functional performance, there are some limitations for the use of the DAFS in this population, including ceiling effects on subscales that are more relevant in AD populations (e.g., time orientation; see McKibbin et al., 2004).

Patterson and colleagues (2001) developed a performance-based measure to be used specifically in middle-aged to elderly, community-dwelling schizophrenic patients with schizophrenia. The UCSD Performance-Based Skills Assessment (UPSA) consists of tasks that were designed to mimic situations that older individuals living in the community frequently encounter. Based on information gathered from the literature and a variety of clinical specialties (e.g., occupational therapy, social work), the test was designed to measure skills in five categories, including Household Chores, Communication, Finances, Transportation, and Planning Recreational Activities. For each skill category, individuals role-play activities that are described by the examiner, who assigns points for correctly completing various aspects of the task. For example, the Household Chores category focuses on cooking and shopping skills. The five-minute task involves preparing a shopping list for a pudding recipe given to the individual by the examiner, and then selecting items necessary to prepare the pudding from an array of items in a mock grocery store. Not all items needed to prepare the pudding are provided in the mock store, and the individual is asked to write down those items that he/she would still need to purchase. Points are given for correct items written on the shopping list. For the Communication category, individuals demonstrate their ability to use a telephone in particular situations (e.g., in an emergency) and respond to a medical appointment confirmation letter. The Finances category involves counting change and paying bills. The Transportation category evaluates the individual's ability to determine a travel route to a predetermined destination using public transportation, also accounting for the cost of the trip, transfers, and other information. The Planning Recreational Activities category involves role-playing two outings to geographically relevant locations, with a description of what he/she would take on the trip, the type of clothes that would be worn on the trip, and how he/she would travel to the destination. The points assigned for performance in each category are used to calculate five subscale scores, which are summed to create a total score (range 0–100).

As predicted, Patterson and colleagues (2001) found that their sample of 50 older patients with schizophrenia and schizoaffective disorders performed worse on the UPSA than 20 demographically similar (in terms of gender and education) normal controls. In examining concurrent validity, the authors found that the UPSA scores significantly correlated with another performance-based measure (DAFS) but not with a self-report measure of well-being that is frequently used in older schizophrenic patients. The authors also reported the results of a hierarchical multiple regression analysis, which revealed that UPSA scores were statistically predicted by severity of global cognitive impairment, as measured by Mini-Mental Status Examination (MMSE; Folstein et al., 1975) scores, and negative symptoms, but not by positive psychotic symptoms.

In the discussion of their results, the authors drew several conclusions regarding performance-based measures, and specifically with regard to their test. They stressed that although self-report can provide valuable information, the data are not specific enough regarding functioning in areas that determine whether a person can live independently. Therefore, the authors concluded that performance-based tests such as the UPSA have advantages over self-report as outcome measures, including the quality, specificity, and reliability of the data obtained. Also, they stated that their findings argue for use of the UPSA in schizophrenic and schizoaffective populations, because the test was tailored to the specific everyday functional problems experienced by these patients.

Numerous studies have been conducted with the UPSA as a measure of functional capacity. For example, Twamley and colleagues (2002) investigated the relationship between cognitive functioning (measured with the DRS and a battery of standardized neuropsychological tests) and the UPSA in older outpatients with psychosis. They reported that all of the cognitive abilities examined were significantly related to UPSA total scores and, similarly, the UPSA subscale scores were significantly related to most cognitive variables. The lack of specific domain relationships was interpreted as evidence for the multifactorial nature of the UPSA tasks (Twamley et al., 2002). However, a more recent study has examined the relationships among neuropsychological performance and indices of two types of functional capacity in schizophrenic patients: social skills were assessed with the Social Skills Performance Assessment (SSPA; involving role plays of social problem situations) and the everyday living skills were assessed with the UPSA (McClure et al., 2007). The two types of functional capacity measures were associated with different cognitive abilities, such that social competence was associated with working memory, episodic memory, and verbal fluency performance, whereas everyday living skills were related to processing speed, episodic memory, and executive functioning. However, the authors reported that the findings provided only modest evidence of specific relationships between functional domains and specific cognitive deficits (McClure et al., 2007).

To further elucidate the relationship of functional capacity to real-world functioning, Bowie and colleagues (2006) studied outpatients with schizophrenia and assessed the relationship between neuropsychological performance, functional capacity (as measured by the UPSA), and real-world functional skills performance (as measured by a caregiver report). Their results provide support for previous reports in the literature regarding the significant correlations between neuropsychological performance and real-world functional outcomes, but demonstrated that when functional capacity is also considered, neuropsychological test scores inconsistently provide additional predictive power in determining real-world functional performance. The authors concluded that functional capacity was the most consistent predictor of real-world functioning, and also noted that additional variance is accounted for by negative and affective symptoms (e.g., depression; Bowie et al., 2006).

Heaton and colleagues (2004) noted the absence of a sensitive, comprehensive, performance-based functional battery for use with other types of disorders, which present with relatively mild neuropsychological impairments. As in the case of the use of the DAFS in schizophrenic patients, if performance-based tests that were developed for use with more severely impaired individuals are used with patients whose cognitive impairment is milder, inaccurate predictions about everyday functioning could result. The functional battery used in this study included the Financial Skills and Shopping measures from the DAFS, supplemented with a newly developed Advanced Finances task that requires individuals to role-play paying bills and managing a checkbook. The greatest level of difficulty in this task involves asking the individual to pay as much on his/her bills as possible, while retaining a certain balance in the checkbook for emergencies. Medication management ability was measured with a modified version of a previously published test (Medication Management Test; MMT; Albert et al., 1999). In a pill-dispensing portion of the test, individuals' ability to dispense a day's dosage and follow a scripted prescription regimen is assessed. Realistic pill bottles with standardized instructions are utilized in this component of the test. In another portion of this test, individuals are instructed to transfer the correct number of pills from the bottles to a medication organizer that holds supply of medications for one week. Another portion of the test is the "medication inference" component, in which individuals respond to questions that can be answered using information provided on the pill bottles and a medication insert. The modified Medication Management Test (MMT-R) only included those items from the original test that have been found to be the most reliable and valid in the population being studied, which consisted of HIV-infected individuals. For the Cooking task, examinees are required to follow recipes and coordinate preparation of a meal. Individuals are given three recipes, and the recipes call for measuring, stirring, and wrapping. The most challenging aspect of this task is determining the order and timing of cooking the items, which ensures that they are completed at the same time. The authors of this study also administered a comprehensive neuropsychological battery, a self-report measure of functioning outside of the laboratory (PAOFI; Chelune et al., 1986), and a modified version of the Lawton and Brody (1969) IADL scale, which has been described above. The authors also collected objective information regarding vocational functioning, including a multimodal, criterion-referenced, standardized battery of vocational tasks that provided information regarding 13 job abilities as defined by the US Department of Labor. All of the various functional measures were summarized as a functional deficit score (FDS), in order to reflect overall impairment on the functional battery. Certain cognitive domains were found to account for most of the unique variance in predictions of IADL failures and failures on the functional battery, namely, learning, abstraction/executive function, and attention/working memory. When included in a model alone, neuropsychological test performance predicted employment status, but it was no longer a significant predictor in multivariate prediction models with functional measures included. The FDS was a unique predictor of each type of outcome measuring everyday functioning, the PAOFI, IADL dependence, and employment status, even when neuropsychological testing and HIV disease stage were included in the models. Heaton and colleagues (2004) suggested that performance-based measures, such as the functional battery used in

their study, can be used to complement neuropsychological testing for determining the presence of syndromic neurocognitive conditions in HIV-infected individuals. The authors noted, however, that besides disease-related impairments of functional capacity, there are other reasons why individuals may fail IADLs in the real world, namely, depression, substance use disorders, and motivational factors. In this study, a measure of depressed mood significantly contributed to the prediction of both subjective and objective measures of everyday functioning.

A Spanish-language version of the functional battery also has been developed at the same research center, and ongoing research is evaluating the cultural relevance of the measures and examining the relationship between neuropsychological test results and performance on functional measures in HIV-infected Spanish speakers (Mindt et al., 2003). Like English speakers in the Heaton et al. (2004) study, neuropsychologically impaired Spanish speakers performed significantly worse on the functional measures than did the neuropsychologically normal Spanish speakers (Mindt et al., 2003). Also, performance on both the neuropsychological battery and the functional assessment were related to indicators of everyday functioning, including employment status. Mindt and her colleagues (2003) concluded that the Spanish version of the functional assessment, with only minor modifications from the original version, is a valid assessment tool for evaluating everyday functioning in monolingual Spanish speakers in the U.S.

Given that there are numerous tasks encompassing global everyday functioning, it may be useful to measure functional capacity specifically for tasks that are particularly relevant for the individual given his/her environmental needs and safety, or for answering the referral question at hand. Targeted measurements of functional capacity could also be useful for directly examining level of functioning in an area likely to be at risk given the nature of impairment. Examples of specific functional evaluations include employment, medication management, and driving.

Objective, criterion-referenced instruments that evaluate an individual's skill level in important areas related to vocational functioning include the MESA SF2 and COMPASS Programs (Valpar International Corporation, 1986, 1992). These programs comprise computerized subtests (Vocabulary, Reading, Spelling, Mathematics, Language Development (Editing), Problem Solving, Short-term Visual Memory, Shape Discrimination, Size Discrimination, and Placing and Tracking) and noncomputerized mechanical tests (Alignment and Driving, Machine Tending, Wiring). Raw scores correspond to ability levels, which are referenced to the US Department of Labor Dictionary of Occupational Titles (DOT; US Department of Labor, 1991). The jobs included in the DOT are assigned profiles that indicate specific levels of abilities needed to perform the job. For the MESA SF2 and COMPASS programs, each item relates to an ability level, and the number of errors committed by an individual within an ability level determines the highest level achieved. The outcome scores from these programs correspond to the number and types of jobs the examinee is considered capable of performing.

Medication management is an important everyday function for numerous types of patient populations. Successful management of medications is particularly challenging and relevant for HIV-infected persons, due to the complicated regimens and serious consequences of nonadherence. Hinkin and colleagues (2002) examined the influence of cognitive impairment on adherence to HIV medication regimens, finding that deficits in executive functioning, attention, and memory were associated with poor adherence, even when accounting for age and history or psychiatric and neurological disorders. However, no performance-based test such as the MMT was included in this study, and addition of such a measure to neuropsychological testing may provide more powerful predictions about the individual's ability (capacity) to adhere. For example, the Medication Management Ability Assessment (MMAA; Patterson et al., 2002) is a modification of the MMT (Albert et al., 1999) that was designed to simulate a medication regimen similar to one that would likely be prescribed to an older individual. The new task involves a role play and differs from the MMT with regard to the types of actions required of the participant (e.g., handing the pills to the tester at a certain time), incorporation of a delay (1 hour between presentation of the prescription regimen and testing), and shorter duration of the test. Importantly, the scoring procedures indicate over- and undermedication (Patterson et al., 2002). The authors reported that older adults with schizophrenia performed significantly worse on the MMAA than a normal comparison group, demonstrating with an objective measure that the patient group had greater difficulty managing medications. Interestingly, the most common error made by the schizophrenic patients was taking fewer pills than prescribed. This finding illustrates how tests of functional capacity may also aid in the development of intervention strategies for medication management, as the process is observed firsthand.

Automobile driving is another important real-world activity that has been assessed with standardized, performance-based tests. In addition to studies of driving abilities in AD (Herrmann et al., 2006; Hunt et al., 1993; Perryman & Fitten, 1994), driving ability has also been examined in the context of Parkinson's disease (Grace et al., 2005) and HIV infection (Marcotte et al., 1999, 2006). Recently, a study of HIV-infected individuals and uninfected controls assessed performance on neuropsychological tests and the Useful Field of View (UFOV), a performance-based, computerized test of visual attention (Marcotte et al., 2006). Poor performance on the UFOV was related to higher accident rates in the past year, and the highest-risk individuals were neuropsychologically impaired, and had poor UFOV performance. The findings indicate that general cognitive status and visual attention specifically are important factors in determining risk for impaired driving (Marcotte et al., 2006). Performance-based measures of driving, such as driving simulators, provide information that might not be captured on a self-reported driving history, such as how an individual would respond to unusual, high-risk situations (e.g., when another driver cuts in front of his/her vehicle unexpectedly).

Conclusions

Estimation of everyday functioning is an important role of neuropsychologists today.

Such predictions have considerable implications for the livelihood, lifestyle, and safety of the individuals under evaluation and their families. As the field of neuropsychology has increasingly focused on estimation of real-world functional abilities, neuropsychologists have utilized traditional measures of cognitive abilities that reveal the individual's pattern of cognitive strengths and weaknesses. With the neuropsychological approach to the prediction of everyday functioning, an assumption is made that if an individual demonstrates an impairment of an ability in the laboratory, that individual will be at risk for functional impairment in real-world tasks that draw upon that ability. Considerable evidence has supported that assumption by showing the association of neuropsychological test results with a variety of functional outcomes.

In addition to the wealth of reported findings, there are several advantages for using standard neuropsychological tests to make predictive statements regarding everyday functioning. Importantly, many neuropsychological tests have demonstrated good psychometric properties. In addition to favorable reliability and validity, normative standards have been developed for many of these tests. The use of normative standards in interpretation of test results involves comparing an individual's test score to a predicted score that would be expected for a neurocognitively normal person with similar demographic characteristics (e.g., age, years of education, ethnicity, and sex). This process reduces the likelihood that misclassification of neurocognitive impairment will occur due to demographic factors, and can help to elucidate whether or not a cognitive deficit is due to acquired brain dysfunction. In addition, test–retest reliability has been examined for most neuropsychological tests. When evaluating an individual over time in order to determine whether his/her cognitive performance is improving or declining (or remaining stable), it is important that the clinician understands what a meaningful discrepancy in scores from one testing session to the next would be. Accordingly, norms for change are available for many neuropsychological tests. Notably, a comprehensive neuropsychological battery provides extensive information regarding the individual's pattern of strengths as well as weaknesses. This information can be important and useful in assisting the individual to compensate for his/her cognitive deficits and could therefore be used in targeting cognitive rehabilitation and interventions.

Although use of demographically-corrected norms in neuropsychological test interpretation is important for determining the nature and severity of acquired impairments (due to disease or injury), the clinician should carefully consider whether corrected or uncorrected scores are best for predicting performance in particular everyday tasks and activities. This is because uncorrected scores (e.g., scaled scores in the normative system of Heaton & Taylor, 2004) reflect absolute level of abilities more directly, compared to the general adult population. Thus, if the everyday activity to be predicted is one that almost all adults in the normal population can perform, uncorrected scores would be preferable. Even then, however, the clinician may first want to establish the likelihood that a loss of ability has occurred (using corrected scores) and then consider whether any such loss is severe enough to interfere in relevant everyday tasks. On the other hand, if the everyday task is sufficiently demanding that only a small proportion of the adult population would be expected to perform it adequately (e.g., pilot, physician, corporate executive), at least education-adjusted norms are likely to be helpful. For example, if a physician has suffered a head injury or is suspected of having early dementia, his/her test performances probably should be compared to normal expectations for a person with a high education level (e.g., 20 years for a doctorate). Again, considerable clinical judgment is required in this interpretation process.

Given the abundance of valuable information that is provided by a comprehensive evaluation, administration of a full battery is recommended whenever a prediction of everyday functioning is to be made. As such, a standard neuropsychological battery could be administered, such as the widely used expanded HRB. The neuropsychologist can also select additional specific tests that tap those abilities that are most relevant to the referral question to supplement the traditional battery.

Although performance-based tests of everyday functional abilities are more face valid, and significant associations have been demonstrated between functional capacity (as measured by performance-based functional tests) and neuropsychological tests, functional capacity tests should not be administered in isolation. That is, we suggest they can best be used to supplement, rather than replace, a comprehensive neuropsychological examination. Results of performance-based functional tests may provide additional information about what real-world activities an individual has difficulty performing, but they do not provide information about how the functional impairment relates to a brain disorder. Further, performance-based functional tests do not provide sufficient insight into the individual's preserved strengths, which is important information for compensation and targeting intervention in cognitive rehabilitation settings.

In addition to the benefits of having the wealth of information that a comprehensive neuropsychological evaluation provides, this approach is also quite efficient in predicting a range of everyday activities. Given that the number of potential everyday tasks of interest is vast, there would not be time to develop and administer functional assessments of all such activities. However, performance-based tests do provide a window into how an individual's cognitive deficits may manifest in specific real-world situations of interest. This could be especially useful for particularly important everyday activities that have implication for health and safety, such as medication management and driving. Additionally, results of performance-based tests could be useful for evaluating the efficacy of cognitive rehabilitation in a more objective manner. As such, performance-based tests can be used to supplement a neuropsychological battery as needed to address the referral question at hand. A review of performance-based measures by Moore et al. (2007) provided recommendations for selecting performance-based measures according to population and specific domain of interest.

Consideration of noncognitive factors appears to be especially important when real-world functioning is worse than expected on the basis of the results of neuropsychological testing and performance-based measures. For example, Heaton and colleagues (2004) demonstrated in an HIV-infected sample that if an individual performed in the normal range on both a neuropsychological battery and a FDS but was still not working, depressive symptoms could be interfering with employment. In addition to depression, other noncognitive factors that can affect everyday functioning include substance use disorders, motivation, and environment-specific factors.

In sum, the neuropsychological approach to the prediction of everyday functioning provides valuable information about individuals' ability to carry out a variety of everyday tasks in the real world. The system of estimating everyday functioning on the basis of neuropsychological test performance is well-supported by evidence in the literature. This approach can be augmented by more recently developed measures of functional capacity, and these performance-based tests can help to elucidate the nature of an individual's functional disability.

References

Albert, S. M., Weber, C. M., & Todak, G. (1999). An observed performance test of medication management ability in HIV: Relation to neuropsychological status and medication adherence outcomes. *AIDS and Behavior, 3*, 121–128.

American Psychiatric Association. (1994). *Diagnostic and statistical manual of mental disorders* (4th ed.). Washington, DC: Author.

Awad, A. G., Voruganti, L. N., & Heslegrave, R. J. (1997). A conceptual model of quality of life in schizophrenia: Description and preliminary clinical validation. *Quality of Life Research: An International Journal of Quality of Life Aspects of Treatment, Care and Rehabilitation, 6*, 21–26.

Bell-McGinty, S., Podell, K., Franzen, M., Baird, A. D., & Williams, M. J. (2002). Standard measures of executive function in predicting instrumental activities of daily living in older adults. *International Journal of Geriatric Psychiatry, 17*, 828–834.

Bowie, C. R., Reichenberg, A., Patterson, T. L., Heaton, R. K., & Harvey, P. D. (2006). Determinants of real-world functional performance in schizophrenia subjects: Correlations with cognition, functional capacity, and symptoms. *American Journal of Psychiatry, 163*, 418–425.

Boyle, P. A., Malloy, P. F., & Salloway, S. (2003). Executive dysfunction and apathy predict functional impairment in Alzheimer disease. *American Journal of Geriatric Psychiatry, 11*, 214–221.

Boyle, P. A., Paul, R. H., Moser, D. J., & Cohen, R. A. (2004). Executive impairments predict functional declines in vascular dementia. *Clinical Neuropsychology, 18*, 75–82.

Cahn-Weiner, D. A., Malloy, P. F., Boyle, P. A., Marran, M., & Salloway, S. (2000). Prediction of functional status from neuropsychological tests in community-dwelling elderly individuals. *Clinical Neuropsychology, 14*, 187–195.

Cahn-Weiner, D. A., Ready, R. E., & Malloy, P. F. (2003). Neuropsychological predictors of everyday memory and everyday functioning in patients with mild Alzheimer's disease. *Journal of Geriatric Psychiatry and Neurology, 16*(2), 84–89.

Carey, C. L, Woods, S. P., Gonzalez, R., Conover, E., Marcotte, T. D., Grant, I., et al. (2004). Predictive validity of global deficit scores in detecting neuropsychological impairment in HIV infection. *Journal of Clinical and Experimental Neuropsychology, 26*, 307–319.

Chaytor, N., & Schmitter-Edgecombe, M. (2003). The ecological validity of neuropsychological tests: A review of the literature on everyday cognitive skills. *Neuropsychology Review, 13*, 181–197.

Chelune, G., Heaton, R., & Lehman, R. (1986). Neuropsychological and personality correlates of patient's complaints of disability. In R. Tarter and G. Goldstein (Eds.), *Advances in Clinical Neuropsychology* (pp. 95–126). New York: New York Plenum Press.

Chelune, G. J., & Moehle, K. A. (1986). Neuropsychological assessment and everyday functioning. In D. Wedding, A. MacNeill Horton, and J. Webster (Eds.), *The Neuropsychology Handbook: Behavioral and Clinical Perspectives* (pp. 489–525). New York: Springer.

Cysique, L. A., Deutsch, R., Atkinson, J. H., Young, C., Marcotte, T. D., Dawson, L., et al. (2007). Incident major depression does not affect neuropsychological functioning in HIV-infected men. *Journal of the International Neuropsychological Society, 12*, 1–11.

Davis, B. A., Martin-Cook, K., Hynan, L. S., & Weiner, M. F. (2006). Caregivers' perceptions of dementia patients' functional ability. *American Journal of Alzheimer's Disease and Other Dementias, 21*, 85–91.

Delis, D. C., Kramer, J. H., Kaplan, E., & Ober, B. A. (1987). *California verbal learning test.* San Antonio, TX: The Psychological Corporation.

Doble, S. E., Fisk, J. D., & Rockwood, K. (1999). Assessing the ADL functioning of persons with Alzheimer's disease: Comparison of family informants' ratings and performance-based assessment findings. *International Psychogeriatrics, 11*, 399–409.

Drachman, D. A., O'Donnell, B. F., Lew, R. A., & Swearer, J. M. (1990). The prognosis in Alzheimer's disease: "How far" rather than "how fast" best predicts the course. *Archives of Neurology, 47*, 851–856.

Dunn, E. J., Searight, H. R., Grisso, T., Margolis, R. B., & Gibbons, J. L. (1990). The relation of the Halstead--Reitan Neuropsychological Battery to functional daily living skills in geriatric patients. *Archives of Clinical Neuropsychology, 5*, 103–117.

Evans, J. D., Heaton, R. K., Paulsen, J. S., Palmer, B. W., Patterson, T., & Jeste, D. V. (2003). The relationship of neuropsychological abilities to specific domains of functional capacity in older schizophrenia patients. *Biological Psychiatry, 53*, 422–430.

Farias, S. T., Harrell, E., Neumann, C., & Houtz, A. (2003). The relationship between neuropsychological performance and daily functioning in individuals with Alzheimer's disease: Ecological validity of neuropsychological tests. *Archives of Clinical Neuropsychology, 18*, 655–672.

Fishman, J. A., & Pasanella, A. K. (1960). College admission-selection studies. *Reviews of Education Research, 30*, 298–310.

Folstein, M. F., Folstein, S. E., & McHugh, P. R. (1975). Mini-mental state: A practical method for grading the cognitive state of patients for the clinician. *Journal of Psychiatric Research, 12*, 189–198.

Franzen, M. D., & Wilhelm, K. L. (1996). Conceptual foundations of ecological validity in neuropsychological assessment. In R. J. Sbordone and C. J. Long (Eds.), *Ecological validity of neuropsychological testing* (pp. 91–112). Boca Raton, FL: St. Lucie.

Goldstein, G. (1996). Functional considerations in neuropsychology In R. J. Sbordone and C. J. Long (Eds.), *Ecological validity of neuropsychological testing* (pp. 75–89). Delray Beach, FL: GR Press/St Lucie Press.

Grace, J., Amick, M. M., D'Abreu, A., Festa, E. K., Heindel, W. C., & Ott, B. R. (2005). Neuropsychological deficits associated with driving performance in Parkinson's and Alzheimer's disease. *Journal of the International Neuropsychological Society, 11*, 766–775.

Green, M. F. (1996). What are the functional consequences of neurocognitive deficits in schizophrenia? *American Journal of Psychiatry, 153*, 321–330.

Guilmette, T. J., & Kastner, M. P. (1996). The prediction of vocational functioning from neuropsychological data. In R. J. Sbordone and C. J. Long (Eds.),

Ecological validity of neuropsychological tests (pp. 387–411). Florida: GR Press/St. Lucie Press.

Harvey, P. D., Davidson, M., Mueser, K. T., Parrella, M., White, L., & Powick, P. (1997). Social-Adaptive Functioning Evaluation (SAFE): A rating scale for geriatric psychiatric patients. *Schizophrenia Bulletin, 23*(1), 131–145.

Harvey, P. D., Moriarity, P. J., Kleinman, L., Coyne, K., Sadowsky, C. H., Chen, M., et al. (2005). The validation of a caregiver assessment of dementia: The Dementia Severity Scale. *Alzheimer Disease and Associated Disorders, 19*, 186–194.

Hathaway, S. R., & McKinley, J. C. (1951). *Minnesota multiphasic personality inventory; manual (Revised)*. San Antonio, TX:Psychological Corporation.

Heaton, R. K., Chelune, G. J., & Lehman, R. A. W. (1978). Using neuropsychological and personality tests to assess the likelihood of patient employment. *Journal of Nervous and Mental Disease, 166*, 408–416.

Heaton, R. K., Marcotte, T. D., Mindt, M. R., Sadek, J., Moore, D. J., & Bentley, H. (2004). The impact of HIV-associated neuropsychological impairment on everyday functioning. *Journal of the International Neuropsychological Society, 10*, 317–331.

Heaton, R. K., Paulsen, J. S., McAdams, L. A., Kuck, J., Zisook, S., Braff, D., et al. (1994). Neuropsychological deficits in schizophrenics: Relationship to age, chronicity, and dementia. *Archives of General Psychiatry, 51*, 469–476.

Heaton, R. K., & Pendleton, M. G. (1981). Use of neuropsychological tests to predict adult patients' everyday functioning. *Journal of Consulting and Clinical Psychology, 49*, 807–821.

Heaton, R. K., & Taylor, M. (2004). *Revised comprehensive norms for an Expanded Halstead-Reitan Battery: Demographically adjusted neurpsychological norms for African American and Caucasian adults*. Lutz, FL: Psychological Assessment Resources, Inc.

Herrmann, N., Rapoport, M. J., Sambrook, R., Hébert, R., McCracken, P., Robillard, A.,et al. (2006). Predictors of driving cessation in mild-to-moderate dementia. *Canadian Medical Association Journal, 175*, 591–595.

Hinkin, C. H., Castellon, S. A., Durvasula, R. S., Hardy, D. J., Lam, M. N., Mason, K. I., et al. (2002). Medication adherence among HIV + adults: Effects of cognitive dysfunction and regimen complexity. *Neurology, 59*, 1944–1950.

Hunt, L., Morris, J. C., Edwards, D., & Wilson, B. (1993). Driving performance in persons with mild senile dementia of the Alzheimer type. *Journal of the American Geriatrics Society, 41*, 747–753.

Jefferson, A. L., Cahn-Weiner, D., Boyle, P., Paul, R. H., Moser, D. J., Gordon, N., et al. (2006). Cognitive predictors of functional decline in vascular dementia. *International Journal of Geriatric Psychiatry, 21*, 752–754.

Klapow, J. C., Evans, J., Patterson, T. L., Heaton, R. K., Koch, W. L., & Jeste, D. V. (1997). Direct assessment of functional status in older patients with schizophrenia. *American Journal of Psychiatry, 154*, 1022–1024.

Kliegel, M., & Zimprich, D. (2005). Predictors of cognitive complaints in older adults: A mixture regression approach. *European Journal of Ageing, 2*, 13–23.

Lavin, D. E. (1965). *The prediction of academic performance*. Oxford, England: Russel Sage Found.

Lawton, M. P., & Brody, E. M. (1969). Assessment of older people: Self-maintaining and instrumental activities of daily living. *Gerontologist, 9*, 179–186.

Lehmann, J. F., DeLateur, B. J., Fowler, R. S. Jr., Warren, C. G., Arnhold, R., Schertzer, G., et al. (1975). Stroke rehabilitation: Outcome and prediction. *Archives of Physical and Medical Rehabilitation, 56*, 383–389.

Loeb, P. A. (1984). Validity of the Community Competence Scale with the elderly. *Dissertation Abstracts International, 45*, 1919.

Loewenstein, D. A., Amigo, E., & Duara, R. (1989). A new scale for the assessment of functional status in Alzheimer's disease and related disorders. *Journals of Gerontology, 4*, 114–121.

Loewenstein, D. A., Arguelles, S., Bravo, M., Freeman, R. Q., Arguelles, T., & Acevedo, A. (2001). Caregivers' judgments of the functional abilities of the Alzheimer's disease patient: A comparison of proxy reports and objective measures. *Journal of Gerontology: Psychological Sciences, 2*, P78–P84.

Long, C. J., & Collins, L. F. (1997). Ecological validity and forensic neuropsychological assessment. In R. J. McCaffrey, A. D. Williams, J. M. Fisher, and L. C. Laing (Eds.), *The practice of forensic neuropsychology: Meeting challenges in the courtroom* (pp. 153–164). New York: Plenum Press.

Marcotte, T. D., Heaton, R. K., Wolfson, T., Taylor, M. J., Alhassoon, O., & Arfaa, K. (1999). The impact of HIV-related neuropsychological dysfunction on driving behavior. *Journal of the International Neuropsychological Society, 5*, 579–592.

Marcotte, T. D., Lazzaretto, D., Cobb, J. S., Roberts, E., Woods, S. P., & Letendre, S. (2006). Visual attention deficits are associated with driving accidents in cognitively-impaired HIV-infected individuals. *Journal of Clinical and Experimental Neuropsychology, 28*, 13–28.

Matarazzo, J. D. (1972). *Wechsler's measurement and appraisal of adult intelligence* (5th ed). Oxford, England: Williams and Wilkins.

Mattis, S. (1988). *Dementia rating scale professional manual*. Odessa, FL: Psychological Assessment Resources.

McClure, M. M., Bowie, C. R., Patterson, T. L., Heaton, R. K., Weaver, C., Anderson, H., et al. (2007). Correlations of functional capacity and neuropsychological performance in older patients with schizophrenia: Evidence for specificity of relationships? *Schizophrenia Research, 89,* 330–338.

McCue, M., Rogers, J. C., & Goldstein, G. (1990). Relationships between neuropsychological and functional assessment in elderly neuropsychiatric patients. *Rehabilitation Psychology, 35,* 91–99.

McKibbin, C. L., Brekke, J. S., Sires, D., Jeste, D. V., & Patterson, T. L. (2004). Direct assessment of functional abilities: Relevance to persons with schizophrenia. *Schizophrenia Research, 72,* 53–67.

Mindt, M. R., Cherner, M., Marcotte, T. D., Moore, D. J., Bentley, H., Esquivel, M. M., et al. (2003). The functional impact of HIV-associated neuropsychological impairment in Spanish-speaking adults: a pilot study. *Journal of Clinical Experimental Neuropsychology, 25,* 1, 122–132.

Moore, D. J., Palmer, B. W., Patterson, T. L., & Jeste, D. V. (2007). A review of performance-based measures of functional living skills. *Journal of Psychiatric Research, 41,* 97–118.

Nadler, J. D., Richardson, E. D., Malloy, P. F., Marran, M. E., & Brinson, M. E. H. (1993). The ability of the Dementia Rating Scale to predict everyday functioning. *Archives of Clinical Neuropsychology, 8,* 449–460.

Newnan, O. S., Heaton, R. K., & Lehman, R. A. W. (1978). Neuropsychological and MMPI correlates of patients' future employment characteristics. *Perceptual and Motor Skills, 46,* 635–642.

Patterson, T. L., Goldman, S., McKibbin, C. L., Hughs, T., & Jeste, D. V. (2001). UCSD performance based skills assessment: Development of a new measure of everyday functioning for severely mentally ill adults. *Schizophrenia Bulletin, 27,* 235–245.

Patterson, T. L., Klapow, J. C., Eastham, J., Heaton, R. K., Evans, J. D., Koch, W. L., et al. (1998). Correlates of functional status in older patients with schizophrenia. *Psychiatry Research, 80,* 41–52.

Patterson, T. L., Lacro, J., & McKibbin, C. L. (2002). Medication management ability assessment: Results from a performance-based measure in older outpatients with schizophrenia. *Journal of Clinical Psychopharmacology, 22,* 11–19.

Perryman, K. M., & Fitten, L. J. (1994). Impact of attentional deficits on driving performance of the elderly and individuals with mild Alzheimer's disease. In J. L. Fitten (Ed.), *Facts and research in gerontology: Dementia and cognitive impairments* (pp. 91–102). New York: Springer Publishing.

Pierson, S. H., & Griffith, N. (2006). Treatment of cognitive impairment in multiple sclerosis. *Behavioral Neurology, 17,* 53–67.

Psychological Corporation. (1997). *WAIS-III and WMS-III technical manual.* San Antonio, TX: Author.

Rao, N., & Kilgore, K. M. (1992). Predicting return to work in traumatic brain injury using assessment scales. *Archives of Physical Medicine and Rehabilitation, 73,* 911–916.

Rao, S. M., Leo, G. J., Ellington, L., & Nauertz, T. (1991). Cognitive dysfunction in multiple sclerosis: II. Impact on employment and social functioning. *Neurology, 41,* 692–696.

Richardson, E. D., Nadler, J. D., & Malloy, P. F. (1995). Neuropsychologic prediction of performance measures on daily living skills in geriatric patients. *Neuropsychology, 9,* 565–572.

Rioch, M. J., & Lubin, A. (1959). Prognosis of social adjustment for mental hospital patients under psychotherapy. *Journal of Consulting Psychology, 23,* 313–318.

Rourke, S. B., Halman, M. H., & Bassel, C. (1999). Neurocognitive complaints in HIV infection and their relationship to depressive symptoms and neuropsychological functioning. *Journal of Clinical and Experimental Neuropsychology, 21,* 737–756.

Searight, H. R., Dunn, E. J., Grisso, J. T., & Margolis, R. B. (1989). Relation of cognitive functioning to daily living skills in a geriatric population. *Psychological Reports, 64,* 399–404.

Tulsky, D. S., & Price, L. R. (2003). The joint WAIS-III and WMS-III factor structure: Development and cross-validation of a six-factor model of cognitive functioning. *Psychological Assessment, 15,* 149–162.

Tupper, D., & Cicerone, K. (1990). Introduction to the neuropsychology of everyday life. In D. Tupper and K. Cicerone (Eds.), *The neuropsychology of everyday life: Assessment and basic competencies* (pp. 3–18). Boston: Kluwer Academic.

Twamley, E. W., Doshi, R. R., Nayak, G. V., Palmer, B. W., Golshan, S., Heaton, R. K., et al. (2002). Generalized cognitive impairments, ability to perform everyday tasks, and level of independence in community living situations of older patients with psychosis. *American Journal of Psychiatry, 159,* 2013–2020.

U.S. Department of Labor. (1991). *Dictionary of occupational titles* (4th ed). Washington, DC: U.S. Government Printing Office.

Valpar International Corporation. (1986). *Microcomputer Evaluation and Screening Assessment (MESA) Short Form 2.* Tuscon, AZ: Author.

Valpar International Corporation. (1992). *Computerized Assessment (COMPASS).* Tucson, AZ: Author.

Van Gorp, W. G., Rabkin, J. G., Ferrando, S. J., Mintz, J., Ryan, E., Borkowski, T., et al. (2007). Neuropsychiatric predictors of return to work in HIV/AIDS. *Journal of the International Neuropsychological Society, 13,* 80–89.

Williams, B. (1994). Patient satisfaction: A valid concept. *Social Science and Medicine, 38,* 509–516.

Woods, S. P., Morgan, E. E., Dawson, M., Scott, J. C., Grant, I., & the HNRC Group. (2006). Action (verb) fluency predicts dependence in instrumental activities of daily living in persons infected with HIV-1. *Journal of Clinical and Experimental Neuropsychology, 28,* 1030–1042.

27

Neuropsychological Performance and the Assessment of Driving Behavior

Thomas D. Marcotte and J. Cobb Scott

There continues to be growing interest in understanding the relationship between neuropsychological functioning and the ability to carry out everyday activities. One such activity, driving an automobile, is an important, complex, and potentially dangerous task that is not only associated with mobility but also often with an individual's sense of identity and quality of life (Fonda et al., 2001; Owsley, 1997). Automobile driving is the primary form of transportation in many areas, due in part to the paucity of public transportation infrastructure (Collia et al., 2003). However, the prominence of driving comes at a cost, as an average of 6 million automobile crashes occur every year in the United States, with approximately 40,000 of these fatal and 2 million resulting in injuries (National Highway Traffic Safety Administration, 2006). Worldwide, the World Health Organization estimates that 1.2 million persons are killed in driving crashes each year, with 50 million injured. Injuries due to traffic crashes are predicted to be third among factors contributing to the global disease and injury burden by 2020, just behind ischemic heart disease and unipolar major depression (World Health Organization, 2004).

While many driving crashes are thought to be preventable, discerning how to prevent crashes presents a complex challenge. Myriad factors can lead to automobile crashes, including inattention, risky decisions or maneuvers, slowed reactions, poor hazard perception, as well as external factors (e.g., other drivers, weather, faulty equipment). A significant body of research has focused on the relationship between driver behaviors and safety errors in healthy individuals, as well as interventions at both the individual and system (e.g., road design, air bags) levels for injury and crash prevention, helping to clarify some of the components that give rise to unsafe (and safe) driving. At the same time that progress is being made in various aspects of driver safety, new technologies abound that compete with the driver's focus of attention. Although cell phones are the most ubiquitous, personal music players (e.g., mp3 players, iPods) and global positioning systems (for navigation), among other infotainment devices, are increasingly finding their way into the driver's activities. And, unfortunately, as developers improve designs so that users require less time to interact with a device (e.g., fewer menu levels), overall risk might increase as users become more inclined to use the product while driving—known as the *usability paradox* (Lee & Strayer, 2004).

While such factors are essential to consider in discussions of driving safety with cognitively normal individuals, impairments in cognitive and motor functioning can drastically increase the probability of safety errors and risky decisions during driving. A variety of neurological (e.g., Alzheimer's disease, multiple sclerosis [MS], HIV), medical (e.g., arthritis), and psychiatric disorders (e.g., antisocial personality disorder), as well as use of licit (e.g., alcohol, benzodiazepines) and illicit (e.g., marijuana) drugs, can influence driving capacity. Thus, recent investigations have attempted to determine the most effective assessment methods for detecting driving deficits and to delineate the driving impairments that might be expected in various clinical populations.

Although not reviewed in detail here, information regarding the specific cognitive abilities affected by certain diseases and disorders may also lead to important interventions to improve driving behavior. In acknowledgment of the dearth of transportation alternatives that are available in many countries, there has been a strong emphasis recently on the development of remediation methods in order to maximize that period over which individuals can drive safely (National Highway Traffic Safety Administration, 1999; Stephens et al., 2005; Wang & Carr, 2004). Such methods may include driver remediation (e.g., retraining), vehicle modifications, technological advances (e.g., impact warning systems), or changes in roadway design (Dickerson et al., 2007). Recent studies have shown driver remediation efforts (Ball et al., 2007; Marottoli et al., 2007; Mazer et al., 2003) and vehicle modifications (Kramer et al., 2007; Ponsford et al., 2008) to be beneficial for certain populations, including those affected by normal aging and individuals recovering from traumatic brain injuries (TBIs) or cerebrovascular accidents.

Given the potential risks to patients and others, it would be understandable to have a bias toward overidentifying individuals as likely to be impaired on the road. Yet a number of studies of neurologic patients have found that a diagnosis alone is not necessarily sufficient cause for a person to lose his or her driver's license (Dubinsky et al., 2000; Molnar et al., 2006). For example, Hunt et al. (1993) found that some individuals with mild Alzheimer's disease continued to have adequate driving skills. Similarly, in our research examining HIV infection, only a subset of those persons with HIV-associated cognitive impairment demonstrated a significant decline in driving performance (Marcotte et al., 2004b). Since the loss of one's license can hamper independent living and driving cessation has been associated with an increase in depressive symptoms in older drivers (Fonda et al., 2001; Marottoli et al., 1997), there remains

a significant need for continued development of valid, and practical, methods of identifying at-risk *individuals*.

Despite the responsibilities frequently placed upon them, clinicians rarely receive formal training in methods for determining driver safety and may be unaware of the potential problems that certain disorders may present for driving (Valcour et al., 2002). This chapter will therefore focus on the literature regarding the relationship between neurocognitive functioning and driving abilities, particularly in neurologic disorders. In order to put this relationship in context, the first section of the chapter will present a general model of driving behavior that addresses the possible levels at which driving abilities could break down, as well as a sampling of the various factors that might contribute to impaired driving. The following section will review clinic-based performance measures, such as neuropsychological tests, that are often used to predict driving performance in clinical populations. In order to facilitate a critical reading of the literature, we will discuss approaches to driving assessments and their relative assets and weaknesses. And lastly we will briefly review some common neuropsychiatric disorders and their impact on driving performance.

A General Model of Driving Behavior

Driving is one of the more complex activities of daily living, requiring intact attention, perception, tracking, choice reactions, sequential movements, judgment, and planning. It is somewhat remarkable, then, that most individuals relatively quickly achieve driving competence (Ogden & Moskowitz, 2004) and are able to maneuver a one-ton vehicle at high speeds down 10-foot lanes while surrounded by vehicles moving at different velocities/directions, unpredictable pedestrians, and countless other hazards.

A number of models of driving behavior have been proposed over the years (Ranney, 1994), emphasizing factors ranging from motivation (e.g., risk avoidance, Fuller, 1984) to information processing (e.g., automaticity, Shiffrin & Schneider, 1977). For this chapter, in order to provide a broad overview of the factors that might affect driving performance, some of these more focused models have been combined into a broad model of driving behavior (Figure 27–1). It is acknowledged that this is a much simplified model and that driving is a dynamic and complicated process. For example, consider the behaviors/abilities involved in simply changing traffic lanes. One must determine when it is safe to glance away from the roadway, track speed and steering while looking at the side mirror and out the driver's window, press the turn signal, determine the speed and positioning of any vehicles adjacent to the driver, accelerate if needed, initiate fine movement of the steering wheel, be ready to respond if a car is in the blind spot, insure that lead cars do not decelerate during the maneuver, and complete the lane change. In addition to the many cognitive factors involved in such a simple lane change (judgment, perception, attentional shifts, processing speed, visual scanning, fine motor skills, reaction time, etc.), other variables could affect the success of the lane change, such as physical limitations, environmental influences (e.g., weather, traffic flow), and vehicle design. However, since the focus of this chapter is primarily on factors internal to the individual, we do not address these latter issues here.

On the right side of Figure 27–1 we show the hierarchical control structure model proposed by Michon (1985). This is one of the more commonly referenced models in the driving literature, and includes strategic, tactical (maneuvering), and operational levels. At the *strategic* level, decisions are made regarding planning for the drive. Such decisions include assessing weather conditions, determining whether the individual feels competent to go on the road, choosing a route, deciding whether to take breaks while driving, and anticipating the steps needed to complete the drive. At the *tactical* level, individuals make decisions about maneuvering the vehicle, including speed, following distance, lane choice, whether to turn on the headlights, as well as whether one should be involved in secondary tasks, such as cell phone use. At the *operational* level, the driver directly maneuvers the vehicle, using the steering wheel, pedals, and so on. One distinguishing aspect of the different levels is the amount of time pressure under which each level takes

place—minutes in the case of the strategic level, seconds for the tactical level, and milliseconds at the operational level. Decisions made at the higher levels can affect the work load at lower levels (e.g., the strategic decision to drive during rush hour can impact the workload at the tactical and operational level), and capacities at the lower levels may inform decisions made at higher levels (slowed reaction time may lead individuals to drive more slowly). Levels overlap during the driving task. For example, maneuvering at the tactical level involves simultaneous actions at the operational level.

To the left of the Michon model in Figure 27–1, we list a number of factors that can affect driving behavior. Individuals start with certain *premorbid cognitive abilities* that may affect driving performance. Some of these are listed in Table 27–1 later in this chapter. Most people have sufficient cognitive capacity to successfully accomplish the tasks that human factors investigators consider essential for safe driving. These include having adequate *situation awareness* ("the perception of elements in the environment within a volume of time and space, the comprehension of their meaning, and the projection of their status in the near future"; see Endsley, 1995), sufficient *hazard perception* (recognizing and predicting potentially hazardous situations, including assessing the magnitude of the hazard), and the ability to make critical driving decisions, such as *gap acceptance* (a driver's determination as to whether a gap between cars for a turn is safe or unsafe, based upon traffic flow, vehicle acceleration capacity, etc.). Most of these factors, of course, involve risk assessment and decision making.

Other factors, including *personality* (e.g., sensation seeking, which can also lead to behaviors that put individuals at risk for CNS insult) and driving *experience*, have been shown to be strong predictors of driving behaviors and can influence or even supersede other factors in determining driving performance. Unsafe (or safe) driving behavior may be influenced by an individual's *motivation* for the behavior at the time, such as speeding to avoid being late to an appointment, opting to eat while on the road, or driving unsafely based on other, overriding needs. In addition, *familiarity with a route* may affect one's driving safety, often in unexpected

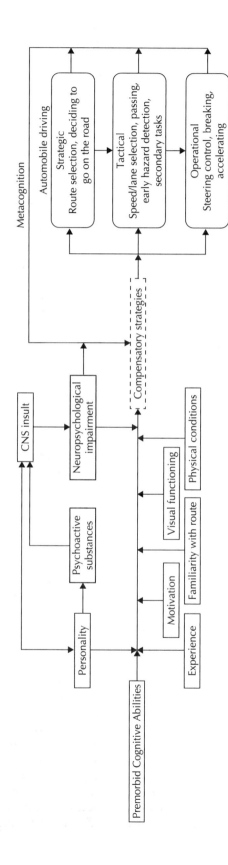

Figure 27–1. General model of driving behavior (incorporating the model from Michon, 1985).

ways, as increased cognitive and attentional demands are placed on the driver attempting to navigate unfamiliar routes. Medically, problems with *visual function* (i.e., impaired vision) and *physical conditions* (e.g., neuropathy, spasticity) can also impact driving ability.

Within this larger context, specific neuropsychological abilities that are needed to perceive and attend to conditions, interpret the situation, make judgments, implement the planned actions, and monitor feedback (Rizzo & Kellison, in press) might be altered by numerous conditions (*CNS insult*), such as normal aging, medical disease, and neurologic disorders, which may reach the level of *neuropsychological impairment*. Cognition can also be affected by use of *psychoactive substances*. CNS insult and prolonged use of psychoactive substances may effect changes in personality, such as increased impulsivity. Adaptation to these conditions can be affected by an individual's *metacognition*, or self-awareness of one's own cognitive and driving abilities. If individuals are aware of their deficits in driving skills, they may utilize *compensatory strategies* (e.g., only driving in certain situations) in an attempt to reduce their driving risk. However, neurocognitive disorders such as Alzheimer's disease also reduce awareness of deficits, potentially leading to underestimates of driving risk. Below, we briefly discuss these factors and their relationship to different driving behaviors.

Factors Impacting Driving Performance

Personality

Personality characteristics have consistently been associated with risky driving in younger and middle-aged adults (Arthur et al., 1991; Dahlen et al., 2005; Tillmann & Hobbs, 1949), as well as older samples (Owsley et al., 2003; Schwebel et al., 2007; cf. Strahan et al., 1997). These personality characteristics are found in nonneurologic disorders, but may be accentuated with cerebral dysfunction, especially involving the frontal lobes, and by certain drugs of abuse, such as methamphetamine (Semple et al., 2005; Simons et al., 2005). A number of studies have shown that impulsivity

is associated with risky driving behaviors such as moving traffic violations, driving under the influence, and crashes (Hilakivi et al., 1989; Paaver et al., 2006). Sensation seeking, defined as enjoying and seeking out exciting, novel, and risky activities (Zuckerman et al., 1972), is moderately correlated with impulsivity (Hur & Bouchard, 1997), and has been shown to predict risky driving behaviors such as speeding, driving under the influence, and reckless driving (Dahlen et al., 2005). Sensation seeking drivers may have higher thresholds for accepted risk or overestimate their driving skills in relation to the perceived level of risk (Jonah, 1997). Importantly, both sensation seeking and impulsivity have strong associations with driving outcomes even when accounting for other cognitive and health-related factors (Arthur et al., 1991), although this relationship may be affected by age (Schwebel et al., 2007) or gender (Oltedal & Rundmo, 2006). Anger and hostility are also constructs that have been associated with risky driving (Deffenbacher et al., 2001; Schwebel et al., 2006).

Experience

It has been hypothesized that novice drivers operate primarily via controlled processing, characterized by slow, effortful processing of information, while experienced drivers use quick, effortless (i.e., automatic) processes to guide behavior (Summala, 1996), and presumably have more resources to dedicate to attentional needs. Novice drivers have elevated crash rates compared to more experienced drivers (Crundall et al., 2003), even when accounting for age differences (Mayhew et al., 2003). It has been suggested that experienced drivers may develop a larger perceptual field of view (Crundall et al., 1999), a quicker response to hazardous stimuli (Wallis & Horswill, 2007), enhanced situational awareness (Gugerty, 1997), or improved ability to more fully scan the field of vision (Underwood, 2007). As noted by van Zomeren et al. (1987), the efficient driver is not the one who reacts quickly to a hazardous situation, but the one who avoids it in the first place. Extensive experience with driving could also potentially create a "reserve," in which the experienced driver could suffer greater brain dysfunction yet remain a reasonably safe driver for a longer period of time. This possibility requires empirical confirmation in direct studies of driving but is indirectly supported by research pointing to preserved cognitive function in dementia in individuals with high levels of cognitive reserve (e.g., Stern, 2006).

Familiarity

With experience, driving behavior in familiar situations may become more automated. It is assumed that individuals drive more safely on familiar routes, since the drivers do not use resources to orient themselves to their surroundings. However, the automaticity of experienced drivers may bring its own hazards. Drivers may be more likely to be involved in fatal crashes on roads on which they frequently travel on (Blatt & Furman, 1998) and may take more risks and thus make more driving errors in familiar versus unfamiliar locations (Rosenbloom et al., 2007). Experienced drivers may also not respond appropriately in potentially risky situations in familiar locales, especially those with ambiguous feedback (Duncan et al., 1991). Therefore, further research is needed to examine the potentially complex relationship between route or setting familiarity and driving safety, especially in individuals with questionable driving skills.

Motivation

Crashes may occasionally come down to the individual's motivation at the time. Driving models focusing on motivation begin with the notion that "driving is self-paced and drivers select the amount of risk they are willing to tolerate in any given situation" (Ranney, 1994). One interesting hypothesis in the Risk Homeostasis model (Wilde, 1982) is that in order to maintain a constant level of risk, drivers will adjust for improvements in safety by driving less cautiously (e.g., some individuals drive faster because of the safety provided by airbags). Some models have been criticized for their primary focus on risk, and it is pointed out that motivation is multifactorial. Regardless, the emphasis on motivation is of interest since it emphasizes that drivers are active decision makers, and not purely passive responders (Ranney, 1994), and one should always keep in mind that drivers are often establishing their priorities, such as speeding to get to a movie on time, deciding to interact with friends in the car rather than focus on the driving task, or driving in poor weather to get badly needed medications at the pharmacy.

Visual Functioning

Safe automobile driving requires effective processing of a multitude of sensory and perceptual information. Although adequate auditory and somatosensory functioning is important to driving, it may be possible to compensate for such deficits. The processing of visual cues, however, is critical as it provides essential information about movement detection, environmental structure, depth perception, optic flow, and the time before collision with other objects. Despite the obvious importance of vision in driving behavior, variable success has been achieved in using traditional visual tests in predicting driving performance. Although widely used, tests of visual acuity and visual field loss have been weakly associated with driving behavior, except in cases of ocular injury, such as cataracts, glaucoma, macular degeneration, or retinal disorders (Owsley & McGwin, 1999; Szlyk et al., 1995), or with hemi- or quandrantanopsia that may occur with strokes, trauma, or tumors (Rizzo & Kellison, 2004). Contrast sensitivity deficits, on the other hand, have shown stronger associations and deserve further study (Marottoli et al., 1998; Owsley & McGwin, 1999). Some important aspects of visual cognition that may affect driving performance, such as motion and object perception, have not been studied extensively and are rarely measured in standard clinical visual assessments (Rizzo & Kellison, 2004).

Physical Conditions

Numerous physical conditions, such as hemiparesis from stroke (Ponsford et al., 2008), spasticity associated with MS (Marcotte et al., 2008), and peripheral neuropathy, among many others, can affect driving performance, although there are studies suggesting that in many cases in which the individual is able to operate a vehicle, cognitive functioning remains central to the evaluation of driving safety (Marshall et al., 2005). A variety of adaptations have been useful in improving driving performance in individuals with physical limitations (Haslegrave, 1991; Lawton et al., 2008).

Psychoactive Substances

Any substance that alters cognition, licit or illicit, can impact driving performance. A thorough review of the effects of such substances on neuropsychological functioning and driving is beyond the scope of this chapter. However, we will briefly note that *prescription medications* for neuropsychiatric conditions can negatively affect driving. For many medications, the greatest impact on driving is during the early stages of use, until tolerance develops. Although some medications reduce driving ability, it is possible that some individuals are better drivers when compared to their untreated condition, although this has rarely been examined. *Benzodiazepines* can affect visual perception, processing speed, coordination, reaction time, memory and attention (Kelly et al., 2004). Epidemiologic studies suggest increased crash risks are associated with benzodiazepine use (Thomas, 1998), and on-road and simulator studies indicate that benzodiazepines reduce steering skills, decision making, braking, and reaction time (Bocca et al., 1999; Moskowitz & Smiley, 1982; van Laar et al., 2001; Verster et al., 2002). Of the *antidepressants*, tricyclic antidepressants have the greatest effects on driving abilities (Rapoport & Banina, 2007), again primarily during the first 1–2 weeks of treatment (Ramaekers, 2003), while the selective serotonin reuptake inhibitors (SSRIs) appear to be less impairing (Ramaekers, 2003; Wingen et al., 2005). There is no research regarding the direct effects of antipsychotics on driving performance, although studies of driving-related psychomotor and cognitive abilities suggest that the atypical neuroleptics may affect driving performance less than conventional neuroleptics (Kagerer et al., 2003).

Nonprescription substances also significantly impact driving skills. *Alcohol*, of course, is the most prevalent drug used recreationally. Alcohol affects driving in the areas of steering control, maintenance of lane position, divided attention, and reduced judgment, among others. Although "driving under the influence" is typically based upon blood alcohol concentrations (BACs) of .05 to 1.0 (50–100 mg/dL), reduced performance is seen at even lower blood alcohol levels (Moskowitz & Robinson, 1988), and there is no clear threshold wherein one transitions from unimpaired to impaired (Ogden & Moskowitz, 2004). Epidemiologically, crash rates increase as legally accepted BAC levels increase (Fell & Voas, 2006). There is minimal information regarding the impact of alcohol on driving abilities in neurologic patients, although it is likely that alcohol's effects are exacerbated in these individuals. Given the extensive research on alcohol and driving, performance at different BAC levels has been used as a benchmark for comparing the effect of other substances on driving (Ramaekers, 2003). Although this offers a useful comparison regarding the relevant effect sizes of these substances, readers should keep in mind the outcomes being assessed. For example, while the inability to maintain lane position is an important (and measurable) complication of alcohol use, other factors (e.g., impaired judgment) are also likely critical in determining an intoxicated individual's crash risk.

Marijuana, or *Cannabis sativa*, can acutely result in reduced learning, attention, processing speed, and psychomotor abilities, depending upon the dose. Driving studies involving cannabis suggest delayed reactions, poor lane tracking (Ramaekers et al., 2004), and poor judgment of speed and distance. Peak psychoactive effects occur approximately 10–20 minutes after smoking, with acute impairment of driving usually subsiding after 3–4 hours (Grotenhermen et al., 2007). Low doses of cannabis result in moderate driving impairment, but this is dramatically increased when alcohol is also consumed (Ramaekers et al., 2004). Since delta-9-tetrahydrocannabinol (THC), the primary psychoactive component of cannabis, can be detected for days or weeks after intake, there has been no clear relationship between urine or blood levels and cognition. With respect to driving laws there is no per se biological limit for the allowable concentration of THC in blood or urine, although preliminary efforts are under way (Grotenhermen et al., 2007). Interestingly, in contrast to alcohol, wherein drivers may have a false sense of self-confidence, subjects ingesting cannabis tend to drive more slowly than when not under the influence, most likely due to their awareness of impairment and increased cautiousness (Grotenhermen 2007; Hindrik et al., 1999). This may not be effective when under time pressure and confronted with unanticipated hazards. Although controlled studies suggest driving impairments with cannabis, the relationship between real-world on-road driving performance and cannabis use remains equivocal.

Small doses of *stimulants* can improve performance on some cognitive tasks, particularly in overcoming fatigue on psychomotor tasks, but it is clear that elevated or long-term doses of drugs such as cocaine and methamphetamine can result in significant cognitive impairments (Jovanovski et al., 2005; Scott et al., 2007). Withdrawal may also result in neuropsychiatric impairments. However, there is little direct research regarding stimulant abuse and driving ability. Field reports of individuals under the influence of stimulants note speeding, poor lane maintenance, agitation, and risk taking (Logan, 1996). In general, low doses of these substances might improve performance in persons who are fatigued, but they do not seem to enhance performance in normal individuals, nor improve functioning on complex tasks (e.g., requiring divided attention) such as driving. Of note, most laboratory studies have used low doses (e.g., of cocaine), and it is anticipated that at higher doses chronic use and withdrawal would result in impaired performance on driving tasks. Methamphetamine, in particular, may be associated with increased risk taking and impulsivity (Gonzalez et al., 2007; Semple et al., 2005). MDMA (3,4-methylenedioxymethamphetamine; Ecstasy) is a popular party drug that may affect attention, perception and memory (Cami et al., 2000). One simulator study found modest effects of MDMA on vehicle control and greater risk taking (Brookhuis et al., 2003). An on-road study found that certain aspects of driving were improved (e.g., maintenance of lane position) with MDMA. whereas others were negatively impacted (e.g., overshooting a lead car's speed decelerations) (Ramaekers et al., 2006).

There is very little research examining the effects of *opiates* such as heroin and methadone on driving performance, although sedation and impairment are the most common side effects of these substances. Long-term maintenance with methadone does not appear to be associated with increased crash risk, after the initial treatment (Lenne et al., 2003).

Neuropsychological Functioning

Driving requires the coordination of a broad range of cognitive and motor skills, as drivers must constantly (1) perceive and attend to stimuli; (2) interpret the situation; (3) decide what, if any, action is needed based on prior experience and perceptual cues; (4) formulate a plan of action in coordination with working memory of the situational factors involved; (5) execute the plan by coordinating muscle movements; (6) process feedback from sensory and perceptual input; and (7) determine whether further action is needed. Usually, these actions are done under time pressure. One can surmise that a number of neuropsychological processes are involved in this sequence of actions. However, the precise contribution of various neurocognitive processes to driving behavior remains murky. In part, this is due to the fact that the study of such processes is often dependent on research examining the association of cognitive *deficits* with driving behavior, as these correlations are generally weak in unimpaired individuals. In addition, driving is an overlearned repertoire of behaviors in which processes often operate in tandem without much directive action, and drivers may be able to overcome some deficits with additional attentional resources or effortful processing. Individuals with intact higher-level abilities to direct and organize (i.e., executive functioning) may be able to overcome deficits in lower-level processes (i.e., psychomotor slowing). Lastly, driving is a dynamic and integrative process, and significant inference must take place to project performance from single, focused measures administered within structured, quiet clinic settings to the rich, and occasionally random, environment of the real world.

Partially due to the complexity of these factors, investigations of the relationship between neuropsychological tests and driving have historically met with mixed results, despite a history of using such tests to predict driving competence. Early studies examined the prediction of driving competence in populations with brain injury or neurologic disease and had inconsistent results, often dependent upon the particular clinical population studied, with predictor (i.e., tests) and criterion variables (i.e., driving tests or driving history) varying widely by study (Galski et al., 1990; O'Neill et al., 1992; Sivak et al., 1981; van Zomeren et al., 1987). In recent years, researchers have utilized more standardized road tests and multimodal assessment approaches, such as combinations of on-road, simulator, medical, and neuropsychological evaluations. In some cases, such efforts have led to increased reliability and validity of criterion variables, although results remain variable.

Neuropsychological tests have been predictive of on-road (Fitten et al., 1995; Hunt et al., 1993; Odenheimer et al., 1994) and driving simulator performance (Marcotte et al., 1999; Rebok et al., 1995; Rizzo et al., 1997; Szlyk et al., 2002) in several studies, while others have found poor relationships between the two (Bieliauskas et al., 1998; Fox et al., 1997). Even in the context of dementia, associations between neuropsychological tests and driving outcomes are inconsistent, despite using tests hypothesized to be particularly sensitive to driving-related skills, such as Trails B or the Clock-Drawing Test (Molnar et al., 2006; Reger et al., 2004). Moreover, the practical utility of most studies is limited, as few studies report cutoff scores for impairment (Molnar et al., 2006).

Thus, no consensus yet exists regarding which neuropsychological measures best identify high-risk drivers. This might occur because neuropsychological tests primarily assess impairment at the strategic or tactical level of driving (Schanke & Sundet, 2000). More likely, it seems that a broad consensus on the relationship is difficult to attain, in part due to varying participant populations, divergent test batteries and sample sizes, and different gold standards regarding what constitutes driving impairment (Molnar et al., 2006; Reger et al., 2004; Withaar et al., 2000). Nonetheless, the general conclusions are that cognitively impaired individuals as a group perform significantly worse than controls on driving measures, and increased levels of cognitive impairment are found in groups involved in traffic crashes (Withaar et al., 2000). The weakness of correlations between cognitive test results and on-road driving performance makes it difficult to determine from neuropsychological tests alone whether cognitively impaired subjects are safe or unsafe drivers. But since no single approach to evaluating driving safety can possibly assess all abilities involved in such a complex activity, neuropsychological tests remain a reasonable modality for evaluating aspects of a patient's fitness to drive, as part of a multidisciplinary assessment.

Table 27–1 presents a summary of hypothesized relationships between general neuropsychological domains and driving behaviors, as structured according to Michon's model (1985). Although deficits in most domains could

Table 27–1. Neurocognitive Abilities Hypothesized To Be Involved at Different Levels of the Driving Task

	Strategic	Tactical	Operational
Attention	✓	λ	λ
Visuospatial abilities	✓	λ	λ
Executive functioning	✓	λ	λ
Working memory		λ	
Learning/memory	✓	λ	
Procedural memory/ knowledge		λ	λ
Processing speed		λ	λ
Psychomotor speed		λ	λ
Language		λ	
Motor			λ

potentially impact driving at each level, we have identified the domains that we suspect are most important at that level. In the following sections we briefly review the findings regarding these domains and driving performance.

As in any evaluation, clinicians should always attend to the examinee's level of alertness, since reduced levels, due to fatigue, sleep disorders, and use of prescription and illicit substances, among other causes, can significantly impact both driving and neuropsychological test performance.

Attention

Attention is often cited as a critical neurocognitive domain in driving. Not only is intact attention a precondition for almost every neurocognitive process (Lezak, 2004), but lapses in attention are one of the most cited reasons for crashes in a number of epidemiological reports, ranging from 15% to 40% of all accidents (e.g., Stutts et al., 2001). Attention is a multidimensional construct, and a number of attentional processes are essential for safe driving. Selective attention is needed to be able to filter out the irrelevant details in a driving environment and focus on more important elements. The ability to divide one's attention effectively is also crucial in order to deal with complex situations, such as driving with distraction from passengers (Rizzo & Kellison, in press), and some consider the inability to divide attention while under time pressure to be one key factor in impaired driving (Brouwer et al., 2002). Sustained attention is needed to continually direct one's cognitive resources to the pertinent aspects of the driving environment and to ensure that the individual is prepared to react with any unexpected occurrences (Brouwer, 2002), since in many instances visual search in driving is bottom-up—drivers waiting to notice a conspicuous target (Cole & Hughes, 1990; Ranney, 1994). Drivers may also schedule "attentional checks," in which they increase attentional resources at key moments (e.g., when deviating from a familiar route) (Ranney, 1994).

The U.S. National Highway Traffic Safety Administration funded a novel observational study, the "100-Car Naturalistic Driving Study," in which 100 cars in Virginia were instrumented with an unobtrusive network of sensors and video cameras (Neale et al., 2005). Data were recorded from 241 drivers over the course of 1 year, who drove a total of over 2 million miles. Despite obtaining drivers with diverse driving histories, 82 crashes (ranging from injury accidents to minimal property damage) and 761 near-crashes were recorded during the study period. The cause of 78% of the crashes and 65% of the near-crashes was characterized upon review as "driver inattention," which included secondary task engagement, inattention to the forward roadway, eye-glances away from the roadway, and lapses of attention due to fatigue. Many of the distractions drawing the attention of the drivers from the critical aspects of the driving tasks were related to operating wireless devices and interacting with passengers. (Which, of course, also draws into question executive functioning [e.g., judgment] in this subset of normal individuals.)

Although lapses of attention are common in cognitively normal drivers, a number of studies have also shown that impairments in attention have significant implications for driving safety across diverse populations (e.g., Galski et al., 1997; Owsley et al., 1998; Ponsford et al., 2008; Reger et al., 2004). While basic attention (e.g., attention span) has shown weak predictive value, complex attentional processes (e.g., divided attention), especially under significant time pressure, have been observed to have strong relationships with driving outcomes in neurologic samples (Brouwer, 2002; Lengenfelder et al., 2002; Uc et al., 2006c). Sustained attention may also have particular relevance for disorders with lapses of consciousness (e.g., seizure disorders) and those that result in excessive fatigue (Brouwer, 2002). Parasuraman and Nestor (1991) have proposed that measures of attention may be most useful in predicting driving safety in aging populations, as older populations are more likely to have attentional deficits, and the driving safety of younger drivers is more likely to be affected by use of substances, personality factors, or risky decision making. More specifically, Duchek and colleagues (1997; Duchek et al., 1998) have argued that selective visual attention may be a particularly critical skill to assess in dementia patients.

The Useful Field of View (UFOV; Ball & Roenker, 1998; Ball et al., 1988) is a sensitive indicator of driving impairment. UFOV is a computerized measure that assesses both divided and selective attention by measuring the amount of time it takes an individual to accurately acquire both central and peripheral visual information without head or eye movements. These abilities are evaluated over extremely brief and focused time points, and therefore not a typical paradigm wherein one needs to attend to multiple tasks over a period of time. In aging groups, poor UFOV performance has been correlated with higher rates of past (Ball et al., 1993) and future automobile crashes (Owsley et al., 1998) and has been associated with poor performance during on-road driving evaluations (Duchek et al., 1998; Myers et al., 2000). UFOV is also significantly reduced in many patient populations, including persons with TBI (Fisk et al., 2002a), MS (Schultheis et al., 2001), stroke (Fisk et al., 2002b; Mazer et al., 2003), HIV (Marcotte et al., 2006), and mild Alzheimer's disease (Duchek et al., 1998). UFOV is commercially available, easy to administer on a PC, and has been shown to provide incremental validity to standard laboratory tests, and thus may offer diagnostic utility to clinicians and researchers (Marcotte et al., 2006).

As with all neuropsychological measures administered within the clinician's office, a potential confound is that brain-injured individuals may be highly motivated and able to muster cognitive resources, and perform better within the structured office environment yet have difficulties over prolonged time periods and in the unstructured driving environment (British Psychological Society, 2001; Lezak, 1995).

Visuospatial Abilities

Driving depends not only on intact vision but also the ability to interpret and integrate the information received. Most neuropsychological research shows these abilities to be one of the most robust predictors of driving outcomes. In fact, visuoperceptual/constructional tasks were shown to have the strongest correlations with driving ability among all neuropsychological domains in a meta-analysis of dementia (Reger et al., 2004). Visuoconstructional tasks such as the WAIS-III Block Design and Figure Copy

tasks (e.g., Rey–Osterrith Complex Figure) are commonly used and have shown modest results, depending on the disorder under study (Amick et al., 2007; Grace et al., 2005; Lundberg et al., 1998; Schanke & Sundet, 2000), as have visuoperceptual measures such as the Benton Revised Retention Test (Hunt et al., 1993) and Benton Visual Form Discrimination Test (Galski et al., 1992). Road sign identification may be an ecologically valid test of visuospatial abilities (Lincoln & Radford, 2008; Uc et al., 2005). Clock drawing (with modified scoring) has also been proposed as a sensitive test for driving outcomes (Freund et al., 2005), although this awaits further study.

Executive Functioning

Executive functions have been extensively discussed, though not necessarily evaluated, as being important to driving ability, as they comprise abilities theoretically essential for driving, including multitasking, planning, organization, decision making, mental flexibility, problem solving, and judgment. For example, prudent decision making is constantly required regarding safe distances (e.g., "gap acceptance") and potential hazards, or, simply, whether conditions are acceptable to drive. In addition, mental flexibility is critical for the executive control of attentional set-shifting, as when drivers glance between the rearview mirror and the roadway. Although executive functions are subserved by distributed neural networks, research generally supports their strong reliance upon the frontal cortex and frontostriatal systems (e.g., Stuss & Alexander, 2007). As such, they can be affected by a variety of neurologic and psychiatric disorders, as well as substance use.

Executive functions have been predictive of driving skills in cognitively normal (e.g., Avolio et al., 1985) and neurological populations (e.g., Daigneault et al., 2002; Marcotte et al., 2004b; van Zomeren et al., 1987; Whelihan et al., 2005). A generally consistent finding is that switching trials of psychomotor sequencing tasks (e.g., Trails B) show moderate associations with driving outcomes (Ball et al., 2006; Grace et al., 2005; cf. Molnar et al., 2006; Szlyk et al., 2002). Other tasks of problem solving and set-shifting have shown less impressive findings. However, getting lost, an integration of visuoperception with executive functioning, is often presumed to be an early sign of trouble with driving (Marottoli, 1997), although few studies examine this hypothesis. Studies using maze navigation tasks or city navigation simulations have shown some promise in predicting fitness to drive (Marcotte et al., 2004b; Ott et al., 2003, 2008a), but as of now most tasks have limited psychometric information.

Executive functioning deficits can potentially affect driving performance over very short time periods. For example, disinhibition may result in generalized risky driving, but may also lead to difficulties in overriding an initiated action (e.g., stopping at a red light once the individual has already started the process of going through the yellow light).

Despite these findings, executive functions have not been examined as extensively as some other neurocognitive domains in the prediction of driving ability. Many components of executive functioning are difficult to measure in the clinic, but it is an area warranting further study (Daigneault et al., 2002).

Working Memory

In order to drive safely, individuals need to briefly store information in working memory about their surroundings and the current task for future use. Although much of driving may be routine, working memory becomes especially important in complex, dynamic situations (Guerrier et al., 1999). Despite this clear relevance to driving ability, few investigations have examined the contributions of working memory to driving outcomes, although some studies have found predictive value with multifactorial tasks that assess working memory among other functions (e.g., Trails B, Grace et al., 2005). Working memory deficits may also contribute to change blindness, or the inability to detect noticeable changes in a visual scene with a brief visual disruption (e.g., blinks, saccades), potentially influencing the ability to detect important variations in traffic (Rizzo & Kellison, 2004).

Learning/Memory

There is evidence that learning and memory performance are associated with driving, especially in individuals with more severe cognitive impairment (Hunt et al., 1993; Odenheimer et al., 1994; Rizzo et al., 1997). However, the associations in normal aging and other disorders (e.g., TBI, Tamietto et al., 2006) have been more modest in comparison to other neurocognitive domains, such as attention (Anstey et al., 2005; McKnight & McKnight, 1999). Although episodic memory (i.e., memory for specific events and information) may not appear to be the most face valid neuropsychological ability for driving, it involves the integration of numerous cognitive processes that may themselves be involved in driving (British Psychological Society, 2001). Alternatively, given that memory tests are some of the more sensitive measures to overall cognitive impairment, the relationship between memory abilities and driving skills may be partially due to memory serving as a proxy for general level of cognitive impairment.

Procedural Memory/Knowledge

Many aspects of the driving task are overlearned and, with time, implemented without conscious attention. As such, driving a car is often cited as an exemplar of procedural memory, or a type of "nondeclarative memory for skills that are not verbalized or consciously inspected" (Loring, 1999). Procedural learning and memory is most closely linked to functioning of the basal ganglia or striatum (Squire, 1993). Previous studies have demonstrated relatively preserved procedural learning in select disorders (Alzheimer's disease, Korsakoff's syndrome), with impairments found in disorders of frontostriatal systems (Parkinson's disease, Huntington's disease). However, few studies have examined procedural memory and driving. One relevant study of two individuals with amnesia, but generally preserved cognition in other domains, found intact driving abilities, consistent with their performance on two procedural learning tasks (Anderson et al., 2007), supporting the notion that for some driving tasks procedural knowledge might be a more important component than declarative memory.

Processing Speed

Swift processing of information is also theoretically critical for driving, although few studies have specifically investigated the contribution of this neurocognitive ability to driving behavior. For example, drivers must not only react to stimuli in the roadway but also effectively process road signs and the pattern of traffic around them. Speed of processing may be an especially critical skill in diseases in which bradyphrenia is a primary symptom, or in disorders that affect the integrity of white matter. To this end, a number of studies have shown that processing-speed deficits are strongly associated with impairments in driving-related abilities in Parkinson's disease (Stolwyk et al., 2006; Uc et al., 2006b; Worringham et al., 2006), HIV infection (Marcotte et al., 1999), and stroke (Galski et al., 1993; Sundet et al., 1995), although these findings are by no means universal (Grace et al., 2005).

There is also evidence that older individuals may have insight regarding declines in speed of information processing, as it has been shown to be predictive of driving cessation in this population (Edwards et al., 2008), although this finding awaits further study. Interestingly, recent data suggest that processing-speed deficits may be partially remediable, and, although the evidence is still preliminary, improvement in driving-related outcomes has been shown with processing-speed training in older adults (Roenker et al., 2003).

In general, simple reaction time measures have not been very sensitive predictors of driving impairments, although choice reaction time measures have been more useful. As noted earlier, while good reaction times may help one get out of a dangerous situation, the good driver avoids those situations in the first place (e.g., consider that adolescents have fast reaction times but high accident rates).

Psychomotor Speed

Psychomotor functioning has been investigated as a potential explanatory factor in driving studies, but it has rarely been a focus except in disorders with prominent motor symptoms (Marcotte et al., 2008). This may be due to the fact that neurocognitive tests often examine psychomotor functioning at the level of fine motor coordination (e.g., Grooved Pegboard Test), whereas driving

may predominantly involve more gross motor skills. In addition, many driving-related motor skills become overlearned with experience, and may be more robust to declines in abilities. The mixed nature of findings, even in diseases with significant psychomotor impairments (e.g., Parkinson's disease), reflects these complications. Nonetheless, it may be beneficial to carry out screening for a broad range of motor abilities, dependent on the disorder, as deficits in psychomotor functioning have proven useful as predictors of driving safety in certain studies (even in the absence of gross motor abnormalities), including those examining Parkinson's disease (Worringham et al., 2006), HIV infection (Marcotte et al., 1999), and aging (Lundberg et al., 1998). In addition, although associations between impairment and driving are inconsistent, one study found that a training program focused on improving speed of movement, coordination, and flexibility among older adults improved driving-related outcomes (Marottoli et al., 2007). More sophisticated and potentially sensitive motor assessments (e.g., motor programming, velocity scaling, forced steadiness, motor disinhibition) may be useful in demarcating the contributions of motor abnormalities to driving behaviors.

Language

In general, measures of language and verbal functioning have yielded mixed results, depending upon the population under study, and severity of impairment. For example, Hunt et al. (1993) found a modest correlation between the Boston Naming Test and driving performance. However, such measures are not considered the most sensitive to driving performance across disorders.

Motor

Measures of pure motor functioning (e.g., finger tapping) are usually of limited utility in predicting driving competence, although they may be of some benefit in assessing neurologic disorders that have significant motor impairments (Grace et al., 2005; Radford et al., 2004).

Mental Status/Screening Tests

The use of cognitive screening tests, such as the Mini-Mental State Examination (MMSE) and Mattis Organic Mental Status Syndrome Examination (MOMSSE), to screen for driving impairments has the same limitations found when using such measures for other types of evaluations: poor sensitivity at the milder ranges of impairment and a lack of clear decision points for those who score in the borderline range. Such measures are typically most useful in mid-to-late stages of dementia (Reger et al., 2004). In addition, most screening measures fail to assess abilities believed to be important for driving (e.g., executive functioning, impulsivity). While a meta-analysis showed that mental status measures had a moderate association with road test scores when dementia and control participants were included, this relationship disappeared when only those with dementia were included (Reger et al., 2004). Thus, screening measures should be used with caution in determining whether individuals are at risk for driving impairments (Lundberg et al., 1997).

A few professional groups have provided guidelines regarding determining when a patient might be an at-risk driver. For example, the American Medical Association (Wang et al., 2003) recommends looking for "red flags" in the patient's history (e.g., medical conditions or medications that may impair driving skills) and reviewing driving history. If problems are suspected, they recommend formally assessing vision, cognition, and motor functioning and provide guidelines and cutoff scores that indicate potential problems. Aspects of vision that should be evaluated include visual acuity (assessed via Snellen chart) and visual fields (assessed via confrontation testing). For cognition, the Trail-Making Test Part B and the Clock-Drawing Test (with Freund Clock Scoring for Driving Competency) are recommended, while the Rapid Pace Walk and Manual Tests of Range of Motion and Motor Strength are recommended for the assessment of motor functioning. Although such guidance is a positive step, the authors acknowledge that other driving-related abilities are missed by this brief evaluation, such as contrast sensitivity, memory, attention, and coordination. In addition, there is little justification for the selection of these tests or for the recommended cutoffs (Molnar et al., 2006).

Metacognition

Metacognition, or the awareness of one's own cognitive (and driving) abilities and processes, can significantly affect driving outcomes. For example, if an individual is not aware of a visuoperceptual deficit, he/she may choose to continue driving or drive less cautiously than if cognizant of the deficit. On the other hand, if aware of deficits, he/she may cease driving or compensate for deficits through various strategies (see below). Studies of the relationships between clinical neuropsychological measures, metacognition, and driver behavior are still in their infancy, although a few studies have shown that awareness of cognitive deficits in TBI is a fairly accurate predictor of driving outcomes (Coleman et al., 2002; Galski et al., 1990). However, emerging evidence also indicates that impaired drivers with various disorders often overestimate their driving abilities (Freund et al., 2005; Lundqvist & Alinder, 2007; Marcotte et al., 2004b; Wild & Cotrell, 2003), although this may improve somewhat with training (Eby et al., 2003). Clinicians should also be aware that certain disorders have a higher prevalence of anosognosia (lack of awareness of impairments), including Alzheimer's disease, stroke, and Korsakoff's amnesia (e.g., Cosentino & Stern, 2005; Orfei et al., 2007).

Compensatory Strategies

Awareness of one's deficits or limitations may lead to compensatory strategies on the part of the driver, such as driving only at certain times (e.g., avoiding night driving) or on particular routes. Studies have shown differential use of compensatory strategies between cognitively impaired and healthy comparison groups (Fisk et al., 2002b; Foley et al., 2000; Rebok et al., 1995; Stutts, 1998; Trobe et al., 1996), indicating that some individuals are aware of their cognitive limitations and adjust accordingly. Yet this relationship seems to be quite complex. Individuals with more severe (Trobe et al., 1996; Valcour et al., 2002) or more prolonged (Gilley et al., 1991) cognitive impairment may reduce their driving involvement more than those with less severity or a shorter duration of impairment. Individuals with medical conditions (e.g., Hakamies-Blomqvist & Siren, 2003), physical performance difficulties (e.g., Edwards et al., 2008), poorer self-rated health (e.g., Anstey et al., 2006), or vision problems (e.g., Freeman et al., 2005) may also cease driving at higher levels. This relationship may be mediated or moderated by other factors, such as gender, availability of public transportation, or availability of other drivers in the household (Freund & Szinovacz, 2002). A common strategy, of course, is driving more slowly, although this in itself may be indicative of impaired driving (Withaar et al., 2000). Another compensatory strategy is driving with a "copilot," or another passenger in the car, who assists with driving-related tasks. This method has been proposed as a potentially helpful method for reducing crash risk (Bedard et al., 1998), although it may be less beneficial in challenging traffic situations (Shua-Haim & Gross, 1996) or in navigating unfamiliar routes (Vrkljan & Polgar, 2007). Nonetheless, many cognitively impaired individuals continue to drive (Valcour et al., 2002), and some compensatory strategies, such as avoiding highway driving, may actually increase crash risk (Baker et al., 2003). For example, unlike highway driving, local driving involves intersections that place even greater emphasis on intact peripheral vision and attention. Evidence is also lacking as to whether compensatory strategies are actually effective in reducing the risk of future crashes (Ball et al., 1998).

Assessment of Driving Capacity— What Measures Constitute "Outcomes" in Driving Studies?

Establishing efficient and accurate assessments of driving impairment poses a significant challenge. There is currently no clear, accepted outcome variable that captures the concept of "impaired driving skills" (Yale et al., 2003), and the best method for assessment remains debated (Marcotte & Scott, 2004). Although on-road evaluations are often used as a gold standard, even by most government testing agencies, they are not universally accepted as such (Brookhuis

et al., 2003). Moreover, many assessments are designed to ensure drivers know and apply certain rules and are generally safe, not to detect specific declines in functioning. In addition, the results of many driving assessments are often determined by a subjective global assessment (e.g., "fit" or "unfit" to drive) that may not encompass all problem areas. Even when driving assessments are standardized and comprehensive, they are often not validated against criterion variables of interest, such as crash involvement or records of violations. Studies that do validate against driving history may have insufficient statistical power, as crashes and violations are relatively rare events and are often underreported (Fox et al., 1998). Reliable, criterion-based cutoffs for failure on many measures are also lacking, leading to imprecise concepts of an "unsafe performance." Furthermore, if a study does find significant differences or an increased risk ratio between clinical and healthy comparison samples, the degree to which *individuals* in the real world are at risk is often not clear.

On the other hand, significant advances in driving assessments have taken place in the last two decades. There has been an increased focus on standardizing on-road evaluations and establishing their reliability and validity, possibly leading to replicable studies (Fox et al., 1998). In addition, researchers have begun to focus on the clinical utility of driving assessments by providing classification statistics such as sensitivity and specificity (e.g., Schultheis et al., 2003). There is also increasing appreciation of the limitations of various assessment of driving safety, leading to innovative assessment methodologies. For example, driving simulators are increasingly affordable, with enhanced technology, graphics, and realism.

Nonetheless, it can be confusing to read the ever-growing literature on driver safety in various medical and neurologic conditions. When evaluating such research, the reader should always keep in mind (1) how the outcome is measured, (2) whether there is any criterion variable with which to correlate the outcome, and (3) how much inference is being made from the results. For example, is performance on a driving simulator assumed to relate to "real-world" driving? If neuropsychological tests are administered, are they correlated with a small portion of driving behavior? Would the impact be different if participants were evaluated within a rich driving environment, which includes ongoing distractions and requires multitasking and vigilance over long periods of time?

There are a variety of methodologies for assessing driving abilities in research and clinical settings, each with its own strengths and limitations. These include evaluating abilities based upon an on-road drive (open and closed course), reviewing recent driving history, and assessing performance on a laboratory-based driving simulator.

Behind the Wheel Evaluations

On-Road Driving Evaluations. On-road evaluations are most often considered the gold standard for identifying impairments in driving abilities, as they provide the greatest face validity, with true sensory feedback and quasi-real-world situations (Withaar et al., 2000). Participants typically drive a standardized route and are scored by driving rehabilitation specialists on tasks such as scanning the environment, maintaining safe distances, and avoiding dangerous or risky maneuvers. Studies that have utilized structured evaluations through clinical ratings have achieved adequate reliability (Akinwuntan et al., 2005a; Hunt et al., 1997b; Marcotte et al., 2004b; Odenheimer et al., 1994). In addition, there has been a movement toward developing empirically based and standardized on-road evaluations for various populations (e.g., Fox et al., 1998), and some researchers have achieved success in establishing such evaluations (e.g., Akinwuntan et al., 2005a).

Despite the clear face validity of on-road tests, questions still remain regarding their ecological and external validity. Few studies have data regarding their criterion validity with relation to future crashes or violations. Participants are usually presented with step-by-step directions, which do not emulate decisions made under real-world conditions, where one must respond to novel or emergency conditions (e.g., a pedestrian appearing in the roadway). Furthermore, evaluations may not be sensitive to certain deficits. For example, directions given during the evaluation may minimize navigational decisions, which in turn may hamper detection of planning and problem-solving deficits (i.e., impairments in executive functions). It has thus been recommended that on-road evaluations include a significant "free-drive" period, in which the examinee drives without direction from the examiner (British Psychological Society, 2001). It is also important to design driving tasks that place demands on executive functions, attention, visual perception, and memory, in order to more effectively cover the broad extent of abilities needed for safe driving in the real world (Uc et al., 2004). In general, due to time and resource constraints, on-road evaluations conducted by governmental agencies are usually less challenging, and therefore likely to be less sensitive, than the longer and more complex evaluations typically conducted by driving rehabilitation specialists.

Objective ratings of on-road driving can also be complicated by the fact that the primary examiner often needs to worry about safety issues (e.g., grabbing the steering wheel during an unsafe maneuver). In part because of this complication, many on-road evaluations yield a clinical impression of driving ability, with limited objective scoring, rather than using extensive scoring schemas. When feasible, a second examiner can offset this limitation. Since these tests entail real-world unpredictability, individuals being assessed on a similar route can encounter disparate scenarios. In addition, unanticipated cueing can take place. For example, Hunt et al. (1997a) found that some mildly impaired patients with Alzheimer's disease slowed at an unregulated intersection, while others did not. In reviewing their data, they noticed that those participants who appropriately slowed were mimicking a car that happened to be in front of them at the time. As with all testing, although undergoing evaluation may result in increased anxiety, it can also lead examinees to maintain their concentration at a higher level than during routine daily driving. Inadvertent cueing may also occur when the examiner unintentionally responds to dangerous situations. Despite these limitations, and the fact that such evaluations engender risk and require significant resources, this methodology provides important insights into how individuals may perform under reasonably controlled, real-life situations.

In addition to these clinically oriented evaluations, some investigators (primarily examining pharmacologic effects) have focused on distinct driving parameters such as the standard deviation of lateral position (a quantitative measure of the degree to which individuals adjust lane position while driving) and time to adaptation to a lead car's changes in speed on public roadways (Kuypers et al., 2006; Ramaekers, 2003).

"Closed-Course" On-Road Driving Evaluations. "Closed-course" evaluations provide the same sensory feedback as normal on-road evaluations but offer an additional level of situational control. These evaluations typically measure basic skills, such as the standard deviation of lateral position, reaction time in braking, or maneuvering through cones or other objects (Galski et al., 1990, 1992; Sivak et al., 1981). Most are conducted without interaction with other vehicles, ensuring a level of control that in-traffic evaluations cannot provide. However, this level of control may preclude evaluation of critical skills that drivers need in the real world, such as decision making or maneuvering in traffic, which may primarily limit the assessment to the operational level of Michon's driving model (1985) and may not evaluate critical skills such as decision making or maneuvering in traffic. Furthermore, it is often not practical to find a location to conduct these evaluations. Given these limitations, "closed-course" evaluations have been recommended only as a precursor to actual on-road assessment (Fox et al., 1998).

Crash History

In order to understand how individuals actually behave in their usual driving environment, investigators often examine a driver's crash history. This methodology provides a fair degree of ecological and external validity by measuring behavior over an extended period of time in a truly real-world setting, thus avoiding some limitations of laboratory-based assessments (i.e., only providing a snapshot of the person's functioning in a contrived environment). In addition, for determining risk this extended sampling also has the advantage of enabling adjustment for an individual's overall amount of driving exposure (i.e., miles driven), although

it has been argued that this may exaggerate the risk for low-mileage groups, since high-mileage groups often accumulate their miles on less congested and simpler roadways (freeways or multilane highways) (Janke, 1991).

Despite the benefits that a review of driving history offers, crashes and violations are rare events, restricting the range of outcome variables. This may limit statistical power and lead to an inadequate number of validation studies. Review of driving history also does not directly inform us of how an individual would perform under unusual (but not rare) situations, such as a pedestrian running into the roadway. In addition, other unidentified factors may affect crash rates (a crash can be caused by another driver, leading to overestimates of driver impairment, or avoided because of the defensive behavior of other drivers, leading to underestimates of driver impairment). Another difficulty concerns the availability of appropriate crash statistics. State motor vehicle records are often difficult to obtain and tend to reflect underreporting of crashes, since most individuals do not report minor crashes (one study found that only 40% of crashes were reported (Insurance Research Council, 1991)). Self-reports of crashes and violations are complicated by possible biases, including the influence of social desirability (i.e., the desire to look unimpaired to the researcher) and the inaccuracy of normal memory, much less the memory impairments seen in neurologic populations. To this end, self-reports of crashes and violations have shown generally modest association with official driving records (Arthur et al., 2005; McGwin et al., 1998).

Driving Simulators

Driving simulators overcome some of the limitations of other approaches and allow researchers to examine driving behavior under more controlled and standardized conditions, and often in greater detail. Whereas most research has focused on using neuropsychological measures to predict real-world driving (i.e., veridicality, or the degree to which performance on laboratory tests relates to performance in the real world), the use of simulators represents an approach that emphasizes verisimilitude, or the degree to which the demands of the measure reflect the demands imparted by the real-world task (Franzen & Wilhelm, 1996; Spooner & Pachana, 2006). Simulator performance has been considered both an outcome, indicative of driving abilities (Liguori et al., 1998; Marcotte et al., 1999; Rizzo et al., 2001; Schultheis et al., 2001; Weiler et al., 2000; Zesiewicz et al., 2002) as well as a useful predictor of on-road performance (Galski et al., 1997; Lee et al., 2003; Marcotte et al., 2004b) and future crashes (e.g., Lew et al., 2005).

Simulations range from as simplistic as having the participant press a pedal when a specified target appears on the screen to full motion systems that provide horizontal and longitudinal travel and nearly 360 degrees of rotation, thus providing the driver with realistic acceleration, braking, and steering cues (e.g., the University of Iowa/National Highway Traffic Safety Administration's National Advanced Driving Simulator; Simulator III at the Swedish National Road and Transport Research Institute). In between these two extremes are high-fidelity, low-cost simulators that are modifiable and provide a feasible option for researchers wishing to measure driving behavior. Hardware for most current simulations include a steering wheel (proprietary or off-the-shelf joystick style), brake/accelerator pedals, and anywhere from a single computer monitor to full field of view projection systems.

Numerous outcome variables can be examined in simulations, such as average speed, speed variability, number of crashes, number of near misses, and reaction time, among others. Methodologies utilized in on-road evaluations, such as tracking the standard deviation of lateral position and car-following behavior, have also been adapted for simulations (Lenne et al., 2003; Marcotte et al., 2008; Moller et al., 2002; Weiler et al., 2000), although the degree to which on-road and simulation performance on these measures are interchangeable remains controversial (Blana & Golias, 2002).

A principal advantage of simulator technology is the ability to place participants into crash avoidance situations (e.g., pedestrians walking into the roadway), wherein they must take evasive action, as well as novel conditions (e.g., fog, mountain driving) that are not reproducible during on-road evaluations (Marcotte et al.,

1999; Rizzo et al., 2001). The replication of such situations are important, because even though much of routine driving involves overlearned behaviors, there are also times when drivers must take quick, decisive action, or anticipate risks and adjust their driving accordingly. This could be considered analogous to piloting an aircraft, in which the vast majority of activities are entirely routine, but during a crisis it is imperative that the pilot/driver be cognitively intact across many domains. Since these responses require higher level and integrated skills such as attention, spatial processing, processing speed, and executive functioning (self-monitoring, judgment), abilities that cannot always be assessed during a directed on-road drive, simulators provide an effective and safe method of evaluation.

Another key advantage of simulators is the ability to perform detailed investigation of driving behavior, and its correlates, under controlled conditions. This includes analyses of specific driving maneuvers in potential crash situations (Rizzo et al., 2001), application of eye movement analyses to infer attentional allocation (Mapstone et al., 2001), and facilitation of high-resolution magnetic resonance imaging studies, such as fMRI (Walter et al., 2001), that might provide insights into the brain regions involved in driving. Preliminary studies also suggest that training on a simulator may generalize to on-road performance in a rehabilitation setting (Akinwuntan et al., 2005b). In addition, performance on simulations may provide additional, independent information above and beyond neuropsychological testing in predicting fitness to drive (Marcotte et al., 2004b).

There remain limitations to simulator technology. Despite tremendous advances in graphics and processing capabilities, simulators still do not fully recreate the multisensory driving experience (i.e., three-dimensional environment, sounds, feel of the roadway, number of typical cars in the road). Interestingly, despite the attention it receives, graphics quality is not necessarily the most salient feature regarding whether participants "buy in" to the experience. Many factors affect how "real" the simulation feels to the participant, including lag time between driver input and car response, screen refresh rates, and the behavior of other simulated vehicles. For example, in our early studies, despite using a single-monitor desktop model with very rudimentary graphics, research participants routinely peered over their shoulders to ensure it was safe to change lanes.

Though participants may take the testing seriously and strive to avoid crashes, they are still aware that a simulator crash will not cause property damage or bodily injury, and thus they may not drive as cautiously as they might in the real world. And, although much information can be garnered from computer simulations, they do not negate the necessity for behavioral observation to fully evaluate the participant's behavior at the time of a crash. Lastly, simulation sickness is a constant concern. As realism increases and participants sense motion but remain seated on a fixed platform, there is a greater likelihood of nausea. This is particularly true for older individuals, especially females. While interventions such as keeping the room cooled and ventilated help, they do not entirely eliminate simulator sickness. And, unfortunately, common medications for motion sickness are of limited use since they may themselves affect driving ability.

The Impact of Neurologic, Psychiatric, and Medical Conditions on Driving Ability

Below we briefly review findings regarding driving and select neuropsychiatric disorders. The usual caveat applies here: the impairments discussed are at the group level and do not *necessarily* apply to individual patients. In addition, findings vary, depending upon the methodology being used to assess driving status (real-world crashes, simple versus complex simulations, on-road assessments).

Normal Aging

Older driver safety is an increasing public health concern. For example, although older drivers in the United States have the lowest crash rate per licensed driver of all age groups, their crash rate per million miles driven is higher than most other age groups (with the exception of the 16- to 20-year-old age group); even more alarming, their fatality rate per crash is higher than any other age group (National Highway Traffic Safety

Administration, 2001, 2004). Slight declines in driving performance have been shown to occur with normal aging (Duchek et al., 2003; Wood, 2002), but there is by no means consensus regarding the extent or even occurrence of such declines (Ball & Owsley, 2003), and while these may result in reduced driving performance, they do not necessarily put the older person into the "impaired driver" category. It has been argued that it is not necessarily age itself but, rather, the specific changes that often accompany aging that are risk factors for increased crashes (Fain, 2003; Fitten, 2003). As such, older age groups are potentially at greater risk of driving impairment due to increased medication use, functional injuries, and medical conditions that affect driving ability, and subgroups with these conditions may increase the average risk for the entire age group (Ball et al., 1998). Declines in one's UFOV have been associated with past (Ball et al., 1993) and future (Owsley et al., 1998) accidents in older adults. In a review of the aging and driving literature, Anstey et al. (2005) identified declines in measures of attention, visuoperception, complex reaction time, and executive functioning as being associated with driving performance, and emphasized the importance of self-monitoring in adjusting for cognitive, visual, and physical deficits.

Neurologic Disease

Alzheimer's Disease. Driving abilities decline in individuals with Alzheimer's disease, even with mild severity (i.e., Clinical Dementia Rating—CDR ≤ 1). This has been found via informant reports (Dubinsky et al., 1992), review of crash records, simulator assessments (Rizzo et al., 1997, 2001), and on-road tests (Fitten et al., 1995; Hunt et al., 1993), although the results have not been entirely consistent (Bieliauskas et al., 1998; Trobe et al., 1996). Driving impairment typically increases significantly over time and tracks with disease severity, although there is variability (Duchek et al., 2003). Proposed predictors of driving performance in Alzheimer's disease have included measures of processing speed (e.g., Trail-Making Test, Part A), attentional switching (e.g., Trail-Making Test, Part B), language (e.g., Boston Naming Test), and higher-order visuoperceptual function (e.g., Rey–O Complex Figure Copy). These have been fairly consistent predictors of on-road performance, even after adjusting for disease status in some cases (Grace et al., 2005; Hunt et al., 1993; Uc et al., 2004, 2006a). Duchek and colleagues (1998) theorized that measures of selective visual attention (visual search errors and UFOV) may be particularly important, and this has been corroborated (Uc et al., 2004). Memory impairment may also be important on driving tasks that make demands upon retrospective memory (Uc et al., 2004). Neither caregiver perception nor patient self-assessment is a consistently good predictor of on-road performance or future crashes in this patient group (Hunt et al., 1993; Wild & Cotrell, 2003). Some consensus meetings have generated specific recommendations regarding dementia and driving. For example, an international workgroup (Lundberg et al., 1997) recommended that individuals with moderate to severe dementia should stop driving, those with mild dementia and functional deterioration should have a specialized driving assessment, and individuals with mild dementia and stable functioning should have periodic follow-ups. However, as with many such guidelines, these recommendations did not include guidance regarding the tools for reaching these classifications.

Parkinson's Disease. Although motor dysfunction is most commonly associated with Parkinson's disease, it can also result in declines in executive functioning and attention, as well as visual functioning. Numerous studies have concluded that driving is impaired in patients with Parkinson's disease, whether assessed via simulator (Madeley et al., 1990), on-road driving (Heikkila & Kallanranta, 2005; Uc et al., 2006c), or accident history (Dubinsky et al., 1991). Driving impairments in patients with Parkinson's disease may be exacerbated by increased task complexity, although there is significant variability among patients (Uc et al., 2006c). Difficulties in set-shifting and cognitive flexibility (e.g., Trail-Making Test, Brixton test), processing speed, and attention (including visual attention, with the UFOV) have been reasonably consistent predictors of performance in this population (Amick et al., 2007; Stolwyk et al., 2006; Uc et al., 2006c; Worringham et al.,

2006). There remains uncertainty regarding the degree to which driving performance does (Zesiewicz et al., 2002), or does not (Wood et al., 2005), relate to common measures of disease progress (i.e., Haehn and Yahr scale and Unified Parkinson's Disease Rating Scale [UPDRS]). In addition to motor and cognitive impairments, sleep abnormalities, such as "sleep attacks," which may occur when patients are fatigued, appear to put patients at increased risk for accidents (Adler & Thorpy, 2005; Hobson et al., 2002; Meindorfner et al., 2005), may be exacerbated by the use of dopamine agonists (Avorn et al., 2005).

Multiple Sclerosis. Cognitive dysfunction occurs in 30%–70% of MS patients, at least at some point during their lifetime (Rao et al., 1991). Memory, attention, processing speed, and executive functioning may be affected, with intellectual functioning and language skills typically preserved (Bobholz & Rao, 2003). From small epidemiologic studies, MS patients have been found to have higher crash rates (Lings, 2002; Schultheis et al., 2002) and, in the laboratory, worse performance on simulators (Kotterba et al., 2003; Marcotte et al., 2008) than controls. Neuromotor symptoms (weakness, sensory disturbance, coordination problems, spasticity), as well as MS-related neurocognitive disturbance may affect driving ability (Schultheis et al., 2001), and MS patients have greater difficulty on the UFOV (Schultheis et al., 2001). Unfortunately, there is limited information relating specific cognitive abilities to driving performance in MS patients. A small on-road study of individuals with MS (Lincoln & Radford, 2008) found measures of attention/concentration (Dot Cancellation), a Road Sign Recognition task, Design Learning, and an information-processing task (Adult Memory and Information-Processing Task B) to be reasonably predictive of on-road failures. A simulator study assessing the ability to maintain lane position while attending to a secondary task found moderate ($r = \sim.5$) correlations with the Trail-Making Test, Digit Symbol, and the Hopkins Verbal Learning Test (Marcotte et al., 2008). Many studies excluded individuals with significant spasticity in order to focus on cognitive issues. However, spasticity, which affects

40%–70% of patients, may also result in specific driving impairments, such as poor speed maintenance, and it may be possible to differentiate the contribution of cognition and spasticity to impairments in specific driving skills (Marcotte et al., 2008). In addition, clinicians should remain cognizant of the possible role that visual dysfunction has on driving performance.

Epilepsy. There is limited data regarding direct assessment of driving in individuals with epilepsy. Although some jurisdictions require health-care providers to report persons with epilepsy who have seizures and want to drive, a consensus statement ("Consensus statements, sample statutory provisions, and model regulations regarding driver licensing and epilepsy. American Academy of Neurology, American Epilepsy Society, and Epilepsy Foundation of America," 1994) was not supportive of mandatory reporting. There is general agreement that individuals with uncontrolled seizures should not drive, and determination regarding permission to drive is in part related to the seizure-free interval, usually recommended to be between 3 and 12 months (Drazkowski, 2007). In addition, antiepileptic medications can result in visual problems, fatigue, and tremors (French et al., 2004), and may affect driving ability.

Traumatic Brain Injury. Although TBIs often result in impairments that might affect driving (e.g., cognitive, perceptual, behavioral), approximately 40%–60% of patients who survive a TBI resume driving. In making this decision, patients often overvalue recovery in physical function and minimize the effects of sustained cognitive and emotional problems (Leon-Carrion et al., 2005). Many return to driving without specific evaluations or medical advice (Fisk et al., 1998; Pietrapiana et al., 2005). The predictors of driving fitness are therefore critical in this population, due to these high rates of driving postinjury and the possibility of recovery with rehabilitation (see below). Unfortunately, studies examining driving fitness in patients recovering from TBI have had inconsistent findings due to the heterogeneous nature of the brain injuries, the broad range of severity, and the differences in time since injury (Tamietto et al., 2006). In many studies, indicators of injury severity, such

as the Glasgow Coma Scale score, length of coma, or posttraumatic amnesia, have been predictive of driving ability (e.g., Korteling & Kaptein, 1996), although some studies have failed to find such associations (e.g., Sivak et al., 1981). While it might be possible to compensate for impairments in speed of processing by reducing speed or using other methods for decreasing time pressure (Schmidt et al., 1996), in some cases patients fail to make these adjustments, resulting in prolonged glances away from the roadway and suggesting limited self-awareness. No specific pattern of neuropsychological deficits predicts driving safety or risk in TBI patients, although neuropsychological tests are generally useful when assessing driving fitness in this population. As with other disorders, clinicians should assess a broad range of cognitive abilities, including executive functions, psychomotor skills, visuospatial ability, processing speed, divided and sustained attention, and working memory, as all have shown predictive power in previous studies (e.g., Coleman et al., 2002; Korteling & Kaptein, 1996). In particular, executive functioning may be useful in predicting driving performance (Coleman et al., 2002), and perhaps the UFOV (Novack et al., 2006). In contrast to Alzheimer's disease, patient and caregiver insight into deficits in TBI patients may be valuable predictors of driving risk (Coleman et al., 2002; Galski et al., 1990; Rapport et al., 1998). Premorbid factors may also play a prominent role in the prediction of driving ability after brain injury. Pietrapiana and colleagues (2005) found that premorbid risky behavioral characteristics and pre-injury driving crashes and violations were critical predictors of crashes over the follow-up period, although retrospective questionnaires were used to probe informants regarding participants' premorbid characteristics. Importantly, studies have begun to emerge showing that a number of TBI patients who undergo intensive, multidisciplinary rehabilitation programs can safely return to driving (Leon-Carrion et al., 2005; Schultheis et al., 2002), although longitudinal studies of the effectiveness of such programs are badly needed.

Stroke. Driving abilities can be significantly diminished by a stroke, with more significant cognitive and motor symptoms leading to worse outcomes (e.g., Schanke & Sundet, 2000). Marshall and colleagues (2007) conducted a review of the predictors of driving ability following stroke. Although methodological quality was wanting in most studies, consistent predictors of on-road driving assessments in poststroke patients were visual field and acuity testing, Trail-Making Test Parts A and B, Rey–O Complex Figure Copy, UFOV, road sign and hazard recognition, and reaction time measures. Older age, the presence of aphasia, and right-sided lesions were also predictive of worse outcomes, while motor function, coordination, and emotional symptoms were judged to need further investigation. There is some evidence that simulator-based training may enhance recovery of driving abilities (Akinwuntan et al., 2005a), although these findings await replication.

HIV/AIDS. Cognitive impairment is a common sequela of HIV infection (Heaton et al., 1995). Despite dramatic reductions in mortality and morbidity with the advent of increasingly effective medications, there are indications that HIV-related neurologic disorders are still prevalent and remain a significant clinical concern (Antinori et al., 2007; Sacktor et al., 2002). Neuropsychological impairments short of severe dementia may result in impaired driving, as assessed via simulator and on-road methodologies (Marcotte et al., 1999, 2004b), with impairments in executive functioning, attention/working memory, and motor abilities being most predictive of driving dysfunction. Poor visual attention (assessed on the UFOV) is associated with increased crashes, particularly in the context of other neuropsychological impairments (Marcotte et al., 2006). Importantly, neuropsychological tests and simulator evaluations may provide unique, independent data regarding the abilities required for intact driving (Marcotte et al., 2004b), and thus a multimodal assessment approach appears most promising in this population.

Psychiatric Disorders

There is a dearth of research directly assessing driving ability in various psychiatric conditions, and it is often difficult to differentiate between driving impairments due to the underlying condition versus the medications aimed at treating the disorder.

An on-road study (Wingen et al., 2006) of individuals with *depression* and receiving SSRI or SNRI medications found that, compared to controls, the treated depressed group had a higher standard deviation of lateral position (weaving) and were also slower to adapt to speed changes in a lead car. Given that prior research suggests that SSRIs do not impair driving after acute repeated doses in healthy controls (Ramaekers, 2003), the authors concluded that the driving difficulties were most likely the result of residual depression rather than the medications. Little research exists with respect to driving performance and *schizophrenia*. A study of 83 older outpatients with schizophrenia (Palmer et al., 2002) found that 43% were currently driving. Using a desktop driving simulation (St Germain et al., 2005), drivers with schizophrenia tended to have more line crossings, collisions, and drove slower compared to controls. The disorder with perhaps the most extensive literature regarding driving performance is *attention-deficit hyperactivity disorder* (ADHD). ADHD includes symptoms of poor sustained attention, distractibility, impaired impulse control, and hyperactivity (American Psychiatric Association, 1994). Simulator (Biederman et al., 2007) and epidemiological (Barkley et al., 2002; Fried et al., 2006) research indicates that persons with ADHD have impaired driving abilities. Individuals with ADHD are more likely to have traffic citations (Jerome et al., 2006) and higher accident rates (Barkley et al., 1993; Cox et al., 2000b). This appears to be especially true for younger individuals with ADHD. Medication improves driving performance on simulators (Barkley et al., 2005; Cox et al., 2000b) and on the road (Cox et al., 2004; Verster et al., 2008). See Barkley and Cox (2007) for a review of the driving and ADHD literature.

Medical Disease

It is beyond the scope of this chapter to review literature on medical disease and driving impairment. However, clinicians should be cognizant that many conditions can affect driving performance, and these may be amplified by neuropsychological impairments. These include conditions such as *cataracts* (Owsley et al., 1999), *mild hepatic encephalopathy* (Bajaj et al., 2008; Wein et al., 2004), *diabetes* (Cox et al., 2000a, 2002), *coronary artery bypass grafting (CABG)* (Ahlgren et al., 2003), *sleep apnea* (Pizza et al., 2008; Vorona & Ware, 2002) and receiving *radiation treatment* (Yuen et al., 2008).

Other Assessment Issues

Assessing Driving History

It is helpful to gather information about driving history and current driving behavior from both the driver and a collateral source, if possible. Information regarding frequency and distance, length of driving episodes, type of roads commonly driven, driving scenarios that are avoided, and the use of "copilots" may prove valuable in understanding a person's driving experience. As noted earlier, although useful, for a variety of reasons (poor memory or awareness, biased reporting), self and other reports may at times not be completely reliable. Table 27–2 provides a list of questions that might be helpful in eliciting possible driving difficulties. Sample questionnaires for gathering information on driving behaviors include the Driving Habits Questionnaire (Ball et al., 1998) and the Dula Dangerous Driving Index (Willemsen et al., 2008).

Retesting

If an evaluation suggests that a patient is capable of continuing to drive, clinicians are confronted with the question of whether the patient should be reevaluated at a later time and, if so, which methodology should be used and over what time interval should the person be reassessed. In the case of AD, the American Academy of Neurology (Dubinsky et al., 2000) recommends that patients with a CDR severity of 1 or greater discontinue driving completely while the patients and family of those with a rating of 0.5 be informed that the individual is at risk and should be evaluated by a qualified driving examiner and reassessed every 6 months. Since up to 30% of individuals with a CDR of 0.5 progress to a score of 1.0 within 1 year (Morris & Cummings, 2005), this follow-up period generally appears appropriate. Although few studies have investigated driving performance longitudinally, in individuals with mild AD, Duchek et al. (2003), Fox et al. (1997), and Ott et al. (2008b) have shown that driving performance can significantly decline from safe to unsafe in only a few years. The longitudinal driving profiles of other conditions await further study.

Informed Consent and Limits to Confidentiality

As in any clinical evaluation, it is important to properly inform the client regarding any limits

Table 27–2. Questions for Assessing Potential Driving Problems

1. Has the driver received any traffic tickets or warnings in the past year or two?
2. Has the driver been in any accidents in the last year or two, even "fender benders"?
3. Does the driver hit curbs or other objects such as the fence or garage more often then he/she used to?
4. Has the driver had more "near misses" or "close calls" lately?
5. Does the driver miss turns or respond slowly to signals or road signs while driving?
6. Does the driver ever get lost?
7. Does the driver have more difficulty when directions need to be followed?
8. Do friends or family members express worry about the person's driving?
9. Do friends or family members ever avoid riding in a car with the driver?
10. Does the driver worry or feel nervous about driving at night, making left turns into oncoming traffic, or driving in unfamiliar places?
11. Does the driver ever describe how pedestrians or other cars "appear out of nowhere"?
12. Does the driver respond slower to unexpected situations?
13. Do other drivers honk at the person when he/she is behind the wheel?
14. Does the driver seem distracted or have a hard time concentrating while driving?
15. Has the driver lost some confidence in his/her driving ability?

(*Source:* Adapted from Eby et al. (2000) and Wang et al. (2003).)

of confidentiality with respect to the reporting of driving-related concerns, and it is recommended that clinicians keep up to date on their local reporting requirements.

Reporting Requirements

Laws in the U.S. vary by state as to whether clinicians are required to report certain medical, psychiatric, and neurological diagnoses to the Department of Motor Vehicles (DMV), health departments, or similar entities. Although most states have regulations regarding impaired drivers, many of the policies are vague, and await clarification via future legal cases. In some states, reporting is required (often with immunity from liability), while in others reporting is either "permitted" or "encouraged." On the basis of court precedent, physicians and psychologists may be held liable for not adequately evaluating driving ability should a crash occur involving dangerous driving on the part of a patient (Pettis, 1992), although valid arguments have been made against this standard (e.g., Pettis & Gutheil, 1993). It is critical that clinicians be conversant with their state's laws regarding reporting procedures. The American Medical Association provides a useful list of the reporting procedures for each state (Wang et al., 2003) (available at http://www.ama-assn.org/ama1/pub/upload/mm/433/chapter8.pdf), although clinicians should request the most current information directly from their state's Department of Motor Vehicles or Medical Advisory Board.

Conclusion

Driving safety is a significant public health concern, and this is reflected in the growing number of research articles in the medical and psychological literature. While it is clear that fitness to drive decreases as the breadth and depth of neuropsychological impairment increases, unfortunately there is still no single cognitive test (or battery of tests) that is clearly predictive of fitness to drive within specific neurologic conditions, let alone across disorders (British Psychological Society, 2001; Withaar et al., 2000).

Driving competence can be reduced by a variety of cognitive impairments, and it is recommended that, in part, the neuropsychological evaluation focus on the types of impairments likely to be encountered based upon the presenting problem (i.e., differential diagnoses). While the choice of tests will vary depending on the suspected cause of driving impairment, tests of visuospatial functioning, psychomotor functioning, processing speed, attention, and executive functioning should ideally be administered. If available in the community and within the resources of the patient, an on-road evaluation by a driving rehabilitation specialist may yield specific areas of driving deficits (a listing of qualified individuals can be found at the Web site for the American Occupational Therapy Association (www.aota.org)). Unfortunately, while failing an on-road test may clearly indicate impaired driving, passing the test does not guarantee driving competency.

In making recommendations, clinicians might consider compensatory strategies, which usually entail either reduction in miles driven (risk exposure) or the avoidance of certain driving situations. Since the loss of driving privileges can significantly affect mobility and independence, clinicians should ideally be ready to discuss alternate transportation options, as well as ways to cope with the psychosocial consequences (Windsor & Anstey, 2006). In addition, it is important that, when feasible, the patient's family be included in the process, as they may potentially provide support with respect to environmental structure and transportation alternatives (Hopewell, 2002). It should be noted that in most jurisdictions the neuropsychologist will *not* be responsible for determining whether individuals should keep their drivers license, but the clinician may need to make his/her best determination as to whether the person should be referred for evaluation by the state licensing agency.

Emerging technologies, such as minimally intrusive eye tracking systems, which measure gaze patterns and allocation of visual attention while driving, may in the future be able to help better clarify driving-related cognitive processes as they occur and perhaps differentiate between unsafe and safe drivers (Sodhi et al., 2002; Underwood et al., 2003). This is also true of in-car systems that track automobile movement and have instrumentation to potentially provide real-time information on driver behavior, strategy, and even decision making. The field has been hampered, in part, by the fact that most investigators use methods and scenarios developed within their own labs, and few assessment methods relating to driving have been widely dispersed for general use. This limits our ability to translate findings across diseases and within comparable cohorts. In addition, basic psychometric data such as test–retest reliabilities have been lacking, with a few exceptions (Hunt et al., 1997b; Marcotte et al., 2004a, 2004b; O'Hanlon et al., 1986; van Laar et al., 1995; Vermeeren & O'Hanlon, 1998). Although in their infancy, there are efforts under way to develop standardized simulations that can be administered across laboratories and patient populations. In addition, new studies using brain imaging technologies may also yield insights into the neural substrates of driving behaviors.

Determining driving ability in *individuals* is one of the most difficult issues facing clinicians, and, although there are promising new developments, predicting real-world competency from behavior in the clinic or lab will likely remain a challenge for many years to come.

Acknowledgments

The authors would like to thank Wade Allen and Abiodun Akinwuntan for their comments on aspects of this chapter. We would also like to thank Rachel Meyer for her help with the literature review and formatting of the document.

References

Adler, C. H., & Thorpy, M. J. (2005). Sleep issues in Parkinson's disease. *Neurology, 64*(12 Suppl 3), S12–S20.

Ahlgren, E., Lundqvist, A., Nordlund, A., Aren, C., & Rutberg, H. (2003). Neurocognitive impairment and driving performance after coronary artery bypass surgery. *European Journal of Cardio-Thoracic Surgery, 23*(3), 334–340.

Akinwuntan, A. E., De Weerdt, W., Feys, H., Baten, G., Arno, P., & Kiekens, C. (2005a). The validity of a road test after stroke. *Archives of Physical Medicine and Rehabilitation, 86*(3), 421–426.

Akinwuntan, A. E., De Weerdt, W., Feys, H., Pauwels, J., Baten, G., Arno, P., et al. (2005b). Effect of simulator training on driving after stroke: A randomized controlled trial. *Neurology, 65*(6), 843–850.

American Psychiatric Association. (1994). *Diagnostic and Statistical Manual of Mental Disorders—Fourth Edition: DSM-IV*. Washington, DC: American Psychiatric Association.

Amick, M. M., Grace, J., & Ott, B. R. (2007). Visual and cognitive predictors of driving safety in Parkinson's disease patients. *Archives of Clinical Neuropsychology, 22*(8), 957–967.

Anderson, S. W., Rizzo, M., Skaar, N., Stierman, L., Cavaco, S., Dawson, J., et al. (2007). Amnesia and driving. *Journal of Clinical and Experimental Neuropsychology, 29*(1), 1–12.

Anstey, K. J., Windsor, T. D., Luszcz, M. A., & Andrews, G. R. (2006). Predicting driving cessation over 5 years in older adults: Psychological well-being and cognitive competence are stronger predictors than physical health. *Journal of the American Geriatrics Society, 54*(1), 121–126.

Anstey, K. J., Wood, J., Lord, S., & Walker, J. G. (2005). Cognitive, sensory and physical factors enabling driving safety in older adults. *Clinical Psychology Review, 25*(1), 45–65.

Antinori, A., Arendt, G., Becker, J. T., Brew, B. J., Byrd, D. A., Cherner, M., et al. (2007). Updated research nosology for HIV-associated neurocognitive disorders. *Neurology, 69*(18), 1789–1799.

Arthur, W., Barrett, G. V., & Alexander, R. A. (1991). Prediction of Vehicular Accident Involvement: A Meta-Analysis. *Human Performance, 4*, 89–105.

Arthur, W., Jr., Bell, S. T., Edwards, B. D., Day, E. A., Tubre, T. C., & Tubre, A. H. (2005). Convergence of self-report and archival crash involvement data: A two-year longitudinal follow-up. *Human Factors, 47*(2), 303–313.

Avolio, B. J., Kroeck, K. G., & Panek, P. E. (1985). Individual-differences in information-processing ability as a predictor of motor-vehicle accidents. *Human Factors, 27*(5), 577–587.

Avorn, J., Schneeweiss, S., Sudarsky, L. R., Benner, J., Kiyota, Y., Levin, R., et al. (2005). Sudden uncontrollable somnolence and medication use in Parkinson disease. *Archives of Neurology, 62*(8), 1242–1248.

Bajaj, J. S., Hafeezullah, M., Hoffmann, R. G., Varma, R. R., Franco, J., Binion, D. G., et al. (2008). Navigation skill impairment: Another dimension of the driving difficulties in minimal hepatic encephalopathy. *Hepatology, 47*(2), 596–604.

Baker, T. K., Falb, T., Voas, R., & Lacey, J. (2003). Older women drivers: Fatal crashes in good conditions. *Journal of Safety Research, 34*(4), 399–405.

Ball, K., Edwards, J. D., & Ross, L. A. (2007). The impact of speed of processing training on cognitive and everyday functions. *Journals of Gerontology. Series B, Psychological Sciences and Social Sciences, 62 Spec No 1*, 19–31.

Ball, K., & Owsley, C. (2003). Driving competence: It's not a matter of age. *Journal of the American Geriatrics Society, 51*(10), 1499–1501.

Ball, K., Owsley, C., Sloane, M. E., Roenker, D. L., & Bruni, J. R. (1993). Visual attention problems as a predictor of vehicle crashes in older drivers. *Investigational Ophthalmology and Visual Science, 34*(11), 3110–3123.

Ball, K., Owsley, C., Stalvey, B., Roenker, D. L., Sloane, M. E., & Graves, M. (1998). Driving avoidance and functional impairment in older drivers. *Accident Analysis and Prevention, 30*(3), 313–322.

Ball, K., & Roenker, D. (1998). *Useful field of view.* San Antonio: The Psychological Corporation.

Ball, K. K., Beard, B. L., Roenker, D. L., Miller, R. L., & Griggs, D. S. (1988). Age and visual search: Expanding the useful field of view. *Journal of the Optical Society of America A. Optics and Image Science, 5*(12), 2210–2219.

Ball, K. K., Roenker, D. L., Wadley, V. G., Edwards, J. D., Roth, D. L., McGwin, G., Jr., et al. (2006). Can high-risk older drivers be identified through performance-based measures in a Department of Motor Vehicles setting? *Journal of the American Geriatrics Society, 54*(1), 77–84.

Barkley, R. A., & Cox, D. (2007). A review of driving risks and impairments associated with attention-deficit/hyperactivity disorder and the effects of stimulant medication on driving performance. *Journal of Safety Research, 38*(1), 113–128.

Barkley, R. A., Guevremont, D. C., Anastopoulos, A. D., DuPaul, G. J., & Shelton, T. L. (1993). Driving-related risks and outcomes of attention deficit hyperactivity disorder in adolescents and young adults: A 3- to 5-year follow-up survey. *Pediatrics, 92*(2), 212–218.

Barkley, R. A., Murphy, K. R., Dupaul, G. I., & Bush, T. (2002). Driving in young adults with attention deficit hyperactivity disorder: Knowledge, performance, adverse outcomes, and the role of executive functioning. *Journal of the International Neuropsychological Society, 8*(5), 655–672.

Barkley, R. A., Murphy, K. R., O'Connell, T., & Connor, D. F. (2005). Effects of two doses of methylphenidate on simulator driving performance in adults with attention deficit hyperactivity disorder. *Journal of Safety Research, 36*(2), 121–131.

Bedard, M., Molloy, D. W., & Lever, J. A. (1998). Factors associated with motor vehicle crashes in cognitively impaired older adults. *Alzheimer Disease and Associated Disorders, 12*(3), 135–139.

Biederman, J., Fried, R., Monuteaux, M. C., Reimer, B., Coughlin, J. F., Surman, C. B., et al. (2007). A laboratory driving simulation for assessment of driving behavior in adults with ADHD: A controlled study. *Annals of General Psychiatry, 6*, 4.

Bieliauskas, L. A., Roper, B. R., Trobe, J., Green, P., & Lacy, M. (1998). Cognitive measures, driving safety, and Alzheimer's disease. *Clinical Neuropsychologist, 12*(2), 206–212.

Blana, E., & Golias, J. (2002). Differences between vehicle lateral displacement on the road and in a fixed-base simulator. *Human Factors, 44*(2), 303–313.

Blatt, J., & Furman, S. M. (1998). Residence location of drivers involved in fatal crashes. *Accident Analysis and Prevention, 30*(6), 705–711.

Bobholz, J. A., & Rao, S. M. (2003). Cognitive dysfunction in multiple sclerosis: A review of recent developments. *Current Opinion in Neurology, 16*(3), 283–288.

Bocca, M. L., Le Doze, F., Etard, O., Pottier, M., L'Hoste, J., & Denise, P. (1999). Residual effect of zolpidem 10 mg and zopiclone 7.5 mg versus flunitrazepam 1 mg and placebo on driving performance and ocular saccades. *Psychopharmacology, 143*(4), 373–379.

British Psychological Society. (2001). *Fitness to drive and cognition: A document of the multi-disciplinary working party on acquired neuropsychological deficits and fitness to drive 1999.* Leicester, UK: The British Psychological Society.

Brookhuis, K. A., De Waard, D., & Fairclough, S. H. (2003). Criteria for driver impairment. *Ergonomics, 46*(5), 433–445.

Brouwer, W. H. (2002). Attention and driving: A cognitive neuropsychological approach. In M. Leclercq and P. Zimmerman (Eds.), *Applied neuropsychology of attention: Theory, diagnosis and rehabilitation* (pp. 230–254). Hove, UK: Psychology Press.

Brouwer, W. H., Withaar, F. K., Tant, M. L., & van Zomeren, A. H. (2002). Attention and driving in traumatic brain injury: A question of coping with time-pressure. *Journal of Head Trauma Rehabilitation, 17*(1), 1–15.

Cami, J., Farre, M., Mas, M., Roset, P. N., Poudevida, S., Mas, A., et al. (2000). Human pharmacology of 3,4-methylenedioxymethamphetamine ("ecstasy"): Psychomotor performance and subjective effects. *Journal of Clinical Psychopharmacology, 20*(4), 455–466.

Cole, B. L., & Hughes, P. K. (1990). Drivers don't search: They just notice. In D. Brogan (Ed.), *Visual search: Proceedings of the First International Conference on Visual Search.* University of Durham, England: Taylor and Francis.

Coleman, R. D., Rapport, L. J., Ergh, T. C., Hanks, R. A., Ricker, J. H., & Millis, S. R. (2002). Predictors of driving outcome after traumatic brain injury. *Archives of Physical Medicine and Rehabilitation, 83*(10), 1415–1422.

Collia, D. V., Sharp, J., & Giesbrecht, L. (2003). The 2001 national household travel survey: A look into the travel patterns of older Americans. *Journal of Safety Research, 34*(4), 461–470.

Consensus statements, sample statutory provisions, and model regulations regarding driver licensing and epilepsy. American Academy of Neurology, American Epilepsy Society, and Epilepsy Foundation of America. (1994). *Epilepsia, 35*(3), 696–705.

Cosentino, S., & Stern, Y. (2005). Metacognitive theory and assessment in dementia: Do we recognize our areas of weakness? *Journal of the International Neuropsychological Society, 11*(7), 910–919.

Cox, D. J., Gonder-Frederick, L. A., Kovatchev, B. P., & Clarke, W. L. (2002). The metabolic demands of driving for drivers with type 1 diabetes mellitus. *Diabetes/Metabolism Research and Reviews, 18*(5), 381–385.

Cox, D. J., Gonder-Frederick, L. A., Kovatchev, B. P., Julian, D. M., & Clarke, W. L. (2000a). Progressive hypoglycemia's impact on driving simulation performance. Occurrence, awareness and correction. *Diabetes Care, 23*(2), 163–170.

Cox, D. J., Humphrey, J. W., Merkel, R. L., Penberthy, J. K., & Kovatchev, B. (2004). Controlled-release methylphenidate improves attention during on-road driving by adolescents with attention-deficit/hyperactivity disorder. *Journal of the American Board of Family Practice, 17*(4), 235–239.

Cox, D. J., Merkel, R. L., Kovatchev, B., & Seward, R. (2000b). Effect of stimulant medication on driving performance of young adults with attention-deficit hyperactivity disorder: A preliminary double-blind placebo controlled trial. *Journal of Nervous and Mental Disease, 188*(4), 230–234.

Crundall, D., Chapman, P., Phelps, N., & Underwood, G. (2003). Eye movements and hazard perception in police pursuit and emergency response driving. *Journal of Experimental Psychology. Applied, 9*(3), 163–174.

Crundall, D., Underwood, G., & Chapman, P. (1999). Driving experience and the functional field of view. *Perception, 28*(9), 1075–1087.

Dahlen, E. R., Martin, R. C., Ragan, K., & Kuhlman, M. M. (2005). Driving anger, sensation seeking, impulsiveness, and boredom proneness in the prediction of unsafe driving. *Accident Analysis and Prevention, 37*(2), 341–348.

Daigneault, G., Joly, P., & Frigon, J. Y. (2002). Executive functions in the evaluation of accident risk of older drivers. *Journal of Clinical and Experimental Neuropsychology, 24*(2), 221–238.

Deffenbacher, J. L., Lynch, R. S., Deffenbacher, D. M., & Oetting, E. R. (2001). Further evidence of reliability and validity for the driving anger expression inventory. *Psychological Reports, 89*(3), 535–540.

Dickerson, A. E., Molnar, L. J., Eby, D. W., Adler, G., Bedard, M., Berg-Weger, M., et al. (2007). Transportation and aging: A research agenda for advancing safe mobility. *Gerontologist, 47*(5), 578–590.

Drazkowski, J. (2007). An overview of epilepsy and driving. *Epilepsia, 48*(Suppl 9), 10–12.

Dubinsky, R. M., Gray, C., Husted, D., Busenbark, K., Vetere-Overfield, B., Wiltfong, D., et al. (1991). Driving in Parkinson's disease. *Neurology, 41*(4), 517–520.

Dubinsky, R. M., Stein, A. C., & Lyons, K. (2000). Practice parameter: Risk of driving and Alzheimer's disease (an evidence-based review): Report of the quality standards subcommittee of the American Academy of Neurology. *Neurology, 54*(12), 2205–2211.

Dubinsky, R. M., Williamson, R. N., Gray, C. S., & Glatt, S. L. (1992). Driving in Alzheimer's disease. *Journal of the American Geriatrics Society, 40*, 1112–1116.

Duchek, J. M., Carr, D. B., Hunt, L., Roe, C. M., Xiong, C., Shah, K., et al. (2003). Longitudinal driving performance in early-stage dementia of the Alzheimer type. *Journal of the American Geriatrics Society, 51*(10), 1342–1347.

Duchek, J. M., Hunt, L., Ball, K., Buckles, V., & Morris, J. C. (1997). The role of selective attention in driving and dementia of the Alzheimer type. *Alzheimer Disease and Associated Disorders, 11*(Suppl 1), 48–56.

Duchek, J. M., Hunt, L., Ball, K., Buckles, V., & Morris, J. C. (1998). Attention and driving performance in Alzheimer's disease. *Journal of Gerontology, 53*(2), P130–P141.

Duncan, J., Williams, P., & Brown, I. (1991). Components of driving skill—experience does not mean expertise. *Ergonomics, 34*(7), 919–937.

Eby, D. W., Molnar, L. J., & Shope, J. T. (2000). *Driving decisions Workbook* (Report UMTRI-2000-14). Ann Abor: University of Michigan, Transportation Research Institute.

Eby, D. W., Molnar, L. J., Shope, J. T., Vivoda, J. M., & Fordyce, T. A. (2003). Improving older driver knowledge and self-awareness through self-assessment: The driving decisions workbook. *Journal of Safety Research, 34*(4), 371–381.

Edwards, J. D., Ross, L. A., Ackerman, M. L., Small, B. J., Ball, K. K., Bradley, S., et al. (2008). Longitudinal predictors of driving cessation among older adults from the ACTIVE clinical trial. *Journals of Gerontology. Series B, Psychological Sciences and Social Sciences, 63*(1), P6–P12.

Endsley, M. R. (1995). Toward a theory of situation awareness in dynamic systems. *Human Factors, 37*(1), 32–64.

Fain, M. J. (2003). Should older drivers have to prove that they are able to drive? *Archives of Internal Medicine, 163*(18), 2126–2128; discussion 2132.

Fell, J. C., & Voas, R. B. (2006). The effectiveness of reducing illegal blood alcohol concentration (BAC) limits for driving: Evidence for lowering the limit to .05 BAC. *Journal of Safety Research, 37*(3), 233–243.

Fisk, G. D., Novack, T., Mennemeier, M., & Roenker, D. (2002a). Useful field of view after traumatic brain injury. *Journal of Head Trauma Rehabilitation, 17*(1), 16–25.

Fisk, G. D., Owsley, C., & Mennemeier, M. (2002b). Vision, attention, and self-reported driving behaviors in community-dwelling stroke survivors. *Archives of Physical Medicine and Rehabilitation, 83*(4), 469–477.

Fisk, G. D., Schneider, J. J., & Novack, T. A. (1998). Driving following traumatic brain injury: Prevalence, exposure, advice and evaluations. *Brain Injury, 12*(8), 683–695.

Fitten, L. J. (2003). Driver screening for older adults. *Archives of Internal Medicine, 163*(18), 2129–2131; discussion 2131.

Fitten, L. J., Perryman, K. M., Wilkinson, C. J., Little, R. J., Burns, M. M., Pachana, N., et al. (1995). Alzheimer and vascular dementias and driving. A prospective road and laboratory study. *Journal of the American Medical Association, 273*(17), 1360–1365.

Foley, D. J., Masaki, K. H., Ross, G. W., & White, L. R. (2000). Driving cessation in older men with incident dementia. *Journal of the American Geriatrics Society, 48*(8), 928–930.

Fonda, S. J., Wallace, R. B., & Herzog, A. R. (2001). Changes in driving patterns and worsening depressive symptoms among older adults. *Journals of Gerontology. Series B, Psychological Sciences and Social Sciences, 56*(6), S343–S351.

Fox, G. K., Bowden, S. C., Bashford, G. M., & Smith, D. S. (1997). Alzheimer's Disease and driving: Prediction and assessment of driving performance. *Journal of the American Geriatrics Society, 45*, 949–953.

Fox, G. K., Bowden, S. C., & Smith, D. S. (1998). On-road assessment of driving competence after brain impairment: Review of current practice and recommendations for a standardized examination. *Archives of Physical Medicine and Rehabilitation, 79*(10), 1288–1296.

Franzen, M. D., & Wilhelm, K. L. (1996). Conceptual foundations of ecological validity in neuropsychological assessment. In R. J. S. C. J. Long (Ed.), *Ecological validity of neuropsychological testing* (pp. 91–112). Boca Raton, FL: St. Lucie Press.

Freeman, E. E., Munoz, B., Turano, K. A., & West, S. K. (2005). Measures of visual function and time to driving cessation in older adults. *Optometry and Vision Science, 82*(8), 765–773.

French, J. A., Kanner, A. M., Bautista, J., Abou-Khalil, B., Browne, T., Harden, C. L., et al. (2004). Efficacy and tolerability of the new antiepileptic drugs I: Treatment of new onset epilepsy: Report of the Therapeutics and Technology Assessment Subcommittee and Quality Standards Subcommittee of the American Academy of Neurology and the American Epilepsy Society. *Neurology, 62*(8), 1252–1260.

Freund, B., Colgrove, L. A., Burke, B. L., & McLeod, R. (2005). Self-rated driving performance among elderly drivers referred for driving evaluation. *Accident Analysis and Prevention, 37*(4), 613–618.

Freund, B., Gravenstein, S., Ferris, R., Burke, B. L., & Shaheen, E. (2005). Drawing clocks and driving cars. *Journal of General Internal Medicine, 20*(3), 240–244.

Freund, B., & Szinovacz, M. (2002). Effects of cognition on driving involvement among the oldest old: Variations by gender and alternative transportation opportunities. *Gerontologist, 42*(5), 621–633.

Fried, R., Petty, C. R., Surman, C. B., Reimer, B., Aleardi, M., Martin, J. M., et al. (2006). Characterizing impaired driving in adults with attention-deficit/hyperactivity disorder: A controlled study. *Journal of Clinical Psychiatry, 67*(4), 567–574.

Fuller, R. (1984). A conceptualization of driving behaviour as threat avoidance. *Ergonomics, 27*(11), 1139–1155.

Galski, T., Bruno, R. L., & Ehle, H. T. (1992). Driving after cerebral hemorrhage: A model with implications for evaluation. *The American Journal of Occupational Therapy, 46*, 324–332.

Galski, T., Bruno, R. L., & Ehle, H. T. (1993). Prediction of behind-the-wheel driving performance in patients with cerebral brain damage: A discriminant function analysis. *American Journal of Occupational Therapy, 47*(5), 391–396.

Galski, T., Ehle, H. T., & Bruno, R. L. (1990). An assessment of measures to predict the outcome of driving evaluations in patients with cerebral damage. *American Journal of Occupational Therapy, 44*(8), 709–713.

Galski, T., Ehle, H. T., & Williams, J. B. (1997). Off-road driving evaluations for persons with cerebral injury: A factor analytic study of pre-driver and simulator testing. *American Journal of Occupational Therapy, 51*(5), 352–359.

Gilley, D. W., Wilson, R. S., Bennett, D. A., Stebbins, G. T., Bernard, B. A., Whalen, M. E., et al. (1991). Cessation of driving and unsafe motor vehicle operation by dementia patients. *Archives of Internal Medicine, 151*(5), 941–946.

Gonzalez, R., Bechara, A., & Martin, E. M. (2007). Executive functions among individuals with methamphetamine or alcohol as drugs of choice: Preliminary observations. *Journal of Clinical and Experimental Neuropsychology, 29*(2), 155–159.

Grace, J., Amick, M. M., D'Abreu, A., Festa, E. K., Heindel, W. C., & Ott, B. R. (2005). Neuropsychological deficits associated with driving performance in Parkinson's and Alzheimer's disease. *Journal of the International Neuropsychological Society, 11*(6), 766–775.

Grotenhermen, F. (2007). The toxicology of cannabis and cannabis prohibition. *Chemistry and Biodiversity, 4*(8), 1744–1769.

Grotenhermen, F., Leson, G., Berghaus, G., Drummer, O. H., Kruger, H. P., Longo, M., et al. (2007). Developing limits for driving under cannabis. *Addiction, 102*(12), 1910–1917.

Guerrier, J. H., Manivannan, P., & Nair, S. N. (1999). The role of working memory, field dependence, visual search, and reaction time in the left turn performance of older female drivers. *Applied Ergonomics, 30*(2), 109–119.

Gugerty, L. J. (1997). Situation awareness during driving: Explicit and implicit knowledge in dynamic spatial memory. *Journal of Experimental Psychology-Applied, 3*(1), 42–66.

Hakamies-Blomqvist, L., & Siren, A. (2003). Deconstructing a gender difference: Driving cessation and personal driving history of older women. *Journal of Safety Research, 34*(4), 383–388.

Haslegrave, C. M. (1991). Driving for handicapped people. *International Disability Studies, 13*(4), 111–120.

Heaton, R. K., Grant, I., Butters, N., White, D. A., Kirson, D., Atkinson, J. H., et al. (1995). The HNRC 500--neuropsychology of HIV infection at different disease stages. HIV Neurobehavioral Research Center. *Journal of the International Neuropsychological Society, 1*(3), 231–251.

Heikkila, V. M., & Kallanranta, T. (2005). Evaluation of the driving ability in disabled persons: A practitioners' view. *Disability and Rehabilitation, 27*(17), 1029–1036.

Hilakivi, I., Veilahti, J., Asplund, P., Sinivuo, J., Laitinen, L., & Koskenvuo, K. (1989). A sixteen-factor personality test for predicting automobile driving accidents of young drivers. *Accident Analysis and Prevention, 21*(5), 413–418.

Hindrik, W., Robbe, J., & O'Hanlon, J. F. (1999). *Marijuana, alcohol, and actual driving performance.*

(Report No. DOT HS 808 939). Washington DC: National Highway Traffic Safety Administration; U.S. Department of Transportation.

Hobson, D. E., Lang, A. E., Martin, W. R., Razmy, A., Rivest, J., & Fleming, J. (2002). Excessive daytime sleepiness and sudden-onset sleep in Parkinson disease: A survey by the Canadian Movement Disorders Group. *Journal of the American Medical Association, 287*(4), 455–463.

Hopewell, C. A. (2002). Driving assessment issues for practicing clinicians. *Journal of Head Trauma Rehabilitation, 17*(1), 48–61.

Hunt, L., Morris, J. C., Edwards, D., & Wilson, B. S. (1993). Driving performance in persons with mild senile dementia of the Alzheimer type. *Journal of the American Geriatrics Society, 41*, 747–753.

Hunt, L. A., Murphy, C. F., Carr, D., Duchek, J. M., Buckles, V., & Morris, J. C. (1997a). Environmental cueing may effect performance on a road test for drivers with dementia of the Alzheimer type. *Alzheimer Disease and Associated Disorders, 11*(Suppl 1), 13–16.

Hunt, L. A., Murphy, C. F., Carr, D., Duchek, J. M., Buckles, V., & Morris, J. C. (1997b). Reliability of the Washington University Road Test. A performance-based assessment for drivers with dementia of the Alzheimer type. *Archives of Neurology, 54*(6), 707–712.

Hur, Y. M., & Bouchard, T. J., Jr. (1997). The genetic correlation between impulsivity and sensation seeking traits. *Behavior Genetics, 27*(5), 455–463.

Insurance Research Council. (1991). *Adequacy of motor vehicle records in evaluating driver performance.* Oak Brook, IL: Insurance Research Council.

Janke, M. K. (1991). Accidents, mileage, and the exaggeration of risk. *Accident Analysis and Prevention, 23*(2–3), 183–188.

Jerome, L., Segal, A., & Habinski, L. (2006). What we know about ADHD and driving risk: A literature review, meta-analysis and critique. *Journal of the Canadian Academy of Child and Adolescent Psychiatry, 15*(3), 105–125.

Jonah, B. A. (1997). Sensation seeking and risky driving: A review and synthesis of the literature. *Accident Analysis and Prevention, 29*(5), 651–665.

Jovanovski, D., Erb, S., & Zakzanis, K. K. (2005). Neurocognitive deficits in cocaine users: A quantitative review of the evidence. *Journal of Clinical and Experimental Neuropsychology, 27*(2), 189–204.

Kagerer, S., Winter, C., Moller, H. J., & Soyka, M. (2003). Effects of haloperidol and atypical neuroleptics on psychomotor performance and driving ability in schizophrenic patients. Results from an experimental study. *Neuropsychobiology, 47*(4), 212–218.

Kelly, E., Darke, S., & Ross, J. (2004). A review of drug use and driving: Epidemiology, impairment, risk factors and risk perceptions. *Drug and Alcohol Review, 23*(3), 319–344.

Korteling, J. E., & Kaptein, N. A. (1996). Neuropsychological driving fitness tests for brain-damaged subjects. *Archives of Physical Medicine and Rehabilitation, 77*(2), 138–146.

Kotterba, S., Orth, M., Eren, E., Fangerau, T., & Sindern, E. (2003). Assessment of driving performance in patients with relapsing-remitting multiple sclerosis by a driving simulator. *European Neurology, 50*(3), 160–164.

Kramer, A. F., Cassavaugh, N., Horrey, W. J., Becic, E., & Mayhugh, J. L. (2007). Influence of age and proximity warning devices on collision avoidance in simulated driving. *Human Factors, 49*(5), 935–949.

Kuypers, K. P., Samyn, N., & Ramaekers, J. G. (2006). MDMA and alcohol effects, combined and alone, on objective and subjective measures of actual driving performance and psychomotor function. *Psychopharmacology, 187*(4), 467–475.

Lawton, C., Cook, S., May, A., Clemo, K., & Brown, S. (2008). Postural support strategies of disabled drivers and the effectiveness of postural support aids. *Applied Ergonomics, 39*(1), 47–55.

Lee, H. C., Cameron, D., & Lee, A. H. (2003). Assessing the driving performance of older adult drivers: On-road versus simulated driving. *Accident Analysis and Prevention, 35*(5), 797–803.

Lee, J. D., & Strayer, D. L. (2004). Preface to the special section on driver distraction. *Human Factors, 46*(4), 583–586.

Lengenfelder, J., Schultheis, M. T., Al-Shihabi, T., Mourant, R., & DeLuca, J. (2002). Divided attention and driving: A pilot study using virtual reality technology. *Journal of Head Trauma Rehabilitation, 17*(1), 26–37.

Lenne, M. G., Dietze, P., Rumbold, G. R., Redman, J. R., & Triggs, T. J. (2003). The effects of the opioid pharmacotherapies methadone, LAAM and buprenorphine, alone and in combination with alcohol, on simulated driving. *Drug and Alcohol Dependence, 72*(3), 271–278.

Leon-Carrion, J., Dominguez-Morales, M. R., & Martin, J. M. (2005). Driving with cognitive deficits: Neurorehabilitation and legal measures are needed for driving again after severe traumatic brain injury. *Brain Injury, 19*(3), 213–219.

Lew, H. L., Poole, J. H., Lee, E. H., Jaffe, D. L., Huang, H. C., & Brodd, E. (2005). Predictive validity of driving-simulator assessments following traumatic brain injury: A preliminary study. *Brain Injury, 19*(3), 177–188.

Lezak, M. D. (1995). *Neuropsychological assessment* (3rd ed.). New York: Oxford University Press.

Lezak, M. D. (2004). *Neuropsychological assessment* (4th ed.). New York: Oxford University Press.

Liguori, A., Gatto, C. P., & Robinson, J. H. (1998). Effects of marijuana on equilibrium, psychomotor performance, and simulated driving. *Behavioural Pharmacology, 9*(7), 599–609.

Lincoln, N. B., & Radford, K. A. (2008). Cognitive abilities as predictors of safety to drive in people with multiple sclerosis. *Multiple Sclerosis, 14*(1), 123–128.

Lings, S. (2002). Driving accident frequency increased in patients with multiple sclerosis. *Acta Neurologica Scandinavica, 105*(3), 169–173.

Logan, B. K. (1996). Methamphetamine and driving impairment. *Journal of Forensic Sciences, 41*(3), 457–464.

Loring, D. W. (1999). *INS Dictionary of Neuropsychology.* New York: Oxford University Press.

Lundberg, C., Hakamies-Blomqvist, L., Almkvist, O., & Johansson, K. (1998). Impairments of some cognitive functions are common in crash-involved older drivers. *Accident Analysis and Prevention, 30*(3), 371–377.

Lundberg, C., Johansson, K., Ball, K., Bjerre, B., Blomqvist, C., Braekhus, A., et al. (1997). Dementia and driving: An attempt at consensus. *Alzheimer Disease and Associated Disorders, 11*(1), 28–37.

Lundqvist, A., & Alinder, J. (2007). Driving after brain injury: Self-awareness and coping at the tactical level of control. *Brain Injury, 21*(11), 1109–1117.

Madeley, P., Hulley, J. L., Wildgust, H., & Mindham, R. H. (1990). Parkinson's disease and driving ability. *Journal of Neurology, Neurosurgery and Psychiatry, 53*(7), 580–582.

Mapstone, M., Rosler, A., Hays, A., Gitelman, D. R., & Weintraub, S. (2001). Dynamic allocation of attention in aging and Alzheimer disease: Uncoupling of the eye and mind. *Archives of Neurology, 58*(9), 1443–1447.

Marcotte, T. D., Corey-Bloom, J., Rosenthal, T. J., Roberts, E., Lampinen, S., & Allen., R. W. (2008). The contribution of cognitive deficits and spasticity to driving performance in Multiple Sclerosi. *Archives of Physical Medicine and Rehabilitation, 89*(9), 1753–1758.

Marcotte, T. D., Heaton, R. K., Wolfson, T., Taylor, M. J., Alhassoon, O., Arfaa, K., et al. (1999). The impact of HIV-related neuropsychological dysfunction on driving behavior. *Journal of the International Neuropsychological Society, 5*(7), 579–592.

Marcotte, T. D., Lazzaretto, D., Scott, J. C., Roberts, E., Woods, S. P., Letendre, S., et al. (2006). Visual attention deficits are associated with driving accidents in cognitively-impaired HIV-infected individuals. *Journal of Clinical and Experimental Neuropsychology, 28,* 13–28.

Marcotte, T. D., & Scott, J. C. (2004). The assessment of driving abilities. *Advances in Transportation Studies: An International Journal,* 79–90.

Marcotte, T. D., Scott, J. C., Lazzaretto, D., & Rosenthal, T. J. (2004a). Long-term stability of standard deviation of lateral position in neurocognitively normal and impaired individuals. *Advances in Transportation Studies: An International Journal, December,* 57–65.

Marcotte, T. D., Wolfson, T., Rosenthal, T. J., Heaton, R. K., Gonzalez, R., Ellis, R. J., et al. (2004b). A multimodal assessment of driving performance in HIV infection. *Neurology, 63*(8), 1417–1422.

Marottoli, R. A. (1997). Crashes: Outcome of choice in assessing driver safety? *Alzheimer Disease and Associated Disorders, 11*(Suppl 1), 28–30.

Marottoli, R. A., Mendes de Leon, C. F., Glass, T. A., Williams, C. S., Cooney, L. M., Jr., Berkman, L. F., et al. (1997). Driving cessation and increased depressive symptoms: Prospective evidence from the New Haven EPESE. Established Populations for Epidemiologic Studies of the Elderly. *Journal of the American Geriatrics Society, 45*(2), 202–206.

Marottoli, R. A., Ness, P. H., Araujo, K. L., Iannone, L. P., Acampora, D., Charpentier, P., et al. (2007). A randomized trial of an education program to enhance older driver performance. *Journals of Gerontology. Series A, Biological Sciences and Medical Sciences, 62*(10), 1113–1119.

Marottoli, R. A., Richardson, E. D., Stowe, M. H., Miller, E. G., Brass, L. M., Cooney, L. M., Jr., et al. (1998). Development of a test battery to identify older drivers at risk for self-reported adverse driving events. *Journal of the American Geriatrics Society, 46*(5), 562–568.

Marshall, S., Man-Son-Hing, M., Molnar, F., Hunt, L., & Finestone, H. (2005). An exploratory study on the predictive elements of passing on-the-road tests for disabled persons. *Traffic Injury Prevention, 6*(3), 235–239.

Marshall, S. C., Molnar, F., Man-Son-Hing, M., Blair, R., Brosseau, L., Finestone, H. M., et al. (2007). Predictors of driving ability following stroke: A systematic review. *Topics in Stroke Rehabilitation, 14*(1), 98–114.

Mayhew, D. R., Simpson, H. M., & Pak, A. (2003). Changes in collision rates among novice drivers during the first months of driving. *Accident Analysis and Prevention, 35*(5), 683–691.

Mazer, B. L., Sofer, S., Korner-Bitensky, N., Gelinas, I., Hanley, J., & Wood-Dauphinee, S. (2003). Effectiveness of a visual attention retraining program on the driving performance of clients with stroke. *Archives of Physical Medicine and Rehabilitation, 84*(4), 541–550.

McGwin, G., Jr., Owsley, C., & Ball, K. (1998). Identifying crash involvement among older drivers: Agreement between self-report and state records. *Accident Analysis and Prevention, 30*(6), 781–791.

McKnight, A. J., & McKnight, A. S. (1999). Multivariate analysis of age-related driver ability and performance deficits. *Accident Analysis and Prevention, 31*(5), 445.

Meindorfner, C., Korner, Y., Moller, J. C., Stiasny-Kolster, K., Oertel, W. H., & Kruger, H. P. (2005). Driving in Parkinson's disease: Mobility, accidents, and sudden onset of sleep at the wheel. *Movement Disorders, 20*(7), 832–842.

Michon, J. (1985). A critical review of driver behavior models: What do we know, what should we do? In L. Evans and R. Schwing (Eds.), *Human behavior and traffic safety* (pp. 485–524). New York: Plenum.

Moller, J. C., Stiasny, K., Hargutt, V., Cassel, W., Tietze, H., Peter, J. H., et al. (2002). Evaluation of sleep and driving performance in six patients with Parkinson's disease reporting sudden onset of sleep under dopaminergic medication: A pilot study. *Movement Disorders, 17*(3), 474–481.

Molnar, F. J., Patel, A., Marshall, S. C., Man-Son-Hing, M., & Wilson, K. G. (2006). Clinical utility of office-based cognitive predictors of fitness to drive in persons with dementia: A systematic review. *Journal of the American Geriatrics Society, 54*(12), 1809–1824.

Morris, J. C., & Cummings, J. (2005). Mild cognitive impairment (MCI) represents early-stage Alzheimer's disease. *Journal of Alzheimer's Disease, 7*(3), 235–239; discussion 255–262.

Moskowitz, H., & Robinson, C. (1988). *Effects of low dose alcohol on driving related skills. A review of the evidence. (Technical Report DOT FT 807 280).* Springfield, VA: National Highway Traffic Safety Administration.

Moskowitz, H., & Smiley, A. (1982). Effects of chronically administered buspirone and diazepam on driving-related skills performance. *Journal of Clinical Psychiatry, 43*(12 Pt 2), 45–55.

Myers, R. S., Ball, K. K., Kalina, T. D., Roth, D. L., & Goode, K. T. (2000). Relation of useful field of view and other screening tests to on-road driving performance. *Perceptual and Motor Skills, 91*(1), 279–290.

National Highway Traffic Safety Administration. (1999). *Safe mobility for older people.* Washington, DC.: U.S. Department of Transportation. Publication No. HS 808 853.

National Highway Traffic Safety Administration. (2001). *Traffic safety facts 2000: Older population.* Washington, DC: U.S. Department of Transportation. Publication No. HS 809 328.

National Highway Traffic Safety Administration. (2004). *Traffic safety facts 2002: A compilation of motor vehicle crash data from the fatality analysis reporting system and the general estimates system.* Washington, DC: U.S. Department of Transportation. Publication No. HS 808 620.

National Highway Traffic Safety Administration. (2006). *Fatality analysis reporting system general estimates system: 2005 data summary.* Washington, DC: U.S. Department of Transportation. Publication No. HS 810 632.

Neale, V. L., Dingus, T. A., Klauer, S. G., Sudweeks, J., & Goodman, M. (2005). *An overview of the 100-car naturalistic study and findings* (No. 05–0400). Washington, DC: National Highway Traffic Safety Administration.

Novack, T. A., Banos, J. H., Alderson, A. L., Schneider, J. J., Weed, W., Blankenship, J., et al. (2006). UFOV performance and driving ability following traumatic brain injury. *Brain Injury, 20*(5), 455–461.

O'Hanlon, J. F., Brookhuis, K. A., Louwerens, J. W., & Volkerts, E. R. (1986). Performance testing as part of drug registration. In J. F. O'Hanlon and J. J. de Gier (Eds.), *Drugs and driving* (pp. 311–330). London: Taylor and Francis.

O'Neill, D., Neubauer, K., Boyle, M., Gerrard, J., Surmon, D., & Wilcock, G. K. (1992). Dementia and driving. *Journal of the Royal Society of Medicine, 85*(4), 199–202.

Odenheimer, G. L., Beaudet, M., Jette, A. M., Albert, M. S., Grande, L., & Minaker, K. L. (1994). Performance-based driving evaluation of the elderly driver: Safety, reliability, and validity. *Journal of Gerontology, 49*(4), M153–M159.

Ogden, E. J., & Moskowitz, H. (2004). Effects of alcohol and other drugs on driver performance. *Traffic Injury Prevention, 5*(3), 185–198.

Oltedal, S., & Rundmo, T. (2006). The effects of personality and gender on risky driving behaviour and accident involvement. *Safety Science, 44*(7), 621–628.

Orfei, M. D., Robinson, R. G., Prigatano, G. P., Starkstein, S., Rusch, N., Bria, P., et al. (2007). Anosognosia for hemiplegia after stroke is a multifaceted phenomenon: A systematic review of the literature. *Brain, 130*(Pt 12), 3075–3090.

Ott, B. R., Festa, E. K., Amick, M. M., Grace, J., Davis, J. D., & Heindel, W. C. (2008a). Computerized maze navigation and on-road performance by drivers with dementia. *Journal of Geriatric Psychiatry and Neurology, 21*(1), 18–25.

Ott, B. R., Heindel, W. C., Papandonatos, G. D., Festa, E. K., Davis, J. D., Daiello, L. A., et al. (2008b). A longitudinal study of drivers with Alzheimer disease. *Neurology, 70*(14), 1171–1178.

Ott, B. R., Heindel, W. C., Whelihan, W. M., Caron, M. D., Piatt, A. L., & DiCarlo, M. A. (2003). Maze test performance and reported driving ability in early dementia. *Journal of Geriatric Psychiatry and Neurology, 16*(3), 151–155.

Owsley. (1997). Clinical and research issues on older drivers: Future directions. *Alzheimer Disease and Associated Disorders, 11*(Suppl 1), 3–7.

Owsley, C., Ball, K., McGwin, G., Jr., Sloane, M. E., Roenker, D. L., White, M., et al. (1998). Visual processing impairment and risk of motor vehicle crash among older adults. *Journal of the American Medical Association, 279*(14), 1083–1088.

Owsley, C., & McGwin, G., Jr. (1999). Vision impairment and driving. *Survey of Ophthalmology, 43*(6), 535–550.

Owsley, C., McGwin, G., Jr., & McNeal, S. F. (2003). Impact of impulsiveness, venturesomeness, and empathy on driving by older adults. *Journal of Safety Research, 34*(4), 353–359.

Owsley, C., Stalvey, B., Wells, J., & Sloane, M. E. (1999). Older drivers and cataract: Driving habits and crash risk. *Journals of Gerontology. Series A, Biological Sciences and Medical Sciences, 54*(4), M203–M211.

Paaver, M., Eensoo, D., Pulver, A., & Harro, J. (2006). Adaptive and maladaptive impulsivity, platelet monoamine oxidase (MAO) activity and risk-admitting in different types of risky drivers. *Psychopharmacology, 186*(1), 32–40.

Palmer, B. W., Heaton, R. K., Gladsjo, J. A., Evans, J. D., Patterson, T. L., Golshan, S., et al. (2002). Heterogeneity in functional status among older outpatients with schizophrenia: Employment history, living situation, and driving. *Schizophrenia Research, 55*(3), 205–215.

Parasuraman, R., & Nestor, P. G. (1991). Attention and driving skills in aging and Alzheimer's disease. *Human Factors, 33*(5), 539–557.

Pettis, R. W. (1992). Tarasoff and the dangerous driver: A look at the driving cases. *Bulletin of the American Academy of Psychiatry and the Law, 20*(4), 427–437.

Pettis, R. W., & Gutheil, T. G. (1993). Misapplication of the Tarasoff duty to driving cases: A call for a reframing of theory. *Bulletin of the American Academy of Psychiatry and the Law, 21*(3), 263–275.

Pietrapiana, P., Tamietto, M., Torrini, G., Mezzanato, T., Rago, R., & Perino, C. (2005). Role of premorbid factors in predicting safe return to driving after severe TBI. *Brain Injury, 19*(3), 197–211.

Pizza, F., Contardi, S., Ferlisi, M., Mondini, S., & Cirignotta, F. (2008). Daytime driving simulation performance and sleepiness in obstructive sleep apnoea patients. *Accident Analysis and Prevention, 40*(2), 602–609.

Ponsford, A. S., Viitanen, M., Lundberg, C., & Johansson, K. (2008). Assessment of driving after stroke-A pluridisciplinary task. *Accident Analysis and Prevention, 40*(2), 452–460.

Radford, K., Lincoln, N., & Lennox, G. (2004). The effects of cognitive abilities on driving in people with Parkinson's disease. *Disability and Rehabilitation, 26*(2), 65–70.

Ramaekers, J. G. (2003). Antidepressants and driver impairment: Empirical evidence from a standard on-the-road test. *Journal of Clinical Psychiatry, 64*(1), 20–29.

Ramaekers, J. G., Berghaus, G., van Laar, M., & Drummer, O. H. (2004). Dose related risk of motor vehicle crashes after cannabis use. *Drug and Alcohol Dependence, 73*(2), 109–119.

Ramaekers, J. G., Kuypers, K. P., & Samyn, N. (2006). Stimulant effects of 3,4-methylenedioxymethamphetamine (MDMA) 75 mg and methylphenidate 20 mg on actual driving during intoxication and withdrawal. *Addiction, 101*(11), 1614–1621.

Ranney, T. A. (1994). Models of driving behavior: A review of their evolution. *Accident Analysis and Prevention, 26*(6), 733–750.

Rao, S. M., Leo, G. J., Bernardin, L., & Unverzagt, F. (1991). Cognitive dysfunction in multiple sclerosis. I. Frequency, patterns, and prediction. *Neurology, 41*(5), 685–691.

Rapoport, M. J., & Banina, M. C. (2007). Impact of psychotropic medications on simulated driving: A critical review. *CNS Drugs, 21*(6), 503–519.

Rapport, L. J., Hanks, R. A., Millis, S. R., & Deshpande, S. A. (1998). Executive functioning and predictors of falls in the rehabilitation setting. *Archives of Physical Medicine and Rehabilitation, 79*(6), 629–633.

Rebok, G. W., Bylsma, F. W., Keyl, P. M., Brandt, J., & Folstein, S. E. (1995). Automobile driving in Huntington's disease. *Movement Disorders, 10*(6), 778–787.

Reger, M. A., Welsh, R. K., Watson, G. S., Cholerton, B., Baker, L. D., & Craft, S. (2004). The relationship between neuropsychological functioning and driving ability in dementia: A meta-analysis. *Neuropsychology, 18*(1), 85–93.

Rizzo, M., & Kellison, I. L. (2004). Eyes, brains, and autos. *Archives of Ophthalmology, 122*(4), 641–647.

Rizzo, M., & Kellison, I. L. (in press). The brain on the road. In T. D. Marcotte and I. Grant (Eds.), *The neuropsychology of Everyday functioning.* New York: Guilford.

Rizzo, M., McGehee, D. V., Dawson, J. D., & Anderson, S. N. (2001). Simulated car crashes at intersections in drivers with Alzheimer disease. *Alzheimer Disease and Associated Disorders, 15*(1), 10–20.

Rizzo, M., Reinach, S., McGehee, D., & Dawson, J. (1997). Simulated car crashes and crash predictors in drivers with Alzheimer disease. *Archives of Neurology, 54*(5), 545–551.

Roenker, D. L., Cissell, G. M., Ball, K. K., Wadley, V. G., & Edwards, J. D. (2003). Speed-of-processing and driving simulator training result in improved driving performance. *Human Factors, 45*(2), 218–233.

Rosenbloom, T., Perlman, A., & Shahar, A. (2007). Women drivers' behavior in well-known versus less familiar locations. *Journal of Safety Research, 38*(3), 283–288.

Sacktor, N., McDermott, M. P., Marder, K., Schifitto, G., Selnes, O. A., McArthur, J. C., et al. (2002). HIV-associated cognitive impairment before and after the advent of combination therapy. *Journal of Neurovirology, 8*(2), 136–142.

Schanke, A. K., & Sundet, K. (2000). Comprehensive driving assessment: Neuropsychological testing and on-road evaluation of brain injured patients. *Scandinavian Journal of Psychology, 41*(2), 113–121.

Schmidt, I. W., Brouwer, W. H., Vanier, M., & Kemp, F. (1996). Flexible adaptation to changing task demands in severe closed head injury patients: A driving simulator study. *Applied Neuropsychology, 3*(3–4), 155–165.

Schultheis, M. T., Garay, E., & DeLuca, J. (2001). The influence of cognitive impairment on driving performance in multiple sclerosis. *Neurology, 56*(8), 1089–1094.

Schultheis, M. T., Garay, E., Millis, S. R., & Deluca, J. (2002). Motor vehicle crashes and violations among drivers with multiple sclerosis. *Archives of Physical Medicine and Rehabilitation, 83*(8), 1175–1178.

Schultheis, M. T., Hillary, F., & Chute, D. L. (2003). The neurocognitive driving test: Applying technology to the assessment of driving ability following brain injury. *Rehabilitation Psychology, 48*(4), 275–280.

Schultheis, M. T., Matheis, R. J., Nead, R., & DeLuca, J. (2002). Driving behaviors following brain injury: Self-report and motor vehicle records. *Journal of Head Trauma Rehabilitation, 17*(1), 38–47.

Schwebel, D. C., Ball, K. K., Severson, J., Barton, B. K., Rizzo, M., & Viamonte, S. M. (2007). Individual difference factors in risky driving among older adults. *Journal of Safety Research, 38*(5), 501–509.

Schwebel, D. C., Severson, J., Ball, K. K., & Rizzo, M. (2006). Individual difference factors in risky driving: The roles of anger/hostility, conscientiousness, and sensation-seeking. *Accident Analysis and Prevention, 38*(4), 801–810.

Scott, J. C., Woods, S. P., Matt, G. E., Meyer, R. A., Heaton, R. K., Atkinson, J. H., et al. (2007). Neurocognitive effects of methamphetamine: A critical review and meta-analysis. *Neuropsychology Review, 17*(3), 275–297.

Semple, S. J., Zians, J., Grant, I., & Patterson, T. L. (2005). Impulsivity and methamphetamine use. *Journal of Substance Abuse Treatment, 29*(2), 85–93.

Shiffrin, R. M., & Schneider, W. (1977). Controlled and automatic human information-processing 2. Perceptual learning, automatic attending, and a general theory. *Psychological Review, 84*(2), 127–190.

Shua-Haim, J. R., & Gross, J. S. (1996). The "co-pilot" driver syndrome. *Journal of the American Geriatrics Society, 44*(7), 815–817.

Simons, J. S., Oliver, M. N., Gaher, R. M., Ebel, G., & Brummels, P. (2005). Methamphetamine and alcohol abuse and dependence symptoms: Associations with affect lability and impulsivity in a rural treatment population. *Addictive Behaviors, 30*(7), 1370–1381.

Sivak, M., Olson, P. L., Kewman, D. G., Won, H., & Henson, D. L. (1981). Driving and perceptual/cognitive skills: Behavioral consequences of brain damage. *Archives of Physical Medicine and Rehabilitation, 62*(10), 476–483.

Sodhi, M., Reimer, B., & Llamazares, I. (2002). Glance analysis of driver eye movements to evaluate distraction. *Behavior Research Methods, Instruments, and Computers, 34*(4), 529–538.

Spooner, D. M., & Pachana, N. A. (2006). Ecological validity in neuropsychological assessment: A case for greater consideration in research with neurologically intact populations. *Archives of Clinical Neuropsychology, 21*(4), 327–337.

Squire, L. R. (1993). *Neuropsychology of memory* (2nd ed.). New York: The Guilford Press.

St Germain, S. A., Kurtz, M. M., Pearlson, G. D., & Astur, R. S. (2005). Driving simulator performance in schizophrenia. *Schizophrenia Research, 74*(1), 121–122.

Stephens, B., McCarthy, D. P., Marsiske, M., Classen, S., Shechtman, O., & Mann, W. C. (2005). International older driver consensus conference on assessment, remediation, and counseling for transportation alternatives: Summary and recommendations. *Physical and Occupational Therapy in Geriatrics, 23*(2/3), 103–121.

Stern, Y. (2006). Cognitive reserve and Alzheimer disease. *Alzheimer Disease and Associated Disorders, 20*(2), 112–117.

Stolwyk, R. J., Charlton, J. L., Triggs, T. J., Iansek, R., & Bradshaw, J. L. (2006). Neuropsychological function and driving ability in people with Parkinson's disease. *Journal of Clinical and Experimental Neuropsychology, 28*(6), 898–913.

Strahan, R. F., Mercier, C. R., Mercier, J. M., & O'Boyle, M. W. (1997). Personality structure of elderly drivers. *Perceptual and Motor Skills, 85*(2), 747–755.

Stuss, D. T., & Alexander, M. P. (2007). Is there a dysexecutive syndrome? *Philosophical Transactions of the Royal Society of London. Series B: Biological Sciences, 362*(1481), 901–915.

Stutts, J. C. (1998). Do older drivers with visual and cognitive impairments drive less? *Journal of the American Geriatrics Society, 46*(7), 854–861.

Stutts, J. C., Reinfurt, D. W., & Rodgman, E. A. (2001). The role of driver distraction in crashes: An analysis of 1995–1999 Crashworthiness Data System Data. *Annual Proceedings/Association for the Advancement of Automotive Medicine, 45*, 287–301.

Summala, H. (1996). Accident risk and driver behaviour. *Safety Science, 22*(1–3), 103–117.

Sundet, K., Goffeng, L., & Hofft, E. (1995). To drive or not to drive: Neuropsychological assessment for driver's license among stroke patients. *Scandinavian Journal of Psychology, 36*(1), 47–58.

Szlyk, J. P., Myers, L., Zhang, Y., Wetzel, L., & Shapiro, R. (2002). Development and assessment of a neuropsychological battery to aid in predicting driving performance. *Journal of Rehabilitation Research and Development, 39*(4), 483–496.

Szlyk, J. P., Seiple, W., & Viana, M. (1995). Relative effects of age and compromised vision on driving performance. *Human Factors, 37*(2), 430–436.

Tamietto, M., Torrini, G., Adenzato, M., Pietrapiana, P., Rago, R., & Perino, C. (2006). To drive or not to drive (after TBI)? A review of the literature and its implications for rehabilitation and future research. *NeuroRehabilitation, 21*(1), 81–92.

Thomas, R. E. (1998). Benzodiazepine use and motor vehicle accidents. Systematic review of reported association. *Canadian Family Physician, 44*, 799–808.

Tillmann, W. A., & Hobbs, G. E. (1949). The accident-prone automobile driver; a study of the psychiatric and social background. *American Journal of Psychiatry, 106*(5), 321–331.

Trobe, J. D., Waller, P. F., Cook-Flannagan, C. A., Teshima, S. M., & Bieliauskas, L. A. (1996). Crashes and violations among drivers with Alzheimer disease. *Archives of Neurology, 53*(5), 411–416.

Uc, E. Y., Rizzo, M., Anderson, S. W., Shi, Q., & Dawson, J. D. (2004). Driver route-following and safety errors in early Alzheimer disease. *Neurology, 63*(5), 832–837.

Uc, E. Y., Rizzo, M., Anderson, S. W., Shi, Q., & Dawson, J. D. (2005). Driver landmark and traffic sign identification in early Alzheimer's disease. *Journal of Neurology, Neurosurgery and Psychiatry, 76*(6), 764–768.

Uc, E. Y., Rizzo, M., Anderson, S. W., Shi, Q., & Dawson, J. D. (2006a). Unsafe rear-end collision avoidance in Alzheimer's disease. *Journal of the Neurological Sciences, 251*(1–2), 35–43.

Uc, E. Y., Rizzo, M., Anderson, S. W., Sparks, J., Rodnitzky, R. L., & Dawson, J. D. (2006b). Impaired visual search in drivers with Parkinson's disease. *Annals of Neurology, 60*(4), 407–413.

Uc, E. Y., Rizzo, M., Anderson, S. W., Sparks, J. D., Rodnitzky, R. L., & Dawson, J. D. (2006c). Driving with distraction in Parkinson disease. *Neurology, 67*(10), 1774–1780.

Underwood, G. (2007). Visual attention and the transition from novice to advanced driver. *Ergonomics, 50*(8), 1235–1249.

Underwood, G., Chapman, P., Brocklehurst, N., Underwood, J., & Crundall, D. (2003). Visual attention while driving: Sequences of eye fixations made by experienced and novice drivers. *Ergonomics, 46*(6), 629–646.

Valcour, V. G., Masaki, K. H., & Blanchette, P. L. (2002). Self-reported driving, cognitive status, and physician awareness of cognitive impairment. *Journal of the American Geriatrics Society, 50*(7), 1265–1267.

van Laar, M., Volkerts, E., & Verbaten, M. (2001). Subchronic effects of the GABA-agonist lorazepam and the 5-HT2A/2C antagonist ritanserin on driving performance, slow wave sleep and daytime sleepiness in healthy volunteers. *Psychopharmacology, 154*(2), 189–197.

van Laar, M. W., van Willigenburg, A. P., & Volkerts, E. R. (1995). Acute and subchronic effects of nefazodone and imipramine on highway driving, cognitive functions, and daytime sleepiness in healthy adult and elderly subjects. *Journal of Clinical Psychopharmacology, 15*(1), 30–40.

van Zomeren, A. H., Brouwer, W. H., & Minderhoud, J. M. (1987). Acquired brain damage and driving: A review. *Archives of Physical Medicine and Rehabilitation, 68*(10), 697–705.

Vermeeren, A., & O'Hanlon, J. F. (1998). Fexofenadine's effects, alone and with alcohol, on actual driving and psychomotor performance. *Journal of Allergy and Clinical Immunology, 101*(3), 306–311.

Verster, J. C., Bekker, E. M., de Roos, M., Minova, A., Eijken, E. J., Kooij, J. J., et al. (2008). Methylphenidate significantly improves driving performance of adults with attention-deficit hyperactivity disorder: A randomized crossover trial. *Journal of Psychopharmacology, 22*(3), 230–237.

Verster, J. C., Volkerts, E. R., & Verbaten, M. N. (2002). Effects of alprazolam on driving ability, memory functioning and psychomotor performance: A randomized, placebo-controlled study. *Neuropsychopharmacology, 27*(2), 260–269.

Vorona, R. D., & Ware, J. C. (2002). Sleep disordered breathing and driving risk. *Current Opinion in Pulmonary Medicine, 8*(6), 506–510.

Vrkljan, B. H., & Polgar, J. M. (2007). Driving, navigation, and vehicular technology: Experiences of older drivers and their co-pilots. *Traffic Injury Prevention, 8*(4), 403–410.

Wallis, T. S., & Horswill, M. S. (2007). Using fuzzy signal detection theory to determine why experienced and trained drivers respond faster than novices in a hazard perception test. *Accident Analysis and Prevention, 39*(6), 1177–1185.

Walter, H., Vetter, S. C., Grothe, J., Wunderlich, A. P., Hahn, S., & Spitzer, M. (2001). The neural correlates of driving. *Neuroreport, 12*(8), 1763–1767.

Wang, C. C., & Carr, D. B. (2004). Older driver safety: A report from the older drivers project. *Journal of the American Geriatrics Society, 52*(1), 143–149.

Wang, C. C., Kosinski, C. J., Schwartzberg, J. G., & Shanklin, A. V. (2003). *Physician's guide to assessing and counseling older drivers.* Washington, DC: National Highway Traffic Safety Administration.

Weiler, J. M., Bloomfield, J. R., Woodworth, G. G., Grant, A. R., Layton, T. A., Brown, T. L., et al. (2000). Effects of fexofenadine, diphenhydramine, and alcohol on driving performance: A randomized placebo-controlled trial in the Iowa Driving Simulator. *Annals of Internal Medicine, 132*, 354–363.

Wein, C., Koch, H., Popp, B., Oehler, G., & Schauder, P. (2004). Minimal hepatic encephalopathy impairs fitness to drive. *Hepatology, 39*(3), 739–745.

Whelihan, W. M., DiCarlo, M. A., & Paul, R. H. (2005). The relationship of neuropsychological functioning to driving competence in older persons with early cognitive decline. *Archives of Clinical Neuropsychology, 20*(2), 217–228.

Wild, K., & Cotrell, V. (2003). Identifying driving impairment in Alzheimer disease: A comparison of self and observer reports versus driving evaluation. *Alzheimer Disease and Associated Disorders, 17*(1), 27–34.

Wilde, G. J. S. (1982). The theory of risk hoeostasis: Implications for safety and health. *Risk Analysis, 2*, 209–225.

Willemsen, J., Dula, C. S., Declercq, F., & Verhaeghe, P. (2008). The Dula Dangerous Driving Index: An investigation of reliability and validity across cultures. *Accident Analysis and Prevention, 40*(2), 798–806.

Windsor, T. D., & Anstey, K. J. (2006). Interventions to reduce the adverse psychosocial impact of driving cessation on older adults. *Clinical Interventions in Aging, 1*(3), 205–211.

Wingen, M., Bothmer, J., Langer, S., & Ramaekers, J. G. (2005). Actual driving performance and psychomotor function in healthy subjects after acute and subchronic treatment with escitalopram, mirtazapine, and placebo: A crossover trial. *Journal of Clinical Psychiatry, 66*(4), 436–443.

Wingen, M., Ramaekers, J. G., & Schmitt, J. A. (2006). Driving impairment in depressed patients receiving long-term antidepressant treatment. *Psychopharmacology, 188*(1), 84–91.

Withaar, F. K., Brouwer, W. H., & van Zomeren, A. H. (2000). Fitness to drive in older drivers with cognitive impairment. *Journal of the International Neuropsychological Society, 6*(4), 480–490.

Wood, J. M. (2002). Age and visual impairment decrease driving performance as measured on a closed-road circuit. *Human Factors, 44*(3), 482–494.

Wood, J. M., Worringham, C., Kerr, G., Mallon, K., & Silburn, P. (2005). Quantitative assessment of driving performance in Parkinson's disease. *Journal of Neurology, Neurosurgery and Psychiatry, 76*(2), 176–180.

World Health Organization. (2004). *World report on road traffic injury prevention*. Geneva: World Health Organization.

Worringham, C. J., Wood, J. M., Kerr, G. K., & Silburn, P. A. (2006). Predictors of driving assessment outcome in Parkinson's disease. *Movement Disorders, 21*(2), 230–235.

Yale, S. H., Hansotia, P., Knapp, D., & Ehrfurth, J. (2003). Neurologic conditions: Assessing medical fitness to drive. *Clinical Medicine and Research, 1*(3), 177–188.

Yuen, H. K., Sharma, A. K., Logan, W. C., Gillespie, M. B., Day, T. A., & Brooks, J. O. (2008). Radiation dose, driving performance, and cognitive function in patients with head and neck cancer. *Radiotherapy and Oncology, 87*(2), 304–307.

Zesiewicz, T. A., Cimino, C. R., Malek, A. R., Gardner, N., Leaverton, P. L., Dunne, P. B., et al. (2002). Driving safety in Parkinson's disease. *Neurology, 59*(11), 1787–1788.

Zuckerman, M., Bone, R. N., Neary, R., Mangelsdorff, D., & Brustman, B. (1972). What is the sensation seeker? Personality trait and experience correlates of the Sensation-Seeking Scales. *Journal of Consulting and Clinical Psychology, 39*(2), 308–321.

28

Neuropsychological Function and Adherence to Medical Treatments

Steven A. Castellon, Charles H. Hinkin, Matthew J. Wright, and
Terry R. Barclay

A recurrent theme throughout this text is that neuropsychological assessment plays an important role in the characterization of various diseases and disorders. The methods to reliably measure cognitive functioning and the signature neuropsychological deficits associated with various disorders have been the traditional focus of most neuropsychology textbooks, this book included. More recently, however, as described in previous chapters, neuropsychologists and their colleagues are striving to bring a better empirical and clinical understanding of the *impact* of neuropsychological compromise on various aspects of "real-world" functioning, including driving, employment status, self-care, and money management. In this chapter, we review another important potential "real-world" consequence of neurocognitive impairment, its impact upon medication adherence.

In the following sections we present an overview of the current knowledge regarding the complex nature of adherence to medication regimens, with a specific focus on neurocognitive factors that are associated with adherence. We start by discussing the importance of adherence in disease control/management and the staggering costs of nonadherence, and review issues related to adherence measurement. The majority of the chapter specifically explores the effect of neurocognitive compromise on medication adherence, including the potential impact of comorbidities such as substance abuse and/or psychiatric disorder that can interact with cognitive dysfunction to affect adherence behavior.

We have chosen to focus on three specific populations, arguably those that have been best studied in regard to adherence and cognition. We will examine findings in both normal and pathological aging and also in HIV/AIDS. The chapter then introduces important theoretical models that have been developed to explain adherence behavior, including theories such as the Health Beliefs Model and Social Action Theory. Finally, we conclude with a brief review and discussion of interventions designed to improve treatment adherence in patients with cognitive compromise.

The Impact and Importance of Adherence

Former United States Surgeon General C. Everett Koop reminded us, "Drugs don't work if patients don't take them," and the clinical and scientific community has spent a lot of energy, time, and money attempting to figure out why some patients do not take their medications. For many medications to be fully beneficial, they require the individual taking them to closely follow a prescribed regimen, and successful adherence is typically associated with a variety of positive outcomes. Unfortunately, poor or suboptimal compliance to medication regimens is surprisingly common, economically staggering, and associated with greatly increased morbidity and mortality, including declines in overall health and increased risk of hospitalization as well as mortality (Callahan &

688

Wolinsky, 1995; Col et al., 1990; Ganguli et al., 2002; Gilmer et al., 2004; Hepke et al., 2004; Huybrechts et al., 2005; Sokol et al., 2005; Vik et al., 2006).

How common is poor adherence? It certainly depends on the specific disease, condition, or population being studied, the length of time that the given group is studied, and the methods used to study them. It also depends, of course, on the definition of adherence that is used, but, if adherence is defined as successfully taking one's expected medications at their expected times, some easily supported generalizations can be made. The literature suggests that adherence to medication regimens is, at best, moderate and almost always declines over time in chronic diseases (Benner et al., 2002; Dunbar-Jacob et al., 2000; Osterberg & Blaschke, 2005). In fact, in spite of association between poor adherence and adverse outcome, rates of compliance are lower than 50% in most studies (for review, see Dunbar-Jacob et al., 2000; Haynes et al., 2003). Adherence rates are often highest in clinical trials due to the increased attention and scrutiny that study participants receive and the more stringent selection criteria driving many trials, but even in clinical trial settings for chronic diseases, adherence rates only rarely exceed 75% (Osterberg & Blaschke, 2005). Rates of adherence are typically higher among patients with acute conditions compared to those with chronic conditions, and medication adherence rates tend to drop rapidly after the first 6 months of treatment (Benner et al., 2002; Haynes et al., 1996; Jackevicius et al., 2002). As we discuss in detail below, when adherence is assessed by means of patient self-report, rates tend to be higher, sometimes markedly so, than when adherence is measured using more objective indicators, such as pill counts or electronic monitoring (Arnsten et al., 2001; Levine et al., 2005).

The financial costs of poor adherence are difficult to accurately estimate but, even according to conservative estimates, impressive. A recent review in *JAMA* suggested that between one-third and two-thirds of all medically oriented hospital admissions were due, at least in part, to poor medication adherence, with an estimated annual cost approaching 100 billion dollars (Osterberg & Blaschke, 2005). Among the severely mentally ill, medication maintenance/

adherence is particularly important, as many patients will suffer symptomatic relapse and will then require hospitalization secondary to poor adherence. For example, the annual health-care costs associated with schizophrenia have been estimated at 32.5 billion dollars, the majority of which have been attributed to the direct or indirect effects of medication nonadherence (Thieda et al., 2003). Many patients, especially the elderly living on fixed incomes, will take less medication than prescribed in an attempt to lower or avoid costs, ironically putting themselves at much higher risk for higher costs secondary to acute illness and/or hospitalization (Briesacher et al., 2007).

Not only are adverse outcomes associated with nonadherence, but several positive outcomes are seen among the medically adherent. Adequate medication adherence can prevent, reduce, or modify the effects of many chronic illnesses and is generally associated with improved health outcomes (Gray et al., 2001; Horwitz et al., 1990). For example, it has been demonstrated that adherence to a consistent antihypertensive therapy is associated with a 35%–40% lower incidence of stroke, a 20%–25% reduction in myocardial infarction, and a more than 50% reduction in heart failure (Neal et al., 2000). A recent review by Sokol and colleagues (2005) found that among four of the leading drivers of health-care costs (diabetes, hypercholesterolemia, high blood pressure, and congestive heart failure), hospitalization rates were significantly lower for patients with high levels of medication adherence and that, for all conditions, a net economic gain—that is, higher costs for medication but lower overall costs, including hospitalization or acute, emergency care—is associated with good adherence as well (Sokol et al., 2005). A review of insurance company patients undergoing diabetes treatment found higher "sense of disease control" and higher overall "sense of well-being" among those who were more adherent—not surprisingly, these patients were also using fewer additional medical care services (Hepke et al., 2004).

Further testimony to the overall salience of medication adherence is the fairly dramatic proliferation of adherence-related research in the last several years, including studies designed to better understand how to improve treatment adherence, or at least modify risk of nonadherence. In fact, the World Health Organization recently published an evidence-based guide for clinicians and others to improve strategies of medication adherence (World Health Organization, 2003), recognizing the magnitude of the deleterious effects of nonadherence. Given the importance of adherence, it is not surprising that there is a rich literature associated with trying to better understand its predictors.

Defining and Measuring Adherence

Adherence can be defined broadly as the extent to which a person's behavior conforms to the advice or directives given them by their physician (Bruer, 1982). As it relates more specifically to pill-taking behavior, adherence is broadly defined as the degree to which patients take medications as prescribed by their health-care providers (Osterberg & Blaschke, 2005). An implied aspect of medication adherence is that medications are taken accurately, with the proper route of administration, in the correct dosage, at the appropriate time, and in accordance with any special instructions (Gould et al., 1999). Although there are several other types of adherence, including faithfully attending health-care appointments, implementing lifestyle changes (e.g., exercise, smoking cessation), and making dietary changes, the main focus of most clinical and research effort regarding adherence has been with pill-taking behavior.

Clearly, determining the causes of poor medication adherence and using that knowledge to structure effective interventions is critically needed. What the existing literature suggests so far is that treatment of nonadherence is a complex, multidetermined problem. Studies have found poor medication adherence to be associated with a host of factors, including cognitive function, substance use, psychiatric disturbance, regimen complexity, medication efficacy, the occurrence of side effects, and the chronicity of the disease/illness/condition being treated. Also, human factors (e.g., packaging and labeling of medication bottles, grade level at which health-related materials are written), physicians' interaction and communication style, patients' financial resources in relation to medication costs, degree of family or social support, patients' beliefs and attitudes regarding health, and level of health literacy have all been shown to impact adherence behavior. Of course, a combination of these factors may interact to impact adherence, and the same patient may show adherence difficulties for different reasons across time (e.g., when first started taking blood pressure medications, forgetfulness secondary to stroke, then, later in the disease course, felt the medication was too expensive and stopped refilling it) or across different medications at the same point in time (e.g., patients do not take their antidepressant medication because they feel it causes side effects, while they consistently skip their blood pressure medication because they do not believe it is really needed).

Adherence Measurement Methodologies

There are a number of techniques that have been used to measure medication adherence, all of which are characterized by unique strengths and weaknesses, with no single measurement gold standard as yet. These can be divided into techniques that are more objective, such as plasma drug levels and electronic measuring devices, and those that are more subjective, such as patient self-report or clinician ratings. Table 28–1 lists several of the methods for measuring adherence, which we briefly discuss below.

Subjective Methods

Self-Report. Self-report is perhaps the most commonly used technique for gathering adherence data. Reliance on patient self-report has several decided strengths, most notably its negligible cost and ease of data collection. However, there are several substantial limitations to this approach. Foremost, multiple studies have shown that many patients may overstate their actual adherence rates. For example, studies of HIV-infected adults have revealed that patient self-report, relative to electronic monitoring techniques, tends to be accurate among patients who candidly admit to poor adherence but may overestimate actual adherence rates by approximately 10%–20% among a large subset of patients

Table 28–1. Methods of Assessing Medication Adherence

Objective measures	Analog measures	Subjective measures
Blood Levels Pro: Plasma drug levels can be used as objective markers of medication adherence. Con: Only useful for recently taken medications; not useful for ascertaining adherence rates unless frequent blood draws are completed.	*Laboratory Performances* Pro: Assesses the ability to self-administer and manage fictitious medications (e.g., sorting, planning for trips). Con: The relationship between laboratory and objective measures is not well studied. Con: Laboratory tasks may not simulate participant's true medication regimen demands.	*Self-Report* Pro: Simple collection (e.g., verbal report, questionnaire endorsements). Con: Biased toward overestimating rates of adherence. Con: Degree of bias often varies as a function of participant characteristics (e.g., personality, motives).
Pill Counts Pro: Straightforward approach given that initial pill count, number of pills to be-taken, and the number of pills remaining after the study period. Con: Participants can easily adjust their pill counts to appear more adherent. This can be reduced by conducting unannounced pill counts.	*Virtual Reality Performances* Pro: Virtual environment can simulate real-world settings in which medication management can be assessed. Con: The association between virtual reality and real-world measures are unclear. Con: Some older participants may have difficulty adapting to the virtual reality environment.	*Clinician Ratings* Pro: Clinical rating scales regarding a participant's acceptance of and level of participation in their medication regimen are easily obtained. Con: Participants often portray their attitudes toward medication adherence as being more favorable than they actually are and clinical ratings tend to overestimate adherence rates.
Electronic Monitoring [Medication Event Monitoring System (MEMS)] Pro: MEMS utilizes pill bottle caps with a microchip that records date, time, and duration of pill bottle opening. Con: The MEMS cap pill bottle is bulky, which can result in participants' removing extra doses from the bottle for later use ("pocket dosing"). Con: MEMS cap use precludes the use of pillbox organizers.		
Pharmacy Refill Records Pro: Cost-effective alternative method for the indirect measurement of adherence. Con: Requires centralized pharmacy records (e.g., Veterans Administration Medical Centers computerized records). Con: Assumes that participants refilling their medications in a timely manner are adherent.		

who claim perfect or near-perfect adherence (Arnsten et al., 2001; Levine et al., 2005).

Pill Counts. Pill counts are another technique that have been used to measure adherence rates. Similar to self-report, the benefits of a

pill count include its minimal cost and ease of data collection. The technique itself is relatively straightforward. If one knows how many pills a patient initially possessed and how many pills they should have ingested in the intervening time period, it is easy to calculate the number of pills that should remain at the end of the study period. Excess doses are therefore considered to reflect doses not taken as prescribed. For example, consider a patient on a regimen of 3 pills/day who begins with 100 pills and returns to clinic 30 days later. If 10 pills remain, that would be interpreted as perfect adherence $(100 - (30 \times 3) = 10)$. While easy for the researcher/clinician to calculate, a decided drawback is that this is easy for patients to calculate as well. Accordingly, prior to their return to clinic, patients may remove extra doses from their pill bottle and thus appear more adherent than is actually the case.

David Bangsberg and his colleagues at UCSF (Bangsberg et al., 2001) have introduced an innovative approach to overcome this limitation. They conduct "unannounced pill counts" and appear at participants' residences without warning to conduct pill counts. They have found this approach to correlate well with biologic outcomes (e.g., HIV viral load). While this methodology works well in a dense urban community, it would be excessively cumbersome for use in sparsely populated rural settings or in a sprawling metropolis without public transportation such as Los Angeles. To overcome such geographical difficulties, Kalichman and colleagues (2007) have adapted this technique and have attempted unannounced pill counts conducted by telephone; they have found this method to correlate highly with unannounced in-person pill counts.

Objective Methods

Electronic Measuring Devices. The above referenced limitations associated with self-report may be particularly pronounced when dealing with individuals with neurocognitive impairment. Patients with dementia frequently encounter difficulty recalling whether they took their prescribed medication. This is especially problematic when self-reported adherence rates are assessed over lengthier time periods. For this reason, the utilization of electronic monitoring devices (e.g., Medication Event Monitoring System [MEMS], Aprex Corp, Union City, California) may provide a more accurate measure of actual adherence rates. MEMS caps employ a computer chip that is embedded in the top of a pill bottle that

automatically records the date, time, and duration of pill bottle opening. Although electronic monitoring devices are not without their own limitations, a number of studies have demonstrated their incremental validity relative to pill counts or self-reports, which frequently overestimate adherence rates. Drawbacks of this method include the bulky nature of the MEMS cap bottle, which precludes inconspicuous transportation of one's medications. This can lead to behavior called "pocket-dosing" in which patients remove an extra dose from their pill bottle to consume at a later point in time rather than carry their pill bottle with them. Also, in the past, the use of MEMS devices has precluded use of daily/weekly pill organizers, although technological advances are now emerging that will overcome this limitation in the future.

Pharmacy Refill Records. Pharmacy refill records have been shown to be a cost-effective means of gathering indirect data regarding medication adherence. This technique is predicated on the assumption that if patients are refilling their medication prescriptions in a timely fashion, then they are more likely to be taking their medication as prescribed as compared to individuals who are tardy in refilling their prescriptions. This approach works best in settings where pharmacy records are centralized and can be easily attained (e.g., in Veterans Administration Medical Centers).

Biologic Markers. Blood levels provide precise quantification of adherence for medications with a long half-life. For example, blood tests are an excellent means for ascertaining lithium levels and, by extension, whether patients with bipolar disorder are indeed taking their lithium carbonate as prescribed. In contrast, blood tests are not as useful for evaluating adherence rates for medications that are rapidly metabolized. In such cases blood levels can detect whether patients have *recently* taken their medications but cannot assist in determining whether patients *typically* take their medication as prescribed.

Laboratory-Based Analog Measures

In addition to assessing actual medication adherence, several investigators have developed laboratory-based measures thought to be reflective of one's ability to adhere to medical recommendations. Coincidentally, two separate groups of investigators (Albert et al., 1999; Gurland et al., 1994) independently developed analog measures of medication management skills by the same name—The Medication Management Test (MMT). Gurland et al.'s version (MMT-Gurland) was initially developed to assess the ability of older adults to self-administer medications, while Albert et al.'s edition (MMT-Albert) was created to assess medication management skills among HIV-infected individuals. Both tests entail sorting, organizing, and making inferences about fictitious medications (e.g., when a prescription would need to be refilled). The MMT-Albert is more in-depth and requires 15–25 minutes to administer; the MMT-Gurland takes approximately 5 minutes to administer. The MMT-Gurland has been shown to be associated with cognitive decline in older adults (Fulmer & Gurland, 1997; Gurland et al., 1994). The MMT-Albert has been associated with cognitive deficits in HIV-infected individuals, specifically difficulties in memory, executive, and motor functioning (Albert et al., 1999, 2003). The MMT-Albert has been further revised by Patterson et al. (2002; Medication Management Ability Assessment; MMAA) and Heaton et al. (2004; Medication Management Test-Revised; MMT-R). Heaton et al.'s adaptation included reordering test items by ascending order of difficulty, rewording some test items and the mock medication insert, as well as reducing the number of fictitious medications (from 5 to 3) and inference items (from 15 to 7). The MMT-R requires approximately 10 minutes to administer and has been shown to correlate with neuropsychological deficits in executive function and memory in HIV-infected individuals (Heaton et al., 2004). To better characterize the possible medication management problems faced by individuals suffering from schizophrenia, the MMAA was modified from the MMT-Albert to better mimic interactions between patients and prescribing physicians (Patterson et al., 2002). It also requires examinees to demonstrate how they would self-administer medications after a 1-hour delay. Performance on the MMAA has been associated with memory and executive abilities of schizophrenic participants (Jeste

et al., 2003; Patterson et al., 2002). Interestingly, the MMAA was recently studied in relationship to a virtual reality (VR) task designed to simulate the medication-taking environment of schizophrenic participants (Baker et al., 2006). Like the MMAA, the experimental VR task correlated with memory and executive functioning, but it also showed significant relationship with sustained attention.

Impact of Cognitive Function on Adherence in Select Populations

Normal Aging

Among elderly individuals, medication adherence is particularly salient as older persons consume a disproportionate amount of prescription medications. In North America, individuals over the age of 65 make up approximately 15% of the population but consume nearly 35%–40% of all prescription medications (Vik et al., 2006). Elderly patients are at much greater likelihood of suffering from chronic disease that will require some degree of adherence to one or more drugs (Gurwitz et al., 2003; Vik et al., 2004; Williams & Kim, 2005). In fact, it has been estimated that upward of 70% of all ambulatory, noninstitutionalized elderly persons take some form of medication, and often multiple medications. Unfortunately, estimates of suboptimal medication adherence among this group of elderly, noninstitutionalized patients approach (or even slightly exceed) 50% in many studies (Barat et al., 2001; Dolder et al., 2003; Gray et al., 2001; Salzman, 1995). As stated above, the risk for adherence failure is accentuated in individuals suffering from chronic diseases, and therefore antihypertensive medications, lipid-lowering drugs, and antiarthritic medications are among the most common victims of nonadherence in elderly individuals (Bennet et al., 2002; Chapman et, al., 2005).

Well known to neuro- and geropsychologists are the cognitive changes that can accompany the aging process. Normal aging often results in some degree of slowing of processing speed, difficulty with more complex or divided attention, and a mild decline in working memory and executive functions (Bennett et al., 2002; Rabbitt & Lowe, 2000). While there is considerable individual variability among elderly individuals across all of these cognitive domains, many adults over the age of 65 will show these characteristic cognitive changes. There is also often some degree of decline in the efficiency of information retrieval, especially for more recently learned information, which can lead to difficulty recalling names and places. Changes in episodic memory retrieval functions often occur with relative sparing of procedural memory and basic memory storage ability (Fleischman & Gabrieli, 1998). Similarly, older adults often show less efficient prospective memory than their younger counterparts (Einstein & McDaniel, 1990). Some of these cognitive changes likely contribute to the difficulties with adherence seen in some older adults (Einstein et al., 1998; Raz, 2000).

In fact, one of the most frequently reported causes for medication nonadherence among the elderly is "forgetfulness" (Brainin, 2001; Leirer et al., 1988). Col and colleagues (1990) reported that poor memory recall had a stronger relationship to treatment nonadherence than did any other of a host of predictors (odds ratio = 7.1) in a nondemented elderly sample. Poor medication adherence may be influenced by two different types of memory deficit, difficulties with retrospective and/or prospective memory. Morell et al. (1990) suggested that patients employ retrospective memory to remember the correct way to take their medication and must use prospective memory to do so at the right time. Morrell and colleagues (1990) reported multiple challenges to successful adherence among older individuals, relative to their younger counterparts. First, older persons showed less efficient recall of drug instructions than did younger controls. Second, while both young and older adults have more difficulty recalling medication regimens as they became more complex, often the older patients are more likely to be on more complex medication regimens. A recent study of predictors of adherence in elderly primary care clinic patients showed that memory scores on a cognitive screening scale were predictive of missed appointments (Mackin & Arean, 2007). It is interesting to note that in this study, while lower memory scores predicted more frequent missed appointments, there was no relationship found between lower memory scores and the patient's self-report of medication adherence (Mackin & Arean, 2007).

Deficits in comprehension have been associated with suboptimal adherence to medication instructions, including those written on the label of the pill bottle, pamphlets accompanying the medications, and those verbally given by the patient's health-care provider (Diehl et al., 1995; Kendrick & Bayne, 1982). For example, Kendrick and Bayne (1982) reported that older adults had difficulty translating instructions seemingly as straightforward as "Take every 6 hours" into a specific medication plan, and Hurd and Butkovich (1986) found that a majority of older individuals made errors when interpreting prescription labels. Similarly, Morrell et al. (1989, 1990) found that about 25% of the information in a medication plan was misunderstood by older adults when they were presented with an array of prescription labels and asked to develop a medication schedule based on the instructions. Others have demonstrated that older adults have particular difficulty with comprehension of text when inferences are required (Cohen, 1981).

In addition to age-related decrements in memory and comprehension abilities, declines in sensorimotor function, attention, and visuoperceptual ability have been shown to be associated with adherence to medication regimens (Conn et al., 1994; Isaac & Tamblyn, 1993; Stilley et al., 2004). Age-related declines in visual functioning have been well documented and include reduced visual acuity, diminished perception of peripheral targets, and poorer color discrimination (Kline & Scialfa, 1997). Deterioration in perceptual acuity may interfere with the patient's ability to discriminate basic information about the medication (s) they are being asked to adhere to, including such factors as pill tablet color and shape (Hurd & Butkovich, 1986). In some cases, impaired motor function may be related to problems with opening medication bottles and effectively cutting/scoring pills (Isaac & Tamblyn, 1993). With regard to attentional abilities, Zacks and Hasher (1997) reported that older adults are less efficient in their ability to both direct and focus their attention as well as to inhibit attention to irrelevant information. Similarly, older adults have been found to be highly susceptible to both internal and external distraction over delays (Rekkas, 2006). Such deficits may be particularly problematic when older individuals are faced with the administration of multiple medications and complex drug regimens. Indeed, noncompliance has been shown to increase dramatically among the elderly in relation to the number of drugs prescribed (Fernandez et al., 2006; Wandless & Davie, 1987). For example, dosage errors in one study increased 15-fold among older patients when the number of drugs prescribed was increased from 1 to 4 (Parkin et al., 1986). Similarly, noncompliance was found to be 3.6 times more prevalent among elderly patients using two or more pharmacies to fill their prescriptions than among those using only one (Col et al., 1990).

Medication adherence also involves working memory and other components of executive functioning. Working memory, the capacity to process, manipulate, and temporarily store new or recently accessed information, has also been found to decline with age (Craik & Jennings, 1992; Park et al., 1996) and therefore negatively impact medication-taking behaviors. In the context of medication management, individuals must keep the intention to take their medicines in working memory while doing other things and must further rely upon these functions to integrate and develop a medication plan for following multiple drug regimens simultaneously. Planning and the ability to monitor the success of that plan and modify the plan if needed are functions that are dependent upon intact executive functioning. Arguably the cognitive domain most implicated in successful adherence to medication regimen is executive functioning (Ownby, 2006), and Insel and colleagues have shown that to be the case in the elderly as well (Insel et al., 2006).

Of course, other noncognitive factors negatively impact adherence among the elderly, some of which may interact with cognitive compromise. Financial factors may be an especially salient concern among the elderly, many of whom are living on reduced and/or fixed income. Many older patients note that they cannot afford to buy one or more of the prescribed medications (Piette & Heisler, 2004) and, consequently, skip or take partial doses of various medications. In some elderly populations, increased social isolation likely impacts adherence, and there is some evidence to suggest that the overall health literacy among the elderly is poorer than that seen in nonelderly populations (Council on Scientific Affairs, 1999). Health literacy will surely impact comprehension of instructions provided by the treatment team (written and oral) and adherence to medical instructions (Baker et al., 1998). As a strong example of the impact of health literacy, a large study of Medicare patients from a managed care plan encompassing four cities showed that a third of their English-speaking and more than one-half of Spanish-speaking respondents had inadequate to marginal health literacy (Gazmararian et al., 1999). In this sample, only 12% of respondents understood the correct timing of dosing medications, and only 16% understood how to take a medication on an empty stomach (Gazmararian et al., 1999).

Dementia

In general, there have been fewer investigations of medication adherence behavior in patients with mild cognitive impairment (MCI) or frank dementia syndromes, although more recently some relevant studies are starting to emerge (Cotrell et al., 2006). A recent large-scale study of medication adherence in elderly individuals from 11 European countries found that the presence of cognitive dysfunction, as measured by fairly broad screening instruments, was associated with increased risk for nonadherence (Cooper et al., 2005). It is impossible to determine the contribution of various types of cognitive dysfunction (e.g., memory versus executive dysfunction versus visuospatial deficits) as the screening measure used produces only an "impairment" score and specifies only the degree, not the specific nature of the impairment detected. These authors noted that the vast majority of those who scored poorly on the cognitive screening measure—in a range suggestive of possible dementia—were not formally diagnosed with a cognitive disorder at the time of the assessment (Cooper et al., 2005). Tierney and her colleagues (2007) recently reported results from a fairly large ($n = 160$) convenience sample of persons over 65 living alone, focusing on the relationship between self-care and neuropsychological functioning. They reported that among those with low scores on the Dementia Rating Scale (DRS), three specific neurocognitive tasks, measuring memory, executive functioning, and conceptualization, were associated with increased risk of having experienced some instance of self-harm or neglect, including medication failures. Indeed, patients with dementing illnesses such as Alzheimer's disease typically have difficulty not only remembering which medications they are taking but also the reason for their use, as a result of disruptions in short-term memory, judgment, insight, and, not infrequently, depression (Ayalon et al., 2006; Mackin & Arean, 2007).

The importance of executive functioning, as alluded to above, cannot be overstated as it relates to adherence. Executive abilities include the ability to plan, initiate, monitor, and inhibit complex, goal-directed behavior. Several studies have found patients with executive functioning deficits are more likely to resist care and are less likely to comply with medication regimens (Allen et al., 2003; Hinkin et al., 2002; Schillerstrom et al., 2005; Stewart et al., 1999). In one study, executive impairment explained 28% of the variance in the performance of activities of daily living in patients with Alzheimer's disease (Boyle et al., 2003).

Several aspects/types of memory require intact executive functions for efficient operation, and some of these tasks may be particularly important for medication adherence. Taking medicines consistently involves developing and implementing a plan to adhere, remembering to adhere (which typically requires both time-based [e.g., take medications at 5:00 p.m.] and event-based prospective remembering [e.g., take medications with food]), and remembering whether the medicine was taken as desired (described as source monitoring). Patients with executive functioning deficits typically show problems with both prospective memory and source monitoring.

Impaired executive functions may contribute to poor medication adherence in a number of ways. For example, individuals with deficits in such higher-order abilities may fail to take their medications because they cannot maintain the cognitive representation related to the need for medication in the face of other events. Similarly, persons with executive dysfunction may fail to organize their schedule in a manner necessary to accommodate medication taking. On the other hand, such individuals may perseverate on medication taking and unintentionally overdose. Moreover, executive deficits may contribute to faulty reasoning that medication adherence is not necessary or that alternative doses or regimens are acceptable.

Additional studies have demonstrated that, in at least some cases, the functional loss associated with executive impairments may be behaviorally mediated by apathy. Indeed, apathy has been associated with executive impairments in patients with various forms of cognitive impairment, including dementia (Castellon et al., 2000; Royall et al., 2000). For example, Boyle et al. (2003) demonstrated that executive impairment and apathy scores contributed to 44% of the variance in instrumental activities of daily living in patients with Alzheimer's disease. Given that executive functions are involved in behaviors associated with motivation, disruption of the neural circuitry maintaining these higher-order processes may lead to apathy and subsequent functional impairment, resistance to care, and impaired decision-making capacity.

HIV/AIDS

Our group has engaged in several studies designed to identify factors that are associated with medication adherence, with a particular emphasis on neurocognitive factors. We present an overview of the primary findings from these studies to illustrate how neurocognitive dysfunction can adversely affect medication adherence in a disease that requires meticulous adherence to an often demanding and unforgiving regimen over extended periods of time. We should mention here that other groups have studied neurocognitive predictors of adherence in HIV/AIDS, either in isolation or in combination with other predictors (e.g., Avants et al., 2001; Solomon & Halkitis, 2007; Wagner, 2002; Waldrop-Valverde et al., 2006). While some have found similar cognitive predictors (e.g., Avants et al., 2001; Solomon & Halkitis, 2007), others have reported somewhat different findings (see Waldrop-Valverde et al., 2006)—perhaps a function of demographic differences seen among the different samples studied and differences in testing battery depth and coverage.

In an early study conducted by our group, we found that medication adherence rates are adversely affected by HIV-associated neurocognitive dysfunction (Hinkin et al., 2002). In this study we administered a battery of neuropsychological tests to a cohort of 137 HIV-infected adults and collected adherence data using an electronic monitoring device (MEMS cap). The mean adherence rate across all 137 participants was 80%. Only 34% (46/137) of participants were classified as good adherers (≥95% of doses taken as scheduled), whereas fully two-thirds of subjects showed suboptimal adherence, often dramatically so. We found that those who were classified as cognitively compromised (global T-score less than 40) had a mean adherence rate of only 70% while neuropsychologically normal subjects' mean adherence rate was 82%. Post hoc analyses revealed that deficits in executive function and higher-order attentional processing were the primary deficits underlying this finding. Surprisingly, in this study memory dysfunction was not related to poor adherence. While the cognitively compromised participants demonstrated poorer adherence in general, this was particularly pronounced when they had to adhere to a more complex medication regimen. As can be seen in Figure 28–1, cognitively compromised subjects who were prescribed complex dosage regimens (defined in that study as a t.i.d schedule) demonstrated the greatest degree of difficulty with adherence. Complex regimens were not nearly as problematic for the neurocognitively intact subjects.

The interplay between person-specific factors and medication-specific factors is of critical importance. Complex regimens, complicated labeling, poorly designed dispensing devices, and so on may all adversely affect medication adherence. However, our data suggests that patients with cognitive and/or physical limitations may be at particular risk. With advancing age, motor and sensory limitations, for example, loss of visual acuity, may affect the ability to read the fine print on medication inserts, and peripheral motor dysfunction can lead to difficulty opening pill bottles. Our group as well as others have also found that advancing age can potentiate the adverse neurocognitive effects of

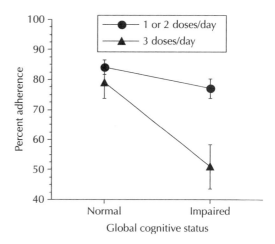

Figure 28–1. Relationship between cognitive status, regimen complexity, and medication adherence among HIV-infected adults.

HIV infection. The impact of age-related neurocognitive dysfunction on medication adherence can also be readily seen. Below we present data showing the interplay of poor adherence, advancing age, and neurocognitive dysfunction (Hinkin et al., 2004). After grouping subjects based on age (using age 50 as a cut point) and adherence rates (≥90% adherence = good adherence; <90% = poor adherence), we found that older subjects who were poor adherers performed disproportionately poorly on neuropsychological testing (See Figure 28–2). Additive effects of other frequently co-occurring risk factors such as Hepatitis C infection, drug use, and psychiatric disturbance can also be expected to similarly interact with neurocognitive dysfunction to adversely affect activities of daily function.

We recently conducted another series of analyses in which we explored the possible moderating effects of age on relationships between neurocognitive functioning, health beliefs, and medication adherence in a sample of 431 HIV-infected participants (Ettenhofer et al., in submission). Adherence to antiretroviral medication was tracked prospectively for approximately 30 days using the MEMS caps electronic monitoring system and self-report. Structural equation modeling (SEM) was used to evaluate models of the variable relationships, with estimates obtained separately for younger individuals (age

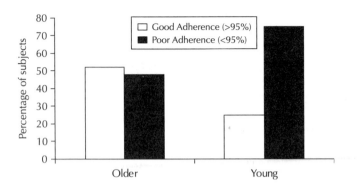

Figure 28–2. Medication adherence in younger (<50 years) and older (≥50 years) HIV-infected adults.

< 50; n = 352) and older individuals (age ≥ 50; n = 79). As can be seen in Figure 28–3 neurocognitive functioning was significantly related to adherence for older participants (r = .38, p < .05), but not for younger participants (r = .09, p > .05). Executive functioning, the cognitive domain that had the strongest loading for both younger and older participants appears to account for much of this relationship. These findings suggest that neurocognitive functioning is a potent predictor of medication adherence for HIV-infected individuals age 50 and over, but not for individuals under age 50. Therefore, age should be considered carefully in research and clinical interventions related to medication adherence in HIV.

Finally, we recently explored the impact of illicit drug use on medication adherence rates among HIV-infected subjects (Hinkin et al., 2007). Among a different cohort of 150 HIV+ subjects, 102 of whom tested urine toxicology positive for illicit drug use, we found that drug-using participants were nearly four times more likely to be classified as poor adherers compared to subjects who tested drug negative. This effect was especially marked among stimulant users who were seven times more likely to fail to adequately adhere to their medication regimen. Recent work coming out of the San Diego HIV Neurobehavioral Research Center shows that methamphetamine-dependent HIV+ adults showed increased rates of both episodic and prospective memory deficits (Carey et al., 2006; Woods et al., 2005), which might partially explain the greater degree of adherence failure in this particular subset of HIV-infected persons.

Psychiatric Status

In many neuromedical populations that show cognitive compromise there is also often some degree of neuropsychiatric dysfunction (Castellon et al., 2001). As an example, in both stroke and several neurodegenerative disorders, depression can be seen as both a direct effect of the disease or disorder (e.g., impact upon neurochemical or neurophysiological function) or may emerge as an indirect effect of the disease, such as reaction to the loss of function and disability. Below, we review the impact of psychiatric disturbance on medication adherence in both idiopathic primary psychiatric diseases (e.g., bipolar disorder, schizophrenia) and then touch upon its impact in populations where neuropsychiatric features are likely to accompany cognitive dysfunction (e.g., stroke, HIV/AIDS, neurodegenerative disease).

Studies have reported nonadherence rates among psychiatric patients ranging from 26% (Drake et al., 1989) to as high as 73% (Razali & Yahya, 1995), often depending on the method used to measure medication adherence. This is particularly problematic given the importance of adherence in preventing disease expression (e.g., symptoms, signs). In depressive disorders, the 1-year relapse rates are as high as 80% in patients not taking antidepressants as compared to 30% for those who adhere, yet some studies have shown that nearly 2 in 3 patients discontinue their medications within 3 months of beginning treatment (Myers & Braithwaite, 1992). Treatment nonadherence is a common reason for psychiatric rehospitalization as well. A study by

Cognition and Medication Adherence among Younger HIV+ Participants

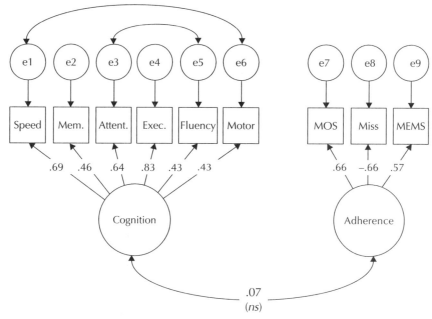

Cognition and Medication Adherence among Olderr HIV+ Participants

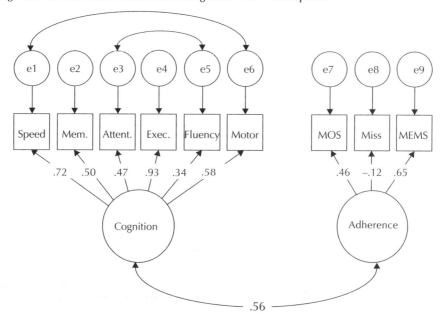

Figure 28–3. Both of these diagrams are from the same multigroup model, 2(48) = 61.67, $p > .05$, RMSEA = .03, NFI = .93, CFI = .98.

Keck and colleagues found that 60% of patients hospitalized with acute mania failed to adhere to their medication regimen in the month prior to hospitalization (Keck et al., 1996).

Psychiatric disturbances, including depression and anxiety, have been associated with poorer medication compliance, to varying degrees, in studies using diverse measures and methodologies (Carney et al., 1995; Edinger et al., 1994; Sensky et al., 1996; Shapiro et al., 1995). For example, a small meta-analysis (12 articles) found that depressed patients were 3 times more likely to be noncompliant with medication and behavioral treatment regimens than their non-depressed counterparts (DiMatteo et al., 2000). Patients with coronary artery disease who also had a diagnosis of major depression adhered to their cardiac medication regimen less than 45% of the time during a brief adherence monitoring phase, while nondepressed CAD patients had 70% adherence (Carney et al., 1995). Wang and colleagues (2002) demonstrated significant effects of depressive symptoms on antihypertensive medication adherence and Ciechanowski and colleagues (2000) found that depressive symptom severity was associated with poorer diet and medication regimen adherence among diabetics. Mood disturbance may interact with health beliefs and other variables, as described below. One study found that health locus of control and social support were each negatively impacted by prominent depressive symptoms and, together, these had an adverse impact on adherence to diet and other health behaviors among patients on chronic hemodialysis (Sensky et al., 1996). Finally, neuropsychiatric dysfunction, including apathy, depression, and hostility, has been related to decreased adherence among the elderly as well (Carney et al., 1995).

Recent studies have revealed that cognitive deficits associated with psychiatric illness may play a role in adherence behaviors. For example, there is evidence that cognitive deficit in some patients with bipolar disorder is enduring and may represent a trait-like variable. Deficits in learning and memory (Cavanagh et al., 2002) and executive functioning (Goldberg et al., 1993; Morice, 1990) have been found consistently, even during the euthymic phase of bipolar illness. Such impairments may have detrimental effects on patients' ability to remember dosing instructions and to appropriately plan and organize a medication-taking regimen. Also, in some diseases, patients with apathy, depression, and other neuropsychiatric symptoms/syndromes are more likely to show neurocognitive deficits, especially executive dysfunction (e.g., Castellon et al., 2000). These patients may be at particularly high risk for adherence failure, with the "double whammy" of neurocognitive and neuropsychiatric issues.

Medication adherence has received increasing attention among researchers and clinicians focused on the severely mentally ill, including schizophrenia and other psychotic disorders. Despite the overwhelming evidence that psychiatric medication is effective in the treatment of their disease, many patients do not take their medications (Dencker & Liberman, 1995; Hale, 1995), and antipsychotic nonadherence is therefore a major barrier to the effective pharmacological treatment of these individuals (Dolder et al., 2004). Several studies have shown that approximately one-third of patients with schizophrenia are fully compliant with medications, one-third are partially compliant, and one-third of patients are entirely noncompliant (Buchanan, 1992; Fleischhacker et al., 1994; Weiden et al., 1995). Moreover, 55% of people with schizophrenia who do not take antipsychotic medication will relapse over the course of a year compared to only 14% of those who comply with their medication regimen (Stephenson et al., 1993). Not surprisingly, multiple investigations have demonstrated that poor medication adherence among patients with schizophrenia is associated with a variety of poor health outcomes, including increased rehospitalization, repeated emergency room visits, worsening of symptoms, and even homelessness (Marder, 1998; Moore et al., 2000; Olfson et al., 2000; Weiden & Olfson, 1995).

Several reviews of the literature on medication adherence in schizophrenia (Fenton et al., 1997; Kampman & Lehtinen, 1999) have identified consistent predictors of poor adherence in this population, including more severe psychopathology, comorbid substance abuse, presence of medication side effects, depressive symptoms, absence of social support from family or friends, practical barriers, such as inability to afford medications, lack of insight, and neurocognitive dysfunction. Although there is substantial heterogeneity among such individuals with regard to the level and pattern of cognitive impairment, some of the most commonly impaired abilities in schizophrenia include attention, working memory, verbal and nonverbal learning, executive functions, and some psychomotor abilities (Heaton & Drexler, 1987; Heinrichs & Zakzanis, 1998; Schwartz et al., 1996; see also Harvey & Keefe, this volume). A major barrier to adherence in this population is related to a lack of insight or inability to understand one's disorder and the need for treatment

(Lacro et al., 2002). Diminished insight, coupled with other cognitive deficits, may decrease patients' ability to adhere to their treatment regimens (Green, 1996; Green et al., 2000).

Psychosocial Models of Adherence

While the main focus of the current chapter is the relationship between cognitive function and medication adherence, it is important to realize that adherence behavior is a complex and dynamic process that can be determined by multiple factors (Remien et al., 2003). Many theories have set forth a combination of internal (e.g., attitudes, health beliefs, motivation) or external influences (e.g., environmental, social) to explain various health-related behaviors, including medication adherence. A detailed review of the various theoretical models of adherence or of all the many adherence-related constructs is well beyond the scope of this chapter. However, we briefly discuss a few of the more important theoretical contributions to the adherence literature.

Health Beliefs Model

The Health Beliefs Model (HBM) was proposed to predict a wide variety of health-related behaviors (Rosenstock, 1974) and has been a focus of numerous studies of medication adherence (Janz & Becker, 1984). The HBM posits that health behaviors, including medication adherence, depend mainly on the desire to avoid illness and the belief that certain actions will prevent or alleviate disease. The model consists of a number of dimensions, including perceived *susceptibility* to illness, perceived illness *severity*, perceived *benefits* of treatment, and perceived *barriers* to treatment compliance. Susceptibility refers to an individual's belief that he or she is at risk of contracting an illness or disease or even the patient's vulnerability to illness in general. Perceived illness severity relates to the patient's belief in the seriousness of contracting an illness and/or of leaving it untreated, including possible social, emotional, and functional consequences. Perceived benefits of treatment refer to beliefs in the efficacy of any actions in reducing disease threat and the impact of living disease free. Finally, perceived barriers to treatment

compliance describes a kind of cost–benefit analysis in which individuals weigh the treatment's effectiveness against potential negative consequences of compliance, such as disruption of daily activities and adverse side effects. HBM theory predicts that those individuals who perceive themselves to be potentially vulnerable to the illness, perceive the consequences of the illness as severe, and are convinced of the efficacy of the proposed treatment regimen are more likely to adhere, especially if they perceive relatively few "costs" associated with adherence (Budd et al., 1996; Smith et al., 1987).

In addition to these four dimensions, the HBM also postulates that diverse demographic, psychosocial, and psychological variables may affect individuals' perceptions and thereby indirectly influence health-related behaviors. The model also states that an individual needs a prompt (e.g., a reminder either of the threat of illness or the action that must be taken against it) before they will engage in health-related behaviors (Weinstein, 1988). These "cues to action" may be internal (e.g., recognition of prodromal symptoms) or external (e.g., comments made by significant others). The HBM has been shown to explain variation in medical regimen adherence behavior in patients with a variety of diseases and disorders, including HIV/AIDS (Barclay et al., 2007), hypertension (Mendoza et al., 2006), diabetes (Harris et al., 1982), heart disease (Mirotznik et al., 1995), epilepsy (Green & Simons-Morton, 1988), mild cognitive impairment (Ownby et al., 2006), and psychiatric disorders including depression and schizophrenia (Adams & Scott, 2000; Cohen et al., 2000). One's health beliefs are dynamic over time and typically will involve the development, modification, and monitoring of health-related cognitions. Individual cognitive capacity may influence the accuracy of one's beliefs, the ability to incorporate new information, and the ability to consistently determine and monitor cause–effect relationships. It stands to reason that acquired cognitive deficits might mediate the relationship between HBM and adherence behavior.

Social Action Theory

Social Action Theory (SAT; Ewart, 1991) addresses the interactions between internal and external factors in the drive toward action or behavior change. SAT holds that contextual factors such as one's physical environment and social and cultural group membership, in combination with various biological factors, will interact to modulate mood and arousal, which impact self-regulatory processes (such as problem solving, motivation, and interactive social factors) that, in turn, lead to action states such as initiating and adhering to one's medication regimen. A large, multisite study of HIV+ individuals taking complex antiretroviral therapy (ART) medications revealed that contextual factors of African American heritage, number of daily doses, symptom difficulty, involvement in a primary relationship, a history of drug use, and a history of homelessness were predictive of poor (<90%) adherence (Johnson et al., 2003). Additionally, poor adherers also reported higher rates of emotional distress. Self-regulatory factors associated with poor adherence were low adherence self-efficacy, difficulty fitting medication schedule into daily routines, problems managing medication side effects, fatigue related to medication adherence, and disbelief in the efficacy of the prescribed ART regimen. This study is consistent with SAT and supports an association between medication adherence and both contextual and self-regulatory factors.

Social Support

Several studies have shown the importance of social support in medication adherence (Berk et al., 2004; DiMatteo, 2004; Simoni et al., 2006; Weaver et al., 2005). The construct of social support can be further parsed into structural and functional factors. Structural factors include the patient's marital status, living arrangement, and density of their social network. Variables such as emotional support, family cohesion, and the amount of practical support reflect functional factors. A meta-analysis by DiMatteo (2004) found that several aspects of functional support were highly associated with better adherence, including the amount of practical and emotional support and family cohesiveness. Structural support factors, including marital status and living arrangement were only modestly related to adherence. Family conflict was negatively related to medication adherence. Results from this meta-analysis would suggest that the mere presence of others in the patient's environment may not always provide a positive impact on adherence—rather it is the amount of perceived and real support provided by those others, whether they be marital partners or friends, that is most predictive of adherence success.

Recent studies of adherence to highly active antiretroviral therapy (HAART) in HIV+ individuals have attempted to delineate the nature of the relationships between social support, affect, and medication adherence with structural equation modeling. One such study (Simoni et al., 2006), showed that social support was positively associated with spirituality and negatively associated with negative affect (e.g., depression), which, in turn, predicted adherence self-efficacy in HIV+ individuals. Adherence self-efficacy was predictive of self-reported adherence, which in turn predicted viral load though the model only accounted for 8% of the total variance in ART adherence. A more compelling study, also utilizing structural equation modeling, demonstrated that the relationship between medication adherence, social support, and affect was mediated by avoidant-coping strategies reported by HIV-infected individuals (Weaver et al., 2005). More specifically, 20% of the variance in medication adherence (measured via MEMS caps) was predicted by negative affect and poor social support as moderated by avoidant coping. The same model also accounted for 44% of the variance in viral load.

Clearly one's health beliefs and attitudes, sense of self-efficacy, treatment expectancies, and degree of social support influence adherence. Also, sociodemographic and contextual factors (e.g., homelessness, ethnic minority status, low income, active substance abuse) play a part in medication adherence. Particularly relevant to the current chapter is that there is yet very little known about the interaction between some of these factors and the presence of neurocognitive deficits on health behaviors. Beyond their direct effect on adherence, cognitive deficits may moderate or mediate the influence of predictors such as treatment expectancies, health beliefs, autonomous health-care management, coping styles, and social support. Indeed, recent data collected from individuals suffering from schizophrenia has shown that difficulties in sustained attention, verbal memory, and executive functioning correlate with their attitudes and beliefs about medications (Kim et al., 2006; Maeda et al., 2006).

Medication Adherence Interventions

Medication adherence problems are fairly widespread among patients with cognitive deficits, including the elderly and/or those with chronic diseases. Interventions aimed at improving adherence are obviously needed in patients with cognitive deficits. Strategies used to increase adherence in these populations include rehabilitation techniques that are aimed at restoring lost function(s) or at improving the patient's current cognitive limitations, or can involve teaching compensatory strategies or providing assistive devices to mediate cognitive limitations. Examples of the latter include pillboxes, medication charts, or personal data assistants (PDA) or voicemail reminder services (see Table 28–2).

Of course, the improved detection and treatment of cognitive deficits may have a positive impact on medication compliance if the cognitive limitations were indeed impacting adherence behavior. In patients with an acquired brain injury (e.g., traumatic brain injury, stroke patients), the natural recovery of function that typically occurs in many of these disorders may lead to better adherence as cognitive deficits improve. By extension, those patients in the early recovery stages of acquired brain injury may be particularly vulnerable to adherence problems, precisely at the time when adherence might be most important. Family or caregiver support may be particularly crucial at this time, especially ensuring that medications are taken as prescribed and routines are developed for pill taking. There are many cognitive rehabilitation techniques that have been set forth to address problems in executive functioning (see Evans, 2003 or Levine et al., 2000), which, as discussed above, are among the most robust predictors of adherence problems. Similarly, memory problems have been addressed by rehabilitation specialists with mixed success, in part dependent upon the nature and severity of the memory

problems being addressed (see Wilson, 2000 and Wilson et al., 2001). For the most part, cognitive rehabilitation or intervention techniques to improve medication management in populations with neuropsychological deficits have not been well studied to date.

On the other hand, compensatory intervention strategies and technologies have received considerable empirical scrutiny. Studies have explored the efficacy of external aids such as pillboxes and pill bottle alarms (Mackowiak et al., 1994; Park et al., 1992), phone/voice mail/pager cues (Leirer et al., 1991), and organizational charts (Park et al., 1992). Haynes and colleagues have reviewed the medication adherence intervention research (Haynes et al., 1996, 2000, 2003) and have consistently observed that successful interventions are typically multifactorial, involving some combination of improving the convenience of care, educating the person and/or family, and cues or reminders to take medication. Also, encouragement of self-monitoring and increasing patient support through counseling, family therapy, and/or supervision, have also been shown to be effective in some instances. However, perhaps the most notable finding from their review of this body of research is that even the effective interventions have not always led to strong, sustained outcomes. For the most part, interventions targeting adherence have typically demonstrated small to medium effect sizes (in the $d \leq 0.25$ range), indicating that significant and lasting behavioral changes with such strategies may be difficult (Haynes et al., 2003).

However, some studies have found reason to be optimistic about a wide variety of compensatory strategies in improving adherence. Park and colleagues (1992) found that older adults who used both an organizer and a chart designed to minimize cognitive effort in taking medications made significantly fewer errors in their medication regimens than did control subjects (nearly a 10-fold decrease, relative to controls—18.3% for controls versus 1.8% for the intervention group). Many other studies have also demonstrated the efficacy of charts, organizers, and written instructions to augment the verbal instruction of physicians (Coe et al., 1984; Lamy et al., 1992). Similarly, color-coded pill bottles matched with a weekly pillbox have

Table 28–2. Obstacles to Medication Adherence

Neurocognitive	Psychological	Demographic/social	Human factors
Attention Deficits	*Psychiatric Disturbance*	*Age*	*Complex Medication*
Learning & Memory	*Substance Abuse/*	In general, youn-	*Regimen*
Deficits	*Dependence*	ger adults tend to	This tends to have a larger
Executive Deficits	Stimulant use is particu-	demonstrate poorer	impact on older adults
Prospective Memory	larly deleterious.	adherence than older	and cognitively compro-
Deficits	Acute substance use	adults.	mised patients.
	effects can also impair	*Poor Social Support*	*Poorly Worded Labeling*
	neurocognitive	*Financial Barriers*	*Poor Visual Acuity*
	functioning.		*Motor Incoordination*
	Counterproductive		
	Health Beliefs		
	e.g., external locus of		
	control, belief that		
	disease is less severe		
	than it is, medications		
	not effective, external		
	health locus of control.		
	Poor Doctor-Patient		
	Relationship		

Interventions to Improve Medication Adherence

Organizational Aides	*Psychiatric screening and*	*Psychoeducation*	*Simplification of medication*
Pillboxes	*treatment*	*regarding age effects*	*regimen*
Medication schedules/	*Psychoeducation &*	*and the impor-*	Reduction in the number of
calendars	*Health Psychology*	*tance of medication*	medications
Mnemonic strategies	*interventions regarding*	*adherence*	Simplification of daily
(e.g., grouping and	*illness*	*Family interventions*	dosing requirements;
studying medica-	*Clinician training,*	*and/or social work*	avoid tid regimens
tion names by daily	*interviewing, and*	*interventions regard-*	*Language-simplified*
does requirements)	*communication skills*	*ing medication*	*medication labels*
External remind-		*regimen support*	*Large print, brail, or audio*
ers Programmed		*Medication scholar-*	*medication labels*
alarms (wrist		*ships, community*	*Easy-to-open pill bottle lids,*
watch; personal		*resource use, social*	*pill bottle openers*
data assistant)		*work intervention*	
Remotely controlled			
reminders (pager,			
phone)			

been demonstrated to enhance compliance in some patients (Martin & Mead, 1982). Finally, Leirer et al. (1991) found a fourfold reduction in episodes of poor adherence when voice mail reminders were used to cue elderly subjects about their medication regimen.

For individuals with vision problems, increasing contrast in written instructions avoiding subtle distinctions among colors, and minimizing the need to discriminate fine detail can help improve adherence. Similarly, studies on the effects of aging suggest that larger font sizes (i.e., 12 or 14 points), conventional font styles, and use of unjustified text are more appropriate

for older adults and those with vision impairments (Drummond et al., 2004; Vanderplas & Vanderplas, 1980). Instructions may also be improved by adding icons or cartoons that highlight important information (Wickens, 1992) as such images tend to be more explicit than text, reducing the need for inferential reasoning (Larkin & Simon, 1987).

Well-designed medication instructions that reduce cognitive demands and motivate the patient may also work to improve adherence (Park et al., 1994). Such instructions may be even more effective if, in addition to explaining how to take medication, they present information that targets incorrect beliefs about the illness or the drug. For example, Carter et al. (1986) found that reminder messages for flu vaccinations improved clinic attendance significantly when they contained information that addressed incorrect beliefs about the side effects and risks of the immunizations.

Others have noted that there are a number of interventions that health-care providers could perform more regularly to potentially increase medication adherence in their patients. These include explaining why particular medications are being prescribed and what outcome is typically expected, including common side effects. When physicians try to anticipate common barriers to adherence such as economic limitations, cognitive impairment, and negative side effects and discuss these potential problems prospectively, this can be effective as well (Bultman & Svarstad, 2000). Providing information about health conditions and medications both verbally and in writing and using an explanatory level consistent with the patient's education and health-care sophistication may improve adherence by improving the patient's knowledge about what they are expected to do (Brown & Segal, 1996). If cognitive limitations might be expected to interfere with the patient's own ability to adhere, then working with the patient's potential caregivers to help *them* understand many of these aforementioned issues has been shown to be effective as well (Ownby et al., 2006). The simple intervention of asking the patient to explain (e.g., to their doctor or nurse) their own understanding of the consequences of not taking medications or how they might cope with adverse side effects can serve the dual-pronged purpose of helping health-care providers detect subtle cognitive problems (e.g., memory, comprehension, language, etc.) or clarify simple misunderstandings that are not necessarily due to cognitive compromise. Finally, attempting to enlist patients' families to assist in providing additional support or supervision of medication taking, has been shown to be effective in improving adherence (DiMatteo, 2004).

Acknowledgments

This chapter includes data gathered as part of two NIH-funded studies (R01 MH58552 and R01 DA13799 awarded to Dr. Hinkin). Additional support was provided by the VA Merit Review program to Drs. Hinkin and Castellon. Drs. Wright and Barclay received support from an NIMH training grant (T32 MH19535). We would like to thank Amanda Gooding and Michelle S. Kim for assistance with manuscript preparation.

References

Adams, J., & Scott, J. (2000). Predicting medical adherence in severe mental disorders. *Acta Psychiatrica Scandinavica, 101,* 119–124.

Albert, S. M., Flater, S. R., Clouse, R., Todak, G., Stern, Y., & Marder, K. (2003). Medication management skill in HIV: I. Evidence for adaptation of medication management strategies in people with cognitive impairment. II. Evidence for a pervasive lay model of medication efficacy. *AIDS and Behavior, 7*(3), 329–338.

Albert, S. M., Weber, C. M., Todak, G., Polanco, C., Clouse, R., McElhiney, M., et al. (1999). An observed performance test of medication management ability in HIV: Relation to neuropsychological status and medication adherence outcomes. *AIDS and Behavior, 3,* 121–128.

Allen, S. C., Jain, M., Ragab, S., & Malik, N. (2003). Acquisition and short-term retention of inhaler techniques require intact executive function in elderly subjects. *Age and Ageing, 32,* 299–302.

Arnsten, J. H., Demas, P. A., Farzadegan, H., Grant, R. W., Gouretvitch, M. N., Chang, C. J., et al. (2001). Antiretroviral therapy adherence and viral suppression in HIV-infected drug users: Comparison of self-report and electronic monitoring. *Clinical Infectious Diseases, 33* (8), 1417–1423.

Avants, S. K., Margolin, A., Warburton, L. A., Hawkins, K. A., & Shi, J. (2001). Predictors of nonadherence to HIV-related medication regimens during methadone stabilization. *American Journal on Addictions/American Academy of Psychiatrists in Alcoholism and Addictions, 10,* 69–78.

Ayalon, L., Ancoli-Israel, S., Stepnowsky, C., Marler, M., Palmer, B.W., Liu, L., et al. (2006). Adherence to continuous positive airway pressure treatment in patients with Alzheimer's disease and obstructive sleep apnea. *American Journal of Geriatric Psychiatry, 14,* 176–180.

Baker, E. K., Kurtz, M. M., & Astur, R. S. (2006). Virtual reality assessment of medication compliance in patients with schizophrenia. *CyberPsychology and Behavior.Special Issue: Virtual and physical toys: Open-ended features for non-formal learning, 9,* 224–229.

Baker, D. W., Parker, R. M., Williams, M. V., & Clark, W. S. (1998). Health literacy and the risk of hospital admission. *Journal of General Internal Medicine, 13*, 791–798.

Bangsberg, D. R., Hecht, F. M., Charlebois, E. D., Chesney, M., & Moss, A. (2001). Comparing objective measures of adherence to HIV antiretroviral therapy: Electronic medication monitors and unannounced pill counts. *AIDS and Behavior, 5*, 275–281.

Barat, I., Andreasen, F., & Damsgaard, E. M. (2001). Drug therapy in the elderly: What doctors believe and patients actually do. *British Journal of Clinical Pharmacology, 51*, 615–622.

Barclay, T. R., Hinkin, C. H., Mason, K. I., Reinhard, M. J., Marion, S. D., Levine, A. J., et al. (2007). Age-associated predictors of medication adherence in HIV+ adults: Health beliefs, self-efficacy, and neurocognitive status. *Health Psychology, 26*, 40–49.

Benner, J. S., Glynn, R. J., Mogun, H., Neumann, P. J., Weinstein, M. C., & Avorn, J. (2002). Long-term persistence in use of statin therapy in elderly patients. *Journal of the American Medical Association, 288*, 455–461.

Bennett, D. A., Wilson, R. S., Schneider, J. A., Evans, D. A., Beckett, L. A., Aggarwal, N. T., et al. (2002). Natural history of mild cognitive impairment in older persons. *Neurology, 23*, 198–205.

Berg, J. S., Dischler, J., Wagner, D. J., Raia, J. J., & Palmer-Shevlin, N. (1993). Medication compliance: A healthcare problem. *Annals of Pharmacotherapy, 27*(Suppl 9), S1–S24.

Berk, M., Berk, L., & Castle, D. (2004). A collaborative approach to the treatment alliance in bipolar disorder. *Bipolar Disorders, 6*, 504–518.

Boyle, P. A., Malloy, P. F., Salloway, S., Cahn-Weiner, D. A., Cohen, R., & Cummings, J. L. (2003). Executive dysfunction and apathy predict functional impairment in Alzheimer's disease. *American Journal of Geriatric Psychiatry, 11*, 214–221.

Brainin, J. (2001). The role of memory strategies in medication adherence among the elderly. *Home Health Care Services Quarterly, 20*, 1–16.

Briesacher, B. A., Gurwitz, J. H., & Soumerai, S. B. (2007). Patients at-risk for cost-related medication nonadherence: A review of the literature. *Journal of General Internal Medicine, 22*, 864–871.

Brown, C. M., & Segal, R. (1996). The effects of health and treatment perceptions on the use of prescribed medication and home remedies among African American and White American hypertensives. *Social Science & Medicine, 43*, 903–917.

Bruer, J. T. (1982). Methodological rigor and citation frequency in patient compliance literature. *American Journal of Public Health, 72*, 297–303.

Buchanan, A. (1992). A two year prospective study of treatment compliance in patient with schizophrenia. *Psychological Medicine, 22*, 787–797.

Budd, R. J., Hughes, I. C., & Smith, J. A. (1996). Health beliefs and compliance with antipsychotic medication. *British Journal of Clinical Psychology, 35*(3), 393–397.

Bultman, D. C., & Svarstad, B. L. (2000). Effects of physician communication style on client medication beliefs and adherence with antidepressant treatment. *Patient Education and Counseling, 40*, 173–185.

Callahan, C. M., & Wolinsky, F. D. (1995). Hospitalization for major depression among older Americans. *Journal of Gerontology, Series A, Biological Science and Medical Science, 50A*, M196–M202.

Carey, C. L., Woods, S. P., Rippeth, J. D., Heaton, R. K., Grant, I., & HIV Neurobehavioral Research Center (HNRC) Group. (2006). Prospective memory in HIV-1 infection. *Journal of Clinical and Experimental Neuropsychology, 28*, 536–548.

Carney, R. M., Freedland, K. E., Eisen, S. A., Rich, M. W., & Jaffe, A. S. (1995). Major depression and medication adherence in elderly patients with coronary artery disease. *Health Psychology, 14*, 88–90.

Carter, W. B., Beach, L. R., & Inui, T. S. (1986). The flu shot study: Using multiattribute utility theory to design a vaccination intervention. Organizational Behavior and Human Decision Processes, 38, 378–391.

Castellon, S. A., Hinkin, C. H., & Satz, P. (2001). Behavioral disorders associated with central nervous system dysfunction. In P. B. Sutker and H. E. Adams (Eds.), *Comprehensive Handbook of Psychopathology* (3rd ed., pp. 813–839). New York: Plenum Press.

Castellon, S. A., Hinkin, C. H., & Myers, H. F. (2000). Neuropsychiatric disturbance is associated with executive dysfunction in HIV-1 infection. *Journal of the International Neuropsychological Society 6*, 336–347.

Cavanagh, J. T., Van Beck, M., Muir, W., & Blackwood, D. H. R. (2002). Case-control study of the neurocognitive function in euthymic patients with bipolar disorder: An association with mania. *British Journal of Psychiatry, 180*, 320–326.

Chapman, R. H., Benner, J. S., Petrilla, A. Tierce, J. C., Collins, S. R., Battleman, D. S., et al. (2005). Predictors of adherence with antihypertensive and lipid-lowering therapy. *Archives of Internal Medicine, 165*, 1147–1152.

Ciechanowski, P. S., Katon, W. J., & Russo, J. E. (2000). Depression and diabetes: Impact of depressive symptoms on adherence, function, and costs. *Archives of Internal Medicine, 160*, 3278–3285.

Coe, R. M., Prendergast, C. G., & Psathas, G. (1984). Strategies for obtaining compliance with medication regimens. *Journal of the American Geriatrics Society, 32,* 589–594.

Cohen, G. (1981). Inferential reasoning in old age. *Cognition, 9,* 59–72.

Cohen, N. L., Parikh, S. V., & Kennedy, S. H. (2000). Medication compliance in mood disorders: Relevance of the Health Belief Model and other determinants. *Primary Care Psychiatry, 6,* 101–110.

Col, N., Fanale, J. E., & Kronholm, P. (1990). The role of medication noncompliance and adverse drug reactions in hospitalizations of the elderly. *Archives of Internal Medicine, 150,* 841–845.

Conn, V., Taylor, S., & Miller, R. (1994). Cognitive impairment and medication compliance. *Journal of Gerontological Nursing, 12,* 41–47.

Cooper, B., Carpenter, I., Katona, C., Schroll, M., Wagner, C., Fialova, D., et al. (2005). The AdHOC study of older adults' adherence to medication in 11 countries. *American Journal of Geriatric Psychiatry, 13,* 1067–1076.

Cotrell, V., Wild, K., & Bader, T. (2006). Medication management and adherence in cognitively impaired older adults. *Journal of Gerontological Social Work, 47,* 32–46.

Craik, F. I. M., & Jennings, J. M. (1992). Human memory. In F. I. M. Craik and T. A. Salthouse (Eds.), *The Handbook of Aging and Cognition.* Hillsdale, NJ (pp. 51–110): Lawrence Erlbaum Associates.

Council on Scientific Affairs (1999). Health literacy report. Ad hoc committee on Health Literacy for the Council of Scientific Affairs, American Medical Association. *JAMA, 281,* 552–557.

Dencker, S. J., & Liberman, R. P. (1995). From compliance to collaboration in the treatment of schizophrenia. *International Clinical Psychopharmacology, 9*(Suppl5), 75–78.

Diehl, M., Willis, S. L., & Schaie, W. (1995). Everyday problem solving in older adults: Observational assessment and cognitive correlates. *Psychology and Aging, 10*(3), 478–491.

Dimatteo, M. R. (2004). Social support and patient adherence to medical treatment: A meta-analysis. *Health Psychology, 23,* 207–218.

Dimatteo, M. R., Lepper, H. S., & Croghan, T. W. (2000). Depression is a risk factor for noncompliance with medical treatment: Meta-analysis of the effects of anxiety and depression on patient adherence. *Archives of Internal Medicine, 160,* 2101–2107.

Dolder, C. R., Lacro, J. P., Warren, K. A., Golshan, S., Perkins, D. O., & Jeste, D. V. (2004). Brief evaluation of medication influences and beliefs: Development and testing of a brief scale for medication adherence. *Journal of Clinical Psychopharmacology, 24*(4), 404–409.

Dolder, C. R., Lacro, J. P., & Jeste, D. V. (2003). Adherence to antipsychotic and non-psychiatric medications in middle-aged and older patients with psychotic disorders. *Psychosomatic Medicine, 65,* 156–162.

Drake, R. E., Osher, F. C., & Wallach, M. A. (1989). Alcohol use and abuse in schizophrenia: A prospective community study. *Journal of Nervous and Mental Disorders, 177,* 408–414.

Drummond, S. R., Drummond, R. S., & Dutton, G. N. (2004). Visual acuity and the ability of the visually impaired to read medication instructions. *British Journal of Ophthalmology, 88*(12), 1541–1542.

Dunbar-Jacob, J., Erlen, J. A., Schlenk, E. A., Ryan, C. M., Sereika, S. M., & Doswell, W. M. (2000). Adherence in chronic disease. *Annual Review of Nursing Research, 18,* 48–90.

Edinger, J. D., Carwile, S., Miller, P., & Hope, V. (1994). Psychological status, syndromatic measures, and compliance with nasal CPAP therapy for sleep apnea. *Perceptual and Motor Skills, 78,* 1116–1118.

Einstein, G. O., & McDaniel, M. A. (1990). Normal aging and prospective memory. *Journal of Experimental Psychology: Learning, Memory, and Cognition, 16,* 717–726.

Einstein, G. O., McDaniel, M. A., Smith, R., & Shaw, P. (1998). Habitual prospective memory and aging: Remembering instructions and forgetting actions. *Psychological Science, 9,* 284–288.

Evans, J. J. (2003). Rehabilitation of executive deficits. In B. A. Wilson (Ed), *Neuropsychological Rehabilitation: Theory and Practice* (pp. 53–70). Lisse, The Netherlands: Swets and Zeitlinger.

Ewart, C. K. (1991). Social action theory for public health psychology. *American Psychologist, 46,* 931–946.

Fenton, W. S., Blyler, C. R., & Heinssen, R. K. (1997). Determinants of mediation compliance in schizophrenia: Empirical and clinical findings. *Schizophrenia Bulletin, 23,* 637–651.

Fernandez, L. C., Baron, F. B., Vazquez, D. B., Martinez, G. T., Urendes, J. J., & Pujol de la Llave, E. (2006). Medication errors and non-compliance in polymedicated elderly patients. *Farmacia Hospitalaria, 30,* 280–283.

Fleischhacker, W. W., Meise, U., Gunther, V., & Kurz, M. (1994). Compliance with antipsychotic drug treatment: Influence of side effects. *Acta Psychiatrica Scandinavica, 89,* 11–15.

Fleischman, D. A., & Gabrieli, J. D. (1998). Repetition priming in normal aging and Alzheimer's disease: A review of findings and theories. *Psychology of Aging, 13,* 88–119.

Fulmer, T., & Gurland, B. (1997). Evaluating the caregiver's intervention in the elder's task performance:

Capacity versus actual behavior. *International Journal of Geriatric Psychiatry, 12*, 920–925.

Ganguli, M., Dodge, H. H., & Mulsant, B. H. (2002). Rates and predictors of mortality in an aging, rural, community-based cohort: The role of depression. *Archives of General Psychiatry, 59*, 1046–1052.

Gazmararian, J. A., Baker, D. W., Williams, M. V., Parker, R. M., Scott, T. L., Green, D. C. et al. (1999). Health literacy among medicare enrollees in a managed care organization. *Journal of the American Medical Association, 281*, 545–551.

Gilmer, T. P., Dolder, C. R., Lacro, J. P, Folsom, D. P., Lindamer, L., Garcia, P., & Jeste, D. V. (2004). Adherence to treatment with antipsychotic medication and healthcare costs among Medicaid beneficiaries with schizophrenia. *American Journal of Psychiatry, 161*, 692–699.

Goldberg, T. E., Gold, J. M., Greeberg, R., Griffin, S., Schulz, S. C., Pickar, D., Kleinman, J. E., & Weinberger, D. R. (1993). Contrasts between patients with affective disorders and patients with schizophrenia on neuropsychological test battery. American Journal of Psychiatry, 150, 1355–1362.

Gould, O. N., McDonald-Miszczak, L., & Gregory, J. (1999). Prediction accuracy and medication instructions: Will you remember tomorrow? *Aging, Neuropsychology, and Cognition, 6*, 141–154.

Gray, S. L., Mahoney, J. E., & Blough, D. K. (2001). Medication adherence in elderly patients receiving home health services following hospital discharge. *Annals of Pharmacotherapy, 35*, 539–545.

Green, L. W., & Simons-Morton, D. G. (1988). Denial, delay and disappointment: Discovering and overcoming the causes of drug errors and missed appointments. *Epilepsy Research, 1*, 7–21.

Green, M. F. (1996). What are the functional consequences of neurocognitive deficits in schizophrenia? *American Journal of Psychiatry, 153*, 321–330.

Green, M. F., Kern, R. S., Braff, D. L., & Mintz, J. (2000). Neurocognitive deficits and functional outcome in schizophrenia: Are we measuring the "right stuff"? *Schizophrenia Bulletin, 26*, 119–136.

Gurland, B. J., Cross, P., Chen, J., & Wilder, D. E. (1994). A new performance test of adaptive cognitive functioning: The medication management (MM) test. *International Journal of Geriatric Psychiatry, 9*, 875–885.

Gurwitz, J. J., Field, T., Harrold, L., Rothschild, J., Debellis, K., Seger, A., et al. (2003). Incidence and preventability of adverse drug events among older persons in the ambulatory setting. *Journal of the American Medical Association, 289*, 141–164.

Hale, A. S. (1995). Atypical antipsychotic and compliance in schizophrenia. *Nordic Journal of Psychiatry, 49*(Suppl 35), 31–39.

Harris, R., Skyler, J. S., Linn, M. W., Pollack, L., & Tewksbury, D. (1982). Relationship between the health belief model and compliance as a basis for intervention in diabetes mellitus. *Pediatric and Adolescent Endocrinology, 10*, 123–132.

Haynes, R. B., Montague, P., Oliver, T., Mc Kibbon, K. A., Brouwers, M. C., & Keneni, R. (2000). Interventions for helping patients to follow prescriptions for medications. *Cochrane Database of Systematic Reviews, 2*, CD000011.

Haynes, R. B., McDonald, H., Garg, A. X., & Montague, P. (2003). Helping patients to follow prescribed treatment: Clinical applications. *Journal of the American Medical Association, 288*, 2880–2883.

Haynes, R. B., McKibbon, K. A., & Kanani, R. (1996). Systematic review of randomized trials of interventions to assist patients to follow prescriptions for medications. *Lancet, 348*, 383–386.

Heaton, R. K., & Drexler, M. (1987). Clinical neuropsychological findings in schizophrenia and aging. In N. E. Miller and G. D. Cohen (Eds.), *Schizophrenia and Aging.* . (pp. 145–161). New York: Guilford Press.

Heaton, R. K., Marcotte, T. D., Rivera-Mindt, M., Sadek, J., Moore, D. J., & the HIV Neurobehavioral Research Center Group. (2004). The impact of HIV-associated neuropsychological impairment on everyday functioning. *Journal of the International Neuropsychological Society, 10*, 317–331.

Heinrichs, R. W., & Zakzanis, K. K. (1998). Neurocognitive deficit in schizophrenia: A quantitative review of the evidence. *Neuropsychology, 12*, 426–445.

Hepke, K.L., Martus, M.T., & Share, D.A. (2004). Costs and utilization associated with pharmaceutical adherence in a diabetic population. *American Journal of Managed Care, 10*, 144–151.

Hinkin, C. H., Barclay, T. R., Castellon, S. A., Levine, A. J., Durvasula, R. S., Marion, S. D., et al. (2007). Drug use and medication adherence among HIV-1 infected individuals. *AIDS and Behavior, 11*, 185–194.

Hinkin, C. H., Castellon, S. A., Durvasula, R. S., Hardy, D. J., Lam, M. N., Mason, K. I., et al. (2002). Medication adherence among HIV+ adults: Effects of cognitive dysfunction and regimen complexity. *Neurology, 59*, 1944–1950.

Hinkin, C. H., Hardy, D. J., Mason, K. I., Castellon, S. A., Durvasula, R. S., Lam, M. N., et al. (2004). Medication adherence in HIV-infected adults: Effect of patient age, cognitive status, and substance abuse. *AIDS, 18*, S19–S25.

Horwitz, R. I., Viscoli, C. M., Berkman, L., Donaldson, R. M., Horwitz, S. M., Murray, C. J., et al. (1990). Treatment adherence and risk of death after a myocardial infarction. *Lancet, 336,* 542–545.

Hurd, P. D., & Butkovich, S. L. (1986). Compliance problems and the older patient: Assessing functional limitations. *Drug Intelligence and Clinical Pharmacy, 20,* 228–231.

Huybrechts, K. F., Ishak, K. J., & Caro, J. J. (2005). Assessment of compliance with osteoporosis treatment and its consequences in a managed care population. *Bone, Epub,* December 1. http://www.sciencedirect.com/science?_ob=ArticleURL&_udi=B6T4Y-4HR72JN-2&_user=4423&_rdoc=1&_fmt=&_orig=search&_sort=d&view=c&_acct=C000059605&_version=1&_urlVersion=0&_userid=4423&md5=1cbce099a9602b01efee460b1d1a1751

Insel, K., Morrow, D., Brewer, B., & Figueredo, A. (2006). Executive function, working memory, and medication adherence among older adults. *Journals of Gerontology: Psychological and Social Sciences, 61,* P102–P107.

Isaac, L. M., & Tamblyn, R. M. (1993). Compliance and cognitive function: A methodological approach to measuring unintentional errors in medication compliance in the elderly. *The Gerontologist, 33,* 772–781

Jackevicius, C. A., Mamdani, M., & Tu, J. V. (2002). Adherence with statin therapy in elderly patients with and without acute coronary syndromes. *Journal of the American Medical Association, 288,* 462–467.

Janz, N. K., & Becker, M. H. (1984). The Health Belief Model: a decade later. *Health Education Quarterly, 11,* 1–47.

Jeste, S. D., Patterson, T. L., Palmer, B. W., Dolder, C. R., Goldman, S., & Jeste, D. V. (2003). Cognitive predictors of medication adherence among middle-aged and older outpatients with schizophrenia. *Schizophrenia Research, 63,* 49–58.

Johnson, M. O., Catz, S. L., Remien, R. H., Rotheram-Borus, M. J., Morin, S. F., Charlebois, E., et al. (2003). Theory-guided, empirically supported avenues for intervention on HIV medication nonadherence: Findings from the healthy living project. *AIDS Patient Care and STDs, 17,* 645–656.

Kalichman, S. C., Amaral, C. M., Stearns, H., White, D., Flanagan, J., Pope, H., et al. (2007). Adherence to antiretroviral therapy assessed by unannounced pill counts conducted by telephone. *Journal of General Internal Medicine, 22,* 1003–1106.

Kampman, O., & Lehtinen, K. (1999). Compliance in psychosis. *Acta Psychiatrica Scandinavica, 100,* 167–175.

Keck, P., McElroy, B., Strakowski, S., Stanton, S. P., Kizer, D., Balistreri, T., et al. (1996). Factors associated with pharmacologic non-compliance in patients with mania. *Journal of Clinical Psychiatry, 57,* 292–297.

Kendrick, R., & Bayne, J. (1982). Compliance with prescribed medication by elderly patients. *Canadian Medical Association Journal, 127,* 961–962.

Kim, S., Shin, I., Kim, J., Yang, S., Shin, H., & Yoon, J. (2006). Association between attitude toward medication and neurocognitive function in schizophrenia. *Clinical Neuropharmacology, 29,* 197–205.

Kline, D. W., & Scialfa, C. T. (1997). Sensory and perceptual functioning: Basic research and human factors implications. In A. D. Fisk and W. A. Rogers (Eds.), *Handbook of Human Factors and the Older Adult* (pp. 27–54). New York: Academic Press.

Lacro, J. P., Dunn, L. B., Dolder, C. R., Leckband, S. G., & Jeste, D. V. (2002). Prevalence of and risk factors for medication nonadherence in patients with schizophrenia: A comprehensive review of recent literature. *Journal of Clinical Psychiatry, 63*(10), 892–909.

Lamy, P. P, Salzman, C., & Nevis-Olesen, J. (1992). Drug prescribing patterns, risks, and compliance guidelines. In C. Salzman (Ed.), *Clinical Geriatric Psychopharmacology* (2nd ed., pp. 15–37). Baltimore, MD: Williams and Wilkins.

Larkin, J. H., & Simon, H. A. (1987). Why a diagram is (sometimes) worth ten thousand words. *Cognitive Science, 11,* 65–99.

Leirer, V. O., Morrow, D. G., Pariante, G. M., & Sheikh, J. L. (1988). Elders' nonadherence, its assessment, and computer assisted instruction for medication recall training. *Journal of the American Geriatric Society, 36,* 877–884.

Leirer, V. O., Morrow, D. G., Tanke, E. D., & Pariante, G. M. (1991). Elders' nonadherence: Its assessment and medication reminding by voice mail. *Gerontologist, 31,* 514–520.

Levine, A. J., Hinkin, C. H., Castellon, S. A., Mason, K. I., Lam, M. N., Perkins, A., et al. (2005). Variations in patterns of highly active antiretroviral therapy (HAART) adherence. *AIDS and Behavior, 9,* 355–362.

Levine, B., Robertson, I. H., Clare, L., Carter, G., Hong, J., Wilson, B. A., et al. (2000). Rehabilitation of executive functioning: an experimental-clinical validation of Goal Management Training. *Journal of the International Neuropsychological Society, 6,* 299–312.

Mackin, R. S., & Arean, P. A. (2007). Cognitive and psychiatric predictors of medical treatment adherence among older adults in primary care clinics. *International Journal of Geriatric Psychiatry, 22,* 55–60.

Mackowiak, E. D., O'Connor, T. W., Jr., Thomason, M., Nighswander, R., Smith, M., Vogenberg, A., et al. (1994). Compliance devices preferred by elderly patients. *American Pharmacy, NS34*, 47–52.

Maeda, K., Kasai, K., Watanabe, A., Henomatsu, K., Rogers, M. A., & Kato, N. (2006). Effect of subjective reasoning and neurocognition on medication adherence for persons with schizophrenia. *Psychiatric Services, 57*, 1203–1205.

Marder, S. R. (1998). Facilitating compliance with antipsychotic medication. *Journal of Clinical Psychiatry, 59*, 21–25.

Martin, D. C., & Mead, K. (1982). Reducing medication errors in a geriatric population. *Journal of the American Geriatrics Society, 4*, 258–260.

McDonnell, P. J., & Jacobs, M. R. (2002). Hospital admissions resulting from preventable adverse drug reactions. *Annals of Pharmacotherapy, 36*, 1331–1336.

Mendoza, P. S., Munoz, P. M., Merino, E. J., & Barriga, O. A. (2006). Determinant factors of therapeutic compliance in elderly hypertensive patients. *Revista Medica de Chile, 134*, 65–71.

Mirotznik, J., Feldman, L., & Stein, R. (1995). The health belief model and adherence with a community center-based, supervised coronary heart disease exercise program. *Journal of Community Health, 20*, 233–247.

Moore, A., Sellwood, W., & Stirling, J. (2000). Compliance and psychological reactance in schizophrenia. *British Psychological Society, 39*, 287–295.

Morice, R. (1990). Cognitive flexibility and prefrontal dysfunction in schizophrenia and mania. *British Journal of Psychiatry, 157*, 50–54.

Morrell, R. W., Park, D. C., & Poon, L. W. (1989). Quality of instructions on prescription drug labels: Effects on memory and comprehension in young and old adults. *Gerontologist, 29*, 345–354.

Morrell, R. W., Park, D. C., & Poon, L. W. (1990). Effects of labeling techniques on memory and comprehension of prescription information in young and old adults. *Journal of Gerontology: Psychological Sciences, 45*, P166–P172.

Myers E.D, & Braithwaite A (1992). Out-patient compliance with antidepressant medication. *British Journal of Psychiatry, 160*, 83–86.

Neal, B., MacMahon, S., & Chapman, N. (2000). Effects of ACE inhibitors, calcium antagonists, and other blood-pressure-lowering drugs: Results of prospectively designed overviews of randomized trials. Blood Pressure Lowering Treatment Trialists' Collaboration. *Lancet, 356*, 1955–1964.

Olfson, M., Mechanic, D., Hansell, S., Boyer, C. A., Walkup, J., & Weiden, P. J. (2000). Predicting medication noncompliance after hospital discharge among patients with schizophrenia. *Psychiatry Services, 51*, 216–222.

Osterberg, L., & Blaschke, T. (2005). Adherence to medication. *New England Journal of Medicine, 353*, 487–497.

Ownby, R. (2006). Medication adherence and cognition: Medical, personal and economic factors influence level of adherence in older adults. *Geriatrics, 61*, 30–35.

Ownby, R. L., Hertzog, C., Crocco, E., & Duara, R. (2006). Factors related to medication adherence in memory disorder clinic patients. *Aging & Mental Health, 10*, 378–385.

Park, D. C., Morrell, R. W., Frieske, D., & Kincaid, D. (1992). Medication adherence behaviors in older adults: Effects of external cognitive supports. *Psychology and Aging, 7*, 252–256.

Park, D. C., Smith, A. D., Lautenschlager, G., Earles, J., Frieske, D., Zwahr, M., et al. (1996). Mediators of long-term memory performance across the life span. *Psychology and Aging, 11*, 621–637.

Park, D. C., Willis, S. L., Morrow, D., Diehl, M., & Gaines, C. L. (1994). Cognitive function and medication usage in older adults. *Journal of Applied Gerontology, 13*, 39–57.

Parkin, D. M., Henney, C. R., Quirk, J., & Crooks, J. (1986). Deviation fro prescribed drug treatment after discharge from hospital. *British Medical Journal, 2*, 686–688.

Patterson, T. L., Lacro, J., McKibbin, C. L., Moscona, S., Hughs, T., & Jeste, D. V. (2002). Medication management ability assessment: Results from a performance-based measure in older outpatients with schizophrenia. *Journal of Clinical Psychopharmacology, 22*, 11–19.

Piette, J. D., & Heisler, M. (2004). Problems due to medication costs among VA and non-VA patients with chronic illnesses. *American Journal of Managed Care, 10*, 861–868.

Rabbitt, P., & Lowe, C. (2000). Patterns of cognitive aging. *Psychology Research, 63*, 308–316.

Raz, N. B. (2000). Aging of the brain and its impact on cognitive performance: Integration of structural and functional findings. In F. I. M. Craik and T. A. Salthouse (Eds.), *The Handbook of Aging and Cognition* (2nd ed. pp. 1–90). Mahwah, NJ: Erlbaum.

Razali, M. S., & Yahya, H. (1995). Compliance with treatment in schizophrenia: A drug intervention program in a developing country. *Acta Psychiatrica Scandinavica, 91*, 331–335.

Rekkas, P. V. (2006). Interference resolution in the elderly: Evidence suggestive of differences in strategy on measures of prepotent inhibition and dual task processing. *Neuropsychology, Development, and Cognition, Section B, Aging, Neuropsychology, and Cognition, 13*(3–4), 341–365.

Remien, R. H., Hirky, A. E., Johnson, M. O., Weinhardt, L. S., Whittier, D., & Minh Le, G. (2003). Adherence to medication treatment: A qualitative study of facilitators and barriers among a diverse sample of HIV+ men and women in four U.S. cities. *AIDS and Behavior, 7,* 61–72.

Rosenstock, I. M. (1974). Historical origins of the health belief model. *Health Education Monographs, 2,* 1–8.

Royall, D. R., Chiodo, L. K., & Polk, M. J. (2000). Correlates of disability among elderly retirees with "subclinical" cognitive impairment. *Journal of Gerontology, Series A, Biological Sciences, 55,* M541–M546.

Salzman, C. (1995). Medication compliance in the elderly. *Journal of Clinical Psychiatry, 56*(Suppl 1), 18–23.

Schillerstrom, J. E., Horton, M. S., & Royall, D. R. (2005). The impact of medical illness on executive function. *Psychosomatics, 46,* 508–516.

Schwartz, B. L., Rosse, R. B., Veazey, C., & Deutsch, S. I. (1996). Impaired motor skill learning in schizophrenia: Implications for corticostriatal dysfunction. *Biological Psychiatry, 39,* 241–248.

Sensky, T., Leger, C., & Gilmour, S. (1996). Psychosocial and cognitive factors associated with adherence to dietary and fluid restriction regimens by people on chronic hemodialysis. *Psychotherapy and Psychosomatics, 65,* 36–42.

Shapiro, P. A., Williams, D., Foray, A., Gelman, I., Wukich, N., & Sciacca, R. (1995). Psychosocial evaluation and prediction of compliance problems and morbidity after heart transplantation. *Transplantation, 60,* 1462–1466.

Simoni, J. M., Frick, P. A., & Huang, B. (2006). A longitudinal evaluation of a social support model of medication adherence among HIV-positive men and women on antiretroviral therapy. *Health Psychology, 25,* 74–81.

Smith, N. A., Ley, P., Seale, J. P., & Shaw, J. (1987). Health beliefs, satisfaction and compliance. *Patient Education and Counseling, 10,* 279–286.

Sokol, M. C., McGuigan, K. A., Verbrugge, R. R., & Epstein, R. S. (2005). Impact of medication adherence on hospitalization risk and healthcare costs. *Medical Care, 43,* 521–530.

Solomon, T. M., & Halkitis, P. N. (2007). Cognitive executive functioning in relation to HIV medication adherence among gay, bisexual, and other men who have sex with men. *AIDS and Behavior,* Epub, July 17, 2007. http://www.springerlink.com/content/k121387545155030/fulltext.html

Stephenson, B. J., Rowe, B. H., Haynes, B., Macharia, W. M., & Leon, G. (1993). Is this patient taking the treatment as prescribed? *Journal of the American Medical Association, 269,* 2779–2781.

Stewart, J. T., Gonzalez-Perez, E, Zhu, Y., & Robinson, B. E. (1999). Cognitive predictors of resistiveness in dementia patients. *American Journal of Geriatric Psychiatry, 7,* 259–263.

Stilley, C. S., Sereika, S., Muldoon, M., Ryan, C. M., & Dunbar-Jacob, J. (2004). Psychological and cognitive function: predictors of adherence with cholesterol lowering treatment. *Annals of Behavioral Medicine, 27,* 117–124.

Thieda, P., Beard, S., Richter, A., & Kane, J. (2003). An economic review of compliance with medication therapy in the treatment of schizophrenia. *Psychiatric Services, 54,* 508–516.

Tierney, M. C., Snow, G., Charles, J., Moineddin, R., & Kiss, A. (2007). Neuropsychological predictors of self-neglect in cognitively impaired older people who live alone. *American Journal of Geriatric Psychiatry, 15,* 140–148.

Vanderplas, J. M., & Vanderplas, J. H. (1980). Some factors affecting legibility of printed materials for older adults. *Perceptual and Motor Skills, 50,* 923–932.

Vik, S. A., Maxwell, C. J., & Hogan, D. B. (2004). Measurement, correlates, and health outcomes of medication adherence among seniors. *Annals of Pharmacotherapy, 38,* 303–312.

Vik, S. A., Hogan, D. B., Patten, S. B., Johnson, J. A., Romonko-Slack, L., & Maxwell, C. J. (2006). Medication nonadherence and subsequent risk of hospitalization and mortality among older adults. *Drugs and Aging, 23,* 345–356.

Wandless, I., & Davie, J. W. (1987). Can drug compliance in the elderly be improved? *British Medical Journal, 1,* 359–361.

Wagner, G. J. (2002). Predictors of antiretroviral adherence as measured by self-report, electronic monitoring, and medication diaries. *AIDS Patient Care and STDs, 16,* 599–608.

Waldrop-Valverde, D., Ownby, R. L., Wilkie, F. L., Mack, A., Kumar, M., & Metsch, L. (2006). Neurocognitive aspects of medication adherence in HIV-positive injecting drug users. *AIDS and Behavior, 10,* 287–297.

Wang, P. S., Bohn, R. L., Knight, E., Glynn, R. J., Mogun, H., & Avorn, J. (2002). Noncompliance with antihypertensive medications: The impact of depressive symptoms and psychosocial factors. *Journal of General Internal Medicine, 17,* 504–511.

Weaver, K. E., Llabre, M. M., Durán, R. E., Antoni, M. H., Ironson, G., Penedo, F. J., et al. (2005). A stress and coping model of medication adherence and viral load in HIV-positive men and women on highly active antiretroviral therapy (HAART). *Health Psychology, 24,* 385–392.

Weiden, P. J., & Olfson, M. (1995). Cost of relapse in schizophrenia. *Schizophrenia Bulletin, 21,* 419–429.

Weiden, P. J., Shaw, E., & Mann, J. (1995). Antipsychotic therapy: Patient preferences and compliance. *Current Approaches in Psychosis, 4*, 1–7.

Weinstein, N. D. (1988). The precaution adoption process. *Health Psychology, 7*, 355–386.

Wickens, C. D. (1992). *Engineering psychology and human performance* (2nd ed.). New York: Harper Collins.

Williams, B. R., & Kim, J. (2005). Medication use and prescribing considerations for elderly patients. *Dental Clinics of North America, 49*, 411–427.

Wilson, B. A. (2000). Compensating for cognitive deficits following brain injury. *Neuropsychological Review, 10*, 233–243.

Wilson, B. A., Emslie, H. C., Quirk, K., & Evans, J. (2001). Reducing everyday memory and planning problems by means of a paging system: A randomized control crossover study. *Journal of Neurology, Neurosurgery, and Psychiatry, 70*, 477–482.

Woods, S. P., Rippeth, J. D., Conover, E., Gongvatana, A., Gonzalez, R., Carey, C., et al. (2005). Deficient strategic control of verbal encoding and retrieval in individuals with methamphetamine dependence. *Neuropsychology, 19*, 35–43.

World Health Organization. (2003).Adherence to long-term therapies: evidence for action. Available at:http://www.who.int/chronic_conditions/adherencereport/en/. (accessed July 3, 2007)

Zacks, R., & Hasher, L. (1997). Cognitive gerontology and attentional inhibition: A reply to Burke and McDowd. *The Journals of Gerontology, Series B, Psychological Science and Social Sciences, 52*, P274–P283.

Author Index

Subject Index